third edition

Financial Markets *and* Institutions

An Introduction to the Risk Management Approach

THE McGRAW-HILL/IRWIN SERIES IN FINANCE, INSURANCE AND REAL ESTATE

Stephen A. Ross
Franco Modigliani Professor of Finance and Economics
Sloan School of Management
Massachusetts Institute of Technology
Consulting Editor

FINANCIAL MANAGEMENT

Adair
Excel Applications for Corporate Finance

Benninga and Sarig
Corporate Finance: A Valuation Approach

Block and Hirt
Foundations of Financial Management
Eleventh Edition

Brealey, Myers, and Allen
Principles of Corporate Finance
Eighth Edition

Brealey, Myers, and Marcus
Fundamentals of Corporate Finance
Fifth Edition

Brooks
FinGame Online 4.0

Bruner
Case Studies in Finance: Managing for Corporate Value Creation
Fifth Edition

Chew
The New Corporate Finance: Where Theory Meets Practice
Third Edition

Chew and Gillan
Corporate Governance at the Crossroads: A Book of Readings

DeMello
Cases in Finance
Second Edition

Grinblatt and Titman
Financial Markets and Corporate Strategy
Second Edition

Helfert
Techniques of Financial Analysis: A Guide to Value Creation
Eleventh Edition

Higgins
Analysis for Financial Management
Eighth Edition

Kester, Ruback, and Tufano
Case Problems in Finance
Twelfth Edition

Ross, Westerfield, and Jaffe
Corporate Finance
Seventh Edition

Ross, Westerfield, Jaffe, and Jordan
Corporate Finance: Core Principles and Applications

Ross, Westerfield, and Jordan
Essentials of Corporate Finance
Fifth Edition

Ross, Westerfield, and Jordan
Fundamentals of Corporate Finance
Seventh Edition

Shefrin
Behavioral Corporate Finance: Decisions that Create Value

Smith
The Modern Theory of Corporate Finance
Second Edition

White
Financial Analysis with an Electronic Calculator
Sixth Edition

INVESTMENTS

Bodie, Kane, and Marcus
Essentials of Investments
Sixth Edition

Bodie, Kane, and Marcus
Investments
Sixth Edition

Cohen, Zinbarg, and Zeikel
Investment Analysis and Portfolio Management
Fifth Edition

Corrado and Jordan
Fundamentals of Investments: Valuation and Management
Third Edition

Hirt and Block
Fundamentals of Investment Management
Eighth Edition

FINANCIAL INSTITUTIONS AND MARKETS

Cornett and Saunders
Fundamentals of Financial Institutions Management

Rose and Hudgins
Bank Management and Financial Services
Sixth Edition

Rose and Marquis
Money and Capital Markets: Financial Institutions and Instruments in a Global Marketplace
Ninth Edition

Santomero and Babbel
Financial Markets, Instruments, and Institutions
Second Edition

Saunders and Cornett
Financial Institutions Management: A Risk Management Approach
Fifth Edition

Saunders and Cornett
Financial Markets and Institutions: An Introduction to the Risk Management Approach
Third Edition

INTERNATIONAL FINANCE

Beim and Calomiris
Emerging Financial Markets

Eun and Resnick
International Financial Management
Fourth Edition

Kuemmerle
Case Studies in International Entrepreneurship: Managing and Financing Ventures in the Global Economy

Levich
International Financial Markets: Prices and Policies
Second Edition

REAL ESTATE

Brueggeman and Fisher
Real Estate Finance and Investments
Twelfth Edition

Corgel, Ling, and Smith
Real Estate Perspectives: An Introduction to Real Estate
Fourth Edition

Ling and Archer
Real Estate Principles: A Value Approach

FINANCIAL PLANNING AND INSURANCE

Allen, Melone, Rosenbloom, and Mahoney
Pension Planning: Pension, Profit-Sharing, and Other Deferred Compensation Plans
Ninth Edition

Altfest
Personal Financial Planning

Crawford
Life and Health Insurance Law
Eighth Edition (LOMA)

Harrington and Niehaus
Risk Management and Insurance
Second Edition

Hirsch
Casualty Claim Practice
Sixth Edition

Kapoor, Dlabay, and Hughes
Focus on Personal Finance: An Active Approach to Help You Develop Successful Financial Skills

Kapoor, Dlabay, and Hughes
Personal Finance
Eighth Edition

third edition

Financial Markets *and* Institutions

An Introduction to the Risk Management Approach

Anthony Saunders
Stern School of Business
New York University

Marcia Millon Cornett
Southern Illinois University

McGraw Hill

Boston Burr Ridge, IL Dubuque, IA Madison, WI New York San Francisco St. Louis
Bangkok Bogotá Caracas Kuala Lumpur Lisbon London Madrid Mexico City
Milan Montreal New Delhi Santiago Seoul Singapore Sydney Taipei Toronto

The McGraw·Hill Companies

Mc Graw Hill

FINANCIAL MARKETS AND INSTITUTIONS:
AN INTRODUCTION TO THE RISK MANAGEMENT APPROACH
International Edition 2007

Published by McGraw-Hill/Irwin, a business unit of The McGraw-Hill Companies, Inc., 1221 Avenue of the Americas, New York, NY, 10020.

10 09 08 07 06 05 04 03 02
20 09 08
CTF BJE

978-007-125986-6 or 007-125986-4 (Powerweb card)

When ordering this title, use ISBN: 978-007-125985-9 or MHID: 007-125985-6 (Powerweb and S&P card)

Printed in Singapore

www.mhhe.com

To my father, Myer Saunders (1919–1998).

—TONY SAUNDERS

To Galen.

—MARCIA MILLON CORNETT

ABOUT THE AUTHORS

Anthony Saunders

Anthony Saunders is the John M. Schiff Professor of Finance and Chair of the Department of Finance at the Stern School of Business at New York University. Professor Saunders received his Ph.D. from the London School of Economics and has taught both undergraduate and graduate level courses at NYU since 1978. Throughout his academic career, his teaching and research have specialized in financial institutions and international banking. He has served as a visiting professor all over the world, including INSEAD, the Stockholm School of Economics, and the University of Melbourne.

Professor Saunders holds positions on the Board of Academic Consultants of the Federal Reserve Board of Governors as well as the Council of Research Advisors for the Federal National Mortgage Association. In addition, Dr. Saunders has acted as a visiting scholar at the Comptroller of the Currency and at the International Monetary Fund. He is editor of the *Journal of Banking and Finance* and the *Journal of Financial Markets, Instruments and Institutions,* as well as the associate editor of eight other journals, including *Financial Management* and the *Journal of Money, Credit and Banking*. His research has been published in all of the major finance and banking journals and in several books. He has just published a new edition of his textbook, with Dr. Marcia Millon Cornett, *Financial Institutions Management: A Risk Management Approach* for McGraw-Hill (fifth edition) as well as a second edition of his book on credit risk measurement for John Wiley & Sons. Professor Saunders was ranked the 16th most prolific author out of more than 5,800 who have published in the seven leading Finance academic journals from 1953 to 2002 and first in the top 16 journals ("Prolific Authors in the Financial Literature: A Half Century of Contributions," *Journal of Finance Literature,* Volume 1, Winter 2005).

Marcia Millon Cornett

Marcia Millon Cornett is the Rehn Professor of Business at Southern Illinois University at Carbondale. She received her B.S. degree in economics from Knox College in Galesburg, Illinois, and her M.B.A. and Ph.D. degrees in finance from Indiana University in Bloomington. Dr. Cornett has written and published several scholarly articles in the areas of bank performance, bank regulation, corporate finance, and investments. Articles authored by Dr. Cornett have appeared in such academic journals as the *Journal of Finance,* the *Journal of Money, Credit, and Banking,* the *Journal of Financial Economics, Financial Management,* and the *Journal of Banking and Finance.* Dr. Cornett also has coauthored two textbooks with Dr. Anthony Saunders of New York University: *Financial Institutions Management,* fifth edition (McGraw-Hill/Irwin, 2006); and *Financial Markets and Institutions,* third edition (McGraw-Hill/Irwin, 2001). She served as a guest editor for the January 2004 special issue of the *Review of Financial Economics* on Commercial Banks: Performance, Regulation, and Market Value. She served as an associate editor of *Financial Management* and is currently an associate editor for the *Journal of Banking and Finance, Journal of Financial Services Research, Multinational Finance Journal, Financial Review, Review of Financial Economics,* and *FMA Online.* Dr. Cornett was listed as the 320th most prolific Finance author out of more than 5,800 who have published in the seven leading Finance academic journals from 1953 to 2002 ("Prolific Authors in the Financial Literature: A Half Century of Contributors," *Journal of Finance Literature,* Volume 1, Winter 2005). Dr. Cornett is currently a member of the Board of Directors and the Finance Committee of the Southern Illinois University Credit Union. Dr. Cornett has also taught at the University of Colorado, Boston College, and Southern Methodist University. She is a member of the Financial Management Association, the American Finance Association, and the Western Finance Association.

PREFACE

The 1990s were characterized as a period in which financial markets in the United States boomed. The Dow Jones Industrial Average rose from a level of 2,800 in January 1990 to more than 11,000 by the end of the decade; this compared to a move from 100 at its inception in 1906 to 2,800 eighty-four years later. However, in the early 2000s, as a result of an economic recession and corporate scandals involving major companies such as Enron, WorldCom, and Tyco, this index fell back below 10,000. Further, several stocks trading in the NASDAQ stock market lost all gains made in the late 1990s. While security values in U.S. financial markets rose dramatically in the 1990s, financial markets in Southeast Asia, South America, and Russia plummeted. More recently, in the early 2000s Argentina's economic and financial system collapsed and its currency fell more than 30 percent in value relative to the U.S. dollar.

Meanwhile, the financial services industry continues to undergo dramatic changes. Not only have the boundaries between traditional industry sectors, such as commercial banking and investment banking, broken down but competition is becoming increasingly global in nature as FIs from Germany, France, and other European countries enter into U.S. financial service markets, and vice versa. Many forces are contributing to this breakdown in interindustry and intercountry barriers, including financial innovation, technology, taxation, and regulation.

As the economic and competitive environments change, attention to profit and, more than ever, risk becomes increasingly important. This book offers a unique analysis of the risks faced by investors and savers interacting through both financial institutions and financial markets, as well as strategies that can be adopted for controlling and better managing these risks. Special emphasis is also put on new areas of operations in financial markets and institutions such as asset securitization, off-balance-sheet activities, and globalization of financial services.

While maintaining a risk measurement and management framework, *Financial Markets and Institutions* provides a broad application of this important perspective. This book recognizes that domestic and foreign financial markets are becoming increasingly integrated and that financial intermediaries are evolving toward a single financial services industry. The analytical rigor is mathematically accessible to all levels of students, undergraduate and graduate, and is balanced by a comprehensive discussion of the unique environment within which financial markets and institutions operate. Important practical tools such as how to issue and trade financial securities and how to analyze financial statements and loan applications will arm students with skills necessary to understand and manage financial market and institution risks in this dynamic environment. While descriptive concepts, so important to financial management (financial market securities, regulation, industry trends, industry characteristics, etc.) are included in the book, ample analytical techniques are also included as practical tools to help students understand the operation of modern financial markets and institutions.

INTENDED AUDIENCE

Financial Markets and Institutions is aimed at the first course in financial markets and institutions at both the undergraduate and M.B.A. levels. While topics covered in this book are found in more advanced textbooks on financial markets and institutions, the explanations and illustrations are aimed at those with little or no practical or academic experience beyond the introductory level finance courses. In most chapters, the main relationships are presented by figures, graphs, and simple examples. The more complicated details and technical problems related to in-chapter discussion are provided in appendixes to the chapters located at the book's Web site (**www.mhhe.com/sc3e**).

ORGANIZATION

Since our focus is on return and risk and the sources of that return and risk in domestic and foreign financial markets and institutions, this book relates ways in which a modern financial manager, saver, and investor can expand return with a managed level of risk to achieve the best, or most favorable, return–risk outcome.

The book is divided into five major sections. Part 1 provides an introduction to the text and an overview of financial markets and institutions. Chapter 1 defines and introduces the various domestic and foreign financial markets and describes the special functions of FIs. This chapter also takes an analytical look at how financial markets and institutions benefit today's economy. In Chapter 2, we provide an in-depth look at interest rates. We first review the concept of time value of money. We then look at factors that determine interest rate levels, as well as their past, present, and expected future movements. Chapter 3 then applies these interest rates to security valuation. In Chapter 4, we describe the Federal Reserve System and how monetary policy implemented by the Federal Reserve affects interest rates and, ultimately, the overall economy.

Part 2 of the text presents an overview of the various securities markets. We describe each securities market, its participants, the securities traded in each, the trading process, and how changes in interest rates, inflation, and foreign exchange rates impact a financial manager's decisions to hedge risk. These chapters cover the money markets (Chapter 5), bond markets (Chapter 6), mortgage markets (Chapter 7), foreign exchange markets (Chapter 8), stock markets (Chapter 9), and derivative securities markets (Chapter 10).

Part 3 of the text summarizes the operations of commercial banks. Chapter 11 describes the key characteristics and recent trends in the commercial banking sector. Chapter 12 describes the financial statements of a typical commercial bank and the ratios used to analyze those statements. This chapter also analyzes actual financial statements for representative commercial banks. Chapter 13 provides a comprehensive look at the regulations under which these financial institutions operate and, particularly, at the effect of recent changes in regulation.

Part 4 of the text provides an overview describing the key characteristics and regulatory features of the other major sectors of the U.S. financial services industry. We discuss other lending institutions (savings institutions, credit unions, and finance companies) in Chapter 14, insurance companies in Chapter 15, securities firms and investment banks in Chapter 16, mutual fund firms in Chapter 17, and pension funds in Chapter 18.

Part 5 concludes the text by examining the risks facing a modern FI and FI managers, and the various strategies for managing these risks. In Chapter 19, we preview the risk measurement and management chapters that follow with an overview of the risks facing a modern FI. We divide the chapters on risk measurement and management along two lines: measuring and managing risks on the balance sheet, and managing risks off the balance sheet. In Chapter 20, we begin the on-balance-sheet risk measurement and management section by looking at credit risk on individual loans and bonds and how these risks adversely impact an FI's profits and value. The chapter also discusses the lending process, including loans made to households and small, medium-size, and large corporations. Chapter 21 covers liquidity risk in financial institutions. This chapter includes a detailed analysis of ways in which FIs can insulate themselves from liquidity risk, and the key role deposit insurance and other guarantee schemes play in reducing liquidity risk.

In Chapter 22, we investigate the net interest margin as a source of profitability and risk, with a focus on the effects of interest rate risk and the mismatching of asset and liability maturities on FI risk exposure. At the core of FI risk insulation is the size and adequacy of the owner's capital stake, which is also a focus of this chapter.

The management of risk off the balance sheet is examined in Chapter 23. The chapter highlights various new markets and instruments that have emerged to allow FIs to better manage three important types of risk: interest rate risk, foreign exchange risk, and credit risk. These markets and instruments and their strategic use by FIs include forwards and futures, options, and swaps.

Finally, Chapter 24 explores ways of removing credit risk from the loan portfolio through asset sales and securitization.

NEW FEATURES

- In-chapter discussions of the many ethical controversies surrounding financial markets and institutions (such as those involving stock market brokers and dealers, commercial banks, investment banks, and mutual funds) have been added to most chapters.
- Ethical Debates boxes have been added to many chapters to highlight specific news stories relating to the ethical controversies involving financial markets and institutions in the early 2000s.
- Discussions of the impact of the Patriot Act and the Sarbanes-Oxley Act on financial institutions management are included in several chapters.
- The impact of the economic slowdown and the subsequent economic recovery in the United States and worldwide on financial markets and institutions is highlighted and discussed in all relevant chapters. This discussion is particularly evident in the first six chapters of the book.
- The impact of historically low interest rates and their eventual increase on financial institutions management is highlighted.
- A discussion of the controversy surrounding the federal government's implicit backing of Fannie Mae and Freddie Mac, and the impact the increased level of risk in these two agencies posed to the U.S. economy in the early 2000s, is added to Chapter 7.
- The latest information pertaining to new capital adequacy rules (or Basel II), which are scheduled for implementation at the end of 2006, has been added to Chapter 13. The discussion includes detailed examples of the calculation of capital adequacy under both Basel I and Basel II.
- The latest changes to deposit insurance premiums charged to financial institutions and insurance coverage for financial institution customers are discussed in Chapter 13.
- Tables and figures in all chapters have been revised to include the most recently available data.
- Sections of the text that include a discussion of international issues and events are highlighted. These sections have been updated to contain the most recent issues pertaining to financial institutions worldwide.
- Appendixes for Chapters 2, 3, 5, 8, 9, 10, 13, 17, 20, and 23 are available at the book's Web site at **www.mhhe.com/sc3e.**
- Search the Site problems included in the body of various chapters and in the end-of-chapter problems have been substantially enhanced. These problems now guide the student through the Web site as they collect the requested data. Further, these problems now ask the student to evaluate the data collected at the Web site.
- Excel problems have been included in the body of various chapters and in the end-of-chapter problems. These problems now ask the student to solve numerical problems similar to those seen in the in-text examples.

ACKNOWLEDGMENTS

We take this opportunity to thank all of those individuals who helped us prepare this third edition. We want to express our appreciation to those instructors whose insightful comments and suggestions were invaluable to us during this revision.

Jack W. Aber
Boston University
Susan Banerjee
Tulane University
James Barth
Auburn University
Peter Basciano
Augusta State University
John R. Becker Blease
University of New Hampshire
Sam Bulmash
University of Southern Florida

Mitch Charkiewicz
Central Connecticut State University
Yew-Mow Chen
San Francisco State University
Erik Devos
SUNY-Binghamton
John Dominick
University of Arkansas
Michael Goldstein
Babson College
Alan E. Grunewald
Michigan State University
Gayle de Haas
Mississippi State University
John Halloran
University of Notre Dame
William C. Handorf
George Washington University
Jean Helwege
Ohio State University
Jann Culvahouse Howell
Iowa State University
Sylvia Hudgins
Old Dominion University
William Jackson
University of North Carolina, Chapel Hill
Bill Lepley
University of Wisconsin, Green Bay
Tim Manuel
University of Montana
Bill Marcum
Wake Forest University
Joe Mascia
Adelphi University
Joseph R. Mason
Drexel University
Clark Maxam
Montana State University
Joe Ogden
SUNY-Buffalo
Evren Ors
Southern Illinois University
Fred Puritz
SUNY-Oneonta
Charles B. Ruscher
University of Arizona
Sherrill Shaffer
University of Wyoming
Richard S. Swasey Jr.
Northeastern University
John Thorton
Kent State University
Jim Tripp
Western Illinois University
George Vlachos
Wayne State University
Dan Walz
Trinity University
Berry Wilson
Pace University
Mei "Miranda" Zhang
Mercer University

We would also like to thank the staff at McGraw-Hill, especially Steve Patterson, Publisher; Christina Kouvelis, Developmental Editor II; Kristin Bradley, Project Manager; Adam Rooke, Designer; Gina Hangos, Production Supervisor; and Kai Chiang, Media Producer. We are also grateful to our secretaries and assistants, Alex Fayman, Jamie John McNutt, and Sharon Moore.

Anthony Saunders

Marcia Cornett

WALKTHROUGH

Chapter Features

The following special features have been integrated throughout the text to encourage student interaction and to aid students in absorbing and retaining the material.

CHAPTER-OPENING OUTLINES

These outlines offer students a snapshot view of what they can expect to learn from each chapter's discussion.

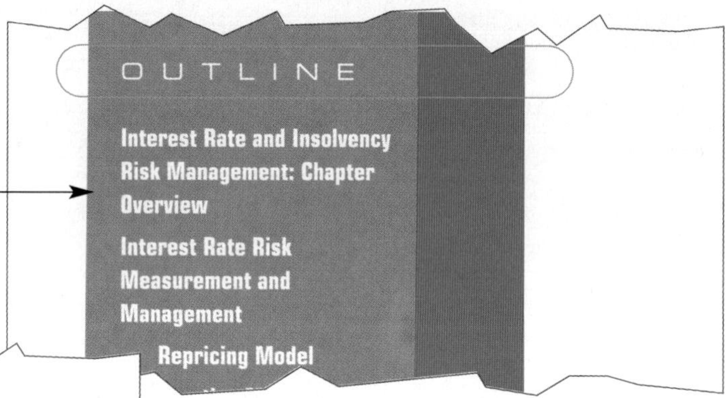

OUTLINE

Interest Rate and Insolvency Risk Management: Chapter Overview

Interest Rate Risk Measurement and Management

Repricing Model

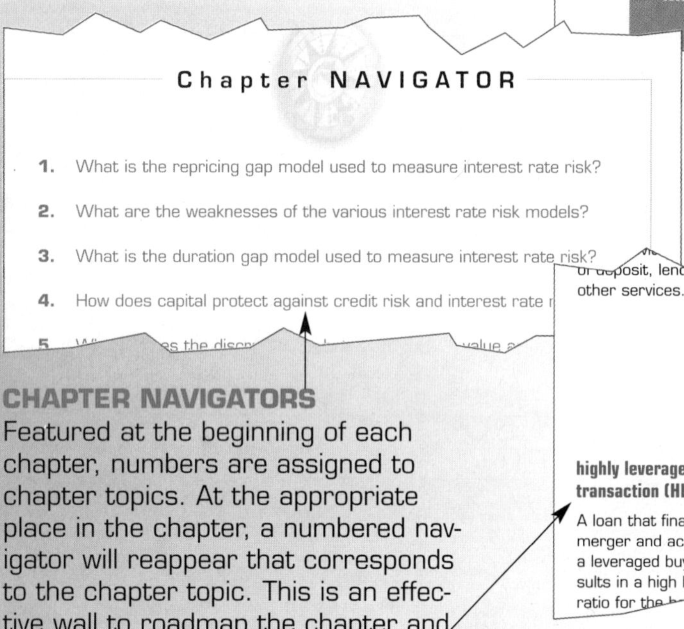

Chapter NAVIGATOR

1. What is the repricing gap model used to measure interest rate risk?
2. What are the weaknesses of the various interest rate risk models?
3. What is the duration gap model used to measure interest rate risk?
4. How does capital protect against credit risk and interest rate r

CHAPTER NAVIGATORS

Featured at the beginning of each chapter, numbers are assigned to chapter topics. At the appropriate place in the chapter, a numbered navigator will reappear that corresponds to the chapter topic. This is an effective wall to roadmap the chapter and connect concepts.

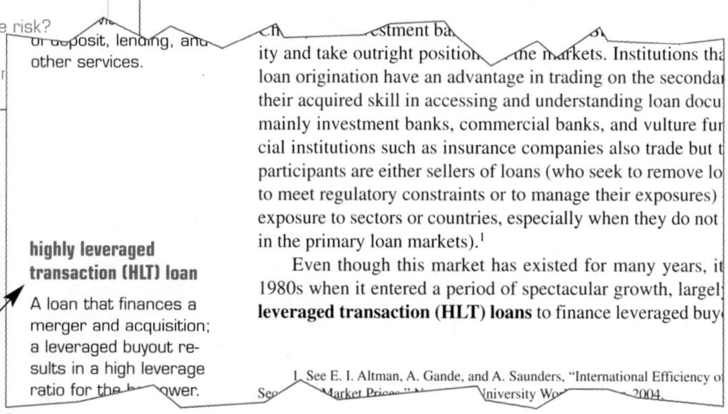

other services.

highly leveraged transaction (HLT) loan
A loan that finances a merger and acquisition; a leveraged buyout results in a high leverage ratio for the

ity and take outright position the markets. Institutions tha loan origination have an advantage in trading on the secondar their acquired skill in accessing and understanding loan docu mainly investment banks, commercial banks, and vulture fu cial institutions such as insurance companies also trade but t participants are either sellers of loans (who seek to remove lo to meet regulatory constraints or to manage their exposures) exposure to sectors or countries, especially when they do not in the primary loan markets).[1]

Even though this market has existed for many years, it 1980s when it entered a period of spectacular growth, largel **leveraged transaction (HLT) loans** to finance leveraged buy

1. See E. I. Altman, A. Gande, and A. Saunders, "International Efficiency o

BOLD KEY TERMS AND A MARGINAL GLOSSARY

The main terms and concepts are emphasized throughout the chapter by the bold key terms and a marginal glossary.

PERTINENT WEB SITE ADDRESSES

Web site addresses are also referenced in the margins throughout each chapter, providing additional resources to aid in the learning process.

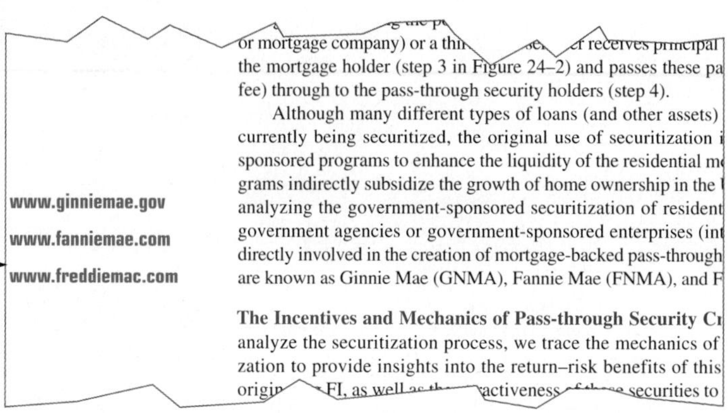

www.ginniemae.gov

www.fanniemae.com

www.freddiemac.com

or mortgage company) or a thi the mortgage holder (step 3 in Figure 24–2) and passes these pa fee) through to the pass-through security holders (step 4).

Although many different types of loans (and other assets) currently being securitized, the original use of securitization i sponsored programs to enhance the liquidity of the residential m grams indirectly subsidize the growth of home ownership in the analyzing the government-sponsored securitization of resident government agencies or government-sponsored enterprises (in directly involved in the creation of mortgage-backed pass-through are known as Ginnie Mae (GNMA), Fannie Mae (FNMA), and F

The Incentives and Mechanics of Pass-through Security C analyze the securitization process, we trace the mechanics of zation to provide insights into the return–risk benefits of this

Pedagogical Features

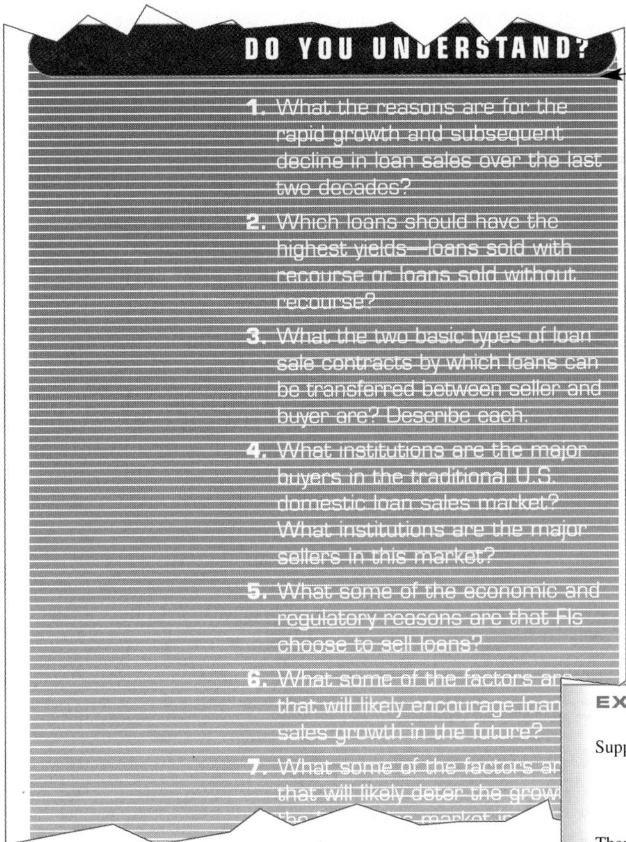

DO YOU UNDERSTAND?

1. What the reasons are for the rapid growth and subsequent decline in loan sales over the last two decades?
2. Which loans should have the highest yields—loans sold with recourse or loans sold without recourse?
3. What the two basic types of loan sale contracts by which loans can be transferred between seller and buyer are? Describe each.
4. What institutions are the major buyers in the traditional U.S. domestic loan sales market? What institutions are the major sellers in this market?
5. What some of the economic and regulatory reasons are that FIs choose to sell loans?
6. What some of the factors are that will likely encourage loan sales growth in the future?
7. What some of the factors are that will likely deter the grow...

"DO YOU UNDERSTAND?" BOXES

These boxes allow students to test themselves on the main concepts presented within each major chapter section.

IN-CHAPTER EXAMPLES

These examples provide numerical demonstrations of the analytical material described in many chapters.

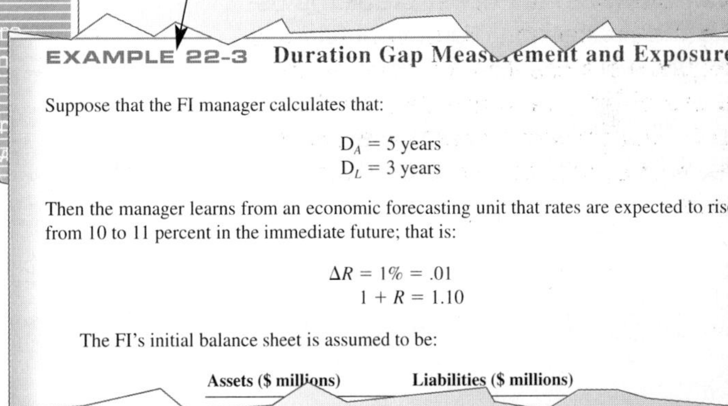

EXAMPLE 22-3 Duration Gap Measurement and Exposure

Suppose that the FI manager calculates that:

$$D_A = 5 \text{ years}$$
$$D_L = 3 \text{ years}$$

Then the manager learns from an economic forecasting unit that rates are expected to rise from 10 to 11 percent in the immediate future; that is:

$$\Delta R = 1\% = .01$$
$$1 + R = 1.10$$

The FI's initial balance sheet is assumed to be:

Assets ($ millions) Liabilities ($ millions)

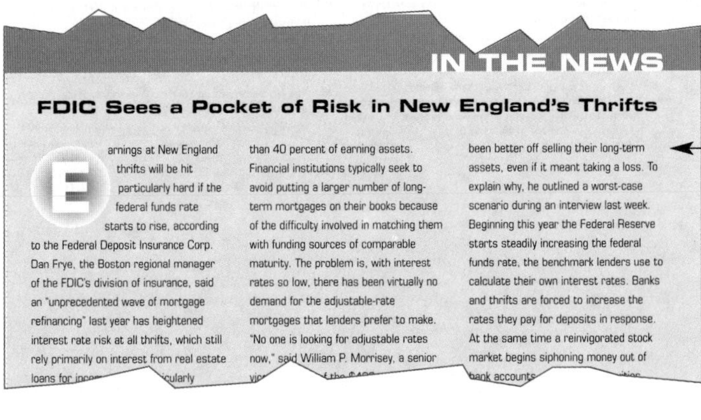

IN THE NEWS

FDIC Sees a Pocket of Risk in New England's Thrifts

Earnings at New England thrifts will be hit particularly hard if the federal funds rate starts to rise, according to the Federal Deposit Insurance Corp. Dan Frye, the Boston regional manager of the FDIC's division of insurance, said an "unprecedented wave of mortgage refinancing" last year has heightened interest rate risk at all thrifts, which still rely primarily on interest from real estate loans for ... than 40 percent of earning assets. Financial institutions typically seek to avoid putting a larger number of long-term mortgages on their books because of the difficulty involved in matching them with funding sources of comparable maturity. The problem is, with interest rates so low, there has been virtually no demand for the adjustable-rate mortgages that lenders prefer to make. "No one is looking for adjustable rates now," said William P. Morrisey, a senior ... been better off selling their long-term assets, even if it meant taking a loss. To explain why, he outlined a worst-case scenario during an interview last week. Beginning this year the Federal Reserve starts steadily increasing the federal funds rate, the benchmark lenders use to calculate their own interest rates. Banks and thrifts are forced to increase the rates they pay for deposits in response. At the same time a reinvigorated stock market begins siphoning money out of bank accounts ...

"IN THE NEWS . . ." BOXES

These boxes demonstrate the application of chapter material to real current events.

WALKTHROUGH

End-of-Chapter Features

EXCEL PROBLEMS

New! These are featured among selected chapters and are denoted by an icon. Spreadsheet templates are available on the book's Web site, **www.mhhe.com/sc3e.**

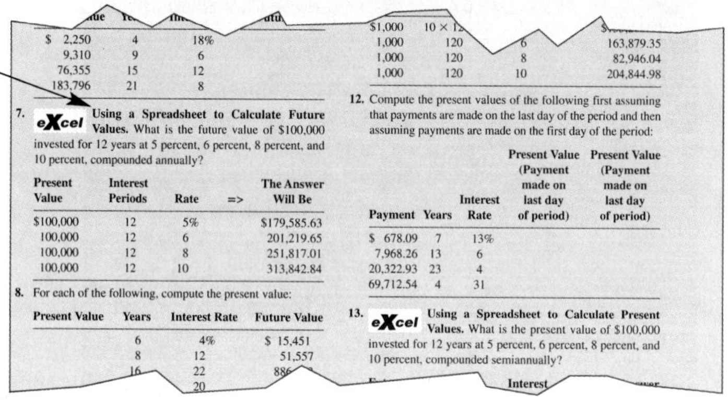

$ 2,250	4	18%	
9,310	9	6	
76,355	15	12	
183,796	21	8	

7. eXcel **Using a Spreadsheet to Calculate Future Values.** What is the future value of $100,000 invested for 12 years at 5 percent, 6 percent, 8 percent, and 10 percent, compounded annually?

Present Value	Interest Periods	Rate	=>	The Answer Will Be
$100,000	12	5%		$179,585.63
100,000	12	6		201,219.65
100,000	12	8		251,817.01
100,000	12	10		313,842.84

8. For each of the following, compute the present value:

Present Value	Years	Interest Rate	Future Value
	6	4%	$ 15,451
	8	12	51,557
	16	22	
		20	

$1,000	10 × 12		
1,000	120	6	163,879.35
1,000	120	8	82,946.04
1,000	120	10	204,844.98

12. Compute the present values of the following first assuming that payments are made on the last day of the period and then assuming payments are made on the first day of the period:

Payment	Years	Interest Rate	Present Value (Payment made on last day of period)	Present Value (Payment made on last day of period)
$ 678.09	7	13%		
7,968.26	13	6		
20,322.93	23	4		
69,712.54	4	31		

13. eXcel **Using a Spreadsheet to Calculate Present Values.** What is the present value of $100,000 invested for 12 years at 5 percent, 6 percent, 8 percent, and 10 percent, compounded semiannually?

S&P PROBLEMS

Based on our exclusive relationship with Standard & Poor's, problems using the Educational Version of Market Insight were created for each appropriate chapter and are denoted by an icon. Students can practice applying real-world data to reinforce their skills.

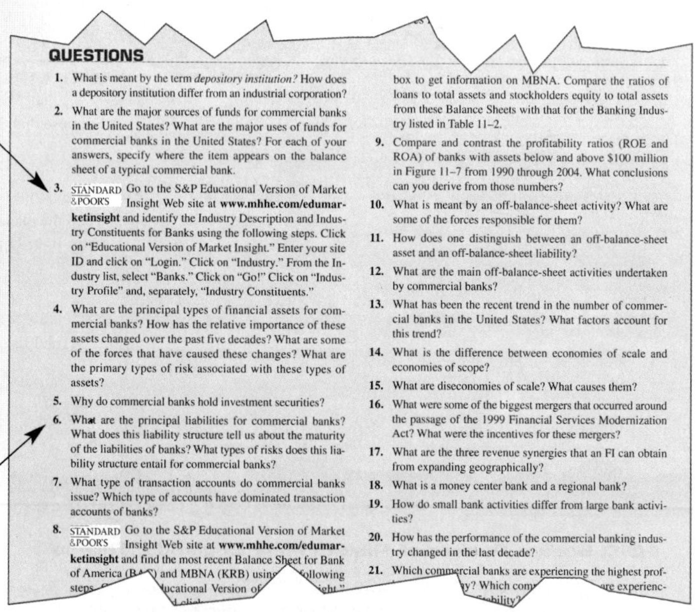

QUESTIONS

1. What is meant by the term *depository institution?* How does a depository institution differ from an industrial corporation?
2. What are the major sources of funds for commercial banks in the United States? What are the major uses of funds for commercial banks in the United States? For each of your answers, specify where the item appears on the balance sheet of a typical commercial bank.
3. STANDARD &POOR'S Go to the S&P Educational Version of Market Insight Web site at **www.mhhe.com/edumarketinsight** and identify the Industry Description and Industry Constituents for Banks using the following steps. Click on "Educational Version of Market Insight." Enter your site ID and click on "Login." Click on "Industry." From the Industry list, select "Banks." Click on "Go!" Click on "Industry Profile" and, separately, "Industry Constituents."
4. What are the principal types of financial assets for commercial banks? How has the relative importance of these assets changed over the past five decades? What are some of the forces that have caused these changes? What are the primary types of risk associated with these types of assets?
5. Why do commercial banks hold investment securities?
6. What are the principal liabilities for commercial banks? What does this liability structure tell us about the maturity of the liabilities of banks? What types of risks does this liability structure entail for commercial banks?
7. What type of transaction accounts do commercial banks issue? Which type of accounts have dominated transaction accounts of banks?
8. STANDARD &POOR'S Go to the S&P Educational Version of Market Insight Web site at **www.mhhe.com/edumarketinsight** and find the most recent Balance Sheet for Bank of America (BAC) and MBNA (KRB) using the following steps. ... Educational Version of ... Insight." ... box to get information on MBNA. Compare the ratios of loans to total assets and stockholders equity to total assets from these Balance Sheets with that for the Banking Industry listed in Table 11–2.
9. Compare and contrast the profitability ratios (ROE and ROA) of banks with assets below and above $100 million in Figure 11–7 from 1990 through 2004. What conclusions can you derive from those numbers?
10. What is meant by an off-balance-sheet activity? What are some of the forces responsible for them?
11. How does one distinguish between an off-balance-sheet asset and an off-balance-sheet liability?
12. What are the main off-balance-sheet activities undertaken by commercial banks?
13. What has been the recent trend in the number of commercial banks in the United States? What factors account for this trend?
14. What is the difference between economies of scale and economies of scope?
15. What are diseconomies of scale? What causes them?
16. What were some of the biggest mergers that occurred around the passage of the 1999 Financial Services Modernization Act? What were the incentives for these mergers?
17. What are the three revenue synergies that an FI can obtain from expanding geographically?
18. What is a money center bank and a regional bank?
19. How do small bank activities differ from large bank activities?
20. How has the performance of the commercial banking industry changed in the last decade?
21. Which commercial banks are experiencing the highest prof... y? Which com... are experienc... ability?

END-OF-CHAPTER PROBLEMS

At least 20 problems per chapter are written for varied levels of difficulty.

ETHICAL DEBATES

Street Braces for Revelations in Settlement

www.powerweb.com/saunders

Ten Wall Street securities firms are bracing for a burst of e-mail messages and other documents suggesting that their stock research was tainted by investment-banking goals, as regulators put the finishing touches on the long-awaited $1.4 billion global research settlement, which is expected to be announced early next week . . . The pact's firm-by-firm allegations will include e-mails from Goldman telecom-sector analysts James Golob and Frank Governali, in which they candidly discuss how investment-banking considerations influenced how many telecom stocks they were recommending in mid-2000 even as the stocks' prices were plummeting. Even Morgan Stanley . . . comes in for criticism for allowing some bullish research reports to sit for as long as six months without an update, according to one p... famil-... the findings ...

portion of the settlement, is expected to be subject voluntarily to a separate set of rules separating its research and investment-banking activities that are more stringent than for other firms involved in the settlement. Three firms paying the most—Citigroup, Merrill Lynch and the Credit Suisse First Boston (CFSB) unit of Credit Suisse Group—also could be hit with securities-fraud charges.

Merrill and CSFB have agreed to pay $200 million in settlement payment. Other firms are paying between $37.5 million and $125 million. The pact also generally includes rules separating research from investment banking; provision of independent research for individual investors; and more disclosure of research ratings and other data ...

ETHICAL DEBATES BOXES

New to this edition, these help students consider and understand the ethical dilemmas pertaining to financial markets and institutions.

SEARCH THE SITE

Go to the Web site of the Office of the Comptroller of the Currency at **www.occ.treas.gov** and find the most recent data on the notional amount of the various types of derivatives contracts outstanding at commercial banks using the following steps.

Click on "Publications"

Click on "Qrtrly. Derivative Fact Sheet"

Click on the most recent date.

Click on "Tables"

This will bring the file onto your computer that contains the relevant data.

SEARCH THE SITE

Now featured within the body of the chapter as well as among the end-of-chapter material in most chapters, these Internet exercises weave the Web, real data, and practical applications with concepts found in the book.

based on U.S. domestic CD ... on ... would probably require additional compensation since it would set returns would be sensitive to LIBOR movements while its sw... to U.S. CD rates.

Currency Swaps

currency swap

A swap used to hedge against foreign exchange rate risk from mismatched currencies on assets and liabilities.

Swaps are long-term contracts that can also be used to hedge a... risk. The following section considers a plain vanilla example o... immunize FIs against foreign exchange rate risk when they ... their assets and liabilities.

Fixed-Fixed Currency Swaps. Consider a U.S. FI with all ... nominated in dollars. It is financing part of its asset portfolio ... four-year, medium-term British pound notes that have a fixed a... By comparison, an FI in the United Kingdom has all its assets d... part... a $100... of four...

INTERNATIONAL ICON

An international icon now appears in the margin to easily communicate where international material is being introduced.

SUPPLEMENTS

FOR THE INSTRUCTOR

Instructor's Resource CD

This comprehensive CD contains all of the following instructor supplements. We have compiled them in electronic format for easier access and convenience. Print copies are available through your McGraw-Hill/Irwin representative. (ISBN 0073041750)

Instructor's Manual

Prepared by Tim Manuel, University of Montana, the Instructor's Manual includes detailed chapter contents and outline, additional examples for use in the classroom, and extensive teaching notes.

Test Bank

Also prepared by Tim Manuel, the Test Bank includes nearly 1,000 additional problems to be used for test material.

Computerized Test Bank

McGraw-Hill's EZ Test is a flexible and easy-to-use electronic testing program. The program allows instructors to create tests from book-specific items. It accommodates a wide range of question types, and instructors may add their own questions. Multiple versions of the test can be created and any test can be exported for use with course management systems such as WebCT, BlackBoard, or PageOut. EZ Test Online is a new service and gives you a place to easily administer your EZ Test-created exams and quizzes online. The program is available for Windows and Macintosh environments.

Solutions Manual

Prepared by co-author Marcia Millon Cornett, the Solutions Manual provides worked-out solutions to the end-of-chapter questions. Author involvement ensures consistency between the solution approaches presented in the text and those in the manual.

PowerPoint

Joseph Ogden, State University of New York–Buffalo, developed the PowerPoint Presentation. It includes full-color slides featuring lecture notes, figures, and tables, which can be easily downloaded and edited.

STUDENT RESOURCES AND ONLINE SUPPORT

Online Learning Center

A wealth of information is available online at **www.mhhe.com/sc3e**. Students will have access to study materials specifically created for this text, interactive quizzes, Excel templates, and much more! Instructors will have access to teaching supports such as electronic files of the ancillary materials and other useful materials. Links to the sites described below will also be provided.

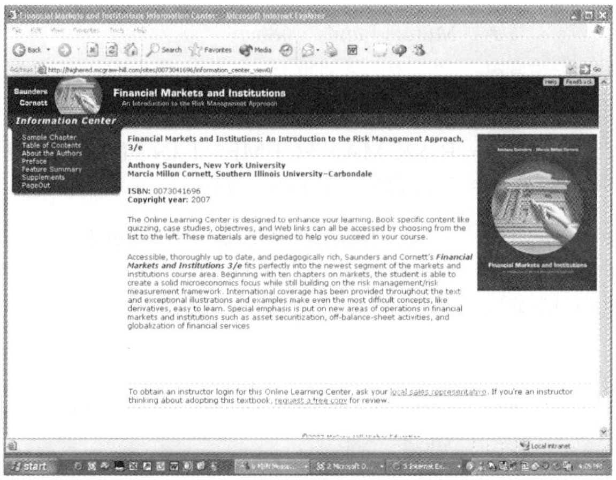

Standard & Poor's Educational Version of Market Insight

McGraw-Hill/Irwin has partnered exclusively with Standard and Poor's to bring you the Educational Version of Market Insight. This rich online resource provides six years of data for 1,000 companies in the renowned COMPUSTAT ® database. S&P problems can be found at the end of relevant chapters of the text. Each new copy of this book includes a card containing a unique password for access to the site. Please visit **www.mhhe.com/edumarketinsight** for access.

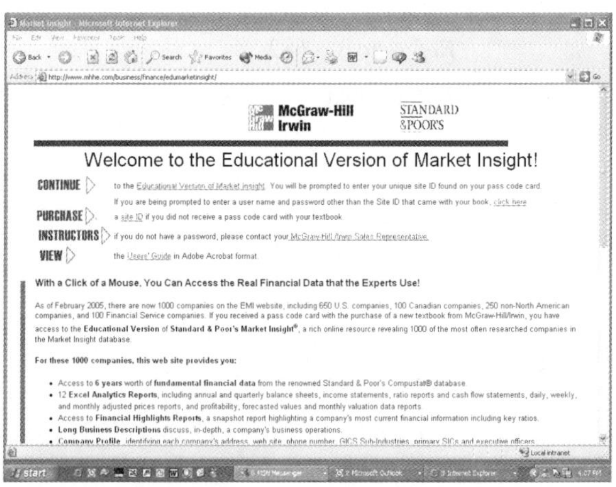

Ethics in Finance PowerWeb

An online site developed to integrate both theoretical and applied ethics into the classroom. It includes current articles, weekly updates with assessment, referred Web links, study tips with self-quizzes, and much more. A passcode card is included with the purchase of a new book for access to this resource. This feature can be found at **www.dushkin.com/powerweb**.

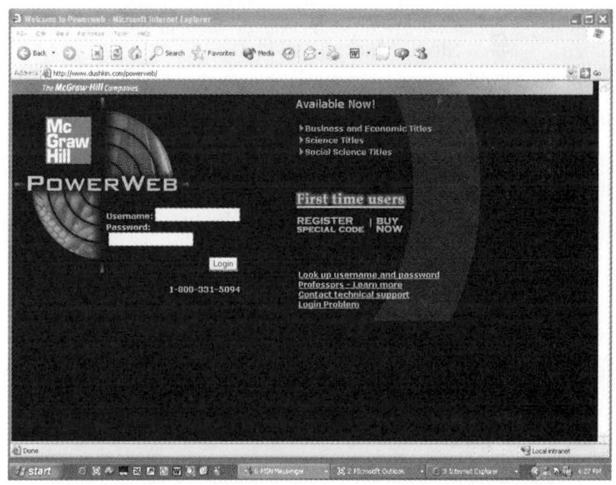

CONTENTS IN BRIEF

CONTENTS

part one

Introduction *and* Overview *of* Financial Markets

Part One of the book provides an introduction to the text and an overview of financial markets. Chapter 1 defines and introduces the various financial markets and describes the special functions of financial institutions. In Chapter 2, we provide an in-depth look at interest rates; Chapter 3 then applies these interest rates to security valuation. In Chapter 4, we describe the Federal Reserve System and how monetary policy implemented by the Federal Reserve affects interest rates, and, ultimately, the overall economy.

OUTLINE

1

Introduction

OUTLINE

Chapter NAVIGATOR

1. What is the difference between primary and secondary markets?
2. What is the difference between money and capital markets?
3. What are foreign exchange markets?
4. What are derivative security markets?
5. What are the different types of financial institutions?
6. What services do financial institutions perform?
7. What risks do financial institutions face?
8. Why are financial institutions regulated?
9. Why are financial markets increasingly becoming global?

WHY STUDY FINANCIAL MARKETS AND INSTITUTIONS? CHAPTER OVERVIEW

In the 1990s, financial markets in the United States boomed. The Dow Jones Industrial Index—a widely quoted index of the values of 30 large corporations (see Chapter 9)—rose from a level of 2,800 in January 1990 to more than 11,000 by the end of the decade; this compares to a move from 100 at its inception in 1906 to 2,800 thirty-four years later. In the early 2000s, as a result of an economic downturn in the United States and elsewhere, this index fell back below 10,000. Further, several stocks traded in the NASDAQ stock market—a second major exchange—lost all gains they made in the late 1990s. While security values in U.S. financial markets rose dramatically in the 1990s, markets in Southeast Asia, South America, and Russia were much more volatile. The Thai baht, for example, fell nearly 50 percent in value relative to the U.S. dollar on July 2, 1997. More recently, in 2002, Argentina's economic and financial system collapsed and its currency fell more than 30 percent in value relative to the U.S. dollar as the government relaxed the peso's one-to-one parity peg to the dollar.

TABLE 1–1 Citigroup Product Lines

Citigroup focuses on nine key product lines. These nine key product lines comprise the entirety of Citigroup.

Credit Cards—World's largest provider of credit cards.
Second quarter '04 net income of $1.012 billion.

Consumer Finance—World's consumer finance leader.
Second quarter '04 net income of $594 million.

Retail Banking—Citibank: highest-rated, leading global brand.
Second quarter '04 net income of $1.156 billion.

Capital Markets & Banking—Number 1 underwriter of combined debt and equity and equity-related transactions.
Second quarter '04 net income of $1.502 billion.

Global Transaction Services*—Leading provider of transaction products; $7.0 trillion in assets under custody.
Second quarter '04 net income of $261 million.

Life Insurance & Annuities—One of the fastest growing life insurers in the United States with expanding international presence.
Second quarter '04 net income of $230 million.

Private Bank—Offers widest range of services to more than 25,000 of the world's most successful and influential families.
Second quarter '04 net income of $152 million.

Asset Management—A leader with $490.5 billion in assets under management.
Second quarter '04 net income of $69 million.

Private Client Services—A leader in managed accounts with $1.087 trillion in total client assets.
Second quarter '04 net income of $209 million.

*Transaction products include the custody and safekeeping of financial investments such as stocks and bonds.
Source: Citigroup Web site, August 2004. **www.citigroup.com**

Meanwhile, the financial institutions industry has gone through a full historical cycle. Originally the banking industry operated as a full-service industry, performing directly or indirectly all financial services (commercial banking, investment banking, stock investing, insurance provision, etc.). In the early 1930s, the economic and industrial collapse resulted in the separation of some of these activities. In the 1970s and 1980s new, relatively unregulated financial services industries sprang up (e.g., mutual funds, brokerage funds) that separated the financial service functions even further. Now, in the early years of the new millennium, regulatory changes, technology, and financial innovation are interacting such that a full set of financial services may again be offered by a single financial institution (FI) such as Citigroup. Table 1–1 lists information on the nine product lines offered by Citigroup. Not only are the boundaries between traditional industry sectors weakening, but competition is becoming global in nature, as German, French, and other international FIs enter into U.S. financial service markets and vice versa.

As economic and competitive environments change, attention to profit and, more than ever, risk becomes increasingly important. This book provides a detailed overview and analysis of the financial system in which financial managers and individual investors operate. Making investment and financing decisions requires managers and individuals to understand the flow of funds throughout the economy as well as the operation and structure of domestic and international financial markets. In particular, the book offers a unique analysis of the risks faced by investors and savers, as well as strategies that can be adopted for controlling and managing these risks. Newer areas of operations such as asset securitization, derivative securities, and internationalization of financial services also receive special emphasis.

This introductory chapter provides an overview of the structure and operations of various financial markets and financial institutions. Financial markets are differentiated by the characteristics (such as maturity) of the financial instruments, or securities that are exchanged. Moreover, each financial market, in turn, depends in part or in whole on financial institutions. Indeed, FIs play a special role in the functioning of financial markets. In particular, FIs often provide the least costly and most efficient way to channel funds to and from financial markets.

OVERVIEW OF FINANCIAL MARKETS

financial markets

The arenas through which funds flow.

Financial markets are structures through which funds flow. Financial markets can be distinguished along two major dimensions: (1) primary versus secondary markets and (2) money versus capital markets. The next sections discuss each of these dimensions.

Primary Markets versus Secondary Markets

1 **Primary Markets.** **Primary markets** are markets in which users of funds (e.g., corporations) raise funds through new issues of financial instruments, such as stocks and bonds. The fund users have new projects or expanded production needs, but do not have sufficient internally generated funds (such as retained earnings) to support these needs. Thus, the fund users issue securities in the external primary markets to raise additional funds. New issues of financial instruments are sold to the initial suppliers of funds (e.g., households) in exchange for funds (money) that the issuer or user of funds needs.[1] Most primary market transactions in the United States are arranged through financial institutions called investment banks—for example, Morgan Stanley or Lehman Brothers—who serve as intermediaries between the issuing corporations (fund users) and investors (fund suppliers). For these public offerings, the investment bank provides the securities issuer (the funds user) with advice on the securities issue (such as the offer price and number of securities to issue) and attracts the initial public purchasers of the securities for the funds user. By issuing primary market securities with the help of an investment bank, the funds user saves the risk and cost of creating a market for its securities on its own (see discussion below). Figure 1–1 illustrates a time line for the primary market exchange of funds for a new issue of corporate bonds or equity. We discuss this process in detail in Chapters 6 and 9.

primary markets

Markets in which corporations raise funds through new issues of securities.

Rather than a public offering (i.e., an offer of sale to the investment public at large), a primary market sale can take the form of a private placement. With a private placement, the securities issuer (user of funds) seeks to find an institutional buyer—such as a pension fund—or group of buyers (suppliers of funds) to purchase the whole issue. Privately placed securities have traditionally been among the most illiquid securities, with only the very largest financial institutions or institutional investors being able or willing to buy and hold them. We discuss the benefits and costs of privately placed primary market sales in detail in Chapter 6.

Primary market financial instruments include issues of equity by firms initially going public (e.g., allowing their equity—shares—to be publicly traded on stock markets for the first time). These first-time issues are usually referred to as **initial public offerings (IPOs).** For example, on April 29, 2004, Google announced a $2.7 billion IPO of its common stock. The company's stock was underwritten by several investment banks, including Morgan Stanley and Credit Suisse First Boston.

initial public offerings (IPOs)

The first public issue of financial instruments by a firm.

Primary market securities also include the issue of additional equity or debt instruments of an already publicly traded firm. For example, in May 2004 Allied Healthcare International announced the sale of an additional 14.5 million shares of common stock (at $4.90 per share) underwritten by investment banks such as SG Cowen & Co. and Friedman Billings Ramsey.

In recent years public confidence in the integrity of the IPO process has eroded significantly. Investigations have revealed that certain underwriters of IPOs have engaged in misconduct contrary to the best interests of investors and the markets. Among the most

1. We discuss the users and suppliers of funds in more detail in Chapter 2.

FIGURE 1–1 Primary and Secondary Market Transfer of Funds Time Line

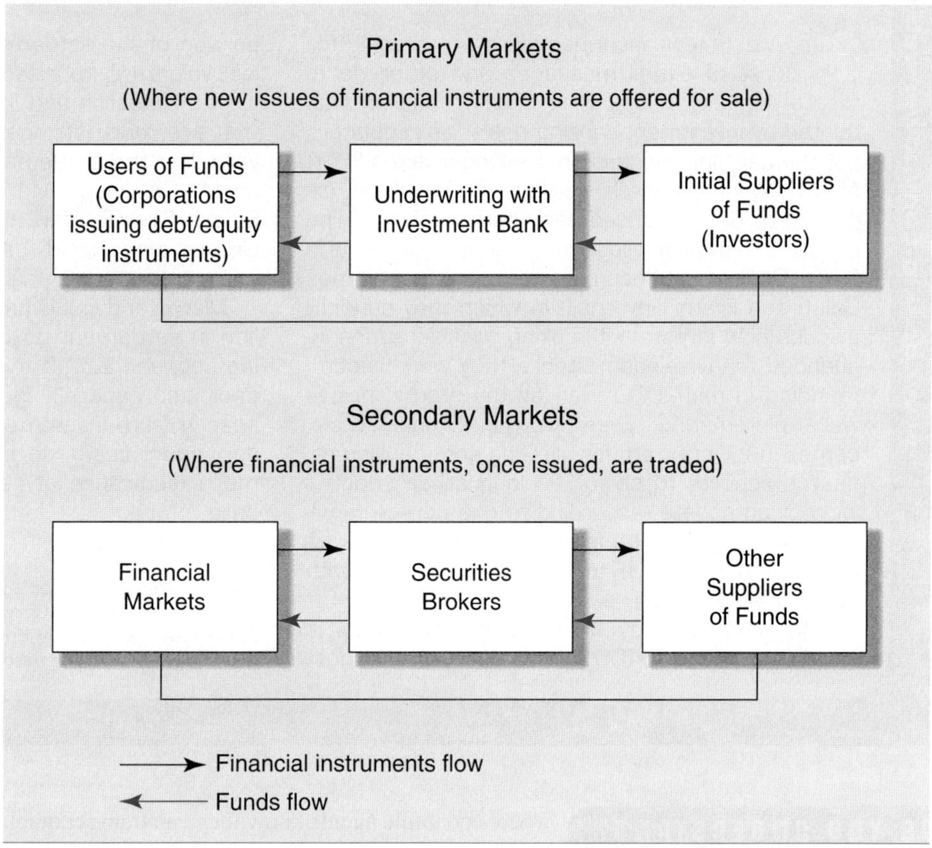

harmful practices that have given rise to public concerns are "spinning" (in which certain underwriters allocate "hot" IPO issues to directors and/or executives of potential investment banking clients in exchange for investment banking business) and "biased" recommendations by research analysts whose compensation is tied to the success of their firms' investment banking business. This culminated in the spring of 2003 with an agreement between securities regulators and 10 of the nation's largest securities firms, in which they agreed to pay a record \$1.4 billion in penalties to settle charges involving investor abuses (see the Ethical Debates box). The settlement centered on civil charges that securities firms routinely issued overly optimistic stock research to investors to gain favor with corporate clients and win their investment banking business. The agreement also settled charges that some major firms improperly allocated IPO shares to corporate executives to win investment banking business from their firms. The agreement has forced brokerage companies to make structural changes in the way they handle research—preventing, for example, analysts from attending certain meetings relating to investment banking.[2]

Secondary Markets. Once financial instruments such as stocks are issued in primary markets, they are then traded—that is, rebought and resold—in secondary markets. For example, on August 6, 2004, 10.9 million shares of ExxonMobil were traded in the secondary stock market. Buyers of secondary market securities are economic agents (consumers, businesses, and governments) with excess funds. Sellers of secondary market financial instruments are economic agents in need of funds. Secondary markets provide a centralized marketplace

2. Within days of this agreement, however, Bears Stearns, one of the 10 firms involved in the settlement, was accused of using its analysts to promote a new stock offering.

www.doskin.com/powerweb

Street Braces for Revelations in Settlement

Ten Wall Street securities firms are bracing for a burst of e-mail messages and other documents suggesting that their stock research was tainted by investment-banking goals, as regulators put the finishing touches on the long-awaited $1.4 billion global research settlement, which is expected to be announced early next week . . . The pact's firm-by-firm allegations will include e-mails from Goldman telecom-sector analysts James Golob and Frank Governali, in which they candidly discuss how investment-banking considerations influenced many telecom stocks they were recommending in mid-2000 even as the stocks' prices were plummeting. Even Morgan Stanley . . . comes in for criticism for allowing some bullish research reports to sit for as long as six months without an update, according to one person familiar with the pact. The findings on Lehman will focus on four or five individuals, including both analysts and managers . . .

The Smith Barney unit of Citigroup, which is slated to pay a $400 million fine, the largest portion of the settlement, is expected to be subject voluntarily to a separate set of rules separating its research and investment-banking activities that are more stringent than for other firms involved in the settlement. Three firms paying the most—Citigroup, Merrill Lynch and the Credit Suisse First Boston (CFSB) unit of Credit Suisse Group—also could be hit with securities-fraud charges.

Merrill and CSFB have agreed to pay $200 million in settlement payment. Other firms are paying between $37.5 million and $125 million. The pact also generally includes rules separating research from investment banking; provision of independent research for individual investors; and more disclosure of research ratings and other data . . .

Source: *The Wall Street Journal*, April 25, 2003, p. C1, by Randall Smith, Susanne Craig, and Charles Gasparino. Reprinted by permission of *The Wall Street Journal*. **www.wsj.com**

DO YOU UNDERSTAND?

1. What allegations were made by regulators against Wall Street securities firms with respect to illegal activities associated with securities underwriting?
2. What fines were assessed against the largest investment banking firms?

where economic agents know they can transact quickly and efficiently. These markets therefore save economic agents the search and other costs of seeking buyers or sellers on their own. Figure 1–1 illustrates a secondary market transfer of funds. When an economic agent buys a financial instrument in a secondary market, funds are exchanged, usually with the help of a securities broker such as Schwab acting as an intermediary between the buyer and the seller of the instrument (see Chapter 9). The original issuer of the instrument (user of funds) is not involved in this transfer. The New York Stock Exchange (NYSE), the American Stock Exchange (AMEX), and the National Association of Securities Dealers Automated Quotation (NASDAQ)[3] system are three well-known examples of secondary markets for trading stocks.[4] We discuss the details of each of these markets in Chapter 9. In addition to stocks and bonds, secondary markets also exist for financial instruments backed by mortgages and other assets (see Chapter 7), foreign exchange (see Chapter 8), and futures and options [i.e., **derivative securities**—financial securities whose payoffs are linked to other, previously issued (or underlying) primary securities (see Chapter 10)]. As we will see in Chapter 10, derivative securities have existed for centuries, but the growth in derivative securities markets occurred mainly in the 1970s, 1980s, and 1990s. As major markets, therefore, the derivative securities markets are among the newest of the financial security markets.

derivative security

A financial security whose payoffs are linked to other, previously issued securities.

secondary market

A market that trades financial instruments once they are issued.

Secondary markets offer benefits to both investors (suppliers of funds) and issuing corporations (users of funds). For investors, secondary markets provide the opportunity to trade securities at their market values quickly as well as to purchase securities with

3. On October 30, 1998, the National Association of Securities Dealers, Inc. (NASD), the world's first electronic stock market, and the American Stock Exchange (AMEX), the nation's second largest floor-based exchange, merged to form the Nasdaq-Amex Market Group. Due to a clash of cultures between the two institutions, the merger was dissolved after just one year.

4. Most bonds are not traded on floor-based exchanges. Rather, FIs trade them over the counter (OTC) using telephone and computer networks (see Chapter 6). For example, less than 1 percent of corporate bonds outstanding are traded on organized exchanges such as the NYSE.

varying risk-return characteristics (see Chapter 2). Corporate security issuers are not directly involved in the transfer of funds or instruments in the secondary market. However, the issuer does obtain information about the current market value of its financial instruments, and thus the value of the corporation as perceived by investors such as its stockholders, through tracking the prices at which its financial instruments are being traded on secondary markets. This price information allows issuers to evaluate how well they are using the funds generated from the financial instruments they have already issued and provides information on how well any subsequent offerings of debt or equity might do in terms of raising additional money (and at what cost).

Trading volume in secondary markets can be large. In the mid-1980s, a NYSE trading day involving 250 million shares was considered to be heavy. In the early 2000s this level of trading was considered quite light. For example, on October 28, 1997, NYSE trading volume exceeded 1 billion shares for the first time ever and trading of this magnitude has occurred several times since. Indeed, on July 24, 2002, trading volume topped 2.8 billion shares, the highest level to date.

Secondary markets offer buyers and sellers liquidity—the ability to turn an asset into cash quickly—as well as information about the prices or the value of their investments. Increased liquidity makes it more desirable and easier for the issuing firm to sell a security initially in the primary market. Further, the existence of centralized markets for buying and selling financial instruments allows investors to trade these instruments at low transaction costs.

Money Markets versus Capital Markets

Money Markets. **Money markets** are markets that trade debt securities or instruments with maturities of one year or less (see Figure 1–2). In the money markets, economic agents with short-term excess supplies of funds can lend funds (i.e., buy money market instruments) to economic agents who have short-term needs or shortages of funds (i.e., they sell money market instruments). The short-term nature of these instruments means that fluctuations in their prices in the secondary markets in which they trade are usually quite small (see Chapters 3 and 19 on interest rate risk). In the United States, money markets do not operate in a specific location—rather, transactions occur via telephones, wire transfers, and computer trading. Thus, most U.S. money markets are said to be **over-the-counter (OTC) markets.**

money markets

Markets that trade debt securities or instruments with maturities of less than one year.

over-the-counter markets

Markets that do not operate in a specific fixed location—rather, transactions occur via telephones, wire transfers, and computer trading.

Money Market Instruments. A variety of money market securities are issued by corporations and government units to obtain short-term funds. These securities include Treasury bills, federal funds, repurchase agreements, commercial paper, negotiable certificates of deposit, and banker's acceptances. Figure 1–3 shows outstanding amounts of money market instruments in the United States in 1990, 2000, and 2004. Notice that in 2004 federal funds and repurchase agreements followed by commercial paper, negotiable CDs, and Treasury bills, had the largest amounts outstanding. Money market instruments and the operation of the money markets are described and discussed in detail in Chapter 5.

Capital Markets. **Capital markets** are markets that trade equity (stocks) and debt (bonds) instruments with maturities of more than one year (see Figure 1–2). The major suppliers of capital market securities (or users of funds) are corporations and governments.

capital markets

Markets that trade debt (bonds) and equity (stocks) instruments with maturities of more than one year.

FIGURE 1–2 Money versus Capital Market Maturities

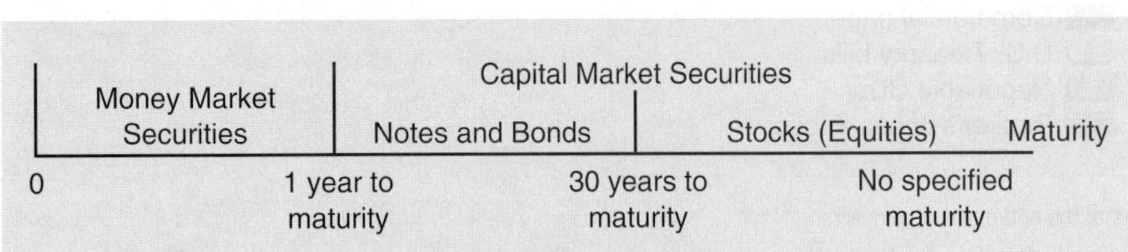

SEARCH THE SITE

Go to the Board of Governors of the Federal Reserve Web site and find the latest information on money market and capital market instruments outstanding.

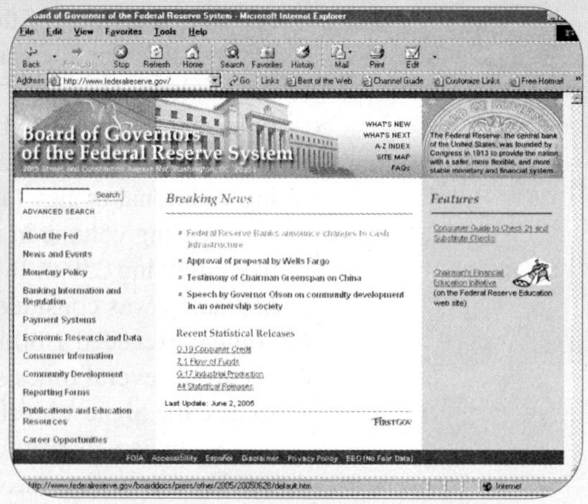

Go to the Federal Reserve Web site at **www.federalreserve.gov**

Click on "Economic Research and Data"

Click on "Statistics: Releases and Historical Data"

Click on "Quarterly Releases: Flow of Funds Accounts of the United States: Releases"

Click on "Current release"

Click on "Level tables"

This will bring up the relevant tables. For example, federal funds and security repurchase agreements are listed in Table L.207; Commercial paper and bankers' acceptances are listed in Table L.208.

Questions

1. What is the most recent dollar value of commercial paper, banker's acceptances, and federal funds and repurchase agreements outstanding?
2. What is the percentage change in each of these since 1990? Since 2004?

FIGURE 1–3 **Money Market Instruments Outstanding**

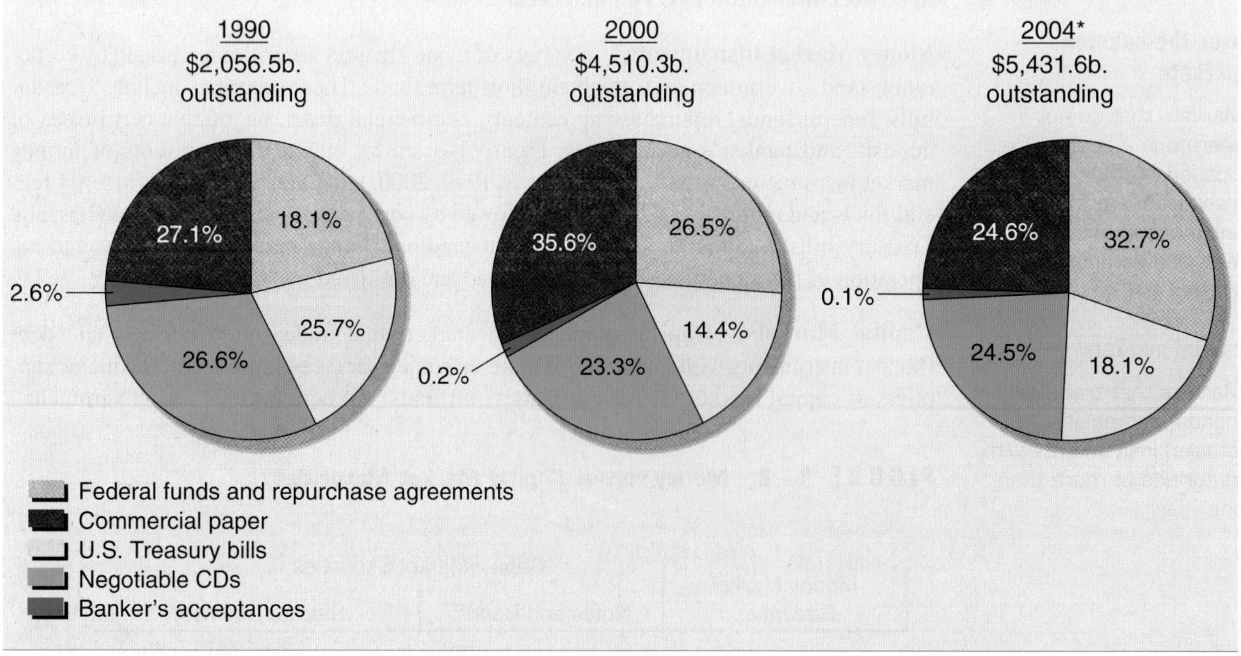

*As of the end of the first quarter.

Source: Federal Reserve Board, "Flow of Fund Accounts," *Statistical Releases,* Washington, DC, various issues. **www.federalreserve.gov**

FIGURE 1–4 Capital Market Instruments Outstanding

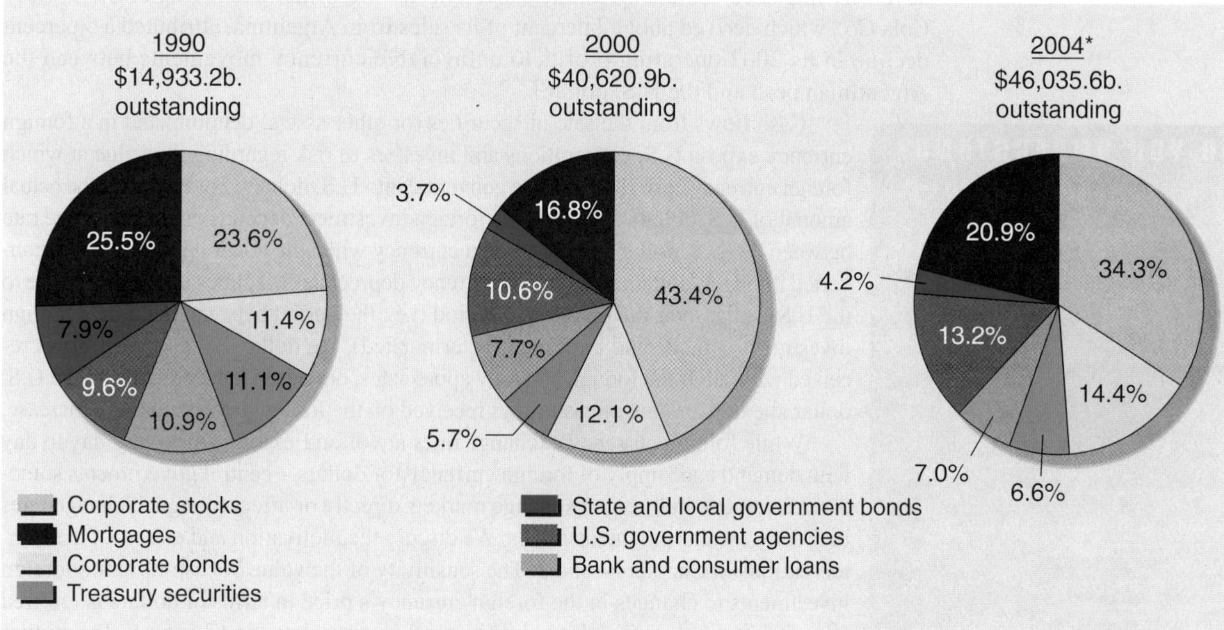

*As of the end of the first quarter.

Source: Federal Reserve Board, "Flow of Fund Accounts," *Statistical Releases,* Washington, DC, various issues. **www.federalreserve.gov**

Households are the major suppliers of funds for these securities. Given their longer maturity, these instruments experience wider price fluctuations in the secondary markets in which they trade than do money market instruments.[5] For example, all else constant, long-term maturity debt instruments experience wider price fluctuations for a given change in interest rates than short-term maturity debt instruments (see Chapter 3).

Capital Market Instruments. Figure 1–4 shows the major capital market instruments and their outstanding amounts by dollar market value. Notice that corporate stocks or equities represent the largest capital market instrument, followed by securitized mortgages and corporate bonds. Securitized mortgages are those mortgages that FIs have packaged together and sold as bonds backed by mortgage cash flows (such as interest and principal repayments—see Chapters 7 and 24). The relative size of the market value of capital market instruments outstanding depends on two factors: number of securities issued and their market prices.[6] One reason for the sharp increase in the value of equities outstanding is the bull market in stock prices in the 1990s. Values have fallen since 2000 as the U.S. economy experienced a downturn and stock prices fell. Capital market instruments and their operations are discussed in detail in Chapters 6, 7, and 9.

Foreign Exchange Markets

3

In addition to understanding the operations of domestic financial markets, a financial manager must also understand the operations of foreign exchange markets and foreign capital markets. Today's U.S.-based companies operate globally. It is therefore essential that financial managers understand how events and movements in financial markets in other countries affect the profitability and performance of their

5. For example, their longer maturities subject these instruments to both higher credit (or bankruptcy) risk and interest rate risk than money market instruments.

6. For example, the market value of equity is the product of the price of the equity times the number of shares that are issued.

own companies. For example, a currency and economic crisis in Argentina in late 2001 adversely impacted some U.S. markets and firms in the winter and spring of 2002. Coca Cola Co., which derived about 2 percent of its sales from Argentina, attributed a 5 percent decline in its 2002 operating profits to unfavorable currency movements between the Argentinian peso and the U.S. dollar.[7]

Cash flows from the sale of securities (or other assets) denominated in a foreign currency expose U.S. corporations and investors to risk regarding the value at which foreign currency cash flows can be converted into U.S. dollars. For example, the actual amount of U.S. dollars received on a foreign investment depends on the exchange rate between the U.S. dollar and the foreign currency when the nondollar cash flow is converted into U.S. dollars. If a foreign currency depreciates (declines in value) relative to the U.S. dollar over the investment period (i.e., the period between the time a foreign investment is made and the time it is terminated), the dollar value of cash flows received will fall. If the foreign currency appreciates, or rises in value, relative to the U.S. dollar, the dollar value of cash flows received on the foreign investment will increase.

While foreign currency exchange rates are often flexible—they vary day to day with demand and supply of foreign currency for dollars—central governments sometimes intervene in foreign exchange markets directly or affect foreign exchange rates indirectly by altering interest rates. We discuss the motivation and effects of these interventions in Chapters 4 and 8. The sensitivity of the value of cash flows on foreign investments to changes in the foreign currency's price in terms of dollars is referred to as *foreign exchange risk* and is discussed in more detail in Chapter 8. Techniques for managing, or "hedging," foreign exchange risk, such as using derivative securities such as foreign exchange (FX) futures, options, and swaps, are discussed in Chapter 23.

DO YOU UNDERSTAND?

1. The difference between primary and secondary markets?
2. The major distinction between money markets and capital markets?
3. What the major instruments traded in the capital markets are?
4. What happens to the dollar value of a U.S. investor's holding of British pounds if the pound appreciates (rises) in value against the dollar?
5. What are derivative security markets?

Derivative Security Markets

Derivative security markets are the markets in which derivative securities trade. A **derivative security** is a financial security (such as a futures contract, option contract, or swap contract) whose payoff is linked to another, previously issued security such as a security traded in the capital or foreign exchange markets. Derivative securities generally involve an agreement between two parties to exchange a standard quantity of an asset or cash flow at a predetermined price and at a specified date in the future. As the value of the underlying security to be exchanged changes, the value of the derivative security changes. While derivative securities have been in existence for centuries, the growth in derivative security markets occurred mainly in the 1970s, 1980s, and 1990s. As major markets, therefore, the derivative security markets are the newest of the financial security markets. We discuss the tremendous growth of derivative security activity in Chapter 10. Derivative security traders can be either users of derivative contracts for hedging (see Chapters 10 and 23) and other purposes or dealers (such as banks) that act as counterparties in trades with customers for a fee.

derivative security markets

The markets in which derivative securities trade.

derivative security

An agreement between two parties to exchange a standard quantity of an asset at a predetermined price on a specified date in the future.

Financial Market Regulation

www.sec.gov

Financial instruments are subject to regulations imposed by regulatory agencies such as the Securities and Exchange Commission (SEC)—the main regulator of securities markets since the passage of the Securities Act of 1934—as well as the exchanges (if any) on which the instruments are traded. For example, the main emphasis of SEC regulations (as stated in the Securities Act of 1933) is on full and fair disclosure of information on securities issues to actual and potential investors. Those firms planning to issue new stocks or bonds to be sold to the public at large (public issues) are required by the SEC to register their securities with the SEC and to fully describe the issue, and any risks associated with the issue, in a legal document called a prospectus.[8] The SEC also monitors trading on the

7. See "U.S. Firms Assess Damage in Argentina," *The Wall Street Journal*, January 9, 2002, p. A10.

8. Those issues not offered to the public at large but rather sold to a few large investors are called private placements and are not subject to SEC regulations (see Chapter 6).

major exchanges (along with the exchanges themselves) to ensure that stockholders and managers do not trade on the basis of inside information about their own firms (i.e., information prior to its public release). SEC regulations are not intended to protect investors against poor investment choices but rather to ensure that investors have full and accurate information available about corporate issuers when making their investment decisions. The SEC has also imposed regulations on financial markets in an effort to reduce excessive price fluctuations. For example, the NYSE operates under a series of "circuit breakers" that require the market to shut down for a period of time when prices drop by large amounts during any trading day. The details of these circuit breaker regulations are listed in Chapter 9.

www.nyse.com

5 OVERVIEW OF FINANCIAL INSTITUTIONS

Financial institutions (e.g., commercial and savings banks, credit unions, insurance companies, mutual funds) perform the essential function of channeling funds from those with surplus funds (suppliers of funds) to those with shortages of funds (users of funds). Chapters 11 through 18 discuss the various types of FIs in today's economy, including (1) the size, structure, and composition of each type of FI, (2) their balance sheets and recent trends, (3) FI performance, and (4) the regulators who oversee each type of FI. Table 1–2 lists and summarizes the FIs discussed in detail in later chapters.

financial institutions

Institutions that perform the essential function of channeling funds from those with surplus funds to those with shortages of funds.

In Table 1–3, we show the changing shares of total assets of FIs in the United States from 1860 to 2004. A number of important trends are clearly evident; most apparent is the decline in the total share of depository institutions—commercial banks and thrifts—since World War II. Specifically, while still the dominant sector of the financial institutions

TABLE 1–2 Types of Financial Institutions

Commercial banks—depository institutions whose major assets are loans and whose major liabilities are deposits. Commercial banks' loans are broader in range, including consumer, commercial, and real estate loans, than are those of other depository institutions. Commercial banks' liabilities include more nondeposit sources of funds, such as subordinate notes and debentures, than do those of other depository institutions.

Thrifts—depository institutions in the form of savings associations, savings banks, and credit unions. Thrifts generally perform services similar to commercial banks, but they tend to concentrate their loans in one segment, such as real estate loans or consumer loans.

Insurance companies—financial institutions that protect individuals and corporations (policyholders) from adverse events. Life insurance companies provide protection in the event of untimely death, illness, and retirement. Property casualty insurance protects against personal injury and liability due to accidents, theft, fire, and so on.

Securities firms and investment banks—financial institutions that underwrite securities and engage in related activities such as securities brokerage, securities trading, and making a market in which securities can trade.

Finance companies—financial intermediaries that make loans to both individuals and businesses. Unlike depository institutions, finance companies do not accept deposits but instead rely on short- and long-term debt for funding.

Mutual funds—financial institutions that pool financial resources of individuals and companies and invest those resources in diversified portfolios of asset.

Pension funds—financial institutions that offer savings plans through which fund participants accumulate savings during their working years before withdrawing them during their retirement years. Funds originally invested in and accumulated in a pension fund are exempt from current taxation.

TABLE 1-3 Percentage Shares of Assets of Financial Institutions in the United States, 1860–2004

	1860	1880	1900	1912	1922	1929	1939	1948	1960	1970	1980	1990	2000	2004†
Commercial banks	71.4%	60.6%	62.9%	64.5%	63.3%	53.7%	51.2%	55.9%	38.2%	37.9%	34.8%	36.8%	35.7%	35.3%
Thrift institutions	17.8	22.8	18.2	14.8	13.9	14.0	13.6	12.3	19.7	20.4	21.4	16.5	10.0	10.6
Insurance companies	10.7	13.9	13.8	16.6	16.7	18.6	27.2	24.3	23.8	18.9	16.1	18.2	16.8	17.6
Investment companies	—	—	—	—	0.0	2.4	1.9	1.3	2.9	3.5	3.6	9.5	17.0	17.0
Pension funds	—	—	0.0	0.0	0.0	0.7	2.1	3.1	9.7	13.0	17.4	11.2	10.7	9.1
Finance companies	—	0.0	0.0	0.0	0.0	2.0	2.2	2.0	4.6	4.8	5.1	5.8	5.8	5.5
Securities brokers and dealers	0.0	0.0	3.8	3.0	5.3	8.1	1.5	1.0	1.1	1.2	1.1	1.3	3.6	4.2
Mortgage companies	0.0	2.7	1.3	1.2	0.8	0.6	0.3	0.1	*	*	0.4	0.6	0.2	0.2
Real estate investment trusts	—	—	—	—	—	—	—	—	0.0	0.3	0.1	0.1	0.2	0.5
Total (percent)	100.0%	100.0%	100.0%	100.0%	100.0%	100.0%	100.0%	100.0%	100.0%	100.0%	100.0%	100.0%	100.0%	100.0%
Total (trillion dollars)	.001	.005	.016	.034	.075	.123	.129	.281	.596	1.328	4.025	8.122	14.650	17.936

Columns may not add to 100% due to rounding.

*Data not available.

†As of June 2004.

Source: Randall Kroszner, "The Evolution of Universal Banking and Its Regulation in Twentieth Century America," in *Universal Banking Financial System Design Reconsidered*, ed. Anthony Saunders and Ingo Walter (Burr Ridge, IL: Irwin, 1996); and Federal Reserve Board, "Flow of Funds Accounts," *Statistical Releases*, various issues. **www.federalreserve.gov**

FIGURE 1–5 Flow of Funds in a World without FIs

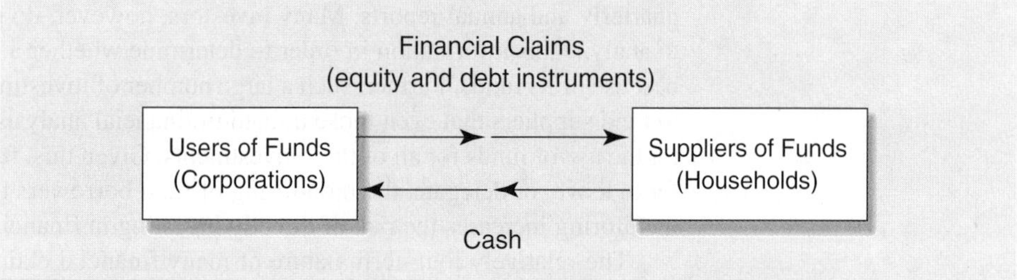

industry, the share of commercial banks declined from 55.9 to 35.3 percent between 1948 and 2004, as the share of thrifts (savings banks, savings associations, and credit unions) fell from 12.3 to 10.6 percent over the same period.[9] Similarly, insurance companies also witnessed a decline in their share, from 24.3 to 17.6 percent. The most dramatic trend involves the increasing share of pension funds and investment companies. Pension funds (private plus state and local) increased their asset share from 3.1 to 9.1 percent, while investment companies (mutual funds and money market mutual funds) increased their share from 1.3 to 17.0 percent over the 1948 to 2004 period.

To understand the important economic function FIs play in the operation of financial markets, imagine a simple world in which FIs did not exist. In such a world, suppliers of funds (e.g., households), generating excess savings by consuming less than they earn, would have a basic choice: They could either hold cash as an asset or directly invest that cash in the securities issued by users of funds (e.g., corporations or households). In general, users of funds issue financial claims (e.g., equity and debt securities) to finance the gap between their investment expenditures and their internally generated savings such as retained earnings. As shown in Figure 1–5, in such a world we have a **direct transfer** of funds (money) from suppliers of funds to users of funds. In return, financial claims would flow directly from users of funds to suppliers of funds.

direct transfer

A corporation sells its stock or debt directly to investors without going through a financial institution.

In this economy without FIs, the level of funds flowing between suppliers of funds (who want to maximize the return on their funds subject to risk) and users of funds (who want to minimize their cost of borrowing subject to risk) through financial markets is likely to be quite low. There are several reasons for this. Once they have lent money in exchange for financial claims, suppliers of funds need to monitor continuously the use of their funds. They must be sure that the user of funds neither steals the funds outright nor wastes the funds on projects that have low or negative returns, since this would lower the chances of being repaid and/or earning a positive return on their investment (such as through the receipt of dividends or interest). Such monitoring is often extremely costly for any given fund supplier because it requires considerable time, expense, and effort to collect this information relative to the size of the average fund supplier's investment.[10]

9. Although commercial bank assets as a percentage of total assets in the financial sector may have declined in recent years, this does not necessarily mean that banking activity has decreased. Indeed, off-balance-sheet activities have replaced some of the more traditional on-balance-sheet activities of commercial banks (see Chapter 12). Further, as is discussed in Part Three of the text, banks are increasingly providing services (such as securities underwriting, insurance underwriting and sales, and mutual fund services) previously performed exclusively by other FIs.

10. Failure to monitor exposes fund suppliers to "agency costs," that is, the risk that the fund users will take actions with the fund supplier's money contrary to the promises contained in the financing agreement. Monitoring costs are part of overall agency costs. That is, agency costs arise whenever economic agents enter into contracts in a world of asymmetric or incomplete information and thus information collection is costly. The more difficult and costly it is to collect information, the more likely it is that contracts will be broken. In this case the fund suppliers could be harmed by the actions taken by the fund users. As discussed below, one solution to this agency problem is for a large number of fund suppliers to place their funds with a single FI who acts as a "delegated" monitor.

As mentioned earlier, the SEC requires and monitors the full and fair disclosure of information on securities to actual or potential investors (suppliers of funds)—such as in quarterly and annual reports. Many investors, however, do not have the financial training to analyze this information in order to determine whether a securities issuer is making the best use of its funds. Further, such a large number of investment opportunities are available to fund suppliers that even those trained in financial analysis rarely have the time to monitor the use of funds for all of their investments. Given this, fund suppliers would likely prefer to leave, or delegate, the monitoring of fund borrowers to others. The resulting lack of monitoring increases the risk of directly investing in financial claims.

liquidity

The ease with which an asset can be converted into cash.

price risk

The risk that an asset's sale price will be lower than its purchase price.

The relatively long-term nature of many financial claims (e.g., mortgages, corporate stock, and bonds) creates a second disincentive for suppliers of funds to hold the direct financial claims issued by users of funds. Specifically, given the choice between holding cash and long-term securities, fund suppliers may well choose to hold cash for **liquidity** reasons, especially if they plan to use their savings to finance consumption expenditures in the near future and financial markets are not very developed, or deep, in terms of the number of active buyers and sellers in the market. Moreover, even though real-world financial markets provide some liquidity services, by allowing fund suppliers to trade financial securities among themselves, fund suppliers face a **price risk** upon the sale of securities. In addition, the secondary market trading of securities involves various transaction costs. The price at which investors can sell a security on secondary markets such as the New York Stock Exchange (NYSE) may well differ from the price they initially paid for the security either because investors change their valuation of the security between the time it was bought and when it was sold and/or because dealers, acting as intermediaries between buyers and sellers, charge transaction costs for completing a trade.[11]

Unique Economic Functions Performed by Financial Institutions

Because of (1) monitoring costs, (2) liquidity costs, and (3) price risk, the average investor may view direct investment in financial claims and markets as an unattractive proposition and prefer to hold cash. As a result financial market activity (and therefore savings and investment) would likely remain quite low.

indirect transfer

A transfer of funds between suppliers and users of funds through a financial intermediary.

However, the financial system has developed an alternative and indirect way for investors (or fund suppliers) to channel funds to users of funds.[12] This is the **indirect transfer** of funds to the ultimate user of funds via FIs. Due to the costs of monitoring, liquidity risk, and price risk, as well as for other reasons explained later, fund suppliers often prefer to hold the financial claims issued by FIs rather than those directly issued by the ultimate users of funds. Consider Figure 1–6, which is a closer representation than Figure 1–5 of the world in which we live and the way funds flow in the U.S. financial system. Notice how financial intermediaries or institutions are standing, or intermediating between, the suppliers and users of funds—that is, channeling funds from ultimate suppliers to ultimate users of funds.

6

How can an FI reduce the monitoring costs, liquidity risks, and price risks facing the suppliers of funds compared to when they directly invest in financial claims? We look at how FIs resolve these cost and risk issues next and summarize them in Table 1–4.

Monitoring Costs. As mentioned above, a supplier of funds who directly invests in a fund user's financial claims faces a high cost of monitoring the fund user's actions in a timely and complete fashion. One solution to this problem is for a large number of small investors to group their funds together by holding the claims issued by an FI. In turn the FI

11. On organized exchanges such as the NYSE, the price difference between a buy and sell price is called the bid-ask spread.

12. We describe and illustrate this flow of funds in Chapter 2.

FIGURE 1–6 **Flow of Funds in a World with FIs**

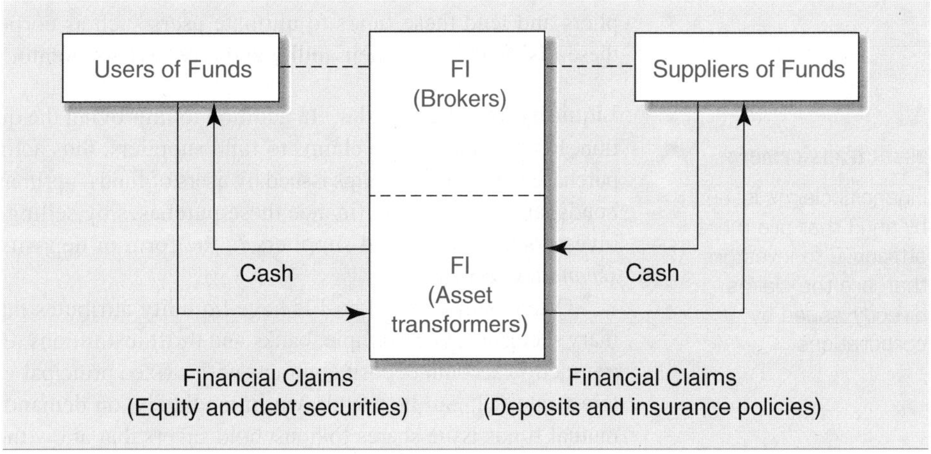

invests in the direct financial claims issued by fund users. This aggregation of funds by fund suppliers in an FI resolves a number of problems. First, the "large" FI now has a much greater incentive to hire employees with superior skills and training in monitoring and who will use this expertise to collect information and monitor the ultimate fund user's actions because the FI has far more at stake than any small individual fund supplier. Second, the monitoring function performed by the FI alleviates the "free-rider" problem that exists when small fund suppliers leave it to each other to collect information and monitor a fund user. In an economic sense, fund suppliers have appointed the FI as a **delegated monitor** to act on their behalf. For example, full-service securities firms such as Morgan Stanley

delegated monitor

An economic agent appointed to act on behalf of smaller investors in collecting information and/or investing funds on their behalf.

TABLE 1–4 **Services Performed by Financial Intermediaries**

Services Benefiting Suppliers of Funds

Monitoring Costs—Aggregation of funds in an FI provides greater incentive to collect a firm's information and monitor actions. The relatively large size of the FI allows this collection of information to be accomplished at a lower average cost (economies of scale).

Liquidity and Price Risk—FIs provide financial claims to household savers with superior liquidity attributes and with lower price risk.

Transaction Cost Services—Similar to economies of scale in information production costs, an FI's size can result in economies of scale in transaction costs.

Maturity Intermediation—FIs can better bear the risk of mismatching the maturities of their assets and liabilities.

Denomination Intermediation—FIs such as mutual funds allow small investors to overcome constraints to buying assets imposed by large minimum denomination size.

Services Benefiting the Overall Economy

Money Supply Transmission—Depository institutions are the conduit through which monetary policy actions impact the rest of the financial system and the economy in general.

Credit Allocation—FIs are often viewed as the major, and sometimes only, source of financing for a particular sector of the economy, such as farming and residential real estate.

Intergenerational Wealth Transfers—FIs, especially life insurance companies and pension funds, provide savers with the ability to transfer wealth from one generation to the next.

Payment Services—Efficiency with which depository institutions provide payment services directly benefits the economy.

carry out investment research on new issues and make investment recommendations for their retail clients (or investors), while commercial banks collect deposits from fund suppliers and lend these funds to ultimate users such as corporations. An important part of these FIs' functions is their ability and incentive to monitor ultimate fund users.

asset transformers

Financial claims issued by an FI that are more attractive to investors than are the claims directly issued by corporations.

Liquidity and Price Risk. In addition to improving the quality and quantity of information, FIs provide further claims to fund suppliers, thus acting as **asset transformers.** FIs purchase the financial claims issued by users of funds—primary securities such as mortgages, bonds, and stocks—and finance these purchases by selling financial claims to household investors and other fund suppliers in the form of deposits, insurance policies, or other *secondary securities.*

Often claims issued by FIs have liquidity attributes that are superior to those of primary securities. For example, banks and thrift institutions (e.g., savings associations) issue transaction account deposit contracts with a fixed principal value and often a guaranteed interest rate that can be withdrawn immediately, on demand, by investors. Money market mutual funds issue shares to household savers that allow them to enjoy almost fixed principal (depositlike) contracts while earning higher interest rates than on bank deposits, and that can be withdrawn immediately by writing a check. Even life insurance companies allow policyholders to borrow against their policies held with the company at very short notice. How can FIs such as depository institutions offer highly liquid, low price-risk securities to fund suppliers on the liability side of their balance sheets while investing in relatively less liquid and higher price-risk securities—such as the debt and equity—issued by fund users on the asset side? Furthermore, how can FIs be confident enough to guarantee that they can provide liquidity services to fund suppliers when they themselves invest in risky assets? Indeed, why should fund suppliers believe FIs' promises regarding the liquidity and safety of their investments?

diversify

The ability of an economic agent to reduce risk by holding a number of securities in a portfolio.

The answers to these three questions lie in FIs' ability to **diversify** away some, but not all, of their investment risk. The concept of diversification is familiar to all students of finance. Basically, as long as the returns on different investments are not perfectly positively correlated, by spreading their investments across a number of assets, FIs can diversify away significant amounts of their portfolio risk. (We discuss the mechanics of diversification in the loan portfolio in Chapter 20.) Indeed, experiments in the United States and the United Kingdom have shown that diversifying across just 15 securities can bring significant diversification benefits to FIs and portfolio managers.[13] Further, for equal investments in different securities, as the number of securities in an FI's asset portfolio increases, portfolio risk falls, albeit at a diminishing rate. What is really going on here is that FIs can exploit the law of large numbers in making their investment decisions, whereas because of their smaller wealth size, individual fund suppliers are constrained to holding relatively undiversified portfolios. As a result, diversification allows an FI to predict more accurately its expected return and risk on its investment portfolio so that it can credibly fulfill its promises to the suppliers of funds to provide highly liquid claims with little price risk. A good example of this is a bank's ability to offer highly liquid, instantly withdrawable demand deposits as liabilities while investing in risky, nontradable, and often illiquid loans as assets. As long as an FI is large enough to gain from diversification and monitoring on the asset side of its balance sheet, its financial claims (its liabilities) are likely to be viewed as liquid and attractive to small savers—especially when compared to direct investments in the capital market.

Additional Benefits FIs Provide to Suppliers of Funds

The indirect investing of funds through FIs is attractive to fund suppliers for other reasons as well. We discuss these below and summarize them in Table 1–4.

13. For a review of such studies, see E. J. Elton and M. J. Gruber, *Modern Portfolio Theory and Investment Analysis*, 6th ed. (New York: John Wiley & Sons, 1998), Chapter 2.

Reduced Transaction Cost. Not only do FIs have a greater incentive to collect information, but also their average cost of collecting relevant information is lower than for the individual investor (i.e., information collection enjoys **economies of scale**). For example, the cost to a small investor of buying a $100 broker's report may seem inordinately high for a $10,000 investment. For an FI with $10 billion of assets under management, however, the cost seems trivial. Such economies of scale of information production and collection tend to enhance the advantages to investors of investing via FIs rather than directly investing themselves.

economies of scale

The concept that cost reduction in trading and other transaction services results from increased efficiency when FIs perform these services.

Nevertheless, as a result of technological advances, the costs of direct access to financial markets by savers are ever falling and the relative benefits to the individual savers of investing through FIs are narrowing. An example is the ability to reduce transactions costs with an **etrade** on the Internet rather than use a traditional stockbroker and paying brokerage fees (see Chapter 9). Another example is the private placement market, in which corporations such as General Electric sell securities directly to investors often without using underwriters. In addition, a number of companies allow investors to buy their stock directly without using a broker. Among well-known companies that have instituted such stock purchase plans are AT&T, Microsoft, Marathon Oil, IBM, Walt Disney Co., and Tribune Co., a Chicago-based entertainment and media company.

etrade

Buying and selling shares on the Internet.

Maturity Intermediation. An additional dimension of FIs' ability to reduce risk by diversification is their greater ability to bear the risk of mismatching the maturities of their assets and liabilities than can small savers. Thus, FIs offer maturity intermediation services to the rest of the economy. Specifically, by maturity mismatching, FIs can produce new types of contracts such as long-term mortgage loans to households, while still raising funds with short-term liability contracts such as deposits. In addition, although such mismatches can subject an FI to interest rate risk (see Chapters 3 and 19), a large FI is better able than a small investor to manage this risk through its superior access to markets and instruments for hedging the risks of such loans (see Chapters 7, 10, 20, and 24).

Denomination Intermediation. Some FIs, especially mutual funds, perform a unique service because they provide services relating to denomination intermediation. Because many assets are sold in very large denominations, they are either out of reach of individual savers or would result in savers holding very undiversified asset portfolios. For example, the minimum size of a negotiable CD is $100,000, while commercial paper (short-term corporate debt) is often sold in minimum packages of $250,000 or more. Individual small savers may be unable to purchase such instruments directly. However, by buying shares in a mutual fund with other small investors, small savers overcome constraints to buying assets imposed by large minimum denomination size. Such indirect access to these markets may allow small savers to generate higher returns (and lower risks) on their portfolios as well.

Economic Functions FIs Provide to the Financial System as a Whole

In addition to the services FIs provide to suppliers and users of funds in the financial markets, FIs perform services that improve the operation of the financial system as a whole. We discuss these next and summarize them in Table 1–4.

The Transmission of Monetary Policy. The highly liquid nature of bank and thrift deposits has resulted in their acceptance by the public as the most widely used medium of exchange in the economy. Indeed, at the core of the three most commonly used definitions of the money supply (see Chapter 4) are bank and/or thrift deposit contracts. Because deposits are a significant component of the money supply, which in turn directly impacts the rate of inflation, depository institutions—particularly commercial banks—play a key role in the *transmission of monetary policy* from the central bank (the Federal Reserve) to the rest of the economy (see Chapter 4 for a detailed discussion of how the Federal Reserve implements

www.federalreserve.gov

monetary policy through depository institutions).[14] Because depository institutions are instrumental in determining the size and growth of the money supply, depository institutions have been designated as the primary conduit through which monetary policy actions by the Federal Reserve impact the rest of the financial sector and the economy in general.

Credit Allocation. Additionally, FIs provide a unique service to the economy in that they are the major source of financing for particular sectors of the economy preidentified by society as being in special need of financing. For example, policymakers in the United States and a number of other countries such as the United Kingdom have identified *residential real estate* as needing special attention. This has enhanced the specialness of those FIs that most commonly service the needs of that sector. In the United States, savings associations and savings banks must emphasize mortgage lending. Sixty-five percent of their assets must be mortgage related for these thrifts to maintain their charter status (see Chapter 14). In a similar fashion, farming is an especially important area of the economy in terms of the overall social welfare of the population. Thus, the U.S. government has directly encouraged financial institutions to specialize in financing this area of activity through the creation of Federal Farm Credit Banks.[15]

DO YOU UNDERSTAND?

1. The three major reasons that suppliers of funds would not want to directly purchase securities?
2. What the asset transformation function of FIs is?
3. What delegated monitoring function FIs perform?
4. What the link is between asset diversification and the liquidity of deposit contracts?
5. What maturity intermediation is?
6. Why the need for denomination intermediation arises?
7. The two major sectors that society has identified as deserving special attention in credit allocation?
8. Why monetary policy is transmitted through the banking system?
9. The payment services that FIs perform?

Intergenerational Wealth Transfers or Time Intermediation. The ability of savers to transfer wealth from their youth to old age as well as across generations is also of great importance to a country's social well-being. Because of this, special taxation relief and other subsidy mechanisms encourage investments by savers in life insurance, annuities, and pension funds. For example, pension funds offer savings plans through which fund participants accumulate tax exempt savings during their working years before withdrawing them during their retirement years.

Payment Services. Depository institutions such as banks and thrifts are also special in that the efficiency with which they provide payment services directly benefits the economy. Two important payment services are check-clearing and wire transfer services. For example, on any given day, over $3 trillion of payments are directed through Fedwire and CHIPS, the two largest wholesale payment wire network systems in the United States. Any breakdowns in these systems would likely produce gridlock to the payment system, with resulting harmful effects to the economy.

Risks Incurred by Financial Institutions

As FIs perform the various services described above, they face many types of risk. Specifically, all FIs hold some assets that are potentially subject to default or credit risk (such as loans, stocks, and bonds). As FIs expand their services to non-U.S. customers or even domestic customers with business outside the United States, they are exposed to both foreign exchange risk and country or sovereign risk as well. Further, FIs tend to mismatch the maturities of their balance sheet assets and liabilities to a greater or lesser extent and are thus exposed to interest rate risk. If FIs actively trade these assets and liabilities rather than hold them for longer-term investments, they are further exposed to market risk or asset price risk. Increasingly, FIs hold contingent assets and liabilities off the balance sheet, which presents an additional risk called off-balance-sheet risk. Moreover, all FIs are exposed to some degree of liability withdrawal or liquidity risk, depending on the type of claims they have sold to liability holders. All FIs are exposed to technology

14. The Federal Reserve is the U.S. central bank charged with promoting economic growth in line with the economy's potential to expand, and in particular, stable prices.

15. The Farm Credit System was created by Congress in 1916 to provide American agriculture with a source of sound, dependable credit at low rates of interest.

TABLE 1–5 Risks Faced by Financial Institutions

1. **Credit Risk**—risk that promised cash flows from loans and securities held by FIs may not be paid in full.
2. **Foreign Exchange Risk**—risk that exchange rate changes can affect the value of an FI's assets and liabilities located abroad.
3. **Country or Sovereign Risk**—risk that repayments from foreign borrowers may be interrupted because of interference from foreign governments.
4. **Interest Rate Risk**—risk incurred by an FI when the maturities of its assets and liabilities are mismatched.
5. **Market Risk**—risk incurred in trading assets and liabilities due to changes in interest rates, exchange rates, and other asset prices.
6. **Off-Balance-Sheet Risk**—risk incurred by an FI as the result of activities related to contingent assets and liabilities.
7. **Liquidity Risk**—risk that a sudden surge in liability withdrawals may require an FI to liquidate assets in a very short period of time and at low prices.
8. **Technology Risk**—risk incurred by an FI when its technological investments do not produce anticipated cost savings.
9. **Operational Risk**—risk that existing technology or support systems may malfunction or break down.
10. **Insolvency Risk**—risk that an FI may not have enough capital to offset a sudden decline in the value of its assets.

risk and operational risk because the production of financial services requires the use of real resources and back-office support systems (labor and technology combined to provide services). Finally, the risk that an FI may not have enough capital reserves to offset a sudden loss incurred as a result of one or more of the risks they face creates insolvency risk for the FI.[16] Chapters 19 through 24 provide an analysis of how FIs measure and manage these risks. We summarize the various risks in Table 1–5.

Regulation of Financial Institutions

8

The preceding section showed that FIs provide various services to sectors of the economy. Failure to provide these services, or a breakdown in their efficient provision, can be costly to both the ultimate suppliers of funds and users of funds as well as to the economy overall. For example, bank failures may destroy household savings and at the same time restrict a firm's access to credit. Insurance company failures may leave household members totally exposed in old age to the cost of catastrophic illnesses and to sudden drops in income on retirement. In addition, individual FI failures may create doubts in savers' minds regarding the stability and solvency of FIs and the financial system in general and cause panics and even withdrawal runs on sound institutions. FIs are regulated in an attempt to prevent these types of market failures and the costs they would impose on the economy and society at large. Although regulation may be socially beneficial, it also imposes private costs, or a regulatory burden, on individual FI owners and managers. Consequently, regulation is an attempt to enhance the social welfare benefits and mitigate the costs of the provision of FI services.

While many regulations restrict competition among industry participants or restrict activities FIs may undertake, recent U.S. regulatory changes have been deregulatory in nature. That is, they have expanded the activities and degree of competition allowed to FIs. As a result, the traditional activities of various institutions have been eroding and many FIs are altering and refining their range of activities. Chapter 13 describes the regulations (past and present) that have been imposed on U.S. FIs.

16. As discussed in Chapter 12, the capital reserves of an FI insulate it against the losses that may occur as a result of its risk exposure.

GLOBALIZATION OF FINANCIAL MARKETS AND INSTITUTIONS

9

Financial markets and institutions in the United States have their counterparts in many foreign countries. Table 1–6 lists U.S. dollar equivalent values of money market and debt securities outstanding in countries throughout the world from 1996 through 2004. Notice that U.S. markets dominate the world debt markets. For example, in 2004 over 26 percent of the world's debt securities were issued in the United States. The next two most active issuers combined (Germany and the United Kingdom) had fewer debt securities outstanding than the U.S. market. While U.S. financial markets have historically been much larger in value size and trading volume than any foreign market, financial markets became truly global in the 1980s as technological improvements resulted in more immediate and cheaper access to real-time data worldwide by domestic and international investors. As a result the volume and values of stocks and other securities traded in foreign markets soared. For example, the value of stocks traded in the Japanese stock market has, at times, exceeded that of stocks traded in the United States. Likewise, foreign bond markets have served as a major source of international capital. For example, **Eurodollar bonds** are dollar-denominated bonds issued mainly in London and other European centers such as Luxembourg. Since they are issued outside U.S. territory,

Eurodollar bond

Dollar-denominated bonds issued mainly in London and other European centers such as Luxembourg.

TABLE 1–6 World Financial Markets, International Debt Outstanding, by Issuer

(in billions of dollars)

	Long-Term Debt			Money Market Securities	
Country	**1996**	**1999**	**2004***	**1999**	**2004***
Argentina	$ 29.0	$ 62.6	$ 87.3	$ 0.4	$ 0.1
Australia	77.4	90.0	179.1	13.1	27.7
Austria	62.5	75.6	169.9	4.5	6.8
Belgium	42.1	61.5	232.6	5.6	21.7
Brazil	23.1	42.9	87.7	3.4	2.2
Canada	177.8	217.1	266.7	5.1	3.4
France	204.4	298.0	700.4	10.4	30.0
Germany	319.8	623.7	1,846.7	60.1	140.8
Hong Kong	15.9	25.5	49.6	12.3	0.6
Ireland	20.0	26.3	97.1	2.9	17.2
Italy	88.6	147.9	534.6	7.9	18.3
Japan	325.6	332.3	264.0	6.0	16.0
Luxembourg	8.4	13.9	34.7	4.4	3.3
Mexico	41.5	61.2	75.4	1.8	0.3
Netherlands	112.2	196.3	539.9	23.5	49.3
Norway	19.5	32.4	62.7	0.8	1.8
South Korea	38.9	49.0	66.2	0.7	2.1
Spain	44.2	107.7	396.5	9.4	13.1
Sweden	99.6	93.4	148.2	4.7	13.9
Switzerland	39.5	80.9	173.0	4.4	15.5
United Kingdom	258.7	436.7	1,085.6	33.6	99.3
United States	372.4	1,286.7	3,118.4	24.1	78.3
Total private sector debt	$2,982.5	$5,105.5	$11,455.8	$260.0	$595.7

*As of the end of the first quarter.

Source: Bank for International Settlements, "International Banking and Financial Market Developments," *Quarterly Review*, various issues. **www.bis.org**

TABLE 1–7 Financial Market Securities Holdings
(in billions of dollars)

	1992	1996	2000	2004*
U.S. Financial Market Instruments Held by Foreign Investors				
Open market paper	$ 12.9	$ 57.9	$ 111.0	$ 158.6
U.S. government securities	595.0	1,293.9	1,772.4	2,361.5
U.S. corporate bonds	251.5	453.2	1,003.9	1,611.6
Loans to U.S. corporate businesses	129.9	126.2	117.3	111.9
Total	989.3	1,931.2	3,004.6	4,243.6
U.S. corporate equities held	329.0	656.8	1,748.3	1,655.4
Total financial assets held	$2,247.0	$4,133.2	$7,369.1	$8,426.6
Foreign Financial Market Instruments Held by U.S. Investors				
Commercial paper	$ 78.4	$ 67.5	$ 120.9	$ 190.0
Bonds	147.2	347.7	504.7	376.9
Bank loans	23.9	43.7	70.7	58.9
U.S. government loans	55.1	50.1	47.3	41.5
Acceptance liabilities to banks	11.3	9.9	3.1	0.0
Total	315.8	518.8	746.7	667.3
Foreign corporate equities held	314.3	876.8	1,787.0	2,040.1
Total financial assets held	$1,712.3	$3,117.0	$5,286.5	$5,295.1

*As of the end of the first quarter.

Source: Federal Reserve Board, "Flow of Fund Accounts," *Statistical Releases*, various issues.

www.federalreserve.gov

Eurodollar bonds are not required to be registered with the U.S. SEC (the regulator of domestic securities' issues). Eurodollar bonds account for over 80 percent of new issues in the international bond market. Globalization of financial markets is also evident in the derivative securities markets (discussed in Chapter 10). Eurodollar futures and options contracts (futures and options in which the underlying index is the three-month Eurodollar deposit rate or the LIBOR rate) are major contributors to these markets, often dominating in terms of the number of contracts and notional value outstanding.[17]

The significant growth in foreign financial markets is the result of several factors. First is the increase in the pool of savings in foreign countries (e.g., the European Union). Second, international investors have turned to U.S. and other markets to expand their investment opportunities and improve their investment portfolio risk and return characteristics. This is especially so as the retirement value of public pension plans has declined in many European countries and investors have turned to private pension plans to boost their long-term savings. Third, information on foreign investments and markets is now more accessible and thorough—for example, via the Internet. Fourth, some U.S. FIs—such as specialized mutual funds—offer their customers opportunities to invest in foreign securities and emerging markets at relatively low transaction costs. Finally, deregulation in many foreign countries has allowed international investors greater access and allowed the deregulating countries to expand their investor bases (e.g., until 1997, foreign investors faced severe restrictions on their ability to buy Korean stocks). As a result of these factors, the overall volume of investment and trading activity in foreign securities is increasing, as is the integration of U.S. and foreign financial markets.

Table 1–7 shows the extent of the growth in foreign investment in U.S. financial markets. From 1992 through 2004, foreign investors' holdings of U.S. financial market

17. For example, on August 4, 2004, 1,070,329 Eurodollar futures contracts were traded on the Chicago Mercantile Exchange, each with a face value of $1 million. U.S. Treasury note futures, each with a face value of $100,000, were the second most active financial future traded, with a volume of 625,360 contracts.

TABLE 1–8 The Largest (in Total Assets) Banks in the World
(in billions of dollars)

Bank	Country	Total Assets
1. Mizuho Financial	Japan	$1,285,471
2. Citigroup	United States	1,264,032
3. UBS Group	Switzerland	1,120,543
4. Crédit Agricole Group	France	1,105,378
5. HSBC Holdings	United Kingdom	1,034,216

Source: *The Banker*, July 1, 2004. **www.thebanker.com**

debt securities outstanding increased 329 percent, from $989.3 billion to $4,243.6 billion, while foreign financial market debt securities held by U.S. investors increased 111 percent, from $315.8 billion to $667.3 billion. From these data it should be evident that while U.S. financial markets dominate world markets, the growth of U.S. financial markets depends more and more on the growth and development of other economies. In turn, the success of other economies depends to a significant extent on their financial market development.

For the same reasons discussed earlier (i.e., monitoring costs, liquidity risk, and price risk), financial institutions are of central importance to the development and integration of markets globally. However, U.S. FIs must now compete not only with other domestic FIs for a share of these markets but increasingly with foreign FIs. Table 1–8 lists the five largest banks in the world, measured by total assets, as of 2004. Only one of these banks is a U.S. bank. Figure 1–7 shows foreign bank offices' assets and liabilities held in the United States from 1992 through 2004. Total foreign bank assets over this period increased from $509.3 billion to $789.4 billion in 2000 before falling back to $736.6 billion in 2004.

The world's most active five banks, on the basis of the percentage of their assets held outside their home countries, are listed in Table 1–9. These include the big Swiss banks (Union Bank of Switzerland and Credit Suisse) as well as one U.S. bank, American Express Bank. Interestingly, although in 2004 Japanese banks occupied 4 of the top 20 banks in the world in terms of asset size, they are absent from the list of banks with the most active international operations. Indeed, domestic problems, including record bad loans (especially in real estate) and a recession, induced Japanese banks to contract their foreign assets and international activities, as well as to merge. For example, in July 2004 Mitsubishi Tokyo Financial Group (Japan's second largest bank) announced that it would seek a merger with UFJ Holdings (Japan's fourth largest bank). The merger created the

TABLE 1–9 Top Global Banks

Bank	Home Country	Percentage of Overseas Business*
1. American Express Bank	United States	86.2%
2. Union Bank of Switzerland	Switzerland	84.4
3. Arab Banking Corporation	Bahrain	82.3
4. Credit Suisse	Switzerland	79.6
5. Standard Charter	United Kingdom	69.6

*Overseas business refers to the percentage of assets banks hold outside their home country.

Source: "Top Global Banks," *The Banker*, February 2003. **www.thebanker.com**

FIGURE 1–7 Foreign Bank Offices Assets and Liabilities Held in the United States
(in billions of dollars)

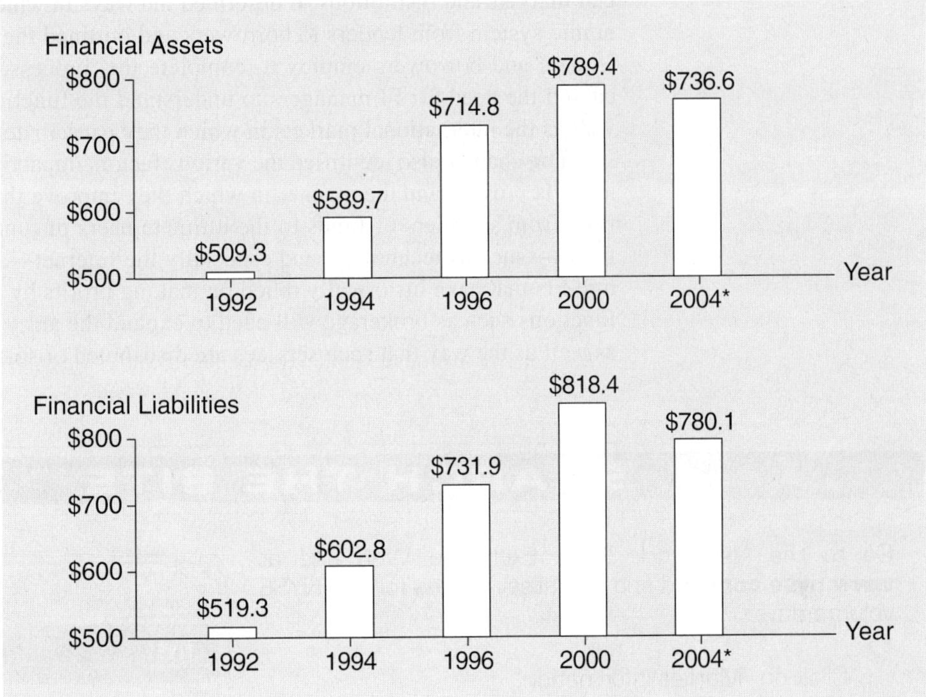

*As of the end of the first quarter.

Source: Federal Reserve Board, "Flow of Fund Accounts," *Statistical Releases,* various issues.

www.federalreserve.gov

world's largest bank with $1.7 trillion in assets.[18] Chapter 13 discusses regulatory differences among countries' FIs and recent changes toward implementing a regulatory "level playing field."

DO YOU UNDERSTAND?

1. What the trends are in the growth of global financial markets since the 1980s?
2. What a Eurodollar bond is?

As a result of the increased globalization of financial markets and institutions, U.S. financial market movements now have a much greater impact on foreign markets than historically. For example, on August 6, 2004, a much weaker than expected increase in new jobs in the United States and record high oil prices sent financial markets around the world reeling. After these announcements the Dow Jones Industrial Average (DJIA) in the United States fell by 1.5 percent, the Financial Times Stock Exchange (FTSE) in the United Kingdom fell 1.7 percent, and the Deutsche Aktienindex (DAX) in Germany fell 2.7 percent. Moreover, foreign financial market movements also have a much greater impact on U.S. markets. For example, on May 15, 2004, as oil prices climbed above $40 a barrel for the first time in 13 years, stock markets fell sharply worldwide. Japan's Nikkei Index fell by 5 percent, the Dow Jones Industrial Average fell below 10,000 for the first time since December 2003, and London's FTSE stock market index suffered its steepest one-day drop in over a year. Thus, the ability of managers to maximize value for an FI's shareholders not only depends on their knowledge of the operations of domestic financial markets and institutions but increasingly on their knowledge of the operations of overseas financial markets and institutions.

18. This bank began formal consolidated operations in 2005.

SUMMARY

This introductory chapter reviewed the basic operations of domestic and foreign financial markets and institutions. It described the ways in which funds flow through an economic system from lenders to borrowers and outlined the markets and instruments that lenders and borrowers employ to complete this process. In addition, the chapter discussed the need for FI managers to understand the functioning of both the domestic as well as the international markets in which they participate.

The chapter also identified the various factors impacting the specialness of the services FIs provide and the manner in which they improve the efficiency with which funds flow from suppliers of funds to the ultimate users of funds. Currently, however, some forces—such as technology and especially the Internet—are so powerful that in the future FIs that have historically relied on making profits by performing traditional special functions such as brokerage will need to expand the array of financial services they sell as well as the way that such services are distributed or sold to their customers.

SEARCH THE SITE

Go to the New York Stock Exchange Web site at **www.nyse.com** and find the latest figures for top NYSE volume days.

Click on "Market Information"

Click on "Data Library"

Click on "Reported Share Volume Records"

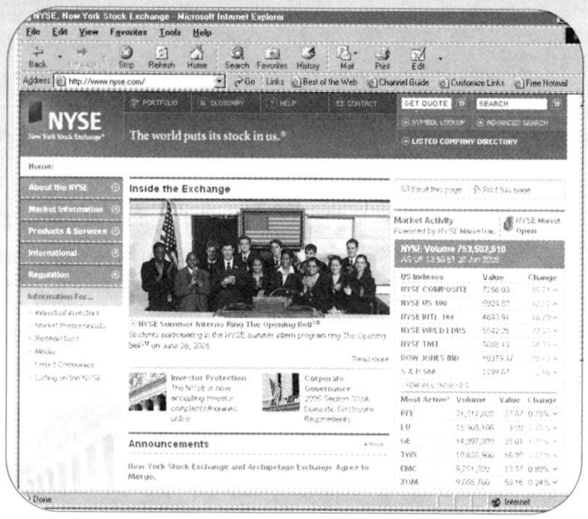

This brings up a file that contains the relevant data.

Questions

1. What is the largest number of daily shares traded on the NYSE? On what day did this occur?
2. Calculate the percentage change in daily trading volume since the 2.8 billion shares traded on July 24, 2002.

QUESTIONS

1. Classify the following transactions as taking place in the primary or secondary markets:
   a. IBM issues $200 million of new common stock.
   b. The New Company issues $50 million of common stock in an IPO.
   c. IBM sells $5 million of GM preferred stock out of its marketable securities portfolio.
   d. The Magellan Fund buys $100 million of previously issued IBM bonds.
   e. Prudential Insurance Co. sells $10 million of GM common stock.
2. Classify the following financial instruments as money market securities or capital market securities:
   a. Bankers Acceptances
   b. Commercial Paper
   c. Common Stock
   d. Corporate Bonds
   e. Mortgages
   f. Negotiable Certificates of Deposit
   g. Repurchase Agreements
   h. U.S. Treasury Bills
   i. U.S. Treasury Notes
   j. Federal Funds
3. How does the location of the money market differ from that of the capital market?
4. Which of the money market instruments has grown fastest since 1990?
5. What are the major instruments traded in capital markets?
6. Why did public confidence in the integrity of the IPO process erode in the early 2000s? What did regulators do to try to reestablish trust?

www.mhhe.com/sc3e

7. STANDARD &POOR'S Go to the S&P Educational Version of Market Insight Web site at **www.mhhe.com/edumarketinsight.** Use the following steps to identify the dollar amount of common stock outstanding for ExxonMobil (XOM). Click on "Educational Version of Market Insight." Enter your Site ID and click on "Login." Click on "Company." In the box marked "Ticker" enter XOM and click on "Go!" Click on "Financial Highlights." This brings up a file that contains the relevant data.
8. If a U.S. bank is holding Japanese yen in its portfolio, what type of exchange rate movement would the bank be most concerned about?
9. What are the different types of financial institutions? Include a description of the main services offered by each.
10. How would economic transactions between suppliers of funds (e.g., households) and users of funds (e.g., corporations) occur in a world without FIs?
11. Why would a world limited to the direct transfer of funds from suppliers of funds to users of funds likely result in quite low levels of fund flows?
12. How do FIs reduce monitoring costs associated with the flow of funds from fund suppliers to fund investors?
13. How do FIs alleviate the problem of liquidity risk faced by investors wishing to invest in securities of corporations?
14. How do financial institutions help individuals to diversify their portfolio risks? Which financial institution is best able to achieve this goal?
15. What is meant by maturity intermediation?
16. What is meant by denomination intermediation?
17. What services do FIs provide to the financial system?
18. Why are FIs regulated?
19. STANDARD &POOR'S Go to the S&P Educational Version of Market Insight Web site at **www.mhhe.com/edumarketinsight.** Use the following steps to identify the Industry Description and Industry Constituents for the following industries: Diversified Banks, Investment Banking & Brokerage, Life & Health Insurance, and Property & Casualty Insurance. Click on "Educational Version of Market Insight." Enter your Site ID and click on "Login." Click on "Industry." From the Industry list, select (one at a time) "Diversified Banks," "Investment Banks & Brokerage," "Life & Health Insurance," and "Property & Casualty." Click on "Go!" Click on "Industry Profile" and, separately, "Industry Constituents." How do the number of firms and the assets sizes of firms vary by industry?
20. What countries have the most international debt securities outstanding?
21. What countries have the largest commercial banks?

www.mhhe.com/sc3e

2

Determinants *of* Interest Rates

OUTLINE

Chapter NAVIGATOR

1. How are interest rates used to determine present and future values?
2. Who are the main suppliers of loanable funds?
3. Who are the main demanders of loanable funds?
4. How are equilibrium interest rates determined?
5. What factors cause the supply and demand curves for loanable funds to shift?
6. How do interest rates change over time?
7. What specific factors determine interest rates?
8. What are the different theories explaining the term structure of interest rates?
9. How can forward rates of interest be derived from the term structure of interest rates?

INTEREST RATE FUNDAMENTALS: CHAPTER OVERVIEW

Nominal interest rates are the interest rates actually observed in financial markets. These nominal interest rates (or just interest rates) directly affect the value (price) of most securities traded in the money and capital markets, both at home and abroad. As will be discussed later, they affect the relationship between spot and forward foreign exchange rates as well.

Changes in interest rates influence the performance and decision making for individual investors, businesses, and governmental units alike. Figure 2–1 illustrates the movement in several key U.S. interest rates over the past 30 years: the prime commercial loan rate, the three-month T-bill rate, the high-grade corporate bond rate, and the

FIGURE 2–1A Key U.S. Interest Rates, 1972–2004

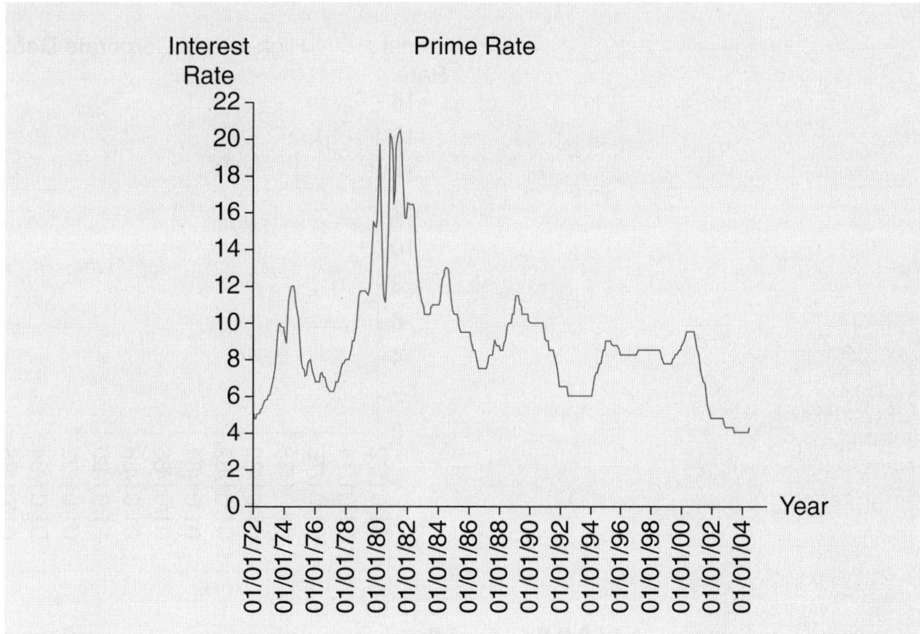

FIGURE 2–1B

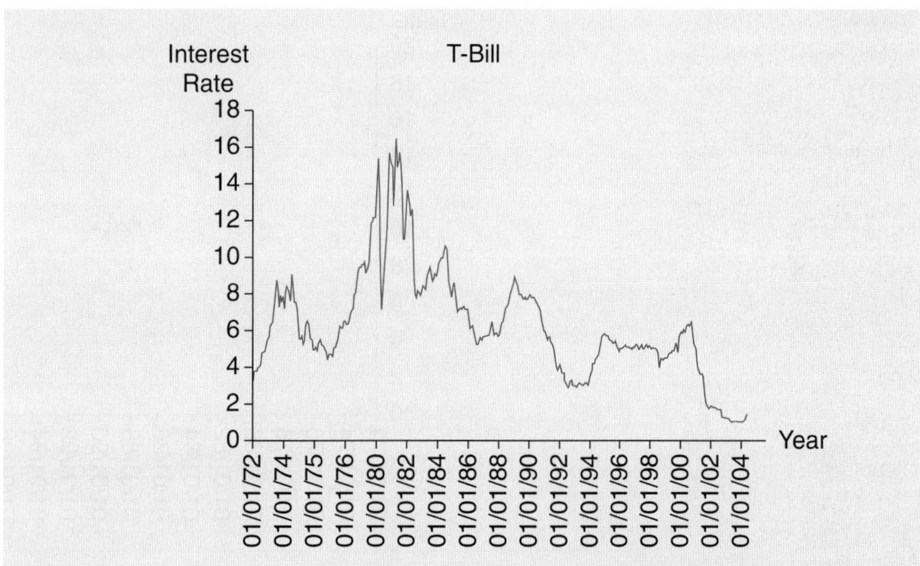

Source: Federal Reserve Board Web site, August 2004. **www.federalreserve.gov**

home mortgage rate. Notice in Figure 2–1 the variability over time in interest rate levels. For example, the prime rate hit highs of over 20 percent in the early 1980s, yet was as low as 4.75 percent in the early 1970s, was well below 10 percent throughout much of the 1990s, and fell back to 4.00 percent in the early 2000s.

nominal interest rates

The interest rates actually observed in financial markets.

This chapter examines the link between the time value of money and interest rates, as well as the factors that drive the level of current and future interest rates. Sections 1 through 6 (as listed in the Chapter Navigator) generally deal with the levels of interest rates, while Sections 7 through 9 are more concerned with differences among various interest rates.

FIGURE 2–1C

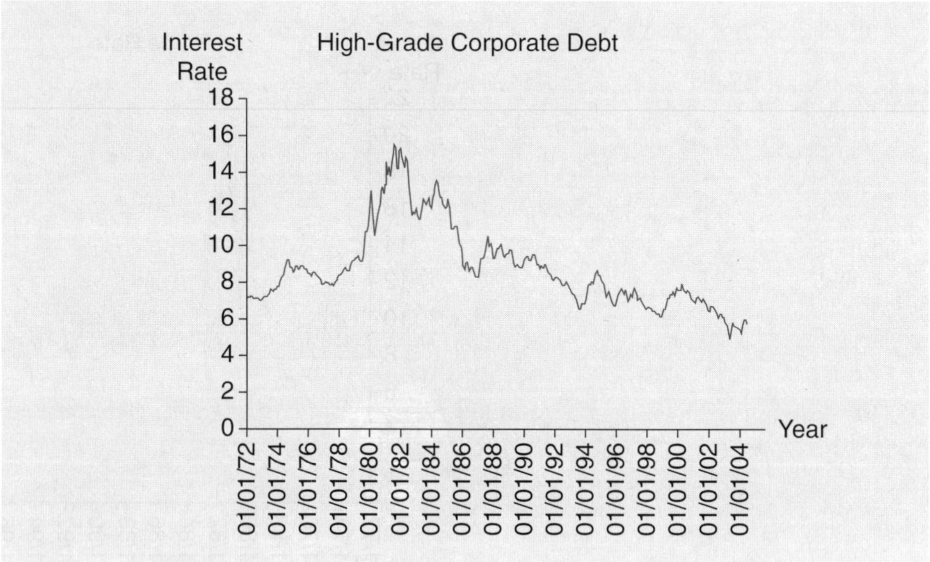

FIGURE 2–1D

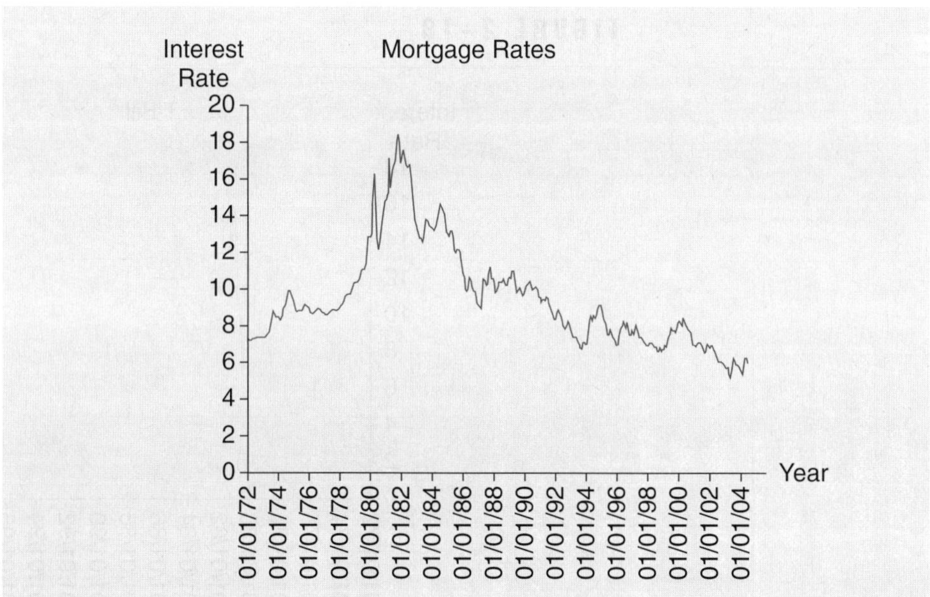

1 TIME VALUE OF MONEY AND INTEREST RATES[1]

Chapter 1 introduced the different types of financial markets that exist and the securities that trade in these markets. Interest rates have a direct and immediate effect on the value of virtually all of these securities—that is, interest rates affect the price or value the seller

1. The time value of money concept is a topic that finance students probably studied in introductory financial management courses. However, its use in the valuation of financial instruments created, traded, and held by financial institutions is critical to financial managers. Therefore, in this chapter, we review and provide a reference guide to the general relationships between interest rates and security valuation. This material can be included or dropped from the chapter reading, depending on the need for review of the material, without harming the continuity of the chapter. In Chapter 3, we use these general relationships to determine values of specific securities (e.g., equities and bonds).

of a security receives and the buyer of a security pays in organized financial markets. In this section, we review the time value of money concepts that link interest rates to the valuation of securities.

Time Value of Money

Time value of money is the basic notion that a dollar received today is worth more than a dollar received at some future date. This is because a dollar received today can be invested and its value enhanced by an interest rate or return such that the investor receives more than a dollar in the future. The interest rate or return reflects the fact that people generally prefer to consume now rather than wait until later. To compensate them for delaying consumption (i.e., saving), they are paid a rate of interest by those who wish to consume more today than their current resources permit (users of funds). Dissavers are willing to pay this rate of interest because they plan to productively use the borrowed funds such that they will earn even more than the rate of interest promised to the savers (suppliers of the funds).

The time value of money concept specifically assumes that any interest or other return earned on a dollar invested over any given period of time (e.g., two, three, four, . . . years) is immediately reinvested—that is, the **interest** return is **compounded.** This is in contrast to the concept of **simple interest,** which assumes that interest returns earned are not reinvested over any given time period.

compound interest

Interest earned on an investment is reinvested.

simple interest

Interest earned on an investment is not reinvested.

EXAMPLE 2-1 Calculation of Simple and Compounded Interest Returns

CALCULATION OF SIMPLE INTEREST RETURN

Suppose you have $1,000 to invest for a period of two years. Currently, default risk-free one-year securities (such as those issued by the U.S. Treasury) are paying a 12 percent interest rate per year, on the last day of each of the two years over your investment horizon. If you earn simple annual interest on this investment, or you do not reinvest the annual (12 percent) interest earned, the value of your investment at the end of the first year is:

$$\begin{aligned}\text{Value in 1 year (simple interest)} &= \text{Principal} + \text{Interest (year 1)}\\ &= \$1{,}000 + \$1{,}000(.12) = \$1{,}000 + \$120\\ &= \$1{,}000(1.12) = \$1{,}120\end{aligned}$$

With simple interest, the $120 in interest earned in year 1 is *not* reinvested in year 2. Rather, you take the $120 in interest out of the investment account and hold it until the end of year 2. Only the original $1,000 investment is carried forward and earns interest in year 2. Thus, the value at the end of the two-year investment horizon is:

$$\begin{aligned}\text{Value in 2 years (simple interest)} &= \text{Principal} + \text{Interest (year 1)} + \text{Interest (year 2)}\\ &= \$1{,}000 + \$1{,}000(.12) + \$1{,}000(.12)\\ &= \$1{,}000 + \$1{,}000(.12)2 = \$1{,}240\end{aligned}$$

Panel A of Figure 2–2 illustrates the value of the investment over the two-year investment horizon using simple interest.

CALCULATION OF COMPOUNDED INTEREST RETURN

If, instead, the annual interest earned is reinvested immediately after it is received at 12 percent (i.e., interest is compounded), the value of the investment at the end of the first year is:

$$\begin{aligned}\text{Value in 1 year (compounded interest)} &= \text{Principal} + \text{Interest (year 1)}\\ &= \$1{,}000 + \$1{,}000(.12) = \$1{,}000 + \$120\\ &= \$1{,}000(1.12) = \$1{,}120\end{aligned}$$

Notice that after the first year of the two-year investment horizon, you have $1,120 whether the investment earns simple or compounded interest. With compounded interest, however, the $120 in interest earned in year 1 is reinvested in year 2. Thus, the whole $1,120 is carried forward and earns interest in year 2. In this case, the value of the investment at the end of the two-year investment horizon is:

$$\begin{aligned}\text{Value in 2 years (compound interest)} &= \text{Principal} + \text{Interest (year 1)} + \text{Interest on original principal (year 2)} + \text{Compounded interest (or interest on interest received in year 1)}\\ &= \$1{,}000 + \$1{,}000(.12) + \$1{,}000(.12) + 1{,}000(.12)(.12)\\ &= \$1{,}000[1 + 2(.12) + (.12)^2] = \$1{,}000(1.12)^2\\ &= \$1{,}254.40\end{aligned}$$

Panel B of Figure 2–2 illustrates the value of the investment over the two-year investment horizon using compounded interest. By compounding interest using time value of money principles, an investor increases his or her return compared to the simple interest return. In the example above using a two-year investment horizon, a 12 percent annual interest rate, and an initial investment of $1,000, the investment is worth $1,254.40 at the end of two years under compounded returns rather than $1,240 using simple interest to calculate returns.

The time value of money concept can be used to convert cash flows earned over an investment horizon into a value at the end of the investment horizon. This is called the investment's future value (*FV*) and is the same as that in the compounded return example above.

FIGURE 2–2 Value of a Two-Year Investment Using Simple Versus Compounded Interest

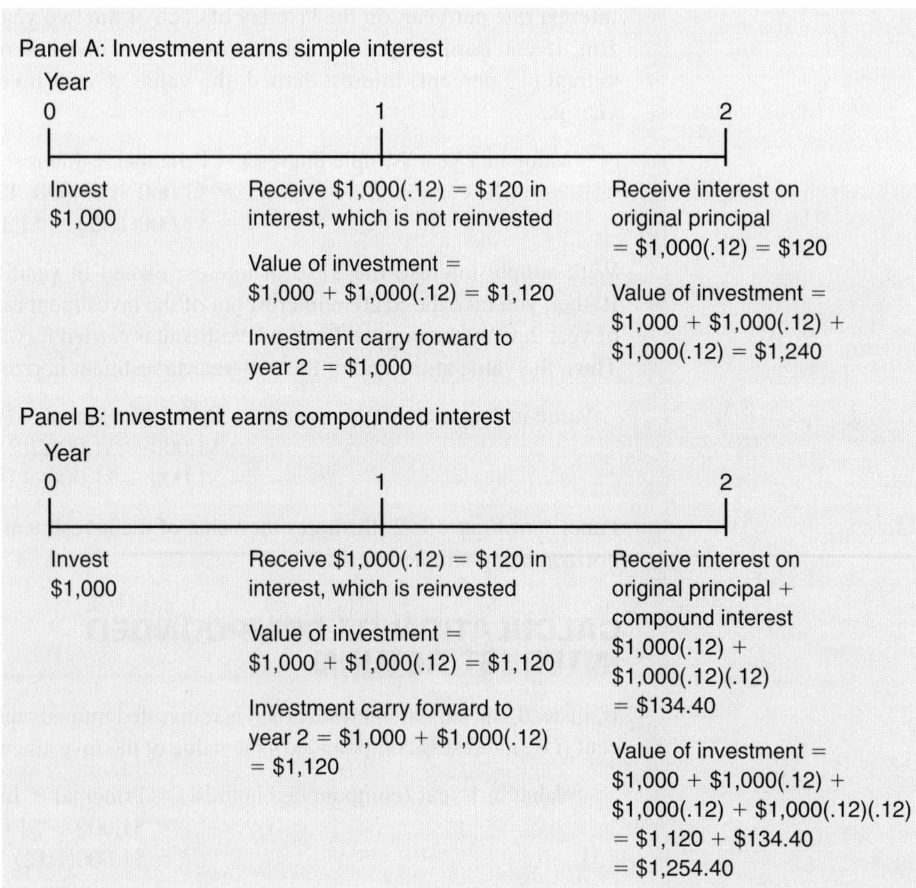

FIGURE 2–3 Time Value of Money Concepts

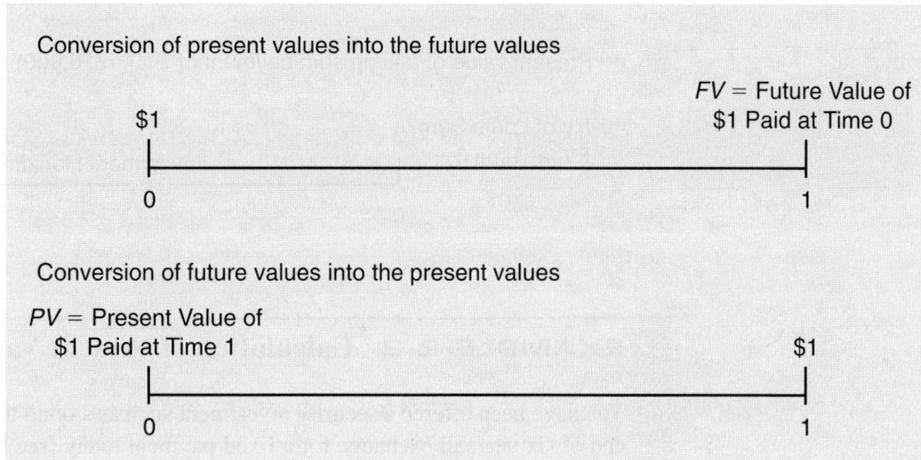

Alternatively, the time value of money concept can be used to convert the value of future cash flows into their current or present values (PV) (i.e., future dollars converted into their equivalent present value or current dollars). We illustrate the FV and PV scenarios in Figure 2–3. Two forms of time value of money calculations are commonly used in finance for security valuation purposes: the value of a lump sum and the value of annuity payments. A **lump sum payment** is a single cash payment received at the beginning or end of some investment horizon (e.g., \$100 at the end of five years). **Annuity** payments are a series of equal cash flows received at fixed intervals over the entire investment horizon (e.g., \$100 a year received each year for five years). In actual practice, "annuity" payments can be paid more frequently than once a year—so that the term *annuity* really means a constant payment received at equal intervals throughout an investment horizon (e.g., twice, three times, . . . a year). We first discuss lump sum time value of money calculations, followed by annuity calculations.

lump sum payment

A single cash flow occurs at the beginning and end of the investment horizon with no other cash flows exchanged.

annuity

A series of equal cash flows received at fixed intervals over the investment horizon.

Lump Sum Valuation

Present Value of a Lump Sum. The present value function converts cash flows received over a future investment horizon into an equivalent (present) value as if they were received at the beginning of the current investment horizon. This is done by discounting future cash flows back to the present using the current market interest rate. The time value of money equation used to calculate this value is illustrated in Figure 2–4 and can be represented as follows.

Present value (PV) of a *lump sum* received at the end of the investment horizon, or future value (FV):

$$PV = FV_t\,[1/(1 + r)]^t = FV_t(PVIF_{r,t}) \quad \textbf{(1)}$$

where

PV = Present value of cash flows
FV_t = Future value of cash flows (lump sum) received in t periods
r = Interest rate earned per period on an investment (equals the nominal annual interest rate, i, divided by the number of compounding periods per year—(e.g., daily, weekly, monthly, quarterly, semiannually)
t = Number of compounding periods in the investment horizon (equals the number of years in the investment horizon times the number of compounding periods per year)
$PVIF_{r,t}$ = Present value interest factor[2] of a lump sum = $[1/(1 + r)]^t$

2. Interest factor formulas are programmed in business calculators—a tool with which every finance student should be familiar. Because there are several variations of business calculators, we do not apply the problems in the text to any one brand of calculator.

FIGURE 2–4 Present Value of a Lump Sum
(invested at the rate of r per period)

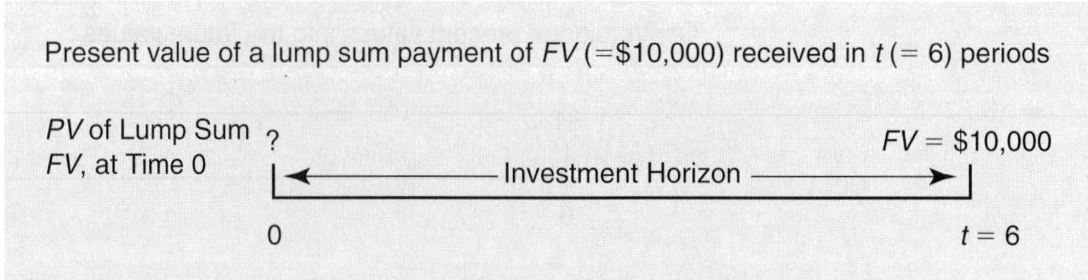

EXAMPLE 2-2 Calculation of Present Value of a Lump Sum

You have been offered a security investment such as a bond that will pay you $10,000 at the end of six years in exchange for a fixed payment today (see Figure 2–4). If the appropriate annual interest rate on the investment is 8 percent compounded annually, the present value of this investment is computed as follows:

$$PV = FV(PVIF_{r,t}) = \$10{,}000\ (PVIF_{8\%,6}) = \$10{,}000\ (.630170) = \$6{,}301.70$$

If the annual interest rate on the investment rises to 12 percent, the present value of this investment becomes:

$$PV = \$10{,}000\ (PVIF_{12\%,6}) = \$10{,}000\ (.506631) = \$5{,}066.31$$

If the annual interest rate on the investment rises to 16 percent, the present value of this investment becomes:

$$PV = \$10{,}000\ (PVIF_{16\%,6}) = \$10{,}000\ (.410442) = \$4{,}104.42$$

Finally, if the annual interest rate on the investment of 16 percent is compounded semiannually (that is, you will receive $t = 12$ (6×2) total interest payments, each calculated as $r = 8$ percent (16 percent $\div$ 2) times the principal value in the investment, where r in this case is the semiannual interest payment) rather than annually, the present value of this investment becomes:

$$PV = \$10{,}000\ (PVIF_{8\%,12}) = \$10{,}000\ (.397114) = \$3{,}971.14$$

Notice from the previous examples that the *present values* of the security investment *decrease as interest rates increase.* For example, as the interest rate rose from 8 percent to 12 percent, the (present) value of the security investment fell $1,235.39 (from $6,301.70 to $5,066.31). As interest rates rose from 12 percent to 16 percent, the value of the investment fell $961.89 (from $5,066.31 to $4,104.42). This is because as interest rates increase, fewer funds need to be invested at the beginning of an investment horizon to receive a stated amount at the end of the investment horizon. This inverse relationship between the value of a financial instrument—for example, a bond—and interest rates is one of the most fundamental relationships in finance and is evident in the swings that occur in financial asset prices whenever major changes in interest rates arise. Indeed, even the hint of an announcement of a change in interest rate targets by the chairman of the Federal Reserve Board (the Fed) (see Chapter 4 for an explanation of when and why the Fed changes interest rate targets) can send financial markets around the world reeling (see In the News box).

Note also that *as interest rates increase,* the *present values* of the investment *decrease at a decreasing rate.* The fall in present value is greater when interest rates rise by 4 percent, from 8 percent to 12 percent, compared to when they rise from 12 percent to 16 percent—the inverse relationship between interest rates and the present value of security investments is neither linear nor proportional.

IN THE NEWS

Wall Street Takes Heart from Greenspan's Words

Waning worries about inflation fuelled a rally on Wall Street yesterday after economic data and a testimony from the Federal Reserve chairman calmed speculation about aggressive rises in interest rates. Alan Greenspan, the Fed chief, repeated that any tightening in monetary policy was "likely to be measured" while a reading of inflation met forecasts.

With two hours to go, the S&P 500 index put on 0.9 percent to 1,135.83 while the Dow Jones Industrial Average added 0.7 percent at 10,405.78. The tech-laden Nasdaq Composite gained 1.8 percent to 2,005.25. While the consumer price index rose at the fastest rate since January 2001, the core CPI, that excludes volatile energy and food expenses, rose only 0.2 percent, in line with expectation . . .

However, the focus was on Mr. Greenspan, who told the Senate that the US central bank anticipates a gradual need to raise borrowing costs. Recent data and other Fed officials' speeches had prompted speculation that Mr. Greenspan and colleagues might be forced to be more aggressive and some economists expected a half-point rise in rates when the Fed meets to decide the matter in two weeks . . .

Higher trading volumes than Wall Street has seen recently fanned hopes that this time, the momentum would last. Mr. Greenspan's testimony overshadowed a busier day for corporate news than the markets have seen in a while, with a few stocks having a significant impact on their respective sectors.

Source: *The Financial Times Limited,* June 16, 2004, p. 48, by Andrei Postolnicu. **www.ft.com**

DO YOU UNDERSTAND?

1. Why stock markets reacted to Federal Reserve chairman Greenspan's statement that any tightening in monetary policy was likely to be measured?
2. How stock markets reacted to this statement?

Finally, from this example notice that the greater the number of compounding periods per year (i.e., semiannually versus annually), the smaller the present value of a future amount.[3]

Future Value of a Lump Sum. The future value of a lump sum equation translates a cash flow received at the beginning of an investment period to a terminal (future) value at the end of an investment horizon (e.g., 5 years, 6 years, 10 years, etc.). The future value (FV) equation is illustrated in Figure 2–5 and can be represented as follows:

Future value of a lump sum received at the beginning of the investment horizon:

$$FV_t = PV(1 + r)^t = PV\,(FVIF_{r,t}) \tag{2}$$

where

$FVIF_{r,t}$ = Future value interest factor of a lump sum = $(1 + r)^t$

FIGURE 2–5 Future Value of a Lump Sum
(invested at the rate of r *per period)*

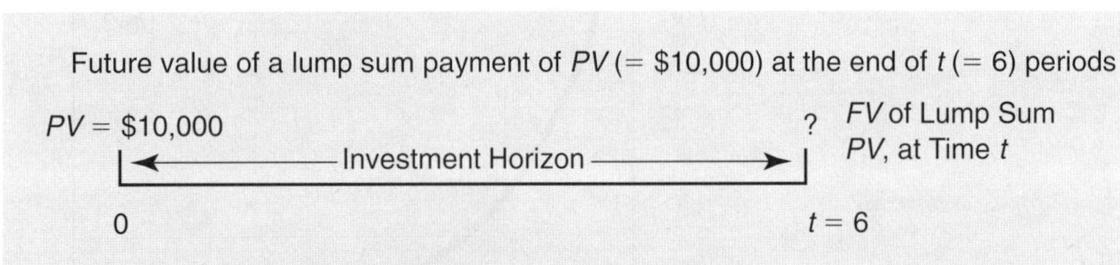

3. The ultimate of compounding periods is instantaneous, or continuous, compounding over the investment horizon (period). In this case the present value formula becomes:

$$PV = FV_t[1/(1 + i/\infty)]^{n\infty} = FV_n(e^{-in})$$

where n is the number of years in the investment horizon (period). Thus, in Example 2–2, if the annual interest rate on the investment is 16 percent compounded continuously, the present value of the $10,000 investment is six years is:

$$PV = \$10,000\,(e^{-.16 \times 6}) = \$10,000\,(.382893) = \$3,828.93$$

EXAMPLE 2-3 Calculation of Future Value of a Lump Sum

You plan to invest \$10,000 today in exchange for a fixed payment at the end of six years (see Figure 2–5). If the appropriate annual interest rate on the investment is 8 percent compounded annually, the future value of this investment is computed as follows:

$$FV = PV\,(FVIF_{r,t}) = \$10{,}000\,(FVIF_{8\%,6}) = \$10{,}000\,(1.586874) = \$15{,}868.74$$

If the annual interest rate on the investment rises to 12 percent, the future value of this investment becomes:

$$FV = \$10{,}000\,(FVIF_{12\%,6}) = \$10{,}000\,(1.973823) = \$19{,}738.23$$

If the annual interest rate on the investment rises to 16 percent, the future value of this investment becomes:

$$FV = \$10{,}000\,(FVIF_{16\%,6}) = \$10{,}000\,(2.436396) = \$24{,}363.96$$

Finally, if the annual interest rate on the investment of 16 percent is compounded semiannually rather than annually (i.e., $r = 16\%/2 = 8\%$ and $t = 6 \times 2 = 12$), the future value of this investment becomes:

$$FV = \$10{,}000\,(FVIF_{8\%,12}) = \$10{,}000\,(2.518170) = \$25{,}181.70$$

Notice that the *future value* of an investment *increases as interest rates increase.* As interest rates rose from 8 percent to 12 percent, the (future) value of the investment of \$10,000 for six years rose by \$3,869.49 (from \$15,868.74 to \$19,738.23). As rates rose from 12 percent to 16 percent, the (future) value of the investment rose \$4,625.73 (from \$19,738.23 to \$24,363.96). Note also that *as interest rates increase, future values increase at an increasing rate.*[4] This is because as interest rates increase, a stated amount of funds invested at the beginning of an investment horizon accumulates to a larger amount at the end of the investment horizon. This is due to the compounding of interest returns. By contrast, as stated earlier, as interest rates increase, the present value of an investment decreases at a decreasing rate. These nonlinear relationships are illustrated in Figure 2–6.

Finally, notice that as the number of compounding periods per year increases, the *future value* of a present amount increases.

FIGURE 2–6 Relation between Interest Rates and Present and Future Values

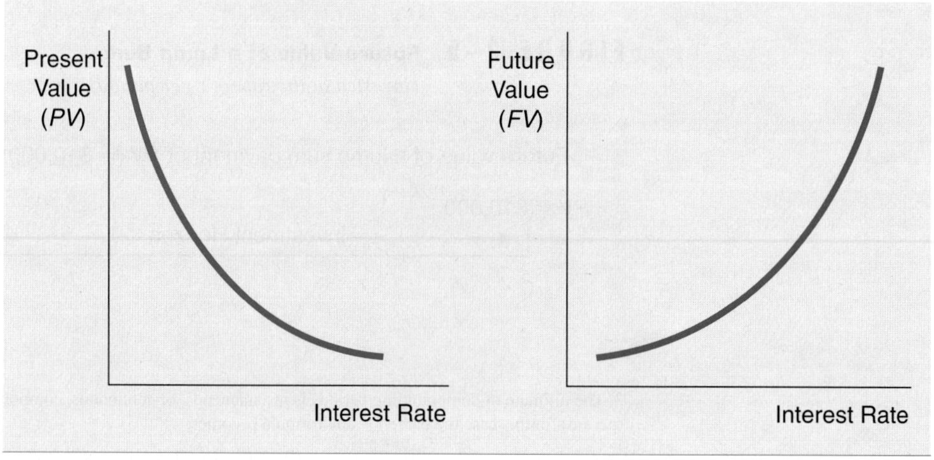

4. That is, as rates go from 8 percent to 12 percent (an increase in interest rates of 4 percent), the future value increases by \$3,869.49; as interest rates go from 12 percent to 16 percent (an increase in interest rates of 4 percent), the future value increases by \$4,625.73.

FIGURE 2–7 Present Value of an Annuity
(invested at the rate of r per period)

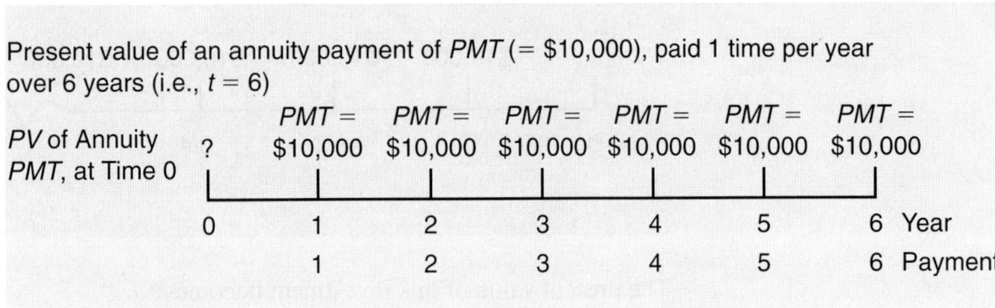

Annuity Valuation

Present Value of an Annuity. The present value of an annuity equation converts a series of equal cash flows received at equal intervals throughout the investment horizon into an equivalent (present) value as if they were received at the beginning of the investment horizon. The time value of money equation used to calculate this value is illustrated in Figure 2–7 and is represented as follows:

Present value (PV) of an annuity stream (PMT) received in the future:

$$PV = PMT \sum_{j=1}^{t} [1/(1+r)]^j = PMT(PVIFA_{r,t}) \tag{3}$$

where

$$PMT = \text{Periodic annuity payment received during an investment horizon}$$
$$PVIFA_{r,t} = \text{Present value interest factor of an annuity}$$
$$= \sum_{j=1}^{t} [(1/(1+r)]^j$$
$$\sum_{j=1}^{t} = \text{Summation sign for addition of all terms from } j = 1 \text{ to } j = t$$

EXAMPLE 2-4 Calculation of Present Value of an Annuity

You have been offered a bond that will pay you $10,000 on the last day of every year for the next six years in exchange for a fixed payment today. We illustrate this investment in Figure 2–7. If the appropriate annual interest rate on the investment is 8 percent, the present value of this investment is computed as follows:

$$\begin{aligned} PV &= PMT\,(PVIFA_{r,t}) \\ &= \$10{,}000\ (PVIFA_{8\%,6}) \\ &= \$10{,}000\ (4.622880) = \$46{,}228.80 \end{aligned}$$

If the investment pays you $10,000 on the last day of every quarter for the next six years (i.e., $r = 8\%/4 = 2\%$ and $t = 6 \times 4 = 24$; see Figure 2–8), the present value of the annuity becomes:

$$\begin{aligned} PV &= \$10{,}000\ (PVIFA_{2\%,24}) \\ &= \$10{,}000\ (18.913926) = \$189{,}139.26 \end{aligned}$$

If the annuity is paid on the first day of each quarter, an extra interest payment would be received for each $10,000 payment. Thus, the time value of money equation for the present value of an annuity becomes:

$$PV = PMT\,(PVIFA_{r,t})(1+r)$$

FIGURE 2–8 Present Value of \$10,000 Received on the Last Day of Each Quarter for Six Years (i.e., $t = 6 \times 4 = 24$)

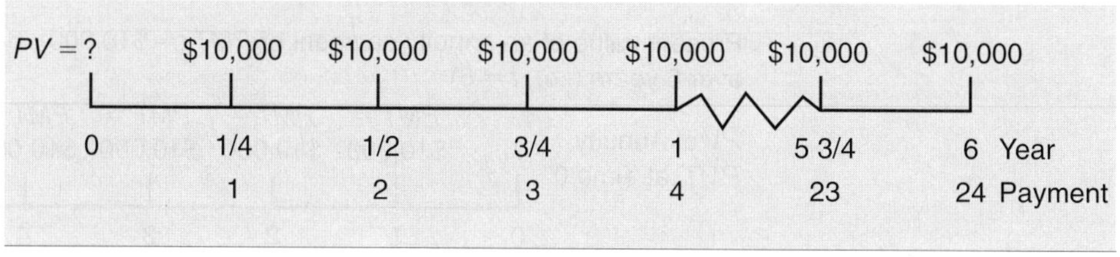

The present value of this investment becomes:

$$PV = \$10{,}000\,(PVIFA_{2\%,24})(1 + .02)$$
$$= \$10{,}000\,(18.913926)(1.02) = \$192{,}922.04$$

Future Value of an Annuity. The future value of an annuity equation converts a series of equal cash flows received at equal intervals throughout the investment horizon into an equivalent future amount at the end of the investment horizon. The equation used to calculate this value is illustrated by the example in Figure 2–9 and is represented as follows:

Future value of an annuity payment stream received over an investment horizon:

$$FV_t = PMT \sum_{j=0}^{t-1} (1 + r)^j = PMT\,(FVIFA_{r,t}) \qquad \textbf{(4)}$$

where

$$FVIFA_{r,t} = \text{Future value interest factor of an annuity payment stream}^5$$
$$= \sum_{j=0}^{t-1} (1 + r)^j$$

EXAMPLE 2-5 Calculation of the Future Value of an Annuity

You plan to invest \$10,000 on the last day of every year for the next six years (as in Figure 2–9). If the interest rate on the investment is 8 percent, the future value of your investment in six years is computed as follows:

$$FV = \$10{,}000\,(FVIFA_{8\%,6})$$
$$= \$10{,}000\,(7.335929) = \$73{,}359.29$$

If the investment pays you \$10,000 on the last day of every quarter for the next six years (i.e., $r = 8\%/4 = 2\%$ and $t = 6 \times 4 = 24$), the future value of the annuity becomes:

$$FV = \$10{,}000\,(FVIFA_{2\%,24})$$
$$= \$10{,}000\,(30.421862) = \$304{,}218.62$$

If the annuity is paid on the first day of each quarter, an extra interest payment would be earned on each \$10,000 investment. Thus, the time value of money equation for the future value of an annuity becomes:

$$FV = PMT(FVIFA_{r,t})(1 + r)$$

Thus, the future value of this investment becomes:

$$FV = \$10{,}000\,(FVIFA_{2\%,24})(1 + .02)$$
$$= \$10{,}000\,(31.030300) = \$310{,}303.00$$

5. Note that the last annuity payment occurs on the last day of the investment horizon. Thus, it earns no interest (i.e., the future value interest factor takes a power of zero). Similarly, the first annuity payment earns only five years of interest. Thus, the future value interest factor takes a power of five. Accordingly, in the future value interest factor of annuity term, j runs from 0 to $t - 1$, or, in this example, $(6 - 1 =)$ 5. In Example 2–4, note that the first annuity payment earns one year of interest. Thus, the present value interest factor term takes a power of one. Likewise, the last annuity payment earns six years of interest. Thus, the present value interest factor takes a power of six. Accordingly, in the present value interest factor of annuity term, j runs from 1 to t, or, in this example, 6.

FIGURE 2–9 Future Value of an Annuity
(invested at the rate of r per period)

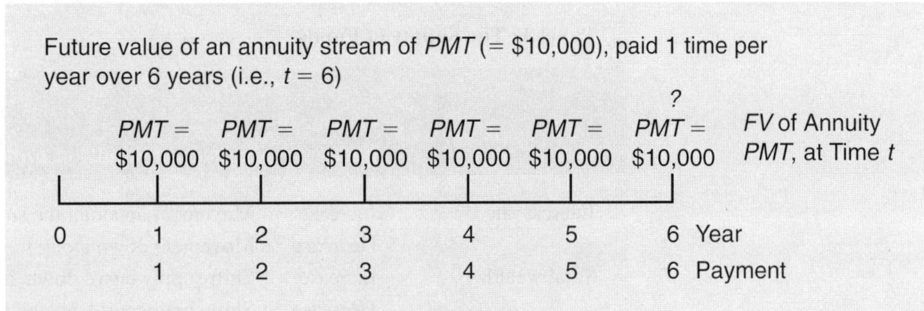

Effective Annual Return

The annual interest rate, i, used in the time value of money equations in Examples 2–2 through 2–5, is the simple (nominal or 12-month) interest rate on the securities. However, if interest is paid or compounded more than once per year, the true annual rate earned or paid will differ from the simple annual rate. The **effective** or **equivalent annual return** (EAR) is the return earned or paid over a 12-month period taking any within-year compounding of interest into account. Specifically, the EAR can be written as follows:

effective or equivalent annual return

Rate earned over a 12-month period taking the compounding of interest into account.

$$EAR = (1 + r)^c - 1 \quad \textbf{(5)}$$

where c = number of compounding periods per year.

In Example 2–2, the EAR on the 16 percent simple return compounded semiannually (i.e., $r = 16\%/2 = 8\%$ and $c = 2$) is computed as:

$$EAR = (1 + .08)^2 - 1 = 16.64\%$$

and in Example 2–4 the EAR on the 8 percent simple return compounded quarterly (i.e., $r = 8\%/4 = 2\%$ and $c = 4$) is computed as:

$$EAR = (1 + .02)^4 - 1 = 8.24\%$$

Thus, for each dollar invested at the beginning of the year, at 16 percent (compounded semiannually) and 8 percent (compounded quarterly) respectively, you would have earned \$0.1664 and \$0.0824 at the end of the year. Accordingly, the EAR provides a more accurate measure of annual returns in time value of money calculations.

DO YOU UNDERSTAND?

1. The difference between simple interest and compounded interest?
2. What should happen to the future value of an annuity stream of cash flows as interest rates increase?
3. How an EAR differs from a simple rate of return?

LOANABLE FUNDS THEORY

So far we have shown the technical details of how interest rates play a part in the determination of the value of financial instruments. Given the impact a change in interest rates has on security values, financial institution and other managers spend much time and effort trying to identify the factors that determine the level of interest rates at any moment in time, as well as what causes interest rate movements over time. One model that is commonly used to explain interest rates and interest rate movements is **loanable funds theory.** The loanable funds theory of interest rate determination views the level of interest rates in financial markets as resulting from factors that affect the supply and demand for loanable funds. This is similar to the way that the prices for goods and services in general are viewed as being the result of the forces of supply and demand for those goods and services. The *supply of loanable funds* is a term commonly used to describe funds provided to the financial markets by net suppliers of funds. The *demand for loanable funds* is a term used to describe the total net demand for funds by fund users. The loanable funds framework categorizes financial market participants—suppliers and demanders of funds—as consumers, businesses, governments,

loanable funds theory

A theory of interest rate determination that views equilibrium interest rates in financial markets as a result of the supply and demand for loanable funds.

TABLE 2–1 Factors that Affect the Supply of and Demand for Loanable Funds for a Financial Security

Panel A: The Supply of Funds

Factor	Change in Factor	Impact on Supply of Funds	Impact on Equilibrium Interest Rate
Interest rate	Increase	Movement up along the supply curve	Increase
	Decrease	Movement down along the supply curve	Decrease
Total wealth	Increase	Shift supply curve down and to the right	Decrease
	Decrease	Shift supply curve up and to the left	Increase
Risk of financial security	Increase	Shift supply curve up and to the left	Increase
	Decrease	Shift supply curve down and to the right	Decrease
Near-term spending needs	Increase	Shift supply curve up and to the left	Increase
	Decrease	Shift supply curve down and to the right	Decrease
Monetary expansion	Increase	Shift supply curve down and to the right	Decrease
	Decrease	Shift supply curve up and to the left	Increase
Economic conditions	Increase	Shift supply curve down and to the right	Decrease
	Decrease	Shift supply curve up and to the left	Increase

Panel B: The Demand for Funds

Factor	Change in Factor	Impact on Demand for Funds	Impact on Equilibrium Interest Rate
Interest rate	Increase	Movement up along the demand curve	Increase
	Decrease	Movement down along the demand curve	Decrease
Utility derived from asset purchased with borrowed funds	Increase	Shift demand curve up and to the right	Increase
	Decrease	Shift demand curve down and to the left	Decrease
Restrictiveness of nonprice conditions	Increase	Shift demand curve down and to the left	Decrease
	Decrease	Shift demand curve up and to the right	Increase
Economic conditions	Increase	Shift demand curve up and to the right	Increase
	Decrease	Shift demand curve down and to the left	Decrease

and foreign participants. Table 2–1 summarizes the factors that affect the supply and demand for loanable funds discussed in this section, their impact on the supply and demand for loanable funds for a specific security, and the impact on the market clearing (or equilibrium) interest rates holding all other factors constant.

2 Supply of Loanable Funds

In general, the quantity of loanable funds supplied increases as interest rates rise. Figure 2–10 illustrates the supply curve for loanable funds. Other factors held constant, more funds are supplied as interest rates increase (the reward for supplying funds is higher). Table 2–2 presents data on the supply of loanable funds from the various groups of market participants from U.S. flow of funds data as of March 2004.

The household sector (consumer sector) is the largest supplier of loanable funds in the United States—$34,860.7 billion in 2004. Households supply funds when they have excess income or want to reallocate their asset portfolio holdings. For example, during times of high economic growth, households may replace part of their cash holdings with earning assets

FIGURE 2–10 Supply of and Demand for Loanable Funds

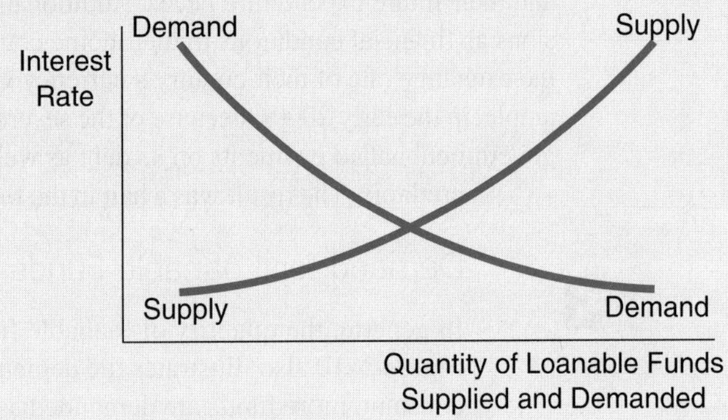

(i.e., by supplying loanable funds in exchange for holding securities). As the total wealth of a consumer increases, the total supply of loanable funds from that consumer will also generally increase. Households determine their supply of loanable funds not only on the basis of the general level of interest rates and their total wealth, but also on the risk of securities investments. The greater the perceived risk of securities investments, the less households are willing to invest at each interest rate. Further, the supply of loanable funds from households also depends on their immediate spending needs. For example, near-term educational or medical expenditures will reduce the supply of funds from a given household.

Higher interest rates will also result in higher supplies of funds from the U.S. business sector ($12,679.2 billion from nonfinancial business and $31,547.9 billion from financial business in 2004) which often has excess cash, or working capital, that it can invest for short periods of time in financial assets. In addition to the interest rates on these investments, the expected risk on financial securities and their businesses' future investment needs will affect their overall supply of funds.

Loanable funds are also supplied by some governments ($12,574.5 billion in 2004). For example, some governments (e.g., municipalities) temporarily generate more cash inflows (e.g., through local taxes) than they have budgeted to spend. These funds can be loaned out to financial market fund users until needed.

Finally, foreign investors increasingly view U.S. financial markets as alternatives to their domestic financial markets ($8,426.7 billion of funds supplied to the U.S. financial markets in 2004). When interest rates are higher on U.S. financial securities than they are on comparable securities in their home countries, foreign investors increase their supply of funds to U.S. markets. Indeed the high savings rates of foreign households (such as Japanese households) has resulted in foreign market participants being major suppliers of funds to U.S. financial markets

TABLE 2-2 Funds Supplied and Demanded by Various Groups *(in billions of dollars)*

	Funds Supplied	Funds Demanded	Net Funds Supplied (Funds Supplied − Funds Demanded)
Households	$34,860.7	$15,197.4	$19,663.3
Business—nonfinancial	12,679.2	30,779.2	−18,100.0
Business—financial	31,547.9	45,061.3	−13,513.4
Government units	12,574.5	6,695.2	5,879.3
Foreign participants	8,426.7	2,355.9	6,070.8

Source: Federal Reserve Board Web site, "Flow of Fund Accounts," June 10, 2004. **www.federalreserve.gov**

in recent years. Similar to domestic suppliers of loanable funds, foreigners assess not only the interest rate offered on financial securities, but also their total wealth, the risk on the security, and their future expenditure needs. Additionally, foreign investors alter their investment decisions as financial conditions in their home countries change relative to the U.S. economy and the exchange rate of their country's currency vis-à-vis the U.S. dollar (see Chapter 8). For example, in the early 2000s, because of the severe financial and economic crisis in Argentina, the government halted payments on its debt as well as debt Argentine companies owed to foreign creditors. The result was a halt in the flow of funds into financial markets in Argentina.

3

Demand for Loanable Funds

In general, the quantity of loanable funds demanded is higher as interest rates fall. Figure 2–10 also illustrates the demand curve for loanable funds. Other factors held constant, more funds are demanded as interest rates decrease (the cost of borrowing funds is lower).

Households (although they are net suppliers of funds) also borrow funds in financial markets ($15,197.4 billion in 2004). The demand for loanable funds by households reflects the demand for financing purchases of homes (with mortgage loans), durable goods (e.g., car loans, appliance loans), and nondurable goods (e.g., education loans, medical loans). Additional nonprice conditions and requirements (discussed below) also affect a household's demand for loanable funds at every level of interest rates.

Businesses demand funds to finance investments in long-term (fixed) assets (e.g., plant and equipment) and for short-term working capital needs (e.g., inventory and accounts receivable) usually by issuing debt and other financial instruments ($30,779.2 billion for nonfinancial businesses and $45,061.3 for financial businesses in 2004). When interest rates are high (i.e., the cost of loanable funds is high), businesses prefer to finance investments with internally generated funds (e.g., retained earnings) rather than through borrowed funds. Further, the greater the number of profitable projects available to businesses, or the better the overall economic conditions, the greater the demand for loanable funds.

Governments also borrow heavily in the markets for loanable funds ($6,695.2 billion in 2004). For example, state and local governments often issue debt instruments to finance temporary imbalances between operating revenues (e.g., taxes) and budgeted expenditures (e.g., road improvements, school construction). Higher interest rates can cause state and local governments to postpone borrowings and thus capital expenditures. Similar to households and businesses, governments' demand for funds varies with general economic conditions. The federal government is also a large borrower partly to finance current budget deficits (expenditures greater than taxes) and partly to finance past deficits. The cumulative sum of past deficits is called the national debt, which in the United States in August 2004 stood at over $7.3 trillion. Thus, the national debt and especially the interest payments on the national debt have to be financed in large part by additional government borrowing. Chapter 4 provides details of how government borrowing and spending impacts interest rates as well as overall economic growth.

www.ustreas.gov

Finally, foreign participants (households, businesses, and governments) also borrow in U.S. financial markets ($2,355.9 billion in 2004). Foreign borrowers look for the cheapest source of dollar funds globally. Most foreign borrowing in U.S. financial markets comes from the business sector. In addition to interest costs, foreign borrowers consider nonprice terms on loanable funds as well as economic conditions in the home country and the general attractiveness of the U.S. dollar relative to their domestic currency (e.g., the euro or the yen). In Chapter 8, we examine how economic growth in domestic versus foreign countries affects foreign exchange rates and foreign investors' demand and supply for funds.

4

Equilibrium Interest Rate

The aggregate supply of loanable funds is the sum of the quantity supplied by the separate fund supplying sectors (e.g., households, business, governments, foreign agents) discussed above. Similarly, the aggregate demand for loanable funds is the sum of the quantity demanded by the separate fund demanding sectors. As illustrated in

SEARCH THE SITE

Go to the United States Treasury and find the latest information available on the size of the U.S. national debt.

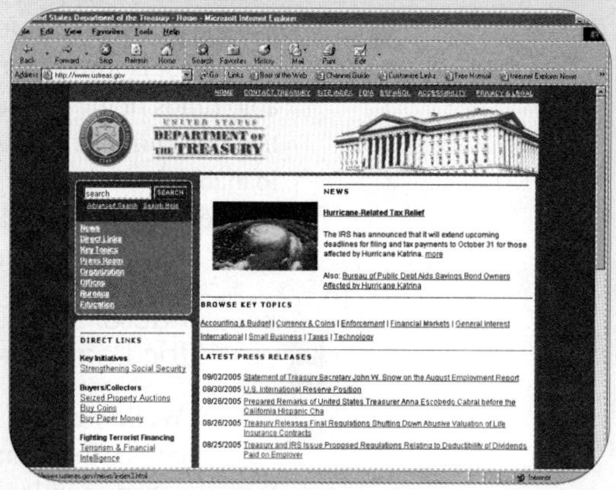

Go to the U.S. Treasury Web site at **www.ustreas.gov**

Click on "Bureaus"

Click on "Bureau of Public Debt"

Click on "The Public Debt"

Click on "Daily amounts to the penny . . ."

This will bring up the relevant tables. For example, on August 2, 2004, the size of the national debt was $7.312 trillion.

Questions

1. What is the most recents dollar value of the U.S. national debt?
2. Calculate the percentage change in the U.S. notional debt since August 12, 2005.

Figure 2–11, the aggregate quantity of funds supplied is positively related to interest rates, while the aggregate quantity of funds demanded is inversely related to interest rates. As long as competitive forces are allowed to operate freely in a financial system, the interest rate that equates the aggregate quantity of loanable funds supplied with aggregate quantity of loanable funds demanded for a financial security, Q^*, is the equilibrium interest rate for that

FIGURE 2–11 Determination of Equilibrium Interest Rates

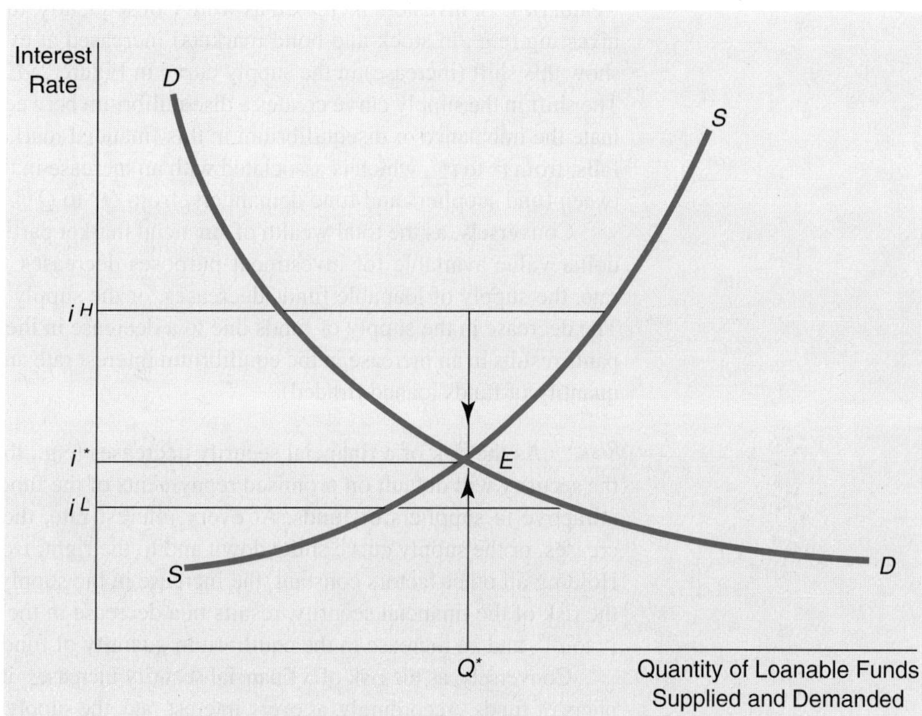

security, i^*, point *E* in Figure 2–11. For example, whenever the rate of interest is set higher than the equilibrium rate, such as i^H, the financial system has a surplus of loanable funds. As a result, some suppliers of funds will lower the interest rate at which they are willing to lend and the demanders of funds will absorb the loanable funds surplus. In contrast, when the rate of interest is lower than the equilibrium interest rate, such as i^L, there is a shortage of loanable funds in the financial system. Some borrowers will be unable to obtain the funds they need at current rates. As a result, interest rates will increase, causing more suppliers of loanable funds to enter the market and some demanders of funds to leave the market. These competitive forces will cause the quantity of funds supplied to increase and the quantity of funds demanded to decrease until a shortage of funds no longer exists.

5 Factors that Cause the Supply and Demand Curves for Loanable Funds to Shift

While we have alluded to the fundamental factors that cause the supply and demand curves for loanable funds to shift, in this section we formally summarize these factors. We then examine how shifts in the supply and demand curves for loanable funds determine the equilibrium interest rate on a specific financial instrument. A shift in the supply or demand curve occurs when the quantity of a financial security supplied or demanded changes at every given interest rate in response to a change in another factor besides the interest rate. In either case, a change in the supply or demand curve for loanable funds causes interest rates to move.

Supply of Funds. We have already described the positive relation between interest rates and the supply of loanable funds along the loanable funds supply curve. Factors that cause the supply curve of loanable funds to shift, at any given interest rate, include the wealth of fund suppliers, the risk of the financial security, future spending needs, monetary policy objectives, and economic conditions.

Wealth. As the total wealth of financial market participants (households, business, etc.) increases, the absolute dollar value available for investment purposes increases. Accordingly, at every interest rate, the supply of loanable funds increases, or the supply curve shifts down and to the right. For example, as the U.S. economy grew in the 1990s, total wealth of U.S. investors increased as well. Consequently, the supply of funds available for investing (e.g., in stock and bond markets) increased at every available interest rate. We show this shift (increase) in the supply curve in Figure 2–12 (a) as a move from *SS* to *SS″*. The shift in the supply curve creates a disequilibrium between demand and supply. To eliminate the imbalance or disequilibrium in this financial market, the equilibrium interest rate falls, from i^* to $i^{*\prime\prime}$, which is associated with an increase in the quantity of funds loaned between fund suppliers and fund demanders, from Q^* to $Q^{*\prime\prime}$.

Conversely, as the total wealth of financial market participants decreases, the absolute dollar value available for investment purposes decreases. Accordingly, at every interest rate, the supply of loanable funds decreases, or the supply curve shifts up and to the left. The decrease in the supply of funds due to a decrease in the total wealth of market participants results in an increase in the equilibrium interest rate and a decrease in the equilibrium quantity of funds loaned (traded).

Risk. As the risk of a financial security decreases (e.g., the probability that the issuer of the security will default on promised repayments of the funds borrowed), it becomes more attractive to suppliers of funds. At every interest rate, the supply of loanable funds increases, or the supply curve shifts down and to the right, from *SS* to *SS″* in Figure 2–12(a). Holding all other factors constant, the increase in the supply of funds, due to a decrease in the risk of the financial security, results in a decrease in the equilibrium interest rate, from i^* to $i^{*\prime\prime}$, and an increase in the equilibrium quantity of funds traded, from Q^* to $Q^{*\prime\prime}$.

Conversely, as the risk of a financial security increases, it becomes less attractive to suppliers of funds. Accordingly, at every interest rate, the supply of loanable funds decreases, or

FIGURE 2–12 The Effect on Interest Rates from a Shift in the Demand Curve for or Supply Curve of Loanable Funds

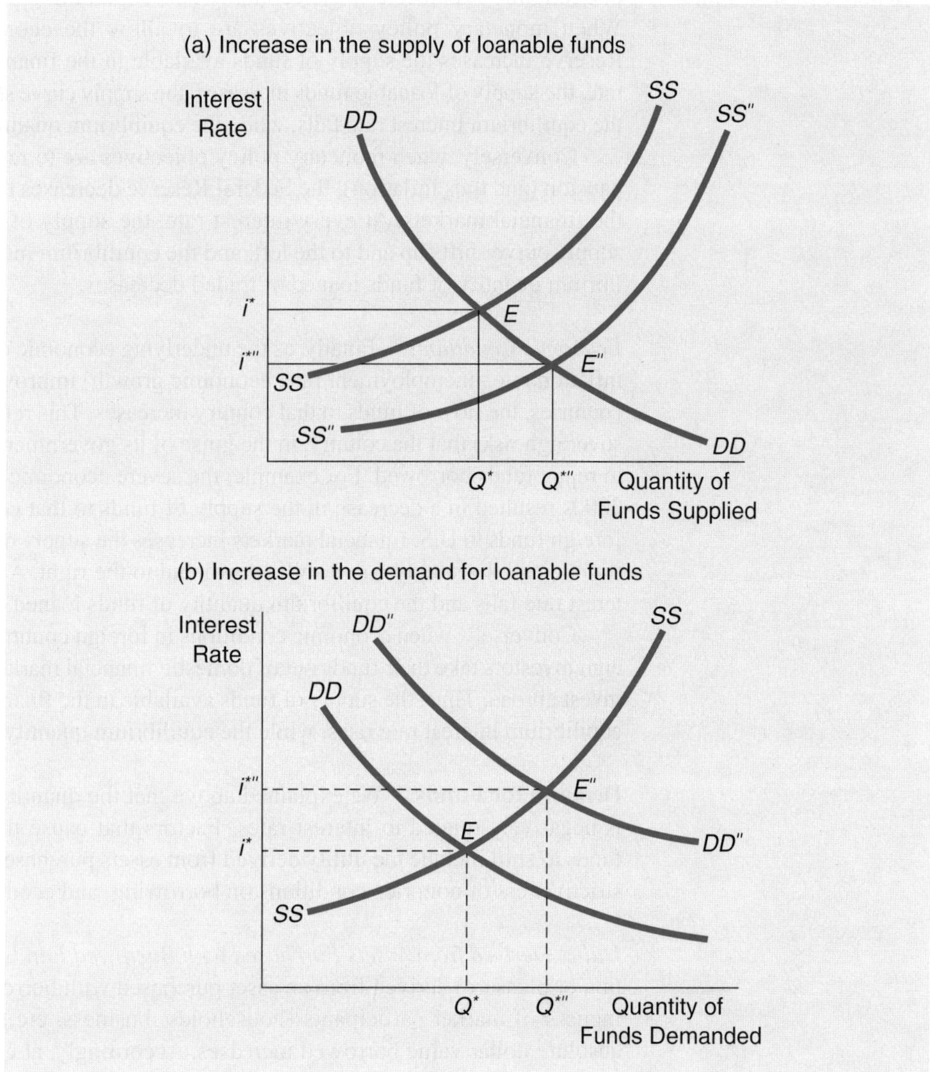

the supply curve shifts up and to the left. Holding all other factors constant, the decrease in the supply of funds due to an increase in the financial security's risk results in an increase in the equilibrium interest rate and a decrease in the equilibrium quantity of funds loaned (or traded).

Near-Term Spending Needs. When financial market participants have few near-term spending needs, the absolute dollar value of funds available to invest increases. For example, when a family's son or daughter moves out of the family home to live on his or her own, current spending needs of the family decrease and the supply of available funds (for investing) increases. At every interest rate, the supply of loanable funds increases, or the supply curve shifts down and to the right. The financial market, holding all other factors constant, reacts to this increased supply of funds by decreasing the equilibrium interest rate and increasing the equilibrium quantity of funds traded.

Conversely, when financial market participants have increased near-term spending needs, the absolute dollar value of funds available to invest decreases. At every interest rate, the supply of loanable funds decreases, or the supply curve shifts up and to the left. The shift in the supply curve creates a disequilibrium in this financial market that results in an increase in the equilibrium interest rate and a decrease in the equilibrium quantity of funds loaned (or traded).

Monetary Expansion. One method used by the Federal Reserve to implement monetary policy is to alter the availability of funds, the growth in the money supply, and thus the rate of economic expansion of the economy (we explain this process in detail in Chapter 4). When monetary policy objectives are to allow the economy to expand, the Federal Reserve increases the supply of funds available in the financial markets. At every interest rate, the supply of loanable funds increases, the supply curve shifts down and to the right, and the equilibrium interest rate falls, while the equilibrium quantity of funds traded increases.

www.federalreserve.gov

Conversely, when monetary policy objectives are to restrict the rate of economic expansion (and thus inflation), the Federal Reserve decreases the supply of funds available in the financial markets. At every interest rate, the supply of loanable funds decreases, the supply curve shifts up and to the left, and the equilibrium interest rate rises, while the equilibrium quantity of funds loaned or traded decreases.

Economic Conditions. Finally, as the underlying economic conditions themselves (e.g., the inflation rate, unemployment rate, economic growth) improve in a country relative to other countries, the flow of funds to that country increases. This reflects the lower risk (country or sovereign risk) that the country, in the guise of its government, will default on its obligation to repay funds borrowed. For example, the severe economic crisis in Argentina in the early 2000s resulted in a decrease in the supply of funds to that country. An increased inflow of foreign funds to U.S. financial markets increases the supply of loanable funds at every interest rate and the supply curve shifts down and to the right. Accordingly, the equilibrium interest rate falls and the equilibrium quantity of funds loaned or traded increases.

Conversely, when economic conditions in foreign countries improve, domestic and foreign investors take their funds out of domestic financial markets (e.g., the United States) and invest abroad. Thus, the supply of funds available in the financial markets decreases and the equilibrium interest rate rises, while the equilibrium quantity of funds traded decreases.

Demand for Funds. We explained above that the quantity of loanable funds demanded is negatively related to interest rates. Factors that cause the demand curve for loanable funds to shift include the utility derived from assets purchased with borrowed funds, the restrictiveness of nonprice conditions on borrowing, and economic conditions.

Utility Derived from Assets Purchased with Borrowed Funds. As the utility (i.e., satisfaction or pleasure) derived from an asset purchased with borrowed funds increases, the willingness of market participants (households, business, etc.) to borrow increases and the absolute dollar value borrowed increases. Accordingly, at every interest rate, the demand for loanable funds increases, or the demand curve shifts up and to the right. For example, suppose a change in jobs takes an individual from Arizona to Minnesota. The individual currently has a convertible automobile. Given the move to Minnesota, the individual's utility from the convertible decreases, while it would increase for a car with heated seats. Thus, with a potential increased utility from the purchase of a new car, the individual's demand for funds in the form of an auto loan increases. We show this shift (increase) in the demand curve in Figure 2–12(b) as a move from DD to DD''. The shift in the demand curve creates a disequilibrium in this financial market. Holding all other factors constant, the increase in the demand for funds due to an increase in the utility from the purchased asset results in an increase in the equilibrium interest rate, from i^* to $i^{*''}$, and an increase in the equilibrium quantity of funds traded, from Q^* to $Q^{*''}$.

Conversely, as the utility derived from an asset purchased with borrowed funds decreases, the willingness of market participants (households, businesses, etc.) to borrow decreases and the absolute dollar amount borrowed decreases. Accordingly, at every interest rate, the demand for loanable funds decreases, or the demand curve shifts down and to the left. The shift in the demand curve again creates a disequilibrium in this financial market. As competitive forces adjust, and holding all other factors constant, the decrease in the demand for funds due to a decrease in the utility from the purchased asset results in a decrease in the equilibrium interest rate and a decrease in the equilibrium quantity of funds loaned or traded.

Restrictiveness on Nonprice Conditions on Borrowed Funds. As the nonprice restrictions put on borrowers as a condition of borrowing decrease, the willingness of market participants to borrow increases and the absolute dollar value borrowed increases. Such nonprice conditions may include fees, collateral, requirements or restrictions on the use of funds (so-called restrictive covenants, see Chapter 6). The lack of such restrictions makes the loan more desirable to the user of funds. Accordingly, at every interest rate, the demand for loanable funds increases, or the demand curve shifts up and to the right, from *DD* to *DD″*. As competitive forces adjust, and holding all other factors constant, the increase in the demand for funds due to a decrease in the restrictive conditions on the borrowed funds results in an increase in the equilibrium interest rate, from *i** to *i*″*, and an increase in the equilibrium quantity of funds traded, from *Q** to *QQ*″*.

Conversely, as the nonprice restrictions put on borrowers as a condition of borrowing increase, market participants' willingness to borrow decreases and the absolute dollar value borrowed decreases. Accordingly, the demand curve shifts down and to the left. The shift in the demand curve results in a decrease in the equilibrium interest rate and a decrease in the equilibrium quantity of funds traded.

Economic Conditions. When the domestic economy experiences a period of growth, such as that in the United States in the 1990s, market participants are willing to borrow more heavily. For example, state and local governments would be more likely to repair and improve decaying infrastructure when the local economy is strong. Accordingly, the demand curve for funds shifts up and to the right. Holding all other factors constant, the increase in the demand for funds due to economic growth results in an increase in the equilibrium interest rate and an increase in the equilibrium quantity of funds traded.

Conversely, when domestic economic growth is stagnant, market participants reduce their demand for funds. Accordingly, the demand curve shifts down and to the left, resulting in a decrease in the equilibrium interest rate and a decrease in the equilibrium quantity of funds traded.

DO YOU UNDERSTAND?

1. Who the main suppliers of loanable funds are?
2. Who the major demanders of loanable funds are?

6

MOVEMENT OF INTEREST RATES OVER TIME

As discussed in the previous section of this chapter, the loanable funds theory of interest rates is based on the supply and demand for loanable funds as functions of interest rates. The equilibrium interest rate (point *E* in Figure 2–11) is only a temporary equilibrium. Changes in underlying factors that determine the demand and supply of loanable funds can cause continuous shifts in the supply and/or demand curves for loanable funds. Market forces will react to the resulting disequilibrium with a change in the equilibrium interest rate and quantity of funds traded in that market. Refer again to Figure 2–12(a), which shows the effects of an *increase in the supply curve* for loanable funds, from *SS* to *SS″* (and the resulting *decrease in the equilibrium interest rate,* from *i** to *i*″*), while Figure 2–12(b) shows the effects of an *increase in the demand curve* for loanable funds, from *DD* to *DD″* (and the resulting *increase in the equilibrium interest rate,* from *i** to *i*″*).

DO YOU UNDERSTAND?

1. What will happen to the equilibrium interest rate when the demand for loanable funds increases?
2. What will happen to the equilibrium interest rate when the supply of loanable funds increases?
3. How supply and demand, together, determine interest rates?

7

DETERMINANTS OF INTEREST RATES FOR INDIVIDUAL SECURITIES

So far we have looked at the general determination of equilibrium (nominal) interest rates for financial securities in the context of the loanable demand and supply theory of the flow of funds. In this section, we examine the specific factors that affect differences in interest rates across the range of real-world financial markets (i.e., differences among interest rates on individual securities, given the underlying level of interest

TABLE 2-3 Factors Affecting Nominal Interest Rates

Inflation—The continual increase in the price level of a basket of goods and services.
Real Interest Rate—nominal interest rate that would exist on a security if no inflation were expected.
Default Risk—risk that a security issuer will default on the security by missing an interest or principal payment.
Liquidity Risk—risk that a security cannot be sold at a predictable price with low transaction costs at short notice.
Special Provisions—provisions (e.g., taxability, convertibility, and callability) that impact the security holder beneficially or adversely and as such are reflected in the interest rates on securities that contain such provisions.
Time to Maturity—length of time a security has until maturity.

rates determined by the demand and supply of loanable funds). These factors include inflation, the "real" interest rate, default risk, liquidity risk, special provisions regarding the use of funds raised by a security's issuance, and the term to maturity of the security. We examine each of these factors in this section and summarize them in Table 2–3.

Inflation

The first factor to affect interest rates is the *actual or expected inflation rate* in the economy. Specifically, the higher the level of actual or expected inflation, the higher will be the level of interest rates. The intuition behind the positive relationship between interest rates and inflation rates is that an investor who buys a financial asset must earn a higher interest rate when inflation increases to compensate for the increased cost of forgoing consumption of real goods and services today and buying these more highly priced goods and services in the future. In other words, the higher the rate of inflation, the more expensive the same basket of goods and services will be in the future. **Inflation** of the general price index of goods and services (IP) is defined as the (percentage) increase in the price of a standardized basket of goods and services over a given period of time. In the United States, inflation is measured using indexes such as the consumer price index (CPI) and the producer price index (PPI). For example, the annual inflation rate using the CPI index between years t and $t + 1$ would be equal to:

inflation

The continual increase in the price level of a basket of goods and services.

$$\text{Inflation } (IP) = \frac{CPI_{t+1} - CPI_t}{CPI_t} \times \frac{100}{1}$$

Real Interest Rates

real interest rate

The interest rate that would exist on a default free security if no inflation were expected.

A **real interest rate** is the interest rate that would exist on a security if no inflation were expected over the holding period (e.g., a year) of a security. As such, it measures society's relative time preference for consuming today rather than tomorrow. The higher society's preference to consume today (i.e., the higher its time value of money or rate of time preference), the higher the real interest rate (RIR) will be.

Fisher Effect. The relationship among real interest rates (*RIR*), expected inflation [Expected (IP)], described above, and nominal interest rates (*i*) is often referred to as the Fisher effect, named for the economist Irving Fisher, who identified these relationships early last century. The Fisher effect theorizes that nominal interest rates observed in financial markets must compensate investors for (1) any reduced purchasing power on funds lent (or principal lent) due to inflationary price changes and (2) an additional premium above the expected rate of inflation for forgoing present consumption (which reflects the real interest rate discussed above).

$$i = \text{Expected } (IP) + RIR \qquad \textbf{(6)}$$

Thus, the nominal interest rate will be equal to the real interest rate only when market participants expect inflation to be zero—Expected $(IP) = 0$. Similarly, nominal interest rates will be equal to the expected inflation rate only when real interest rates are zero. Note that we can rearrange the nominal interest rate equation to show the determinants of the real interest rate:

Often the Fisher effect formula is written as:

$$i = RIR + \text{Expected } (IP) + [RIR \times \text{Expected } (IP)]$$

where $RIR \times$ Expected (IP) is the inflation premium for the loss of purchasing power on the promised nominal interest rate payments due to inflation. For small values of RIR and Expected (IP) this term is negligible. The approximation formula in Equation 7 assumes these values are small.

$$RIR = i - \text{Expected } (IP) \qquad (7)$$

EXAMPLE 2-6 Calculations of Real Interest Rates

The one-year Treasury bill rate in 2001 averaged 3.49 percent and inflation (measured by the consumer price index) for the year was 1.60 percent. If investors had expected the same inflation rate as that actually realized (i.e., 1.60 percent), then according to the Fisher effect the real interest rate for 2001 was:

$$3.49\% - 1.60\% = 1.89\%$$

The one-year T-bill rate in 2003 was 1.24 percent, while the CPI for the year was 1.90 percent, which implies a real interest rate of −0.66 percent, that is, the real interest rate was actually negative.

stats.bls.gov/cpi/home.htm

Figure 2–13 shows the nominal interest rate (one-year T-bill rate) versus the change in the CPI from 1962 through 2004. Because the expected inflation rate is difficult to estimate accurately, the real interest rate can be difficult to measure accurately as well, since investors' expectations are not always realized. A 2004 study by Ibbotson Associates found that inflation over the period 1926 to 2003 averaged 3.03 percent per year, from 1926 to 1965 inflation averaged 1.56 percent per year, for the last 20 years it averaged 3.07 percent, and for the last 10 years inflation averaged 2.45 percent. As a result, Treasury bills provided a negative real rate in every holding period except for the last 10 and 20 years. Specifically, the real rate on Treasury bills over the period 1926 to 2003 averaged –1.02 percent per year, from 1926 to 1965 averaged –1.49 percent per year, for the last 20 years it averaged 0.15 percent, and for the last 10 years it averaged 0.15 percent.[6]

Default or Credit Risk

default risk

The risk that a security issuer will default on that security by being late on or missing an interest or principal payment.

Default risk is the risk that a security issuer will default on making its promised interest and principal payments to the buyer of a security. The higher the default risk, the higher the interest rate that will be demanded by the buyer of the security to compensate him or her for this default (or credit) risk exposure. Not all securities exhibit default risk. For example, U.S. Treasury securities are regarded as having no default risk since they are issued by the U.S. government, and the probability of the U.S. government defaulting on its debt payments is practically zero given its taxation powers and its ability to print currency. Some borrowers, however, such as corporations or individuals, have less predictable cash flows (and no taxation powers), and therefore investors charge them an interest rate risk premium reflecting their perceived probability of default and the potential recovery of the amount loaned. The difference between a quoted interest rate on a security (security j) and a Treasury security

6. Ibbotson Associates, *Stocks, Bonds, Bills, and Inflation 2004 Yearbook* (Chicago: Ibbotson Associates, 2004).

FIGURE 2–13 **Nominal Interest Rates versus Inflation**

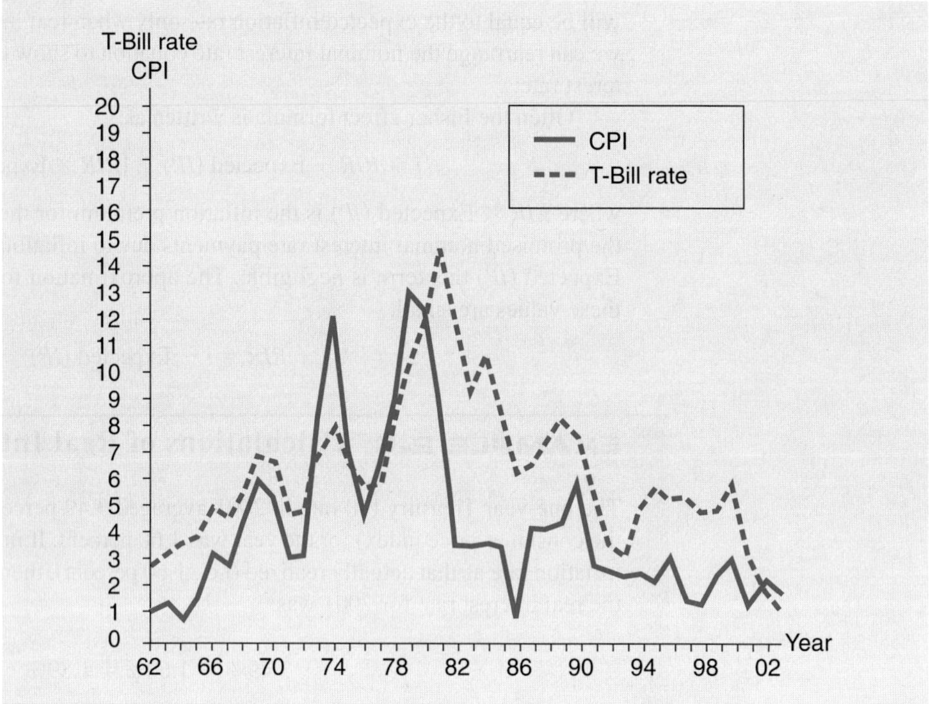

Source: Federal Reserve Board Web site and U.S. Department of Labor Web site, August 2004.
www.federalreserve.gov and **stats.bls.gov/cpi/home.htm**

with similar maturity, liquidity, tax, and other features (such as callability or convertibility) is called a *default* or *credit risk premium* (DRP_j). That is:

$$DRP_j = i_{jt} - i_{Tt} \tag{8}$$

where

www.moodys.com

i_{jt} = interest rate on a security issued by a non-Treasury issuer (issuer j) of maturity m at time t

i_{Tt} = interest rate on a security issued by the U.S. Treasury of maturity m at time t

www.standardandpoors.com

The default risk on many corporate bonds is evaluated and categorized by various bond rating agencies such as Moody's and Standard & Poor's. (We discuss these ratings in more detail in Chapter 6.) For example, in December 2003, the 10-year Treasury interest rate, or yield, was 4.01 percent. On Aaa-rated and Baa-rated corporate debt interest rates were 5.66 percent and 6.76 percent, respectively. Thus, the average default risk premiums on the Aaa-rated and Baa-rated corporate debt were:

$$DRP_{Aaa} = 5.66\% - 4.01\% = 1.65\%$$
$$DRP_{Baa} = 6.76\% - 4.01\% = 2.75\%$$

Figure 2–14 presents these risk premiums from 1977 through 2004. Notice from this figure and Figure 2–13 that default risk premiums tend to increase when the economy is contracting and decrease when the economy is expanding. For example, from 1981 to 1982 real interest rates (T-bills—CPI in Figure 2–13) increased from 5.90 percent to 8.47 percent. Over the same period, default risk premiums on Aaa-rated bonds increased from 0.25 percent to 0.78 percent and on Baa-rated bonds from 2.12 percent to 3.10 percent.

Liquidity Risk

A highly liquid asset is one that can be sold at a predictable price with low transaction costs and thus can be converted into its full market value at short notice. The interest rate

FIGURE 2–14 Default Risk Premium on Corporate Bonds

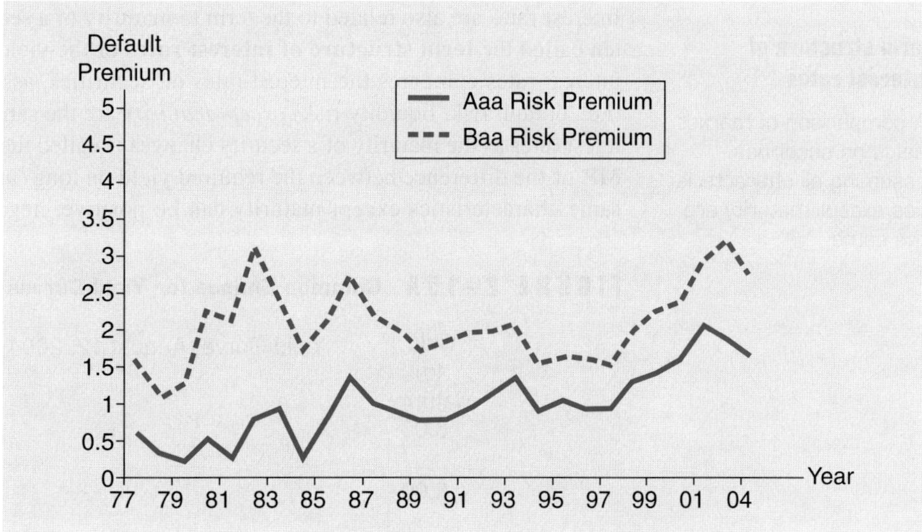

Source: Federal Reserve Board Web site, August 2004. **www.federalreserve.gov**

liquidity risk

The risk that a security can be sold at a predictable price with low transaction costs on short notice.

on a security reflects its relative liquidity, with highly liquid assets carrying the lowest interest rates (all other characteristics remaining the same). Likewise, if a security is illiquid, investors add a **liquidity risk** premium (LRP) to the interest rate on the security. In the United States, liquid markets exist for most government securities and the stocks and some bonds issued by large corporations. Many bonds, however, do not trade on a regular basis or on organized exchanges such as the NYSE. As a result, if investors wish to sell these bonds quickly, they may get a lower price than they could have received if they had waited to sell the bonds. Consequently, investors demand a liquidity premium on top of all other premiums to compensate for the bond's lack of liquidity and the potential price discount from selling it early.

A different type of liquidity risk premium may also exist (see below) if investors dislike long-term securities because their prices (present values) are more sensitive to interest rate changes than short-term securities (see Chapter 3). In this case, a higher liquidity risk premium may be added to a security with a longer maturity simply because of its greater exposure to price risk (loss of capital value) on a security as interest rates change.

Special Provisions or Covenants

Numerous special provisions or covenants that may be written into the contracts underlying the issuance of a security also affect the interest rates on different securities (see Chapter 6). Some of these special provisions include the security's taxability, convertibility, and callability.

For example, for investors, interest payments on municipal securities are free of federal, state, and local taxes. Thus, the interest rate demanded by a municipal bond holder is smaller than that on a comparable taxable bond—for example, a Treasury bond, which is taxable at the federal level but not at the state or local (city) levels, or a corporate bond, whose interest payments are taxable at the state and local levels as well as federal levels.

A convertible (special) feature of a security offers the holder the opportunity to exchange one security for another type of the issuer's security at a preset price. Because of the value of this conversion option, the convertible security holder requires a lower interest rate than a comparable nonconvertible security holder (all else equal). In general, special provisions that provide benefits to the security holder (e.g., tax-free status and convertibility) are associated with lower interest rates, and special provisions that provide benefits to the security issuer (e.g., callability, by which an issuer has the option to retire—call—a security prior to maturity at a preset price) are associated with higher interest rates.

Term to Maturity

term structure of interest rates

A comparison of market yields on securities, assuming all characteristics except maturity are the same.

Interest rates are also related to the term to maturity of a security.[7] This relationship is often called the **term structure of interest rates** or the yield curve. The term structure of interest rates compares the interest rates on securities, assuming that all characteristics (i.e., default risk, liquidity risk) *except maturity* are the same. The change in required interest rates as the maturity of a security changes is called the maturity premium (MP). The MP, or the difference between the required yield on long- and short-term securities of the same characteristics except maturity can be positive, negative, or zero. The interest or

FIGURE 2–15A Common Shapes for Yield Curves on Treasury Securities

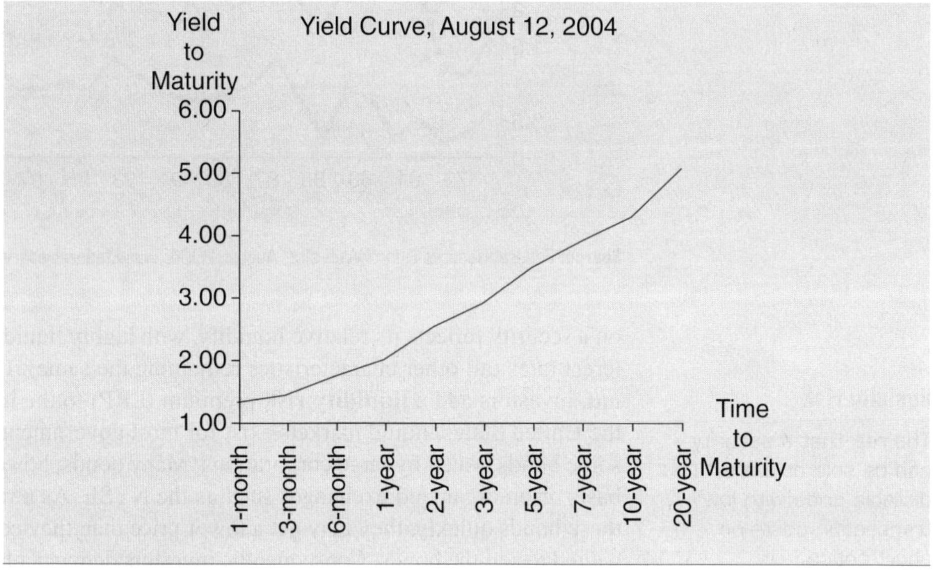

FIGURE 2–15B

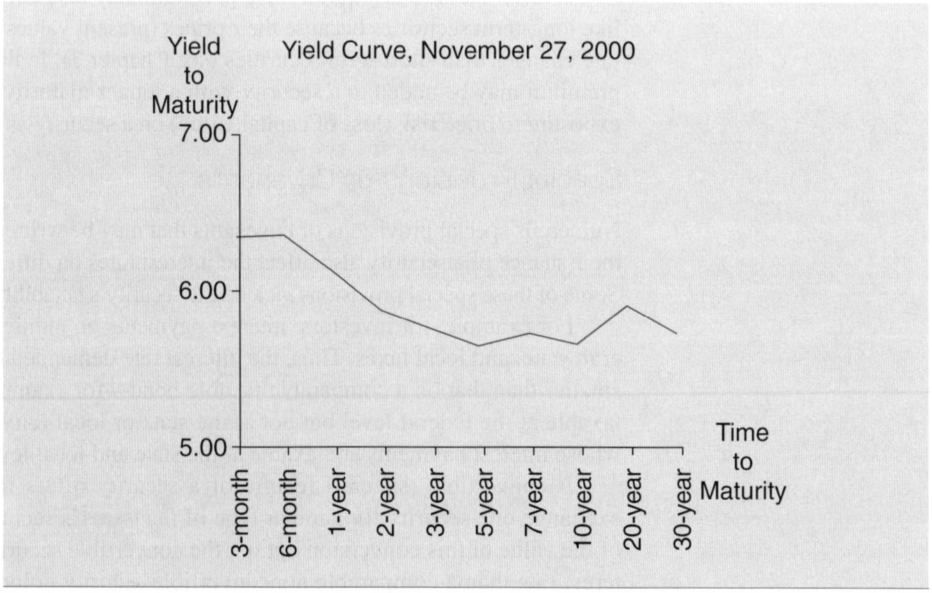

Source: U.S. Treasury, Daily Treasury Yield Curves, various states. **www.ustreas.gov**

7. As we discuss in Chapter 3, only debt securities have an identifiable maturity date; equity securities do not.

FIGURE 2–15C

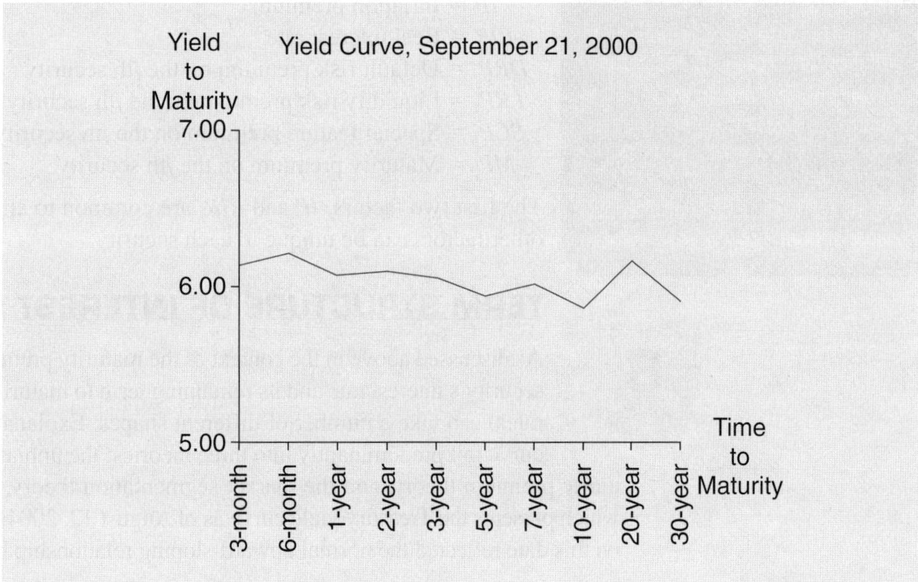

yield to maturity curve for U.S. Treasury securities is the most frequently reported and analyzed yield to maturity curve. The shape of the yield curve on Treasury securities has taken many forms over the years, but the three most common shapes are shown in Figure 2–15. In graph (a), the yield curve on August 12, 2004, yields rise steadily with maturity when the yield curve is upward sloping. This is the most common yield curve, so that on average the MP is positive. Graph (b) shows an inverted or downward-sloping yield curve, reported on November 27, 2000, for which yields decline as maturity increases. Inverted yield curves do not generally last very long. Finally, graph (c) shows a flat yield curve, reported on September 21, 2000, in which the yield to maturity is virtually unaffected by the term to maturity.[8]

Note that these yield curves may reflect factors other than investors' preferences for the maturity of a security, since in reality there may be liquidity differences among the securities traded at different points along the yield curve. For example, newly issued 20-year Treasury bonds offer a rate of return less than (seasoned issues) 10-year Treasury bonds if investors prefer new ("on the run") securities to previously issued ("off the run") securities. Specifically, since (historically) the Treasury only issues new 10-year notes and 20-year bonds at the long end of the maturity spectrum, an existing 10-year Treasury bond would have to have been issued 10 years previously (i.e., it was originally a 20-year bond when it was issued 10 years previously). The increased demand for the newly issued "liquid" 20-year Treasury bonds relative to the less liquid 10-year Treasury bonds can be large enough to push the equilibrium interest rate on the 20-year Treasury bonds below that on the 10-year Treasury bonds and even below short-term rates. In the next section, we review three major theories that are often used to explain the shape of the yield to maturity curve.

Putting the factors that impact interest rates in different markets together, we can use the following general equation to determine the factors that functionally impact the fair interest rate (i_j^*) on an individual (jth) financial security:

$$i_j^* = f(IP, RIR, DRP_j, LRP_j, SCP_j, MP_j) \tag{9}$$

8. Yield curves from the last 15 years can be viewed at **stockcharts.com/charts/yieldcurve.html.** A look at this Web site reveals how infrequently inverted or flat yield curves occur.

DO YOU UNDERSTAND?

1. What the difference is between inflation and real interest rates?
2. What should happen to a security's equilibrium interest rate as the security's liquidity risk increases?
3. What term structure of interest rates means?

where

IP = Inflation premium
RIR = Real interest rate
DRP_j = Default risk premium on the jth security
LRP_j = Liquidity risk premium on the jth security
SCP_j = Special feature premium on the jth security
MP_j = Maturity premium on the jth security

The first two factors, IP and RIR, are common to all financial securities, while the other factors can be unique to each security.

TERM STRUCTURE OF INTEREST RATES

8

As discussed above in the context of the maturity premium, the relationship between a security's interest rate and its remaining term to maturity (the term structure of interest rates) can take a number of different shapes. Explanations for the shape of the yield curve fall predominantly into three theories: the unbiased expectations theory, the liquidity premium theory, and the market segmentation theory. Review again Figure 2–15(a), which presents the Treasury yield curve as of August 12, 2004. As can be seen, the yield curve on this date reflected the normal upward-sloping relationship between yield and maturity.

Unbiased Expectations Theory

According to the unbiased expectations theory of the term structure of interest rates, at a given point in time the yield curve reflects the market's current expectations of future short-term rates. As illustrated in Figure 2–16, the intuition behind the unbiased expectations theory is that if investors have a four-year investment horizon, they could either buy a current, four-year bond and earn the current or spot yield on a four-year bond (${}_1\bar{R}_4$ if held to maturity) each year, or could invest in four successive one-year bonds (of which they only know the current one-year spot rate (${}_1\bar{R}_1$), but form expectations of the unknown future one-year rates [$E({}_2\tilde{r}_1)$, $E({}_3\tilde{r}_1)$, and $E({}_4\tilde{r}_1)$]). Note that each interest rate term has two subscripts, for example, ${}_1\bar{R}_4$. The first subscript indicates the period in which the security is bought, so that 1 represents the purchase of a security in period 1. The second subscript indicates the maturity on the security, so that 4 represents the purchase of a security with a four-year life. Similarly, $E({}_3\tilde{r}_1)$ is the expected return on a security with a one-year life purchased in period 3.

In equilibrium, the return to holding a four-year bond to maturity should equal the expected return to investing in four successive one-year bonds. If this equality does not hold, an arbitrage opportunity exists. For example, if the investor could earn more on the one-year bond investments, he could short (or sell) the four-year bond, use the proceeds to buy the four successive one-year bonds, and earn a guaranteed profit over the four-year investment horizon. Thus, according to the unexpected expectations hypothesis, if future one-year rates are expected to rise each successive year into the future, then the yield curve will slope upwards. Specifically, the current four-year T-bond rate or return will exceed the three-bond rate, which will exceed the two-year bond rate, and so on. Similarly, if future one-year rates are expected to remain constant each successive year into the future, then the four-year bond rate will be equal to the three-year bond rate—that is, the term structure of interest rates will remain

FIGURE 2–16 Unbiased Expectation Theory of the Term Structure of Interest Rates

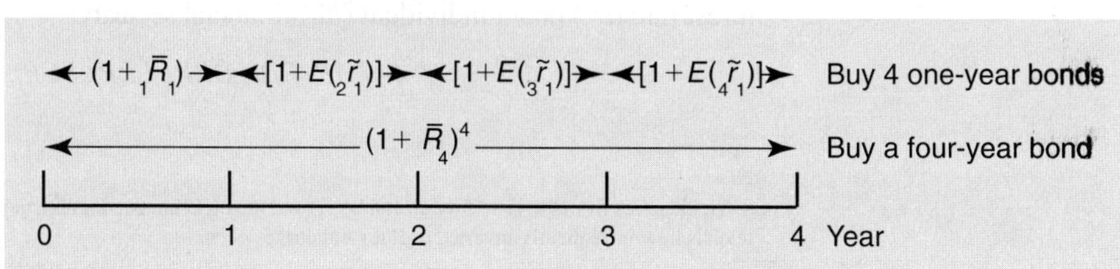

constant over the relevant time period. Specifically, the unbiased expectation theory posits that current long-term interest rates are geometric averages of current and expected *future* short-term interest rates. The mathematical equation representing this relationship is:

$$(1 + {}_1\bar{R}_N)^N = (1 + {}_1\bar{R}_1)(1 + E({}_2\tilde{r}_1)) \ldots (1 + E({}_N\tilde{r}_1)) \quad \textbf{(10)}$$

therefore:

$${}_1\bar{R}_N = [(1 + {}_1\bar{R}_1)(1 + E({}_2\tilde{r}_1)) \ldots (1 + E({}_N\tilde{r}_1))]^{1/N} - 1$$

where

${}_1\bar{R}_N$ = Actual N-period rate today (i.e., the first day of year 1)
N = Term to maturity, $N = 1, 2, \ldots, 4, \ldots$
${}_1\bar{R}_1$ = Actual current 1-year rate today
$E({}_i\tilde{r}_1)$ = Expected one-year rates for years, $i = 2, 3, 4, \ldots, N$ in the future

Notice, as above, that uppercase interest rate terms, ${}_1\bar{R}_t$, are the actual current interest rates on securities purchased today with a maturity of t years. Lowercase interest rate terms, ${}_t\tilde{r}_1$, are estimates of future one-year interest rates starting t years into the future.

EXAMPLE 2-7 Construction of a Yield Curve Using the Unbiased Expectations Theory of the Term Structure of Interest Rates

Suppose that the current one-year rate (one-year spot rate) and expected one-year T-bond rates over the following three years (i.e., years 2, 3, and 4, respectively) are as follows:

$${}_1\bar{R}_1 = 1.94\%,\ E({}_2\tilde{r}_1) = 3.00\%,\ E({}_3\tilde{r}_1) = 3.74\%,\ E({}_4\tilde{r}_1) = 4.10\%$$

Using the unbiased expectations theory, current (or today's) rates for one-, two-, three-, and four-year maturity Treasury securities should be:

$${}_1\bar{R}_1 = 1.94\%$$
$${}_1\bar{R}_2 = [(1 + .0194)(1 + .03)]^{1/2} - 1 = 2.47\%$$
$${}_1\bar{R}_3 = [(1 + .0194)(1 + .03)(1 + .0374)]^{1/3} - 1 = 2.89\%$$
$${}_1\bar{R}_4 = [(1 + .0194)(1 + .03)(1 + .0374)(1 + .041)]^{1/4} - 1 = 3.19\%$$

and the current yield to maturity curve will be upward sloping as shown:

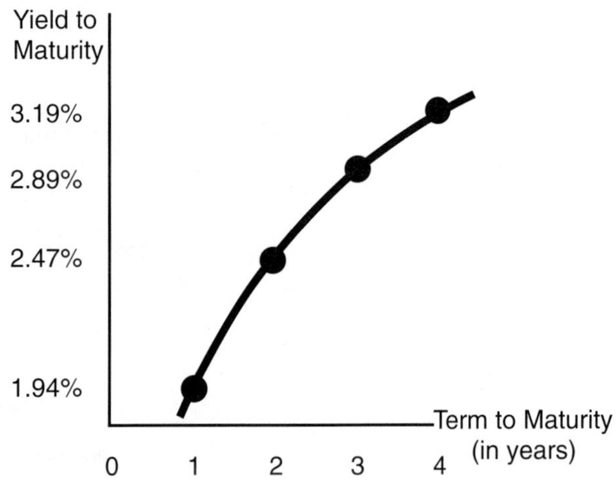

This upward-sloping yield curve reflects the market's expectation of persistently rising one-year (short-term) interest rates over the future horizon.[9]

9. That is, $E({}_4\tilde{r}_1) > E({}_3\tilde{r}_1) > E({}_2\tilde{r}_1) > {}_1\bar{R}_1$

Liquidity Premium Theory

The second theory, the liquidity premium theory of the term structure of interest rates, is an extension of the unbiased expectations theory. It is based on the idea that investors will hold long-term maturities only if they are offered at a premium to compensate for future uncertainty in a security's value, which increases with an asset's maturity. Specifically, in a world of uncertainty, short-term securities provide greater marketability (due to their more active secondary market) and have less price risk (due to smaller price fluctuations for a given change in interest rates) than long-term securities. As a result, investors prefer to hold shorter-term securities because they can be converted into cash with little risk of a capital loss, i.e., a fall in the price of the security below its original purchase price. Thus, investors must be offered a liquidity premium to buy longer-term securities which have a higher risk of capital losses. This difference in price or liquidity risk can be directly related to the fact that longer-term securities are more sensitive to interest rate changes in the market than are shorter-term securities—see Chapter 3 for a discussion on bond interest rate sensitivity and the link to a bond's maturity or duration. Because the longer the maturity on a security the greater its risk, the liquidity premium increases as maturity increases.

The liquidity premium theory states that long-term rates are equal to geometric averages of current and expected short-term rates (as under the unbiased expectations theory), plus liquidity risk premiums that increase with the maturity of the security. Figure 2–17 illustrates the differences in the shape of the yield curve under the unbiased expectations hypothesis versus the liquidity premium hypothesis. For example, according to the liquidity

FIGURE 2–17 Yield Curve under the Unbiased Expectations Hypotheses (UEH) versus the Liquidity Premium Hypothesis (LPH)

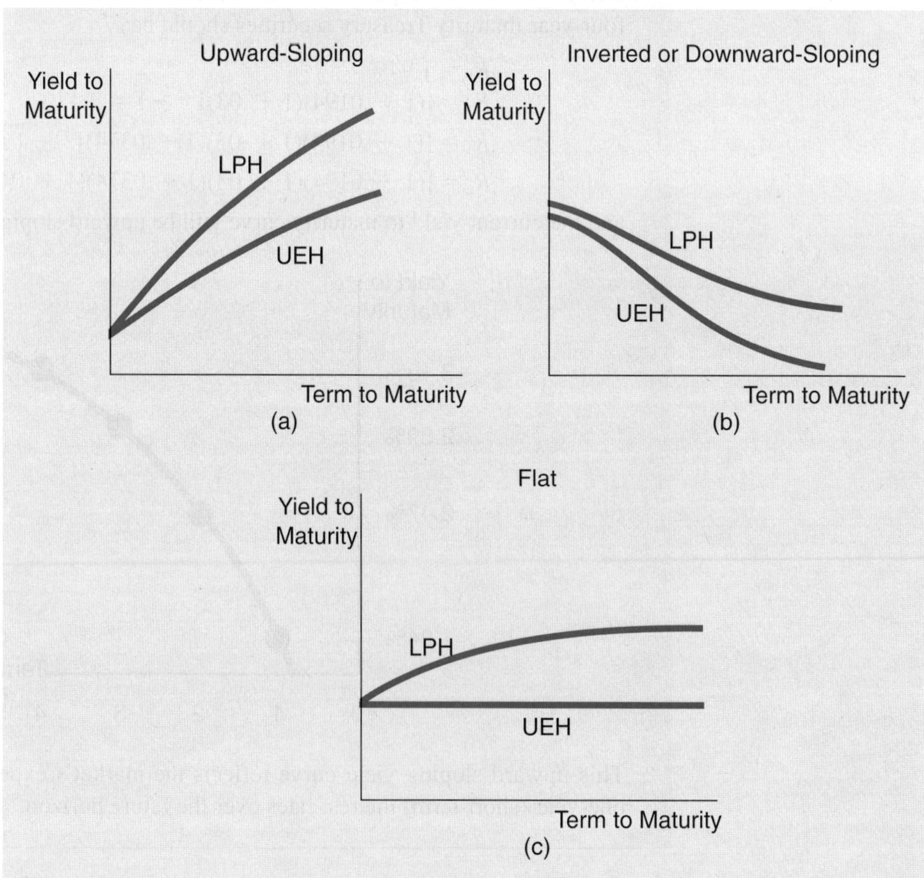

premium theory, an upward-sloping yield curve may reflect investors' expectations that future short-term rates will be flat, but because liquidity premiums increase with maturity, the yield curve will nevertheless be upward sloping. Indeed, an upward-sloping yield curve may reflect expectations that future interest rates will rise, be flat, or even fall, as long as the liquidity premium increases with maturity fast enough to produce an upward-sloping yield curve. The liquidity premium theory may be mathematically represented as:

$$ {}_1\bar{R}_N = [(1 + {}_1\bar{R}_1)(1 + E({}_2\tilde{r}_1) + L_2) \ldots (1 + E({}_N\tilde{r}_1) + L_N)]^{1/N} - 1 \qquad \textbf{(11)} $$

where

L_t = Liquidity premium for a period t
$L_2 < L_3 < \ldots L_N$

The Appendix to this chapter (located at the book's Web site, **www.mhhe.com/sc3e** provides an example in which we construct a yield curve using the liquidity premium hypothesis.

Market Segmentation Theory

The market segmentation theory argues that individual investors and FIs have specific maturity preferences, and to get them to hold securities with maturities other than their most preferred requires a higher interest rate (maturity premium). Accordingly, the market segmentation theory does not consider securities with different maturities as perfect substitutes. Rather, individual investors and FIs have preferred investment horizons (habitats) dictated by the nature of the liabilities they hold. For example, banks might prefer to hold relatively short-term U.S. Treasury bonds because of the short-term nature of their deposit liabilities, while insurance companies may prefer to hold long-term U.S. Treasury bonds because of the long-term nature of their life insurance contractual liabilities. Accordingly, interest rates are determined by distinct supply and demand conditions within a particular maturity segment (e.g., the short end and long end of the bond market). The market segmentation theory assumes that investors and borrowers are generally unwilling to shift from one maturity sector to another without adequate compensation in the form of an interest rate premium. Figure 2–18 demonstrates how changes in the supply curve for short- versus long-term bond segments of the market results in changes in the shape of the yield to maturity curve. Specifically in Figure 2–18, the higher the yield on securities (the lower the price), the higher the demand for them.[10] Thus, as the *supply* of securities *decreases in the short-term* market and *increases in the long-term* market, the *slope* of the yield curve *becomes steeper.* If the *supply* of *short-term* securities had *increased* while the *supply* of *long-term* securities had *decreased,* the *yield curve would have a flatter slope* and might even have sloped downward. Indeed, the large-scale repurchases of long-term Treasury bonds (i.e., reductions in supply) by the U.S. Treasury in early 2000 has been viewed as the major cause of the inverted yield curve that appeared in February 2000.

www.ustreas.gov

DO YOU UNDERSTAND?

1. What the three explanations are for the shape of the yield curve? Discuss each and compare them.

9 FORECASTING INTEREST RATES

As seen in the time value of money examples at the beginning of this chapter, as interest rates change, so do the values of financial securities. Accordingly, the ability to predict or forecast interest rates is critical to the profitability of financial institutions and individual investors alike. For example, if interest rates rise, the value of investment portfolios of FIs and individuals will fall, resulting in a loss of wealth. Thus, interest rate forecasts are extremely important for the financial wealth of both FIs and individuals. The discussion of the unbiased expectations hypothesis in the previous section of this chapter indicated that the shape of the yield curve is determined by the market's current expectations of future

10. In general, the price and yield on a bond are inversely related. Thus, as the price of a bond falls (becomes cheaper), the demand for the bond will rise. This is the same as saying that as the yield on a bond rises, it becomes cheaper and the demand for it increases.

FIGURE 2–18 Market Segmentation and Determination of the Slope of Yield Curve

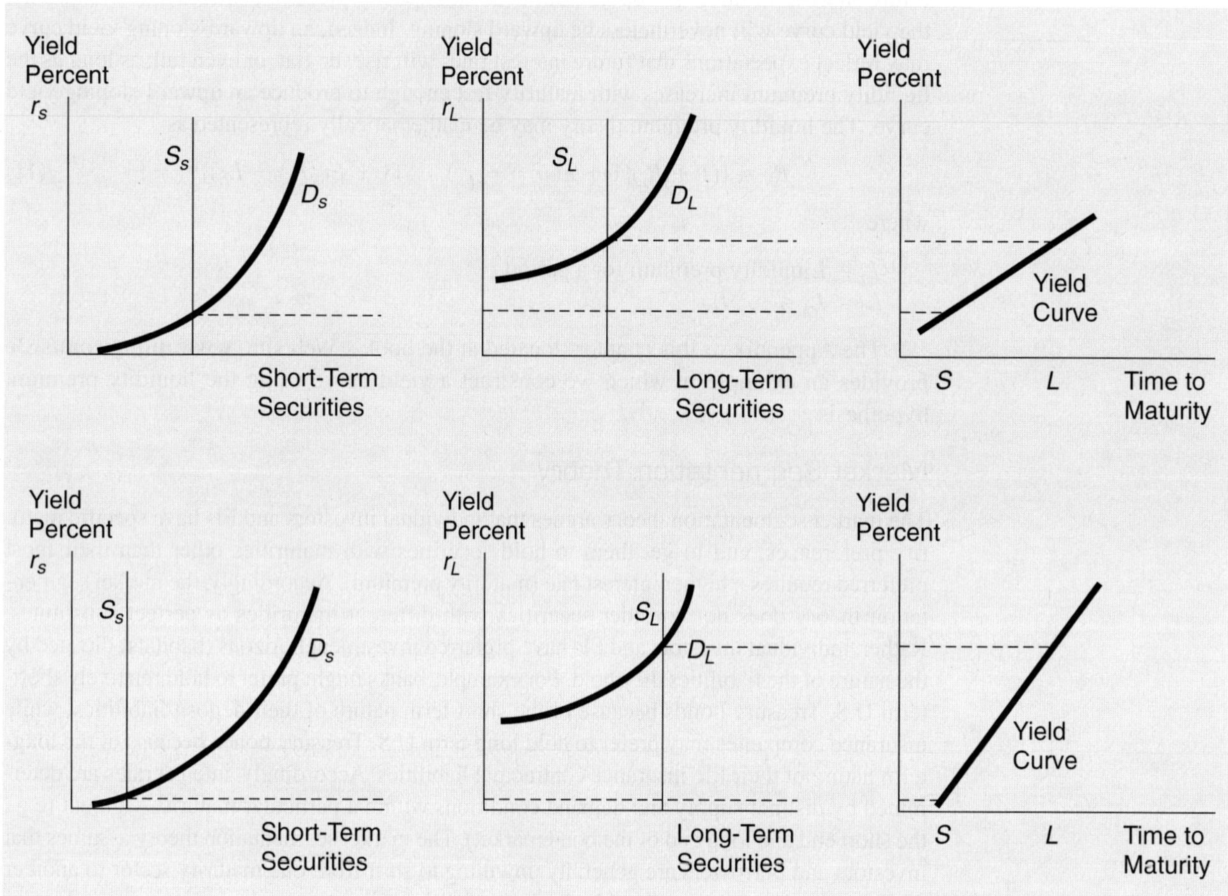

short-term interest rates. For example, an upward-sloping yield curve suggests that the market expects future short-term interest rates to increase. Given that the yield curve represents the market's current expectations of future short-term interest rates, the unbiased expectations hypothesis can be used to forecast (short-term) interest rates in the future (i.e., forward one-year interest rates). A **forward rate** is an expected or "implied" rate on a short-term security that is to be originated at some point in the future. Using the equations representing unbiased expectations theory, the market's expectation of forward rates can be derived directly from existing or actual rates on securities currently traded in the spot market.

forward rate

An expected rate (quoted today) on a security that originates at some point in the future.

EXAMPLE 2–8 Calculation of Implied Forward Rates on One-Year Securities Using the Unbiased Expectations Hypothesis

To find an implied forward rate on a one-year security to be issued one year from today, the unbiased expectations hypothesis equation can be rewritten as follows:

$${}_1\bar{R}_2 = [(1 + {}_1\bar{R}_1)(1 + ({}_2f_1))]^{1/2} - 1$$

where

${}_2f_1$ = Expected one-year rate for year 2, or the implied forward one-year rate for next year

Therefore, ${}_2f_1$ is the market's estimate of the expected one-year rate for year 2. Solving for ${}_2f_1$, we get:

$${}_2f_1 = [(1 + {}_1\bar{R}_2)^2/(1 + {}_1\bar{R}_1)] - 1$$

In general, we can find the one-year forward rate for any year, N years into the future using the following equation:

$$_Nf_1 = [(1 + {_1\bar{R}_N})^N/(1 + {_1\bar{R}_{N-1}})^{N-1}] - 1 \quad \textbf{(12)}$$

DO YOU UNDERSTAND?

1. What a forward rate is?
2. How an implied forward rate can be obtained from current short and long-term interest rates?

For example, on August 16, 2004, the existing or current (spot) one-year, two-year, three-year, and four-year zero-coupon Treasury security rates were as follows:

$$_1\bar{R}_1 = 1.94\%,\ {_1\bar{R}_2} = 2.54\%,\ {_1\bar{R}_3} = 3.17\%,\ {_1\bar{R}_4} = 3.44\%$$

Using the unbiased expectations theory, one-year forward rates on zero-coupon Treasury bonds for years 2, 3, and 4 as of August 16, 2004, were:

$$_2f_1 = [(1.0254)^2/(1.0194)] - 1 = 3.144\%$$
$$_3f_1 = [(1.0317)^3/(1.0254)^2] - 1 = 4.444\%$$
$$_4f_1 = [(1.0344)^4/(1.0317)^3] - 1 = 4.254\%$$

Thus, the expected one-year rate, one year in the future, was 3.144 percent; the expected one-year rate, two years into the future, was 4.444 percent; and the expected one-year rate three years into the future was 4.254 percent.

SUMMARY

This chapter reviewed the determinants of nominal interest rates and their effects on security prices and values in domestic and foreign financial markets. It described the way funds flow through the financial system from lenders to borrowers and how the level of interest rates and its movements over time are determined. The chapter also introduced theories regarding the determination of the shape of the term structure of interest rates.

SEARCH THE SITE

Go to the Federal Reserve Board's Web site and get the latest rates on 10-year T-bond and Aaa- and Baa-rated corporate bonds.

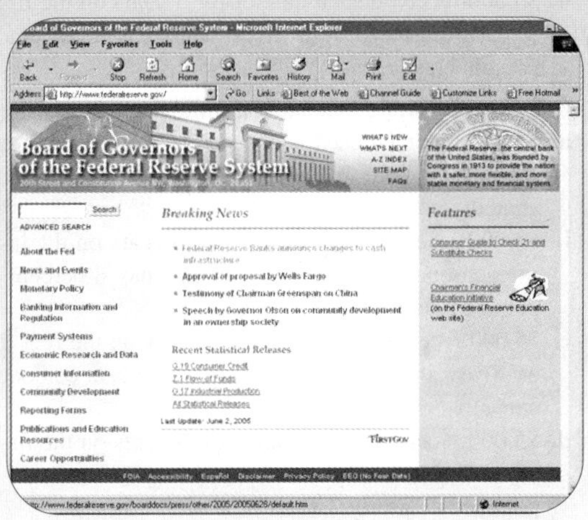

Go to the Federal Reserve's Web site at **www.federalreserve.gov**

Click on "Economic Research and Data"

Click on "Statistics: Releases and Historical Data"

Click on "Weekly Releases: Selected Interest Rates: Releases"

Click on the most recent date.

This will bring the file onto your computer that contains the relevant data.

Questions

1. Calculate the percentage change in the 10-year T-bond and Aaa- and Baa-rated corporate bonds since March 2004.
2. Calculate the current spread of Aaa- and Baa-rated corporate bonds over the 10-year T-bond rate. How have these spreads changed over the last two years?

www.mhhe.com/sc3e

QUESTIONS

1. What is the difference between simple interest and compound interest?
2. Calculate the present value of $5,000 received five years from today if your investments pay
   a. 6 percent compounded annually
   b. 8 percent compounded annually
   c. 10 percent compounded annually
   d. 10 percent compounded semiannually
   e. 10 percent compounded quarterly

   What do your answers to these questions tell you about the relation between present values and interest rates and between present values and the number of compounding periods per year?
3. Calculate the future value in five years of $5,000 received today if your investments pay
   a. 6 percent compounded annually
   b. 8 percent compounded annually
   c. 10 percent compounded annually
   d. 10 percent compounded semiannually
   e. 10 percent compounded quarterly

   What do your answers to these questions tell you about the relation between future values and interest rates and between future values and the number of compounding periods per year?
4. Calculate the present value of the following annuity streams:
   a. $5,000 received each year for 5 years on the last day of each year if your investments pay 6 percent compounded annually.
   b. $5,000 received each quarter for 5 years on the last day of each quarter if your investments pay 6 percent compounded quarterly.
   c. $5,000 received each year for 5 years on the first day of each year if your investments pay 6 percent compounded annually.
   d. $5,000 received each quarter for 5 years on the first day of each quarter if your investments pay 6 percent compounded quarterly.
5. Calculate the future value of the following annuity streams:
   a. $5,000 received each year for 5 years on the last day of each year if your investments pay 6 percent compounded annually.
   b. $5,000 received each quarter for 5 years on the last day of each quarter if your investments pay 6 percent compounded quarterly.
   c. $5,000 received each year for 5 years on the first day of each year if your investments pay 6 percent compounded annually.
   d. $5,000 received each quarter for 5 years on the first day of each quarter if your investments pay 6 percent compounded quarterly.
6. For each of the following, compute the future value:

Present Value	Years	Interest Rate	Future Value
$ 2,250	4	18%	
9,310	9	6	
76,355	15	12	
183,796	21	8	

7. **eXcel** **Using a Spreadsheet to Calculate Future Values.** What is the future value of $100,000 invested for 12 years at 5 percent, 6 percent, 8 percent, and 10 percent, compounded annually?

Present Value	Periods	Interest Rate	=>	The Answer Will Be
$100,000	12	5%		$179,585.63
100,000	12	6		201,219.65
100,000	12	8		251,817.01
100,000	12	10		313,842.84

8. For each of the following, compute the present value:

Present Value	Years	Interest Rate	Future Value
	6	4%	$ 15,451
	8	12	51,557
	16	22	886,073
	25	20	550,164

9. **eXcel** **Using a Spreadsheet to Calculate Present Values.** What is the present value of $100,000 invested for 12 years at 5 percent, 6 percent, 8 percent, and 10 percent compounded annually?

Future Value	Periods	Interest Rate	=>	The Answer Will Be
$100,000	12	5%		$55,683.74
100,000	12	6		49,696.94
100,000	12	8		39,711.38
100,000	12	10		31,863.08

10. Compute the future values of the following first assuming that payments are made on the last day of the period and then assuming payments are made on the first day of the period:

Payment	Years	Interest Rate	Future Value (Payment made on last day of period)	Future Value (Payment made on first day of period)
$ 123	13	13%		
4,555	8	8		
74,484	5	10		
167,332	9	1		

11. **eXcel** **Using a Spreadsheet to Calculate Future Value of Annuities.** What is the future value of $1,000 invested each month for 10 years at 5 percent, 6 percent, 8 percent, and 10 percent, compounded monthly?

Annuity Payment	Periods	Interest Rate	=>	The Answer Will Be
$1,000	10 × 12 = 120	5%		$155,282.28
1,000	120	6		163,879.35
1,000	120	8		182,946.04
1,000	120	10		204,844.98

12. Compute the present values of the following first assuming that payments are made on the last day of the period and then assuming payments are made on the first day of the period:

Payment	Years	Interest Rate	Present Value (Payment made on last day of period)	Present Value (Payment made on first day of period)
\$ 678.09	7	13%		
7,968.26	13	6		
20,322.93	23	4		
69,712.54	4	31		

13. eXcel **Using a Spreadsheet to Calculate Present Values.** What is the present value of \$100,000 invested for 12 years at 5 percent, 6 percent, 8 percent, and 10 percent, compounded semiannually?

Future Value	Periods	Interest Rate	=>	The Answer Will Be
\$100,000	12 × 2 =24	5%		\$55,287.54
100,000	24	6		49,193.37
100,000	24	8		39,012.15
100,000	24	10		31,006.79

14. What is the future value of \$950 paid on the last day of each 6 months for 12 years assuming an interest rate of 11 percent compounded semiannually?

15. Calculate the effective annual return on an investment offering a 12 percent interest rate, compounded monthly.

16. Who are the suppliers of loanable funds?

17. Who are the demanders of loanable funds?

18. What factors cause the supply of funds curve to shift?

19. What factors cause the demand for funds curve to shift?

20. A particular security's equilibrium rate of return is 8 percent. For all securities, the inflation risk premium is 1.75 percent and the real interest rate is 3.5 percent. The security's liquidity risk premium is .25 percent and maturity risk premium is .85 percent. The security has no special covenants. Calculate the security's default risk premium.

21. If we observe a one-year Treasury security rate higher than the two-year Treasury security rate, what can we infer about the one-year rate expected one year from now?

22. The current one-year Treasury-bill rate is 5.2 percent, and the expected one-year rate 12 months from now is 5.8 percent. According to the unbiased expectations theory, what should be the current rate for a two-year Treasury security?

23. Suppose that the current one-year rate (one-year spot rate) and expected one-year T-bill rates over the following three years (i.e., years 2, 3, and 4, respectively) are as follows:

$$_1\bar{R}_1 = 6\%,\ E(_2\tilde{r}_1) = 7\%,\ E(_3\tilde{r}_1) = 7.5\%,\ E(_4\tilde{r}_1) = 7.85\%$$

Using the unbiased expectations theory, calculate the current (long-term) rates for one-, two-, three-, and four-year-maturity Treasury securities. Plot the resulting yield curve.

24. Suppose we observe the following rates: $_1\bar{R}_1 = 8\%$, $_1\bar{R}_2 = 10\%$. If the unbiased expectations theory of the term structure of interest rates holds, what is the one-year interest rate expected one year from now, $E(_2\tilde{r}_1)$?

25. Suppose we observe the three-year Treasury security rate ($_1\bar{R}_3$) to be 12 percent, the expected one-year rate next year—$E(_2\tilde{r}_1)$—to be 8 percent, and the expected one-year rate the following year—$E(_3\tilde{r}_1)$—to be 10 percent. If the unbiased expectations theory of the term structure of interest rates holds, what is the one-year Treasury security rate?

26. A recent edition of *The Wall Street Journal* reported interest rates of 2.25 percent, 2.60 percent, 2.98 percent, and 3.25 percent for three-year, four-year, five-year, and six-year Treasury note yields, respectively, According to the unbiased expectation theory of the term structure of interest rates, what are the expected one-year rates for years 4, 5, and 6?

27. How does the liquidity premium theory of the term structure of interest rates differ from the unbiased expectations theory? In a normal economic environment, that is, an upward-sloping yield curve, what is the relationship of liquidity premiums for successive years into the future? Why?

28. Based on economists' forecasts and analysis, one-year Treasury bill rates and liquidity premiums for the next four years are expected to be as follows:

$$_1\bar{R}_1 = 5.65\%$$
$$E(_2\tilde{r}_1) = 6.75\% \qquad L_2 = 0.05\%$$
$$E(_3\tilde{r}_1) = 6.85\% \qquad L_3 = 0.10\%$$
$$E(_4\tilde{r}_1) = 7.15\% \qquad L_4 = 0.12\%$$

Using the liquidity premium hypothesis, plot the current yield curve. Make sure you label the axes on the graph and identify the four annual rates on the curve both on the axes and on the yield curve itself.

29. Suppose we observe the following rates: $_1\bar{R}_1 = .10$, $_1\bar{R}_2 = .14$, and $E(_2\tilde{r}_1) = .10$. If the liquidity premium theory of the term structure of interest rates holds, what is the liquidity premium for year 2?

30. If you note the following yield curve in *The Wall Street Journal,* what is the one-year forward rate for the period beginning two years from today, $_2f_1$ according to the unbiased expectations hypothesis?

Maturity	Yield
One day	2.00%
One year	5.50
Two years	6.50
Three years	9.00

31. A recent edition of *The Wall Street Journal* reported interest rates of 6 percent, 6.35 percent, 6.65 percent, and 6.75 percent for three-year, four-year, five-year, and six-year Treasury notes, respectively. According to the unbiased expectations hypothesis, what are the expected one-year rates for years 4, 5, and 6 (i.e., what are $_4f_1$, $_5f_1$, and $_6f_1$)?

32. Assume the current interest rate on a one-year Treasury bond ($_1\bar{R}_1$) is 4.50 percent, the current rate on a two-year Treasury bond ($_1\bar{R}_2$) is 5.25 percent, and the current rate on a three-year Treasury bond ($_1\bar{R}_3$) is 6.50 percent. If the unbiased expectations theory of the term structure of interest rates is correct, what is the one-year interest rate expected on Treasury bills during year 3 ($E(_3\tilde{r}_1)$ or $_3f_1$)?

APPENDIX 2A: Construction of a Yield Curve Using the Liquidity Premium Theory of the Term Structure of Interest Rates

View this appendix at

www.mhhe.com/sc3e

www.mhhe.com/sc3e

3

Interest Rates *and* Security Valuation

Chapter NAVIGATOR

1. What are the differences in the required rate of return, the expected rate of return, and the realized rate of return?
2. How are bonds valued?
3. How are security prices affected by interest rate changes?
4. How do the maturity and coupon rate on a security affect its price sensitivity to interest rate changes?
5. What is duration?
6. How do maturity, yield to maturity, and coupon interest affect the duration of a security?
7. What is the economic meaning of duration?

OUTLINE

INTEREST RATES AS A DETERMINANT OF FINANCIAL SECURITY VALUES: CHAPTER OVERVIEW

In Chapter 2, we introduced the basic concepts of time value of money and how time value of money equations can be used to convert cash flows received or paid over an investment horizon into either a present value or future value. Of particular importance was the fact that interest rate levels, and changes in interest rate levels, affect security values. We also reviewed the factors that determine the level of interest rates, changes in interest rates, and interest rate differences among securities (e.g., default risk, callability).

With this understanding of how and why interest rates change, in this chapter we apply time value of money principals to the valuation of specific financial securities, paying particular attention to the change in a security's value when interest rates change. We examine how characteristics specific to a financial security (e.g., its coupon rate and remaining time

TABLE 3–1 Various Interest Rate Measures

Coupon Rate—interest rate on a bond instrument used to calculate the annual cash flows the bond issuer promises to pay the bond holder.

Required Rate of Return—interest rate an investor should receive on a security given its risk. Required rate of return is used to calculate the fair present value on a security.

Expected Rate of Return—interest rate an investor would receive on a security if he or she buys the security at its current market price, receives all expected payments, and sells the security at the end of his or her investment horizon.

Realized Rate of Return—actual interest rate earned on an investment in a financial security. Realized rate of return is a historical (ex post) measure of the interest rate.

to maturity) also influence a financial security's price.[1] We conclude the chapter with an analysis of the duration of a security. Duration, which measures the weighted-average time to maturity of an asset or liability, using the present values of the cash flows as weights, also has economic meaning as the sensitivity of an asset or liability's value or price to a small interest rate change. The valuation and duration models reviewed in this chapter are used by traders to determine whether to transact in the various financial markets we discuss in Chapters 5 through 10.

1 VARIOUS INTEREST RATE MEASURES

In Chapter 2, we presented a general discussion of interest rates and how they are determined. The term *interest rates* can actually have many different meanings depending on the time frame used for analysis and the type of security being analyzed. In this chapter, we start off by defining the different interest rate measures employed in the valuation of financial securities by market participants. These definitions are summarized in Table 3–1. In the body of the chapter we apply these rates to the valuation of bonds (bond markets and their operations are discussed in detail in Chapter 6). In Appendix 3A to this chapter, located at the book's Web site (**www.mhhe.com/sc3e**), we apply these rates to the valuation of stocks (stock markets and their operations are discussed in Chapter 9).

Coupon Rate

coupon interest rate

Interest rate used to calculate the annual cash flow the bond issuer promises to pay the bond holder.

One variation on the meaning of the term *interest rate* specific to debt instruments is the **coupon interest rate** paid on a bond. As discussed in detail in the next section, the coupon rate on a bond instrument is the annual (or periodic) cash flow that the bond issuer contractually promises to pay the bond holder. This coupon rate is only one component of the overall return (required, expected, or realized rate of return) the bond holder earns on a bond, however. As discussed below, required, expected, or realized rates of return incorporate not only the coupon payments but all cash flows on a bond investment, including full and partial repayments of principal by the issuer.

Required Rate of Return

Market participants use time value of money equations to calculate the fair present value of a financial security over an investment horizon. As we discussed in Chapter 2 and will see later on in this chapter, this process involves the discounting of all projected cash

1. Security valuation is a topic that finance students probably studied in introductory financial management courses. However, these models are critical tools for traders of financial securities and managers of financial institutions. Therefore, in this chapter we review and provide a reference guide to the general pricing relationships. This material can be included or dropped from the chapter reading, depending on the need for review of the material, without harming the continuity of the chapter.

required rate of return

The interest rate an investor should receive on a security, given its risk.

flows (*CFs*)[2] on the security at an appropriate interest rate. The interest rate used to find the fair present value of a financial security is called the **required rate of return** (*rrr*). This interest rate is a function of the various risks associated with a security (discussed in Chapter 2) and is thus the interest rate the investor *should* receive on the security given its risk (default risk, liquidity risk, etc.). The required rate of return is thus an ex ante (before the fact) measure of the interest rate on a security. The *fair present value* (*FPV*) is determined by the following formula:

$$FPV = \frac{\widetilde{CF}_1}{(1 + rrr)^1} + \frac{\widetilde{CF}_2}{(1 + rrr)^2} + \frac{\widetilde{CF}_3}{(1 + rrr)^3} + \cdots + \frac{\widetilde{CF}_n}{(1 + rrr)^n}$$

where

rrr = Required rate of return
$\widetilde{CF}_t$ = Cash flow projected in period t ($t = 1, \ldots, n$)
$\sim$ = Indicates that projected cash flow is uncertain (because of default and other risks)
n = Number of periods in the investment horizon

Once an *FPV* is calculated, market participants then compare this fair present value with the *current market price* (*P*) at which the security is trading in a financial market. If the current market price of the security (*P*) is less than its fair value (*FPV*), the security is currently undervalued. The market participant would want to buy more of this security at its current price. If the current market price of the security is greater than its fair present value, the security is overvalued. The market participant would not want to buy this security at its current price. If the fair present value of the security equals its current market price, the security is said to be fairly priced given its risk characteristics. In this case, *FPV* equals *P*.

EXAMPLE 3–1 Application of Required Rate of Return

A bond you purchased two years ago for \$890 is now selling for \$925. The bond paid \$100 per year in coupon interest on the last day of each year (the last payment made today). You intend to hold the bond for four more years and project that you will be able to sell it at the end of year 4 for \$960. You also project that the bond will continue paying \$100 in interest per year. Given the risk associated with the bond, its required rate of return (*rrr*) over the next four years is 11.25 percent. Accordingly, the bond's fair present value is:

$$FPV = \frac{100}{(1 + .1125)^1} + \frac{100}{(1 + .1125)^2} + \frac{100}{(1 + .1125)^3} + \frac{100 + 960}{(1 + .1125)^4}$$
$$= \$935.31$$

Given the current selling price of the bond, \$925, relative to the fair present value, \$935.31, this bond is currently undervalued.

expected rate of return

The interest rate an investor would earn on a security if he or she buys the security at its current market price, receives all promised or expected payments on the security, and sells the security at the end of his or her investment horizon.

Expected Rate of Return

The **expected rate of return** (*Err*) on a financial security is the interest rate a market participant *would* earn by buying the security at its *current market price* (*P*), receiving all the projected cash flow payments ($\widetilde{CF}$s) on the security, and selling the security when the security matures at the end of the participant's investment horizon. Thus, the expected

2. The projected cash flows used in these equations may be those promised by the security issuer or expected cash flows estimated by the security purchaser (or some other analyst) from a probability distribution of the possible cash flows received on the security. In either case, the cash flows received are not ex ante known with perfect certainty because of default and other risks.

TABLE 3–2 The Relation between Required Rate of Return and Expected Rate of Return

$Err \geqslant rrr$, or $P \leqslant FPV$	The present value of the cash flows received on the security is greater than or equal to that required to compensate for the risk incurred from investing in the security. Thus, buy this security.
$Err < rrr$, or $P > FPV$	The present value of the cash flows received on the security is less than that required to compensate for the risk incurred from investing in the security. Thus, do not buy this security.

rate of return is also an ex ante measure of the interest rate on a security. However, the expected rate of return on an investment is based on the current market price rather than fair present value. As discussed above, these may or may not be equal.

Again, time value of money equations are used to calculate the expected rate of return on a security. In this case, the current market price of the security is set equal to the present value of all projected cash flows received on the security over the investment horizon. The expected rate of return is the discount rate in the present value equations that just makes the present value of projected cash flows equal to its current market price (P).[3] That is:

$$P = \frac{\widetilde{CF}_1}{(1 + Err)^1} + \frac{\widetilde{CF}_2}{(1 + Err)^2} + \frac{\widetilde{CF}_3}{(1 + Err)^3} + \cdots + \frac{\widetilde{CF}_n}{(1 + Err)^n}$$

where

Err = Expected rate of return
$\widetilde{CF}_t$ = Cash flow projected in period t ($t = 1, \ldots, n$)
n = Number of periods in the investment horizon
~ = Indicates that cash flows in the future are uncertain

Once an expected rate of return (Err) on a financial security is calculated, the market participant compares this expected rate of return to its required rate of return (rrr). If the expected rate of return is greater than the required rate of return, the projected cash flows on the security are greater than is required to compensate for the risk incurred from investing in the security. Thus, the market participant would want to buy more of this security. If the expected rate of return is less than the required rate of return, the projected cash flows from the security are less than those required to compensate for the risk involved. Thus, the market participant would not want to invest more in the security.[4] We summarize these relationships in Table 3–2.

EXAMPLE 3–2 Application of Expected Rate of Return

Refer to information in Example 3–1 describing a bond you purchased two years ago for \$890. Using the current market price of \$925, the expected rate of return on the bond over the next four years is calculated as follows:

$$925 = \frac{100}{(1 + Err)^1} + \frac{100}{(1 + Err)^2} + \frac{100}{(1 + Err)^3} + \frac{100 + 960}{(1 + Err)^4}$$

$$\Rightarrow Err = 11.607\%$$

Given that the required return on the bond is 11.25 percent, the projected cash flows on the bond are greater than is required to compensate you for the risk on the bond.

3. We are also assuming that any cash flows on the investment can be reinvested to earn the same expected rate of return.

4. Note also that by implication, if $Err > rrr$, then the market price of a security (P) is less than its fair present value (FPV) and vice versa if $Err < rrr$.

Required versus Expected Rates of Return: The Role of Efficient Markets

We have defined two ex ante (before the fact) measures of interest rates. The *required* rate of return is used to calculate a *fair* present value of a financial security, while the *expected* rate of return is a discount rate used in conjunction with the *current* market price of a security to calculate an ex ante (or before the fact) return. As long as financial markets are efficient (see below), the current market price of a security tends to equal its fair price present value. This is the case most of the time. However, when an event occurs that unexpectedly changes interest rates or a characteristic of a financial security (e.g., an unexpected dividend increase, an unexpected decrease in default risk), the current market price of a security can temporarily diverge from its fair present value. When investors determine a security is undervalued (i.e., its current market price is less than its fair present value), demand for the security increases, as does its price. Conversely, when investors determine a security is overvalued (i.e., its current market price is greater than its fair present value), they will sell the security, resulting in a price drop. The speed with which financial security prices adjust to unexpected news, so as to maintain equality with the fair present value of the security, is referred to as **market efficiency.** We examine the three forms of market efficiency (weak form, semistrong form, and strong form) in Chapter 9.

market efficiency

The process by which financial security prices move to a new equilibrium when interest rates or a security-specific characteristic changes.

Realized Rate of Return

Required and expected rates of return are interest return concepts pertaining to the returns expected or required just prior to the investment being made. Once made, however, the market participant is concerned with how well the financial security actually performs. The **realized rate of return** (rr) on a financial security is the interest rate *actually* earned on an investment in a financial security. The realized rate of return is thus a historical interest rate of return—it is an ex post (after the fact) measure of the interest rate on the security.

realized rate of return

The actual interest rate earned on an investment in a financial security.

To calculate a realized rate of return (rr), all cash flows actually paid or received are incorporated in time value of money equations to solve for the realized rate of return. By setting the price actually paid for the security (P) equal to the present value of the realized cash flows ($RCF_1, RCF_2, \ldots, RCF_n$), the realized rate of return is the discount rate that just equates the purchase price to the present value of the realized cash flows. That is:

DO YOU UNDERSTAND?

1. The difference between a required rate of return and an expected rate of return?
2. The difference between the coupon rate on a bond and the realized rate of return on a bond?

$$P = \frac{RCF_1}{(1+rr)^1} + \frac{RCF_2}{(1+rr)^2} + \cdots + \frac{RCF_n}{(1+rr)^n}$$

where

RCF_t = Realized cash flow in period t ($t = 1, \ldots, n$)
rr = Realized rate of return on a security

If the realized rate of return (rr) is greater than the required rate of return (rrr), the market participant actually earned more than was needed to be compensated for the ex ante or expected risk of investing in the security. If the realized rate of return is less than the required rate of return, the market participant actually earned less than the interest rate required to compensate for the risk involved.

EXAMPLE 3-3 Application of Realized Rate of Return

Consider again the bond investment described in Examples 3–1 and 3–2. Using your original purchase price, \$890, and the current market price on this bond, the realized rate of return you have earned on this bond over the last two years is calculated as follows:

$$890 = \frac{100}{(1+rr)^1} + \frac{100+925}{(1+rr)^2}$$

$$\Rightarrow rr = 13.08\%$$

BOND VALUATION

The valuation of a bond instrument employs time value of money concepts. The fair value of a bond reflects the present value of all cash flows promised or projected to be received on that bond discounted at the required rate of return (*rrr*). Similarly, the expected rate of return (*Err*) is the interest rate that equates the current market price of the bond with the present value of all promised cash flows received over the life of the bond. Finally, a realized rate of return (*rr*) on a bond is the actual return earned on a bond investment that has already taken place. We again will limit our present discussion of bond valuation to required and expected rates of return. Appendix 3A to this chapter, found on the book's Web site (**www.mhhe.com/sc3e**), reviews the valuation of equity instruments (such as common stock). Promised cash flows on bonds come from two sources: (1) interest or coupon payments paid over the life of the bond and (2) a lump sum payment (face or par value) when a bond matures.

coupon bonds

Bonds that pay interest based on a stated coupon rate. The interest paid or coupon payments per year is generally constant over the life of the bond.

zero-coupon bonds

Bonds that do not pay interest.

2

Bond Valuation Formula Used to Calculate Fair Present Values

Most bonds pay a stated coupon rate of interest to the holders of the bonds. These bonds are called **coupon bonds.** The interest, or coupon, payments per year, INT, are generally constant (are fixed) over the life of the bond.[5] Thus, the fixed interest payment is essentially an annuity paid to the bond holder periodically (normally semiannually) over the life of the bond. Bonds that do not pay coupon interest are called **zero-coupon bonds.** For these bonds, INT is zero. The face or par value of the bond, on the other hand, is a lump sum payment received by the bond holder when the bond matures. Face value is generally set at $1,000 in the U.S. bond market.

Using time value of money formulas, and assuming that the bond issuer makes its promised semiannual coupon and principal payments, the present value of the bond can be written as:[6]

$$V_b = \frac{INT/2}{(1 + i_d/2)^1} + \frac{INT/2}{(1 + i_d/2)^2} + p + \frac{INT/2}{(1 + i_d/2)^{2N}} + \frac{M}{(1 + i_d/2)^{2N}}$$

$$= \frac{INT}{2}\sum_{t=1}^{2N}\left(\frac{1}{1 + i_d/2}\right)^t + \frac{M}{(1 + i_d/2)^{2N}}$$

$$= \frac{INT}{(2)}(PVIFA_{i_d/2,2N}) + M(PFIV_{i_d/2,2N})$$

where

V_b = Present value of the bond
M = Par or face value of the bond
INT = Annual interest (or coupon) payment per year on the bond; equals the par value of the bond times the (percentage) coupon rate
N = Number of years until the bond matures
i_d = Annual interest rate used to discount cash flows on the bond
$PVIF$ = Present value interest factor of a lump sum payment
$PVIFA$ = Present value interest factor of an annuity stream

5. Variable rate bonds pay interest that is indexed to some broad interest rate measure (such as Treasury bill rates) and thus experience variable coupon payments. Income bonds pay interest only if the issuer has sufficient earnings to make the promised payments. Index (or purchasing power) bonds pay interest based on an inflation index. Both these types of bonds, therefore, can have variable interest payments.

6. More generally for bonds that pay interest other than semiannually:

$$V_b = \frac{INT}{m}(PVIFA_{i_d/m,Nm}) + M(PVIF_{i_d/m,Nm})$$

where m = Number of times per year interest is paid.

EXAMPLE 3-4 Calculation of the Fair Value of a Coupon Bond

You are considering the purchase of a \$1,000 face value bond that pays 10 percent coupon interest per year, with the coupon paid semiannually (i.e., \$50 (=1,000(.1)/2) over the first half of the year and \$50 over the second half of the year). The bond matures in 12 years (i.e., the bond pays interest (12 × 2 =) 24 times before it matures). If the required rate of return (*rrr*) on this bond is 8 percent (i.e., the periodic discount rate is (8%/2 =) 4 percent), the fair market value of the bond is calculated as follows:

$$V_b = \frac{1{,}000(.1)}{2}(PVIFA_{8\%/2,12(2)}) + 1{,}000(PVIF_{8\%/2,12(2)})$$
$$= 50(15.24696) + 1{,}000(.39012) = \$1{,}152.47$$

or an investor would be willing to pay no more than \$1,152.47 for this bond.[7,8]

If the required rate of return on this bond is 10 percent, the fair market value of the bond is calculated as follows:

$$V_b = \frac{1{,}000(.1)}{2}(PVIFA_{10\%/2,12(2)}) + 1{,}000(PVIF_{10\%/2,12(2)})$$
$$= 50(13.79864) + 1{,}000(.31007) = \$1{,}000.00$$

or an investor would be willing to pay no more than \$1,000.00 for this bond.

If the required rate of return on this bond is 12 percent, the fair market value of the bond is calculated as follows:

$$V_b = \frac{1{,}000(.1)}{2}(PVIFA_{12\%/2,12(2)}) + 1{,}000(PVIF_{12\%/2,12(2)})$$
$$= 50(12.55036) + 1{,}000(.24698) = \$874.50$$

or an investor would be willing to pay no more than \$874.50 for this bond.

In the preceding example, notice that when the required rate of return (rrr) on the bond is 8 percent, the fair value of the bond, \$1,152.47, is greater than its face value of \$1,000. When this relationship between the fair value and the face value of a bond exists, the bond is referred to as a **bond** that should sell at a **premium.** This premium occurs because the coupon rate on the bond is greater than the required rate of return on the bond (a 10 percent coupon rate versus an 8 percent required rate of return in our example). When the required rate of return on the bond is 12 percent, the present value of the bond is less than its face value, and the bond is referred to as a **bond** that should sell at a **discount.** This discount occurs because the coupon rate on the bond is less than the required rate of return on the bond.

premium bond

A bond in which the present value of the bond is greater than its face value.

discount bond

A bond in which the present value of the bond is less than its face value.

7. If the bond paid interest once per year (i.e., $m = 1$) rather than twice, the bond's fair market value is calculated as:

$$V_b = 1{,}000(.1)(PVIFA_{8\%,12}) + 1{,}000(PVIF_{8\%,12}) = \$1{,}150.72.$$

8. These pricing formulas are programmed in business calculators. Because there are several variations of business calculators, we do not apply the problems in the text to any one brand of calculator.

TABLE 3–3 Description of a Premium, Discount, and Par Bond

Premium Bond—when the *coupon rate* on a bond is greater than the *required rate of return* on the bond, the *fair present value* is greater than the *face value* of the bond.
When the *coupon rate* on a bond is greater than the *yield to maturity* on the bond, the *current market price* is greater than the *face value* of the bond.

Discount Bond—when the *coupon rate* on a bond is less than the *required rate of return* on the bond, the *fair present value* is less than the *face value* of the bond.
When the *coupon rate* on a bond is less than the *yield to maturity* on the bond, the *current market price* is less than the *face value* of the bond.

Par Value—when the *coupon rate* on a bond is equal to the *required rate of return* on the bond, the *fair present value* is equal to the *face value* of the bond.
When the *coupon rate* on a bond is equal to the *yield to maturity* on the bond, the *current market price* is equal to the *face value* of the bond.

par bond

A bond in which the present value of the bond is equal to its face value.

Finally, when the required rate of return on the bond is 10 percent, the present value of the bond is equal to its face value, and the bond is referred to as a **bond** that should sell at **par.** This par occurs because the coupon rate on the bond is equal to the required rate of return on the bond. To achieve the required rate of return on the bond, the bond holder experiences neither a gain nor a loss on the difference between the purchase price of the bond and the face value received at maturity. We summarize the scenarios for premium, discount,[9] and par bonds in Table 3–3.

It should be noted that the designation as a premium, discount, or par bond does not necessarily assist a bond holder in the decision to buy or sell a bond. This decision is made on the basis of the relationship between the fair present value and the actual current market price of the bond. Rather, premium, discount, and par bonds are descriptive designations regarding the relationship between the fair present value of the bond and its face value. As stated above, the fair present value of the bond will equal the bond's price only in an efficient market where prices instantaneously adjust to new information about the security's value.

Bond Valuation Formula Used to Calculate Yield to Maturity

yield to maturity

The return or yield the bond holder will earn on the bond if he or she buys it at its current market price, receives all coupon and principal payments as promised, and holds the bond until maturity.

The present value formulas can also be used to find the expected rate of return (*Err*) or, assuming all promised coupon and principal payments are made with a probability of 100 percent, what is often called the **yield to maturity** (ytm) on a bond (i.e., the return the bond holder would earn on the bond if he or she buys the bond at its current market price, receives all coupon and principal payments as promised, and holds the bond until maturity). The yield to maturity calculation implicitly assumes that all coupon payments periodically received by the bond holder can be reinvested at the same rate—that is, reinvested at the calculated yield to maturity.[10]

Rewriting the bond valuation formula, where V_b is the current market price that has to be paid to buy the bond, we can solve for the yield to maturity (ytm) on a bond as follows (where we write ytm instead of Err):

$$V_b = \frac{INT/2}{(1 + ytm/2)^1} + \frac{INT/2}{(1 + ytm/2)^2} + \cdots + \frac{INT/2}{(1 + ytm/2)^{2N}} + \frac{M}{(1 + ytm/2)^{2N}}$$

$$= \frac{INT}{2}(PVIFA_{ytm/2,2N}) + M(PVIF_{ytm/2,2N})$$

9. The term discount bond is also used to denote a zero-coupon bond.

10. As discussed in Appendix 3B to this chapter (located at the book's Web site, **www.mhhe.com/sc3e**), if coupon payments are reinvested at less (more) than this rate, the yield to maturity will be lower (higher) than that calculated in this section. This concept will be key to understanding interest rate risk discussed later in the text (Chapters 22 and 23).

TABLE 3–4 Summary of Factors that Affect Security Prices and Price Volatility When Interest Rates Change

Interest Rate—there is a negative relation between interest rate changes and present value (or price) changes on financial securities.

As interest rates increase, security prices decrease at a decreasing rate.

Time Remaining to Maturity—the shorter the time to maturity for a security, the closer the price is to the face value of the security.

The longer the time to maturity for a security, the larger the price change of the security for a given interest rate change.

The maturity effect described above increases at a decreasing rate.

Coupon Rate—the higher a security's coupon rate, the smaller the price change on the security for a given change in interest rates.

EXAMPLE 3–5 Calculation of the Yield to Maturity on a Coupon Bond

You are considering the purchase of a $1,000 face value bond that pays 11 percent coupon interest per year, paid semiannually (i.e., $550 (= $1,000(.11)/2) per semiannual period). The bond matures in 15 years and has a face value of $1,000. If the current market price of the bond is $931.176, the yield to maturity (or *Err*) is calculated as follows:

$$931.176 = \frac{1{,}000(.11)}{2}(PVIFA_{ytm/2,15(2)}) + 1{,}000(PVIF_{ytm/2,15(2)})$$

Solving for *ytm*,[11] the yield to maturity (or expected rate of return) on the bond is 12 percent.[12] Equivalently, you would be willing to buy the bond only if the required rate of return (*rrr*) was no more than 12 percent.

DO YOU UNDERSTAND?

1. What the difference is between a zero-coupon bond and a coupon bond?
2. What the difference is between a discount bond, a premium bond, and a par bond?
3. How the difference between the yield to maturity on a bond and the coupon rate on the bond will cause the bond to sell at a premium or a discount?

As already discussed in this chapter and in Chapter 2, the variability of financial security prices depends on interest rates and the characteristics of the security. Specifically, the factors that affect financial security prices include interest rate changes, the time remaining to maturity, and the coupon rate. We evaluate next the impact of each of these factors as they affect bond prices. Table 3–4 summarizes the major relationships we will be discussing.

IMPACT OF INTEREST RATE CHANGES ON SECURITY VALUES

3

Refer back to Example 3–4. Notice in this example that present values of the cash flows on bonds decreased as interest rates increased. Specifically, when the required rate of return increased from 8 percent to 10 percent, the fair present value of the bond fell from $1,152.47 to $1,000, or by 13.23 percent ((1,000 − 1,152.47)/1,152.47). Similarly, when the required rate of return increased from 10 percent to 12 percent, the fair present value of the bond fell from $1,000 to $874.50, or by 12.55 percent ((874.50 − 1,000)/1,000). This is the inverse relationship between present values

11. Business calculators are programmed to easily solve for the yield to maturity on a security.

12. The yield to maturity is the nominal return on the bond. Its effective annual return is calculated as (see Chapter 2):

$$EAR = (1 + ytm/2)^2 - 1 = (1 + .12/2)^2 - 1 = 12.36\%$$

FIGURE 3–1 Relation between Interest Rates and Bond Values

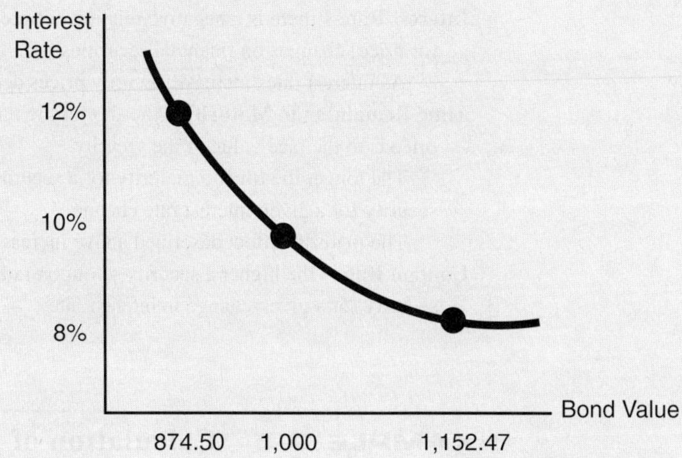

and interest rates we discussed in Chapter 2. While the examples refer to the relation between fair values and required rates of returns, the inverse relation also exists between current market prices and expected rates of return—as yields on bonds increase, the current market prices of bonds decrease. We illustrate this inverse relation between interest rates on bonds and the present value of bonds in Figure 3–1.

Notice too from the earlier example that the inverse relationship between bond prices and interest rates is not linear. Rather, the percentage change in the present value of a bond to a given change in interest rates is smaller when interest rates are higher. When the required rate of return on the bond increased from 8 percent to 10 percent (a 2 percent increase), the fair present value on the bond decreased by 13.23 percent. However, another 2 percent increase in the required rate of return (from 10 percent to 12 percent) resulted in a fair present value decrease of only 12.55 percent. The same nonlinear relation exists for current market prices and yield to maturities. Thus, as interest rates increase, present values of bonds (and bond prices) decrease at a decreasing rate. This is illustrated in Figure 3–1.

The relationship between interest rates and security values is important for all types of investors. Financial institutions (FIs) such as commercial banks, thrifts, and insurance companies are affected because the vast majority of the assets and liabilities held by these firms are financial securities (e.g., loans, deposits, investment securities). When required rates of return rise (fall) on these securities, the fair present values of the FI's asset and liability portfolios decrease (increase) by possibly different amounts, which in turn affects the fair present value of the FI's equity (the difference between the fair present value of an FI's assets and liabilities).

For example, suppose an FI held the 8 percent required return bond evaluated in Example 3–4 (10 percent coupon interest per year paid semiannually, 12 years remaining to maturity, and face value of $1,000) in its asset portfolio and had partly financed the asset purchase by issuing the 10 percent required return bond evaluated in Example 3–4 (the same bond characteristics as above except that the required rate of return is 10 percent) as part of its liability portfolio. In the example, we calculated the fair present values of these bonds as $1,152.47 and $1,000, respectively. The market value balance sheet of the FI is shown in Table 3–5. The market value of the FI's equity is $152.47 ($1,152.47 − $1,000)—the difference between the market values of the FI's assets and liabilities. This can also be thought of as the value of the FI's equity owners' contribution to the financing of the purchase of the asset. If the required rate of return increases by 2 percent on both of these bonds (to 10 percent on the bond in the asset portfolio and to 12 percent on the bond in the liability portfolio),

DO YOU UNDERSTAND?

1. What happens to the fair present value of a bond when the required rate of return on the bond increases?
2. What happens to the fair present value of a bond when the required rate of return on the bond decreases?

TABLE 3–5 Balance Sheet of an FI before and after an Interest Rate Increase

(a) Balance Sheet before the Interest Rate Increase

Assets		Liabilities and Equity	
Bond (8% required rate of return)	$1,152.47	Bond (10% required rate of return)	$1,000
		Equity	$152.47

(b) Balance Sheet after 2 Percent Increase in the Interest Rates

Assets		Liabilities and Equity	
Bond (10% required rate of return)	$1,000	Bond (12% required rate of return)	$874.50
		Equity	$125.50

the fair present values of the asset and liability portfolios fall to $1,000 and $874.50, respectively. As a result, the value of the FI's equity falls to $125.50 ($1,000 − $874.50)—see Table 3–5. Implicitly, the equity owners of the FI have lost $26.97 ($152.47 − $125.50) of the value of their ownership stake in the FI. We examine the measurement and management of an FI's interest rate risk in more detail in Chapter 22.

In this section we presented an example in which a change in interest rates results in a decrease in an FI's asset and liability values, and thus equity value. In the next two sections we look at how the maturity of, and coupon rate on, a security affects the size of the value changes for a given change in interest rates.

4

IMPACT OF MATURITY ON SECURITY VALUES

price sensitivity

The percentage change in a bond's present value for a given change in interest rates.

An important factor that affects the degree to which the price of a bond changes (or the price sensitivity of a bond changes) as interest rates change is the time remaining to maturity on the bond. A bond's **price sensitivity** is measured by the percentage change in its present value for a given change in interest rates. The larger the percentage change in the bond's value for a given interest rate change, the larger the bond's price sensitivity. Specifically, as is explained below, the shorter the time remaining to maturity, the closer a bond's price is to its face value. Also, the further a bond is from maturity, the more sensitive the price (fair or current) of the bond as interest rates change. Finally, the relationship between bond price sensitivity and maturity is not linear. As the time remaining to maturity on a bond increases, price sensitivity increases but at a decreasing rate. Table 3–6 presents the bond information we will be using to illustrate these relationships.

Maturity and Security Prices

Table 3–6 lists the present values of 10 percent (compounded semiannually) coupon bonds with a $1,000 face value and 12 years, 14 years, and 16 years, respectively, remaining to maturity. We calculate the fair present value of these bonds using an 8 percent, 10 percent, and 12 percent required rate of return. Notice that for each of these bonds, the closer the bond is to maturity, the closer the fair present value of the bond is to the $1,000 face value. This is true regardless of whether the bond is a premium, discount, or par bond. For example, at an 8 percent interest rate, the 12-year, 14-year, and 16-year bonds have present

TABLE 3–6 The Impact of Time to Maturity on the Relation between a Bond's Fair Present Value and Its Required Rate of Return

	12 Years to Maturity			14 Years to Maturity			16 Years to Maturity		
Required Rate of Return	Fair Price*	Price Change	Percentage Price Change	Fair Price*	Price Change	Percentage Price Change	Fair Price*	Price Change	Percentage Price Change
8%	$1,152.47			$1,166.63			$1,178.74		
		−$152.47	−13.23%		−$166.63	−14.28%		−$178.74	−15.16%
10%	1,000.00			1,000.00			1,000.00		
		−125.50	−12.55		−134.06	−13.41		−140.84	−14.08
12%	874.50			865.94			859.16		

*The bond pays 10% coupon interest compounded semiannually and has a face value of $1,000.

values of $1,152.47, $1,166.63, and $1,178.74, respectively. The intuition behind this is that nobody would pay much more than the face value of the bond and any remaining (in this case semiannual) coupon payments just prior to maturity since these are the only cash flows left to be paid on the bond. Thus, the time value effect is reduced as the maturity of the bond approaches. Many people call this effect the pull to par—bond prices and fair values approach their par values (e.g., $1,000) as time to maturity declines towards zero.

Maturity and Security Price Sensitivity to Changes in Interest Rates

The Percentage Price Change columns in Table 3–6 provide data to examine the effect time to maturity has on bond price sensitivity to interest rates change. From these data we see that the longer the time remaining to maturity on a bond, the more sensitive are bond prices to a given change in interest rates. (Note again that all bonds in Table 3–6 have a 10 percent coupon rate and a $1,000 face value.) For example, the fair present value of the 12-year bond falls 13.23 percent (i.e., ($1,000 − $1,152.47)/$1,152.47 = −.1323 = −13.23%) as the required rate of return increases from 8 percent to 10 percent. The same 2 percent increase (from 8 percent to 10 percent) in the required rate of return produces a larger 14.28 percent drop in the fair present value of the 14-year bond, and the 16-year bond's fair present value drops 15.16 percent. This same trend is demonstrated when the required rate of return increases from 10 percent to 12 percent—the longer the bond's maturity, the greater the percentage decrease in the bond's fair present value.

The same relationship occurs when analyzing expected rates of return (or yields to maturity) and the current market price of the bond—the longer the time to maturity on a bond, the larger the change in the current market price of a bond for a given change in yield to maturity.

Incremental Changes in Maturity and Security Price Sensitivity to Changes in Interest Rates. A final relationship we can examine from Table 3–6 is that between incremental changes in time remaining to maturity and incremental changes in security price sensitivity to a given change in interest rates. Specifically, notice that the maturity effect described above is not linear. For example, a 2 percent increase in the required rate of return (from 8 percent to 10 percent) on the 12-year bond produces a 13.23 percent (i.e., ($1,000 − $1,152.47)/$1,152.47 = −.1323 = −13.23%) decrease in the bond's fair present value. The same 2 percent increase (from 8 percent to 10 percent) in the 14-year bond produces a 14.28 percent decrease in the fair present value. The difference, as we move from a 12-year to a 14-year maturity, is 1.05 percent (14.28% − 13.23%). Increasing the time to maturity two more years

DO YOU UNDERSTAND?

1. What happens to a bond's price as it approaches maturity?
2. What happens to a bond's price sensitivity for a given change in interest rates as its time to maturity increases? decreases?

FIGURE 3–2 The Impact of a Bond's Maturity on Its Interest Rate Sensitivity

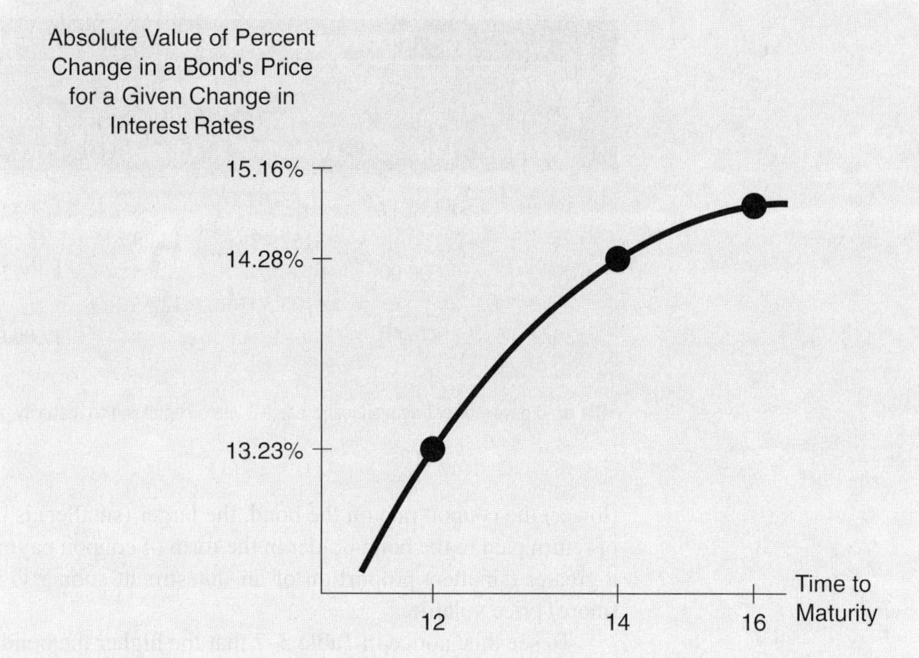

(from 14 years to 16 years) produces an increase in price sensitivity of .88 percent (−14.28% − (−15.16%)). While price sensitivity for a given increase in interest rates increases with maturity, the increase is nonlinear (decreasing) in maturity. We illustrate this relationship in Figure 3–2, as the required rate of return increases from 8 percent to 10 percent.

IMPACT OF COUPON RATES ON SECURITY VALUES

4 Another factor that affects the degree to which the price sensitivity of a bond changes as interest rates change is the bond's coupon rate. Specifically, the higher the bond's coupon rate, the higher its present value at any given interest rate. Also, the higher the bond's coupon rate, the smaller the price changes on the bond for a given change in interest rates. These relationships hold when evaluating either required rates of return and the resulting fair present value of the bond or expected rates of return and the current market price of the bond. To understand these relationships better, consider again the bonds in Example 3–4. Table 3–7 summarizes the bond values and value changes as interest rates change.

Coupon Rate and Security Price

In Table 3–7, we first list the fair present values of the bonds analyzed in Example 3–4. We then repeat the present value calculations using two bonds with identical characteristics except for the coupon rate: 10 percent versus 12 percent. Notice that the fair present value of the 10 percent coupon bond is lower than that of the 12 percent coupon bond at every required rate of return. For example, when the required rate of return is 8 percent, the fair value of the 10 percent coupon bond is $1,152.47 and that of the 12 percent coupon bond is $1,304.94.

Coupon Rate and Security Price Sensitivity to Changes in Interest Rates

Table 3–7 also demonstrates the effect a bond's coupon rate has on its price sensitivity to a given change in interest rates. The intuition behind this relation is as follows. The higher

TABLE 3–7 The Impact of Coupon Rate on the Relation between a Bond's Fair Present Value and Its Required Rate of Return

	10 Percent Coupon Bond			12 Percent Coupon Bond		
Required Rate of Return	Fair Price*	Price Change	Percentage Price Change	Fair Price*	Price Change	Percentage Price Change
8%	$1,152.47			$1,304.94		
		−$152.47	−13.23%		−$166.95	−12.79%
10%	1,000.00			1,137.99		
		−125.50	−12.55		−137.99	−12.13
12%	874.50			1,000.00		

*The bond pays interest semiannually, has 12 years remaining to maturity, and has a face value of $1,000.

(lower) the coupon rate on the bond, the larger (smaller) is the portion of the required rate of return paid to the bond holder in the form of coupon payments. Any security that returns a greater (smaller) proportion of an investment sooner is more (less) valuable and less (more) price volatile.

To see this, notice in Table 3–7 that the higher the bond's coupon rate, the smaller the bond's price sensitivity for any given change in interest rates. For example, for the 10 percent coupon bond, a 2 percent increase in the required rate of return (from 8 percent to 10 percent) results in a 13.23 percent decrease in the bond's fair price. A further 2 percent increase in the required rate of return (from 10 percent to 12 percent) results in a smaller 12.55 percent decrease in the fair price.

DO YOU UNDERSTAND?

1. Whether a high or low coupon-rate bond experiences a larger price change if interest rates increase?
2. Whether a high or low coupon-rate bond experiences a larger price change if interest rates decrease?

For the 12 percent coupon bond, notice that the 2 percent increase in the required rate of return (from 8 percent to 10 percent) results in a 12.79 percent decrease in the bond's fair price, while an increase in the required rate of return from 10 percent to 12 percent results in a lower 12.13 percent decrease in the bond's fair price. Thus, price sensitivity on a bond is negatively related to the level of the coupon rate on a bond. The higher the coupon rate on the bond, the smaller the decrease in the bond's fair price for a given increase in the required rate of return on the bond.

We illustrate this relationship in Figure 3–3. The high coupon-paying bond is less susceptible to interest rate changes than the low coupon-paying bond. This is represented in Figure 3–3 by the slope of the line representing the relation between interest rates and bond prices. The sensitivity of bond prices is smaller (the slope of the line is flatter) for high-coupon bonds than for low-coupon bonds.

DURATION

5

In this section, we show that the price sensitivity of a bond, or the percent change in the bond's fair present value, for a given change in interest rates (as discussed above) can be more directly measured by a concept called duration (or Macauley's duration). We also show that duration produces an accurate measure of the price sensitivity of a bond to interest rate changes for relatively small changes in interest rates. The duration measure is a less accurate measure of price sensitivity the larger the change in interest rates. **Duration** is the *weighted-average* time to maturity on a financial security using the relative present values of the cash flows as weights. On a time value of money basis, duration measures the period of time required to recover the initial investment in a bond. Any cash flows received prior to the period of a bond's duration reflect the recovery of the initial investment, while cash flows received after the period of a bond's measured duration and before its maturity are the profits or returns earned by the investor. In addition

duration

The weighted-average time to maturity on an investment.

FIGURE 3–3 The Impact of a Bond's Coupon Rate on Its Interest Rate Sensitivity

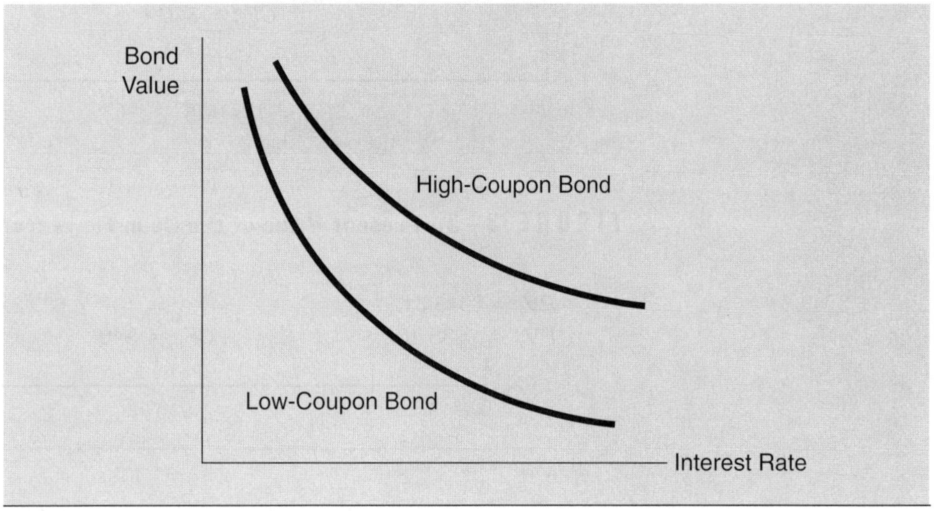

elasticity

The percentage change in the price of a bond for a given change in interest rates.

to being a measure of the average life of an asset or liability, duration also has *economic* meaning as the sensitivity, or **elasticity,** of that asset's or liability's value to small interest rate changes (either required rate of return or yield to maturity).[13] Duration describes the percentage price, or present value, change of a financial security for a given (small) change in interest rates. Thus, rather than calculating present value changes resulting from interest rate changes, as we did in the previous sections, the duration of a financial security can be used to directly calculate the price change.

In this section, we present the basic arithmetic needed to calculate the duration of an asset or liability. Then we analyze the economic meaning of the number we calculate for duration and explain why duration, as a measure of interest rate sensitivity, is most accurate only for small changes in interest rates. Appendix 3B to this chapter located at the book's Web site **(www.mhhe.com/sc3e)**, looks at how duration can be used to immunize an asset or liability against interest rate risk.

A Simple Illustration of Duration

Duration is a measure that incorporates the time of arrival of all cash flows on an asset or liability along with the asset or liability's maturity date. To see this, consider a bond with one year remaining to maturity, a \$1,000 face value, an 8 percent coupon rate (paid semiannually), and an interest rate (either required rate of return or yield to maturity) of 10 percent. The promised cash flows from this bond are illustrated in Figure 3–4. The bond holder receives the promised cash flows (CF) from the bond issuer at the end of one half year and at the end of one year.

$CF_{1/2}$ is the \$40 promised payment of (semiannual) coupon interest (\$1,000 $\times$ 8% $\times$ ½) received after six months. CF_1 is the promised cash flow at the end of year 1; it is equal to the second \$40 promised (semiannual) coupon payment plus the \$1,000 promised payment of face value. To compare the relative sizes of these two cash flow payments—since duration measures the weighted-average time to maturity of a bond—we should put them in the same dimensions, because \$1 of principal or interest received at the end of one year is worth less to an investor in terms of time value of money than is \$1 of principal or

13. In this sense, duration is to bonds what beta is to stocks. That is, beta is the change in the price of a security for a given change in the rate of return on a market portfolio. Thus, both duration and beta are measures of systematic risk.

FIGURE 3–4 Promised Cash Flows on the One-Year Bond

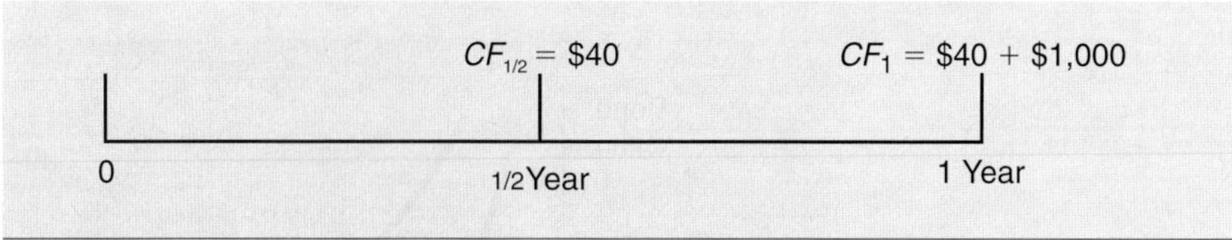

FIGURE 3–5 Present Value of the Cash Flows from the Bond

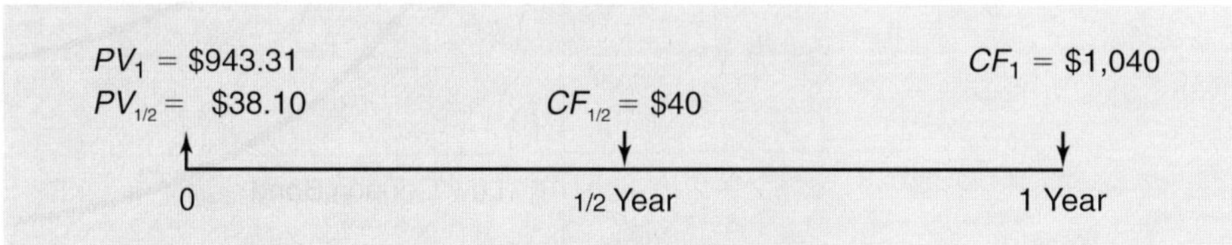

interest received at the end of six months. Assuming that the current interest rate is 10 percent per year, we calculate the present values (PV) of the two cash flows (CF) as:

$$\begin{aligned} CF_{1/2} &= \$40 & PV_{1/2} &= \$40/(1.05) = \$38.10 \\ CF_1 &= \$1{,}040 & PV_1 &= \$1{,}040/(1.05)^2 = \$943.31 \\ CF_{1/2} + CF_1 &= \$1{,}080 & PV_{1/2} + PV_1 &= \$981.41 \end{aligned}$$

Note that since $CF_{1/2}$, the cash flows received at the end of one half year, are received earlier, they are discounted at $(1 + R/2)$ (where R is the current annual interest rate on the bond); this discount factor is smaller than the discount rate applied to the cash flow received at the end of the year $(1 + R/2)^2$. Figure 3–5 summarizes the *PVs* of the cash flows from the bond.[14]

The bond holder receives some cash flows at one half year and some at one year (see Figure 3–5). Intuitively, duration is the weighted-average maturity on the portfolio of zero-coupon bonds, one that has payments at one-half year and at the end of the year (year 1) in this example. Specifically, duration analysis weights the time at which cash flows are received by the relative importance in *present value terms* of the cash flows arriving at each point in time. In present value terms, the relative importance of the cash flows arriving at time $t = \frac{1}{2}$ year and time $t = 1$ year are as follows:

Time (t)	Weight (X)
½ year	$X_{1/2} = \dfrac{PV_{1/2}}{PV_{1/2} + PV_1} = \dfrac{38.10}{981.41} = .0388 = 3.88\%$
1 year	$X_1 = \dfrac{PV_1}{PV_{1/2} + PV_1} = \dfrac{943.31}{981.41} = .9612 = 96.12\%$
	$1.0 \quad 100\%$

In present value terms, the bond holder receives 3.88 percent of the cash flows on the bond with the first coupon payment at the end of six months ($t_{1/2}$) and 96.12 percent with the second payment of coupon plus face value at the end of the year (t_1). By definition, the sum of the (present value) cash flow weights must equal 1:

$$X_{1/2} + X_1 = 1$$
$$.0388 + .9612 = 1$$

14. Here we use the Treasury formula for calculating the present values of cash flows on a security that pays cash flows semiannually. We use $1/(1 + \frac{1}{2}R)^2$ to discount the one-year cash flow rather than $1/(1 + R)$. This approach is more accurate, since it reflects the semiannual payment and compounding of interest on the bond.

We can now calculate the duration (D), or the weighted-average time to maturity of the bond, using the present value of its cash flows as weights:

$$D_L = X_{1/2} \times (t_{1/2}) + X_1 \times (t_1)$$
$$= .0388 \times (\tfrac{1}{2}) + .9612 \times (1) = .9806 \text{ years}$$

Thus, although the maturity of the bond is one year, its duration or average life in a cash flow sense is only .9806 years. On a time value of money basis, the initial investment in the bond is recovered after .9806 years. After that time, the investor earns a profit on the bond. Duration is less than maturity because in present value terms, 3.88 percent of the cash flows are received during the year.

A General Formula for Duration

You can calculate the duration for any fixed-income security that pays interest annually using the following formula:

$$D = \frac{\sum_{t=1}^{N} \frac{CF_t \times t}{(1+R)^t}}{\sum_{t=1}^{N} \frac{CF_t}{(1+R)^t}} = \frac{\sum_{t=1}^{N} PV_t \times t}{\sum_{t=1}^{N} PV_t}$$

where

D = Duration measured in years
t = 1 to N, the period in which a cash flow is received
N = Number of years to maturity
CF_t = Cash flow received on the security at end of period t
R = Yield to maturity (ytm) or current required market rate of return (rrr) on the investment
PV_t = Present value of the cash flow received at the end of the period t

For bonds that pay interest semiannually, the duration equation becomes:[15]

$$D = \frac{\sum_{t=1/2}^{N} \frac{CF_t \times t}{(1+R/2)^{2t}}}{\sum_{t=1/2}^{N} \frac{CF_t}{(1+R/2)^{2t}}}$$

where $t = \tfrac{1}{2}, 1, 1\tfrac{1}{2}, \ldots, N$.

Notice that the denominator of the duration equation is the present value of the cash flows on the security (which in an efficient market will be equal to the current market price). The numerator is the present value of each cash flow received on the security multiplied or weighted by the length of time required to receive the cash flow. To help you fully understand this formula, we look at some examples next.

15. In general, the duration equation is written as:

$$D = \frac{\sum_{t=1/m}^{N} \frac{CF_t \times t}{(1+R/m)^{mt}}}{\sum_{t=1/m}^{N} \frac{CF_t}{(1+R/m)^{mt}}}$$

where m = number of times per year interest is paid.

EXAMPLE 3-6 The Duration of a Four-Year Bond

Suppose that you have a bond that offers a coupon rate of 10 percent paid semiannually (or 5 percent paid every 6 months). The face value of the bond is $1,000, it matures in four years, its current yield to maturity (*R*) is 8 percent, and its current price is $1,067.34. See Table 3–8 for the calculation of its duration. As the calculation indicates, the duration, or weighted-average time to maturity, on this bond is 3.42 years. In other words, on a time value of money basis, the initial investment of $1,067.34 is recovered after 3.42 years. Between 3.42 years and maturity (4 years), the bond produces a profit or return to the investor. Table 3–9 shows that if the annual coupon rate is lowered to 6 percent, the duration of the bond rises to 3.60 years. Since 6 percent annual coupon payments are smaller than 10 percent coupon payments, it takes longer to recover the initial investment with the 6 percent coupon bond. In Table 3–10, duration is calculated for the original 10 percent coupon bond, assuming that its yield to maturity (discount rate) increases from 8 percent to 10 percent. Now duration falls from 3.42 years (in Table 3–8) to 3.39 years. The higher the yield to maturity on the bond, the more the investor earns on reinvested coupons and the shorter the time needed to recover his or her initial investment. Finally, as the maturity on a bond decreases, in this case to 3 years in Table 3–11, duration falls to 2.67 years (i.e., the shorter the maturity on the bond, the more quickly the initial investment is recovered).

The Duration of a Zero-Coupon Bond. Zero-coupon bonds sell at a discount from face value on issue and pay their face value (e.g., $1,000) on maturity. These bonds have no intervening cash flows, such as coupon payments, between issue and maturity. The current price that an investor is willing to pay for such a bond, assuming semiannual compounding of interest, is equal to the present value of the single, fixed (face value) payment on the bond that is received on maturity (here, $1,000):

$$P = 1{,}000/(1 + R/2)^{2N}$$

where

R = Required semiannually compounded yield to maturity
N = Number of years to maturity
P = Price

TABLE 3-8 Duration of a Four-Year Bond with 10 Percent Coupon Paid Semiannually and 8 Percent Yield

t	CF_t	$\frac{1}{(1+4\%)^{2t}}$	$\frac{CF_t}{(1+4\%)^{2t}}$	$\frac{CF_t \times t}{(1+4\%)^{2t}}$
½	50	0.9615	48.08	24.04
1	50	0.9246	46.23	46.23
1½	50	0.8890	44.45	66.67
2	50	0.8548	42.74	85.48
2½	50	0.8219	41.10	102.75
3	50	0.7903	39.52	118.56
3½	50	0.7599	38.00	133.00
4	1,050	0.7307	767.22	3,068.88
			1,067.34	3,645.61

$$D = \frac{3{,}645.61}{1{,}067.34} = 3.42 \text{ years}$$

TABLE 3–9 Duration of a Four-Year Bond with 6 Percent Coupon Paid Semiannually and 8 Percent Yield

t	CF_t	$\frac{1}{(1+4\%)^{2t}}$	$\frac{CF_t}{(1+4\%)^{2t}}$	$\frac{CF_t \times t}{(1+4\%)^{2t}}$
½	30	0.9615	28.84	14.42
1	30	0.9246	27.74	27.74
1½	30	0.8890	26.67	40.00
2	30	0.8548	25.64	51.28
2½	30	0.8219	24.66	61.65
3	30	0.7903	23.71	71.13
3½	30	0.7599	22.80	79.80
4	1,030	0.7307	752.62	3,010.48
			932.68	3,356.50

$$D = \frac{3{,}356.50}{932.68} = 3.60 \text{ years}$$

TABLE 3–10 Duration of a Four-Year Bond with 10 Percent Coupon Paid Semiannually and 10 Percent Yield

t	CF_t	$\frac{1}{(1+5\%)^{2t}}$	$\frac{CF_t}{(1+5\%)^{2t}}$	$\frac{CF_t \times t}{(1+5\%)^{2t}}$
½	50	0.9524	47.62	23.81
1	50	0.9070	45.35	45.35
1½	50	0.8638	43.19	64.78
2	50	0.8227	41.14	82.28
2½	50	0.7835	39.18	97.95
3	50	0.7462	37.31	111.93
3½	50	0.7107	35.53	124.36
4	1,050	0.6768	710.68	2,842.72
			1,000.00	3,393.18

$$D = \frac{3{,}393.18}{1{,}000.00} = 3.39 \text{ years}$$

TABLE 3–11 Duration of a Three-Year Bond with 10 Percent Coupon Paid Semiannually and 8 Percent Yield

t	CF_t	$\frac{1}{(1+4\%)^{2t}}$	$\frac{CF_t}{(1+4\%)^{2t}}$	$\frac{CF_t \times t}{(1+4\%)^{2t}}$
½	50	0.9615	48.08	24.04
1	50	0.9246	46.23	46.23
1½	50	0.8890	44.45	66.67
2	50	0.8548	42.74	85.48
2½	50	0.8219	41.10	102.75
3	1,050	0.7903	829.82	2,489.46
			1,052.42	2,814.63

$$D = \frac{2{,}814.63}{1{,}052.42} = 2.67 \text{ years}$$

Because the only cash flow received on these securities is the final payment at maturity (time N), the following must be true:

$$D_{zc} = N_{zc}$$

That is, the duration of a zero-coupon instrument equals its maturity. Note that it is only for zero-coupon bonds that duration and maturity are equal. Indeed, for any bond that pays some cash flows prior to maturity, its duration will always be less than its maturity.

EXAMPLE 3-7 The Duration of a Zero-Coupon Bond

Suppose that you have a zero-coupon bond with a face value of \$1,000, a maturity of four years, and a current yield to maturity of 8 percent compounded semiannually. Since the bond pays no interest, the duration equation consists of only one term—cash flows at the end of year 4:

t	CF_4	$\frac{1}{(1+8\%/2)^{2\times4}}$	$\frac{CF_4}{(1+8\%/2)^{2\times4}}$	$\frac{CF_4 \times 4}{(1+4\%/2)^{2\times4}}$
4	\$1,000	0.7307	730	2,923

$$D = 2{,}923/730 = 4 \text{ years}$$

or duration equals the maturity of the zero-coupon bond.

Features of Duration

6 The preceding examples suggest several important features of duration relating to the time remaining to maturity, yield to maturity, and coupon interest of the underlying bond being analyzed. These features are summarized in Table 3–12.

Duration and Coupon Interest. A comparison of Tables 3–8 and 3–9 indicates that the higher the coupon or promised interest payment on the bond, the lower its duration. This is due to the fact that the larger the coupon or promised interest payment, the more quickly investors receive cash flows on a bond and the higher are the present value weights of those cash flows in the duration calculation. On a time value of money basis, the investor recoups his or her initial investment faster when coupon payments are higher.

Duration and Yield to Maturity. A comparison of Tables 3–8 and 3–10 also indicates that duration decreases as yield to maturity increases. This makes intuitive sense since the higher the yield to maturity on the bond, the lower the present value cost of waiting to receive the later cash flows on the bond. Higher yields to maturity discount later cash flows more heavily, and the relative importance, or weights, of those later cash flows decline when compared to cash flows received earlier.

TABLE 3-12 Features of Duration

1. The higher the coupon or promised interest payment on a security, the lower is its duration.
2. The higher the yield on a security, the lower is its duration.
3. Duration increases with maturity at a decreasing rate.

TABLE 3–13 Duration of a Two-Year Bond with 10 Percent Coupon Paid Semiannually and 8 Percent Yield

t	CF_t	$\frac{1}{(1+4\%)^{2t}}$	$\frac{CF_t}{(1+4\%)^{2t}}$	$\frac{CF_t \times t}{(1+4\%)^{2t}}$
½	50	0.9615	48.08	24.04
1	50	0.9246	46.23	46.23
1½	50	0.8890	44.45	66.67
2	1,050	0.8548	897.54	1,795.08
			1,036.30	1,932.02

$$D = \frac{1{,}932.02}{1{,}036.30} = 1.86 \text{ years}$$

FIGURE 3–6 Discrepancy between Maturity and Duration on a Coupon Bond

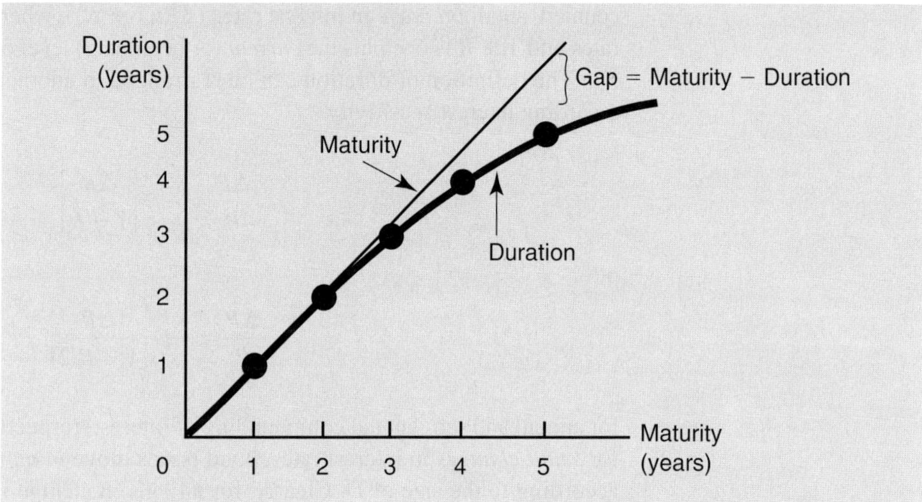

Duration and Maturity. A comparison of Tables 3–8, 3–11, and 3–13 indicates that duration increases with the maturity of a bond, but at a *decreasing* rate. As maturity of a 10 percent coupon bond decreases from four years to three years (Tables 3–8 and 3–11), duration decreases by 0.75 years, from 3.42 years to 2.67 years. Decreasing maturity for an additional year, from three years to two years (Tables 3–11 and 3–13), decreases duration by 0.81 years from 2.67 years to 1.86 years. Notice too that for a coupon bond, the longer the maturity on the bond the larger the discrepancy between maturity and duration. Specifically, the two-year maturity bond has a duration of 1.86 years (0.14 years less than its maturity), while the three-year maturity bond has a duration of 2.67 years (0.33 years less than its maturity), and the four-year maturity bond has a duration of 3.42 years (0.58 years less than its maturity). Figure 3–6 illustrates this relation between duration and maturity for our 10 percent coupon (paid semiannually), 8 percent yield bond.

7

Economic Meaning of Duration

So far we have calculated duration for a number of different bonds. In addition to being a measure of the average life of a bond, duration is also a direct measure of its interest rate sensitivity, or elasticity.[16] In other words, the larger the numerical

16. In Chapter 22, we also make the direct link between duration and the interest rate sensitivity of an asset or liability or of an FI's entire portfolio (i.e., its duration gap). We show how duration can be used to immunize a security or portfolio of securities against interest rate risk.

value of duration (D), the more sensitive the price of that bond to (small) changes or shocks in interest rates. The specific relationship between these factors for securities with annual compounding of interest is represented as:[17]

$$\frac{\Delta P/P}{\Delta R/(1 + R)} = -D$$

For securities with semiannual receipt (compounding) of interest, it is represented as:

$$\frac{\Delta P/P}{\Delta R/(1 + R/2)} = -D$$

The economic interpretation of this equation is that the number D is the interest elasticity, or sensitivity, of the bond's price to small interest rate (either required rate of return or yield to maturity) changes. The negative sign in front of the D indicates the inverse relationship between interest rate changes and price changes. That is, $-D$ describes the percentage fair or current value *decrease*—capital loss—on the security ($\Delta P/P$) for any given (discounted) small *increase* in interest rates ($\Delta R/(1 + R)$), where ΔR is the change in interest rates and $1 + R$ is one plus the *current* (or beginning) level of interest rates.

The definition of duration can be rearranged in another useful way for interpretation regarding interest sensitivity:

$$\frac{\Delta P}{P} = -D\left[\frac{\Delta R}{1 + R}\right]$$

or

$$\frac{\Delta P}{P} = -D\left[\frac{\Delta R}{1 + R/2}\right]$$

for annual and semiannual compounding of interest, respectively. This equation shows that for *small changes* in interest rates, bond prices move *in an inversely proportional* manner according to the size of D. Clearly, for any given change in interest rates, long duration securities suffer a larger capital loss (or receive a higher capital gain) should interest rates rise (fall) than do short duration securities.[18]

modified duration

Duration divided by 1 plus the interest rate.

The duration equation can be rearranged, combining D and $(1 + R)$ into a single variable $D/(1 + R)$, to produce what practitioners call **modified duration** (MD). For annual compounding of interest:

$$\frac{\Delta P}{P} = -MD \times \Delta R$$

where

$$MD = \frac{D}{1 + R}$$

For semiannual compounding of interest:

$$\frac{\Delta P}{P} = -MD \times \Delta R$$

17. In what follows, we use the Δ (change) notation instead of d (derivative notation) to recognize that interest rate changes tend to be discrete rather then infinitesimally small. For example, in real-world financial markets the smallest observed rate change is usually one basis point, or 1/100 of 1 percent.

18. By implication, gains and losses under the duration model are *symmetric*. That is, if we repeated the above examples but allowed interest rates to decrease by one basis point annually (or ½ basis point semiannually), the percentage increase in the price of the bond ($\Delta P/P$) would be proportionate with D. Further, the capital gains would be a mirror image of the capital losses for an equal (small) decrease in interest rates.

where

$$MD = \frac{D}{1 + R/2}$$

This form is more intuitive because we multiply *MD* by the simple change in interest rates rather than the discounted change in interest rates as in the general duration equation. Next, we use duration to measure the price sensitivity of different bonds to small changes in interest rates.

The Interest-Paying Bond.

EXAMPLE 3–8 Four-Year Bond

Consider a four-year bond with a 10 percent coupon paid semiannually (or 5 percent paid every 6 months) and an 8 percent yield to maturity (the discount rate). According to calculations in Table 3–8, the bond's duration is $D = 3.42$ years. Suppose that the yield to maturity increases by 10 basis points (1/10 of 1 percent) from 8 to 8.10 percent; then, using the semiannual compounding version of the duration model shown above, the percentage change in the bond's price is:

$$\frac{\Delta P}{P} = -(3.42)\left[\frac{.001}{1.04}\right]$$
$$= -.00329$$

or

$$= -0.329\%$$

The bond price had been $1,067.34, which was the present value of a four-year bond with a 10 percent coupon and an 8 percent yield to maturity. However, the duration model predicts that the price of this bond would fall by 0.329 percent, or by $3.51, to $1,063.83 after the increase in the yield to maturity on the bond of 10 basis points.[19]

With a lower coupon rate of 6 percent, as shown in Table 3–9, the bond's duration, *D*, is 3.6 and the bond price changes by:

$$\frac{\Delta P}{P} = -(3.60)\left[\frac{.001}{1.04}\right] = -.00346$$

or

$$= -0.346\%$$

for a 10-basis-point increase in the yield to maturity for each semiannual period. The bond's price drops by 0.346 percent, or by $3.23, from $932.68 (reported in Table 3–9) to $929.45. Notice again that, all else held constant, the higher the coupon rate on the bond, the shorter the duration of the bond and the smaller the percentage decrease in a bond's price for a given increase in interest rates.

Large Interest Rate Changes and Duration

It needs to be stressed here that duration accurately measures the price sensitivity of financial securities only for *small* changes in interest rates of the order of one or a few basis points

19. That is, a price fall of 0.329 percent in this case translates into a dollar fall of $3.51. To calculate the dollar change in value, we can rewrite the equation as $\Delta P = (P)(-D)((\Delta R)/(1 + R/2)) = (\$1{,}067.34)(-3.42)(.001/1.04) = \$3.51$.

FIGURE 3–7 Duration Estimated versus True Bond Price

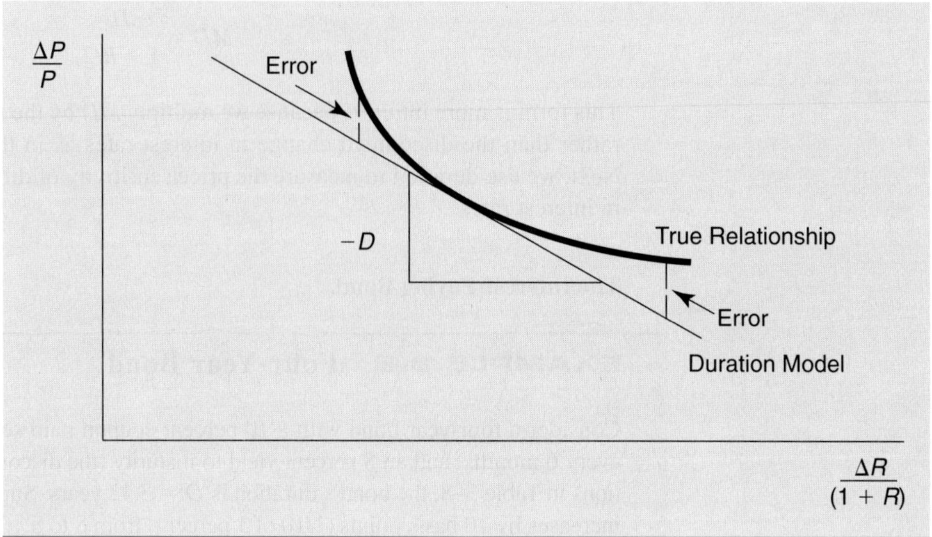

DO YOU UNDERSTAND?

1. When the duration of an asset is equal to its maturity?
2. What the denominator of the duration equation measures?
3. What the numerator of the duration equation measures?
4. What the duration of a zero-coupon bond is?
5. Which has the longest duration, a 30-year, 8 percent yield to maturity, zero-coupon bond, or a 30-year, 8 percent yield to maturity, 5 percent coupon bond?
6. What the relationship is between the duration of a bond and its interest elasticity?

(a basis point is equal to one-hundredth of 1 percent). Suppose, however, that interest rate shocks are much larger, of the order of 2 percent or 200 basis points or more. While such large changes in interest rates are not common, this might happen in a financial crisis or if the central bank (see Chapter 4) suddenly changes its monetary policy strategy. In this case, duration becomes a less accurate predictor of how much the prices of bonds will change, and therefore, a less accurate measure of the price sensitivity of a bond to changes in interest rates. Figure 3–7 is a graphic representation of the reason for this. Note the difference in the change in a bond's price due to interest rate changes according to the proportional duration measure (D), and the "true relationship," using time value of money equations of Chapter 2 (and discussed earlier in this chapter) to calculate the exact present value change of a bond's price to interest rate changes.

Specifically, duration predicts that the relationship between an interest rate change and a security's price change will be proportional to the security's D (duration). By precisely calculating the exact or true change in the security's price, however, we would find that for large interest rate increases, duration overpredicts the *fall* in the security's price, and for large interest rate decreases, it underpredicts the *increase* in the security's price. Thus, duration misestimates the final value of a security following a large change (either positive or negative) in interest rates. Further, the duration model predicts symmetric effects for rate increases and decreases on a bond's price. As Figure 3–7 shows, in actuality, the *capital loss effect* of large rate increases tends to be smaller than the *capital gain effect* of large rate decreases. This is the result of a bond's price–interest rate relationship exhibiting a property called **convexity** rather than *linearity*, as assumed by the simple duration model. Intuitively, this is because the sensitivity of the bond's price to a change in interest rates depends on the *level* from which interest rates change (i.e., 6 percent, 8 percent, 10 percent, 12 percent). In particular, the higher the level of interest rates, the smaller a bond's price sensitivity to interest rate changes.

convexity

The degree of curvature of the price–interest rate curve around some interest rate level.

EXAMPLE 3–9 Calculation of the Change in a Security's Price Using the Duration versus the Time Value of Money Formula

To see the importance of accounting for the effects of convexity in assessing the impact of large interest rate changes, consider the four-year, $1,000 face value bond with a 10 percent coupon paid semiannually and an 8 percent yield. In Table 3–8 we found this bond has a duration of 3.42 years, and its current price is $1,067.34 at a yield of 8 percent. We represent this as point *A* in Figure 3–8. If rates rise from 8 to 10 percent, the duration model predicts that the bond price will fall by 6.577 percent; that is:

$$\frac{\Delta P}{P} = -3.42(.02/1.04) = -6.577\%$$

or from a price of $1,067.34 to $997.14 (see point *B* in Figure 3–8). However, calculating the exact change in the bond's price after a rise in yield to 10 percent, we find its true value is:

$$V_b = 50(PVIFA_{10\%/2,4(2)}) + 1{,}000(PVIFA_{10\%/2,4(2)}) = \$1{,}000$$

This is point *C* in Figure 3–8. As you can see, the true or actual fall in price is less than the predicted fall by $2.86. The reason for this is the natural convexity to the price-yield curve as yields rise.

Reversing the experiment reveals that the duration model would predict the bond's price to rise by 6.577 percent if yields fell from 8 to 6 percent, resulting in a predicted price of $1,137.54 (see point *D* in Figure 3–8). By comparison, the true or actual change in price can be computed as $1,140.39 by estimating the present value of the bond's coupons and its face value with a 6 percent yield (see point E in Figure 3–8). The duration model has underpredicted the bond price increase by $2.85 ($1,140.39 − $1,137.54).

An important question for managers of financial institutions and individual savers is whether the error in the duration equation is big enough to be concerned about. This depends on the size of the interest rate change and the size of the portfolio under management. Clearly, for a large portfolio the error will also be large.

FIGURE 3–8 Price-Yield Curve for the Four-Year 10 Percent Coupon Bond

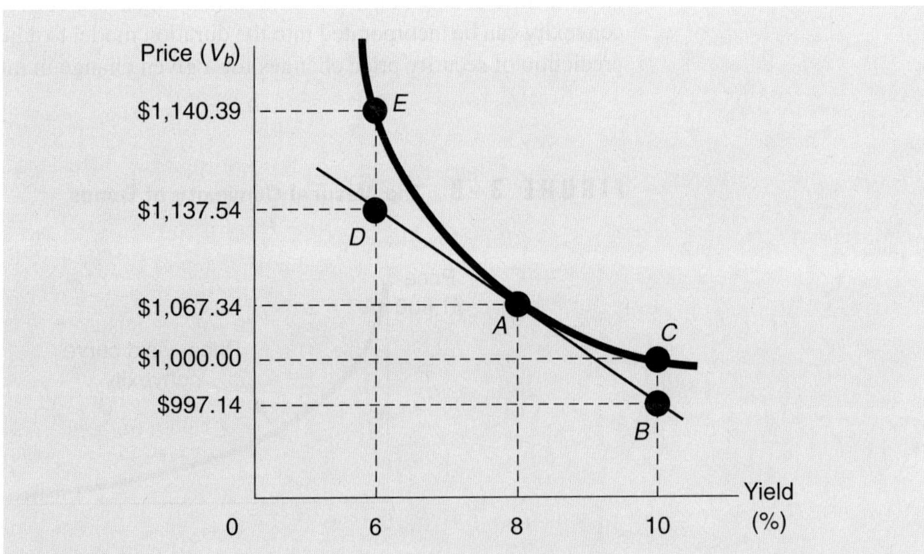

Note that convexity is a desirable feature for an investor or FI manager to capture in a portfolio of assets. Buying a bond or a portfolio of assets that exhibits a lot of convexity or curvature in the price–yield curve relationship is similar to buying partial interest rate risk insurance. Specifically, high convexity means that for equally large changes of interest rates up and down (e.g., plus or minus 2 percent), the capital gain effect of a rate decrease more than offsets the capital loss effect of a rate increase.

So far, we have established the following three characteristics of convexity:

1. Convexity is desirable. The greater the convexity of a security or portfolio of securities, the more insurance or interest rate protection an investor or FI manager has against rate increases and the greater the potential gains after interest rate falls.
2. Convexity diminishes the error in duration as an investment criterion. The larger the interest rate changes and the more convex a fixed-income security or portfolio, the greater the error the investor or FI manager faces in using just duration (and duration matching) to immunize exposure to interest rate shocks.
3. All fixed-income securities are convex. The price of a bond can never be less than zero.

To illustrate the third characteristic, we can take the four-year, 10 percent coupon, 8 percent yield bond and look at two extreme price–yield scenarios. What is the price on the bond if yields fall to zero, and what is its price if yields rise to some very large number such as infinity? Where $R = 0$:

$$V_b = \frac{50}{(1+0)^1} + \frac{50}{(1+0)^2} + \cdots + \frac{1{,}050}{(1+0)^8} = \$1{,}400$$

The price is just the simple undiscounted sum of the coupon values and the face value of the bond. Since yields can never go below zero, \$1,400 is the maximum possible price for the bond. Where $R = \infty$:

$$V_b = \frac{50}{(1+\infty)^1} + \frac{50}{(1+\infty)^2} + \cdots + \frac{1{,}050}{(1+\infty)^8} = \$0$$

As the yield goes to infinity, the bond price falls asymptotically toward zero, but by definition a bond's price can never be negative. Thus, zero must be the minimum bond price (see Figure 3–9). In Appendix 3C to this chapter, located at the book's Web site (**www.mhhe.com/sc3e**), we look at how to measure convexity and how this measure of convexity can be incorporated into the duration model to adjust for or offset the error in the prediction of security price changes for a given change in interest rates.

FIGURE 3–9 **The Natural Convexity of Bonds**

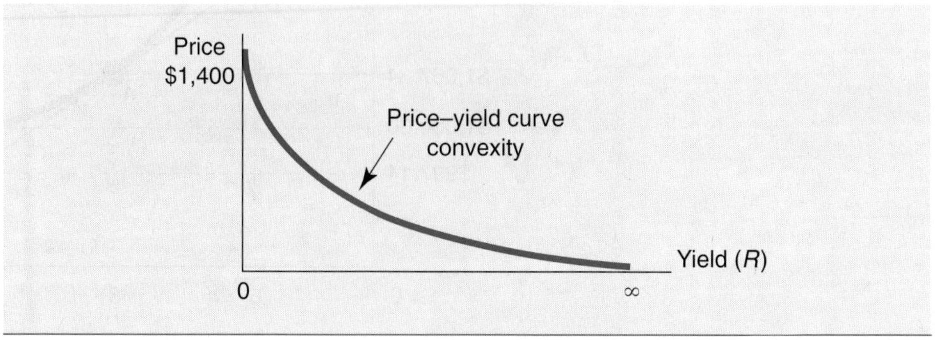

SUMMARY

This chapter applied the time value of money formulas presented in Chapter 2 to the valuation of financial securities such as equities and bonds. With respect to bonds, we included a detailed examination of how changes in interest rates, coupon rates, and time to maturity affect their price and price sensitivity. We also presented a measure of bond price sensitivity to interest rate changes, called duration. We showed how the value of duration is affected by various bond characteristics, such as coupon rates, interest rates, and time to maturity.

QUESTIONS

1. You bought a bond five years ago for $935 per bond. The bond is now selling for $980. It also paid $75 in interest per year, which you reinvested in the bond. Calculate the realized rate of return earned on this bond.
2. Refer again to the bond information in Question 1. You expect to hold the bond for three more years, then sell it for $990. If the bond is expected to continue paying $75 per year over the next three years, what is the expected rate of return on the bond during this period?
3. Johnson Motors' bonds have 10 years remaining to maturity. Interest is paid annually, the bonds have a $1,000 par value, and the coupon rate is 8 percent. The bonds have a yield to maturity of 9 percent. What is the current market price of these bonds?
4. eXcel **Using a Spreadsheet to Calculate Bond Values.** What is the value of $1,000 bond with a 12-year maturity and an 8 percent coupon rate (paid semiannually) if the required return is 5 percent, 6 percent, 8 percent, and 10 percent?

Face Value	Total Payments	Periodic Coupon Payment	Required Return	=>	The Bond Value Will Be
$1,000	12 × 2 = 24	1,000(.08)/2 = 40	5%		$1,268.27
1,000	24	40	6		1,169.36
1,000	24	40	8		1,000.00
1,000	24	40	10		862.01

5. A 10-year, 12 percent semiannual coupon bond, with a par value of $1,000 sells for $1,100. What is the bond's yield to maturity?
6. eXcel **Using a Spreadsheet to Calculate Yield to Maturity.** What is the yield to maturity on the following bonds; all have a maturity of 10 years, a face value of $1,000, and a coupon rate of 9 percent (paid semiannually). The bonds current market values are $945.50, $987.50, $1,090.00, and $1,225.875, respectively.

Market Value	Total Payments	Periodic Coupon Payment	Face Value	=>	The Yield to Maturity Will Be
945.50	10×2 = 20	1,000(.09)/2 = 45	$1,000		9.87%
987.50	20	45	1,000		9.19
1,090.00	20	45	1,000		7.69
1,225.875	20	45	1,000		5.97

7. Galen Corporation has a bond issue outstanding with an annual coupon rate of 7 percent paid quarterly and 4 years remaining until maturity. The par value of the bond is $1,000. Determine the current value of the bond if market conditions justify a 14 percent, compounded quarterly, required rate of return.
8. You have just been offered a bond for $863.73. The coupon rate is 8 percent payable annually, and interest rates on new issues with the same degree of risk are 10 percent. You want to know how many more interest payments you will receive, but the party selling the bond cannot remember. If the par value is $1,000, how many interest payments remain?
9. A bond you are evaluating has a 10 percent coupon rate (compounded semiannually), a $1,000 face value, and is 10 years from maturity.
   a. If the required rate of return on the bond is 6 percent, what is its fair present value?
   b. If the required rate of return on the bond is 8 percent, what is its fair present value?
   c. What do your answers to parts (a) and (b) say about the relation between required rates of return and fair values of bonds?
10. For each of the following situations, identify whether a bond would be considered a premium bond, a discount bond, or a par bond.
    a. A bond's current market price is greater than its face value.
    b. A bond's coupon rate is equal to its yield to maturity.
    c. A bond's coupon rate is less than its required rate of return.
    d. A bond's coupon rate is less than its yield to maturity.
    e. A bond's coupon rate is greater than its yield to maturity.
    f. A bond's fair present value is less than its face value.
11. Calculate the yield to maturity on the following bonds.
    a. A 9 percent coupon (paid semiannually) bond, with a $1,000 face value and 15 years remaining to maturity. The bond is selling at $985.
    b. An 8 percent coupon (paid quarterly) bond, with a $1,000 face value and 10 years remaining to maturity. The bond is selling at $915.
    c. An 11 percent coupon (paid annually) bond, with a $1,000 face value and 6 years remaining to maturity. The bond is selling at $1,065.
12. Calculate the fair present values of the following bonds, all of which pay interest semiannually, have a face value of $1,000, have 12 years remaining to maturity, and have a required rate of return of 10 percent.
    a. The bond has a 6 percent coupon rate.
    b. The bond has an 8 percent coupon rate.

www.mhhe.com/sc3e

c. The bond has a 10 percent coupon rate.
d. What do your answers to parts (a) through (c) say about the relation between coupon rates and present values?

13. Repeat parts (a) through (c) of Question 12 using a required rate of return on the bond of 8 percent. What do your calculations imply about the relation between the coupon rates and bond price volatility?

14. Calculate the fair present value of the following bonds, all of which have a 10 percent coupon rate (paid semiannually), face value of $1,000, and a required rate of return of 8 percent.
a. The bond has 10 years remaining to maturity.
b. The bond has 15 years remaining to maturity.
c. The bond has 20 years remaining to maturity.
d. What do your answers to parts (a) through (c) say about the relation between time to maturity and present values?

15. Repeat parts (a) through (c) of Question 14 using a required rate of return on the bond of 11 percent. What do your calculations imply about the relation between time to maturity and bond price volatility?

16. STANDARD &POOR'S Go to the S&P Market Insight Web site at **www.mhhe.com/edumarketinsight** and find the long-term debt outstanding for Alcoa Inc. (AA) and Target Corp. (TGT) using the following steps:
Click on "Educational Version of Market Insight"
Enter your Site ID and Click on "Login"
Click on "Company"
Enter "AA" in the "Ticker" box and click on "Go!"
Click on "Excel Analytics"
Click on "FS Ann. Balance Sheet"
This will download the Balance Sheet for Alcoa, which contains the balances for Fixed Income Securities (or long-term debt). Repeat the process by entering "TGT" in the "Ticker" box to get information on Target. If interest rates increase, what will happen to the market values of this debt?

17. What is the economic meaning of duration?

18. a. What is the duration of a two-year bond that pays an annual coupon of 10 percent and has a current yield to maturity of 12 percent? Use $1,000 as the face value.
b. What is the duration of a two-year zero-coupon bond that is yielding 11.5 percent? Use $1,000 as the face value.
c. Given these answers, how does duration differ from maturity?

19. Consider the following two banks:
Bank 1 has assets composed solely of a 10-year, 12 percent coupon, $1 million loan with a 12 percent yield to maturity. It is financed with a 10-year, 10 percent coupon, $1 million CD with a 10 percent yield to maturity.
Bank 2 has assets composed solely of a 7-year, 12 percent, zero-coupon bond with a current value of $894,006.20 and a maturity value of $1,976,362.88. It is financed by a 10-year, 8.275 percent coupon, $1,000,000 face value CD with a yield to maturity of 10 percent.
All securities except the zero-coupon bond pay interest annually.
a. If interest rates rise by 1 percent (100 basis points), how do the values of the assets and liabilities of each bank change?
b. What accounts for the differences between the two banks' accounts?

20. Consider the following.
a. What is the duration of a five-year Treasury bond with a 10 percent semiannual coupon selling at par?
b. What is the duration of the above bond if the yield to maturity (ytm) increases to 14 percent? What if the ytm increases to 16 percent?
c. What can you conclude about the relationship between duration and yield to maturity?

21. Consider the following.
a. What is the duration of a four-year Treasury bond with a 10 percent semiannual coupon selling at par?
b. What is the duration of a three-year Treasury bond with a 10 percent semiannual coupon selling at par?
c. What is the duration of a two-year Treasury bond with a 10 percent semiannual coupon selling at par?
d. What conclusions can you draw from these results between duration and maturity?

22. What is the duration of a zero coupon bond that has 8 years to maturity? What is the duration if the maturity increases to 10 years? If it increases to 12 years?

23. Suppose that you purchase a bond that matures in five years and pays a 13.76 percent coupon rate. The bond is priced to yield 10 percent.
a. Show that the duration is equal to four years.
b. Show that if interest rates rise to 11 percent next year and your investment horizon is four years from today, you will still earn a 10 percent yield on your investment.

24. An insurance company is analyzing the following three bonds, each with 5 years to maturity, and is using duration as its measure of interest rate risk:
a. $10,000 par value, coupon rate = 8%, ytm = .10
b. $10,000 par value, coupon rate = 10%, ytm = .10
c. $10,000 par value, coupon rate = 12%, ytm = .10
What are the durations of each of the three bonds?

25. How is duration related to the interest elasticity of a fixed-income security? What is the relationship between duration and the price of a fixed-income security?

26. You have discovered that when the required return of a bond you own fell by 0.50 percent from 9.75 percent to 9.25 percent, the price rose from $975 to $995. What is the duration of this bond?

The following questions are related to Appendix 3A material in this chapter, located at the book's Web site (**www.mhhe.com/sc3e**).

27. Calculate the present value on a stock that pays $5 in dividends per year (with no growth) and has a required rate of return of 10 percent.

28. A stock you are evaluating paid a dividend last year of $2.50. Dividends have grown at a constant rate of 1.5 percent over the last 15 years and you expect this to continue.
a. If the required rate of return on the stock is 12 percent, what is its fair present value?

www.mhhe.com/sc3e

b. If the required rate of return on the stock is 15 percent, what is its expected price four years from today?

29. You are considering the purchase of a stock that is currently selling at $64 per share. You expect the stock to pay $4.50 in dividends next year.

a. If dividends are expected to grow at a constant rate of 3 percent per year, what is your expected rate of return on this stock?

b. If dividends are expected to grow at a constant rate of 5 percent per year, what is your expected rate of return on this stock?

c. What do your answers to parts (a) and (b) say about the impact of dividend growth rates on expected rate of returns on stocks?

30. A stock you are evaluating is expected to experience supernormal growth in dividends of 8 percent over the next six years. Following this period, dividends are expected to grow at a constant rate of 3 percent. The stock paid a dividend of $5.50 last year and the required rate of return on the stock is 10 percent. Calculate the stock's fair present value.

APPENDIX 3A: Equity Valuation

View this appendix at
www.mhhe.com/sc3e

APPENDIX 3B: Duration and Immunization

View this appendix at
www.mhhe.com/sc3e

APPENDIX 3C: More on Convexity

View this appendix at
www.mhhe.com/sc3e

www.mhhe.com/sc3e

4

The Federal Reserve System, Monetary Policy, *and* Interest Rates

OUTLINE

Chapter NAVIGATOR

1. What are the major functions of the Federal Reserve System?
2. What is the structure of the Federal Reserve System?
3. What are the monetary policy tools used by the Federal Reserve?
4. How do monetary policy changes affect key economic variables?
5. How do U.S. monetary policy initiatives affect foreign exchange rates?
6. What have been some of the recent challenges experienced by major central banks outside of the United States?

MAJOR DUTIES AND RESPONSIBILITIES OF THE FEDERAL RESERVE SYSTEM: CHAPTER OVERVIEW

The Federal Reserve (the Fed) is the central bank of the United States. Founded by Congress under the Federal Reserve Act in 1913, the Fed's original duties were to provide the nation with a safer, more flexible, and more stable monetary and financial system. This was needed following a number of banking crises and panics that had occurred in the first decade of the 20th century (particularly 1907) and the last decades of the 19th century. As time passed, additional legislation, including the Banking Act of 1935, the Full Employment Act of 1946, and the Full Employment and Balanced Growth Act of 1978 (also called the Humphrey-Hawkins Act), revised and supplemented the original purposes and objectives of the Federal Reserve System. These objectives included economic growth in line with the economy's potential to expand, a high level of employment, stable prices, and moderate long-term interest rates.

The Federal Reserve System is an independent central bank in that its decisions do not have to be ratified by the president or another member of the executive branch of the U.S. government. The system is, however, subject to oversight by the U.S. Congress under its authority to coin money. Further, the Federal Reserve is required to work within the framework of the overall objectives of economic and financial policies established by the U.S. government.

1

The Federal Reserve System has evolved into one of the most powerful economic bodies in the world. As mentioned in previous chapters, even the hint of a change in interest rate policy by the Fed can have an impact on markets around the world. Its duties incorporate four major functions: (1) conducting monetary policy, (2) supervising and regulating depository institutions, (3) maintaining the stability of the financial system, and (4) providing payment and other financial services to the U.S. government, the public, financial institutions, and foreign official institutions.

In this chapter, we present an overview of the Federal Reserve System. We start with a basic description, highlighting its organization and structure. We then examine the monetary policy tools available to the Fed and how the Fed uses these tools to influence the U.S. money supply and interest rates both domestically and internationally. Finally, we look at the impact of U.S. monetary policy on foreign exchange rates.

2

STRUCTURE OF THE FEDERAL RESERVE SYSTEM

The Federal Reserve System consists of 12 Federal Reserve Banks located in major cities throughout the United States and a seven-member Board of Governors located in Washington, D.C. This structure was implemented in 1913 to spread power along regional lines, between the private sector and the government, and among bankers, businesspeople, and the public. Federal Reserve Banks and the Federal Reserve Board of Governors together comprise and operate the Federal Open Market Committee (FOMC), which is responsible for the formulation and implementation of monetary policy.

www.federalreserve.gov

Organization of the Federal Reserve System

The Federal Reserve System is divided into 12 Federal Reserve districts that are the "operating arms" of the central banking system (see Figure 4-1). Each district has one main Federal Reserve Bank, some of which also have branches in other cities within the district (identified in Figure 4–1). In addition to carrying out the functions for the central banking system as a whole, each Reserve bank acts as a depository institution for the banks in its district. In terms of total assets, the three largest Federal Reserve Banks are the New York, Chicago, and San Francisco banks. Together these three banks hold over 50 percent of the total assets (discussed later) of the Federal Reserve System. The New York Federal Reserve Bank is generally considered the most important of the Federal Reserve Banks because so many of the largest U.S. and international banks are located in the New York district (the so-called money center banks).

www.newyorkfed.org

Federal Reserve Banks operate under the general supervision of the Board of Governors of the Federal Reserve based in Washington, D.C. Each Federal Reserve Bank has its own nine-member Board of Directors that oversees its operations: six are elected by member banks in the district (three are professional bankers and three are businesspeople) and three are appointed by the Federal Reserve Board of Governors (directors in this group are prohibited from being employees, officers, or stockholders of a member bank). These nine directors are responsible for appointing the president of their Federal Reserve Bank.

Nationally chartered banks, those chartered by the federal government through the Office of the Comptroller of the Currency (OCC),[1] are required to become members of the Federal Reserve System (FRS). State-chartered banks (those not chartered by the OCC) can also elect to become FRS members if they meet the standards set by the FRS.[2] The primary advantage of FRS membership is direct access to the federal funds wire transfer network for interbank borrowing and lending of reserves (discussed below). Commercial banks that become members of the FRS are required to buy stock in their Federal Reserve district bank. Thus, Federal Reserve Banks are quasipublic (part private, part government)

www.occ.treas.gov

1. The Office of the Comptroller of the Currency (OCC) charters, regulates, and supervises national banks in the United States to ensure a safe, sound, and competitive banking system (see Chapters 11 and 13).

2. These state-chartered banks are called state-chartered member banks. State-chartered banks that are not members of the FRS are called state-chartered nonmember banks (see Chapter 11).

FIGURE 4–1 Federal Reserve Districts

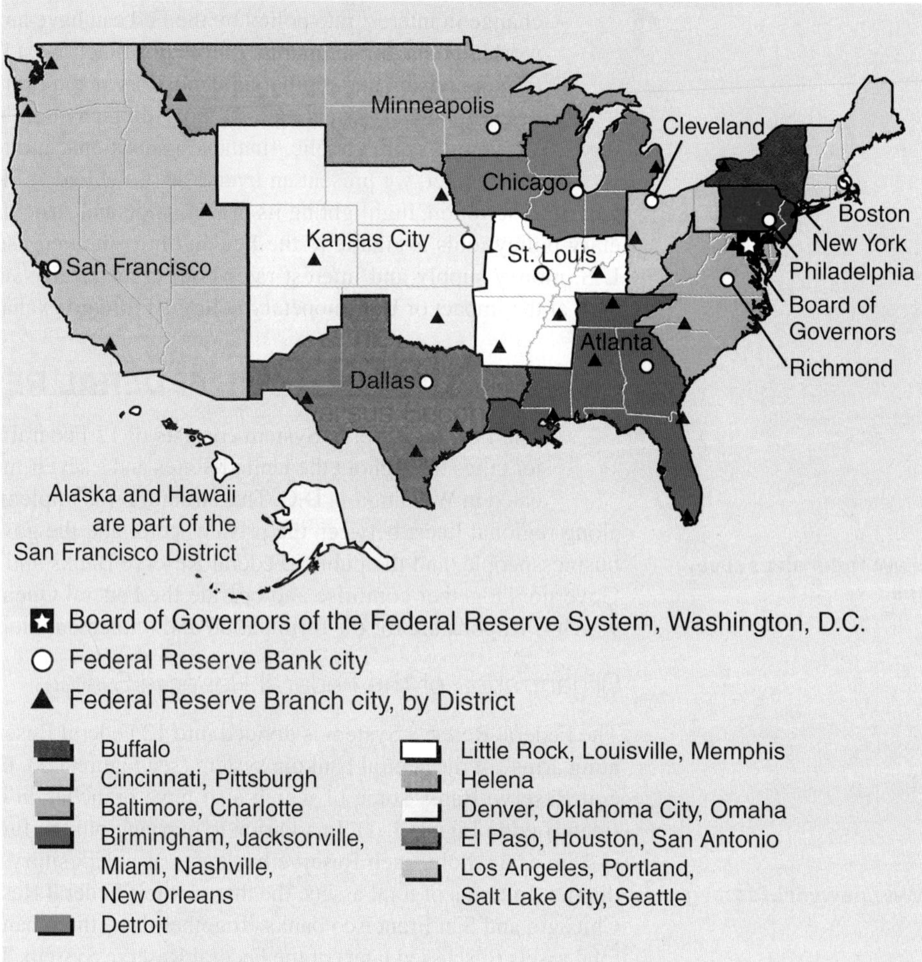

Source: Federal Reserve Board Web site, "The Structure of the Federal Reserve System," October 2004. **www.federalreserve.gov**

entities owned by member commercial banks in their district. Their stock, however, is not publicly traded and pays a predetermined dividend (at a maximum rate of 6 percent annually). Approximately 40 percent of all U.S. banks (holding over 80 percent of the total assets in the U.S. banking system) are currently members of the Federal Reserve System.

Federal Reserve Banks operate as nonprofit organizations. They generate income primarily from three sources: (1) interest earned on government securities acquired in the course of Federal Reserve open market transactions (see below), (2) interest earned on reserves that banks are required to deposit at the Fed (see reserve requirements below), and (3) fees from the provision of payment and other services to member depository institutions.

Board of Governors of the Federal Reserve System

The Board of Governors of the Federal Reserve (also called the Federal Reserve Board) is a seven-member board headquartered in Washington, D.C. Each member is appointed by the president of the United States and must be confirmed by the Senate. Board members serve a nonrenewable 14-year term.[3] Board members are often individuals with Ph.D.

3. The length of the term is intended to limit the president's control over the Fed and thus to reduce political pressure on Board members; the nonrenewable nature of an appointment prevents any incentives for governors to take actions that may not be in the best interests of the economy yet may improve their chances of being reappointed.

degrees in economics and/or an extensive background in economic research and political service, particularly in the area of banking. Board members' terms are staggered so that one term expires every other January. The president designates two members of the Board to be the chairman and vice chairman for four-year terms. The Board usually meets several times per week. As they carry out their duties, members routinely confer with officials of other government agencies, representatives of banking industry groups, officials of central banks of other countries, members of Congress, and academics.

The primary responsibilities of the Federal Reserve Board are the formulation and conduct of monetary policy and the supervision and regulation of banks. All seven Board members sit on the Federal Open Market Committee, which makes key decisions affecting the availability of money and credit in the economy (see below). For example, the Federal Reserve Board, through the FOMC, can and usually does set money supply and interest rate targets. The Federal Reserve Board also sets bank reserve requirements (discussed in Chapter 13) and reviews and approves the discount rates (see below) set by the 12 Federal Reserve Banks.

The Federal Reserve Board also has primary responsibility for the supervision and regulation of (1) all bank holding companies (their nonbank subsidiaries and their foreign subsidiaries), (2) state-chartered banks that are members of the Federal Reserve System (state-chartered member banks), and (3) Edge Act and agreement corporations (through which U.S. banks conduct foreign operations).[4] The Fed also shares supervisory and regulatory responsibilities with state supervisors and other federal supervisors (e.g., the OCC, the FDIC), including overseeing both the operations of foreign banking organizations in the United States and the establishment, examination, and termination of branches, commercial lending subsidiaries, and representative offices of foreign banks in the United States. The Board approves member bank mergers and acquisitions and specifies permissible nonbank activities of bank holding companies. The Board is also responsible for the development and administration of regulations governing the fair provision of consumer credit (e.g., the Truth in Lending Act, the Equal Credit Opportunity Act).

www.occ.treas.gov

www.fdic.gov

The chairman of the Federal Reserve Board often advises the president of the United States on economic policy and serves as the spokesperson for the Federal Reserve System in Congress and to the public. All Board members share the duties of conferring with officials of other government agencies, representatives of banking industry groups, officials of the central banks of other countries, and members of Congress.

Federal Open Market Committee

Federal Open Market Committee (FOMC)

The major monetary policy-making body of the Federal Reserve System.

The **Federal Open Market Committee (FOMC)** is the major monetary policy-making body of the Federal Reserve System. As alluded to above, the FOMC consists of the seven members of the Federal Reserve Board of Governors, the president of the Federal Reserve Bank of New York, and the presidents of four other Federal Reserve Banks (on a rotating basis). The chairman of the Board of Governors is also the chair of the FOMC. The FOMC is required to meet at least four times each year in Washington, D.C. However, eight regularly scheduled meetings have been held each year since 1980.

open market operations

Purchases and sales of U.S. government and federal agency securities by the Federal Reserve.

The main responsibilities of the FOMC are to formulate policies to promote full employment, economic growth, price stability, and a sustainable pattern of international trade. The FOMC seeks to accomplish this by setting guidelines regarding open market operations. **Open market operations**—the purchase and sale of U.S. government and federal agency securities—is the main policy tool that the Fed uses to achieve its monetary targets (although the operations themselves are normally carried out by traders at the Federal Reserve Bank of New York–see below). The FOMC also sets ranges for the

4. An Edge Act corporation is a subsidiary of a federally chartered domestic bank holding company that generally specializes in financing international transactions. An agreement corporation operates like an Edge Act but is a subsidiary of a state-chartered domestic bank. Created by the Edge Act of 1919, Edge Act corporations are exempt from certain U.S. bank regulations, thus allowing U.S. banks to compete against foreign banks on an even level. For example, Edge Act corporations are exempt from prohibitions on investing in equities of foreign corporations. Ordinarily, U.S. banks are not allowed to undertake such investments.

TABLE 4–1 Functions Performed by the Federal Reserve Banks

Assistance in the Conduct of Monetary Policy—Federal Reserve Bank (FRB) presidents serve on the Federal Open Market Committee (FOMC). FRBs set and change discount rates.
Supervision and Regulation—FRBs have supervisory and regulatory authority over the activities of banks located in their district.
Government Services—FRBs serve as the commercial bank for the U.S. Treasury.
New Currency Issue—FRBs are responsible for the collection and replacement of damaged currency from circulation.
Check Clearing—FRBs process, route, and transfer funds from one bank to another as checks clear through the Federal Reserve System.
Wire Transfer Services—FRBs and their member banks are linked electronically through the Federal Reserve Communications System.
Research Services—each FRB has a staff of professional economists who gather, analyze, and interpret economic data and developments in the banking sector in their district and economywide.

growth of the monetary aggregates, sets the federal funds rate (see below), and directs operations of the Federal Reserve in foreign exchange markets (see Chapter 8). In addition, although reserve requirements and the discount rate are not specifically set by the FOMC, their levels are monitored and guided by the FOMC. Associated with each meeting of the FOMC is the release of the Beige Book. The Beige Book summarizes information on current economic conditions by Federal Reserve district. Information included in the Beige Book is drawn from reports from bank directors, interviews with key business leaders, economists, market experts, and other sources. Meetings of the FOMC are some of the most closely watched economic meetings in the world. As the FOMC formulates and implements monetary policy, not only do its actions affect the U.S. economy, but economies worldwide.

Functions Performed by Federal Reserve Banks

As part of the Federal Reserve System, Federal Reserve Banks perform multiple functions. These include assistance in the conduct of monetary policy, supervision and regulation of member banks, and the provision of services such as new currency issue, check clearing, wire transfer, and research services to the federal government, member banks, or the general public. We summarize these functions in Table 4–1. The In the News box summarizes how the Federal Reserve provided extraordinary services in many of these areas in response to the terrorist attacks on the United States on September 11, 2001.

DO YOU UNDERSTAND?

1. What steps were taken by the Federal Reserve after the terrorist attacks in the United States in September 2001?
2. Why the Federal Reserve took these steps?

Assistance in the Conduct of Monetary Policy. As mentioned above, a primary responsibility of the Federal Reserve System is to influence the monetary (and financial) conditions in U.S. financial markets and thus the economy. Federal Reserve Banks assist in this process in several ways. First, as discussed above, 5 of the 12 Federal Reserve Bank presidents serve on the Federal Open Market Committee (FOMC), which determines monetary policy with respect to the open market sale and purchase of government securities and, therefore, interest rates.[5] Second, the Boards of Directors of each Federal Reserve Bank set and change the **discount rate** (the interest rate on loans made by Federal Reserve Banks to depository institutions). As discussed above, any discount rate change must be reviewed by the Board of Governors of the Federal Reserve. For example, in an attempt

discount rate

The interest rate on loans made by Federal Reserve Banks to depository institutions.

5. The president of the New York Federal Reserve Bank always sits on the FOMC. The other four positions are allocated to the other Federal Reserve districts on a rotating annual basis.

The September 11 terrorist attack on the World Trade Center and the Pentagon was not only a human tragedy but also an event with potentially serious ramifications for the economy. Although the airline and insurance industries face severe long-term problems as a result of the attack, the event posed an immediate threat to the entire economy by disrupting the payments and financial systems. Specifically, while the attack increased firms' and individuals' demand for liquidity, heightened uncertainty and the possibility of falling asset prices also threatened to reduce lending by banks and other intermediaries. Significant disruption to the payments system of lending has the potential to slow economic activity markedly.

In response to the attack, the Federal Reserve provided additional liquidity through several channels to help restore confidence and ensure the continued functioning of the financial and payments systems. First, the Fed's New York Trading Desk injected an unusual amount of liquidity through repurchase agreements (repos) . . . the Fed held $61 billion of securities acquired under repurchase agreements on September 12, versus an average of $27 billion on the previous ten Wednesdays and about $12 billion on September 13, 2000. Second, the Federal Reserve lent money directly to banks through the discount window. The $45 *billion* in discount loans outstanding on September 12 dwarfed the $59 million average of the previous 10 Wednesdays. Third, the Federal Reserve—along with the Comptroller of the Currency–urged banks to restructure loans for borrowers with temporary liquidity problems. To assist such restructuring, the Fed stood ready with additional funds. Fourth, because transportation difficulties prevented checks from being cleared in a timely manner, the Federal Reserve extended almost $23 billion in check "float" on September 12, some 30 times the average float over each of the 10 previous Wednesdays. Fifth, the Federal Reserve quickly established or extended "swap lines" with foreign central banks, such as the European Central Bank, the Bank of England, and the Bank of Canada. These accords enable central banks to temporarily exchange currencies to meet liquidity needs in foreign currencies. For example, the Fed and the European Central Bank might swap dollars for euros for a specified period of time, to enable the ECB to loan dollars to branches of European banks operating in the United States. Finally, the FOMC reduced the federal funds rate target by 1/2 percentage point, to 3 percent, early on Monday, September 17, while retaining the balance of risks toward economic weakness in its public statement. This action was interpreted as a confidence-boosting measure for the reopening of the New York Stock Exchange later that morning.

Deposits at Federal Reserve Banks conveniently summarize the liquidity provided to the economy. On September 12, this measure stood at $102 billion, more than 5 times the average of the previous 10 Wednesdays. As in previous periods of financial stress (e.g., the crash of 1987, the Russian default of 1998, and the Y2K scare) the Federal Reserve's action helped ensure the smooth functioning of the payments and financial systems, thereby minimizing the economic repercussions of the tragedy.

Source: *Monetary Trends,* The Federal Reserve Bank of St. Louis, November 2001, p. 1, by Christopher J. Neely.

to stimulate the U.S. economy and prevent a severe economic recession, the Federal Reserve approved 11 decreases in the discount (and federal funds) rate in 2001 (see discussion below). These loans are transacted through each Federal Reserve Bank's **discount window** and involve the discounting of eligible short-term securities in return for cash loans. Federal Reserve Bank Boards also have discretion in deciding which banks qualify for discount window loans.

discount window

The facility through which Federal Reserve Banks issue loans to depository institutions.

Supervision and Regulation. Each Federal Reserve Bank has supervisory and regulatory authority over the activities of state-chartered member banks and bank holding companies located in their districts. These activities include (1) the conduct of examinations and inspections of member banks, bank holding companies, and foreign bank offices by teams of bank examiners; (2) the authority to issue warnings (e.g., cease and desist orders should some banking activity be viewed as unsafe or unsound); and (3) the authority to

TABLE 4–2 Number and Value of Checks Cleared by the Federal Reserve

Year	Number of Checks Cleared (in millions)	Value of Checks Cleared (in billions of dollars)
1920	424	$ 149.8
1930	905	324.9
1940	1,184	280.4
1950	1,955	856.9
1960	3,419	1,154.1
1970	7,158	3,331.7
1980	15,716	8,038.0
1990	18,598	12,519.2
2000	16,994	13,849.0
2003	15,806	15,431.0

Source: Federal Reserve Board Web site, "Payment Systems," various dates. **www.federalreserve.gov**

approve various bank and bank holding company applications for expanded activities (e.g., mergers and acquisitions).

Government Services. As discussed above, the Federal Reserve serves as the commercial bank for the U.S. Treasury (U.S. government). Each year government agencies and departments deposit and withdraw billions of dollars from U.S. Treasury operating accounts held by Federal Reserve Banks. For example, it is the Federal Reserve Banks that receive deposits relating to federal unemployment taxes, individual income taxes withheld by payroll deduction, and so on. Further, some of these deposits are not protected by deposit insurance and must be fully collateralized at all times. It is the Federal Reserve Banks that hold collateral put up by government agencies. Finally, Federal Reserve Banks are responsible for the operation of the U.S. savings bond scheme, the issuance of Treasury securities, and other government-sponsored securities (e.g., Fannie Mae, Freddie Mac—see Chapter 7). Federal Reserve Banks issue and redeem savings bonds and Treasury securities, deliver government securities to investors, provide for a wire transfer system for these securities (the Fedwire), and make periodic payments of interest and principal on these securities.

New Currency Issue. Federal Reserve Banks are responsible for the collection and replacement of currency (paper and coin) from circulation. They also distribute new currency to meet the public's need for cash. For example, at the end of 1999, the Fed increased the printing of currency to meet the estimated $697 billion demand for currency resulting from the Y2K scare. As noted in the In the News box, in September 2001 the Fed lent additional money to banks in response to the terrorist attacks on the United States. The $45 billion lent at that time compares to an average of $59 million in discount window loans outstanding during the previous 10 weeks.

Check Clearing. Over 60 billion checks are written in the United States each year. About 15 billion of these checks are deposited in the same institution on which the check was written (called "on-us" checks). The Federal Reserve System operates a central check-clearing system for U.S. banks, routing interbank checks to depository institutions on which they are written and transferring the appropriate funds from one bank to another. About 40 percent of these interbank checks, approximately 16 billion per year, are processed by this system.[6] Table 4–2 shows the number and value of checks collected by the Federal Reserve Banks from 1920 through 2003. The number of checks cleared through

6. The remainder are processed through private check-clearing systems.

TABLE 4–3 Number and Value of Fedwire Transactions Processed by the Federal Reserve

Year	Number of Transactions (in millions)	Value of Transactions (in billions of dollars)
1920	0.5	$ 30.9
1930	2.0	198.9
1940	0.8	92.1
1950	1.0	509.2
1960	3.0	2,428.1
1970	7.0	12,332.0
1980	43.0	78,594.9
1990	62.6	199,067.2
2000	108.3	379,756.4
2003	123.3	436,706.3

Source: Federal Reserve Board Web site, "Payment Systems," various dates. **www.federalreserve.gov**

the system peaked in 2000 with almost 17 billion checks cleared. However, industry consolidation and greater use of electronic products has resulted in a reduction in the number of checks written and thus cleared through the Federal Reserve system. All depository institutions have accounts with the Federal Reserve Bank in their district for this purpose.

In October 2004, new legislation allowed banks to destroy checks after taking a digital image that is then processed electronically. The Check 21 Act, enacted by Congress and the Federal Reserve, begins the process of moving to a paperless environment. Check 21 authorizes the use of a substitute check (Image Replacement Document) for settlement. The new law is designed to encourage the adoption of electronic check imaging. It was prompted partly by the September 11 attacks, which grounded the cargo airplanes that fly 42 billion checks a year around the United States, threatening to disrupt the financial system. Further, the decline in overall check volume, caused by industry consolidation and greater use of electronic products, has brought a rise in processing costs. As banks look for ways to reduce operating costs, switching to electronic processing of checks will save as much as $3 billion a year for the banking industry. For customers, the implications are mixed. Because checks will be processed much more quickly, check writers will lose the "float" of several days between the time checks are deposited and when they are debited from the account.

Wire Transfer Services. The Federal Reserve Banks and their member banks are linked electronically through the Federal Reserve Communications Systems. This network allows these institutions to transfer funds and securities nationwide in a matter of minutes. Two electronic (wire) transfer systems are operated by the Federal Reserve: Fedwire and the Automated Clearinghouse (ACH). Fedwire is a network linking more than 6,000 domestic banks with the Federal Reserve System. Banks use this network to make deposit and loan payments, to transfer book entry securities among themselves, and to act as payment agents on behalf of large corporate customers.[7] Fedwire transfers are typically large dollar payments (averaging over $3.5 million per transaction). Table 4–3 shows the number and dollar value of Fedwire transactions processed by Federal Reserve banks from 1920 through 2003. The Automated Clearinghouse (ACH) was developed jointly by the private sector and the Federal Reserve System in the early 1970s and has evolved as a nationwide method

7. A second major wire transfer service is the Clearing House Interbank Payments System (CHIPS). CHIPS operates as a private network, independent of the Federal Reserve. At the core of the CHIPS system are approximately 100 large U.S. and foreign banks acting as correspondent banks for smaller domestic and international banks in clearing mostly international transactions in dollars.

TABLE 4–4 Number and Value of ACH Transactions Processed by the Federal Reserve

Year	Number of Transactions (in millions)	Value of Transactions (in billions of dollars)
1975	6	$ 92.9
1980	227	286.6
1990	1,435	4,660.5
2000	4,651	14,024.0
2003	6,502	16,762.0

Source: Federal Reserve Board Web site, "Payment Systems," various dates. **www.federalreserve.gov**

to electronically process credit and debit transfers of funds. Table 4–4 shows the number and dollar value of ACH transactions processed by Federal Reserve Banks from 1975 through 2003.

Research Services. Each Federal Reserve Bank has a staff of professional economists who gather, analyze, and interpret economic data and developments in the banking sector as well as the overall economy. These research projects are often used in the conduct of monetary policy by the Federal Reserve.

Balance Sheet of the Federal Reserve

Table 4–5 shows the balance sheet for the Federal Reserve System as of June 2004. The conduct of monetary policy by the Federal Reserve involves changes in the assets and

TABLE 4–5 Balance Sheet of the Federal Reserve
(in billions of dollars)

Assets		
Gold and foreign exchange	$ 30.4	3.8%
SDR certificates	2.2	0.3
Treasury currency	36.0	4.5
Federal Reserve float	0.2	0.0
Federal Reserve loans to domestic banks	0.3	0.0
Security repurchase agreements	33.5	4.1
U.S. Treasury securities	687.4	85.1
U.S. government agency securities	0.0	0.0
Miscellaneous assets	17.8	2.2
Total assets	$807.8	100.0%
Liabilities and Equity		
Depository institution reserves	$ 29.6	3.7%
Vault cash of commercial banks	43.4	5.4
Deposits due to federal government	6.3	0.8
Deposits due to rest of the world	0.3	0.0
Currency outside banks	689.7	85.4
Miscellaneous liabilities	29.3	3.6
Federal Reserve Bank stock	9.2	1.1
Total liabilities and equity	$807.8	100.0%

Source: Federal Reserve Board, "Flow of Fund Accounts," Monetary Authority, September 2004, p. L.108. **www.federalreserve.gov**

SEARCH THE SITE

Go to the Federal Reserve Board's Web site and get the latest data on the number and volume of Fedwire and ACH transactions processed by the Fed.

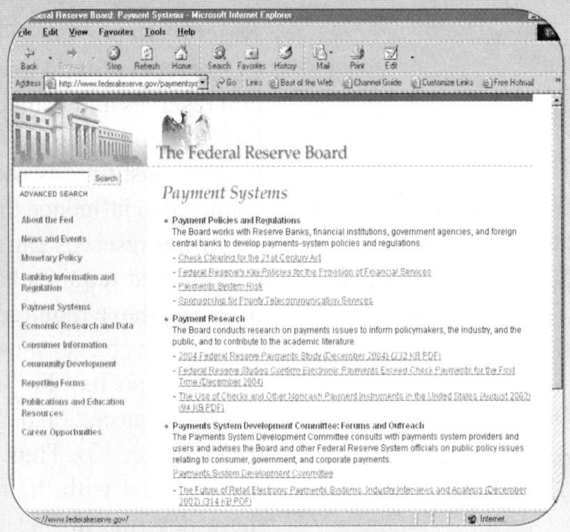

Go to the Federal Reserve's Web site at **www.federalreserve.gov**

Click on "Payment Systems"

Click on "Fedwire and National Settlement Services"

Click on "Annual Data"

Under Fedwire Funds Services, click on "Data Table." This will bring the file onto your computer that contains the relevant data.

Repeat these steps clicking on "Automated Clearinghouse Services" after "Payment Systems"

Click on "Annual Data"

Under Commercial Automated Clearinghouse Transactions Processed by the Federal Reserve, click on "Data Table." This will bring the file onto your computer that contains the relevant data.

Go back one step and then under Government Automated Clearinghouse Transactions Processed by the Federal Reserve, click on "Data Table"

These two files together contain the relevant data.

Questions

1. What are the current levels of the number and volume of Fedwire and ACH transactions processed?
2. Calculate the percentage change in each of these since 2003, reported in Tables 4–3 and 4–4.

liabilities of the Federal Reserve System, which are reflected in the Federal Reserve System's balance sheet.

reserves

Depository institutions' vault cash plus reserves deposited at Federal Reserve Banks.

monetary base

Currency in circulation and reserves (depository institution reserves and vault cash of commercial banks) held by the Federal Reserve.

Liabilities. The major liabilities on the Fed's balance sheet are currency in circulation and **reserves** (depository institution reserve balances in accounts at Federal Reserve Banks plus vault cash on hand at commercial banks). Their sum is often referred to as the Fed's **monetary base** or **money base.** We can represent these as follows:

Reserves—depository institution reserve balances at the Fed plus vault cash.
Money base—currency in circulation plus reserves.

As we show below, changes in these accounts are the major determinants of the size of the nation's money supply–increases (decreases) in either or both of these balances (e.g., currency in circulation or reserves) will lead to an increase (decrease) in the money supply (see below for a definition of the U.S. money supply).

Currency Outside Banks. The largest liability, in terms of percent of total liabilities and equity, of the Federal Reserve System is currency in circulation (85.4 percent of total liabilities and equity). At the top of each Federal Reserve note ($1 bill, $5 bill, $10 bill, etc.) is the seal of the Federal Reserve Bank that issued it. Federal Reserve notes are basically IOUs from the issuing Federal Reserve Bank to the bearer. In the U.S., Federal Reserve notes are recognized as the principal medium of exchange, and therefore function as money (see Chapter 1).

Reserve Deposits. The second largest liability on the Federal Reserve's balance sheet (9.1 percent of total liabilities and equity) is commercial bank reserves (depository institution reserves and vault cash of commercial banks). All banks hold reserve accounts at their local Federal Reserve Bank. These reserve holdings are used to settle accounts between depository institutions when checks and wire transfers are cleared (see above). Reserve accounts also influence the size of the money supply (as described below).

required reserves

Reserves the Federal Reserve requires banks to hold.

excess reserves

Additional reserves banks choose to hold.

Total reserves can be classified into two categories: (1) **required reserves** (reserves that the Fed requires banks to hold by law) and (2) **excess reserves** (additional reserves over and above required reserves) that banks choose to hold themselves. Required reserves are reserves banks must hold by law to back a portion of their customer transaction accounts (deposits). For example, the Federal Reserve currently requires 10 cents of every dollar of transaction deposit accounts at U.S. commercial banks to be backed with reserves (see Chapter 13). Thus, required reserves expand or contract with the level of transaction deposits and with the required reserve ratio set by the Federal Reserve Board. Because these deposits do not earn interest, banks try to keep excess reserves to a minimum.[8] Excess reserves, on the other hand, may be lent by banks to other banks that do not have sufficient reserves on hand to meet their required levels. As the Federal Reserve implements monetary policy, it uses the market for excess reserves.

Assets. The major assets on the Federal Reserve's balance sheet are Treasury securities, Treasury currency, and gold and foreign exchange. While loans to domestic banks are quite a small portion of the Federal Reserve's assets, they play an important role in implementing monetary policy (see below).

DO YOU UNDERSTAND?

1. What the main functions of Federal Reserve Banks are?
2. What the main responsibilities of the Federal Reserve Board are?
3. How the FOMC implements monetary policy?
4. What the main assets and liabilities in the Federal Reserve System are?

Treasury Securities. Treasury securities (85.1 percent of total assets) are the Fed's holdings of securities issued by the U.S. Treasury (U.S. government). The Fed's open market operations involve the buying and selling of these securities. An increase (decrease) in Treasury securities held by the Fed leads to an increase (decrease) in the money supply.

Gold and Foreign Exchange and Treasury Currency. The Federal Reserve holds Treasury gold certificates that are redeemable at the U.S. Treasury for gold. The Fed also holds small amounts of Treasury-issued coinage and foreign-denominated assets to assist in foreign currency transactions or currency swap agreements with the central banks of other nations.

Loans to Domestic Banks. As mentioned earlier, depository institutions in need of additional funds can borrow at the Federal Reserve's discount window (discussed in detail below). The interest rate or discount rate charged on these loans is often lower than other interest rates in the short-term money markets (see Chapter 5). As we discuss below, in January 2003 the Fed implemented changes to its discount window lending policy that increased the cost of discount window borrowing but eased the requirements on which

8. The minimum daily average reserves that a bank must maintain are computed as a percentage of the daily average net transaction accounts held by the bank over the two-week computation period, called the reserve computation period. Transaction accounts include all deposits on which an account holder may make withdrawals (for example, demand deposits, NOW accounts, and share draft accounts—offered by credit unions). Transaction account balances are reduced by demand balances due from U.S. depository institutions and cash items in process of collection to obtain net transaction accounts. Under the current set of regulations, a lag of 30 days exists between the beginning of the reserve computation period and the beginning of the reserve maintenance period (over which deposits at the Federal Reserve Bank must meet or exceed the required reserve target less vault cash).Thus, the bank's reserve manager knows the value of its target reserves with perfect certainty throughout the reserve maintenance period. See Chapter 13 for more specific details.

depository institutions can borrow. As part of this change, the discount window rate was increased so that it would be higher than the fed funds rate. As a result, (discount) loans to domestic banks are normally a relatively small portion of the Fed's total assets.[9]

3 MONETARY POLICY TOOLS

In the previous section of this chapter, we referred briefly to tools or instruments that the Federal Reserve uses to implement its monetary policy. These included open market operations, the discount rate, and reserve requirements. Regardless of the tool the Federal Reserve uses to implement monetary policy, the major link by which monetary policy impacts the macroeconomy occurs through the Federal Reserve influencing the market for bank reserves (required and excess reserves held as depository institution reserves balances in accounts at Federal Reserve Banks plus vault cash on hand of commercial banks). Specifically, the Federal Reserve's monetary policy seeks to influence either the demand for, or supply of, excess reserves at depository institutions and in turn the money supply and the level of interest rates. Specifically, a change in excess reserves resulting from the implementation of monetary policy triggers a sequence of events that affect such economic factors as short-term interest rates, long-term interest rates, foreign exchange rates, the amount of money and credit in the economy, and ultimately the levels of employment, output, and prices.

Depository institutions trade excess reserves held at their local Federal Reserve Banks among themselves. Banks with excess reserves—whose reserves exceed their required reserves—have an incentive to lend these funds (generally overnight) to banks in need of reserves since excess reserves held in the vault or on deposit at the Federal Reserve earn no interest. The rate of interest (or price) on these interbank transactions is a benchmark interest rate, called the federal funds rate or **fed funds rate,** which is used in the United States to guide monetary policy. The fed funds rate is a function of the supply and demand for federal funds among banks and the effects of the Fed's trading through the FOMC.

fed funds rate

The interest rate on short-term funds transferred between financial institutions, usually for a period of one day.

In implementing monetary policy, the Federal Reserve can take one of two basic approaches to affect the market for bank excess reserves: (1) it can target the quantity of reserves in the market based on the FOMC's objectives for the growth in the monetary base (the sum of currency in circulation and reserves) and, in turn, the money supply (see below), or (2) it can target the interest rate on those reserves (the fed funds rate). The actual approach used by the Federal Reserve has varied according to considerations such as the need to combat inflation or the desire to encourage sustainable economic growth (we discuss the various approaches below). Since 1993, the FOMC has implemented monetary policy mainly by targeting interest rates (mainly using the fed funds rate as a target). As mentioned earlier, to reduce the effects of an economic slowdown in the United States, the Fed decreased the fed funds rate 11 times in 2001.

Even into August 2003 the FOMC took the unusual step of foreshadowing its future policy course by announcing that the historically low interest rates could be maintained for a considerable period. Although the FOMC did not specify the length of the considerable period, it was not until the summer of 2004 that the Fed increased the fed funds rate (initially by 0.25 percent).

In this section, we explore the tools or instruments used by the Fed to implement its monetary policy strategy.[10] Figure 4–2 illustrates the monetary policy implementation process that we will be discussing in more detail below.

9. Such loans could increase rapidly in a major financial crisis or panic (such as the stock market crash of October 1987 and the terrorist attacks in September 2001).

10. In addition to the tools described here, the Fed (as well as the Federal Deposit Insurance Corporation and the Office of the Comptroller of the Currency) can indirectly affect the money supply by signaling to bankers to tighten or loosen credit availability. Further, changes in other types of regulations such as capital requirements can affect the money supply.

FIGURE 4–2 Federal Reserve Monetary Policy Activities

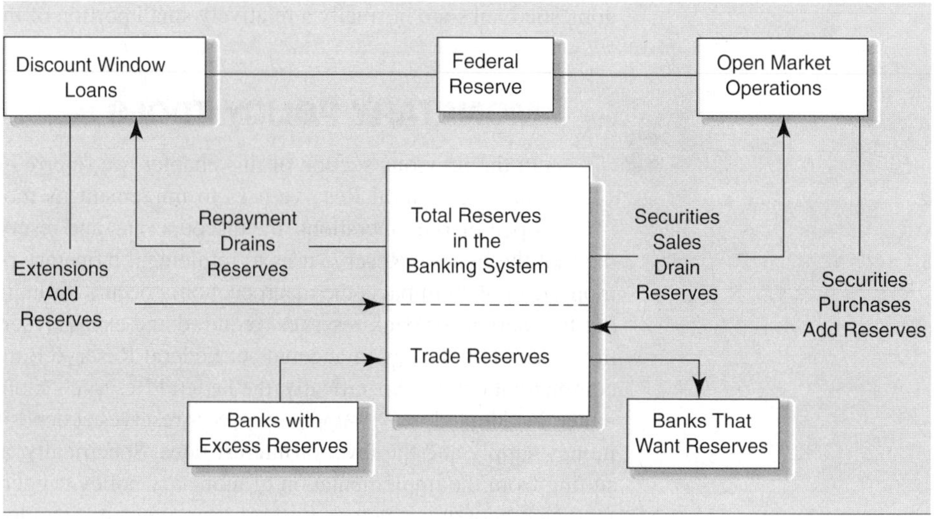

Source: Federal Reserve Board Web site, "Purposes & Functions," April 2002. **www.federalreserve.gov**

www.newyorkfed.org

Federal Reserve Board Trading Desk

Unit of the Federal Reserve Bank of New York through which open market operations are conducted.

policy directive

Statement sent to the Federal Reserve Board Trading Desk from the FOMC that specifies the money supply target.

Open Market Operations

When a targeted monetary aggregate or interest rate level is determined by the FOMC, it is forwarded to the **Federal Reserve Board Trading Desk** at the Federal Reserve Bank of New York (FRBNY) through a statement called the **policy directive.** The manager of the Trading Desk uses the policy directive to instruct traders on the daily amount of open market purchases or sales to transact. Open market operations are the Federal Reserves' purchases or sales of securities in the U.S. Treasury securities market. This is an over-the-counter market in which traders are linked to each other electronically (see Chapter 5).

To determine a day's activity for open market operations, the staff at the FRBNY begins each day with a review of developments in the fed funds market since the previous day and a determination of the actual amount of reserves in the banking system the previous day. The staff also reviews forecasts of short-term factors that may affect the supply and demand of reserves on that day. With this information, the staff decides the level of transactions needed to obtain the desired fed funds rate. The process is completed with a daily conference call to the Monetary Affairs Division at the Board of Governors and one of the four voting Reserve Bank presidents (outside of New York) to discuss the FRBNY plans for the day's open market operations. Once a plan is approved, the Trading Desk is instructed to execute the day's transactions.

Open market operations are particularly important because they are the primary determinant of changes in bank excess reserves in the banking system and thus directly impact the size of the money supply and/or the level of interest rates (e.g., the fed funds rate). When the Federal Reserve purchases securities, it pays for the securities by either writing a check on itself or directly transferring funds (by wire transfer) into the seller's account. Either way, the Fed credits the reserve deposit account of the bank that sells it (the Fed) the securities. This transaction increases the bank's excess reserve levels. When the Fed sells securities, it either collects checks received as payment or receives wire transfers of funds from these agents (such as banks) using funds from their accounts at the Federal Reserve Banks to purchase securities. This reduces the balance of the reserve account of a bank that purchases securities. Thus, when the Federal Reserve sells (purchases) securities in the open market, it decreases (increases) banks' (reserve account) deposits at the Fed.

EXAMPLE 4–1 Purchases of Securities by the Federal Reserve

Suppose the FOMC instructs the FRBNY Trading Desk to purchase $500 million of Treasury securities. Traders at the FRBNY call primary government securities dealers of major commercial and investment banks (such as Goldman Sachs and Morgan Stanley),[11] who provide a list of securities they have available for sale, including the denomination, maturity, and the price on each security. FRBNY traders then seek to purchase the target number of securities (at the desired maturities and lowest possible price) until they have purchased the $500 million. The FRBNY then notifies its government bond department to receive and pay the sellers for the securities it has purchased. The securities dealer sellers (such as banks) in turn deposit these payments in their accounts held at their local Federal Reserve Bank. As a result of these purchases, the Treasury securities account balance of the Federal Reserve System is increased by $500 million and the total reserve accounts maintained by these banks and dealers at the Fed is increased by $500 million. We illustrate these changes to the Federal Reserve's balance sheet in Table 4-6. In addition, there is also an impact on commercial bank balance sheets. Total reserves (assets) of commercial banks will increase by $500 million due to the purchase of securities by the Fed, and demand deposits (liabilities) of the securities dealers (those who sold the securities) at their banks will increase by $500 million.[12] We also show the changes to commercial banks' balance sheets in Table 4–6.

Note the Federal Reserve's purchase of Treasury securities has increased the total supply of bank reserves in the financial system. This in turn increases the ability of banks to make new loans and create new deposits.

EXAMPLE 4–2 Sale of Securities by the Federal Reserve

Suppose the FOMC instructs the FRBNY Trading Desk to sell $500 million of securities. Traders at the FRBNY call government securities dealers who provide a list of securities they are willing to buy, including the price on each security. FRBNY traders sell securities to these dealers at the highest prices possible until they have sold $500 million. The FRBNY then notifies its government bond department to deliver the securities to, and receive payment from, the buying security dealers. The securities dealers pay for these securities by drawing on their deposit accounts at their commercial banks. As a result of this sale, the Treasury securities account balance for the Federal Reserve System is decreased by $500 million (reflecting the sale of $500 million in Treasury securities) and the reserve accounts maintained at the Fed by commercial banks that handle these securities transactions for the dealers are decreased by $500 million. The changes to the Federal Reserve's balance sheet would in this case have the opposite sign (negative) as those illustrated in Table 4–6. In addition, total reserves of commercial banks will decrease by $500 million due to the purchase of securities from the Fed, and demand deposits of the securities dealers at their banks will decrease by $500 million (reflecting the payments for the securities by the securities dealers). Commercial banks' balance sheet changes would have the opposite sign as those illustrated in Table 4–6 for a purchase of securities.

11. As of October 2004, there were 22 primary securities dealers trading, on average, $545 billion of securities per day.

12. In reality, not all of the $500 million will generally be deposited in demand deposit accounts of commercial banks, and commercial banks will not generally hold all of the $500 million in reserve accounts of Federal Reserves Banks. We relax these simplifying assumptions and look at the effect on total reserves and the monetary base later in the chapter.

TABLE 4-6 Purchase of Securities in the Open Market

Change in Federal Reserve's Balance Sheet			
Assets		**Liabilities**	
Treasury securities	+ $500m.	Reserve account of securities dealers' banks	+ $500m.
Change in Commercial Bank Balance Sheets			
Assets		**Liabilities**	
Reserve accounts at Federal Reserve	+ $500m.	Securities dealers' demand deposit accounts at banks	+ $500m.

Note that the Federal Reserve's sale of Treasury or other government securities has decreased the total supply of bank reserves in the financial system. This in turn decreases the ability of banks to make loans and create new deposits.

While the Federal Reserve conducts most of its open market operations using Treasury securities, other government securities can be used as well. Treasury securities are used most because the secondary market for such securities is highly liquid and there is an established group of primary dealers who also trade extensively in the secondary market. Thus, the Treasury securities market can absorb a large number of buy and sell transactions without experiencing significant price fluctuations.

At times, the Federal Reserve may want to *temporarily* increase (or decrease) the aggregate level of bank reserves for reasons other than directly impacting monetary targets or interest rates. For example, holiday deposit withdrawals can create temporary imbalances in the level of bank reserves. In this case, the Trading Desk often uses **repurchase agreements** or repos to offset such temporary shortfalls in bank reserves and liquidity. With a repo, the Fed purchases government securities from a dealer or a bank with an agreement that the seller will repurchase them within a stated period of time (generally 1 to 15 days) as specified in the repurchase agreement.

repurchase agreements

Open market transactions in which the Trading Desk purchases government securities with an agreement that the seller will repurchase them within a stated period of time.

When a repurchase agreement is used, the level of bank reserves rises as the securities are sold. They are then reduced when the dealers repurchase their securities a few days later. The return to the Fed for letting the dealer borrow funds in exchange for the securities (and the cost to the dealer for borrowing the funds) is the difference between the original prices and the repurchase price of the securities. When the Fed wants to conduct a temporary open market sale, it enters a reverse repurchase agreement (or a matched sale-purchase transaction). In this case, the Fed sells securities to the dealer with the agreement to buy them back at a higher price later. The Fed uses repurchase agreements and reverse repurchase agreements to bring about a temporary change in the level of reserves in the system or to respond to some event that the Fed thinks could have a significant but short-lived effect on the economy. The objective of such repurchase agreements is to smooth out fluctuations in bank reserves and thus in the nation's money supply and to avoid adverse impacts on interest rates.

The Discount Rate

The discount rate is the second monetary policy tool or instrument used by the Federal Reserve to control the level of bank reserves (and thus the money supply or interest rates). As defined above, the discount rate is the rate of interest Federal Reserve Banks charge on loans to depository institutions in their district. The Federal Reserve can influence the level and price of reserves by changing the discount rate it charges on these loans.

Specifically, changing the discount rate signals to the market and the economy that the Federal Reserve would like to see higher or lower rates in the economy. Thus, the discount rate is like a signal of the FOMC's intentions regarding the tenor of monetary policy. For example, raising the discount rate signals that the Fed would like to see a tightening of monetary conditions and higher interest rates in general (and a relatively lower amount of borrowing). Lowering the discount rate signals a desire to see more expansionary monetary conditions and lower interest rates in general.

For two reasons, the Federal Reserve has rarely used the discount rate as a monetary policy tool. First, it is difficult for the Fed to predict changes in bank discount window borrowing when the discount rate changes. There is no guarantee that banks will borrow more (less) at the discount window in response to a decrease (increase) in the discount rate. Thus, the exact direct effect of a discount rate change on the money supply is often uncertain. Second, because of its "signaling" importance, a discount rate change often has great effects on the financial markets. For example, the unexpected 0.50 percent decrease in the Fed's discount rate on January 3, 2001, resulted in a 299.60 point increase in the Dow Jones Industrial Average, one of the largest one-day point gains in the history of the Dow. Moreover, virtually all interest rates respond in the same direction (if not the same amount) to the discount rate change. For example, Figure 4–3 shows the correlation in four major U.S. interest rates (discount rate, prime rate (the rate banks charge to large corporations for short-term loans), three-month CD rate, and three-month T-bill rate) from 1990 through August 2004.

In general, discount rate changes are used only when the Fed wants to send a strong message to financial markets to show that it is serious about wanting to implement new monetary policy targets. For example, Federal Reserve Board members commented that the January 3, 2001 discount rate change was taken in light of further weakening of sales and production, tight conditions in some segments of financial markets, and high energy prices sapping household and business purchasing power. Thus, this drop in the discount rate and the 10 rate drops that followed in 2001 were intended to signal the Fed's strong and persistent intention to allow the money supply to increase and to stimulate economic growth.

FIGURE 4–3 Various U.S. Interest Rates

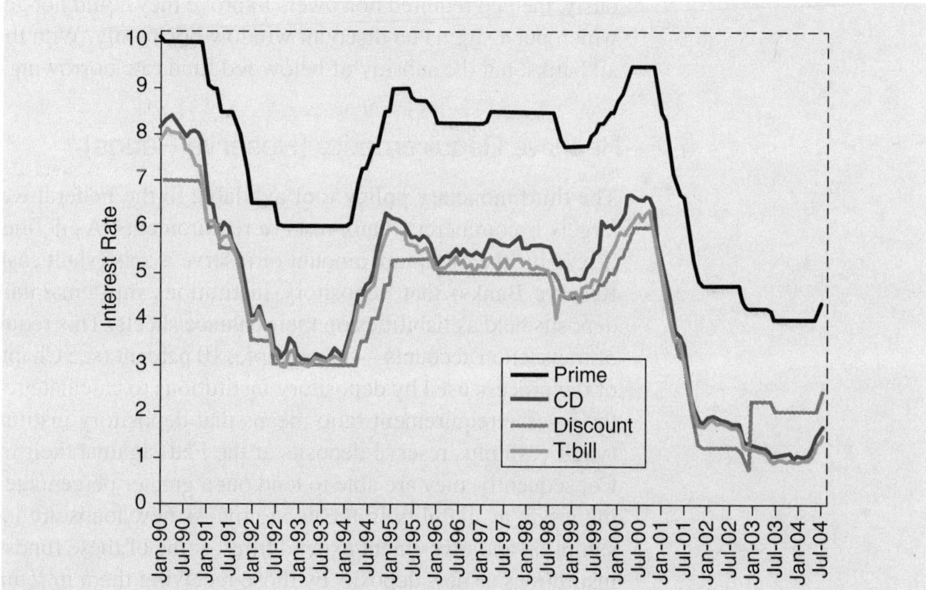

Source: Federal Reserve Board Web site, "Research and Data," October 2004. **www.federalreserve.gov**

Historically, discount window lending was limited to depository institutions with severe liquidity needs. The discount window rate, which was set below the fed funds rate, was charged on loans to depository institutions only under emergency or special liquidity situations (see Figure 4–3, 1990–2002). However, in January 2003, the Fed implemented changes to its discount window lending that increased the cost of borrowing but eased the terms. Specifically, three lending programs are now offered through the Fed's discount window. Primary credit is available to generally sound depository institutions on a very short-term basis, typically overnight, at a rate above the Federal Open Market Committee's target rate for federal funds. Primary credit may be used for any purpose, including financing the sale of fed funds. Primary credit may be extended for periods of up to a few weeks to depository institutions in generally sound financial condition that cannot obtain temporary funds in the financial markets at reasonable terms. Secondary credit is available to depository institutions that are not eligible for primary credit. It is extended on a very short-term basis, typically overnight, at a rate that is above the primary credit rate. Secondary credit is available to meet backup liquidity needs when its use is consistent with a timely return to a reliance on market sources of funding or the orderly resolution of a troubled institution. Secondary credit may not be used to fund an expansion of the borrower's assets. The Federal Reserve's seasonal credit program is designed to assist small depository institutions in managing significant seasonal swings in their loans and deposits. Seasonal credit is available to depository institutions that can demonstrate a clear pattern of recurring intrayearly swings in funding needs. Eligible institutions are usually located in agricultural or tourist areas. Under the seasonal program, borrowers may obtain longer-term funds from the discount window during periods of seasonal need so that they can carry fewer liquid assets during the rest of the year and make more funds available for local lending.

With the change, discount window loans to healthy banks would be priced at 1 percent above the fed funds rate rather than below, as it generally was in the period preceding January 2003. Note in Figure 4–3 the jump in the discount window rate in January 2003. Loans to troubled banks would cost 1.5 percent above the fed funds rate. The changes were intended not to change the Fed's use of the discount window to implement monetary policy, but to significantly increase the discount rate while making it easier to get a discount window loan. By increasing banks' use of the discount window as a source of funding, the Fed hopes to reduce volatility in the fed funds market as well. The change also allows healthy banks to borrow from the Fed regardless of the availability of private funds. Previously, the Fed required borrowers to prove they could not get funds from the private sector, which put a stigma on discount window borrowing. With the changes, the Fed will lend to all banks, but the subsidy of below fed fund rate borrowing will be gone.

Reserve Requirements (Reserve Ratios)

The third monetary policy tool available to the Federal Reserve to achieve its monetary targets is commercial bank reserve requirements. As defined above, reserve requirements determine the minimum amount of reserve assets (vault cash plus bank deposits at Federal Reserve Banks) that depository institutions must maintain by law to back transaction deposits held as liabilities on their balance sheets. This requirement is usually set as a ratio of transaction accounts—for example, 10 percent (see Chapter 13 for a detailed description of the process used by depository institutions to calculate required reserves). A decrease in the reserve requirement ratio means that depository institutions may hold fewer reserves (vault cash plus reserve deposits at the Fed) against their transaction accounts (deposits). Consequently, they are able to lend out a greater percentage of their deposits, thus increasing credit availability in the economy. As new loans are issued and used to finance consumption and investment expenditures, some of these funds spent will return to depository institutions as new deposits by those receiving them in return for supplying consumer and investment goods to bank borrowers. In turn, these new deposits, after deducting the appropriate reserve requirement, can be used by banks to create additional loans, and so on. This process continues until the banks' deposits have grown sufficiently large such that banks willingly hold their *current* reserve balances at the new lower reserve ratio. Thus, a decrease in the reserve requirement results in a multiplier increase in the supply of bank deposits and thus the money supply. The multiplier effect can be written as follows:

$$\text{Change in bank deposits} = (1/\text{new reserve requirement}) \\ \times \text{ increase in reserves created by reserve requirement change}$$

Conversely, an increase in the reserve requirement ratio means that depository institutions must hold more reserves against the transaction accounts (deposits) on their balance sheet. Consequently, they are able to lend out a smaller percentage of their deposits than before, thus decreasing credit availability and lending, and eventually, leading to a multiple contraction in deposits and a decrease in the money supply. Now the multiplier effect is written as:

$$\text{Change in bank deposits} = (1/\text{new reserve requirement}) \\ \times \text{ decrease in reserves created by reserve requirement change}$$

EXAMPLE 4-3 Increasing the Money Supply by Lowering Banks' Reserve Requirements on Transaction Accounts

City Bank currently has $400 million in transaction deposits on its balance sheet. The current reserve requirement, set by the Federal Reserve, is 10 percent. Thus, City Bank must have reserve assets of at least $40 million ($400 million × .10) to back its deposits. In this simple framework, the remaining $360 million of deposits can be used to extend loans to borrowers. Table 4–7, Panel A, illustrates the Federal Reserve's and City Bank's balance sheets, assuming City Bank holds all of its reserves at the Fed, (i.e., City Bank has no vault cash).

If the Federal Reserve decreases the reserve requirement from 10 percent to 5 percent, City Bank's minimum reserve requirement decreases by $20 million, from $40 million to $20 million ($400 million × .05). City Bank can now use $20 million of its reserves at its local Federal Reserve Bank (since these are now excess reserves that earn no interest) to make new loans. Suppose, for simplicity, that City Bank is the only commercial bank (in practice, the multiplier effect described below will work the same except that deposit growth will be spread over a number of banks). Those who borrow the $20 million from the bank will spend the funds on consumption and investment goods and services and those who produce and sell these goods and services will redeposit the $20 million in funds received from their sale at their bank (assumed here to be City Bank). We illustrate this redeposit of funds in Figure 4–4. As a result, transaction deposits City Bank's balance sheet changes to $420 million (shown in Panel B of Table 4–7). Because of the $20 million increase in transaction account deposits, City Bank now must increase its reserves held at the Federal Reserve Bank by $1 million ($20 million × .05) but still has $19 million in excess reserves with which to make more new loans from the additional deposits of $20 million (see row 2 in Figure 4–4).

Assuming City Bank continues to issue new loans and that borrowers continue to spend the funds from their loans, and those receiving the loanable funds (in exchange for the sale of goods and services) redeposit those funds in transaction deposits at City Bank, City Bank's balance sheet will continue to grow until there are no excess reserves held by City Bank (Panel C in Table 4–7). The resulting change in City Bank's deposits will be:

$$\text{Change in bank deposits} = (1/.05) \times (40\text{m} - 20\text{m}) = \$400\text{m}$$

For this to happen, City Bank must willingly hold the $40 million it has as reserves. This requires City Bank's balance sheet (and its deposits) to double in size as a result of the reserve requirement decrease from 10 percent to 5 percent (i.e., $800 million deposits × .05 = $40 million).

TABLE 4–7 Lowering the Reserve Requirement

Panel A: Initial Balance Sheets

Federal Reserve Bank			
Assets		**Liabilities**	
Securities	$40m.	Reserve accounts	$40m.

City Bank			
Assets		**Liabilities**	
Loans	$360m.	Transaction deposits	$400m.
Reserve deposits at Fed (10% of deposits)	40m.		

Panel B: Balance Sheet Immediately after Decrease in Reserve Requirement

Federal Reserve Bank			
Assets		**Liabilities**	
Securities	$21m.	Reserve accounts	$21m.

City Bank			
Assets		**Liabilities**	
Loans	$380m.	Transaction deposits	$420m.
Reserve deposits at Fed (5% of deposits)	21m.		
Cash (from liquidated reserves)	19m.		

Panel C: Balance Sheet after All Changes Resulting from Decrease in Reserve Requirement

Federal Reserve Bank			
Assets		**Liabilities**	
Securities	$40m.	Reserve accounts	$40m.

City Bank			
Assets		**Liabilities**	
Loans	$760m.	Transaction deposits	$800m.
Reserve deposits at Fed (5% of deposits)	40m.		

While the deposit multiplier effect has been illustrated here using the example of a change in reserve requirements, it also holds when other monetary policy tools or instruments are changed as well (e.g., open market operations). For example, suppose the FOMC instructs the FRBNY Trading Desk to purchase $200 million in U.S. Treasury securities. If the reserve requirement is set at 10 percent, the $200 million open market purchase will result in an increase in bank reserves of $200 million, and ultimately, via the multiplier (1/.1), an increase in bank deposits and the money supply of $2 billion:

$$1/.1 \times \$200 \text{ million} = \$2{,}000 \text{ million} = \$2 \text{ billion}$$

We have made some critical assumptions about the behavior of banks and borrowers to simplify our illustration of the impact of a change in open market operations and reserve

FIGURE 4–4 Deposit Growth Multiplier

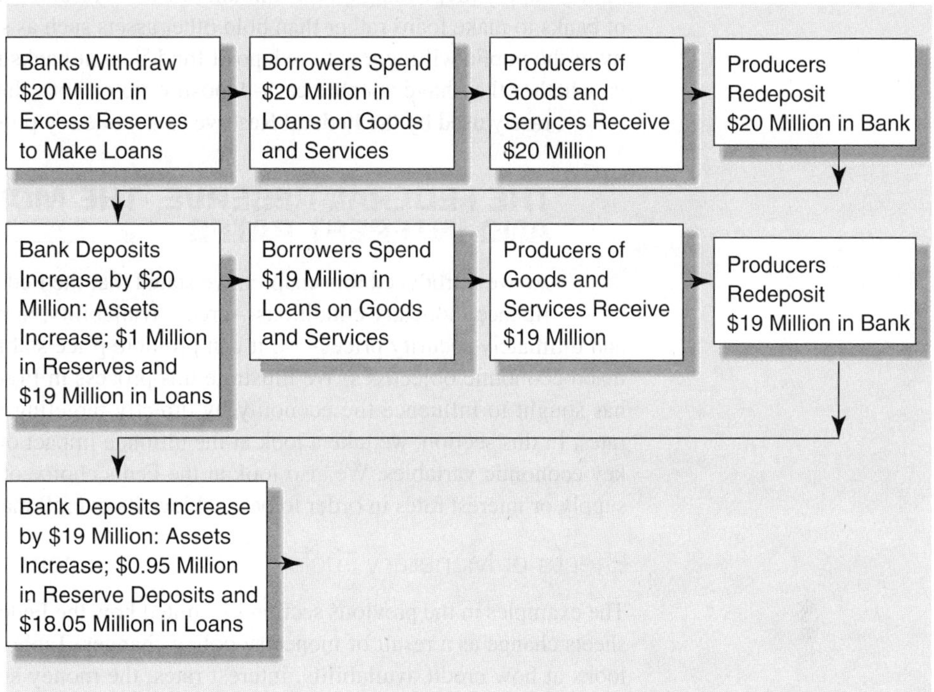

requirements on bank deposits and the money supply. In Example 4–3 we assumed that City Bank was the only bank, that it converts all (100 percent) of its excess reserves into loans, that all (100 percent) of these funds are spent by borrowers, and that all are returned to City Bank as "new" transaction deposits. If these assumptions are relaxed, the overall impact of a decrease in the reserve requirement ratio, or increase in excess reserves from an open market operation, on the amount of bank deposits and the money supply will be smaller than illustrated above and the precise effect of a change in the reserve base on the money supply is less certain.[13] Nevertheless, as long as some portion of the excess reserves created by the decrease in the reserve requirement are converted into loans and some portion of these loans after being spent are returned to the banking system in the form of transaction deposits, a decrease in reserve requirements will result in a multiple (that is, greater than one) increase in bank deposits, the money supply, and credit availability.

DO YOU UNDERSTAND?

1. What the major policy tools used by the Federal Reserve to influence the economy are?
2. What the impact is on credit availability and the money supply if the Federal Reserve purchases securities?
3. Why the Federal Reserve is unique in its ability to change the money supply through monetary policy tools?

Conversely, if the Federal Reserve increases reserve requirement ratios, depository institutions must convert some loans on their balance sheet back into reserves held at their local Federal Reserve Bank. The overall result is that an increase in the reserve requirements will result in a multiple decline in credit availability, bank deposits, and the money supply (i.e., the multiplier effect described above will be reversed). Again, the overall effect on the money supply is not fully predictable.

13. For example, in Example 4–3, if only 90 percent of any funds lent by City Bank are returned to the bank in the form of transaction deposits and 10 percent is held in cash, then the resulting change in City Bank's deposits will be:

$$\text{Change in bank deposits} = [1/(\text{new reserve requirement} + c)] \times \text{change in reserves created by reserve requirement change}$$

where c = the public's cash-to-deposit ratio or preference for holding cash outside banks relative to bank deposits = .1 (or 10/100). Thus, City Bank's change in deposits = [1/(0.5 + .1)] × (40m − 20m) = $133.33 million.

Because changes in reserve requirements can result in unpredictable changes in the money supply (depending on the amount of excess reserves held by banks, the willingness of banks to make loans rather than hold other assets such as securities, and the predictability of the public willingness to redeposit funds lent at banks instead of holding cash—that is, whether they have a stable cash-deposit ratio or not), the reserve requirement is very rarely used by the Federal Reserve as a monetary policy tool.

4 THE FEDERAL RESERVE, THE MONEY SUPPLY, AND INTEREST RATES

As we introduced this chapter, we stated that the Federal Reserve takes steps to influence monetary conditions—credit availability, interest rates, the money supply, and ultimately security prices—so it can promote price stability (low inflation) and other macroeconomic objectives. We illustrate this process in Figure 4–5. Historically, the Fed has sought to influence the economy by directly targeting the money supply or interest rates. In this section, we take a look at the ultimate impact of monetary policy changes on key economic variables. We also look at the Fed's choice of whether to target the money supply or interest rates in order to best achieve its overall macroeconomic objectives.

Effects of Monetary Tools on Various Economic Variables

The examples in the previous section illustrated how the Federal Reserve and bank balance sheets change as a result of monetary policy changes. Table 4–8 goes one step further and looks at how credit availability, interest rates, the money supply, and security prices are

FIGURE 4–5 The Process of Monetary Policy Implementation

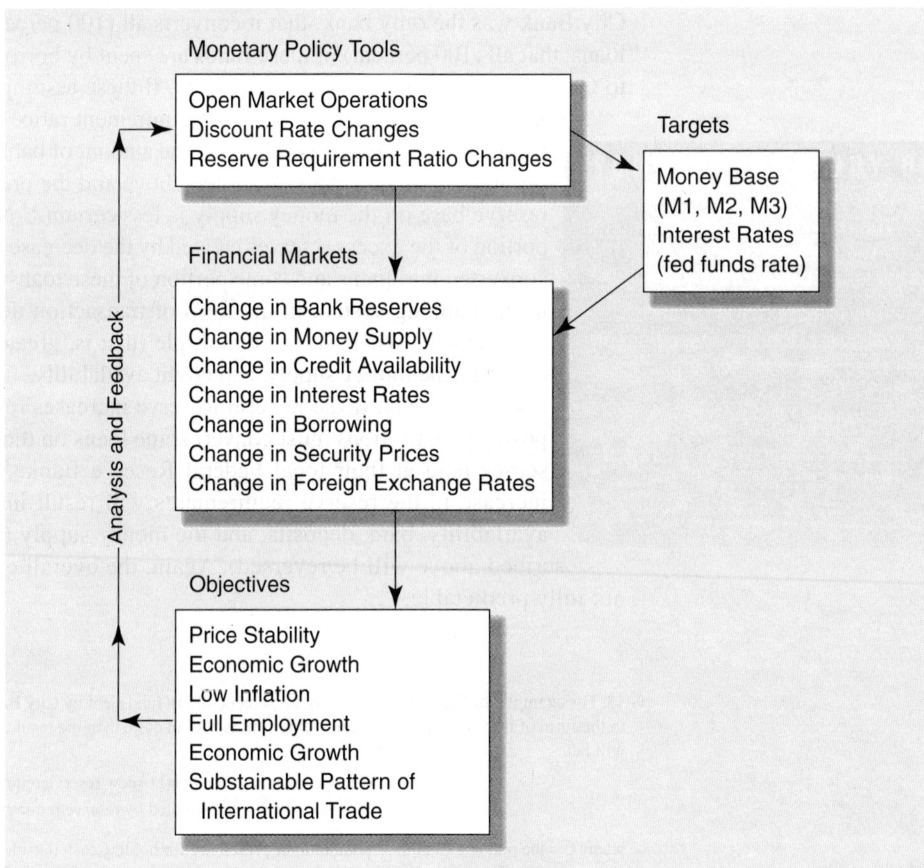

TABLE 4–8 The Impact of Monetary Policy on Various Economic Variables

	Expansionary Activities	Contractionary Activities
Impact on:		
Reserves	↑	↓
Credit availability	↑	↓
Money supply	↑	↓
Interest rates	↓	↑
Security prices	↑	↓

affected by these monetary policy actions. To do this, we categorize monetary policy tool changes into expansionary activities versus contractionary activities.

Expansionary Activities. We described above the three monetary policy tools that the Fed can use to increase the money supply: open market purchases of securities, discount rate decreases, and reserve requirement ratio decreases. All else held constant, when the Federal Reserve purchases securities in the open market, the reserve accounts of banks increase. When the Fed lowers the discount rate, this generally results in a lowering of interest rates in the economy. Finally, a decrease in the reserve requirements, all else constant, results in an increase in bank reserves.

In two of the three cases (open market operations and reserve requirement changes), an increase in reserves results in an increase in bank deposits and the money supply. One immediate effect of this is that interest rates fall and security prices start to rise (see Chapters 2 and 3). In the third case (a discount rate change), the impact of a lowering of interest rates is more direct. Lower interest rates encourage borrowing from banks. Economic agents spend more when they can get cheaper funds. Households, businesses, and governments are more likely to invest in fixed assets (e.g., housing, plant, and equipment). Households increase their purchases of durable goods (e.g., automobiles, appliances). State and local government spending increases (e.g., new road construction, school improvements). Finally, lower domestic interest rates relative to foreign rates can result in a drop in the (foreign) exchange value of the dollar relative to other currencies.[14] As the dollar's (foreign) exchange value drops, U.S. goods become relatively cheaper compared to foreign goods. Eventually, U.S. exports increase. The increase in spending from all of these market participants results in economic expansion, stimulates additional real production, and may cause the inflation rate (defined in Chapter 2) to rise. Ideally, the expansionary policies of the Fed are meant to be conducive to real economic expansion (economic growth, full employment, sustainable international trade) without price inflation. Indeed, price stabilization (low inflation) can be viewed as the primary policy objective of the Fed.

Contractionary Activities. We also described three monetary policy tools that the Fed can use in a contractionary fashion: open market sales of securities, discount rate increases, and reserve requirement ratio increases. All else constant, when the Federal Reserve sells securities in the open market, reserve accounts of banks decrease. When the Fed raises the discount rate, interest rates generally increase in the open market, making borrowing more expensive. Finally, an increase in the reserve requirement ratio, all else constant, results in a decrease in excess reserves for all banks and limits the availability of funds for additional loans.

In all three cases, interest rates will tend to rise. Higher interest rates discourage credit availability and borrowing. Economic participants spend less when funds are expensive.

14. See the discussion of the interest rate parity theorem in Chapter 8.

TABLE 4–9 Federal Reserve Monetary Policy Targets

Target	Years
Fed funds rate targeted using bank reserves to achieve target	1970–October 1979
Nonborrowed reserves targeted	October 1979–October 1982
Borrowed reserves targeted	October 1983–July 1993
Fed funds rate targeted (rate announced)	July 1993–present

Households, businesses, and governments are less likely to invest in fixed assets. Households decrease their purchases of durable goods. State and local government spending decreases. Finally, an increase in domestic interest rates relative to foreign rates may result in an increase in the (foreign) exchange value (rate) of the dollar. As the dollar's exchange rate increases, U.S. goods become relatively expensive compared to foreign goods. Eventually, U.S. exports decrease.

Money Supply versus Interest Rate Targeting

As shown in Table 4–9, the Federal Reserve has varied between its use of the money supply and interest rates as the target variable used to control economic activity in the United States. Panel A of Figure 4–6 illustrates the targeting of money supply (such as M1),[15] while Panel B of Figure 4–6 shows the targeting of interest rates. For example, letting the demand curve for money be represented as M_D in Panel A of Figure 4–6, suppose the FOMC sets the target M1 money supply (currency and checkable deposits)[16] at a level that is consistent with 5 percent growth, line M_S in Panel A of Figure 4-6. At this M_S level, the FOMC expects the equilibrium interest rate to be i^*. However, unexpected increases or decreases in production, or changes in inflation, may cause the demand curve for money to shift up and to the right, M_D', or down and to the left, M_D''. Accordingly, interest rates will fluctuate between i' and i''. Thus, targeting the money supply can lead to periods of relatively high volatility in interest rates.

In Panel B of Figure 4-6, suppose instead the FOMC targets the interest rate, $i_T =$ 6 percent. If the demand for money falls, to M_D'', interest rates will fall to $i'' = 5$ percent with no intervention by the Fed. In order to maintain the target interest rate, the FOMC has to conduct monetary policy actions (such as open market sales of U.S. securities) to lower bank reserves and the money supply (to M_S'). This reduction in the money supply will maintain the target interest rate at $i_T = 6$ percent. As should be obvious from these graphs and the discussion, the Federal Reserve can successfully target *only one of these two variables* (money supply or interest rates) at any one moment. If the money supply is the target variable used to implement monetary policy, interest rates must be allowed to fluctuate relatively freely. By contrast, if an interest rate (such as the fed funds rate) is the target, then bank reserves and the money supply must be allowed to fluctuate relatively freely.

15. M1 ($1,341.2 billion outstanding in September 2004) consists of (1) currency outside the U.S. Treasury, Federal Reserve Banks, and the vaults of depository institutions; (2) traveler's checks of nonbank issuers; (3) demand deposits at all commercial banks other than those owed to depository institutions, the U.S. government, and foreign banks and official institutions, less cash items in the process of collection and Federal Reserve float; (4) other checkable deposits (OCDs). M2 ($6,298.5 billion outstanding in September 2004) consists of M1 plus (1) savings and small time deposits (time deposits in amounts of less than $100,000) and (2) other nondeposit obligations of depository institutions. M3 ($9,278.9 billion outstanding in September 2004) consists of M2 plus (1) large time deposits (in amounts of $100,000 or more) issued by all depository institutions and (2) other nondeposit obligations of depository institutions.

16. Remember that the money base is currency in circulation plus reserves (depository institution reserves balances in accounts at Federal Reserve Banks plus vault cash on hand of commercial banks). Thus, the money base is a part (subset) of the M1 money supply.

FIGURE 4–6 Targeting Money Supply versus Interest Rates

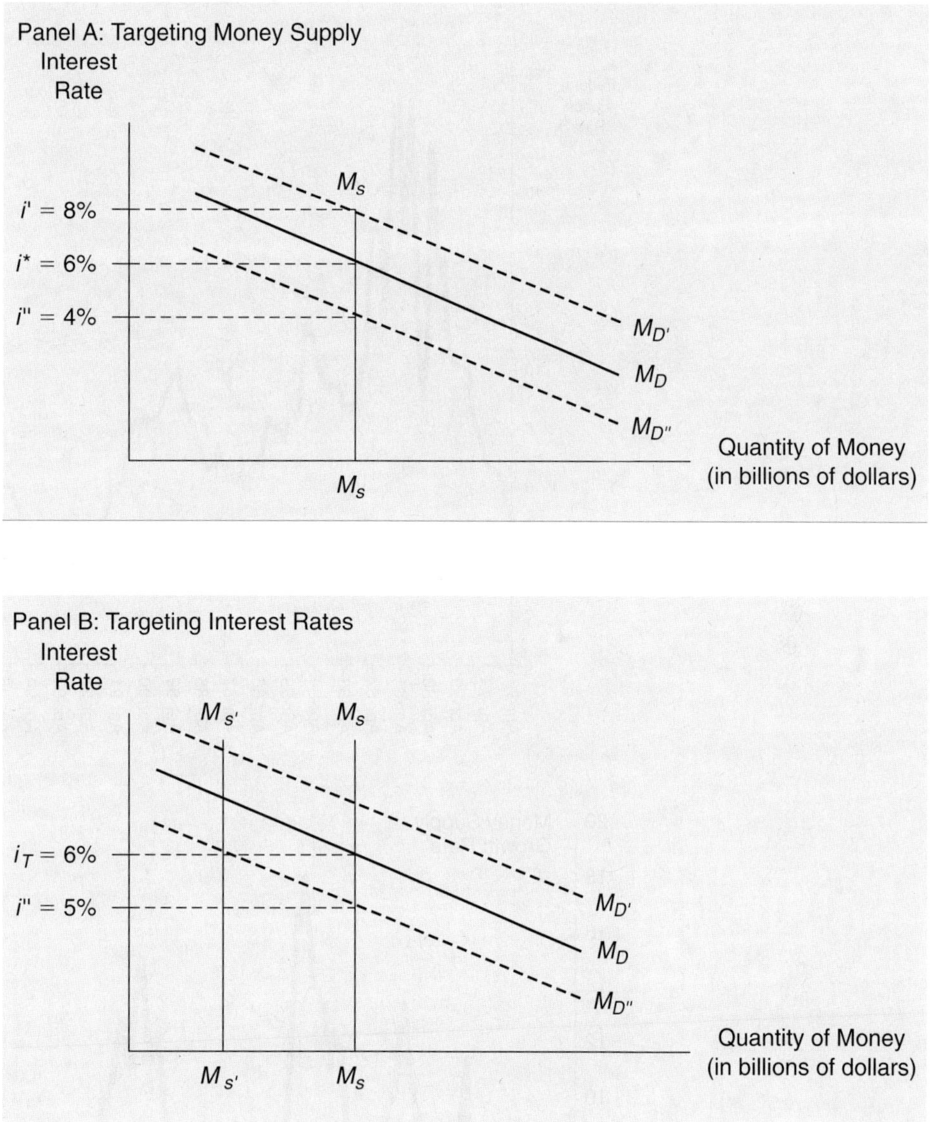

In the 1970s, the Fed implemented its monetary policy strategy by targeting the federal funds rate. However, during the 1970s, interest rates rose dramatically (see Figure 4–7). The Fed responded to these interest rate increases by increasing the money supply, which led to historically high levels of inflation (e.g., over 10 percent in the summer of 1979). With rapidly rising inflation, Paul Volcker (chairman of the Federal Reserve Board at the time) felt that interest rate targets were not doing an appropriate job in constraining the demand for money (and the inflationary side of the economy). Thus, on October 6, 1979, the Fed chose to completely refocus its monetary policy, moving away from interest rate targets toward targeting the money supply itself, and in particular bank reserves—so-called nonborrowed reserves, which are the difference between total reserves and reserves borrowed through the discount window (see the earlier discussion in this chapter).

Growth in the money supply, however, did not turn out to be any easier to control. For example, the Fed missed its M1 growth rate targets in each of the first three years in which

FIGURE 4–7 Federal Funds Rates and Annualized Money Supply Growth Rates, 1977–August 2004

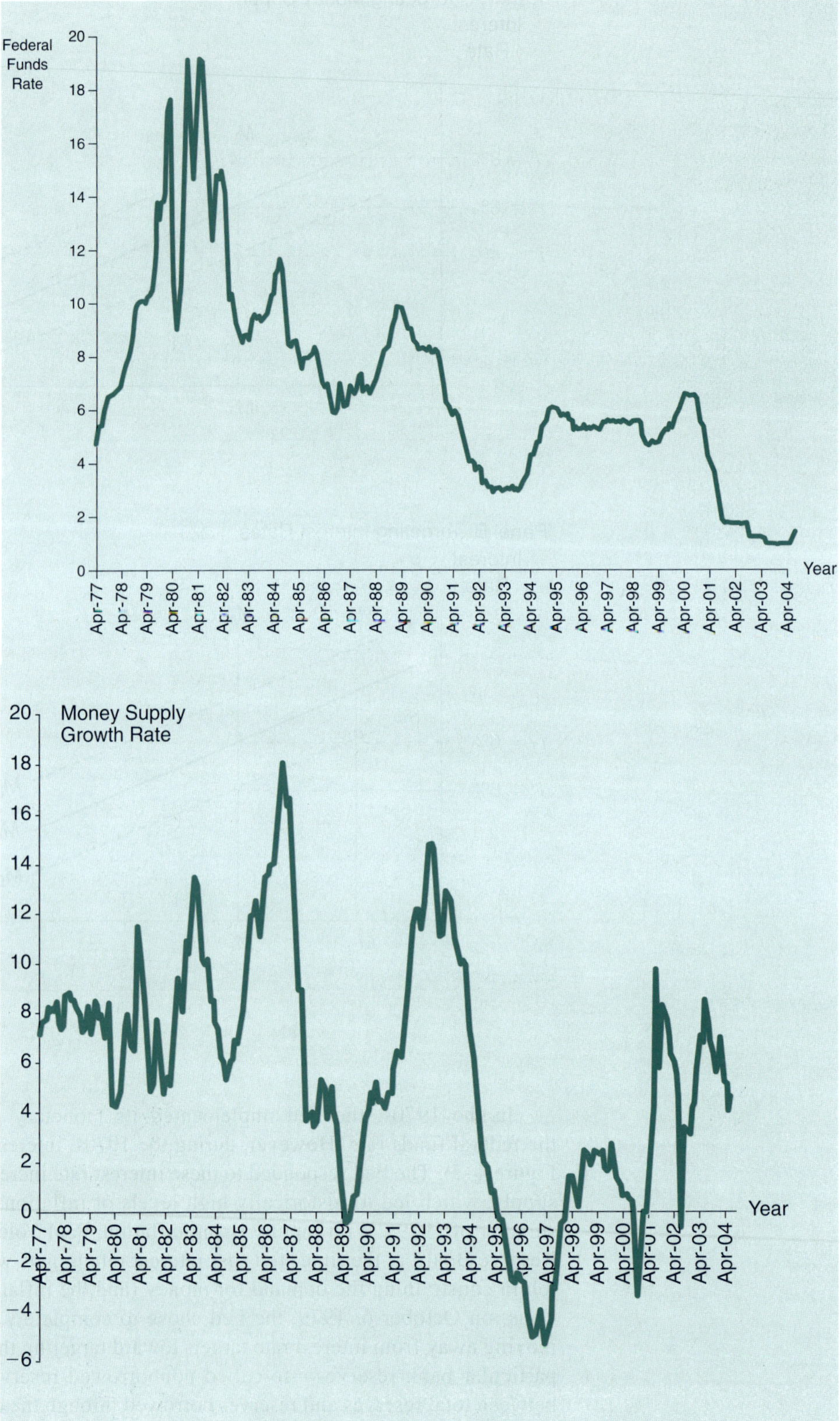

Source: Federal Reserve Board Web site,"Research and Data," September 2004. **www.federalreserve.gov**

DO YOU UNDERSTAND?

1. What actions the Federal Reserve can take to promote economic expansion? Describe how each affects credit availability, interest rates, money supply, and security prices.
2. What actions the Federal Reserve can take to contract the U.S. economy? Describe how each affects credit availability, interest rates, money supply, and security prices.
3. Why the simultaneous targeting of the money supply and interest rates is sometimes impossible to achieve?

reserve targeting was used. Further, in contrast to expectations, volatility in the money supply growth rate grew as well (see Figure 4–7). Thus, in October 1982, the Federal Reserve abandoned its policy of targeting nonborrowed reserves for a policy of targeting borrowed reserves (those reserves banks borrow from the Fed's discount window).

The borrowed reserve targeting system lasted from October 1982 until 1993, when the Federal Reserve announced that it would no longer target bank reserves and money supply growth at all. At this time, the Fed announced that it would use interest rates—the federal funds rate—as the main target variable to guide monetary policy (initially setting the target rate at a constant 3 percent). Under the current regime, and contrary to previous tradition such as in the 1970s, the Fed simply announces whether the federal funds rate target has been increased, decreased, or left unchanged after every monthly FOMC meeting—previously, the federal funds rate change had been kept secret. This announcement is watched very closely by financial market participants who, as demonstrated in In the News boxes in previous chapters, react quickly to any change in the fed funds rate target.

INTERNATIONAL MONETARY POLICIES AND STRATEGIES

As discussed in Chapter 2, foreign investors are major participants in the financial markets. As such, the Federal Reserve considers economic conditions of other major countries—for example, Japan—when assessing and conducting its monetary policy for the U.S. economy. The Fed's actions regarding international monetary policy initiatives are most effective if it coordinates its activities and policies with the central banks of other countries. In this section, we look at how U.S. monetary policy initiatives affect foreign exchange rates.

5

Impact of U.S. Monetary Policy on Foreign Exchange Rates

Central banks in major countries often make commitments to each other about institutional aspects of their intervention (or nonintervention) in the foreign exchange markets. This is done through various forums, including meetings such as the Group of 7 (the meeting of senior government representatives from the seven major industrialized countries of the world). The current U.S. approach is to generally allow exchange rates to fluctuate freely. However, central banks can influence their country's exchange rates by buying and selling currencies, especially if they perceive the market has become unstable (a process called **foreign exchange intervention**). For example, in June 1999, the Bank of Japan (Japan's central bank) bought $5 billion U.S. dollars for yen in the currency markets, thus increasing the supply of yen. The reason for this was that there was wide concern among central bankers that the yen's exchange rate was appreciating (rising) too fast against the dollar and this might be a deterrent to Japanese exports and the movement of the Japanese economy out of recession. The purchase, conducted when Japanese markets were closed for a public holiday, caused the yen to fall in value relative to the dollar, from 120 yen per dollar (i.e., .00833 dollar per yen) to as high as 122.52 yen per dollar (i.e., .00816 dollar per yen—see Figure 4–8).

www.boj.or.jp/en

foreign exchange intervention

Commitments between countries about the institutional aspects of their intervention in the foreign exchange markets.

The process of foreign exchange intervention is similar to that of open market purchases and sales of Treasury securities (described earlier). Instead of purchasing or selling securities, the Federal Reserve purchases or sells some of its holdings of foreign currency reserves (listed as part of gold and foreign exchange in Table 4–5) in the foreign exchange markets (see Chapter 8). Specifically, when the Federal Reserve sells domestic currency to purchase foreign currency (e.g., the Japanese yen) in the foreign exchange market,[17] it results in an increase in the Fed's "gold and foreign exchange" and "deposits due to rest of the world" accounts (see Table 4–5). Further, since the Fed's purchasing of yen supplies more dollars to outside holders, this transaction increases the money supply in the United States.

17. This transaction is completed by the Foreign Exchange Desk at the Federal Reserve Bank of New York.

FIGURE 4–8 Exchange Rate of Japanese Yen for U.S. Dollars in Response to Bank of Japan Intervention

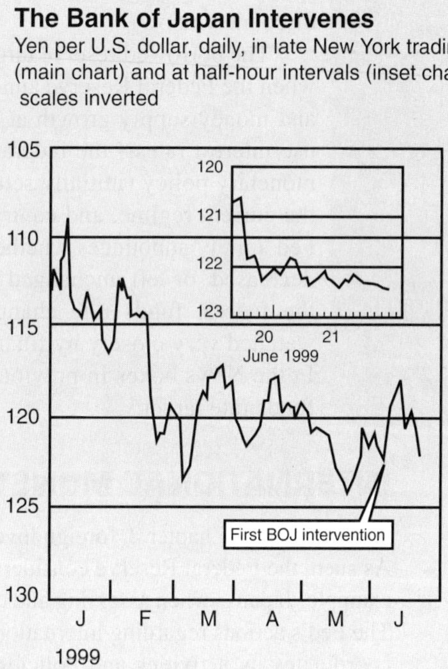

Source: *The Wall Street Journal*, June 22, 1999, p. A16. Reprinted by permission of *The Wall Street Journal*, **www.wsj.com**

DO YOU UNDERSTAND?

1. How central banks intervene in foreign exchange markets?

For example, as shown in Figure 4–9, if the Federal Reserve decides to purchase ¥5 billion Japanese yen for dollars, the transaction results in an increase in the U.S. money supply and a decrease in the supply of Japanese yen. Thus, the supply curve for the foreign currency (the Japanese yen) shifts up and to the left, from $S_¥$ to $S'_¥$, and the equilibrium foreign exchange rate of U.S. dollars for Japanese yen (i.e., US\$/¥) rises from US\$/¥ to US\$/¥′ in Figure 4–9—that is, the foreign currency (Japanese yen) appreciates in value relative to the U.S. dollar such that US\$/¥ increases (or the U.S. dollar depreciates in value relative to the Japanese yen such that ¥/US\$ decreases). Conversely, when the Federal Reserve purchases domestic currency using foreign exchange as payment, the transaction results in a decrease in the U.S. money supply and an increase in the supply of the foreign currency. As a result, the foreign currency depreciates in value relative to the U.S. dollar or the U.S. dollar appreciates in value relative to the foreign currency.

EXAMPLE 4-4 Purchase of Foreign Assets by Selling Domestic Currency

Suppose the Federal Reserve decides to purchase \$5 billion worth of foreign currency in exchange for \$5 billion of its deposit accounts at the Federal Reserve. The Fed's purchase of foreign currency results in two balance sheet changes. First, the Fed's holdings of foreign exchange increase by \$5 billion. Second, the Fed increases its dollar deposit accounts of the foreign currency sellers by \$5 billion. Thus, the Fed's purchase of foreign currency and the payment with dollar deposits at the Fed result in a \$5 billion increase in U.S. bank reserves. Finally, the increase in the U.S. money supply and decrease in the supply of Japanese yen will result in an appreciation of the Japanese yen relative to the U.S. dollar.

FIGURE 4–9 **Changes in the Equilibrium Foreign Exchange Rate in Response to Purchase of Japanese Yen with U.S. Dollars**

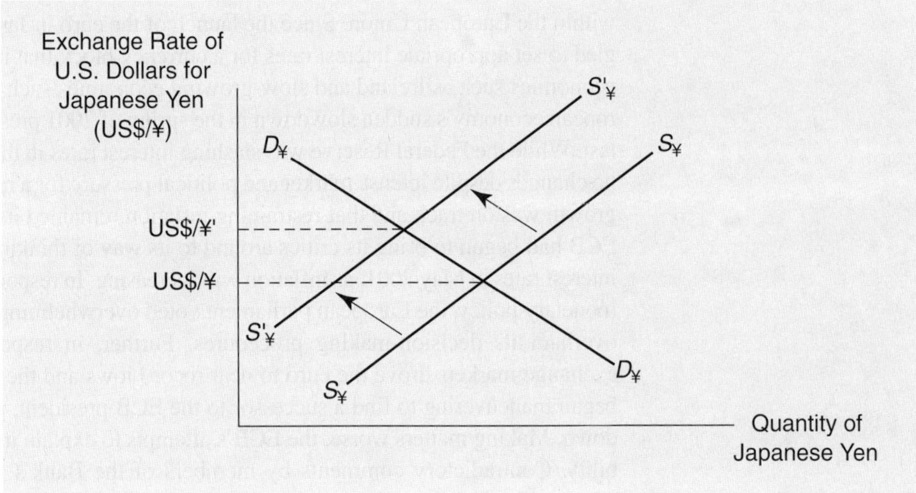

Challenges of Other Major Central Banks

6

The Bank of Japan. Like the Federal Reserve, other major countries have central banks that are charged with promoting economic growth and stability in their countries. For example, after years of financial and economic stagnation, in March 2001, the Bank of Japan (BOJ) announced that it would no longer target the uncollateralized overnight call rate, which is similar to the U.S. fed funds rate. Instead, the BOJ now targets the outstanding balance of current accounts at the BOJ, which is similar to the reserve component of the U.S. monetary base, and stated a goal of increasing the current account balances by 25 percent (from 4 to 5 trillion yen) by the end of 2001.[18] The result was that the government flooded the market with yen in an attempt to stimulate the economy. However, the economic news remained grim. In 2001, to October, industrial production fell by 11.9 percent, while retail sales fell by 4.9 percent. Further, the yen depreciated, falling nearly 20 percent to 132 yen against the dollar over the last quarter of 2001. The economy continued to contract and prices in Japan fell 4 percent in 2001 from 2000. In this deflationary environment, with long term nominal interest rates at 1.5 to 2 percent, Japan's real interest rates were as high as 6 percent—way too high to stimulate the growth Japan so badly needed. The result was that the BOJ had no choice but to release even more yen in hopes of stimulating the economy and halting the deflationary cycle.

www.boj.or.jp/en

The Japanese authorities also sought to smooth excess volatility in the yen with large-scale intervention in 2003 and at the start of 2004. The Bank of Japan spent ¥20,000 billion in 2003 and ¥15,000 billion in the first quarter of 2004 on intervention. By mid-2004 the efforts of the BOJ appeared to be working. Japan's economy posted annualized growth of more than 6 percent in the first two quarters of 2004 as an upturn sparked by export growth during 2003 spread through the economy. Japan's economy continued to recover through the summer of 2004. Industrial production rose, corporate profitability improved, and exports boomed. Consumer spending, previously a weak spot in the economy, also gradually increased. Moreover, in 2004 Japan's central bank kept its loose monetary policy unchanged, leaving the financial system flush with enough cash to fuel the rebound. For example, the BOJ left its target for liquidity, or the extra cash it keeps for commercial banks, in a range of ¥30 trillion ($271 billion) to ¥35 trillion ($316 billion). It also kept its monthly purchases of government bonds at ¥1.2 trillion ($11 billion).

www.ecb.int

The European Central Bank. On January 1, 1999, twelve major European countries pegged their exchange rates together to create a single currency, called the European currency

18. Because the overnight call loan rate was approximately 0.15 percent when the BOJ announced its change in policy, many argued that low interest rates left the BOJ with little room to ease further, and thus forced this change in policy.

unit, or euro. The ECU became the official currency in these 12 countries on January 1, 2002. As these countries tied their currencies and their economies together, it is the European Central Bank (ECB) that has been charged with promoting and maintaining economic growth within the European Union. Since the launch of the euro in January 1999, the ECB has struggled to set appropriate interest rates for a currency block that includes relatively fast-growing economies such as Ireland and slow-growing economies such as Germany and Italy. The European economy's sudden slowdown in the spring of 2001 presented the ECB with its first big test. While the Federal Reserve was slashing interest rates in the United States, the ECB made no changes despite intense market and political pressure for a reduction. The bank insisted that growth was on track and that restraining inflation remained its chief priority.[19] Just when the ECB had begun to bring its critics around to its way of thinking it reversed its policy, cutting interest rates in May 2001, as inflation was increasing. In response to its seemingly "irrational" monetary policy, the European parliament voted overwhelmingly to recommend that the ECB overhaul its decision-making procedures. Further, in response to ECB actions, foreign exchange markets drove the euro to near record lows and the European Union governments began maneuvering to find a successor to the ECB president, putting pressure on him to step down. Making matters worse, the ECB's attempts to explain its strategy further hurt its credibility. Contradictory comments by members of the Bank's governing council left market watchers baffled about the prospects for interest rate cuts they felt were badly needed.

Even worse, the ECB faced growing criticism over its monetary policy. Alone among major central banks, the ECB follows a two-tier strategy for containing inflation: targeting growth of the money supply (called M3) and monitoring economic activity including inflation, output, and other economic indicators. Most central banks have abandoned rigid money supply targeting, believing there is no clear short-term relation between the growth of money and inflation. The ECB's view is that indicators of economic activity in the euro zone are still in their infancy and difficult to reliably assess, while its M3 data are reliable.

DO YOU UNDERSTAND?

1. The problems facing the Bank of Japan and its attempts to address these problems?
2. How the European Central Bank has performed during its first few years of operation?

At the core of the ECB's problem lies the inherent dilemma of managing a single currency with a single monetary policy for 12 different countries whose growth and inflation rates have differed since the introduction of the euro in 1999. For example, although the overall euro-area inflation rate was 2.8 percent in July 2001, national rates varied from a high of 5.2 percent in the Netherlands to a low of 2.2 percent in France. However, over time the economies of the 12 nations began to behave more alike. For example, the difference in growth rates in the fastest growing member of the euro zone and the slowest narrowed from 8.1 percent in 1999 to about 3.4 percent in 2001. Further, inflation and unemployment rates across Europe moved closer together, and wage levels and living standards in the euro zone's poorer countries (such as Portugal and Greece) began to catch up with those of the more prosperous countries. More and more the countries moved in the same economic cycle, which is what the economic and monetary union was meant to make happen.

As a result, in early 2003, the ECB downgraded the importance of the money supply in its monetary policy strategy. The ECB now defines an inflation target, stating that inflation should not exceed 2 percent over the medium term. The ECB also added that in the pursuit of price stability it will aim to maintain inflation rates close to 2 percent over the medium term. These seemingly contradictory statements again brought controversy for the ECB. The first statement defined price stability as a rate of inflation of at most 2 percent over the medium term. This definition came under increasing criticism for giving the ECB an incentive to push inflation below 2 percent, thereby increasing the risk of deflation, especially in those countries where inflation was already significantly lower than the 2 percent euro-zone average. The second statement could mean that the ECB shifted to a medium-term target of 2 percent for the rate of inflation. Thus, instead of creating clarity with its 2003 change in monetary policy, the ECB managed to create some confusion about its true intentions.

The Bank of China. China represents the world's second largest economy. Thus, changes in the growth, productivity, inflation, and interest rates in China are felt worldwide. The country has long pursued a stable monetary policy, which helped its economy grow at an extremely fast

19. See "What's Wrong with the ECB? " *Institutional Investor,* September 2001, p. 64, by Tom Buerkle.

pace. During the early 2000s China accounted for one-third of global economic growth, twice as much as did the United States. In 2003, for example, China's official GDP growth rate surged to 9.7 percent, and some economists stated it was as high as 13 percent. China's economy expanded another 9.7 percent in the first three months of 2004, well above the government target of 7 percent. Indeed, growth was so rapid that Chinese government officials and economists were afraid that the economy could be overheated. Such rapid growth presented greater pressure from inflation (a problem faced by the U.S. central bank—the Fed—in the late 1990s).

In May of 2004, the Bank of China (the central bank) announced that it was closely watching inflation and expected consumer prices to climb in the second quarter of the year. The bank promised forceful measures to cool things down, but what the bank would or could do was not clear. Rumors were rife that the Bank of China might raise interest rates for the first time in nine years. However, the bank stopped short of giving any clear indication of an early adjustment in interest rates. Instead, the government took moves to increase bank reserve requirements and took administrative measures such as price curbs and strict land policies to reduce fixed investment and credit growth. In mid-2005 China considered loosening the yuan's peg to the U.S. dollar (which had been set at 8.28 yuans to the dollar since 1994) to slow economic growth. Allowing the yuan to appreciate relative to the dollar would increase inputs and cool the overheating economy.

The challenge facing the Chinese would be difficult for policymakers anywhere: to slow the economy enough to ensure sustainable growth, but not so much as to cause a damaging crash, the much-feared hard landing. But the task of China's policymakers was doubly difficult because they have far fewer tools at their disposal than their counterparts in developed countries. For example, the thousands of state-owned firms, as well as the banking system, respond very little to pricing signals or interest rate changes.

SUMMARY

This chapter described the Federal Reserve System in the United States. The Federal Reserve is the central bank charged with conducting monetary policy, supervising and regulating depository institutions, maintaining the stability of the financial system, and providing specific financial services to the U.S. government, the public, and financial institutions. We reviewed the structure under which the Fed provides these functions, the monetary policy tools it uses, and the impact of monetary policy changes on credit availability, interest rates, money supply, security prices, and foreign exchange rates.

SEARCH THE SITE

Go to the Federal Reserve Board Web site and find the latest information available on the prime rate, the three-month CD rate, the discount rate, and the three-month T-bill rate using the following steps.

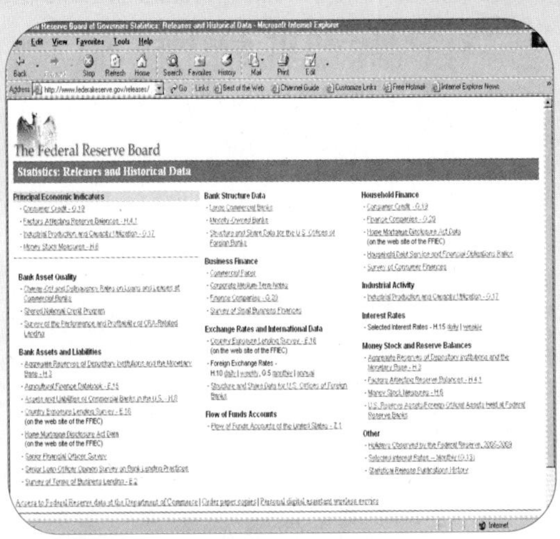

Go to the Federal Reserve Board's Web site at **www.federalreserve.gov/releases**

Click on "Selected Interest Rates: Weekly"

Click on the most recent date. The data will be in this file on your computer screen.

Questions

1. What are the current levels for each of these interest rates?
2. Calculate the percentage change in each of these rates since March 2004.

www.mhhe.com/sc3e

QUESTIONS

1. Describe the functions performed by Federal Reserve Banks.
2. Define the discount window and the discount rate.
3. Describe the structure of the Board of Governors of the Federal Reserve System.
4. What are the primary responsibilities of the Federal Reserve Board?
5. What are the primary responsibilities of the Federal Open Market Committee?
6. What are the major liabilities of the Federal Reserve System? Describe each.
7. What are the major assets of the Federal Reserve System? Describe each.
8. What are the tools used by the Federal Reserve to implement monetary policy?
9. Suppose the Federal Reserve instructs the Trading Desk to purchase $1 billion of securities. Show the result of this transaction on the balance sheets of the Federal Reserve System and commercial banks.
10. Suppose the Federal Reserve instructs the Trading Desk to sell $850 million of securities. Show the result of this transaction on the balance sheets of the Federal Reserve System and commercial banks.
11. Explain how a decrease in the discount rate affects credit availability and the money supply.
12. Why does the Federal Reserve rarely use the discount rate to implement its monetary policy?
13. What changes did the Fed implement to its discount window lending policy in the early 2000s?
14. Bank Three currently has $600 million in transaction deposits on its balance sheet. The Federal Reserve has currently set the reserve requirement at 10 percent of transaction deposits.
    a. If the Federal Reserve decreases the reserve requirement to 8 percent, show the balance sheet of Bank Three and the Federal Reserve System just before and after the full effect of the reserve requirement change. Assume Bank Three withdraws all excess reserves and gives out loans, and that borrowers eventually return all of these funds to Bank Three in the form of transaction deposits.
    b. Redo part (a) using a 12 percent reserve requirement.
15. National Bank currently has $500 million in transaction deposits on its balance sheet. The current reserve requirement is 10 percent, but the Federal Reserve is decreasing this requirement to 8 percent.
    a. Show the balance sheet of the Federal Reserve and National Bank if National Bank converts all excess reserves to loans, but borrowers return only 50 percent of these funds to National Bank as transaction deposits.
    b. Show the balance sheet of the Federal Reserve and National Bank if National Bank converts 75 percent of its excess reserves to loans and borrowers return 60 percent of these funds to National Bank as transaction deposits.
16. The FOMC has instructed the FRBNY Trading Desk to purchase $500 million in U.S. Treasury securities. The Federal Reserve has currently set the reserve requirement at 5 percent of transaction deposits. Assume U.S. banks withdraw all excess reserves and give out loans.
    a. Assume also that borrowers eventually return all of these funds to their banks in the form of transaction deposits. What is the full affect of this purchase on bank deposits and the money supply?
    b. What is the full effect of this purchase on bank deposits and the money supply if borrowers only return 95 percent of these funds to their banks in the form of transaction deposits?
17. Which of the monetary tools available to the Federal Reserve is most often used? Why?
18. Describe how expansionary activities conducted by the Federal Reserve impact credit availability, the money supply, interest rates, and security prices. Do the same for contractionary activities.
19. How does the purchase and sale of domestic currency to sell and buy foreign currency in the foreign exchange market affect the Federal Reserve's balance sheet, the money supply, and foreign exchange rates?
20. Suppose the Federal Reserve purchases $10 billion worth of foreign currency in exchange for deposit accounts at the Federal Reserve. Show the changes that result from this transaction on the Fed's balance sheet.

part two

Securities Markets

Part Two of the book presents an overview of the various securities markets. We describe each securities market, its participants, the securities traded in each, and the trading process in each. These chapters cover the money markets (Chapter 5), bond markets (Chapter 6), mortgage markets (Chapter 7), foreign exchange markets (Chapter 8), stock markets (Chapter 9), and derivative securities markets (Chapter 10).

OUTLINE

5

Money Markets

OUTLINE

Chapter NAVIGATOR

1. What are money markets?
2. What are the major types of money market securities?
3. What is the process used to issue Treasury securities?
4. Who are the main participants in money markets?
5. To what extent do foreign investors participate in U.S. money markets?
6. What are the major developments in Euro money markets?

DEFINITION OF MONEY MARKETS: CHAPTER OVERVIEW

1

Money markets exist to transfer funds from individuals, corporations, and government units with short-term excess funds (suppliers of funds) to economic agents who have short-term needs for funds (users of funds). Specifically, in **money markets,** short-term debt instruments (those with an original maturity of one year or less) are issued by economic units that require short-term funds and are purchased by economic units that have excess short-term funds. Once issued, money market instruments trade in active secondary markets. Capital markets serve a similar function for market participants with excess funds to invest for periods of time longer than one year and/or who wish to borrow for periods longer than one year. Market participants who concentrate their investments in capital market instruments also tend to invest in some money market securities so as to meet their short-term liquidity needs. The secondary markets for money market instruments are extremely important, as they serve to reallocate the (relatively) fixed amounts of liquid funds available in the market at any particular time. At the end of 2004 these markets had over $5,260 billion in financial claims outstanding.

IN THE NEWS

Products "Set to Become Popular" Short-Term Funds

Short-term funds, money market funds that invest in assets of up to a year in order to deliver higher returns, are expected to increase in popularity, Moody's Investors Service, the credit rating agency, said yesterday. . . . These funds invest in medium to top-rated fixed income paper and money market securities with average maturities of up to 365 days.

"The driver has been the low interest rates of recent years," said Douglas Rivkin, senior credit officer at Moody's. "Institutional investors have been seeking better returns for their balances. They can do five to 30 basis points in yield better than money market funds." Short-term funds have attracted more than $500 billion in assets this year in the U.S. market, according to estimates from iMoneyNet quoted by Moody's.

"The money invested in short-term funds does not yet compare with the some $2,000 billion invested in money market mutual funds (but) we expect to see additional growth in this cash management asset class."

Source: *Financial Times,* October 8, 2004, p. 45, by Charles Batchelor. **www.ftbusiness.com**

DO YOU UNDERSTAND?

1. The size of the growth in short-term funds in the early 2000s?
2. Why investments in short-term funds have grown in the early 2000s?

In this chapter, we present an overview of money markets. We define and review the various money market instruments that exist, the new issue and secondary market trading process for each, and the market participants trading these securities. We also look at international money markets and instruments, taking a particularly close look at the Euro markets.

MONEY MARKETS

money markets

Markets that trade debt securities or instruments with maturities of less than one year.

opportunity cost

The forgone interest cost from the holding of cash balances when they are received.

default risk

The risk of late or nonpayment of principal or interest.

The need for money markets arises because the immediate cash needs of individuals, corporations, and governments do not necessarily coincide with their receipts of cash. For example, the federal government collects taxes quarterly; however, its operating and other expenses occur daily. Similarly, corporations' daily patterns of receipts from sales do not necessarily occur with the same pattern as their daily expenses (e.g., wages and other disbursements). Because excessive holdings of cash balances involve a cost in the form of forgone interest, called **opportunity cost,** those economic units with excess cash usually keep such balances to the minimum needed to meet their day-to-day transaction requirements. Consequently, holders of cash invest "excess" cash funds in financial securities that can be quickly and relatively costlessly converted back to cash when needed with little risk of loss of value over the short investment horizon. Money markets are efficient in performing this service in that they enable large amounts of money to be transferred from suppliers of funds to users of funds for short periods of time both quickly and at low cost to the transacting parties. In general, a money market instrument provides an investment opportunity that generates a higher rate of interest (return) than holding cash, but it is also very liquid and (because of its short maturity) has relatively low default risk.

1

Notice, from the description above, that money markets and money market securities or instruments have three basic characteristics. First, money market instruments are generally sold in large denominations (often in units of $1 million to $10 million). Most money market participants want or need to borrow large amounts of cash, so that transactions costs are low relative to the interest paid. The size of these initial transactions prohibits most individual investors from investing directly in money market securities. Rather, individuals generally invest in money market securities indirectly, with the help of financial institutions such as money market mutual funds or short-term funds (see the In the News box).

Second, money market instruments have low **default risk;** the risk of late or nonpayment of principal and/or interest is generally small. Since cash lent in the money markets

DO YOU UNDERSTAND?

1. What the three characteristics common to money market securities are?
2. Why it is difficult for individual investors to be involved in the initial sale of a money market security?

must be available for a quick return to the lender, money market instruments can generally be issued only by high-quality borrowers with little risk of default.

Finally, money market securities must have an original maturity of one year or less. Recall from Chapter 3 that the longer the maturity of a debt security, the greater is its interest rate risk and the higher is its required rate of return. Given that adverse price movements resulting from interest rate changes are smaller for short-term securities, the short-term maturity of money market instruments helps lower the risk that interest rate changes will significantly affect the security's market value and price.

YIELDS ON MONEY MARKET SECURITIES

For many of the money market securities discussed below, returns are measured and quoted in a manner that does not allow them to be evaluated using the time value of money equations. For example, some securities' interest rates or returns are based on a 360-day year, while others are based on a 365-day year. It is therefore inappropriate to compare annual interest rates on the various money market securities as well as on short-term and long-term securities without adjusting their interest rates for differences in the securities' characteristics.

Effective Annual Return

The quoted annual nominal interest rate (i) on money market securities with a maturity of less than one year can be converted to an effective annual interest return (EAR) using the following equation:[1]

$$EAR = \left(1 + \frac{i}{365/h}\right)^{365/h} - 1$$

where h = number of days to maturity.

EXAMPLE 5-1 Calculation of EAR on a Money Market Security

Suppose you can invest in a money market security that matures in 75 days and offers a 7 percent annual interest rate. The effective annual interest return on this security is:

$$EAR = \left(1 + \frac{.07}{365/75}\right)^{365/75} - 1 = 7.20\%$$

Discount Yields

Some money market instruments (e.g., Treasury bills and commercial paper) are bought and sold on a discount basis. That is, instead of directly received interest payments over the investment horizon, the return on these securities results from the purchase of the security at a discount from its face value (P_0) and the receipt of face value (P_f) at maturity, as we show in the following time line.

$$\begin{array}{lcr} P_0 & \text{———————————} & P_f \\ 0 & & \text{Maturity} \\ & & \text{(days)} \end{array}$$

Further, yields on these securities normally use a 360-day year rather than a 365-day year to calculate interest return. Interest rates on discount securities, or discount yields (i_{dy}), are quoted on a discount basis using the following equation:

$$i_{dy} = [(P_f - P_0)/P_f](360/h)$$

1. This equation assumes that as these short-term securities mature they can be reinvested for the remainder of the year at the same interest rate.

where

P_f = Face value
P_0 = Discount price of the security
h = Number of days until maturity

There are several features of a discount yield that make it difficult to compare with yields on other (nondiscount) securities—for example, U.S. Treasury bonds—that pay a (coupon) interest payment semiannually. The annual interest rate on nondiscount securities (such as U.S. Treasury bonds) is often referred to as the nominal or bond equivalent yield (i_{bey}).[2] The bond equivalent yield used for comparison with a discount money market instrument of short (less than one year) maturity can be calculated as follows:

$$i_{bey} = [(P_f - P_0)/P_0](365/h)$$

Notice the discount yield uses the terminal price, or the security's face value (P_f), as the base price in calculating an annualized interest rate. By contrast, bond equivalent yields are based on the purchase price (P_0) of a security. Further, and as already mentioned, discount yields often use a 360-day rather than a 365-day year to compute interest returns. An appropriate comparison of interest rates on discount securities versus nondiscount securities, adjusting for both the base price and days in the year differences, requires converting a discount yield into a bond equivalent yield in the following manner:

$$i_{bey} = i_{dy}(P_f / P_0)\ (365/360)$$

Finally, neither of these interest rates considers the effects of compounding of interest during the less than one year investment horizon. The *EAR* on a discount security would be calculated by applying the calculated bond equivalent yield (i_{bey}) for the discount security to the *EAR* equation, as illustrated in Example 5–1 (i.e., setting i equal to i_{bey} in Example 5–1).

EXAMPLE 5-2 Comparison of Discount Yield, Bond Equivalent Yield, and EAR

Suppose you can purchase a \$1 million Treasury bill that is currently selling on a discount basis (i.e., with no explicit interest payments) at 97½ percent of its face value. The T-bill is 140 days from maturity (when the \$1 million will be paid). Depending on the setting in which you are interested, any one of the following three yields or interest rates could be appropriate:

Discount yield: $i_{dy} = [(\$1\text{m.} - \$975{,}000)/\$1\text{m.}](360/140) = 6.43\%$

Bond equivalent yield: $i_{bey} = [(\$1\text{m.} - \$975{,}000)/\$975{,}000](365/140) = 6.68\%$

EAR: $EAR = [1 + .0668/(365/140)]^{365/140} - 1 = 6.82\%$

Single-Payment Yields

Some money market securities (e.g., jumbo CD, fed funds) pay interest only once during their lives: at maturity. Thus, the single-payment security holder receives a terminal payment consisting of interest plus the face value of the security, as we show in the following time line. Such securities are special cases of the pure discount securities that only pay the face value on maturity.

Invest \$1 ———————— Receive \$1 + Interest
0 ———————— Maturity (days)

Further, quoted nominal interest rates on single-payment securities (or single-payment yield, i_{spy}) normally assume a 360-day year. In order to compare interest rates on these securities with others, such as U.S. Treasury bonds, that pay interest based on a 365-day year, the nominal interest rate must be converted to a bond equivalent yield in the following manner:

$$i_{bey} = i_{spy}(365/360)$$

2. We describe nominal yields and bond valuation in detail in Chapter 3.

Further, allowing for interest rate compounding, the EAR for single-payment securities must utilize the bond equivalent yield as follows:

$$EAR = \left[1 + i_{spy}\frac{365/360}{365/h}\right]^{365/h} - 1$$

$$EAR = [1 + i_{bey}/(365/h)]^{365/h} - 1$$

EXAMPLE 5-3 Comparison of Single-Payment Yield, Bond Equivalent Yield, and EAR

Suppose you can purchase a $1 million jumbo CD that is currently 105 days from maturity. The CD has a quoted annual interest rate of 5.16 percent for a 360-day year. The bond equivalent yield is calculated as:

$$i_{bey} = 5.16\%(365/360) = 5.232\%$$

The EAR on the CD is calculated as:

$$EAR = [1 + (.05232)/(365/105)]^{365/105} - 1 = 5.33\%$$

DO YOU UNDERSTAND?

1. What characteristics of a bond equivalent yield prevent it from being directly compared to an EAR?

Table 5–1 lists various money market instruments and their quoted interest rates, as reported in *The Wall Street Journal* for November 9, 2004. As we proceed with the discussion of the various money market instruments, pay particular attention to the convention used to state returns in the various money markets. For example, Treasury bill rates are stated as discount yields and use a 360-day year. Federal funds and repurchase agreements are stated on a bond equivalent yield basis but use a 360-day year. Commercial paper, negotiable certificates of deposit, and bankers acceptance yields are quoted as discount yields. Differences in the convention used to calculate yields must be considered particularly when comparing returns across various securities.

MONEY MARKET SECURITIES

2

A variety of money market securities are issued by corporations and government units to obtain short-term funds. These securities include Treasury bills, federal funds, repurchase agreements, commercial paper, negotiable certificates of deposit, and banker's acceptances. In this section, we look at the characteristics of each of these. Table 5–2 defines each of the money market securities and Table 5–3 lists the amounts of each outstanding and the interest rate on each of these instruments in 1990 and 2004.

Treasury Bills

Treasury bills
Short-term obligations of the U.S. government issued to cover government budget deficits and to refinance maturing government debt.

www.federalreserve.gov

Treasury bills (T-bills) are short-term obligations of the U.S. government issued to cover current government budget shortfalls (deficits)[3] and to refinance maturing government debt. In 2004 there were $981.9 billion of Treasury bills outstanding. As discussed in Chapter 4, T-bills (and other Treasury securities) are also used by the Federal Reserve as a tool in conducting monetary policy through open market operations. T-bills are sold through an auction process (described below). Original maturities are 13 weeks or 26 weeks, and they are issued in denominations of multiples of $1,000. The minimum allowable denomination for a T-bill bid is $1,000. A typical purchase in the newly issued T-bill market is a round lot of $5 million. However, existing T-bills can be bought and sold

3. The excess of U.S. government expenditures minus revenues.

TABLE 5–1 Various U.S. Money Market Security Rates

Money Rates

Tuesday, November 9, 2004

The key U. S. and foreign annual interest rates below are a guide to general levels but don't always represent actual transactions.

Commercial Paper

Yields paid by corporations for short-term financing, typically for daily operation

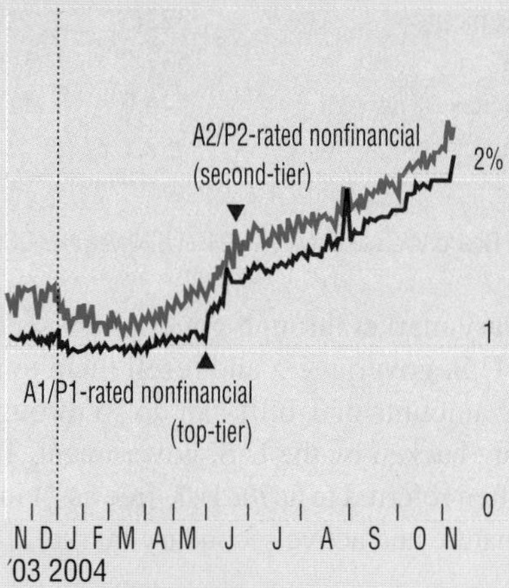

Source: Federal Reserve

Prime Rate: 4.75% (effective 09/22/04). The base rate on corporate loans posted by at least 75% of the nation's 30 largest banks.
Discount Rate (Primary): 2.75% (effective 09/21/04).
Federal Funds: 1.875% high, 1.640% low, 1.750% near closing bid, 1.875% offered. Effective rate: 1.79%. Source: Prebon Yamane (USA) Inc. Federal-funds target rate: 1.750% (effective 09/21/04).
Call Money: 3.50% (effective 09/22/04).
Commercial Paper: Placed directly by General Electric Capital Corp.: 2.02% 30 to 44 days; 2.04% 45 to 59 days; 2.14% 60 to 89 days; 2.20% 90 to 119 days; 2.25% 120 to 149 days; 2.30% 150 to 179 days; 2.37% 180 to 209 days; 2.42% 210 to 239 days; 2.46% 240 to 270 days.
Euro Commercial Paper: Placed directly by General Electric Capital Corp.: 2.05% 30 days; 2.11% two months; 2.12% three months; 2.13% four months; 2.16% five months; 2.18% six months.
Dealer Commercial Paper: High-grade unsecured notes sold through dealers by major corporations: 2.04% 30 days; 2.13% 60 days; 2.21% 90 days.
Certificates of Deposit: 2.05% one month; 2.22% three months; 2.40% six months.
Bankers Acceptances: 2.04% 30 days; 2.16% 60 days; 2.22% 90 days; 2.28% 120 days; 2.36% 150 days; 2.42% 180 days. Source: Prebon Yamane (USA) Inc.
Eurodollars: 2.07% - 2.04% one month; 2.19% - 2.15% two months; 2.25% - 2.21% three months; 2.31% - 2.27% four months; 2.38% - 2.34% five months; 2.44% - 2.40% six months. Source: Prebon Yamane (USA) Inc.
London Interbank Offered Rates (Libor): 2.09125% one month; 2.27375% three months; 2.46375% six months; 2.76625% one year. Effective rate for contracts entered into two days from date appearing at top of this column.
Euro Libor: 2.10013% one month; 2.17000% three months; 2.23738% six months; 2.37750% one year. Effective rate for contracts entered into two days from date appearing at top of this column.
Euro Interbank Offered Rates (Euribor): 2.101% one month; 2.170% three months; 2.239% six months; 2.380% one year. Source: Reuters.
Foreign Prime Rates: Canada 4.25%; European Central Bank 2.00%; Japan 1.375%; Switzerland 2.60%; Britain 4.75%.
Treasury Bills: Results of the Monday, November 8, 2004, auction of short-term U.S. government bills, sold at a discount from face value in units of $1,000 to $1 million: 2.045% 13 weeks; 2.260% 26 weeks. Tuesday, November 9, 2004 auction: 1.900% 4 weeks.
Overnight Repurchase Rate: 1.75%. Source: Garban Intercapital.
Freddie Mac: Posted yields on 30-year mortgage commitments. Delivery within 30 days 5.47%, 60 days 5.52%, standard conventional fixed-rate mortgages: 2.875%, 2% rate capped one-year adjustable rate mortgages.
Fannie Mae: Posted yields on 30 year mortgage commitments (priced at par) for delivery within 30 days 5.52%, 60 days 5.57%, standard conventional fixed-rate mortgages; 3.35%, 6/2 rate capped one-year adjustable rate mortgages. Constant Maturity Debt Index: 2.221% three months; 2.428% six months; 2.672% one year.
Merrill Lynch Ready Assets Trust: 1.20%.
Consumer Price Index: September, 189.9, up 2.5% from a year ago. Bureau of Labor Statistics.

Source: *The Wall Street Journal*, November 10, 2004, p. C12. Reprinted by permission of *The Wall Street Journal*. **www.wsj.com**

TABLE 5–2 Money Market Instruments

Treasury Bills—short-term obligations issued by the U.S. government.

Federal Funds—short-term funds transferred between financial institutions usually for no more than one day.

Repurchase Agreements—agreements involving the sale of securities by one party to another with a promise to repurchase the securities at a specified date and price.

Commercial Paper—short-term unsecured promissory notes issued by a company to raise short-term cash.

Negotiable Certificates of Deposit—bank-issued time deposit that specifies an interest rate and maturity date and is negotiable (saleable on a secondary market).

Banker Acceptances—time drafts payable to a seller of goods, with payment guaranteed by a bank.

TABLE 5–3 Money Market Instruments Outstanding, December 1990 and 2004
(in billions of dollars)

	Amount Outstanding		Rate of Return	
	1990	2004	1990	2004
Treasury bills	$527.0	$981.9	6.68%	2.15%
Federal funds and repurchase agreements	372.3	1,585.1	7.31	1.83
Commercial paper	537.8	1,309.7	8.14	1.89
Negotiable certificates of deposit	546.9	1,379.4	8.13	2.28
Banker's acceptance	52.1	4.4	7.95	2.04

Source: Federal Reserve Board Web site, May 1991 and November 2004, various tables. **www.federalreserve.gov**

in an active secondary market through government securities dealers who purchase Treasury bills from the U.S. government and resell them to investors. Thus, investors wanting to purchase smaller amounts of T-bills can do so through a dealer for a fee.

Because they are backed by the U.S. government, T-bills are virtually default risk free. In fact, T-bills are often referred to as *the* risk-free asset in the United States. Further, because of their short-term nature and active secondary market, T-bills have little liquidity risk.

The New Issue and Secondary Market Trading Process for Treasury Bills. The U.S. Treasury has a formal process by which it sells new issues of Treasury bills through its regular **Treasury bill auctions.** Every week (usually on a Thursday), the amount of new 13-week and 26-week T-bills the Treasury will offer for sale is announced. Bids may be submitted by government securities dealers, financial and nonfinancial corporations, and individuals and must be received by a Federal Reserve Bank (over the Internet (through Treasury Direct), by phone, or by paper form) by the deadline of 1 P.M. on the Monday following the auction announcement. Allocations and prices are announced the following morning (Tuesday) and the T-bills are delivered on the Thursday following the auction.

Treasury bill auctions

The formal process by which the U.S. Treasury sells new issues of Treasury bills.

www.ustreas.gov

Submitted bids can be either competitive bids or noncompetitive bids. As of 1998, all successful bidders (both competitive and noncompetitive) are awarded securities at the same price, which is the price equal to the lowest price of the competitive bids accepted (as will be explained below). Prior to this, Treasury security auctions were discriminatory auctions in that different successful bidders paid different prices (their bid prices). Appendix A to this chapter, located at the book's Web site (**www.mhhe.com/sc3e**), discusses the reasons behind the change and the benefits to the U.S. Treasury from a single price auction.

Competitive bids specify the desired quantity of T-bills and the bid price. The highest bidder receives the first allocation (allotment) of T-bills, and subsequent bids are filled in decreasing order of the bid until all T-bills auctioned that week are distributed. The price paid by all bidders is, then, the lowest price of the accepted competitive bidders. Any competitive bidder can submit more than one bid. However, no bidder can legally receive more than 35 percent of the T-bills involved in any auction. This rule limits the ability of one bidder to "squeeze" the market. Competitive bids are generally used by large investors and government securities dealers, and make up the majority of the auction market. Table 5–4 shows the results of the Treasury auction on November 8, 2004. At this auction, 50.73 and 53.27 percent of the submitted bids were accepted for the 13- and 26-week T-bills, respectively.

Figure 5–1 illustrates the T-bill auction for the 13-week T-bills. The highest accepted bid on the 13-week T-bills was 99.4975 percent of the face value of the T-bills. Bids were filled at prices below the high. The lowest accepted bid price was 99.48875 percent. The median accepted bid price was 99.4925 percent. All bidders who submitted prices *above* 99.48875 percent (categories 1 through 5 in Figure 5–1) were awarded in full (winning bids) at a price of 99.48875 percent. Thus, those who submitted a bid at a price greater than

TABLE 5–4 Treasury Auction Results, November 8, 2004

	13-Week Treasury Bill Auction	26-Week Treasury Bill Auction
Bids tendered (in millions)	$37,959.1	$33,988.5
Bids accepted (in millions)	$19,254.8	$18,104.7
Noncompetitive bids (in millions)	$1,745.3	$895.5
Price	99.48875%	98.86372%
High Price	99.49750%	98.87881%
Low price	99.48875%	98.86372%
Median price	99.49250%	98.86875%

Source: Department of Treasury Web site, Bureau of Public Debt, November 8, 2004. **www.ustreas.gov**

99.48875 percent paid less than their bid price yet received their full allocation of T-bills requested. Bidders who submitted a price below 99.48875 percent (categories 7 and beyond in Figure 5–1) received no allocation of the auctioned T-bills. A portion, but not all, of the bids submitted at 99.48875 were filled (category 6 in Figure 5–1). Bids submitted at 99.48875 were filled on a pro rata (proportional) basis until the supply available was exhausted.

With noncompetitive bids, the bidder indicates the quantity of T-bills he or she wants to buy and agrees to pay the lowest price of the winning competitive bids. Noncompetitive bidders get a preferential allocation—that is, all these bids are met before the remaining T-bills are allocated to the competitive bidders. Notice, from Table 5–4, that 10.06 percent ($1,745.3m./$19,254.8m.) and 4.95 percent ($895.5m./$18,104.7m.), respectively, of the accepted bids at the November 8, 2004, Treasury auction were noncompetitive for 13- and 26-week T-bills. This resulted in a supply of T-bills available to competitive bidders (S_C) that is lower than the total supply (S_T), because of the preferential bidding status of noncompetitive bidders (i.e., noncompetitive bidders always receive a 100 percent allocation of their bids). Noncompetitive bids are limited to $1 million or less and allow small investors to participate in the T-bill auction market without incurring large risks. Small investors who are unfamiliar with money market interest rate movements can use a noncompetitive bid to avoid bidding a price too low to receive any of the T-bills.

The secondary market for T-bills is the largest of any U.S. money market security. At the heart of this market are those securities dealers designated as primary government securities dealers by the Federal Reserve Bank of New York (consisting of 22 financial institutions) who purchase the majority of the T-bills sold competitively at auction and who

www.newyorkfed.org

FIGURE 5–1 Treasury Auction Results

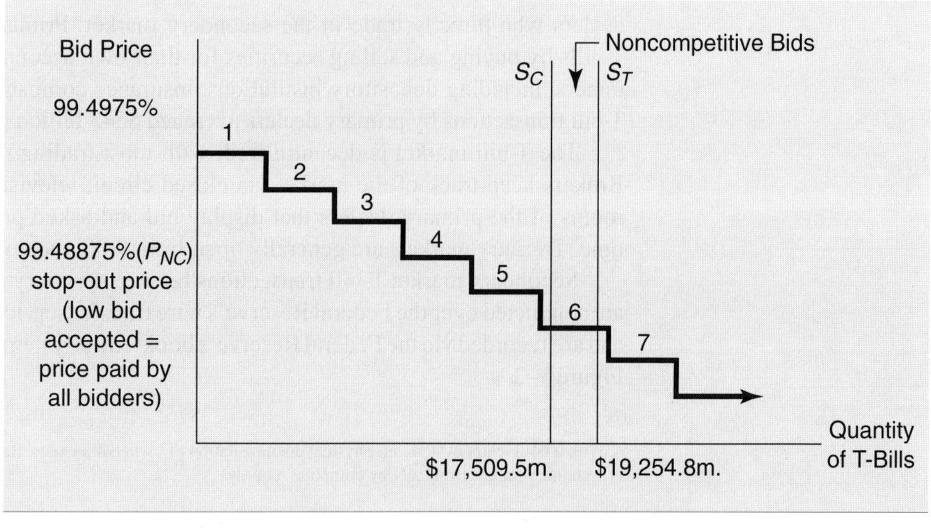

FIGURE 5–2 Secondary Market Treasury Bill Transaction

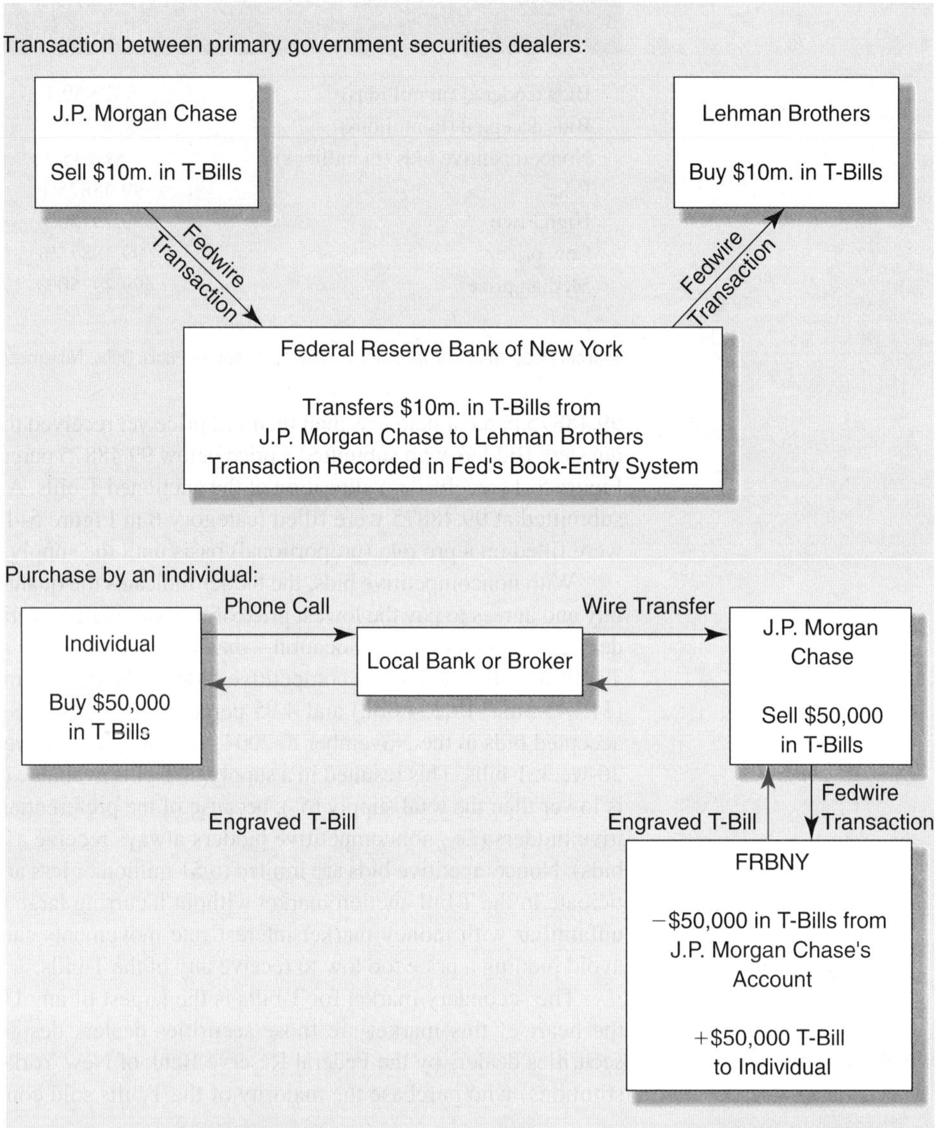

create an active secondary market. In addition, there are many (approximately 500) smaller dealers who directly trade in the secondary market. Primary dealers make a market for T-bills by buying and selling securities for their own account and by trading for their customers, including depository institutions, insurance companies, pension funds, and so on. T-bill transactions by primary dealers averaged $545 billion per day in November 2004.

The T-bill market is decentralized, with most trading transacted over the telephone. Brokers keep track of the market via closed circuit television screens located in trading rooms of the primary dealers that display bid and asked prices available at any point in time. Treasury markets are generally open from 9:00 A.M. to 3:30 P.M. EST.

Secondary market T-bill transactions between primary government securities dealers are conducted over the Federal Reserve's wire transfer service—Fedwire (see Chapter 4)—and are recorded via the Federal Reserve's book-entry system.[4] We illustrate a transaction in Figure 5–2.

4. With a book-entry system, no physical documentation of ownership exists. Rather, ownership of Treasury securities is accounted for electronically by computer records.

SEARCH THE SITE

Go to the Bureau of Public Debt Web site at **www.publicdept.treas.gov** and find the latest information on 13-week and 26-week Treasury bill auctions.

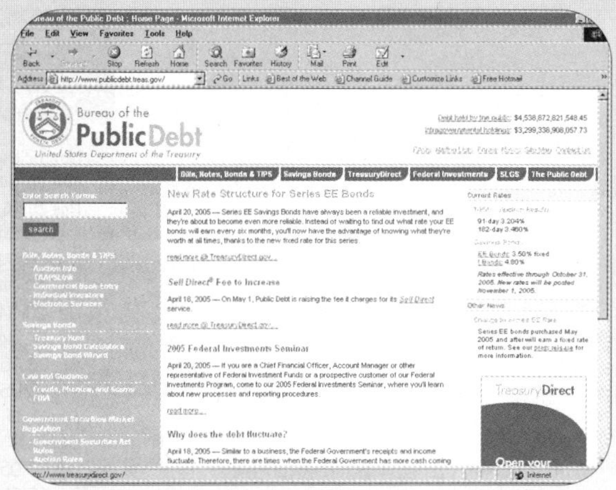

Under "Bills, Notes, Bonds–Tips," click on "Auction Info"

Click on "200X" (most current year)

Click on "Auction Results Press Releases"

Click on "13-week Bill" and then "26-week Bill"

Under the most recent date, click on "*Results*"

This will bring up the relevant tables.

Questions

1. What are the high, low, and median prices on the most recent issues?
2. What is the dollar value of tendered and accepted bids for the most recent issues?
3. What is the dollar value of noncompetitive bids on the most recent issues?

www.newyorkfed.org

For example, if J.P. Morgan Chase wants to sell \$10 million of T-bills to Lehman Brothers, J.P. Morgan Chase would instruct its district Federal Reserve Bank—the Federal Reserve Bank of New York (FRBNY)—to electronically transfer the (book-entry) T-bills, via the Fedwire, from its account to Lehman Brothers (also in the district of the FRBNY). The transaction would be recorded in the Fed's book-entry system with no physical transfer of paper necessary. An individual wanting to purchase \$50,000 of T-bills in the secondary market must contact his or her bank or broker. A bank or broker that is not a primary government securities dealer or a secondary market dealer must contact (via phone, fax, or wire) one of these dealers (e.g., J.P. Morgan Chase) to complete the transaction. The T-bill dealer will instruct its local Federal Reserve Bank to increase (credit) its T-bill account at the Fed. In exchange for the investor's \$50,000, these securities are subsequently recorded in the dealer's book-entry system as an issue held for the investor. T-bill dealers maintain records identifying owners of all Treasury securities held in its account in the book-entry system.

Treasury Bill Yields. As we discussed above, Treasury bills are sold on a discount basis. Rather than directly paying interest on T-bills (the coupon rate is zero), the government issues T-bills at a discount from their par (or face) value. The return comes from the difference between the purchase price paid for the T-bill and the face value received at maturity. Table 5–5 lists T-bill rates as quoted in *The Wall Street Journal* for trading on November 10, 2004. Column 1 in the quote lists the maturity date of the T-bill (note the maximum maturity is less than one year). Column 2 specifies the remaining number of days until each T-bill matures. For example, at the close of trading on November 10, 2004, the T-bill maturing on November 26, 2004, would trade for an additional 16 days. Column 3, labeled BID, is the discount yield (defined below) on the T-bill given the current selling price available to T-bill holders (i.e., the price dealers are willing to pay T-bill holders to purchase their T-bills for them). Column 4, labeled ASKED, is the discount yield based on the current purchase price set by dealers that is available to investors (i.e., potential T-bill buyers). The percentage difference in the ask

TABLE 5–5 Treasury Bill Rates

(1)	(2)	(3)	(4)	(5)	(6)
Treasury Bills					
MATURITY	DAYS TO MAT	BID	ASKED	CHG	ASK YLD
Nov 12 04	2	1.63	1.62	0.04	1.64
Nov 18 04	8	1.82	1.81	0.03	1.84
Nov 26 04	**16**	**1.86**	**1.85**	**0.01**	**1.85**
Dec 02 04	22	1.84	1.83	–	1.86
Dec 09 04	29	1.88	1.87	–	1.90
Dec 16 04	36	1.84	1.83	–	1.86
Dec 23 04	43	1.91	1.90	0.03	1.93
Dec 30 04	50	1.92	1.91	–	1.94
Jan 06 05	57	1.92	1.91	0.02	1.94
Jan 13 05	64	1.94	1.93	–	1.96
Jan 20 05	**71**	**1.94**	**1.93**	**−0.01**	**1.96**
Jan 27 05	78	1.95	1.94	–	1.98
Feb 03 05	85	2.01	2.00	–	2.04
Feb 10 05	92	2.04	2.03	–	2.07
Feb 17 05	99	2.05	2.04	–	2.08
Feb 24 05	106	2.05	2.04	–	2.03
Mar 03 05	113	2.10	2.09	–	2.13
Mar 30 05	120	2.12	2.11	–	2.15
Mar 17 05	127	2.12	2.11	–	2.16
Mar 24 05	134	2.14	2.13	–	2.18
Mar 31 05	141	2.14	2.13	–	2.18
Apr 07 05	148	2.18	2.17	–	2.22
Apr 14 05	**155**	**2.20**	**2.19**	**0.01**	**2.24**
Apr 21 05	162	2.21	2.20	–	2.25
Apr 28 05	169	2.23	2.22	–	2.27
May 05 05	176	2.23	2.22	–	2.28
May 12 05	183	2.25	2.24	−0.01	2.30

Source: *The Wall Street Journal*, November 11, 2004, p. C15. Reprinted by permission of *The Wall Street Journal*. **www.wsj.com**

and bid yields is known as the spread. The spread is essentially the profit the dealers make in return for conducting the trade for investors. It is part of the transaction cost incurred by investors for the trade. Column 5, labeled CHG, is the change in the Asked (discount) yield from the previous day's closing yield. Finally, the last column (column 6), labeled ASK YLD, is the Asked discount yield converted to a bond equivalent yield. As discussed above, the discount yield (*dy*) on a T-bill is calculated as follows:

$$i_{\text{T-bill}}\,(dy) = \frac{P_f - P_0}{P_f} \times \frac{360}{h}$$

EXAMPLE 5–4 Calculating a Treasury Bill Asked Discount Yield

Suppose that you purchase the 155-day T-bill maturing on April 14, 2005, for \$9,905.71. The T-bill has a face value of \$10,000. The T-bill's Asked discount yield is reported as:

$$i_{\text{T-bill}}\,(dy) = \frac{\$10{,}000 - 9{,}905.71}{\$10{,}000} \times \frac{360}{155} = 2.19\%$$

Thus, 2.19 percent is the asked discount yield on this T-bill reported in Table 5–5.

As described above, the discount yield differs from a true rate of return (or bond equivalent yield) for two reasons: (1) the base price used is the face value of the T-bill and not the purchase price of the T-bill, and (2) a 360-day year rather than a 365-day year is used. The bond equivalent yield uses a 365-day year and the purchase price, rather than the face value of the T-bill, as the base price. Thus, the formula for a bond equivalent yield on a T-bill, $i_{\text{T-bill}}\ (bey)$, is:

$$i_{\text{T-bill}}\ (bey) = \frac{P_f - P_0}{P_0} \times \frac{360}{h}$$

For example, the bond equivalent yield (or ASK YLD reported in Table 5–5) in Example 5–4 is calculated as:[5]

$$i_{\text{T-bill}} = \frac{\$10,000 - \$9,905.71}{\$9,905.71} \times \frac{360}{155} = 2.24\%$$

A Treasury bill's price (such as that used in the examples above) can be calculated from the quote reported in the financial press (e.g., *The Wall Street Journal*) by rearranging the yield equations listed above. Specifically, for the asked discount yield, the required market ask price would be:

$$P_0 = P_f - \left[i_{\text{T-bill}}(dy) \times \frac{h}{360} \times P_f\right]$$

and for the bond equivalent yield:

$$P_0 = P_f / \left[1 = \left(i_{\text{T-bill}}(bey) \times \frac{h}{365}\right)\right]$$

EXAMPLE 5-5 Calculation of Treasury Bill Price from a *Wall Street Journal* Quote

From Table 5–5, the asked (or discount) yield on the T-bill maturing on January 20, 2005, (or 71 days from November 10, 2004), is 1.93 percent. The T-bill price for these T-bills is calculated as:

$$P_0 = \$10,000 - \left[.0193 \times \frac{71}{360} \times \$10,000\right] = \$9,961.94$$

or using the ASK YLD (or the bond equivalent yield) on the T-bill, 1.96 percent:

$$P_0 = \$10,000 / \left[1 + \left(.0196 \times \frac{71}{365}\right)\right] = \$9,962.02$$

Federal Funds

federal funds

Short-term funds transferred between financial institutions, usually for a period of one day.

Federal funds (fed funds) are short-term funds transferred between financial institutions, usually for a period of one day. For example, commercial banks trade fed funds in the form of excess reserves held at their local Federal Reserve Bank. That is, one commercial bank may be short of reserves, requiring it to borrow excess reserves from another bank that has a surplus. The institution that borrows fed funds incurs a liability on its balance sheet, "federal funds purchased," while the institution that lends the fed funds records an asset, "federal

5. Remember, from above, that the effective annual return (over a 12-month investment period) on this T-bill is:

$$(1 + .0224/(365/155))^{365/155} - 1 = 2.25\%$$

federal funds rate

The interest rate for borrowing fed funds.

funds sold." The overnight (or one day) interest rate for borrowing fed funds is the **federal funds rate.** The fed funds rate is a function of the supply and demand for federal funds among financial institutions and the effects of the Federal Reserve's trading through the FOMC (as discussed in Chapter 4).

Federal Funds Yields. Federal funds (fed funds) are single-payment loans—they pay interest only once, at maturity. Further, fed funds transactions take the form of short-term (mostly overnight) *unsecured* loans. Quoted interest rates on fed funds, i_{ff}, assume a 360-day year. Therefore, to compare interest rates on fed funds with other securities such as Treasury bills, the quoted fed funds interest rate must be converted into a bond equivalent rate or yield, i_{bey}.

EXAMPLE 5-6 Conversion of Federal Funds Rate of Interest to a Bond Equivalent Rate

From Table 5–1, the overnight fed funds rate on November 9, 2004, was 1.875 percent. The conversion of the fed funds rate to a bond equivalent rate is calculated as follows:

$$i_{bey} = i_{ff}(365/360)$$
$$= 1.875\%\ (365/360) = 1.901\%$$

In addition to being the cost of unsecured, overnight, interbank borrowing, the federal funds rate is of particular importance because, as was discussed in Chapter 4, it is a focus or target rate in the conduct of monetary policy.

Trading in the Federal Funds Market. The fed funds market is a highly liquid and flexible source of funding for commercial banks and savings banks. Commercial banks, especially the largest commercial banks, conduct the vast majority of transactions in the fed funds market. Fed funds transactions are created by banks borrowing and lending excess reserves held at their Federal Reserve Bank (see Chapter 4), using Fedwire, the Federal Reserve's wire transfer network, to complete the transaction. Banks with excess reserves lend fed funds, while banks with deficient reserves borrow fed funds.

Federal funds transactions can be initiated by either the lending or the borrowing bank, with negotiations between any pair of commercial banks taking place directly over the telephone. Alternatively, trades can be arranged through fed funds brokers (such as Garban Ltd. and RMJ Securities Corp), who charge a small fee for bringing the two parties to the fed funds transaction together.[6]

correspondent banks

Banks with reciprocal accounts and agreements.

Figure 5–3 illustrates a fed funds transaction. For example, a bank that finds itself with $75 million in excess reserves (e.g., J.P. Morgan Chase) can call its **correspondent banks** (banks with which it has reciprocal accounts and agreements)[7] to see if they need overnight reserves. The bank will then sell its excess reserves to those correspondent banks that offer the highest rates for these fed funds (e.g., Bank of America). When a transaction is agreed upon, the lending bank (J.P. Morgan Chase) instructs its district Federal Reserve Bank (e.g., the FRBNY) to transfer the $75 million in excess reserves to the borrowing bank's (Bank of America) reserve account at its Federal Reserve Bank (e.g., the Federal Reserve Bank of San Francisco). The Federal Reserve System's wire transfer network, Fedwire, is used to complete the transfer of funds. The next day, the funds are transferred back, via Fedwire, from the borrowing bank to the lending bank's

6. Brokerage fees are often as low as 50 cents per $1 million transacted.

7. Correspondent bank relations are discussed in more detail in Chapter 12.

FIGURE 5–3 Federal Funds Transaction

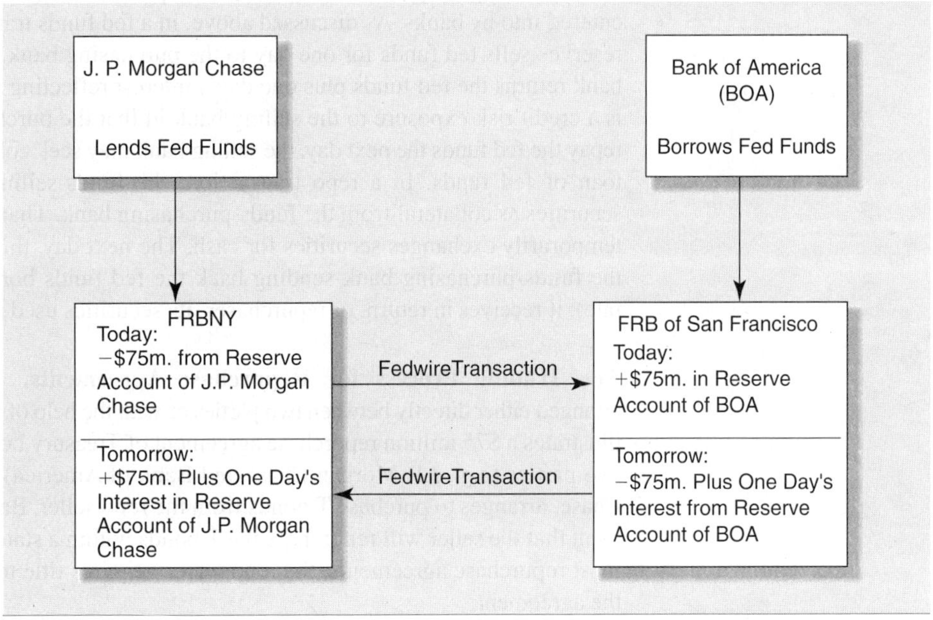

reserve account at the Federal Reserve Bank plus one day's interest.[8] Overnight fed funds loans will likely be based on an oral agreement between the two parties and are generally unsecured loans.

Repurchase Agreements

repurchase agreement

An agreement involving the sale of securities by one party to another with a promise to repurchase the securities at a specified price and on a specified date.

reverse repurchase agreement

An agreement involving the purchase of securities by one party from another with the promise to sell them back.

A **repurchase agreement** (repo or RP) is an agreement involving the sale of securities by one party to another with a promise to repurchase the securities at a specified price and on a specified date in the future. Thus, a repurchase agreement is essentially a collateralized fed funds loan, with the collateral backing taking the form of securities. The securities used most often in repos are U.S. Treasury securities (e.g., T-bills) and government agency securities (e.g., Fannie Mae). A **reverse repurchase agreement** (reverse repo) is an agreement involving the purchase (buying) of securities by one party from another with the promise to sell them back at a given date in the future.

Because the parties in every repurchase agreement transaction have opposite perspectives, the titles repo and reverse repo can be applied to the same transaction. That is, a given transaction is a repo from the point of view of the securities' seller and a reverse repo from the point of view of the securities' buyer. Whether a transaction is termed a *repo* or a *reverse repo* generally depends on which party initiated the transaction. Most repos have very short terms to maturity (generally from 1 to 14 days), but there is a growing market for longer-term 1- to 3-month repos. Repos with a maturity of less than one week generally involve denominations of $25 million or more. Longer-term repos are more often in denominations of $10 million.

Many commercial firms, with idle funds in their deposit accounts at banks, use repos as a way to earn a small return until these funds are needed. In this case the firm uses its

8. Increasingly, participants in the fed funds markets do not hold balances at the Federal Reserve (e.g., commercial banks that do not belong to the Federal Reserve System). In this case, the fed funds transaction is settled in immediately available funds—fed funds on deposit at the lending bank that may be transferred or withdrawn with no delay. A federal funds broker, typically a commercial bank, matches up institutions using a telecommunications network that links federal funds brokers with participating institutions. Upon maturity of the fed funds loan, the borrowing bank's fed funds demand deposit account at the lending bank is debited for the total value of the loan and the borrowing bank pays the lending bank an interest payment for the use of the fed funds. Most of these fed funds transactions are for more than $5 million (they averaged around $45 million in the early 2000s) and usually have a one- to seven-day maturity.

idle funds to buy T-bills from its bank. The bank then agrees to repurchase the T-bills in the future at a higher price. However, most repos are collateralized fed funds transactions entered into by banks. As discussed above, in a fed funds transaction, the bank with excess reserves sells fed funds for one day to the purchasing bank. The next day, the purchasing bank returns the fed funds plus one day's interest reflecting the fed funds rate. Since there is a credit risk exposure to the selling bank in that the purchasing bank may be unable to repay the fed funds the next day, the selling bank may seek collateral backing for the one-day loan of fed funds. In a repo transaction, the funds-selling bank receives government securities as collateral from the funds-purchasing bank. That is, the funds-purchasing bank temporarily exchanges securities for cash. The next day, this transaction is reversed, with the funds-purchasing bank sending back the fed funds borrowed plus interest (the repo rate); it receives in return, or repurchases, its securities used as collateral in the transaction.

The Trading Process for Repurchase Agreements. Repurchase agreements are arranged either directly between two parties or with the help of brokers and dealers. Figure 5–4 illustrates a $75 million repurchase agreement of Treasury bonds arranged directly between two parties (e.g., J.P. Morgan Chase and Bank of America). The repo buyer, J.P. Morgan Chase, arranges to purchase T-bonds from the repo seller, Bank of America, with an agreement that the seller will repurchase the T-bonds within a stated period of time—one day. In most repurchase agreements, the repo buyer acquires title to the securities for the term of the agreement.

Once the transaction is agreed upon, the repo buyer, J.P. Morgan Chase, instructs its district Federal Reserve Bank (the FRBNY) to transfer $75 million in excess reserves, via Fedwire, to the repo seller's reserve account. The repo seller, Bank of America, instructs its district Federal Reserve Bank (the FRB of San Francisco) to transfer $75 million from its T-bond account via securities Fedwire to the repo buyer's T-bond account. Upon maturity of the repo (one day in this example), these transactions are reversed. In addition, the repo

FIGURE 5–4 A Repurchase Agreement Transaction

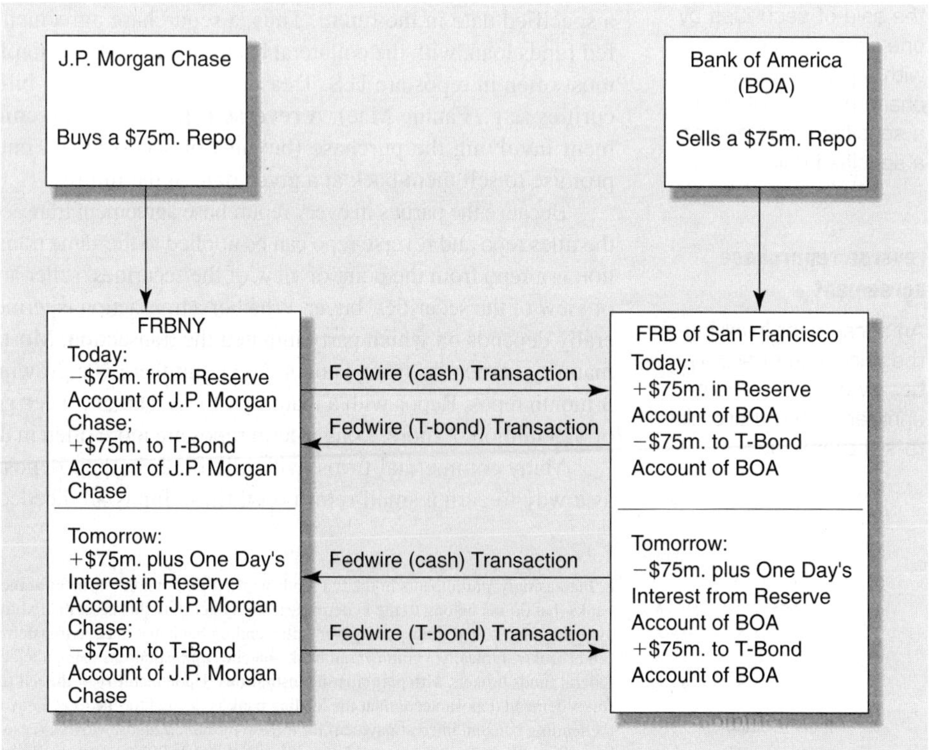

seller transfers additional funds (representing one day's interest) from its reserve account to the reserve account of the repo buyer.

As noted in Chapter 4, repurchase agreements are used by the Federal Reserve to help it conduct open market operations as part of its overall monetary policy strategy. When monetary adjustments are intended to be temporary (such as smoothing out fluctuations in interest rates or the money supply), the Fed uses repurchase agreements with dealers or banks. The maturities of the repos used by the Federal Reserve are rarely longer than 15 days. Government securities dealers—such as the largest investment and commercial banks—engage in repos to manage their liquidity and to take advantage of anticipated changes in interest rates.

Repurchase Agreement Yields. Because Treasury securities back repurchase agreements, they are low credit risk investments and have lower interest rates than uncollateralized fed funds.[9] The spread between the rate on collateralized repos versus uncollateralized fed funds has usually been in the order of 0.25 percent, or 25 basis points. The yield on repurchase agreements is calculated as the annualized percentage difference between the initial selling price of the securities and the contracted (re)purchase price (the selling price plus interest paid on the repurchase agreement), using a 360-day year. Specifically:

$$i_{RA} = \frac{P_f - P_0}{P_0} \times \frac{360}{h}$$

where

P_f = Repurchase price of the securities (equals the selling price plus interest paid on the repurchase agreement)
P_0 = Selling price of the securities
h = Number of days until the repo matures

EXAMPLE 5-7 Calculation of a Yield on a Repurchase Agreement

Suppose a bank enters a reverse repurchase agreement in which it agrees to buy Treasury securities from one of its correspondent banks at a price of \$10,000,000, with the promise to sell these securities back at a price of \$10,002,986 (\$10,000,000 plus interest of \$2,986) after five days. The yield on this repo to the bank is calculated as follows:

$$i_{RA} = \frac{\$10{,}002{,}986 - \$10{,}000{,}000}{\$10{,}000{,}000} \times \frac{360}{5} = 2.15\%$$

Because of their common use as a source of overnight funding and the fact that repos are essentially collateralized fed funds, the Federal Reserve generally classifies federal funds and repurchase agreements together in its statistical data. Together, these amounted to \$1,585.1 billion outstanding in 2004 (see Table 5–3).

Some notable differences exist, however, between repurchase agreements and fed funds. For example, repurchase agreements are less liquid than fed funds since they can only be arranged after an agreed upon type of collateral is posted (i.e., repos are hard to arrange at the close of the banking day, whereas fed funds can be arranged at very short notice, even a few minutes). Further, nonbanks are more frequent users of repurchase agreements.

9. There is a one-day interest rate risk that may impact credit risk if interest rates suddenly rise so that the market value of the collateral backing the repo falls. To avoid the risk many repo transactions require a securities "haircut" to be imposed at the time of the transaction—more securities are used to back the cash part of the transaction. For example, Bank A may send \$100 million in cash to Bank B. In turn, Bank B sends \$105 million in securities as collateral to back the cash loan from A.

FIGURE 5–5 Commercial Paper and Prime Rate, 1973–2004

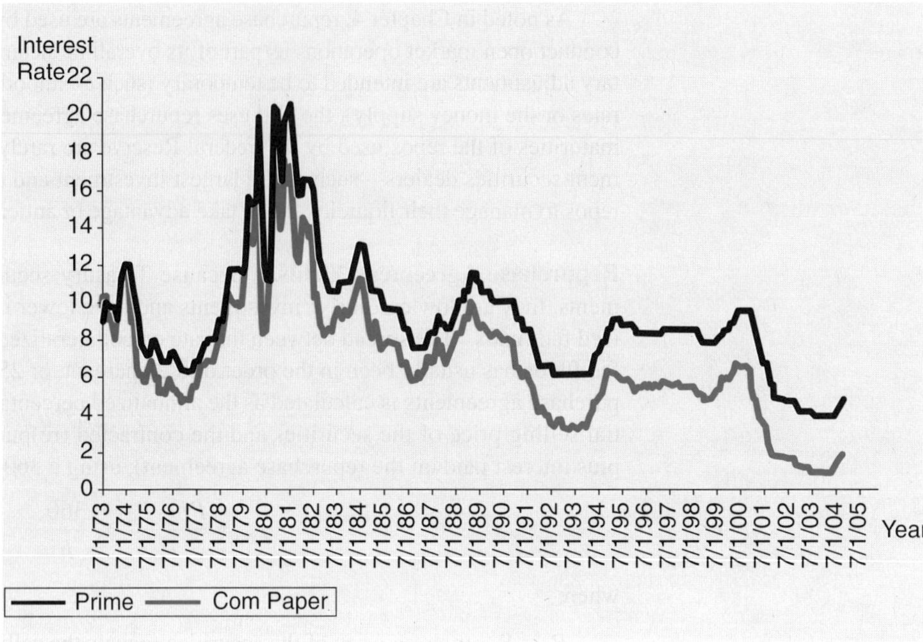

Source: Federal Reserve Board Web site, "Selected Interest Rates," November 2004. **www.federalreserve.gov**

Commercial Paper

commercial paper

An unsecured short-term promissory note issued by a company to raise short-term cash, often to finance working capital requirements.

Commercial paper is an unsecured short-term promissory note issued by a corporation to raise short-term cash, often to finance working capital requirements. Commercial paper is the largest (in terms of dollar value outstanding) of the money market instruments, with \$1,309.7 billion outstanding as of 2004. One reason for such large amounts of commercial paper outstanding is that companies with strong credit ratings can generally borrow money at a lower interest rate by issuing commercial paper than by directly borrowing (via loans) from banks. Indeed, although business loans were the major asset on bank balance sheets between 1965 and 1990, they have dropped in importance since 1990. This trend reflects the growth of the commercial paper market. Figure 5–5 illustrates the difference between commercial paper rates and the prime rate for borrowing from banks from 1973 through November 2004.[10] Notice that in the late 1990s, as the U.S. economy thrived and default risk on the highest quality borrowers decreased, the spread between the prime rate and commercial paper rate increased.

www.sec.gov

Commercial paper is generally sold in denominations of \$100,000, \$250,000, \$500,000, and \$1 million. Maturities generally range from 1 to 270 days—the most common maturities are between 20 and 45 days. This 270-day maximum is due to a Securities and Exchange Commission (SEC) rule that securities with a maturity of more than 270 days must go through the time-consuming and costly registration process to become a public debt offering (i.e., a corporate bond). Commercial paper can be sold directly by the issuers to a buyer such as a mutual fund (a direct placement) or can be sold indirectly by dealers in the commercial paper market. The dollar value (in thousands of dollars) of each method of issue from 1991 through November 2004, is reported in Figure 5–6.

10. It should be noted, however, that the best borrowers from banks can borrow below prime. Prime rate in today's banking world is viewed as a rate to be charged to an average borrower—best borrowers pay prime rate minus some spread.

FIGURE 5–6 Direct versus Dealer Placements of Commercial Paper

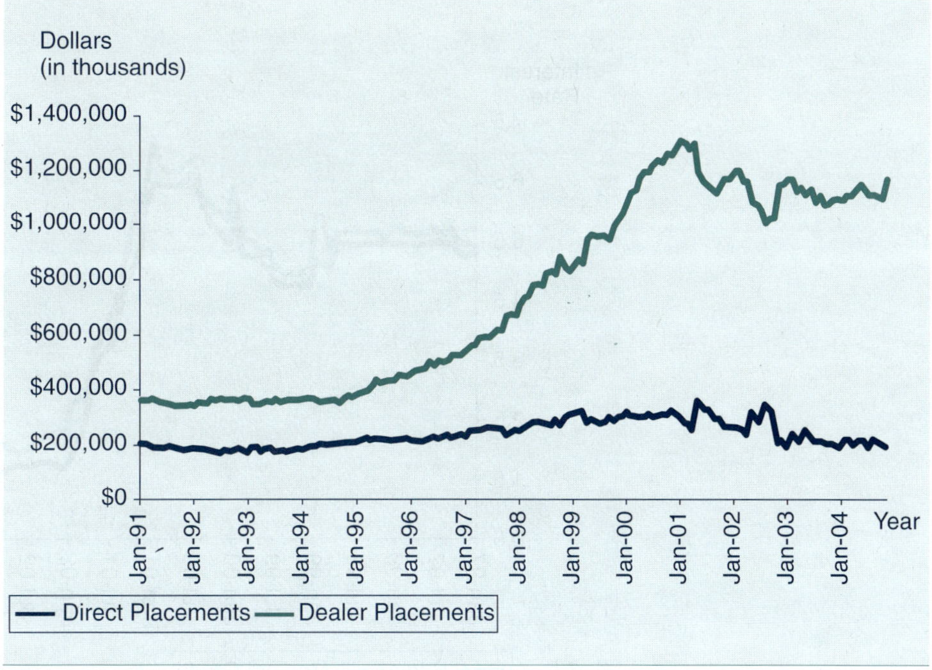

Source: Federal Reserve Board Web site, "Research and Data," November 2004. **www.federalreserve.gov**

Commercial paper is generally held by investors from the time of issue until maturity. Thus, there is no active secondary market for commercial paper.[11] Because commercial paper is not actively traded and because it is also unsecured debt, the credit rating of the issuing company is of particular importance in determining the marketability of a commercial paper issue. Credit ratings provide potential investors with information regarding the ability of the issuing firm to repay the borrowed funds, as promised, and to compare the commercial paper issues of different companies. Several credit rating firms rate commercial paper issues (e.g., Standard & Poor's, Moody's, and Fitch IBCA, Inc.). Standard & Poor's rates commercial paper from A-1 for highest quality issues to D for lowest quality issues, while Moody's rates commercial paper from P-1 for highest quality issues to "not rated" for lowest quality issues. Virtually all companies that issue commercial paper obtain ratings from at least one rating services company, and most obtain two rating evaluations.

www.standardandpoors.com

www.moodys.com

In the early 2000s, the slowdown in the U.S. economy resulted in ratings downgrades for some of the largest commercial paper issuers. For example, the downgrade of General Motors and Ford from a tier-one to tier-two commercial paper issuer had a huge impact on the commercial paper markets. Tyco International, another major commercial paper issuer, fell from a tier-one to a tier-three issuer, a level for which there is virtually no demand. The result is that these commercial paper issuers were forced to give up the cost advantage of commercial paper and to move to the long-term debt markets to ensure they have access to cash. Thus, while still the largest money market instrument outstanding, the decrease in the number of eligible commercial paper issuers in the early 2000s resulted in a decrease in the size of the commercial paper market for the first time in 40 years.[12] This decrease can be seen in Figure 5–6.

The better the credit rating on a commercial paper issue, the lower the interest rate on the issue. The spread between the interest rate on medium grade commercial paper and prime grade commercial paper is shown in Figure 5–7. During the 1990s, the spread was generally

11. This is partly because any dealer that issues (underwrites) commercial paper of a given company will generally buy back that commercial paper should a buyer wish to sell it. Thus, in general, underwriters act as counterparties in any secondary market trade.

12. See "Falling Short," *The Economist,* March 30, 2002, pp. 65–66.

FIGURE 5–7 Rates on Prime versus Medium Grade Commercial Paper, 1997–2004

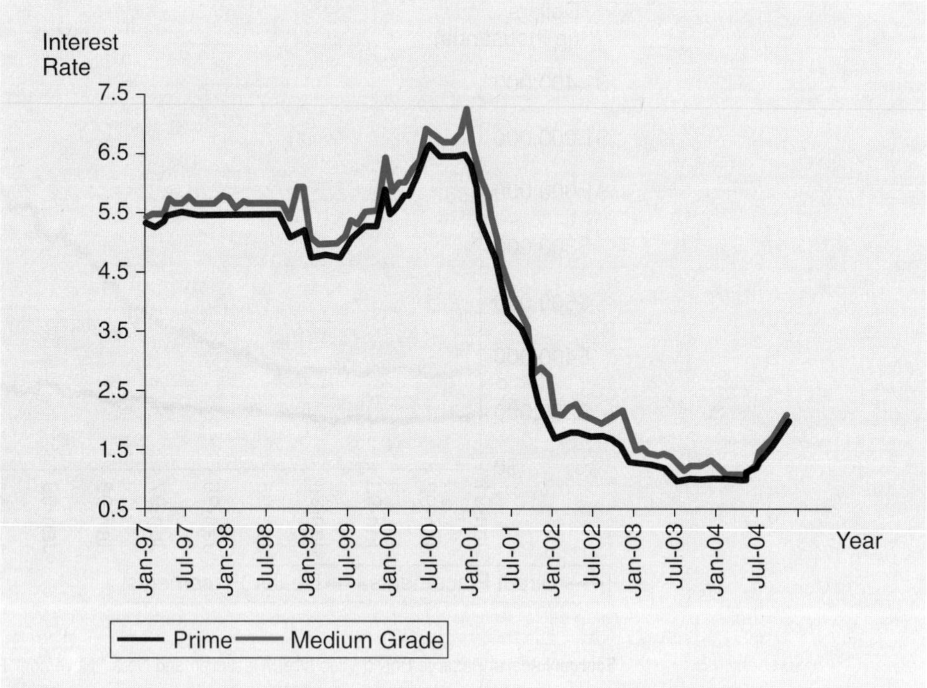

Source: Federal Reserve Board Web site, "Research and Data," November 2004. **www.federalreserve.gov**

on the order of 0.22 percent (22 basis points) per year. From June 2001 through June 2003, as the economy slowed, the spread increased to an average of 0.38 percent per year.

Commercial paper issuers with lower than prime credit ratings often back their commercial paper issues with a line of credit obtained from a commercial bank. In these cases, the bank agrees to make the promised payment on the commercial paper if the issuer cannot pay off the debt on maturity. Thus, a letter of credit backing commercial paper effectively substitutes the credit rating of the issuer with the credit rating of the bank. This reduces the risk to the purchasers of the paper and results in a lower interest rate (and high credit rating) on the commercial paper. In other cases, an issuer arranges a line of credit with a bank (a loan commitment) and draws on this line if it has insufficient funds to meet the repayment of the commercial paper issue at maturity. As commercial paper issuers' credit ratings fell with the downturn in the economy in the early 2000s, however, banks found these previously low-risk standby letters of credit to be less attractive. Banks tended to provide these letters of credit only if the customer also promised to use the bank for other, more lucrative business opportunities (e.g., loans).

The Trading Process for Commercial Paper. Commercial paper is sold to investors either directly (about 15 percent of all issues in 2004—see Figure 5–6), using the issuer's own sales force (e.g., GMAC), or indirectly through brokers and dealers (about 85 percent of all issues in 2004), such as major bank subsidiaries that specialize in investment banking activities (so-called Section 20 subsidiaries) and investment banks underwriting the issues.[13] Commercial paper underwritten and issued through brokers and dealers is more expensive to the issuer, usually increasing the cost of the issue by one-tenth to one-eighth of a percent, reflecting an underwriting cost. In return, the dealer guarantees, through a firm commitment underwriting, the sale of the whole issue. To help achieve this goal, the dealer contacts prospective buyers of the commercial paper, determines the appropriate discount rate on the

13. Commercial bank subsidiaries have been allowed to underwrite commercial paper only since 1987.

commercial paper, and relays any special requests for the commercial paper in terms of specific quantities and maturities to the issuer. When a company issues commercial paper through a dealer, a request made at the beginning of the day by a potential investor (such as a money market mutual fund) for a particular maturity is often completed by the end of the day.

When commercial paper is issued directly from an issuer to a buyer, the company saves the cost of the dealer (and the underwriting services) but must find appropriate investors and determine the discount rate on the paper that will place the complete issue. When the firm decides how much commercial paper it wants to issue, it posts offering rates to potential buyers based on its own estimates of investor demand. The firm then monitors the flow of money during the day and adjusts its commercial paper rates depending on investor demand.

Commercial Paper Yields. Like Treasury bills, yields on commercial paper are quoted on a discount basis—the discount return to commercial paper holders is the annualized percentage difference between the price paid for the paper and the par value using a 360-day year. Specifically:

$$i_{cp}(dy) = \frac{P_f - P_0}{P_f} \times \frac{360}{h}$$

and when converted to a bond equivalent yield:

$$i_{cp}(bey) = \frac{P_f - P_0}{P_0} \times \frac{365}{h}$$

EXAMPLE 5-8 Calculation of the Yield on Commercial Paper

Suppose an investor purchases 95-day commercial paper with a par value of \$1,000,000 for a price of \$994,854. The discount yield (*dy*) on the commercial paper is calculated as:

$$i_{cp}(dy) = \frac{\$1{,}000{,}000 - \$994{,}854}{\$1{,}000{,}000} \times \frac{360}{95} = 1.95\%$$

and the bond equivalent yield (*bey*) is:

$$i_{cp}(bey) = \frac{\$10{,}000{,}000 - \$994{,}854}{994{,}854} \times \frac{365}{95} = 1.99\%$$

Negotiable Certificates of Deposits

negotiable certificate of deposit

A bank-issued, fixed maturity, interest-bearing time deposit that specifies an interest rate and maturity date and is negotiable.

bearer instrument

An instrument in which the holder at maturity receives the principal and interest.

A **negotiable certificate of deposit** (CD) is a bank-issued time deposit that specifies an interest rate and maturity date and is negotiable (i.e., salable) in the secondary market. As of December 2004, there were \$1,379.4 billion of negotiable CDs outstanding. A negotiable CD is a **bearer instrument**—whoever holds the CD when it matures receives the principal and interest. A negotiable CD can be traded any number of times in secondary markets; therefore, the original buyer is not necessarily the owner at maturity.[14] Negotiable CDs have denominations that range from \$100,000 to \$10 million; \$1 million is the most common denomination. The large denominations make negotiable CDs too large for most individuals to buy. However, negotiable CDs are often purchased by money market mutual funds (see Chapter 17), which pool funds of individual investors and allow this group to indirectly purchase negotiable CDs. Negotiable CD maturities range from two weeks to one year, with most having a maturity of one to four months.

14. By contrast, retail CDs with face values under \$100,000 are not traded. Thus, a negotiable CD is more "liquid" to an investor than a retail CD or time deposit.

While CDs have been used by banks since the early 1900s, they were not issued in a negotiable form until the early 1960s. Because of rising interest rates in the 1950s and significant interest rate penalties charged on the early withdrawal of funds invested in CDs, large CDs became unattractive to deposit holders. The result was a significant drop in deposits at banks (disintermediation). In 1961, First National City Bank of New York (now known as Citigroup) issued the first negotiable CD, and money market dealers agreed to make a secondary market in them. These negotiable CDs were well received and helped banks regain many of their lost deposits. Indeed, the success of negotiable CDs helped bank managers focus more actively on managing the liability side of their portfolios (see Chapter 21).

The Trading Process for Negotiable Certificates of Deposit. Banks issuing negotiable CDs post a daily set of rates for the most popular maturities of their negotiable CDs, normally 1, 2, 3, 6, and 12 months. Then, subject to its funding needs, the bank tries to sell as many CDs to investors who are likely to hold them as investments rather than sell them to the secondary market.

In some cases, the bank and the CD investor directly negotiate a rate, the maturity, and the size of the CD. Once this is done, the issuing bank delivers the CD to a custodian bank specified by the investor. The custodian bank verifies the CD, debits the amount to the investor's account, and credits the amount to the issuing bank. This is done through the Fedwire system by transferring fed funds from the custodian bank's reserve account at the Fed to the issuing bank's reserve account.

The secondary market for negotiable CDs allows investors to buy existing negotiable CDs rather than new issues. While it is not a very active market, the secondary market for negotiable CDs is made up of a linked network of approximately 15 brokers and dealers using telephones to transact. The secondary market is predominantly located in New York City, along with most of the brokers and dealers.

The mechanics of the secondary market are similar to those of the primary market for negotiable CDs. Certificates are physically transported between traders or their custodian banks. The custodian bank verifies the certificate and records the deposit in the investor's account. Most transactions executed in the morning are usually settled the same day; most transactions executed later in the day are settled the next business day.

Negotiable CD Yields. Negotiable CD rates are negotiated between the bank and the CD buyer. Large, well-known banks can offer CDs at slightly lower rates than smaller, less well-known banks. This is due partly to the lower perceived default risk and greater marketability of well-known banks and partly to the belief that larger banks are often "too big to fail"—regulators will bail out troubled large banks and protect large depositors beyond the explicit ($100,000) deposit cap under the current FDIC insurance program (see Chapter 13). Interest rates on negotiable CDs are generally quoted on an interest-bearing basis using a 360-day year. CDs with a maturity of more than one year generally pay interest semiannually.

EXAMPLE 5-9 Calculation of the Secondary Market Value of a Negotiable CD

A bank has issued a 6-month, $1 million negotiable CD with a 4.1 percent annual interest rate. Thus, the CD holder will receive:

$$FV = \$1\text{m.}(1 + .041/2) = \$1{,}020{,}500$$

in six months in exchange for $1 million deposited in the bank today.

Immediately after the CD is issued, the market rate on the $1 million CD rises to 4.6 percent. As a result, the secondary market price of the $1 million face value CD decreases as follows:

$$PV = 1{,}020{,}500/(1 + .046/2) = \$997{,}556$$

Banker's Acceptances

banker's acceptance

A time draft payable to a seller of goods, with payment guaranteed by a bank.

A **banker's acceptance** is a time draft payable to a seller of goods, with payment guaranteed by a bank. There were $4.4 billion banker's acceptances outstanding in 2004. Time drafts issued by a bank are orders for the bank to pay a specified amount of money to the bearer of the time draft on a given date.

The Trading Process for Banker's Acceptances. Many banker's acceptances arise from international trade transactions and the underlying letters of credit (or time drafts) that are used to finance trade in goods that have yet to be shipped from a foreign exporter (seller) to a domestic importer (buyer). Foreign exporters often prefer that banks act as guarantors for payment before sending goods to domestic importers, particularly when the foreign supplier has not previously done business with the domestic importer on a regular basis. In the United States, a majority of all acceptances are originated in New York, Chicago, and San Francisco. The U.S. bank insures the international transaction by stamping "Accepted" on a time draft written against the letter of credit between the exporter and the importer, signifying its obligation to pay the foreign exporter (or its bank) on a specified date should the importer fail to pay for the goods. Foreign exporters can then hold the banker's acceptance (the accepted time draft written against the letter of credit) until the date specified on the letter of credit. If they have an immediate need for cash, they can sell the acceptance before that date at a discount from the face value to a buyer in the money market (e.g., a bank). In this case, the ultimate bearer will receive the face value of the banker's acceptance on maturity. We describe this process in more detail in Appendix B to this chapter located at the book's Web site (**www.mhhe.com/sc3e**).

Because banker's acceptances are payable to the bearer at maturity, they can and are traded in secondary markets. Maturities on banker's acceptances traded in secondary markets range from 30 to 270 days. Denominations of banker's acceptances are determined by the size of the original transaction (between the domestic importer and the foreign exporter). Once in the secondary markets, however, banker's acceptances are often bundled and traded in round lots, mainly of $100,000 and $500,000.

Only the largest U.S. banks are active in the banker's acceptance market. Because the risk of default is very low (essentially an investor is buying a security that is fully backed by commercial bank guarantees), interest rates on banker's acceptances are low. Specifically, there is a form of double protection underlying banker's acceptances that reduces their default risk. Since both the importer and the importer's bank must default on the transaction before the investor is subject to risk, the investor is also protected by the value of the goods imported to which he or she now has a debtor's claim—the goods underlying the transaction can be viewed as collateral. Like T-bills and commercial paper, banker's acceptances are sold on a discounted basis.

DO YOU UNDERSTAND?

1. How Treasury bills are first issued?
2. What federal funds are?
3. What the two types of federal funds transactions are? Describe each.
4. What security is mainly used in repurchase agreements?
5. Why the negotiable CD market was created?
6. What the process is by which a banker's acceptance is created?

Comparison of Money Market Securities

Having reviewed the different money market securities, it should be obvious that the different securities have a number of characteristics in common: large denominations, low default risk, and short maturities. It should also be noted that these securities are quite different in terms of their liquidity. For example, Treasury bills have an extensive secondary market. Thus, these money market securities can be converted into cash quickly and with little loss in value. Commercial paper, on the other hand, has no organized secondary market. These cannot be converted into cash quickly unless resold to the original dealer/underwriter, and conversion may involve a relatively higher cost. Federal funds also have no secondary market trading, since they are typically overnight loan transactions and are not intended as investments to be held beyond very short horizons (thus, the lack of a secondary market is inconsequential). Indeed, longer-horizon holders simply roll over their holdings or, in the case of those in need of liquidity, simply do not renew their fed funds loans. Bank negotiable CDs can also be traded on secondary markets, but in recent years trading has been relatively inactive, as most negotiable

CDs are being bought by "buy and hold" oriented money market mutual funds, as are banker's acceptances.

MONEY MARKET PARTICIPANTS

The major money market participants are the U.S. Treasury, the Federal Reserve, commercial banks, money market brokers and dealers, corporations, and other financial institutions such as mutual funds. Table 5–6 summarizes the role (issuer or investor) each of these participants plays in the markets for the various money market securities.

The U.S. Treasury

www.ustreas.gov

The U.S. Treasury raises significant amounts of funds in the money market when it issues T-bills. T-bills are the most actively traded of the money market securities. T-bills allow the U.S. government to raise money to meet unavoidable short-term expenditure needs prior to the receipt of tax revenues. Tax receipts are generally concentrated around quarterly dates, but government expenditures are more evenly distributed over the year.

The Federal Reserve

www.federalreserve.gov

The Federal Reserve is a key (arguably the most important) participant in the money markets. The Federal Reserve holds T-bills (as well as T-notes and T-bonds) to conduct open market transactions—purchasing T-bills when it wants to increase the money supply, and selling T-bills when it wants to decrease the money supply. The Federal Reserve often uses

TABLE 5–6 Money Market Participants

Instrument	Principal Issuer	Principal Investor
Treasury bills	U.S. Treasury	Federal Reserve System Commercial banks Mutual funds Brokers and dealers Other financial institutions Corporations
Federal funds	Commercial banks	Commercial banks
Repurchase agreement	Federal Reserve System Commercial banks Brokers and dealers Other financial institutions	Federal Reserve System Commercial banks Mutual funds Brokers and dealers Other financial institutions Corporations
Commercial paper	Commercial banks Other financial institutions Corporations	Brokers and dealers Mutual funds Corporations Other financial institutions
Negotiable CDs	Commercial banks	Brokers and dealers Mutual funds Corporations Other financial institutions
Banker's acceptances	Commercial banks	Commercial banks Brokers and dealers Corporations

repurchase agreements and reverse repos to temporarily smooth interest rates and the money supply. Moreover, the Fed targets the federal funds rate as part of its overall monetary policy strategy, which can in turn affect other money market rates. Finally, the Fed operates the discount window, which it can use to influence the supply of bank reserves to commercial banks and ultimately the demand for and supply of fed funds and repos.

Commercial Banks

Commercial banks are the most diverse group of participants in the money markets. As Table 5–6 shows, banks participate as issuers and/or investors of almost all money market instruments discussed above. For example, banks are the major issuers of negotiable CDs, banker's acceptances, federal funds, and repurchase agreements.

The importance of banks in the money markets is driven in part by their need to meet reserve requirements imposed by regulation. For example, during periods of economic expansion, heavy loan demand can produce reserve deficiencies for banks (i.e., their actual reserve holdings are pushed below the minimums required by regulation). Additional reserves can be obtained by borrowing fed funds from other banks, engaging in a repurchase agreement, selling negotiable CDs, or selling commercial paper.[15] Conversely, during contractionary periods, many banks have excess reserves that they can use to purchase Treasury securities, trade fed funds, engage in a reverse repo, and so on.

Money Market Mutual Funds

Money market mutual funds purchase large amounts of money market securities and sell shares in these pools based on the value of their underlying (money market) securities (see Chapter 17). In doing so, money market mutual funds allow small investors to invest in money market instruments. At the end of 2004, money market mutual funds had $1,912.3 billion invested in short-term financial securities—such as repurchase agreements, negotiable CDs, open market paper (mostly commercial paper), and U.S. government securities. Money market mutual funds provide an alternative investment opportunity to interest-bearing deposits at commercial banks.[16]

Brokers and Dealers

Brokers' and dealers' services are important to the smooth functioning of money markets. We have alluded to various categories of brokers and dealers in this chapter. First are the 22 primary government security dealers. This group of participants plays a key role in marketing new issues of Treasury bills (and other Treasury securities). Primary government securities dealers also make the market in Treasury bills, buying securities from the Federal Reserve when they are issued and selling them in the secondary market. Secondary market transactions in the T-bill markets are transacted in the trading rooms of these primary dealers. These dealers also assist the Federal Reserve when it uses the repo market to temporarily increase or decrease the supply of bank reserves available.

The second group of brokers and dealers are money and security brokers. The five major brokers in this group are Cantor Fitzgerald Securities Corp., Garban-Intercapital, Liberty, RMJ Securities Corp., and Hill Farber. When government securities dealers trade with each other, they often use this group of brokers as intermediaries. These brokers also play a major role in linking buyers and sellers in the fed funds market and assist secondary trading in

15. Only bank holding companies such as Citigroup can issue commercial paper. However, funds so borrowed can be lent (downstreamed) to bank subsidiaries such as Citibank. Currently, the Federal Reserve imposes reserve requirements on such transactions.

16. Indeed, the short maturity of these asset holdings is an objective of these funds so as to retain the depositlike nature of their liabilities (called shares). The major difference between deposits and money market mutual fund (MMMF) shares is that interest-bearing deposits (below $100,000) are fully insured by the FDIC, whereas MMMF shares are not. Moreover, because of bank regulatory costs (such as reserve requirements, capital adequacy requirements, and deposit insurance premiums), bank deposits generally offer lower interest rates or returns than noninsured money market mutual funds. Thus, the net gain in switching to a money market mutual fund is a higher return in exchange for the loss of FDIC deposit insurance coverage. Many investors appeared willing to give up FDIC insurance coverage to obtain additional returns in the late 1990s and early 2000s.

other money market securities as well. These brokers never trade for their own account, and they keep the names of dealers involved in trades they handle confidential.

The third group of brokers and dealers are the thousands of brokers and dealers who act as intermediaries in the money markets by linking buyers and sellers of money market securities (see Chapter 16). This group of brokers and dealers often act as the intermediaries for smaller investors who do not have sufficient funds to invest in primary issues of money market securities or who simply want to invest in the money markets.

Corporations

Nonfinancial and financial corporations raise large amounts of funds in the money markets, primarily in the form of commercial paper. The volume of commercial paper issued by corporations has been so large that there is now more commercial paper outstanding than any other type of money market security. Because corporate cash inflows rarely equal their cash outflows, they often invest their excess cash funds in money market securities, especially T-bills, repos, commercial paper, negotiable CDs, and banker's acceptances.

Other Financial Institutions

Because their liability payments are relatively unpredictable, property-casualty (PC) insurance companies, and to a lesser extent life insurance companies, must maintain large balances of liquid assets (see Chapter 15). To accomplish this, insurance companies invest heavily in highly liquid money market securities, especially T-bills, repos, commercial paper, and negotiable CDs.

Since finance companies are not banks and cannot issue deposits, they raise large amounts of funds in the money markets (see Chapter 14), especially through the issuance of commercial paper.

DO YOU UNDERSTAND?

1. Who the major money market participants are?
2. Which money market securities commercial banks issue?
3. What services brokers and dealers provide for money market participants?

INTERNATIONAL ASPECTS OF MONEY MARKETS

While U.S. money markets are the largest and most active in the world, money markets across the world have been growing in size and importance. Two forms of growth include (1) U.S. money market securities bought and sold by foreign investors and (2) foreign money market securities. In conjunction with this increased worldwide interest in U.S. money market securities, some of the largest U.S. financial institutions that trade in money markets for themselves and their customers have opened offices in London, Tokyo, and beyond, most recently through mergers and acquisitions. For example, in October 2003 Citigroup acquired 5 percent of Shanghai Pudong Development Bank, China's ninth-largest commercial bank, which has a network of 270 outlets across the country's major metropolitan areas, with the option of increasing its stake in the future.

5 As a result of the growth in money markets worldwide, the flow of funds across borders in various countries has grown as international investors move their funds to money markets offering the most attractive yields. Table 5–7 lists the total amounts of various U.S. money market securities held by foreign investors from 1994 through 2004. Figure 5–8 shows the U.S. dollar equivalent amounts of money market instruments traded in international money markets as of June 2004, by the currency of issue and type of instrument issued. Table 5–8 shows the variation in central bank interest rates (discount rates for lender of last resort loans) in several countries in 2004.

Euro Money Markets

6 Because of the importance of the U.S. dollar relative to other currencies, many international financial contracts call for payment in U.S. dollars—the U.S. dollar is still the major international medium of exchange. As a result, foreign governments and businesses have historically held a store of funds (deposits) denominated in dollars outside of the United States. Further, U.S. corporations conducting international trade often

TABLE 5-7 Foreign Investments in U.S. Money Market Instruments
(in billions of dollars)

	1994	1997	2000	2004
Treasury securities[†]	$632.6	$1,251.8	$1,222.0	$1,805.1
Repurchase agreements	46.6	90.8	91.3	552.0
Negotiable CDs	56.3	73.6	107.2	165.4
Open market paper[‡]	24.9	77.8	111.0	115.5

[†]Includes Treasury bills, notes, and bonds.

[‡]Commercial paper and banker's acceptances.

Source: Federal Reserve Board Web site, "Flow of Fund Accounts," September 2004. **www.federalreserve.gov**

DO YOU UNDERSTAND?

1. What the major U.S. money market securities held by foreign investors are?
2. Which currencies most international money market instruments are issued in?

hold U.S. dollar deposits in foreign banks overseas to facilitate expenditures and purchases. These dollar-denominated deposits held offshore in U.S. bank branches overseas and in other (foreign) banks are called Eurodollar deposits (Eurodollar CDs) and the market in which they trade is called the **Eurodollar market.** Eurodollars may be held by governments, corporations, and individuals from anywhere in the world and are not directly subject to U.S. bank regulations, such as reserve requirements and deposit insurance premiums (or protection). As a result, the rate

Eurodollar market

The market in which Eurodollars trade.

FIGURE 5-8 Worldwide Money Market Instruments Outstanding

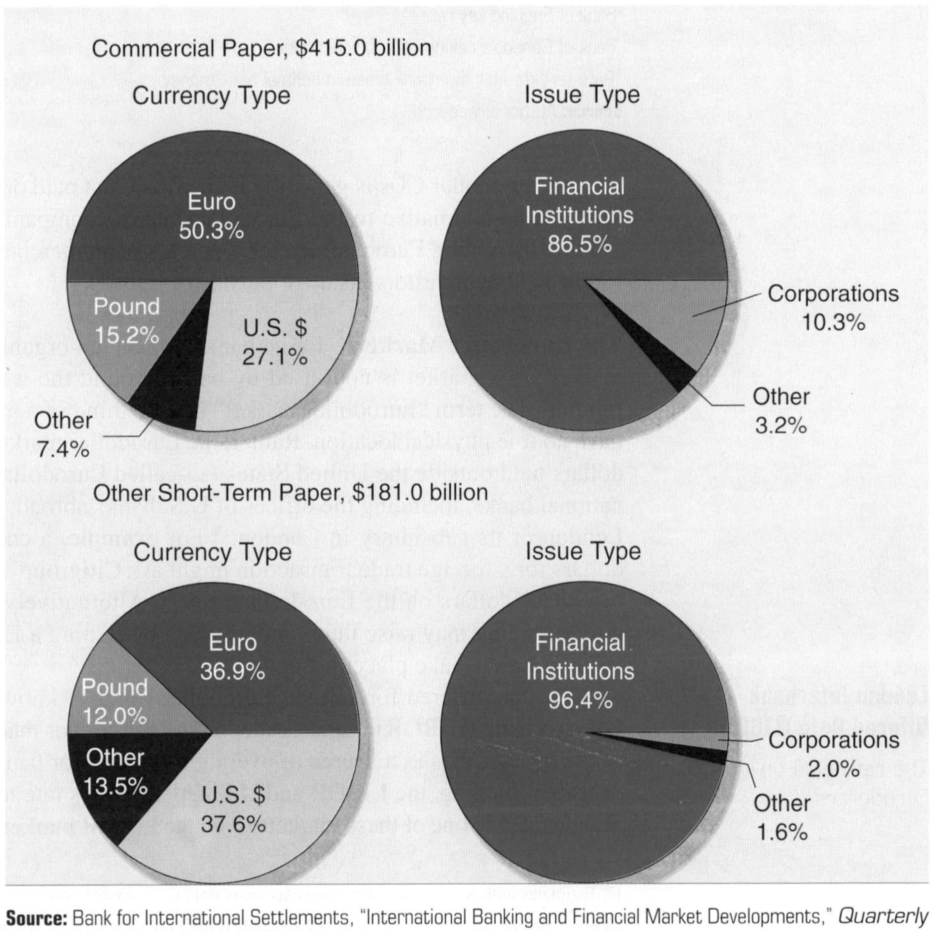

Source: Bank for International Settlements, "International Banking and Financial Market Developments," *Quarterly Review,* September 2004. **www.bis.org**

TABLE 5-8 Selected Central Bank Interest Rates

	New Rate		Previous Rate	
Country/Interest Rate	Percent Per Year	Applicable From	Percent Per Year	Applicable From
1. EU countries				
Euro area	2	June '03	2.5	Mar. '03
Denmark				
Discount rate	2	June '03	2.15	Mar. '03
Sweden				
Deposit rate	1¾	Nov. '04	1¼	July '04
Repurchase rate	2.5	Nov. '04	2.0	July '04
United Kingdom				
Repurchase rate†	4.75	Aug. '04	4½	June '04
2. Switzerland				
Three-month LIBOR target	¼–1¼	Sep. '04	0–1	June '04
3. Non-European countries				
Canada‡				
Discount rate	2½	Oct. '04	2¼	Sep. '04
Japan				
Discount rate	0.10	Sep. '01	0.25	Mar. '01
United States				
Federal funds rate§	2	Nov. '04	1.75	Sep. '04

†Bank of England key rate.
‡Bank of Canada's ceiling rate for call money.
§Rate targeted for interbank trade in central bank money.
Source: Author's research.

paid on Eurodollar CDs is generally higher than that paid on U.S.-domiciled CDs (see below). As an alternative to the Eurodollar market, companies can also obtain short-term funding by issuing Eurocommercial paper. Eurocommercial paper is issued in Europe but can be held by investors inside or outside of Europe.

The Eurodollar Market. Large banks in London organized the interbank Eurodollar market. This market is now used by banks around the world as a source of overnight funding. The term "Eurodollar market" is something of a misnomer because the markets have no true physical location. Rather, the Eurodollar market is simply a market in which dollars held outside the United States (so-called Eurodollars) are tracked among multinational banks, including the offices of U.S. banks abroad, such as Citigroup's branch in London or its subsidiary in London.[17] For example, a company in Italy needing U.S. dollars for a foreign trade transaction might ask Citigroup's subsidiary in London to borrow these dollars on the Eurodollar market. Alternatively, a Greek bank needing U.S. dollar funding may raise the required funds by issuing a Eurodollar CD. Most Eurodollar transactions take place in London.

London Interbank Offered Rate (LIBOR)

The rate paid on Eurodollars.

The rate offered for sale on Eurodollar funds is known as the **London Interbank Offered Rate (LIBOR).** Funds traded in the Eurodollar market are often used as an alternative to fed funds as a source of overnight funding for banks.[18] As alternative sources of overnight funding, the LIBOR and U.S. federal funds rate tend to be very closely related. Should rates in one of these markets (e.g., the LIBOR market) decrease relative to the other

17. Estimates indicate that more than twice as many dollars are traded outside than within U.S. borders.

18 Also, the rate paid by banks buying these funds is the London Interbank Bid Rate (LIBID). The spread between LIBOR and LIBID is small, rarely exceeding 12.5 basis points.

FIGURE 5–9 Overnight Interest Rates, 1997–2004

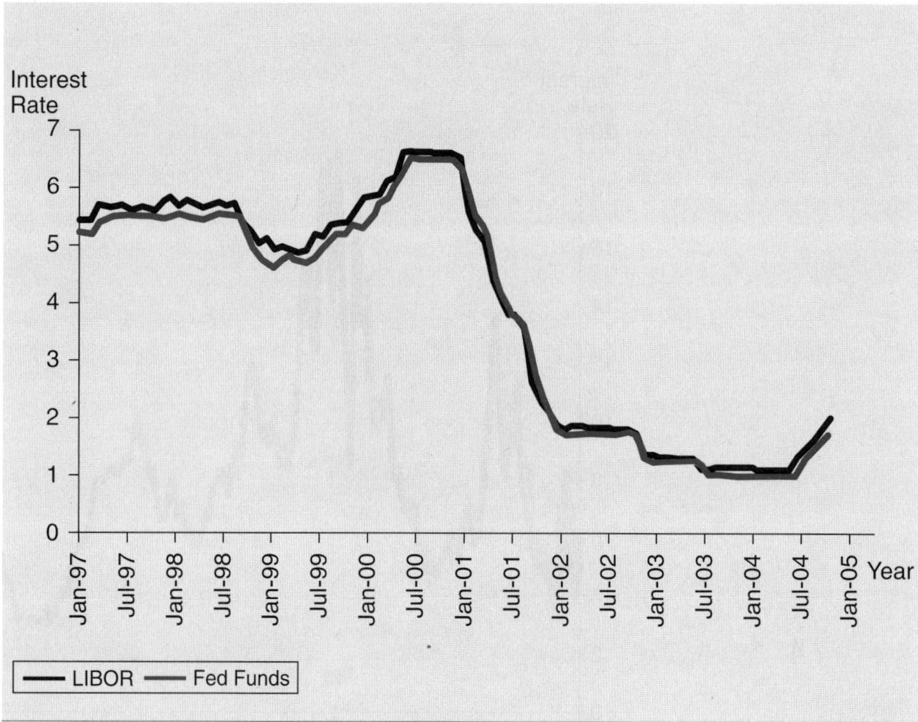

Source: Fannie Mae Web site, November 2004. **www.fanniemae.com**

(e.g., the fed funds market), overnight borrowers will borrow in the LIBOR market rather than the fed funds market. As a result, the LIBOR will increase with this increased demand and the fed funds rate will decrease with the decline in demand. This will make the difference between the two rates quite small, although not equal, as is discussed below. The ease of transacting in both markets makes it virtually costless to use one market versus the other. Indeed, the LIBOR rate is frequently used by major banks in the United States as a base rate on commercial and industrial loans.

While they are close substitutes for overnight funding, the fed funds rate is generally lower than the LIBOR. This difference is due to the low-risk nature of U.S. bank deposits versus foreign bank deposits. U.S. bank deposits are covered by deposit insurance up to certain levels. Moreover, there is a perception that large U.S. bank depositors and large U.S. banks are implicitly insured via a "too big to fail" (or TBTF) guarantee. Such guarantees lower U.S. bank risk and thus the cost of borrowing in the fed funds market. Foreign banks have no such explicit or implicit guarantees. As a result, LIBOR is generally higher than the fed funds rate, reflecting slightly higher default risk. The fed funds rate and LIBOR between 1997 and 2004 are plotted in Figure 5–9. The spread of the LIBOR over the fed funds rate averaged 0.12 percent over the early part of this period (1997–1999), and the correlation between the movements in the two rates was 92 percent. After 1999 the spread was only 0.01 percent and the fed funds rate sometimes exceeded the LIBOR rate after July 2001. As noted above, the increased demand for Eurodollars relative to fed funds as a source of overnight funding has, at times, outweighed the effect of the deposit insurance and TBTF guarantees. The result is that the fed funds rate has, at times, risen above the LIBOR rate. The correlation between the movement in the two rates was 95 percent after 1999.

Initially, most short-term adjustable-rate business loans were tied to the U.S. fed funds rate. However (as seen below), the tremendous growth of the Eurodollar market has resulted in the LIBOR becoming the standard rate by which loan rates are now priced. For example,

FIGURE 5–10 Three-Month U.S. Bank Issued versus Eurodollar CD Rates, 1971–2004

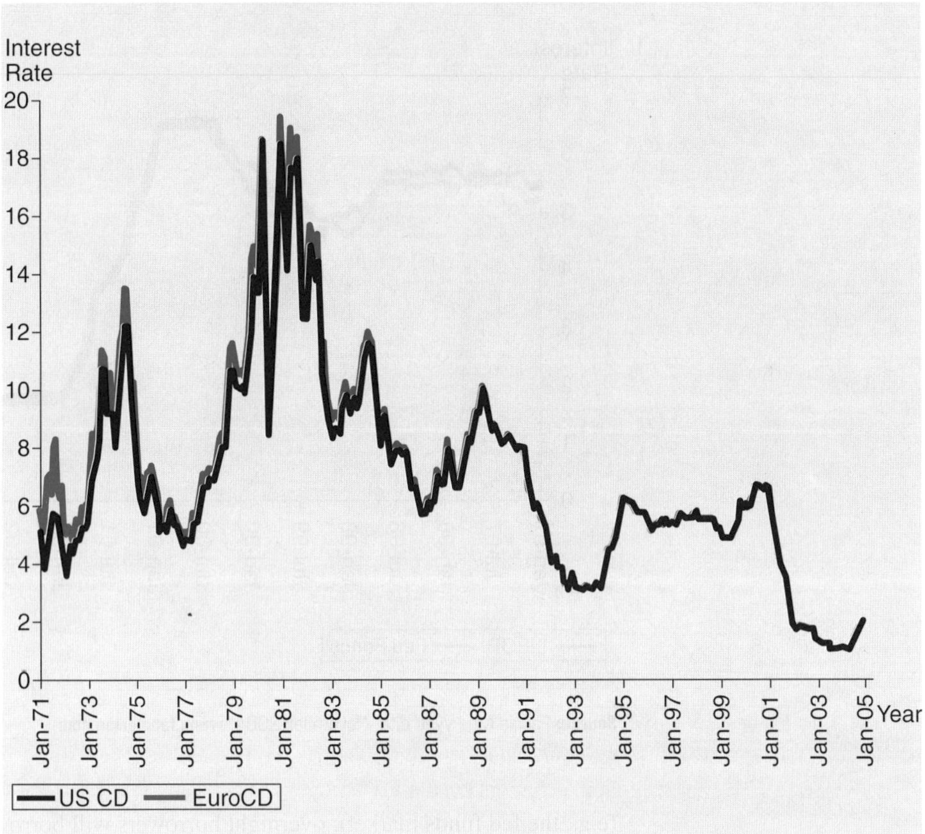

Source: Federal Reserve Board Web site, "Research and Data,"November 2004. **www.federalreserve.com**

Eurodollar CDs

Dollar-denominated deposits in non-U.S. banks.

the commercial paper market in the United States now quotes rates as a spread over the LIBOR rate rather than over the Treasury bill rate.

Eurodollar Certificates of Deposit. **Eurodollar certificates of deposits** (CDs) are U.S. dollar–denominated CDs in foreign banks. Maturities on Eurodollar CDs are less than one year, and most have a maturity of one week to six months. Because these securities are deposited in non-U.S. banks, Eurodollar CDs are not subject to reserve requirements in the same manner as U.S. deposits (although the reserve requirement on U.S. CDs was set to zero at the beginning of 1991).

Figure 5–10 shows the difference between three-month Eurodollar and U.S. bank issued–CDs from 1971 through 2004. As can be seen in this figure, prior to the 1990s, the Eurodollar CD paid consistently higher interest rates than U.S. CDs. In the 1990s, after the reserve requirement on CDs was set to zero, it is difficult to distinguish the Eurodollar CD rate from the U.S. CD rate. Indeed, during the 1990s and early 2000, the average rate paid on three-month Eurodollar CDs was 3.62 percent and on three-month U.S. CDs was 3.63 percent. The correlation on the movements in the two rates was 0.99988—that is, returns on three-month Eurodollar CDs and U.S. CDs were virtually identical in the 1990s and early 2000s.

DO YOU UNDERSTAND?

1. What the difference is between a Eurodollar CD, Euronote, CD and Eurocommercial paper?
2. What the relation is between the federal funds rate and the LIBOR?

Eurocommercial paper

Eurosecurities issued in Europe by dealers of commercial paper without involving a bank.

Eurocommercial Paper. **Eurocommercial paper** (Euro-CP) is issued in Europe by dealers of commercial paper without involving a bank. The Eurocommercial paper rate is

TABLE 5–9 Eurocommercial Paper Outstanding, 1995–2004
(in billions of U.S. dollars)

	Amount Outstanding			
	1995	1998	2001	2004
Eurocommercial paper	$87.0	$132.9	$243.1	$414.9
Currency type				
U.S. dollar	55.7	77.9	102.7	112.5
Euro-area currencies*	9.1	24.1	80.5	208.6
Japanese yen	2.1	3.5	13.6	4.2
Pound sterling	N/A	N/A	29.1	63.1
Other currencies	20.0	27.3	17.2	26.5
Issuer nationality				
Germany	14.4	28.3	108.6	142.4
United Kingdom	9.2	26.1	48.8	98.6
United States	19.5	22.0	50.9	78.1
Japan	18.0	6.6	11.6	16.8
Other developed countries	55.8	91.5	176.2	263.5
Other	15.6	26.6	13.0	13.4

*The BIS used the deutsche mark in 1995.

Source: Bank for International Settlements, "International Banking and Financial Market Developments," *Quarterly Review*, various issues. **www.bis.org**

generally about one-half to 1 percent above the LIBOR rate. Foreign commercial paper markets are new and small relative to U.S. commercial paper markets. Eurocommercial paper is issued in local currencies as well as in U.S. dollars. Table 5–9 lists the amount of Eurocommercial paper outstanding in the international money markets from 1995 through 2004 by currency and nationality of issuer. Notice that with the introduction of the European Currency Unit in 1999, Eurocommercial paper denominated in Euro area currencies increased significantly. By 2004, more than 50 percent of all Eurocommercial paper outstanding was denominated in euros. In comparison, U.K. (British pound sterling) issuances comprised 15 percent of all Eurocommercial paper issuances, while U.S dollar–denominated new issuances fell to 27 percent of the total. Projections are that with the full introduction of the euro in 2002 replacing the EC unit currencies, the euro money market will only continue to grow.

SUMMARY

In this chapter, we reviewed money markets, which are markets that trade debt securities with original maturities of one year or less. The need for money markets arises because cash receipts do not always coincide with cash expenditures for individuals, corporations, and government units. Because holding cash involves an opportunity cost, holders of excess cash invest these funds in money market securities. We looked at the various money market securities available to short-term investors and the major borrowers and issuers of each. We also outlined the processes by which each of these securities are issued and traded in secondary markets. We concluded the chapter by examining international issues involving money markets, taking a particular look at Euro money markets.

www.mhhe.com/sc3e

SEARCH THE SITE

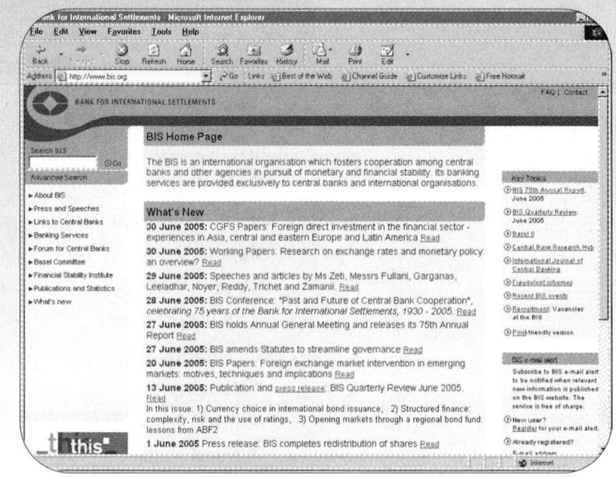

Go to the Bank for International Settlements Web site **at www.bis.org** and update the data for international Money Market Instruments Outstanding in Table 5–9 using the following steps.

Click on "BIS Quarterly Review"

Click on "Statistical Annex Read"

Click on "Securities Markets"

This will bring up a file to your computer that contains the relevant data: Table 13A Money Market Instruments.

Questions

1. What is the most recent value of money market instruments outstanding by currency type and issuer type?
2. How have these numbers changed since 2004 as reported in Table 5–9?

QUESTIONS

1. What are the three characteristics common to money market securities?
2. What is the difference between a discount yield and a bond equivalent yield? Which yield is used for Treasury bill quotes?
3. Why can discount yields not generally be compared to yields on other (nondiscount) securities?
4. What is the discount yield, bond equivalent yield, and effective annual return on a $1 million Treasury bill that currently sells at 97 3/8 percent of its face value and is 65 days from maturity?
5. Calculate the bond equivalent yield and effective annual return yield on a jumbo CD that is 115 days from maturity and has a quoted nominal yield of 6.56 percent.
6. Describe the T-bill auction process.
7. What is the difference between a competitive bid and a noncompetitive bid in a T-bill auction?
8. You would like to purchase a Treasury bill that has a $10,000 face value and is 68 days from maturity. The current price of the Treasury bill is $9,875. Calculate the discount yield on this Treasury bill.
9. Suppose you purchase a T-bill that is 125 days from maturity for $9,765. The T-bill has a face value of $10,000.
   a. Calculate the T-bill's quoted discount yield.
   b. Calculate the T-bill's bond equivalent yield.
10. Refer to Table 5–5.
    a. Calculate the ask price of the T-bill maturing on January 6, 2005, as of November 10, 2004.
    b. Calculate the bid price of the T-bill maturing on March 17, 2005, as of November 10, 2004.
11. *eXcel* **Using a Spreadsheet to Calculate T-bill Prices:** What is the bid price of a $10,000 face value T-bill with a bid rate of 2.23 percent if there are 10, 25, 50, 100, and 250 days to maturity?

Face Value	Bid Rate	Days to Maturity	=>	The Answer Will Be
$10,000	2.23%	10		$9,993.81
10,000	2.23	25		9,984.51
10,000	2.23	50		9,969.03
10,000	2.23	100		9,938.06
10,000	2.23	250		9,845.14

12. A T-bill that is 225 days from maturity is selling for $95,850. The T-bill has a face value of $100,000.
    a. Calculate the discount yield and bond equivalent yield on the T-bill.
    b. Calculate the discount yield and bond equivalent yield on the T-bill if it matures in 300 days.
13. *eXcel* **Using a Spreadsheet to Calculate T-bill Yield:** What is the quoted yield of a $10,000 face value T-bill with a market price of $8,885 if there are 10, 25, 50, 100, and 250 days to maturity?

Face Value	Market Price	Days to Maturity	=>	The Answer Will Be
$10,000	$8,885	10		4.014%
10,000	8,885	25		1.606
10,000	8,885	50		0.803
10,000	8,885	100		0.401
10,000	8,885	250		0.161

14. What are federal funds? How are they recorded on the balance sheets of commercial banks?
15. Describe the two types of fed funds transactions.
16. If the overnight fed funds rate is quoted as 2.25 percent, what is the bond equivalent rate? Calculate the bond equivalent rate on fed funds if the quoted rate is 3.75 percent.
17. What is the difference between a repurchase agreement and a reverse repurchase agreement?
18. Suppose a bank enters a repurchase agreement in which it agrees to buy Treasury securities from a correspondent bank at a price of $24,950,000, with the promise to buy them back at a price of $25,000,000.
    a. Calculate the yield on the repo if it has a 7-day maturity.
    b. Calculate the yield on the repo if it has a 21-day maturity.
19. Why do commercial paper issues have an original maturity of 270 days or less?
20. Why do commercial paper issuers almost always obtain a rating of their issues?
21. You can buy commercial paper of a major U.S. corporation for $495,000. The paper has a face value of $500,000 and is 45 days from maturity. Calculate the discount yield and bond equivalent yield on the commercial paper.
22. What is the process through which negotiable CDs are issued?
23. You have just purchased a four-month, $500,000 negotiable CD, which will pay a 5.5 percent annual interest rate.
    a. If the market rate on the CD rises to 6 percent, what is its current market value?
    b. If the market rate on the CD falls to 5.25 percent, what is its current market value?
24. Describe the process by which a banker's acceptance is created.
25. Who are the major issuers of and investors in money market securities?
26. What are Eurodollar CDs and Eurocommercial paper?

APPENDIX 5A: Single versus Discriminating Price Treasury Auctions

View this appendix at www.mhhe.com/sc3e

APPENDIX 5B: Creation of a Banker's Acceptance

View this appendix at www.mhhe.com/sc3e

www.mhhe.com/sc3e

6

Bond Markets

OUTLINE

Chapter NAVIGATOR

1. What are the major bond markets?
2. What are the characteristics of the various bond market securities?
3. Who are the major bond market participants?
4. What types of securities trade in international bond markets?

DEFINITION OF BOND MARKETS: CHAPTER OVERVIEW

Equity (stocks) and debt (notes, bonds, and mortgages) instruments with maturities of more than one year trade in **capital markets.** In the next several chapters, we look at characteristics of the different capital markets, starting in this chapter with bond markets.[1] In Chapter 7, we look at the mortgage markets (e.g., mortgage-backed securities, asset-backed securities), and in Chapter 9, we describe the equity markets.

Bonds are long-term debt obligations issued by corporations and government units. Proceeds from a bond issue are used to raise funds to support long-term operations of the issuer (e.g., for capital expenditure projects). In return for the investor's funds, bond issuers promise to pay a specified amount in the future on the maturity of the bond (the face value) plus coupon interest on the borrowed funds (the coupon rate times the face value of the bond). If the terms of the repayment are not met by the bond issuer, the bond holder (investor) has a claim on the assets of the bond issuer.

Bond markets are markets in which bonds are issued and traded. They are used to assist in the transfer of funds from individuals, corporations, and government units with excess funds to corporations and government units in need of long-term debt funding. Bond markets are traditionally classified into three types: (1) Treasury notes and bonds, (2) municipal bonds, and (3) corporate bonds. Figure 6–1 shows the distribution of each type

1. Although both notes and bonds are issued by agents such as the U.S. government, their characteristics (e.g., coupon rate) other than maturity are generally the same. In this chapter, the term *bond* will mean bonds and notes in general, except where we distinguish notes by their special maturity features. For example, U.S. Treasury notes have maturities of over one year up to 10 years. U.S. Treasury bonds have maturities from over 10 years to 30 years at the time of issue.

capital markets

Markets that trade debt (bonds and mortgages) and equity (stocks) instruments with maturities of more than one year.

bonds

Long-term debt obligations issued by corporations and government units.

bond markets

Markets in which bonds are issued and traded.

FIGURE 6–1 Bond Market Instruments Outstanding, 1994–2004

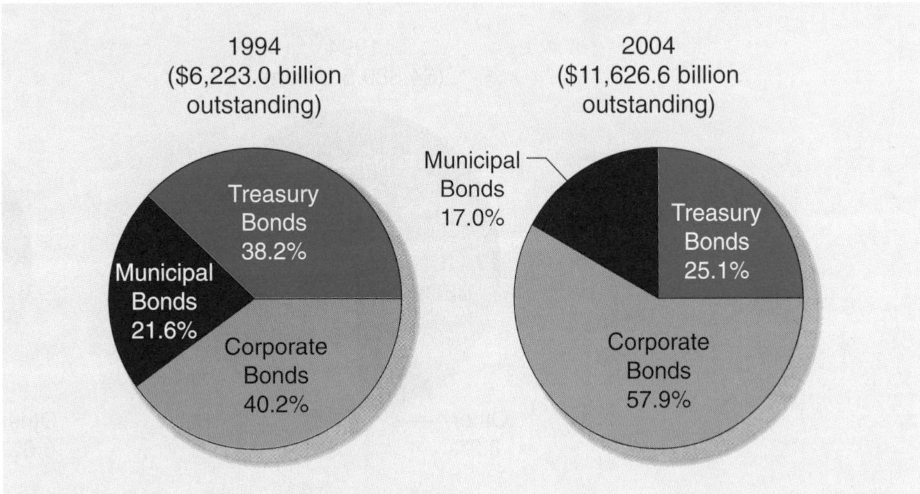

Source: Federal Reserve Board Web site, "Flow of Funds Accounts," various issues. **www.federalreserve.gov**

outstanding in 1994 and 2004. In this chapter, we look at the characteristics of the various bond securities (including the trading process in bond markets), the participants in the bond markets, and international bond markets and securities.

BOND MARKET SECURITIES

Government units and corporations are the major bond security issuers. Figure 6–1 shows that the dollar amount of bond securities issued by these groups has increased 86.8 percent, from $6,223.0 billion in 1994 to $11,626.6 billion in 2004. In this section, we look at the bond market securities issued by each of these issuers: Treasury notes and bonds, municipal bonds, and corporate bonds.

Treasury Notes and Bonds

Treasury notes and bonds

Long-term bonds issued by the U.S. Treasury to finance the national debt and other federal government expenditures.

Treasury notes and bonds (T-notes and T-bonds) are issued by the U.S. Treasury to finance the national debt and other federal government expenditures ($2,920.8 billion outstanding in September 2004). The national debt (*ND*) reflects the historical accumulation of annual federal government deficits or expenditures (*G*) minus taxes (*T*) over the last 200-plus years, as follows:

$$ND_t = \sum_{t=1}^{N} (G_t - T_t)$$

www.ustreas.gov

Figure 6–2 shows the composition of the U.S. national debt from 1994 through 2004. Notice that over this period, approximately 40 to 50 percent of the U.S. national debt consisted of Treasury notes and bonds.[2] Notice also that as the U.S. economy boomed in the late 1990s

2. Included as part of the U.S. national debt are government account securities. These include U.S. savings securities, dollar-denominated foreign government securities issued by the U.S. Treasury directly to foreign governments, federal insurance fund securities, federal retirement fund securities, and others.

FIGURE 6–2 Composition of the U.S. National Debt

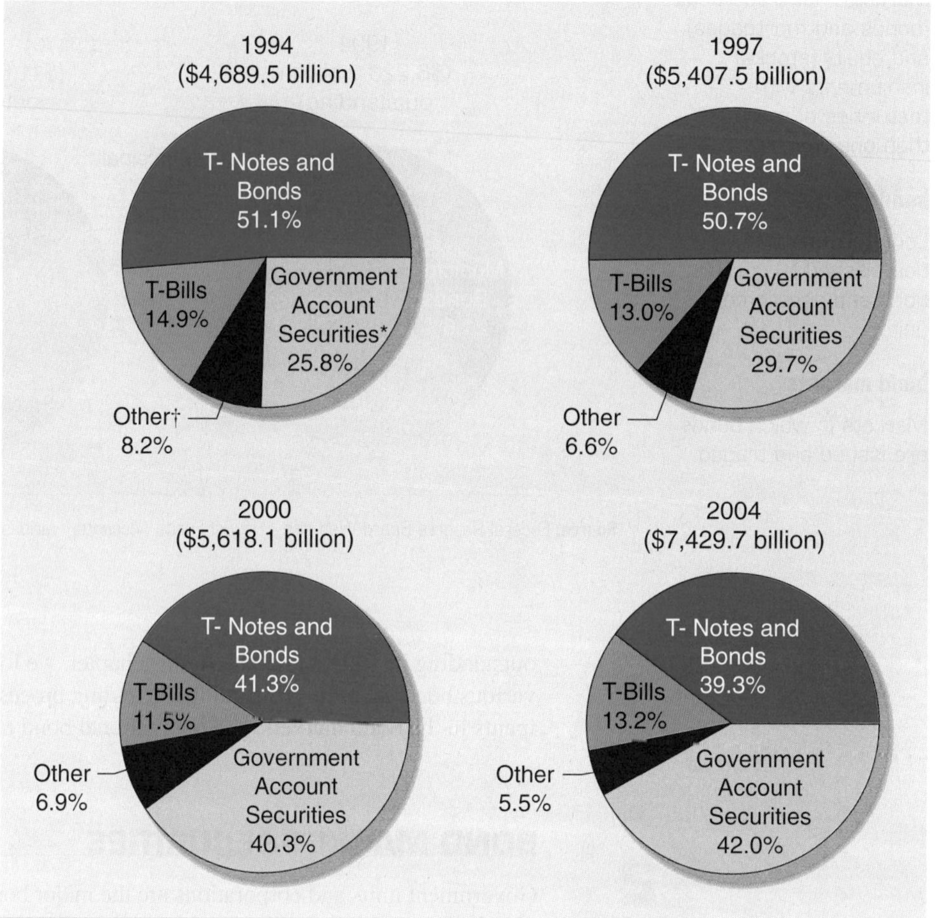

*Includes securities held by government trust funds, revolving funds, and special funds such as Social Security and government pension funds.

†Includes U.S. savings securities, dollar-denominated foreign government securities issued by the U.S. Treasury directly to foreign governments, and other.

Source: U.S. Treasury Department, *Treasury Bulletin,* November 2004. **www.ustreas.gov**

and the U.S. budget deficit shrank, the amount of public debt outstanding in the form of U.S. Treasury securities decreased from a year-end high of $3.44 trillion in 1997 to $2.97 trillion in 2000. However, as the U.S. budget deficit grew in the early 2000s, so did the level of outstanding U.S. Treasury securities, to $3.9 trillion by 2004.

Like T-bills, T-notes and bonds are backed by the full faith and credit of the U.S. government and are, therefore, default risk free. As a result, T-notes and bonds pay relatively low rates of interest (yields to maturity) to investors. T-notes and bonds, however, are not completely risk free. Given their longer maturity (i.e., duration), these instruments experience wider price fluctuations than do money market instruments as interest rates change (and thus are subject to interest rate risk—see Chapter 22). Further, many of the older issued bonds and notes—"off the run" issues—may be less liquid than newly issued bonds and notes—"on the run" issues—in which case they may bear an additional premium for illiquidity risk. Figure 6–3 shows the pattern of 10-year T-note yields versus 3-month T-bill yields from 1980 through 2004.

SEARCH THE SITE

Go to the Bureau of the Public Debt Web site at **www.publicdebt.treas.gov** and find the latest information available on the composition of the U.S. national debt using the following steps.

Click on "The Public Debt Online"

Under the section Monthly Statement of the Public Debt, click on "Summary page"

This will bring up the relevant tables.

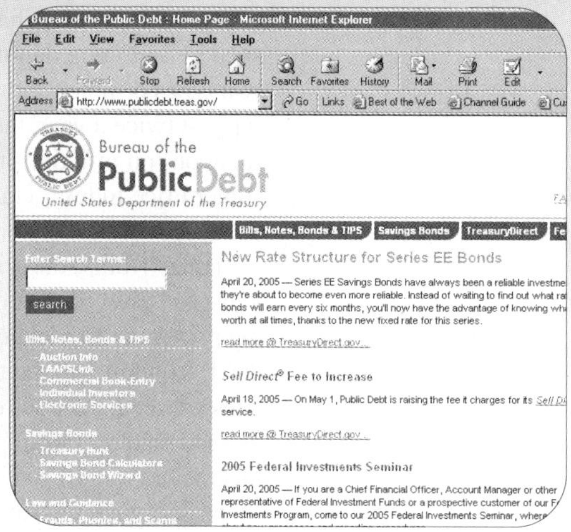

Questions

1. How has this number changed since 2004 reported in Figure 6–2?
2. Calculate the percentage of the national debt comprised of T-notes and bonds, T-bills, government account securities, and other securities.

FIGURE 6–3 **T-Bill versus T-Note Yields, 1980–2004**

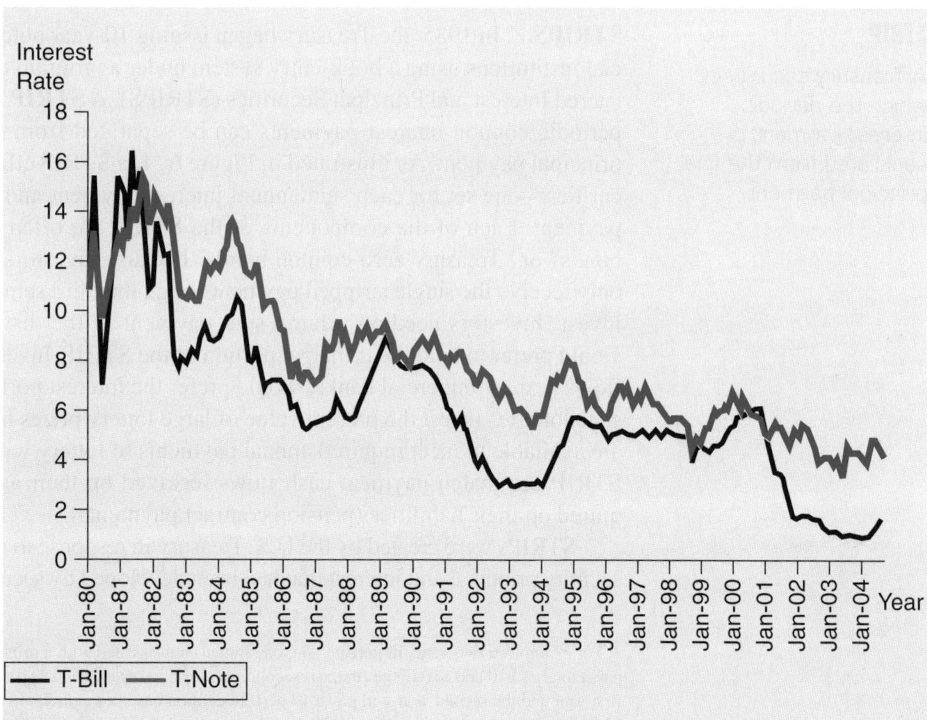

Source: Federal Reserve Board Web site, "Research and Data," November 2004. **www.federalreserve.gov**

In contrast to T-bills, which are sold on a discount basis from face value (see Chapter 5), T-notes and T-bonds pay coupon interest (semiannually). Further, T-bills have an original maturity of one year or less. Treasury notes have original maturities from over 1 to 10 years, while T-bonds have original maturities from over 10 years. T-notes and bonds are issued in minimum denominations of $1,000, or in multiples of $1,000. The Treasury issues two types of notes and bonds: fixed principal and inflation-indexed. While both types pay interest twice a year, the principal value used to determine the percentage interest payment (coupon) on inflation-indexed bonds is adjusted to reflect inflation (measured by the Consumer Price Index). Thus, the semiannual coupon payments and the final principal payment are based on the inflation-adjusted principal value of the security.[3]

Like T-bills, once issued T-notes and T-bonds trade in very active secondary markets. Table 6–1 presents part of a T-note and T-bond (including Treasury STRIPS—see below) closing price/interest yield quote sheet from *The Wall Street Journal* for trading on November 9, 2004. Column 1 in the table lists the coupon rate on the Treasury security. Note that coupon rates are set at intervals of 0.125 (or $\frac{1}{8}$ of 1) percent. Column 2 is the month and year the note or bond matures (an "n" after the year means that the security is a T-note—i.e., having an original maturity of 10 years or less). Column 3, labeled BID, is the close of the day selling price (in percentage terms) available to T-note and bond holders (i.e., the price dealers are willing to pay T-note and bond holders for their Treasury securities). Prices are quoted as percentages of the face value on the Treasury security, in 32nds. For example, using a face value of $1,000, the bid price on the 6.750 percent coupon, May 05 T-note was $1,022.1875 ($102\frac{7}{32}\% \times \$1{,}000$). Column 4, labeled ASKED, is the close of the day purchase price available to investors. Column 5, labeled CHG, is the change in the asked price from the previous day's close in 32nds—that is, the June 2009 T-note's price decreased by $\frac{1}{32}$ from the previous day. Finally, the last column, labeled ASK YLD, is the asked price converted into a rate of return (yield to maturity) on the T-note or T-bond. This yield is calculated using the yield to maturity formulas found in Chapter 3—it is the interest rate or yield (using semiannual compounding) that makes the price of the security just equal to the present value of the expected coupon and face value cash flows on the bond (where this yield is the single discount rate that makes this equality hold).

STRIP

A Treasury security in which the periodic interest payment is separated from the final principal payment.

STRIPS. In 1985, the Treasury began issuing 10-year notes and 30-year bonds[4] to financial institutions using a book-entry system under a program titled Separate Trading of Registered Interest and Principal Securities (STRIPS). A **STRIP** is a Treasury security in which periodic coupon interest payments can be separated from each other and from the final principal payment. As illustrated in Figure 6–4, a STRIP effectively creates two sets of securities—one set for each semiannual interest payment and one set for the final principal payment. Each of the components of the STRIP are often referred to as "Treasury zero bonds" or "Treasury zero-coupon bonds" because investors in the individual components only receive the single stripped payments (e.g., the third semiannual coupon) in which they invest. Investors needing a lump sum payment in the distant future (e.g., life insurers) would prefer to hold the principal portion of the STRIP. Investors wanting nearer-term cash flows (e.g., commercial banks) would prefer the interest portions of the STRIP. Also, some state lotteries invest the present value of large lottery prizes in STRIPS to be sure that funds are available to meet required annual payments to lottery winners. Pension funds purchase STRIPS to match payment cash flows received on their assets (STRIPS) with those required on their liabilities (pension contract payments).

STRIPs were created by the U.S. Treasury in response to the separate trading of Treasury security principal and interest that had been developed by securities firms. Specifically, in the

3. For example, a two-year, 10 percent coupon (annual) bond issued with a principal value (face value) of $1,000 will pay a total of $10 and $10 in the first and second years. An indexed (annual) bond when inflation is 10 percent in the first year and the second year will pay a 10 percent coupon based on principal values of $1,000 (1.1) = $1,100 and $1,000 $(1.1)^2$ = $1,210, respectively. That is, the first year coupon will be 10% × $1,100 = $11 and the second year coupon will be 10% × $1,210 = $12.10.

4. The U.S. Treasury stopped issuing 30-year bonds in 2001. However, the treasury reviewed the assurance of 30-year bonds in 2006.

TABLE 6–1 Treasury Note and Bond Quote

Treasury Bonds, Notes and Bills

November 9, 2004

Explanatory Notes

Representative Over-the-Counter quotation based on transactions of $1 million or more. Treasury bond, note and bill quotes are as of mid-afternoon. Colons in bid-and-asked quotes represent 32nds; 101:01 means 101 1/32. Net changes in 32nds. n-Treasury note. i-Inflation-Indexed issue. Treasury bill quotes in hundredths, quoted on terms of a rate of discount. Days to maturity calculated from settlement date. All yields are to maturity and based on the asked quote. Latest 13-week and 26-week bills are boldfaced. For bonds callable prior to maturity, yields are computed to the earliest call date for issues quoted above par and to the maturity date for issues below par. *When issued.
Source: eSpeed/Cantor Fitzgerald

U.S. Treasury strips as of 3 p.m. Eastern time, also based on transactions of $1 million or more. Colons in bid and asked quotes represent 32nds; 99:01 means 99 1/32. Net changes in 32nds. Yields calculated on the asked quotation. ci-stripped coupon interest. bp-Treasury bond, stripped principal. np-Treasury note, stripped principal. For bonds callable prior to maturity, yields are computed to the earliest call date for issues quoted above par and to the maturity date for issues below par.
Source: Bear, Stearns & Co. via Street Software Technology Inc.

Government Bonds & Notes

RATE	MATURITY MO/YR	BID	ASKED	CHG	ASK YLD
5.875	Nov 04n	100:01	100:02	–1	0.12
7.875	Nov 04n	100:02	100:03	–1	0.94
11.625	Nov 04	100:03	100:04	–1	1.21
2.000	Nov 04n	100:00	100:01	...	1.42
1.750	Dec 04n	100:00	100:00	1	1.74
1.625	Jan 05n	99:29	99:30	...	1.90
7.500	Feb 05n	101:14	101:15	...	1.87
1.500	Feb 05n	99:26	99:27	...	1.96
1.625	Mar 05n	99:25	99:26	...	2.11
1.625	Apr 05n	99:22	99:23	...	2.23
6.500	May 05n	102:04	102:05	...	2.25
6.750	**May 05n**	**102:07**	**102:08**	–1	2.29
12.000	May 05	104:30	104:31	–1	2.22
1.250	May 05n	99:14	99:15	1	2.22
1.125	Jun 05n	99:08	99:09	...	2.26
1.500	Jul 05n	99:13	99:14	1	2.29
6.500	Aug 05n	103:03	103:04	...	2.34
10.750	Aug 05	106:10	106:11	...	2.31
2.000	Aug 05n	99:21	99:22	...	2.37
1.625	Sep 05n	99:09	99:10	...	2.39
1.625	Oct 05n	99:06	99:07	...	2.44
5.750	Nov 05n	103:08	103:09	...	2.44
5.875	Nov 05n	103:12	103:13	–1	2.45
1.875	Nov 05n	99:11	99:12	...	2.46
1.875	Dec 05n	99:08	99:09	–1	2.50
1.875	Jan 06n	99:06	99:07	...	2.53
5.625	Feb 06n	103:26	103:27	...	2.51
9.375	Feb 06	108:14	108:15	–1	2.51
1.625	Feb 06n	98:25	98:26	...	2.56
1.500	Mar 06n	98:16	98:17	...	2.57
2.250	Apr 06n	99:14	99:15	...	2.62
2.000	May 06n	99:02	99:03	...	2.61
4.625	May 06n	102:29	102:30	–1	2.62
6.875	May 06n	106:08	106:09	–1	2.61
2.500	May 06n	99:23	99:24	...	2.65
2.750	Jun 06n	100:02	100:03	–1	2.68
7.000	**Jul 06n**	**107:00**	**107:01**	...	**2.69**
2.750	**Jul 06n**	**100:01**	**100:02**	...	**2.71**
2.375	Aug 06n	99:12	99:13	–1	2.71
2.375	Aug 06n	99:10	99:11	–1	2.74
2.500	Sep 06n	99:15	99:16	...	2.77
6.500	Oct 06n	106:30	106:31	...	2.76
2.500	**Oct 06n**	**99:12**	**99:13**	**–1**	**2.80**
2.625	Nov 06n	99:20	99:21	...	2.79
3.500	Nov 06n	101:10	101:11	–1	2.80
3.375	Jan 07i	106:24	106:25	–5	0.25
2.250	Feb 07n	98:20	98:21	–1	2.86
6.250	Feb 07n	107:11	107:12	–1	2.86
6.625	May 07n	108:28	108:29	...	2.92
4.375	May 07n	103:14	103:15	–1	2.93
3.125	May 07n	100:13	100:14	...	2.94
2.750	Aug 07n	99:10	99:11	1	3.00
3.250	Aug 07n	100:20	100:21	–1	2.99
6.125	Aug 07n	108:07	108:08	–1	2.99
3.000	Nov 07n	99:24	99:25	–2	3.07
3.625	Jan 08i	109:25	109:26	–4	0.51
3.000	Feb 08n	99:19	99:20	...	3.12
5.500	Feb 08n	107:09	107:10	–1	3.12
2.625	May 08n	98:04	98:05	...	3.18
5.625	May 08n	108:01	108:02	...	3.18
3.250	Aug 08n	100:00	100:01	1	3.24
3.125	Sep 08n	99:15	99:16	1	3.26
3.125	Oct 08n	99:12	99:13	1	3.29
3.375	Nov 08n	100:06	100:07	...	3.31
4.750	Nov 08n	105:12	105:13	...	3.30
3.375	Dec 08n	100:04	100:05	...	3.33
3.250	Jan 09n	99:18	99:19	...	3.35
3.875	Jan 09i	112:23	112:24	–5	0.77
3.000	Feb 09n	98:16	98:17	...	3.37
2.625	Mar 09n	96:28	96:29	–1	3.39
3.125	Apr 09n	98:27	98:28	...	3.40
3.875	May 09n	101:27	101:28	...	3.42
5.500	May 09n	108:26	108:27	...	3.37
4.000	**Jun 09n**	**102:09**	**102:10**	**–1**	**3.45**
3.625	Jul 09n	100:20	100:21	...	3.47
3.500	Aug 09n	100:02	100:03	...	3.48
6.000	Aug 09n	111:00	111:00	...	3.47
3.375	Sep 09n	99:14	99:15	...	3.49
3.375	**Oct 09n**	**99:11**	**99:12**	...	**3.51**
10.375	Nov 09	100:04	100:05	–1	0.02
4.250	Jan 10i	116:13	116:14	–5	0.98
6.500	Feb 10n	113:29	113:30	...	3.57
11.750	Feb 10	102:16	102:17	–1	2.04
0.875	Apr 10i	99:03	99:04	–3	1.04
10.000	May 10	103:30	103:31	...	2.16
5.750	Aug 10n	110:21	110:22	...	3.67
12.750	Nov 10	110:08	110:09	–1	2.40
3.500	Jan 11i	113:24	113:25	–4	1.18
5.000	Feb 11n	106:25	106:26	1	3.77
13.875	May 11	116:18	116:19	–1	2.61
5.000	Aug 11n	106:23	106:24	1	3.86
14.000	Nov 11	122:03	122:04	–1	2.64
3.375	Jan 12i	113:25	113:26	–5	1.35
4.875	Feb 12n	105:27	105:28	...	3.94
3.000	Jul 12i	111:07	111:08	–4	1.45
4.375	Aug 12n	102:13	102:14	...	4.01
4.000	Nov 12n	99:25	99:26	...	4.03
10.375	Nov 12	120:23	120:24	1	3.11
3.875	Feb 13n	98:20	98:21	...	4.07
3.625	May 13n	96:26	96:27	...	4.07
1.875	Jul 13i	102:05	102:06	–4	1.60
4.250	Aug 13n	100:25	100:26	–1	4.14
12.000	Aug 13	130:20	130:21	–1	3.27
4.250	Nov 13n	100:19	100:20	...	4.17
2.000	Jan 14i	102:25	102:26	–4	1.67
4.000	Feb 14n	98:18	98:19	–1	4.18
4.750	May 14n	104:07	104:08	–1	4.20
13.250	May 14	140:18	140:19	–1	3.46
2.000	Jul 14i	102:17	102:18	–5	1.71
4.250	**Aug 14n**	**100:08**	**100:09**	...	**4.21**
12.500	Aug 14	139:02	139:03	–2	3.51
11.750	Nov 14	137:08	137:09	–1	3.56
11.250	Feb 15	157:23	157:24	–1	4.25
10.625	Aug 15	154:00	154:00	–1	4.30
9.875	Nov 15	147:29	147:30	–1	4.35
9.250	Feb 16	142:26	142:27	–1	4.39
7.250	May 16	125:00	125:00	–1	4.45
7.500	Nov 16	127:18	127:19	–1	4.50
8.750	May 17	140:00	140:00	–1	4.53
8.875	Aug 17	141:16	141:17	–1	4.55
9.125	May 18	145:01	145:02	–2	4.61
9.000	Nov 18	144:12	144:13	–1	4.65
8.875	Feb 19	143:08	143:09	–2	4.68
8.125	Aug 19	135:26	135:27	–2	4.72
8.500	Feb 20	140:15	140:16	–3	4.74
8.750	May 20	143:17	143:18	–2	4.75
8.750	Aug 20	143:26	143:27	–2	4.76
7.875	Feb 21	134:07	134:08	–2	4.81
8.125	May 21	137:12	137:13	–1	4.81
8.125	Aug 21	137:18	137:19	–2	4.83
8.000	Nov 21	136:11	136:12	–2	4.84
7.250	Aug 22	127:25	127:26	–1	4.89
7.625	Nov 22	132:17	132:18	–1	4.89
7.125	Feb 23	126:16	126:17	–2	4.91
6.250	Aug 23	115:29	115:30	–2	4.94
7.500	Nov 24	132:10	132:11	–3	4.94
2.375	Jan 25i	103:15	103:16	–1	2.16
7.625	Feb 25	134:01	134:02	–4	4.94
6.875	Aug 25	124:18	124:19	–3	4.96
6.000	Feb 26	113:03	113:04	–4	4.99
6.750	Aug 26	123:06	123:07	–5	4.99
6.500	Nov 26	120:00	120:00	–5	4.99
6.625	Feb 27	121:21	121:22	–4	5.00
6.375	Aug 27	118:15	118:16	–5	5.00
6.125	Nov 27	115:05	115:06	–5	5.01
3.625	Apr 28i	125:26	125:27	–5	2.21
5.500	Aug 28	106:20	106:21	–5	5.02
5.250	Nov 28	103:06	103:07	–5	5.02
5.250	Feb 29	103:09	103:10	–5	5.01
3.875	Apr 29i	131:13	131:14	–8	2.20
6.125	Aug 29	115:21	115:22	–5	5.01
6.250	May 30	117:24	117:25	–7	5.01
5.375	**Feb 31**	**106:11**	**106:12**	**–6**	**4.94**
3.375	Apr 32i	125:22	125:23	–6	2.13

U.S. Treasury Strips

MATURITY		TYPE	BID	ASKED	CHG	ASK YLD
Nov	04	ci	100:00	100:00	...	1.86
Nov	04	bp	99:31	99:31	...	1.95
Nov	04	np	100:00	100:00	...	1.82
Jan	05	ci	99:23	99:23	...	1.63
Feb	05	ci	99:16	99:16	...	1.92
Feb	05	np	99:16	99:16	...	2.00
Apr	05	ci	99:05	99:05	...	2.03
May	05	ci	98:31	98:31	...	2.07
May	05	bp	98:27	98:27	...	2.30
May	05	np	98:27	98:27	...	2.30
May	05	np	98:27	98:27	...	2.30
Jul	05	ci	98:23	98:23	...	1.91
Aug	05	ci	98:11	98:11	...	2.20
Aug	05	bp	98:07	98:07	...	2.37
Aug	05	np	98:07	98:07	...	2.38
Oct	05	ci	97:28	97:28	...	2.34
Nov	05	ci	97:21	97:21	...	2.37
Nov	05	np	97:17	97:17	...	2.48
Nov	05	np	97:17	97:17	...	2.48
Jan	06	ci	97:16	97:16	...	2.16
Feb	06	ci	96:30	96:30	...	2.49
Feb	06	bp	96:28	96:28	...	2.53
Feb	06	np	96:29	96:29	...	2.51
Apr	06	ci	96:15	96:15	...	2.55
May	06	ci	96:06	96:06	...	2.59
May	06	np	96:04	96:04	...	2.63
May	06	np	96:05	96:05	...	2.61
Jul	06	ci	96:07	96:07	...	2.31
Jul	06	np	95:20	95:20	...	2.69
Aug	**06**	**ci**	**95:16**	**95:16**	...	**2.64**
Aug	**06**	**np**	**95:11**	**95:11**	...	**2.72**
Oct	06	np	94:26	94:26	...	2.79
Oct	06	ci	94:30	94:30	...	2.72
Nov	06	ci	94:21	94:21	...	2.75
Nov	06	np	94:17	94:17	...	2.82
Nov	06	np	94:17	94:17	...	2.81
Feb	07	ci	93:26	93:26	...	2.84
Feb	07	np	93:25	93:25	...	2.87
May	07	ci	92:30	92:30	...	2.94
May	07	np	92:30	92:30	...	2.94
May	07	np	92:30	92:30	...	2.94
Aug	07	ci	91:30	91:30	...	3.07
Aug	07	np	92:03	92:03	...	3.01
Aug	07	np	92:03	92:03	...	3.01
Nov	07	ci	91:07	91:07	...	3.08
Nov	07	np	91:08	91:08	...	3.07
Feb	08	ci	90:13	90:13	1	3.12
Feb	08	np	90:10	90:10	1	3.16
Feb	08	np	90:11	90:11	1	3.14
May	08	ci	89:14	89:14	1	3.20
May	08	np	89:15	89:15	1	3.20
Aug	08	ci	88:21	88:21	1	3.23
Aug	08	np	88:17	88:17	1	3.27
May	08	np	89:16	89:16	1	3.19
Nov	08	ci	87:17	87:17	1	3.35
Nov	08	np	87:18	87:18	1	3.34
Nov	08	np	87:18	87:18	1	3.34
Feb	09	ci	86:17	86:17	1	3.42
Feb	09	np	86:20	86:20	1	3.40
May	09	ci	85:20	85:20	1	3.47
May	09	np	85:27	85:27	1	3.41
May	09	np	85:21	85:21	1	3.46
Aug	09	ci	84:20	84:20	1	3.54
Aug	09	np	84:21	84:21	1	3.53
Nov	09	ci	83:29	83:29	1	3.54
Nov	09	bp	83:07	83:07	1	3.70
Feb	10	ci	82:21	82:21	2	3.65
Feb	10	np	82:20	82:20	–1	3.66
May	10	ci	81:23	81:23	2	3.70
Aug	10	ci	80:22	80:22	2	3.76
Aug	10	np	80:24	80:24	4	3.75
Nov	10	ci	80:02	80:02	2	3.73
Feb	11	ci	78:13	78:13	...	3.92
Feb	11	np	78:24	78:24	1	3.85
May	11	ci	77:14	77:14	...	3.97
Aug	11	ci	76:13	76:13	...	4.03
Aug	11	np	76:24	76:24	...	3.95
Nov	11	ci	75:17	75:17	...	4.05
Feb	12	ci	74:16	74:16	...	4.10
Feb	12	np	74:27	74:27	...	4.03
May	12	ci	73:15	73:15	...	4.15
Aug	12	ci	72:13	72:13	...	4.20
Aug	12	np	73:00	73:00	...	4.10
Nov	12	ci	71:14	71:14	...	4.24
Nov	12	np	72:06	72:06	...	4.11
Feb	13	ci	70:16	70:16	...	4.28
Feb	13	np	71:08	71:08	...	4.15
May	13	ci	69:17	69:17	...	4.32
May	13	np	70:19	70:19	...	4.14
Aug	13	ci	68:19	68:19	...	4.35
Aug	13	np	69:11	69:11	...	4.22
Nov	13	ci	67:22	67:22	...	4.38
Nov	13	np	68:12	68:12	...	4.26
Feb	14	ci	66:22	66:22	...	4.42
Feb	14	np	67:20	67:20	...	4.27
May	14	ci	65:24	65:24	...	4.46
May	14	np	66:22	66:22	...	4.31
Aug	14	ci	64:26	64:26	...	4.49
Nov	14	ci	63:27	63:27	...	4.53

Source: *The Wall Street Journal,* Friday, November 10, 2004, p. C15. Reprinted by permission of *The Wall Street Journal.* **www.wsj.com**

FIGURE 6–4 Creation of a Treasury STRIP

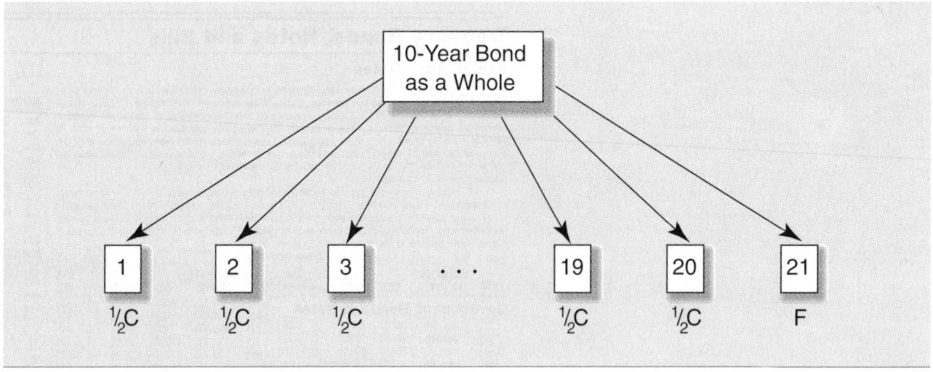

early 1980s, Merrill Lynch introduced Treasury Investment Growth Receipts (TIGRs). Merrill Lynch purchased Treasury securities, stripped them into one security representing the principal component only and a separate security for each coupon payment, and put these individual securities up for resale. The Treasury's creation of the STRIP was meant to offer a competitive product to the market.

www.ml.com

The U.S. Treasury does not issue STRIPs directly to investors. Rather, stripped Treasury notes and bonds may be purchased only through financial institutions and government securities brokers and dealers, who create the STRIP components after purchasing the original T-notes or T-bonds (whole) in Treasury auctions (see below). After the STRIP components have been created, by requesting that the Treasury separate each coupon and face value payment on each bond and recording them as separate securities in its book-entry computer system, they can be sold individually in the secondary markets.[5]

EXAMPLE 6–1 Creation of a STRIP

Suppose the Treasury issues a five-year T-note with a par value of $10,000 and an 8 percent coupon rate (paid semiannually, or $400 is paid to the holder every six months for the next five years) to Citigroup. Citigroup decides to convert the bond into a set of stripped securities by requesting the Treasury to separate the coupons and face value of the note into separate securities on its computer system (basically giving each coupon and face value a separate I.D. or CUSIP number). This means that Citigroup can then sell 11 different securities: 10 securities associated with each of the semiannual coupon payments of $400 and one that pays $10,000 (the face or principal value) in five years to outside investors. We show the value of each of these securities in Table 6–2, assuming the yield to maturity on each of the stripped securities is 7.90 percent, and is the same as the bond sold "whole."

Notice that the total present value of the 11 different securities involved with the STRIP is the same as that of the original T-note before it is stripped, $10,040.65. However, in general, the bank (Citigroup) will try to sell the 11 stripped securities for a greater total present value than the bond as a whole. The reason for this is that many investors desire particular maturity zero-coupon bonds to meet investment goals and needs. Such goals and needs (such as duration targets—see below) are often harder to achieve through buying whole T-notes or T-bonds. Consequently, investors are willing to pay a higher price and thus accept a yield lower than 7.90 percent on the stripped investments. As a result, the total price Citigroup would get from selling the 11 STRIPS would exceed $10,040.65.

5. Once a bond is stripped, if an investor purchases each coupon and face value component at a later time, he or she can ask the Treasury to reconstitute the original bond on its computer system. Thus, the Treasury STRIP program is highly flexible and STRIPS can be reconstituted as whole bonds.

TABLE 6-2 Present Value of STRIP Components of a 10-Year T-Note with an 8 Percent Coupon Rate and 7.90 Percent Yield to Maturity

Maturity on Security (in years)	Cash Flow Received at Maturity	Present Value of Cash Flow at 7.90 Percent
0.5	$ 400	$ 384.80
1.0	400	370.18
1.5	400	356.11
2.0	400	342.58
2.5	400	329.56
3.0	400	317.04
3.5	400	304.99
4.0	400	293.40
4.5	400	282.25
5.0	400	271.53
5.0	10,000	6,788.21
Total		$10,040.65

As mentioned above, STRIPs are attractive investments to investors desiring particular maturity zero-coupon bonds to meet investment goals and needs. For example, STRIPs are used as investment securities for individual retirement accounts, Keogh plans, and pension funds. Frequently, managers of these types of financial institutions face the problem of structuring their asset investments so they can pay a given cash amount to policyholders in some future period. The classic example of this is an insurance policy that pays the holder some lump sum when the holder reaches retirement age. The risk to the life insurance company manager is that interest rates on the funds generated from investing the holder's premiums could fall. Thus, the accumulated returns on the premiums invested might not meet the target or promised amount. In effect, the insurance company would be forced to draw down its reserves and net worth to meet its payout commitments. (See Chapter 15 for a discussion of this risk.) To immunize or protect itself against interest rate risk, the insurer can invest in Treasury zero-coupon bonds (or STRIPS).

EXAMPLE 6-2 Using a STRIP to Immunize against Interest Rate Risk

Suppose that it is 2007 and an insurer must make a guaranteed payment to an investor in five years, 2012. For simplicity, we assume that this target guaranteed payment is $1,469,000, a lump sum policy payout on retirement, equivalent to investing $1,000,000 at an annually compounded rate of 8 percent over five years.

To immunize or protect itself against interest rate risk, the insurer needs to determine which investments would produce a cash flow of exactly $1,469,000 in five years, regardless of what happens to interest rates in the immediate future. By investing in a five-year maturity (and duration) Treasury zero-coupon bond (or STRIP), the insurance company would produce a $1,469,000 cash flow in five years, no matter what happens to interest rates in the immediate future.

Given a $1,000 face value and an 8 percent yield and assuming annual compounding, the current price per five-year STRIP is $680.58 per bond:

$$P = 680.58 = \frac{1,000}{(1.08)^5}$$

If the insurer buys 1,469 of these bonds at a total cost of $1,000,000 in 2007, these investments would produce $1,469,000 on maturity in five years. The reason is that the duration of this bond portfolio exactly matches the target horizon for the insurer's future liability to its policyholders. Intuitively, since the STRIP pays no intervening cash flows or coupons, future changes in interest rates have no reinvestment income effect. Thus, the return would be unaffected by intervening interest rate changes.

Most T-note and T-bond issues are eligible for the STRIP program. The components of a STRIP are sold with minimum face values of $1,000 and in increasing multiples of $1,000 (e.g., $2,000, $3,000). Thus, the par amount of the securities must be an amount that will produce semiannual coupon payments of $1,000 or a multiple of $1,000. The original Treasury note and bond issues that are eligible for the STRIP program are usually limited to those with large par values.

The T-note and bond quote list in Table 6–1 includes a portion of the Treasury STRIPS that traded on November 9, 2004. Look at the two rows for STRIPS maturing in August 2006. The first column of the quote lists the month and year the STRIP matures (e.g., Aug 06). The second column, labeled TYPE, indicates whether the instrument represents the coupon payments (ci) or the note's principal value (np) from the original Treasury note. Columns 3 and 4 list the bid and asked prices for the STRIPS. Like the quote for other Treasury securities (discussed above), the BID is the close of the day selling price (in percentage terms) available to STRIP holders (i.e., the price dealers are willing to pay T-note and bond holders for their Treasury securities). Prices are quoted as percentages of the face value on the Treasury security, in 32nds. The ASKED price is the close of the day purchase price available to investors. Column 5, labeled CHG, is the change in the asked price from the previous day's close in 32nds. Finally, the last column, labeled ASK YLD, is the asked price converted into a rate of return (yield to maturity) on the STRIP. This yield is calculated using the yield to maturity formulas found in Chapter 3, that is, it is the interest rate or yield (using semiannual compounding to correspond with the semiannual coupon payments that are "stripped" from each other and the final principal payment) that makes the price of the security just equal to the present value of the expected coupon or face value cash flows on the STRIP.

EXAMPLE 6–3 Calculation of Yield on a STRIP

For the principal (np) STRIP maturing in August 2006 (reported in Table 6–1), the ASKED price at the close on Tuesday, November 9, 2004 (or present value) is 95:11 (= $95^{11}/_{32}$, or 95.34375 percent). Settlement occurs two business days after purchase, so you receive actual ownership on Thursday, November 11, 2004. When the STRIP matures, on August 15, 2006 (in 1.764384 years), the STRIP holder will receive 100 percent of the face value (or future value). Using semiannual compounding, the yield to maturity (ytm), or ASK YLD is calculated as:

$$95^{11}/_{32}\% = 100\%(1 + ytm/2)^{2 \times 1.764384}$$

Solving for *ytm*, we get:

$$ytm = 2.72\%$$

Treasury Note and Bond Yields. Treasury note and bond yield to maturities and prices are calculated using bond valuation formulas presented in Chapter 3. The general bond valuation formula is:

$$V_b = \frac{INT}{m}(PVIFA_{i_d/m,Nm}) + M(PVIF_{I_d/m,Nm})$$

where

V_b = Present value of the bond
M = Par or face value of the bond
INT = Annual interest (or coupon) payment on the bond, equals the par value times the coupon rate
N = Number of years until the bond matures
m = Number of times per year interest is paid
i_d = Interest rate used to discount cash flows on the bond

EXAMPLE 6-4 Calculation of a T-Note Price from a *Wall Street Journal* Quote

From Table 6–1, there were two T-notes outstanding on November 9, 2004 (with a settlement date of November 11, 2004), with a maturity on July 15, 2006 (i.e., they were 1.67945 years from maturity). The first T-note had a coupon rate of 7.000 percent and an ASK YLD of 2.69 percent (*The Wall Street Journal* lists yields and prices to $^1/_{100}$ of 1 percent). Using the bond valuation formula, the ASKED price on the bond should have been:

$$V_b = \frac{7.000\%}{2}(PVIFA_{2.69\%/2,1.67945(2)}) + 100(PVIF_{2.69\%/2,1.67945(2)})$$
$$= 107.0312$$

or to the nearest $^1/_{32}$, $107^1/_{32}$. The ASKED quote reported in *The Wall Street Journal* was indeed $107^1/_{32}$.

For the second July 2006 maturity T-note, the coupon rate was 2.750 percent and the yield was 2.71 percent. The ASKED price on the bond should have been (and was):

$$V_b = \frac{2.750\%}{2}(PVIFA_{2.71\%/2,1.67945(2)}) + 100(PVIF_{2.71\%/2,1.67945(2)})$$
$$= 100.0652$$

or to the nearest $^1/_{32}$, $100^2/_{32}$.

accrued interest

That portion of the coupon payment accrued between the last coupon payment and the settlement day.

Accrued Interest. When an investor buys a T-note or T-bond between coupon payments, the buyer must compensate the seller for that portion of the coupon payment accrued between the last coupon payment and the settlement day (normally, settlement takes place 1 to 2 days after a trade). This amount is called **accrued interest.** Thus, at settlement, the buyer must pay the seller the purchase price of the T-note or T-bond plus accrued interest. The sum of these two is often called the *full price* or *dirty price* of the security. The price without the accrued interest added on is called the *clean price.*

Accrued interest on a T-note or T-bond is based on the actual number of days the bond was held by the seller since the last coupon payment:

$$\text{Accrued interest} = \frac{INT}{2} \times \frac{\text{Actual number of days since last coupon payment}}{\text{Actual number of days in coupon period}}$$

EXAMPLE 6-5 Calculation of Accrued Interest and Yield to Maturity on a Bond

On August 2, 2007, you purchase a $10,000 T-note that matures on May 15, 2013 (settlement occurs two days after purchase, so you receive actual ownership of the bond on August 4, 2007). The coupon rate on the T-note is 5.875 percent and the current price quoted on the bond is 101-11 (or 101.34375 percent of the face value of the T-note). The last coupon payment occurred on May 15, 2007 (81 days before settlement), and the next coupon payment will be paid on November 15, 2007 (103 days from settlement). We illustrate this time line in Figure 6–5.

The accrued interest due to the seller from the buyer at settlement is calculated as:

$$(5.875\%/2) \times 81/184 = 1.29314\%$$

of the face value of the bond, or $129.3134. The dirty price of this transaction is:

$$\text{Clean price} + \text{Accrued interest} = \text{Dirty price}$$

$$101.34375\% + 1.29314\% = 102.63689\%$$

of the face value of the bond, or $10,263.689 per $10,000 face value bond.

The yield to maturity (which is based on the clean price) on the bond received on August 4, 2007, and maturing on May 15, 2013 (a total of 5 years and 285 days, or 5.7808 years) is:

$$101.34375\% = \frac{5.875\%}{2}(PVIFA_{ytm/2,\,5.7808(2)}) + 100(PVIF_{ytm/2,\,5.7808(2)})$$

Solving for the yield to maturity, we get 5.632 percent.

Notice that as the purchase date approaches the coupon interest payment date, the accrued interest due to the seller from the buyer increases. Just before a coupon payment date the buyer pays the seller fractionally less than the full coupon payment. However, as the accrued interest portion of the dirty price of the note increases, the clean price of the note decreases to offset this, keeping the overall price of the note to the buyer constant. This is illustrated in Figure 6–6.

Treasury Inflation Protection Securities (TIPS). In January 1997, the U.S. Treasury began issuing inflation-indexed bonds called Treasury Inflation Protection Securities (TIPS), which provide returns tied to the inflation rate. Like the fixed-coupon bonds issued by the Treasury, the coupon rate on TIPS is determined by the auction process described below. However, unlike the fixed-principal bonds, the principal value of a TIPS bond can increase (or decrease) by the amount of U.S. inflation (or deflation) as measured by the percentage change in the Consumer Price Index (CPI) every six months. This principal is

FIGURE 6–5 Timeline Used to Determine Accrued Interest on a Bond

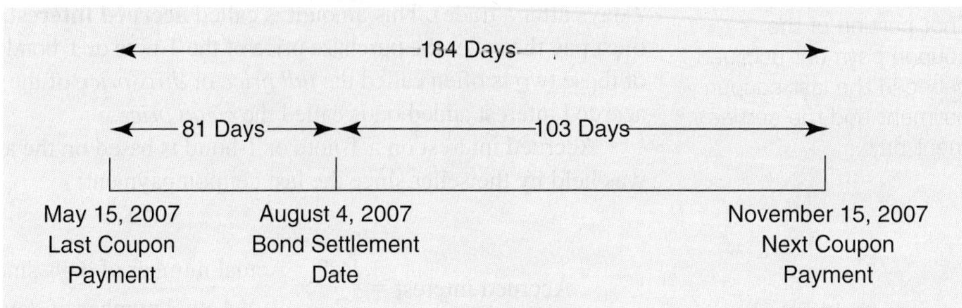

FIGURE 6–6 Dirty Price of Treasury Note

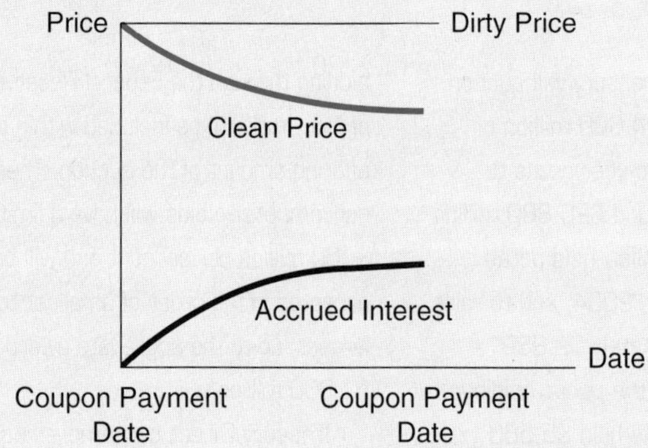

called the inflation-adjusted principal. TIPS bonds are used by investors who wish to earn a rate of return on their investments that keeps up with the inflation rate over time.

To see how TIPS bonds work, consider an investor who, on January 1, 2007, purchases a TIPS bond with an original principal of \$100,000, a 4 percent annual (or 2 percent semiannual) coupon rate, and 10 years to maturity. The inflation-adjusted principal at the end of the first six months, on June 30, 2007, is found by multiplying the original par value (\$100,000) by the semiannual inflation rate. Thus, if the semiannual inflation rate during the first six months is 0.5 percent, the principal amount used to determine the first coupon payment is adjusted upward by 0.5 percent (\$100,000 × 1.005), to \$100,500. Therefore, the first coupon payment, paid on June 30, 2007, is \$2,010 (\$100,500 × 2.0%). The inflation-adjusted principal at the beginning of the second six months is \$100,500. Suppose that the semiannual inflation rate for the second six-month period is 1 percent. Then the inflation-adjusted principal at the end of the second six months (on December 31, 2007), and the principal amount used to determine the second coupon payment, is adjusted upward by 1 percent (\$100,500 × 1.01), to \$101,505. The coupon payment to the investor for the second six-month period is the inflation-adjusted principal on this coupon payment date (\$101,505) times the semiannual coupon rate (2 percent). Thus, on December 31, 2007, the investor receives a coupon payment of \$2,030.10 (\$101,505 × 2.0%).

Primary and Secondary Market Trading in Treasury Notes and Bonds. As in primary market T-bill sales, the U.S. Treasury sells T-notes and T-bonds through competitive and noncompetitive Treasury auctions (see Chapter 5). Table 6–3 shows a recent auction pattern for T-note and T-bond new issues. The Treasury issues a press release about a week before each auction announcing the details of the auction, including the auction date, the amount to be sold, and other details about the securities to be issued (see In the News box).

TABLE 6–3 Auction Pattern for Treasury Notes and Bonds

Security	Purchase Minimum	General Auction Schedule
2-year note	\$1,000	Monthly
3-year note	\$1,000	February, May, August, November
5-year note	\$1,000	February, May, August, November
10-year note	\$1,000	February, May, August, November
30-year bond	\$1,000	February, August

Source: U.S. Treasury Web site, Bureau of Public Debt, November 2004. **www.ustreas.gov**

Treasury to Auction $24,000 Million of Two-Year Notes

The Treasury will auction $24,000 million of two-year notes to refund $26,880 million of publicly held notes maturing October 31, 2004, and to raise new cash of approximately $2,880 million. In addition to the public holdings, Federal Reserve Banks hold $5,560 million of the maturing notes for their own accounts, which may be refunded by issuing an additional amount of the new security.

Up to $1,000 million in noncompetitive bids from Foreign and International Monetary Authority (FIMA) accounts bidding through the Federal Reserve Bank of New York will be included within the offering amount of the auction. These noncompetitive bids will have a limit of $100 million per account and will be accepted in the order of smallest to largest, up to the aggregate award limit of $1,000 million.

Treasury Direct customers requested that we reinvest their maturing holdings of approximately $483 million into the two-year note.

The auction will be conducted in the single-price auction format. All competitive and noncompetitive awards will be at the highest yield of accepted competitive tenders. The allocation percentage applied to bids awarded at the highest yield will be rounded up to the next hundredth of a whole percentage point, e.g., 17.13 percent.

The notes being offered today are eligible for the STRIPS program.

This offering of Treasury securities is governed by the terms and conditions set forth in the Uniform Offering Circular for the Sale and Issue of Marketable Book-Entry Treasury Bills, Notes, and Bonds (31 CFR Part 356, as amended).

Details about the new security are given in the attached offering highlights.

Attachment

HIGHLIGHTS OF TREASURY OFFERINGS TO THE PUBLIC OF TWO-YEAR NOTES TO BE ISSUED NOVEMBER 1, 2004

October 25, 2004

Offering Amount . . . . $24,000 million
Maximum Award (35% of Offering Amount) . . . . $8,400 million
Maximum Recognized Bid at a Single Yield . . . . $8,400 million
NLP Reporting Threshold . . . . $8,400 million

Description of Offering:
Term and type of security . . . . 2-year notes
Series U-2006
CUSIP number . . . . 912828 CY 6
Auction date . . . . October 27, 2004
Issue date . . . . November 1, 2004
Dated date . . . . October 31, 2004
Maturity date . . . . October 31, 2006
Interest date . . . . Determined based on the highest accepted competitive bid
Yield . . . . Determined at auction
Interest payment dates . . . . April 30 and October 31
Minimum bid amount and multiples $1,000
Accrued interest payable by investor . . . . Determined at auction
Premium or discount . . . . Determined at auction

STRIPS Information:

Minimum amount required $1,000

Corpus CUSIP number . . . . .912820 KW 6

Due date(s) and CUSIP number(s)
for additional TINT(s) . . . . .October 31, 2006 – 912833 3N 8

Submission of bids:

Noncompetitive bids:

Accepted in full up to $5 million at the highest accepted yield.

Foreign and International Monetary Authority (FIMA) bids: Noncompetitive bids submitted through the Federal Reserve banks as agents for FIMA accounts. Accepted in order of size from smallest to largest with no more than $100 million awarded per account. The total noncompetitive amount awarded to Federal Reserve Banks as agents for FIMA accounts will not exceed $1,000 million. A single bid that would cause the limit to be exceeded will be partially accepted in the amount that brings the aggregate award total to the $1,000 million limit. However, if there are two or more bids of equal amounts that would cause the limit to be exceeded, each will be prorated to avoid exceeding the limit.

Competitive bids:

(1) Must be expressed as a yield with three decimals, e.g., 7.123%.

(2) Net long position for each bidder must be reported when the sum of the total bid amount, at all yields, and the net long position is $2 billion or greater.

(3) Net long position must be determined as of one-half hour prior to the closing time for receipt of competitive tenders.

Receipt of Tenders:

Noncompetitive tenders: Prior to 12:00 noon Eastern Daylight Saving time on auction day.

Competitive tenders: Prior to 1:00 p.m. Eastern Daylight Saving time on auction day.

Payment Terms: By charge to a funds account at Federal Reserve Bank on issue date, or payment of full par amount with tender. *Treasury Direct* customers can use the Pay Direct feature which authorizes a charge to their account of record at their financial institution on issue date.

Source: U.S. Treasury Web site, Bureau of Public Debt, November 19, 2004. **www.ustreas.gov**

www.federalreserve.gov

Bids may be submitted by government securities dealers, businesses, and individuals through a Federal Reserve Bank until noon Eastern time for noncompetitive bids and 1 P.M. Eastern time for competitive bids on the day of the auction. Awards are announced the following day. Table 6–4 shows the results of the two-year T-note auction of October 27, 2004. At this auction, 56.90 percent (or $29,559.73 million) of the submitted bids ($51,949.97 million) were accepted. Further, 4.11 percent ($742.34 million) of the accepted bids at the October 27, 2004 Treasury auction were noncompetitive. The auction is a single-bid auction—all bidders pay the same price, which is the price equal to the lowest price of the competitive bids accepted.[6]

6. Similar to Treasury bill auctions (discussed in Chapter 5), this single-price auction process went into effect in 1998. Prior to this the Treasury used a discriminatory auction process. Appendix 5A (located at the book's Web site **www.mhhe.com/sc3e**) compares the two types of auction.

TABLE 6-4 Announcement of Treasury Auction Results, October 27, 2004

PUBLIC DEBT NEWS

Department of the Treasury • Bureau of the Public Debt • Washington, DC 20239

TREASURY SECURITY AUCTION RESULTS
BUREAU OF THE PUBLIC DEBT - WASHINGTON DC

FOR IMMEDIATE RELEASE
October 27, 2004

CONTACT: Office of Financing
202-504-3550

RESULTS OF TREASURY'S AUCTION OF 2-YEAR NOTES

Interest Rate:	2 1/2%	Issue Date:	November 01, 2004
Series:	U-2006	Dated Date:	October 31, 2004
CUSIP No:	912828CY4	Maturity Date:	October 31, 2006

High Yield: 2.590% Price: 99.825825

All noncompetitive and successful competitive bidders were awarded securities at the high yield. Tenders at the high yield were allotted 37.24%. All tenders at lower yields were accepted in full.

Accrued interest of $ 0.06906 per $1,000 must be paid for the period from October 31, 2004 to November 01, 2004.

AMOUNTS TENDERED AND ACCEPTED (in thousands)

Tender Type	Tendered	Accepted
Competitive	$ 45,648,000	$ 23,257,762
Noncompetitive	742,337	742,337
FIMA (noncompetitive)	0	0
SUBTOTAL	46,390,337	24,000,099 1/
Federal Reserve	5,559,633	5,559,633
TOTAL	$ 51,949,970	$ 29,559,732

Median yield 2.560%: 50% of the amount of accepted competitive tenders was tendered at or below that rate. Low yield 2.450%: 5% of the amount of accepted competitive tenders was tendered at or below that rate.

Bid-to-Cover Ratio = 46,390,337 / 24,000,099 = 1.93

1/ Awards to TREASURY DIRECT = $583,001,000

Source: U.S. Treasury Web site, Bureau of Public Debt, November 20, 2004. **www.ustreas.gov**

DO YOU UNDERSTAND?

1. What the difference is between a competitive and noncompetitive Treasury auction bid?
2. What percentage of a Treasury auction offering may be awarded to any single bidder?

Figure 6–7 illustrates the auction results for the two-year T-notes. The highest price offered on the two-year T-notes was 100.097 percent (or a yield of 2.45 percent) of the face value of the T-notes. Bids were filled at prices below the high. The lowest accepted bid price was 99.8258 percent (or a yield of 2.59 percent). At this price, all $29,559.73 million in two-year T-notes offered were sold. All bidders who submitted prices above 99.8258 percent (categories 1 through 5 in Figure 6–7) were awarded in full (winning bids) at the low price accepted (i.e., 99.8258 percent). Bidders who submitted a price below 99.8258 percent (categories 7 and beyond in Figure 6–7) received no allocation of the auctioned T-notes. A portion, but not all, of the bids submitted at 99.8258 were filled (category 6 in Figure 6–7). These bids are filled pro rata at this price. For example, if total bids in category 6 were $100 million, but only $25 million in notes remained to be allocated to competitive bidders (given the S_C supply curve in Figure 6–7), each bidder would receive 25 percent ($\frac{1}{4}$) of his or her bid quantity at this price. All of the $742.34 million noncompetitive bids were accepted at a price of 99.8258 percent (which is equal to the low price paid by the winning competitive bidders).

Most secondary market trading of Treasury notes and bonds occurs directly through broker and dealer trades (see Chapters 5 and 16). For example, according to the Federal Reserve

FIGURE 6–7 Treasury Auction Results

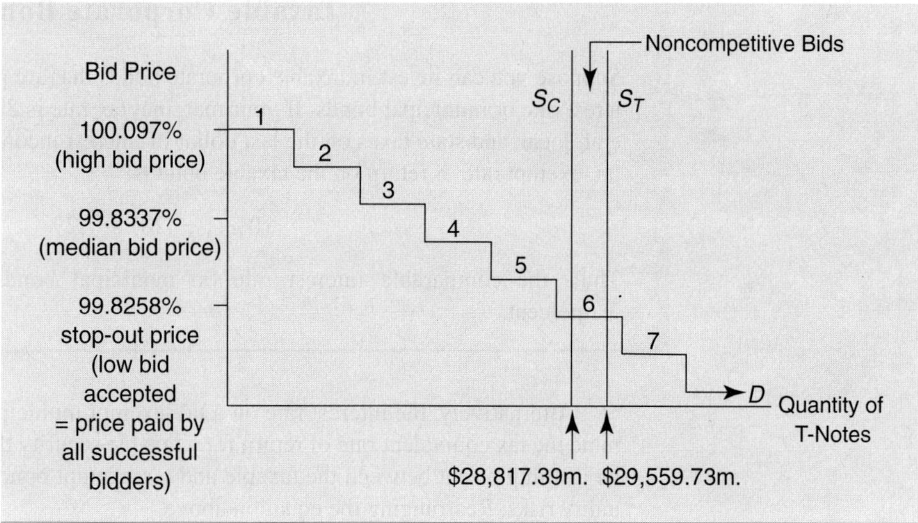

Bank of New York, the average daily trading volume in T-note and T-bond issues for the week ended November 12, 2004 was $552.67 billion. The Treasury quotes in Table 6–1 show just a small number of the Treasury securities that traded on November 9, 2004. The full quote listed in *The Wall Street Journal* shows the hundreds of different Treasury securities that trade daily.

Municipal Bonds

municipal bonds

Securities issued by state and local (e.g., county, city, school) governments.

Municipal bonds are securities issued by state and local (e.g., counties, cities, schools) governments ($1,977.2 billion outstanding in 2004) either to fund temporary imbalances between operating expenditures and receipts or to finance long-term capital outlays for activities such as school construction, public utility construction, or transportation systems. Tax receipts or revenues generated from a project are the source of repayment on municipal bonds.

Municipal bonds are attractive to household investors since interest payments on municipal bonds (but not capital gains) are exempt from federal income taxes and most state and local income taxes (in contrast, interest payments on Treasury securities are exempt only from state and local income taxes). As a result, the interest borrowing cost to the state or local government is lower, because investors are willing to accept lower interest rates on municipal bonds relative to comparable taxable bonds such as corporate bonds.

Municipal Bond Yields. To compare returns from tax-exempt municipal bonds with those on fully taxable corporate bonds, the after-tax (or equivalent tax-exempt) rate of return on a taxable bond can be calculated as follows:

$$i_a = i_b(1 - t)$$

where

i_a = After-tax (equivalent tax-exempt) rate of return on a taxable corporate bond
i_b = Before-tax rate of return on a taxable bond
t = Marginal income tax rate of the bond holder (i.e., the sum of his or her marginal federal, state, and local taxes)[7]

7. Treasury securities are exempt from federal taxes. Thus, the after-tax return on a Treasury security is calculated as:

$$i_a = i_b(1 - t_L)$$

where t_L = the sum of local and state tax rates.

EXAMPLE 6-6 Comparison of Municipal Bonds and Fully Taxable Corporate Bond Rates

Suppose you can invest in taxable corporate bonds that are paying a 10 percent annual interest rate or municipal bonds. If your marginal tax rate is 28 percent (i.e., the sum of federal, local, and state taxes on the last dollar of interest income), the after-tax or equivalent tax-exempt rate of return on the taxable bond is:

$$10\%(1 - .28) = 7.2\%$$

Thus, the comparable interest rate on municipal bonds of similar risk would be 7.2 percent.

Alternatively, the interest rate on a tax-exempt municipal bond can be used to determine the tax equivalent rate of return for a taxable security that would cause an investor to be just indifferent between the taxable and tax-exempt bonds of the same default and liquidity risks. Rearranging the equation above,

$$i_b = i_a/(1 - t)$$

EXAMPLE 6-7 Conversion of a Municipal Bond Rate to a Tax Equivalent Rate

You are considering an investment in a municipal bond that is paying $i_a = 6.5$ percent annually. If your marginal tax rate (t) is 21 percent, the tax equivalent rate of interest on this bond (i_b) is:

$$8.223\% = 6.5\%/(1 - .21)$$

general obligation bonds

Bonds backed by the full faith and credit of the issuer.

Two types of municipal bonds exist: general obligation bonds and revenue bonds. Table 6–5 shows the amount of both issued in 1990 through 2004. **General obligation (GO) bonds** are backed by the full faith and credit of the issuer—that is, the state or local government promises to use all of its financial resources (e.g., its taxation powers) to repay the bond. GO bonds have neither specific assets pledged as collateral backing the bond nor a specific revenue stream identified as a source of repayment of the bond's principal and interest. Because the taxing authority of the government issuer is promised to ensure repayment, the issuance of new GO bonds generally requires local taxpayer approval. Possibly because of this requirement, and taxpayers' reluctance to have their taxes increased, general obligation bonds represent a small portion of municipal bonds issued (38 percent in 2004).

TABLE 6–5 General Obligation and Revenue Bonds Issued, 1990 through 2004

(in billions of dollars)

	1990	2001	2004
General obligation bonds	$39,610	$100,519	$129,447
Revenue bonds	81,295	170,047	207,960

Source: Federal Reserve Bulletin, Table 1.45, May 1992, May 2002, and May 2004. **www.federalreserve.gov**

revenue bonds

Bonds sold to finance a specific revenue-generating project, backed by cash flows from that project.

Revenue bonds are sold to finance a specific revenue-generating project and are backed by cash flows from that project. For example, a revenue bond may be issued to finance an extension of a state highway. To help pay off the interest and principal on that bond, tolls collected from the use of the highway may be pledged as collateral. If the revenue from the project is insufficient to pay interest and retire the bonds on maturity as promised—perhaps because motorists are reluctant to use the highway and pay the tolls—general tax revenues may not be used to meet these payments. Instead, the revenue bond goes into default and bond holders are not paid. Thus, revenue bonds are generally riskier than GO bonds.

Municipal bonds are typically issued in minimum denominations of $5,000. Although trading in these bonds is less active than that of Treasury bonds, a secondary market exists for municipal bonds. Table 6–6 lists a municipal bond quote sheet from *The Wall Street Journal* on November 19, 2004. Column 1 lists the (local) government issuer. Column 2 lists the coupon rate (generally paid semiannually) on the bond issue. Column 3, labeled MAT, is the maturity date of the bond issue. Column 4, labeled PRICE, is the bond price in percentage terms (i.e., 101.503 = 101.503 percent of the face value). Column 5, labeled CHG, is the change in the price from the previous day's close. Column 6, labeled BID YLD, is the yield to maturity on the municipal bond based on the current selling price available to the municipal bond holder. As discussed above, these yields are not taxed at the federal, state, or local levels and are thus not comparable to corporate bond yields.

Municipal bonds are not default risk free. Defaults on municipal bonds peaked in 1990 at $1.4 billion, due mainly to a major economic recession in the United States. Unlike Treasury securities, for which the federal government (in the worst case) can raise taxes or print money to make promised payments, state and local governments are limited to their local tax and revenue base as sources of funds for municipal bond repayment.

The Trading Process for Municipal Bonds. The initial (primary market) sale for municipal bonds (and corporate bonds, discussed below) occurs either through a public offering, using an investment bank serving as a security underwriter, or through a private placement to a small group of investors (often financial institutions). Generally, when a large state or local governmental unit issues municipals to the public, many investment banks are interested in

TABLE 6–6 Municipal Bond Quote

Tax-Exempt Bonds

Representative prices for several active tax-exempt revenue and refunding bonds, based on institutional trades, but may not reflect actual transactions. Yield is to maturity. n-new.
Source: The Bond Buyer/Standard & Poor's Securities Evaluations. All rights reserved.

ISSUE	COUPON	MAT	PRICE	CHG	BID YLD
Atlanta GA psgr fac chg	5.000	01-01-34	101.503	+.160	4.81
Atlanta GA wtr/wastewtr 04	5.000	11-01-43	100.778	+.157	4.90
Atlanta GA wtr/wastewtr 04	5.000	11-01-37	101.645	+.158	4.79
Berkeley Co Sch SC	5.000	12-01-28	100.250	+.144	4.97
Burlington KS poll Sr04	5.300	06-01-31	105.764	+.157	4.56
CA Infr&EcoDevBayAr toll	5.000	07-01-36	102.243	+.142	4.68
Chicago IL GO Sr 04A	5.000	01-01-34	101.458	+.148	4.80
ChicagoIL genarpt 3rdref	5.250	01-01-34	102.248	+.147	4.94
Clark Co NV arpt syst rv	5.000	07-01-36	101.121	+.153	4.85
Clark Co NV ind dev rev bd	5.000	12-01-33	100.154	+.156	4.98
Dallas ISD Tex sch ref bd	5.000	08-15-31	102.003	+.156	4.74
DallasFtWorthTX JointRv0	5.000	11-01-32	100.083	+.205	4.99
Denver Sch Dist Colo	4.500	12-01-28	96.926	+.280	4.71
Illinois Finance Auth hosp	5.500	08-15-43	103.327	+.154	5.07
Metro Washington Arpt DC	5.000	10-01-34	100.079	+.224	4.99
MetropolitanTransAthNY	5.000	11-15-31	102.046	+.133	4.69
Miami-DadeCoFLAviationRv	5.000	10-01-37	101.528	+.156	4.81
Miami-DadeCoFLAviationRv	4.750	10-01-36	95.205	+.454	5.05
Montgomery Co OH Sr04	5.000	05-01-30	100.822	+.150	4.89
NJ Econ DevAuth motor veh	5.000	07-01-29	103.076	+.156	4.60
NJ Econ DevAuth motor veh	5.000	07-01-34	102.661	+.155	4.66
NYC gen oblig bds Fiscal 05	5.000	11-01-34	101.123	+.157	4.86
NYC Muni Wtr Fin Auth	5.000	06-15-39	101.203	+.153	4.84
Orlando Orange Co Exprwy	5.000	07-01-35	102.172	+.142	4.69
Penn St Pub Sch Bldg	5.000	06-01-33	101.947	+.141	4.72
Penn Turnpke Comm Rv	5.000	12-01-34	102.497	+.160	4.69
Port Auth NY&NJ consol	5.125	05-01-34	102.092	+.175	4.89
Puerto Rico ElecPwrAuth	5.125	07-01-29	102.907	+.142	4.71
Puerto Rico Pub Bldgs	5.000	07-01-36	100.984	+.153	4.87
Puerto Rico Pub Bldgs	5.250	07-01-33	103.976	+.156	4.74
Puerto Rico pub impr GO	5.000	07-01-34	101.098	+.153	4.86
Puerto Rico pub impr GO	5.000	07-01-29	101.367	+.153	4.82
Sacramento Co Sanit Dist	5.000	12-01-35	102.538	+.161	4.68
Sales Tx Asset Rec Corp NY	5.000	10-15-32	102.669	+.159	4.66
Sales Tx Asset Rec Corp NY	5.000	10-15-29	102.910	+.160	4.63
SaltRiver Prj Agri Imprv	4.750	01-01-32	100.062	+.219	4.74
SaltRiver Prj Agri Imprv	5.000	01-01-31	102.271	+.135	4.66
TexasTpkeAuthRvBds	5.000	08-15-42	100.247	+.127	4.96
Univ of CA limited proj	4.800	05-15-34	98.941	+.308	4.87
Univ of CA limited proj	4.875	05-15-37	100.511	+.139	4.80

Source: The *Wall Street Journal*, November 19, 2004, p. B6. Reprinted by permission of *The Wall Street Journal*. **www.wsj.com**

TABLE 6–7 Top Municipal Bond Underwriters*

Underwriter	Principal Amount (in millions of dollars)	Market Share	Number of Issues
UBS Financial Services	$35,811.6	13.5%	631
Citigroup	30,092.8	11.3	476
Lehman Brothers	22,021.1	8.3	170
Merrill Lynch	18,708.8	7.1	208
Goldman Sachs	18,081.6	6.8	132
J.P. Morgan Securities	17,685.0	6.7	324
Bear, Stearns	15,464.1	5.8	133
Morgan Stanley	14,695.8	5.5	179
RBC Dain Rauscher	11,157.6	4.2	533
Banc of America Securities	10,403.2	3.9	327
Industry totals	$265.5 billion		

*Through September 2004.

Source: Thomson Financial Securities Data, November 2004. **www.tfibcm.com**

underwriting the bonds and the municipals can generally be sold in a national market. Total dollar volume of these new issues was $265.5 billion in the first three quarters of 2004, down from $289 billion in the first three quarters of 2003. Table 6–7 lists the activity of the top 10 municipal bond underwriters in 2004.

firm commitment underwriting

The issue of securities by an investment bank in which the investment bank guarantees the issuer a price for newly issued securities by buying the whole issue at a fixed price from the issuer. It then seeks to resell these securities to suppliers of funds (investors) at a higher price.

Firm Commitment Underwriting. Public offerings of municipal (and corporate, see below) bonds are most often made through an investment banking firm (see Chapter 16) serving as the underwriter. Normally, the investment bank facilitates this transfer using a **firm commitment underwriting,** illustrated in Figure 6–8. The investment bank guarantees the municipality (or corporation for a corporate bond) a price for newly issued bonds by buying the whole issue at a fixed price from the municipal issuer (the bid price). The investment bank then seeks to resell these securities to suppliers of funds (investors) at a higher price (the offer price). As a result, the investment bank takes a risk that it may not be able to resell the securities to investors at a higher price. This may occur if prices of municipal bonds suddenly fall due to an unexpected change in interest rates or negative information being released about the creditworthiness of the issuing municipality. If this occurs, the investment bank takes a loss on its underwriting of the security. However, the municipal issuer is protected by being able to sell the whole issue.

The investment bank can purchase the bonds through competitive bidding against other investment bankers or through direct negotiation with the issuer. In a competitive sale, the issuer invites bids from a number of underwriters. The investment bank that submits the highest bid to the issuer wins the bid. The underwriter may use a syndicate of other underwriters and investment banks to distribute (sell) the issue to the public. Most state and local governments require a competitive municipal bond issue to be announced in a trade publication, such as the *Bond Buyer*. With a negotiated sale, the investment bank obtains

FIGURE 6–8 Firm Commitment Underwriting of a Municipal or Corporate Bond Issue

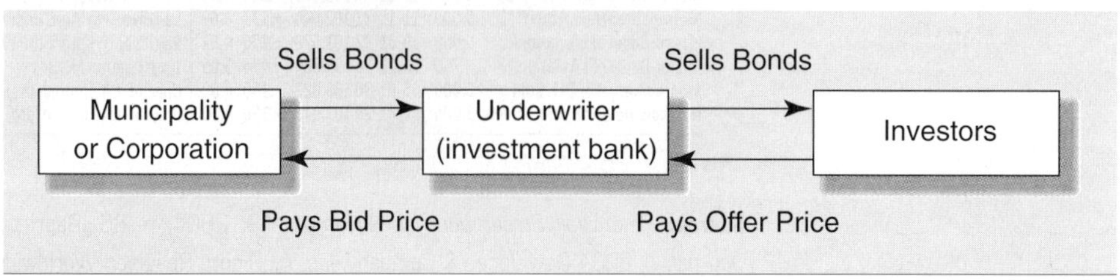

the exclusive right to originate, underwrite, and distribute the new bonds through a one-on-one negotiation process. With a negotiated sale, the investment bank provides the origination and advising services to the issuers. Most states require that GO bonds be issued through competitive bids.

best-efforts offering

The issue of securities in which the investment bank does not guarantee a price to the issuer and acts more as a placing or distribution agent on a fee basis related to its success in placing the issue.

Best-Efforts Offering. Some municipal (and corporate) securities are offered on a **best-efforts** basis in which the investment bank does not guarantee a firm price to the issuer (as with a firm commitment offering) and acts more as a placing or distribution agent for a fee. With best-efforts offerings, the investment bank incurs no risk of mispricing the security since it seeks to sell the bonds at the price it can get in the market. In return the investment bank receives a fee. Further, the investment bank offers the securities at a price originally set by the municipality. Thus, the investment bank does not incur the expense of establishing the market price for the customer. Often, knowing that the investment bank has not put any of its own funds into the issue, investors in best-efforts issues are not willing to pay as much for the bonds as with a firm commitment issue.

private placement

A security issue placed with one or a few large institutional buyers.

Private Placement. In a **private placement,** a municipality (or corporation), sometimes with the help of an investment bank, seeks to find a large institutional buyer or group of buyers (usually fewer than 10) to purchase the whole issue. To protect smaller individual investors against a lack of disclosure, the Security and Exchange Act of 1934 requires publicly traded securities to be registered with the Securities and Exchange Commission (SEC). Private placements, on the other hand, can be unregistered and can be resold only to large, financially sophisticated investors (see below). These large investors supposedly possess the resources and expertise to analyze a security's risk.

Privately placed bonds (and stocks) have traditionally been among the most illiquid securities in the bond market, with only the very largest financial institutions or institutional investors being able or willing to buy and hold them in the absence of an active secondary market. In April 1990, however, the Securities and Exchange Commission amended its Regulation 144A. This allowed large investors to begin trading these privately placed securities among themselves even though, in general, privately placed securities do not satisfy the stringent disclosure and informational requirements that the SEC imposes on approved publicly registered issues. Rule 144A private placements may now be underwritten by investment banks on a firm commitment basis. Of the total $351.96 billion in private debt (municipal and corporate) placements in the first three quarters of 2004, $328.12 billion (93.2 percent) were Rule 144A placements. Credit Suisse First Boston was the lead underwriter of Rule 144A debt placements in 2004 (underwriting $48.82 billion, 14.9 percent of the total placements).

Issuers of privately placed bonds tend to be less well known (e.g., medium-sized municipalities and corporations). As a result of a lack of information on these issues, and the resulting possibility of greater risk, interest rates paid to holders of privately placed bonds tend to be higher than on publicly placed bond issues. Although Rule 144A has improved the liquidity of privately placed bonds, this market is still less liquid than the public placement market. Another result of the increased attention to this market by investment banks is that the interest premiums paid by borrowers of privately placed issues over public issues have decreased.

Although the SEC defined large investors as those with assets of $100 million or more—which excludes all but the very wealthiest household savers—it is reasonable to ask how long this size restriction will remain. As they become more sophisticated and the costs of information acquisition fall, savers will increasingly demand access to the private placement market. In such a world, savers would have a choice not only between the secondary securities from financial institutions and the primary securities publicly offered by municipalities and corporations but also between publicly offered (registered) securities and privately offered (unregistered) securities.

Secondary Market Trading. The secondary market for municipal bonds is thin (i.e., trades are relatively infrequent). Thin trading is mainly a result of a lack of information on bond issuers, as well as special features (such as covenants) that are built into those bond's contracts. Information on municipal bond issuers (particularly of smaller government units) is generally more costly to obtain and evaluate, although this is in part offset by bond rating agencies (see below). In a similar fashion, bond rating agencies generate information about corporate and sovereign (country) borrowers as well.

Corporate Bonds

corporate bonds

Long-term bonds issued by corporations.

bond indenture

The legal contract that specifies the rights and obligations of the bond issuer and the bond holders.

Corporate bonds are all long-term bonds issued by corporations ($6,728.6 billion outstanding in 2004, some 57.9 percent of all outstanding long-term bonds). The minimum denomination on publicly traded corporate bonds (which, in contrast to privately placed corporate bonds, require SEC registration) is $1,000, and coupon-paying corporate bonds generally pay interest semiannually.

The **bond indenture** is the legal contract that specifies the rights and obligations of the bond issuer and the bond holders. The bond indenture contains a number of covenants associated with a bond issue. These bond covenants describe rules and restrictions placed on the bond issuer and bond holders. As described below, these covenants include such rights for the bond issuer as the ability to call the bond issue and restrictions as to limits on the ability of the issuer to increase dividends. By legally documenting the rights and obligations of all parties involved in a bond issue, the bond indenture helps lower the risk (and therefore the interest cost) of the bond issue. All matters pertaining to the bond issuer's performance regarding any debt covenants as well as bond repayments are overseen by a trustee (frequently a bank trust department) who is appointed as the bond holders' representative or "monitor." The signature of a trustee on the bond is a guarantee of the bond's authenticity. The trustee also acts as the transfer agent for the bonds when ownership changes as a result of secondary market sales and when interest payments are made from the bond issuer to the bond holder. The trustee also informs the bond holders if the firm is no longer meeting the terms of the indenture. In this case, the trustee initiates any legal action on behalf of the bond holders against the issuing firm. In the event of a subsequent reorganization or liquidation of the bond issuer, the trustee continues to act on behalf of the bond holders to protect their principal.

www.nyse.com

Table 6–8 presents a bond market quote sheet from *The Wall Street Journal* for November 9, 2004, for corporate bonds traded on the New York Stock Exchange (NYSE). Quotes are listed by dollar volume of trading, from highest to lowest. Look at the third quote posted in Table 6–8. Column 1 of the quote lists the issuer (Kraft Foods). Column 2 lists the coupon rate (4 percent). Column 3 lists the maturity date (October 1, 2008). Column 4, labeled LAST PRICE, is the closing price (in percent) of the bond on November 9 (100.292%). Column 5, labeled LAST YIELD, is the yield to maturity (see Chapter 3) on the bond (3.917%) using the LAST PRICE. Column 6, labeled *EST SPREAD, is the difference between the yield (in basis points) on the corporate bond and a similar maturity Treasury security (40 = .40%). Column 7, labeled UST†, lists the maturity (in years) of the Treasury security used to determine the spread (five-year note). Column 8, labeled EST $ VOL (000's), is the trading volume for the bond in thousands of dollars (130,423 = $130,423,000).

bearer bonds

Bonds with coupons attached to the bond. The holder presents the coupons to the issuer for payments of interest when they come due.

registered bond

A bond in which the owner is recorded by the issuer and the coupon payments are mailed to the registered owner.

Bond Characteristics. Corporate (and Treasury) bonds have many different characteristics that differentiate one issue from another. We list and briefly define these characteristics in Table 6–9, and we describe them in detail below.

Bearer versus Registered Bonds. Corporate bonds can be bearer bonds or registered bonds. With **bearer bonds,** coupons are attached to the bond and the holder (bearer) at the time of the coupon payment gets the relevant coupon paid on presentation to the issuer (i.e., gets the bond coupon "clipped"). With a **registered bond,** the bond holder's (or owner's) identification information is kept in an electronic record by the issuer and the coupon payments are mailed or wire-transferred to the bank account of the registered owner. Because of the

TABLE 6–8 Corporate Bond Market Quote

Corporate Bonds

Tuesday, November 9, 2004

Forty most active fixed-coupon corporate bonds

(1) COMPANY (TICKER)	(2) COUPON	(3) MATURITY	(4) LAST PRICE	(5) LAST YIELD	(6) *EST SPREAD	(7) UST†	(8) EST $ VOL (000's)
Goldman Sachs Group (GS)	6.600	Jan 15, 2012	111.904	4.628	42	10	183,115
Ford Motor Credit (F)	7.250	Oct 25, 2011	107.338	5.944	173	10	141,752
Kraft Foods (KFT)	**4.000**	**Oct 01, 2008**	**100.292**	**3.917**	**40**	**5**	**130,423**
General Motors (GM)	8.375	Jul 15, 2033	104.550	7.968	303	30	127,929
Ford Motor Co (F)	7.450	Jul 16, 2031	98.250	7.603	266	30	120,549
XL Capital Ltd (XL)	5.250	Sep 15, 2014	98.869	5.398	117	10	115,277
Time Warner (TWX)	6.875	May 01, 2012	112.842	4.806	58	10	114,682
Ford Motor Credit (F)	7.000	Oct 01, 2013	105.529	6.180	197	10	113,778
Morgan Stanley (MWD)	4.000	Jan 15, 2010	98.928	4.231	71	5	111,841
Kraft Foods (KFT)	5.625	Nov 01, 2011	105.874	4.628	42	10	109,405
General Electric (GE)	5.000	Feb 01, 2013	102.634	4.610	40	10	107,302
Time Warner (TWX)	7.700	May 01, 2032	118.498	6.278	134	30	99,094
Wells Fargo (WFC)	5.125	Sep 15, 2016	100.209	5.100	88	10	98,420
General Electric Capital (GE)	6.750	Mar 15, 2032	115.259	5.647	71	30	89,488
Morgan Stanley (MWD)	4.750	Apr 01, 2014	97.440	5.096	88	10	89,438
Sprint Capital (FON)	7.625	Jan 30, 2011	116.301	4.577	35	10	86,315
Goldman Sachs Group (GS)	4.750	Jul 15, 2013	98.847	4.914	71	10	83,936
General Motors Acceptance (GM)	8.000	Nov 01, 2031	103.417	7.697	277	30	80,007
Viacom (VIA)	5.625	Aug 15, 2012	106.356	4.638	41	10	77,880
BellSouth (BLS)	6.550	Jun 15, 2034	105.797	6.123	119	30	77,422
Viacom (VIA)	6.625	May 15, 2011	112.088	4.462	24	10	77,070
Merck (MRK)	2.500	Mar 30, 2007	97.693	3.520	44	3	76,900
General Motors Acceptance (GM)	6.875	Aug 28, 2012	102.988	6.380	217	10	76,677
Merck (MRK)	5.950	Dec 01, 2028	101.279	5.850	91	30	76,025
J.P. Morgan Chase (JPM)	5.250	May 30, 2007	104.464	3.401	32	3	75,487
General Motors Acceptance (GM)	7.250	Mar 02, 2011	105.425	6.194	198	10	72,393
CIT Group (CIT)	4.125	Nov 03, 2009	99.484	4.241	73	5	72,095
Ford Motor Credit (F)	5.625	Oct 01, 2008	102.594	4.881	136	5	70,022
COX Communications (COX)	4.625	Jun 01, 2013	94.082	5.502	128	10	69,084
Gillette (G)	3.800	Sep 15, 2009	99.980	3.803	30	5	68,635
Citigroup (C)	3.625	Feb 09, 2009	99.249	3.818	30	5	67,764
Comcast Cable Communications (CMCSA)	8.875	May 01, 2017	128.505	5.656	145	10	64,105
XL Capital Finance (Europe) PLC (XL)	6.500	Jan 15, 2012	109.260	4.948	73	10	62,910
Nordea Bank AB (NBHSS)	5.250	Nov 30, 2012	103.632	4.702	50	10	62,600
General Motors Acceptance (GM)	5.850	Jan 14, 2009	102.023	5.300	178	5	60,762
Bank of America (BAC)	5.250	Dec 01, 2015	101.727	5.044	85	10	60,275
Liberty Media (L)	5.700	May 15, 2013	101.114	5.534	134	10	60,270
Comcast Holdings (CMCSA)	7.625	Feb 15, 2008	111.385	3.861	35	5	60,169
National Rural Utilities Cooperative Finance (NRUC)	7.250	Mar 01, 2012	115.264	4.748	53	10	57,618
General Motors Acceptance (GM)	6.875	Sep 15, 2011	103.309	6.270	205	10	55,410
AT&T Wireless Services (CNG)	8.750	Mar 01, 2031	131.926	6.258	131	30	53,400

Volume represents total volume for each issue; price/yield data are for trades of $1 million and greater. * Estimated spreads, in basis points (100 basis points is one percentage point), over the 2, 3, 5, 10 or 30-year hot run Treasury note/bond. 2-year: 2.500 10/06; 3-year: 3.000 11/07; 5-year: 3.375 10/09; 10-year: 4.250 08/14; 30-year: 5.375 02/31. †Comparable U.S. Treasury issue.

Source: MarketAxess Corporate BondTicker

Source: *The Wall Street Journal*, November 10, 2004, p. C12. Reprinted by permission of *The Wall Street Journal*. **www.wsj.com**

TABLE 6–9 Bond Characteristics

Bearer Bonds—bonds on which coupons are attached. The bond holder presents the coupons to the issuer for payments of interest when they come due.

Registered Bonds—with a registered bond, the owner's identification information is recorded by the issuer and the coupon payments are mailed to the registered owner.

Term Bonds—bonds in which the entire issue matures on a single date.

Serial Bonds—bonds that mature on a series of dates, with a portion of the issue paid off on each.

Mortgage Bonds—bonds that are issued to finance specific projects that are pledged as collateral for the bond issue.

Equipment Trust Certificates—bonds collateralized with tangible non–real estate property (e.g., railcars and airplanes).

Debentures—bonds backed solely by the general credit of the issuing firm and unsecured by specific assets or collateral.

Subordinated Debentures—unsecured debentures that are junior in their rights to mortgage bonds and regular debentures.

Convertible Bonds—bonds that may be exchanged for another security of the issuing firm at the discretion of the bond holder.

Stock Warrants—bonds that give the bond holder an opportunity to purchase common stock at a specified price up to a specified date.

Callable Bonds—bonds that allow the issuer to force the bond holder to sell the bond back to the issuer at a price above the par value (at the call price).

Sinking Fund Provisions—bonds that include a requirement that the issuer retire a certain amount of the bond issue each year.

lack of security with bearer bonds, they have largely been replaced by registered bonds in the United States.

term bonds

Bonds in which the entire issue matures on a single date.

serial bonds

Bonds that mature on a series of dates, with a portion of the issue paid off on each.

Term versus Serial Bonds. Most corporate bonds are **term bonds,** meaning that the entire issue matures on a single date. Some corporate bonds (and most municipal bonds), on the other hand, are **serial bonds,** meaning that the issue contains many maturity dates, with a portion of the issue being paid off on each date. For economic reasons, many issuers like to avoid a "crisis at maturity." Rather than having to pay off one very large principal sum at a given time in the future (as with a term issue), many issuers like to stretch out the period over which principal payments are made—especially if the corporation's earnings are quite volatile.

mortgage bonds

Bonds issued to finance specific projects, which are pledged as collateral for the bond issue.

Mortgage Bonds. Corporations issue **mortgage bonds** to finance specific projects that are pledged as collateral for the bond issue. Thus, mortgage bond issues are secured debt issues.[8] Bond holders may legally take title to the collateral to obtain payment on the bonds if the issuer of a mortgage bond defaults. Because mortgage bonds are backed with a claim to specific assets of the corporate issuer, they are less risky investments than unsecured bonds. As a result, mortgage bonds have lower yields to bond holders than unsecured bonds. Equipment trust certificates are bonds collateralized with tangible (movable) non–real estate property such as railcars and airplanes.

debentures

Bonds backed solely by the general credit of the issuing firm, unsecured by specific assets or collateral.

subordinated debentures

Bonds that are unsecured and are junior in their rights to mortgage bonds and regular debentures.

Debentures and Subordinated Debentures. Bonds backed solely by the general creditworthiness of the issuing firm, unsecured by specific assets or collateral, are called **debentures.** Debenture holders generally receive their promised payments only after the secured debt holders, such as mortgage bond holders, have been paid. **Subordinated debentures** are also unsecured, and they are junior in their rights to mortgage bonds and regular debentures. In the event of a default, subordinated debenture holders receive a cash distribution only after all nonsubordinated debt has been repaid in full. As a result, subordinated bonds are the riskiest type of bond and generally have higher yields than nonsubordinated bonds. In many cases, these bonds are termed *high-yield* or *junk bonds* because of their below investment grade credit ratings (see below).

convertible bonds

Bonds that may be exchanged for another security of the issuing firm at the discretion of the bond holder.

Convertible Bonds. **Convertible bonds** are bonds that may be exchanged for another security of the issuing firm (e.g., common stock) at the discretion of the bond holder. If the market value of the securities the bond holder receives with conversion exceeds the market value of the bond, the bond holder can return the bonds to the issuer in exchange for the new securities and make a profit. As a result, conversion is an attractive option or feature to bond holders. Thus, convertible bonds are hybrid securities involving elements of both debt and equity. They give the bond holder an investment opportunity (an option) that is not available with nonconvertible bonds. As a result, the yield on a convertible bond is usually lower (generally, 2 to 5 percentage points) than that on a nonconvertible bond:

$$i_{cvb} = i_{ncvb} - op_{cvb}$$

where

i_{cvb} = Rate of return on a convertible bond
i_{ncvb} = Rate of return on a nonconvertible bond
op_{cvb} = Value of the conversion option to the bond holder

8. Open-end mortgage bonds allow the firm to issue additional bonds in the future, using the same assets as collateral and giving the same priority of claim against those assets. Closed-end mortgage bonds prohibit the firm from issuing additional bonds using the same assets as collateral and giving the same priority of claim against those assets.

EXAMPLE 6-8 Analysis of a Convertible Bond

In 2007, Titan Corporation had a convertible bond issue outstanding. Each bond, with a face value of $1,000, could be converted into common shares at a rate of 285.71 shares of stock per $1,000 face value bond (the conversion rate), or $3.50 per share. In June 2007, Titan's common stock was trading (on the NYSE) at $9.375 per share. While this might look like conversion would be very profitable, Titan's convertible bonds were trading at 267.875 percent of the face value of the bond, or $2,678.75.

To determine whether or not it is profitable to convert the bonds into common stock in Titan Corp., the conversion value of each bond can be calculated as:

$$\text{Conversion value} = \frac{\text{Current market price of common}}{\text{stock received on conversion}} \times \text{Conversion rate}$$

If a bond holder were to convert Titan Corp. bonds into stock, each bond (worth $2,678.75) could be exchanged for 285.71 shares of stock worth $9.375. The conversion value of the bonds is:

$$\$9.375 \times 285.71 = \$2,678.53$$

Thus, there is virtually no difference in dollar value of the investment to the investor if he or she holds Titan's debt or its common stock equivalent.

Figure 6–9 illustrates the value of a convertible bond as a function of the issuing firm's asset value. The horizontal axis plots the firm's value, which establishes an upper bound for the value of the convertible bond (since it cannot trade for more than the value of the firm's assets). Thus, the value of the issuing firm line that bisects the figure at a 45° angle also represents the issuing firm's value and sets an upper bound for the value of the convertible bond. In addition, the figure plots the values of the firm's convertible and nonconvertible bonds. At low firm values, the values of both bonds drop off as bankruptcy becomes more likely. Note that the nonconvertible bond's value does not increase at higher firm asset values since bond holders receive only their promised payments and no more. However, the convertible bond values rise directly with the firm's asset value. Specifically, at low firm asset values the convertible bond value acts more like a nonconvertible bond, trading at only a slight premium

FIGURE 6–9 **Value of a Convertible Bond**

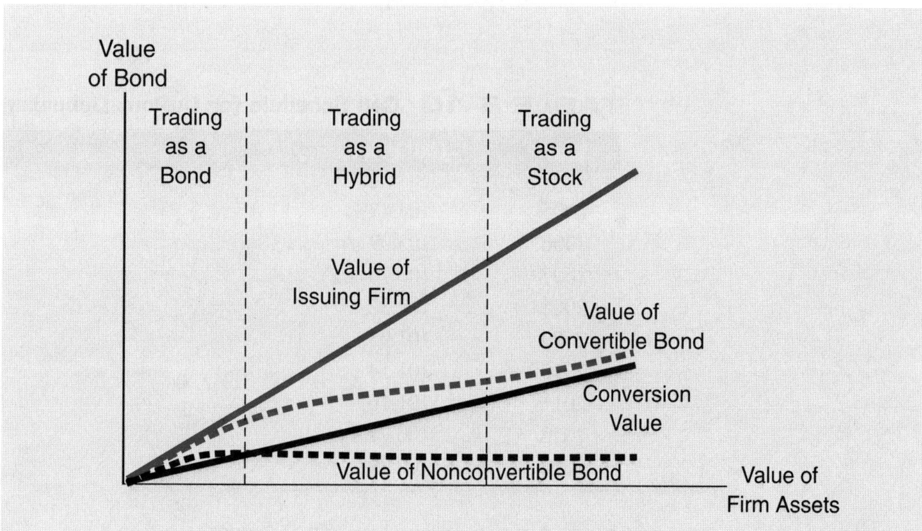

over the nonconvertible bond. When the issuing firm's value is high, however, the convertible will act more like a stock, selling for only a slight premium over the conversion value. In the middle range, the convertible bond will trade as a hybrid security, acting partly like a bond and partly like a stock.

Most convertible bond issues are set up so that it is not initially profitable to convert to stock. Usually the stock price must increase 15 to 20 percent before it becomes profitable to convert the bond to the new security.

stock warrants

Bonds issued with stock warrants attached giving the bond holder an opportunity to purchase common stock at a specified price up to a specified date.

Stock Warrants. Bonds can also be issued with **stock warrants** attached. Similar to convertible bonds, bonds issued with stock warrants attached give the bond holder an opportunity to detach the warrants to purchase common stock at a prespecified price up to a prespecified date. In this case, however, if the bond holder decides to purchase the stock (by returning or exercising the warrant), the bond holder does not have to return the underlying bond to the issuer (as under a convertible bond). Instead, he or she keeps the bond and pays for additional stock at a price specified in the warrant. Bond holders will exercise their warrants if the market value of the stock is greater than the price at which the stock can be purchased through the warrant. Further, the bond holder may sell the warrant rather then exercise it, while maintaining ownership of the underlying bond. Risky firms commonly attach stock warrants to their bonds to increase the bonds' marketability. Rather than paying extremely high interest rates or accepting very restrictive bond covenants, the firm attaches stock warrants to the bonds in order to get investors to buy them.

call provision

A provision on a bond issue that allows the issuer to force the bond holder to sell the bond back to the issuer at a price above the par value (or at the call price).

call premium

The difference between the call price and the face value on the bond.

Callable Bonds. Many corporate bond issues include a **call provision,** which allows the issuer to require the bond holder to sell the bond back to the issuer at a given (call) price—usually set above the par value of the bond. The difference between the call price and the face value on the bond is the **call premium.** Many callable bond issues have a deferred call provision in which the right to call the bond is deferred for a period of time after the bond is issued (generally 10 years). Bonds are usually called in when interest rates drop (and bond prices rise) so that the issuer can gain by calling in the old bonds (with higher coupon rates) and issuing new bonds (with lower coupon rates).

For example, in 2004, DuPont had a $300 million callable debenture issue outstanding. The face value of each bond was $1,000. The issue, with a maturity date of January 15, 2023, was callable as a whole or in part not less than 30 days nor more than 60 days following January 15 of each year between the years 2005 and 2013, as listed in Table 6–10. Thus, if the bonds are called in 2008, the bond holder will receive $1,023.20 (102.32% × $1,000) per bond called in. Note that as the bond approaches maturity, the call premium declines. The closer the bond is to maturity, the smaller the premium required for forcing bond holders to give up the bonds early.

TABLE 6–10 Call Schedule for DuPont Debenture Due 2023

Year	Call Price
2005	103.47%
2006	103.09
2007	102.70
2008	102.32
2009	101.93
2010	101.54
2011	101.16
2012	100.77
2013	100.39

Source: DuPont Corporation, Annual Report, 2005.

A call provision is an unattractive feature to bond holders, since the bond holder may be forced to return the bond to the issuer before he or she is ready to end the investment and the investor can only reinvest the funds at a lower interest rate. As a result, callable bonds have higher yields (generally between 0.05 and 0.25 percent) than comparable noncallable bonds:

$$i_{ncb} = i_{cb} - op_{cb}$$

where

i_{ncb} = Rate of return on a noncallable bond
i_{cb} = Rate of return on a callable bond
op_{cb} = Value of the issuer's option to call the debt early

sinking fund provision

A requirement that the issuer retire a certain amount of the bond issue each year.

Sinking Fund Provisions. Many bonds have a **sinking fund provision,** which is a requirement that the issuer retire a certain amount of the bond issue early over a number of years, especially as the bond approaches maturity. The bond issuer provides the funds to the trustee by making frequent payments to a sinking fund. This sinking fund accumulates in value and is eventually used to retire the entire bond issue at maturity or to periodically retire a specified dollar amount of bonds either by purchasing them in the open market or by randomly calling bonds to be retired. In this case, the selected bonds are called and redeemed. Once the bonds are called they cease to earn interest. The bond holders must surrender their bonds to receive their principal.[9] For example, in 2004 May Department Stores Co. had a sinking fund debenture issue outstanding that required that the firm put $12.5 million per year from 1999 through 2017 (19 years) into a sinking fund, so that a total of $237.5 million of the $250 million principal on the bonds would be accumulated before maturity.

Since it reduces the probability of default at the maturity date, a sinking fund provision is an attractive feature to bond holders. Thus, bonds with a sinking fund provision are less risky to the bond holder and generally have lower yields than comparable bonds without a sinking fund provision.

The Trading Process for Corporate Bonds. Primary sales of corporate bond issues occur through either a public sale (issue) or a private placement in a manner identical to that discussed for municipal bonds (see above). In the first three quarters of 2004, a total of $3,927.8 billion of (corporate and municipal) debt was issued, of which $351.96 billion was privately placed.

There are two secondary markets in corporate bonds: the exchange market (e.g., the NYSE) and the over-the-counter (OTC) market. The major exchange for corporate bonds is the New York Stock Exchange Fixed Income Market. Most of the trading on the NYSE's bond market is completed through its Automated Bond System (ABS), which is a fully automated trading and information system that allows subscribing firms to enter and execute bond orders through terminals in their offices. Users receive immediate execution reports and locked-in prices on their trades. Notice, however, the small amount of trading volume reported for NYSE bonds in Table 6–8. The average daily dollar value of bond trading totaled $13.5 billion in 2004 in a market with $6.73 trillion of bonds outstanding. This is because less than 1 percent of all corporate bonds trade on exchanges such as the NYSE.

Most bonds are traded OTC among major bond dealers such as Salomon Smith Barney and UBS Paine Webber. The OTC direct, interdealer market totally dominates trading in corporate bonds. Virtually all large trades are carried out on the OTC market, even for bonds listed on an exchange, such as the NYSE bond market. Thus, prices reported on the exchanges (like those in Table 6–8) are generally considered to be inexact estimates of prices associated with large transactions. Thus, in contrast to Treasury securities, secondary market trading of corporate bonds can involve a significant degree of liquidity risk.

9. If the bond holder does not turn the bonds in for redemption, they continue to be outstanding and are obligations of the issuer. However, the issuer's obligation is limited to refunding only the principal, since interest payments stopped on the call date.

TABLE 6–11 Bond Credit Ratings

Explanation	Moody's	S&P
Best quality; smallest degree of risk	Aaa	AAA
High quality; slightly more long-term	Aa1	AA+
risk than top rating	Aa2	AA
	Aa3	AA−
Upper medium grade; possible impairment	A1	A+
in the future	A2	A
	A3	A−
Medium grade; lack outstanding investment	Baa1	BBB+
characteristics	Baa2	BBB
	Baa3	BBB−
Speculative issues; protection may be	Ba1	BB+
very moderate	Ba2	BB
	Ba3	BB−
Very speculative; may have small assurance	B1	B+
of interest and principal payments	B2	B
	B3	B−
Issues in poor standing; may be in default	Caa	CCC
Speculative in a high degree; with marked shortcomings	Ca	CC
Lowest quality; poor prospects of attaining	C	C
real investment standing		D

Source: Moody's and Standard & Poor's Web sites. **www.moodys.com; www.standardandpoors.com**

Bond Ratings

As mentioned above, the inability of investors to get information pertaining to the risk, especially default risk, on bonds, at a reasonable cost, can result in thinly traded markets. In Chapter 3, we examined the impact of interest rate risk (i.e., interest rate changes) on bond prices. Specifically, we demonstrated that bonds with longer maturities (durations) and low coupon rates experience larger price changes for a given change in interest rates than bonds with short maturities and high coupon rates (i.e., bonds with longer maturities and lower coupon rates are subject to greater interest rate risk). As important, bond investors also need to measure the degree of default risk on a bond.

Large bond investors, traders, and managers often evaluate default risk by conducting their own analysis of the issuer, including an assessment of the bond issuer's financial ratios (see Chapter 20) and security prices. Small investors are not generally capable of generating the same extensive information and thus frequently rely on bond ratings provided by the bond rating agencies. The two major bond rating agencies are Moody's and Standard & Poor's (S&P).[10] Both companies rank bonds based on the perceived probability of issuer default and assign a rating based on a letter grade. Table 6–11 summarizes these rating systems and provides a brief definition of each. The highest credit quality (lowest default risk) that rating agencies assign is a triple-A (Aaa for Moody's and AAA for S&P). Bonds with a triple-A rating have the lowest interest spread over similar maturity Treasury securities. As the assessed default risk increases, Moody's and S&P lower the credit rating assigned on a bond issue, and the interest spread over similar maturity Treasuries paid to bond holders generally increases.[11] Figure 6–10 shows the

www.moodys.com

www.standardandpoors.com

10. Other credit rating agencies include Fitch IBCA, Inc. (**www.fitchibca.com**) and Duff and Phelps Credit Rating Services (**www.dufflle.com**).

11. Note that S&P and Moody's sometimes disagree on ratings (recently differences occur about 15 percent of the time). When this occurs, a bond is said to have a "split" rating.

FIGURE 6–10 **Rates on Treasury Bonds, Aaa-Rated Bonds, and Baa-Rated Bonds**

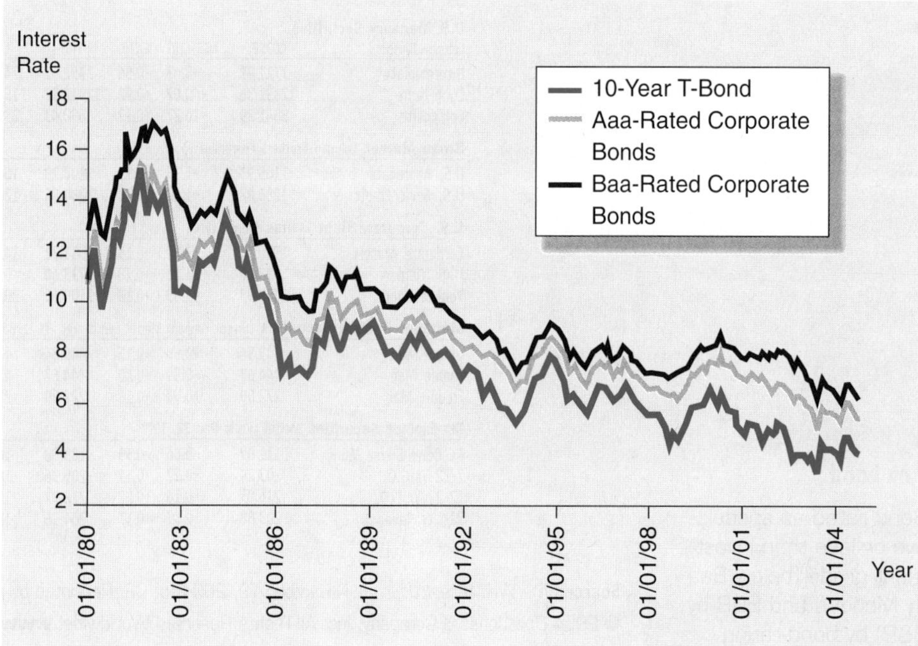

Source: Federal Reserve Board Web site, "Research and Data," November 2004. **www.federalreserve.gov**

rates on 10-year Treasury securities versus Aaa-rated and Baa-rated bonds from 1980 through October 2004. The risk premium over this period on Aaa-rated bonds was 1.06 percent and on Baa-rated bonds was 2.16 percent. The cumulative default rates on these bonds over a 10-year period after issuance is 0.03 percent on Aaa-rated bonds and 9.63 percent on Baa-rated bonds.[12]

Rating agencies consider several factors in determining and assigning credit ratings on bond issues. For example, a financial analysis is conducted of the issuer's operations and its needs, its position in the industry, and its overall financial strength and ability to pay the required interest and principal on the bonds. Rating agencies analyze the issuer's liquidity, profitability, debt capacity, and more recently its corporate governance structure (following the passage of the Sarbanes-Oxley Act in 2002—see Chapter 9). Then for each particular issue, rating agencies evaluate the nature and provisions of the debt issue (e.g., the covenants and callability of the bond) and the protection afforded by, and relative position of, the debt issue in the event of bankruptcy, reorganization, or other arrangements under the laws of bankruptcy and other laws affecting creditors' rights. However, in recent years rating agencies have been criticized as slow to react. Perhaps the best example of this was the failure to downgrade Enron (the second-largest corporate bankruptcy in U.S. history) in the months leading up to its failure in 2001.

As a practical matter, a bond needs to be rated if it is to be used as an investment vehicle by certain institutional investors. Bonds rated Baa or better by Moody's and BBB or better by S&P are considered to be investment-grade bonds. Financial institutions (e.g., banks,

12. See E. I. Altman and B. Karlin, "Default and Returns on High-Yield Bonds: Analysis through 2003 and Default Outlook," working paper, New York University Salomon Center, May 2004. A cumulative default rate reflects annual default rates over time. If a bond has a 99 percent chance of surviving default in the first year of its life and 98 percent in its second year, then the two-year cumulative default rate (CDR) = 1 − [(.99) × (.98)] = .0298, or 2.98%.

TABLE 6–12 Major Bond Market Indexes

Major Bond Indexes

U.S. Treasury Securities Lehman Brothers	CLOSE	NET CHG	% CHG	52-WEEK HIGH	52-WEEK LOW	52-WEEK % CHG	YTD % CHG
Intermediate	7711.97	+3.43	+0.04	7752.62	7414.07	+3.18	+2.90
Long-term	12831.36	+40.62	+0.32	12912.12	11522.05	+7.58	+7.83
Composite	8841.39	+10.27	+0.12	8890.43	8374.44	+4.39	+4.27
Broad Market Lehman Brothers (preliminary)							
U.S. Aggregate	1105.93	+1.35	+0.11	1108.18	1040.43	+5.78	+4.10
U.S. Gov't/Credit	1280.02	+1.68	+0.12	1284.86	1202.77	+5.81	+4.01
U.S. Corporate Debt Issues Merrill Lynch							
Corporate Master	1510.34	+2.20	+0.15	1511.31	1410.52	+5.60	+4.98
High Yield	713.60	+1.28	+0.18	713.60	635.21	+12.34	+9.29
Yankee Bonds	1098.53	+1.43	+0.13	1100.66	1029.81	+5.09	+4.67
Mortgage-Backed Securities current coupon; Merrill Lynch: Dec. 31, 1986=100							
Ginnie Mae	445.84	+0.68	+0.15	445.84	413.50	+6.18	+5.84
Fannie Mae	444.67	+0.89	+0.20	444.67	416.12	+5.07	+4.67
Freddie Mac	272.09	+0.50	+0.18	272.09	254.70	+5.45	+4.88
Tax-Exempt Securities Merrill Lynch; Dec. 22, 1999							
6% Bond Buyer Muni	111.09	-0.66	-0.59	133.88	104.94	-0.31	-1.03
7-12 Yr G.O.	203.24	+0.22	+0.11	205.36	187.76	+4.96	+3.90
12-22 Yr G.O.	216.03	+0.16	+0.07	218.02	199.83	+5.49	+4.30
22+ Yr Revenue	203.88	+0.35	+0.17	204.36	188.50	+5.16	+3.91

Source: *The Wall Street Journal*, November 19, 2004, p. C2. Reprinted by permission of *The Wall Street Journal*. **www.wsj.com**

junk bond

Bond rated as speculative or less than investment grade (below Baa by Moody's and BBB by S&P) by bond-rating agencies.

insurance companies) are generally prohibited by state and federal law from purchasing anything but investment-grade bond securities.[13] Bonds rated below Baa by Moody's and BBB by S&P are considered to be speculative-grade bonds and are often termed **junk bonds,** or high-yield bonds.[14] The issuance of speculative bonds was rare prior to the economic downturn of the late 1970s. Given the risk involved with speculative bonds and the ready availability of investment-grade bonds, investment banks had a difficult time marketing the more speculative bonds to primary bond market investors. The market grew significantly in the late 1990s, with smaller and medium-sized firms, unqualified to issue investment-grade debt securities, issuing long-term debt in this market. For example, in 1990, $503.3 million in corporate "high-yield" straight debt was issued. In just the first three quarters of 2004, $117.5 billion was issued.

DO YOU UNDERSTAND?

1. What the different classifications of bonds are? Describe each.
2. What a STRIP security is?
3. What the process is through which Treasury notes and bonds are issued in the primary markets?
4. What the difference is between a general obligation bond and a revenue bond?
5. What the difference is between a firm commitment and a best-efforts bond issue offering?
6. What the characteristics are that differentiate corporate bonds?
7. What factors are used to determine a firm's bond issue rating?

Bond Market Indexes

Table 6–12 lists major bond market indexes as of November 18, 2004. Data in this table give investors general information on returns of bonds from various types of issuers (e.g., Treasuries, municipals, and corporate bonds) and various maturities. The indexes are those managed by major investment banks (e.g., Lehman Brothers, Merrill Lynch) and reflect both the monthly capital gain and loss on bonds in the index plus any interest (coupon) income earned. Changes in the values of these broad market indexes can be used by bond traders to evaluate changes in the investment attractiveness of bonds of different types and maturities.

13. For example, the Financial Institutions Reform, Recovery, and Enforcement Act of 1989 rescinded the ability of savings associations to purchase and hold below-investment-grade bonds (see Chapter 13).

14. A bond downgraded from investment-grade status (e.g., BBB) to junk bond status (e.g., B) is called a "fallen angel."

FIGURE 6–11 Bond Market Securities Held by Various Groups of Market Participants, September 2004

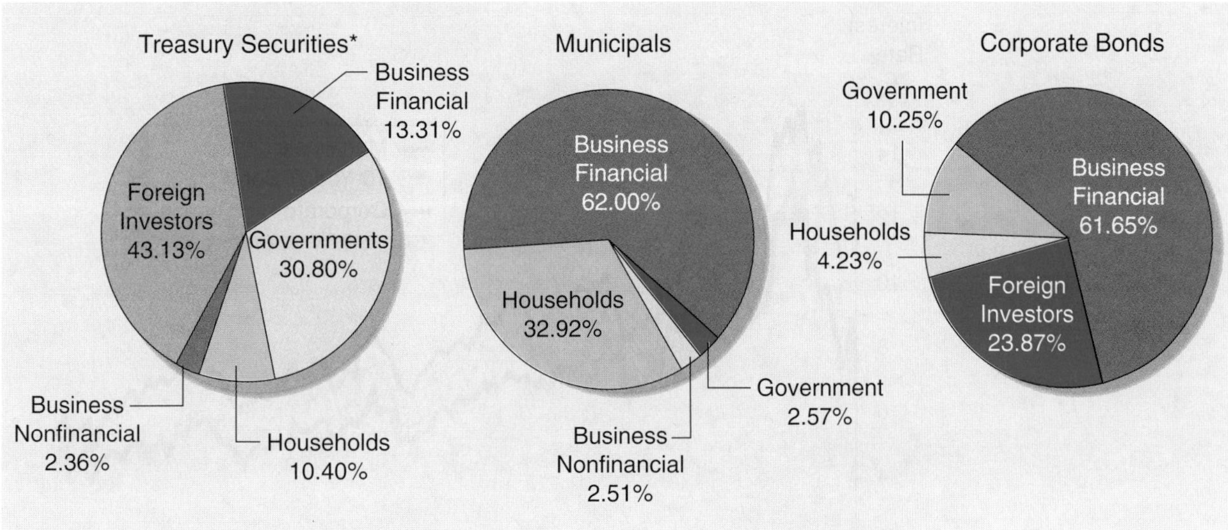

*Includes Treasury bills, notes, and bonds.

Source: Federal Reserve Board Web site, "Flow of Funds Accounts," November 2004. **www.federalreserve.gov**

BOND MARKET PARTICIPANTS

Bond markets bring together suppliers and demanders of long-term funds. We have just seen that the major issuers of debt market securities are federal, state, and local governments and corporations. The major purchasers of capital market securities are households, businesses, government units, and foreign investors. Figure 6–11 shows the percentage of each type of bond security held by each of these groups. Notice that financial firms called "business financial" (e.g., banks, insurance companies, mutual funds) are the major suppliers of funds for two of the three types of bonds. Financial firms hold 13.31 percent of all Treasury notes and bonds, 62.00 percent of municipal bonds, and 61.65 percent of the corporate bonds outstanding. In addition to their direct investment reported in Figure 6–11, households often deposit excess funds in financial firms (such as mutual bond funds and pension funds) that use these funds to purchase bond market securities. Thus, much of the business and financial holdings of bond securities shown in Figure 6–11 reflects indirect investments of households in the bond market.

DO YOU UNDERSTAND?

1. Who the major purchasers of bond market securities are?

COMPARISON OF BOND MARKET SECURITIES

www.stlouisfed.org

Figure 6–12 shows the yield to maturity on various types of bonds (e.g., 10-year Treasury bonds, municipal bonds, and high-grade corporate bonds) from 1980 through 2004. While the general trends in yields were quite similar over this period (i.e., yield changes are highly correlated), yield spreads among bonds can vary as default risk, tax status, and marketability change. For example, yield spread differences can change when characteristics of a particular type of bond are perceived to be more or less favorable to the bond holder (e.g., relative changes in yield spreads can result when the default risk increases for a firm that has one bond issue with a sinking fund provision and another issue without a sinking fund issue). Economic conditions can also cause bond yield spreads to vary over time. This is particularly true during periods of slow economic growth (e.g., 1982 and 1989–1991), as investors require higher default risk premiums.

DO YOU UNDERSTAND?

1. What events can cause yield spreads on bond securities to change?

FIGURE 6–12 Yields on Bond Market Securities, 1980–2004

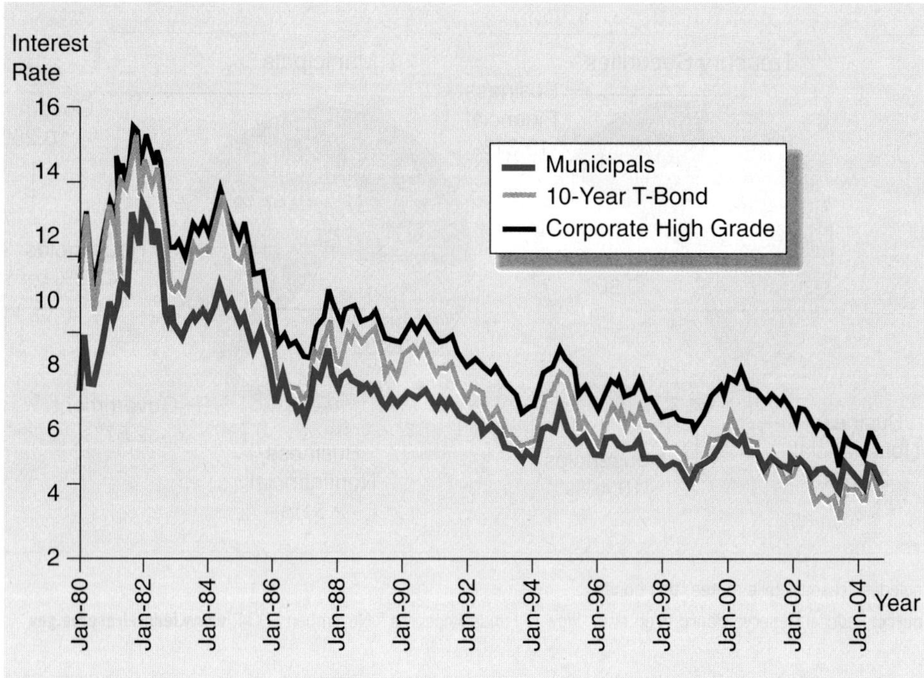

Source: Federal Reserve Board Web site, "Research and Data," November 2004. **www.federalreserve.gov**

The St. Louis Federal Reserve Bank offers free online access to its database (called FRED) of U.S. economic and financial data, including daily U.S. interest rates, monetary business indicators, exchange rates, balance of payments, and regional economic data.

INTERNATIONAL ASPECTS OF BOND MARKETS

4

International bond markets are those markets that trade bonds that are underwritten by an international syndicate, offer bonds to investors in different countries, issue bonds outside the jurisdiction of any single country, and offer bonds in unregistered form. The rapid growth in international bond markets in recent years can be seen in Table 6–13, which lists the dollar volume of new issues of international bond securities from 1994 through 2004. Much of this growth has been driven by investors' demand for international securities and international portfolio diversification (e.g., the growth of specialized U.S. mutual funds that invest in offshore bond issues). In just seven years, new issues have grown from \$253.6 billion (in 1994) to \$1,472.4 billion (in 2003) and \$868.5 billion (in just the first half of 2004). The majority of this growth has been debt issued by developed countries (e.g., the U.S. and Europe). Notice the drop in debt securities issued by Japan and by "Other countries" (i.e., emerging market countries such as Thailand and Singapore) after the economic crisis in Southeast Asia in 1997. For example, (net) new debt issues for Japan were negative in every year reported in Table 6–13 except the first six months of 2004 (meaning that more Japanese notes and bonds were redeemed than issued). New debt issues in "Other countries" fell from \$89.2 billion in 1997 to \$42.8 billion in 2004 before rising to \$66.9 billion in 2003 and \$42.8 billion in the first half of 2004. Notice also the sharp increase in new euro-denominated debt issues in 1997, \$257.9 billion, as investors attempted to position themselves before the introduction of the euro in 1999. This number rose even higher, to \$559.9 billion in 2000, \$756.2 billion in 2003, and \$444.9 billion in the first six months of 2004, as the euro began circulating. Indeed, in the fourth

TABLE 6–13 International Debt Securities Issued, 1994–2004
(in billions of U.S. dollars)

	1994	1997	2000	2003	2004*
Total net issues	$253.6	$573.3	$1,243.4	$1,472.4	$868.5
Money market instruments	3.3	19.8	152.1	75.4	37.6
Bonds and notes	250.3	553.5	1,091.3	1,397.0	830.9
Developed countries	205.5	449.0	1,163.1	1,365.9	802.7
Euro area	167.1	257.9	559.9	756.2	444.9
Japan	−5.9	−0.4	−25.8	−1.0	17.3
United States	22.9	176.9	467.2	275.6	133.3
Offshore centers	7.2	14.5	15.0	16.3	5.9
Other countries	32.5	89.2	42.8	66.9	42.8
International institutions	8.5	20.6	22.6	23.2	17.1
Financial institutions	136.1	360.0	802.8	1,188.6	699.4
Public sector	103.1	89.0	267.9	170.5	150.8
Corporate issuers	14.4	124.3	172.7	113.3	18.3

*Through second quarter.
Source: Bank for International Settlements, Quarterly Review, various issues. **www.bis.org**

quarter of 2001, just before the full implementation of the euro, debt securities issued by euro-area countries rose 75 percent compared to third quarter issuances, from $66 billion to $155 billion. In contrast, debt securities issued in the United States decreased 8 percent (from $222 billion in the third quarter of 2001 to $210 billion in the fourth quarter) and net Japanese issuances were negative in both quarters.

Table 6–14 lists the values of international debt outstanding by currency and type (e.g., floating-rate, straight fixed-rate, and equity-related debt) from 1995 through 2004. In June 2004, international bonds and notes outstanding totaled over $11.7 trillion, compared to $2.2 trillion in 1995. Straight fixed-rate securities dominate the market, mainly because of the strong demand for dollar and euro currency assets. Floating-rate notes were second in size, partly as a result of interest rate uncertainty in the late 1990s and early 2000s.

Notice that prior to 2004 a majority of international debt instruments were denominated in U.S. dollars. For example, in December 2000, some 53.3 percent of the floating-rate debt, 48.0 percent of the straight fixed-rate debt, and 53.6 percent of the equity-related debt was denominated in U.S. dollars. The U.S. dollar was the currency of choice as an international medium of exchange and store of value. However, euro-denominated debt outstanding surpassed the U.S. dollar as the main currency in which international debt is denominated. In 2004, 51.5 percent of floating-rate debt, 41.0 percent of straight fixed-rate debt, and 38.5 percent of equity-related debt outstanding was issued in euros. Thus, since its introduction the euro has surpassed the Japanese yen and the U.S. dollar as the lead currency with which debt issues are denominated. Notice too from Table 6–14 that the markets for emerging-country bonds (other currencies) have recovered from the Asian crisis of the late 1990s. Fear of losses on holdings of these emerging market bonds sparked a wide selloff in the emerging markets in the late 1990s and early 2000s.[15]

15. For example, Argentina had severe economic and financial problems in the early 2000s that culminated in an $82 billion default in government bonds in 2002. However, Argentina's problems did not seem to spread to other Latin American countries, nor did they cause significant disruption in global financial markets. Most of Argentina's creditors appeared to have been successful in reducing their exposures to acceptable levels in the months preceding defaults of Argentine debt issues. As a result, creditors were able to absorb the default without having to sell off a large number of other sovereign bonds to cover Argentine-related losses.

TABLE 6–14 International Bonds and Notes Outstanding, 1995–2004
(in billions of U.S. dollars)

Type; Sector and Currency	1995	1997	2000	2004*
Total Issues	$2,209.3	$3,322.8	$5,884.0	$11,736.0
Floating Rate	326.2	735.7	1,482.9	3,112.7
U.S. dollar	181.5	442.1	790.0	1,111.8
Euro	44.2	130.9	471.9	1,604.3
Japanese yen	27.0	69.6	86.3	105.4
Pound sterling	N/A	N/A	112.4	224.5
Other currencies	73.6	93.0	22.3	66.7
Financial institutions	203.2	535.0	1,288.7	2,899.9
Government and state agencies	61.9	83.1	90.9	96.3
International institutions	18.4	26.9	21.3	24.9
Corporate issuers	42.8	90.7	82.0	91.7
Straight Fixed Rate	1,712.4	2,389.8	4,158.8	8,267.4
U.S. dollar	490.8	890.2	1,994.5	3,446.3
Euro	214.4	693.1	1,225.6	3,386.3
Japanese yen	315.4	368.7	352.2	356.2
Pound sterling	N/A	N/A	331.9	623.4
Other currencies	691.9	437.7	254.6	455.2
Financial institutions	501.4	894.8	2,068.7	5,485.5
Government and state agencies	492.8	621.3	1,080.3	1,123.3
International institutions	268.3	272.6	353.5	488.4
Corporate issuers	449.3	601.1	656.3	1,170.3
Equity Related†	170.7	197.4	242.3	355.9
U.S. dollar	83.1	123.0	129.8	148.6
Euro	10.7	25.0	74.6	136.9
Japanese yen	7.4	14.8	16.6	39.2
Pound sterling	N/A	N/A	8.8	11.6
Other currencies	69.5	34.7	12.4	19.6
Financial institutions	32.5	45.3	115.4	163.6
Government and state agencies	0.4	5.9	2.1	4.6
International institutions	—	0.1	0.2	—
Corporate issuers	137.7	146.1	124.6	187.7

*As of June.

†Convertible bonds and bonds with equity warrants.

N/A = not available.

Source: Bank for International Settlements, *Quarterly Review*, various issues. **www.bis.org**

DO YOU UNDERSTAND?

1. The major currency in which international bonds are denominated?
2. What group of market participants is the major issuer of international debt?

Figure 6–13 illustrates the distribution of international bonds by type of issuer (e.g., financial institutions, governments). Financial institutions issue the vast majority of floating-rate bonds (93.2 percent) and most of the straight fixed-rate bonds (66.3 percent). Financial institutions had been hampered in 1998 by concerns over their exposures to lower-rated countries. The stabilization of market conditions in 1999 and the early 2000s made it easier for U.S. and European financial institutions to issue new debt securities. Public sector issues were largely accounted for by U.S. financing agencies and a few emerging market issues. Corporations, as might be expected, issue the majority of the equity-related bonds (52.7 percent).

FIGURE 6–13 Distribution of International Bonds Outstanding by Type of Issuer, June 2004

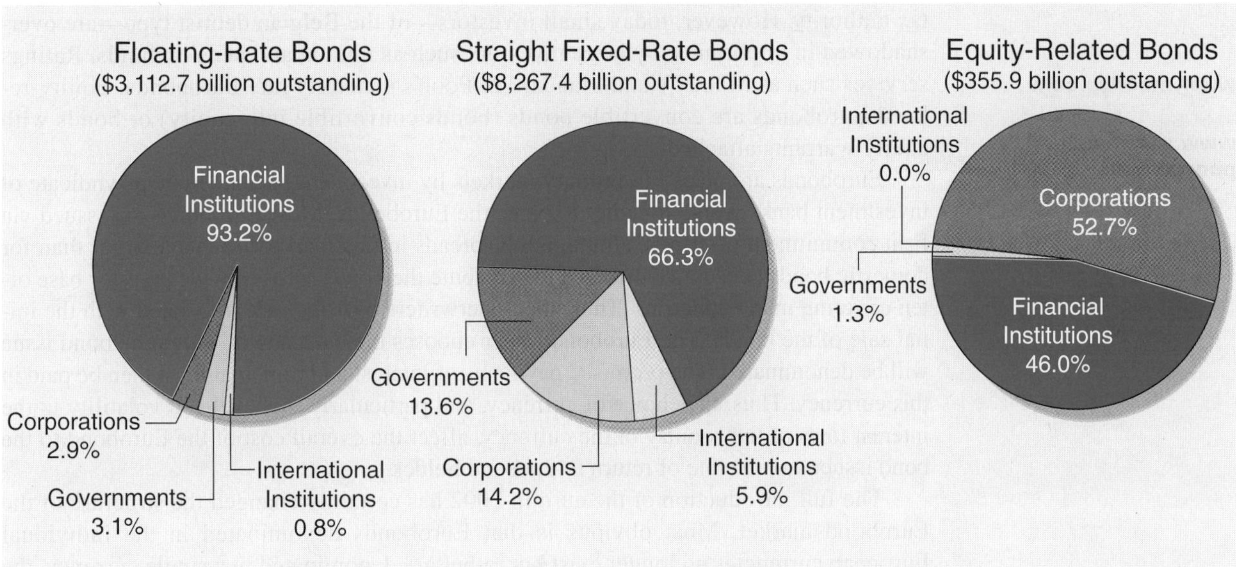

Source: Bank for International Settlements, *Quarterly Review*, September 2004. **www.bis.org**

EUROBONDS, FOREIGN BONDS, AND BRADY AND SOVEREIGN BONDS

International bonds can also be classified into three main groups: Eurobonds, foreign bonds, and Brady and sovereign bonds.

Eurobonds

Eurobonds are long-term bonds issued and sold outside the country of the currency in which they are denominated (e.g., dollar-denominated bonds issued in Europe or Asia)[16]. Perhaps confusingly, the term *Euro* simply implies the bond is issued outside the country in whose currency the bond is denominated. Thus, "Euro"-bonds are issued in countries outside of Europe and in currencies other than the euro. Indeed, the majority of issues are still in U.S. dollars and can be issued in virtually any region of the world. Eurobonds were first sold in 1963 as a way to avoid taxes and regulation. U.S. corporations were limited by regulations on the amount of funds they could borrow domestically (in the United States) to finance overseas operations, while foreign issues in the United States were subject to a special 30 percent tax on their coupon interest. In 1963, these corporations created the Eurobond, by which bonds were denominated in various currencies and were not directly subject to U.S. regulation. Even when these regulations were abandoned, access to a new and less-regulated market by investors and corporations created sufficient demand and supply for the market to continue to grow.

Eurobonds are generally issued in denominations of $5,000 and $10,000. They pay interest annually using a 360-day year (floating-rate Eurobonds generally pay interest every six months on the basis of a spread over some stated rate, usually the LIBOR rate). Eurobonds are generally *bearer* bonds and are traded in the over-the-counter markets, mainly in London and Luxembourg. Historically, they have been of interest to smaller investors who want to shield the ownership of securities from the tax authorities.

16. A Eurobond does not have to be issued in Europe.

The classic investor is the "Belgian dentist" who would cross the border to Luxembourg on the coupon date to collect his coupons without the knowledge of the Belgian tax authority. However, today small investors—of the Belgian dentist type—are overshadowed in importance by large investors such as mutual and pension funds. Ratings services such as Moody's and Standard & Poor's generally rate Eurobonds. Equity-related Eurobonds are convertible bonds (bonds convertible into equity) or bonds with equity warrants attached.

www.moodys.com

www.standardandpoors.com

Eurobonds are placed in primary markets by investment banks. Often, a syndicate of investment banks works together to place the Eurobonds. Most Eurobonds are issued via firm commitment offerings, although the spreads in this market are much larger than for domestic bonds because of the need to distribute the bonds across a wide investor base often covering many countries. Thus, the underwriters bear the risk associated with the initial sale of the bonds. The Eurobond issuer chooses the currency in which the bond issue will be denominated. The promised payments of interest and principal must then be paid in this currency. Thus, the choice of currency, and particularly the level and volatility in the interest rates of the country of the currency, affect the overall cost of the Eurobond to the bond issuer and the rate of return to the bond holder.

The full introduction of the euro in 2002 has certainly changed the structure of the Eurobond market. Most obvious is that Eurobonds denominated in the individual European currencies no longer exist but rather are denominated in a single currency, the euro. Further, liquidity created by the consolidation of European currencies allows for the demand and size of euro-denominated Eurobond issues to increase. Such growth was exhibited early in the life of the euro (or the European currency unit (ECU) prior to 2002) as the volume of new Euro debt issues in the first and second quarter of 1999 rose 32 percent and 43 percent, respectively, from the same periods in 1998. In January 1999, a record $415 billion in long-term Eurobonds were issued. In 2000 and 2001, a total of $989.1 billion long-term Eurobonds were issued, and in 2003 alone $756.2 billion of long-term Eurobonds were issued. Finally, Eurobond yields across the European countries should vary only slightly, which should improve euro-denominated securities' marketability even further.

Foreign Bonds

Foreign bonds are long-term bonds issued by firms and governments outside of the issuer's home country and are usually denominated in the currency of the country in which they are issued rather than in their own domestic currency—for example, a Japanese company issuing a dollar-denominated public bond rather than a yen-denominated bond in the United States. Foreign bonds were issued long before Eurobonds and, as a result, are frequently called traditional international bonds. Countries sometimes name their foreign bonds to denote the country of origin. For example, foreign bonds issued in the United States are called Yankee bonds, foreign bonds issued in Japan are called Samurai bonds, and foreign bonds issued in the United Kingdom are called Bulldog bonds.

Brady Bonds and Sovereign Bonds

Brady bonds

Bonds that are swapped for an outstanding loan to a less developed country.

Brady bonds were created in the mid-1980s through International Monetary Fund (IMF) and central bank–sponsored programs under which U.S. and other banks[17] exchanged their dollar loans to emerging market countries for dollar bonds issued by the relevant countries (e.g., the Philippines, Mexico, Brazil). These bonds had a much longer maturity than that promised on the original loans and a lower promised original coupon (yield) than the interest rate on the

17. Major market makers include the Dutch ING Bank, Lehman Brothers, Salomon Smith Barney, Citibank, J. P. Morgan Chase, Bankers Trust, and Merrill Lynch.

TABLE 6–15 Loan for Bond Swaps Achieved through the Brady Plan
(in billions of dollars)

Country	1998	2004
Argentina	$29.9	$6.8
Brazil	45.6	17.8
Bulgaria	8.1	2.4
Costa Rica	0.5	0.4
Cote d'Ivoire	2.4	2.2
Dominican Republic	0.5	0.5
Ecuador	8.0	0.0
Mexico	33.0	1.3
Nigeria	5.8	1.4
Peru	10.6	2.5
Philippines	4.5	1.1
Poland	14.0	2.8
Russia	24.1	0.0
Uruguay	0.6	0.5
Venezuela	19.3	7.7
Total	202.2	47.4

Source: J. A. Penicock Jr., "Emerging Market Debt," working paper, Conference on Integrated Risk and Return Management for Insurance Companies, New York Salomon Center, May 1999, and World Bank Web site, November 2004. **www.worldbank.org**

original loan. In many cases, the bond's principal and interest payments have been partially backed by U.S. T-bonds as collateral to improve their attractiveness to investors.[18] Once banks and other financial institutions have swapped loans for bonds, they can sell them on the secondary market.

Approximately $211.1 billion of less developed countries (LDC) loans had been converted into bonds under the Brady Plan by 1998, with the top issuers being Brazil (22.1 percent), Mexico (16.0 percent), Argentina (14.5 percent), Russia (11.7 percent), and Venezuela (12.1 percent). Table 6–15 lists the size of loan for Brady bond swaps through 1998 and the amount still outstanding in 2004. These bond-for-loan swap programs seek to restore LDCs' creditworthiness and thus the value of bank holdings of such debt by creating longer-term, lower-fixed-interest, but more liquid securities in place of shorter-term, floating-rate loans.[19]

DO YOU UNDERSTAND?

1. What Eurobonds are?
2. How Brady bonds are created?
3. What sovereign bonds are?

More recently, as the credit quality of some LDCs has improved, some Brady bonds have been converted back into **sovereign bonds,** whereby U.S. Treasury bond collateral backing is removed and the creditworthiness of the country is substituted instead. For example, in April 2003 Mexico sold $2.5 billion of sovereign bonds to help finance the repurchase of the country's U.S. dollar–denominated Brady bonds. Spreads over Treasuries on these bonds are much higher than on Brady bonds (often in the 4 percent plus range). However, countries save by not having to pledge U.S. dollar Treasury bonds as collateral against principal and interest payments.

sovereign bonds

A bond that is swapped for an outstanding loan to a less developed country (LDC), in which the U.S. Treasury secondary collateral backing is removed and the creditworthiness of the country is substituted instead.

18. For example, the face value payment of a 30-year Brady bond may be backed by the issuing government placing a 30-year U.S. zero-coupon T-bond as collateral in an escrow account. Should the issuing government default on its Brady bond, investors would have a claim to the 30-year zero-coupon Treasury bond as collateral.

19. However, even after restructuring their debt into Brady bonds, Russia and Ecuador defaulted on their outstanding Brady bonds in 1999.

SUMMARY

This chapter looked at the domestic and international bond markets. We defined and discussed the three types of bonds available to long-term debt investors: Treasury notes and bonds, municipal bonds, and corporate bonds. We also reviewed the process through which bonds trade in both primary and secondary bond markets. International bond markets have grown dramatically in recent years. We documented and offered some reasons for this growth. We concluded the chapter with a description of the different types of international bonds: the traditional foreign bonds, the relatively new Eurobonds, Brady bonds, and sovereign bonds.

SEARCH THE SITE

Go to the Bank for International Settlements Web site at **www.bis.org** and find the most recent data on the issue of new international debt and the current distribution of international bonds by type of issuer using the following steps.

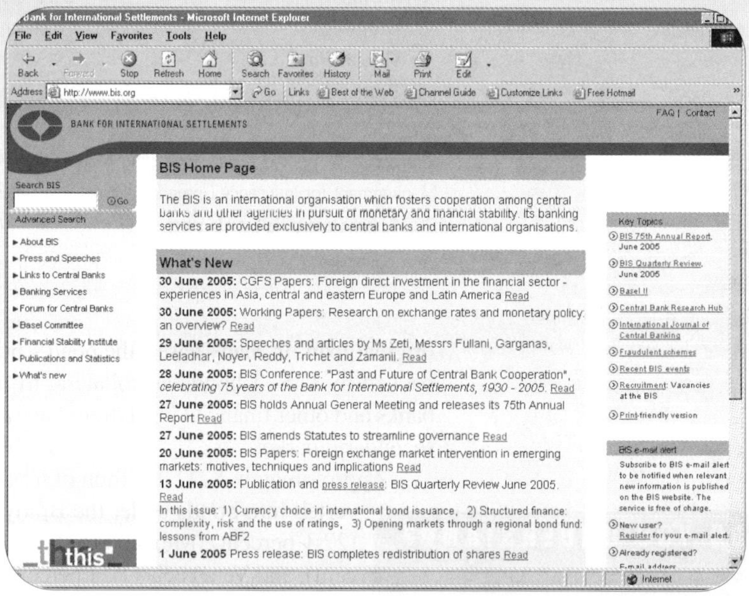

Click on "BIS Quarterly Review"

Click on "Statistical annex Read"

Click on "securities market"

This will bring the file onto your computer that contains the relevant data in Tables 12B and 13B.

Questions

1. How have these values changed since 2004 reported in Tables 6–13 and 6–14?
2. Calculate the percentage of floating rate, straight fixed rate, and equity related bonds issued in U.S. dollars and Euros.

QUESTIONS

1. What are capital markets and how do bond markets fit into the definition of capital markets?
2. What is the difference between T-bills, T-notes, and T-bonds?
3. Refer to the T-note and T-bond quote in Table 6–1.
   - **a.** What is the asking price on the 9.25 percent February 2016 T-bond if the face value of the bond is $10,000?
   - **b.** What is the bid price on the 6.5 percent August 2005 T-note if the face value of the bond is $10,000?
4. Refer again to Table 6–1.
   - **a.** Verify the ASKED price on the 2.750 percent July 2006 T-note for Tuesday, November 9, 2004. The ASK YLD on the note is 2.71 percent and the note matures on July 31, 2006. Settlement occurs two business days after purchase; i.e., you would take possession of the note on November 11, 2004.
   - **b.** Verify the ASK YLD on the 4.00 percent February 2014 T-note for Tuesday, November 9, 2004. The ASKED price is 98:19 and the note matures on February 28, 2014.

5. What is a STRIP? Who would invest in a STRIP?

6. Refer to Table 6–1.
   a. Verify the Tuesday, November 9, 2004 ASK YLD on the principal (np) STRIP maturing in November 2006. Use a two-day settlement period from the date of purchase (i.e., ownership occurs on November 6, 2004). The STRIP matures on November 30, 2006.
   b. Verify the ASKED price on the principal (np) STRIP maturing in August 2009, i.e., the STRIP matures on August 15, 2009.

7. On October 5, 2007, you purchase a $10,000 T-note that matures on August 15, 2018 (settlement occurs two days after purchase, so you receive actual ownership of the bond on October 7, 2007). The coupon rate on the T-note is 4.375 percent and the current price quoted on the bond is 105:08 (or 105.25% of the face value of the T-note). The last coupon payment occurred on May 15, 2007 (145 days before settlement), and the next coupon payment will be paid on November 15, 2007 (39 days from settlement).
   a. Calculate the accrued interest due to the seller from the buyer at settlement.
   b. Calculate the dirty price of this transaction.
   c. Calculate the yield to maturity (based on the clean price) on the bond received on October 7, 2007, and maturing on August 15, 2018 (or in 10.8603 years).

8. You can invest in taxable bonds that are paying a 9.5 percent annual rate of return or a municipal bond paying a 7.75 percent annual rate of return. If your marginal tax rate is 21 percent, which security bond should you buy?

9. A municipal bond you are considering as an investment currently pays a 6.75 percent annual rate of return.
   a. Calculate the tax equivalent rate of return if your marginal tax rate is 28 percent.
   b. Calculate the tax equivalent rate of return if your marginal tax rate is 21 percent.

10. What is the difference between general obligation bonds and revenue bonds?

11. Refer to Table 6–6.
    a. On November 9, 2004, what were the coupon rate, price, and yield on municipal bonds issued by the Texas Turnpike-Authority?
    b. What was the price, on November 8, 2004, on Montgomery County, Ohio bonds maturing in May 2030?

12. Refer to Table 6–8.
    a. What was the price on the Ford Motor Credit Corporation 7.25 percent coupon bonds on November 9, 2004?
    b. What was the dollar volume of trading in General Electric 5.0 percent coupon bonds maturing in 2013 on November 9, 2004?
    c. What was the price on CIT Group bonds on November 4, 2004?

13. eXcel **Using a Spreadsheet to Calculate Bond Values:** What is the bond quote for a $1,000 face value bond with an 8 percent coupon rate (paid semiannually) and a required return of 7.5 percent if the bond is 6.48574, 8.47148, 10.519, and 14.87875 years from maturity?

Face Value	Total Payments	Periodic Coupon Payment	Required Return	=>	The Bond Value Will Be
100%	6.48574 × 2 = 12.97148	8%/2 = 4%	7.5%		102-17%
100	8.47148 × 2 = 16.94296	4	7.5		103-03
100	10.519 × 2 = 21.0380	4	7.5		103-19
100	14.87875 × 2 = 29.7575	4	7.5		104-14

14. What is the difference between bearer bonds and registered bonds?

15. What is the difference between term bonds and serial bonds?

16. Which type of bond—a mortgage bond, a debenture, or a subordinated debenture—generally has the
    a. Highest cost to the bond issuer?
    b. Least risk to the bond holder?
    c. Highest yield to the bond holder?

17. What is a convertible bond? Is a convertible bond more or less attractive to a bond holder than a nonconvertible bond?

18. Hilton Hotels Corp. has a convertible bond issue outstanding. Each bond, with a face value of $1,000, can be converted into common shares at a rate of 61.2983 shares of stock per $1,000 face value bond (the conversion rate), or $16.316 per share. Hilton's common stock is trading (on the NYSE) at $15.90 per share and the bonds are trading at $975.
    a. Calculate the conversion value of each bond.
    b. Determine if it is currently profitable for bond holders to convert their bonds into shares of Hilton Hotel common stock.

19. What is a callable bond? Is a call provision more or less attractive to a bond holder than a noncallable bond?

20. Explain the meaning of a sinking fund provision on a bond issue.

21. What is the difference between an investment-grade bond and a junk bond?

22. STANDARD &POOR'S Go to the S&P Educational Version of Market Insight Web site at **www.mhhe.com/edumarketinsight** and find the S&P credit rating for Boeing Corp. (BA) and Texas Instruments (TXN) using the following steps. Click on "Educational Version of Market Insight." Enter your Site ID and click on "Login." Click on "Company." In the box marked "Ticker" enter BA and click on "Go!" Under Compustat Reports click on "Financial Hlts." This brings up a file that contains the relevant data. Repeat this process using the ticker TXN.

23. What is the difference between a Eurobond and a foreign bond?

24. How are Brady bonds created?

Mortgage Markets

OUTLINE

Chapter NAVIGATOR

1. What is the difference between a mortgage and a mortgage-backed security?
2. What are the main types of mortgages issued by financial institutions?
3. What are the major characteristics of a mortgage?
4. How is a mortgage amortization schedule determined?
5. What are some of the new innovations in mortgage financing?
6. What is a mortgage sale?
7. What is a pass-through security?
8. What is a collateralized mortgage obligation?
9. Who are the major mortgage holders in the United States?
10. What are the trends in the international securitization of mortgages?

MORTGAGES AND MORTGAGE-BACKED SECURITIES: CHAPTER OVERVIEW

Mortgages are loans to individuals or businesses to purchase a home, land, or other real property. As of September 2004, there were $10.13 trillion of primary mortgages outstanding, held by various financial institutions such as banks and mortgage companies. Figure 7–1 lists the major categories of mortgages and the amount of each outstanding in 1994 and 2004. Home mortgages (one to four families) are the largest loan category (76.7 percent of all mortgages in 2004), followed by commercial mortgages (used to finance specific projects that are pledged as collateral for the mortgage—16.1 percent), multifamily dwellings (5.8 percent), and farms (1.4 percent).

FIGURE 7–1 Mortgage Loans Outstanding

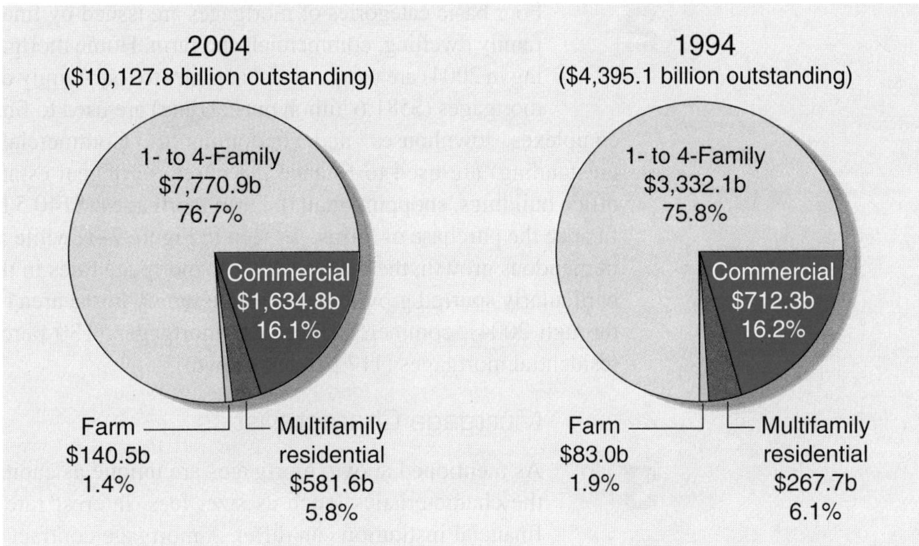

Source: Federal Reserve Board Web site, "Flow of Fund Accounts," March 1995 and December 2004. **www.federalreserve.gov**

Many mortgages, particularly residential mortgages, are subsequently **securitized** by the mortgage holder—they are packaged and sold as assets backing a publicly traded or privately held debt instrument. Securitization allows financial institutions' (FIs') asset portfolios to become more liquid, reduces interest rate risk and credit risk, provides FIs with a source of fee income, and helps reduce the effects of regulatory constraints such as capital requirements, reserve requirements, and deposit insurance premiums on FI profits (see Chapter 13). Currently, approximately 60 percent of home mortgages are securitized.

mortgages

Loans to individuals or businesses to purchase a home, land, or other real property.

securitized

Securities are packaged and sold as assets backing a publicly traded or privately held debt instrument.

We examine mortgage markets separately from bond and stock markets for several reasons. First, mortgages are backed by a specific piece of real property. If the borrower defaults on a mortgage, the financial institution can take ownership of the property. Only mortgage bonds are backed by a specific piece of property that allows the lender to take ownership in the event of a default. All other corporate bonds and stock give the holder a general claim to a borrower's assets. Second, there is no set size or denomination for primary mortgages. Rather, the size of each mortgage depends on the borrower's needs and ability to repay. Bonds generally have a denomination of $1,000 or a multiple of $1,000 per bond and shares of stock are generally issued in (par value) denominations of $1 per share. Third, primary mortgages generally involve a single investor (e.g., a bank or mortgage company). Bond and stock issues, on the other hand, are generally held by many (sometimes thousands of) investors. Finally, because primary mortgage borrowers are often individuals, information on these borrowers is less extensive and unaudited. Bonds and stocks are issued by publicly traded corporations that are subject to extensive rules and regulations regarding information availability and reliability.

In this chapter, we look at the characteristics and operations of the mortgage and mortgage-backed securities markets. We look at different types of mortgages and the determination of mortgage payments. (We look at the processes used by financial institutions to evaluate mortgage loan applicants in Chapter 20.) We also discuss the agencies owned or sponsored by the U.S. government that help securitize mortgage pools. We briefly describe the major forms of mortgage-backed securities and discuss the process of securitization. More complete details of the securitization process are provided in Chapter 24. We conclude the chapter with a look at international investors in mortgages and mortgage-backed securities markets, as well as trends in international securitization of mortgage assets.

PRIMARY MORTGAGE MARKET

2

Four basic categories of mortgages are issued by financial institutions: home, multifamily dwelling, commercial, and farm. Home mortgages ($7,770.9 billion outstanding in 2004) are used to purchase one- to four-family dwellings. Multifamily dwelling mortgages ($581.6 billion outstanding) are used to finance the purchase of apartment complexes, townhouses, and condominiums. Commercial mortgages ($1,634.8 billion outstanding) are used to finance the purchase of real estate for business purposes (e.g., office buildings, shopping malls). Farm mortgages ($140.5 billion outstanding) are used to finance the purchase of farms. As seen in Figure 7–1, while all four areas have experienced tremendous growth, the historically low mortgage rates in the 1990s and early 2000s have particularly spurred growth in the single family home area (133 percent growth from 1994 through 2004), commercial business mortgages (130 percent growth), and multifamily residential mortgages (117 percent growth).

Mortgage Characteristics

3

As mentioned above, mortgages are unique as capital market instruments because the characteristics (such as size, fees, interest rate) of each mortgage held by a financial institution can differ. A mortgage contract between a financial institution and a borrower must specify all of the characteristics of the mortgage agreement.

When a financial institution receives a mortgage application, it must determine whether the applicant qualifies for a loan. (We describe this process in Chapter 20.) Because most financial institutions sell or securitize their mortgage loans in the secondary mortgage market (discussed below), the guidelines set by the secondary market buyer for acceptability, as well as the guidelines set by the financial institution, are used to determine whether or not a mortgage borrower is qualified. Further, the characteristics of loans to be securitized will generally be more standardized than those that are not to be securitized. When mortgages are not securitized, the financial institution can be more flexible with the acceptance/rejection guidelines it uses and mortgage characteristics will be more varied.

lien

A public record attached to the title of the property that gives the financial institution the right to sell the property if the mortgage borrower defaults.

Collateral. As mentioned in the introduction, all mortgage loans are backed by a specific piece of property that serves as collateral to the mortgage loan. As part of the mortgage agreement, the financial institution will place a **lien** against a property that remains in place until the loan is fully paid off. A lien is a public record attached to the title of the property that gives the financial institution the right to sell the property if the mortgage borrower defaults or falls into arrears on his or her payments. The mortgage is secured by the lien—that is, until the loan is paid off, no one can buy the property and obtain clear title to it. If someone tries to purchase the property, the financial institution can file notice of the lien at the public recorder's office to stop the transaction.

down payment

A portion of the purchase price of the property a financial institution requires the mortgage borrower to pay up front.

Down Payment. As part of any mortgage agreement, a financial institution requires the mortgage borrower to pay a portion of the purchase price of the property (a **down payment**) at the closing (the day the mortgage is issued). The balance of the purchase price is the face value of the mortgage (or the loan proceeds).

Down payments decrease the probability that the borrower will default on the mortgage. A mortgage borrower who makes a large down payment is less likely to walk away from the house should property values fall, leaving the mortgage unpaid. As seen in the In the News box, the drop in real estate values in Texas in the 1980s caused many mortgage borrowers to walk away from their homes and mortgages, as well as many mortgage lenders to fail.

DO YOU UNDERSTAND?

1. The condition of savings and loans associations in Texas in the mid and late 1980s?
2. What factors caused the massive lender failures?

The size of the down payment depends on the financial situation of the borrower. Generally, a 20 percent down payment is required (i.e., the loan-to-value ratio may be no more than 80 percent). Borrowers that put up less than 20 percent are required

Texas S&L Toll: 80% Likely to Need Aid

The Texas thrift crisis, which has already claimed 87 of the state's savings institutions, has not hit rock bottom yet. Amid rising interest rates and a continuing drop in real estate values comes this sobering prediction: Only one out of five savings and loan associations is expected to survive without federal assistance. "The crisis is worsening at an accelerated pace," said Stuart Chesley, chairman of the Texas Savings and Loan League. "We are unable to contain the losses."

The ailing Federal Savings and Loan Insurance Corp. spent $24.5 billion last year to rescue 87 Texas S&Ls, or about one-third of the state total. But at least 70 more are insolvent and still in need of assistance. And an additional 68 Texas thrifts are in danger of failing, according to a study prepared by Ferguson & Co. for the Texas Savings and Loan League. That would leave 54 survivors, or 19 percent of the 279 savings associations that were operating in Texas last March . . .

For many Texas thrift executives, the crisis will bring an end to their institutions and their careers. Dozens upon dozens of managers are throwing their hands up in the face of plummeting real estate values and loan demand. For the national thrift industry, the Texas crisis paints a picture of what could happen in other overbuilt markets. "To a lesser extent, what we are seeing in Texas probably will be repeated elsewhere," said consultant William Ferguson, principal of Ferguson & Co., Irving, Tex.

Collapsing real estate loans and property values are at the heart of the Texas crisis. The twin evils are symptoms of a vastly overbuilt market. The poor performance of the expected survivors—arguably the most conservative lenders—illustrates the troubles of the overall industry. The state's 54 strongest thrifts experienced a 45 percent increase in repossessed assets during the nine months ended Sept. 30, according to Ferguson & Co.

Losses at these thrifts—largely spurred by loan-loss provisions and write-downs—equaled 53 percent of the group's total profits from the previous two years. Retained earnings for the group fell by 24 percent. "We still are seeing significant devaluations in Texas real estate," said James Pledger, Texas savings and loan commissioner. "The depth of the economic hole in this state is hard to comprehend." Damage from the real estate implosion promises to keep regulators on the defensive. Up to 138 more Texas thrifts with combined assets of about $40 billion may need federal assistance before the Texas crisis has run its course.

www.american banker.com

Source: *The American Banker*, February 15, 1989 p.1, by Steve Klinkerman.

private mortgage insurance

Insurance contract purchased by a mortgage borrower guaranteeing to pay the financial institution the difference between the value of the property and the balance remaining on the mortgage.

to purchase **private mortgage insurance** (PMI). (Technically, the insurance is purchased by the lender (the financial institution) but paid for by the borrower, generally as part of the monthly payment.) In the event of default, the PMI issuer (such as Norwest Mortgage Company) guarantees to pay the financial institution the difference between the value of the property and the balance remaining on the mortgage. As payments are made on the mortgage, or if the value of the property increases, a mortgage borrower can eventually request that the PMI requirement be removed. Every financial institution differs in its requirements for removing the PMI payment from a mortgage. However, in most cases financial institutions require a waiting period of one to two years after the loan's origination date, proof through an approved appraiser that the loan-to-value ratio is less than 80 percent, on-time payments during the waiting period, and a letter from the borrower requesting that the PMI be removed from the loan.

federally insured mortgages

Mortgages originated by financial institutions, with repayment guaranteed by either the Federal Housing Administration (FHA) or the Veterans Administration (VA).

Insured versus Conventional Mortgages. Mortgages are classified as either federally insured or conventional. **Federally insured mortgages** are originated by financial institutions, but repayment is guaranteed (for a fee of 0.5 percent of the loan amount) by either the Federal Housing Administration (FHA) or the Veterans Administration (VA). In order to qualify, FHA and VA mortgage loan applicants must meet specific requirements set by these government agencies (e.g., VA-insured loans are available only to individuals who served and were honorably discharged from military service in the United States). Further, the maximum size of the mortgage is limited (the limit varies by state and is based on the cost of housing). For example, in 2005, FHA loan limits on single-family homes ranged from $160,176 to $290,319, depending on location and cost of living. FHA or VA mortgages require either a very low or zero down payment. (FHA mortgages require as little as a 3 percent down payment.)

conventional mortgages

Mortgages issued by financial institutions that are not federally insured.

Conventional mortgages are mortgages held by financial institutions and are not federally insured (but as already discussed, they generally are required to be privately insured if the borrower's down payment is less than 20 percent of the property's value). Secondary market mortgage buyers will not generally purchase conventional mortgages that are not privately insured and that have a loan-to-value ratio of greater than 80 percent.

Mortgage Maturities. A mortgage generally has an original maturity of either 15 or 30 years. Until recently, the 30-year mortgage was the one most frequently used. However, the 15-year mortgage has grown in popularity. Mortgage borrowers are attracted to the 15-year mortgage because of the potential saving in total interest paid (see below). However, because the mortgage is paid off in half the time, monthly mortgage payments are higher on a 15-year than on a 30-year mortgage.

Financial institutions find the 15-year mortgage attractive because of the lower degree of interest rate risk on a 15-year relative to a 30-year mortgage. To attract mortgage borrowers to the 15-year maturity mortgage, financial institutions generally charge a lower interest rate on a 15-year mortgage than a 30-year mortgage.

Most mortgages allow the borrower to prepay all or part of the mortgage principal early without penalty. In general, the monthly payment is set at a fixed level to repay interest and principal on the mortgage by the maturity date (i.e., the mortgage is fully **amortized**). We illustrate this payment pattern for a 15-year fixed-rate mortgage in Figure 7–2. However, other mortgages have interest rates and thus payments that vary.

amortized

A mortgage is amortized when the fixed principal and interest payments fully pay off the mortgage by its maturity date.

In addition to 15- and 30-year fixed-rate and variable-rate mortgages, financial institutions sometimes offer **balloon payment mortgages.** A balloon payment mortgage requires a fixed monthly interest payment (and, sometimes, principal payments) for a three-to-five year period. Full payment of the mortgage principal (the balloon payment) is then required at the end of the period, as illustrated for a five-year balloon payment mortgage in Figure 7–2. Because they normally consist of interest only, the monthly payments prior to maturity are lower than those on an amortized loan (i.e., a loan that requires periodic repayments of principal and interest). Generally, because few borrowers save enough funds to pay off the mortgage in three to five years, the mortgage principal is refinanced at the

balloon payment mortgage

Mortgage that requires a fixed monthly interest payment for a three- to five-year period. Full payment of the mortgage principal (the balloon payment) is then required at the end of the period.

FIGURE 7–2 Fixed-Rate versus Balloon Payment Mortgage

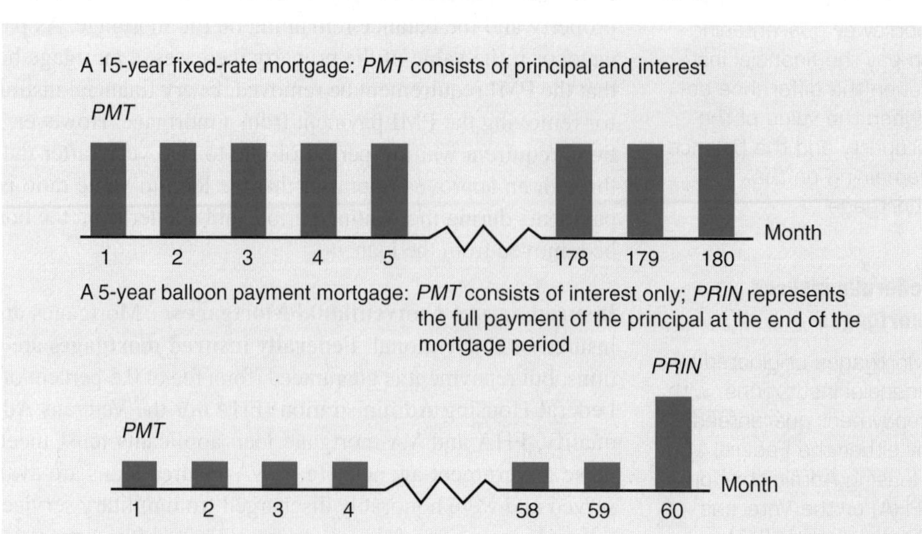

FIGURE 7–3 30-Year Mortgage versus 10-Year Treasury Rates

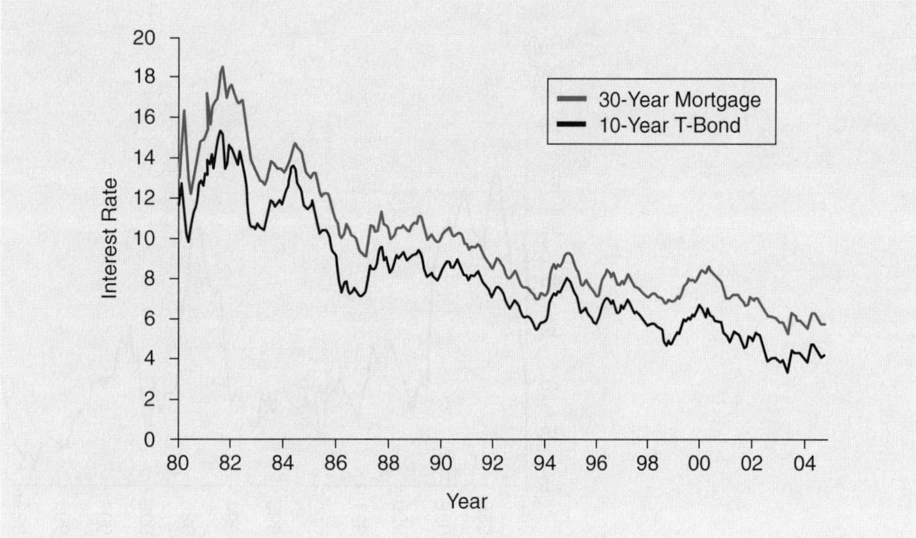

Source: Federal Reserve Board Web site, "Research and Data," December 2004. **www.federalreserve.gov**

current mortgage interest rate at the end of the balloon loan period (refinancing at maturity is not, however, guaranteed). Thus, with a balloon mortgage the financial institution essentially provides a long-term mortgage in which it can periodically revise the mortgage's characteristics.

Interest Rates. Possibly the most important characteristic identified in a mortgage contract is the interest rate on the mortgage. Mortgage borrowers often decide how much to borrow and from whom solely by looking at the quoted mortgage rates of several financial institutions. In turn, financial institutions base their quoted mortgage rates on several factors. First, they use the market rate at which they obtain funds (e.g., the fed funds rate or the rate on certificates of deposit). The market rate on available funds is the base rate used to determine mortgage rates. Figure 7–3 illustrates the trend in mortgage interest rates and 10-year Treasury bond rates from 1980 through 2004. The rate on a specific mortgage is also adjusted for other factors (e.g., whether the mortgage specifies a fixed or variable (adjustable) rate of interest and whether the loan specifies discount points and other fees)—see below.

fixed-rate mortgage

A mortgage that locks in the borrower's interest rate and thus the required monthly payment over the life of the mortgage, regardless of how market rates change.

adjustable-rate mortgage

A Mortgage in which the interest rate is tied to some market interest rate. Thus, the required monthly payments can change over the life of the mortgage.

Fixed- versus Adjustable-Rate Mortgages. Mortgage contracts specify whether a fixed or variable rate of interest will be paid by the borrower. A **fixed-rate mortgage** locks in the borrower's interest rate and thus required monthly payments over the life of the mortgage, regardless of how market rates change. In contrast, the interest rate on an **adjustable-rate mortgage** (ARM) is tied to some market interest rate or interest rate index. Thus, the required monthly payments can change over the life of the mortgage. ARMs generally limit the change in the interest rate allowed each year and during the life of the mortgage (called *caps*). For example, an ARM might adjust the interest rate based on the average Treasury bill rate plus 1.5 percent, with caps of 1.5 percent per year and 4 percent over the life of the mortgage.

Figure 7–4 shows the percentage of ARMs relative to all mortgages closed from 1987 through 2004. Mortgage borrowers generally prefer fixed-rate loans to ARMs, particularly when interest rates in the economy are low. If interest rates rise, ARMs may cause borrowers to be unable to meet the promised payments on the mortgage. In contrast, most mortgage lenders prefer ARMs. When interest rates rise, ARM payments on their mortgage assets will rise. Since deposit rates and other liability rates too will be rising, it will be easier for financial institutions to pay the higher interest rates to their depositors when they

FIGURE 7–4 ARMs' Share of Total Loans Closed, 1987–2004

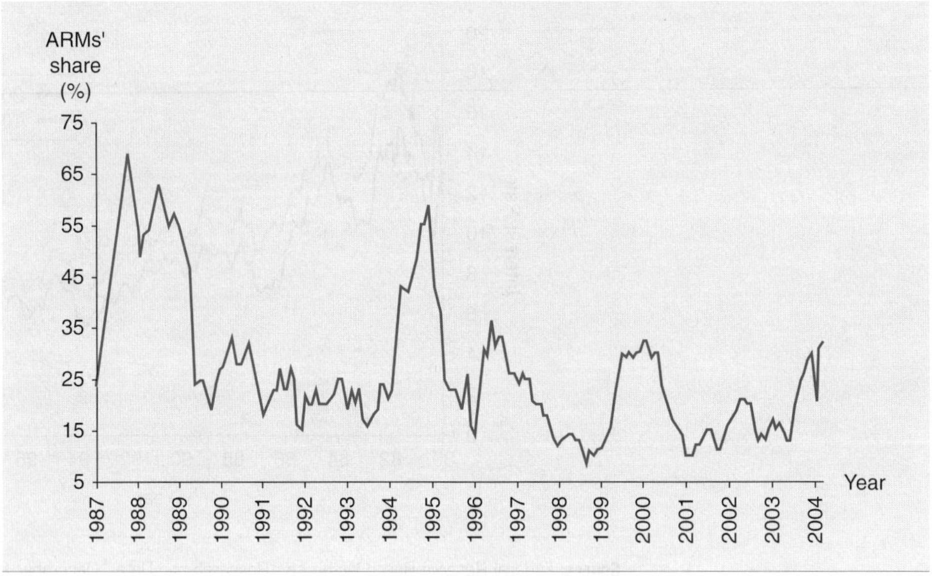

Source: Federal Housing Finance Board Web site, December 2004. **www.fhfb.gov**

issue ARMs. However, higher interest payments mean mortgage borrowers may have trouble making their payments. Thus, default risk increases. As a result, while ARMs reduce a financial institution's interest rate risk, they also increase their default risk.

Note from Figure 7–4 the behavior of the share of ARMs to fixed-rate mortgages over two recent periods—1997 to 1999 and late 2000 through spring 2004—when interest rates fell dramatically. Notice that borrowers' preferences for fixed-rate mortgages prevailed over these two periods, as a consistently low percentage of total mortgages closed were ARMs (over these periods the percentage of ARMs to total mortgages issued averaged only 17 percent and 14 percent, respectively).

discount points

Interest payments made when the loan is issued (at closing). One discount point paid up front is equal to 1 percent of the principal value of the mortgage.

Discount Points. **Discount points** (or more often just called points) are fees or payments made when a mortgage loan is issued (at closing). One discount point paid up front is equal to 1 percent of the principal value of the mortgage. For example, if the borrower pays 2 points up front on a $100,000 mortgage, he or she must pay $2,000 at the closing of the mortgage. While the mortgage principal is $100,000, the borrower effectively has received $98,000. In exchange for points paid up front, the financial institution reduces the interest rate used to determine the monthly payments on the mortgage. The borrower determines whether the reduced interest payments over the life of the loan outweigh the up-front fee through points. This decision depends on the period of time the borrower expects to hold the mortgage (see below).

Other Fees. In addition to interest, mortgage contracts generally require the borrower to pay an assortment of fees to cover the mortgage issuer's costs of processing the mortgage. These include such items as costs of:

Application fee. Covers the issuer's initial costs of processing the mortgage application and obtaining a credit report.
Title search. Confirms the borrower's legal ownership of the mortgaged property and ensures there are no outstanding claims against the property.
Title insurance. Protects the lender against an error in the title search.
Appraisal fee. Covers the cost of an independent appraisal of the value of the mortgaged property.

SEARCH THE SITE

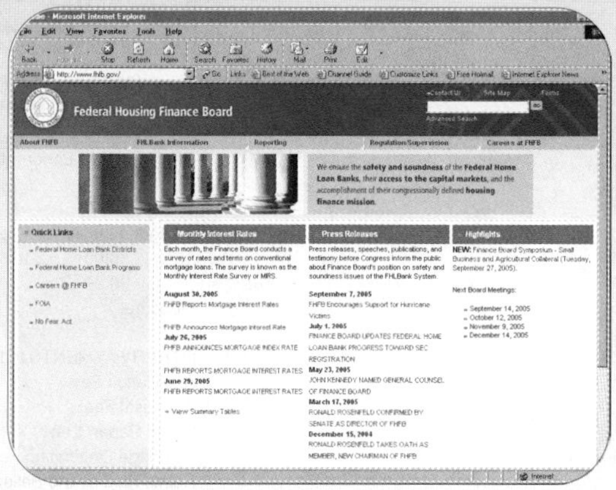

Go to the Federal Housing Finance Board's Web site and find the latest information available on the percentage of mortgages issued as adjustable- and fixed-rate mortgages.

Go to the Federal Housing Finance Board Web site at **www.fhfb.gov.**

Under "Monthly Interest Rate" click on "View Summary Tables"

Click on "—By Property Type"

This will download an EXCEL file on to your computer that will contain data on fixed- versus adjustable-rate mortgage originations.

Questions

1. Calculate the most recent percentage of mortgages issued as adjustable rate mortgages.
2. What has happened to interest rates since 2004 to cause this percentage to change from that in Figure 7–4?

Loan origination fee. Covers the remaining costs to the mortgage issuer for processing the mortgage application and completing the loan.

Closing agent and review fees. Cover the costs of the closing agent who actually closes the mortgage.

Other costs. Any other fees, such as VA loan guarantees, FHA or private mortgage insurance.

Figure 7–5 presents a sample closing statement in which the various fees are reported and the payment required by the borrower at closing is determined.

Mortgage Refinancing. Mortgage refinancing occurs when a mortgage borrower takes out a new mortgage and uses the proceeds obtained to pay off the current mortgage. Mortgage refinancing involves many of the same details and steps involved in applying for a new mortgage and can involve many of the same fees and expenses. Mortgages are most often refinanced when a current mortgage has an interest rate that is higher than the current interest rate. As coupon rates on new mortgages fall, the incentive for mortgage borrowers to pay off old, high coupon rate mortgages and refinance at lower rates increases. Figure 7–6 shows the percentage of mortgage originations that involved refinancings from 1990 through 2004. Notice that as mortgage rates fall (see Figure 7–3) the percentage of mortgages that are refinancings increases. For example, as mortgage rates fell in the early 2000s, refinancings increased to over 70 percent of all mortgages originated.

By refinancing the mortgage at a lower interest rate, the borrower pays less each month—even if the new mortgage is for the same amount as the current mortgage. Traditionally, the decision to refinance involves balancing the savings of a lower monthly payment against the costs (fees) of refinancing. However, refinancing adds transaction and recontracting costs. Origination costs or points for new mortgages, along with the cost of appraisals and credit checks, frequently arise as well. An often-cited rule of thumb is that the interest rate for a new mortgage should be 2 percentage points below the rate on the current mortgage for refinancing to make financial sense.

FIGURE 7–5 Mortgage Closing Statement

Borrower(s): Manuel Goodperson, Manuela Goodperson — Date: 02/05/2007
Lender: Starpointe Savings Bank Peasant Run Plaza Warre
Property: 321 Main St. Watchung, NJ 07060

Type of Mortgage FHA ( ) GI ( ) Convent. ( )	Amount of Loan	$106,400.00
Additional Funds made available by: $		
	Total A	$106,400.00

PAYMENTS to Lender (to establish escrow reserve)				
Taxes	3 months @	$ 172.50	$	517.50
Insurance	3 months @	$ 28.92	$	86.76
Mortgage Insurance Premium	2 months @	$ 69.16	$	138.32
0.00			$	
0.00			$	
Flood Ins.			$	44.08
		Total B	$	786.66
OTHER PAYMENTS to Lender				
Application Fee			$	54.00
Appraisal Fee			$	500.00
Credit Report Fee			$	
Mortgage Origination Fee			$	564.00
Points Paid by the Seller(s)			$	
Processing Fee			$	
Interest on Loan to			$	629.66
			$	
			$	
			$	
		Total C	$	1,747.66
PAYMENTS to Others				
Current Taxes & Assessments			$	
Title Search & Examination			$	
Survey			$	415.00
Title Insurance Policies			$	932.00
Hazard Insurance			$	
Recording Fees			$	8.11
Attorney Fees			$	750.00
Realty Transfer Fee or Tax			$	
Broker's Commission			$	
Mortgage Cancellation Fee			$	
Pay off of Mortgage Loan(s)			$	1,000.00
Balance due to Seller(s)			$	104,482.00
			$	
			$	
			$	
		Total D	$	107.587.11

Total B, C, and D	$110,121.43
Overpayment returned to Borrower (A less total B, C, and D)	$ −3,721.43

0 Year Mortgage @ % per year monthly payment payable day of each month commencing 02/05/2007

Principal & Interest	$
1/12 Taxes (Estimated)	$
1/12 Insurance	$
1/12 Mortgage Insurance Premium	$
Total	$

This statement has been examined by us and explained to our complete satisfaction. We have been given a copy of this statement. We authorize and direct that the closing attorney distribute the funds as set forth above.

Borrower Manuel Goodperson

Closing Attorney
Larry Lawyer, Esq

Borrower Manuela Goodperson

Mortgage Amortization

amortization schedule

Schedule showing how the monthly mortgage payments are split between principal and interest.

The fixed monthly payment made by a mortgage borrower generally consists partly of repayment of the principal borrowed and partly of the interest on the outstanding (remaining) balance of the mortgage. In other words, these fixed payments fully amortize (pay off) the mortgage by its maturity date. During the early years of the mortgage, most of the fixed monthly payment represents interest on the outstanding principal and a small amount represents a payoff of the outstanding principal. As the mortgage approaches maturity, most of the payment represents a payoff of the outstanding principal and a small amount represents interest. An **amortization schedule** shows how the fixed monthly payments are split between principal and interest.

FIGURE 7–6 Mortgage Refinancings as a Percentage of All Mortgages Originated, 1990–2004

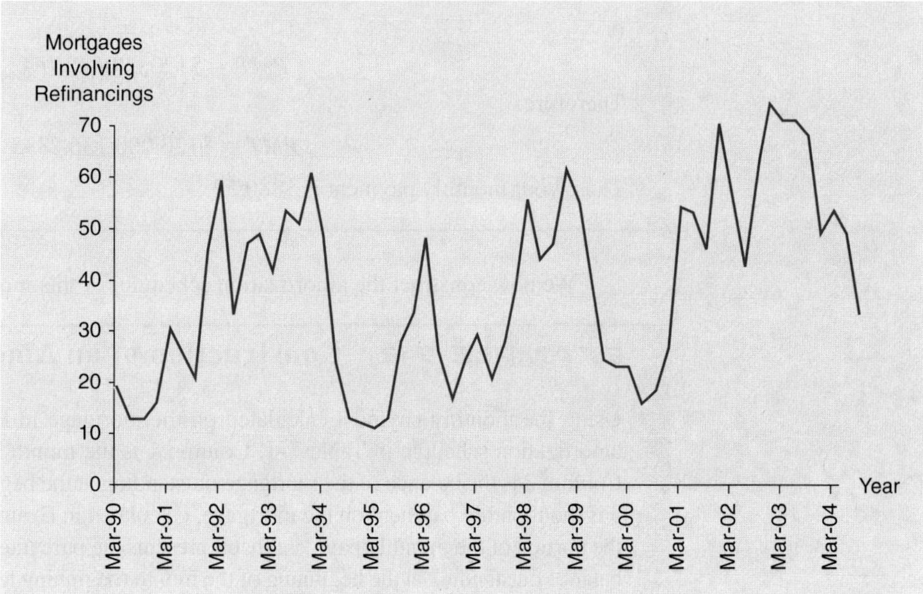

Source: Mortgage Bankers Association Web site, December 2004. **www.mbaa.org**

EXAMPLE 7–1 Calculation of Monthly Mortgage Payments

You plan to purchase a house for \$150,000 using a 30-year mortgage obtained from your local bank. The mortgage rate offered to you is 8 percent with zero points. In order to forgo the purchase of private mortgage insurance, you will make a down payment of 20 percent of the purchase price (\$30,000 = .20 × \$150,000) at closing and borrow \$120,000 through the mortgage.

The monthly payments on this mortgage are calculated using the time value of money formulas presented in Chapter 2. Specifically, the amount borrowed through the mortgage represents a present value of the principal, and the monthly payments represent a monthly annuity payment. The equation used to calculate your fixed monthly mortgage payments to pay off the \$120,000 mortgage at an 8 percent annual (8%/12 = .6667% monthly) interest rate over 30 years (or 30 × 12 = 360 payments) is as follows:[1]

$$PV = PMT \sum_{j=1}^{t} \left(\frac{1}{1 + r} \right)^j$$

$$= PMT\,(PVIFA_{r,t})$$

where

PV = Principal amount borrowed through the mortgage
PMT = Monthly mortgage payment
$PVIFA$ = Present value interest factor of an annuity
r = Monthly interest rate on the mortgage (equals the nominal annual interest rate, i, divided by 12 (months per year))
t = Number of months (payments) over the life of the mortgage

1. Mortgage valuation is very similar to bond valuation discussed in Chapter 3. Recall the formula to determine the present value of a bond:

$$V_b = INT(PVIFA_{r,t}) + M(PVIF_{r,t})$$

Both securities require periodic annuity payments of interest. However, mortgages generally require that a portion of the principal be included with each payment. With bonds, the full principal amount borrowed, M, is generally paid when the bond matures.

For the mortgage in this example:

$$\$120{,}000 = PMT(PVIFA_{.6667\%,360})$$

or:

$$PMT = \$120{,}000/(PVIFA_{.6667\%,360})$$

Therefore:

$$PMT = \$120{,}000/136.2835 = \$880.52$$

Thus, your monthly payment is $880.52.

We now construct the amortization schedule for this mortgage.

EXAMPLE 7–2 Construction of an Amortization Schedule

Using the monthly payment calculated on the mortgage in Example 7–1, we construct an amortization schedule in Table 7–1. Column 1 is the month in the 360-month loan period. Column 2 is the balance of the mortgage outstanding at the beginning of each month. Column 3 is the monthly payment on the mortgage, calculated in Example 7–1. Column 4, Interest, is the portion of the monthly payment that represents the pure interest payment based on the loan balance outstanding at the beginning of the month (beginning loan balance × 8%/12). Column 5, Principal, is the portion of the monthly payment that represents the repayments of the mortgage's principal (monthly payment – monthly interest, or in this example for month 1, $880.52 – $800 = $80.52). Column 6 is the balance of the mortgage principal outstanding at the end of the month. This value becomes the beginning balance in the next month.

Notice that the total payments made by the mortgage borrower over the 30-year life of the mortgage are $316,987.20. Of this amount $120,000 is repayment of the original principal. Thus, the borrower pays a total of $196,978.20 in interest over the life of the mortgage. Figure 7–7 illustrates the proportion of each payment that is interest versus principal. Notice that during the early years the majority of each payment is interest and very little goes toward the payment of principal. As the mortgage approaches maturity the majority of each payment is principal and very little goes to paying interest.

TABLE 7–1 Amortization Schedule for a 30-Year Mortgage

(1) Month	(2) Beginning Loan Balance	(3) Payment	(4) Interest	(5) Principal	(6) Ending Loan Balance
1	$120,000.00	$880.52	$800.00	$80.52	$119,919.48
2	119,919.48	880.52	799.46	81.06	119,838.42
•	•	•	•	•	•
•	•	•	•	•	•
119	105,623.54	880.52	704.16	176.36	105,447.18
120 (10 years)	105,447.18	880.52	702.98	177.54	105,269.64
•	•	•	•	•	•
•	•	•	•	•	•
239	73,359.08	880.52	489.06	391.46	72,967.62
240 (20 years)	72,967.62	880.52	486.45	394.07	72,573.55
•	•	•	•	•	•
•	•	•	•	•	•
359	1,743.58	880.52	11.63	868.89	874.69
360 (30 years)	874.69	880.52	5.83	874.69	0
Total		$316,987.20	$196,987.20	$120,000.00	

FIGURE 7–7 Amortization of a 30-Year Mortgage

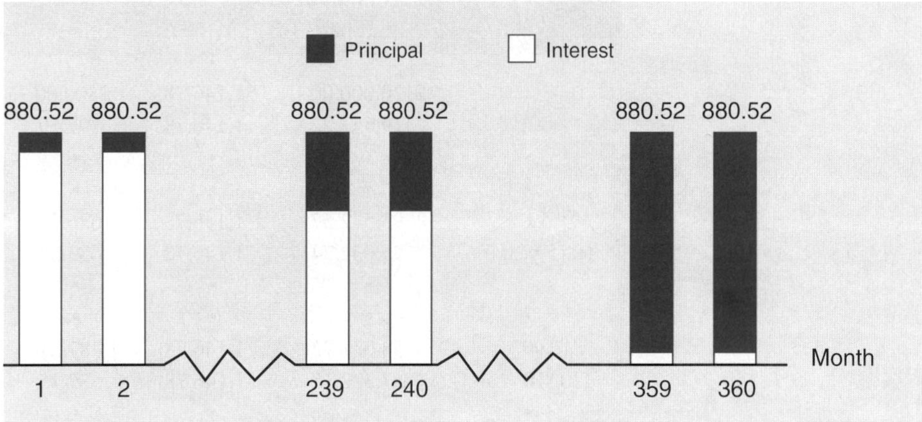

As discussed above, an advantage of a 15-year mortgage to a mortgage borrower is that the total interest paid on a 15-year mortgage is smaller than that paid on a 30-year mortgage.

EXAMPLE 7-3 Comparison of Interest Paid on a 15-Year versus a 30-Year Mortgage

Using the information in Example 7–1 but changing the loan maturity to 15 years (180 months), the monthly payment on the \$120,000 mortgage loan is:

$$\$120{,}000 = PMT(PVIFA_{.6667\%,180})$$

or:

$$PMT = \$120{,}000/(PVIFA_{.6667\%,180})$$

Therefore:

$$PMT = \$120{,}000/104.6406 = \$1{,}146.78$$

Solving for *PMT*, your monthly mortgage payment is \$1,146.78. Table 7–2 shows the corresponding loan amortization schedule.

Total payments on the 15-year mortgage are \$206,420.85, of which \$86,420.85 is interest. This compares to interest of \$196,978.20 on the 30-year mortgage (a difference of \$110,557.35). The mortgage borrower's interest payments are reduced significantly with the 15-year mortgage relative to the 30-year mortgage. However, the borrower must pay \$1,146.78 per month with the 15-year mortgage compared to \$880.52 with the 30-year mortgage, a difference of \$266.26 per month. This may be difficult if his or her income level is not very high.

Another factor that affects the amortization of a loan is whether the borrower pays discount points up front in exchange for a reduced interest rate and, consequently, reduced monthly payments.

TABLE 7-2 Amortization Schedule for a 15-Year Mortgage

Month	Beginning Loan Balance	Payment	Interest	Principal	Ending Loan Balance
1	$120,000.00	$1,146.78	$800.00	$ 346.78	$119,653.22
2	119,653.22	1,146.78	797.69	349.09	119,304.13
•	•	•	•	•	•
•	•	•	•	•	•
59	95,542.57	1,146.78	636.95	509.83	95,032.74
60 (5 years)	95,032.74	1,146.78	633.55	513.23	94,519.51
•	•	•	•	•	•
•	•	•	•	•	•
199	58,081.72	1,146.78	387.21	759.57	57,322.15
120 (10 years)	57,322.15	1,146.78	382.15	764.63	56,557.52
•	•	•	•	•	•
•	•	•	•	•	•
179	2,270.83	1,146.78	15.14	1,131.64	1,139.19
180 (15 years)	1,139.19	1,146.78	7.59	1,139.19	0
Total		$206,420.85	$86,420.85	$120,000.00	

EXAMPLE 7-4 Analyzing the Choice between Points and Monthly Payments of Interest

You plan to purchase a house for $150,000 using a 30-year mortgage obtained from your local bank. You will make a down payment of 20 percent of the purchase price, in this case, equal to $30,000. Thus, the mortgage loan amount will be $120,000. Your bank offers you the following two options for payment:

Option 1: Mortgage rate of 8 percent (or 8%/12 = .6667% per month) and zero points.
Option 2: Mortgage rate of 7.75 percent (or 7.75%/12 = .6458% per month) and 2 points ($2,400 = $120,000 × .02).

If option 2 is chosen, you receive $117,600 at closing ($120,000 − $2,400), although the mortgage principal is $120,000.

To determine the best option, we first calculate the monthly payments for both options as follows:

Option 1: $\$120{,}000 = PMT\,(PVIFA_{.6667\%,360}) \rightarrow PMT = \$880.52$
Option 2: $\$120{,}000 = PMT\,(PVIFA_{.6458\%,360}) \rightarrow PMT = \$859.69$

In exchange for $2,400 up front, option 2 reduces your monthly mortgage payments by $20.83. The present value of these savings (evaluated at 7.75 percent) over the 30 years is:

$$PV = \$20.83\,(PVIFA_{.6458\%,360}) = \$2{,}907.54$$

Option 2 is the better choice. The present value of the monthly savings, $2,907.54, is greater than the points paid up front, $2,400.

Suppose, however, you plan on paying off the loan in 15 years (180 months) even though the mortgage has a 30-year maturity. Now the monthly savings from option 2 have a present value of:

$$PV = \$20.83\,(PVIFA_{.6458\%,180}) = \$2{,}212.95$$

Option 1 becomes the better deal. The present value of the monthly savings, $2,212.95, is less than the points paid up front, $2,400.

To find the point (number of years) at which you are indifferent between the two options, you solve the following equation:

$$\$2{,}400 = \$20.83\ (PVIF_{.6458\%,\,X})$$

Solving for X gives 211 months, or 17.6 years. Thus, if you plan on paying off the mortgage in 17.6 years or less, option 1 is the better deal. If you plan on paying off the mortgage in more than 17.6 years, option 2 is preferred.

---

automatic rate-reduction mortgages

Mortgages in which the lender automatically lowers the rate on an existing mortgage when prevailing rates fall.

Notice that the choice of points (and lower monthly payments) versus no points (and higher monthly payments) depends on how long the mortgage borrower takes to pay off the mortgage. Specifically, the longer the borrower takes to pay off the mortgage, the more likely he or she is to choose points and a lower mortgage rate. Thus, by offering points, the mortgage lender decreases the probability that the mortgage borrower will prepay the mortgage—paying the mortgage off early reduces the present value of the monthly savings to the mortgage borrower.

Other Types of Mortgages

5 New methods of creative financing have been developed by financial institutions to attract mortgage borrowers. These include automatic rate-reduction mortgages, graduated-payment mortgages, growing-equity mortgages, second mortgages, shared-appreciation mortgages, equity-participation mortgages, and reverse-annuity mortgages.

graduated-payment mortgages

Mortgages in which borrowers make small payments early in the life of the mortgage. Payments then increase over the first 5 to 10 years, and finally payments level off at the end of the mortgage period.

Automatic Rate-Reduction Mortgages. As the name suggests, with automatic rate-reduction mortgages, the lender automatically lowers the rate on an existing mortgage when prevailing rates fall. Unlike variable-rate mortgages, while the interest rate on an automatic rate-reduction mortgage can be adjusted downward, it will not be increased if prevailing rates increase. Thus, interest rates on automatic rate-reduction mortgages can only fall. Mortgage lenders offer automatic rate-reduction mortgages as a way of keeping their mortgage customers from refinancing their mortgages with another mortgage lender when mortgage rates fall.

growing-equity mortgages

Mortgages in which the initial payments are the same as on a conventional mortgage, but they increase over a portion or the entire life of the mortgage. In contrast to GPMs, which do not affect the time until the mortgage is paid off, the incremental increase in monthly payments on GEMs reduces the principal on the mortgage more quickly. This reduces the actual life of the mortgage.

Graduated-Payment Mortgages. **Graduated-payment mortgages** (GPMs) allow mortgage borrowers to make small payments early in the life of the mortgage. The payments then increase over the first 5 to 10 years, and finally payments level off at the end of the mortgage period. GPMs are used by households that expect their incomes to rise along with the GPM payment. GPMs are also used by homeowners who plan to move or refinance quickly. They allow borrowers to qualify for a larger loan than they could get with a conventional mortgage. The risk to the borrower and the financial institution is that, if the expected income increase does not occur, the borrower may default on the mortgage. GPMs are not an extremely common type of mortgage, but some financial institutions (such as Allied Home Mortgage) that do significant business in this area have a separate Web site to provide information on their GPMs.

Growing-Equity Mortgages. **Growing-equity mortgages** (GEMs) are mortgages in which the initial payments are the same as on a conventional mortgage, but they increase over a portion or the entire life of the mortgage. In contrast to GPMs, which do not affect the time until the mortgage is paid off, the incremental increase in monthly payments on GEMs reduces the principal on the mortgage more quickly. This reduces the actual life of the mortgage. Thus, GEMs are used by borrowers who want to pay off a mortgage in a shorter period of time than stated in the mortgage contract and, like GPMs, borrowers who expect their incomes to rise over the life of the mortgage. Although GEMs represent only a small part of the mortgage loan market, the reduced term and faster repayment of the mortgage principal make GEMs more attractive to lenders than a standard fixed-rate loan. Like GPMs default occurs on the mortgage if the borrower misses a payment.

second mortgages

Loans secured by a piece of real estate already used to secure a first mortgage.

home equity loan

Loans that let customers borrow on a line of credit secured with a second mortgage on their homes.

shared-appreciation mortgage

Allows a home buyer to obtain a mortgage at an interest rate below current market rates in exchange for a share in any appreciation in the property value. If the property is eventually sold for more than the original purchase price, the financial institution is entitled to a portion of the gain.

equity-participation mortgage

A mortgage that is similar to a SAM except that an outside investor shares in the appreciation of the property rather than the financial institution.

reverse-annuity mortgage

A mortgage for which a mortgage borrower receives regular monthly payments from a financial institution rather than making them. When the RAM matures (or the borrower dies) the borrower (or the estate of the borrower) sells the property to retire the debt.

Second Mortgages. **Second mortgages** are loans secured by a piece of real estate already used to secure a first mortgage. Should a default occur, the second mortgage holder is paid only after the first mortgage is paid off. As a result, interest rates on second mortgages are higher than on first mortgages.

About 15 percent of all primary mortgage holders also have second mortgages. Second mortgages provide mortgage borrowers with a way to use the equity they have built up in their homes as collateral on another mortgage, thus allowing mortgage borrowers to raise funds without having to sell their homes. Financial institutions often offer **home equity loans** that let customers borrow on a line of credit secured with a second mortgage on their homes. The dollar value of home equity loans issued by U.S. depository institutions and outstanding in September 2004 was $459.8 billion, compared to a total of $2,242.5 billion in total home mortgage loans. Further, the rate of interest financial institutions charged on home equity loans was 7.06 percent compared to 5.42 percent on 15-year fixed-rate first mortgage loans.

Interest on all mortgages (first, second, and home equity) secured by residential real estate is tax deductible. Interest on other types of individual loans—such as consumer loans—is not eligible for a tax deduction.

Shared-Appreciation Mortgages. Introduced in the early 1980s, a **shared-appreciation mortgage** (SAM) allows a home buyer to obtain a mortgage at an interest rate below current market rates (as much as 2 percent) in exchange for a share (given to the lender) in any appreciation in the property value. Thus, the borrower's monthly mortgage payments are smaller. However, if the property is eventually sold for more than the original purchase price, the financial institution is entitled to a portion of the gain. The financial institution has bought, in effect, a call option on the value of the house compared to its purchase price (with the house buyer being viewed as the seller of that option). SAMs are used mainly when interest rates are high because they allow borrowers who would not qualify for high interest rate (high monthly payment) mortgages to do so. Although SAM originations have been small, financial institutions that issue SAMs experience about half the interest rate risk on SAMs compared to conventional fixed-rate mortgages.

Equity-Participation Mortgages. An **equity-participation mortgage** (EPM) is similar to a SAM except that an outside investor shares in the appreciation of the property rather than the financial institution that issues the mortgage. The investor either provides a portion of the down payment on the property or provides monthly payments. While not used much in the early 2000s when interest rates were low, EPMs were very popular in the 1980s when interest rates peaked. EPMs allowed otherwise nonqualifying homeowners to obtain a mortgage.

Reverse-Annuity Mortgages. With a **reverse-annuity mortgage** (RAM), a mortgage borrower receives regular monthly payments from a financial institution rather than making them. When the RAM matures (or the borrower dies), the borrower (or the borrower's estate) sells the property to retire the debt. RAMs were designed as a way for retired people to live on the equity they have built up in their homes without the necessity of selling the homes. Maturities on RAMs are generally set such that the borrower will likely die prior to maturity.

As the U.S. population ages, RAMs are growing in popularity. Because so many people retire asset rich and income poor, RAMs present a way for seniors to unlock some of the value tied up in their home to boost their income. Funds received from a RAM may be used for any purpose including meeting housing expenses (such as taxes, insurance, and maintenance expenses), as well as other living expenses. RAMs provide a way for retired homeowners to maintain financial independence as well as ownership of their home, but

DO YOU UNDERSTAND?

1. What the function of a lien placed on a mortgage contract is?
2. When private mortgage insurance is required for a mortgage?
3. What the difference is between an insured mortgage and a conventional mortgage?
4. What the typical mortgage maturity is?
5. What graduated-payment mortgages are?

they are more costly than more conventional types of mortgages. Thus, RAMs are attractive mainly to older homeowners who have accumulated substantial equity in their homes.

SECONDARY MORTGAGE MARKETS

After financial institutions originate mortgages, they often sell or securitize them in the secondary mortgage market. In 2004, over 60 percent of all residential mortgages were securitized in this fashion. The sale/securitization of mortgages in the secondary mortgage markets reduces the liquidity risk, interest rate risk, and credit risk experienced by the originating financial institution compared to keeping the mortgage in its asset portfolio. For example, depository institutions obtain the majority of their funds from short-term deposits. Holding long-term fixed-rate mortgages in their asset portfolios subjects them to interest rate risk, particularly if interest rates are expected to increase (see Chapter 22). Moreover, selling/securitizing mortgages can generate fee income for the mortgage-originating financial institution and helps reduce the effects of regulatory constraints (see Chapter 13). In this section, we introduce and provide an overview of the secondary mortgage markets. We look at these markets in more detail, including how financial institutions can use these markets to hedge credit risk on their balance sheets in Chapter 24.

Many financial institutions such as mortgage companies prefer to concentrate on the servicing of mortgages rather than the long-term financing of them, which occurs if they are kept on the balance sheet. For example, in the second quarter of 2004 New Century Financial Corp., one of the largest mortgage finance companies, originated \$12.3 billion of mortgages and sold \$10.3 billion of them in the secondary mortgage markets. The loan originator may also act as a servicer, collecting payments from mortgage borrowers and passing the required interest and principal payments through to the secondary market investor. The servicer also keeps the formal records of all transactions pertaining to the mortgage. In return for these services, the financial institution collects a monthly fee. Mortgage servicers generally charge fees ranging from 1/4 to 1/2 percent of the mortgage balance. Financial institutions can remove mortgages from their balance sheets through one of two mechanisms. First, they can pool their recently originated mortgages together and sell them in the secondary mortgage market. Second, financial institutions can issue mortgage-backed securities, creating securities that are backed by their newly originated mortgages (i.e., securitization of mortgages).

History and Background of Secondary Mortgage Markets

The secondary mortgage markets were created by the federal government to help boost U.S. economic activity during the Great Depression. In the 1930s, the government established the Federal National Mortgage Association (FNMA or Fannie Mae) to buy mortgages from thrifts so that these depository institutions could make more mortgage loans. The government also established the Federal Housing Administration (FHA) and the Veterans Administration (VA) to insure certain mortgage contracts against default risk (described earlier). This made it easier to sell/securitize mortgages. Financial institutions originated the mortgages and secondary market buyers did not have to be as concerned with a borrower's credit history or the value of collateral backing the mortgage since they had a federal government guarantee protecting them against default risk.

www.fanniemae.com

www.va.com

By the late 1960s, fewer veterans were obtaining guaranteed VA loans. As a result, the secondary market for mortgages declined. To encourage continued expansion in the housing market, the U.S. government created the Government National Mortgage Association (GNMA or Ginnie Mae) and the Federal Home Loan Mortgage Corporation (FHLMC or Freddie Mac), which provided direct or indirect guarantees that allowed for the creation of mortgage-backed securities (see below).

www.ginniemae.gov

www.freddiemac.com

As the secondary mortgage markets have evolved, a wide variety of mortgage-backed securities have been developed to allow primary mortgage lenders to securitize their mortgages and to allow a thriving secondary market for mortgages to develop. The organizations involved in the secondary mortgage markets (e.g., GNMA, FNMA) differ in the types of mortgages included in the mortgage pools, security guarantees (or insurance), and payment patterns on the securities.

Mortgage Sales

6

Financial institutions have sold mortgages and commercial real estate loans among themselves for more than 100 years. In fact, a large part of **correspondent banking** involves small banks making loans that are too big for them to hold on their balance sheets—either for lending concentration risk or capital adequacy reasons—and selling parts of these loans to large banks with whom they have had a long-term deposit and lending correspondent relationship. In turn, large banks often sell parts of their loans, called *participations,* to smaller banks.

correspondent banking

A relationship between a small bank and a large bank in which the large bank provides a number of deposit, lending, and other services.

mortgage sale

Sale of a mortgage originated by a bank with or without recourse to an outside buyer.

recourse

The ability of a loan buyer to sell the loan back to the originator should it go bad.

A **mortgage sale** occurs when a financial institution originates a mortgage and sells it with or without recourse to an outside buyer. If the mortgage is sold without recourse, the financial institution not only removes it from its balance sheet but also has no explicit liability if the mortgage eventually goes bad. Thus, the buyer of the mortgage (not the financial institution that originated the loan) bears all the credit risk.[2] If, however, the mortgage is sold with **recourse,** under certain conditions the buyer can return the mortgage to the selling financial institution; therefore, the financial institution retains a contingent credit risk liability. In practice, most mortgage sales are without recourse. For example, in 2003, thrifts sold \$628 billion of the primary mortgages from their asset portfolios: \$498 billion (79.3 percent) of these were sold without recourse. Mortgage sales usually involve no creation of new types of securities, such as those described below. We discuss loan sales in more detail in Chapter 24.

A major reason that financial institutions sell loans is to manage their credit risk better (see Chapter 20). Mortgage sales remove assets (and credit risk) from the balance sheet and allow a financial institution to achieve better asset diversification. Additionally, mortgage sales allow financial institutions to improve their liquidity risk and interest rate risk situations. Other than risk management, however, financial institutions are encouraged to sell loans for a number of other economic (generation of fee income) and regulatory reasons (including reducing the cost of reserve requirements and reducing the cost of holding capital requirement against mortgages).[3] The benefits of loan sales are discussed in detail in Chapter 24.

A wide array of potential buyers and sellers of mortgage loans exist. The five major buyers of primary mortgage loans are domestic banks, foreign banks, insurance companies and pension funds, closed-end bank loan mutual funds, and nonfinancial corporations. The major sellers of mortgage loans are money center banks, small regional or community banks, foreign banks, and investment banks. We discuss the motivations of each in Chapter 24.

Mortgage-Backed Securities

In this section, we introduce the three major types of mortgage-backed securities—the pass-through security, the collateralized mortgage obligation (CMO), and the mortgage-backed bond. In Chapter 24, we provide a detailed analysis of these securities and the processes by which these mortgage-backed securities are created.

Pass-through securities and CMOs are securitized mortgages. Securitization of mortgages involves the pooling of a group of mortgages with similar characteristics, the removal of these mortgages from the balance sheet, and the subsequent sale of interests in the mortgage pool to secondary market investors. Securitization of mortgages results in the creation of mortgage-backed securities (e.g., government agency securities, collateralized

2. Although the buyer's credit risk is reduced if the mortgage is federally insured against default risk.

3. Under the current BIS scheme (see Chapter 13), this is 2.8 percent for most residential mortgages.

TABLE 7–3 Government-Related Mortgage-Backed Pass-Through Securities Outstanding
(in billions of dollars)

	1995	1998	2000	2004
GNMA	$ 472.3	$ 537.4	$ 611.5	$ 572.1
FNMA	583.0	834.5	1,057.7	1,816.0
FHLMC	515.1	646.5	822.3	1,190.0
Private mortgage issuers	292.8	536.6	740.7	1,152.3
Total	$1,863.2	$2,582.0	$3,232.2	$4,730.4

Source: Federal Reserve Bulletin, various issues, Table 1.54, p. A35. **www.federalreserve.gov**

mortgage obligations), which can be traded in secondary mortgage markets. For example, there were $4.73 trillion in outstanding mortgage securitization pools at the end of 2004. The ability of mortgage issuers to remove mortgages (and the accompanying credit risk and interest rate risk) from their balance sheets has added billions of dollars to mortgage markets and resulted in lower rates and fees to mortgage borrowers.

Pass-Through Securities. Financial institutions frequently pool the mortgages and other assets they originate and offer investors an interest in the pool in the form of *pass-through certificates or securities.* **Pass-through mortgage securities** "pass through" promised payments of principal and interest on pools of mortgages created by financial institutions to secondary market investors (mortgage-backed security bond holders) holding an interest in these pools. After a financial institution accepts mortgages, it pools them and sell interests in these pools to pass-through security holders. Each pass-through mortgage security represents a fractional ownership share in a mortgage pool.[4] Thus, a 1 percent owner of a pass-through mortgage security issue is entitled to a 1 percent share of the principal and interest payments made over the life of the mortgages underlying the pool of securities. The originating financial institutions (e.g., bank or mortgage company) or a third-party servicer receives principal and interest payments from the mortgage holder and passes these payments (minus a servicing fee) through to the pass-through security holders.

pass-through mortgage securities

Mortgage-backed securities that "pass through" promised payments of principal and interest on pools of mortgages created by financial institutions to secondary market participants holding interests in the pools.

Three agencies, either government-owned or government-sponsored, are directly involved in the creation of mortgage-backed pass-through securities. Informally, they are known as Ginnie Mae (GNMA), Fannie Mae (FNMA), and Freddie Mac (FHLMC). Private mortgage issuers, such as banks and thrifts, also purchase mortgage pools, but they do not conform to government-related issuer standards. Table 7–3 reports the amount of mortgaged-backed pass-through securities outstanding for each from 1995 through 2004.

www.ginniemae.gov

GNMA. The Government National Mortgage Association (GNMA), or Ginnie Mae, began in 1968 when it split off from the Federal National Mortgage Association (FNMA). GNMA is a government-owned agency with two major functions: sponsoring mortgage-backed securities programs by financial institutions such as banks, thrifts, and mortgage bankers and acting as a guarantor to investors in mortgage-backed securities regarding the timely pass-through of principal and interest payments from the financial institution or mortgage servicer to the bond holder. In other words, GNMA provides **timing insurance**. In acting as a sponsor and payment-timing guarantor, GNMA supports only those pools of mortgage loans whose default or credit risk is insured by one of three government agencies: the Federal Housing Administration (FHA), the Veterans Administration (VA), and the Farmers Home Administration (FMHA). Mortgage loans insured by these agencies target

timing insurance

A service provided by a sponsor of pass-through securities (such as GNMA) guaranteeing the bond holder interest and principal payments at the calendar date promised.

4. This is a simplification. In actual practice, the mortgages are first sold (placed) in a "special purpose vehicle" (SPV) off the balance sheet, and it is this SPV that issues the bonds backed by the mortgages.

groups that might otherwise be disadvantaged in the housing market, such as low-income families, young families, and veterans. As such, the maximum mortgage under the FHA/VA/FMHA–GNMA securitization program is capped. The cap was $359,650 for a single family home in 2004.

GNMA securities are issued in minimum denominations of $25,000. The minimum pool size for GNMA single-family mortgages is $1 million. Once a pool of mortgages is packaged by a financial institution in accordance with GNMA specifications, pass-through securities can be issued. Cash flows of interest and principal received from the original mortgages are used to pay the promised payments on the GNMA securities. The mortgages from the pool are used as collateral, guaranteeing the promised payments to the GNMA holders.

GNMA requires that all of the mortgages in a pool used to back a particular GNMA pass-through security issue have the same interest rate. Secondary market purchasers of GNMA pass-through securities generally receive 0.50 percent less than the rate on the underlying mortgages. The 0.50 percent is divided between the financial institution that services the mortgages and GNMA, which charges a fee for the provision of its timing insurance.

www.fanniemae.com

FNMA. Originally created in 1938, the Federal National Mortgage Association (FNMA or Fannie Mae) is the oldest of the three mortgage-backed security-sponsoring agencies. It is now a private corporation owned by shareholders, with its stock traded on the New York Stock Exchange. However, in the minds of many investors, it still has implicit government backing, which makes it equivalent to a government-owned agency. Indeed, the fact that FNMA has a secured line of credit available from the U.S. Treasury should it need funds in an emergency supports this view. As a result, FNMA bonds are rated AAA. FNMA is a more active agency than GNMA in creating pass-through securities. GNMA merely sponsors such programs and guarantees the timing of payments from financial institution servicers to GNMA investors; FNMA actually helps create pass-throughs by buying and holding mortgages on its balance sheet; it also issues bonds directly to finance those purchases.

Specifically, FNMA creates mortgage-backed securities (MBSs) by purchasing packages of mortgage loans from banks and thrifts; it finances such purchases by selling MBSs to outside investors such as life insurers or pension funds. In addition, FNMA engages in swap transactions by which it swaps MBSs with a bank or thrift for original mortgages. Since FNMA guarantees securities in regard to the full and timely payment of interest and principal, the financial institution receiving the MBSs can then resell them in the capital market or can hold them in its own portfolio. Unlike GNMA, FNMA securitizes conventional mortgage loans, as well as FHA/VA insured loans, as long as the conventional loans have acceptable loan-to-value or collateral ratios not normally exceeding 80 percent. Conventional loans with high loan-to-value ratios usually require that the mortgages be insured with private mortgage insurance (see earlier discussion) before they are accepted into FNMA securitization pools.

www.freddiemac.com

FHLMC. The Federal Home Loan Mortgage Corporation (FHLMC), or Freddie Mac (FMAC), performs a similar function to that of FNMA except that its major securitization role has historically involved thrifts. Like FNMA, FHLMC is a stockholder-owned corporation with a line of credit from the U.S. Treasury. Thus, its bonds are also rated AAA. Further, like FNMA, it buys mortgage pools from financial institutions and swaps MBSs for loans. FHLMC also sponsors conventional mortgage pools and mortgages that are not federally insured as well as FHA/VA mortgage pools and guarantees timely payment of interest and ultimate payment of principal on the securities it issues.

Private Mortgage Pass-Through Issuers. Private mortgage pass-through issuers (such as commercial banks, thrifts, and private conduits) purchase nonconforming mortgages (e.g., mortgages that exceed the size limit set by government agencies, such as the $359,650 cap

TABLE 7–4 Pass-Through Securities Quote Sheet

Mortgage-Backed Securities

Indicative, not guaranteed; from Bear Stearns Cos./Street Pricing Service

(1) RATE		(2) PRICE (JAN) (PTS-32DS)	(3) PRICE CHANGE (32DS)	(4) AVG LIFE (YEARS)	(5) SPRD TO AVG LIFE (YEARS)	(6) SPREAD CHANGE (BPS)	(7) PSA (PREPAY SPEED)	(8) YIELD TO MAT*
30-year								
FMAC GOLD	5.5%	101-17	+02	4.7	157	-1	357	5.10
FMAC GOLD	6.0%	103-07	-02	2.6	150	-1	636	4.60
FMAC GOLD	6.5%	104-27	-02	1.8	58	-3	750	3.44
FNMA	5.5%	101-15	+02	4.6	156	-1	364	5.08
FNMA	6.0%	103-10	-01	2.4	131	-1	704	4.34
FNMA	6.5%	104-29	-02	1.6	26	-3	799	3.07
GNMA **	5.5%	101-31	+02	4.9	143	-4	325	5.01
GNMA **	6.0%	103-16	-02	2.6	138	-1	574	4.48
GNMA **	6.5%	105-07	-01	2.0	70	-4	648	3.65
15-year								
FMAC GOLD	5.0%	101-17	+02	4.4	112	-2	278	4.58
FNMA	5.0%	101-18	+02	4.2	109	-2	298	4.52
GNMA **	5.0%	102-13	+01	4.3	89	-2	275	4.34

*Extrapolated from benchmarks based on projections from Bear Stearns prepayment model, assuming interest rates remain unchanged. ** Government guaranteed.

Source: *The Wall Street Journal,* December 8, 2004, p. C9. Reprinted by permission of *The Wall Street Journal.* **www.wsj.com**

set by the FHA), pool them, and sell pass-through securities on which the mortgage collateral does not meet the standards of a government-related mortgage issuer. There are a limited number of private conduits—Prudential Home, Residential Funding Corporation, GE Capital Mortgages, Ryland/Saxon Mortgage Countrywide, Chase Mortgage Finance, and Citigroup/Citibank Housing. Private mortgage pass-through securities must be registered with the SEC and are generally rated by a rating agency (such as Moody's) in a manner similar to corporate bonds.

Mortgaged-Backed Pass-Through Quotes. Table 7–4 presents a quote sheet for mortgage-backed pass-through securities traded on December 7, 2004. The quote lists the trades by issuer (e.g., GNMA, FNMA). Column 1 of the quote lists the sponsor of the issue (e.g., FMAC, FNMA, GNMA), the stated maturity of the issue (30 years or 15 years), the mortgage coupons on the mortgages in each pool (e.g., 5.5 percent), and information about the maximum delay between the receipt of interest by the servicer/sponsor and the actual payment of interest to bond holders. The "GOLD" next to FMAC indicates a maximum stated delay of 55 days. The current market price of a bond is shown in column 2, with the daily price change in column 3. Both prices are in percentages, and the number after the dash is in 32nds (e.g., 101-17 = $101\frac{17}{32}$). Column 4 shows the average life of the bond reflecting the prepayment patterns of homeowners in the pool as estimated by one investment bank (Bear Stearns). Notice these pools of 15- and 30-year mortgages have an expected weighted-average life[5] of no more than 4.9 years. The fifth column in the quote is a measure of the yield spread of the mortgage-backed security over a Treasury bond with the same average life, and column 6 reports the spread change for the day. Column 7 is a measure of the estimated prepayment speed. The prepayment speeds are shown relative to those normally occurring on pass-through securities as estimated by the Public Securities Association (PSA). Thus, 357 PSA (prepayment speed) means that these MBS mortgage holders are prepaying over $3\frac{1}{2}$ times quicker than the speed that normally would be expected. One possible reason for this is that current interest rates are low and many mortgage holders are

5. The weighted-average life of these securities is not the same as duration, which measures the weighted-average time to maturity based on the relative present values of cash flows as weights. Rather, the weighted-average life is a significant simplification of the duration measure that seeks to concentrate on the expected timing of repayments of principal; i.e., it is the weighted-average time over which principal repayments will be received.

prepaying early to refinance new mortgages at lower rates. We discuss prepayment risk and prepayment speeds as estimated by the PSA in greater detail in Chapter 24. Finally, the last column (8) is the yield to maturity on the mortgage-backed pass-through security. This yield is calculated using the yield to maturity formulas found in Chapter 3, given the contractual income, principal cash flows, and the expected prepayment pattern (based on projections made by Bear Stearns).

Government Sponsorship and Oversight of FNMA and Freddie Mac. As mentioned above, while neither FNMA nor Freddie Mac is fully backed by the U.S. government, both are sponsored by the U.S. government. For example, both have a secured line of credit available from the U.S. Treasury. The implicit guarantee afforded by this government sponsorship leads investors to believe the government would step in if the agencies had trouble. This, in turn, allows FNMA and Freddie Mac to borrow more cheaply than virtually all other mortgage issuers.

This special relationship between FNMA, Freddie Mac, and the U.S. government, and the subsidy that goes with this relationship, sparked a public policy debate in the early 2000s. Many have raised concerns that these two government-sponsored enterprises **(GSEs)** may not be the most efficient mechanisms for subsidizing housing. Yet both GSEs have experienced persistently high profit, arguably the result of the "federal" guarantee or subsidy. As a result, some regulators have argued that FNMA and Freddie Mac be fully privatized by cutting their links to U.S. government guarantees. Others have called for the creation of new U.S. government–sponsored competitors to FNMA and Freddie Mac so as to reduce the size of the government subsidy going to these two GSEs.

GSE

A government-sponsored enterprise such as Fannie Mae and Freddie Mac.

www.hud.gov

www.ofheo.gov

Another issue of concern relates to the safety and soundness of these GSEs. The U.S. government sponsorship of FNMA and Freddie Mac creates the potential for moral hazard (increased risk-taking behavior) and raises concerns as to the problems that would arise if these GSEs became financially distressed or even insolvent. In response to these concerns, the U.S. government assigned two safety and soundness regulators to focus exclusively on these housing GSEs: the Department of Housing and Urban Development (HUD) and the Office of Federal Housing Enterprise Oversight (OFHEO). Further, in 2002 (in the wake of the Enron collapse) regulators introduced legislation that would require FNMA and Freddie Mac to register their bonds with the Securities and Exchange Commission (SEC). To date these GSEs are exempt from SEC disclosure rules. Federal Reserve chairman Alan Greenspan expressed his concern that banks that sell derivatives to FNMA and Freddie Mac might be taking on too much risk because these banks believe the GSEs are implicitly supported by the government.[6] In response, both FNMA and Freddie Mac started reporting more information about their derivatives positions to investors.[7]

In the early 2000s, these two agencies came under fire for several reasons. First, in September 2002 Fannie Mae was criticized for allowing a sharp increase in interest rate risk to exist on its balance sheet. The Office of Federal Housing Enterprise Oversight (OFHEO), a main regulator of Fannie Mae, required Fannie Mae to submit weekly reports to the OFHEO on the company's exposure to interest rate risk. The OFHEO also instructed Fannie Mae to keep regulators apprised of any challenges associated with returning its interest rate risk measure to more acceptable levels, and it warned that the office might take additional action if Fannie Mae's management's effectiveness in lowering interest rate risk suffered adverse developments. Despite these actions, Fannie Mae reported a 52 percent drop in net income for 2003, attributed to wide swings in the value of derivative contracts used to hedge interest rate risk.

6. For example, both agencies are major purchasers of credit derivatives such as credit swaps (see Chapter 23) and paid premiums in 2002 of around $2,800 per $1 million of protection. By comparison, Merrill Lynch was paying $10,000 per million—see, "The Debt Nobody Frets Over," *International Herald Tribune,* May 22, 2002, p. 12.

7. See "Fannie Mae and Freddie Mac Pressed Again, This Time on Disclosure and Derivatives," *New York Times,* April 25, 2002, p. C2, by Alex Beresson and "Freddie Mac, Fannie Mae Face Disclosure Rules," *The Wall Street Journal,* July 2, 2002, p. A2.

In October 2003, Fannie Mae and Freddie Mac came under new criticism for allegedly overcharging lenders for services they provide. The overcharges came in the fees that the companies collect from banks, thrifts, and other lenders for guaranteeing repayment of their mortgages. If true, the overcharges hurt mortgage lenders, squeezing their profit margins and perhaps home buyers, too, as lenders increased mortgage interest rates to recover the increased fees. Later that same month Fannie Mae announced that it miscalculated the value of its mortgages, forcing it to make a $1.1 billion restatement of its stockholders equity. Earlier in the year Freddie Mac announced a $4.5 billion misstatement of its earnings. Although both were claimed to be computational errors, the episodes reinforced fears that Fannie Mae and Freddie Mac managers lack the necessary skills to operate their massive and complex businesses, which some investors and political critics worry could pose risk to the nation's financial system if not properly managed. In the fall of 2004, these apparent errors led to an investigation by the OFHEO into the accounting practices of both GSEs. The OFHEO found evidence that Fannie Mae's accounting practices had been designed to skirt accepted accounting practices, smooth earnings, and, in at least one case, increase bonuses to executives. In September 2004, Freddie Mac admitted that it distorted its financial statements to give investors a picture of smooth earnings and agreed to pay a $125 million civil penalty for using derivative transactions and other accounting practices to make earnings look less volatile.

Finally, in February 2004, Federal Reserve chairman Alan Greenspan stated that Fannie Mae and Freddie Mac pose very serious risks to the U.S. financial system and urged Congress to curb their growth sooner rather than later. The fear is that the two agencies used their implicit federal backing to assume more risk and finance expansion through increased debt. Such actions create a source of systematic risk for the U.S. financial system.

As a result of these problems and the potential risk to the financial system, in July 2004 the Treasury Department was given the authority to limit future debt issuance by Fannie Mae and Freddie Mac. This was seen as a positive step in curbing the enormous growth, financed through borrowing, of the GSEs and a way to reduce fears among government officials, competitors of the GSEs, and investors that the two agencies posed growing risks to the financial system. Further, in 2004 the U.S. Senate proposed a bill that would create a new independent regulator of Fannie Mae and Freddie Mac with broad authority to determine the companies' safety and soundness, capital standards, and new lines of business, and even to decide the companies' ultimate fate in the event of insolvency. The OFHEO followed up the Senate's actions by drafting a rule that would spell out how it could take over and wind down Fannie Mae and Freddie Mac's operations if they ever get into financial trouble. Adoption of that rule would send a strong signal to investors that the two agencies are not fully guaranteed by the U.S. government and not immune from market forces.[8]

8 **Collateralized Mortgage Obligations.** Although pass-throughs are still the primary mechanism for securitization, the **collateralized mortgage obligation (CMO)** is a second vehicle for securitizing financial institution assets that is increasingly used. Innovated in 1983 by FHLMC and First Boston, the CMO is a device for making mortgage-backed securities more attractive to certain types or classes of investors. The CMO does this by repackaging the cash flows from mortgages and pass-through securities in a different fashion.

collateralized mortgage obligation (CMO)

A mortgage-backed bond issued in multiple classes or tranches.

A pass-through security gives each investor a pro rata share of any interest and principal cash flows on a mortgage pool. By contrast, a CMO can be viewed as a multiclass pass-through with a number of different bond holder classes or **tranches.** Unlike a pass-through, which has no guaranteed annual coupon, each bond holder class in a CMO has a different

tranche

A bond holder class associated with a CMO.

8. See "Fannie, Freddie Face a Tough Plan," by John D. McKinnon, *The Wall Street Journal,* March 29, 2004, p. A2; "Regulators Hit Fannie, Freddie with New Assault," by James R. Hagerty, *The Wall Street Journal,* April 28, 2004, p. A1; "Fannie, Freddie May Get Limits," by John D. McKinnon and James R. Hagerty, *The Wall Street Journal,* July 16, 2004, p. C1; "Regulator Details a Wide Range of Accounting Problems at Fannie," by James R. Hagerty, John D. McKinnon, and Dawn Kopecki, *The Wall Street Journal,* September 23, 2004, p. A1.

guaranteed coupon (paid semiannually) just as a regular T-bond. More importantly, the allocation of any excess cash flows over and above the guaranteed coupon payments due to increased mortgage prepayments go toward retiring the principal outstanding of only one class of bond holders, leaving all other classes prepayment protected for a period of time.[9] CMOs give investors greater control over the maturity of the mortgage-backed securities they buy. By comparison, for pass-throughs, the mortgage-backed security holder has a highly uncertain maturity date due to the risk of very rapid prepayments (called *prepayment risk by the mortgagees*).

mortgage- (asset-) backed bonds

Bonds collateralized by a pool of assets.

Mortgage-Backed Bond. **Mortgage- (asset-) backed bonds** (MBBs) are the third type of mortgage-backed security. These bonds differ from pass-throughs and CMOs in two key dimensions. First, while pass-throughs and CMOs help financial institutions remove mortgages from their balance sheets, MBBs normally remain on the balance sheet. Second, pass-throughs and CMOs have a direct link between the cash flows on the underlying mortgages and the cash flows on the bond instrument issued. By contrast, the relationship for MBBs is one of collateralization rather than securitization; the cash flows on the mortgages backing the bond are not necessarily directly connected to interest and principal payments on the MBB.

Essentially, a financial institution issues an MBB to raise long-term low-cost funds. MBB holders have a first claim to a segment of the financial institution's mortgage assets. Practically speaking, the financial institution segregates a group of mortgage assets on its balance sheet and pledges this group of assets as collateral against the MBB issue.

A trustee normally monitors the segregation of assets and ensures that the market value of the collateral exceeds the principal owed to MBB holders. Financial institutions back most MBB issues by excess collateral. This excess collateral backing of the bond, in addition to the priority rights of the bond holders, generally ensures the sale of these bonds with a high investment grade credit rating (BBB or better). In contrast, the financial institution, when evaluated as a whole, could be rated as BB or even lower. A high credit rating results in lower coupon payments than would be required if significant default risk had lowered the credit rating.

Weighed against the benefits of MBB issuance are a number of costs. The first cost is that MBBs tie up mortgages on the financial institution's balance sheet for a long time. This decreases the asset portfolio's liquidity. Second, balance sheet illiquidity is enhanced by the need to overcollateralize MBBs to ensure a high-quality credit risk rating for the issue. Third, by keeping the mortgages on the balance sheet, the financial institution continues to be liable for capital adequacy and reserve requirement taxes. Because of these costs, MBBs are the least used of the three basic vehicles of securitization.

DO YOU UNDERSTAND?

1. Which loans should have the highest yields—loans sold with recourse or loans sold without recourse?
2. The three forms of mortgage loan securitization? What are the major differences in the three forms?
3. Why an investor in a securitized asset who is concerned about prepayment risk would prefer a CMO over a pass-through security?

PARTICIPANTS IN THE MORTGAGE MARKETS

9 In this chapter, we have demonstrated that financial institutions are critical in the operations of both the primary and secondary mortgage markets. Some financial institutions (e.g., banks, savings institutions) contribute mainly to the primary mortgage markets. Others (e.g., mortgage companies) contribute to both the primary and secondary markets. Figure 7–8 shows the distribution of mortgages outstanding in 1992 and 2004 by type of mortgage holder—the ultimate investor.

Notice in Figure 7–8 the growth in the importance of mortgage securitization pools over the period (40.42 percent of all mortgages outstanding in 1992 versus 52.42 percent in 2004).

9. Some CMOs, however, are issued with planned amortization class (PAC) bonds. PAC bonds offer a fixed principal redemption schedule that is met as long as prepayments on the underlying mortgages remain within a certain range. PACs are designated to protect CMO investors against prepayment risk. See discussion in Chapter 24.

FIGURE 7–8 Mortgages Outstanding by Type of Holder, 1992 and 2004

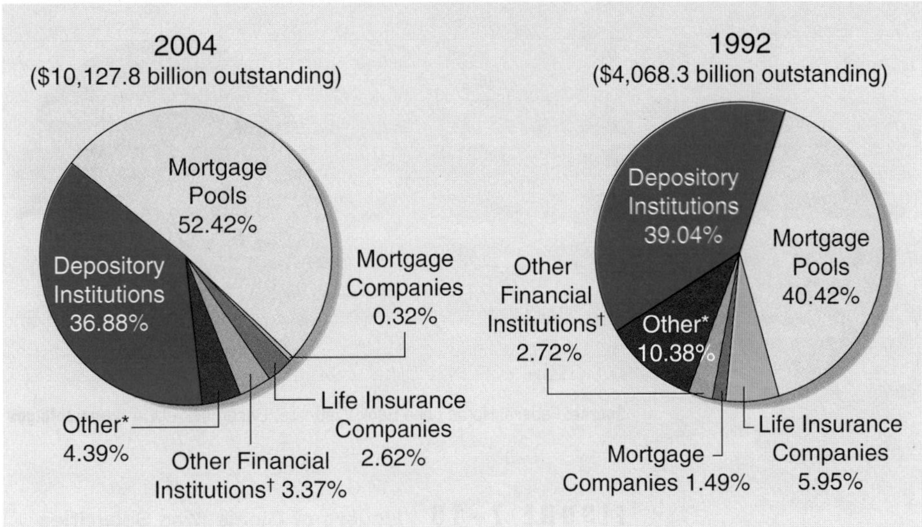

*Includes households, businesses, state and local governments, and the federal government.

†Includes other insurance companies, pension funds, finance companies, and REITs.

Source: Federal Reserve Board Web site, "Flow of Fund Accounts," September 2004. **www.federalreserve.gov**

Remember that government-sponsored mortgage pools were virtually nonexistent before the establishment of GNMA in 1968. By contrast, mortgages held by life insurance companies, households, businesses, and the federal government have fallen as a percentage of the total pool of mortgages outstanding (5.95 percent for life insurance companies in 1992 versus 2.62 percent in 2004; 10.38 percent for households, businesses, and government in 1992 versus 4.39 percent in 2004).

Notice that the actual holdings of mortgages by specialized mortgage companies (such as Sierra Pacific Mortgage Company and Greenwich Home Mortgage Corp. of New Jersey) are small (1.49 percent in 1992 and 0.32 percent in 2004). Mortgage companies, or mortgage bankers, are financial institutions[10] that originate mortgages and collect payments on them. Unlike a bank or thrift, mortgage companies typically do not hold on to the mortgages they originate. Instead, they sell the mortgages they originate but continue to service the mortgages by collecting payments and keeping records on each loan. Mortgage companies earn income to cover the costs of originating and servicing the mortgages from the servicing fees they charge the ultimate buyers of mortgages. Figure 7–9 shows the distribution of one- to four-family mortgage originations; mortgage companies originated 28.3 percent of all home mortgages in 2004. Mortgage companies are major originators of FHA- and VA-insured mortgage pass-throughs sponsored by GNMA. Figure 7–10 shows the distribution of issuers of GNMA securities; mortgage companies issued over half of all GNMA securities in 2004. What should be evident from these figures is that despite originating such a large volume in the mortgage market, the reason for the small investments in mortgages by mortgage companies (as seen in Figure 7–7) is that, while mortgage companies are major *originators* of home mortgages, they generally do not *hold* the mortgage loans in their asset portfolios for a long period of time. Rather, mortgage companies *sell* or *securitize* most of the mortgages they originate in the secondary market.

DO YOU UNDERSTAND?

1. Who the major holders of mortgages in the United States are?
2. Why mortgage companies hold such a small portion of the mortgage market on their balance sheets?

10. Most of these mortgage companies are finance companies, which are discussed in Chapter 14.

FIGURE 7–9 **One- to Four-Family Mortgage Originations**

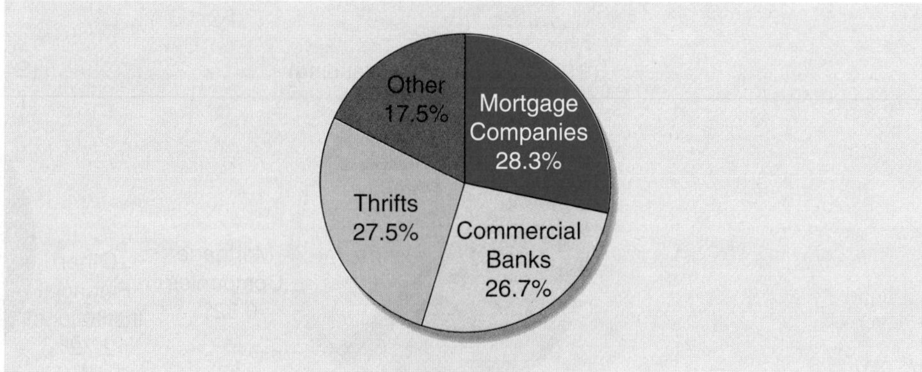

Source: Federal Home Loan Bank Web site, December 2004. **www.fhfb.gov**

FIGURE 7–10 **Issuers of Ginnie Mae Securities**

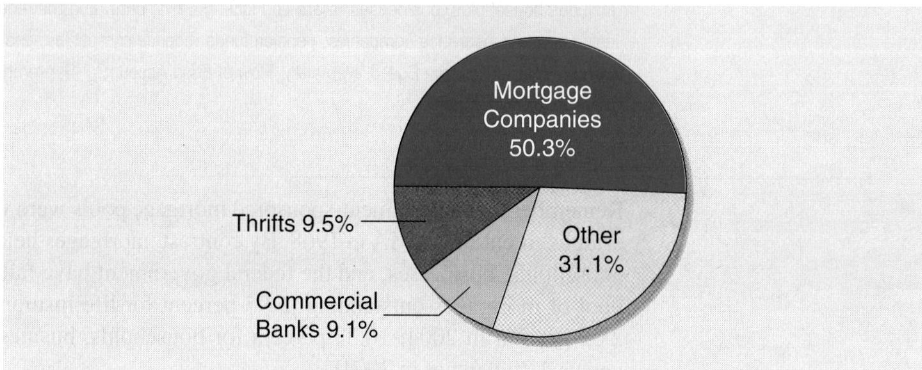

Source: Ginnie Mae Web site, December 2004. **www.ginniemae.gov**

INTERNATIONAL TRENDS IN SECURITIZATION

10

Demand by International Investors for U.S. Mortgage-Backed Securities

International investors participate in U.S. mortgage and mortgage-backed securities markets. Table 7–5 lists the dollar value of primary mortgages issued and held by foreign banking offices in the United States between 1992 and 2004. Notice that the value of mortgages held by foreign banks has decreased over this period by 71 percent (from \$51.6 billion in 1992 to \$15.5 billion in 2004). This compares to primary mortgages issued and held by domestic depository institutions of \$3,734.9 billion in 2004 (see Figure 7–8)—foreign bank offices issue and hold less than 0.5 percent of the total primary mortgage market in the United States.

International Mortgage Securitization

While they have not evolved to the level of U.S. mortgage markets, securitization vehicles have also been developed for mortgages in countries other than the United States. After the United States, Europe is the world's second-largest and most developed securitization market. Although a form of securitization has been in existence in Europe in the German and Danish mortgage markets since the 1700s, securitization as we currently know it

TABLE 7-5 Foreign Investments in U.S. Mortgage Markets
(in billions of dollars)

	1992	1995	1998	2000	2004
Mortgages held by foreign banking offices in the United States	$51.6	$35.1	$20.6	$17.1	$15.5

Source: Federal Reserve Board Web site, "Flow of Fund Accounts," various issues. **www.federalreserve.gov**

DO YOU UNDERSTAND?

1. What the trends in securitization of assets in Europe have been?

emerged outside the United State only in the mid-1980s. The original growth of "modern" securitization in Europe was based largely upon the activities of a small number of centralized lenders in the booming U.K. residential mortgage market of the late 1980s.

Since mid-1993, the number of European originators of securitized assets has continued to grow, as have the types of assets that can be securitized and the investor base. Further, securitization costs have fallen, and legislative and regulatory changes in European countries have supported this market's growth. The volume of European securitizations skyrocketed in 1996 and 1997, when European countries securitized a total of $41.5 billion assets. Despite the world economic crisis in 1998, the European securitization market fell only slightly to $38.4 billion. More than $22 billion of securitized vehicles were issued in just the first half of 1999 alone, including $3.5 billion in international deals from Japan. Japan and Europe accounted for $16 billion of the first quarter total. Latin America and the emerging markets (still struggling with economic crises) lagged behind, with issues totaling $7.0 billion.

The European securitization market topped $218 billion in 2003 and $192 billion in the first nine months of 2004. The United Kingdom is the biggest issuer of mortgage-backed securities with over 30 percent of the European market. Germany is second, but far behind the United Kingdom, with 5 percent of the European market.[11] In Europe, the factors driving the securitization market include the conversion to a single currency (a factor driving many European markets at the beginning of the 21st century), the effects of globalization of all markets, and the spread of U.S.-style financial securities. The single currency, the euro, has accentuated the increased trend in securitization in Europe; issuers are able to securitize combined assets in the Euro with minimal currency risk while benefiting from a bigger and more diversified pool of buyers. Future expectations are that securitized assets will be denominated almost exclusively in dollars and euros, with euros potentially becoming more liquid than the dollar.

In Russia, mortgage lending has grown in the early 2000s, following the enactment of many crucial laws that were meant to encourage mortgage loans. Such basic laws as the right to own property and land, the right to sell it, and the right to pledge it as security for a mortgage did not exist in Russia until recently. In addition, a Federal Mortgage Agency was set up and mortgage terms have become more favorable. The maximum term on a mortgage was extended to 20 years from 5 and interest rates in Russia fell from 24 percent to 15 percent. In addition, a secondary mortgage market was created. DeltaCredit, a private Russian-U.S. joint venture, started operating as Russia's first specialized mortgage bank. The International Finance Corporation extended a $20 million credit line to DeltaCredit for housing finance in 2002 and another $66 million in 2003. In October 2003 five more international banks announced their intention to enter the Russian mortgage market. As of 2003 mortgage lending in Russia totaled around $200 million. Estimates suggest that this can grow to $10 billion to $30 billion. The huge demand for more and better housing, coupled with fast progress in the mortgage market, should boost household credit in coming years.[12]

11. See "Europe at an Interesting Crossroads," *Asset Securitization Report,* November 2004.

12. See "The Beginning of Russia's Mortgage Boom," *Quest Economics Database,* November 30, 2003.

SUMMARY

In this chapter, we examined the primary and secondary mortgage markets. For several reasons, mortgages are analyzed separately from other capital market securities (e.g., bonds and stocks). We identified several characteristics associated with mortgages and various categories of primary mortgage markets. We also provided an overview of the secondary mortgage markets.

Securitization of mortgages allows financial institutions to reduce interest rate risk exposure experienced when mortgages are left in the asset portfolios for the entire life of the mortgage. We look at the details of the securitization process in a risk-return framework in Chapter 24.

SEARCH THE SITE

Go to the Federal Reserve Board's Web site at **www.federalreserve.gov** and find the most recent data on Mortgage Loans Outstanding.

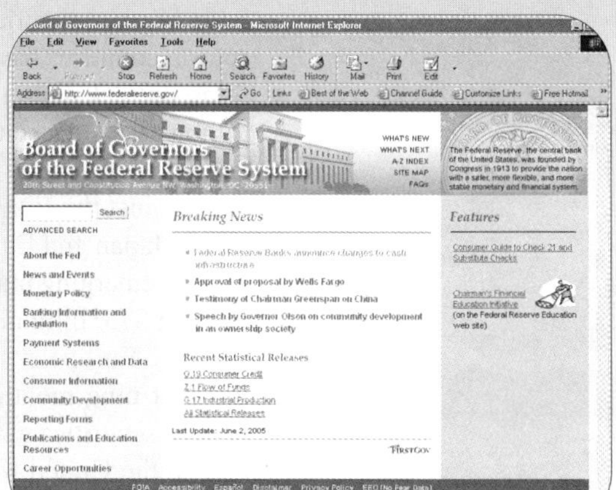

Click on "Economic Research and Data"

Click on "Statistics: Releases and Historical Data"

Click on "Flow of Fund Accounts of the United States, Releases"

Click on the most recent date.

Click on "Level tables"

This downloads a file onto your computer that contains the relevant data in Table L217.

Questions

1. What is the current dollar value of mortgage loans outstanding? How has this value changed since 2004 reported in Figure 7–1?

2. Calculate the percentage of mortgage loans outstanding comprised of 1- to 4-family, multifamily residential, commercial, and farm loans?

QUESTIONS

1. Why are mortgage markets studied as a separate capital market?
2. What are the four major categories of mortgages and what percentage of the overall market does each entail?
3. What is the purpose of putting a lien against a piece of property?
4. Explain the difference between a federally insured mortgage and a conventional mortgage.
5. Explain the difference between a fixed-rate mortgage and an adjustable-rate mortgage. Include a discussion of mortgage borrowers' versus mortgage lenders' preferences for each.
6. You plan to purchase a $100,000 house using a 30-year mortgage obtained from your local credit union. The mortgage rate offered to you is 8.25 percent. You will make a down payment of 20 percent of the purchase price.
   a. Calculate your monthly payments on this mortgage.
   b. Calculate the amount of interest and, separately, principal paid in the 25th payment.
   c. Calculate the amount of interest and, separately, principal paid in the 225th payment.
   d. Calculate the amount of interest paid over the life of this mortgage.
7. You plan to purchase a $175,000 house using a 15-year mortgage obtained from your local bank. The mortgage rate offered to you is 7.75 percent. You will make a down payment of 20 percent of the purchase price.
   a. Calculate your monthly payments on this mortgage.

b. Calculate the amount of interest and, separately, principal paid in the 60th payment.
c. Calculate the amount of interest and, separately, principal paid in the 180th payment.
d. Calculate the amount of interest paid over the life of this mortgage.

8. You plan to purchase an $80,000 house using a 15-year mortgage obtained from your local bank. The mortgage rate offered to you is 8.00 percent. You will make a down payment of 20 percent of the purchase price.
   a. Calculate your monthly payments on this mortgage.
   b. Calculate the amount of interest and, separately, principal paid in the 127th payment.
   c. Calculate the amount of interest and, separately, principal paid in the 159th payment.
   d. Calculate the amount of interest paid over the life of this mortgage.

9. eXcel **Using a Spreadsheet to Calculate Mortgage Payments:** What is the monthly payment on a $150,000, 15-year mortgage if the mortgage rate is 5.75 percent? 6.25 percent? 7.5 percent? 9 percent?

Present Value	Periods	Interest Rate	=>	The Payment Will Be
$150,000	15 × 12	5.75%/12		$1,245.62
150,000	15 × 12	6.25%/12		1,286.13
150,000	15 × 12	7.50%/12		1,390.52
150,000	15 × 12	9.00%/12		1,521.40

10. eXcel **Using a Spreadsheet to Calculate Mortgage Payments:** What is the monthly payment on a $150,000, 30-year mortgage if the mortgage rate is 5.75 percent? 6.25 percent? 7.5 percent? 9 percent?

Present Value	Periods	Interest Rate	=>	The Payment Will Be
$150,000	30 × 12	5.75%/12		$ 875.36
150,000	30 × 12	6.25%/12		923.58
150,000	30 × 12	7.50%/12		1,048.82
150,000	30 × 12	9.00%/12		1,206.93

11. You plan to purchase a house for $115,000 using a 30-year mortgage obtained from your local bank. You will make a down payment of 20 percent of the purchase price.
   a. Your bank offers you the following two options for payment:
      Option 1: Mortgage rate of 9 percent and zero points.
      Option 2: Mortgage rate of 8.85 percent and 2 points.
      Which option should you choose?
   b. Your bank offers you the following two options for payments:
      Option 1: Mortgage rate of 10.25 percent and 1 point.
      Option 2: Mortgage rate of 10 percent and 2.5 points.
      Which option should you choose?

12. What is the difference between a graduated-payment mortgage and a growing-equity mortgage?
13. What is the difference between a shared-appreciation mortgage and an equity-participation mortgage?
14. How did the U.S. secondary mortgage markets evolve?
15. What is a mortgage sale? How does a mortgage sale differ from the securitization of mortgage?
16. What is a pass-through security?
17. What is the Government National Mortgage Association? How does this organization play a role in secondary mortgage markets?
18. What is the Federal National Mortgage Association? How does this organization play a role in secondary mortgage markets?
19. STANDARD &POOR'S Go to the S&P Educational Version of Market Insight Web site at **www.mhhe.com/edumarketinsight** and find the debt-to-equity ratio for the Federal Home Loan Mortgage Corp (FRE) and Fannie Mae (FNM) using the following steps: Click on "Educational Version of Market Insight" Enter your Site ID and click on "Login" Click on "Company" In the box marked "Ticker" enter FRE and click on "Go!" Click on "Excel Analytics" Click on "FS Ann. Balance Sheet"

    This brings up a file that contains the relevant data: total liabilities and total shareholders' equity. Repeat this process using the ticker FNM.
20. Describe a collateralized mortgage obligation. How is a CMO created?
21. What is a mortgage-backed bond? Why do financial institutions issue MBBs?

8 Foreign Exchange Markets

OUTLINE

Chapter NAVIGATOR

1. What are foreign exchange markets and foreign exchange rates?
2. What are the world's largest foreign exchange markets?
3. What is the euro and how/why was it created?
4. What is the difference between a spot foreign exchange transaction and a forward foreign exchange transaction?
5. How can return and risk be measured on foreign exchange transactions?
6. What is the role of financial institutions in foreign exchange transactions?
7. What is the relation between interest rates, inflation, and exchange rates?

FOREIGN EXCHANGE MARKETS AND RISK: CHAPTER OVERVIEW

In addition to understanding the operations of domestic financial markets, a financial manager must also understand the operations of foreign exchange markets and foreign capital markets. Today's U.S.-based companies operate globally. It is therefore essential that financial managers understand how events and movements in financial markets in other countries affect the profitability and performance of their own companies. For example, a currency and economic crisis in Argentina in late 2001 adversely impacted some U.S. markets and firms in the winter and spring of 2002. Coca Cola Co., which derived about 2 percent of its sales from Argentina, attributed a 5 percent decline in its 2002 operating profits to unfavorable currency movements between the Argentinian peso and the U.S. dollar.[1]

Indeed, U.S. imports of foreign goods exceeded $2.0 trillion in 2004, while exports totaled $1.5 trillion. Trades of this magnitude would not be possible without a market where investors can easily buy and sell foreign currencies. Additionally, as firms and investors increase the volume of transactions in foreign currencies, hedging foreign exchange risk has

1. See "U.S. Firms Assess Damage in Argentina," *The Wall Street Journal*, January 9, 2002, p. A10.

become a more important activity. Financial managers, therefore must understand how events in other countries in which they operate affect cash flows received from or paid to other countries and thus their company's or FI's profitability. Foreign exchange markets are the markets in which traders of foreign currencies transact most efficiently and at the lowest cost. As a result, foreign exchange markets facilitate foreign trade, facilitate raising capital in foreign markets, facilitate the transferring of risk between participants, and facilitate speculation on currency values.

foreign exchange markets

Markets in which cash flows from the sale of products or assets denominated in a foreign currency are transacted.

foreign exchange rate

The price at which one currency can be exchanged for another currency.

foreign exchange risk

Risk that cash flows will vary as the actual amount of U.S. dollars received on a foreign investment changes due to a change in foreign exchange rates.

Cash flows from the sale of products, services, or assets denominated in a foreign currency are transacted in **foreign exchange** (FX) **markets**. A **foreign exchange rate** is the price at which one currency (e.g., the U.S. dollar) can be exchanged for another currency (e.g., the Swiss franc) in the foreign exchange markets. These transactions expose U.S. corporations and investors to **foreign exchange risk** as the cash flows are converted into and out of U.S. dollars. The actual amount of U.S. dollars received on a foreign transaction depends on the (foreign) exchange rate between the U.S. dollar and the foreign currency when the nondollar cash flow is received (and exchanged for U.S. dollars) at some future date. If the foreign **currency** declines (or **depreciates**) in value relative to the U.S. dollar over the period between the time a foreign investment is made and the time it is liquidated, the dollar value of the cash flows received will fall. If the foreign **currency** rises (or **appreciates**) in value relative to the U.S. dollar, the dollar value of the cash flows received on the foreign investment increases.

In this chapter, we examine the operations of foreign exchange markets. We start with a brief look at the history of foreign exchange markets. We define and describe the spot and forward foreign exchange transaction process. We also look at balance of payment accounts that summarize a country's foreign transactions.

BACKGROUND AND HISTORY OF FOREIGN EXCHANGE MARKETS

Foreign exchange markets have existed for some time as international trade and investing have resulted in the need to exchange currencies. The type of exchange rate system used to accomplish this exchange, however, has changed over time. For example, from 1944 to 1971, the Bretton Woods Agreement called for the exchange rate of one currency for another to be fixed within narrow bands around a specified rate with the help of government intervention. The Bretton Woods Agreement, however, led to a situation in which some currencies (such as the U.S. dollar) became very overvalued and others (such as the German mark) became very undervalued. The Smithsonian Agreement of 1971 sought to address this situation. Under this agreement, major countries allowed the dollar to be devalued and the boundaries between which exchange rates could fluctuate were increased from 1 to 2¼ percent.

currency depreciation

When a country's currency falls in value relative to other currencies, meaning the country's goods become cheaper for foreign buyers and foreign goods become more expensive for foreign sellers.

currency appreciation

When a country's currency rises in value relative to other currencies, meaning that the country's goods are more expensive for foreign buyers and foreign goods are cheaper for foreign sellers (all else constant).

In 1973, under the Smithsonian Agreement II, the exchange rate boundaries were eliminated altogether. This effectively allowed exchange rates of major currencies to float freely. This free-floating foreign exchange rate system is still partially in place. However, as discussed in Chapter 4, central governments may still intervene in the foreign exchange markets directly to change the direction of exchange rates and currencies by altering interest rates to affect the value of their currency relative to others. Moreover, in 1992 twelve major European countries and the Vatican City pegged their exchange rates together to create a single currency, called the euro.[2]

Until 1972, the interbank foreign exchange market was the only channel through which spot and forward (see below) foreign exchange transactions took place. The interbank market involves electronic trades between major banks (such as between J.P. Morgan Chase and HSBC) around the world. This market is over the counter (OTC) and thus has no regular trading hours, so that currencies can be bought or sold somewhere around the world 24 hours a day. Major banks operating in the interbank foreign exchange market are

2. The 12 countries are Austria, Belgium, Finland, France, Germany, Greece, Ireland, Italy, Luxembourg, Netherlands, Portugal, and Spain.

referred to as market makers, since they trade in the major currencies on a more or less continuous basis. When extremely large transactions occur, foreign exchange brokers may be used to find investors for part of the transactions. Smaller banks do not deal directly in the interbank foreign exchange market. Rather, they have arrangements to transact with larger banks. Corporations and individuals that want to trade in foreign currencies also usually transact through their main bank.

Since 1972, organized markets such as the International Money Market (IMM) of the Chicago Mercantile Exchange (CME) have developed derivatives trading in foreign currency futures and options. However, the presence of such a well-developed interbank market for foreign exchange forward contracts has hampered the development of the futures market for foreign exchange trading. For example, while foreign currency trading has grown significantly since 1972, trading in the forward market continues to be much larger than the futures market (on the order of 20 times the daily volume measured by value of trades).

The major differences between the interbank foreign exchange market and organized trading on exchanges include the market location, the standardization of contracts, the standardization of delivery dates, and the differences in the way contracts are settled. While the interbank forward market is a worldwide market with no geographic boundaries, the principal futures market is the IMM in Chicago. Futures market contracts trade in the major currencies (e.g., the euro, British pound) with contracts expiring on the third Wednesday of March, June, September, and December. In contrast, forward market contracts can be entered into on any currency, with maturity stated as a given number of days for delivery of the currency in the future. The futures market (the IMM of the CME) determines the size of futures contracts on foreign currencies, and all contracts must be of these sizes. In the forward market, contract size is negotiated between the bank and the customer. Finally, less than 1 percent of all futures contracts are completed by delivery of the foreign currency. Rather, profit or loss on the futures contract is settled daily between the trader and the exchange, and many traders sell their contracts prior to maturity (see Chapter 10). In contrast, delivery of the foreign currency occurs on the contract's maturity in over 90 percent of forward contracts.

In 1982, the Philadelphia Stock Exchange (PHLX) began trading currency options. By 1988, currency options were trading in volumes as high as $4 billion per day in underlying value. Currency options put the PHLX on international maps, bringing trading interest from Europe, the Pacific Rim, and the Far East and leading the exchange to be the first securities exchange to open international offices in money centers overseas. Currency options made the Philadelphia Stock Exchange an around-the-clock operation. In September 1987, Philadelphia was the first securities exchange in the United States to introduce an evening trading session, chiefly to accommodate increasing demand for currency options in the Far East. In January 1989, the exchange responded to growing European demand by adding an early morning session. Finally, in September 1990, the PHLX became the first exchange in the world to offer around-the-clock trading by bridging the gap between the night session and the early morning hours.

DO YOU UNDERSTAND?

1. What the Bretton Woods Agreement did to the ability of foreign exchange rates to fluctuate freely?
2. What the euro is?

2 The foreign exchange markets have become among the largest of all financial markets, with turnover exceeding $1.9 trillion per day in 2004. London continues to be the largest center for trading in foreign exchange; it handles almost twice the daily volume of New York, the second-largest market. Third-ranked Tokyo handles approximately one-third the volume of London. Moreover, the FX market is essentially a 24-hour market, moving from Tokyo, London, and New York throughout the day. Therefore, fluctuations in exchange rates and thus FX trading risk exposure continues into the night even when some FI operations are closed.

3 **The Introduction of the Euro.** The euro is the name of the European Union's (EU's) single currency. It started trading on January 1, 1999, when exchange rates among the currencies of the original 11 participating countries were fixed, although domestic currencies (e.g., the Italian lira and French franc) continued to circulate and be used for transactions within each country. By January 1, 2002, domestic currencies started to be phased out and euro notes and coins began circulating within

12 EU countries (and the Vatican City). The eventual creation of the euro had its origins in the creation of the European Community (EC): a consolidation of three European communities in 1967 (the European Coal and Steel Community, the European Economic Market, and the European Atomic Energy Community). The emphasis of the EC was both political and economic. Its aim was to break down trade barriers within a common market and create a political union among the people of Europe. The Maastricht Treaty of 1993 set out stages for transition to an integrated monetary union among the EC participating countries, referred to as the European Monetary Union (EMU). Some of the main stipulations of the Maastricht Treaty included the eventual creation of a single currency (the euro), the creation of an integrated European system of central banks, and the establishment of a single European Central Bank (ECB).

While the creation of the euro has had a significant effect throughout Europe, it is also expected to have a notable impact on the global financial system. For example, in the first decade of the 2000s, as the U.S. experienced an increasing national debt, rapid consumer spending, and a current account deficit big enough to bankrupt most other countries (see below), the euro increased in value by 35 percent against the U.S. dollar. In November 2004, as the dollar depreciated in value against the euro, Russia's Central Bank said it was considering replacing some of the U.S. dollars in its reserves with euros. Asian central banks hinted that they would soon do the same. The Chinese Central Bank had already substituted some of its dollars for euros.[3] Indeed, the euro is fast becoming the world's second most important currency for international transactions behind the dollar and some predict, given the combined size of the "euro-economies" (particularly if the United Kingdom eventually replaces the pound sterling with the euro), may even compete against the dollar as the premier international currency. The main impact of the establishment of the euro on foreign exchange markets has been on trading volume. On January 1, 1999, the consolidation of the original 11 currencies into a fixed exchange rate regime immediately eliminated 8 percent of global foreign exchange turnover. This decline was not subsequently recovered by an increase in trading in the euro compared to its predecessor currencies.

FOREIGN EXCHANGE RATES AND TRANSACTIONS

Foreign Exchange Rates

As mentioned above, a foreign exchange rate is the price at which one currency (e.g., the U.S. dollar) can be exchanged for another currency (e.g., the Swiss franc). Table 8–1 lists the exchange rates between the U.S. dollar and other currencies as of 4:00 p.m. eastern standard time on December 16, 2004 (and December 15, 2004). Foreign exchange rates are listed in two ways: U.S. dollars received for one unit of the foreign currency exchanged (U.S. $ EQUIVALENT) and foreign currency received for each U.S. dollar exchanged (CURRENCY PER U.S. $). For example, the exchange rate of U.S. dollars for Canadian dollars on December 16, 2004, was .8109 (US$/C$), or U.S. $.8109 could be received for each Canadian dollar exchanged. Conversely, the exchange rate of Canadian dollars for U.S. dollars was 1.2332 (C$/US$), or 1.2332 Canadian dollars could be received for each U.S. dollar exchanged.

Notice that the U.S. $ EQUIVALENT exchange rates, or the rate of U.S. dollars for the foreign currency, are simply the inverse of the CURRENCY PER U.S. $ exchange rates, or the rate of exchange of foreign currency for U.S. dollars and vice versa. For example, US$/C$ = .8109 = 1/(C$/US$) = 1/1.2332, and C$/US$ = 1.2332 = 1/(US$/C$) = 1/.8109. This is the case for both spot and forward exchange rates in Table 8–1.

3. See "The Disappearing Dollar," *The Economist*, December 4, 2004.

TABLE 8–1 Foreign Currency Exchange Rates

Source: Reuters

Exchange Rates

December 16, 2004

The foreign exchange mid-range rates below apply to trading among banks in amounts of $1 million and more, as quoted at 4 p.m. Eastern time by Reuters and other sources. Retail transactions provide fewer units of foreign currency per dollar.

	U.S. $ EQUIVALENT		CURRENCY PER U.S. $	
Country	**Thu**	**Wed**	**Thu**	**Wed**
Argentina (Peso)-y	.3346	.3359	2.9886	2.9771
Australia (Dollar)	.7573	.7639	1.3205	1.3091
Bahrain (Dinar)	2.6526	2.6526	.3770	.3770
Brazil (Real)	.3647	.3669	2.7420	2.7255
Canada (Dollar)	.8109	.8165	1.2332	1.2247
1-month forward	.8108	.8163	1.2333	1.2250
3-months forward	.8107	.8162	1.2335	1.2252
6-months forward	.8111	.8167	1.2329	1.2244
Chile (Peso)	.001727	.001741	579.04	574.38
China (Renminbi)	.1208	.1208	8.2781	8.2781
Colombia (Peso)	.0004231	.0004203	2363.51	2379.25
Czech. Rep. (Koruna)				
Commercial rate	.04323	.04375	23.132	22.857
Denmark (Krone)	.1782	.1803	5.6117	5.5463
Ecuador (US Dollar)	1.0000	1.0000	1.0000	1.0000
Egypt (Pound)-y	.1608	.1608	6.2201	6.2201
Hong Kong (Dollar)	.1286	.1286	7.7760	7.7760
Hungary (Forint)	.005377	.005456	185.98	183.28
India (Rupee)	.02283	.02285	43.802	43.764
Indonesia (Rupiah)	.0001077	.0001081	9285	9251
Israel (Shekel)	.2305	.2313	4.3384	4.3234
Japan (Yen)	.009546	.009591	104.76	104.26
1-month forward	.009565	.009612	104.55	104.04
3-months forward	.009607	.009651	104.09	103.62
6-months forward	.009676	.009721	103.35	102.87
Jordan (Dinar)	1.4104	1.4104	.7090	.7090
Kuwait (Dinar)	3.3891	3.3932	.2951	.2947
Lebanon (Pound)	.0006607	.0006607	1513.55	1513.55
Malaysia (Ringgit)-b	.2632	.2632	3.7994	3.7994
Malta (Lira)	3.0734	3.1039	.3254	.3222
Mexico (Peso)				
Floating rate	.0888	.0894	11.2562	11.1832
New Zealand (Dollar)	.7107	.7183	1.4071	1.3922
Norway (Krone)	.1614	.1634	6.1958	6.1200
Pakistan (Rupee)	.01674	.01675	59.737	59.702
Peru (new Sol)	.3061	.3061	3.2669	3.2669
Philippines (Peso)	.01775	.01777	56.338	56.275
Poland (Zloty)	.3192	.3232	3.1328	3.0941
Russia (Ruble)-a	.03587	.03589	27.878	27.863
Saudi Arabia (Riyal)	.2667	.2666	3.7495	3.7509
Singapore (Dollar)	.6068	.6100	1.6480	1.6393
Slovak Rep. (Koruna)	.03419	.03461	29.248	28.893
South Africa (Rand)	.1730	.1744	5.7803	5.7339
South Korea (Won)	.0009456	.0009421	1057.53	1061.46
Sweden (Krona)	.1473	.1493	6.7889	6.6979
Switzerland (Franc)	.8639	.8763	1.1575	1.1412
1-month forward	.8651	.8776	1.1559	1.1395
3-months forward	.8677	.8801	1.1525	1.1362
6-months forward	.8721	.8844	1.1467	1.1307
Taiwan (Dollar)	.03089	.03084	32.373	32.425
Thailand (Baht)	.02550	.02549	39.216	39.231
Turkey (Lira)	.00000071	.00000071	1408451	1408451
U.K. (Pound)	1.9318	1.9435	.5177	.5145
1-month forward	1.9279	1.9394	.5187	.5156
3-months forward	1.9208	1.9326	.5206	.5174
6-months forward	1.9118	1.9235	.5231	.5199
United Arab (Dirham)	.2723	.2723	3.6724	3.6724
Uruguay (Peso)				
Financial	.03760	.03760	26.596	26.596
Venezuela (Bolivar)	.000521	.000521	1919.39	1919.39
SDR	1.5415	1.5380	.6487	.6502
Euro	1.3248	1.3404	.7548	.7460

Special Drawing Rights (SDR) are based on exchange rates for the U.S., British, and Japanese currencies. Source: International Monetary Fund.

a-Russian Central Bank rate. b-Government rate. y-Floating rate.

Source: *The Wall Street Journal,* December 17, 2004, p. B7. Reprinted by permission of *The Wall Street Journal.* **www.wsj.com**

Foreign Exchange Transactions

spot foreign exchange transactions

Foreign exchange transactions involving the immediate exchange of currencies at the current (or spot) exchange rate.

There are two types of foreign exchange rates and foreign exchange transactions: spot and forward. **Spot foreign exchange transactions** involve the immediate exchange of currencies at the current (or spot) exchange rate—see Figure 8–1. Spot transactions can be conducted through the foreign exchange division of commercial banks or a nonbank foreign currency dealer. For example, a U.S. investor wanting to buy British pounds through a local bank on December 16, 2004, essentially has the dollars transferred from his or her bank account to the dollar account of a pound seller at a rate of $1 per .5177 pound (or $1.9318 per pound).[4] Simultaneously, pounds are transferred from the seller's account into an account designated by the U.S. investor. If the dollar depreciates in value relative to the pound (e.g., $1 per .5136 pound or $1.9470 per pound), the value of the pound investment, if converted back into U.S. dollars, increases. If the dollar appreciates in value relative to the pound (e.g., $1 per .5196 pound or $1.9246 per pound), the value of the pound investment, if converted back into U.S. dollars, decreases.

The appreciation of a country's currency (or a rise in its value relative to other currencies) means that the country's goods are more expensive for foreign buyers and foreign goods are cheaper for foreign sellers (all else constant). Thus, when a country's currency appreciates, domestic manufacturers find it harder to sell their goods abroad and foreign manufactures find it easier to sell their goods to domestic purchasers. Conversely, depreciation of a country's currency (or a fall in its value relative to other currencies) means the country's goods become cheaper for foreign buyers and foreign goods become more expensive for foreign sellers. Figure 8–2 shows the pattern of exchange rates between the U.S.

4. In actual practice, settlement—exchange of currencies—occurs normally two days after a transaction.

FIGURE 8–1 Spot versus Forward Foreign Exchange Transaction

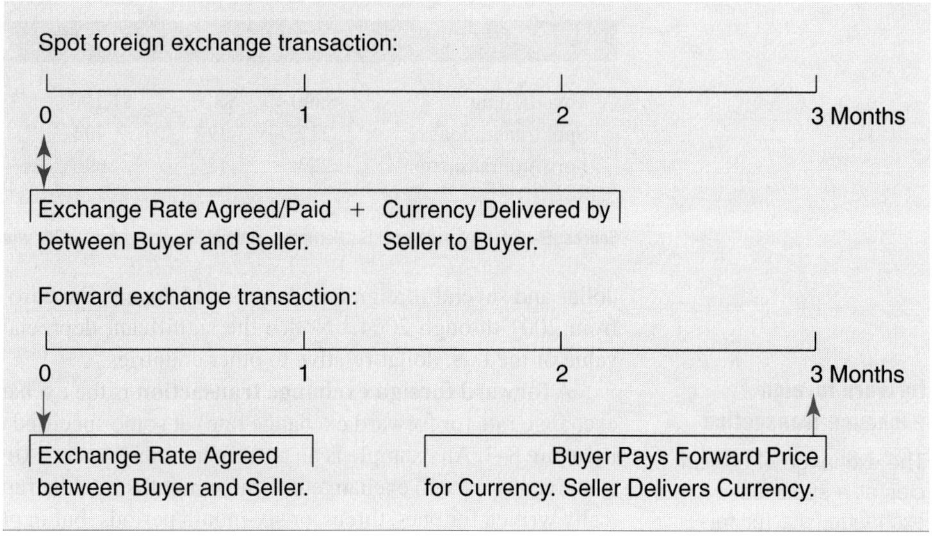

FIGURE 8–2 Exchange Rate of the U.S. Dollar with Various Foreign Currencies*

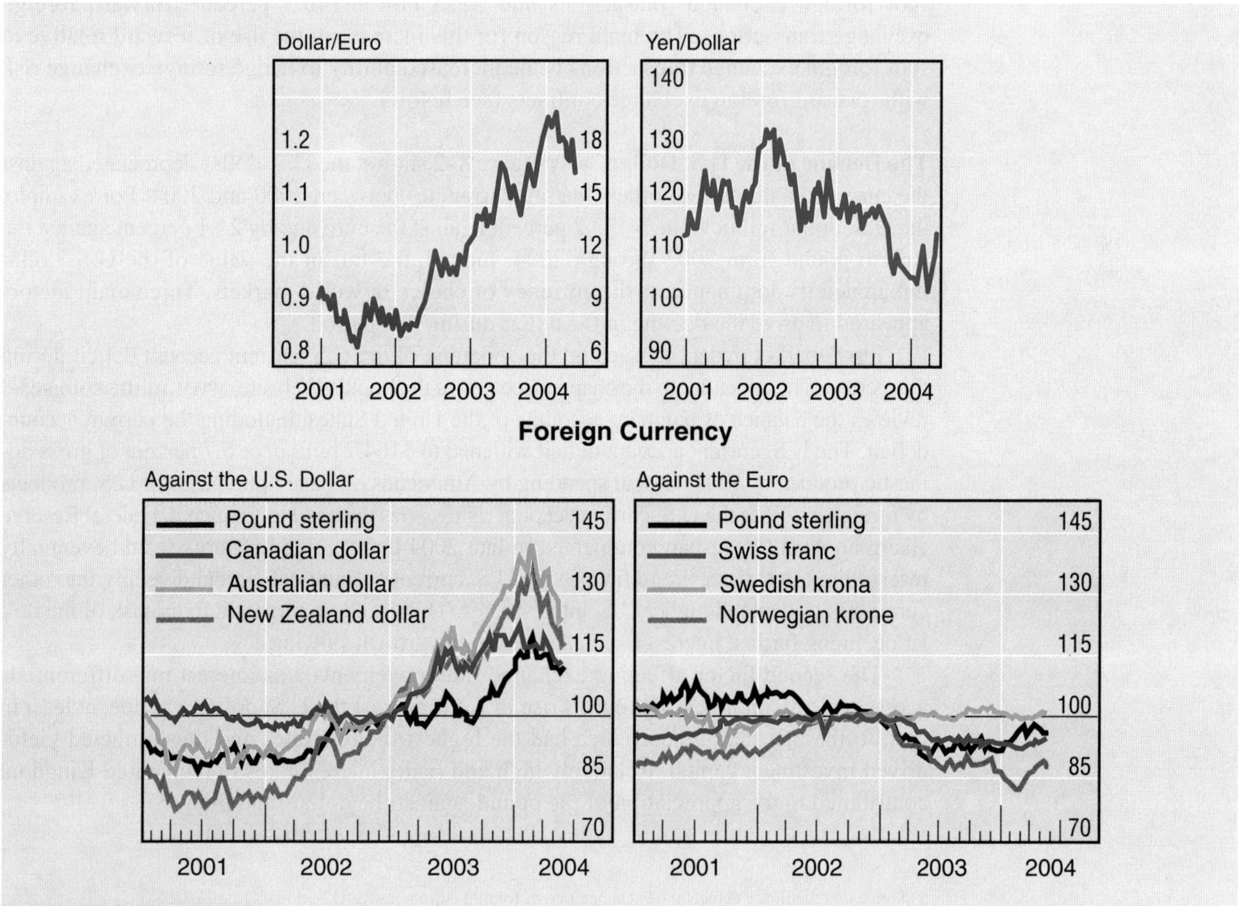

*Vertical axes are the value of the foreign currency against the U.S. dollar.

Source: Bank for International Settlements, Annual Report, June 2004. **www.bis.org**

TABLE 8–2 Foreign Exchange Market Trading
(in billions of U.S. dollars)

	1989	1992	1995	1998	2000	2004
Total trading	$590	$820	$1,190	$1,490	$1,200	$1,880
Spot transactions	317	394	494	568	387	621
Forward transactions	273	426	696	922	813	1,259

Source: Bank for International Settlements, Annual Report, June 2004. **www.bis.org**

dollar and several foreign currencies and between the euro and several foreign currencies from 2001 through 2004.[5] Notice the significant depreciation, in 2003 and 2004, in the value of the U.S. dollar relative to other countries.

forward foreign exchange transaction

The exchange of currencies at a specified exchange rate (or forward exchange rate) at some specified date in the future.

A **forward foreign exchange transaction** is the exchange of currencies at a specified exchange rate (or forward exchange rate) at some specified date in the future, as illustrated in Figure 8–1. An example is an agreement today (at time 0) to exchange dollars for pounds at a given (forward) exchange rate three months into the future. Forward contracts are typically written for one-, three-, or six-month periods, but in practice they can be written over any given length of time.

Of the $1.88 trillion in average daily trading volume in the foreign exchange markets in 2004, $621 billion (33.0 percent) involved spot transactions while $1,259 billion (67.0 percent) involved forward transactions. This compares to 1989 where (as shown in Table 8–2) average daily trading volume was $590 billion; $317 billion (53.7 percent) of which was spot foreign exchange transactions and $273 billion (46.3 percent) forward foreign exchange transactions. The main reason for this increase in the use of forward relative to spot foreign exchange transactions is the increased ability to hedge foreign exchange risk with forward foreign exchange contracts (see below).

The Decline of the U.S. Dollar. As Figure 8–2 shows, the U.S. dollar depreciated against the euro and a number of other floating currencies between 2000 and 2004. For example, the U.S. dollar fell in value by 33.2 percent against the euro and by 24.1 percent against the British pound from 2002 through 2004. Indeed, the fall in the value of the U.S. dollar threatened its dominance as the currency of choice in world markets. Three main factors appeared to drive the decline in the dollar during this period.

First, market traders focused on the widening of the U.S. current account deficit during this period. The appendix to the chapter (located at the book's Web site, **www.mhhe.com/sc3e**) reviews the balance of payment accounts of the United States, including the current account deficit. The U.S. current account deficit widened to $164.7 billion, or 5.7 percent of gross domestic product, in 2004. Global spending by Americans outpaced purchases of U.S. products by foreigners. With the U.S. current account rising, so is the need to finance it. Federal Reserve chairman Alan Greenspan commented in late 2004 that foreign investors would eventually reach a limit in their desire to finance the U.S. current account deficit and diversify into other currencies or demand higher U.S. interest rates. This could, in turn, add to the risk of the dollar declining further, interest rising, and economic growth slowing.

The second factor affecting exchange rate movements was interest rate differentials across major economies. The euro's rise in value against the U.S. dollar was due, at least in part, to the fact that the euro area had the highest interest rates and thus attracted yield-driven investment capital. Relatively high and rising interest rates in the United Kingdom contributed to the appreciation of the pound against the dollar (and the yen) as well.[6]

5. Notice that the figure depicts the exchange rate of foreign currencies for U.S. dollars (e.g., ¥/US$).

6. Carry trades were a popular mechanism facilitating investors' search for yield. These trades involve borrowing in a low-yielding currency and investing in a high-yielding currency. A main funding currency was the U.S. dollar. The main recipients of the borrowed funds included the pound and the euro.

A third factor affecting the exchange rates was a high volume of central bank intervention relative to past practice, especially in Asian countries. These actions kept upward pressure on the local currencies but helped to devalue the U.S. dollar. For example, the Japanese Ministry of Finance purchased $316 billion of U.S. assets between January 2003 and March 2004 (many times the purchases in earlier years). Chinese monetary authorities bought dollar reserves while trying to preserve its fixed exchange rate with the U.S. dollar. In India, Korea, and Taiwan, dollar reserves also rose substantially as monetary authorities tried to limit the appreciation of their currencies against the U.S. dollar.

As of 2004, the U.S. government had taken little action to stem the depreciation of the U.S. dollar. A cheap dollar makes products exported from other countries more expensive in global markets relative to U.S.-made products. Further, a cheap dollar allows U.S. companies to offer cheaper products in foreign markets. The resulting increase in exports and decrease in imports should help narrow the U.S. trade deficit. Further, these currency trends hurt the sales of competing non-U.S. companies in countries with strong currencies, such as Europe and the United Kingdom. Indeed, the fall in the U.S. dollar in the last half of 2004 was predicted to result in a ½ percent decrease in Europe's economic growth rate for the year.

5

Return and Risk of Foreign Exchange Transactions

This section discusses the extra dimensions of return and risk from foreign exchange transactions. The section also explores ways that financial institutions can hedge foreign exchange risk.

Measuring Risk and Return on Foreign Exchange Transactions. The risk involved with a spot foreign exchange transaction is that the value of the foreign currency may change relative to the U.S. dollar. Further, foreign exchange risk is introduced by adding foreign currency assets and liabilities to an FI's portfolio. Like domestic assets and liabilities, returns result from the contractual income from or costs paid on a security. With foreign assets and liabilities, however, returns are also affected by changes in foreign exchange rates.

EXAMPLE 8–1 Foreign Exchange Risk

Suppose that on December 16, 2004, a U.S. firm plans to purchase 3 million Swiss francs' (Sf) worth of Swiss bonds from a Swiss FI in one month's time. The Swiss FI wants payment in Swiss francs. Thus, the U.S. firm must convert dollars into Swiss francs. The spot exchange rate for December 16, 2004 (reported in Table 8–1) of U.S. dollars for Swiss francs is .8639, or one franc costs $.8639 in dollars. Consequently, the U.S. firm must convert:

$$\text{U.S.\$/Sf exchange rate} \times \text{Sf 3 million} = .8639 \times \text{Sf 3m} = \$2{,}591{,}700$$

into Swiss francs today.

One month after the conversion of dollars to Swiss francs, the Swiss bond purchase deal falls through and the U.S. firm no longer needs the Swiss francs it purchased at $.8639 per franc. The spot exchange rate of the Swiss franc to the dollar has fallen or depreciated over the month so that the value of a franc is worth only $.8514, or the exchange rate is $.8514 per franc. The U.S. dollar value of 3 million Swiss francs is now only:

$$.8514 \times \text{Sf 3 million} = \$2{,}554{,}200$$

The depreciation of the Swiss franc relative to the dollar over the month has caused the U.S. firm to suffer a $37,500 ($2,554,200 − $2,591,700) loss due to exchange rate fluctuations.

To avoid such a loss in the spot markets, the U.S. FI could have entered into a forward transaction, which is the exchange of currencies at a specified future date and a specified exchange rate (or forward exchange rate). Forward exchange rates for December 16, 2004, are also listed in Table 8–1. As mentioned above, forward contracts are typically written for a one-, three-, or six-month period from the date the contract is written, although they can be written for any time period from a few days to many years. For example, if the U.S. investor had entered into a one-month forward contract selling the Swiss franc on December 16, 2004, at the same time it purchased the spot francs, the U.S. investor would have been guaranteed an exchange rate of .8651 U.S. dollars per Swiss franc, or 1.1559 Swiss francs per U.S. dollar, on delivering the francs to the buyer in one month's time. If the U.S. FI had sold francs one month forward at .8651 on December 16, 2004, it would have largely avoided the loss of \$37,500 described in Example 8–1. Specifically, by selling 3 million francs forward, it would have received:

$$.8651 \times \text{Sf } 3 \text{ million} = \$2{,}595{,}300$$

at the end of the month suggesting a small net profit of \$2,595,300 − \$2,591,700 = \$3,600 on the combined spot and forward transactions. Essentially, by using the one-month forward contract, the FI hedges (or insures itself) against foreign currency risk in the spot market.

As discussed below, financial institutions, and particularly commercial banks, are the main participants in the foreign exchange markets. When issuing a foreign-currency-denominated liability or buying a foreign-currency-denominated asset an FI will do so only if the expected return is positive.

EXAMPLE 8-2 Calculating the Return of Foreign Exchange Transactions of a U.S. FI

Suppose that a U.S. FI has the following assets and liabilities:

Assets	Liabilities
\$100 million U.S. loans (one year) in dollars	\$200 million U.S. CDs (one year) in dollars
\$100 million equivalent U.K. loans (one year) (loans made in pounds)	

The U.S. FI is raising all of its \$200 million liabilities in dollars (one-year CDs), but it is investing 50 percent in U.S. dollar assets (one-year maturity loans) and 50 percent in U.K. pound sterling assets (one-year maturity loans).[7] In this example, the FI has matched the maturity (M) or duration (D) of its assets (A) and liabilities (L):

$$(M_A = M_L = D_A = D_L = 1 \text{ year})$$

but has mismatched the currency composition of its asset and liability portfolios. Suppose that the promised one-year U.S. dollars CD rate is 8 percent, to be paid in dollars at the end of the year, and that one-year, credit risk–free loans in the United States are yielding 9 percent. The FI would have a positive spread of 1 percent from investing domestically. Suppose, however, that credit risk–free one-year loans are yielding 15 percent in the United Kingdom.

To invest \$100 million (of the \$200 million in CDs issued) in one-year loans in the United Kingdom, the U.S. FI engages in the following transactions:

1. At the beginning of the year, it sells \$100 million for pounds on the spot currency markets. If the exchange rate is \$1.60 to £1, this translates into \$100 million/1.6 = £62.5 million.
2. It takes the £62.5 million and makes one-year U.K. loans at a 15 percent interest rate.

7. For simplicity, we ignore the leverage or net worth aspects of the FI's portfolio.

3. At the end of the year, pound revenue from these loans will be £62.5(1.15) = £71.875 million.[8]
4. It repatriates these funds back to the United States at the end of the year—that is, the U.S. FI sells the £71.875 million in the foreign exchange market at the spot exchange rate that exists at that time, the end of the year spot rate.

Suppose that the spot foreign exchange rate has not changed over the year—it remains fixed at \$1.60/£1. Then the dollar proceeds from the U.K. investment are:

$$\text{£}71.875 \text{ million} \times \$1.60/\text{£}1 = \$115 \text{ million or as a return}$$

$$\frac{\$115 \text{ million} - \$100 \text{ million}}{\$100 \text{ million}} = 15\%$$

Given this, the weighted or average return on the FI's portfolio of investments would be:

$$(.5)(.09) + (.5)(.15) = .12, \text{ or } 12\%$$

This exceeds the cost of the FI's CDs by 4 percent (12% − 8%).

Suppose, however, that the pound had fallen (depreciated) in value against the U.S. dollar from \$1.60/£1 at the beginning of the year to \$1.45/£1 at the end of the year, when the FI needed to repatriate the principal and interest on the loan. At an exchange rate of \$1.45/£1, the pound loan revenues at the end of the year translate into:

$$\text{£}71.875 \text{ million} \times \$1.45/\text{£}1 = \$104.22 \text{ million}$$

or as a return on the original dollar investment of:

$$\frac{\$104.22 - \$100}{\$100} = .0422 = 4.22\%$$

The weighted return on the FI's asset portfolio would be:

$$(.5)(.09) + (.5)(.0422) = .0661 = 6.61\%$$

In this case, the FI actually has a loss or a negative interest margin (6.61% − 8% = −1.39%) on its balance sheet investments.

The reason for the loss is that the depreciation of the pound from \$1.60 to \$1.45 has offset the attractively high yield on British pound sterling loans relative to domestic U.S. loans. If the pound had instead appreciated (risen in value) against the dollar over the year—say, to \$1.70/£1—the U.S. FI would have generated a dollar return from its U.K. loans of:

$$\text{£}71.875 \times \$1.70 = \$122.188 \text{ million}$$

or a percentage return of 22.188 percent.

The U.S. FI would receive a double benefit from investing in the United Kingdom, a high yield on the domestic British loans and an appreciation in pounds over the one-year investment period.

Hedging Foreign Exchange Risk. Since a manager cannot know in advance what the pound/dollar spot exchange rate will be at the end of the year, a portfolio imbalance or investment strategy in which the bank is *net long* \$100 million in pounds (or £62.5 million) is risky. As we discussed, the British loans would generate a return of 22.188 percent if the pound appreciated from \$1.60 to \$1.70 but would produce a return of only 4.22 percent if the pound were to depreciate in value against the dollar to \$1.45.

In principle, an FI manager can better control the scale of its FX exposure in either of two major ways: on-balance-sheet hedging and off-balance-sheet hedging. On-balance-sheet hedging involves making changes in the on-balance-sheet assets and liabilities to protect FI profits from FX risk. Off-balance-sheet hedging involves no on-balance-sheet changes but rather involves taking a position in forward or other derivative securities to hedge FX risk.

8. No default risk is assumed.

On-Balance-Sheet Hedging. The following example illustrates how an FI manager can control FX exposure by making changes on the balance sheet.

EXAMPLE 8-3 Hedging on the Balance Sheet

Suppose that instead of funding the $100 million investment in 15 percent British loans with U.S. CDs, the FI manager funds the British loans with $100 million equivalent one-year pound sterling CDs at a rate of 11 percent. Now the balance sheet of the FI would be as follows:

Assets	Liabilities
$100 million U.S. loans (9%)	$100 million U.S. CDs (8%)
$100 million U.K. loans (15%) (loans made in pounds)	$100 million U.K. CDs (11%) (deposits raised in pounds)

In this situation, the FI has both a matched maturity and foreign currency asset– liability book. We might now consider the FI's profitability or spreads between the return on assets and cost of funds under two scenarios: first, when the pound depreciates in value against the dollar over the year from $1.60/£1 to $1.45/£1, and second, when the pound appreciates in value during the year from $1.60/£1 to $1.70/£1.

1. The Depreciating Pound. When the pound falls in value to $1.45/£1, the return on the British loan portfolio is 4.22 percent. Consider what happens to the cost of $100 million in pound liabilities in dollar terms:

1. At the beginning of the year, the FI borrows $100 million equivalent in pounds CDs for one year at a promised interest rate of 11 percent. At an exchange rate of $1.60/£1, this is a pound equivalent amount of borrowing of $100 million/1.6 = £62.5 million.
2. At the end of the year, the FI must pay the pound CD holders their principal and interest, £62.5 million (1.11) = £69.375 million.
3. If the pound had depreciated to $1.45/£1 over the year, the repayment in dollar terms would be $100.59 million (=£69.375 million times $1.45/£1), or a dollar cost of funds of 0.59 percent.

Thus, at the end of the year, the following occurs:

Average return on assets:

$$(0.5)(0.9) + (0.5)(.0422) = .0661 = 6.61\%$$

$$\text{U.S. asset return} + \text{U.K. asset return} = \text{Overall return}$$

Average cost of funds:

$$(0.5)(.08) + (0.5)(.0059) = .04295 = 4.295\%$$

$$\text{U.S. cost of funds} + \text{U.K. cost of funds} = \text{Overall cost}$$

Net return:

$$\text{Average return on assets} - \text{Average cost of funds}$$

$$6.61\% - 4.295\% = 2.315\%$$

2. The Appreciating Pound. When the pound appreciates over the year from $1.60/£1 to $1.70/£1, the return on British loans equals 22.188 percent. Now consider the dollar cost of British one-year CDs at the end of the year when the U.S. FI must pay the principal and interest to the CD holder:

$$£69.375 \text{ million} \times \$1.70/£1 = \$117.9375 \text{ million}$$

or a dollar cost of funds of 17.9375 percent. Thus, at the end of the year:

Average return on assets:

$$(0.5)(.09) + (0.5)(.22188) = .15594, \text{ or } 15.594\%$$

Average cost of funds:

$$(0.5)(.08) + (0.5)(.179375) = .12969, \text{ or } 12.969\%$$

Net return:

$$15.594\% - 12.969\% = 2.625\%$$

Thus, by directly matching its foreign asset and liability book, an FI can lock in a positive return or profit spread whichever direction exchange rates change over the investment period. For example, even if domestic U.S. banking is a relatively low-profit activity (i.e., there is a low spread between the return on assets and the cost of funds), the FI could be very profitable overall. Specifically, it could lock in a large positive spread—if it exists—between deposit rates and loan rates in foreign markets. In our example, a 4 percent positive spread occurred between British one-year loan rates and deposit rates compared to only a 1 percent spread domestically.

Note that for such imbalances in domestic spreads and foreign spreads to continue over long periods of time, financial service firms would have to face significant barriers to entry into foreign markets. Specifically, if real and financial capital is free to move, FIs would increasingly withdraw from the U.S. market and reorient their operations toward the United Kingdom. Reduced competition would widen loan deposit interest spreads in the United States, and increased competition would contract U.K. spreads until the profit opportunities from overseas activities disappeared.

Hedging with Forwards. Instead of matching its \$100 million foreign asset position with \$100 million of foreign liabilities, the FI might have chosen to remain with a currency mismatch on the balance sheet. Instead, as a lower-cost alternative, it could hedge by taking a position in the forward or other derivative markets for foreign currencies—for example, the one-year forward market for selling pounds for dollars. Any forward position taken would not appear on the balance sheet; it would appear as a contingent off-balance-sheet claim, which we describe as an item below the bottom line in Chapter 12. The role of the forward FX contract is to offset the uncertainty regarding the future spot rate on pounds at the end of the one-year investment horizon. Instead of waiting until the end of the year to transfer pounds back into dollars at an unknown spot rate, the FI can enter into a contract to sell forward its *expected* principal and interest earnings on the loan at today's known forward exchange rate for dollars/pounds, with delivery of pound funds to the buyer of the forward contract taking place at the end of the year. Essentially, by selling the expected proceeds on the pound loan forward at a known (forward FX) exchange rate today, the FI removes the future spot exchange rate uncertainty and thus the uncertainty relating to investment returns on the British loan.

EXAMPLE 8-4 Hedging with Forwards

Consider the following transactional steps when the FI hedges its FX risk by immediately selling its expected one-year pound loan proceeds in the forward FX market:

1. The U.S. FI sells \$100 million for pounds at the spot exchange rate today and receives \$100 million/1.6 = £62.5 million.
2. The FI then immediately lends the £62.5 million to a British customer at 15 percent for one year.
3. The FI also sells the expected principal and interest proceeds from the pound loan forward for dollars at today's forward rate for one-year delivery. Let the current forward

one-year exchange rate between dollars and pounds stand at \$1.55/£ or at a 5 cent discount to the spot rate; as a percentage discount:

$$(\$1.55 - \$1.60)/\$1.6 = -3.125\%$$

This means that the forward buyer of pound promises to pay:

$$£62.5 \text{ million } (1.15) \times \$1.55/£ = £71.875 \times \$1.55/£ = \$111.406 \text{ million}$$

to the FI (the forward seller) in one year when the FI delivers the £71.875 million proceeds of the loan to the forward buyer.

4. In one year, the British borrower repays the loan to the FI plus interest in pounds (£71.875 million).
5. The FI delivers the £71.875 million to the buyer of the one-year forward contract and receives the promised \$111.406 million.

Barring the pound borrower's default on the loan or the pound forward buyer's reneging on the forward contract, the FI knows from the very beginning of the investment period that it has locked in a guaranteed return on the British loan of:

$$\frac{\$111.406\text{m.} - \$100\text{m.}}{\$100\text{m.}} = .11406, \text{ or } 11.406\%$$

Specifically, this return is fully hedged against any dollar/pound exchange rate changes over the one-year holding period of the loan investment. Given this return on British loans, the overall expected return on the FI's asset portfolio is:

$$(.5)(.09) + (.5)(.11406) = .10203, \text{ or } 10.203\%$$

Since the cost of funds for the FI's \$200 million U.S. CDs is an assumed 8 percent, it has been able to lock in a return spread over the year of 2.203 percent regardless of spot exchange rate fluctuations between the initial overseas (loan) investment and repatriation of the foreign loan proceeds one year later.

In the preceding example, it is profitable for the FI to drop domestic U.S. loans and to hedge foreign U.K. loans, since the hedged dollar return on foreign loans of 11.406 percent is so much higher than the 9 percent for domestic loans. As the FI seeks to invest more in British loans, it needs to buy more spot pounds. This drives up the spot price of pounds in dollar terms to more than \$1.60/£1. In addition, the FI could sell more pounds forward (the proceeds of these pound loans) for dollars, driving the forward rate to below \$1.55/£1. The outcome would widen the dollar forward–spot exchange rate difference on pounds, making forward hedged pounds investments less attractive than before. This process would continue until the U.S. cost of FI funds just equals the forward hedged return on British loans—that is, the FI could make no further profits by borrowing in U.S. dollars and making forward contract–hedged investments in U.K. loans (see also the discussion below on the interest rate parity theorem).

Role of Financial Institutions in Foreign Exchange Transactions

6

Foreign exchange market transactions, like corporate bond and money market transactions, are conducted among dealers mainly over the counter (OTC) using telecommunication and computer networks. Foreign exchange traders are generally located in one large trading room at a bank or other FI where they have access to foreign exchange data and telecommunications equipment. Traders generally specialize in just a few currencies.

A major structural change in foreign exchange trading has been the growing share of electronic brokerage in the interbank markets at the expense of direct dealing (and telecommunication). Online foreign exchange trading is increasing and the transnational nature of

TABLE 8–3 Liabilities to and Claims on Foreigners Reported by Banks in the United States, Payable in Foreign Currencies
(millions of dollars, end of period)

Item	1993	1996	1999	2002	2004†
Banks' liabilities	$78,259	$103,383	$88,537	$80,543	$68,189
Banks' claims (assets)	62,017	66,018	67,365	71,724	89,485
Claims of banks' domestic customers*	12,854	10,978	20,826	35,923	20,593

Note: Data on claims exclude foreign currencies held by U.S. monetary authorities.

*Assets owned by customers of the reporting bank located in the United States that represents claims on foreigners held by reporting banks for the accounts of the domestic customers.

†As of September.

Source: *Treasury Bulletin,* various issues. **www.ustreas.gov**

the electronic exchange of funds makes secure, Internet-based trading an ideal platform. Online trading portals—terminals where currency transactions are being executed—are a low-cost way of conducting spot and forward foreign exchange transactions. In 2004, some 85 to 95 percent of interbank trading in major currencies was conducted by using electronic brokerage. This compares to 50 percent in 1998 and 20 to 30 percent in 1995. Two companies, Reuters and EBS, currently dominate the market for the provision of electronic trading platforms, software, FX quotation systems. Reuters speculates that the number of global FIs using online trading systems will grow from 200 banks in 2003 to 700 banks by 2007.[9] Electronic brokers automatically provide traders with the best prices available to them. Traders using traditional methods typically needed to contact several dealers to obtain market price information.[10]

Since 1982, when Singapore opened its FX market, foreign exchange markets have operated 24 hours a day. When the New York market closes, trading operations in San Francisco are still open; when trading in San Francisco closes, the Hong Kong and Singapore markets open; when Tokyo and Singapore close, the Frankfurt market opens; an hour later, the London market opens; and before these markets close, the New York market reopens.

The nation's largest commercial banks are major players in foreign currency trading and dealing, with large money center banks such as Citigroup and J. P. Morgan Chase also taking significant positions in foreign currency assets and liabilities. Smaller banks maintain lines of credit with these large banks for foreign exchange transactions.

Table 8–3 lists the outstanding dollar value of U.S. banks' foreign assets and liabilities for the period 1993 to September 2004. The September 2004 figure for foreign assets was $89.5 billion, with foreign liabilities of $68.2 billion. Notice that except for 2004, U.S. banks had more liabilities to than claims on (assets) foreigners. Thus, if the dollar depreciates relative to foreign currencies, more dollars (converted into foreign currencies) will be needed to pay off the liabilities and U.S. banks would experience a loss due to foreign exchange risk. The reverse was true in 2004.

Table 8–4 gives the categories of foreign currency positions (or investments) of all U.S. banks in five major currencies in September 2004. Columns 1 and 2 of Table 8–4 refer to the assets and liabilities denominated in foreign currencies that are held in the portfolios of U.S.

9. See "The Institutional Investor Guide to Foreign Exchange as an Asset Class," by Conrad Steinmann, *Institutional Investor*, February 2003, p. 4.

10. In May 2002, the U.S. Justice Department announced it was investigating a group of the world's largest banks (including Citigroup, J.P. Morgan Chase, and Credit Suisse Group) for allegedly using their online trading service to restrict competition in the foreign currency markets. See "U.S. Probes Whether Big Banks Stifled Rivals in Currency Trading," by John R. Wilke, *The Wall Street Journal,* May 15, 2002, p. A1.

TABLE 8–4 Monthly U.S. Bank Positions in Foreign Currencies and Foreign Assets and Liabilities, 2004
(in currency of denomination)

	(1) Assets	(2) Liabilities	(3) FX Bought*	(4) FX Sold*	(5) Net Position†
Canadian dollars (millions)	100,911	94,089	407,029	415,855	−2,004
Japanese yen (billions)	43,504	43,541	196,313	199,094	−2,818
Swiss francs (millions)	50,961	54,110	490,979	503,769	−15,939
British pounds (millions)	208,746	199,404	653,994	645,438	17,898
Euros (millions)	1,049,526	995,969	2,053,300	2,077,367	29,490

*Includes spot, future, and forward contracts.

†Net position = Assets − Liabilities + FX bought − FX sold

Source: *Treasury Bulletin,* December 2004, pp. 100–114. **www.ustreas.gov**

banks. Columns 3 and 4 refer to foreign currency trading activities (the spot and forward foreign exchange contracts bought—a long position—and sold—a short position —in each major currency). Foreign currency trading dominates direct portfolio investments. Even though the aggregate trading positions appear very large—for example, U.S. banks bought 196,313 billion yen—their overall or net exposure positions can be relatively small (e.g., the net position in yen was −2,004 billion yen).

A financial institution's overall net foreign exchange (FX) exposure in any given currency can be measured by its net book or position exposure, which is measured in column 5 of Table 8–4 as:

$$\begin{aligned}\text{Net exposure}_i &= (\text{FX assets}_i - \text{FX liabilities}_i) + (\text{FX bought}_i - \text{FX sold}_i)\\ &= \text{Net foreign assets}_i + \text{Net FX bought}_i\\ &= \text{Net position}_i\end{aligned}$$

where

i = ith country's currency

Clearly, a financial institution could match its foreign currency assets to its liabilities in a given currency and match buys and sells in its trading book in that foreign currency to reduce its foreign exchange net exposure to zero and thus avoid foreign exchange risk. It could also offset an imbalance in its foreign asset–liability portfolio by an opposing imbalance in its trading book so that its **net exposure** position in that currency would also be zero.

net exposure

A financial institution's overall foreign exchange exposure in any given currency.

net long (short) in a currency

A position of holding more (fewer) assets than liabilities in a given currency.

Notice in Table 8–4 that U.S. banks' net foreign exchange exposures in December 2004 varied across currencies: They carried a positive net exposure position in British pounds and euros, while they had a negative net exposure position in Canadian dollars, Japanese yen, and Swiss francs. A *positive* net exposure position implies that a U.S. financial institution is overall **net long in a currency** (i.e., the financial institution has purchased more foreign currency than it has sold). The institution would profit if the foreign currency appreciates in value against the U.S. dollar, but also faces the risk that the foreign currency will fall in value against the U.S. dollar, the domestic currency. A *negative* net exposure position implies that a U.S. financial institution is **net short** (i.e., the financial institution has sold more foreign currency than it has purchased) in a foreign currency. The institution would profit if the foreign currency depreciates in value against the U.S. dollar, but faces the risk that the foreign currency could rise in value against the dollar. Thus, failure to maintain a fully balanced position in any given currency exposes a U.S. financial institution to fluctuations in the foreign exchange rate of that currency against the dollar. Indeed, the greater the volatility of foreign exchange rates given any net exposure position, the greater the fluctuations in value of a financial institution's foreign exchange portfolio (see also Chapter 19, where we discuss market risk). An FI's net position

SEARCH THE SITE

Go to the Financial Management service of the United States Treasury at **www.fms.treas.gov** and find the latest information available on the Monthly U.S. Bank Positions in Foreign Currencies and Foreign Assets and Liabilities.

Click on "Treasury Bulletin"

Click on the latest issue date

This will bring up the Table of Contents. Scroll down to and click on "Foreign Currency Positions." This will bring up the Monthly U.S. Bank Positions in Foreign Currencies and Foreign Assets and Liabilities.

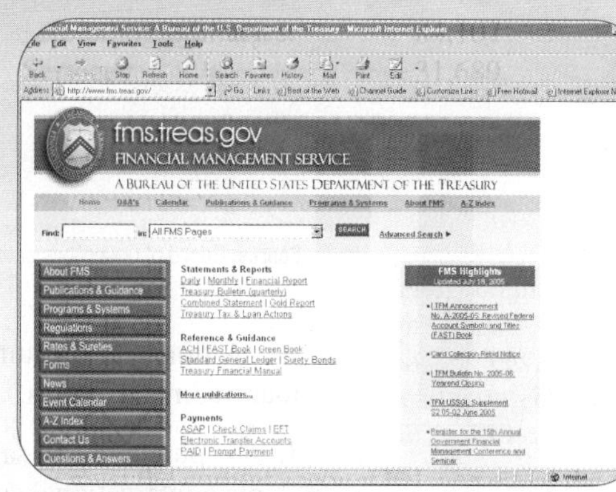

Questions

1. Calculate the net foreign exchange exposure of U.S. banks to the Canadian dollar, Japanese yen, Swiss franc, British pound, and the euro?
2. What do the values say about the foreign exchange exposure of U.S. banks to these currencies?

in a currency may not be completely under its own control. For example, even though an FI may feel that a particular currency will fall in value relative to the U.S. dollar, it may hold a positive net exposure in that currency because of many previous business loans issued to customers in that country. Thus, it is important that the FI manager recognize the potential for future foreign exchange losses, and undertake hedging or risk management strategies like those described above (in Example 8–4), when making medium- and long-term decisions in nondomestic currencies.

We have given the foreign exchange exposures for U.S. banks only, but most large nonbank financial institutions also have some foreign exchange exposure either through asset-liability holdings or currency trading. The absolute sizes of these exposures are smaller than for major U.S. money center banks. The reasons for this are threefold: smaller asset sizes, prudent person concerns,[11] and regulations.[12] Table 8–5 shows international versus U.S.-based assets held by private pension funds from 1989 to 2004.

The levels of claims in foreign currencies and positions in foreign currencies held by financial institutions have increased in recent years, as has the level of foreign currency trading. Average daily trading volume in foreign exchange markets rose to $1.9 trillion in 2004, an increase of 36 percent since 2001. The increased trading activity during this period was due to a number of factors, including the presence of trends and higher volatility in foreign exchange markets, which led to investments in currencies that experienced a persistent trend of appreciation (such as the euro). This volatility also resulted in an increase in hedging activity, which further increased currency trades. Also, as discussed above, interest rate differentials across countries resulted in investments in high-interest-rate currencies financed with short positions in low-interest-rate currencies. As cross-border investments increased, investors increasingly used foreign exchange markets as an asset class—that is, as an alternative investment to bonds and stocks.

11. *Prudent person concerns*, which require financial institutions to adhere to investment and lending policies, standards, and procedures that a reasonable and prudent person would apply with respect to a portfolio of investments and loans to avoid undue risk of loss and obtain a reasonable return, are especially important for pension funds.

12. For example, New York State restricts foreign asset holdings of New York–based life insurance companies to less than 10 percent of their assets.

TABLE 8-5 Foreign versus U.S.-Based Assets Held by Private Pension Funds *(in billions of U.S. dollars)*

	1989	1994	1999	2004
Total assets	$1,629.4	$2,433.8	$4,355.0	$4,145.5
Foreign assets	137.8	227.1	289.9	328.2
U.S.-based assets	1,419.6	2,206.7	4,065.1	3,817.3

Source: Board of Governors of the Federal Reserve, *Flow of Funds Accounts*, various issues. **www.federalreserve.gov**

A financial institution's position in the foreign exchange markets generally reflects four trading activities:

1. The purchase and sale of foreign currencies to allow customers to partake in and complete international commercial trade transactions.
2. The purchase and sale of foreign currencies to allow customers (or the financial institution itself) to take positions in foreign real and financial investments.
3. The purchase and sale of foreign currencies for hedging purposes to offset customer (or financial institution) exposure in any given currency.
4. The purchase and sale of foreign currencies for speculative purposes through forecasting or anticipating future movements in foreign exchange rates.

open position

An unhedged position in a particular currency.

In the first two activities, the financial institution normally acts as an *agent* on behalf of its customers for a fee but does not assume the foreign exchange risk itself. J.P. Morgan Chase is a dominant supplier of foreign exchange trading to retail customers in the United States. As of December 31, 2003, the aggregate value of J.P. Morgan Chase's notional or principal amounts of foreign exchange contracts totaled $10,129 billion (i.e., over $10 trillion). In the third activity, the financial institution acts defensively as a hedger to reduce foreign exchange exposure. For example, it may take a short (sell) position in the foreign exchange of a country to offset a long (buy) position in the foreign exchange of that same country. Thus, foreign exchange risk exposure essentially relates to **open** (or speculative) **positions** taken by the FI, the fourth activity. A financial institution usually creates open positions by taking an unhedged position in a foreign currency in its foreign exchange trading with other financial institutions. The Federal Reserve estimates that 200 financial institutions are active market makers in foreign currencies in the U.S. foreign exchange market, with about 30 commercial and investment banks making a market in the five most important currencies (as the Ethical Debates box highlights, the Fed monitors to ensure the legality of these market makers). Financial institutions can make speculative trades directly with other financial institutions or arrange them through specialist foreign exchange brokers. The Federal Reserve Bank of New York estimates that approximately 44 percent of speculative or open position trades are accomplished through specialized brokers who receive a fee for arranging trades between financial institutions. Speculative trades can be instituted through a variety of foreign exchange instruments. Spot currency trades are the most common, with financial institutions seeking to make a profit on the difference between buy and sell prices (i.e., movements in the purchase and sale prices over time). However, financial institutions can also take speculative positions in foreign exchange forward contracts, futures, and options (see Chapter 10).

DO YOU UNDERSTAND?

1. What the difference is between a spot and forward foreign exchange market transaction?
2. Which of the following two loans is more attractive: (a) one-year U.S. dollar bank loans yielding 10 percent, or (b) U.K. sterling loans yielding 15 percent? The cost of one-year U.S. dollar CDs is 8 percent. The dollar/pound spot exchange is $1.50/£1 and the one-year forward exchange rate is $1.48/£1.
3. What the two ways are in which an FI manager can hedge foreign exchange risk?
4. What the four major foreign exchange trading activities performed by financial institutions are?

7

INTERACTION OF INTEREST RATES, INFLATION, AND EXCHANGE RATES

As global financial markets and financial institutions and their customers have become increasingly interlinked, so have interest rates, inflation, and foreign exchange rates. For example, higher domestic interest rates may attract foreign

www.duskin.com/powerweb

Fed Fines UBS $100 Million for Money-Transfer Violations

The U.S. Federal Reserve said it fined UBS AG, Europe's biggest bank, $100 million for engaging in dollar-bill transactions with countries—like Cuba—that are subject to U.S. trade sanctions. Employees of UBS in Zurich engaged in transfers of U.S. bank notes with financial institutions in Cuba, Libya, Iran, and the former Yugoslavia, in violation of a contract with the Federal Reserve Bank of New York . . . the $100 million civil penalty was among the three biggest ever levied by the Fed.

Several banks operate such currency facilities internationally for the Fed to ensure a steady supply of U.S. currency around the world. The facilities ship and receive huge bundles of dollar-denominated bills for their foreign bank customers, who pay fees for this service. The Fed terminated its contract with UBS in October after its investigation found efforts to cover up the dealings. UBS said it "recognizes that very serious mistakes were made, accepts the sanctions and expresses its regret." The Switzerland-based bank said it sacked or disciplined a dozen employees and shut down its bank-note trading . . .

In an order assessing the $100 million penalty, the Fed said its contract banned currency dealings with countries under U.S. sanction. In addition to breaking that prohibition, the Fed said that employees of the bank took actions "aimed at concealing those banknote transactions" from the Fed, including "falsification of monthly reports" that UBS submitted to the Fed. A new release from Switzerland's bank regulator, the Federal Banking Commission, said that the falsification involved manipulating statistical data in order to hide the prohibited transactions.

The Federal Reserve's investigation began after a cache of U.S. currency was discovered in occupied Iraq. The Fed inquiry showed that the dollars had originally been transferred to UBS. It isn't clear how the dollars got from UBS to Iraq. But the enquiry established that the UBS currency-exchanges division was engaging in intermittent transactions with parties in the four banned countries. The deals involved $5 billion to $10 billion between 1996 and 2003.

Source: *The Wall Street Journal,* May 11, 2004, p. A3, by John D. McKinnon and Marcus Walker. Reprinted by permission of *The Wall Street Journal,* **www.wsj.com**

DO YOU UNDERSTAND?

1. What charges were brought up against UBS by the Federal Reserve?
2. What the illegal activities undertaken by UBS employees were?

financial investment and impact the value of the domestic currency. In this section, we look at the effect that inflation (or the change in the price level of a given set of goods and services, defined earlier, in Chapter 2, as the variable *IP*) in one country has on its foreign currency exchange rates—purchasing power parity (PPP). We also examine the links between domestic and foreign interest rates and spot and forward foreign exchange rates—interest rate parity (IRP).

Purchasing Power Parity

One factor affecting a country's foreign currency exchange rate with another country is the relative inflation rate in each country (which, as shown below, is directly related to the relative interest rates in these countries). Specifically, in Chapter 2, we showed that:

$$i_{US} = IP_{US} + RIR_{US}$$

and

$$i_S = IP_S + RIR_S$$

where

i_{US} = Interest rate in the United States
i_S = Interest rate in Switzerland (or another foreign country)
IP_{US} = Inflation rate in the United States
IP_S = Inflation rate in Switzerland (or another foreign country)
RIR_{US} = Real rate of interest in the United States
RIR_S = Real rate of interest in Switzerland (or another foreign country)

Assuming real rates of interest (or rates of time preference) are equal across countries:

$$RIR_{US} = RIR_S$$

then:

$$i_{US} - i_S = IP_{US} - IP_S$$

The (nominal) interest rate spread between the United States and Switzerland reflects the difference in inflation rates between the two countries.

As relative inflation rates (and interest rates) change, foreign currency exchange rates that are not constrained by government regulation should also adjust to account for relative differences in the price levels (inflation rates) between the two countries. One theory that explains how this adjustment takes place is the theory of **purchasing power parity (PPP)**. According to PPP, foreign currency exchange rates between two countries adjust to reflect changes in each country's price levels (or inflation rates and implicitly interest rates) as consumers and importers switch their demands for goods from relatively high inflation (interest) rate countries to low inflation (interest) rate countries. Specifically, the PPP theorem states that the change in the exchange rate between two countries' currencies is proportional to the difference in the inflation rates in the two countries. That is:

purchasing power parity (PPP)

The theory explaining the change in foreign currency exchange rates as inflation rates in the countries change.

$$IP_{US} - IP_S = \Delta S_{US/S}/S_{US/S}$$

where

$S_{US/S}$ = Spot exchange rate of U.S. dollars for Swiss francs (or another currency)

Thus, according to PPP the most important factor determining exchange rates is the fact that in open economies, differences in prices (and by implication, price level changes with inflation) drive trade flows, and thus demand for and supplies of currencies.

EXAMPLE 8-5 Application of Purchasing Power Parity

Suppose that the current spot exchange rate of U.S. dollars for Russian rubles, $S_{US/R}$, is .17 (i.e., 0.17 dollars, or 17 cents, can be received for 1 ruble). The price of the Russian-produced goods increases by 10 percent (i.e., inflation in Russia, IP_R, is 10 percent) and the U.S. price index increases by 4 percent (i.e., inflation in the United States, IP_{US}, is 4 percent). According to PPP, the 10 percent rise in the price of Russian goods combined relative to 4 percent rise in the price of U.S. goods results in a depreciation of the Russian ruble (by 6 percent). Specifically, the exchange rate of Russian rubles to U.S. dollars should fall, so that:[13]

$$\text{U.S. inflation rate} - \text{Russian inflation rate} = \frac{\text{Change in spot exchange rate of U.S. dollars for Russian rubles}}{\text{Initial spot exchange rate of U.S. dollars for Russian rubbles}}$$

or:

$$IP_{US} - IP_R = \Delta S_{US/R}/S_{US/R}$$

Plugging in the inflation and exchange rates, we get:

$$.04 - .10 = \Delta S_{US/R}/S_{US/R} = \Delta S_{US/R}/.17$$

or:

$$-.06 = S_{US/R}/.17$$

and:

$$\Delta S_{US/R} = -(.06) \times .17 = -.0102$$

13. This is the relative version of the PPP theorem. There are other versions of the theory (such as absolute PPP and the law of one price); however, the version shown here is the one most commonly used.

Thus, it takes 1.02 cents less to receive a ruble (or 15.98 cents [17 cents − 1.02 cents], or .1598 of $1, can be received for 1 ruble). The Russian ruble depreciates in value by 6 percent against the U.S. dollar as a result of its higher inflation rate.[14]

law of one price

An economic rule which states that in an efficient market identical goods and services produced in different countries should have a single price.

The theory behind purchasing power parity is that in the long run exchange rates should move toward rates that would equalize the prices of an identical basket of goods and services in any two countries. This is also known as the **law of one price,** an economic concept which states that in an efficient market, if countries produce a good or service that is identical to that in other countries, that good or service must have a single price, no matter where it is purchased. This is the thinking behind *The Economist*'s "Big Mac" index, proposed in 1986 as a lighthearted measure of whether currencies are at their correct level. The "basket" in the Big Mac index is a McDonald's Big Mac, which is produced locally in almost 120 countries. The Big Mac PPP is the exchange rate that would leave a burger in any country costing the same as in America. For example, in 2004, the average price of a Big Mac in four American cities was $2.90 (including tax). In Japan a Big Mac costs ¥262. Dividing this by the American price of $2.90 produces a dollar PPP against the yen of ¥90, compared with its current rate of ¥113, suggesting that the yen is 20 percent undervalued. In contrast, the euro (based on a weighted average of Big Mac prices in the euro area) is 13 percent overvalued. Interestingly, all emerging-market currencies are undervalued against the dollar. The Big Mac index was never intended as a precise forecasting tool. Burgers are not "traded" across borders as the PPP theory demands; prices are distorted by differences in the cost of nontradable goods and services, such as property rents. Yet these very failings make the Big Mac index useful, since looked at another way it can help to measure countries' differing costs of living. That a Big Mac is cheap in China does not in fact prove that the yuan is being held massively below its fair value. It is quite natural for average prices to be lower in poorer countries and therefore for their currencies to appear cheap.

Interest Rate Parity

We discussed above that foreign exchange spot market risk can be reduced by entering into forward foreign exchange contracts. Table 8–1 lists foreign exchange rates on December 16, 2004. Notice that spot rates and forward rates differ. For example, the spot exchange rate between the Canadian dollar and U.S. dollar was .8109 on December 16, 2004, meaning that one Canadian dollar could be exchanged on December 16, 2004, for .8109 U.S. dollars. The six-month forward rate between the two currencies on December 16, 2004, however, was .8111. This forward exchange rate is determined by the spot exchange rate and the interest rate differential between the two countries.

interest rate parity theorem (IRPT)

The theory that the domestic interest rate should equal the foreign interest rate minus the expected appreciation of the domestic currency.

The relationship that links spot exchange rates, interest rates, and forward exchange rates is described as the **interest rate parity theorem (IRPT).** Given that investors have an opportunity to invest in domestic or foreign markets, the IRPT implies that, by hedging in the forward exchange rate market, an investor should realize the same returns, whether investing domestically or in a foreign country—that is, the hedged dollar return on foreign investments just equals the return on domestic investments. Mathematically, the IRPT can be expressed as:

$$1 + i_{USt} = (1/S_t) \times (1 + i_{UKt}) \times F_t$$

Return on U.S. investment = Hedged return on foreign (U.K.) investment

14. A 6 percent fall in the ruble's value translates into a new exchange rate of .1598 dollar per ruble if the original exchange rate between dollars and rubles was .17.

where

$1 + i_{USt}$ = 1 plus the interest rate on a U.S. investment maturing at time t
$1 + i_{UKt}$ = 1 plus the interest rate on a U.K. investment maturing at time t
S_t = \$/£ spot exchange rate at time t
F_t = \$/£ forward exchange rate at time t

Rearranging, the IRPT can be expressed as:

$$(i_{USt} - i_{UKt})/(1 + i_{UKt}) = (F_t - S_t)/S_t$$

As can be seen, if interest rates in the United States and a foreign country are the same (i.e., $i_{USt} = i_{UKt}$) so that the left-hand side of the equation is zero, then the forward rate should equal the spot exchange rate ($F_t = S_t$) since the right-hand side of the equation equals zero. If U.S. interest rates are higher than foreign rates, the forward dollar value of the foreign currency will be greater than the spot dollar value, since investors can earn more over the investment horizon in the United States than in the foreign market. If U.S. interest rates are lower than foreign rates, the forward dollar value of the foreign currency will be less than the spot dollar value, since investors can earn more in foreign markets than in U.S. markets.

EXAMPLE 8-6 An Example of the Interest Rate Parity Theorem at Work

Suppose that on December 16, 2004, a U.S. citizen has excess funds available to invest in either U.S. or British bank time deposits. It is assumed that both types of deposits are credit or default risk free and that the investment horizon is one month. The interest rate available on British pound one-month time deposits, i_{UK}, is 0.5 percent monthly. The spot exchange rate of U.S. dollars for British pounds on December 16, 2004 (from Table 8–1) is \$1.9318/£, and the one-month forward rate is \$1.9279/£. According to the IRPT, the interest rate on comparable U.S. one-month time deposits should be:

$$1 + i_{US} = (1/1.9318) \times (1 + .005) \times 1.9279 = 1.002971$$

or 0.2971 percent. We can rearrange this relationship as shown above as:

$$\frac{.002971 - .005}{1 + .0005} = \frac{1.9279 - 1.9318}{1.9318}$$

$$-.002019 = -.002019$$

Thus, the discounted spread between domestic and foreign interest rates is, in equilibrium, equal to the percentage spread between forward and spot exchange rates.

DO YOU UNDERSTAND?

1. What the term *purchasing power parity* means?
2. What the interest rate parity condition is? How does it relate to the existence or nonexistence of arbitrage opportunities?

Suppose that, in the preceding example, the annual rate on U.S. time deposits was 0.35 percent per month (rather than 0.2971 percent). In this case, it would be profitable for the investor to put any excess funds into U.S. rather than U.K. time deposits. In fact, a riskfree (or arbitrage) investment opportunity now exists and will result in a flow of funds out of U.K. time deposits into U.S. time deposits. According to the IRPT, this flow of funds would quickly drive up the U.S. dollar for British pound spot exchange rate until the potential risk-free profit opportunities from investment in U.S. deposits is eliminated. Thus, any arbitrage opportunity should be small and fleeting.[15] Any long-term violations of this relationship are likely to occur only if major imperfections exist in international deposit markets, including barriers to cross-border financial flows.

15. In addition, as funds flow out of U.K. time deposits, banks in the United Kingdom would have an incentive to raise interest rates. By comparison, as funds flow into U.S. banks, the banks would have the incentive to lower interest rates. Further, as funds flow to the United States, British investors would sell dollars forward for pounds (in addition to buying more spot dollars). While the purchase of spot dollars leads to an appreciation in the spot dollar rate, the sale of dollars forward for pounds will lead to a depreciation in the forward rate (F_t). These two effects, combined with the effect on the spot rate of \$/£, would once again equate the returns on domestic and foreign investments.

SUMMARY

In this chapter, we reviewed foreign exchange markets. Foreign exchange markets have grown to be among the largest of the world's financial markets. We reviewed the trading process in this market, paying particular attention to the role played by financial institutions in the operations of the foreign exchange market. In the appendix to the chapter we look at balance of payment accounts, which summarize the trading activity of one country with all others.

SEARCH THE SITE

Go to the Department of Commerce Web site at **www.bea.doc.gov** and find the most recent balance of payment data for the United States.

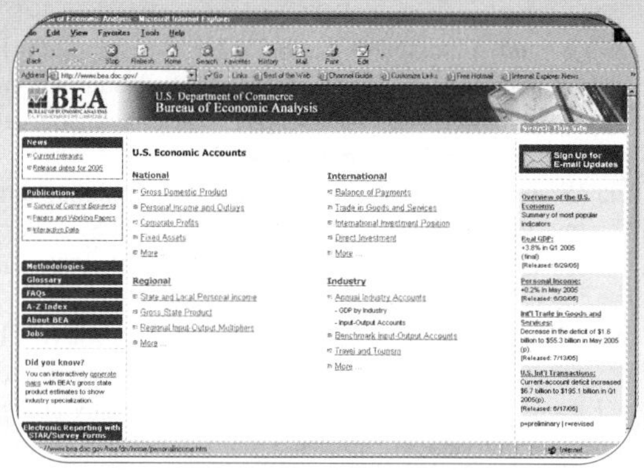

Once at the Web site, under "International," click on "Balance of Payments"

Click on "Latest news release"

This will bring up a table with the U.S. Balance of Payments.

Questions

1. Identify the most recent balances of U.S. current accounts and their components.
2. Does the U.S. currently have a surplus or a deficit on its current accounts?

QUESTIONS

1. How did the Bretton Woods and the Smithsonian Agreements affect the ability of foreign exchange rates to float freely? How did the elimination of exchange boundaries in 1973 affect the ability of foreign exchange rates to float freely?
2. Refer to Table 8–1.
   a. What was the spot exchange rate of Canadian dollars for U.S. dollars on December 16, 2004?
   b. What was the six-month forward exchange rate of Canadian dollars for U.S. dollars on December 16, 2004?
   c. What was the three-month forward exchange rate of U.S. dollars for Swiss francs on December 15, 2004?
3. Refer to Table 8–1.
   a. On November 16, 2004, you purchased a British pound–denominated CD by converting $1 million to pounds at a rate of .5262 pounds for U.S. dollars. It is now December 16, 2004. Has the U.S. dollar appreciated or depreciated in value relative to the British pound?
   b. Using the information in part (a), what is your gain or loss on the investment in the CD? Assume no interest has been paid on the CD.
4. On December 16, 2004, you convert 500,000 U.S. dollars to Japanese yen in the spot foreign exchange market and purchase a one-month forward contract to convert yen into dollars. How much will you receive in U.S. dollars at the end of the month? Use the data in Table 8–1 for this problem.
5. Bank USA recently purchased $10 million worth of euro-denominated one-year CDs that pay 10 percent interest annually. The current spot rate was 1.30/$.
   a. Is Bank USA exposed to an appreciation or depreciation of the dollar relative to the euro?
   b. What will be the return on the one-year CD if the dollar appreciates relative to the euro such that the spot rate at the end of the year is 1.20/$?
   c. What will be the return on the one-year CD if the dollar depreciates relative to the euro such that the spot rate at the end of the year is 1.40/$?

www.mhhe.com/sc3e

6. Bankone issued $200 million worth of one-year CDs in Brazilian reals at a rate of 6.50 percent. The exchange rate at the time of the transaction was Brazilian real 1/$.
   a. Is Bankone exposed to an appreciation or depreciation of the U.S. dollar relative to the Brazilian real?
   b. What will be the percentage cost to Bankone on this CD if the dollar depreciates relative to the Brazilian real such that the exchange rate between the currencies is Brazilian real 1.2/$ at the end of the year?
   c. What will be the percentage cost to Bankone on this CD if the dollar appreciates relative to the Brazilian real such that the exchange rate between the currencies is Brazilian real 0.9/$ at the end of the year?

7. Sun Bank USA has purchased a 16 million one-year Australian dollar loan that pays 12 percent interest annually. The spot rate of U.S. dollars for Australian dollars is 0.625. It has funded this loan by accepting a British pound (BP)–denominated deposit for the equivalent amount and maturity at an annual rate of 10 percent. The current spot rate of U.S. dollars for British pounds is 1.60.
   a. What is the net interest income earned in dollars on this one-year transaction if the spot rate of U.S. dollars for Australian dollars and U.S. dollars for BPs at the end of the year are 0.588 and 1.848, respectively?
   b. What should the spot rate of U.S. dollars for BPs be at the end of the year in order for the bank to earn a net interest income of $200,000 (disregarding any change in principal values)?

8. North Bank has been borrowing in the U.S. markets and lending abroad, thereby incurring foreign exchange risk. In a recent transaction, it issued a one-year $2 million CD at 6 percent and is planning to fund a loan in British pounds at 8 percent for a 2 percent expected spread. The spot rate of U.S. dollars for British pounds is 1.45.
   a. However, new information now indicates that the British pound will depreciate such that the spot rate of U.S. dollars for British pounds is 1.43 by year end. What should the bank charge on the loan to maintain the 2 percent spread?
   b. The bank has an opportunity to hedge using one-year forward contracts at 1.46 U.S. dollars for British pounds. What is the spread if the bank hedges its forward foreign exchange exposure?
   c. How should the loan rates be increased to maintain the 2 percent spread if the bank intends to hedge its exposure using the forward rates?

9. eXcel **Using a Spreadsheet to Calculate Foreign Exchange Risk:** Suppose that on January 18, 2007, a U.S. firm plans to purchase 3 million euros' (€) worth of French bonds from a French FI in one month's time. The French FI wants payment in euros. Thus, the U.S. firm must convert dollars into euros. The spot exchange rate for January 18, 2007, of U.S. dollars to euros is 1.6545, or one euro costs $1.6545 in dollars. Consequently, the U.S. firm must convert:

   U.S.$/€ exchange rate × €3 million =
   1.6545 × €3m. = $4,963,500

   into euros today. One month after the conversion of dollars to euros, the French bond purchase deal falls through and the U.S. firm no longer needs the euros it purchased at $1.6545 per euro. Calculate the gain/loss on the bond to the U.S. firm if the spot exchange rate of U.S. dollars to euros is 1.7555, 1.6545, 1.6135, and 1.5845 at the end of the month.

Price at Beginning of Month	U.S. $ to € Exchange Rate at End of Month	Price at End of Month	=> The Gain/Loss Will Be
$4,963,500	1.7555	1.7555×€3 million = $5,266,500	$5,266,500 − $4,963,500 = $330,300
4,963,500	1.6545	1.6545×€3 million = $4,963,500	$4,963,500 − $4,963,500 = $0
4,963,500	1.6135	1.6135×€3 million = $4,840,500	$4,840,500 − $4,963,500 = −$123,00
4,963,500	1.5845	1.5845×€3 million = $4,753,500	$4,753,500 − $4,963,500 = −$210,000

10. How are foreign exchange markets open 24 hours per day?

11. Citibank holds $23 million in foreign exchange assets and $18 million in foreign exchange liabilities. Citibank also conducted foreign currency trading activity in which it bought $5 million in foreign exchange contracts and sold $12 million in foreign exchange contracts.
    a. What is Citibank's net foreign assets?
    b. What is Citibank's net foreign exchange bought?
    c. What is Citibank's net foreign exposure?

12. What are the major foreign exchange trading activities performed by financial institutions?

13. If the interest rate in the United Kingdom is 8 percent, the interest rate in the United States is 10 percent, the spot exchange rate is $1.75/£, and interest rate parity holds, what must be the one-year forward exchange rate?

14. Suppose all of the conditions in Question 12 hold except that the forward rate of exchange is also $1.75/£. How could an investor take advantage of this situation?

15. If a bundle of goods in Japan costs ¥4,000,000 while the same goods and services cost $40,000 in the United States, what is the current exchange rate of U.S. dollars for yen? If, over the next year, inflation is 6 percent in Japan and 10 percent in the United States, what will the goods cost next year? Will the dollar depreciate or appreciate relative to the yen over this time period?

16. What is the implication for cross-border trades if it can be shown that interest rate parity is maintained consistently across different markets and different currencies?

17. What are some reasons why interest rate parity may not hold in spite of the economic forces that should ensure the equilibrium relationship?

18. One form of the interest rate parity equation appears as $1 + r_{ust} = (1/S_t) \times (1 + r_{ukt}) \times F_t$ where both the spot and forward rates are expressed in terms of dollars for pounds or direct exchange rates. How would the equation be written if the exchange rates were indirect—that is, pounds for dollars?

19. Assume that annual interest rates are 8 percent in the United States and 4 percent in Switzerland. An FI can borrow (by issuing CDs) or lend (by purchasing CDs) at these rates. The spot rate is $0.60/Sf.
    a. If the forward rate is $0.64/Sf, how could the bank arbitrage using a sum of $1 million? What is the spread earned?
    b. At what forward rate is this arbitrage eliminated?

The following questions are related to Appendix 8A material in this chapter, see **www.mhhe.com/sc3e**

20. Why has the United States held a trade deficit for most of the 1990s and early 2000s? Make sure you distinguish between the import versus export of goods and services.

21. The following table lists balance of payment current accounts for country A.

Current Accounts		
1. Exports of goods, services, and income		$168,953
2. Goods, adjusted, excluding military	$92,543	
3. Services	45,689	
4. Income receipts on U.S. assets abroad	30,721	
5. Imports of goods, services, and income		−150,936
6. Goods, adjusted, excluding military	−84,107	
7. Services	−31,689	
8. Income payments on foreign assets in the United States	−35,140	
9. Unilateral transfers, net		−9,421

a. What is country A's total current accounts?
b. What is country A's balance on goods?
c. What is country A's balance on services?
d. What is country A's balance on investment income?

22. Why must the current account balance equal the value of the capital account balance (in opposite sign)?

APPENDIX 8A: Balance of Payment Accounts

View this appendix at
www.mhhe.com/sc3e

www.mhhe.com/sc3e

9 Stock Markets

OUTLINE

Chapter NAVIGATOR

1. What are the major characteristics of common stock?
2. What are the major characteristics of preferred stock?
3. What is the process by which common stock is issued in primary markets?
4. What are the major secondary stock markets?
5. What is the process by which a trade takes place in the stock markets?
6. What are the major stock market indexes?
7. Who are the major stock market participants?
8. What are the three forms of market efficiency?
9. What are the major characteristics of international stock markets?

THE STOCK MARKETS: CHAPTER OVERVIEW

Stock markets allow suppliers of funds to efficiently and cheaply get equity funds to public corporations (users of funds). In exchange, the fund users (firms) give the fund suppliers ownership rights in the firm as well as cash flows in the form of dividends. Thus, corporate stock or equity serves as a source of financing for firms, in addition to debt financing or retained earnings financing. In the 1990s, the market value of corporate stock outstanding increased faster than any other type of financial security. Figure 9–1 shows the market value of corporate stock issued in the United States from 1994 through 2004 by type of issuer. Notice that from 1994 through 2004, stock values increased 147 percent (increasing 170 percent from 1994 through 2000 before falling 13.6 percent in value in 2001 as the U.S. economy hit a downturn) compared to 86.8 percent growth in bond values (see Figure 6–1) and 130.4 percent growth in primary mortgage market values (see Figure 7–1).

FIGURE 9–1 Market Value of Common Stock Outstanding, by Type of Issuer

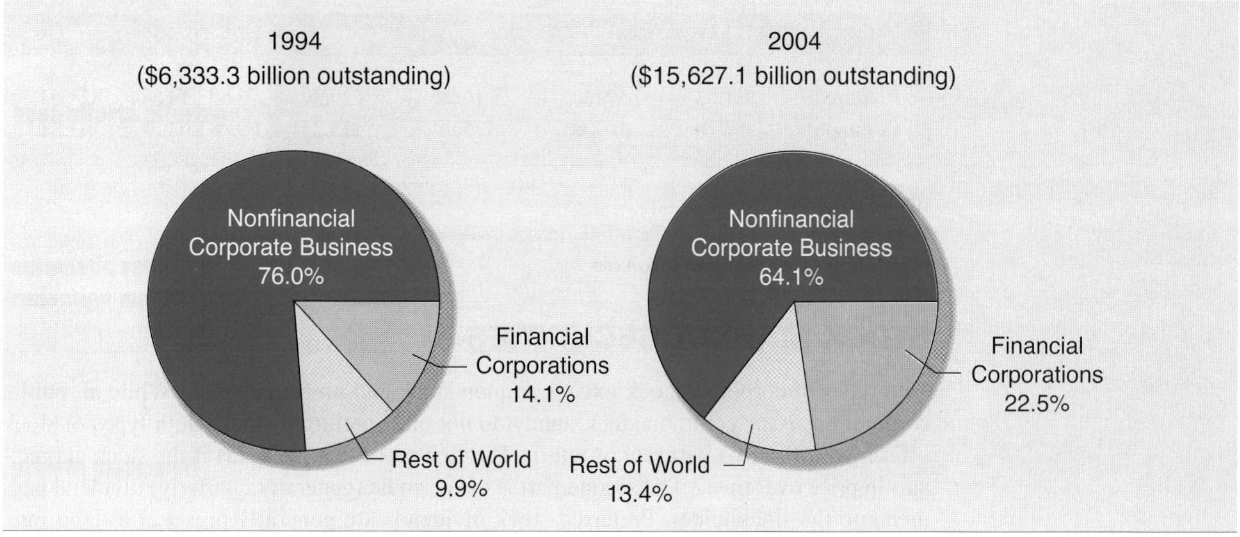

Source: Federal Reserve Board, Web site, "Flow of Fund Accounts," various issues. **www.federalreserve.gov**

Legally, holders of a corporation's common stock or equity have an ownership stake in the issuing firm that reflects the percentage of the corporation's stock they hold. Specifically, corporate stockholders have the right to a share in the issuing firm's profits, as in dividend payments, after the payment of interest to bond holders and taxes. They also have a residual claim on the firm's assets if the company fails or is dissolved after all debt and tax liabilities are paid. Bond holders, on the other hand, are creditors of the issuing firm. They have no direct ownership interest in the firm, but they have a superior claim to the firm's earnings and assets relative to that of stockholders.

Further, common stockholders have voting privileges on major issues in the firm such as the election of the board of directors. It is the board of directors that oversees the day-to-day operations of the firm. The board is charged with ensuring that the firm is being run so as to maximize the value of the firm (i.e., the value of its equity and debt claims). Thus, while stockholders have no direct control over a firm's day-to-day operations, they do decide on who will oversee these operations and they can replace the board when they feel the firm is not being run efficiently from a value-maximizing perspective.

The secondary market for corporate stock is the most closely watched and reported of all financial security markets. Daily television and newspaper reports include recaps of the movements in stock markets (both in the United States and abroad). This is because stock market movements are sometimes seen as predictors of economic activity and performance. This is also because corporate stocks may be the most widely held of all financial securities. Most individuals own stocks either directly or indirectly through pension fund and mutual fund investments, and thus their economic wealth fluctuates closely with that of the stock market.

In this chapter, we present a description of equity or stock securities and the markets in which they trade. We begin with a description of the different types of corporate stock. We next look at how they are sold to the public and then traded; first in primary markets (the original sale) and then in secondary markets (the markets for resale). We also review the major stock market indexes. We look at the participants in stock markets and other issues relating to those markets (such as the link between stock market indexes and the overall economic activity, the efficiency of the stock market, and regulations covering stock market operations). We conclude the chapter with an examination of international participation in U.S. stock markets and some characteristics of foreign stock markets.

TABLE 9–1 New Securities Issued
(in billions of dollars)

	1992	1998	2000	2001	2003	2004*
Preferred	\$21.33	\$21.20	\$ 16.91	\$ 29.30	\$33.14	\$21.54
Common	57.10	107.60	175.79	115.25	81.03	93.81

*Through September.

Source: Federal Reserve Bulletin, Table 1.46, various issues, and Thompson Financial Web site.
www.federalreserve.gov; www.tfibcm.com

STOCK MARKET SECURITIES

Two types of corporate stock exist: common stock and preferred stock. While all public corporations issue common stock, many do not offer preferred stock. Both types of stock offer investors a two-part rate of return. The first part is capital gains if the stock appreciates in price over time.[1] The second part is the periodic (generally quarterly) dividend payments to the stockholder. Preferred stock dividends are generally preset at a fixed rate, while common stock dividends vary over time and are thus more uncertain (see below). Thus, the return to a stockholder over a period $t - 1$ to t can be written as:

$$R_t = \frac{P_t - P_{t-1}}{P_{t-1}} + \frac{D_t}{P_{t-1}}$$

where

P_t = Stock price at time t

D_t = Dividends paid over time $t - 1$ to t

$\frac{P_t - P_{t-1}}{P_{t-1}}$ = Capital gain over time $t - 1$ to t

$\frac{D_t}{P_{t-1}}$ = Return from dividends paid over time $t - 1$ to t

EXAMPLE 9–1 Calculation of Return on a Stock

Suppose you owned a stock over the last year. You originally bought the stock for \$40 (P_{t-1}) and just sold it for \$45 (P_t). The stock also paid an annual dividend of \$4 on the last day of the year. Your return on the stock investment can be calculated as follows:

$$R_1 = \frac{\$45 - \$40}{\$40} + \frac{\$4}{\$40}$$
$$= 12.5\% + 10.0\% = 22.5\%$$

or your return on the stock over the last year was 22.5 percent, 12.5 percent from capital gains and 10.0 percent from dividends.

We also looked at the calculation of the rate of return on corporate stocks in the Appendix 3A to Chapter 3, located at the book's Web site (**www.mhhe.com/sc3e**).

Table 9–1 shows the annual issuance of new common and preferred stock sold to new and existing stockholders from 1992 through 2004. Notice that preferred stock represents a small but growing portion of the new issue market (16 percent in 1995 and 1998 and 29 percent in 2003). Indeed, the majority of public corporations do not have preferred stock outstanding.

1. If the stock price falls, then the stock is subject to capital losses.

Common Stock

Common stock is the fundamental ownership claim in a public corporation. Many characteristics of common stock differentiate it from other types of financial securities (e.g., bonds, mortgages, preferred stock). These include (1) discretionary dividend payments, (2) residual claim status, (3) limited liability, and (4) voting rights. These characteristics are described next.

common stock

The fundamental ownership claim in a public corporation.

Dividends. While common stockholders can potentially receive unlimited dividend payments if the firm is highly profitable, they have no special or guaranteed dividend rights. Rather, the payment and size of dividends are determined by the board of directors of the issuing firm (who are elected by the common stockholders). Further, unlike interest payments on debt, a corporation does not default if it misses a dividend payment to common stockholders. Thus, common stockholders have no legal recourse if dividends are not received, even if a company is highly profitable and chooses to use these profits to reinvest in new projects and firm growth.[2]

Another drawback with common stock dividends, from an investor's viewpoint, is that they are taxed twice—once at the firm level (at the corporate tax rate, by virtue of the fact that dividend payments are not tax deductible from the firm's profits or net earnings) and once at the personal level (at the personal income tax rate). Investors can partially avoid this double taxation effect by holding stocks in growth firms that reinvest most of their earnings to finance growth rather than paying larger dividends. Generally, earnings growth leads to stock price increases. Thus, stockholders can sell their stock for a profit and pay capital gains tax rather than ordinary income in the form of dividends. Under current tax laws, capital gains tax rates are lower than ordinary income tax rates. For example, in the early 2000s through the middle of the first decade, ordinary income tax rates ranged from 15 percent to 38.6 percent of an individual's taxable income. Long-term (a 12-month or longer investment horizon) capital gains tax rates were capped at 20 percent.

In the context of the return equation above, the reinvestment of earnings (rather than payment of dividends) affects both return components: capital gains and dividends. By reinvesting earnings (rather than paying dividends), the dividend component of returns, D_t/P_{t-1}, decreases. However, the reinvestment of earnings generally results in a relatively larger increase in the capital gains component, $(P_t - P_{t-1})/P_{t-1}$.

EXAMPLE 9-2 Payment of Dividends versus Reinvestment of Earnings

A corporation has after-(corporate) tax earnings that would allow a \$2 dividend per share to be paid to its stockholders. If these dividends are paid, the firm will be unable to invest in new projects, and its stock price, currently \$50 per share, probably would not change. The return to the firm's stockholders in this case is:

$$R_t = \frac{50 - 50}{50} + \frac{2}{50} = 4\%$$

Suppose a stockholder bought the stock at the beginning of the year (at \$50) and sold it at the end of the year (at \$50). The stockholder's ordinary income tax rate is 31 percent and capital gains tax rate is 20 percent. The return to the stockholder in this case is all in the form of ordinary income (dividends). Thus, the after-tax rate of return to the stockholder is $4\%(1 - .31) = 2.76\%$.

Alternatively, rather than pay dividends, the firm can use the earnings to invest in new projects that will increase the overall value of the firm such that the stock price will rise to

2. Eventually, of course, such profits will be paid out—in the extreme case on dissolution of the corporation.

$52 per share. The return to the firm's stockholders in this case is:

$$R_t = \frac{52 - 50}{50} + \frac{0}{50} = 4\%$$

In this case, the return to the stockholder is all in the form of capital gains, and is thus taxed at a rate of 20 percent. Thus, the after-tax rate of return to the stockholder is 4% (1 − .20) = 3.2%.

residual claim

In the event of liquidation, common stockholders have the lowest priority in terms of any cash distribution.

Residual Claim. Common stockholders have the lowest priority claim on a corporation's assets in the event of bankruptcy—they have a **residual claim.** Only after all senior claims are paid (i.e., payments owed to creditors such as the firm's employees, bond holders, the government (taxes), and preferred stockholders) are common stockholders entitled to what assets of the firm are left. The residual claim feature associated with common stock makes it riskier than bonds as an investable asset.

limited liability

No matter what financial difficulties the issuing corporation encounters, neither it nor its creditors can seek repayment from the firm's common stockholders. This implies that common stockholder losses are limited to the original amount of their investment.

Limited Liability. One of the most important characteristics of common stock is its limited liability feature. Legally, **limited liability** implies that common stockholder losses are limited to the amount of their original investment in the firm, I in Figure 9–2, if the company's asset value falls to less than the value of the debt it owes, point B. That is, the common stockholders' personal wealth held outside their ownership claims in the firm are unaffected by bankruptcy of the corporation—even if the losses of the firm exceed its total common stock ownership claims. In contrast, sole proprietorship or partnership stock interests mean the stockholders may be liable for the firm's debts out of their total private wealth holdings, W in Figure 9–2, if the company gets into financial difficulties and its losses exceed the stockholders ownership claims in the firm. This is the case of "unlimited" liability.

Voting Rights. A fundamental privilege assigned to common stock is voting rights. While common stockholders do not exercise control over the firm's daily activities (these activities are overseen by managers hired to act in the best interests of the firm's common stockholders and bond holders), they do exercise control over the firm's activities indirectly through the election of the board of directors. For example, in 2004 Walt Disney Co. shareholders were unhappy with many actions of the company's management, especially CEO and board chairman Michael Eisner. Problems included dropping viewer ratings at Disney-owned ABC and the breakdown of talks with Pixar Animation Studios, which had provided some of Disney's most successful movies in the past years. Eisner stepped down as chairman of the board of Disney after 43.4 percent of all shareholders voted to remove him from the board at the March 3 shareholder meeting. Six months later Eisner also announced his resignation as Disney's CEO.

dual-class firms

Two classes of common stock are outstanding, with differential voting rights assigned to each class.

The typical voting rights arrangement is to assign one vote per share of common stock. However, some corporations are organized as **dual-class firms,** in which two classes of common stock are outstanding, with different voting rights assigned to each class. For example, inferior voting rights have been assigned by (1) limiting the number of votes per share on one class relative to another (e.g., Alberto-Culver Class A shares are entitled to one-tenth vote per share, while Class B shares are entitled to one vote per share), (2) limiting the fraction of the board of directors that one class could elect relative to another (e.g., ICH Corp. allowed one vote per share on both its common and Class B stock, but common shares elect 20 percent of the board, while Class B stockholders elect 80 percent of the board), or (3) a combination of these two (e.g., American Fructose Class A shares elect 25 percent of the board and have one vote per share on all other matters, while Class B shares elect 75 percent of the board and have 10 votes per share on all other matters). To offset the reduced voting rights, inferior

FIGURE 9–2 The Limited Liability Effect

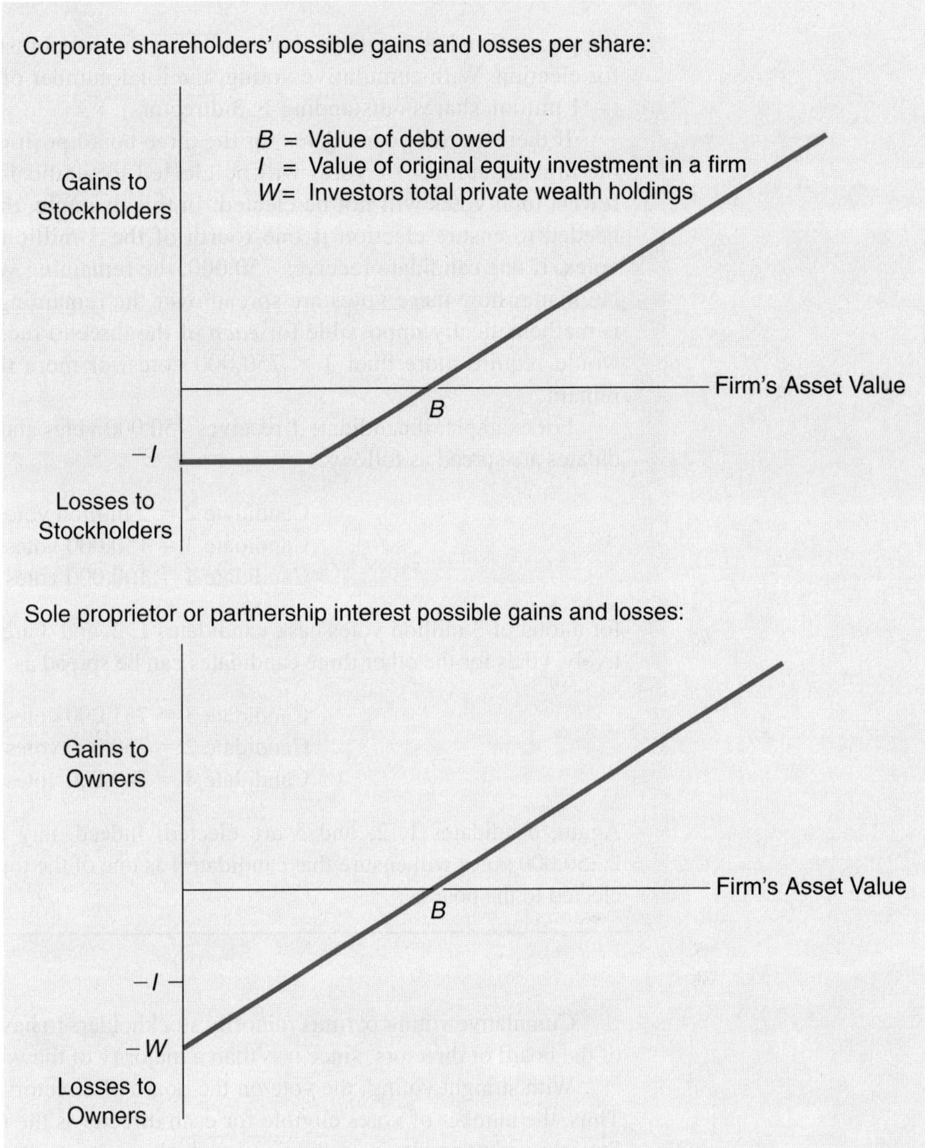

class shares are often assigned higher dividend rights. For example, no dividend is paid on the Class B common shares of Alberto Culver unless an equal or greater dividend is paid on the Class A stock.

cumulative voting

All directors up for election are voted on at the same time. The number of votes assigned to each stockholder equals the number of shares held multiplied by the number of directors to be elected.

Shareholders exercise their voting rights, electing the board of directors by casting votes at the issuing firm's annual meeting or by mailing in a proxy vote (see below). Two methods of electing a board of directors are generally used: cumulative voting and straight voting. Cumulative voting is required by law in some states (e.g., California and Illinois) and is authorized in others. With **cumulative voting,** all directors up for election, as nominated by the shareholders and selected by a committee of the board, are voted on at the same time. The number of votes assigned to each stockholder equals the number of shares held multiplied by the number of directors to be elected. A shareholder may assign all of his or her votes to a single candidate for the board or may spread them over more than one candidate. The candidates with the highest number of total votes are then elected to the board.

EXAMPLE 9-3 Cumulative Voting of a Board of Directors

Suppose a firm has 1 million shares of common stock outstanding and three directors up for election. With cumulative voting, the total number of votes available is 3,000,000 (= 1 million shares outstanding × 3 directors).

If there are four candidates for the three board positions, the three candidates with the highest number of votes will be elected to the board and the candidate with the fewest total votes will not be elected. In this example, the minimum number of votes needed to ensure election is one-fourth of the 3 million votes available, or 750,000 votes. If one candidate receives 750,000, the remaining votes together total 2,250,000. No matter how these votes are spread over the remaining three director candidates, it is mathematically impossible for *each* of the three to receive *more than* 750,000. This would require more than 3 × 750,000 votes, or more than the 2,250,000 votes that remain.

For example, if candidate 1 receives 750,000 votes and votes for the other three candidates are spread as follows:

Candidate 2 = 2 million votes
Candidate 3 = 150,000 votes
Candidate 4 = 100,000 votes

for a total of 3 million votes cast, candidates 1, 2, and 3 are elected to the board. Alternatively, votes for the other three candidates can be spread as:

Candidate 3 = 751,000 votes
Candidate 2 = 750,000 votes
Candidate 4 = 749,000 votes

Again, candidates 1, 2, and 3 are elected. Indeed, any distribution of the remaining 2,250,000 votes will ensure that candidate 1 is one of the top three vote getters and will be elected to the board.

Cumulative voting permits minority stockholders to have some real say in the election of the board of directors, since less than a majority of the votes can affect the outcome.

With straight voting, the vote on the board of directors occurs one director at a time. Thus, the number of votes eligible for each director is the number of shares outstanding. Straight voting results in a situation in which an owner of over half the voting shares can elect the entire board of directors.

proxy

A voting ballot sent by a corporation to its stockholders. When returned to the issuing firm, a proxy allows stockholders to vote by absentee ballot or authorizes representatives of the stockholders to vote on their behalf.

Proxy Votes. Most shareholders do not attend the annual meetings. Most corporations anticipate this and routinely mail proxies to their stockholders prior to the annual meeting. A completed **proxy** returned to the issuing firm allows stockholders to vote by absentee ballot or authorize representatives of the stockholders to vote on their behalf. It is estimated that, on average, less than 40 percent of the total possible votes are cast at corporate meetings. However, use of the Internet may increase this number in the future. By 2006, most U.S. firms (such as Alcoa, Federated Investors, and Morgan Stanley Dean Witter) were putting proxy statements online and allowing votes to be cast via the Internet. The entire documentation delivery process can be electronically automated with the use of services such as EquiServe or Automatic Data Processing's (ADP's) ProxyVote. Official documentation is delivered in electronic form, to shareholders, who log onto the system with a control number or personal identification number and vote for or against the resolutions presented. By the mid-2000s, the average firm offering on-line voting received almost 10 percent of its votes electronically.

Preferred Stock

2

Preferred stock is a hybrid security that has characteristics of both a bond and a common stock. Preferred stock is similar to common stock in that it represents an ownership interest in the issuing firm, but like a bond it pays a fixed periodic (dividend) payment. Preferred stock is senior to common stock but junior to bonds. Therefore, preferred stockholders are paid only when profits have been generated and all debt holders have been paid (but before common stockholders are paid). Like common stock, if the issuing firm does not have sufficient profits to pay the preferred stock dividends, preferred stockholders cannot force the firm into bankruptcy. Further, if the issuing firm goes bankrupt, preferred stockholders are paid their claim only after all creditors have been paid, but before common stockholders are paid.

preferred stock

A hybrid security that has characteristics of both bonds and common stock.

Dividends on preferred stock are generally fixed (paid quarterly) and are expressed either as a dollar amount or a percentage of the face or par value of the preferred stock.

EXAMPLE 9-4 Calculation of Preferred Stock Dividends

Suppose you own a preferred stock that promises to pay an annual dividend of 5 percent of the par (face) value of the stock (received in quarterly installments). If the par value of the stock is $100, the preferred stockholder will receive:

$$\text{Annual dividends} = \$100 \times .05 = \$5$$

or:

$$\text{Quarterly dividend} = \$5 \div 4 = \$1.25$$

at the end of each quarter.

Alternatively, the preferred stock could promise to pay an annual dividend of $5 per year in quarterly installments.

nonparticipating preferred stock

Preferred stock in which the dividend is fixed regardless of any increase or decrease in the issuing firm's profits.

cumulative preferred stock

Preferred stock in which missed dividend payments go into arrears and must be made up before any common stock dividends can be paid.

participating preferred stock

Preferred stock in which actual dividends paid in any year may be greater than the promised dividends.

noncumulative preferred stock

Preferred stock in which dividend payments do not go into arrears and are never paid.

Preferred stockholders generally do not have voting rights in the firm. An exception to this rule may exist if the issuing firm has missed a promised dividend payment. For example, preferred stock in Pitney Bowes, Inc., has no voting rights except when dividends are in arrears for six quarterly payments. In this case, preferred stockholders can elect one-third of the board of directors.

Typically, preferred stock is nonparticipating and cumulative. **Nonparticipating preferred stock** means that the preferred stock dividend is fixed regardless of any increase or decrease in the issuing firm's profits. **Cumulative preferred stock** means that any missed dividend payments go into arrears and *must* be made up before *any* common stock dividends can be paid.

In contrast, **participating preferred stock** means that actual dividends paid in any year may be greater than the promised dividends. In some cases, if the issuing firm has an exceptionally profitable year, preferred stockholders may receive some of the high profits in the form of an extra dividend payment. In others, the participating preferred stock pays and changes dividends along the same lines as common stock dividends. For example, RISCORP, Inc., has participating preferred stock outstanding that pays dividends equal to those on its common stock. If **preferred stock is noncumulative,** missed dividend payments do not go into arrears and are never paid. For example, G & L Realty, Inc.'s preferred stock entitles stockholders to monthly dividends based on an annual rate of $2.45 per share. If a dividend payment is missed, the dividends do not go into arrears. Noncumulative preferred stock is generally unattractive to prospective preferred stockholders. Thus, noncumulative preferred stock generally has some other special features (e.g., voting rights) to make up for this drawback.

Corporations find preferred stock beneficial as a source of funds because, unlike coupon interest on a bond issue, dividends on preferred stock can be missed without fear of bankruptcy proceedings. Additionally, preferred stock is beneficial to an issuing firm's

FIGURE 9–3 Primary Market Stock Transaction

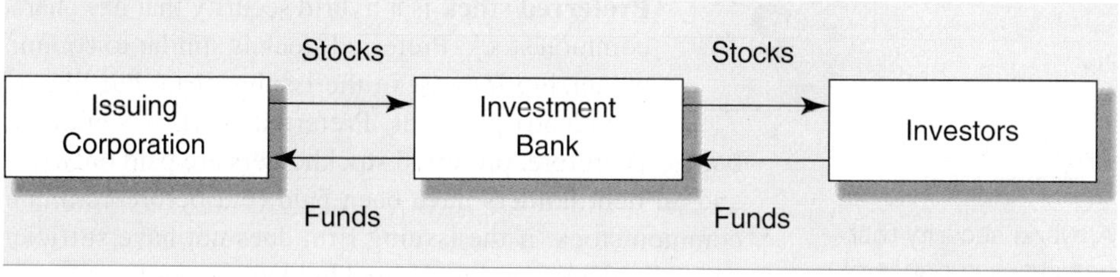

debt holders. Funds raised through a preferred stock issue can be used by the firm to fund the purchase of assets that will produce income needed to pay debt holders before preferred stockholders can be paid.

However, preferred stock also has its drawbacks for corporations. The first drawback is that, if a preferred dividend payment is missed, new investors may be reluctant to make investments in the firm. Thus, firms are generally unable to raise any new capital until all missed dividend payments are paid on preferred stock. In addition, preferred stockholders must be paid a rate of return consistent with the risk associated with preferred stock (i.e., dividend payments may be delayed). Therefore, preferred stock may be a costlier source of funding for the issuing firm than bonds.[3]

A second drawback of preferred stock from the issuing firm's viewpoint is that, unlike coupon interest paid on corporate bonds, dividends paid on preferred stock are not a tax-deductible expense—preferred dividends are paid out of after-tax earnings. This raises the cost of preferred stock relative to bonds for a firm's shareholders. Specifically, this difference in the tax treatment between coupon interest on debt and preferred stock dividends affects the net profit available to common stockholders of the firm.

DO YOU UNDERSTAND?

1. What common stock is?
2. What some of the drawbacks are of dividends paid on common stock from the stockholders' point of view?
3. What the difference is between cumulative voting and straight voting of the board of directors?
4. What preferred stock is? How is preferred stock similar to common stock and bonds?

PRIMARY AND SECONDARY STOCK MARKETS

Before common stock can be issued by a corporation, shares must be authorized by a majority vote of both the board of directors and the firm's existing common stockholders. Once authorized, new shares of stock are distributed to existing and new investors through a primary market sale with the help of investment banks. Once issued, the stocks are traded in secondary stock markets (such as the NYSE or NASDAQ—see below).

In this section, we examine the process involved with the primary sale of corporate stock. We also describe the secondary markets, the process by which stocks trade in these markets, and the indexes that are used to summarize secondary stock market value changes.

Primary Markets

3

Primary markets are markets in which corporations raise funds through *new* issues of stocks. The new stock securities are sold to initial investors (suppliers of funds) in exchange for funds (money) that the issuer (user of funds) needs. As illustrated in Figure 9–3, most primary market transactions go through investment banks (e.g., Morgan Stanley or Lehman Brothers—see Chapter 16), which serve as the intermediary between the issuing corporations (fund users) and ultimate investors (fund suppliers) in securities.

primary markets
Markets in which corporations raise funds through new issues of securities.

3. Nevertheless, the cost of preferred stock is lowered because *corporate* investors in preferred stock can shelter up to 70 percent of their dividends against taxes. Some of these tax savings may be "passed back" to the issuing firm in the form of lower required gross dividends. Thus, debt may or may not be a lower cost vehicle for the issuing firm depending on the value of this tax shield to corporate investors.

net proceeds

The guaranteed price at which the investment bank purchases the stock from the issuer.

gross proceeds

The price at which the investment bank resells the stock to investors.

underwriter's spread

The difference between the gross proceeds and the net proceeds.

syndicate

The process of distributing securities through a group of investment banks.

originating house

The lead bank in the syndicate, which negotiates with the issuing company on behalf of the syndicate.

Like the primary sale of bonds (discussed in Chapter 6), the investment bank can conduct a primary market sale of stock using a firm commitment underwriting (where the investment bank guarantees the corporation a price for newly issued securities by buying the whole issue at a fixed price from the corporate issuer) or a best efforts underwriting basis (where the underwriter does not guarantee a price to the issuer and acts more as a placing or distribution agent for a fee). In a firm commitment underwriting, the investment bank purchases the stock from the issuer for a guaranteed price (called the **net proceeds**) and resells them to investors at a higher price (called the **gross proceeds**). The difference between the gross proceeds and the net proceeds (called the **underwriter's spread**) is compensation for the expenses and risks incurred by the investment bank with the issue. In the 1990s, the underwriter's gross spread on first-time equity issues (i.e., private firms going public—the initial public offering or IPO) averaged 7.65 percent and on seasoned equity issues (i.e., publicly traded firms issuing additional shares) averaged 5.67 percent.[4] We discuss these costs in more detail in Chapter 16.

Often an investment bank will bring in a number of other investment banks to help sell and distribute a new issue—called a **syndicate.** For example, the "tombstone" in Figure 9–4 announcing the issue of 5 million shares of common stock in Roper Industries, Inc., lists the syndicate of six investment banks involved in the initial issue. The investment banks are listed according to their degree of participation in the sale of new shares. The lead bank (or "Sole Book-Running Manager") in the syndicate (Merrill Lynch), which directly negotiated with the issuing company on behalf of the syndicate, is called the **originating house.** Once an issue is arranged and its terms set, each member of the syndicate is assigned a given number of shares in the issue for which it is responsible for selling. Shares of stock issued through a syndicate of investment banks spreads the risk associated with the sale of the stock among several investment banks. A syndicate also results in a larger pool of potential outside investors, increasing the probability of a successful sale and widening the scope of the investor base.

A primary market sale may be a first-time issue by a private firm going public (i.e., allowing its equity, some of which was held privately by managers and venture capital investors, to be *publicly* traded in stock markets for the first time). These first-time issues are also referred to as initial public offerings (IPOs—see Chapter 16). For example, in 2004, Google, Inc., announced a $1.67 billion IPO of its common stock, one of the largest high-tech IPOs in history. Alternatively, a primary market sale may be a seasoned offering, in which the firm already has shares of the stock trading in the secondary markets. In both cases, the issuer receives the proceeds of the sale and the primary market investors receive the securities. Like the primary sales of corporate bond issues, corporate stocks may initially be issued through either a public sale (where the stock issue is offered to the general investing public) or a private placement (where stock is sold privately to a limited number of large investors).

In recent years public confidence in the integrity of the IPO process has eroded significantly. Investigations have revealed that certain underwriters of IPOs have engaged in misconduct contrary to the best interests of investors and the markets. Among the most harmful practices giving rise to public concerns are "spinning" (in which certain underwriters allocate "hot" IPO issues to directors and/or executives of potential investment banking clients in exchange for investment banking business) and "biased" recommendations by research analysts (whose compensation is tied to the success of their firms' investment banking business). This culminated in the spring of 2003 with an agreement between securities regulators and 10 of the nation's largest securities firms, in which they agreed to pay a record $1.4 billion in penalties to settle charges involving investor abuses. The settlement centered on civil charges that securities firms routinely issued overly optimistic stock research to investors to gain favor with corporate clients and win their investment banking business.

4. See A. Gande, M. Puri, and A. Saunders, "Bank Entry, Competition and the Market for Corporate Securities Underwriting," *Journal of Financial Economics,* 1999, pp. 165–195; and I. Lee, S. Lockhead, J. Ritter, and Q. Zhao, "The Cost of Raising Capital," *Journal of Financial Research,* Spring 1996, pp. 59–74.

FIGURE 9–4 **Tombstone Announcing the Issuance of Common Stock**

This announcement is under no circumstances to be construed as an offer to sell or as a solicitation of an offer to buy any of these securities.
The offering is made only by the Prospectus Supplement and the Prospectus to which it relates.

New Issue **December 7, 2004**

5,000,000 Shares

ROPER

Common Stock

Price $60.10 Per Share

Copies of the Prospectus Supplement and the Prospectus to which it relates may be obtained in any State or jurisdiction in which this announcement is circulated from only such of the undersigned or other dealers or brokers as may lawfully offer these securities in such State or jurisdiction.

Sole Book-Running Manager

Merrill Lynch & Co.

JPMorgan **Wachovia Securities**

Robert W. Baird & Co.

Friedman Billings Ramsey **KeyBanc Capital Markets**

Source: Roper, Inc., prospectus.

The agreement also settled charges that some major firms improperly allocated IPO shares to corporate executives to win investment banking business from their firms. The agreement forces brokerage companies to make structural changes in the way they handle research—preventing, for example, analysts from attending certain meetings relating to investment banking.[5]

5. Within days of this agreement, however, Bears Stearns, one of the 10 firms party to the settlement, was accused of using its analysts to promote a new stock offering.

preemptive rights

A right of existing stockholders in which new shares must be offered to existing shareholders first in such a way that they can maintain their proportional ownership in the corporation.

Corporate law in some states, and some corporate charters, gives shareholders **preemptive rights** to the new shares of stock when they are issued. This means that before a seasoned offering of stock can be sold to outsiders, the new shares must first be offered to existing shareholders in such a way that they can maintain their proportional ownership in the corporation. A "rights offering" generally allows existing stockholders to purchase shares at a price slightly below the market price. Stockholders can then exercise their rights (buying the allotted shares in the new stock) or sell them. The result can be a low-cost distribution of new shares for a firm (i.e., the issuing firm avoids the expense of an underwritten offering).

EXAMPLE 9-5 Calculation of Shares Purchased through a Rights Offering

Suppose you own 1,000 shares of common stock in a firm with 1 million total shares outstanding. The firm announces its plan to sell an additional 500,000 shares through a rights offering. Thus, each shareholder will be sent 0.5 right for each share of stock owned. One right can then be exchanged for one share of common stock in the new issue.

Your current ownership interest is 0.1 percent (1,000/1 million) prior to the rights offering and you receive 500 rights (1,000 × 0.5) allowing you to purchase 500 of the new shares. If you exercise your rights (buying the 500 shares), your ownership interest in the firm after the rights offering is still 0.1 percent ((1,000 + 500)/(1 million + 500,000)). Thus, the rights offering ensures that every investor can maintain his or her fractional ownership interest in the firm.

Suppose the market value of the common stock is $40 before the rights offering, or the total market value of the firm is $40 million ($40 × 1 million), and the 500,000 new shares are offered to current stockholders at a 10 percent discount, or for $36 per share. The firm receives $18 million. The market value of the firm after the rights offering is $58 million (the original $40 million plus the $18 million from the new shares), or $38.67 per share ($58 million ÷ 1.5 million).

Your 1,000 shares are worth $40,000 ($40 × 1,000) before the rights offering, and you can purchase 500 additional shares for $18,000 ($36 × 500). Thus, your total investment in the firm after the rights offering is $58,000, or $38.67 per share ($58,000 ÷ 1,500).

Suppose you decide not to exercise your preemptive right. Since each right allows a stockholder to buy a new share for $36 per share when the shares are worth $38.67, the value of one right should be $2.67. Should you sell your rights rather than exercise them, you maintain your original 1,000 shares of stock. These have a value after the rights offering of $38,667 (1,000 × 38.67). You could also sell your rights to other investors for $1,333 (500 × $2.67). As a result, you have a total wealth level of $40,000—you have lost no wealth.

In 2004, PriceSmart announced a rights offering to its common stockholders intended to raise $110 million in new stock at a subscription price of $7.00 per share—that is, to issue 15.787 million new shares of common stock. Prior to the rights offering, PriceSmart had 10,524,000 shares of common stock outstanding, and each shareholder received 1 right for each share of stock owned. PriceSmart common stock traded between $7.25 and $9.25 per share during the period of the rights offering. Thus, right holders could purchase new shares in PriceSmart at a discount of between $0.25 and $2.25 from the market price of the stock. These rights could be sold by PriceSmart common stockholders to other investors. Rights are similar to options in that they give the holder the option, but not the obligation, to buy the stock at a fixed price (see Chapter 10). The rights holder has the option of buying the new shares at the stated price, selling the rights to other investors, or letting the rights expire at the end of the offering period unused.

In a public sale of stock, once the issuing firm and the investment bank have agreed on the details of the stock issue, the investment bank must get SEC approval in accordance

FIGURE 9–5 **Getting Shares of Stock to the Investing Public**

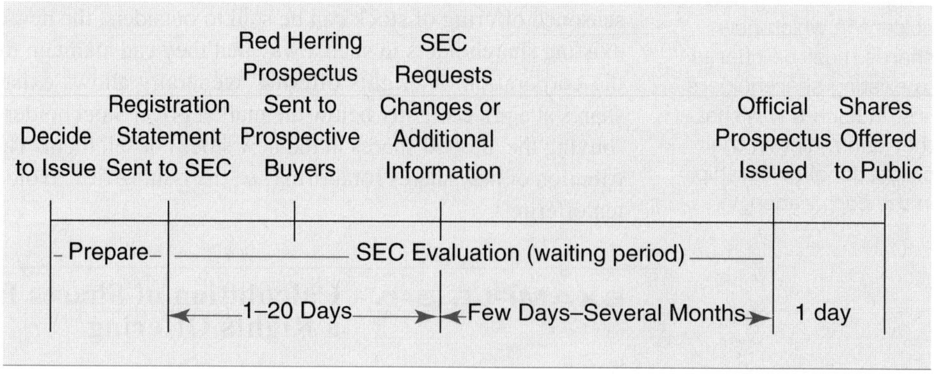

with the Securities and Exchange Act of 1934. Registration of a stock can be a lengthy process. We illustrate the process in Figure 9–5. The process starts with the preparation of the registration statement to be filed with the SEC. The registration statement includes information on the nature of the issuer's business, the key provisions and features of the security to be issued, the risks involved with the security, and background on the management. The focus of the registration statement is on full information disclosure about the firm and the securities issued to the public at large. At the same time that the issuer and its investment bank prepare the registration statement to be filed with the SEC, they prepare a preliminary version of the public offering's prospectus called the **red herring prospectus.** The red herring prospectus is similar to the registration statement but is distributed to potential equity buyers. It is a preliminary version of the official or final prospectus that will be printed upon SEC registration of the issue.

red herring prospectus

A preliminary version of the prospectus describing a new security issue distributed to potential buyers prior to the security's registration.

After submission of the registration statement, the SEC has 20 days to request additional information or changes to the registration statement. It generally takes about 20 days for the SEC to approve a new security issue. First-time or infrequent issuers can sometimes wait up to several months for SEC registration, especially if the SEC keeps requesting additional information and revised red herring prospectuses. This period of review is called the waiting period. However, companies that know the registration process well can generally obtain registration in a few days.

Once the SEC is satisfied with the registration statement, it registers the issue. At this point, the issuer (along with its investment bankers) sets the final selling price on the shares, prints the official prospectus describing the issue, and sends it to all potential buyers of the issue. Upon issuance of the prospectus (generally the day following SEC registration), the shares can be sold.

The period of time between the company's filing of the registration statement with the SEC and the selling of shares is referred to as the "quiet period." Historically, the issuing company could send no written communication to the public during the quiet period other than information regarding the normal course of business. Once a company registered with the SEC for a public offering it could engage in oral communication only. That meant the company executives could go on so-called roadshows to solicit investors or have brokers call potential investors to discuss the offering. But they could not provide any written communication, such as faxes or letters, or give interviews about the company's offering. These rules, adopted in 1933, did not foresee new technology, such as the Internet and e-mail. Moreover, these outdated rules may have hurt investors by giving them too little information. Thus, in October 2004, the SEC proposed a rule change giving large companies (market capitalization of at least $700 million or with at least $1 billion in debt) more freedom to communicate with investors during the quiet period. Specifically, these companies would be allowed to communicate with investors at any time prior to a public offering through

FIGURE 9–6 **Getting Shelf Registrations to the Investing Public**

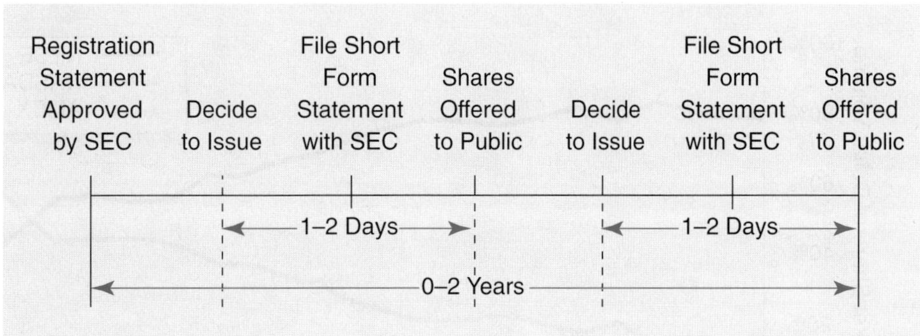

e-mail, letters, even TV ads as long as the information is also filed with the SEC. Such communication was previously prohibited.

Further, in January 2005, the SEC proposed an overhaul in the issuing process for stock IPOs that would facilitate greater use of the Internet to disseminate information to the markets. Although the use of the Internet was not forbidden by the SEC, current rules put issuers in legal jeopardy if they depart from the formal written prospectuses and face-to-face roadshows. Under the new proposed rules, the SEC would formally allow Internet broadcasts of roadshows. These online broadcasts would be open to all investors, not just the chosen few invited to previously closed-door presentations. In fact, the proposed rules encourage broad Internet roadshow dissemination, giving investment banks that open them to the public a break from certain filing requirements. Furthermore, issuers and investment bankers would be able to forgo sending final offering prospectuses to IPO investors. Under the SEC's proposal, issuers would still have to distribute preliminary (red herring) prospectuses to potential investors. But realizing that most investors get offering documents electronically anyway, the SEC wanted to allow issuers to e-mail investors when a stock price is set, tell them their allocations, and point out that a formal prospectus would soon be filed with the SEC.

www.sec.gov

shelf registration

Allows firms that plan to offer multiple issues of stock over a two-year period to submit one registration statement summarizing the firm's financing plans for the period.

secondary stock markets

The markets in which stocks, once issued, are traded—rebought and resold.

In order to reduce the time and cost of registration, yet still protect the public by requiring issuers to disclose information about the firm and the security to be issued, the SEC passed a rule in 1982 allowing for "shelf registration." As illustrated in Figure 9–6, **shelf registration** allows firms that plan to offer multiple issues of stock over a two-year period to submit one registration statement as described above (called a master registration statement). The registration statement summarizes the firm's financing plans for the two-year period. Thus, the securities are shelved for up to two years until the firm is ready to issue them. Once the issuer and its investment bank decide to issue shares during the two-year shelf registration period, they prepare and file a short form statement with the SEC. Upon SEC approval, the shares can be priced and offered to the public usually within one or two days of deciding to take the shares "off the shelf."

Thus, shelf registration allows firms to get stocks onto the market quickly (e.g., in one or two days) if they feel conditions (especially the price they can get for the new stock) are right, without the time lag generally associated with full SEC registration. For example, in January 2005, Array BioPharma, Inc., announced a public offering of 6 million shares of its common stock under its shelf registration filed with the SEC. UBS Investment Bank led the underwriting of shares that were sold just days after this announcement.

Secondary Markets

Secondary stock markets are the markets in which stocks, once issued, are traded—that is, bought and sold by investors. The New York Stock Exchange

FIGURE 9–7 **Dollar Volume of Trading on the NYSE, AMEX, and NASDAQ**

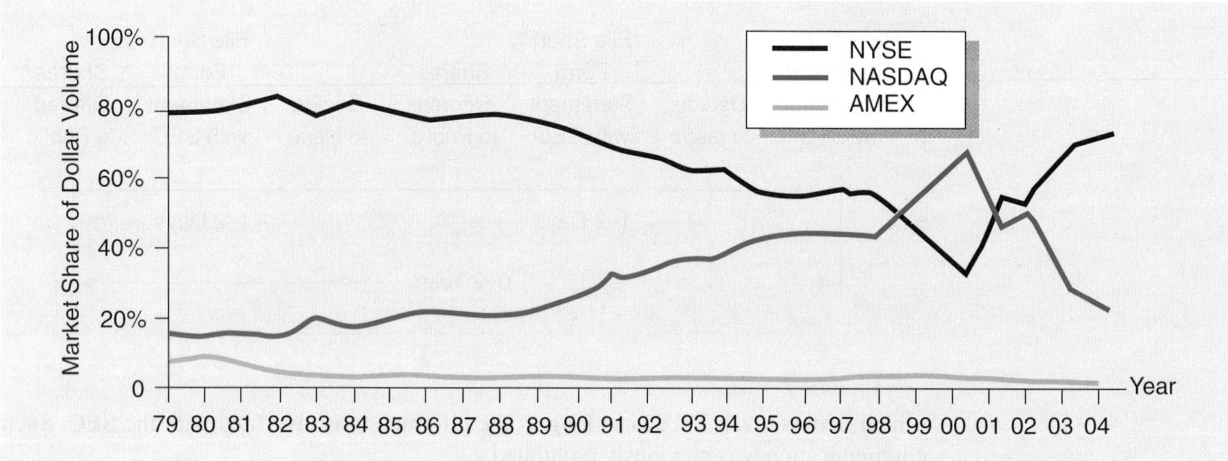

Source: NASDAQ Web site, various dates. **www.nasdaq.com**

(NYSE) and the National Association of Securities Dealers Automated Quotation (NASDAQ) system are well-known examples of secondary markets in stocks.[6]

When a transaction occurs in a secondary stock market, funds are exchanged, usually with the help of a securities broker or firm acting as an intermediary between the buyer and the seller of the stock. The original issuer of the stock is not involved in this transfer of the stocks or the funds. In this section, we look at the major secondary stock markets, the process by which a trade occurs, and the major stock market indexes.

www.nyse.com

www.amex.com

www.nasdaq.com

Stock Exchanges. The three major U.S. stock markets are the New York Stock Exchange (NYSE), the National Association of Securities Dealers Automated Quotation (NASDAQ) system, and the American Stock Exchange (AMEX). Figures 9–7, 9–8, and 9–9 present data comparing the three stock markets. Figure 9–7 shows dollar volume of trading in each market from 1979 through 2004; Figure 9–8 shows share volume in each market from 1975 through 2004; and Figure 9–9 shows the number of companies listed in each market from 1975 through 2004. Obvious from these trading volume and listing figures is that while the NYSE is the premier stock market and the NASDAQ is a strong second market, activity on the AMEX is dropping on all accounts. Other smaller stock exchanges include the Pacific Stock Exchange, the Chicago Stock Exchange, the Philadelphia Stock Exchange, the Boston Stock Exchange, and the Cincinnati Stock Exchange. These account for no more than 5 percent of daily U.S. stock market volume.

Note that the total market value of shares listed in these markets was over $21 trillion at the end of 2004. Although this market looks huge, this represents the value of all stocks ever issued by firms that did not go bankrupt. For example, of this total market value, just over $115 billion of new shares was issued in 2004 (see Table 9–1).

The New York Stock Exchange. Worldwide, the New York Stock Exchange (NYSE) is the most well known of all the organized exchanges in the United States. Over 2,700 different stocks are listed and traded on the NYSE. Table 9–2 summarizes the market activity in the NYSE (as well as the AMEX and NASDAQ) as of the end of 2004. The dollar volume of trading in average daily 2004 was $45.9 billion on 1.5 billion shares traded.

6. On October 30, 1998, the National Association of Securities Dealers, Inc. (NASD) (which at the time owned the NASDAQ market, the world's first electronic stock market) and the American Stock Exchange (AMEX), the nation's second largest floor-based exchange, merged to form the Nasdaq-Amex Market Group. At the time, the two markets shared Web sites, made joint press statements, and collaborated on marketing plans. NASDAQ was also to help develop state-of-the-art technology for AMEX. However, after less than a year there was a clash of cultures between the two markets. In 2000, the NASD sold its ownership of NASDAQ, maintaining its ownership of AMEX. In March 2002, the NASD unsuccessfully approached the NYSE asking it to consider the purchase of AMEX. Unable to find an outside buyer, in 2005 AMEX members purchased the exchange from the NASD.

FIGURE 9–8 Annual Share Volume of Trading on the NYSE, AMEX, and NASDAQ

(in millions of shares traded)

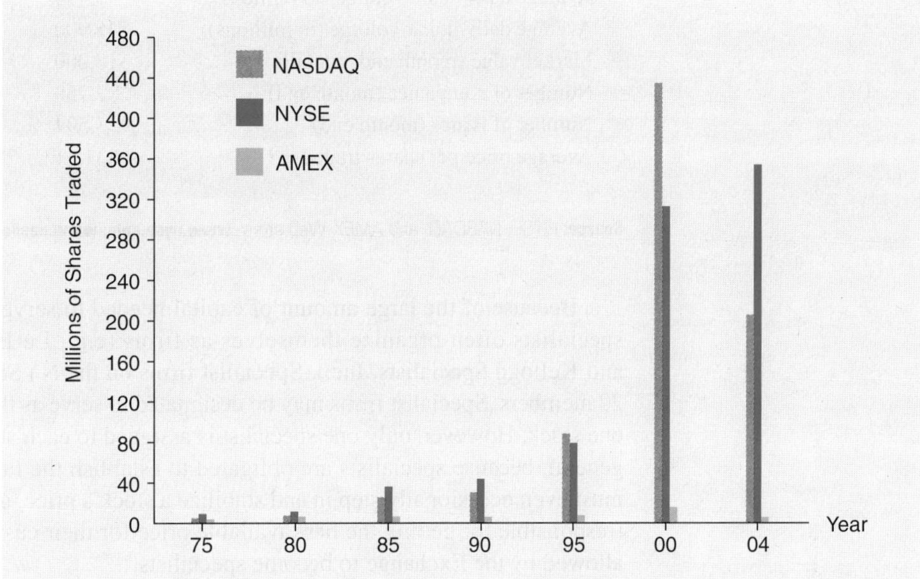

Source: NYSE, NASDAQ, and AMEX Web sites, various dates. **www.nyse.com; www.nasdaq.com; www.amex.com**

5

The Trading Process. All transactions occurring on the NYSE occur at a specific place on the floor of the exchange (called a **trading post**)—see Figure 9–10. Each stock is assigned a special market maker (a **specialist**). The market maker is like a monopolist with the power to arrange the market for the stock. In return, the specialist has an affirmative obligation to stabilize the order flow and prices for the stock in times when the market becomes turbulent (e.g., when there is a large imbalance of sell orders, the specialist has an obligation to buy the stock to stabilize the price).

trading post

A specific place on the floor of the exchange where transactions on the NYSE occur.

specialists

Exchange members who have an obligation to keep the market going, maintaining liquidity in their assigned stock at all times.

FIGURE 9–9 Number of Companies Listed on NYSE, AMEX, and NASDAQ

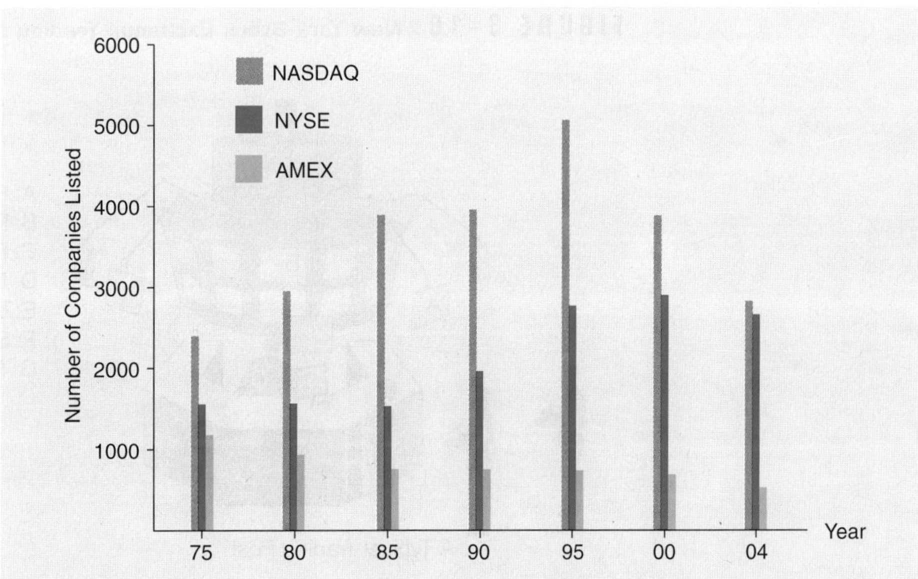

Source: NYSE, NASDAQ, and AMEX Web sites, various dates. **www.nyse.com; www.nasdaq.com; www.amex.com**

TABLE 9–2 Market Activity on the NYSE, AMEX, and NASDAQ

	NYSE	AMEX	NASDAQ
Average daily share volume (in millions)	1,494	69	1,073
Average daily dollar volume (in millions)	$45,900	$2,477	$20,894
Market value (month end) (in billions)	$18,000	$411	$2,990
Number of companies (month end)	2,758	655	3,293
Number of issues (month end)	3,594	807	3,503
Average price per shares traded	$31.51	$36.14	$19.46

Source: NYSE, NASDAQ, and AMEX Web sites. **www.nyse.com; www.nasdaq.com; www.amex.com**

Because of the large amount of capital needed to serve the market-making function, specialists often organize themselves as firms (e.g., Le Branche & Co., Spear, Leeds and Kellogg Specialists, Inc.). Specialist firms on the NYSE range in size from 2 to over 20 members. Specialist firms may be designated to serve as the market maker for more than one stock. However, only one specialist is assigned to each stock listed on the exchange. In general, because specialists are obligated to establish the fair market price of a stock and must even occasionally step in and stabilize a stock's price, underwriters/investment banks (responsible for getting the best available price for their customers' new issues) are rarely allowed by the Exchange to become specialists.

Three types of transactions can occur at a given post: (1) brokers trade on behalf of customers at the "market" price (market order); (2) limit orders are left with a specialist to be executed; and (3) specialists transact for their own account. These types of trades are discussed in more detail below. As of December 2004, 323 firms had representatives "seated" on the floor of the NYSE (230 of the total 1,366 seats dealt with trades sent from the public) at a price of $1.0 million per seat, a nine-year low for a NYSE seat. In 1999 during the stock market boom, the price of a seat rose to $2.6 million. By mid-2005, the price of a seat had risen to $3.0 million.

Generally, as illustrated in Figure 9–11, when individuals want to transact on the NYSE, they contact their broker (such as Merrill Lynch). The broker then sends the order to its representative at the exchange (called a commission broker) or to a floor broker (working for themselves) to conduct the trade with the appropriate specialist or market

FIGURE 9–10 New York Stock Exchange Trading Post

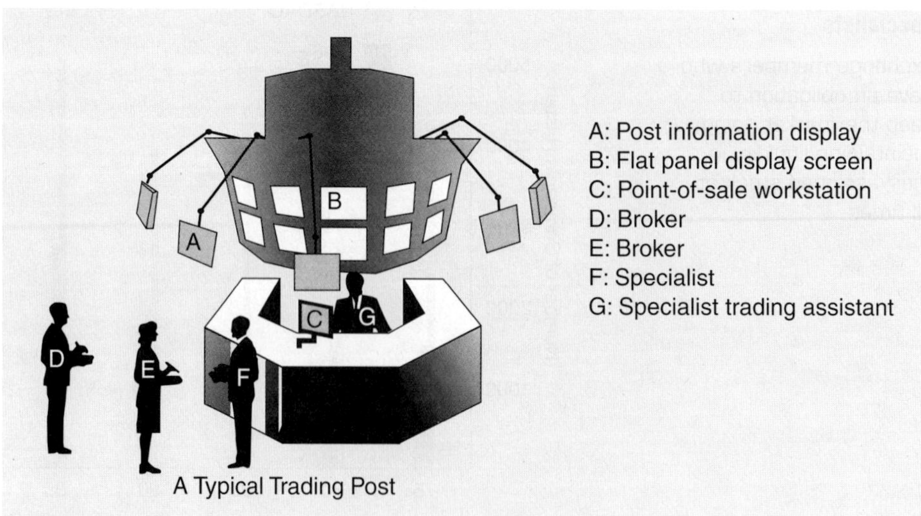

Source: The New York Stock Exchange Web site, August 1999. **www.nyse.com**

FIGURE 9–11 Purchase of a Stock on the NYSE

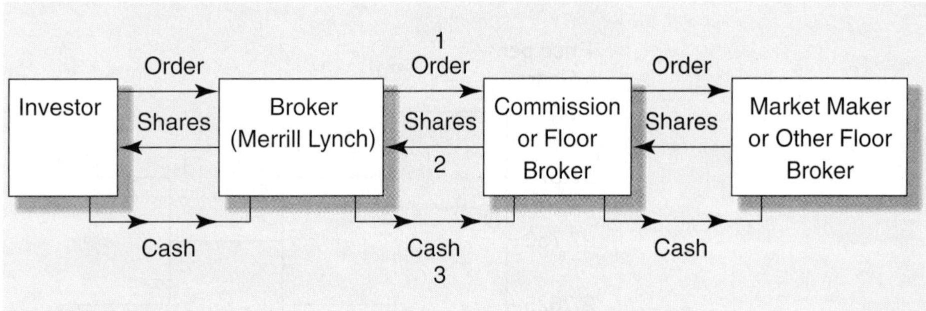

maker in the stock. Large brokerage firms generally own several "seats" on the floor filled by their commission brokers trading orders for the firm's clients or its own accounts. One of the specialist's jobs is to execute orders for floor and commission brokers. However, these brokers can transact at a post with others without specialist participation. Specialists participate in only about 10 percent of all shares traded. Also, orders are increasingly coming from the public using online (Internet) trading, bypassing the commission broker and going directly to the floor broker (see Chapter 16).

Once the transaction is completed (generally in less than 15 minutes), the investor's broker is contacted and the trade is confirmed. Generally, the transaction is settled in three days (so-called settlement at T + 3)—that is, the investor has three days to pay for the stock and the floor or commission broker has three days to deliver the stock to the investor's broker.

market order

An order to transact at the best price available when the order reaches the post.

The vast majority of orders sent to floor or commission brokers are of two types: market orders or limit orders. A **market order** is an order for the broker and the market specialist to transact at the best price available when the order reaches the post. The floor or commission broker will go to the post and conduct the trade. Before 2005, the best price meant that brokers were required to enter only their very best bid and offer prices for a stock at a specified time into a public electronic database of stock quotes. In 2004, the SEC proposed an overhaul of the rules that radically altered the way the best price would be established: Brokers seeking the best price on a trade would have to enter all their bids and offers for a stock into the public database. This would enable other brokers who want to fill orders, including large block trades, to "sweep" all markets for the best price and to simultaneously execute trades in the same stock across different markets. The so-called intermarket sweep would allow brokers to pick off the best prices among all accessible quotes. So a customer (like an individual investor) who wants to buy shares of stock could get chunks of that order filled at the best price across various markets. The change introduces more computerization into the trading process and reduces the amount of NYSE trading conducted via the auction system overseen by specialist firms.

limit order

An order to transact at a specified price.

A **limit order** is an order to transact only at a specified price (the limit price). When a floor or commission broker receives a limit order, he or she will stand by the post with the order if the current price is near the limit price. When the current price is not near the limit price, a floor or commission broker does not want to stand at the post for hours (and even days) waiting for the current price to equal the limit price on this single limit order. In this case, the floor broker enters the limit order on the order book of the specialist at the post. The specialist, who is at the post at all times when the market is open, will monitor the current price of the stock and conduct the trade when, and if, it equals the limit price. Some limit orders are submitted with time limits. If the order is not filled by the time date for expiration, it is deleted from the market maker's book.[7] The third type of trade is that of a specialist trading for his or her own account.

7. Similar to a limit order, a stop order is an order to sell a stock when its price falls to a particular point.

FIGURE 9–12 Price on a Market Order versus a Limit Order

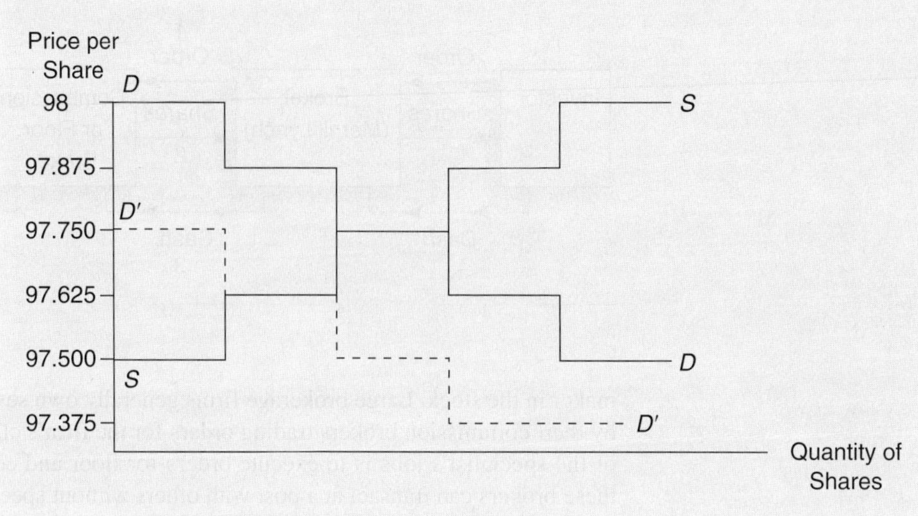

Figure 9–12 illustrates the link between a market order and a limit order. When a market order is placed, the transaction occurs at the current market price, $97.75 per share, determined by the intersection of investors' aggregate supply (*S*) of and demand (*D*) for the stock. If the limit order price (e.g., $97.625 per share) differs from the current market price, the order is placed on the specialist's book. If supply and/or demand conditions change (e.g., the demand curve in Figure 9–12 falls to *D*′) such that the market price falls to $97.625 per share, the specialist completes the limit order and notifies the floor broker who submitted the order.

Program Trading. The NYSE has defined program trading as the simultaneous buying and selling of a portfolio of at least 15 different stocks valued at more than $1 million, using computer programs to initiate the trades. For example, program trading can be used to create portfolio insurance. A program trader can take a long position in a portfolio of stocks and a short position in a stock index futures contract (see Chapter 10). Should the market value of the stock portfolio fall, these losses are partly offset by the position in the futures contract. The timing of these trades is determined by the computer program.

Program trading has been criticized for its impact on stock market prices and increased volatility. For example, on Tuesday, April 25, 1997, the Dow Jones Industrial Average (DJIA), discussed below, rose 173.38 points, at the time the biggest price increase in the 1990s. That day saw no significant new economic information and, while several companies announced earnings results that were better than expected, these announcements were not significant enough on their own to explain the large price increase. Rather, it was computer-driven program trading that was given the credit for the large change in the index. On June 27, 1994, a single program trade executed on the NYSE pushed the DJIA down almost 30 points. The program trade took place around noon on a trading day that saw less then 300 million shares traded. This trade was followed by two other sell orders via program trades. Together, the three program trades drove the DJIA down 55 points before ending the day down 34 points to 3708. Critics argue that whenever the market has a disturbance and investors are hesitant to trade, program traders accelerate activity and have a significant impact on stock market values.

As a result of the potential for increased volatility created by program trading, the New York Stock Exchange introduced trading curbs (or circuit breakers) on trading. Trading curbs are limitations placed on trading when the DJIA falls significantly. For example in the first quarter of 2005, a 1,050-point drop in the DJIA before 2 p.m. would halt trading for one hour or for 30 minutes if the drop occurred between 2 and 2:30 p.m.; and a drop occurring at 2:30 p.m. or later would have no effect. A 2,150-point drop in the DJIA before 1 p.m. would halt trading for two hours; for one hour if the drop occurs between 1 and 2 p.m.; and the remainder of the day if the drop occurs at 2:30 p.m. or later. A 3,200-point drop in the DJIA would halt trading for the remainder of the day regardless of when the decline occurs.

In the late 1980s, about 15 million shares were traded per day on the NYSE as program trades. At the end of 2004, average daily volume of program trading was 811.5 million shares (44.9 percent of the total average daily volume). The most active program traders are investment banks (e.g., UBS, Morgan Stanley) conducting trades for their own accounts or those of their customers (e.g., insurance companies, hedge funds, pension funds). Much of this program trading involves index funds (e.g., Vanguard's 500 Index Fund, which seeks to replicate the S&P 500 Index—see below) and futures contracts on various indexes (e.g., S&P 500 Index futures—see Chapter 10). Investment in these index funds grew in the 1980s and 1990s as a result of the relatively poor performance (in terms of returns) of specialized mutual funds (see Chapter 17) and the strong performance in the major indexes.

Stock Market Quote. Table 9–3 presents a small part of a NYSE stock quote list from *The Wall Street Journal* summarizing trading on Thursday, December 30, 2004. Column 1 lists the year-to-date percentage change in the stock price (e.g., Amerisource Berger Corporation's stock price increased 4.3 percent between January 1 and December 30, 2004). Columns 2 and 3 of the stock quote show the high and low closing price on the listed stocks over the previous (from December 30, 2004) 52 weeks. Share prices and price changes are recorded in cents. As of September 2000, the NYSE started phasing in decimalization of stock quotes in which equity securities prices were quoted in a decimal format—$64.50, with increments of one cent per share. Column 4 lists the name of the corporation and its ticker symbol. When trades are recorded on a stock, the ticker symbol is used rather than the company name. Column 5, labeled DIV, is the annual dividend per share based on the most recent dividend payment (e.g., Amerisource Berger Corp. paid dividends of $0.10 per share on its common stock during the 12 months preceding December 30, 2004). Column 6, labeled YLD %, is the dividend yield on the stock (equal to the annual dividends per year divided by the closing stock price (e.g., for Amerisource Berger Corp., .10 ÷ 58.54 = 0.2 percent)). Column 7 is the firm's P/E ratio—the ratio of the company's closing price to earnings per share over the previous year (e.g., Amerisource Berger Corp.'s P/E ratio is reported to be 14; Amerisource Berger's price—the numerator of the P/E ratio—is reported as 58.54; thus, Amerisource Berger Corp.'s earnings per share—the denominator of the P/E ratio—over the period December 2003 through December 2004 must have been $4.18 per share: $E = P \div P/E = \$58.54 \div 14$). The P/E ratio is used by traders as an indicator of the relative value of the stock. High P/E ratio stocks reflect the market's expectation of growth in earnings. Should earnings expectations fail to materialize, these stocks will see a price drop. Low P/E ratio stocks generally have low earnings growth expectations. Column 8, VOL 100s, lists the day's trading volume in 100s of shares (e.g., 1,566,900 shares of Amerisource Berger Corp. traded on December 30, 2004). Normally, shares are traded in "round" lots of 100. Column 9, CLOSE, is the price on the last transaction to occur (the close) on December 30, 2004. Finally, Column 10, NET CHG, is the change in the closing price from the previous day's closing price (in cents).

www.amex.com

The American Stock Exchange. The American Stock Exchange (AMEX), located in New York, generally lists stocks of smaller firms that are of national interest. It is organized as a floor broker-specialist market-maker system like the NYSE. As of December 2004, stocks of 807 issues were trading on the AMEX. Figures 9–7 through 9–9 show the diminishing size and importance of the AMEX. Average daily share volume on the AMEX in December 2004 (69 million shares), as seen in Table 9–2, was approximately 4 percent of the shares traded on the NYSE. Average daily dollar volume on the AMEX in December 2004 ($2,477 million) was 5 percent of that on the NYSE.

TABLE 9-3 Stock Market Quote, December 30, 2004

(1) YTD % CHG	(2) 52-WEEK HI	(3) 52-WEEK LO	(4) STOCK (SYM)	(5) DIV	(6) YLD %	(7) PE	(8) VOL 100s	(9) CLOSE	(10) NET CHG
4.3	64.50	49.74	AmeriSrcBrg ABC	.10	.2	14	15669	58.54	0.54
10.7	40.47	27.77	AmeronInt AMN	.80	2.1	42	148	38.41	-0.32
29.9	45.99	34.63	AmerUsGp A AMH	.40	.9	11	1675	45.44	-0.24
47.7	36.23	22.99	Ametek AME s	.24	.7	...	3741	35.65	-0.03
-7.2	21.56	10.70	AMN Hlthcare AHS		...	28	544	15.92	-0.03
7.2	14.51	12.50	AmpcoPgh AP	.40	2.7	98	32	14.66	0.16
14.6	37.52	27.90	Amphenol APH s		...	22	1619	36.64	0.04
46.5	24	15.27	AMREP AXR	.40e	1.7	11	22	23.20	-0.38
6.4	27	21.91	AmSoBcp ASO	1.00f	3.8	15	4596	26.08	0.14
-15.8	17.33	9.62	Amvescap AVZ	.33e	2.7	...	333	12.41	0.12
27.1	71.55	48	AnadrkPete APC	.56	.9	11	10658	64.85	-0.27
-18.9	52.37	31.36	AnalogDevcs ADI	.24	.6	25	20925	37.03	0.39
23.6	27.77	21.10	↑Angelica AGL	.44	1.6	49	138	27.19	-0.03
-22.5	48.25	29.91	↑AngGldAsh ADS AU	.75e	2.1	...	6689	36.17	-0.33
-3.4	54.74	49.42	AnheuserB BUD	.98	1.9	19	13006	50.87	0.21
47.5	39.35	24.28	AnixterIntl AXE	1.50e	4.1	23	2226	36.20	-0.10
7.7	21.22	15.94	AnnalyMtg NLY	2.00	10.1	10	10352	19.82	0.12
-18.1	31.43	19.98	AnnTaylor ANN s		...	14	6936	21.30	-0.02
17.7	42.39	27.01	AnteonIntl ANT		...	31	2402	42.43	0.28
11.4	13.10	10.38	↑AnthracitCap AHR	1.12	9.1	28	1388	12.33	-0.05
-23.5	14.28	10.01	AnworthMtg ANH	1.08	10.1	8	3455	10.65	...
-1.3	29.44	18.15	AON Cp AOC	.60	2.5	11	6078	23.64	...
24.6	55.16	36.79	↑ApacheCp APA s	.32	.6	12	9437	50.54	-0.07
12.6	38.80	26.45	↑ApartmtInv AIV	2.40	6.2	33	3645	38.83	0.03
-28.0	14.30	3.60	Applica APN		...	dd	3881	5.47	0.12
1.3	24.44	17.76	ApBioApplera ABI	.17	.8	23	5064	20.98	0.13
72.4	32	13.13	ApldIndTch AIT s	.37	1.4	21	2560	27.42	-0.16
17.3	34.95	26.25	ApriaHlthcr AHG		...	15	3315	33.40	-0.38
37.1	54.89	36.71	AptarGp ATR	.60	1.1	22	303	53.47	0.10
10.9	24.11	18.90	AquaAmer WTR	.52f	2.1	30	1857	24.51	0.51
9.7	4.86	2.25	Aquila ILA		...	dd	7340	3.72	0.01
7.6	39.61	28.36	Aracruz ADS ARA	2.18e	5.8	20	736	37.70	0.05
-3.5	29.35	21.18	Aramark RMK	.22f	.8	19	3797	26.47	-0.10
-5.8	45.90	31.29	Arbitron ARB		...	21	919	39.30	-0.21
20.7	24.56	18.05	ArborRltyTr ABR n	.78e	3.2	...	341	24.75	0.21
11.7	30.87	23.41	ArchChem ARJ	.80	2.8	22	366	28.65	0.18
11.6	39	26.20	ArchCoal ACI	.32	.9	19	6784	34.80	-0.31
46.9	22.31	14.90	ArcherDan ADM	.30	1.3	24	12583	22.36	0.43
38.5	38.25	25.67	ArcstneSmt ASN	1.72a	4.6	17	9536	37.74	0.09
22.3	37.82	25.85	↑ArdenRlty ARI	2.02	5.4	45	2225	37.12	0.07

How to Read the Stock Tables

The following explanations apply to the New York and American exchange listed issues and the Nasdaq Stock Market. NYSE and Amex prices are composite quotations that include trades on the Chicago, Pacific, Philadelphia, Boston and National (NSX) exchanges and reported by the National Association of Securities Dealers.

Boldfaced quotations highlight those issues whose price changed by 5% or more if their previous closing price was $2 or higher.

Underlined quotations are those stocks with large changes in volume, per exchange, compared with the issue's average trading volume. The calculation includes common stocks of $5 a share or more with an average volume over 65 trading days of at least 5,000 shares. The underlined quotations are for the 40 largest volume percentage leaders on the NYSE and the Nasdaq National Market. It includes the 20 largest volume percentage gainers on the Amex.

YTD percentage change reflects the stock price percentage change for the calendar year to date, adjusted for stock splits and dividends over 10%.

The 52-week high and low columns show the highest and lowest price of the issue during the preceding 52 weeks plus the current week, but not the latest trading day. These ranges are adjusted to reflect stock payouts of 1% or more, and cash dividends or other distributions of 10% or more.

Dividend/Distribution rates, unless noted, are annual disbursements based on the last monthly, quarterly, semiannual, or annual declaration. Special or extra dividends or distributions, including return of capital, special situations or payments not designated as regular are identified by footnotes.

Yield is defined as the dividends or other distributions paid by a company on its securities, expressed as a percentage of price.

The P/E ratio is determined by dividing the closing market price by the company's diluted per-share earnings, as available, for the most recent four quarters. Charges and other adjustments usually are excluded when they qualify as extraordinary items under generally accepted accounting rules.

Sales figures are the unofficial daily total of shares traded, quoted in hundreds (two zeros omitted; f-four zeros omitted.)

Exchange ticker symbols are shown for all New York and American exchange common stocks, and Dow Jones News/Retrieval symbols are listed for Class A and Class B shares listed on both markets. Nasdaq symbols are listed for all Nasdaq NMS issues. A more detailed explanation of Nasdaq ticker symbols appears with the NMS listings.

Footnotes:
↑-New 52-week high.
↓-New 52-week low.
a-Extra dividend or extras in addition to the regular dividend.
b-indicates annual rate of the cash dividend and that a stock dividend was paid.
c-Liquidating dividend.
cc-P/E ratio is 100 or more.
dd-Loss in the most recent four quarters.
e-Indicates a dividend was declared in the preceding 12 months, but that there isn't a regular dividend rate. Amount shown may have been adjusted to reflect stock split, spinoff or other distribution.
FD-First day of trading.
f-Annual rate, increased on latest declaration.
g-Indicates the dividend and earnings are expressed in Canadian money. The stock trades in U.S. dollars. No yield or P/E ratio is shown.
gg-Special sales condition; no regular way trading.
h-Does not meet continued listing standards
i-indicates amount declared or paid after a stock dividend or split.
j-Indicates dividend was paid this year, and that at the last dividend meeting a dividend was omitted or deferred.
k-Indicates dividend declared this year on cumulative issues with dividends in arrears.
lf-Late filing
m-Annual rate, reduced on latest declaration.
n-Newly issued in the past 52 weeks. The high-low range begins with the start of trading and doesn't cover the entire period.
p-Initial dividend; no yield calculated.
pf-Preferred.
pp-Holder owes installment(s) of purchase price.
pr-Preference.
q-Temporary exemption from Nasdaq requirements.
r-Indicates a cash dividend declared in the preceding 12 months, plus a stock dividend.
rt-Rights.
s-Stock split or stock dividend, or cash or cash equivalent distribution, amounting to 10% or more in the past 52 weeks. The high-low price is adjusted from the old stock. Dividend calculations begin with the date the split was paid or the stock dividend occured.
stk-Paid in stock in the last 12 months. Company doesn't pay cash dividend.
t-NYSE bankruptcy
un-Units.
v-Trading halted on primary market.
vj-In bankruptcy or receivership or being reorganized under the Bankruptcy Code, or securities assumed by such companies.
wd-When distributed.
wi-When issued.
wt-Warrants.
ww-With warrants.
x-Ex-dividend, ex-distribution, ex-rights or without warrants.
z-Sales in full, not in 100s.

Source: *The Wall Street Journal*, December 31, 2004, p. C5. Reprinted by permission of *The Wall Street Journal*. **www.wsj.com**

www.nasdaq.com

The NASDAQ and OTC Market. Securities not sold on one of the organized exchanges such as the NYSE and AMEX are traded over the counter (OTC). Unlike the centralized NYSE and AMEX exchanges, the over-the-counter markets do not have a physical trading floor. Rather, transactions are completed via an electronic market. The NASDAQ (National Association of Securities Dealers Automated Quotation) market is the world's first electronic stock market. The NASDAQ system provides continuous trading for the most active stocks traded over the counter. Indeed, as seen in Figures 9–7 through 9–9, the NASDAQ currently has more firms listed than the NYSE. Further, during the tech boom in the late 1990s, the dollar and share volume of trading on the NASDAQ exceeded that on the NYSE. As the tech boom crashed in the early 2000s, however, the NYSE again saw the greatest dollar and share volume of trading.

5 The NASDAQ market is primarily a dealer market, in which dealers are the market makers who stand ready to buy or sell particular securities. Unlike the NYSE (or AMEX), many dealers, in some cases more than 20, will make a market for a single stock—that is, quote a bid (buy) and ask (sell) price. There are no limits on the number of stocks a NASDAQ market maker can trade or on the number of market makers in a particular stock. A NASDAQ broker or dealer may also be a member of an organized exchange (e.g., the NYSE). Moreover, the original underwriter of a new issue can also become the dealer in the secondary market—unlike the NYSE, which seeks a separation between underwriters and dealers.[8] Anyone who meets the fairly low capital requirements for market makers on the NASDAQ can register to be a broker-dealer.

An individual wanting to make a trade contacts his or her broker. The broker then contacts a dealer in the particular security to conduct the transaction. In contrast to the NYSE and AMEX, the NASDAQ structure of dealers and brokers results in the NASDAQ being a negotiated market (e.g., quotes from several dealers are usually obtained before a transaction is made). When a request for a trade is received, a dealer will use the NASDAQ electronic communications network (ECN) to find the dealers providing the inside quotes—the lowest ask and the highest bid. The dealer may also request the quotes of every market maker in the stock. The dealer initiating the trade will then contact the dealer offering the best price and execute the order. The dealer will confirm the transaction with the investor's broker and the customer will be charged that quote plus a commission for the broker's services. Like exchange trading, online (Internet) trading services now allow investors to trade directly with a securities dealer without going through a personal broker.

Because of a lack of liquidity in the NASDAQ market after the 1987 market crash, and the negative impact this had on the ability of small traders to transact in this market, NASDAQ implemented a mandatory system, the Small Order Execution System (SOES), to provide automatic order execution for individual traders with orders of less than or equal to 1000 shares. Market makers must accept SOES orders, which means small investors and traders are provided with excellent liquidity. The SOES allows small investors and traders to compete on a level playing field for access to NASDAQ orders and execution.

For even smaller firms, NASDAQ maintains an electronic "OTC bulletin board," which is not part of the NASDAQ market but is a means for brokers and dealers to get and post current price quotes over a computer network. Roughly 30,000 stocks trade on the over-the-counter market, which allows any security to be traded. The OTC market is not a formal exchange. There are no membership requirements for trading or listing requirements for securities. Thousands of brokers register with the SEC as dealers in OTC securities, quoting prices at which they are willing to buy or sell securities. A broker executes a trade by contacting a dealer listing an attractive quote. The smallest stocks are listed on "pink sheets" distributed through the National Association of Securities Dealers. These OTC quotations of stock are recorded manually and published daily on pink sheets by which dealers communicate their interest in trading at various prices.

8. A study by K. Ellis, R. Michaely, and M. O'Hara, "When the Underwriter Is the Market Maker: An Examination of Trading in the IPO Aftermarket," *Journal of Finance,* 2002, pp. 1039–1074, finds that the lead underwriter always becomes a market maker in a new issue and, in fact, becomes the most active dealer in issues it brings to the NASDAQ market.

Choice of Market Listing. Firms listed with the NYSE and AMEX markets must meet the listing requirements of the exchange. The requirements are extensive and can be found at the Web sites of the exchanges. The basic qualifications are based on such characteristics as firm market value, earnings, total assets, number of shares outstanding, number of shareholders, and trading volume. An NYSE-listed firm may also have its securities listed on regional exchanges. There are several reasons that NYSE listing is attractive to a firm: improved marketability of the firm's stock (making it more valuable); publicity for the firm, which could result in increased sales; and improved access to the financial markets, as firms find it easier to bring new issues of listed stock to the market.

The requirements for AMEX listing are generally less stringent than those for the NYSE. Thus, AMEX-listed firms tend to be smaller, less well known (therefore less traded), and often younger than NYSE firms.

Firms that do not meet the requirements for NYSE or AMEX exchange listing trade on the NASDAQ. Thus, most NASDAQ firms are smaller, of regional interest, or unable to meet the listing requirements of the organized exchanges. Many NASDAQ companies are newly registered public issues with only a brief history of trading. Over time, many of these apply for NYSE listing. Not all companies eligible to be listed on the NYSE actually do so. Some companies—for example, Microsoft—believe that the benefits of exchange listing (improved marketability, publicity) are not significant. Others prefer not to release the financial information required by the exchanges for listing.

Electronic Communication Networks and Online Trading. The major stock markets currently open at 9:30 a.m. eastern standard time and close at 4:00 p.m. eastern standard time. Extended-hours trading involves any securities transaction that occurs outside these regular trading hours. Almost all extended-hours trading is processed through computerized alternative trading systems (ATS), also known as electronic communications networks (ECNs) such as Archipelago, the Island, and Instinet. Nine equity ECNs are currently in operation. ECNs are computerized systems that automatically match orders between buyers and sellers and serve as an alternative to traditional market making and floor trading. They are also the major vehicles for extended-hours trading. ECNs account for approximately 38 percent of all NASDAQ transactions and almost all extended-hours trading, which averages 70 million shares per day. The majority of stocks traded on ECNs are NASDAQ-listed securities. Regulations limit the trading of exchanged-listed (e.g., NYSE) stocks on ECNs. However, these securities are beginning to find their way onto ECNs as several exchange-related rules are relaxed. ECNs were initially developed as private trading systems for institutional investors and brokers. However, they have opened their systems in varying degrees to include a greater number of institutions as well as individual investors. In April 2005, the NYSE announced that it would acquire Archipelago and the NASDAQ announced that it would acquire Instinet. Pressure on traditional markets like the NYSE and NASDAQ to match the rise of cheaper, faster computer systems for electronically matching stock trades of investors (like those used by Archipelago and Instinet) drove these acquisitions.

As a result of the increased availability of computer technology to individual as well as professional traders in the 1990s, online stock trading via the Internet became one of the biggest growth areas for financial service firms in the late 1990s and into the 2000s. For example, the number of online investment accounts in the United States increased from 3 million in 1997 to 18 million in 2000. However, with the drop in the stock markets after March 2001, growth in online trading activity fell. For example, the number of individuals who traded on the Internet on a typical day decreased 67 percent between March 2001 and September 2002. As the stock market improved in 2003, Internet trading again increased. At the end of 2004, online investment accounts numbered 11 million. However, 6 of 10 online traders stated that they wanted the option of speaking with a broker in person.[9] Online trading is an area of stock trading that is not likely to go away. The Internet will continue to produce opportunities for investors to communicate with their financial advisors and enact trades without incurring the cost of an office visit. For example, the top-level accounts offered by E*Trade now enable customers to view all of

9. See "Online Trading: Investors Take Charge," by Lynn Woods, *Kiplinger's Personal Finance,* January 2003, p. 28.

TABLE 9–4 Major Stock Market Indexes

Major Stock Indexes

Dow Jones Averages	DAILY HIGH	LOW	CLOSE	NET CHG	% CHG	52-WEEK HIGH	LOW	% CHG	YTD % CHG
30 Industrials	10850.18	10799.71	10800.30	- 28.89	- 0.27	10854.54	9749.99	+ 3.31	+ 3.31
20 Transportations	3823.96	3798.74	3808.60	- 1.69	- 0.04	3811.62	2750.80	+26.66	+26.66
15 Utilities	337.79	335.99	336.86	+ 0.70	+ 0.21	336.86	261.89	+26.21	+26.21
65 Composite	3417.78	3404.54	3405.08	- 3.77	- 0.11	3412.44	2852.12	+13.47	+13.47
Dow Jones Indexes									
Wilshire 5000	12010.55	11980.87	11987.82	+ 5.84	+ 0.05	11987.82	10293.52	+11.00	+11.00
US Total Market	290.31	289.60	289.74	+ 0.11	+ 0.04	289.74	250.37	+10.30	+10.30
US Large-Cap	260.80	260.08	260.11	- 0.02	- 0.01	260.21	229.69	+ 7.75	+ 7.75
US Mid-Cap	371.00	369.73	370.71	+ 0.66	+ 0.18	370.71	301.79	+18.47	+18.47
US Small-Cap	415.36	414.18	414.85	+ 0.31	+ 0.07	415.01	335.75	+15.98	+15.98
US Growth	1094.80	1091.99	1092.49	+ 0.31	+ 0.03	1092.49	944.85	+ 6.94	+ 6.94
US Value	1526.69	1522.96	1523.39	+ 0.16	+ 0.01	1523.39	1308.11	+12.88	+12.88
Global Titans 50	195.90	195.22	195.27	+ 0.07	+ 0.04	195.41	176.36	+ 5.77	+ 5.67
Asian Titans 50	119.72	117.62	119.55	+ 1.93	+ 1.64	119.55	98.30	+13.19	+13.22
DJ STOXX 50	2781.86	2774.47	2774.77	- 2.74	- 0.10	2804.06	2541.84	+ 4.30	+ 4.30
Nasdaq Stock Market									
Nasdaq Comp	2182.37	2176.40	2178.34	+ 1.34	+ 0.06	2178.34	1752.49	+ 8.73	+ 8.73
Nasdaq 100	1628.74	1621.58	1623.76	- 1.19	- 0.07	1627.46	1304.43	+10.62	+10.62
Biotech	774.21	771.13	771.88	- 0.89	- 0.12	845.11	622.19	+ 6.59	+ 6.59
Computer	968.10	965.11	965.49	+ 0.45	+ 0.05	1012.13	768.60	+ 3.27	+ 3.27
Standard & Poor's Indexes									
500 Index	1216.47	1213.41	1213.55	+ 0.10	+ 0.01	1213.55	1063.23	+ 9.14	+ 9.14
MidCap 400	664.73	661.95	664.50	+ 1.53	+ 0.23	664.50	549.51	+15.36	+15.36
SmallCap 600	329.86	328.92	329.01	- 0.29	- 0.09	329.58	263.47	+21.67	+21.67
SuperComp 1500	272.90	272.24	272.32	+ 0.06	+ 0.02	272.32	236.65	+10.11	+10.11
New York Stock Exchange and Others									
NYSE Comp	7265.41	7242.22	7253.56	+ 11.32	+ 0.16	7253.56	6217.06	+12.63	+12.63
NYSE Financial	7508.23	7476.92	7492.91	+ 15.90	+ 0.21	7492.91	6322.00	+12.23	+12.23
Russell 2000	654.45	652.99	653.06	- 0.28	- 0.04	654.57	517.10	+17.26	+17.26
Value Line	405.34	404.05	404.84	+ 0.66	+ 0.16	404.84	332.98	+11.63	+11.63
Amex Comp	n.a.	n.a.	1430.07	+ 3.34	+ 0.23	1426.73	1160.18	+21.86	+21.86

Source: *The Wall Street Journal,* Friday, December 31, 2004, p. C2. Reprinted by permission of The Wall Street Journal © 2004 Dow Jones & Company, Inc. All Rights Reserved Worldwide. **www.wsj.com**

their E*Trade accounts. A client with multiple brokerage accounts as well as bank accounts can view balances for all of these accounts. Customers can also see, in real time, the value of each account, the total value of all accounts together, and how account values have changed.

Stock Market Indexes

6

A stock market index is the composite value of a group of secondary market-traded stocks. Movements in a stock market index provide investors with information on movements of a broader range of secondary market securities. Table 9–4 shows a listing of some major stock market indexes as of December 30, 2004. Figure 9–13 shows the trends in some of these indexes (the Dow Jones Industrial Average, the NYSE Composite Index,[10] the S&P Composite Index, the NASDAQ Composite Index, and the Wilshire 5000 Index) from 1989 through 2004. Notice that movements in these indexes are highly correlated over the 15-year period. Notice also that the correlation of the NASDAQ index deviated from the others in the late 1990s and early 2000s as technology stocks (listed mainly on the NASDAQ) soared in value (rising from 2300 in January 1999 to over 5000 by March 2000) then fell back to 1423 in September 2001. Indeed, notice that after a five-year period of unprecedented growth (1995–2000) for all of these indexes, the early 2000s, and the downturn in the U.S. economy, produced little growth of these indexes. As the U.S. economy picked up through the first decade of the 2000s, however, all four indexes grew steadily.

www.dowjones.com

www.nyse.com

www.standardandpoors.com

www.nasdaq.com

www.wilshire.com

10. Figure 9–13 does not incorporate the change in base value from 50 to 5,000 on the NYSE Composite Index on December 31, 2002 (see below).

FIGURE 9–13 **DJIA, NYSE Composite Index, S&P Composite Index, NASDAQ Composite Index, and Wilshire 5000 Index Values**

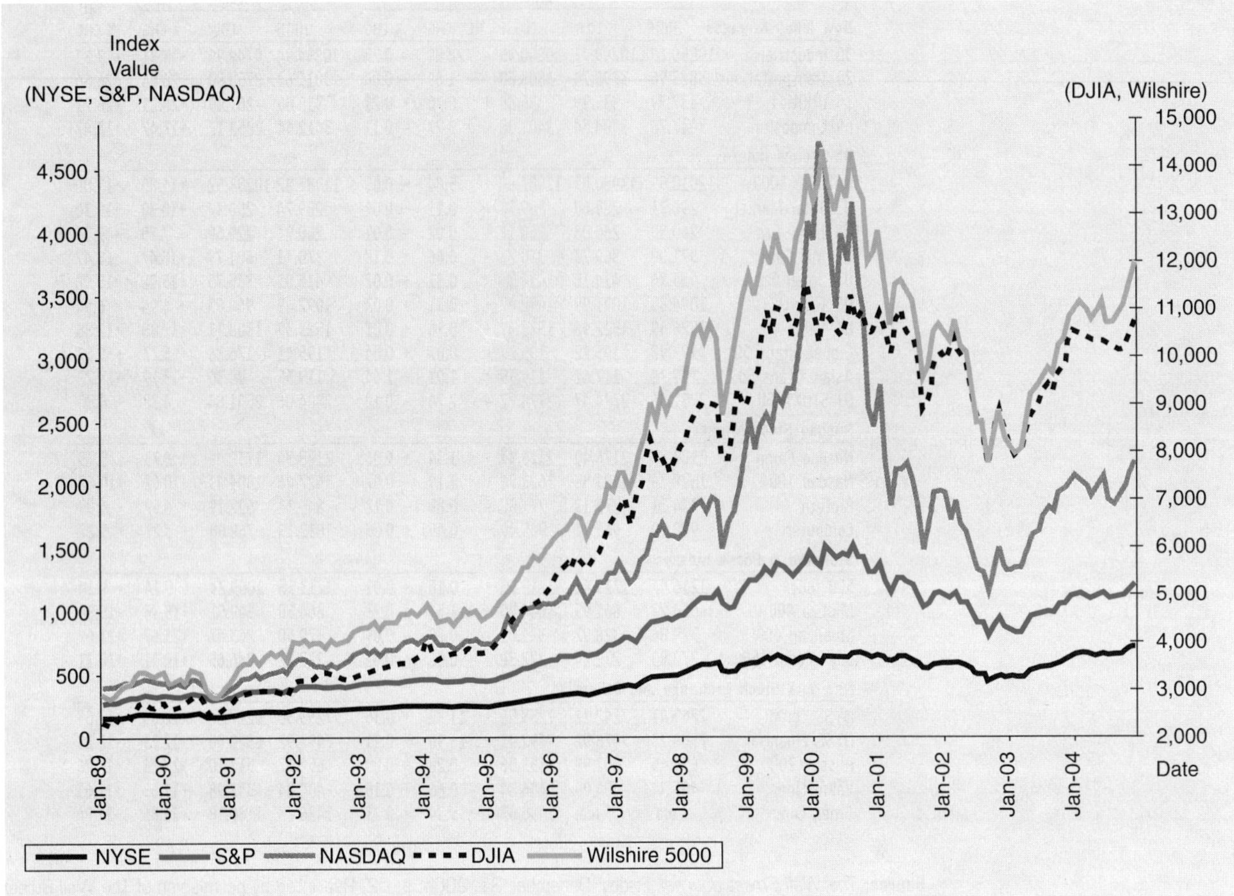

Source: Dow Jones, the New York Stock Exchange, Standard & Poor's, NASDAQ, and Wilshire Web sites, various dates.

The Dow Jones Industrial Average. The Dow Jones Industrial Average (the DJIA or the Dow) is the most widely reported stock market index. The DJIA was first published in 1896 as an index of 12 industrial stocks. In 1928, the Dow was expanded to include the values of 30 large (in terms of sales and total assets) corporations selected by the editors of *The Wall Street Journal* (owned by Dow Jones & Company). In choosing companies to be included in the DJIA, the editors look for the largest companies with a history of successful growth and with interest among stock investors. The composition of the DJIA was most recently revised in April 2004, when AT&T, Eastman Kodak, and International Paper were replaced by American International Group (AIG), Pfizer, and Verizon Communications. Table 9–5 lists the 30 NYSE and NASDAQ corporations included in the DJIA. Dow Jones and Company has also established and publishes indexes of 20 transportation companies, 15 utility companies, and a composite index consisting of all 65 companies in the industrial, transportation, and utility indexes.

Dow indexes are *price-weighted averages,* meaning that the stock *prices* of the companies in the indexes are added together and divided by an adjusted value, (or divisor) as follows:

$$\sum_{i=1}^{30} P_{it}/\text{Divisor}$$

where

P_{it} = Price of each stock in the Dow index on day t

TABLE 9–5 Dow Jones Industrial Average Companies

Altria Group (formerly Philip Morris)	IBM
Aluminum Company of America	Intel
American Express	Johnson & Johnson
American International Group (AIG)	J. P. Morgan Chase
Boeing	McDonald's
Caterpillar	Merck
Citigroup	Microsoft
Coca-Cola	Minnesota Mining & Manufacturing (3M)
DuPont	Pfizer
Exxon Mobil	Procter & Gamble
General Electric	SBC Communications
General Motors	United Technologies
Hewlett-Packard	Verizon Communications
Home Depot	Wal-Mart
Honeywell	Walt Disney

Source: Dow Jones & Company Web site, December 2004. **www.dowjones.com**

The divisor was set at 30 in 1928, but due to stock splits, stock dividends, and changes in the 30 firms included in the index, this value dropped to 0.13532775 by the end of 2004.

The NYSE Composite Index. In 1966, the NYSE established the NYSE Composite Index to provide a comprehensive measure of the performance of the overall NYSE market. The index consists of all common stocks listed on the NYSE. In addition to the composite index, NYSE stocks are divided into four subgroups: industrial, transportation, utility, and financial companies. The indexed value of each group is also reported daily.

The NYSE is a *value-weighted index,* meaning that the *current market values* (stock price × number of shares outstanding) of all stocks in the index are added together and divided by their value on a base date. Any changes in the stocks included in the index are incorporated by adjusting the base value of the index. To modernize and align the index methodology with those used in other indexes, the NYSE revised its NYSE Composite Index in January 2003. At this time the composite was recalculated to reflect a new base value of 5,000 rather than the original base value of 50 set in December 1965.

DO YOU UNDERSTAND?

1. What the purpose of a rights offering is?
2. What the major secondary stock markets in the United States are?
3. What the major U.S. stock indexes are?

The Standard & Poor's 500 Index. Standard & Poor's established the S&P 500 index (a value-weighted index) consisting of the stocks of 500 of the largest U.S. corporations listed on the NYSE and the NASDAQ. The NYSE stocks included in the S&P 500 index account for over 80 percent of the total market value of all stocks listed on the NYSE. Thus, movements in the S&P 500 Index are highly correlated with those of the NYSE Composite Index (the correlation between the two indices was .96 from 1989 through June 2004—see Figure 9–13). Standard & Poor's also reports subindexes consisting of industrials and utilities in the S&P 500 Index.

The NASDAQ Composite Index. Established in 1971, the NASDAQ Composite Index (a value-weighted index) consists of three categories of NASDAQ companies: industrials, banks, and insurance companies. All stocks traded through the NASDAQ in these three industries are included. NASDAQ also reports separate indexes based on industrials, banks, insurance companies, computers, and telecommunications companies.

The Wilshire 5000 Index. The Wilshire 5000 Index was created in 1974 (when computers made the daily computation of such a large index possible) to track the value of the entire

SEARCH THE SITE

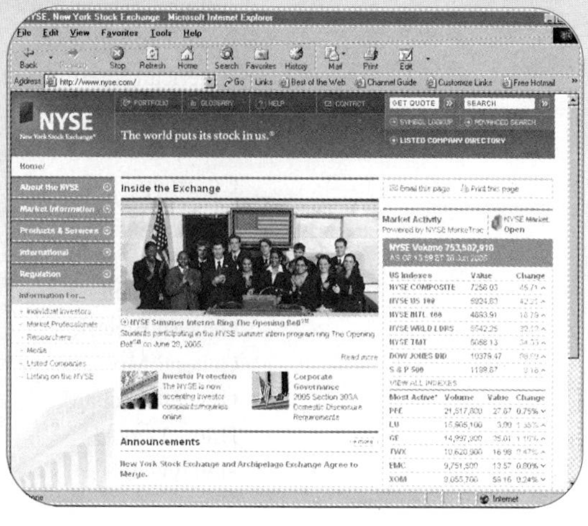

Go to the NYSE Web site at **www.nyse.com** and find the most recent information on the NYSE market indexes.

Under "Market Information" click on "Indexes"

This will bring up the summary of the NYSE indexes.

Questions

1. What is the high and low value for the NYSE Composite Index over the last year?
2. Calculate the percentage change in the NYSE Composite and NYSE Financial Indices over the last year.

stock market. It is the broadest stock market index and possibly the most accurate reflection of the overall stock market. The Wilshire 5000 Index contains virtually every stock that meets three criteria: the firm is headquartered in the United States; the stock is actively traded in a U.S.-based stock market; and the stock has widely available price information (which rules out the smaller OTC stocks from inclusion). Though the index started with 5,000 firms, it currently includes more than 6,700 stocks. Like the NYSE Composite Index, the S&P 500 Index, and the NASDAQ Composite Index, the Wilshire 5000 Index is a value-weighted index. The Wilshire 5000 Index has the advantage that it is the best index to track the path of the U.S. stock market. Since it includes essentially every public firm, it is highly representative of the overall market. However, because it is so diverse, determining which sectors or asset classes (technology, industrial, small-cap, large-cap, etc.) are moving the market is impossible.

EXAMPLE 9-6 Price-Weighted versus Value-Weighted Indexes

Suppose a stock index contains stock of four firms: W, X, Y, and Z. The stock prices for the four companies are \$50, \$25, \$60, and \$5, respectively, and the firms have 100 million, 400 million, 200 million, and 50 million shares outstanding, respectively. If the index is price-weighted, its initial value, *PWI*, is calculated as:

$$\begin{aligned} PWI &= \sum_{i=1}^{4} P_{it}/4 \\ &= (\$50 + \$25 + \$60 + \$5)/4 \\ &= 140/4 \\ &= 35 \end{aligned}$$

If the index is value-weighted, its initial value, *VWI*, is:

$$\begin{aligned} VWI &= \sum_{i=1}^{4} (P_{it} \times \text{number of shares outstanding})/4 \\ &= ((\$50 \times 100\text{m}) + (\$25 \times 400\text{m}) + (\$60 \times 200\text{m}) + (\$5 \times 50\text{m}))/4 \\ &= \$6{,}812.5 \text{ million} \end{aligned}$$

If the next day, share prices change to \$55, \$24, \$62, and \$6, respectively, the price-weighted index value changes to:

$$
\begin{aligned}
PWI &= \sum_{i=1}^{4} P_{it}/4 \\
&= (\$55 + \$24 + \$62 + \$6)/4 \\
&= 147/4 \\
&= 36.75
\end{aligned}
$$

and the percentage change in the index is (36.75 – 35)/35 = 5 percent. The value-weighted index is now:

$$
\begin{aligned}
VWI &= \sum_{i=1}^{4} (P_{it} \times \text{number of shares outstanding})/4 \\
&= ((\$55 \times 100\text{m}) + (\$24 \times 400\text{m}) + (\$62 \times 200\text{m}) + (\$6 \times 50\text{m}))/4 \\
&= \$6{,}950 \text{ million}
\end{aligned}
$$

and the percentage change in this index is (6,950 – 6,812.5)/6,812.5 = 2.02 percent.

If, after the market closes, company W undergoes a two-for-one split, its stock price falls to \$55/2 = \$27.50 and the number of shares increases to 200 million. The prices now sum to \$119.50. At the same time the divisor on the price-weighted index adjusts such that:

$$
\begin{aligned}
\text{Divisor} &= 119.5/36.75 \\
&= 3.2517
\end{aligned}
$$

Thus, the value of the price-weighted index remains at:

$$
\begin{aligned}
PWI &= \sum_{i=1}^{4} P_{it}/3.2517 \\
&= (\$27.50 + \$24 + \$62 + \$6)/3.2517 \\
&= 119.5/3.2517 \\
&= 36.75
\end{aligned}
$$

Further, the value-weighted index remains unchanged at 6950. Both indexes are unaffected by the stock split. Apparent from this example, however, is that the firms included in the index and the weighting process used affect values of the reported changes in the overall stock market.

STOCK MARKET PARTICIPANTS

7

Table 9–6 shows the holdings of corporate stock from 1994 through 2004 by type of holder. Households are the single largest holders of corporate stock (holding 39.2 percent of all corporate stock outstanding in 2004). Mutual funds and private and public pension funds are also prominent in the stock markets (holding 22.0 percent, 9.8 percent, and 7.5 percent of the \$15.63 trillion in corporate stock outstanding, respectively).

As a result of the tremendous increase in stock values in the 1990s, most individuals in the United States either directly own corporate stock or indirectly own stock via investments in mutual funds and pension funds. Figure 9–14 shows the age distribution of adult stockholders by percentage of all shareholders and percentage of shares owned. While over 50 percent of all stockholders are under 45 years of age, this group owns just 23.0 percent of all stock outstanding. The major investors (holding 53.0 percent of all stock outstanding) are those 37.3 percent of the market participants between 45 and 64 years old.

DO YOU UNDERSTAND?

1. Who the major holders of stock are?
2. What age group of individual investors hold the largest percentage of stock outstanding?

Table 9–7 reports characteristics of adult investors in the stock markets, classified as All Adults, Baby Boomers (born between 1947 and 1962), and Senior Citizens (those 65 years and older). Approximately 34 percent of stock investors are employed as professionals or executives, while 38 percent have a college degree.

TABLE 9–6 Holders of Corporate Stock
(in billions of dollars)

	1994	1997	2000	2002	2004	Percent of 2004 Total
Household sector	$3,070.9	$5,689.6	$7,317.1	$5,045.2	$6,132.7	39.2%
State and local governments	10.6	79.0	115.1	80.3	87.6	0.6
Rest of world	397.7	919.5	1,748.3	1,260.8	1,670.3	10.7
Depository institutions	180.6	331.4	315.2	213.7	260.1	1.7
Life insurance companies	246.1	558.6	940.8	708.9	962.4	6.2
Other insurance companies	112.1	186.0	194.3	152.3	187.5	1.2
Private pension funds	996.3	1,863.9	2,195.1	1,096.7	1,536.3	9.8
Public pension funds	557.4	1,431.7	1,335.1	918.3	1,180.3	7.5
Mutual funds	709.6	2,018.7	3,292.5	2,286.2	3,431.7	22.0
Closed-end funds	31.9	50.2	35.7	33.7	70.8	0.4
Brokers and dealers	20.1	51.9	77.2	74.9	107.5	0.7

Source: Federal Reserve Board Web site, various issues. **www.federalreserve.gov**

The mean family income of stock investors is $84,900, and the mean value of investors' overall investment portfolios is $148,500. Baby boomers have smaller investment portfolios, $115,800, than the average, and senior citizens are the largest group of investors, with a mean investment portfolio valued at $267,700.

OTHER ISSUES PERTAINING TO STOCK MARKETS

Economic Indicators

In Appendix 3A to Chapter 3, located at the book's Web site (**www.mhhe.com/sc3e**), we used time value of money equations to determine the fair value of a stock. Specifically, we saw that the fair value of a stock today (P_0) could be represented as:

$$P_0 = \frac{D_1}{(1 + i_s)^1} + \frac{D_2}{(1 + i_s)^2} + \cdots + \frac{D_\infty}{(1 + i_s)^\infty}$$

FIGURE 9–14 Distribution of Common Stock Ownership by Age

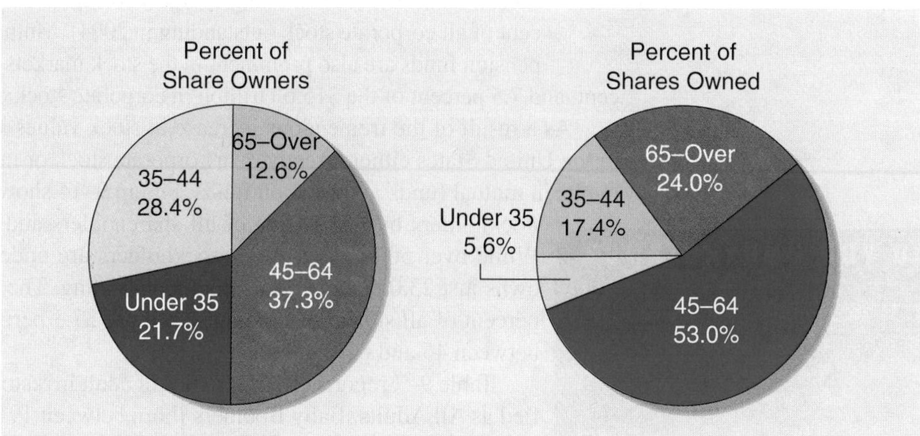

Source: *NYSE Shareownership,* New York Stock Exchange, 2000. **www.nyse.com**

TABLE 9–7 Profiles of Adult Stockholders

	All Adults	Baby Boomers	Senior Citizens
Employed:	77.0%	87.8%	20.7%
Occupation (conditional on working):			
Professional/Executive	33.8	39.1	37.3
Clerical, technical, or sales	20.3	21.9	16.8
Education:			
Completed college	38.0	39.4	33.6
Any postgraduate work	15.9	16.6	16.0
Family status:			
Married	82.0	85.6	72.8
Widowed	3.2	0.5	17.9
Portfolio attributes:			
Has brokerage account	30.5	29.3	45.6
Willing to take risk	82.3	83.8	61.5
Owns IRA or Keogh	51.4	49.1	69.0
Owns mutual fund	31.9	30.4	45.7
Only one stock owned	13.4	10.4	14.9
Median age	44	43	71
Median family income (000s)	$57.0	$64.0	$40.0
Mean family income (000s)	$84.9	$94.1	$68.1
Median portfolio value (000s)	$28.0	$31.0	$63.0
Mean portfolio value (000s)	$148.5	$115.8	$267.7
Mean number of stocks held	2.3	1.9	4.7
Mean number of stocks held if hold stocks directly	3.4	2.1	5.2

Notes: Tabulations from the 1998 Survey of Consumer Finances. Baby boomer shareholders are those born between 1947 and 1962. Senior citizen shareholders are those aged 65 and above in 1998.

Source: *NYSE Shareownership*, The New York Stock Exchange, 2002. **www.nyse.com**

The present value of a stock today is the discounted (at a rate i_s) sum of the expected future dividends (D_i) to be paid on the stock. As expected future dividends increase (decrease), stock prices should increase (decrease). Appendix 9A to this chapter (located at the book's Web site, **www.mhhe.com/sc3e**) reviews the Capital Asset Pricing Model used to determine an appropriate interest rate at which to discount these dividends.

To the extent that today's stock values reflect expected future dividends, stock market indexes might be used to forecast future economic activity. An increase (decrease) in stock market indexes today potentially signals the market's expectation of higher (lower) corporate dividends and profits and, in turn, higher (lower) economic growth. To the extent that the market's assessment of expected dividends is correct, stock market indexes can be predictors of economic activity. Indeed, stock prices are one of the 10 variables included in the index of leading economic indicators used by the Federal Reserve as it formulates economic policy (see Chapter 4).[11]

www.federalreserve.gov

Figure 9–15 shows the relation between stock market movements (using the DJIA) and economic cycles in the United States. Notice some recessionary periods (represented in Figure 9–15 by the shaded bars) were indeed preceded by a decline in stock market

11. The other indicators include average weekly hours of manufacturing production workers; average weekly initial claims for unemployment insurance; manufactures' new orders, consumer goods and materials; vendor performance, slower diffusion index; manufacturers' new orders, nondefense capital goods; building permits for new private housing units; money supply; interest rate spread, 10-year Treasury bonds less fed funds; and index of consumer expectations. These data, tabulated by the National Bureau of Economic Research (NBER), are available in the *Survey of Current Business*.

FIGURE 9–15 The Relation between Stock Market Movements and Economic Activity

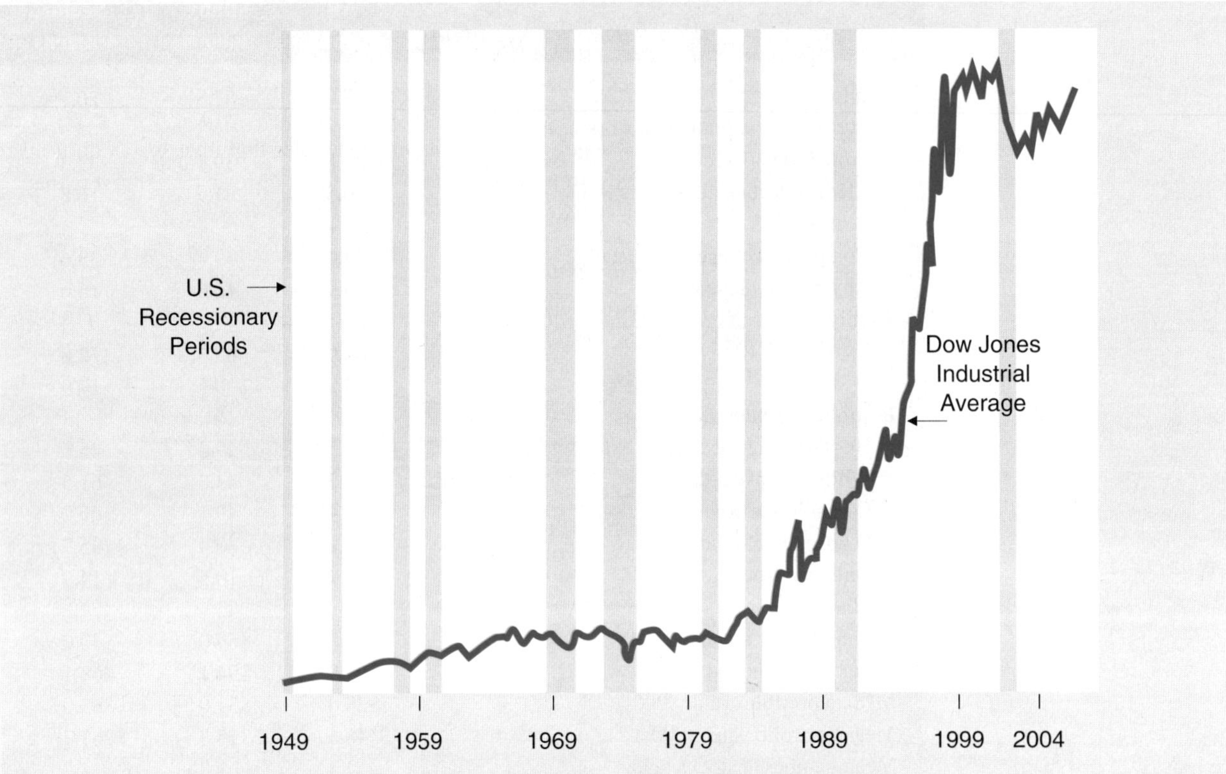

Source: Dow Jones & Company Web site and National Bureau of Economic Research Web site, December 2004. **www.dowjones.com; www.nber.org**

index values; other recessionary periods were not preceded by a decline in stock market index values. Figure 9–15 suggests that stock market movements are not consistently accurate predictors of economic activity. In fact, a study by researchers at the Federal Reserve Bank of Kansas City found that only 11 of 27 recessions in the United States between 1900 and 1987 were preceded by declines in stock market values.[12]

Market Efficiency

8

As discussed above (and in Chapter 3), theoretically, the *current* market price of a stock equals the present value of its expected future dividends (or the *fair* market value of the security). However, when an event occurs that unexpectedly changes interest rates or a characteristic of the company (e.g., an unexpected dividend increase or decrease in default risk), the current market price of a stock can temporarily diverge from its fair present value. When market traders determine that a stock is undervalued (i.e., the current price of the stock is less than its fair present value), they will purchase the stock, thus driving its price up. Conversely, when market traders determine that a stock is overvalued (i.e., its current price is greater than its fair present value), they will sell the stock, resulting in a price decline.

market efficiency

The speed with which financial security prices adjust to unexpected news pertaining to interest rates or a stock-specific characteristic.

The degree to which financial security prices adjust to "news" and the degree (and speed) with which stock prices reflect information about the firm and factors that affect firm value is referred to as **market efficiency**.[13] Three measures (weak form, semistrong form, and strong form market efficiency) are commonly used to measure the degree of

12. See Byron Higgins, "Is a Recession Inevitable This Year?" *Economic Review,* Federal Reserve Bank of Kansas City, January 1988, pp. 3–16.

13. While we discuss market efficiency in the context of stock markets, it also applies to the speed with which any security's price changes in response to new information.

stock market efficiency. The measures differ in the type of information or news (e.g., public versus private, historic versus nonhistoric) that is impounded into stock prices.

Weak Form Market Efficiency. According to the weak form of market efficiency, current stock prices reflect all historic price and volume information about a company. Old news and trends are already impounded in historic prices and are of no use in predicting today's or future stock prices. Thus, weak form market efficiency concludes that investors cannot make more than the fair (required) return using information based on historic price movements.

Empirical research on weak form market efficiency generally confirms that markets are weak form efficient. Evidence suggests that successive price changes are generally random and that the correlation between stock prices from one day to the next is virtually zero. Thus, historical price and volume trends are of no help in predicting future price movements (and technical analysis has no value as a trading strategy).

Semistrong Form Market Efficiency. The semistrong form market efficiency hypothesis focuses on the speed with which public information is impounded into stock prices. According to the concept of semistrong form market efficiency, as public information arrives about a company, it is immediately impounded into its stock price. For example, semistrong form market efficiency states that a common stock's value should respond immediately to unexpected news announcements by the firm regarding its future earnings. Thus, if an investor calls his or her broker just as the earnings news is released, that investor cannot earn an abnormal return. Prices have already (immediately) adjusted. According to semistrong form market efficiency, investors cannot make more than the fair (required) return by trading on public news releases.

Since historical information is a subset of all public information, if semistrong form market efficiency holds, weak form market efficiency must hold as well. However, it is possible for weak form market efficiency to hold when semistrong form market efficiency does not. This implies that investors can earn abnormal returns by trading on current public news releases. The quicker the stock market impounds this information, the smaller any abnormal returns will be.

Semistrong form market efficiency has been examined by testing how security prices react to unexpected news releases or announcement "events" (event studies—see Appendix 9B to this chapter located at the book's Web site (**www.mhhe.com/sc3e**)). Some specific announcements that have been tested include macroeconomic events such as interest rate changes and firm-specific announcements such as earnings and dividend changes, stock splits, brokerage house buy and sell recommendations, and mergers and acquisitions. Financial markets have generally been found to immediately reflect information from news announcements.

Strong Form Market Efficiency. The strong form of market efficiency states that stock prices fully reflect all information about the firm, both public and private. Thus, according to strong form market efficiency, even learning private information about the firm is of no help in earning more than the required rate of return. As individuals[14] get private information about a firm, the market has already reacted to it and has fully adjusted the firm's common stock price to its new equilibrium level. Thus, strong form market efficiency implies that there is no set of information that allows investors to make more than the fair (required) rate of return on a stock.

If strong form market efficiency holds, semistrong form market efficiency must hold as well. However, semistrong form market efficiency can hold when strong form market efficiency does not. This implies that private information can be used to produce abnormal returns, but as soon as the private or inside information is publicly released, abnormal returns are unobtainable.

14. How institutional investors factor into efficient markets raises questions. Many consider institutional investors to have private information that results from better analysis of public information and greater resources. Obviously, whether these institutions can expect to discover the private information and thus expect to earn abnormal returns in the long run is an issue. Indeed, whether the information set of institutions belongs in the semistrong or strong form group is arguable.

Because private information is not observable, testing for strong form market efficiency is difficult. As a result, there are few studies testing its validity. The limited empirical tests of strong form market efficiency examine information available to insiders. Generally, studies have found that corporate insiders (e.g., directors, officers, and chairs) do earn abnormal returns from trading and that the more informed the insider, the more often abnormal returns are earned. Therefore, information possessed by corporate insiders can be used in trading to earn abnormal returns.

Because private information can be used to earn abnormal returns, laws prohibit investors from trading on the basis of private information (insider trading) although they can trade, like any investor, based on publicly available information about the firm. For example, in June 2002 the FBI and SEC arrested Dr. Samuel Waksal on criminal charges of trying to sell ImClone stock and tipping off family members and friends (including Martha Stewart) after learning that regulators would reject his company's promising cancer drug. Dr. Waksal and Ms. Stewart were sentenced to jail terms (of seven years and five months, respectively) as a result of this insider trading. To try to ensure that insider trading does not occur, publicly traded companies are required to file monthly reports with the Securities and Exchange Commission reporting every purchase and sale of the company's securities by officers and directors of the company. Even with this information, identifying trades driven by private (inside) as opposed to public information is often hard.

Stock Market Regulations

www.sec.gov

Stock markets and stock market participants are subject to regulations imposed by the Securities and Exchange Commission (SEC) as well as the exchanges on which stocks are traded. The main emphasis of SEC regulations is on full and fair disclosure of information on securities issues to actual and potential investors. The two major regulations that were created to prevent unfair and unethical trading practices on security exchanges are the Securities Act of 1933 and the Securities Exchange Act of 1934. The 1933 Act required listed companies to file a registration statement and to issue a prospectus that details the recent financial history of the company when issuing new stock. The 1934 Act established the SEC as the main administrative agency responsible for the oversight of secondary stock markets by giving the SEC the authority to monitor the stock market exchanges and administer the provisions of the 1933 Act. SEC regulations are not intended to protect investors against poor investment choices but rather to ensure that investors have full and accurate information available when making their investment decisions.

For example, in October 2000, the SEC adopted Regulation FD (Fair Disclosure) to combat selective disclosure. Selective disclosure occurs when stock issuers release nonpublic information about their company to selected persons, such as securities analysts or institutional investors, before disclosing the information to the general public. This practice undermines the integrity of the securities markets and reduces investor confidence in the fairness of the markets. Selective disclosure also may create conflicts of interests for securities analysts, who may have an incentive to avoid making negative statements about an issuer for fear of losing their access to selectively disclosed information. Regulation FD requires that any material information released by a firm be done so to the general public and not selectively.

In 2001 a number of securities firms received tremendous publicity concerning conflicts of interest between analysts' research recommendations on buying or not buying stocks and whether the firm played a role in underwriting the securities of the firm the analysts were recommending. After an investigation by the New York State's attorney general, Merrill Lynch agreed to pay a fine of $100 million and to follow procedures more clearly separating analysts' recommendations (and their compensation) from the underwriting activities of the firm. Major Wall Street firms were also investigated (see below). This investigation was triggered by the dramatic collapse of many new technology stocks while analysts were still making recommendations to buy or hold them.

Subsequent to these investigations, the SEC instituted rules requiring Wall Street analysts to vouch that their stock picks are not influenced by investments banking colleagues and that analysts disclose details of their compensation that would flag investors to any possible conflicts. Evidence that analysts have falsely attested to the independence of their work could be used to institute enforcement actions. Violators could face a wide array of sanctions, including fines and penalties such as a suspension or a bar from the securities industry. In addition, the SEC proposed that top officials from all public companies sign off on financial statements.

Along with these changes instituted by the SEC, the U.S. Congress passed the Sarbanes-Oxley Act in July 2002. This act created an independent auditing oversight board under the SEC, increased penalties for corporate wrongdoers, forced faster and more extensive financial disclosure, and created avenues of recourse for aggrieved shareholders. Further, in 2002 the NYSE took actions intended to heighten corporate governance standards on domestic NYSE-listed companies. Key changes included requirements on companies to have a majority of independent directors, to adopt corporate governance guidelines and codes of ethics and business conduct, to have shareholders' approval of all equity-based compensation plans, and to have CEOs annually certify information given to investors. The goal of the legislation was to prevent deceptive accounting and management practices and to bring stability to jittery stock markets battered in the summer of 2002 by corporate governance scandals of Enron, Global Crossings, Tyco, WorldCom, and others.

In the spring of 2003 an agreement was announced between regulators and 10 of the nation's largest securities firms to pay a record $1.4 billion in penalties to settle charges involving investor abuses. The long-awaited settlement centered on civil charges that securities firms routinely issued overly optimistic stock research to investors in order to gain favor with corporate clients and win their investment banking business. The agreement also settled charges that at least two big firms, Citigroup and Credit Suisse First Boston, improperly allocated IPO shares to corporate executives to win banking business from their firms. The SEC and other regulators, including the NASD, the NYSE, and state regulators, unveiled multiple examples of how Wall Street stock analysts tailored their research reports and ratings to win investment banking business. The Wall Street firms agreed to the settlement without admitting or denying any wrongdoing. The agreement forced brokerage companies to make structural changes in the way they handle research—preventing, for example, analysts from attending certain investment banking meetings with bankers. The agreement also required securities firms to have separate reporting and supervisory structures for their research and banking operations and required that analysts' pay be tied to the quality and accuracy of their research, rather than the amount of investment banking business they generate.

This was not the end, however. Investors of several companies sued investment banks for actions taken to mislead investors such as falsifying financial statements and hiding debt. Seeking to end these suits, investment banks settled many of them. For example, in June 2005, J.P. Morgan Chase paid $2.2 billion and Citigroup paid $2 billion to investors of Enron to settle a class-action lawsuit filed by this group. This followed a $2 billion payout to investors of WorldCom by J.P. Morgan Chase to settle a similar lawsuit.

The SEC has delegated certain regulatory responsibilities to the markets (e.g., NYSE or NASDAQ). In these matters, the NYSE and NASDAQ are self-regulatory organizations. Specifically, the NYSE has primary responsibility for the day-to-day surveillance of trading activity. It monitors specialists to ensure adequate compliance with their obligation to make a fair and orderly market; monitors all trading to guard against unfair trading practices; monitors broker-dealer activity with respect to minimum net capital requirements, standards, and licensing; and enforces various listing and disclosure requirements.

www.nyse.com

In October 2003, the SEC criticized the NYSE for failing to police its specialists and ignoring blatant violations in which investors were cheated out of millions of dollars in trades involving more than two billion shares over the 2001–2003 period. The confidential report painted a picture of a floor trading system riddled with abuses, with specialist firms routinely placing their own trades ahead of those of customers, and of an NYSE that was ill-equipped or unwilling to address the problems. The report concluded that when the NYSE did act on investor abuses, it often did little more than admonish the specialists in a letter or assess a small fine. In response to the criticism, the NYSE agreed to make improvements to curb alleged abuses. Actions by the NYSE against trading abuses did pick up in 2004. For example, in June 2004, the NYSE fined ($100,000) and suspended (for six weeks) an executive at Morgan Stanley who oversaw large stock trades. The NYSE alleged that the executive placed trades to bolster a stock in the firm's own trading account in order to limit losses Morgan Stanley would take on the stock. In November 2004, the NYSE warned firms on the floor to monitor closely communications they have with corporate executives to make sure the firms do not leak market-moving information or succumb to improper pressure to manipulate prices. NYSE rules require specialists to give companies periodic updates on their stocks' trading. But the companies' executives are not allowed to call specialists during trading hours, which had happened on at least one occasion, prompting the NYSE warning. Finally, in December 2004 Knight Securities was fined $79 million in penalties to settle an investigation pertaining to the cheating of stock clients over a three-year period from 1999 to 2001. Regulators alleged that Knight Trading Group traders routinely delayed filling clients' stock orders to trade for the firm's own account, pocketing commissions of several dollars per share rather than the standard pennies per share.

DO YOU UNDERSTAND?

1. Whether movements in stock market indexes are always accurate predictors of changes in economic activity?
2. What the difference is between weak form, semistrong form, and strong form market efficiency?
3. What the purpose of regulations imposed on the stock market participants by the SEC is?

The National Association of Securities Dealers (NASD) has the primary responsibility for regulating brokers and dealers on the NASDAQ market. It requires its members to meet certain standards of conduct in issuing and selling securities and monitors members to prevent them from profiting unreasonably at the expense of their customers. The NASD also conducts field examinations of its member firms at least once a year and can censure, fine, suspend, or expel a broker-dealer from the NASD if violations are found.

INTERNATIONAL ASPECTS OF STOCK MARKETS

The U.S. stock markets are the world's largest. However, European markets are becoming an increasing force, and with the full implementation of a common currency, the euro, in 2002, they should continue to grow in importance. Figure 9–16 shows the proportion of stock market capitalization among major countries in 1988, 2000, and 2004. The U.S. dominance in the stock markets is best seen in 2000 and 2004. Note also the stock market developments in Europe and the Pacific Basin countries from 1988 to 2000. While the European markets have increased their market share (from 20.93

FIGURE 9–16 Worldwide Stock Market Capitalization

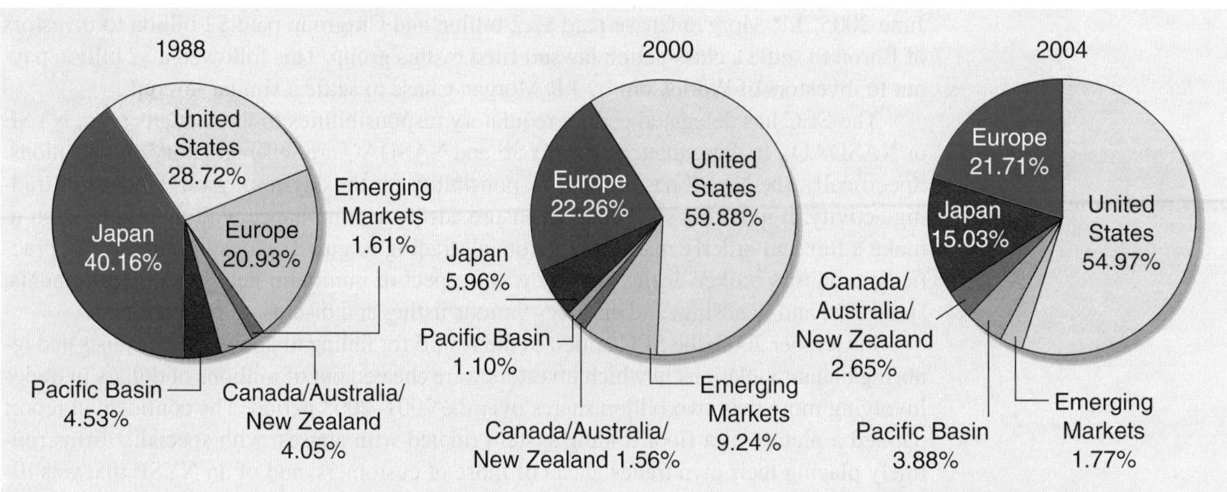

Source: *Emerging Stock Markets Fact Book, 1998 and 2001*; International Finance Corporation, December 2004. **www.ifc.org**

to 21.71 percent of the total), the Asian economic problems that started in 1997 reduced the value of these markets significantly (for example, Japanese and Pacific Basin stock markets decreased from 40.16 and 4.53 percent in 1988 to 5.96 and 1.10 percent in 2000 of the worldwide stock markets, respectively, before recovering to 15.03 and 3.88 percent, respectively, as the economies recovered).

From an investor's viewpoint, international stock markets are attractive because some risk can be eliminated (diversified away—see Chapter 20) by holding the stocks issued by corporations in foreign countries. For example, while a stock issued by a corporation in one country might be reduced in value by a recessionary slowdown, increases in the value of stocks issued by a corporation in another country (that is experiencing economic growth or an appreciation in the foreign exchange rate of its currency) can offset those losses. A recent (1976–1999) look at correlations in stock returns in the United States, Europe, and the Pacific Basin countries shows that diversification opportunities do indeed exist.[15] For example, the correlation coefficient on (local currency) stock returns in the United States versus the United Kingdom was 0.50, and in the United States versus Hong Kong was 0.37.[16]

EXAMPLE 9-7 Returns from International Portfolio Diversification

Suppose you owned stock in a U.S. company and a U.K. company. U.S. dollars were converted to British pounds last year to make the investment, and pounds were converted back to dollars as you liquidated the investment. Also suppose the exchange rate of British pounds into U.S. dollars was 1.8081 last year and is now 1.8909. Thus, the pound appreciated relative to the dollar over the investment period. The details of the two stock investments are as follows:

	U.S. Stock	U.K. Stock		U.S. Dollar Equivalent for U.K. Stocks
Purchase price, P_{t-1}^C	\$50	£60	=	\$108.486
Sale price, P_t^C	\$48	£64	=	\$121.0176
Dividends, D_t^C	\$1.50	£2.50	=	\$4.72725

The return on the U.S. company's stock was:

$$R_t^{US} = \frac{\$48 - \$50}{\$50} + \frac{\$1.5}{\$50} = -1\%$$

and the return on the U.K. company's stock, ignoring the change in the exchange rate, was:

$$R_t^{UK} = \frac{£64 - £60}{£60} + \frac{£2.5}{£60} = 10.83\%$$

On a U.S. dollar equivalent basis the return was:

$$R_t^{UK} = \frac{\$121.0176 - \$108.486}{\$108.486} + \frac{\$4.72725}{108.486} = 15.91\%$$

The loss on the U.S. stock, 1 percent, was offset by an increase in the value of the U.K. stock, reflecting both an increase in its local market value and an appreciation in the pound relative to the dollar.

15. See A. Sarkar and K. Li, "Should U.S. Investors Hold Foreign Stocks?" *Current Issues,* Federal Reserve Bank of New York, March 2002.

16. A correlation coefficient of 1 means the returns move exactly together; a correlation coefficient of 0 means there is no relation in the return movements, and a correlation of negative 1 means the returns move in exactly the opposite direction.

While international diversification eliminates some risks, it introduces others. For example, for smaller investors, information about foreign stocks is less complete and timely than that for U.S. stocks. Further, international investments introduce foreign exchange risk (see Chapter 8) and political (or sovereign) risk (see Chapter 19).

As seen in Table 9–6 (Rest of world), foreign investors held $1,670.3 billion (or 10.7 percent) of the outstanding stock issued in the United States. Moreover, foreign companies issued $2,094.0 billion of the stocks in the United States (see Figure 9–1). Facilitating U.S. investment in stocks of foreign corporations is the creation of the American Depository Receipt (ADR). An ADR is a certificate that represents ownership of a foreign stock. An ADR is typically created by a U.S. bank, which buys stock in foreign corporations in their domestic currencies and places them with a custodian. The bank then issues dollar ADRs backed by the shares of the foreign stock. Each ADR is a claim on a given number of shares of stock held by the bank. These ADRs are then traded in the United States, in dollars, on and off the organized exchanges. The major attraction to U.S. investors is that ADRs are claims to foreign companies that trade on domestic (U.S.) exchanges *and* in dollars. Global Depository Receipts (GDRs) are similar to ADRs, but are issued worldwide.

There are currently over 2,000 ADRs of foreign corporations available to U.S. investors (mainly listed on the NYSE, the AMEX, or the NASDAQ). ADR trading volume in 2004 (through November) exceeded 33.4 billion shares and the average daily volume was $3.46 billion. The Bank of New York is the main issuer of ADRs. Through ADRs, over 20 percent of the shares of the top 100 non-U.S. companies (such as Nokia and Royal Dutch Petroleum) ranked by U.S. sales were owned by U.S. residents.

A further advantage of ADRs to U.S. investors is that the SEC requires companies with ADRs trading in the United States to file financial statements that are consistent with U.S. generally accepted accounting principles (GAAP). Thus, unlike direct investments in foreign corporations on their local exchanges, investors in ADRs can obtain and review significant amounts of (audited) information on the foreign firm that appears in a currency, language, and format familiar to U.S. investors.

Similar to domestically traded stock, U.S. investment banks underwrite and sell stock issues globally. For example, Aspreva Pharmaceuticals issued 8,280,000 of its common shares in March 2005; 5,865,000 were issued in the United States and 2,415,000 in international markets. An internationally placed stock issue is attractive to an issuing firm because the shares of stock can reach a much larger market than if they were placed strictly in the United States. Foreign investors (with investment needs that differ from U.S. investors) may buy these stocks even when U.S. investors may not. Foreign issues of stock can also help enhance the international reputation of the firm. This is especially important to firms that concentrate at least a part of their business in international trade.

As noted earlier, U.S. stock exchanges are regulated by the SEC on some matters and are self-regulated organizations for others. Stock market structures in Japan, Canada, Hong Kong, and Australia are similar to the U.S. structure. These exchanges are self-regulating, with the government mainly playing the role of monitor. In Canada, Hong Kong, and Australia, the exchanges determine which securities are listed and the criteria that firms must meet for membership. In Japan, the Ministry of Finance must approve all listed securities.

In France, Belgium, Spain, and Italy, governments exercise the major control over the operations and activities of the exchanges. Membership on these exchanges may require government approval or licensing, and to insure against insolvency government agencies set minimum capital requirements. In Germany, Switzerland, Austria, and Sweden, the majority of the exchange trading is conducted through banks, reflecting regulatory and government policy.

As mentioned earlier, prices on U.S. stock markets are determined continuously throughout the trading day as brokers submit orders. Stock markets in Canada, Japan, Hong Kong, and most of Europe also use continuous trading. Stock markets in Germany and Austria use call-based trading, in which orders are batched for simultaneous execution at the same price and at a particular time during the day.

Only the Montreal Stock Exchange uses a specialist system of trading directly similar to that of the NYSE. The Amsterdam Stock Exchange gives certain firms the specialists duties for small and medium-sized trades. Large trades, however, are transacted directly by the parties involved. On the Toronto Stock Exchange, market makers are similar to specialists. These traders are selected by the exchange to trade for their own accounts and to create an orderly price flow in stocks that the exchange assigns them. These traders are obligated to post bid and ask prices throughout the day and to keep their bid-ask spreads small.

All other continuous trading markets in the world use a competitive dealer system of trading similar to that used by NASDAQ. For example, the London International Stock Exchange allows any well-capitalized firm that follows the regulations to act as a dealer for any security. Market makers publish firm bid-ask quotes for their stocks. One difference in this market is that for a limit order, only the broker-dealer that accepts the order from a customer knows about it. The computerized trading system does not record the existence of an order. The dealer then executes the order when his or her own price reaches the requested level. The Tokyo Stock Exchange uses a variation of the competitive dealer system, in which a broker functions as an intermediary between the dealers and the brokers who are members of the exchange. The brokers cannot buy or sell for their own accounts but can only arrange transactions among dealers, conduct trading auctions, and match buy and sell orders submitted by brokers for their clients.

DO YOU UNDERSTAND?

1. What percentage of the world's capital markets are represented by U.S. stocks?
2. What an ADR is?

SUMMARY

In this chapter, we examined corporate stocks and stock markets. Holders of corporate (preferred and common) stock have an ownership interest in the issuing firm based on the percentage of stock held. Stock markets are the most watched and reported of the financial markets. We described the major characteristics of corporate stocks—for example, dividend rights, residual claim status, limited liability, and voting rights of stockholders. We also looked at the primary and secondary markets for stocks, including a description of the trading process. While the NYSE has historically been the major stock market exchange in the United States, we showed that the NASDAQ system is increasing in importance.

We also looked at stock market indexes as predictors of future economic activity, reviewed the speed with which stock market prices adjust to new information, and described the major regulations governing stock market trading. We concluded the chapter with a brief look at international stock market activity—foreign investments in U.S. corporate stocks and U.S. investments in foreign corporate stocks.

SEARCH THE SITE

Go to the Federal Reserve Board's Web site and find the most recent data on the market value of common stock outstanding, by type of issue and by holder.

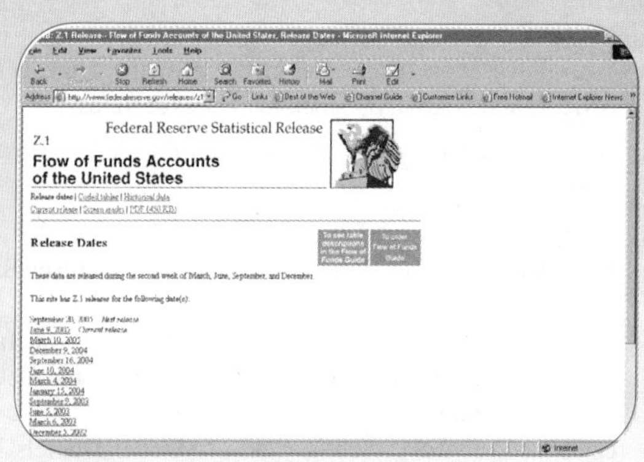

Go to the Federal Reserve Board's Web site at **www.federalreserve.gov/releases/Z1**

Click on the most recent date.

Click on "Level Tables."

This will download a file onto your computer that will contain the data on the market value of common stock outstanding, Table L213.

Questions

1. What is the market value of common stock currently outstanding? Calculate the percentage change in this value since 2004, reported in Figure 9–1.
2. What is the percentage of common stock outstanding issued by nonfinancial corporate businesses, financial corporations, and the rest of the world?

www.mhhe.com/sc3e

QUESTIONS

1. Why are the stock markets the most watched and reported of the financial security markets?
2. What are some characteristics associated with dividends paid on common stock?
3. What is meant by the statement "common stockholders have a residual claim on the issuing firm's assets"?
4. What is a dual-class firm? Why do firms typically issue dual classes of common stock?
5. Suppose a firm has 15 million shares of common stock outstanding and six candidates are up for election to five seats on the board of directors.
   a. If the firm uses cumulative voting to elect its board, what is the minimum number of votes needed to ensure election to the board?
   b. If the firm uses straight voting to elect its board, what is the minimum number of votes needed to ensure election to the board?
6. What is the difference between nonparticipating and participating preferred stock?
7. What is the difference between cumulative and noncumulative preferred stock?
8. Suppose you own 50,000 shares of common stock in a firm with 2.5 million total shares outstanding. The firm announces a plan to sell an additional 1 million shares through a rights offering. The market value of the stock is $35 before the rights offering and the new shares are being offered to existing shareholders at a $5 discount.
   a. If you exercise your preemptive rights, how many of the new shares can you purchase?
   b. What is the market value of the stock after the rights offering?
   c. What is your total investment in the firm after the rights offering? How is your investment split between original shares and new shares?
   d. If you decide not to exercise your preemptive rights, what is your investment in the firm after the rights offering? How is this split between old shares and rights?
9. What have been the trends in the growth of the NYSE, AMEX, and NASDAQ stock market exchanges?
10. What is a market order? What is a limit order? How are each executed?
11. Refer to the stock market quote in Table 9–3.
    a. What was the closing stock price for Anheuser-Busch Corp. on December 30, 2004?
    b. What were the high and low prices at which Ann Taylor stores traded between December 31, 2003 and December 30, 2004?
    c. What was the dividend yield on Archer Daniels Midland stock as of December 30, 2004?
12. STANDARD &POOR'S Go to the S&P Markets Insight Web site and find stock market data for Pfizer Inc. (PFE) using the following steps. Go to the S&P Educational Version of Market Insight Web site at **www.mhhe.com/edumarketinsight.** Click on "Educational Version of Market Insight." Enter your site ID and click on "Login." Click on "Company." In the box marked "Ticker" enter PFE and click on "Go!" Under Compustat Reports click on "Company Profile." This brings up a file that contains the relevant data.
13. STANDARD &POOR'S Go to the S&P Market Insight Web site and find forecasted stock prices for Microsoft Corp. (MSFT) using the following steps. Go to the S&P Educational Version of Market Insight Web site at **www.mhhe.com/edumarketinsight.** Click on "Educational Version of Market Insight." Enter your site ID and click on "Login." Click on "Company." In the box marked "Ticker" enter MSFT and click on "Go!" Click on "Exel Analytics." Click on "Forecasted Vals." This brings up a file that contains the relevant data.
14. eXcel **Using a Spreadsheet to Calculate Stock Returns:** At the beginning of the year, you purchased a share of stock for $50. Over the year the dividends paid on the stock were $4.50 per share. Calculate the return on a stock if the price of the stock at the end of the year is $40, $48, $50, and $55.

Price at Beginning of Year	Dividends	Price at End of Year	=>	The Return Is
$50	$4.50	$40		−11.00%
50	4.50	48		5.00
50	4.50	50		9.00
50	4.50	55		19.00

15. What are the major U.S. stock market indexes?
16. Who are the major holders of corporate stock?
17. STANDARD &POOR'S Go to the S&P Market Insight Web site and look up the industry profile for Consumer Electronics using the following steps. Go to the S&P Educational Version of Market Insight Web site at **www.mhhe.com/edumarketinsight.** Click on "Educational Version of Market Insight." Enter your site ID and click on "Login." Click on "Industry." Under Industry select Consumer Electronics and click on "Go!" Click on "GICS Sub-Industry Profile." This brings up a file that contains the relevant data. How does this industry's performance compare to the S&P 500 Index?
18. Are stock market indexes consistently accurate predictors of economic activity?
19. Describe the three forms of stock market efficiency.
20. What are circuit breakers used by the NYSE?
21. What is an ADR? How is an ADR created?

APPENDIX 9A: The Capital Asset Pricing Model

View this appendix at
www.mhhe.com/sc3e

APPENDIX 9B: Event Study Tests

View this appendix at
www.mhhe.com/sc3e

10

Derivative Securities Markets

OUTLINE

Chapter NAVIGATOR

1. What are forward and future contracts?
2. How is a futures transaction conducted?
3. What information can be found in a futures quote?
4. What are option contracts?
5. What information can be found in an options quote?
6. Who are the main regulators of futures and options markets?
7. What is an interest rate swap?
8. What are caps, floors, and collars?
9. What are the biggest derivative securities markets globally?

DERIVATIVE SECURITIES: CHAPTER OVERVIEW

A **derivative security** is a financial security whose payoff is linked to another, previously issued security. Derivative securities generally involve an agreement between two parties to exchange a standard quantity of an asset or cash flow at a predetermined price and at a specified date in the future. As the value of the underlying security to be exchanged changes, the value of the derivative security changes. A securitized asset such as a mortgage-backed security (see Chapter 7) is a derivative security in that its value is based on the value of an underlying security (e.g., a mortgage). Option contracts are also derivatives since their value depends on the price of some underlying security (e.g., a stock) relative to a reference (or strike) price. **Derivative securities markets** are the markets in which derivative securities trade. While derivative securities have been in existence for centuries, the growth in derivative securities markets occurred mainly in the 1970s, 1980s, and 1990s. As major markets, therefore, the derivative securities markets are the newest of the financial security markets.

derivative security

An agreement between two parties to exchange a standard quantity of an asset at a predetermined price at a specified date in the future.

derivative securities markets

The markets in which derivative securities trade.

www.cme.com

www.federalreserve.gov

www.cbot.com

The first of the modern wave of derivatives to trade were foreign currency futures contracts. These contracts were introduced by the International Monetary Market (IMM), a subsidiary of the Chicago Mercantile Exchange (CME), in response to the introduction of floating exchange rates between currencies of different countries following the Smithsonian Agreements of 1971 and 1973 (see Chapter 8).

The second wave of derivative security growth was with interest rate derivative securities. Their growth was mainly in response to increases in the volatility of interest rates in the late 1970s and after, as the Federal Reserve started to target nonborrowed reserves (see Chapter 4) rather than interest rates. Financial institutions such as banks and savings institutions had many rate-sensitive assets and liabilities on their balance sheets. As interest rate volatility increased, the sensitivity of the net worth (equity) of these institutions to interest rate shocks increased as well. In response, the Chicago Board of Trade (CBT) introduced, in the 1970s, numerous short-term and long-term interest rate futures contracts, and in the 1980s, stock index futures and options. Accordingly, financial institutions are the major participants in the derivative securities markets. Financial institutions can be either users of derivative contracts for hedging (see Chapter 23) or dealers that act as counterparties in trades with customers for a fee. Approximately 640 U.S. banks use derivatives and only five large dealer banks—J. P. Morgan Chase, Bank of America Corp., Citigroup Inc., First Union Corp., and Wells Fargo—account for some 95 percent of the derivatives that user banks hold.[1]

A third wave of derivative security innovations occurred in the 1990s with credit derivatives (e.g., credit forwards, credit risk options, and credit swaps). For example, a credit forward is a forward agreement that hedges against an increase in default risk on a loan (a decline in the credit quality of a borrower) after the loan rate is determined and the loan is issued. In September 2004, the notional value of credit derivatives held by U.S. banks was approximately $1,909 billion. These derivative securities have become particularly useful for managing credit risk of emerging-market countries and credit portfolio risk in general.[2]

In addition to trading on traditional exchanges such at the CME and the CBT (which maintain "open outcry" trading pits, where trading is conducted using hand waving and shouting), the early 2000s saw the rise in derivative trading on electronic exchanges. For example, in October 2004, the CME announced the billionth trade on its Globex electronic trading platform. In the third quarter of 2004, electronic trading of derivative security was 61 percent of total volume, up from 52 percent in the second quarter of 2004. In 2004 Eurex, the world's largest derivatives exchange, launched a fully electronic exchange in the United States. Based in Chicago, this exchange offers futures and options on U.S. Treasury notes and 30-year Treasury bonds as well as 2-, 5-, and 10-year contracts on euro interest rate contracts. The CBT, concerned that its Treasury contracts were under threat, introduced improved technology of its own, reduced transaction costs, and established a new common trading link with the CME.

In this chapter, we present an overview of the derivative securities markets. We look at the markets for forwards, futures, options, swaps, and some special derivative contracts (caps, floors, and collars). We define the various derivative securities and focus on the markets themselves—their operations and trading processes. In Chapter 23, we describe how these securities can be used to manage and hedge the foreign exchange, interest rate, and credit risks of financial institutions.

FORWARDS AND FUTURES

1

To present the essential nature and characteristics of forward and futures contracts and markets, we compare them with spot contracts. We define each in Table 10–1.

1. See Office of the Comptroller of the Currency, "Bank Derivatives Report," Third Quarter, September 2004.

2. Enron Corp. was among the top 20 dealers in the credit derivatives market in the early 2000s. Enron's derivatives trading liabilities to third parties were estimated at around $18.7 billion in late 2001. In fact, Enron's extensive use of credit derivatives, not just its accounting practices, may lie at the root of the energy giant's slide into the largest bankruptcy in U.S. history. Enron used profits from its credit derivatives trading operation to mask losses in its other businesses. Enron made billions trading derivatives, but lost billions on virtually everything else it did.

TABLE 10–1 Spot, Forward, and Futures Contracts

Spot Contract—agreement made between a buyer and a seller at time 0 for the seller to deliver the asset immediately and the buyer to pay for the asset immediately.

Forward Contract—agreement between a buyer and a seller at time 0 to exchange a nonstandardized asset for cash at some future date. The details of the asset and the price to be paid at the forward contract expiration date are set at time 0. The price of the forward contract is fixed over the life of the contract.

Futures Contract—agreement between a buyer and a seller at time 0 to exchange a standardized asset for cash at some future date. Each contract has a standardized expiration and transactions occur in a centralized market. The price of the futures contract changes daily as the market value of the asset underlying the futures fluctuates.

Spot Markets

spot contract

An agreement to transact involving the immediate exchange of assets and funds.

A **spot contract** is an agreement between a buyer and a seller at time 0, when the seller of the asset agrees to deliver it immediately and the buyer agrees to pay for that asset immediately.[3] Thus, the unique feature of a spot market is the immediate and simultaneous exchange of cash for securities, or what is often called *delivery versus payment.* A spot bond quote of \$97 for a 20-year maturity bond is the price the buyer must pay the seller, per \$100 of face value, for immediate (time 0) delivery of the 20-year bond.

Spot transactions occur because the buyer of the asset believes its value will increase in the immediate future (over the investor's holding period). If the value of the asset increases as expected, the investor can sell the asset at its higher price for a profit. For example, if the 20-year bond increases in value to \$99 per \$100 of face value, the investor can sell the bond for a profit of \$2 per \$100 of face value.

Forward Markets

forward contract

An agreement to transact involving the future exchange of a set amount of assets at a set price.

Forward Contracts. A **forward contract** is a contractual agreement between a buyer and a seller at time 0 to exchange a prespecified asset for cash at some later date. Market participants take a position in forward contracts because the future (spot) price or interest rate on an asset is uncertain. Rather than risk that the future spot price will move against them—that the asset will become more expensive to buy in the future—forward traders pay a financial institution a fee to arrange a forward contract. Such a contract lets the market participant hedge the risk that future spot prices on an asset will move against him or her by guaranteeing a future price for the asset *today.*

For example, in a three-month forward contract to deliver \$100 face value of 10-year bonds, the buyer and seller agree on a price and amount today (time 0), but the delivery (or exchange) of the 10-year bond for cash does not occur until three months into the future. If the forward price agreed to at time 0 was \$98 per \$100 of face value, in three months' time the seller delivers \$100 of 10-year bonds and receives \$98 from the buyer. This is the price the buyer must pay and the seller must accept no matter what happens to the spot price of 10-year bonds during the three months between the time the contract was entered into and the time the bonds are delivered for payment (i.e., whether the spot price falls to \$97 or below or rises to \$99 or above).

In Chapter 8, we discussed the market for forward foreign currency exchange contracts, which allows market participants to buy or sell a specified currency for a specified price at a specified date (e.g., one-month, three-month, or six-month contracts are standard).

3. Technically, physical settlement and delivery may take place one or two days after the contractual spot agreement in bond markets. In equity markets, delivery and cash settlement normally occurs three business days after the spot contract agreement ($T + 3$ settlement).

Forward contracts can also be based on a specified interest rate (e.g., LIBOR) rather than a specified asset (called forward rate agreements, or FRAs). The buyer of an FRA agrees to pay the contract rate based on some notional principal amount (e.g., \$1 million)—he or she buys the notional amount at the stated interest rate. The seller of an FRA agrees to sell the funds to the buyer at the stated rate. For example, for a three-month FRA written today with a notional value of \$1 million and a contract rate of 5.70 percent, the buyer of the FRA agrees to pay 5.70 percent (the current three-month LIBOR rate) to borrow \$1 million starting three months from now. The seller of the FRA agrees to lend \$1 million to the buyer at 5.70 percent starting three months from now. If interest rates rise in the next three months, the FRA buyer benefits from the FRA. He or she can borrow \$1 million at the rate stated on the FRA (5.70 percent) rather than the higher market rate (say, 7 percent).

Forward contracts often involve underlying assets that are nonstandardized, because the terms of each contract are negotiated individually between the buyer and the seller (e.g., a contract between Bank A to buy from Bank B, six months from now, \$1 million in 30-year Treasury bonds with a coupon rate of 6.25 percent). As a result, the buyer and seller involved in a forward contract must locate and deal directly with each other in the over-the-counter market to set the terms of the contract rather than transacting the sale in a centralized market (such as a futures market exchange).

Forward Markets. Commercial banks (see Chapter 11) and investment banks and broker-dealers (see Chapter 16) are the major forward market participants, acting as both principals and agents. These financial institutions make a profit on the spread between the price at which they buy and sell the asset underlying the forward contracts.

Each forward contract is originally negotiated between the financial institution and the customer, and therefore the details of each (e.g., price, expiration, size, delivery date) can be unique. As the forward market has grown over the last decade, however, traders have begun making secondary markets in some forward contracts, communicating the buy and sell price on the contracts over computer networks. As of September 2004, U.S. commercial banks held over \$8.15 trillion of forward contracts that were listed for trading in the over-the-counter markets. The advent of this secondary market trading has resulted in an increase in the standardization of forward contracts. It has also become increasingly easy to get out of a forward position by taking an offsetting forward position in the secondary market. Secondary market activity in forward contracts has made them more attractive to firms and investors that had previously been reluctant to get locked into a forward contract until expiration. Secondary market activity has also resulted in a situation in which the differences between forward and future contracts have significantly narrowed.

Futures Markets

futures contract

An agreement to transact involving the future exchange of a set amount of assets for a price that is settled daily.

marked to market

Describes the prices on outstanding futures contracts that are adjusted each day to reflect current futures market conditions.

Futures Contracts. A **futures contract** is normally traded on an organized exchange such as the New York Futures Exchange (NYFE). A futures contract, like a forward contract, is an agreement between a buyer and a seller at time 0 to exchange a standardized, prespecified asset for cash at some later date. Thus, a futures contract is very similar to a forward contract. One difference between forwards and futures is that forward contracts are bilateral contracts subject to counterparty default risk, but the default risk on futures is significantly reduced by the futures exchange guaranteeing to indemnify counterparties against credit or default risk. Another difference relates to the contract's price, which in a forward contract is fixed over the life of the contract (e.g., \$98 per \$100 of face value for three months to be paid on expiration of the forward contract), whereas a futures contract is **marked to market** daily. This means that the contract's price is adjusted each day as the futures price for the contract changes and the contract approaches expiration. Therefore, actual daily cash settlements occur between the buyer and seller in response to these price changes (this is called marking-to-market). This can be compared to a forward contract, for which cash payment from buyer to seller occurs only at the end

initial margin

A deposit required on futures trades to ensure that the terms of any futures contract will be met.

maintenance margin

The margin a futures trader must maintain once a futures position is taken. If losses on the customer's futures position occur and the level of the funds in the margin account drop below the maintenance margin, the customer is required to deposit additional funds into his or her margin account, bringing the balance back up to the initial margin.

leveraged investment

An investment in which traders post and maintain only a small portion of the value of their futures position in their accounts. The vast majority of the investment is borrowed from the investor's broker.

of the contract period. Marking these contracts to market ensures that both parties to the futures contract maintain sufficient funds in their account to guarantee the eventual payoff when the contract matures. For the buyers of the futures contract, marking to market can result in unexpected payments from their account if the price of the futures contract moves against them.

Brokerage firms require their customers to post only a portion of the value of the futures contracts, called an **initial margin,** any time they request a trade. The amount of the margin varies according to the type of contract traded and the quantity of futures contracts traded (e.g., 5 percent of the value of the underlying asset). Minimum margin levels are set by each exchange. If losses on the customer's futures position occur (when their account is marked to market at the end of the trading day) and the level of the funds in the margin account drops below a stated level (called the **maintenance margin**), the customer receives a margin call. A margin call requires the customer to deposit additional funds into his or her margin account, bringing the balance back up to the initial level. The maintenance margin is generally about 75 percent of the initial margin. If the margin is not maintained, the broker closes out (sells) the customer's futures position. Any amount of cash received above the initial margin may be withdrawn by the customer from his or her account. Brokerage firms are responsible for ensuring that their customers maintain the required margin requirements.

Because futures traders must post and maintain only a small portion of the value of their futures position in their accounts (e.g., 4 percent of the value of the contracts), these **investments** are highly **leveraged.** That is, the vast majority of the investment is "borrowed" from the investor's broker. This high degree of leverage, combined with the marking to market feature of these contracts, can require the payment of large, unexpected cash flows from the investor to the broker if the price of the futures contracts moves against the investor.

EXAMPLE 10-1 The Impact of Marking to Market and Margin Requirements on Futures Investments

Suppose an investor has a \$1 million position in T-bond futures. The investor's broker requires a maintenance margin of 4 percent, or \$40,000 (\$1m. × .04), which is the amount currently in the investor's account. Suppose also that the value of the futures contracts drops by \$50,000 to \$950,000. The investor will now be required to hold \$38,000 (\$950,000 × .04) in his account (or he has a \$2,000 surplus). Further, because futures contracts are marked to market, the investor's broker will make a margin call to the investor requiring him to immediately send a check for \$50,000 − \$2,000, or \$48,000, leaving him with account balance of \$38,000 at his broker for the \$950,000 T-bond future position. Thus, as stated above, the marking to market feature of futures contracts can lead to unexpected cash outflows for a futures investor.

In a futures contract, like a forward contract, a person or firm makes a commitment to deliver an asset (such as foreign exchange) at some future date. If a counterparty were to default on a futures contract, however, the exchange would assume the defaulting party's position and payment obligations. Consider the case of Barings, the 200-year-old British merchant bank that failed as a result of trading losses in February 1995. In this case, Barings (specifically, one trader, Nick Leeson) bought \$8 billion worth of futures on the Japanese Nikkei Stock Market Index, betting that the Nikkei index would rise. For a number of reasons, the index actually fell and the bank lost more than \$1.2 billion on its trading position over a period of one month. When Barings was unable to meet its margin calls on Nikkei Index futures traded on the Singapore futures exchange (SIMEX)

ETHICAL DEBATES

www.dushkin.com/powerweb

Big Australian Bank Widens Probe

Widening its investigation into a rogue-trading scandal, National Australia Bank Ltd. said foreign-currency trading losses could rise to as much as 600 million Australian dollars ($485 million). The big Australian bank's Chief Executive Frank Cicutto ordered that a probe into unauthorized trading of foreign-currency options be expanded into other market operations, such as commodities, spot currency, and interest rates. While the focus continues to be on bogus trades from its foreign-currency options desk, NAB hopes the broader review of its entire trading floor will inject confidence into its market operation.

Details of the wider investigation emerged as NAB raised its estimate of a pretax loss arising from unauthorized foreign-currency options trades since October by A$5 million to A$185 million. Analysis already expect known losses to wipe out the bank's entire fiscal 2004 earnings growth . . . Four NAB employees were suspended last week in connection with the allegations of unauthorized trading. The federal police and bank-sector regulators also are investigating.

Source: *The Wall Street Journal*, January 20, 2004, p. A12, by Erick Johnston. **www.wsj.com**

in 1995, the exchange stood ready to assume Barings' futures contracts and ensure that no counterparty lost money. Thus, unless a systematic financial market collapse threatens an exchange itself, futures are essentially default risk free. In addition, the default risk of a futures contract is less than that of a forward contract for at least four reasons: (1) daily marking to market of futures (so that there is no buildup of losses or gains), (2) margin requirements on futures that act as a security bond should a counterparty default, (3) price movement limits that spread extreme price fluctuations over time, and (4) default guarantees by the futures exchange itself. The Ethical Debates box highlights a more recent example of a rogue trader's actions that led to large losses at National Australia Bank.

DO YOU UNDERSTAND?

1. How a rogue trader at National Australia Bank caused losses of A$185 million for the bank?
2. What option position taken by National Australia Bank created these losses?

Futures Markets. Futures trading occurs on organized exchanges—for example, the Chicago Board of Trade (CBT) and the Chicago Mercantile Exchange (CME). Financial futures market trading was introduced in 1972 with the establishment of foreign exchange future contracts on the International Money Market (IMM). By 2005, five major exchanges existed in the United States[4] and several exchanges exist abroad.[5] Table 10–2 lists the characteristics of some of the most widely traded financial futures contracts. Table 10–3 lists the average month-end contracts outstanding, number of contracts traded, and number of contracts settled from 1992 through 2003. The terms of futures contracts (e.g., contract size, delivery month, trading hours, minimum price fluctuation, daily price limits, and process used for delivery) traded in the United States are set by the exchange and are subject to the approval of the Commodity Futures Trading Commission (CFTC), the principal regulator of futures markets. For example, the contract terms for 30-year T-bond futures are listed in Table 10–4.

www.cbot.com

www.cme.com

www.cftc.gov

In recent years, "off-market" trading systems have sprung up in which institutional investors and money managers can continue to trade during, as well as after, futures exchanges operating hours. Indeed, trading volume in off-market currencies, interest rate swaps, and Eurodollars has grown an estimated 3 to 10 times faster than trading volume on futures exchanges.

4. These include the Chicago Board of Trade, the Chicago Mercantile Exchange, the New York Futures Exchange, the MidAmerica Commodity Exchange, and the Kansas City Board of Trade.

5. These include the London International Financial Futures Exchange (LIFFE), the Singapore Exchange (SGX), the Marchè a Terme International de France (MATIF), and the Montreal Exchange.

TABLE 10-2 Characteristics of Actively Traded Futures Contracts

Type of Futures	Contract Size	Exchange*	Open Interest
Interest Rates			
Treasury bonds	$100,000	CBT	631,291
Treasury notes	$100,000	CBT	1,688,804
Treasury notes—5 year	$100,000	CBT	1,146,364
Treasury notes—2 year	$200,000	CBT	265,181
Federal funds—30 days	$5,000,000	CBT	342,948
Eurodollars	$1,000,000	CME	7,062,495
Short sterling	£500,000	LIFFE	1,317,857
Eurolibor-3 month	Euro 1,000,000	LIFFE	2,731,469
Euroswiss-3 month	Sfr 1,000,000	LIFFE	265,205
Canadian banker's acceptances	C$1,000,000	ME	291,712
Commonwealth T-bonds—3 year	A$100,000	SFE	328,388
Euroyen	¥100,000,000	SGX	343,003
German Euro-government bonds—5 year	Euro 100,000	EUREX	759,612
German Euro-government bonds—10 year	Euro 100,000	EUREX	1,209,789
Currency			
Japanese yen	¥12,500,000	CME	157,988
Canadian dollar	C$100,000	CME	70,945
British pound	£62,500	CME	67,679
Swiss franc	Sfr 125,000	CME	53,537
Australian dollar	A$100,000	CME	64,094
Euro FX	Euro 125,000	CME	141,853
Index			
DJIA	$10 times average	CBT	48,135
S&P 500 index	$250 times index	CME	683,891
Mini S&P index	$50 times index	CME	832,200
Nasdaq 100	$100 times index	CME	66,075
Mini Nasdaq100	$20 times index	CME	320,564
Russell 1000	$500 times index	NYBOT	74,899
Share price index	A$25 times index	SFE	160,405
CAC-40 stock index	Euro 10 times index	MATIF	480,167
FT-SE 100 index	£10 times index	LIFFE	466,212
DJ Euro Stoxx 50 index	Euro 10 times index	EUREX	1,491,682

*CBT = Chicago Board of Trade, CME = Chicago Mercantile Exchange, LIFFE = London International Financial Futures Exchange, ME = Montreal Exchange, MATIF = Marchè a Terme International de France, SFE = Sydney Futures Exchange, SGX = Singapore Exchange Ltd., EUREX = The European Derivatives Market.

Source: *The Wall Street Journal*, January 10, 2005, p. C11. Reprinted by permission of *The Wall Street Journal*. **www.wsj.com**

open-outcry auction

Method of futures trading where traders face each other and "cry out" their offer to buy or sell a stated number of futures contracts at a stated price.

2

Trading on the largest exchanges such as the CBT takes place in trading "pits." A trading pit consists of circular steps leading down to the center of the pit. Traders for each delivery date on a futures contract informally group together in the trading pit. Futures trading occurs using an **open-outcry auction** method where traders face each other and "cry out" their offers to buy or sell a stated number of futures contracts at a stated price.

TABLE 10-3 Futures Market Activity, 1992–2003

	1992	1995	2000	2003
Average month end contracts outstanding (in thousands):				
Financial instruments	2,037.8	3,749.8	5,454.9	9,117.1
Currencies	385.5	299.2	402.7	499.0
Number of contracts traded (in millions):				
Financial instruments	148.2	259.0	297.0	760.3
Currencies	38.7	24.3	20.0	30.0
Number of contracts maturing (in thousands):				
Financial instruments	965.4	1,939.9	3,151.5	7,115.8
Currencies	503.1	521.5	722.3	682.1

Source: Commodity Futures Trading Commission, January 2000 and 2005. **www.cftc.gov**

floor broker

Exchange members who place trades from the public.

professional traders

Exchange members who trade for their own account.

position traders

Exchange members who take a position in the futures market based on their expectations about the future direction of the prices of the underlying assets.

day traders

Exchange members who take a position within a day and liquidate it before day's end.

scalpers

Exchange members who take positions for very short periods of time, sometimes only minutes, in an attempt to profit from this active trading.

Only futures exchange members are allowed to transact on the floor of futures exchanges. Trades from the public are placed with a **floor broker.** When an order is placed, a floor broker may trade with another floor broker or with a professional trader. **Professional traders** are similar to specialists on the stock exchanges in that they trade for their own account. Professional traders are also referred to as position traders, day traders, or scalpers. **Position traders** take a position in the futures market based on their expectations about the future direction of prices of the underlying assets. **Day traders** generally take a position within a day and liquidate it before day's end. **Scalpers** take positions for very short periods of time, sometimes only minutes, in an attempt to profit from this active trading. Scalpers do not have an affirmative obligation to provide liquidity to futures markets but do

TABLE 10-4 Contract Terms for 30-Year Treasury Bond Futures

Trading Unit: One U.S. Treasury bond having a face value at maturity of $100,000.

Deliverable Grades: U.S. Treasury bonds that, if callable, are not callable for at least 15 years from the first day of the delivery month or, if not callable, have a maturity of at least 15 years from the first day of the delivery month. The invoice price equals the futures settlement price times a conversion factor plus accrued interest. The conversion factor is the price of the delivered bond ($1 par value) to yield 6 percent.

Tick Size: 1/32 of a point ($31.25/contract); par is on the basis of 100 points.

Price Quote: Points ($1,000) and thirty-seconds of a point; for example 80-16 equals $80^{16}/_{32}$.

Contract Months: March, June, September, December.

Last Trading Day: Seventh business day preceding the last business day of the delivery month.

Last Delivery Day: Last business day of the delivery month.

Delivery Method: Federal Reserve book-entry wire-transfer system.

Trading Hours: Open Outcry—7:20 a.m.–2:00 p.m. Chicago time, Mon.–Fri.
Electronic—7:00 p.m.–4:00 p.m. Chicago time Sun.-Fri.

Trading in expiring contracts closes at noon (Chicago time) on the last trading day.

Ticker Symbols: Open Auction—US
Electronic—ZB

Daily Price Limit: None.

Source: Chicago Board of Trade Web site, January 2005. **www.cbot.com**

FIGURE 10–1 Clearinghouse Function in Futures Markets

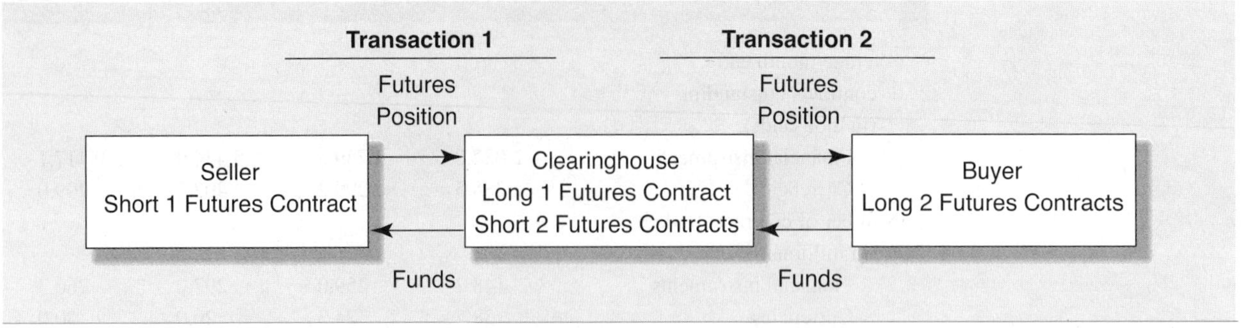

so in expectation of earning a profit. Scalpers' profits are related to the bid-ask spread and the length of time a position is held. Specifically, it has been found that scalper trades held longer than three minutes, on average, produce losses to scalpers. Thus, this need for a quick turnover of a scalper's position enhances futures market liquidity and is therefore valuable.[6]

long position
A purchase of a futures contract.

short position
A sale of a futures contract.

clearinghouse
The unit that oversees trading on the exchange and guarantees all trades made by the exchange traders.

Similar to trading in the stock market, futures trades may be placed as market orders (instructing the floor broker to transact at the best price available) or limit orders (instructing the floor broker to transact at a specified price). The order may be for a purchase of the futures contract in which the futures holder takes a **long position** in the futures contract, or the order may be for a sale of the futures contract in which the futures holder takes a **short position** in the futures contract.

Once a futures price is agreed upon in a trading pit, the two parties do not complete the deal with each other but rather (as illustrated in Figure 10–1) with the clearinghouse overseeing the exchange. The exchange's clearinghouse guarantees all trades made by exchange traders. The **clearinghouse** breaks up every trade into a buy and sell transaction and takes the opposite side of the transaction, becoming the buyer for every futures contract seller (transaction 1 in Figure 10–1) and the seller for every futures contract buyer (transaction 2 in Figure 10–1). Thus, the clearinghouse ensures that all trading obligations are met. Clearinghouses are able to perform their function as guarantor of an exchange's futures contracts by requiring all member firms to deposit sufficient funds (from customers' margin accounts) to ensure that the firm's customers will meet the terms of any futures contract entered into on the exchange.

3 Table 10–5 shows a futures quote from *The Wall Street Journal* for January 10, 2005. The three types of financial futures contracts are interest rate futures, currency futures, and equity stock index futures. The underlying asset on an interest rate futures contract is a bond or a short-term fixed-interest security's price or interest rate (e.g., Treasury securities, Eurodollar CDs); on a currency contract it is an exchange rate (e.g., yen to U.S. dollar); and on an index futures contract it is a major U.S. or foreign stock market index (e.g., the Dow Jones Industrial Average—see Chapter 9). Look at the quote for Treasury bond interest rate futures contracts. The bold heading of each quote contains information about the underlying deliverable asset (e.g., Treasury bonds) on the futures contract, the exchange on which the futures is traded (e.g., CBT), the face value of a contract (e.g., \$100,000), and the basis for the quoted prices (e.g., pts 32nds of 100%, or 112–11 = $112\frac{11}{32}\%$). Each row of the quote provides information for a specific delivery month (e.g., Mar = March 2005). The first column of the quote lists the delivery month. The second through fourth columns, labeled OPEN, HIGH, and LOW, are the opening price,

6. See W.L. Silber, "Marketmaker Behavior in an Auction Market: An Analysis of Scalpers in Futures Markets," *Journal of Finance*, September 1984, pp. 937–53.

TABLE 10-5 Futures Quote

Interest Rate Futures

Treasury Bonds (CBT)-$100,000; pts 32nds of 100%

	OPEN	HIGH	LOW	SETTLE	CHG	LIFETIME HIGH	LIFETIME LOW	OPEN INT
Mar	112-09	112-15	112-00	112-11	8	114-02	100-25	612,141
June	111-16	111-20	111-10	111-16	8	113-07	100-00	18,941
Sept	109-31	109-31	109-31	110-26	8	111-02	109-31	195

Est vol;147,946; vol Fri 379,969; open int 631,291, +18,215.

Treasury Notes (CBT)-$100,000; pts 32nds of 100%

	OPEN	HIGH	LOW	SETTLE	CHG	LIFETIME HIGH	LIFETIME LOW	OPEN INT
Mar	111-14	111-16	11-085	11-125	.5	13-165	04-315	1,651,390
June	10-185	110-20	110-13	110-16	.5	12-145	109-10	36,636
Sept	110-07	110-07	110-04	10-065	2.5	110-22	09-235	778

Est vol 427,231; vol Fri 968,424; open int 1,688,804, +38,116.

5 Yr. Treasury Notes (CBT)-$100,000; pts 32nds of 100%

	OPEN	HIGH	LOW	SETTLE	CHG	LIFETIME HIGH	LIFETIME LOW	OPEN INT
Mar	109-01	109-01	108-27	08-305	−1.0	10-275	108-17	1,123,831
June	108-17	108-17	08-155	08-155	−1.0	110-06	08-095	22,533

Est vol 245,270; vol Fri 550,876; open int 1,146,364, +13,173.

2 Yr. Treasury Notes (CBT)-$200,000; pts 32nds of 100%

	OPEN	HIGH	LOW	SETTLE	CHG	LIFETIME HIGH	LIFETIME LOW	OPEN INT
Mar	04-165	04-175	104-15	04-167	−.7	05-022	04-147	265,181

Est vol 27,944; vol Fri 57,609; open int 265,181, +6,425.

30 Day Federal Funds (CBT)-$5,000,000; 100 - daily avg.

	OPEN	HIGH	LOW	SETTLE	CHG	LIFETIME HIGH	LIFETIME LOW	OPEN INT
Jan	97.755	97.760	97.755	97.755	...	98.945	97.750	132,057
Feb	97.50	97.50	97.49	97.50	...	98.87	97.38	123,598
Mar	97.41	97.42	97.40	97.41	−.01	98.65	97.20	42,894
Apr	97.25	97.25	96.25	97.24	−.01	97.80	96.25	34,662
May	97.06	97.06	97.04	97.05	−.02	97.66	97.04	8,108
June	97.03	97.04	97.02	97.02	−.02	97.70	97.02	1,017

Est vol 24,662; vol Fri 39,816; open int 342,948, −887

10 Yr. Interest Rate Swaps (CBT)-$100,000; pts 32nds of 100%

	OPEN	HIGH	LOW	SETTLE	CHG	LIFETIME HIGH	LIFETIME LOW	OPEN INT
Mar	110-02	110-03	109-26	109-30	1	111-19	108-09	36,142

Est vol 440; vol Fri 290; open int 36,142, −77.

10 Yr. Muni Note Index (CBT)-$1,000 x index

	OPEN	HIGH	LOW	SETTLE	CHG	LIFETIME HIGH	LIFETIME LOW	OPEN INT
Mar	104-11	104-13	104-08	104-12	6	105-05	101-27	2 685

Est vol 332; vol Fri 717; open int 2,685,-+531.
Index: Close 105-14; Yield 4.326.

1 Month Libor (CME)-$3,000,000; pts of 100%

	OPEN	HIGH	LOW	SETTLE	CHG	YIELD	CHG	OPEN INT
Jan	97.50	97.50	97.50	97.50	...	2.50		23,005
Feb	97.39	97.39	97.38	97.38	...	2.62		15,455
Mar	97.18	97.18	97.18	97.18	−.01	2.82	.01	5,646
Apr	97.02	97.02	97.02	97.02	−.02	2.98	.02	1,185

Est vol 1,921, vol Fri 2,994; open int 45,984, +1,109

Eurodollar (CME)-$1,000,000; pts of 100%

	OPEN	HIGH	LOW	SETTLE	CHG	YIELD	CHG	OPEN INT
Jan	97.34	97.34	97.33	97.33	...	2.67	...	74,450
Feb	97.18	97.18	97.18	97.18	...	2.82	...	8,016
Mar	97.06	97.06	97.03	97.04	−.01	2.96	.01	1.072.293
June	96.74	96.74	96.71	96.72	−.01	3.28	.01	1.167.365
Sept	96.48	96.49	96.44	96.47	−.01	3.53	.01	1,080,285
Dec	96.29	96.30	96.24	96.27	−.02	3.73	.02	807,488
Mr06	96.17	96.18	96.12	96.15	−.01	3.85	.01	603,927
June	96.08	96.08	96.03	96.06	−.01	3.94	.01	427,781
Sept	95.99	96.01	95.95	95.98	−.01	4.02	.01	312,914
Dec	95.90	95.93	95.86	95.89	−.01	4.11	.01	271,139
Mr07	95.83	95.85	95.79	95.82	−.01	4.18	.01	180,265
June	95.76	95.76	95.72	95.74	−.01	4.26	.01	160,047
Sept	95.68	95.69	95.65	95.67	−.01	4.33	.01	125,473
Dec	95.60	95.60	95.56	95.59	...	4.41	...	120,327
Mr08	95.53	95.54	95.50	95.52	...	4.48	...	96,701
June	95.45	95.46	95.43	95.44	...	4.56	...	103,718
Sept	95.37	95.38	95.35	95.36	...	4.64	...	95,510
Dec	95.28	95.28	95.26	95.27	...	4.73	...	85,283
Mr09	95.21	95.22	95.19	95.20	...	4.80	...	66,313
June	95.12	95.13	95.10	95.12	.01	4.88	−.01	59,362
Sept	95.04	95.05	95.02	95.04	.01	4.96	−.01	50,398
Dec	94.94	94.96	94.93	94.95	.01	5.05	−.01	29,002
Mr10	94.88	94.90	94.88	94.89	.01	5.11	−.01	13,739
June	94.81	94.83	94.81	94.83	.02	5.17	−.02	9,478
Sept	94.74	94.76	94.74	94.76	.03	5.24	−.03	7,788
Dec	94.65	94.67	94.65	94.67	.03	5.33	−.03	7,959
Mr11	94.60	94.62	94.60	94.62	.02	5.38	−.02	5,967
June	94.55	94.57	94.55	94.57	.02	5.43	−.02	5,432
Sept	94.50	94.52	94.50	94.52	.02	5.48	−.02	4,408
Dec	94.42	94.44	94.42	94.44	.03	5.56	−.03	2,010

Est vol 394,719; vol Fri 2,178,312; open int 7,062,495, +164,238.

Euroyen (CME)-¥100,000,000; pts of 100%

	OPEN	HIGH	LOW	SETTLE	CHG	LIFETIME HIGH	LIFETIME LOW	OPEN INT
Mar	99.90	99.90	99.90	99.90	...	99.91	99.27	51,335
June	99.90	99.90	99.90	99.90	.01	99.90	99.16	33,651
Sept	99.86	99.86	99.86	99.86	...	99.87	98.98	7,739
Dec	99.82	99.82	99.82	99.82	.01	99.83	98.90	8,222
Mr06	99.75	99.76	99.75	99.76	.01	99.76	98.84	7,267

Est vol 2,733; vol Fri 41; open int 115,390, +781.

Short Sterling (LIFFE)-£500,000; pts of 100%

	OPEN	HIGH	LOW	SETTLE	CHG	LIFETIME HIGH	LIFETIME LOW	OPEN INT
Jan	...	...	...	95.13	...	95.10	95.10	1,200
Mar	95.14	95.16	95.13	95.15	.01	96.38	93.29	238,562
June	95.20	95.26	95.20	95.24	.02	96.30	95.18	258,004
Sept	95.24	95.30	95.23	95.28	.02	96.23	94.06	243,955
Dec	95.24	95.30	95.22	95.28	.02	96.15	94.06	195,890
Mr06	95.19	95.28	95.19	95.26	.02	96.10	94.05	110,280
June	95.18	95.28	95.18	95.26	.03	95.97	94.04	98,941
Sept	95.20	95.27	95.20	95.25	.03	95.75	94.20	71,174
Dec	95.20	95.25	95.20	95.24	.03	95.83	94.21	43,451
Mr07	95.20	95.22	95.20	95.23	.03	95.82	94.20	23,310
June	95.20	95.22	95.20	95.22	.03	95.73	94.21	17,602
Sept	95.19	95.20	95.19	95.20	.03	95.62	94.21	10,080

Est vol 145,632; vol Fri 264,224; open int 1,317,857, +34,869.

Long Gilt (LIFFE)-£100,000; pts of 100%

	OPEN	HIGH	LOW	SETTLE	CHG	LIFETIME HIGH	LIFETIME LOW	OPEN INT
Mar	111.65	111.88	111.60	111.83	.06	112.65	109.67	194,963

Est vol 26,064; vol Fri 59,539; open int 194,963, +1,950.

3 Month Euribor (LIFFE)-€1,000,000; pts of 100%

	OPEN	HIGH	LOW	SETTLE	CHG	LIFETIME HIGH	LIFETIME LOW	OPEN INT
Jan	97.86	97.86	97.86	97.86	...	97.86	97.76	34,561
Feb				97.85	...	97.85	97.74	11,530
Apr	97.78	97.81	97.78	97.80	...	97.81	97.74	1,952
May	97.74	97.79	97.74	97.76	...	97.79	97.70	300
June	97.69	97.73	97.69	97.72	.01	97.79	94.29	576,765
Sept	97.56	97.61	97.54	97.60	.02	97.71	94.29	370,415
Dec	97.42	97.47	97.40	97.46	.02	97.61	94.41	366,070
Mr06	97.32	97.38	97.30	97.36	.02	97.53	94.40	260,164
June	97.21	97.26	97.18	97.24	.02	97.42	94.66	219,568
Sept	97.10	97.15	97.08	97.14	.02	97.31	94.58	150,577
Dec	96.97	97.03	96.96	97.02	.02	97.16	94.62	98,016
Mr07	96.90	96.96	96.90	96.95	.03	97.07	94.57	48,159
June	96.82	96.89	96.82	96.88	.03	96.98	94.57	26,054
Sept	96.75	96.81	96.75	96.80	.03	96.88	95.26	23,051
Dec	96.66	96.71	96.66	96.71	.03	96.77	95.18	11,953
Mr08	96.62	96.66	96.62	96.67	.04	96.71	95.31	3,674
June	96.60	96.60	96.60	96.61	.04	96.60	95.12	1,948

Est vol 482,471; vol Fri 835,141; open int 2,731,469, +2,307.

3 Month Euroswiss (LIFFE)-CHF 1,000,000; pts of 100%

	OPEN	HIGH	LOW	SETTLE	CHG	LIFETIME HIGH	LIFETIME LOW	OPEN INT
Mar	99.18	99.21	99.18	99.20	.01	99.23	97.90	107,400
June	99.00	99.05	98.99	99.03	.01	99.08	97.74	66,755
Sept	98.80	98.87	98.80	98.84	.02	98.95	97.75	48,253
Dec	98.63	98.71	98.63	98.67	.03	98.80	97.68	27,140
Mr06	98.52	98.57	98.52	98.54	.03	98.66	97.63	8,610
June	98.41	98.41	98.41	98.41	.04	98.54	97.51	4,143
Sept	98.28	98.28	98.28	98.29	.04	98.43	97.91	2,795

Est vol 33,028; vol Fri 16,383; open int 265,205, +2,859.

Canadian Bankers Acceptance (ME)-CAD 1,000,000

	OPEN	HIGH	LOW	SETTLE	CHG	LIFETIME HIGH	LIFETIME LOW	OPEN INT
Mar	97.34	97.34	97.30	97.30	−0.03	97.74	94.45	101,617
June	97.14	97.14	97.09	97.09	−0.04	97.44	95.30	122,730
Sept	96.94	96.94	96.87	96.87	−0.06	97.25	95.21	42,954
Dec	96.73	96.73	96.67	96.67	−0.06	97.08	95.43	12,711
Mr06	96.50	96.52	96.49	96.48	−0.03	96.83	95.16	5,859
June	96.28	96.28	96.26	96.26		96.65	95.33	5,097

Est vol 43,729; vol Fri 75,467; open int 291,712, +36,788

10 Yr. Canadian Govt. Bonds (ME)-CAD 100,000

	OPEN	HIGH	LOW	SETTLE	CHG	LIFETIME HIGH	LIFETIME LOW	OPEN INT
Mar	111.62	111.65	111.41	111.54	−0.03	112.76	110.05	127,435

Est vol 7,138; vol Fri 12,188; open int 127,435, +1,897

3 Yr. Commonwealth T-Bonds (SFE)-AUD 100,000

	OPEN	HIGH	LOW	SETTLE	CHG	LIFETIME HIGH	LIFETIME LOW	OPEN INT
Mar	94.77	94.83	94.74	94.77	−0.01	95.11	94.65	328,388

Est vol 41,687; vol Fri 48,207; open int 328,388, −9,099.

Euroyen (SGX)-¥100,000,000; pts of 100%

	OPEN	HIGH	LOW	SETTLE	CHG	LIFETIME HIGH	LIFETIME LOW	OPEN INT
Mar	99.90	99.90	99.90	99.90		99.91	99.18	103,011
June	99.90	99.90	99.89	99.90	0.01	99.90	99.10	94,727
Sept	99.86	99.86	99.86	99.86	0.01	99.87	98.95	45,033
Mr06	99.75	99.75	99.75	99.75		99.77	98.84	28,307

Est vol 1,110; vol Fri 3,903; open int 343,003, +1,353.

5 Yr. Euro-BOBL (EUREX)-€100,000; pts of 100%

	OPEN	HIGH	LOW	SETTLE	CHG	LIFETIME HIGH	LIFETIME LOW	OPEN INT
Mar	113.13	113.33	113.07	113.22	0.06	113.76	110.63	742,492
June	112.31	112.31	112.31	112.42	0.06	112.82	111.28	17,120

vol Mon 497,761; open int 759,612, +4,621.

10 Yr. Euro-BUND (EUREX)-€100,000; pts of 100%

	OPEN	HIGH	LOW	SETTLE	CHG	LIFETIME HIGH	LIFETIME LOW	OPEN INT
Mar	119.13	119.48	119.07	119.33	0.14	119.97	112.75	1,206,555
June	118.19	118.53	118.19	118.40	0.14	118.93	113.45	3,234

vol Mon 815,285; open int 1,209,789, −4,171.

2 Yr. Euro-SCHATZ (EUREX)-€100,000; pts of 100%

	OPEN	HIGH	LOW	SETTLE	CHG	LIFETIME HIGH	LIFETIME LOW	OPEN INT
Mar	106.10	106.18	106.07	106.13	0.03	106.41	105.52	675,089

vol Mon 364,341; open int 675,263, +26,128.

Currency Futures

Japanese Yen (CME)-¥12,500,000; $ per ¥

	OPEN	HIGH	LOW	SETTLE	CHG	LIFETIME HIGH	LIFETIME LOW	OPEN INT
Mar	.9580	.9651	.9580	.9641	.0072	.9885	.8873	137,751
June	na	.9717	.9699	.9711	.0072	.9917	.9040	20,084

Est vol 12,086; vol Fri 55,229; open int 157,988, −1,357.

Canadian Dollar (CME)-CAD 100,000; $ per CAD

	OPEN	HIGH	LOW	SETTLE	CHG	LIFETIME HIGH	LIFETIME LOW	OPEN INT
Mar	.8111	.8208	.8101	.8184	.0072	.8526	.7150	66,547
June	.8179	.8211	.8112	.8190	.0072	.8495	.7150	3,096
Sept	.8190	.8206	.8190	.8200	.0072	.8490	.7160	768

Est vol 7,776; vol Fri 34,917; open int 70,945, +578.

British Pound (CME)-£62,500; $ per £

	OPEN	HIGH	LOW	SETTLE	CHG	LIFETIME HIGH	LIFETIME LOW	OPEN INT
Mar	1.8628	1.8718	1.8625	1.8689	.0057	1.9446	1.7321	67,626

Est vol 4,890; vol Fri 34,667; open int 67,679, −6,192.

Swiss Franc (CME)-CHF 125,000; $ per CHF

	OPEN	HIGH	LOW	SETTLE	CHG	LIFETIME HIGH	LIFETIME LOW	OPEN INT
Mar	.8468	.8510	.8461	.8485	.0018	.8892	.7853	53,358
June	...	...	...	.8529	.0018	.8920	.8529	112

Est vol 5,586; vol Fri 29,659; open int 53,537, +2,721.

Australian Dollar (CME)-AUD 100,000; $ per AUD

	OPEN	HIGH	LOW	SETTLE	CHG	LIFETIME HIGH	LIFETIME LOW	OPEN INT
Mar	.7536	.7573	.7529	.7545	.0026	.7879	.6400	63,328
June	...	...	...	.7499	.0026	.7785	.6670	344

Est vol 1,898; vol Fri 15,414; open int 64,094, −2,895.

Mexican Peso (CME)-MXN 500,000; $ per MXN

	OPEN	HIGH	LOW	SETTLE	CHG	LIFETIME HIGH	LIFETIME LOW	OPEN INT
Jan	...	...	...	.08882	00030	.08910	.08770	63
Mar	.08772	.08802	.08755	.08797	00030	.08890	.08200	68,521
June	.08665	.08665	.08665	.08670	00030	.08735	.08160	1,243

Est vol 4,140; vol Fri 24,210; open int 70,109, +4,067.

Euro/US Dollar (CME)-€125,000; $ per €

	OPEN	HIGH	LOW	SETTLE	CHG	LIFETIME HIGH	LIFETIME LOW	OPEN INT
Mar	1.3063	1.3132	1.3061	1.3098	.0036	1.3687	1.1363	139,081
June	1.3124	1.3155	1.3107	1.3122	.0036	1.3699	1.1750	1,388

Est vol 46,172; vol Fri 204,156; open int 141,853, +2,394.

Euro/US Dollar (NYBOT)-€200,000; $ per €

	OPEN	HIGH	LOW	SETTLE	CHG	LIFETIME HIGH	LIFETIME LOW	OPEN INT
Mar	...	...	...	1.3100	.0034	1.3643	1.2930	449

Est vol 425; vol Fri 327; open int 449, +22.

Euro/Japanese Yen (NYBOT)-€100,000; ¥ per €

	OPEN	HIGH	LOW	SETTLE	CHG	LIFETIME HIGH	LIFETIME LOW	OPEN INT
Mar	136.30	136.45	135.79	135.79	−.67	140.94	135.79	19,713

Est vol 5,304; vol Fri 6,335; open int 19,713, −1,565.

Euro/British Pound (NYBOT)-€100,000; £ per €

	OPEN	HIGH	LOW	SETTLE	CHG	LIFETIME HIGH	LIFETIME LOW	OPEN INT
Mar	.7010	.7018	.7008	.7011	−.0003	.7140	.6892	6,107

Est vol 465; vol Fri 658; open int 6,109, −42.

Index Futures

DJ Industrial Average (CBT)-$10 x index

	OPEN	HIGH	LOW	SETTLE	CHG	LIFETIME HIGH	LIFETIME LOW	OPEN INT
Mar	10614	10672	10585	10628	29	10875	9720	48,094

Est vol 4,271; vol Fri 7,588; open int 48,135, −773.
Idx prl: Hi 10663.74; Lo 10582.38; Close 10621.03, +17.07.

Mini DJ Industrial Average (CBT)-$5 x index

	OPEN	HIGH	LOW	SETTLE	CHG	LIFETIME HIGH	LIFETIME LOW	OPEN INT
Mar	10613	10673	10585	10628	29	10878	9705	53,818

Vol Mon 96,267; open int 53,837, −1,511.

DJ-AIG Commodity Index (CBT)-$100 x index

	OPEN	HIGH	LOW	SETTLE	CHG	LIFETIME HIGH	LIFETIME LOW	OPEN INT
Jan	...	...	...	480.3	1.3	507.5	464.9	670

Est vol 464; vol Fri 54; open int 697, +22.
Idx prl: Hi 146.670; Lo 144.384; Close 144.572, +.360.

S&P 500 Index (CME)-$250 x index

	OPEN	HIGH	LOW	SETTLE	CHG	LIFETIME HIGH	LIFETIME LOW	OPEN INT
Mar	118710	119670	118550	119170	540	122120	84380	663,690
June	119750	120200	118930	119570	540	122700	95750	11,111

Est vol 38,217; vol Fri 36,338; open int 683,891, +300.

TRAKRS Long-Short Tech (CME)-$1 x index

	OPEN	HIGH	LOW	SETTLE	CHG	LIFETIME HIGH	LIFETIME LOW	OPEN INT
July	36.79	37.31	36.68	36.89	.21	45.25	19.76	153,940

Est vol 270; vol Fri 0; open int 153,940, unch.
Idx prl: Hi 37.17; Lo 36.26; Close 36.70, +.39.

Russell 2000 (CME)-$500 x index

	OPEN	HIGH	LOW	SETTLE	CHG	LIFETIME HIGH	LIFETIME LOW	OPEN INT
Mar	613.40	624.50	612.80	620.00	7.25	658.50	517.25	20,796

Est vol 1,848; vol Fri 1,380; open int 20,796, +89.
Idx prl: Hi 623.30; Lo 613.21; Close 617.74, +4.53.

Russell 1000 (NYBOT)-$500 x index

	OPEN	HIGH	LOW	SETTLE	CHG	LIFETIME HIGH	LIFETIME LOW	OPEN INT
Mar	635.75	640.00	635.75	638.75	3.00	655.00	630.50	74,899

Est vol 274; vol Fri 216; open int 74,899, −4.
Idx prl: Hi 640.57; Lo 634.96; Close 638.09, +2.51.

NYSE Composite Index (NYBOT)-$50 x index

	OPEN	HIGH	LOW	SETTLE	CHG	LIFETIME HIGH	LIFETIME LOW	OPEN INT
Mar	7080.00	7080.00	7080.00	7085.00	20.00	7252.00	6980.00	1,169

Est vol 1; vol Fri 14; open int 1,169, +4.
Idx prl: Hi 7106.97; Lo 7055.54; Close 7081.70, +24.19.

U.S. Dollar Index (NYBOT)-$1,000 x index

	OPEN	HIGH	LOW	SETTLE	CHG	LIFETIME HIGH	LIFETIME LOW	OPEN INT
Mar	83.63	83.63	83.21	83.36	−.36	93.07	80.48	16,183
June	83.60	83.50	83.40	83.40	−.36	90.80	80.67	2,039

Est vol 2,061; vol Fri 7,407; open int 18,277, −1,451.
Idx prl: Hi 83.61; Lo 83.13; Close 83.29, −.31.

Nikkei Stock Average (CME)-$5 x index

	OPEN	HIGH	LOW	SETTLE	CHG	LIFETIME HIGH	LIFETIME LOW	OPEN INT
Mar	11445.	11510.	11440.	11470.	35	12190.	10490.	31,110

Est vol 3,077; vol Fri 3,917; open int 31,167, −218.
Index Closed.

Share Price Index (SFE)-AUD 25 x index

	OPEN	HIGH	LOW	SETTLE	CHG	LIFETIME HIGH	LIFETIME LOW	OPEN INT
Mar	4070.0	4087.0	4058.0	4078.0	6.0	4094.0	3390.0	151,246
June	4084.0	4097.0	4077.0	4092.0	7.0	4097.0	3407.0	3.421
Sept	4084.0	4102.0	4083.0	4097.0	5.0	4102.0	3398.0	3,008

Est vol 10,109; vol Fri 10,372; open int 160,405, +772.
Index: Hi na; Lo na; Close 4074.9, +11.7.

CAC-40 Stock Index (MATIF)-€10 x index

	OPEN	HIGH	LOW	SETTLE	CHG	LIFETIME HIGH	LIFETIME LOW	OPEN INT
Jan	3874.0	3887.5	3861.5	3880.0	−1.5	3890.5	3727.0	375,732
Feb	3891.5	3892.5	3871.0	3886.0	−1.5	3892.5	3740.0	1,192
Mar	3891.5	3894.0	3875.5	3891.5	−1.5	3900.0	3548.5	88,044

Est vol 41,800; vol Fri 63,685; open int 480,167, +17,521.
Index: Hi 3890.39; Lo 3860.15; Close 3877.82, −0.14.

Source: *The Wall Street Journal*, January 11, 2005, p. C11. Reprinted by permission of *The Wall Street Journal*. **www.wsj.com**

high price, and low price at which trades occurred during the day (e.g., 112–09 = 112$^{9}/_{32}$% of \$100,000 = \$112,281.25 at the open of trading on January 10, 2005). The fifth column, labeled SETTLE, is a representative price at which a trade occurs at the end of the day.[7] If trading in a futures contract is active, the settle price is the price on the last trade of the day. If, however, the contract does not trade actively, the settlement price is determined by a committee of the exchange immediately after the market's close. The settlement price is the price used to determine the value of a trader's position at the end of each trading day. The sixth column, labeled CHG, is the change in the futures price quote from the previous day's settlement price. Columns 7 and 8, labeled LIFETIME HIGH and LOW, are the highest and lowest prices at which a trade has occurred over the life of the futures contract. Finally, the last column, labeled OPEN INT, is the **open interest,** or total number of futures contract outstanding at the beginning of the day. The bottom line of the futures quote lists the estimated trading volume for the day (e.g., 147,946 contracts), the volume of trading in the contract the previous day (e.g., 379,969), and the number of contracts outstanding for that type (T-bonds), regardless of expiration month (e.g., 631,291).

open interest

The total number of the futures, put option, or call option contracts outstanding at the beginning of the day.

A holder of a futures contract has two choices for liquidating his or her position: liquidate the position before the futures contract expires, or hold the futures contract to expiration. To liquidate before the expiration date, the futures holder simply calls his or her broker and requests an offsetting trade to his or her original position, an opposite position. For example, if the original transaction was a buy or long position, the trader can sell or short the same futures contract. Thus, any losses on the buy position will be exactly offset by gains on the sell position over the remaining life (time) to expiration of the contract. Generally, a vast majority (99 percent in the early 2000s) of all futures positions are liquidated before maturity.

If the futures holder keeps the futures contract to expiration, the parties will either (as specified in the futures contract) conduct a cash settlement where the traders exchange cash based on the final price of the underlying asset relative to the futures price, or the futures holder will take delivery of the underlying asset (e.g., a T-bond) from the futures seller.

DO YOU UNDERSTAND?

1. What the difference is between a spot contract, a forward contract, and a futures contract?
2. What the major futures exchanges in the United States are?
3. What position traders, day traders, and scalpers are?
4. When a futures trader would buy (long) a futures contract? Sell (short) a futures contract?

Profit and Loss on a Futures Transaction. In Table 10–5, a March 2005 Treasury bond futures contract traded on the CBT could be bought (long) or sold (short) on January 10, 2005, for 112$^{11}/_{32}$ (or 112.34375) percent of the face value of the T-bond. The minimum contract size on one of these futures is \$100,000, so a position in one contract can be taken at a price of \$112,343.75.

The subsequent profit or loss from a position in March 2005 T-bonds taken on January 10, 2005, is graphically described in Figure 10–2. A long position in the futures market produces a profit when the value of the underlying T-bond increases (i.e., interest rates fall between January 10, 2005, and the March expiration).[8] A short position in the futures will produce a profit when the value of the underlying T-bond decreases (i.e., interest rates rise). For example, if the T-bond futures price falls to 111–16 percent (or 111$^{16}/_{32}$% = 111.5%) of the face value between January 10, 2005, and the March expiration, the long position incurs a loss of \$843.75 ((111.5% − 112.34375%) × \$100,000), while the short position incurs a gain of \$843.75.[9]

7. One model that explains how futures prices are determined is the cost of carry model. This model asserts that the futures price equals the spot price on the underlying asset plus the cost of carrying the asset over the life of the futures contract. Carrying costs include any financing costs of purchasing the underlying asset (e.g., interest costs) plus any storage, insurance, and transportation costs. For financial futures the costs of storage, insurance, and transportation are negligible.

8. Notice that if rates move in an opposite direction from that expected, losses are incurred on the futures position. That is, if rates rise and futures prices drop, the long investor loses on his or her futures position. Similarly, if rates fall and futures prices rise, the short investor loses on his or her futures position.

9. It should be noted that a risk in trading of derivatives is that favorable price moves may occur after the derivative contract matures. For example, if the T-bond futures price falls to 114–6 on April 1, 2005, the March T-bond contract would have matured and the long futures trader would have incurred no profit.

FIGURE 10–2 **Profit or Loss on a Futures Position in Treasury Bonds Taken on January 10, 2005**

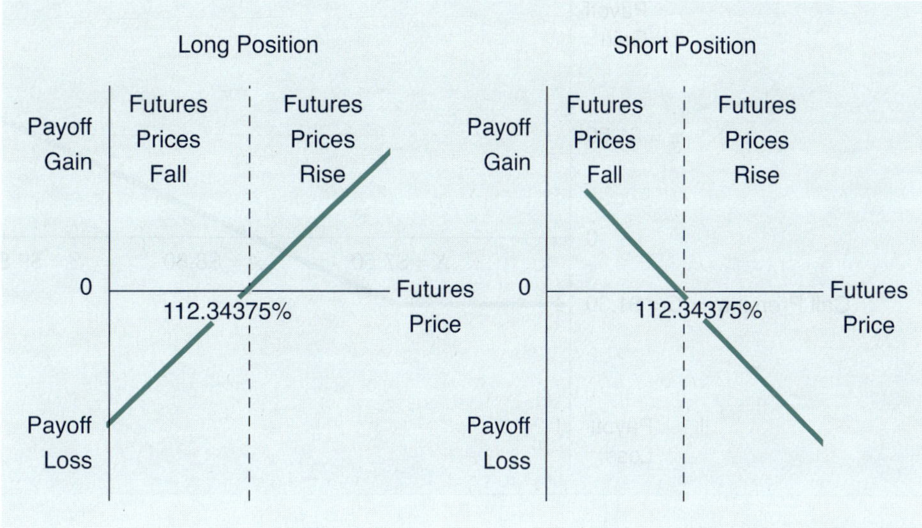

OPTIONS

4

An **option** is a contract that gives the holder the right, but not the obligation, to buy or sell an underlying asset at a prespecified price for a specified time period. An **American option** gives the option holder the right to buy or sell the underlying asset at *any time* before and on the expiration date of the option. A **European option** (e.g., options on the S&P 500 Index) gives the option holder the right to buy or sell the underlying option *only* on the expiration date. Most options traded on exchanges in the United States and abroad are American options. Options are classified as either call options or put options. We discuss both of these below, highlighting their payoffs in terms of price movements on the underlying asset.

option

A contract that gives the holder the right, but not the obligation, to buy or sell the underlying asset at a specified price within a specified period of time.

American option

An option that can be exercised at any time before and on the expiration date.

European option

An option that can be exercised only on the expiration date.

call option

An option that gives a purchaser the right, but not the obligation, to buy the underlying security from the writer of the option at a prespecified exercise price on a prespecified date.

Call Options

A **call option** gives the purchaser (or buyer) the right to buy an underlying security (e.g., a stock) at a prespecified price called the *exercise* or *strike* price (X). In return, the buyer of the call option must pay the writer (or seller) an up-front fee known as a *call premium* (C). This premium is an immediate negative cash flow for the buyer of the call option. However, he or she potentially stands to make a profit should the underlying stock's price be greater than the exercise price (by an amount exceeding the premium) when the option expires. If the price of the underlying stock is greater than X (the option is referred to as "in the money"), the buyer can exercise the option, buying the stock at X and selling it immediately in the stock market at the current market price, greater than X. If the price of the underlying stock is less than X when the option expires (the option is referred to as "out of the money"), the buyer of the call would not exercise the option (i.e., buy the stock at X when its market value is less than X). In this case, the option expires unexercised. The same is true when the underlying stock price is equal to X when the option expires (the option is referred to as "at the money"). The call buyer incurs a cost C (the call premium) for the option, and no other cash flows result.

Buying a Call Option. The profit or loss from buying a call option is illustrated in Figure 10–3. As Figure 10–3 shows, if, as the option expires, the price of the stock underlying the option is S, the buyer makes a profit of π, which is the difference between the stock's price (S, e.g., \$9.80) and the exercise price of the option (X, e.g., \$7.50) minus the

FIGURE 10–3 Payoff Function for the Buyer of a Call Option on a Stock

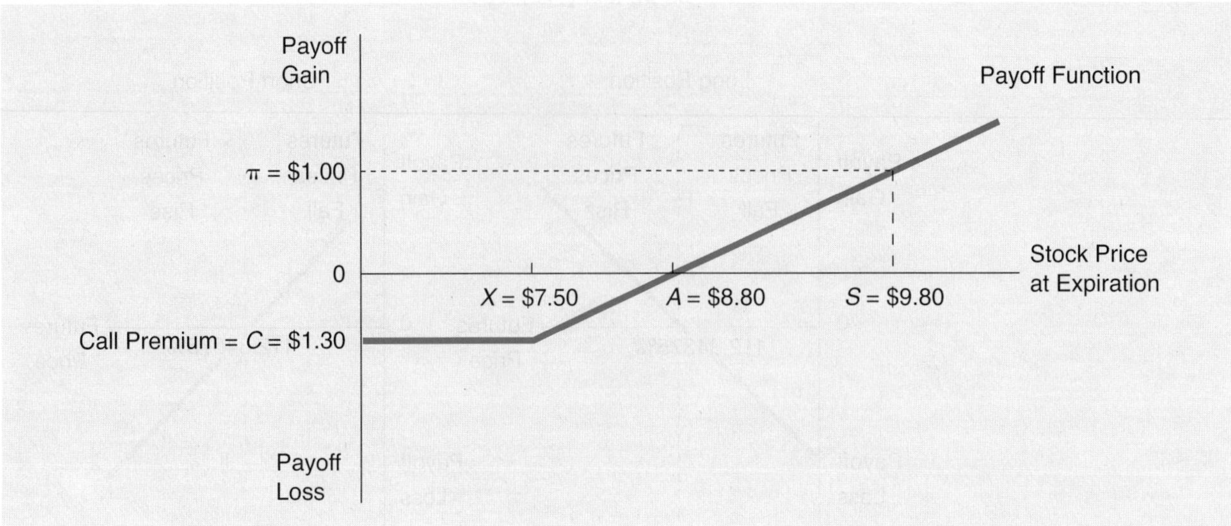

call premium paid to the writer of the option (C, e.g., \$1.30). If the underlying stock's price is A (i.e., \$8.80) as the option expires, the buyer of the call has just broken even because the net proceeds from exercising the call ($A - X = \$8.80 - \$7.50 = \$1.30$) just equals the premium payment for the call (C, or \$1.30 in this case).

Notice two important things about call options in Figure 10–3:

1. As the underlying stock's price rises, the call option buyer has a large profit potential: The higher the underlying stock's price at expiration, the larger the profit on the exercise of the option, that is, if $S = \$9.80$, then $\pi = \$9.80 - \$7.50 - \$1.30 = \$1$.
2. As the underlying stock's price falls, the call option buyer has a higher potential for losses, but they are limited to the call option premium. If the underlying stock's price at expiration is below the exercise price, X, the call buyer is not obligated to exercise the option. Thus, the buyer's losses are limited to the amount of the up-front premium payment (C, or \$1.30 in this case) made to purchase the call option.

Thus, buying a call option is an appropriate position when the underlying asset's price is expected to rise.[10]

Writing a Call Option. The writer of a call option sells the option to the buyer (or is said to take a short position in the option). In writing a call option on a stock, the writer or seller receives an up-front fee or premium (C, e.g., \$1.30) and must stand ready to sell the underlying stock to the purchaser of the option at the exercise price, X, (e.g., \$7.50). Note the payoff from writing a call option on a stock in Figure 10–4.

Notice two important things about this payoff function:

1. As the underlying stock's price falls, the potential for a call option writer to receive a positive payoff (or profit) increases. If the underlying stock's price is less than the exercise price (X) at expiration, the call option buyer will not exercise the option. The call option writer's profit has a maximum value equal to the call premium (C, or \$1.30 in this case) charged up front to the buyer of the option.

10. Traders using options get extra leverage on their investments. For example, suppose that a stock price is \$32 and an investor who feels that this price will rise buys call options with an exercise price of \$35 for \$0.50 per option. If the price does not go above \$35 during the life of the option, the investor will lose \$0.50 per option (or 100 percent of the investment). However, if the price rises to \$40, the investor will realize a profit of \$4.50 per option (or 900 percent of the original investment).

FIGURE 10–4 Payoff Function for the Writer of a Call Option on a Stock

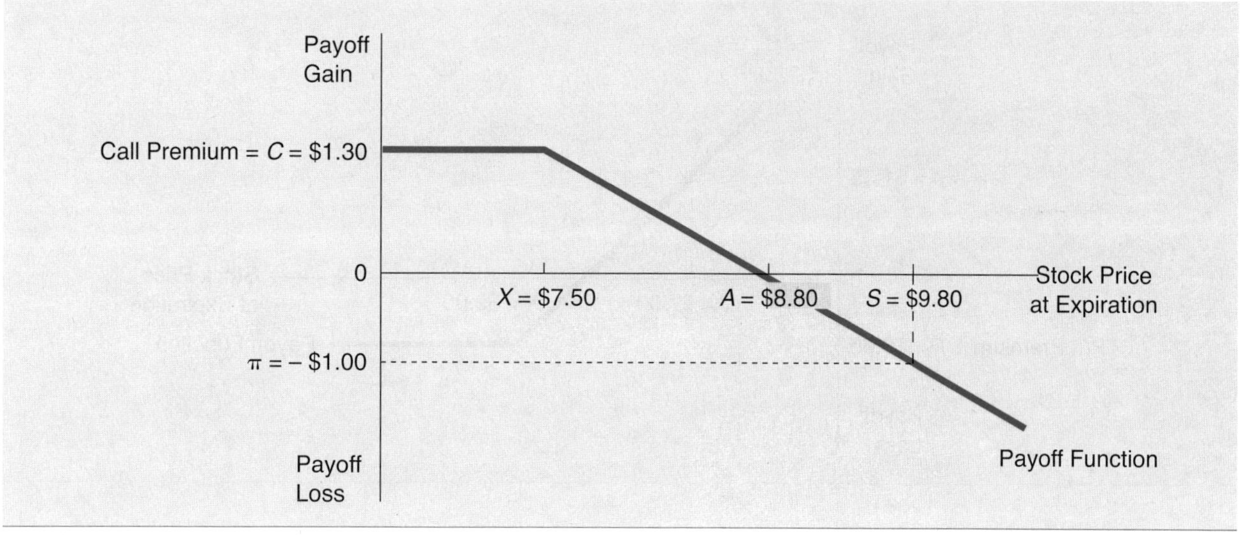

2. As the underlying stock's price rises, the call option writer has unlimited loss potential. If the underlying stock's price (*S*, e.g., \$9.80) is greater than the exercise price (*X*, e.g., \$7.50) at expiration, the call option buyer will exercise the option, forcing the option writer to buy the underlying stock at its high market price and then sell it to the call option buyer at the lower exercise price. That is, if $S = \$9.80$, then $\pi = \$1.30 - \$9.80 + \$7.50 = -\$1$. Since stock prices are theoretically unbounded in the upward direction, these losses could be very large.

Thus, writing a call option is an appropriate position when the underlying asset's price is expected to fall. Caution is warranted, however, because profits are limited but losses are potentially unlimited. A rise in the underlying stock's price to *S* results in the writer of the option losing π (in Figure 10–4).

Put Options

put option

An option that gives a purchaser the right, but not the obligation, to sell the underlying security to the writer of the option at a prespecified price on a prespecified date.

A **put option** gives the option buyer the right to sell an underlying security (e.g., a stock) at a prespecified price to the writer of the put option. In return, the buyer of the put option must pay the writer (or seller) the put premium (*P*). If the underlying stock's price is less than the exercise price (*X*) when the option expires (the put option is "in the money"), the buyer will buy the underlying stock in the stock market at less than *X* and immediately sell it at *X* by exercising the put option. If the price of the underlying stock is greater than *X* when the option expires (the put option is "out of the money"), the buyer of the put option never exercises the option (i.e., selling the stock at *X* when its market value is more than *X*). In this case, the option expires unexercised. This is also true if the price of the underlying stock is equal to *X* when the option expires (the put option is trading "at the money"). The put option buyer incurs a cost *P* for the option, and no other cash flows result.

Buying a Put Option. The buyer of a put option on a stock has the right (but not the obligation) to sell the underlying stock to the writer of the option at an agreed exercise price (*X*, e.g., \$9.00). In return for this option, the buyer of the put option pays a premium (*P*, e.g., \$0.65) to the option writer. We show the potential payoffs to the buyer of the put option in Figure 10–5. Note the following:

1. The lower the price of the underlying stock at the expiration of the option, the higher the profit to the put option buyer upon exercise. For example, if stock prices fall to *D* (=\$7.00) in Figure 10–5, the buyer of the put option can purchase the underlying stock in the stock

FIGURE 10–5 Payoff Function for the Buyer of a Put Option on a Stock

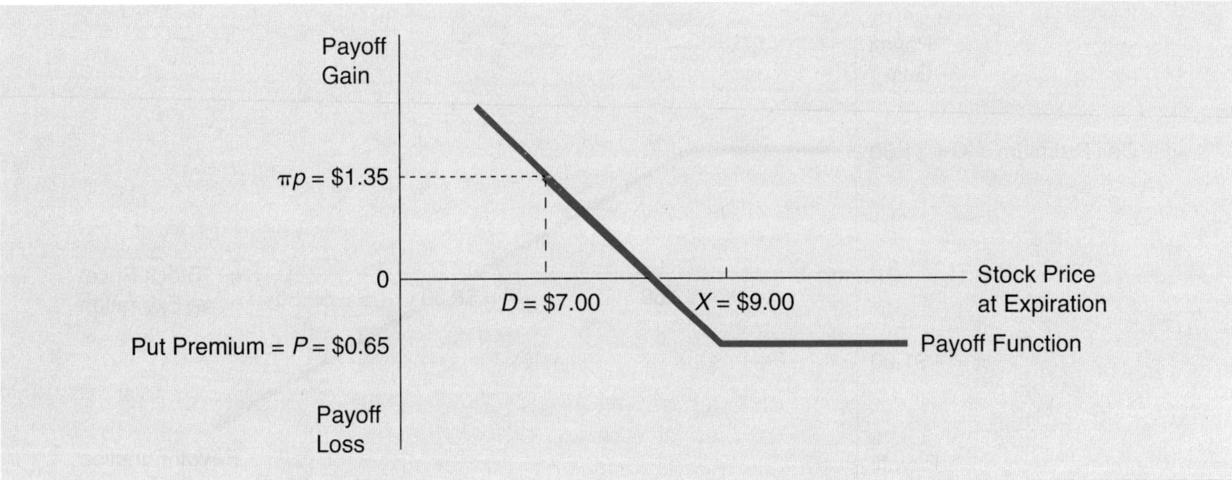

market at D = \$7.00 and put it (sell it) back to the writer of the put option at the higher exercise price X = \$9.00. As a result, after deducting the cost of the put premium, P = \$0.65, the buyer makes a profit of πp (= −\$7.00 − \$0.65 + \$9.00 = \$1.35) in Figure 10–5.

2. As the underlying stock's price rises, the probability that the buyer of a put option has a negative payoff increases. If the underlying stock's price is greater than the exercise price (X = \$9.00) at expiration, the put option buyer will not exercise the option. As a result, his or her maximum loss is limited to the size of the up-front put premium (P = \$0.65 in this case) paid to the put option writer.

Thus, buying a put option is an appropriate position when the price on the underlying asset is expected to fall.

Writing a Put Option. The writer or seller of a put option receives a fee or premium (P, e.g., \$0.65) in return for standing ready to buy the underlying stock at the exercise price (X, e.g., \$9.00) should the buyer of the put choose to exercise the option at expiration. See the payoff function for writing a put option on a stock in Figure 10–6. Note the following:

1. When the underlying stock's price rises, the put option writer has an enhanced probability of making a profit. If the underlying stock's price is greater than the exercise price (X = \$9.00) at expiration, the put option buyer will not exercise the option. The put option writer's maximum profit, however, is constrained to equal the put premium (P, or \$0.65 in this case).
2. When the underlying stock's price falls, the writer of the put option is exposed to potentially large losses. If the price of the underlying stock is below the exercise price (e.g., D = \$7.00 in Figure 10–6), the put option buyer will exercise the option, forcing the option writer to buy the underlying stock from the option buyer at the exercise price (X = \$9.00) when it is worth only D = \$7.00 in the stock market (i.e., if D = \$7.00, then πp = \$0.65 − \$9.00 + \$7.00 = −\$1.35). The lower the stock's price at expiration relative to the exercise price, the greater the losses to the option writer.

Thus, writing a put option is an appropriate position if the price on the underlying asset is expected to rise. However, profits are limited and losses are potentially large.

Notice from the above discussion that an option holder has three ways to liquidate his or her position. First, if conditions are never profitable for an exercise (the option remains "out of the money"), the option holder can let the option expire unexercised. Second, if conditions are right for exercise (the option is "in the money"), the holder can take the opposite side of the transaction: thus, an option buyer can sell options on the underlying asset with the same exercise price and the same expiration date. Third, if conditions are right for exercise, the

FIGURE 10–6 **Payoff Function for the Writer of a Put Option on a Stock**

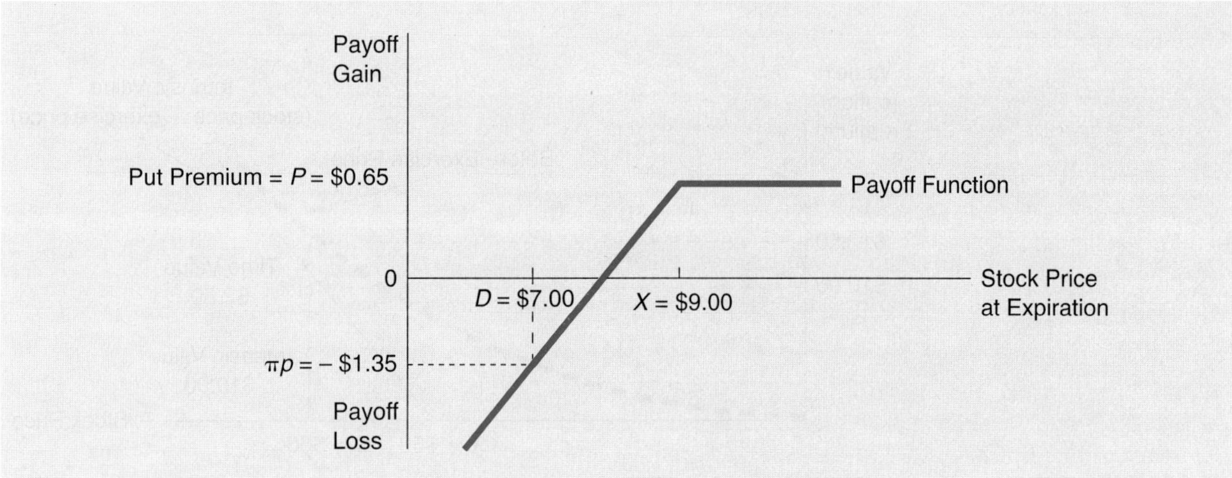

option holder can exercise the option, enforcing the terms of the option. For an American option, this exercise can theoretically occur any time before the option expires, while for a European option this exercise can occur only as the option expires, that is, on its maturity.

Option Values

The model most commonly used by practitioners and traders to price and value options is the Black–Scholes pricing model. The Black–Scholes model examines five factors that affect the price of an option:

1. The spot price of the underlying asset
2. The exercise price on the option
3. The option's exercise date
4. Price volatility of the underlying asset
5. The risk-free rate of interest

We show how to calculate an option's time value and, in turn, its overall value for any price of the underlying asset (at any point in time prior to maturity for a European option) using Black–Scholes option pricing model in the appendix to this chapter located at the book's Web site (**www.mhhe.com/sc3e**). In the body of the text we discuss these factors and the intuition behind their effect on an option's value.

Notice in the discussion above that we examined the profit and loss from exercising an option *at expiration*. The profit and loss on an option was a function of the spot price of the option's underlying asset and the exercise price on the option. The difference between the underlying asset's spot price and an option's exercise price is called the option's **intrinsic value.** For a call option, the intrinsic value is:

intrinsic value of an option

The difference between an option's exercise price and the underlying asset's price.

Stock price − Exercise price	if Stock price > Exercise price (option is in the money)
Zero	if Stock price ≤ Exercise price (option is out of the money)

For a put option, the intrinsic value is:

Exercise price − Stock price	if Stock price < Exercise price (option is in the money)
Zero	if Stock price ≥ Exercise price (option is out of the money)

At expiration, an option's value is equal to its intrinsic value.

FIGURE 10–7 The Intrinsic Value versus the Before-Exercise Value of a Call Option

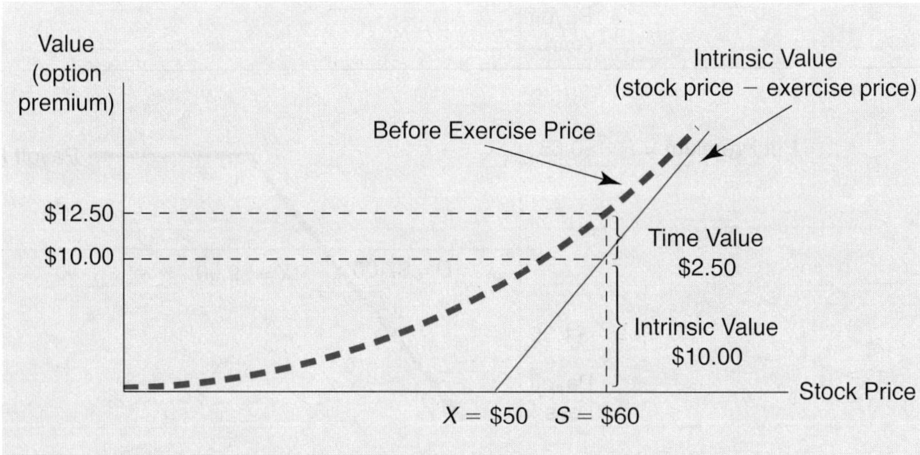

We limit the analysis of the profit and loss on an option to exercise at expiration because research has found that it is generally not optimal to exercise an option before its expiration date because of its potential "time value" (see below).[11] Specifically, exercising a call option early (prior to expiration) is only appropriate if the value of the option before expiration is always less than its intrinsic value, which is rarely the case.

Figure 10–7 illustrates the time value effect for a call option. For example, suppose you have a call option on a stock with an exercise price of $50 and an expiration in three months. The underlying stock's price is currently $60. The intrinsic value of the option is $10 ($60 − $50). The option is currently selling on the Chicago Board of Trade for $12.50. Thus, the value of the call option is greater than its intrinsic value by $2.50. The difference between an option's price (or premium) and its intrinsic value is called its **time value.** If you exercise the option today (prior to expiration), you receive the intrinsic value but give up the time value (which in this example is $2.50).

time value of an option

The difference between an option's price (or premium) and its intrinsic value.

The time value of an option is the value associated with the probability that the intrinsic value *could* increase (if the underlying asset's price moves favorably) between the option's purchase and the option's expiration date itself. The time value of an option is a function of the price volatility of the underlying asset and the time until the option matures (its expiration date). As price volatility increases, the chance that the stock will go up or down in value increases. The owner of the call option benefits from price increases but has limited downside risk if the stock price decreases, since the loss of value of an option can never exceed the call premium. Thus, over any given period of time, the greater the price volatility of the underlying asset, the greater the chance the stock price will increase and the greater the time value of the option. Further, the greater the time to maturity, the greater (longer in time) the opportunity for the underlying stock price to increase; thus, the time value of the option increases.

It is this "time value" that allows an out of the money option to have value and trade on the option markets. As noted above, a call option is out of the money if the exercise price is greater than the underlying stock's price, or the intrinsic value of the option is zero. This option still has "time" value and will trade at a positive price or premium, however, if investors believe that prior to the option's expiration, the stock price might increase (to a value greater than the exercise price). As an option moves toward expiration, its time value goes to zero. At any point in time, the time value of an option can be calculated by subtracting its intrinsic value (e.g., $10) from its current market price or premium (e.g., $12.50).

11. See J. Cox and M. Rubinstein, *Options Markets* (Englewood Cliffs, NJ: Prentice-Hall, 1985).

SEARCH THE SITE

Go to the Commodity Futures Trading Commission Web site at **www.cftc.gov** and find the most recent information on the futures and options volume.

Click on "Reports & Publications"

Click on "FY 200X Annual Report to Congress" under "Commission Reports"

This will download a file on to your computer that will contain data on futures contracts outstanding, traded, and maturing. The data are in the Appendices to the Annual Report.

Questions

1. Calculate the percentage change in average month end futures contracts outstanding, number of futures contracts outstanding, and number of futures contracts maturing since 2003 reported in Table 10–3.
2. Calculate the percentage change in average month end option contracts outstanding and number of option contracts traded since 2003 reported in Table 10–6.

The risk-free rate of interest affects the value of an option in a less than clear-cut way. All else constant, as the risk-free rate increases, the growth rate of the stock price increases. Recall from Chapter 3 that as the risk-free rate of interest increases, the required rate (and ultimately realized rate) of return increases on all investments. The result is greater stock price growth. However, the present value of any future cash flows received by the option holder decreases. For a call option, the first effect tends to increase the price of the option, while the second effect tends to decrease the price. It can be shown that the first effect always dominates the second effect. That is, the price of a call option always increases as the risk-free rate increases. Conversely, the two effects both tend to decrease the value of a put option. Thus, the price of a put option decreases as the risk-free rate increases.

Option Markets

www.cboe.com

The Chicago Board of Options Exchange (CBOE) opened in 1973. It was the first exchange devoted solely to the trading of stock options. In 1982, financial futures options contracts (options on financial futures contracts, e.g., Treasury bond futures contracts) started trading. Options markets have grown rapidly since the mid-1980s.

www.liffe.com

Table 10–6 shows the level of trading activity in the options markets from 1992 through 2003. Table 10–7 lists the characteristics of some of the most active option contracts. The largest option exchange is the Chicago Board Options Exchange (CBOE).[12] The first option exchanges abroad were the European Options Exchange and the London International Financial Futures Exchange (LIFFE). Options exchanges have more recently been opened in Paris, Sweden, Switzerland, Germany, and Japan. As with futures trading, many options also trade over the counter. Thus, the volume of trading in options is more than what is reported in the option quotes (see below) for the organized exchanges.

12. Other major exchanges are the American Stock Exchange, CBT, CME, IMM, Pacific Stock Exchange, Philadelphia Exchange, New York Stock Exchange, and the Financial Instrument Exchange of the New York Cotton Exchange.

TABLE 10–6 Options Market Activity, 1992–2003

	1992	1995	2000	2003
Average month-end contracts outstanding (in thousands)	1,585.8	3,285.4	4,007.5	12,857.4
Number of contracts traded (in thousands)	39,928.1	65,502.6	64,695.8	173,915.2

Source: Commodity Futures Trading Commission Web site, January 2000 and 2005. **www.cftc.gov**

The trading process for options is similar to that for futures contracts. An investor desiring to take an option position calls his or her broker and places an order to buy or sell a stated number of call or put option contracts with a stated expiration date and exercise price. The broker directs this order to its representative on the appropriate exchange for execution. Most trading on the largest exchanges such as the CBOE takes place in trading pits, where traders for each delivery date on an option contract informally group together. Like futures contracts, options trading generally occurs using an open-outcry auction method.

Only option exchange members are allowed to transact on the floor of option exchanges. Trades from the public are placed with a floor broker, professional trader, or a market maker for the particular option being traded. Option trades may be placed as market orders (instructing the floor broker to transact at the best price available) or limit orders (instructing the floor broker to transact at a specified price).

Once an option price is agreed upon in a trading pit, the two parties electronically send the details of the trade to the option clearinghouse (the Options Clearing Corporation), which breaks up trades into buy and sell transactions and takes the opposite side of each transaction—becoming the seller for every option contract buyer and the buyer for every option contract seller. The broker on the floor of the options exchange confirms the transaction with the investor's broker.

In the early 2000s, the CBOE increased the speed at which orders can be placed, executed, and filled by equipping floor brokers with hand-held touch-screen computers that allow them to route and execute orders more easily and efficiently. For example, when a broker selects an order from the workstation, an electronic trading card appears on the hand-held computer screen. The electronic card allows the broker to work the order and enter necessary trade information (e.g., volume, price, opposing market makers). When the card (details of the transaction) is complete, the broker can execute the trade with the touch of a finger. Once the broker has submitted the trade, the system simultaneously sends a "fill" report to the customer and instantaneously transmits this data to traders worldwide.

Table 10–8 shows portions of an option quote table from *The Wall Street Journal* for January 10, 2005. (*The Wall Street Journal* no longer lists individual stock option quotes. The stock option quote listed in Table 10–8 is taken from *The Wall Street Journal Online.*) Three types of options trade: stock options, stock index options, and options on futures contracts. More "exotic" or special types of options (e.g., credit options—see Chapter 23) tend to trade over the counter rather than on organized exchanges. We discuss the three major types of exchange-traded options next.

5 **Stock Options.** The underlying asset on a stock option contract is the stock of a publicly traded company. One option generally involves 100 shares of the underlying company's stock. As mentioned earlier, options on U.S. option exchanges are American options. Look at the options quotes for American Airlines (AMR) in Table 10–8. The first line lists the name of the company and its closing stock price for the day (e.g., \$8.79). The first column is the expiration month on the option (e.g., Jan = January 2005). The second column lists the strike or exercise price on the different options on American Airlines stock (e.g., \$6 and \$7.50). Note that the same stock can have many different call and put options differentiated by expiration and strike price. Further, the quote gives

TABLE 10–7 Characteristics of Actively Traded Options

Type of Option	Exchange*	Contract Traded
Stock options	CBOE	Stock options
	AM	Stockoptions
	PB	Stock options
	PC	Stock options
	NY	Stock options
Stock index options	CBOE	Dow Jones Industrial Average
	CBOE	Dow Jones Transportation Average
	CBOE	Dow Jones Utility Average
	CBOE	Nasdaq 100
	CBOE	Russell 2000
	CBOE	S&P 100 Index
	CBOE	S&P 500 Index
	AM	Euro Top 100
	AM	Hong Kong Index
	AM	Major Market Index
	AM	S&P Midcap
	PB	Gold/Silver
	PB	Oil Service
	PB	PHLX KBW Bank
	PB	Utility Index
Financial futures options:		
Interest rate	CBT	T-bonds
	CBT	T-notes
	CBT	T-notes—5 year
	CME	Eurodollar
	CME	Mid-Curve Eurodollar—1 year
	LIFFE	Eurolibor
	EUREX	Euro Bond
Currency	CME	Japanese yen
	CME	Canadian dollar
	CME	British pound
	CME	Swiss franc
	CME	Euro FX
Stock index	CBT	DJIA
	CME	S&P 500 Index

*CBOE = Chicago Board of Option Exchange, AM = American Exchange, PB = Philadelphia Stock Exchange, PC = Pacific Stock Exchange, NY = New York Stock Exchange, CBT = Chicago Board of Trade, CME = Chicago Mercantile Exchange, LIFFE = London International Financial Futures Exchange, and EUREX = The European Derivatives Market.

Source: *The Wall Street Journal,* January 11, 2005, p. C11. Reprinted by permission of *The Wall Street Journal.* **www.wsj.com**

an indication of whether the call and put options are trading in, out of, or at the money. For example, as shown in Figure 10–8, the American Airlines call option with an exercise price of $7.50 is trading in the money ($7.50 is less than the current stock price, $8.79), while the call options with an exercise price of $10 are trading out of the money ($10 is greater than the current stock price, $8.79). The exact opposite holds for the put options. That is, the put option with an exercise price of $7.50 is trading out of the money ($7.50 is less than the current stock price, $8.79), while the put options with an exercise price of $10 are trading in the

TABLE 10–8 Option Quote, January 10, 2005

STOCK OPTIONS

Prices at close January 10, 2005

A M R (AMR)							Underlying stock price*: 8.79
		Call			Put		
Expiration	Strike	Last	Volume	Open Interest	Last	Volume	Open Interest
May	6.00	3.30	12	578	0.45	20	4175
Jan	7.50	1.30	60	17062	0.15	138	58909
Feb	8.00	1.35	1	2018	...	...	2490
May	8.00	1.81	20	757	...	...	1994
Aug	8.00	...	...	453	1.45	10	390
Jan	9.00	0.35	150	15656	0.65	25	6894
Feb	9.00	0.75	224	2723	1.00	500	3314
May	9.00	1.30	5	635	...	...	2968
Aug	9.00	1.75	10	111	...	...	132
Jan	10.00	0.10	65	55461	1.30	490	64476
Feb	10.00	0.30	595	4272	1.66	8	9452
May	10.00	0.95	50	2926	...	...	33385
Aug	10.00	1.35	21	459	...	...	243
Feb	11.00	0.15	37	4123	2.30	15	5366
Feb	12.00	0.10	40	5065	...	...	1643
Jan	12.50	...	...	19720	3.80	20	15853
Feb	13.00	0.05	3000	5967	...	...	231
May	13.00	0.25	6	530	...	...	56
Aug	13.00	0.55	10	363	...	...	15
Aug	20.00	0.05	12	116	...	...	...

**Underlying stock price* represents listed exchange price only. It may not match the composite closing price.

FUTURES OPTIONS

STRIKE CALLS-SETTLE PUTS-SETTLE

Interest Rate

T-Bonds (CBT)

$100,000; points and 64ths of 100%

Price	Feb	Mar	Apr	Feb	Mar	Apr
110	2-27	2-52	...	0-05	0-30	1-09
111	1-36	2-05	2-02	0-14	0-47	1-34
112	0-54	1-29	1-33	0-32	1-07	2-01
113	0-22	0-61	1-06	1-00	1-39	...
114	0-07	0-37	0-49	1-49	2-15	...
115	0-02	0-22	0-33	2-44	2-63	...

Est vol 40,597;
Fr vol 27,753 calls 37,460 puts
Op int Fri 242,355 calls 343,663 puts

T-Notes (CBT)

$100,000; points and 64ths of 100%

Price	Feb	Mar	Apr	Feb	Mar	Apr
109	...	2-33	...	0-01	0-08	0-34
110	1-28	1-43	1-23	0-03	0-18	0-55
111	0-39	0-63	0-53	0-14	0-38	1-21
112	0-08	0-31	0-29	0-47	1-06	...
113	0-01	0-12	0-15	1-39	1-51	...
114	0-01	0-04	0-07	...	2-43	...

Est vol 192,801 Fr 122,929 calls 162,054 puts
Op int Fri 907,025 calls 1,235,899 puts

5 Yr Treas Notes (CBT)

$100,000; points and 64ths of 100%

Price	Feb	Mar	Apr	Feb	Mar	Apr
10800	0-63	...	...	0-02	0-13	0-33
10850	0-35	0-50	0-45	0-06	0-22	0-46
10900	0-15	0-32	0-30	0-18	0-34	...
10950	0-04	0-17	0-19	0-39	0-52	1-20
11000	0-01	0-09	...	1-04	1-12	...
11050	0-01	0-04	...	1-35	1-39	...

Est vol 77,636 Fr 17,815 calls 57,440 puts
Op int Fri 174,627 calls 497,173 puts

Eurodollar (CME)

$ million; pts. of 100%

Price	Jan	Feb	Mar	Jan	Feb	Mar
9675	...	...	.290	.000	.000	.000
9700	.040	.057	.065	.000	.017	.025
9725	.000	.005	.010	.210	.215	.220
9750	.000	.000	.000	.460	...	.460
9775	.000	...	.000	...	...	.710
9800	.000	...	.000	.960	...	.960

Est vol 809,507;
Fr vol 207,031 calls 664,280 puts
Op int Fri 5,123,572 calls 5,237,907 puts

Index

Mini DJ Industrial Avg (CBT)

$5 times premium

Price	Jan	Feb	Mar	Jan	Feb	Mar
104	2.48	3.09	3.63	0.20	0.81	1.35
105	1.65	2.38	2.94	0.37	1.10	1.66
106	0.98	1.75	2.34	0.70	1.47	2.06
107	0.50	1.24	1.80	1.22	1.96	2.52
108	0.22	0.82	1.35	1.94	2.54	3.07
109	0.09	0.51	0.98	2.81	3.23	3.70

Est vol 1,474 Fr 903 calls 1,229 puts
Op int Fri 10,976 calls 11,174 puts

S&P 500 Stock Index (CME)

$250 times premium

Price	Jan	Feb	Mar	Jan	Feb	Mar
1180	17.20	25.50	32.20	5.50	13.80	20.60
1185	13.80	22.40	29.20	7.10	15.70	22.50
1190	10.70	19.60	26.30	9.00	17.90	24.60
1195	8.10	17.00	23.50	11.40	20.30	26.80
1200	6.00	14.60	20.90	14.30	22.90	29.20
1205	4.20	12.30	18.50	17.50	25.60	31.70

Est vol 19,977 Fr 7,747 calls 12,644 puts
Op int Fri 145,329 calls 295,519 puts

STRIKE CALLS-SETTLE PUTS-SETTLE

Currency

Japanese Yen (CME)

12,500,000 yen; cents per 100 yen

Price	Feb	Mar	Jun	Feb	Mar	Jun
9550	1.51	1.89	...	0.60	0.98	...
9600	1.22	1.61	2.78	0.81	1.20	1.68
9650	0.97	1.37	2.52	1.06	1.46	1.92
9700	0.76	1.16	2.29	1.35	1.75	2.18
9750	0.59	0.98	...	1.68	2.07	...
9800	0.45	0.83	1.87	...	2.41	2.75

Est vol 474 Fr 1,627 calls 1,346 puts
Op int Fri 30,020 calls 27,715 puts

Canadian Dollar (CME)

100,000 Can.$, cents per Can.$

Price	Feb	Mar	Jun	Feb	Mar	Jun
8100	1.35	1.68	2.41	0.51	0.84	1.52
8150	1.04	1.38	0.00	0.70	1.04	...
8200	0.78	1.12	1.87	0.94	1.28	1.97
8250	0.58	0.91	...	1.24	1.57	0.00
8300	0.42	0.74	1.45	1.58	1.90	2.54
8350	0.30	0.59	1.28	...	2.24	...

Est vol 1,472 Fr 568 calls 988 puts
Op int Fri 11,113 calls 9,653 puts

British Pound (CME)

62,500 pounds; cents per pound

Price	Feb	Mar	Jun	Feb	Mar	Jun
1850	...	3.52	...	0.97	1.64	3.61
1860	...	2.96	4.10	1.34	2.07	4.06
1870	1.72	2.40	3.62	1.83	2.51	4.57
1880	1.30	1.95	...	2.41	3.06	0.00
1890	0.96	1.56	2.79	3.07	3.66	5.72
1900	0.70	1.23	2.43	3.80	4.33	6.35

Est vol 260 Fr 236 calls 1,380 puts
Op int Fri 3,696 calls 3,463 puts

Swiss Franc (CME)

125,000 francs; cents per franc

Price	Feb	Mar	Jun	Feb	Mar	Jun
8400	...	1.91	...	...	1.06	1.73
8450	...	...	...	0.83	...	...
8500	0.92	1.38	...	1.07	1.53	...
8550	...	...	...	1.36	1.81	2.44
8600	0.54	0.97	2.01	1.69	2.12	2.71
8650	0.40	...	...	2.05	2.43	...

Est vol 37 Fr 151 calls 766 puts
Op int Fri 1,317 calls 1,199 puts

Euro Fx (CME)

125,000 euros; cents per euro

Price	Feb	Mar	Jun	Feb	Mar	Jun
13000	1.88	2.50	3.87	0.90	1.52	2.66
13050	...	2.23	...	1.12	1.75	2.89
13100	1.36	1.98	3.37	1.38	2.00	3.15
13150	1.13	1.74	3.13	1.65	2.26	3.41
13200	0.92	1.53	2.91	1.94	2.55	3.68
13250	0.75	1.33	2.69	2.27	2.84	3.96

Est vol 2,814 Fr 11,706 calls 18,371 puts
Op int Fri 44,975 calls 54,080 puts

STOCK INDEX OPTIONS

DJ INDUS AVG(DJX)

STRIKE	VOL	LAST	NET CHG	OPEN INT
Mar 88p	16	0.10	...	5,192
Mar 92p	20	0.15	...	3,133
Mar 94p	20	0.20	...	2,029
Mar 98p	3	0.40	...	7,871
Jan 100c	21	6.40	-0.20	10,381
Mar 100c	2	7.20	-1.20	8,541
Mar 100p	199	0.60	-0.10	12,510
Jan 101c	75	5.60	...	3,438
Feb 101p	14	0.30	-0.10	2,065
Jan 102c	10	4.10	-1.50	2,288
Feb 102c	2	4.20	-0.80	11
Jan 103c	102	3.20	...	8,432
Jan 103p	983	0.10	-0.10	3,417
Feb 103p	1,018	0.50	-0.25	678
Mar 103p	65	1.05	0.20	1,552
Jan 104c	55	2.40	-0.30	2,649
Jan 104p	561	0.20	-0.05	4,667
Feb 104p	88	0.65	-0.20	1,315
Mar 104c	3	3.70	...	4,230
Mar 104p	1,008	1.35	-0.20	4,455
Jan 105c	24	1.75	...	35,601
Jan 105p	389	0.35	-0.20	30,529
Feb 105c	41	2.30	-0.05	1,769
Feb 105p	515	1.10	-0.15	574
Mar 105p	4	1.70	-0.25	870
Jan 106c	352	0.80	-0.20	10,689
Jan 106p	311	0.80	0.05	6,954
Feb 106c	476	1.80	0.10	2,017
Feb 106p	869	1.65	0.20	1,343
Mar 106c	275	2.35	0.10	11,459
Mar 106p	227	2.15	-0.10	8,277
Jan 107c	303	0.35	-0.15	13,040
Jan 107p	260	1.30	-0.20	6,677
Feb 107c	544	1.25	-0.25	1,256
Feb 107p	13	2.10	0.20	524
Jan 108c	1,354	0.20	...	10,981
Jan 108p	13	2	0.20	6,564
Feb 108c	1,303	0.85	0.05	5,629
Feb 108p	50	2.35	-0.65	1,740
Mar 108c	253	1.35	-0.15	6,731
Mar 108p	73	2.90	-0.30	744
Jan 109c	46	0.10	-0.05	2,519
Jan 109p	10	2.55	-0.45	3,342
Feb 109c	10	0.50	...	7,964
Mar 109c	105	0.95	-0.50	196
Jan 110c	15	0.05	...	5,644
Jan 110p	1	4	0.10	4,432
Feb 110c	600	0.30	-0.05	4,772
Mar 110c	40	0.75	-0.10	5,386
Mar 110p	30	4.20	0.40	92
Mar 112c	20	0.35	...	6,843

Call Vol.........7,563 Open Int..309,681
Put Vol......... 9,043 Open Int..288,605

S & P 500(SPX)

STRIKE	VOL	LAST	NET CHG	OPEN INT
Jan 975p	100	0.05	-0.05	7,096
Feb 1005p	370	0.40	-0.20	11,777
Jan 1025p	9,095	0.10	-0.05	20,978
Mar 1025c	40	169.80	0.80	629
Mar 1025p	9,352	1.65	...	74,228
Jan 1050c	10	145.20	9.70	237
Feb 1050c	54	140	1.90	308
Feb 1050p	1,410	0.75	-0.05	13,329
Mar 1050p	1	2.25	-0.25	26,793
Jan 1075p	73	0.15	-0.05	37,065
Feb 1075c	1	116	-0.40	97
Feb 1075p	266	1.25	-0.35	16,187
Mar 1075p	177	3.20	-0.80	34,916
Jan 1100c	9	89	2.00	7,444
Jan 1100p	1,438	0.25	-0.05	28,311
Feb 1100p	1,340	1.70	-0.80	18,443
Mar 1100c	40	99	7.00	10,893
Mar 1100p	855	5	-1.00	63,982
Jan 1110p	10	0.25	-0.20	56,081
Jan 1115p	500	0.25	-0.15	14,381
Jan 1120p	518	0.30	-0.30	3,134
Jan 1125c	5	68.50	1.60	10,869
Jan 1125p	1,435	0.45	-0.25	33,730
Feb 1125c	50	70.30	3.70	2,035
Feb 1125p	151	3.30	-0.70	17,239
Mar 1125p	966	7.50	-1.50	46,629
Jan 1130c	2	56.20	1.20	87
Jan 1130p	100	0.60	-0.25	9,150
Feb 1130p	153	4.10	-0.50	602
Jan 1135c	20	60.90	2.30	2,385
Jan 1135p	27	0.45	-0.55	5,386
Jan 1140c	10	55.70	5.20	1,638
Jan 1140p	179	0.60	-0.60	8,614
Feb 1140p	69	4.80	-1.60	742
Jan 1145p	54	1	-0.35	14,030
Jan 1150c	160	41.20	2.20	7,398
Jan 1150p	2,047	1.10	-0.90	43,306
Feb 1150p	859	6.40	-1.70	11,132
Mar 1150c	1	50.40	-2.30	13,597
Mar 1150p	4,976	12.50	-1.30	36,357
Jan 1155p	262	1.40	-0.60	2,388
Jan 1160c	7	31.50	0.80	1,629
Jan 1160p	674	1.80	-1.20	12,377
Jan 1165c	10	27.10	1.90	67
Jan 1165p	264	2.80	-0.80	6,837
Jan 1170p	743	3.50	-1.50	17,142
Mar 1170p	43	18	-1.30	1,705
Jan 1175c	239	20	2.30	23,086
Jan 1175p	1,330	4.40	-2.40	36,948
Feb 1175c	279	27.70	-1.00	7,499
Feb 1175p	167	12.10	-2.40	15,316
Mar 1175c	380	35.20	2.70	27,927
Mar 1175p	680	19	-1.00	27,692
Jan 1180c	277	17.50	3.50	1,700
Jan 1180p	633	5.50	-2.80	17,112
Mar 1180c	418	32	0.90	1,107
Mar 1180p	40	18.90	-4.60	2,418
Jan 1185c	425	11.90	0.90	3,019
Jan 1185p	948	8	-2.50	10,074
Feb 1185c	16	20	...	3,761
Feb 1185p	899	16	-2.00	5,573
Jan 1190c	532	10	1.50	4,767
Jan 1190p	1,071	9.10	-3.90	11,299
Jan 1195c	214	7	0.50	3,120
Jan 1195p	470	13	-2.50	6,466
Jan 1200c	7,216	5.50	0.70	53,033
Jan 1200p	1,025	16	-3.00	44,381
Feb 1200c	2,597	13.50	1.00	19,260
Feb 1200p	79	22	-4.00	12,697
Mar 1200c	2,964	21.30	1.30	51,436
Mar 1200p	2,339	29	-3.50	39,521
Jan 1205c	283	3.40	-0.60	2,971
Jan 1205p	20	16	-7.00	5,120
Mar 1205p	20	32.70	-0.30	2,948
Jan 1210c	559	2.50	0.25	12,691
Jan 1210p	146	19.90	-4.90	5,281
Mar 1210c	40	18	1.60	16,147
Jan 1215c	324	1.70	-0.05	11,441
Mar 1215c	2	15	0.30	1,740
Jan 1220c	1,341	1	-0.25	7,668
Jan 1220p	153	33	1.00	2,625
Jan 1225c	1,501	0.75	0.05	23,879
Jan 1225p	42	36.60	-0.30	2,950
Feb 1225c	285	5.20	-0.50	12,342
Feb 1225p	27	39	-5.50	2,284
Mar 1225c	772	10.80	-0.20	32,571
Mar 1225p	31	41	-5.30	4,242
Jan 1230c	2,319	0.45	-0.35	9,548
Jan 1235c	356	0.35	-0.35	10,903
Jan 1235p	30	45.70	-2.80	513
Jan 1245c	110	0.30	-0.10	2,794
Feb 1245c	1	2.50	0.05	2,370
Jan 1250c	255	0.20	...	23,077
Jan 1250p	5	58.70	-0.30	2,500
Feb 1250c	126	2	0.10	12,382
Feb 1250p	5	64.70	-0.50	1,832
Mar 1250c	213	4.90	0.20	25,784
Feb 1255c	22	1.40	-0.25	1,055
Jan 1275p	150	85.20	4.20	876
Feb 1275c	86	0.55	-0.35	5,725
Feb 1275p	5	88.20	4.20	284
Mar 1275c	21	2	...	12,132
Jan 1300c	152	0.05	...	34,044
Jan 1300p	54	107.80	12.80	273
Mar 1300c	312	0.70	-0.30	23,687
Mar 1300p	50	106.90	22.40	2,668
Mar 1350c	2	0.35	0.20	2,514

Call Vol.........53,446 Open Int.1,237,912
Put Vol......... 84,482 Open Int.2,643,247

Source: *The Wall Street Journal*, January 11, 2005, pp. C11. Reprinted by permission of *The Wall Street Journal*. **www.wsj.com**

money ($10 is greater than the current stock price, $8.79). Columns 3 through 5 give data on the call options: call price or premium (e.g., LAST) of the option (e.g., $3.30, or one May call option with an exercise price of $6 would cost $3.30 × 100 = $330),[13] volume (e.g., 12 call options traded on January 10, 2005), and open interest (e.g., 578 May call options with

13. Times 100 since each option contract is for 100 shares.

FIGURE 10–8 **In the Money and Out of the Money Options**

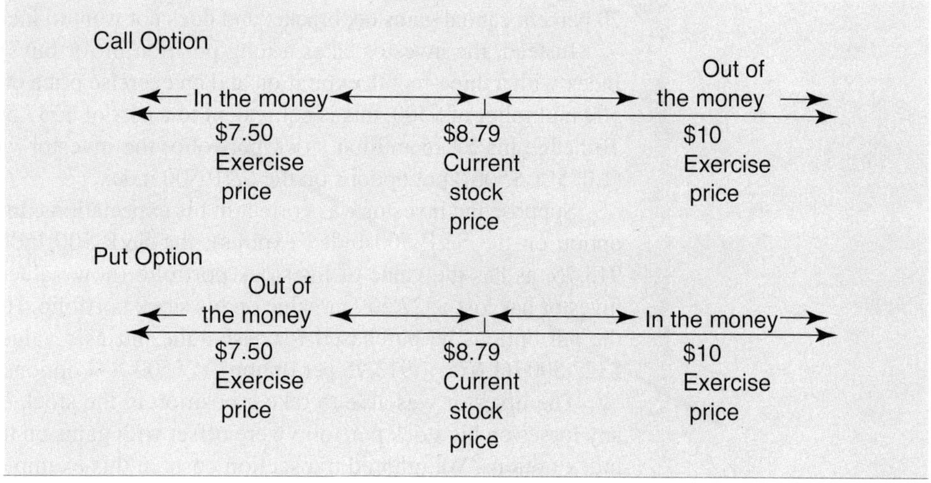

a $6 strike price were outstanding at the open of trading on January 10, 2005). Columns 6 through 8 list the same type of data for put options traded.

Stock Index Options. The underlying asset on a stock index option is the value of a major stock market index (e.g., the DJIA or the S&P 500 Index—see Chapter 9). An investor would buy a call (put) option on a stock index when he or she thinks the value of the underlying stock market index will rise (fall) by the expiration date of the option. If the index does indeed rise above (fall below) the exercise price on the option, the call (put) option holder can profit by an amount equal to the intrinsic value when the option expires. A difference between a stock option and a stock index option is that at expiration, the stock index option holder cannot settle the option contract with the actual purchase or sale of the underlying stock index. Rather, at expiration, stock index options are settled in cash (i.e., the option holder receives the intrinsic value if the option is in the money and nothing if the option is out of the money). Except for the S&P 500 (which is a European option), stock index options are American options.

Options on stock indexes allow investors to invest indirectly in a diversified portfolio that replicates a major market index (e.g., the S&P 500 Index). If an investor thinks the S&P 500 Index will rise in the future, he or she can buy a call option on the S&P 500 Index. If the S&P 500 Index does rise, the value of the call option also rises. Thus, the investor can earn returns based directly on the S&P 500 Index without investing the large amounts of money needed to directly buy every stock in the index.

The dollar value associated with each stock index option is established by a particular multiplier—the value of a stock index option is equal to the index times its multiplier. For example, the multiplier on the S&P 500 index option is 500, on the S&P 100 index option is 100, on the DJIA option is 100, and on the NYSE Composite index option is 500. Thus, if an S&P 500 index option has an exercise price of 1,050, the dollar amount involved with the exercise of this option is 1,050 × $500 = $525,000.

Options on stock indexes also give investors a way to hedge their existing stock portfolios.

EXAMPLE 10-2 Using a Stock Index Option to Hedge a Stock Portfolio

Suppose that over the last seven years an investor's stock portfolio increased in value from $250,000 to $2.15 million. The stock portfolio was originally set up to (virtually) replicate the S&P 500 Index. The investor believes that due to expected rising interest rates in the next three months, stock market indexes (including the S&P 500 Index, currently at 1,075.0) will soon experience sharp declines in value and his stock portfolio will experience the same percentage drop in value. The investor has thought of liquidating his stock portfolio but is in the 20 percent capital gains tax bracket and does not want to incur such high tax payments.

Instead, the investor takes a long position in (or buys) put options on the S&P 500 Index with a three-month expiration and an exercise price of 1,075. Incorporating the S&P 500 multiplier of $500, this is equivalent to a cost of $537,500 (1,075 × $500) per option. To hedge his $2.15 million stock portfolio, the investor would buy 4 ($2.15 million ÷ (1,075 × $500)) put options on the S&P 500 index.

Suppose the investor was correct in his expectations. In three months' time (as the put option on the S&P 500 Index expires), the S&P 500 Index has dropped 15 percent to 913.75, as has the value of his stock portfolio (now valued at $1,827,500 million). The investor has lost $322,500 in value on his stock portfolio. However, the investor can settle the put options he purchased for cash—the intrinsic value at the option's expiration is $322,500 ((1,075 − 913.75 per option) × $500 × 4 options).

The investor was able to take a position in the stock index option market such that any losses on his stock portfolio were offset with gains on the put option position in stock index options. We ignored transaction costs in this example (i.e., the premiums required to purchase the four put options), but they would be small relative to the losses the investor would have incurred had he not hedged his stock portfolio with stock index options.

5 Stock index option quotes (in Table 10–8) list the underlying index (e.g., DJ INDUS AVG = DJIA). The first column lists the expiration month of the option contract and the second column lists the exercise price, often listed in some submultiple of the actual value of the index (e.g., 100 = 10,000 for the DJIA), including a designation for put, p, or call, c, options traded. Column 3 is the trading volume (e.g., 21 = 21 options traded). Column 4 lists the settlement price (or premium) on the option (e.g., 6.4 means the price of one January 2005 call option with an exercise price of 100 is $6.4 × 100 = $640), and Column 5 is the change in this settlement price (or premium) from the previous day (e.g., −0.20). Finally, the last column of the quote table reports the number of contracts outstanding at the beginning of the day (e.g., 10,381).

Options on Futures Contracts. The underlying asset on a futures option is a futures contract (e.g., $100,000 Treasury bond futures—discussed above). The buyer of a call (put) option on a futures contract has the right to buy (sell) the underlying futures contract before expiration (i.e., an American option). The seller of a call (put) option on a futures contract creates the obligation to sell (buy) the underlying futures contract on exercise by the option buyer. If exercised, a call (put) option holder can buy (sell) the underlying futures contracts at the exercise price. Options on futures can be more attractive to investors than options on an underlying asset when it is cheaper or more convenient to deliver futures contracts on the asset rather then the actual asset. For example, trading options on T-bond futures contracts rather than options on T-bonds ensures that a highly liquid asset will be delivered and that problems associated with accrued interest and the determination of which long-term bond to deliver are avoided. Another advantage is that price information about futures contracts (the underlying asset on the option) is generally more readily available than price information on the T-bonds themselves (T-bond price information can be obtained only by surveying bond dealers). Options are currently written on interest rate, currency, and stock index futures contracts.

5 Look at the first futures option quote listed in Table 10–8 (for T-bonds). The bold heading for each quote lists the type of option (e.g., on T-bond futures contracts), face value of each option contract (e.g., $100,000), and the basis for the quote (e.g., "points and 64ths of 100%" means 2−27 = 2 $^{27}/_{64}$%). Each row in the quote then lists trading results for a specific exercise price (e.g., 110, 111). Column 1 lists the strike price (e.g., 110 = 110%); Columns 2 through 4 list settlement prices on call options traded,

by expiration month of the option contract (e.g., February, March, and April). The last three columns list settlement prices for the various expiration put options.[14]

DO YOU UNDERSTAND?

1. What the difference is between a call option and a put option?
2. When an option trader would want to buy a call option on a stock?
3. When an option trader would want to buy a put option on a stock?
4. What the three types of options traded in the United States are?

6

REGULATION OF FUTURES AND OPTIONS MARKETS

The Commodity Futures Trading Commission (CFTC), formed in 1974, is the primary regulator of futures markets. The CFTC's major mission is to protect the trading public by seeking to prevent misrepresentations and/or market manipulation by exchange participants. The CFTC approves new or proposed contracts to ensure they have an economic purpose, conducts economic studies of the markets, enforces the rules set by the individual exchanges, and provides regulatory surveillance of futures market participants. The CFTC also monitors futures trading in an attempt to identify market manipulation. One way the CFTC monitors trading is by obtaining information on positions of all large market participants in an attempt to identify unusual activity. The CFTC also puts limits on the number of futures contracts any trader can hold and monitors the time stamping of trades, where traders must record the time at which a trade occurs to identify irregularities.

www.cftc.gov

www.sec.gov

The Securities and Exchange Commission (SEC) is the main regulator of stock options in which delivery is based on a stock or stock index (e.g., stock options and stock index options). The CFTC is the main regulator of options on futures contracts in which delivery involves a futures contract. For example, the SEC regulates trading of S&P 500 futures options traded on the CBT, the value of which is determined by the value of the S&P 500 Index, but the CFTC regulates trading of S&P 500 futures options traded on the CME, the value of which is determined by the futures contract on the S&P 500 Index. This distinction has often caused confusion for both regulators and traders alike.

DO YOU UNDERSTAND?

1. Who the main regulators of futures and option exchanges are?

The individual futures and option exchanges also set and enforce many rules on their members designed to ensure the smooth operations and financial solvency of the exchange. As mentioned above, exchanges also are responsible for setting trading procedures, hours of trading, contract characteristics, margin requirements, and so on for contracts traded on the individual exchanges.

7

SWAPS

swap

An agreement between two parties to exchange assets or a series of cash flows for a specific period of time at a specified interval.

A **swap** is an agreement between two parties (called counterparties) to exchange specified periodic cash flows in the future based on some underlying instrument or price (e.g., a fixed or floating rate on a bond or note). Like forward, futures, and option contracts, swaps allow firms to better manage their interest rate, foreign exchange, and credit risks. Swaps were introduced in the early 1980s, and the market for swaps has grown enormously in recent years. Figure 10–9 shows the growth in the notional value of swaps outstanding from 1987 through 2004. Of the $164.49 trillion outstanding in 2004, the notional value of swap contracts outstanding by U.S. commercial banks (by far the major participant in the swap markets) was $52.91 trillion in September 2004. The five generic types of swaps are interest rate swaps, currency swaps, credit risk swaps, commodity swaps, and equity swaps.[15] The asset or instrument underlying the swap may change, but the basic principle of a swap agreement is the same in that it involves the transacting parties restructuring their asset or liability cash flows in a preferred direction. In this section, we consider the role of the two major generic types of swaps—interest rate and currency. We look at other types of swaps and describe the ability of swaps to hedge various kinds of risk in more detail in Chapter 23.

14. Contracts with other maturities also trade but are not reported in *The Wall Street Journal.*

15. There are also *swaptions,* which are options to enter into a swap agreement at some preagreed contract terms (e.g., a fixed rate of 10 percent) at some time in the future in return for the payment of an up-front premium.

FIGURE 10–9 Notional Value of Swaps Outstanding

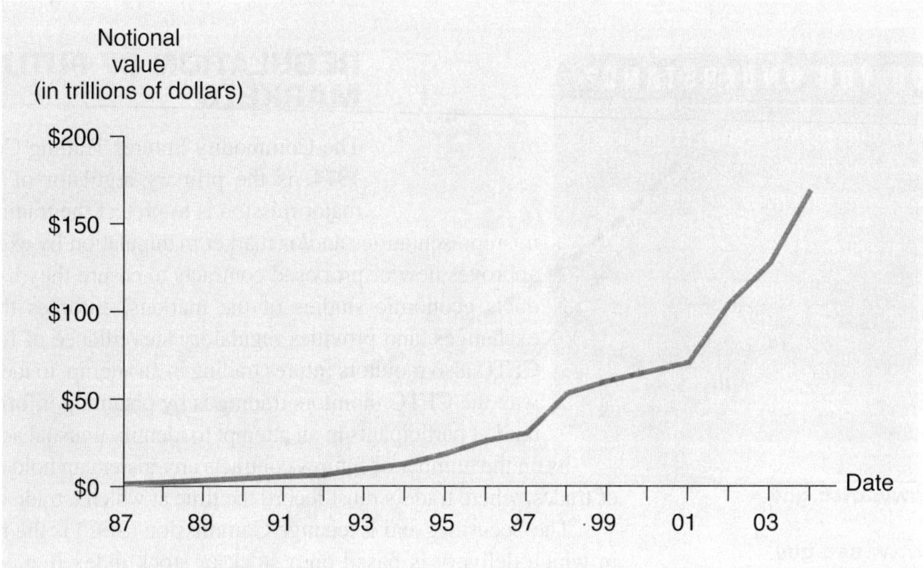

Interest Rate Swaps

interest rate swap

An exchange of fixed-interest payments for floating-interest payments by two counterparties.

swap buyer

By convention, a party that makes the fixed-rate payments in an interest rate swap transaction.

notional principal

The principal amount involved in a swap.

swap seller

By convention, a party that makes the floating-rate payments in an interest rate swap transaction.

By far the largest segment of the swap market comprises **interest rate swaps.** Conceptually, an interest rate swap is a succession of forward contracts on interest rates arranged by two parties.[16] As such, it allows the swap parties to put in place long-term protection (sometimes for as long as 15 years) against interest rate risk (see Chapter 22). The swap reduces the need to "roll over" contracts from old ones into new ones if futures or forward contracts had been relied on to achieve such long-term hedging protection.[17]

In a swap contract, the **swap buyer** agrees to make a number of fixed interest rate payments based on a principal contractual amount (called the **notional principal**) on periodic settlement dates to the **swap seller.** The swap seller, in turn, agrees to make floating-rate payments, tied to some interest rate, to the swap buyer on the same periodic settlement dates. In undertaking this transaction, the party that is the fixed-rate payer is seeking to transform the variable-rate nature of its liabilities into fixed-rate liabilities to better match the fixed returns earned on its assets. Meanwhile, the party that is the variable-rate payer seeks to turn its fixed-rate liabilities into variable-rate liabilities to better match the variable returns on its assets.

EXAMPLE 10–3 Hedging Interest Rate Risk with an Interest Rate Swap

To explain the role of a swap transaction in protecting a firm against interest rate risk, we use a simple example of an interest rate swap. Consider two financial institutions. The first is a money center bank that has raised $50 million of its funds by issuing five-year, medium-term notes with 7 percent annual fixed coupons (see Table 10–9). On the asset side of its portfolio, the bank makes commercial and industrial (C&I) loans whose rates are indexed to annual changes in the London Interbank Offered Rate (LIBOR). Banks index

16. For example, a four-year swap with annual swap dates involves four net cash flows between the parties to a swap. This is essentially similar to arranging four forward rate agreement (FRA) contracts: a one-year, a two-year, a three-year, and a four-year contract.

17. For example, futures contracts are offered usually with a maximum maturity of two years or less.

TABLE 10–9 Money Center Bank Balance Sheet

Assets		Liabilities	
C & I loans (rate indexed to LIBOR)	$50 million	Medium-term notes (coupons) fixed at 7% annually	$50 million

most large commercial and industrial loans to either LIBOR or the federal funds rate in the money market.

As a result of having floating-rate loans and fixed-rate liabilities in its asset–liability structure, the money center bank is exposed to interest rate risk. Specifically, if interest rates decrease, the bank's interest income decreases, since the variable interest return on loans (assets) will fall relative to the fixed cost of its funds (liabilities).

One way for the bank to hedge the risk of this exposure is to alter the interest rate sensitivity of its liabilities by transforming them into floating-rate liabilities that better match the (floating) rate sensitivity of its asset portfolio. The bank can make changes either on or off the balance sheet. On the balance sheet, the bank could attract an additional $50 million in short-term deposits that are indexed to the LIBOR rate in a manner similar to its loans. The proceeds of these deposits can be used to pay off its medium-term notes. This reduces the difference in the interest rate sensitivity between the bank's assets and liabilities. Alternatively, the bank could go off the balance sheet and sell an interest rate swap—that is, enter into a swap agreement to make the floating-rate payment side of a swap agreement.

The second party to the swap in this example is a thrift institution (a savings bank) that has invested $50 million in fixed interest rate residential mortgage assets of long maturity. To finance this residential mortgage portfolio, the savings bank has had to rely on short-term certificates of deposit with an average duration of one year (see Table 10–10). On maturity, these CDs must be "rolled over" at the current market rate.

Consequently, the savings bank's asset–liability balance sheet structure is the reverse of the money center bank's—if interest rates increase, the bank's interest expense increases. Since its assets (mortgages) are fixed rate, while its liabilities (deposits) are floating, the bank's net income falls.

The savings bank could hedge this interest rate risk exposure by transforming the short-term floating-rate nature of its liabilities into fixed-rate liabilities that better match the long-term maturity structure of its assets by either on- or off-balance-sheet hedging. On the balance sheet, the thrift could issue long-term notes (or bonds) with a maturity equal (or close to equal) that on the mortgages. The proceeds of the sale of the notes can be used to pay off the CDs. As a result, it would be funding long-term mortgages with long-term notes. Alternatively, the thrift could go off the balance sheet and buy a swap—that is, the thrift could enter into a swap agreement to make the fixed-rate payment side of a swap agreement.

The opposing balance sheet and interest rate risk exposures of the money center bank and the savings bank provide the necessary conditions for an interest rate swap agreement between the two parties. This swap agreement can be arranged directly by the two parties themselves—for example, by direct telephone contact. However, it is likely that a third financial institution—another commercial bank or an investment bank—would act either as a broker or an agent, receiving a fee[18] for bringing the two parties together or intermediating fully by accepting the credit risk exposure and guaranteeing the cash flows underlying the swap contract. We illustrate these swap transactions in Figure 10–10. By acting as a principal as well as an agent in arranging the swap, the third party financial institution can add a credit risk premium to the fee. However, the credit risk exposure of a swap to a financial institution is somewhat less than

18. One way the fees are reflected is in swap bid-ask spreads. For example, a bank can either make fixed-rate payments (buy a swap) or receive fixed-rate payments (sell a swap). Generally, the fixed rate for selling a swap is set at a margin above the fixed rate for buying.

TABLE 10–10 Savings Bank Balance Sheet

Assets		Liabilities	
Fixed-rate mortgages	$50 million	Short-term CDs (one year)	$50 million

FIGURE 10–10 A Swap Transaction

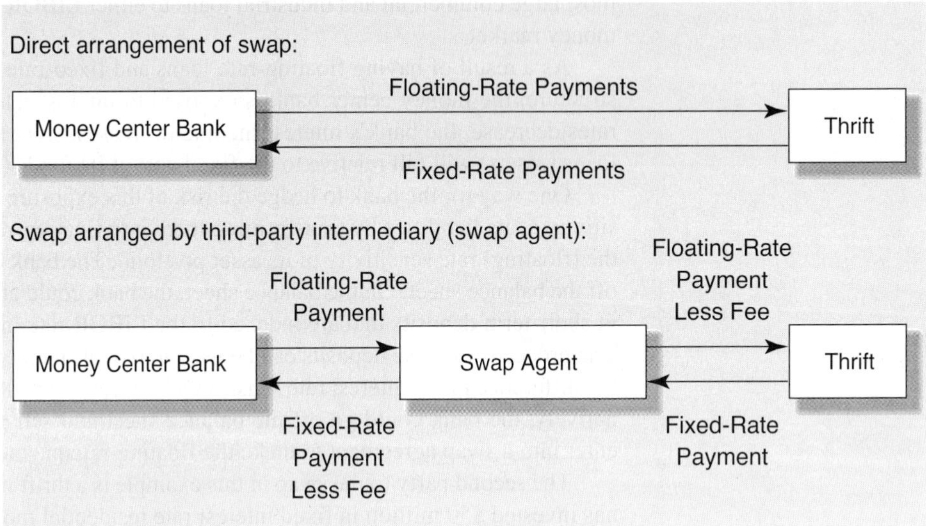

FIGURE 10–11 Fixed-Floating Rate Swap

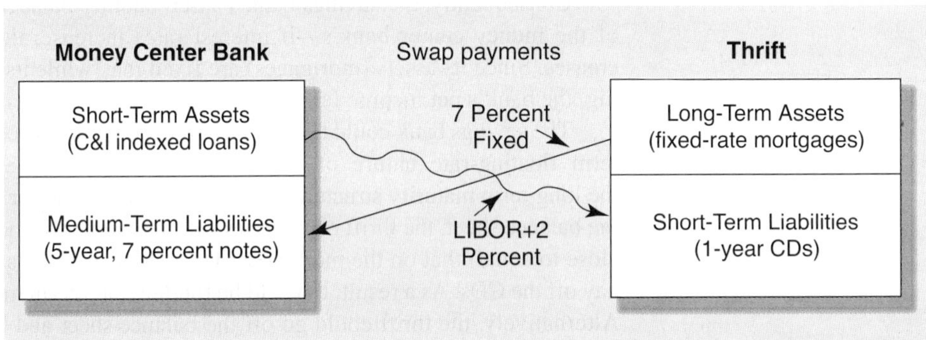

that on a loan (see Chapter 23). Conceptually, when a third-party financial institution fully intermediates the swap, that institution is really entering into two separate swap agreements—in this example, one with the money center bank and one with the savings bank.

The swap agreement that is arranged might dictate that the thrift send fixed payments of 7 percent per annum of the notional $50 million value of the swap to the money center bank, each year for five years, to allow the money center bank to cover fully the coupon interest payments on its note issue. In return, the money center bank sends annual payments indexed to the one-year LIBOR, for five years, to help the thrift better cover the cost of refinancing its one-year renewable CDs. Suppose that the money center bank agrees to send the thrift annual payments at the end of each year equal to the one-year LIBOR plus 2 percent.[19] We depict this fixed-floating rate swap transaction in Figure 10–11.

As a result of the swap, the money center bank has transformed its five-year, fixed-rate liability notes into a variable-rate liability matching the variability of returns on its C&I

19. These rates implicitly assume that this is the cheapest way each party can hedge its interest rate exposure. For example, LIBOR plus 2 percent is the lowest cost way that the money center bank can transform its fixed-rate liabilities into floating-rate liabilities.

loans. Further, through the interest rate swap, the money center bank effectively pays LIBOR plus 2 percent for its financing. The thrift has also transformed its variable-rate CDs into fixed-rate payments similar to those received on its fixed-rate mortgages.

Currency Swaps

currency swap

A swap used to hedge against exchange rate risk from mismatched currencies on assets and liabilities.

Interest rate swaps are long-term contracts that can be used to hedge interest rate risk exposure. This section considers a simple example of how **currency swaps** can be used to immunize or hedge against exchange rate risk when firms mismatch the currencies of their assets and liabilities.

Fixed-Fixed Currency Swaps. Consider a U.S. financial institution with all of its fixed-rate assets denominated in dollars. It is financing part of its asset portfolio with a £100 million issue of five-year, medium-term British pound sterling notes that have a fixed annual coupon of 6 percent. By comparison, a financial institution in the United Kingdom has all its assets denominated in pounds; it is partly funding those assets with a $200 million issue of five-year, medium-term dollar notes with a fixed annual coupon of 6 percent.

These two financial institutions are exposed to opposing currency risks. The U.S. institution is exposed to the risk that the dollar will depreciate (decline in value) against the pound over the next five years, which would make it more costly to cover the annual coupon interest payments and the principal repayment on its pound-denominated note liabilities. On the other hand, the U.K. institution is exposed to the risk that the dollar will appreciate against the pound, making it more difficult to cover the dollar coupon and principal payments on its five-year, $200 million note liabilities.

These financial institutions can hedge their exposures either on or off the balance sheet. Assume that the dollar/pound exchange rate is fixed at $2/£1. On the balance sheet, the U.S. financial institution can issue $200 million in five-year, medium-term dollar notes. The proceeds of the sale can be used to pay off the £100 million of five-year, medium-term pound notes. Similarly, the U.K. financial institution can issue £100 million in five-year, medium-term pound notes, using the proceeds to pay off the $200 million of five-year, medium-term dollar notes. Both institutions have taken actions on the balance sheet so that they are no longer exposed to movements in the exchange rate between the two currencies (i.e., their assets and liabilities are currency matched).

EXAMPLE 10-4 Expected Cash Flows on Fixed-Fixed Currency Swap

Alternatively, the U.K. and U.S. financial institutions can enter into a currency swap by which the U.K. institution sends annual payments in pounds to cover the coupon and principal repayments of the U.S. financial institution's pound sterling note issue, and the U.S. financial institution sends annual dollar payments to the U.K. financial institution to cover the interest and principal payments on its dollar note issue.[20] We summarize this currency swap in Figure 10–12. As a result of the swap, the U.K. financial institution transforms its fixed-rate dollar liabilities into fixed-rate pound liabilities that better match the fixed-rate pound cash flows from its asset portfolio. Similarly, the U.S. financial institution transforms fixed-rate pound liabilities into fixed-rate dollar liabilities that better match the fixed-rate dollar cash flows on its asset portfolio. In undertaking this exchange of cash flows, the two parties normally agree on a fixed exchange rate for the cash flows at the beginning of the period.[21] In this example, the fixed exchange rate is $2/£1.

20. In a currency swap, both principal and interest payments are usually included as part of the swap agreement. For interest rate swaps, it is usual to include only interest rate payments. The reason for this is that both principal and interest are exposed to foreign exchange risk.

21. As with interest rate swaps, this exchange rate reflects the contracting parties' expectations as to future exchange rate movements.

FIGURE 10–12 Fixed-Fixed Pound/Dollar Currency Swap

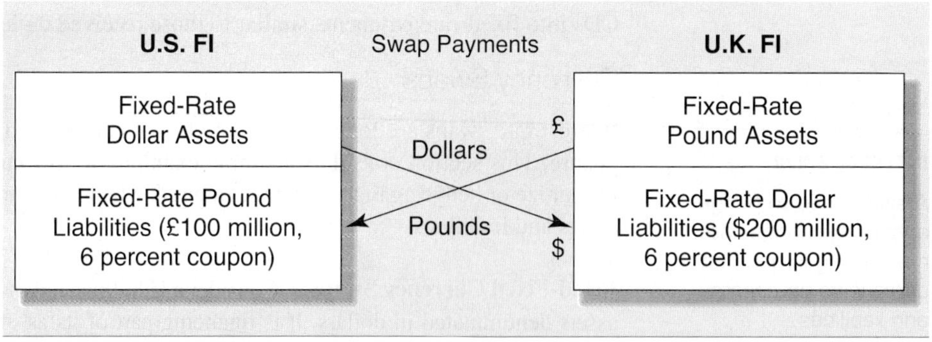

Note in the example above that should the exchange rate change from the rate agreed in the swap ($2/£1), either one or the other side would be losing in the sense that a new swap might be entered into at a more favorable exchange rate to one party. Specifically, if the dollar were to appreciate against the pound over the life of the swap, the agreement would become more costly for the U.S. financial institution. If, however, the dollar depreciated, the U.K. financial institution would find the agreement increasingly costly over the swap's life.

Swap Markets

Swap transactions are generally heterogeneous in terms of maturities, indexes used to determine payments, and timing of payments—there is no standardized contract. Swap dealers exist to serve the function of taking the opposite side of each transaction in order to keep the swap market liquid by locating or matching counterparties or, in many cases, taking one side of the swap themselves. In a direct swap between two counterparties, each party must find another party having a mirror image financing requirement—for example, a financial institution in need of swapping fixed-rate payments, made quarterly for the next 10 years, on $25 million in liabilities must find a counterparty in need of swapping $25 million in floating-rate payments made quarterly for the next 10 years. Without swap dealers, the search costs of finding such counterparties to a swap can be significant.

A further advantage of swap dealers is that they generally guarantee swap payments over the life of the contract. If one of the counterparties defaults on a direct swap, the other counterparty is no longer adequately hedged against risk and may have to replace the defaulted swap with a new swap at less favorable terms (replacement risk). By booking a swap with a swap dealer, a default by a counterparty will not affect the other counterparty. The swap dealer incurs any costs associated with the default (the fee or spread charged by the swap dealer to each party in a swap incorporates this default risk).[22] Commercial and investment banks have evolved as the major swap dealers, mainly because of their close ties to the financial markets and their specialized skills in assessing credit risk. Each swap market dealer manages a large "book" of swaps listing its swap positions. As a result, swap dealers can also diversify some of their risk exposure away.

In contrast to futures and options markets, swap markets are governed by very little regulation—there is no central governing body overseeing swap market operations. However, the International Swaps and Derivatives Association (ISDA) is a global trade association with over 600 member institutions (including most of the world's major financial institutions) from some 47 countries that sets codes and standards for swap markets. Established in 1985, the ISDA establishes, reviews, and updates the code of standards (the language and provisions) for swap documentation. The ISDA also acts as the spokesgroup for the industry on regulatory changes and issues, promotes the development of risk management practices for swap dealers (for example, the ISDA was instrumental in helping to develop the guidelines

www.isda.org

www.federalreserve.gov

www.fdic.gov

22. For interest rate swaps where the dealer intermediates, a different (higher) fixed rate will be set for receiving fixed rate payments compared to paying fixed rate.

set by the Basle committee on capital adequacy in financial institutions—see Chapter 13), provides a forum for informing and educating swap market participants about relevant issues, and sets standards of commercial conduct for its members.

DO YOU UNDERSTAND?

1. Which party in a swap is the swap buyer and which party is the swap seller?
2. What the difference is between an interest rate swap and a currency swap?

Further, because commercial banks are the major swap dealers, the swap markets are subject, indirectly, to regulations imposed by the Board of Governors of the Federal Reserve, the FDIC, and other bank regulatory agencies charged with monitoring bank risk. For example, commercial banks must include swap risk exposure when calculating risk-based capital requirements (see Chapter 13). To the extent that swap activity is part of a bank's overall business, swap markets are monitored for abuses. Investment banks and insurance companies have recently become bigger players in the swap markets, however, and these dealers are subject to few regulations on their swap dealings.

CAPS, FLOORS, AND COLLARS

8

Caps, floors, and collars are derivative securities that have many uses, especially in helping an FI to hedge interest rate risk. In general, FIs purchase interest rate caps if they are exposed to losses when interest rates rise. Usually, this happens if FIs are funding assets with floating-rate liabilities such as notes indexed to the London Interbank Offered Rate (or some other floating cost of funds) and they have fixed-rate assets or they are net long in bonds. By contrast, FIs purchase floors when they have fixed costs of debt and have variable or floating rates (returns) on assets or they are net short in bonds. Finally, FIs purchase collars to finance cap or floor positions or are concerned about excessive interest rate volatility.

cap

A call option on interest rates, often with multiple exercise dates.

Buying a **cap** means buying a call option or a succession of call options on interest rates.[23] Specifically, if interest rates rise above a cap rate, which acts in a similar fashion to a strike price in an option contract, the seller of the cap—usually a bank—compensates the buyer—for example, another financial institution—in return for an up-front premium. Suppose that two firms enter a two-year cap agreement with a notional value of $1 million. The cap rate is 10 percent and payments are settled once a year based on year-end interest rates. For the interest rate movements shown in Figure 10–13, the cap writer owes the cap buyer (11% − 10%) × $1 million, or $10,000, at the end of year 1, and (12% − 10%) × $1 million, or $20,000, at the end of year 2. As a result, buying an interest rate cap is like

FIGURE 10–13 **Hypothetical Path of Interest Rates during a Cap Agreement**

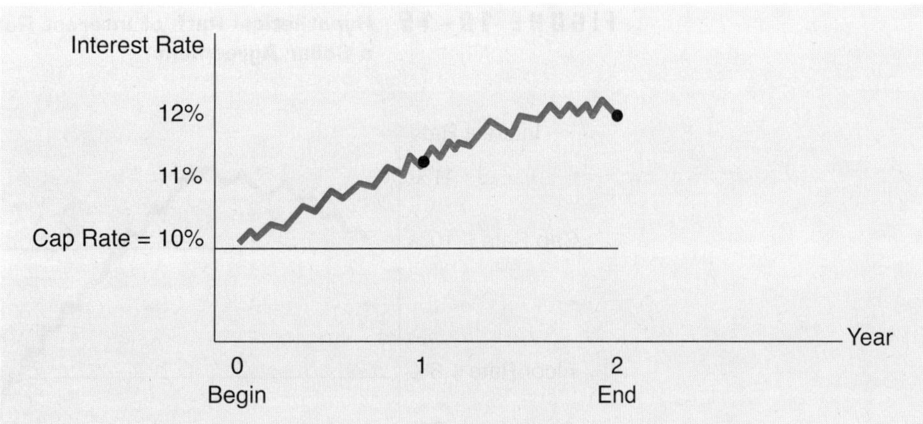

23. Note that a cap can be viewed as a call option on interest rates (as discussed here) or as a put option on bond prices, since rising interest rates mean falling bond prices. Similarly, a floor (discussed in the next paragraph) can be viewed as a put option on interest rates or a call option on bond prices. We follow market convention and discuss caps and floors as options on interest rates rather than on bond prices.

buying insurance against an (excessive) increase in interest rates. A cap agreement can have one or many exercise dates.

floor

A put option on interest rates, often with multiple exercise dates.

Buying a **floor** is similar to buying a put option on interest rates. If interest rates fall below the floor rate, the seller of the floor compensates the buyer in return for an up-front premium. For example, suppose that two financial institutions enter a two-year floor agreement with a notional value of $1 million. The floor rate is 8 percent, and payments are settled once a year based on year-end rates. For the interest rate movements shown in Figure 10–14, the floor writer owes the floor buyer (8% − 7%) × $1 million, or $10,000, at the end of year 1, and (8% − 6%) × $1 million, or $20,000, at the end of year 2. As with caps, floor agreements can have one or many exercise dates.

collar

A position taken simultaneously in a cap and a floor.

A **collar** occurs when a firm takes a simultaneous position in a cap and a floor, usually *buying* a cap and *selling* a floor. The idea here is that the firm wants to hedge itself against rising rates but wants to finance the cost of the cap. One way to do this is to sell a floor and use the premiums earned on the floor to pay the premium on the purchased cap. For example, suppose that a financial institution enters into a two-year collar agreement with a notional value of $1 million. The floor rate is 8 percent and the cap rate is 10 percent. Payments are settled once a year based on year-end rates. For the interest rate movements shown in Figure 10–15, the collar buyer, the financial institution, gains (11% − 10%) × $1 million, or $10,000, at the end

FIGURE 10–14 **Hypothetical Path of Interest Rates during a Floor Agreement**

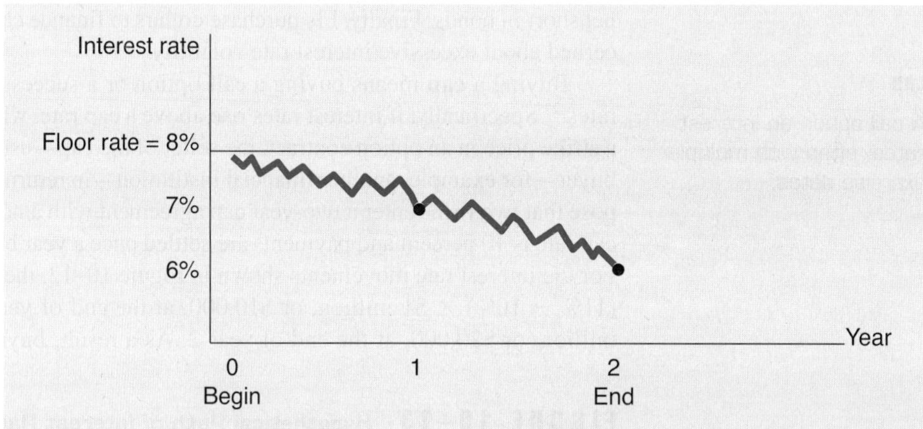

FIGURE 10–15 **Hypothetical Path of Interest Rates during a Collar Agreement**

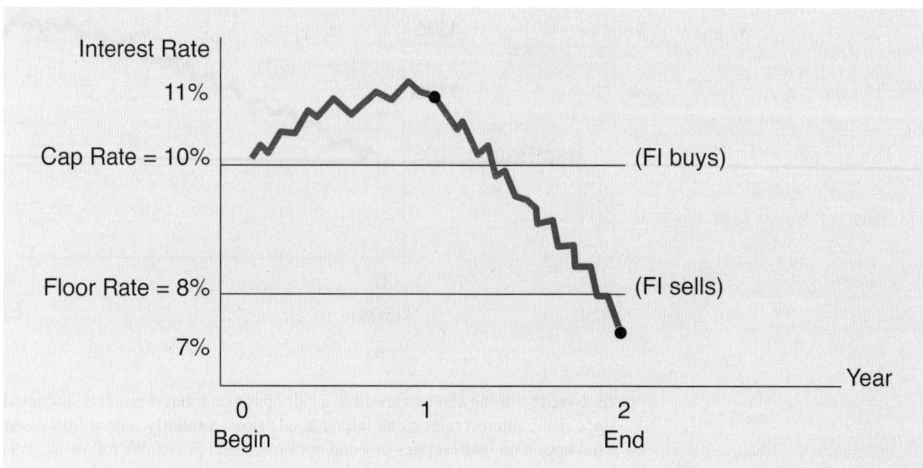

DO YOU UNDERSTAND?

1. What the difference is between a cap and a collar?
2. The conditions under which a firm would buy a floor?

of year 1. However, since the financial institution has written or sold a floor to another financial institution to finance the cap purchase, it pays (8% − 7%) × \$1 million, or \$10,000, at the end of year 2.

Many firms invested in caps and collars in the mid-2000s in expectation that interest rates would increase. For example, in 2004 Deutsche Bank arranged a \$900 million collar for Aluminum Bahrain, which wanted to hedge a large portfolio against interest rate increases with minimal costs.

INTERNATIONAL ASPECTS OF DERIVATIVE SECURITIES MARKETS

9

Tables 10–11 and 10–12 report the amount of global over-the-counter (OTC) and exchange-traded derivative securities from 1999 through 2004. Notice global OTC trading far outweighs exchange trading. The total notional amount of outstanding OTC contracts was \$220.06 trillion in 2004 compared to exchange-traded contracts which totaled \$48.99 trillion in 2004. In both markets interest rate contracts dominated: \$164.63 trillion in notional value in the OTC markets and \$45.36 trillion on exchanges.

U.S. markets and currencies continue to dominate global derivative securities markets. On organized exchanges, North American markets traded \$27.90 trillion of the \$48.99 trillion contracts outstanding in 2004. In the OTC markets, \$24.55 trillion of the currency contracts,

TABLE 10–11 Amounts of Global Derivative Securities Outstanding on the OTC Market

(in billions of dollars)

Contract	1999	2001	2004
Total Contracts	\$88,202	\$111,115	\$220,058
Foreign Exchange Contracts:	14,344	16,748	26,997
By currency:			
Canadian dollar	647	593	968
Euro	4,667	6,368	10,312
Japanese yen	4,236	4,178	6,516
Pound sterling	2,242	2,315	4,614
Swiss franc	880	800	1,344
U.S. dollar	12,834	15,410	24,551
Other	2,746	3,689	5,687
Interest Rate Contracts:	60,091	77,513	164,626
By currency:			
Canadian dollar	825	781	1,298
Euro	20,692	26,185	63,006
Japanese yen	12,391	11,799	21,103
Pound sterling	4,588	6,215	11,867
Swiss franc	1,414	1,362	2,651
U.S. dollar	16,510	27,422	57,827
Other	3,195	3,673	6,872
Equity-Linked Contracts:	1,809	1,881	4,520
By currency:			
U.S. equities	516	376	867
European equities	1,040	1,353	2,768
Japanese equities	124	56	447
Other equities	129	97	438

Source: Bank for International Settlements, Quarterly Review, June 2002 and December 2004. **www.bis.org**

TABLE 10–12 Derivative Financial Instruments Trade on Organized Exchanges
(in billions of dollars)

Contract	1999	2001	2004
Futures:			
All markets:	$8,294.2	$9,633.5	$17,661.8
Interest rate	7,913.9	9,234.0	17,024.8
Currency	36.7	65.6	84.1
Equity index	343.5	334.0	552.9
North America:	3,553.2	5,906.4	9,777.9
Europe:	2,379.2	2,444.5	5,533.8
Asia and Pacific:	2,149.8	1,202.0	2,200.7
Other markets:	211.9	80.4	149.4
Options:			
All markets:	5,258.7	14,083.7	31,330.3
Interest rate	3,755.5	12,492.6	28,335.0
Currency	22.4	27.4	37.2
Equity index	1,480.8	1,563.7	2.958.1
North America:	3,377.1	10,292.2	18,119.7
Europe:	1,603.2	3,698.0	12,975.4
Asia and Pacific:	240.7	62.8	169.6
Other markets:	37.7	30.8	65.6

Source: Bank for International Settlements, Quarterly Review, June 2002 and December 2004. **www.bis.org**

DO YOU UNDERSTAND?

1. Which are the largest derivative securities markets globally?
2. In which currencies most global derivative securities are denominated?

$57.83 trillion of the interest rate contracts, and $0.9 trillion of the equity-linked contracts were denominated in U.S. dollars.

The euro and European derivative securities markets, however, are now a strong second behind the United States. In 2004 European exchange markets traded $18.51 trillion of the total $48.99 trillion contracts. In the OTC markets, $10.3 trillion of the currency contracts $63.01 trillion of the interest rate contracts, and $2.77 trillion of the equity-linked contracts were denominated in the euro or European currencies. In fact, in 1999 and 2004, more interest rate contracts on the OTC were euro-denominated than U.S. dollar-denominated.

As has been seen in earlier chapters on other financial markets, the continued economic and financial problems in Japan have resulted in a drop in the value of derivative securities traded on Japanese exchanges and denominated in the Japanese yen. Overall, Asian and Pacific derivative security exchanges have seen a drop in amounts outstanding, falling to $2.37 trillion in 2004. In the OTC derivatives security markets $6.52 trillion of the currency contracts, $21.10 trillion of interest rate contracts, and $0.45 trillion of the equity-linked contracts were denominated in the yen in 2004.

SUMMARY

In this chapter, we introduced the major derivative securities and the markets in which they trade. Derivative securities (forwards, futures, options, and swaps) are securities whose value depends on the value of an underlying asset but whose payoff is not guaranteed with cash flows from these assets. Derivative securities can be used as investments on which a trader hopes to directly profit or as hedge instruments used to protect the trader against risk from another asset or liability held. We examined the characteristics of the various securities and the markets in which each trade. We look at how these securities are used by financial institutions to hedge various risks in Chapter 23.

www.mhhe.com/sc3e

SEARCH THE SITE

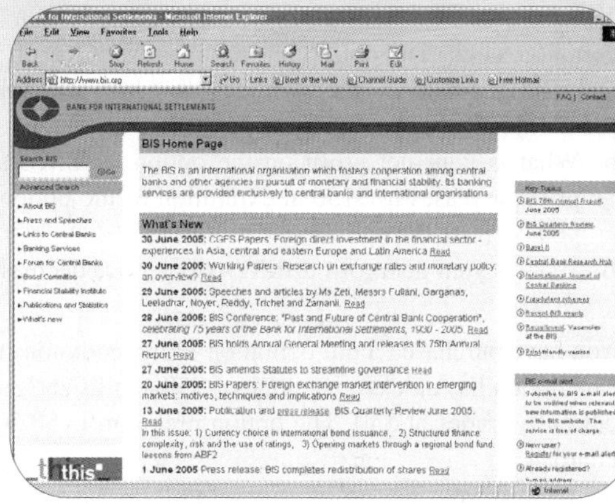

Go to the Bank for International Settlements Web site at **www.bis.org** and find the most recent data on the amount of derivatives traded worldwide over the counter and on organized exchanges using the following steps.

Click on "BIS Quarterly Review."

Click on "Statistical Annex Read."

Click on "Derivatives Markets."

This downloads a file onto your computer that contains the relevant data.

Questions

1. By what percentage have these values changed since 2004 as reported in Tables 10–11 and 10–12?
2. What countries are currently the biggest traders of derivative securities?

QUESTIONS

1. What is a derivative security?
2. What is the difference between a spot contract, a forward contract, and a futures contract?
3. What are the functions of floor brokers and professional traders on the futures exchanges?
4. What is the purpose of requiring a margin on a futures or option transaction? What is the difference between an initial margin and a maintenance margin?
5. When is a futures or option trader in a long versus a short position in the derivative contract?
6. What is the meaning of a Treasury bond futures price quote of 103–13?
7. Refer to Table 10–5.
   a. What was the settlement price on the December 2006 Eurodollar futures contract on Monday, January 10, 2005?
   b. How many 30-day federal funds futures contracts traded on Friday, January 7, 2005?
   c. What is the face value on a Swiss franc currency futures contract on January 10, 2005?
   d. What was the settlement price on the March 2005 DJIA futures contract on January 7, 2005?
8. Refer to Table 10–5.
   a. If you think two-year Treasury note prices will fall between January 10, 2005, and June 2005, what type of futures position would you take?
   b. If you think inflation in Japan will increase by more than that in the United States between January and March 2005, what type of futures position would you take?
   c. If you think stock prices will fall between January and June 2005, what type of position would you take in the June S&P 500 Index futures contract? What happens if stock prices actually rise?
9. Suppose you purchase a Treasury bond futures contract at a price of 95 percent of the face value, $100,000.
   a. What is your obligation when you purchase this futures contract?
   b. Assume that the Treasury bond futures price falls to 94 percent. What is your loss or gain?
   c. Assume that the Treasury bond futures price rises to 97. What is your loss or gain?
10. eXcel **Using a Spreadsheet to Calculate Profit and Loss on Futures Transactions:** At the beginning of the quarter, you purchased a $100,000 Treasury bond futures contract for 108–12. Calculate the profit on the futures contract if the price at the end of the quarter is 106–16, 108–20, 110–8, and 112–02.

Price at Beginning of Quarter	Price at End of Quarter	=>	The Profit or Loss Is
$100,000 × 108.375 = 108,375	$100,000 × 106.5 = 106,500		−$1,875
100,000 × 108.375 = 108,375	100,000 × 108.625 = 108,625		$250
100,000 × 108.375 = 108,375	100,000 × 110.25 = 110,250		1,875
100,000 × 108.375 = 108,375	100,000 × 112.0625 = 112,062.5		3,687.5

11. What is an option? How does an option differ from a forward or futures contract?
12. What is the difference between a call option and a put option?
13. What must happen to the price of the underlying T-bond futures contract for the purchaser of a call option on T-bond futures to make money? How does the writer of the call option make money?

www.mhhe.com/sc3e

14. What must happen to the price of the underlying stock for the purchaser of a put option on the stock to make money? How does the writer of the put option make money?

15. You have taken a long position in a call option on IBM common stock. The option has an exercise price of $136 and IBM's stock currently trades at $140. The option premium is $5 per contract.

a. What is your net profit on the option if IBM's stock price increases to $150 at expiration of the option and you exercise the option?

b. What is your net profit if IBM's stock price decreases to $130?

16. You have purchased a put option on Pfizer common stock. The option has an exercise price of $38 and Pfizer's stock currently trades at $40. The option premium is $0.50 per contract.

a. What is your net profit on the option if Pfizer's stock price does not change over the life of the option?

b. What is your net profit on the option if Pfizer's stock price falls to $34 and you exercise the option?

17. What are the three ways an option holder can liquidate his or her position?

18. Refer to Table 10–8.

a. How many American Airlines January 7.50 put options were outstanding at the open of trading on Monday, January 10, 2005?

b. What was the closing price of a T-note March 109 futures call option on January 10, 2005?

c. How many call options on the S&P 500 Stock Index futures contract traded on Friday, January 7, 2005?

d. What was the open interest on March 2005 put options (with an exercise price of 92) on the DJ Industrial Average stock index on January 10, 2005?

19. What factors affect the value of an option?

20. Who are the major regulators of futures and options markets?

21. What is a swap?

22. What is the difference between an interest rate swap and a currency swap?

23. Which party is the swap buyer and which is the swap seller in a swap transaction?

24. A commercial bank has fixed-rate long-term loans in its asset portfolio and variable-rate CDs in its liability portfolio. Bank managers believe interest rates will increase in the future. What side of a fixed-floating rate swap would the commercial bank need to take to protect against this interest rate risk?

25. An insurance company owns $50 million of floating-rate bonds yielding LIBOR plus 1 percent. These loans are financed with $50 million of fixed-rate guaranteed investment contracts (GICs) costing 10 percent. A finance company has $50 million of auto loans with a fixed rate of 14 percent. The loans are financed with $50 million in CDs at a variable rate of LIBOR plus 4 percent.

a. What is the risk exposure of the insurance company?

b. What is the risk exposure of the finance company?

c. What would be the cash flow goals of each company if they were to enter into a swap agreement?

d. Which company would be the buyer and which company would be the seller in the swap?

e. Diagram the direction of the relevant cash flows for the swap arrangement.

26. A commercial bank has $200 million of floating-rate loans yielding the T-bill rate plus 2 percent. These loans are financed with $200 million of fixed-rate deposits costing 9 percent. A savings bank has $200 million of mortgages with a fixed rate of 13 percent. They are financed with $200 million in CDs with a variable rate of T-bill rate plus 3 percent.

a. Discuss the type of interest rate risk each institution faces.

b. Propose a swap that would result in each institution having the same type of asset and liability cash flows.

c. Show that this swap would be acceptable to both parties.

27. An American firm has British pound-denominated accounts payable on its balance sheet. Managers believe the exchange rate of British pounds to U.S. dollars will depreciate before the accounts will be paid. What type of currency swap should the firm enter?

28. What is the difference between a cap, a floor, and a collar? When would a firm enter any of these derivative security positions?

APPENDIX 10A: Black-Scholes Option Pricing Model

View this appendix at
www.mhhe.com/sc3e

part three

Commercial Banks

Part Three of the text summarizes the operations of commercial banks. Chapter 11 describes the key characteristics and recent trends in the commercial banking sector. Chapter 12 describes the financial statements of a typical commercial bank and the ratios used to analyze those statements. Chapter 13 provides a comprehensive look at the regulations under which these financial institutions operate and, particularly, at the effect of recent changes in regulations.

OUTLINE

11 Commercial Banks

Industry Overview

OUTLINE

Chapter NAVIGATOR

1. What is a commercial bank?
2. What are the main assets held by commercial banks?
3. What are the main liabilities held by commercial banks?
4. What types of off-balance-sheet activities do commercial banks undertake?
5. What factors have motivated the significant decrease in the number of commercial banks?
6. How has the commercial banking industry performed in recent years?
7. How has technology affected the operations of commercial banks?
8. Who are the main regulators of commercial banks?
9. What are the world's biggest banks?

COMMERCIAL BANKS AS A SECTOR OF THE FINANCIAL INSTITUTIONS INDUSTRY: CHAPTER OVERVIEW

The products that modern financial institutions sell and the risks they face are becoming increasingly similar, as are the techniques they use to measure and manage these risks. The two panels in Table 11–1 indicate the products sold by the financial services industry in 1950 and in 2006. The largest (in dollar value of assets) FI group is commercial banks, also called *depository institutions* because a significant proportion of their funds come from customer deposits. Savings institutions and credit unions (discussed in Chapter 14) are also depository institutions. Chapters 11 through 13 describe commercial banks, their financial statements, and the regulations that govern their operations.

As we examine the structure of commercial banks and their financial statements, notice a distinguishing feature between them and nonfinancial firms illustrated in Figure 11–1. Specifically, commercial banks' major assets are loans (financial assets) and their major

TABLE 11–1 Products Sold by the U.S. Financial Services Industry

	Function							
				Lending		Underwriting Issuance of		
Institution	Payment Services	Savings Products	Fiduciary Services	Business	Consumer	Equity	Debt	Insurance and Risk Management Products
1950								
Depository institutions	X	X	X	X	X			
Insurance companies		X		*				
Finance companies				*	X			X
Securities firms		X	X			X	X	
Pension funds		X						
Mutual funds		X						
2006								
Depository institutions	X	X	X	X	X	X	X	X
Insurance companies	X	X	X	X	X	X	X	X
Finance companies	X	X	X	X	X	†	†	X
Securities firms	X	X	X	X	X	X	X	X
Pension funds		X	X	X				X
Mutual funds	X	X	X					X

*Minor involvement

†Selective involvement via affiliates

liabilities are deposits. Just the opposite is true for nonfinancial firms, whose deposits are listed as assets on their balance sheets and whose loans are listed as liabilities. In contrast to commercial banks, nonfinancial firms' major assets are nonfinancial (tangible) assets such as buildings and machinery. Indeed, as illustrated in Figure 11–2, commercial banks provide loans to, and accept deposits from, nonfinancial firms (and individuals), while nonfinancial firms provide deposits to, and obtain loans from, commercial banks.

FIGURE 11–1 Differences in Balance Sheets of Commercial Banks and Nonfinancial Firms

Commercial Banks		Nonfinancial Firms	
Assets	Liabilities and Equity	Assets	Liabilities and Equity
Loans	Deposits	Deposits	Loans
Other financial assets		Other financial assets	
Other nonfinancial assets	Other liabilities and equity	Other nonfinancial assets	Other liabilities and equity

FIGURE 11–2 Interaction between Commercial Banks and Nonfinancial Firms

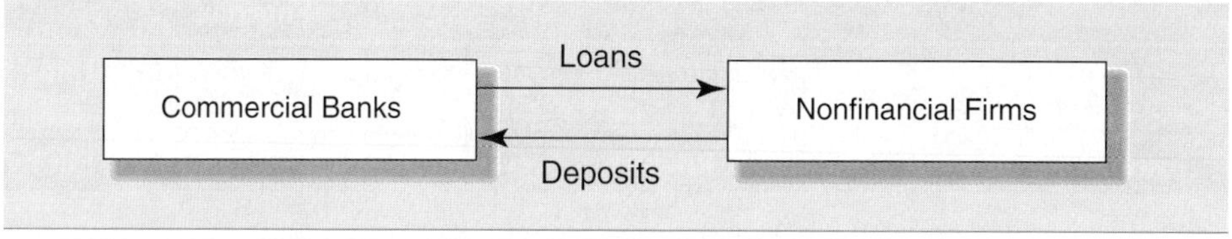

As we discussed in Chapter 1, depository institutions, and commercial banks in particular, perform several services that are essential to the efficient functioning of the financial markets in the United States. For example, because deposits are a significant component of the money supply, commercial banks play a key role in the transmission of monetary policy for the central bank to the rest of the economy. Further, commercial banks are special in that the efficiency with which they provide payment services directly benefits the economy. Finally, commercial banks offer maturity intermediation services to the economy. Specifically, by maturity mismatching, commercial banks can produce new types of contracts such as long-term mortgage loans to households while still raising funds with short-term liability contracts such as deposits. Because of the vital nature of the services they provide, commercial banks are regulated to protect against a disruption in the provision of these services and the cost this would impose on the economy and society at large. Our attention in this chapter focuses on (1) the size, structure, and composition of the commercial banking industry, (2) its balance sheets and recent trends, (3) the industry's recent performance, and (4) its regulators.

DEFINITION OF A COMMERCIAL BANK

Commercial banks represent the largest group of depository institutions measured by asset size. They perform functions similar to those of savings institutions and credit unions—they accept deposits (liabilities) and make loans (assets). As we discuss in more detail in Chapter 14, commercial banks are distinguishable from savings institutions and credit unions, however, in the size and composition of their loans and deposits. Specifically, while deposits are the major source of funding, commercial bank liabilities usually include several types of *non* deposit sources of funds (such as subordinated notes and debentures). Moreover, their loans are broader in range, including consumer, commercial, international, and real estate loans. Commercial banks are regulated separately from savings institutions and credit unions. Within the banking industry, the structure and composition of assets and liabilities also vary significantly for banks of different asset sizes.

DO YOU UNDERSTAND?

1. What the three categories of depository institutions are?
2. What distinguishes a commercial bank from other types of depository institutions?

BALANCE SHEETS AND RECENT TRENDS

Chapter 12 provides a detailed discussion of the financial statements (balance sheets and income statements) of commercial banks and how financial statements are used by regulators, stockholders, depositors, and creditors to evaluate bank performance. In this chapter, we present a brief introduction to the commercial bank industry balance sheets and their recent performance, highlighting trends in each.

Assets

Consider the aggregate balance sheet (in Table 11–2) and the percentage distributions (in Figure 11–3) for all U.S. commercial banks as of 2004. The majority of the assets held by commercial banks are loans. Total loans amounted to $4,739.8 billion, or 57.5 percent of total assets, and fell into four broad classes: business or commercial and industrial loans; commercial and residential real estate loans; individual loans,

TABLE 11-2 Balance Sheet
(all U.S. commercial banks, in billions of dollars)

Assets			
Total cash assets			$416.9
U.S. government securities		$1,047.4	
Federal funds and repurchase agreements		384.6	
Other		447.3	
Investment securities			1,879.3
Interbank loans		193.6	
Loans excluding interbank		4,624.3	
Commercial and industrial	$ 890.1		
Real estate	2,544.9		
Individual	806.3		
All other	383.0		
Less: Reserve for loan losses		78.1	
Total loans			4,739.8
Other assets			1,208.4
Total assets			$8,244.4
Liabilities and Equity			
Transaction accounts		$ 716.9	
Nontransaction accounts		4,689.1	
Total deposits			$5,406.0
Borrowings			1,769.6
Other liabilities			247.4
Total liabilities			$7,423.0
Equity			821.4

Source: Federal Deposit Insurance Corporation, *Statistics on Banking,* Third Quarter 2004. **www.fdic.gov**

FIGURE 11–3 Distribution of Commercial Bank Assets, Liabilities, and Equity, September 2004

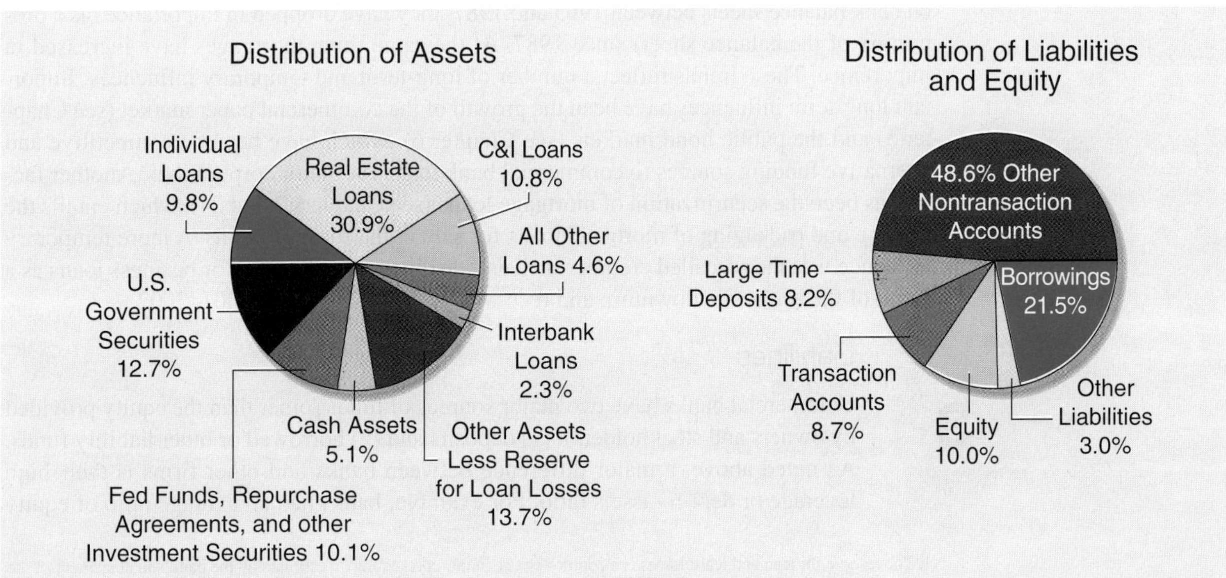

Source: Federal Deposit Insurance Corporation, *Quarterly Banking Profile,* Third Quarter 2004. **www.fdic.gov**

such as consumer loans for auto purchases and credit card loans; and all other loans, such as loans to emerging-market countries.[1]

Investment securities consist of items such as interest-bearing deposits purchased from other FIs, federal funds sold to other banks, repurchase agreements (RPs or repos),[2] U.S. Treasury and agency securities, municipal securities issued by states and political subdivisions, mortgage-backed securities, and other debt and equity securities. In 2004, the investment portfolio totaled \$1,879.3 billion, or 22.8 percent of total assets. U.S. government securities such as U.S. Treasury bonds totaled \$1,047.4 billion, with other securities making up the remainder. Investment securities generate interest income for the bank and are also used for trading and liquidity management purposes. Many investment securities held by banks are highly liquid, have low default risk, and can usually be traded in secondary markets (see Chapter 12).

While loans are the main revenue-generating assets for banks, investment securities provide banks with liquidity. Unlike manufacturing companies, commercial banks and other financial institutions are exposed to high levels of liquidity risk. Liquidity risk is the risk that arises when a financial institution's liability holders such as depositors demand cash for the financial claims they hold with the financial institution. Because of the extensive levels of deposits held by banks (see below), they must hold significant amounts of cash and investment securities to make sure they can meet the demand from their liability holders if and when they liquidate the claims they hold.

A major inference we can draw from this asset structure (and the importance of loans in this asset structure) is that the major risks faced by modern commercial bank managers are credit or default risk, liquidity risk, interest rate risk, and, ultimately, insolvency risk (see Chapters 19 through 24). Because commercial banks are highly leveraged and therefore hold little equity (see below) compared to total assets, even a relatively small amount of loan defaults can wipe out the equity of a bank, leaving it insolvent. Losses such as those due to defaults are charged off against the equity (stockholders' stake) in a bank. Additions to the reserve for loan and lease losses account (and, in turn, the expense account "provisions for losses on loans and leases") to meet *expected* defaults reduce retained earnings and, thus, reduce equity of the bank (see Chapter 12). *Unexpected* defaults (e.g., due to a sudden major recession) are meant to be written off against the remainder of the bank's equity (e.g., its retained earnings and funds raised from share offerings). We look at recent loan performance below.

Figure 11–4 shows broad trends over the 1951–2005 period in the four principal earning asset areas of commercial banks: business loans (or commercial and industrial loans), securities, mortgages, and consumer loans. Although business loans were the major asset on bank balance sheets between 1965 and 1987, they have dropped in importance (as a proportion of the balance sheet) since 1987. At the same time, mortgages have increased in importance. These trends reflect a number of long-term and temporary influences. Important long-term influences have been the growth of the commercial paper market (see Chapter 5) and the public bond markets (see Chapter 6), which have become competitive and alternative funding sources to commercial bank loans for major corporations. Another factor has been the securitization of mortgage loans (see Chapters 7 and 24), which entails the pooling and packaging of mortgage loans for sale in the form of bonds. A more temporary influence was the so-called credit crunch and decline in the demand for business loans as a result of the economic downturn and recession in 1989–1992 and 2001–2002.

Liabilities

3

Commercial banks have two major sources of funds (other than the equity provided by owners and stockholders): (1) deposits and (2) borrowed or other liability funds. As noted above, a major difference between banks and other firms is their high leverage or debt-to-assets ratio. For example, banks had an average ratio of equity

1. The reserve for loan and lease losses is a contra-asset account representing an estimate by the bank's management of the percentage of gross loans (and leases) that will have to be "charged-off" due to future defaults (see Chapter 12).

2. Federal funds and repos are described in detail in Chapter 5.

FIGURE 11–4 Portfolio Shift: U.S. Commercial Banks' Financial Assets

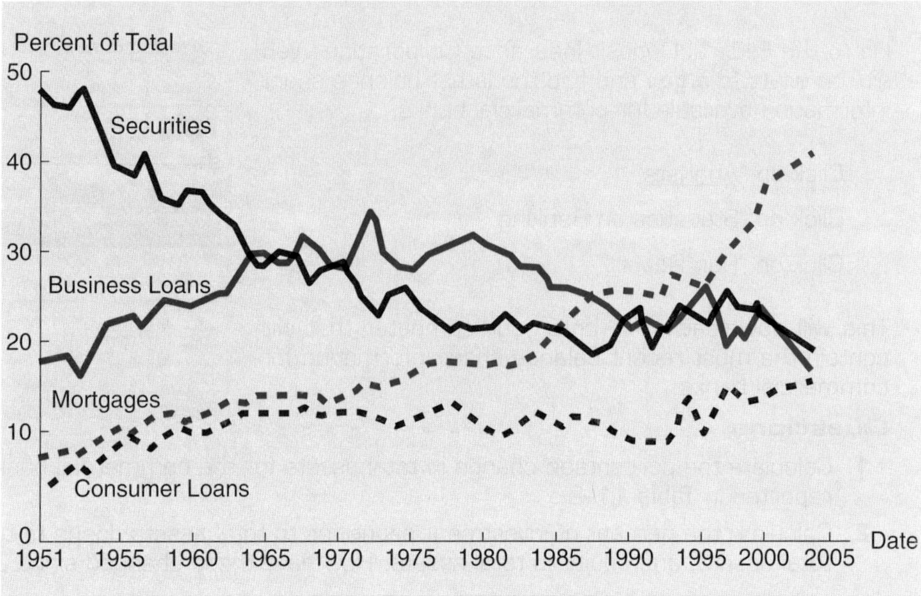

Source: Federal Deposit Insurance Corporation, *Statistics on Banking*, various issues. **www.fdic.gov**

to assets of 10.0 percent in 2004; this implies that 90.0 percent of assets were funded by debt, either deposits or borrowed funds.

Note that in Table 11–2, which shows the aggregate balance sheet of U.S. banks, in September 2004, deposits amounted to \$5,406.0 billion (65.5 percent of total assets) and borrowings and other liabilities were \$1,769.4 and \$247.4 billion (21.5 percent and 3.0 percent of total assets), respectively. Of the total stock of deposits, transaction accounts represented 13.3 percent of total deposits (and 8.7 percent of total assets), or \$716.9 billion. **Transaction accounts** are checkable deposits that either bear no interest (demand deposits) or are interest bearing (most commonly called negotiable order of withdrawal accounts or **NOW accounts**). Since their introduction in 1980, interest-bearing checking accounts, especially NOW accounts, have dominated the transaction accounts of banks. Nevertheless, since limitations are imposed on the ability of corporations to hold such accounts,[3] and NOW accounts often have minimum balance requirements, noninterest-bearing demand deposits are still held. The second major segment of deposits is retail or household savings and time deposits, normally individual account holdings of less than \$100,000. Important components of bank retail savings accounts are small nontransaction accounts, which include passbook savings accounts and retail time deposits. Small nontransaction accounts compose 59.0 percent of total deposits (and 48.6 percent of total assets). However, this disguises an important trend in the supply of these deposits to banks. Specifically, the amount held of retail savings and time deposits has been falling in recent years, largely as a result of competition from money market mutual funds.[4] These funds pay a competitive rate of interest based on wholesale money market rates by pooling and investing funds (see Chapter 17) while requiring relatively small-denomination investments.

transaction accounts

The sum of noninterest-bearing demand deposits and interest-bearing checking accounts.

NOW account

An interest-bearing checking account.

The third major segment of deposit funds is large time deposits (\$100,000 or more);[5] these deposits amounted to \$679.6 billion, or approximately 12.6 percent of total deposits

3. However, legislation is pending in the U.S. Congress to repeal this Depression-era ban on interest-bearing business checking accounts.

4. See U.S. General Accounting Office, "Mutual Funds: Impact on Bank Deposits and Credit Availability," GAO/GGD-95-230 (Washington, DC: Government Printing Office, 1995).

5. \$100,000 is the cap for explicit coverage under FDIC provided deposit insurance. We discuss this in more detail in Chapter 13.

SEARCH THE SITE

Go to the Federal Deposit Insurance Corporation Web site at **www.fdic.gov** and find the latest balance sheet information available for commercial banks.

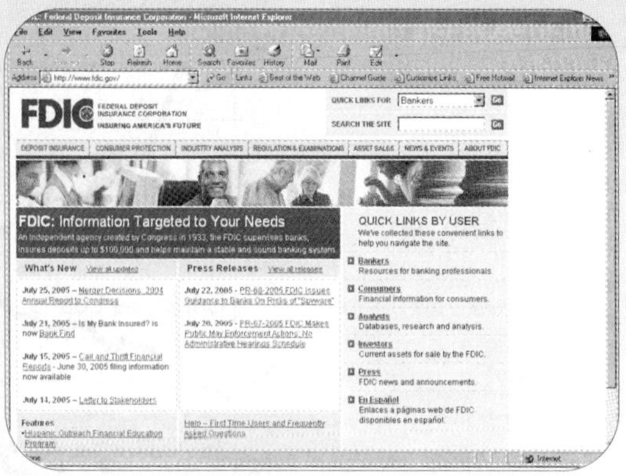

Click on "Analysts"

Click on "Statistics on Banking"

Click on "Run Report"

This will download a file onto your computer that will contain the most recent balance sheet information for commercial banks.

Questions

1. Calculate the percentage change in total assets for the commercial bank industry since 2004 reported in Table 11–2.
2. Calculate the percent of investment securities to total assets, loans to total assets, deposits to total assets, and equity to total assets. How have these changed since 2004?

negotiable CDs

Fixed-maturity interest-bearing deposits with face values of $100,000 or more that can be resold in the secondary market.

(and 8.2 percent of total assets) in 2004. These are primarily **negotiable certificates of deposit** (deposit claims with promised interest rates and fixed maturities of at least 14 days) that can be resold to outside investors in an organized secondary market. As such, they are usually distinguished from retail time deposits by their negotiability and secondary market liquidity.

Nondeposit liabilities comprise borrowings and other liabilities that total 24.5 percent of total assets, or $2,017.0 billion. These categories include a broad array of instruments, such as purchases of federal funds (bank reserves) on the interbank market and repurchase agreements (temporary swaps of securities for federal funds) at the short end of the maturity spectrum, to the issuance of notes and bonds at the longer end (see Chapters 5 and 6). We discuss commercial banks' use of each of these in Chapter 12.

Overall, the liability structure of banks' balance sheets tends to reflect a shorter maturity structure than that of their asset portfolio. Further, relatively more liquid instruments such as deposits and interbank borrowings are used to fund relatively less liquid assets such as loans. Thus, interest rate risk—or maturity mismatch risk—and liquidity risk are key exposure concerns for bank managers (see Chapters 19 through 24).

Equity

Commercial bank equity capital (10.0 percent of total liabilities and equity in 2004) consists mainly of common and preferred stock (listed at par value), surplus[6] or additional paid-in capital, and retained earnings. Regulators require banks to hold a minimum level of equity capital to act as a buffer against losses from their on- and off-balance-sheet activities (see Chapter 13). Because of the relatively low cost of deposit funding, banks tend to hold equity close to the minimum levels set by regulators. As we discuss in Chapters 13 and 22, this impacts banks' exposure to risk and their ability to grow—both on and off the balance sheet—over time.

4 Off-Balance-Sheet Activities

The balance sheet itself does not reflect the total scope of bank activities. Banks conduct many fee-related activities off the balance sheet. Off-balance-sheet (OBS) activities are

6. Surplus or additional paid-in capital shows the difference between the stock's par value and what the original stockholders paid when they bought the newly issued shares.

becoming increasingly important, in terms of their dollar value and the income they generate for banks—especially as the ability of banks to attract high-quality loan applicants and deposits becomes ever more difficult. OBS activities include issuing various types of guarantees (such as letters of credit), which often have a strong insurance underwriting element, and making future commitments to lend. Both services generate additional fee income for banks. Off-balance-sheet activities also involve engaging in derivative transactions—futures, forwards, options, and swaps.

off-balance-sheet (OBS) asset

When an event occurs, this item moves onto the asset side of the balance sheet or income is realized on the income statement.

off-balance-sheet liability

When an event occurs, this item moves onto the liability side of the balance sheet or an expense is realized on the income statement.

Under current accounting standards, such activities are not shown on the current balance sheet. Rather, an item or activity is an **off-balance-sheet asset** if, when a contingent event occurs, the item or activity moves onto the asset side of the balance sheet or an income item is realized on the income statement. Conversely, an item or activity is an **off-balance-sheet liability** if, when a contingent event occurs, the item or activity moves onto the liability side of the balance sheet or an expense item is realized on the income statement.

By undertaking off-balance-sheet activities, banks hope to earn additional fee income to complement declining margins or spreads on their traditional lending business. At the same time, they can avoid regulatory costs or "taxes" since reserve requirements and deposit insurance premiums are not levied on off-balance-sheet activities (see Chapter 13). Thus, banks have both earnings and regulatory "tax-avoidance" incentives to undertake activities off their balance sheets.

Off-balance-sheet activities, however, can involve risks that add to the overall insolvency exposure of a financial intermediary (FI). Indeed, the failure of the U.K. investment bank Barings and the bankruptcy of Orange County in California in the 1990s have been linked to FIs' off-balance-sheet activities in derivatives. More recently, the 1997–1998 Asian crisis left banks that had large positions in the Asian-related derivative securities markets with large losses. For example, Chase Manhattan Corp. announced a 1998 third quarter earnings decrease of 15 percent due to losses in global markets, including derivative securities. More recently, following a $638 million loss for the third quarter of 2001, the departure of its chief financial officer, and a Securities and Exchange Commission inquiry, Enron Corp. drew down about $3 billion from a credit line with J.P. Morgan Chase and Citigroup and was in talks about obtaining a new multibillion-dollar line from various other banks. J.P. Morgan and Citigroup, alone, were eventually exposed to $2.25 billion in losses on their off-balance-sheet dealings with Enron. Also in 2001, Allied Irish Banks incurred a $750 million loss from foreign exchange derivative trades by a rogue trader, and in 2004 unauthorized trading of foreign currency options at National Australian Bank resulted in a loss of $85 million. Off-balance-sheet activities and instruments have risk-reducing as well as risk-increasing attributes, and, when used appropriately, they can reduce or hedge an FI's interest rate, credit, and foreign exchange risks.

We show the notional, or face, value of bank OBS activities, and their distribution and growth, for 1992 to 2004 in Table 11–3. Notice the relative growth in the notional dollar value of OBS activities in Table 11–3. By 2004, the notional value of OBS bank activities was $92,047.8 billion compared to the $8,244.4 billion value of on-balance-sheet activities. The notional or face value of OBS activities does not accurately reflect the risk to the bank undertaking such activities. The potential for the bank to gain or lose on the contract is based on the possible change in the market value of the contract over the life of the contract rather than the notional or face value of the contract, normally less than 3 percent of the notional value of an OBS contract.[7]

The use of derivative contracts accelerated during the 1992–2004 period and accounted for much of the growth in OBS activity. Figure 11–5 shows that this growth has occurred for all types of derivative contracts: futures and forwards, swaps, and options. As we discuss in detail in Chapter 23, the significant growth in derivative securities activities by commercial banks has been a direct response to the increased interest rate risk, credit risk, and foreign exchange risk exposures they have faced, both domestically and internationally. In particular,

7. The market value of a swap (today) is the difference between the present value of the cash flows (expected) to be received minus the present value of cash flows expected to be paid.

TABLE 11-3 Aggregate Volume of Off-Balance-Sheet Commitments and Contingencies by U.S. Commercial Banks, Annual Data as of December
(in billions of dollars)

	1992	1998	2004	Distribution 2004	Percentage Increase from 1992 through 2004
Commitments to lend	$1,272.0	$3,478.7	$5,686.4	6.2%	347.0%
Future and forward contracts (exclude FX)					
On commodities and equities	26.3	122.3	123.7	0.1	370.3
On interest rates	1,738.1	4,817.7	6,923.0	7.5	298.3
Notional amount of credit derivatives	8.6	129.2	1,909.3	2.1	25,815.3
Standby contracts and other option contracts					
Option contracts on interest rates	1,012.7	5,071.0	15,340.8	16.7	14,148.4
Option contracts on foreign exchange	494.8	1,719.5	1,627.2	1.8	228.9
Option contracts on commodities	60.3	406.6	1,020.2	1.1	15,918.7
Commitments to buy FX (includes $U.S.), spot, and forward	3,015.5	5,724.9	4,969.2	5.4	64.8
Standby LCs and foreign office guarantees	162.5	240.5	391.3	0.4	140.8
(Amount of these items sold to others via participations)	(14.9)	(25.4)	(66.5)		
Commercial LCs	28.1	32.7	29.5	0.0	5.0
Participations in acceptances	1.0	0.9	0.9	0.0	−10.0
Securities borrowed or lent	107.2	371.9	1,073.1	1.2	901.0
Other significant commitments and contingencies	25.7	40.8	44.0	0.0	71.2
Notional value of all outstanding swaps	2,122.0	10,164.0	52,909.2	57.5	23,933.6
Total, including memoranda items	$10,200.3	$32,320.7	$92,047.8	100%	802.4
Total assets (on-balance-sheet items)	$3,476.4	$5,182.8	$8,244.4		137.2

FX = Foreign exchange, LC = Letter of credit.

Sources: FDIC, *Statistics on Banking,* various issues. **www.fdic.gov**

these contracts offer banks a way to hedge these risks without having to make extensive changes on the balance sheet.

Although the simple notional dollar value of OBS items overestimates their risk exposure amounts, the increase in these activities is still nothing short of phenomenal.[8] Indeed,

8. This overestimation of risk exposure occurs because the risk exposure from a contingent claim (such as an option) is usually less than its face value (see Chapter 12).

FIGURE 11–5 Derivative Contracts Held by Commercial Banks, by Product*

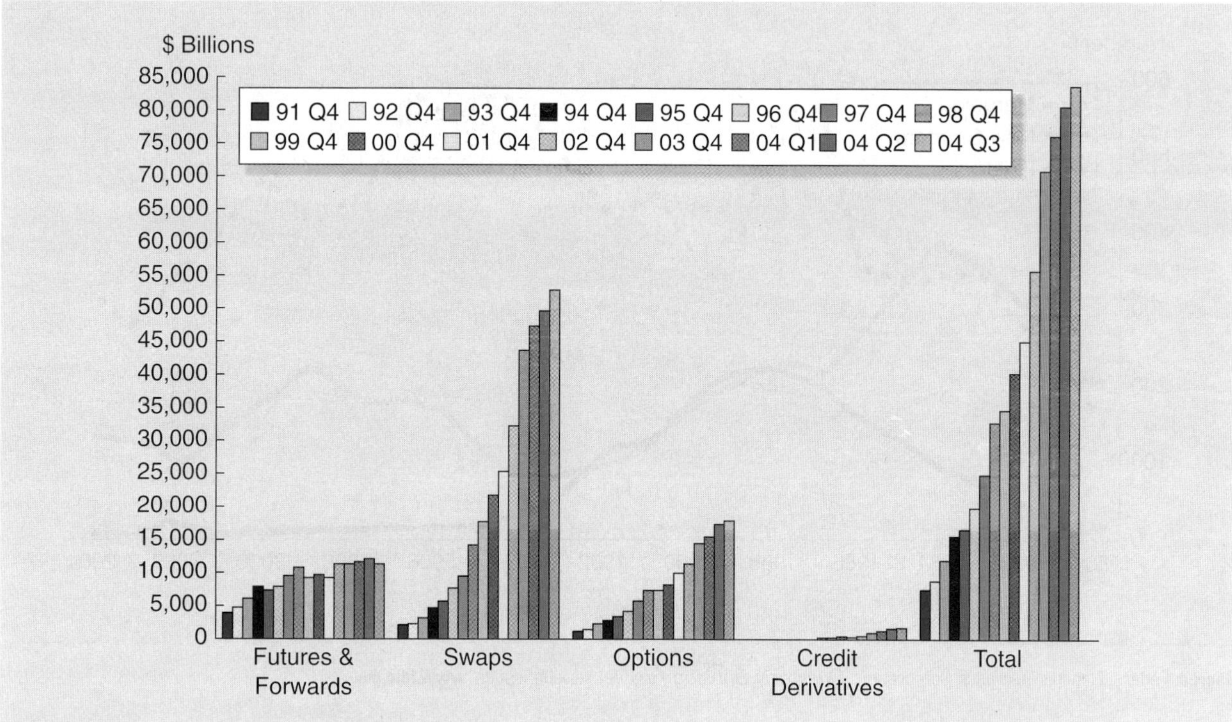

*In billions of dollars; notional amount of futures, total exchange-traded options, total swaps. Note that data after 1994 do not include spot FX in the total notional amount of derivatives.

Credit derivatives were reported for the first time in the first quarter of 1997. Currently, the Call Report does not differentiate credit derivatives by product, which have therefore been added as a separate category. As of 1997, credit derivatives have been included in the sum of total derivatives in this chart.

Source: FDIC, *Statistics on Banking,* September 2004. **www.fdic.gov**

this phenomenal increase has pushed regulators into imposing capital requirements on such activities and into explicitly recognizing an FI's solvency risk exposure from pursuing such activities. We describe these capital requirements in Chapter 13.

As noted in Table 11–3 and Figure 11–5, major types of OBS activities for U.S. banks include loan commitments, letters of credit, loans sold, and derivative securities. A loan commitment is a contractual commitment to loan a certain maximum amount to a borrower at given interest rate terms over some contractual period in the future (e.g., one year). Letters of credit are essentially guarantees that FIs sell to underwrite the future performance of the buyers of the guarantees. Commercial letters of credit are used mainly to assist a firm in domestic and international trade. The FI's role is to provide a formal guarantee that it will pay for the goods shipped or sold if the buyer of the goods defaults on its future payments. Standby letters of credit cover contingencies that are potentially more severe, less predictable or frequent, and not necessarily trade related. Loans sold are loans that the FI originated and then sold to other investors that (in some cases) can be returned to the originating institution in the future if the credit quality of the loans deteriorates. Derivative securities are futures, forward, swap, and option positions taken by the bank for hedging and other purposes (see Chapter 10). We discuss each of these in Chapter 12.

Other Fee-Generating Activities

Commercial banks engage in other fee-generating activities that cannot easily be identified from analyzing their on- and off-balance-sheet accounts. Two of these include trust services and correspondent banking.

FIGURE 11–6 **Structural Changes in the Number of Commercial Banks, 1980–2004.**

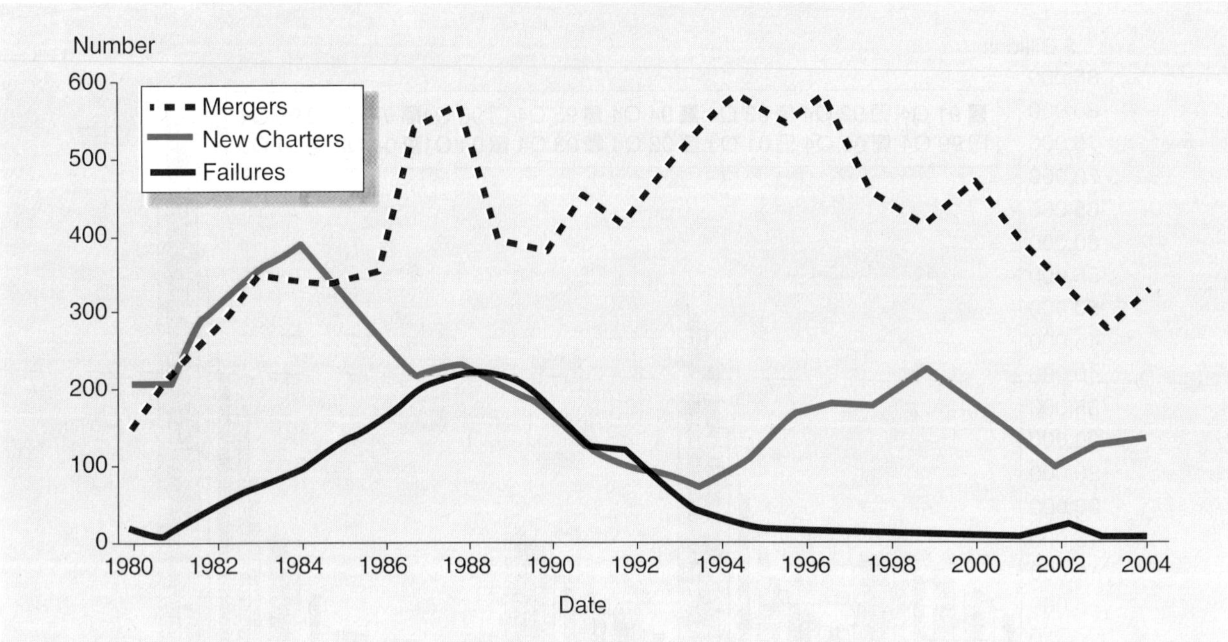

Source: Federal Deposit Insurance Corporation, *Quarterly Banking Profile,* various issues. **www.fdic.gov**

Trust Services. The trust department of a commercial bank holds and manages assets for individuals or corporations. Only the largest banks have sufficient staff to offer trust services. Individual trusts represent about one-half of all trust assets managed by commercial banks. These trusts include estate assets and assets delegated to bank trust departments by less financially sophisticated investors.[9] Pension fund assets are the second largest group of assets managed by the trust departments of commercial banks. The banks manage the pension funds, act as trustees for any bonds held by the pension funds, and act as transfer and disbursement agent for the pension funds. We discuss pension funds in more detail in Chapter 18.

DO YOU UNDERSTAND?

1. What major assets commercial banks hold?
2. What the major sources of funding for commercial banks are?
3. What OBS assets and liabilities are?
4. What other types of fee generating activities banks participate in?

Correspondent Banking. Correspondent banking is the provision of banking services to other banks that do not have the staff resources to perform the services themselves. These services include check clearing and collection, foreign exchange trading, hedging services, and participation in large loan and security issuances. Correspondent banking services are generally sold as a package of services. Payment for the services is generally in the form of noninterest-bearing deposits held at the bank offering the correspondent services (see Chapter 12).

5 SIZE, STRUCTURE, AND COMPOSITION OF THE INDUSTRY

As of September 2004, the United States had 7,660 commercial banks. Even though this may seem to be a large number, in fact the number of banks has been decreasing. For example, in 1984, the number of banks was 14,483; in 1989, it was 12,744. Figure 11–6 illustrates the number of bank mergers, bank failures, and new charters for the period 1980 through 2004. Notice that much of the change in the size, structure, and composition of this industry is the result of mergers and acquisitions. As we discuss in Chapter 13, strict regulations imposed on commercial banks over much of the last century limited geographical diversification opportunities. As a result, commercial bank operational

9. In recent years, banks have converted many of their trust portfolios into mutual funds.

TABLE 11–4 Large U.S. Bank Mergers, 1990–2004

Year	Banks	Price Paid for Target (in billions of dollars)
1990	Citizens & Southern/Sovran Financial	$ 2.05
1991	Chemical/Manufacturers Hanover	2.04
1991	Bank America/Security Pacific	4.21
1996	Chase Manhattan/Chemical Bank	11.36
1996	Wells Fargo/First Interstate	11.20
1997	Nations Bank/Barnett Banks	15.50
1997	First Bank System/US Bancorp	19.20
1998	Bank America/Nations Bank	66.62
1998	Wells Fargo/Norwest	31.71
1998	Deutsche Bank/Bankers Trust*	10.28
1999	Fleet Financial/Bank Boston	16.02
1999	Firstar/Mercantile Bancorp	10.69
1999	HSBC/Republic New York*	10.30
2000	J.P. Morgan/Chase	33.50
2000	Firstar/U.S. Bancorp	21.00
2001	First Union/Wachavia	13.10
2004	Bank of America/Fleet Financial	43.00
2004	J.P. Morgan Chase/Bank One	60.00
2005	Bank of America/MBNA	35.00

*International acquisitions.

Source: Authors' research.

megamerger

The merger of banks with assets of $1 billion or more.

economies of scale

The degree to which a firm's average unit costs of producing financial services fall as its output of services increase—for example, cost reduction in trading and other transaction services resulting from increased efficiency when these services are performed by FIs.

economies of scope

The degree to which a firm can generate cost synergies by producing multiple financial service products.

X efficiencies

Cost savings due to the greater managerial efficiency of the acquiring firm.

areas were often narrow (and specialized) and the number of commercial banks was large. It was not until the 1980s and 1990s that regulators (such as the Federal Reserve or state banking authorities) allowed banks to merge with other banks across state lines (interstate mergers), and it has only been since 1994 that Congress has passed legislation (the Reigle-Neal Act) easing branching by banks across state lines. Finally, it has only been since 1987 that banks have possessed powers to underwrite corporate securities. (Full authority to enter the investment banking (and insurance) business was received only with the passage of the Financial Services Modernization Act in 1999.) We discuss the impact that changing regulations have had on the ability of commercial banks to merge and branch in Chapter 13. Table 11–4 lists some of the largest bank mergers in recent years.

Economies of Scale and Scope

An important reason for the consolidation of the banking industry is the search by banks to exploit potential cost and revenue economies of scale and scope. Indeed, **megamergers** (mergers involving banks with assets of $1 billion or more) are often driven by the desire of managers to achieve greater cost and revenue economies or savings. Cost economies may result from **economies of scale** (where the unit or average cost of producing the bank's services falls as the size of the bank expands), **economies of scope** (where banks generate synergistic cost savings through joint use of inputs such as computer systems in producing multiple products), or managerial efficiency sources (often called **X efficiencies**[10] because they are difficult to specify in a quantitative fashion).

Economies of Scale. As financial firms become larger, the potential scale and array of the technology in which they can invest generally expands The largest FIs generally have

10. X efficiencies are those cost savings not directly due to economies of scope or economies of scale. As such, they are usually attributed to superior management skills and other difficult-to-measure managerial factors. To date, the explicit identification of what composes these efficiencies remains to be established in the empirical banking literature.

the largest expenditures on technology-related innovations. For example, the Tower Group (a consulting firm specializing in information technology) estimated that technology expense as a percentage of noninterest expense would be as high as 22 percent at the largest U.S. banks in the period 1999–2004. As discussed below, Internet banking is sure to be one of the major factors shaping the banking industry in the 21st century. The Internet offers financial institutions a channel to customers that enables them to react quickly to customer needs, bring products to the market quickly, and respond more effectively to changing business conditions. However, this capability will come at a cost to financial institutions as they invest in the necessary technology.

If enhanced or improved technology lowers an FI's average costs of financial service production, larger FIs may have an economy of scale advantage over smaller financial firms. Economies of scale imply that the unit or average cost of producing FI services in aggregate (or some specific activity such as deposits or loans) falls as the size of the FI expands. For example, First Union Corporation's $3.2 billion acquisition of Signet Banking Corporation was billed as a cost-saving acquisition. Because of overlapping operations in similar product areas with Signet, First Union said it expected annual cost savings of approximately $240 million. First Union and Signet had significant back-office operations in Virginia that could be combined and consolidated. The consolidation of such overlapping activities would lower the average costs for the combined (larger) bank. Similarly, the 2004 merger of J.P. Morgan Chase with Bank One was projected to save $2.2 billion on before-tax expenses in the three years after the merger, with job cuts estimated to be 10,000 out of a combined workforce of 140,000.

The long-run implication of economies of scale on the banking sector is that the largest and most cost-efficient banks will drive out smaller financial institutions, leading to increased large-firm dominance and concentration in financial services production. Such an implication is reinforced if time-related operating or technological improvements increasingly benefit larger banks more than smaller banks. For example, satellite technology and supercomputers, in which enormous technological advances are being made, may be available to the largest banks only. The effect of improving technology over time, which is biased toward larger projects, is to decrease the average costs of producing FI services over time but with a larger decrease for large banks.

Technology investments are risky, however. If their future revenues do not cover their costs of development, they reduce the value of the bank and its net worth to the bank's owners. On the cost side, large-scale investments may result in excess capacity problems and integration problems as well as cost overruns and cost control problems. Then, small banks with simple and easily managed computer systems, and those leasing time on large banks' computers without bearing the fixed costs of installation and maintenance, may have an average cost advantage. In this case, technological investments of large-size banks result in higher average costs of financial service production, causing the industry to operate under conditions of **diseconomies of scale.**

diseconomies of scale

The costs of joint production of FI services are higher than they would be if they were produced independently.

Wells Fargo & Co.'s purchase of First Interstate Bancorp (in April 1996) is an example of potential diseconomies of scale due to the inability to integrate technologies of the two banks and a failure of a back-office system. Wells Fargo wanted to make the merger process easy for First Interstate customers by allowing them to use up their old checks and deposit forms. Unfortunately, due to the merger, customer account numbers had been changed and Wells Fargo's computer system had trouble keeping up with the integrated check-clearing system. Some deposits were not posted to the proper account and there was a deluge of improperly bounced checks. Further, Wells Fargo's back-office operations were thinly staffed and unable to find where all the misplaced deposits had gone. More than a year after the purchase, Wells Fargo was still having organization and systems problems integrating First Interstate. Promising to reimburse all customers for its accounting mistakes, Wells Fargo eventually corrected the problem, incurring an operating loss of some $180 million.

Cost Economies of Scope. FIs are multiproduct firms producing services involving different technological and personnel needs. Investments in one financial service area (such as lending) may have incidental and synergistic benefits in lowering the costs to produce financial services in other areas (such as securities underwriting or brokerage). Similarly, computerization allows the storage of important information on customers and their needs that can be used by more than one service area. FIs' abilities to generate synergistic cost savings through joint use of inputs in producing multiple products is called economies of scope, as opposed to economies of scale (see above). In 1999, regulators passed the Financial Services Modernization Act, which repealed laws that prohibited mergers between commercial banks and investment banks (as well as insurance companies). The bill, touted as the biggest change in the regulation of financial institutions in over 60 years, created a "financial services holding company" that can engage in banking activities *and* securities *and* insurance underwriting.

The result of this regulation and the rulings leading up to it was a number of mergers and acquisitions between commercial and investment banks in 1997 through 2004. Some of the largest mergers included UBS's $12.0 billion purchase of Paine Webber in 2000, Credit Suisse First Boston's 2000 purchase of Donaldson Lufkin Jenrette for $11.5 billion in 2000, Citicorp's $83 billion merger with Travelers Group in April 1998 (partially divested in 2002), Bankers Trust's April 1997 acquisition of Alex Brown for $1.7 billion, and Bank of America's June 1997 purchase of Robertson Stephens for $540 million (resold to Bank of Boston for $800 million in April 1998).[11] In each case the banks stated that one motivation for the acquisition was the desire to establish a presence in the securities business as laws separating investment banking and commercial banking were changing. Also noted as a motivation in these acquisitions was the opportunity to expand business lines, taking advantage of economies of scale and scope to reduce overall costs and merge the customer bases of the respective commercial and investment banks involved in the acquisitions.

Revenue Economies of Scope. In addition to economies of scope on the cost side, economies of scope (or synergies) on the revenue side can emanate from mergers and acquisitions. For example, CEOs of both J.P. Morgan and Chase Manhattan stated that the success of their merger to form J.P. Morgan Chase was dependent on revenue growth. The merger combined J.P. Morgan's greater array of financial products with Chase's broader client base. The merger added substantially to many businesses (such as equity underwriting, equity derivatives, and asset management) that Chase had been trying to build on its own through smaller deals and also gave it a bigger presence in Europe where investment and corporate banking are fast-growing businesses. Four years later, in 2004, J.P. Morgan Chase (which had been operating in only four states) acquired Bank One, its first USA credit card operations, and a massive retail network of about 1,800 branches concentrated in the Midwest.

Revenue synergies have three potential dimensions. First, acquiring an FI in a growing market may produce new revenues. Second, the acquiring bank's revenue stream may become more stable if the asset and liability portfolio of the acquired (target) institution exhibits different product, credit, interest rate, and liquidity risk characteristics from the acquirer's. For example, real estate loan portfolios have shown very strong regional cycles. Specifically, in the 1980s, U.S. real estate declined in value in the Southeast, then in the Northeast, and then in California with a long and variable lag. Thus, a geographically diversified real estate portfolio may be far less risky than one in which both acquirer and target specialize in a single region.[12] Third, expanding into markets that are less than fully competitive offers an opportunity for revenue enhancement. That is, banks may be able to identify and expand geographically into those markets in which *economic rents* potentially exist but in which regulators will not view such entry as potentially anticompetitive. Indeed, to the extent that geographic expansions are viewed as enhancing an FI's monopoly power

11. Citing slower growth and lower profits than expected in 2002 Citigroup sold off 20 percent of the Travelers Property Casualty unit to the public and distributed the remaining 80 percent to Citigroup shareholders. Citigroup continues to have other insurance subsidiaries. Further, in April 2002 FleetBoston (the combined Fleet Financial and Bank of Boston) announced that the bank would sell off Robertson Stephens. FleetBoston stated the sale was the result of sagging profits in the investment banking industry and a desire to concentrate on its core business-lending to medium-size businesses, money management, and retail banking.

12. As a result, the potential revenue diversification gains for more geographically concentrated mergers such as the 1991 merger of Bank of America and Security Pacific are likely to be relatively low because both are heavily exposed to California real estate loans.

TABLE 11–5 U.S. Bank Asset Concentration, 1984 versus 2004

	2004				1984			
	Number	Percent of Total	Assets*	Percent of Total	Number	Percent of Total	Assets*	Percent of Total
All FDIC-insured commercial banks	7,660		$8,244.4		14,483		$2,508.9	
1. Under $100 million	3,755	49.0%	194.6	2.4%	12,044	83.2%	404.2	16.1%
2. $100 million–$1 billion	3,458	45.2	927.8	11.2	2,161	14.9	513.9	20.5
3. $1–$10 billion	360	4.7	971.3	11.8	254	1.7	725.9	28.9
4. $10 billion or more	87	1.1	6,150.7	74.6	24	0.2	864.7	34.5

*In billions of dollars.

Source: General Accounting Office, *Interstate Banking,* GAO/GGD, 95–35, December 1994, p. 101; and *FDIC Quarterly Banking Profile,* Third Quarter 2004. **www.fdic.gov**

by generating excessive rents, regulators may act to prevent a merger unless it produces potential efficiency gains that cannot be reasonably achieved by other means.[13] In recent years, the ultimate enforcement of antimonopoly laws and guidelines has fallen to the U.S. Department of Justice. In particular, the Department of Justice has established guidelines regarding the acceptability or unacceptability of acquisitions based on the potential increase in concentration in the market in which an acquisition takes place.

www.usdoj.gov

Bank Size and Concentration

community bank

A bank that specializes in retail or consumer banking.

retail banking

Consumer-oriented banking, such as providing residential and consumer loans and accepting smaller deposits.

wholesale banking

Commercial-oriented banking, such as providing commercial and industrial loans funded with purchased funds.

regional or superregional bank

A bank that engages in a complete array of wholesale commercial banking activities.

federal funds market

An interbank market for short-term borrowing and lending of bank reserves.

money center bank

A bank that relies heavily on nondeposit or borrowed sources of funds.

Interestingly, a comparison of asset concentration by bank size (see Table 11–5) indicates that the recent consolidation in banking appears to have reduced the asset share of the smallest banks (under $1 billion) from 36.6 percent in 1984 to 13.6 percent in 2004. These small or **community banks**—with less than $1 billion in asset size—tend to specialize in **retail** or consumer **banking,** such as providing residential mortgages and consumer loans, and accessing the local deposit base. Clearly, this group of banks is decreasing both in number and importance.

The relative asset share of the largest banks (over $1 billion in size), on the other hand, increased from 63.4 percent in 1984 to 86.4 percent in 2004. The largest 10 U.S. banks as of January 2005 are listed in Table 11–6. Large banks engage in a more complete array of **wholesale** commercial **banking** activities, encompassing consumer and residential lending as well as commercial and industrial lending (C&I loans) **regionally, superregionally,** and nationally. In addition, big banks have access to the markets for purchased funds, such as the interbank or **federal funds market,** to finance their lending and investment activities. Some of the very biggest banks are often classified as being **money center banks.** Currently five banking organizations make up the money center bank group: Bank of New York, Deutsche Bank (through its U.S. acquisition of Bankers Trust), Citigroup, J. P. Morgan Chase, and HSBC Bank USA (formerly Republic NY Corporation).[14]

It is important to note that asset or lending size does not necessarily make a bank a money center bank. For example, Bank of America Corporation, with $1,089.3 billion in assets in 2005 (the third largest U.S. bank organization), is not a money center bank, but HSBC Bank USA (with only $316.1 billion in assets) is a money center bank. The classification as a money center bank is partly based on the physical location of the bank and partly based on its heavy reliance on nondeposit or borrowed sources of funds. Specifically, a money center bank is a bank located in a major financial center (e.g., New York) and heavily relies on both national and international money markets for its source of funds. In fact,

13. U.S. Department of Justice, "Horizontal Merger Guidelines," April 2, 1992.

14. Bankers Trust was purchased by Deutsche Bank (a German bank) in 1998. The Bankers Trust name, however, has been retained for U.S. operations. Republic NY Corporation was purchased by HSBC (a British bank) in 1999. Republic NY Bank was renamed HSBC Bank USA.

TABLE 11-6 Top Ten U.S. Banks Listed by Total Asset Size, First Quarter 2005

Bank	Total Assets (in billions of dollars)
Citigroup	$1,436.6
J.P. Morgan Chase	1,138.5
Bank of America	1,089.3
Wachovia	436.7
Wells Fargo	421.5
Taunus*	321.4
HSBC North America	316.1
U.S. Bancorp	192.8
National City Corp.	136.4
Citizens Financial Group	134.4

*Formerly Bankers Trust. A subsidiary of Deutsche Bank.

Source: Federal Reserve Board Web site, National Information Center. January 2005. **www.federalreserve.gov**

because of its extensive retail branch network,[15] Bank of America tends to be a net supplier of funds on the interbank market (federal funds market). By contrast, money center banks such as J. P. Morgan Chase have no retail branches.

Bank Size and Activities

interest rate spread

The difference between lending and deposit rates.

net interest margin

Interest income minus interest expense divided by earning assets.

Bank size has traditionally affected the types of activities and financial performance of commercial banks. Small banks generally concentrate on the retail side of the business—making loans and issuing deposits to consumers and small businesses. In contrast, large banks engage in both retail and wholesale banking and often concentrate on the wholesale side of the business. Further, small banks generally hold fewer off-balance-sheet assets and liabilities than large banks. For example, while small banks issue some loan commitments and letters of credit, they rarely hold derivative securities. Large banks' relatively easy access to purchased funds and capital markets compared to small banks' access is a reason for many of these differences. For example, large banks with easier access to capital markets operate with lower amounts of equity capital than do small banks. Also, large banks tend to use more purchased funds (such as fed funds) and have fewer core deposits (deposits such as demand deposits that are stable over short periods of time, see Chapter 12) than do small banks. At the same time, large banks lend to larger corporations. This means that their **interest rate spreads** (i.e., the difference between their lending rates and deposit rates) and **net interest margins** (i.e., interest income minus interest expense divided by earning assets) have usually been narrower than those of smaller regional banks, which are more sheltered from competition in highly localized markets and lend to smaller, less sophisticated customers.

DO YOU UNDERSTAND?

1. What economies of scale and scope are?
2. What the three dimensions to revenue synergy gains are?
3. What the features are that distinguish a money center bank from other banks?
4. Which size banks generally have the highest ROA? ROE?

In addition, large banks tend to pay higher salaries and invest more in buildings and premises than small banks do. They also tend to diversify their operations and services more than small banks do. Large banks generate more noninterest income (i.e., fees, trading account, derivative security, and foreign trading income) than small banks. Although large banks tend to hold less equity, they do not necessarily return more on their assets. However, as the barriers to regional competition and expansion in banking have fallen in recent years, the largest banks have generally improved their return on equity (ROE) and return on asset (ROA) performance relative to small

15. In 2004 Bank of America had over 4,500 branches nationwide.

FIGURE 11–7 ROA and ROE on Different Size Banks, 1990–2004

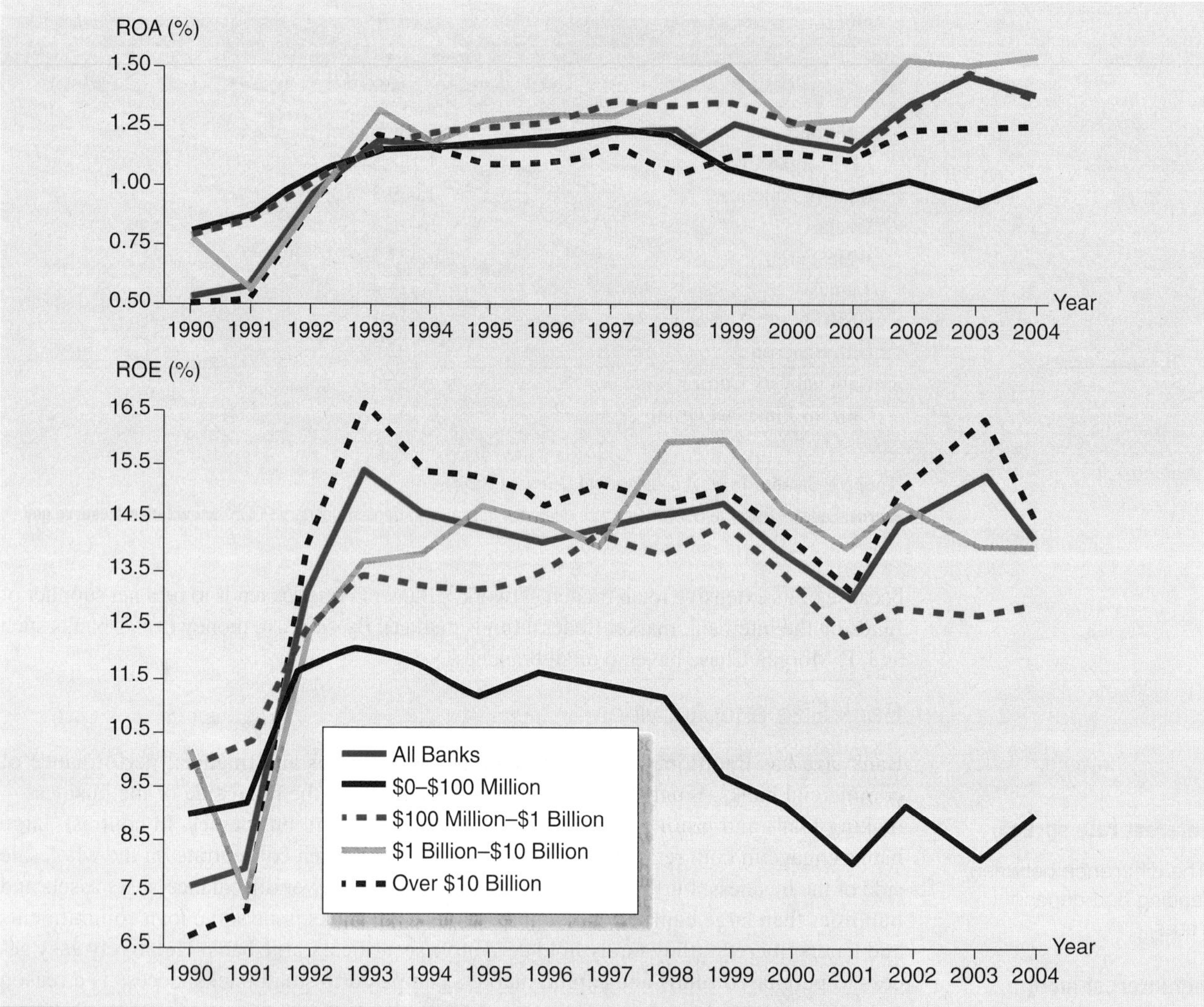

Source: Federal Deposit Insurance Corporation, *Quarterly Banking Profile,* various issues. **www.fdic.gov**

banks (see Figure 11–7).[16] We discuss the impact of size on bank financial statements and performance in more detail in Chapter 12.

INDUSTRY PERFORMANCE

6

Table 11–7 presents selected performance ratios for the commercial banking industry for 1989 through September 2004. With the economic expansion in the U.S. economy and falling interest rates throughout most of the 1990s, U.S. commercial banks flourished for most of the 1990s. In 1999 commercial bank earnings were a record $71.6 billion. More than two-thirds of all U.S. banks reported an ROA of 1 percent or higher, and the average ROA for all banks was 1.31 percent, up from 1.19 percent for the year 1998. This, despite continued financial problems in Southeast Asia, Russia, and South America. With the economic downturn in the early 2000s, bank performance deteriorated slightly. For example,

16. ROA is calculated as net income divided by the book value of total assets for the bank. ROE is calculated as net income divided by common equity of the bank and measures the return to the bank's common stockholders. We discuss ROA and ROE in more detail in Chapter 12.

TABLE 11–7 Selected Indicators for U.S. Commercial Banks, 1989, 1993 through September 2004

	2004*	2003	2001	1999	1997	1995	1993	1989
Number of institutions	7,660	7,770	8,080	8,579	9,143	9,940	10,958	12,709
Return on assets (%)	1.31	1.40	1.15	1.31	1.24	1.17	1.22	0.49
Return on equity (%)	14.01	15.31	13.09	14.02	14.71	14.68	15.67	7.71
Noncurrent loans to total assets (%)	0.59	0.77	0.92	0.63	0.66	0.85	1.61	2.30
Net charge-offs to loans (%)	0.61	0.89	0.94	0.61	0.64	0.49	0.85	1.16
Asset growth rate (%)	10.34	7.41	5.20	5.38	9.54	7.53	5.72	5.38
Net operating income growth (%)	4.22	14.95	−1.61	20.40	12.48	7.48	35.36	−38.70
Number of failed/assisted institutions	3	3	3	7	1	6	42	206

*Through September 30, ratios annualized where appropriate. Asset growth is for 12 months ending September 2004.

Source: FDIC, *Quarterly Banking Profile,* various dates; and *Historical Statistics,* 1989. **www.fdic.gov**

commercial banks' string of eight consecutive years of record earnings ended in 2000 as their net income fell to $71.2 billion. Banks' provision for loan losses rose to $9.5 billion in the fourth quarter of 2000, an increase of $3.4 billion (54.7 percent) from the level of a year earlier. This was the largest quarterly loss provision since the fourth quarter of 1991. Finally, the average ROA was 1.19 percent in 2000, down from 1.31 percent in 1999.

This downturn was short-lived, however. In 2001, net income of $74.3 billion easily surpassed the old record of $71.6 billion and net income rose further to $106.3 billion in 2003. Moreover, in 2003, both ROA and ROE reached all-time highs of 1.40 and 15.34 percent, respectively. For the first three quarters of 2004, ROA and ROE were again high at 1.31 and 14.01 percent, respectively. The two main sources of earnings strength in 2003 were higher noninterest income (up $18.9 billion, 10.3 percent) and lower loan loss provisions (down $14.2 billion, or 27.6 percent). The greatest improvement in profitability occurred at large institutions, whose earnings had been depressed in the early 2000s by credit losses on loans to corporate borrowers and by weakness in market-sensitive noninterest revenue. Only 5.7 percent of all institutions were unprofitable in 2003, the lowest proportion since 1997. In 2004, a combination of continued strength in consumer loan demand and growing demand for commercial loans added to the strength of earnings. The third quarter of 2004 saw the sixth time in seven quarters that industry earnings set a new record. Further, at the end of September **noncurrent loans** fell to their lowest level since the end of 2000.

noncurrent loans

Loans past due 90 days or more and loans that are not accruing interest because of problems of the borrower.

Several explanations have been offered for the strong performance of commercial banks during the early 2000s. First, the Federal Reserve cut interest rates 13 times during this period. Lower interest rates made debt cheaper to service and kept many households and small firms borrowing. Second, lower interest rates made home purchasing more affordable. Thus, the housing market boomed throughout the period. Third, the development of new financial instruments such as credit derivatives and mortgage-backed securities helped banks shift credit risk from their balance sheets to financial markets and other FIs such as insurance companies. Finally, improved information technology has helped banks manage their risk better. Nevertheless, the question still remains, what will happen to this industry if and when interest rates rise? If historical patterns hold, bank stocks should be highly vulnerable to rising interest rates. For example, after fairly modest increases in interest rates in 2004, mortgage originations (which totaled $3.3 trillion in 2003) fell to $1.6 trillion in 2004.

net charge-offs

Actual losses on loans and leases.

net operating income

Income before taxes and extraordinary items.

The performance in the late 1990s and even the early 2000s is quite an improvement from the recessionary and high interest rate conditions in which the industry operated in the late 1980s. As reported in Table 11–7, the average ROA and ROE for commercial banks in the early 2000s was as high as 1.40 and 15.31 percent, respectively, compared to 1989 when ROA and ROE averaged 0.49 percent and 7.71 percent, respectively. Noncurrent loans to assets ratio and **net charge-offs** (actual losses on loans and leases) to loans ratio averaged 0.59 percent and 0.61 percent, respectively, in 2004, versus 2.30 percent and 1.16 percent, respectively, in 1989. **Net operating income** (income before taxes and extraordinary items) grew at an annualized rate of 14.95 percent in 2003 versus a *drop* of 38.70 percent in 1989. Finally, note that in 2004 (through September), three U.S. commercial banks failed versus 206 in 1989. As a result of such massive losses and failures in the industry, several regulations were proposed and enacted to prevent such occurrences from happening again. (We discuss the major changes in regulations and their impact in Chapter 13.) As a result of these changes and the generally strong U.S. economy, in the last decade or so the commercial banking industry essentially has gone from the brink of disaster to a period of almost unprecedented profit and stability.

DO YOU UNDERSTAND?

1. What the trends in ROA and ROE have been in the commercial banking industry over the last fifteen years?
2. What the trend in loan performance has been in the commercial banking industry over the last fifteen years?

TECHNOLOGY IN COMMERCIAL BANKING

Certain to affect the future performance of commercial banks (as well as all financial institutions) is the extent to which banks adopt the newest technology, including the extent to which industry participants embrace the Internet and online banking. Technological innovation has been a major concern of all types of financial institutions in recent years. Since the 1980s, banks, insurance companies, and investment companies have sought to improve operational efficiency with major investments in internal and external communications, computers, and an expanded technological infrastructure. Internet and wireless communications technologies are having a profound effect on financial services. These technologies are more than just new distribution channels—they are a completely different way of providing financial services. Indeed, a global financial service firm such as Citigroup has operations in more than 100 countries connected in real time by a proprietary-owned satellite system.

Technology is important because well-chosen technological investments have the potential to increase both the FI's net interest margin—or the difference between interest income and interest expense—and other net income. Therefore, technology can directly improve profitability. The following subsections focus on some specific technology-based products found in modern retail and wholesale banking. Note that this list is far from complete.

Wholesale Banking Services

Probably the most important area in which technology has impacted wholesale or corporate customer services is a bank's ability to provide cash management or working capital services. Cash management service needs have largely resulted from (1) corporate recognition that excess cash balances result in a significant opportunity cost due to lost or forgone interest and (2) corporate need to know cash or working capital positions on a real-time basis. Among the services that modern banks provide to improve the efficiency with which corporate clients manage their financial positions are these:

1. *Controlled disbursement accounts.* An account feature that allows almost all payments to be made in a given day to be known in the morning. The bank informs the corporate client of the total funds it needs to meet disbursements, and the client wire-transfers the amount needed. These checking accounts are debited early each day so that corporations can obtain an early insight into their net cash positions.
2. *Account reconciliation.* A checking feature that records which of the firm's checks have been paid by the bank.
3. *Lockbox services.* A centralized collection service for corporate payments to reduce the delay in check clearing, or the **float.** In a typical lockbox arrangement, a local bank sets up a lockbox at the post office for a corporate client located outside the area. Local customers mail payments to the lockbox rather than to the out-of-town corporate headquarters. The bank collects these checks several times per day and deposits them directly into the customer's account. Details of the transaction are wired to the corporate client.
4. *Electronic lockbox.* Same as item 3 but the customer receives online payments for public utilities and similar corporate clients.
5. *Funds concentration.* A service that redirects funds from accounts in a large number of different banks or branches to a few centralized accounts at one bank.

float

The interval between the deposit of a check and when funds become available for depositor use—that is, the time it takes a check to clear at a bank.

6. *Electronic funds transfer.* Includes overnight payments via CHIPS or Fedwire, automated payment of payrolls or dividends via automated clearinghouses (ACHs), and automated transmission of payment messages by SWIFT, an international electronic message service owned and operated by U.S. and European banks that instructs banks to make specific payments.
7. *Check deposit services.* Encoding, endorsing, microfilming, and handling customers' checks.
8. *Electronic initiation of letters of credit.* Allows customers in a network to access bank computers to initiate letters of credit.
9. *Treasury management software.* Allows efficient management of multiple currency and security portfolios for trading and investment purposes.
10. *Electronic data interchange.* A specialized application of electronic mail, allowing businesses to transfer and transact invoices, purchase orders, and shipping notices automatically, using banks as clearinghouses.
11. *Facilitating business-to-business e-commerce.* A few of the largest commercial banks have begun to offer firms the technology for electronic business-to-business commerce. The banks are essentially automating the entire information flow associated with the procurement and distribution of goods and services among businesses.
12. *Electronic billing.* Provides the presentment and collection services for companies that send out substantial volumes of recurring bills. Banks combine the e-mail capability of the Internet to send out bills with their ability to process payments electronically through the interbank payment networks.
13. *Verifying identities.* Using encryption technology a bank certifies the identities of its own account holders and serves as the intermediary through which its business customers can verify the identities of account holders at other banks.
14. *Assisting small business entries in e-commerce.* Helps smaller firms in setting up the infrastructure—interactive Web site and payment capabilities—for engaging in e-commerce.

Retail Banking Services

Retail customers have demanded efficiency and flexibility in their financial transactions. Using only checks or holding cash is often more expensive and time-consuming than using retail-oriented electronic payment technology and, increasingly, the Internet. Some of the most important retail payment product innovations include the following:

1. *Automated teller machines (ATMs).* Allow customers 24-hour access to their checking accounts. They can pay bills as well as withdraw cash from these machines. In addition, if the bank's ATMs are part of a bank network (such as CIRRUS, PLUS, or HONOR), retail depositors can gain direct nationwide—and in many cases international—access to their deposit accounts by using the ATMs of other banks in the network to draw on their accounts.
2. *Point-of-sale (POS) debit cards.* Allow customers who choose not to use cash, checks, or credit cards for purchases to buy merchandise using debit card/point-of-sale (POS) terminals. The merchant avoids the check float and any delay in payment associated with credit card receivables since the bank offering the debit card/POS service immediately and directly transfers funds from the customer's deposit account to the merchant's deposit account at the time of card use. Unlike check or credit card purchases, the use of a debit card results in an immediate transfer of funds from the customer's account to the merchant's account.[17] Moreover, the customer never runs up a debit to the card issuer, as is common with a credit card.

17. In the case of bank-supplied credit cards, the merchant normally is compensated very quickly but not instantaneously (usually in one or two days) by the credit card issuer. The bank then holds an account receivable against the card user. However, even a short delay can represent an opportunity cost for the merchant.

3. *Preauthorized debits/credits.* Includes direct deposit of payroll checks into bank accounts and direct payments of mortgage and utility bills.
4. *Paying bills via telephone.* Allows direct transfer of funds from the customer's bank account to outside parties either by voice command or by touch-tone telephone.
5. *Online banking.* Allows customers to conduct retail banking and investment services offered via the Internet.[18,19] Connects customers to their deposit and brokerage accounts and provides such services as electronic securities trading and bill-paying service via personal computers.[20]
6. *Smart cards (stored-value cards).* Allow the customer to store and spend money for various transactions using a card that has a chip storage device, usually in the form of a strip. These have become increasingly popular at universities.

Early entrants into Internet banking have been banks that have introduced new technology in markets with demographic and economic characteristics that help ensure customer acceptance, such as urban banks with a strong retail orientation that have tailored their Internet offering to their retail customers. For example, in 2003 Wells Fargo said its online banking customer base jumped 52 percent over 2002 levels, Bank of America reported a 50 percent increase to 6.2 million online customers, and Bank One saw a 65 percent increase to 2.2 million online customers. Banks that have invested in Internet banking, as a complement to their existing services, have performed similar to those without Internet banking, despite relatively high initial technology-related expenses. In particular, these banks generally have higher noninterest income (which offsets any increased technology expenses). Further, the risk of banks offering Internet-related banking products appears to be similar to the risk of those banks without Internet banking.

In addition to the development of Internet banking as a complement to the traditional services offered by commercial banks, a new segment of the industry has arisen that consists of Internet-only banks. That is, these banks have no "brick and mortar" facilities, or are "banks without walls." In these banks, all business is conducted over the Internet. However, Internet-only banks have yet to capture more than a small fraction of the banking market. While ATMs and Internet banking may potentially lower bank operating costs compared to employing full-service tellers, the inability of machines to address customers' concerns and questions flexibly may drive retail customers away; revenue losses may counteract any cost-saving effects. Customers still want to interact with a person for many transactions. For example, a survey of the home buying and mortgage processing by the Mortgage Bankers Association (in the early 2000s) found that, while 73 percent of home buyers used the Internet to obtain information on mortgage interest rates, only 12 percent applied for a mortgage via the Internet and only 3 percent actually closed on a mortgage on the Internet. As new technology is implemented, banks cannot ignore the issue of service quality and convenience. Indeed, the survival of small banks in the face of growing nationwide branching may well be due in part to customers' beliefs that overall service quality is higher with tellers who provide a human touch rather then the Internet banking and ATMs more common at bigger banks. Even Internet-only banks are recognizing this as "virtual" banks such as Atlanta's Net Bank added 42 "bricks" (branches) in 2001. Further, a new type of customer service will be needed; customers

18. In October 1998, Citigroup announced a new Internet service covering all areas of retail financial services. This will require it to scrap its existing computer systems and build a whole new infrastructure. The new service will be known as E-Citi (*see* "Citibank Sets New On-Line Bank System," by Saul Hansell, *New York Times,* October 5, 1998, pp. C1–C4).

19. K. Furst, W. W. Lang, and D. E. Nolle found that, as of the third quarter of 1999, while only 20 percent of U.S. national banks offered Internet banking, these transactions accounted for almost 90 percent of the national banking system's assets and 84 percent of the total number of small deposit accounts. See "Internet Banking: Developments and Prospects," Office of the Comptroller of the Currency, Economic and Policy Analysis Working Paper 2000–9, September 2000.

20. For example, the U.S. Postal Service estimates that $2.4 billion was spent on postage for bills and bank statements in 1995 and that electronic billing will save $900 million of that within 10 years. See "Paying Bills without Any Litter," by Saul Hansell, *New York Times,* July 5, 1996, pp. D1–D3.

require prompt, well-informed support on technical issues as they increasingly conduct their financial business electronically.[21]

This increased use of technology by bank customers also creates technology (or operational) risk that can arise whenever existing technology malfunctions. For example, a failure of a bank-office system occurred in September 2001 when Citibank's (a subsidiary of Citigroup) ATM system crashed for an extended period of time. Citibank's 2,000 nationwide ATMs, its debit card system and its online banking functions went down for almost two business days. More recently, in June 2005 Bank of America notified customers that their accounts might be at risk after former bank employees allegedly sold customers' private information, Citigroup announced that computer tapes containing personal information on 3.9 million customers were lost, and a computer-security breach at a company that processes credit card transactions exposed more than 40 million bank card customers to possible fraud. Even though such technology breakdowns are rare, their occurrence can cause major dislocations in the banks involved and potentially disrupt the financial system in general.

REGULATORS

8

Chapter 13 provides a detailed description of the regulations governing commercial banks and their impact on the banking industry. This section describes the regulators who develop, implement, and monitor these regulations. Unlike other countries that have one or sometimes two regulators, U.S. banks may be subject to the supervision and regulations of as many as four separate regulators. These regulators provide the common rules and regulations under which banks operate. They also monitor banks to ensure they abide by the regulations imposed. As discussed in Chapter 4, it is the regulators' job to, among other things, ensure the safety and soundness of the banking system. The key commercial bank regulators are the Federal Deposit Insurance Corporation (FDIC), the Office of the Comptroller of the Currency (OCC), the Federal Reserve System (FRS), and state bank regulators. The next sections discuss the principal role that each plays.

Federal Deposit Insurance Corporation

www.fdic.gov

Established in 1933, the Federal Deposit Insurance Corporation (FDIC) insures the deposits of commercial banks.[22] In so doing, it levies insurance premiums on banks, manages the deposit insurance fund (which is generated from those premiums and their reinvestment), and conducts bank examinations. In addition, when an insured bank is closed, the FDIC acts as the receiver and liquidator, although the closure decision itself is technically made by the bank's chartering or licensing agency (see below). Because of problems in the thrift industry and the insolvency of the savings association insurance fund (FSLIC) in 1989 (see Chapter 13), the FDIC now manages both the commercial bank insurance fund and the savings association insurance fund. The Bank Insurance Fund is called *BIF* and the savings association fund is called the Savings Association Insurance Fund, or *SAIF* (see Chapter 14). The number of FDIC-BIF insured banks and the division between nationally and state-chartered banks is shown in Figure 11–8.

Office of the Comptroller of the Currency

www.occ.treas.gov

The Office of the Comptroller of the Currency (OCC) is the oldest U.S. bank regulatory agency. Established in 1863, it is organized as a subagency of the U.S. Treasury. Its primary function is to charter national banks as well as to close them. In addition, the OCC examines national banks and has the power to approve or disapprove their merger applications. Instead of seeking a national charter, however, banks can seek to be chartered by 1 of 50 individual state bank regulatory agencies.

21. See "Out with the Old, In with the New," by Justyn Trenner, *The Banker,* May 2000, pp. 110–11.

22. Virtually all U.S. banks are members of the FDIC's insurance fund.

FIGURE 11–8 Bank Regulators

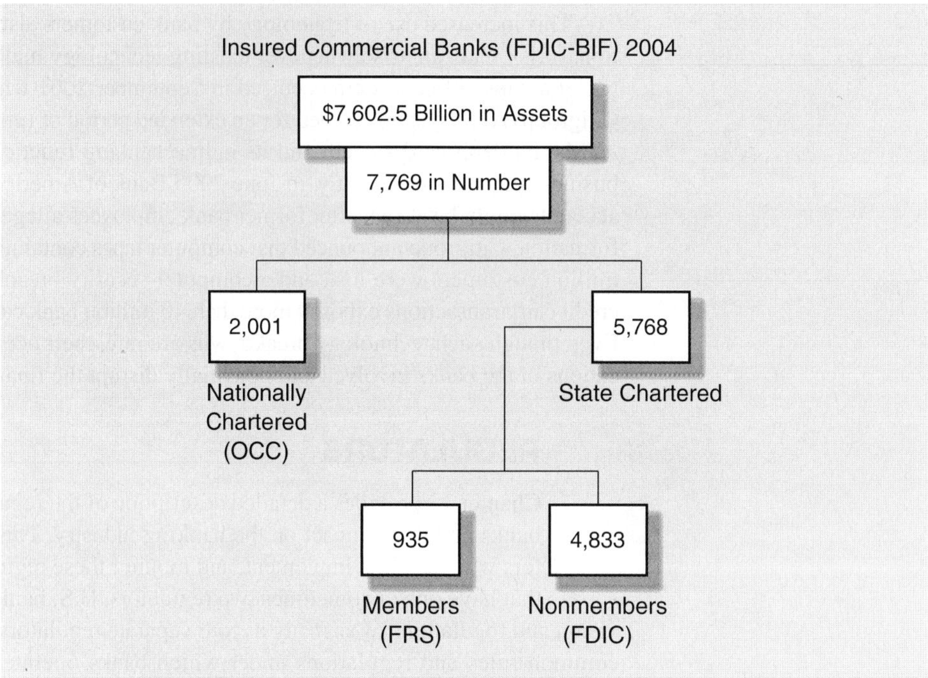

Source: FDIC, *Statistics on Banking,* Fourth Quarter 2004. **www.fdic.gov**

dual banking system

The coexistence of both nationally and state-chartered banks, as in the United States.

Historically, state-chartered banks have been subject to fewer regulations and restrictions on their activities than national banks. This lack of regulatory oversight was a major reason many banks chose not to be nationally chartered. Many more recent regulations (such as the Depository Institutions Deregulation and Monetary Control Act of 1980) attempted to level the restrictions imposed on federal and state-chartered banks (see Chapter 13). Not all discrepancies, however, were changed and state chartered banks are still generally less heavily regulated than nationally chartered banks. The choice of being a nationally chartered or state-chartered bank lies at the foundation of the **dual banking system** in the United States. Most large banks, such as Citibank, choose national charters, but others have state charters. For example, Morgan Guaranty, the money center bank subsidiary of J. P. Morgan Chase, is chartered as a state bank under State of New York law. In 2004, 2,001 banks were *nationally* chartered and 5,768 were *state* chartered, representing 25.8 percent and 74.2 percent, respectively, of all commercial bank assets.[23]

Federal Reserve System

www.federalreserve.gov

In addition to being concerned with the conduct of monetary policy, the Federal Reserve, as this country's central bank, also has regulatory power over some banks and, where relevant, their holding company parents. All 2,001 nationally chartered banks shown in Figure 11–8 are automatically members of the Federal Reserve System (FRS). In addition, 935 of the state-chartered banks have also chosen to become members. Since 1980, all banks have had to meet the same noninterest-bearing reserve requirements whether they are members of the FRS or not. The primary advantage of FRS membership is

23. In early 2004 the regulation of banks by federal versus state regulators came under debate. In January 2004, the OCC proclaimed that it alone has the right to draft and enforce rules that govern not only nationally chartered bank holding companies, but also the more than 2,000 banks that operate as subsidiaries of these holding companies. The move outraged state regulators, who claimed the OCC was attempting to preempt states' authority and grab power. See "House Panel Attacks Regulator Battling the States over Banks," by Jathon Sapsford, *The Wall Street Journal,* February 26, 2004, p. C5.

direct access to the federal funds wire transfer network for nationwide interbank borrowing and lending of reserves. Finally, many banks are often owned and controlled by parent **holding companies**—for example, Citigroup is the parent holding company of Citibank (a national bank). Because the holding company's management can influence decisions taken by a bank subsidiary and thus influence its risk exposure, the FRS regulates and examines bank holding companies as well as the banks themselves.

DO YOU UNDERSTAND?

1. Who the major regulators of commercial banks are?
2. Which of all commercial banks the OCC regulates?

holding company

A parent company that owns a controlling interest in a subsidiary bank or other FI.

State Authorities

As mentioned above, banks may choose to be state-chartered rather than nationally chartered. State-chartered commercial banks are regulated by state agencies. State authorities perform functions similar to those the OCC performs for national banks.

GLOBAL ISSUES

9

For the reasons discussed in earlier chapters, financial institutions are of central importance to the development and integration of markets globally. However, U.S. financial institutions must now compete not only with other domestic financial institutions for a share of these markets but increasingly with foreign financial institutions. Table 11–8 lists the 20 largest banks in the world, measured by total assets, as of 2004. Only 3 of the top 20 banks are U.S. banks. The three-way merger between the Industrial Bank of Japan, Fuji Bank, and Dai-Ichi Kangyo Bank in 2000 created the world's largest banking group, Mizohu Financial Group, with assets of over $1,285 billion.[24] Table 11–9 lists foreign bank offices' assets and liabilities held in the United States from 1992 through 2004. Total foreign bank assets over this period increased from $509.3 billion to $850.9 billion in 2001 before falling to $645.8 billion in 2004.[25] The world's most globally active banks, based on the percentage of their assets held outside their home countries, include the big Swiss banks (Union Bank of Switzerland with 76.8 percent of its business outside of Switzerland in the early 2000s and Credit Suisse with 72.9 percent of its business outside of Switzerland in the early 2000s) as well as one U.S. bank, American Express Bank. The two largest U.S. banks, Citigroup and J.P. Morgan Chase, ranked 28th (with 36.41 percent of their business overseas) and 29th (with 35.34 percent of their business overseas in the early 2000s), respectively.

Advantages and Disadvantages of International Expansion

International expansion has six major advantages.

Risk Diversification. As with domestic geographic expansions, an FI's international activities potentially enhance its opportunity to diversify the risk of its earnings flows. Often domestic earnings flows from financial services are strongly linked to the state of the domestic economy. Therefore, the less integrated the economies of the world are, the greater is the potential for earnings diversification through international expansions.[26]

Economies of Scale. To the extent that economies of scale exist, an FI can potentially lower its average operating costs by expanding its activities beyond domestic boundaries.

24. This bank began formal consolidated operations in 2002.

25. A. N. Berger, Q. Dai, S. Ongena, and D. C. Smith, in "To What Extent Will the Banking Industry be Globalized? A Study of Bank Nationality and Reach in 20 European Nations," working paper, Federal Reserve Board, May 2002, examine the choice of the locale of the provider of bank services for foreign affiliates of multinational corporations operating in 20 European nations. They find that foreign affiliates of multinational companies choose host nation banks for cash management services more often than home-nation or third-nation banks. They also find that if a host nation is the choice of nationality, then the firm is much less likely to choose a global bank.

26. This, of course, assumes that stockholders are sufficiently undiversified to value FIs diversifying on their behalf.

TABLE 11-8 The 20 Largest (in Total Assets) Banks in the World
(in millions of dollars)

Bank	Country	Total Assets
1. Mizuho Financial Group	Japan	$1,285,471
2. Citigroup	United States	1,264,032
3. UBS Group	Switzerland	1,120,543
4. Crédit Agricole Mutual	France	1,105,378
5. HSBC Holdings	United Kingdom	1,034,216
6. Deutsche Bank	Germany	1,014,845
7. BNP Paribas	France	988,982
8. Mitsibushi Tokyo Financial Group	Japan	974,950
9. Sumitomo Mitsui Financial Group	Japan	950,448
10. Royal Bank of Scotland	United Kingdom	806,207
11. Barclays Bank	United Kingdom	791,292
12. Credit Suisse Group	Switzerland	777,849
13. J.P. Morgan Chase	United States	770,912
14. UFJ Holdings	Japan	753,631
15. Bank of America	United States	736,445
16. ING Bank	Netherlands	684,004
17. Société Generale	France	681,218
18. ABN-AMRO Bank	Netherlands	667,636
19. HSBC	United Kingdom	650,721
20. Industrial and Commercial Bank of China	China	637,829

Source: *The Banker*, July 1, 2004. **www.thebanker.com**

TABLE 11-9 Foreign Bank Offices' Assets and Liabilities Held in the United States
(in millions of dollars)

	1992	1994	1996	2000	2001	2002	2004*
Financial assets	$509.3	$589.7	$714.8	$789.4	$850.9	$801.1	$645.8
Financial liabilities	519.3	602.8	731.9	818.4	883.9	838.4	691.9

*As of September.

Source: Federal Reserve Board, "Flow of Funds Accounts," Statistical Releases, various issues. **www.federalreserve.gov**

Innovations. An FI can generate extra returns from new product innovations if it can sell such services internationally rather than just domestically. For example, consider complex financial innovations, such as securitization, caps, floors, and options, that FIs have innovated in the United States and sold to new foreign markets with few domestic competitors until recently.[27]

Funds Source. International expansion allows an FI to search for the cheapest and most available sources of funds. This is extremely important with the very thin profit margins in domestic and international wholesale banking. It also reduces the risk of fund shortages (credit rationing) in any one market.

27. One reason that Sumitomo Bank took a limited partnership stake in Goldman Sachs in 1986 was to acquire knowledge and expertise about the management and valuation of complex financial instruments.

Customer Relationships. International expansions also allow an FI to maintain contact with and service the needs of domestic multinational corporations. Indeed, one of the fundamental factors determining the growth of FIs in foreign countries has been the parallel growth of foreign direct investment and foreign trade by globally oriented multinational corporations from the FI's home country.

Regulatory Avoidance. To the extent that domestic regulations such as activity restrictions and reserve requirements impose constraints or taxes on the operations of an FI, seeking low-regulatory, low-tax countries can allow an FI to lower its net regulatory burden and to increase its potential net profitability.

In contrast, international expansion has three major disadvantages.

Information/Monitoring Costs. Although global expansions allow an FI the potential to better diversify its geographic risk, the absolute level of exposure in certain areas such as lending can be high, especially if the FI fails to diversify in an optimal fashion. For example, the FI may fail to choose a loan portfolio combination on its efficient portfolio frontier (see Chapter 20). Foreign activities may also be riskier for the simple reason that monitoring and information collection costs are often higher in foreign markets. For example, Japanese and German accounting standards differ significantly from the generally accepted accounting principles (GAAP) that U.S. firms use. In addition, language, legal, and cultural issues can impose additional transaction costs on international activities. Finally, because the regulatory environment is controlled locally and regulation imposes a different array of net costs in each market, a truly global FI must master the various rules and regulations in each market.

Nationalization/Expropriation. To the extent that an FI expands by establishing a local presence through investing in fixed assets such as branches or subsidiaries, it faces the political risk that a change in government may lead to the nationalization of those fixed assets.[28] If foreign FI depositors take losses following a nationalization, they may seek legal recourse from the FI in U.S. courts rather than from the nationalizing government. For example, the resolution of the outstanding claims of depositors in Citicorp's branches in Vietnam following the Communist takeover and expropriation of those branches took many years.

Fixed Costs. The fixed costs of establishing foreign organizations may be extremely high. For example, a U.S. FI seeking an organizational presence in the London banking market faces real estate prices significantly higher than in New York. Such relative costs can be even higher if an FI chooses to enter by buying an existing U.K. bank rather than establishing a new operation, because of the cost of acquiring U.K. equities (i.e., paying an acquisition premium). These relative cost considerations become even more important if the expected volume of business to be generated, and thus the revenue flows, from foreign entry are uncertain. The failure of U.S. acquisitions of U.K. merchant banks to realize expected profits following the 1986 deregulation in the United Kingdom is a good example of unrealized revenue expectations vis-à-vis the high fixed costs of entry and the costs of maintaining a competitive position.[29]

Global Banking Performance

While U.S. depository institution performance deteriorated only slightly in the early 2000s, not all countries faired as well. In April 2001, the Japanese government announced plans for a government-backed purchase of ¥11,000 billion ($90 billion) of shares of Japanese banks

28. Such nationalizations have occurred with some frequency in African countries.

29. However, U.S. banks and securities firms have fared better since the Canadian deregulation of securities business in 1987 (see "Canada's Borrowing with Its Fat Fees Lures Wall Street," by Clyde H. Farnsworth, *The New York Times,* April 15, 1995, p. D1).

as part of an increasingly desperate drive to avert a banking collapse, recover from a 16-year low in the levels of Japanese equity markets, and stem the country's decline into recession. This was the third major attempt to bail out the banking system since 1998. Previous attempts were unsuccessful. For example, in March 2001, Fitch Investors Service (a major international rating agency) put 19 of the biggest Japanese banks on their credit watch list. The purchase of bank shares was intended to offset losses from the writing off of bad loans (estimated to be as high as ¥32,000 billion ($260 billion)) in bank portfolios. Foreign financial institutions were also solicited in attempts to assist in the prevention of a complete financial collapse in Japan. For instance, in October 2003, Goldman Sachs set up an investment fund to buy as much as ¥1 trillion ($9.1 billion) in nonperforming loans from the Sumitomo Mitsui Banking Corporation. Earlier, in January 2003, Goldman had agreed to buy ¥150.3 billion ($1.4 billion) of preferred shares from Sumitomo. Merrill Lynch and Deutsche Bank also bought troubled assets from Japanese banks. These efforts, along with a strengthening Japanese economy, appear to have averted a disastrous crisis. By the end of 2003 Japanese banks posted their largest earnings in years.[30]

In China, however, the banking industry deteriorated in the early 2000s. China's four state-run banks had about $120 billion in nonperforming loans, accounting for about 21 percent of total loans. Private economists put the percentage of nonperforming loans closer to 50 percent of total loans. Looking to clean up its troubled banking sector, the China Banking Regulatory Commission unveiled a comprehensive plan to overhaul the country's banking system, one that included a shift by China from restricting overseas competition to allowing it. The plan gives foreign banks greater scope to operate. Measures include raising the ceiling on foreign ownership in Chinese financial institutions from 15 percent to 20 percent for a single investor, expanding the number of cities where foreign branches can conduct some local currency business, and easing capital requirements for branches.

Also experiencing trouble in the early 2000s were Germany's largest banks, which were experiencing their worst downturn since World War II. German banks' problems were due to mounting bad loans, a result of nearly a decade of low growth and high unemployment in Germany, as well as plummeting corporate profits and share prices. Further, small local banks increasingly competed for loan business, contributing to a crisis for the country's biggest banks. Backed by government guarantees on their own borrowing, small banks enjoyed high credit ratings and a low cost of funds. This resulted in a tradition of low lending rates that left these banks with 67 percent of the small business loan market and 39 percent of all checking accounts. Without a constant stream of loan income, the large German banks were heavily reliant on trading and fee income from their securities business.

In Russia in the early 2000s, regulations were tightened to limit financial crime. As a result Russia was dropped from an international money-laundering blacklist. Before the changes, Russia was considered one of the chief conduits of illegal funds into the world financial system. In an attempt to alter this status, Russia's central bank enforced new rules. For example, banks are now required to report their capital adequacy and risky assets on a daily basis rather than quarterly and are being encouraged to move from Russian to international accounting standards. Regulators also audited banks as part of preparations for a new deposit insurance plan. Central bank officials predicted that 300 banks would not be allowed into the deposit insurance plan. The downside of the increased regulations was that in trying to clean up the banking industry, the central bank increased the fragility of Russia's banks. Knowing that several banks would not be insured, anxious depositors kept all-night vigils outside bank offices. In early July 2004, Guta Bank, the 22nd largest bank in Russia, closed its doors and stopped allowing withdrawals. Interest rates on the interbank market loans soared as first-tier banks stopped lending to riskier, smaller banks. While not as severe as the crisis in 1998, the Russian banking system remains in a fragile state.

DO YOU UNDERSTAND?

1. What the major advantages of international expansion to an FI are?
2. What the major disadvantages of international expansion to an FI are?
3. What the advantages and disadvantages of an FI's international expansion are?
4. Why do you think so few U.S. banks have established branches in Russia?

30. See "Respite for Japanese Banks," *The Wall Street Journal*, November 26, 2003, p. C12, and "Japan's Banks Post Profits," by Jason Singer, *The Wall Street Journal*, May 25, 2004, p. C14.

SUMMARY

This chapter provided an overview of the major activities of commercial banks and recent trends in the banking industry. Commercial banks rely heavily on deposits to fund their activities, although borrowed funds are becoming increasingly important for the largest institutions. Historically, commercial banks have concentrated on commercial or business lending and on investing in securities. Differences between the asset and liability portfolios of commercial banks and other financial institutions, however, are being eroded due to competitive forces, consolidation, regulation, and changing financial and business technology. Indeed, in the 2000s, the largest group of assets in commercial bank portfolios were mortgage related. The chapter examined the relatively large decline in the number of commercial banks in the last decade and reviewed reasons for the recent wave of bank mergers. Finally, the chapter provided an overview of this industry's performance over the last decade and discussed several global issues in commercial banking.

SEARCH THE SITE

Go to the FDIC Web site at **www.fdic.gov.** Find the most recent breakdown of U.S. bank asset concentrations using the following steps.

Click on "Analysts."

From there click on "FDIC Quarterly Banking Profile" and then click on "Quarterly Banking Profile: Commercial Bank Section."

Then click on "TABLE III-A. Full Year 200X, FDIC-Insured Commercial Banks."

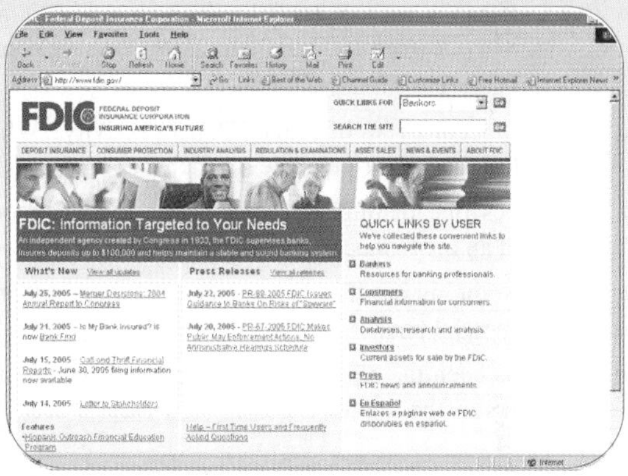

This will bring the files up on your computer that contain the relevant data.

Questions

1. How has the number and dollar value of assets held by commercial bank changed since 2004 reported in Table 11–5?
2. Calculate the percentage change in small (less than $1 billion in asset size) versus large (greater than $1 billion in asset size) banks since 2004 reported in Table 11–5.

QUESTIONS

1. What is meant by the term *depository institution?* How does a depository institution differ from an industrial corporation?
2. What are the major sources of funds for commercial banks in the United States? What are the major uses of funds for commercial banks in the United States? For each of your answers, specify where the item appears on the balance sheet of a typical commercial bank.
3. STANDARD &POOR'S Go to the S&P Educational Version of Market Insight Web site at **www.mhhe.com/edumarketinsight** and identify the Industry Description and Industry Constituents for Banks using the following steps. Click on "Educational Version of Market Insight." Enter your site ID and click on "Login." Click on "Industry." From the Industry list, select "Banks." Click on "Go!" Click on "Industry Profile" and, separately, "Industry Constituents."
4. What are the principal types of financial assets for commercial banks? How has the relative importance of these assets changed over the past five decades? What are some of the forces that have caused these changes? What are the primary types of risk associated with these types of assets?
5. Why do commercial banks hold investment securities?
6. What are the principal liabilities for commercial banks? What does this liability structure tell us about the maturity

of the liabilities of banks? What types of risks does this liability structure entail for commercial banks?

7. What type of transaction accounts do commercial banks issue? Which type of accounts have dominated transaction accounts of banks?

8. STANDARD &POOR'S Go to the S&P Educational Version of Market Insight Web site at **www.mhhe.com/edumarketinsight** and find the most recent Balance Sheet for Bank of America (BAC) and MBNA (KRB) using the following steps. Click on "Educational Version of Market Insight." Enter your site ID and click on "Login." Click on "Company." Enter "BAC" in the "Ticker:" box and click on "Go!" Click on "FS Ann. Balance Sheet." This will download the Balance Sheet for Bank of America which contains the balances for Loans, Total Assets, and Stockholders Equity. Repeat the process by entering "KRB" in the "Ticker:" box to get information on MBNA. Compare the ratios of loans to total assets and stockholders equity to total assets from these Balance Sheets with that for the Banking Industry listed in Table 11–2.

9. Compare and contrast the profitability ratios (ROE and ROA) of banks with assets below and above $100 million in Figure 11–7 from 1990 through 2004. What conclusions can you derive from those numbers?

10. What is meant by an off-balance-sheet activity? What are some of the forces responsible for them?

11. How does one distinguish between an off-balance-sheet asset and an off-balance-sheet liability?

12. What are the main off-balance-sheet activities undertaken by commercial banks?

13. What has been the recent trend in the number of commercial banks in the United States? What factors account for this trend?

14. What is the difference between economies of scale and economies of scope?

15. What are diseconomies of scale? What causes them?

16. What were some of the biggest mergers that occurred around the passage of the 1999 Financial Services Modernization Act? What were the incentives for these mergers?

17. What are the three revenue synergies that an FI can obtain from expanding geographically?

18. What is a money center bank and a regional bank?

19. How do small bank activities differ from large bank activities?

20. How has the performance of the commercial banking industry changed in the last decade?

21. Which commercial banks are experiencing the highest profitability and why? Which commercial banks are experiencing the lowest profitability?

22. STANDARD &POOR'S Go to the S&P Educational Version of Market Insight Web site at **www.mhhe.com/edumarketinsight** and look up the Industry Financial Highlights as posted by S&P for banks using the following steps. Click on "Educational Version of Market Insight." Enter your site ID and click on "Login." Click on "Industry." From the Industry list, select "Banks." Click on "Go!" Click on any/all of the items listed under "Industry Financial Highlights."

23. What technologically related wholesale and retail services do banks offer their customers?

24. Who are the major regulators of commercial banks? Which banks does each agency regulate?

25. What are the major functions performed by the FDIC?

26. What are the main advantages of being a member of the Federal Reserve System?

27. What are the advantages and disadvantages of international expansion?

12

Commercial Banks' Financial Statements *and* Analysis

Chapter NAVIGATOR

1. What are the four major categories of assets on a commercial bank's balance sheet?
2. What are core deposits and purchased funds?
3. What off-balance-sheet activities do commercial banks undertake?
4. What are the major categories on a commercial bank's income statement?
5. What ratios can be used to analyze a commercial bank?

OUTLINE

WHY EVALUATE THE PERFORMANCE OF COMMERCIAL BANKS? CHAPTER OVERVIEW

Unlike other private corporations, commercial banks (CBs) are unique in the special services they perform (e.g., assistance in the implementation of monetary policy) and the level of regulatory attention they receive (see Chapters 1 and 13). CBs are, as a result, unique in the types of assets and liabilities they hold. Like any for-profit corporation, however, the ultimate measure of a CB's performance is the value of its common equity to its shareholders. This chapter discusses the financial statements of these institutions. Managers, stockholders, depositors, regulators, and other parties use performance, earnings, and other measures obtained from financial statements to evaluate commercial banks. For example, the In The News box looks at how regulators use financial statement data to evaluate the overall safety and soundness of a bank. As we proceed through the chapter, notice the extent to which regulators' evaluation of the overall safety and soundness of a bank (or their assignment of a so-called CAMELS rating) depends on financial statement data. Given the extensive level of regulation and the accompanying requirements for public availability of financial information, the financial statements of commercial banks are ideal candidates to use in examining the performance of depository institutions.

DO YOU UNDERSTAND?

1. What CAMELS stands for and how each category is evaluated?
2. What each of the five CAMELS categories signifies?

The CAMELS Evaluation Components

The Uniform Financial Institutions Rating System (UFIRS) was adopted by the Federal Financial Institutions Examination Council (FFIEC) on November 13, 1979. Under the 1997 revision of the UFIRS, each financial institution is assigned a composite rating based on an evaluation and rating of six essential components of an institution's financial condition and operations that are summarized in a composite "CAMELS" rating. The acronym CAMELS stands for Capital Adequacy, Asset Quality, Management, Earnings, Liquidity, and Sensitivity to Market Risk.

An institution's *Capital Adequacy* is evaluated in relation to the volume of risk assets; the volume of marginal and inferior quality assets; the bank's growth experience, plan and prospects; and the strength of management. Consideration is also given to an institution's capital ratios relative to its peer group, its earnings retention, its dividend policies and its access to capital markets or other appropriate sources of financial assistance.

Asset Quality is evaluated by the level, distribution and severity of adversely classified assets; the level and distribution of nonaccrual and reduced-rate assets; the adequacy of the allowance for loan losses; and management's demonstrated ability to administer and collect problem credits. In addition, examiners evaluate the volume of concentrations of credit, trends in asset quality, volume of out-of-territory loans, level and severity of other real estate held and the bank's underwriting standards.

Management is evaluated against virtually all factors considered necessary to operate the bank within accepted banking practices and in a safe and sound manner. Thus, management is evaluated in relation to technical competence; leadership and administrative ability; compliance with banking regulations and statutes; adequacy of, and compliance with, internal policies and controls; and whether the board has a plan covering management succession. The assessment of management also takes into account the quality of internal controls, operating procedures and all lending, investment, and other operating policies. Finally, examiners review and assess the composition, experience level, abilities and involvement of the officers, directors and shareholders.

Earnings are evaluated with respect to their ability to cover losses and provide adequate capital protection; trends; peer group comparisons; the quality and composition of net income; and the degree of reliance on interest-sensitive funds. Consideration is also given to the bank's dividend payout ratio, the rate of growth of retained earnings and the adequacy of bank capital. The adequacy of provisions to the allowance for loan losses, and the extent to which extraordinary items, securities transactions and tax effects contribute to net income, are also assessed.

Liquidity is evaluated in relation to the volatility of deposits; the frequency and level of borrowings, use of brokered deposits, technical competence relative to the structure of liabilities, availability of assets readily convertible into cash; and access to money markets or other ready sources of funds. The overall effectiveness of asset-liability management is considered, as well as the adequacy of, and compliance with, established liquidity policies. The nature, volume and anticipated use of credit commitments are also factors that are weighed.

The *Sensitivity to Market Risk* component reflects the degree to which changes in interest rates, foreign exchange rates, commodity prices, or equity prices can adversely affect a financial institution's earnings or economic capital. When evaluating this component, consideration should be given to: management's ability to identify, measure, monitor, and control market risk; the institution's size; the nature and complexity of its activities; and the adequacy of its capital and earnings in relation to its level of market risk exposure.

CAMELS ratings range from 1 to 5.

Composite "1"—Institutions in this group are basically sound in every respect.

Composite "2"—Institutions in this group are fundamentally sound, but may reflect modest weaknesses correctable in the normal course of business.

Composite "3"—Institutions in this category exhibit financial, operational or compliance weaknesses ranging from moderately severe to unsatisfactory.

Composite "4"—Institutions in this group have an immoderate volume of serious financial weaknesses or a combination of other conditions that are unsatisfactory.

Composite "5"—This category is reserved for institutions with an extremely high immediate or near term probability of failure.

Source: Federal Deposit Insurance Corporation, DOS Manual of Examination Policies, February 2005. **www.fdic.gov**

This chapter uses commercial banks to illustrate a return on equity (ROE) framework as a method of evaluating depository institutions' profitability. The ROE framework decomposes this frequently used measure of profitability into its various component parts to identify existing or potential financial management and risk exposure problems.[1] The fact that bank size and/or niche (i.e., the financial market segment the bank specializes in servicing) may affect the evaluation of financial statements is also highlighted.

FINANCIAL STATEMENTS OF COMMERCIAL BANKS

report of condition

Balance sheet of a commercial bank reporting information at a single point in time.

report of income

Income statement of a commercial bank reporting revenues, expenses, net profit or loss, and cash dividends over a period of time.

Financial information on commercial banks is reported in two basic documents. The **report of condition** (or balance sheet) presents financial information on a bank's assets, liabilities, and equity capital. The balance sheet reports a bank's condition at a single point in time. The **report of income** (or the income statement) presents the major categories of revenues and expenses (or costs) and the net profit or loss for a bank over a period of time. Financial statements of commercial banks must be submitted to regulators and stockholders at the end of each calendar quarter—March, June, September, and December. The Federal Financial Institutions Examination Council (FFIEC), based in Washington, D.C., prescribes uniform principles, standards, and report forms for depository institutions.[2]

All financial institutions, and particularly commercial banks, are also engaging in an increased level of off-balance-sheet (OBS) activities. These activities produce income (and sometimes losses) for the FI that are reported on the income statement. This chapter summarizes off-balance-sheet activities (and the risks involved with such activities), which are discussed in more detail in Chapters 19 and 23.

www.ffiec.gov

To evaluate the performance of commercial banks, we use two bank holding companies of varying sizes and market niches: North Fork Bancorporation and Bank of America Corporation.

www.northforkbank.com

North Fork Bancorp (NFB) is a publicly traded commercial bank holding company headquartered in Melville, New York; in 2004, it had $63.29 billion in assets. It is Long Island's largest independent commercial bank, operating 255 branch locations throughout New York, Connecticut, and New Jersey. NFB, by emphasizing retail banking, has been one of the most efficient and profitable banks in the country. **Retail banks** focus on individual consumer banking relationships, such as residential mortgages and consumer loans on the asset side of the portfolio, and individual demand, NOW, savings, and time deposits on the liability side. In contrast, **wholesale banks** focus their business activities on business banking relationships; they hold more business loans and fewer mortgages and consumer loans and use fewer consumer deposits and more purchased funds than retail banks do. In addition to providing a range of personal and commercial banking products, NFB also offers an array of financial services, including trust, asset management, brokerage services, and related annuity and mutual fund products. NFB invests heavily in real estate loans and attempts to fund assets as much as possible with core deposits. At the end of 2004, multifamily and residential mortgage loans constituted almost 90 percent of the bank's loan portfolio. In 1998, NFB acquired New York Bancorp, which increased its then size to $10.1 billion in assets and 108 branch locations. In 2000, NFB acquired JSB Financial, Inc. and Commercial Bank of New York to bring the bank to $17.0 billion in assets. Finally, in late 2004, NFB acquired Green Point Financial Corporation, one of the largest mortgage originators in the United States, to bring it to its current size.

retail bank

A bank that focuses its business activities on consumer banking relationships.

wholesale bank

A bank that focuses its business activities on commercial banking relationships.

www.bankofamerica.com

Bank of America Corporation (BOA), headquartered in Charlotte, North Carolina, is the nation's third largest bank, with assets of $1,064 billion as of 2004. The merger of Bank of America and FleetBoston Financial in 2004 brought the bank's asset value to above

1. This decomposition is often termed *DuPont* analysis.

2. The financial statements reported by banks use book value accounting concepts; i.e., assets, liabilities, and equity accounts are generally reported at their original cost or book value. An alternative accounting method frequently discussed for use by banks is market value accounting. We discuss the issues, consequences of, and current status of the use of market value accounting in Chapter 22.

$1 trillion, with more than 5,880 offices in the United States and offices in 35 countries supporting clients across 150 countries. Bank of America operates nationally in many business lines, including retail and wholesale banking, investment and trust management, and credit card company business. Bank of America has created the nation's largest ATM network with 16,500 ATMs engaging in more than 2.3 trillion transactions per day, is the nation's largest debit card issuer with nearly 17 million cards outstanding, is the nation's leading small business lender, and is the number one institution in number of relationships, investment banking, treasury management, syndications, secured and unsecured credit, and leasing to middle-market U.S. companies.

Balance Sheet Structure

Table 12–1 presents December 31, 2004, balance sheet information for the two commercial bank holding companies (hereafter called *banks*). As stated in Chapter 11, many banks are owned by parent bank holding companies. One-bank holding companies control only one subsidiary commercial bank; multiple-bank holding companies control two or more subsidiary commercial banks (see Chapter 13). The financial statements reported in this chapter are for the consolidated multiple-bank holding company, which includes the parent holding company plus bank subsidiaries. These data are taken from the Federal Deposit Insurance Corporation call reports and are available at the Federal Reserve Bank of Chicago Web site. Pay particular attention to the fact that, unlike manufacturing corporations, the majority of a commercial bank's assets are financial assets rather than physical or fixed assets (such as buildings or machines). Additionally, a relatively large portion of a commercial bank's liabilities are short-term deposits and borrowings. In general, banks have higher leverage than manufacturing corporations do.

www.fdic.gov

www.chicagofed.org

1

Assets. A bank's assets are grouped into four major subcategories: (1) cash and balances due from other depository institutions, (2) investment securities, (3) loans and leases, and (4) other assets. Investment securities and loans and leases are the bank's earning assets. Cash and balances due from depository institutions (item 5 in Table 12–1) consist of vault cash, deposits at the Federal Reserve (the central bank), deposits at other financial institutions, and cash items in the process of collection. None of these items generates much income for the bank, but each is held because they perform specific functions.

Cash and Balances Due from Other Depository Institutions. Vault cash (item 1) is composed of the currency and coin needed to meet customer withdrawals. Deposits at the Federal Reserve (item 2) are used primarily to meet legal reserve requirements (see Chapter 13), to assist in check clearing, wire transfers, and the purchase or sale of Treasury securities. Deposits at other financial institutions (item 3) are primarily used to purchase services from those institutions. These banks generally purchase services such as check collection, check processing, fed funds trading, and investment advice from **correspondent banks** (see below). Cash items in the process of collection (item 4) are checks written against accounts at other institutions that have been deposited at the bank. Credit is given to the depositor of these checks only after they clear.

correspondent bank

A bank that provides services to another commercial bank.

Investment Securities. Investment securities (item 12 in Table 12–1) consist of items such as interest-bearing deposits at other FIs, federal funds sold, repurchase agreements (RPs or repos), U.S. Treasury and agency securities, securities issued by states and political subdivisions (municipals), mortgage-backed securities, and other debt and equity securities. These securities generate some income for the bank and are used for liquidity risk management purposes. Investment securities are highly liquid,[3] have low default risk, and

3. Not all of a bank's investment securities can be sold immediately. Some securities, such as U.S. Treasury securities and municipals, can be pledged against certain types of borrowing by the bank and, therefore, must remain on the bank's books until the debt obligation is removed or another security is pledged as collateral.

TABLE 12-1 Balance Sheet for Two Commercial Banks on December 31, 2004
(in millions of dollars)

	North Fork Bancorp*	Bank of America*
Assets		
1. Vault cash	$255.47	$6,457.30
2. Deposits at Federal Reserve	39.25	399.02
3. Deposits at other financial institutions	229.32	(1,910.90)
4. Cash items in process of collection	483.48	19,433.38
5. Cash balances due from depository institutions	$1,007.52	$24,378.80
6. Interest-bearing deposits at other FIs	61.44	19,101.12
7. Federal funds sold and RPs	2,667.90	73,604.82
8. U.S. Treasury and U.S. agency securities	685.47	336.39
9. Securities issued by states and political subdivisions	965.42	4,061.64
10. Mortgage-backed securities	12,671.04	172,690.84
11. Other debt and equity securities	821.98	18,498.14
12. Investment securities	$17,873.25	$288,292.95
13. Commercial and industrial loans	2,743.47	93,542.24
14. Loans secured by real estate	31,714.60	299,056.78
15. Consumer loans	1,532.62	99,060.62
16. Other loans	235.03	52,324.42
17. Leases	144.28	19,708.07
18. Gross loans and leases	$36,370.00	$563,692.13
19. Less: Unearned income	35.12	—
20. Reserve for loan and lease losses	211.11	9,050.75
21. Net loans and leases	$36,123.77	$554,641.38
22. Premises and fixed assets	414.89	6,662.60
23. Other real estate owned	19.06	124.79
24. Investments in unconsolidated subsidiaries	10.87	3,455.08
25. Intangible assets	6,260.08	49,379.16
26. Other	1,582.97	136,809.46
27. Other assets	$8,287.87	$196,431.09
28. Total assets	$63,292.41	$1,063,744.22
Liabilities and Equity Capital		
29. Demand deposits	$2,427.27	$76,162.16
30. NOW accounts	568.18	15,243.66
31. MMDAs	12,593.06	243,440.77
32. Other savings deposits	11,295.55	105,753.40
33. Deposits in foreign offices	—	110,129.01
34. Retail CDs	4,951.80	65,937.20
35. Core deposits	$31,835.86	$616,666.20
36. Wholesale CDs	2,526.48	58,716.89
37. Total deposits	$34,362.34	$675,383.09
38. Federal funds purchased and RPs	13,292.95	106,741.81
39. Other borrowed funds	4,975.80	85,720.38
40. Subordinated notes and debentures	184.47	12,502.65
41. Other liabilities	842.78	73,327.58
42. Total liabilities	$53,658.34	$953,675.51
43. Preferred stock	—	—
44. Common stock	5.60	2,907.19
45. Surplus and paid-in capital	8,293.75	84,958.48
46. Retained earnings	1,334.72	22,235.34
47. Other equity capital	—	(32.30)
48. Total equity capital	$9,634.07	$110,068.71
49. Total liabilities and equity capital	$63,292.41	$1,063,744.22

*Values are taken from the 2004 FDIC report of condition data tapes and available at the Federal Reserve Bank of Chicago Web site. **www.chicagofed.org**

can usually be traded in secondary markets. Banks generally maintain significant amounts of these securities to ensure that they can easily meet liquidity needs that arise unexpectedly.[4] However, because the revenue generated from investment securities is low compared to that from loans and leases, many (particularly larger) banks attempt to minimize the amount of investment securities they hold.

Short-maturity (less than one year to maturity) investments include interest-bearing deposits at other FIs (item 6), federal funds sold and repurchase agreements (item 7), and U.S. Treasury bills and agency securities (item 8). Returns on these investments vary directly with changes in market interest rates. Although banks with excess cash reserves invest some of this in interest-earning liquid assets such as T-bills and short-term securities, they have the option to lend excess reserves for short intervals to other banks seeking increased short-term funding. The interbank market for excess reserves is called the federal funds (fed funds) market. In the United States, federal funds are short-term uncollateralized loans made by one bank to another; more than 90 percent of such transactions have maturities of one day. Repurchase agreements (RPs or repos) can be viewed as collateralized federal funds transactions. In a federal funds transaction, the bank with excess reserves sells fed funds for one day to the purchasing bank. The next day, the purchasing bank returns the fed funds plus one day's interest, reflecting the fed funds rate. Since credit risk exposure exists for the selling bank, because the purchasing bank may be unable to repay the fed funds the next day, the seller may seek collateral backing for the one-day fed funds loan. In an RP transaction, the funds-selling bank receives government securities as collateral from the funds-purchasing bank—that is, the funds-purchasing bank temporarily exchanges securities for cash. The next day, this transaction is reversed—the funds-purchasing bank sends back the fed funds it borrowed plus interest (the RP rate); it receives in return (or repurchases) its securities used as collateral in the transaction.

www.ginniemae.gov

www.fanniemae.com

www.freddiemac.com

Long-maturity investments such as U.S. Treasury bonds and U.S. agency securities (item 8), municipals (item 9), mortgage-backed securities (item 10), and most other securities (item 11) usually offer somewhat higher expected returns than short-maturity investments since they are subject to greater interest rate risk exposure—see Chapter 22. U.S. Treasury securities and Government National Mortgage Association (agency) bonds are fully backed by the U.S. government and thus carry no default risk. Other U.S. government agency securities, such as those of the Federal National Mortgage Association and the Federal Home Loan Mortgage Corporation, are not directly backed by the full faith and credit of the U.S. government and therefore carry some default risk (see Chapter 7). Municipal securities held by commercial banks are generally high-rated, investment-grade (i.e., low-risk) securities, issued by municipalities as either general obligation or revenue bonds.[5] Interest paid on municipals is exempt from federal income tax obligations. Mortgage-backed securities include items such as collateralized mortgage obligations and mortgage-backed bonds (see Chapter 7). Other investment securities include investment-grade corporate bonds, foreign debt securities, and securities such as U.S. Treasury securities and municipals held for short-term trading purposes. These trading account securities earn interest for the bank and generate capital gains or losses from changes in the market values of these securities.[6]

Loans. Loans (items 13–16 in Table 12–1) are the major items on a bank's balance sheet and generate the largest flow of revenue income. However, loans are also the least liquid

4. Most investment securities are debt rather than equity instruments because current regulations generally prohibit banks from owning equity securities as investments. Banks can hold equity securities only if they are acquired as collateral on a loan or if they are stocks issued by the Federal Reserve Bank.

5. Payments of principal and interest on general obligation bonds are backed by the full faith, credit, and taxing authority of the issuer. Payments of principal and interest on revenue bonds are backed only by the revenues generated from the facility or project that the proceeds of the bonds are financing.

6. Investment securities included in the bank's trading portfolio and designated as *trading securities* or *available-for-sale securities* are listed on the balance sheet at their *market value*. All other items on the balance sheet are listed at their *book values*.

asset item and the major source of credit and liquidity risk for most banks. Leases (item 17) are used as alternatives to loans when the bank, as owner of a physical asset, allows a customer to use an asset in return for periodic lease payments. Loans are categorized as commercial and industrial (C&I) loans (item 13), loans secured by real estate (item 14), individual or consumer loans (item 15), and other loans (item 16). Foreign loans often carry an additional risk for the bank—called *country* or *sovereign risk* (see Chapters 8 and 19).

Commercial and Industrial Loans. C&I loans are used to finance a firm's capital needs, equipment purchases, and plant expansion. They can be made in quite small amounts such as $100,000 to small businesses or in packages as large as $10 million or more to major corporations. Commercial loans can be made at either fixed rates or floating rates of interest. The interest rate on a fixed-rate loan is set at the beginning of the contract period. This rate remains in force over the loan contract period no matter what happens to market rates. The interest rate on a floating-rate loan can be adjusted periodically according to a formula so that the interest rate risk is transferred in large part from the bank to the borrower. As might be expected, longer-term loans are more likely to be made under floating-rate contracts than are relatively short-term loans. In addition, commercial loans can be made for periods as short as a few weeks to as long as eight years or more. Traditionally, short-term commercial loans (those with an original maturity of one year or less) are used to finance firms' working capital needs and other short-term funding needs, while long-term commercial loans are used to finance credit needs that extend beyond one year, such as the purchase of real assets (machinery), new venture start-up costs, and permanent increases in working capital. Commercial loans can be secured or unsecured. A *secured loan* (or asset-backed loan) is backed by specific assets of the borrower, while an *unsecured loan* (or junior debt) gives the lender only a general claim on the assets of the borrower should default occur.

Real Estate Loans. Real estate loans are primarily mortgage loans and some revolving home equity loans (see Chapter 7). For banks (as well as savings institutions), residential mortgages are the largest component of the real estate loan portfolio; until recently, however, commercial real estate mortgages had been the fastest-growing component of real estate loans. Residential mortgages are very long-term loans with an average maturity of approximately 25 years. As with C&I loans, the characteristics of residential mortgage loans differ widely. As discussed in Chapter 7, these include the size of loan, the loan-to-value ratio, and the maturity of the mortgage. Other important characteristics are the mortgage interest (or commitment) rate and fees and charges on the loan, such as commissions, discounts, and points paid by the borrower or the seller to obtain the loan. In addition, the mortgage rate differs according to whether the mortgage has a fixed rate or a floating rate, also called an *adjustable rate*.

Consumer Loans. A third major category of loans is the individual or consumer loan—for example, personal and auto loans. Commercial banks, finance companies, retailers, savings banks, and gas companies also provide consumer loan financing through credit cards such as Visa, MasterCard, and proprietary credit cards issued by companies such as Sears and AT&T.

Other Loans. Other loans include a wide variety of borrowers and types such as loans to nonbank financial institutions, state and local governments, foreign banks, and sovereign governments. Each loan category entails a wide variety of characteristics that must be evaluated to determine the risk involved, whether the bank should grant the loan, and, if so, at what price. We discuss the evaluation methods in Chapter 20.

Unearned Income and Allowance for Loan and Lease Losses. Unearned income (item 19) and the allowance (reserve) for loan and lease losses (item 20) are contra-asset accounts that are deducted from gross loans and leases on the balance sheet to create net loans and leases (item 21). Unearned income is the amount of income that the bank has received on a loan from a customer but has not yet recorded as income on the income statement. Over the life of the loan, the bank earns (or accrues) interest income and accordingly transfers it out of unearned income into interest income. The allowance for loan and lease losses is an estimate by the bank's management of the amount of the gross loans (and leases) that will not be repaid to the bank. Although the maximum amount of the reserve is influenced by tax laws, the bank's management actually sets the level based on loan growth and recent loan loss experience. The allowance for loan losses is an accumulated reserve that is adjusted each period as management recognizes the possibility of additional bad loans and makes appropriate provisions for such losses. Actual losses are then deducted from, and recoveries are added to (referred to as **net write-offs**), their accumulated loan and lease loss reserve balance.

net write-offs

Actual loan losses less loan recoveries.

Investment securities plus net loans and leases are the **earning assets** of a depository institution. It is these items on the balance sheet that generate interest income and some of the noninterest income described below.

earning assets

Investment securities plus net loans and leases.

Other Assets. Other assets on the bank's balance sheet (item 27) consist of items such as premises and fixed assets (item 22), other real estate owned (collateral seized on defaulted loans—item 23), investments in unconsolidated subsidiaries (item 24), intangible assets (i.e., goodwill and mortgage servicing rights—item 25), and other (i.e., deferred taxes, prepaid expenses, and mortgage servicing fees receivable—item 26). These accounts are generally a small part of the bank's overall assets.

Liabilities. A bank's liabilities consist of various types of deposit accounts and other borrowings used to fund the investments and loans on the asset side of the balance sheet. Liabilities vary in terms of their maturity, interest payments, check-writing privileges, and deposit insurance coverage.

Deposits. Demand deposits (item 29) are transaction accounts held by individuals, corporations, partnerships, and governments that pay no explicit interest. Corporations are prohibited from using deposits other than demand deposits (e.g., NOW accounts) for transaction account purposes. This group therefore constitutes the major holders of demand deposits. Since 1980, all banks in the United States have been able to offer checkable deposits that pay interest and are withdrawable on demand; they are called *negotiable order of withdrawal accounts* or **NOW accounts**[7] (item 30). The major distinction between these instruments and traditional demand deposits is that these instruments require the depositor to maintain a minimum account balance to earn interest. If the minimum balance falls below some level, such as $500, the account formally converts to a status equivalent to a demand deposit and earns no interest. Also, there are restrictions on corporations holding NOW accounts.

NOW account

Negotiable order of withdrawal account is similar to a demand deposit but pays interest when a minimum balance is maintained.

Money market deposit accounts or **MMDAs** (item 31) are an additional liability instrument that banks can use. To make banks competitive with the money market mutual funds offered by groups such as Vanguard and Fidelity, the MMDAs they offer must be liquid. In the United States, MMDAs are checkable but subject to restrictions on the number of checks written on each account per month, the number of preauthorized automatic transfers per month, and the minimum denomination of the amount of each check. In addition, MMDAs impose minimum balance requirements on depositors. The Federal Reserve does not require banks to hold cash reserves against MMDAs. Accordingly, banks generally pay higher rates on MMDAs than on NOW accounts. **Other savings deposits** (item 32) are all savings accounts other than MMDAs (i.e., regular passbook accounts) with no set maturity and no check-writing privileges. Like MMDAs, savings accounts currently carry zero reserve requirements.

MMDAs

Money market deposit accounts with retail savings accounts and some limited checking account features.

other savings deposits

All savings accounts other than MMDAs.

7. Super-NOW accounts have very similar features to NOW accounts but require a larger minimum balance.

Some banks separate foreign from domestic deposits on the balance sheet (item 33). Foreign deposits are not explicitly covered by FDIC-provided deposit insurance guarantees (see Chapter 13). These deposits are generally large and held by corporations with a high level of international transactions and activities.

retail CDs

Time deposits with a face value below $100,000.

wholesale CDs

Time deposits with a face value of $100,000 or more.

negotiable instrument

An instrument whose ownership can be transferred in the secondary market.

brokered deposits

Wholesale CDs obtained through a brokerage house.

The major categories of time deposits are retail certificates of deposit (CDs) and wholesale CDs. **Retail CDs** (item 34) are fixed-maturity instruments with face values under $100,000. Although the size, maturity, and rates on these CDs are negotiable, most banks issue standardized retail CDs. **Wholesale CDs** (item 36) (discussed also in Chapter 5) were created by banks in the early 1960s as a contractual mechanism to allow depositors to liquidate their position in these CDs by selling them in the secondary market rather than having to hold them to maturity or requesting that the bank cash in the deposit early (which involves a penalty cost for the depositor). Thus, a depositor can sell a relatively liquid instrument without causing adverse liquidity risk exposure for the bank. Consequently, the unique feature of wholesale CDs is not so much their large minimum denomination size of $100,000 or more but the fact that they are **negotiable instruments**. That is, they can be resold by title assignment in a secondary market to other investors. This means, for example, that if IBM had bought a $1 million three-month CD from J.P. Morgan Chase, but for unexpected liquidity reasons needed funds after only one month passed, it could sell this CD to another outside investor in the secondary market. This does not impose any obligation on J.P. Morgan Chase in terms of an early funds withdrawal request. Wholesale CDs obtained through a brokerage or investment house rather than directly from a customer are referred to as **brokered deposits.**[8] CDs held in foreign offices and denominated in dollars are referred to as *Eurodollar deposits* (see Chapter 5).

Borrowed Funds. The liabilities described above are all deposit liabilities, reflecting deposit contracts issued by banks in return for cash. However, banks not only fund their assets by issuing deposits but borrow in various markets for purchased funds. Since the funds generated from these purchases are not deposits, they are subject to neither reserve requirements (as with demand deposits and NOW accounts) nor deposit insurance premium payments to the FDIC (as with all the domestic deposits described earlier).[9] The largest market available for purchased funds is the federal funds market (item 38). As we discussed earlier, a bank with excess reserves can sell them in the fed funds market, recording them as an asset on the balance sheet. The bank that purchases fed funds shows them as a liability on its balance sheet. As with the fed funds market, the RP market (item 38) is a highly liquid and flexible source of funds for banks needing to increase their liabilities and to offset deposit withdrawals. Moreover, like fed funds, these transactions can be rolled over each day if the counterparty is willing. The major difference in flexibility of liability management for fed funds and RPs is that a fed funds transaction can be entered into at virtually any time in the banking day. In general, it is difficult to transact an RP borrowing late in the day since the bank sending the fed funds must be satisfied with the type and quality of the securities' collateral proposed by the borrowing bank. Although this collateral is normally T-bills, T-notes, T-bonds, and mortgage-backed securities, the maturities and other features, such as callability or coupons, may be unattractive to the fund seller.

Fed funds and RPs have been the major sources of borrowed funds, but banks have utilized other borrowing (item 39) sources to supplement their flexibility in liability management. Four of these sources are banker's acceptances (BAs), commercial paper, medium-term notes, and discount window loans. Banks often convert off-balance-sheet letters of credit into on-balance-sheet BAs by discounting the letter of credit when the

8. These are often purchased in $100,000 increments. For example, a broker may receive $1 million from an investor and break this up into 10 lots of $100,000 CDs that are placed (brokered out) at 10 different banks. Thus, effectively, the full $1 million is covered by FDIC deposit insurance.

9. Foreign deposits are not subject to deposit insurance premiums. However, in the exceptional event of a very large failure in which all deposits are protected, under the 1991 FDICIA, the FDIC is required to levy a charge on surviving large banks proportional to their total asset size. To the extent that assets are partially funded by foreign liabilities, this is an implied premium on foreign deposits.

holder presents it for acceptance (see Chapter 5). In addition, these BAs may be resold to money market investors. As a result, BA sales to the secondary market are an additional funding source. Although a bank subsidiary itself cannot issue commercial paper, its parent holding company can—that is, Citigroup can issue commercial paper but Citibank cannot. This provides banks owned by holding companies—most of the largest banks in the United States—with an additional funding source, since the holding company can "downstream" funds generated from its commercial paper sales to its bank subsidiary. Finally, banks facing temporary liquidity crunches can borrow from the central bank's discount window at the discount rate. Since this rate is not market determined and usually lies below fed funds and government security rates, it offers a very attractive borrowing opportunity to a bank with deficient reserves as the reserve maintenance period comes to an end (see Chapter 13).[10]

A number of banks in search of stable sources of funds with low withdrawal risk have begun to issue subordinated notes and debentures (item 40), often in the five- to seven-year range. These notes are especially attractive because they are subject to neither reserve requirements nor deposit insurance premiums, and some can serve as (Tier 2) capital for the bank to satisfy Federal Reserve regulations regarding minimum capital requirements (see Chapter 13).

core deposits

Deposits of the bank that are stable over short periods of time and thus provide a long-term funding source to a bank.

purchased funds

Rate-sensitive funding sources of the bank.

2

Some banks separate core deposits from purchased funds on their balance sheets. The stable deposits of the bank are referred to as **core deposits** (item 35). These deposits are not expected to be withdrawn over short periods of time and are therefore a more permanent source of funding for the bank. Core deposits are also the cheapest funds banks can use to finance their assets. Because they are both a stable and low-cost source of funding, core deposits are the most frequently used source of funding by commercial banks. Core deposits generally are defined as demand deposits, NOW accounts, MMDAs, other saving accounts, and retail CDs. **Purchased funds** are more expensive and/or volatile sources of funds because they are highly rate sensitive—these funds are more likely to be immediately withdrawn or replaced as rates on competitive instruments change. Further, interest rates on these funds, at any point in time, are generally higher than rates on core deposits. Purchased funds are generally defined as brokered deposits, wholesale CDs, deposits at foreign offices, fed funds purchased, RPs, and subordinated notes and debentures.

Other Liabilities. Banks also list other liabilities (item 41) that do not require interest to be paid. These items consist of accrued interest, deferred taxes, dividends payable, minority interests in consolidated subsidies, and other miscellaneous claims.

Equity Capital. The bank's equity capital (item 47) consists mainly of preferred (item 43) and common (item 44) stock (listed at par value), surplus or additional paid-in capital (item 45), and retained earnings (item 46). Regulations require banks to hold a minimum level of equity capital to act as a buffer against losses from their on- and off-balance-sheet assets (see Chapter 13).

Off-Balance-Sheet Assets and Liabilities

3

Off-balance-sheet (OBS) items are *contingent* assets and liabilities that *may* affect the future status of a financial institution's balance sheet. OBS activities are less obvious and often invisible to financial statement readers because they usually appear "below the bottom line," frequently as footnotes to accounts. As part of the quarterly financial reports submitted to regulators, schedule L lists the notional dollar size of OBS activities of banks. We briefly summarized the OBS activities of commercial banks in Chapter 11. In this chapter, we introduce the items as they appear off the FI's balance sheet.

10. Although the low rate makes the discount window an attractive place to borrow, banks do not use it often because such borrowings are intended for use only as a last resort (see Chapter 4).

TABLE 12–2 Off-Balance-Sheet Activities for Two Commercial Banks on December 31, 2004
(in millions of dollars)

	North Fork Bancorp*	Bank of America*
Commitments and Contingencies		
1. Loan commitments	$ 5,967.39	$ 572,568.75
2. Commercial letters of credit	16.48	5,874.68
3. Standby letters of credit	339.30	64,979.82
4. Loans sold	—	468.55
Notional Amounts for Derivatives†		
5. Forwards and futures	$ 4,678.82	$ 2,243,068.56
6. Options	1,950.50	2,612,771.26
7. Interest rate swaps	632.47	12,124,562.28
8. Total	$13,584.96	$17,624,293.90

*Values are taken from the 2004 FDIC Report of Condition data tapes available at the Federal Reserve Bank of Chicago Web site. **www.chicagofed.org**

†Notional amounts reflect the face value of the contracts entered into.

Although OBS activities are now an important source of fee income for many FIs, they have the potential to produce positive as well as negative *future* cash flows. Some OBS activities can involve risks that add to the institution's overall risk exposure; others can hedge or reduce their interest rate, credit, and foreign exchange risks. A depository institution's performance and solvency are also affected by the management of these items. Off-balance-sheet activities can be grouped into four major categories: loan commitments, letters of credit, loans sold, and derivative securities. The OBS activities for North Fork Bancorp and Bank of America are reported in Table 12–2.

loan commitment

Contractual commitment to loan to a firm a certain maximum amount at given interest rate terms.

up-front fee

The fee charged for making funds available through a loan commitment.

commitment fee

The fee charged on the unused component of a loan commitment.

Loan Commitments. These days, most commercial and industrial loans are made by firms that take down (or borrow against) prenegotiated lines of credit or loan commitments rather than borrow cash immediately in the form of spot loans. A **loan commitment** agreement (item 1 in Table 12–2) is a contractual commitment by a bank or another FI (such as an insurance company) to loan to a customer a certain maximum amount (say, $10 million) at given interest rate terms (say, 12 percent). The loan commitment agreement also defines the length of time over which the borrower has the option to take down this loan. In return for making this loan commitment, the bank may charge an **up-front fee** (or facility fee) of, say, 1/8 percent of the commitment size, or $12,500 in this example. In addition, the bank must stand ready to supply the full $10 million at any time over the commitment period—for example, one year. Meanwhile, the borrower has a valuable option to take down any amount between $0 and $10 million over the commitment period. The bank may also charge the borrower a **commitment fee** on any unused commitment balances at the end of the period. In this example, if the borrower takes down only $8 million over the year and the fee on *unused* commitments is 1/4 percent, the bank generates additional revenue of 1/4 percent times $2 million, or $5,000.

Note that only when the borrower actually draws on the commitment do the loans made under the commitment appear on the balance sheet. Thus, only when the $8 million loan is taken down exactly halfway through the one-year commitment period (i.e., six months later) does the balance sheet show the creation of a new $8 million loan. We illustrate the transaction in Figure 12–1. When the $10 million commitment is made at time 0, nothing shows on the balance sheet. Nevertheless, the bank must stand ready to supply the full $10 million in loans on any day within the one-year commitment period—at time 0 a

FIGURE 12–1 **Loan Commitment Transaction**

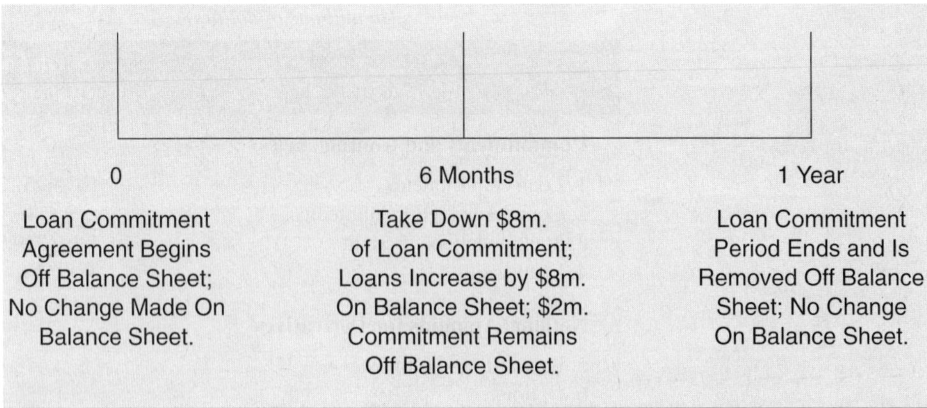

new contingent claim on the resources of the bank is created. At time 6 months, when the $8 million is drawn down, the balance sheet will reflect this as an $8 million loan.

commercial letters of credit

Contingent guarantees sold by an FI to underwrite the trade or commercial performance of the buyers of the guarantees.

standby letters of credit

Guarantees issued to cover contingencies that are potentially more severe and less predictable than contingencies covered under trade-related or commercial letters of credit.

Commercial Letters of Credit and Standby Letters of Credit. In selling **commercial letters of credit** (LCs—item 2 in Table 12–2) and **standby letters of credit** (SLCs—item 3) for fees, banks add to their contingent future liabilities. Both LCs and SLCs are essentially *guarantees* to underwrite performance that a depository institution sells to the buyers of the guarantees (such as a corporation). In economic terms, the depository institution that sells LCs and SLCs is selling insurance against the frequency or severity of some particular future event occurring. Further, similar to the different lines of insurance sold by property-casualty insurers, LC and SLC contracts differ as to the severity and frequency of their risk exposures. We look next at the risk exposure from engaging in LC and SLC activities off the balance sheet.

Commercial Letters of Credit. Commercial letters of credit are widely used in both domestic and international trade. For example, they ease the shipment of grain between a farmer in Iowa and a purchaser in New Orleans or the shipment of goods between a U.S. importer and a foreign exporter. The bank's role is to provide a formal guarantee that payment for goods shipped or sold will be forthcoming regardless of whether the buyer of the goods defaults on payment. We show a very simple LC example in Figure 12–2 for an international transaction between a U.S. importer and a German exporter.

Suppose that the U.S. importer sent an order for $10 million worth of machinery to a German exporter, as shown in step 1 of Figure 12–2. However, the German exporter may

FIGURE 12–2 **Simple Letter of Credit Transaction**

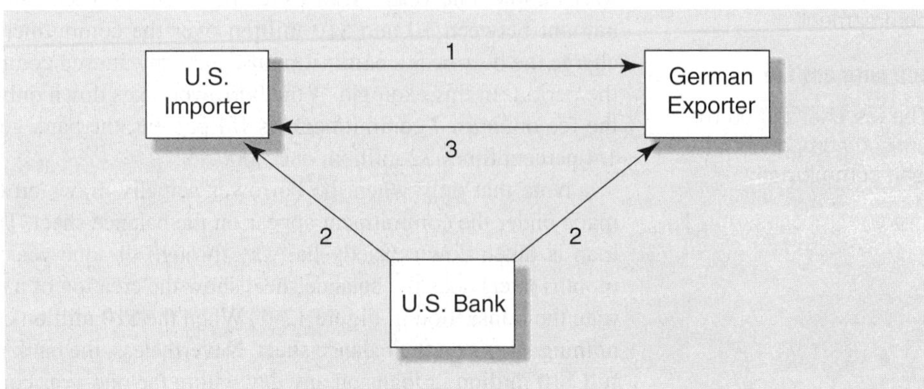

be reluctant to send the goods without some assurance or guarantee of being paid once the goods are shipped. The U.S. importer may promise to pay for the goods in 90 days, but the German exporter may feel insecure either because it knows little about the creditworthiness of the U.S. importer or because the U.S. importer has a low credit rating (i.e., B or BB). To persuade the German exporter to ship the goods, the U.S. importer may have to turn to a large U.S. bank with which it has developed a long-term customer relationship. In its role as a lender and monitor, the U.S. bank can better appraise the U.S. importer's creditworthiness. The U.S. bank can issue a contingent payment guarantee—that is, an LC to the German exporter on the importer's behalf—in return for an LC fee paid by the U.S. importer. In our example, the bank would send the German exporter an LC guaranteeing payment for the goods in 90 days regardless of whether the importer defaults on its obligation to the German exporter (step 2 in Figure 12–2). Implicitly, the bank is replacing the U.S. importer's credit risk with its own credit risk guarantee. For this substitution to work effectively, the bank, in guaranteeing payment, must have a higher credit standing or better credit quality reputation than the U.S. importer. Once the bank issues the LC and sends it to the German exporter, the exporter ships the goods to the U.S. importer (step 3 in Figure 12–2).[11] The probability is very high that in 90 days' time the U.S. importer will pay the German exporter for the goods sent and the bank keeps the LC fee as profit. The fee is perhaps 10 basis points of the face value of the letter of credit, or \$10,000 in this example.

A small probability exists, however, that the U.S. importer will be unable to pay the \$10 million in 90 days and will default. Then the bank is obliged to make good on its guarantee. The cost of such a default could mean that the bank must pay \$10 million, although it would have a creditor's claim against the importer's assets to offset this loss. Clearly, the fee should exceed the expected default risk on the LC, which equals the probability of default times the expected payout on the LC after adjusting for the bank's ability to reclaim assets from the defaulting importer and any monitoring costs.

Standby Letters of Credit. Standby letters of credit perform an insurance function similar to commercial and trade letters of credit. The structure and type of risk covered differ, however. FIs may issue SLCs to cover contingencies that are potentially more *severe,* less *predictable* or frequent, and not necessarily trade related. These contingencies include performance bond guarantees by which an FI may guarantee that a real estate development will be completed in some interval of time. Alternatively, the FI may offer default guarantees to back an issue of commercial paper or municipal revenue bonds to allow issuers to achieve a higher credit rating and a lower funding cost than otherwise.

Without credit enhancements, for example, many firms would be unable to borrow in the commercial paper market (see Chapter 5) or would have to borrow at a higher funding cost. P1 borrowers, who offer the highest quality commercial paper, normally pay 40 basis points less than P2 borrowers, the next quality grade. By paying a fee of perhaps 25 basis points to a bank, an FI guarantees to pay commercial paper purchasers' principal and interest on maturity should the issuing firm itself be unable to pay. The SLC backing of commercial paper issues normally results in the paper's placement in the lowest default risk class (P1) and the issuer's savings of up to 15 basis points on issuing costs—40 basis points (the P2 − P1 spread) minus the 25-basis-point SLC fee equals 15 basis points.

Note that in selling the SLCs, banks are competing directly with another of their OBS products, loan commitments. Rather than buying an SLC from a bank to back a commercial paper issue, the issuing firm might pay a fee to a bank to supply a loan commitment. This loan commitment would match the size and maturity of the commercial paper issue—for example, a \$100 million ceiling and 45-day maturity. If, on maturity, the commercial paper issuer had insufficient funds to repay the commercial paper holders, the issuer has the right to take down the \$100 million loan commitment and to use these funds

11. As discussed in Chapter 5, the German exporter may also receive a banker's acceptance written against the letter of credit.

to meet repayments on the commercial paper. Often, the up-front fees on such loan commitments are less than those on SLCs; therefore, many firms issuing commercial paper prefer to use loan commitments.

Finally, remember that U.S. banks are not the only issuers of SLCs. Not surprising, property-casualty insurers have an increasingly important business line of performance bonds and financial guarantees. The growth in these lines for property-casualty insurers has come at the expense of U.S. banks. Moreover, foreign banks increasingly are taking a share of the U.S. market in SLCs. The reason for the loss in this business line by U.S. banks is that to sell guarantees such as SLCs credibly, the seller must have a better credit rating than the customer. In recent years, few U.S. banks or their parent holding companies have had AA ratings or better. Other domestic FIs and foreign banks, on the other hand, have more often had AA ratings or better. High credit ratings not only make the guarantor more attractive from the buyer's perspective, but also make the guarantor more competitive because its cost of funds is lower than that of less creditworthy FIs.

loans sold

Loans originated by the bank and then sold to other investors that can be returned to the originating institution.

recourse

The ability to put an asset or loan back to the seller should the credit quality of that asset deteriorate.

Loans Sold. **Loans sold** (item 4 in Table 12–2) are loans that a bank originated and then sold to other investors that may be returned (sold with **recourse**) to the originating institution in the future if the credit quality of the loans deteriorates. We discuss the types of loans that banks sell, their incentives to sell, and the way in which they can sell them in more detail in Chapter 24. Banks and other FIs increasingly originate loans on their balance sheets, but rather than holding the loans to maturity, they quickly sell them to outside investors. These outside investors include other banks, insurance companies, mutual funds, or even corporations. In acting as loan originators and loan sellers, banks are operating more as loan brokers than as traditional asset transformers (see Chapters 1 and 11).

When an outside party buys a loan with absolutely no recourse to the seller of the loan should the loan eventually go bad, loan sales have no OBS contingent liability implications for banks. Specifically, *no recourse* means that if the loan the bank sells should go bad, the buyer of the loan must bear the full risk of loss. In particular, the buyer cannot go back to the seller or originating bank to seek payment on the bad loan. Suppose that the loan is sold with recourse. Then, loan sales present a long-term off-balance-sheet or contingent credit risk to the seller. Essentially, the buyer of the loan holds an option to put the loan back to the seller, which the buyer can exercise should the credit quality of the purchased loan materially deteriorate. In reality, the recourse or nonrecourse nature of loan sales is often ambiguous. For example, some have argued that banks generally are willing to repurchase bad no-recourse loans to preserve their reputations with their customers. Obviously, reputation concerns may extend the size of a selling bank's contingent liabilities from OBS activities.

derivative securities

Futures, forward, swap, and option positions taken by the FI for hedging or other purposes.

Derivative Contracts. **Derivative securities** (items 5 to 7 in Table 12–2) are the futures, forward, swap, and option positions taken by a bank for hedging and other purposes (see Chapters 10 and 23). We discussed the tremendous growth of derivative securities activity in Chapter 11. Banks can be either users of derivative contracts for hedging (see Chapter 10 and 23) and other purposes or dealers that act as counterparties in trades with customers for a fee. It has been estimated that some 600 U.S. banks use derivatives and that five large dealer banks—J.P. Morgan Chase, Bank of America, Citigroup, First Union, and Wells Fargo—account for some 95 percent of the derivatives that user banks hold.[12]

Contingent credit risk is likely to be present when banks expand their positions in futures, forward, swap, and option contracts. This risk relates to the fact that the counterparty to one of these contracts may default on payment obligations, leaving the bank unhedged and having to replace the contract at today's interest rates, prices, or exchange rates, which may be relatively unfavorable. In addition, such defaults are most likely to occur when the counterparty is losing heavily on the contract and the bank is in the money on the contract. This type of default risk is much more serious for forward contracts than for futures contracts. This is because forward contracts are nonstandard contracts entered into bilaterally by negotiating parties, such as two banks, and all cash flows are required to be paid at one

12. See OCC Bank Derivative Report, Third Quarter 2004 and Chapter 10.

time (on contract maturity). Thus, they are essentially over-the-counter (OTC) arrangements with no external guarantees should one or the other party default on the contract (see Chapter 10). By contrast, futures contracts are standardized contracts guaranteed by organized exchanges such as the New York Futures Exchange (NYFE). Futures contracts, like forward contracts, make commitments to deliver foreign exchange (or some other asset) at some future date. If a counterparty were to default on a futures contract, however, the exchange would assume the defaulting party's position and payment obligations.

Option contracts can also be traded over the counter (OTC) or bought/sold on organized exchanges. If the options are standardized options traded on exchanges, such as bond options, they are virtually default risk free.[13] If they are specialized options purchased OTC, such as interest rate caps (see Chapter 10), some elements of default risk exist.[14] Similarly, swaps are OTC instruments normally susceptible to default risk (see Chapter 10).[15] In general, default risk on OTC contracts increases with the time to maturity of the contract and the fluctuation of underlying prices, interest rates, or exchange rates.[16]

Other Fee-Generating Activities

Commercial banks engage in other fee-generating activities that cannot easily be identified from analyzing their on- and off-balance-sheet accounts. These include trust services, processing services, and correspondent banking.

Trust Services. The trust department of a commercial bank holds and manages assets for individuals or corporations. Only the largest banks have sufficient staff to offer trust services. Individual trusts represent about one-half of all trust assets managed by commercial banks. These trusts include estate assets and assets delegated to bank trust departments by less financially sophisticated investors. Pension fund assets are the second largest group of assets managed by the trust departments of commercial banks. The banks manage the pension funds, act as trustees for any bonds held by the pension funds, and act as transfer and disbursement agents for the pension funds.

Processing Services. Commercial banks have traditionally provided financial data processing services for their business customers. These services include managing a customer's accounts receivable and accounts payable. Similarly, bank cash management services include the provision of lockbox services where customers of a firm send payments to a post office box managed by a bank, which opens, processes, collects, and deposits checks within a very short time (sometimes as short as one hour) in the business customer's account. Banks also provide personalized services for both large and small companies, including moving funds from savings accounts that earn interest to transactions accounts that do not earn interest as firms need to make payments. The larger commercial banks have broadened their range of business services to include management consulting, data processing, and information systems or other technological services. Information systems and software marketed by commercial banks assist clients in collecting, analyzing, and reporting data effectively and efficiently.

Correspondent Banking. Correspondent banking is the provision of banking services to other banks that do not have the staff resources to perform the service themselves. These

13. Note that the options still can be subject to interest rate risk; see the discussion in Chapter 23.

14. Under an interest rate cap, the seller, in return for a fee, promises to compensate the buyer should interest rates rise above a certain level. If rates rise much more than expected, the cap seller may have an incentive to default to truncate the losses. Thus, selling a cap is similar to a bank's selling interest rate risk insurance (see Chapter 10 for more details).

15. In a swap, two parties contract to exchange interest rate payments or foreign exchange payments. If interest rates (or foreign exchange rates) move a good deal, one party can face considerable future loss exposure, creating incentives to default.

16. Reputational considerations and the need for future access to markets for hedging deter the incentive to default (see Chapter 23 as well). However, most empirical evidence suggests that derivative contracts have reduced FI risk. See for example, G. Gorton and R. Rosen, "Banks and Derivatives," University of Pennsylvania Wharton School, working paper, February 1995. Gorton and Rosen find that swap contracts have generally reduced the systematic risk of the U.S. banking system.

services include check clearing and collection, foreign exchange trading, hedging services, and participation in large loan and security issuances. Correspondent banking services are generally sold as a package of services. Payment for the services is generally in the form of noninterest bearing deposits held at the bank offering the correspondent services.

Income Statement

4 See Table 12–3 for the report of income or income statement for North Fork Bancorp and Bank of America for the 2004 calendar year. The report of income identifies the interest income and expenses, net interest income, provision for loan losses, noninterest income and expenses, income before taxes and extraordinary items, and net income for the *year* for the banks earned from the on- and off-balance-sheet activities described above. As we discuss the income statement, notice the direct relationship between it and the balance sheet (both on- and off-). The composition of an FI's assets and liabilities, combined with the interest rates earned or paid on them, directly determines the interest income and expense on the income statement. In addition, because the assets and liabilities of FIs are mainly financial, most of the income and expense items reported on the income statement are interest rate related (rather than reflecting sales prices and cost of goods sold, as seen with manufacturing corporations).

Interest Income. The income statement for a commercial bank first shows the sources of interest income (item 13). Interest and fee income on loans and leases (item 6 in Table 12–3) is the largest interest income-producing category. Subcategories are often listed on the income statement (items 1–4) for each category of loan listed earlier. Most banks also list income from leases (item 5) as a separate item. Interest from investment securities held (item 12) is also included as interest income. These too may be listed by subcategories (items 7–11) described earlier. Interest income is recorded on an accrued basis (see earlier discussion). Thus, loans on which interest payments are past due can still be recorded as generating income for a bank.[17] Interest income is taxable, except for that on municipal securities and tax-exempt income from direct lease financing. Tax-exempt interest can be converted to a taxable equivalent basis as follows:

$$\text{Taxable equivalent interest income} = \frac{\text{Interest income}}{1 - \text{Bank's tax rate}}$$

Interest Expenses. Interest expense (item 23) is the second major category on a bank's income statement. Items listed here come directly from the liability section of the balance sheet: interest on deposits (item 19) [NOW accounts (item 14), MMDAs and other savings (item 15), foreign deposits (item 16), retail CDs (item 17), and wholesale CDs (item 18)], and interest on fed funds (item 20), RPs (item 20), and other borrowed funds (item 21). Interest on subordinated notes and debentures (item 22) is generally reported as a separate item.

Net Interest Income. Total interest income minus total interest expense is listed next on the income statement as net interest income (item 24). Net interest income is an important tool in assessing the bank's ability to generate profits and control interest rate risk (see below).

Provision for Loan Losses. The provision for loan losses (item 25) is a noncash, tax-deductible expense. The provision for loan losses is the current period's allocation to the allowance for loan losses listed on the balance sheet. This item represents the bank management's prediction of loans at risk of default for the period. While the loans remain on the bank's balance sheet, the expected losses from any bad loans affect net income and equity on the income statement and balance sheet, respectively. As mentioned earlier, the size of the provision is determined by management, and in the United States it is subject to a maximum allowable tax deductible amount set by the Internal Revenue Service.

17. A bank can recognize income for at least 90 days after the due date of the interest payment.

TABLE 12-3 Income Statement for Two Commercial Banks for 2004
(in millions of dollars)

	North Fork Bancorp*	Bank of America*
Interest Income		
1. Income on C&I loans	$ 139.29	$ 5,815.84
2. Income on real estate loans	895.11	13,827.56
3. Income on consumer loans	93.51	8,284.55
4. Income on other loans	5.04	1,706.23
5. Income on leases	5.93	928.58
6. Interest and fees on loans and leases	$1,138.88	$30,562.76
7. Interest on deposits at other institutions	0.30	352.70
8. Interest on fed funds and RPs	10.27	866.91
9. Interest on U.S. Treasury and agency securities	6.41	8.18
10. Interest on mortgage-backed securities	354.87	6,748.01
11. Interest on municipals and other debt and equity securities	64.06	2,528.98
12. Interest income on investment securities	$ 435.91	$10,504.78
13. Total interest income	$1,574.79	$41,067.54
Interest Expense		
14. Interest on NOW accounts	17.33	103.69
15. Interest on MMDA accounts and other savings	98.97	1,942.78
16. Interest on foreign deposits	—	1,955.13
17. Interest on retail CDs	34.75	1,554.12
18. Interest on wholesale CDs	31.30	1,269.15
19. Interest on deposit accounts	$ 182.35	$ 6,824.87
20. Interest on fed funds and RPs	107.14	2,120.84
21. Interest on other borrowed funds	87.96	2,017.94
22. Interest on subordinated notes and debentures	1.99	275.96
23. Total interest expense	$379.44	$11,239.61
24. Net interest income	$1,195.35	$29,827.93
25. Provision for loan losses	27.19	3,555.41
Noninterest Income		
26. Income from fiduciary activities	3.32	1,004.52
27. Service charges on deposit accounts	100.02	6,706.28
28. Gains from trading assets and liabilities	61.59	3,541.11
29. Other noninterest income	70.59	8,718.82
30. Total noninterest income	$ 235.52	$19,970.73
Noninterest Expense		
31. Salaries and employee benefits	289.76	11,117.40
32. Expenses of premises and fixed assets	100.77	3,463.50
33. Other noninterest expense	145.15	9,980.09
34. Total noninterest expense	$ 535.68	$24,560.99
35. Income before taxes and extraordinary items	$ 868.00	$21,682.26
36. Applicable income taxes	304.57	6,885.90
37. Extraordinary items	—	—
38. Net income	$ 563.43	$14,796.36

*Values are taken from the 2004 FDIC Report of Condition data tapes available at the Federal Reserve Bank of Chicago Web site. **www.chicagofed.org**

EXAMPLE 12-1 The Relationship between Allowance for Loan Losses, Provision for Loan Losses, and Loan Balances

At the beginning of the month, a bank has $1 million in its loan portfolio and $50,000 in the allowance for loan losses (see Panel A of Figure 12–3). During the month, management estimates that an additional $5,000 of loans will not be paid as promised. Accordingly, the bank records an expense to loan loss provision (which reduces net income and thus retained earnings and equity of the bank) and increases the allowance for loan losses to $55,000 on the balance sheet (see Panel B in Figure 12–3). Notice that the loan is still listed as an asset on the bank's balance sheet at this time. After another month, management feels there is no chance of recovering on the loan and writes the $5,000 loan off its books. At this time, loans are reduced by $5,000 as is the allowance for loan losses (see Panel C in Figure 12–3). Notice when the loan is considered unrecoverable and actually removed from the balance sheet, there is no impact on the bank's income or equity value.

FIGURE 12–3 The Relationship between Allowance for Loan Losses, Provision for Loan Losses, and Loan Balances

Panel A: Beginning of Month 1

Assets		Liabilities and Equity	
Securities	$ 250,000	Deposits	$ 700,000
Gross Loans	1,000,000	Common Stock	200,000
Less: Allowance		Ret. Earnings	300,000
for Loan Losses	$50,000	Total Equity	500,000
Net Loans	$950,000	Total	$1,200,000
Total Assets	$1,200,000		

Panel B: End of Month 1

Assets		Liabilities and Equity	
Securities	$ 250,000	Deposits	$ 700,000
Gross Loans	1,000,000	Common Stock	200,000
Less: Allowance		Ret. Earnings	295,000
for Loan Losses	$55,000	Total Equity	495,000
Net Loans	$945,000	Total	$1,195,000
Total Assets	$1,195,000		

Panel A: End of Month 2

Assets		Liabilities and Equity	
Securities	$ 250,000	Deposits	$ 700,000
Gross Loans	995,000	Common Stock	200,000
Less: Allowance		Ret. Earnings	295,000
for Loan Losses	$50,000	Total Equity	495,000
Net Loans	$945,000	Total	$1,195,000
Total Assets	$1,195,000		

Noninterest Income. Noninterest income (item 30) includes all other income received by the bank as a result of its on- and off-balance-sheet activities and is becoming increasingly important as the ability to attract core deposits and high-quality loan applicants becomes more difficult. Included in this category is income from fiduciary activities (for example, earnings from operating a trust department—item 26), service charges on deposit accounts (generally the largest source of noninterest income—item 27), other gains (losses) and fees from trading assets and liabilities (from marketable instruments and OBS derivative instruments—item 28), and other noninterest income (fee income from OBS loan commitments and letters of credit, and revenue from one-time transactions such as sales of real estate owned, loans, premises, and fixed assets—item 29).

The sum of interest income and noninterest income is referred to as the bank's **total operating income** or *total revenue*. Total operating income for a bank is equivalent to total sales in a manufacturing firm and represents the bank's income received from all sources.

total operating income

The sum of the interest income and noninterest income.

Noninterest Expense. Noninterest expense (item 34) items consist mainly of personnel expenses and are generally large relative to noninterest income. Items in this category include salaries and employee benefits (item 31), expenses of premises and fixed assets (i.e., utilities, depreciation, and deposit insurance—item 32), and other (expenses of one-time transactions such as losses on sale of real estate, loans, and premises—item 33).

Income before Taxes and Extraordinary Items. Net interest income minus provisions for loan losses plus noninterest income minus noninterest expense produces the operating profit or income before taxes and extraordinary items for the bank (item 35).

Income Taxes. All federal, state, local, and foreign income taxes due from the bank are listed next on the income statement (item 36). Some of this amount may have been paid to the Internal Revenue Service (IRS) and the remainder is recorded as a liability (deferred taxes) to be paid to the IRS later.

Extraordinary Items. Extraordinary items and other adjustments (item 37) are events or transactions that are both unusual and infrequent. This includes such things as effects of changes in accounting rules, corrections of accounting errors made in previous years, and equity capital adjustments (losses from a major disaster such as an earthquake in an area where earthquakes are not expected to occur in the foreseeable future).

Net Income. Income before taxes and extraordinary items minus income taxes plus (or minus) extraordinary items results in the net income for the bank (item 38). Net income is the *bottom line* on the income statement.

Direct Relationship between the Income Statement and the Balance Sheet

As mentioned earlier, banks' financial statements are directly related (more so than for nonfinancial companies). That is, the items on the income statement are determined by the balance sheet assets and liabilities along with the interest rates on each item. This direct relationship between the two financial statements can be seen by depicting the income statement as follows:

$$NI = \sum_{n=1}^{N} r_n A_n - \sum_{m=1}^{M} r_m L_m - P + NII - NIE - T$$

DO YOU UNDERSTAND?

1. The difference between a wholesale bank and a retail bank?
2. What the trade-offs are in holding a large proportion of short-term securities, such as T-bills, versus long-term securities, such as loans?
3. What the trade-offs are in issuing short-term deposit accounts such as demand deposits and retail CDs, versus long-term deposits and other funding sources, such as wholesale CDs and long-term debt?
4. What the major difference is between a commercial letter of credit and a standby letter of credit?
5. What counterparty risk in a forward contract means?
6. Which is riskier for a bank, loan sales with recourse or loan sales without recourse?
7. What the nature of the relationship is between balance sheet and income statement items?
8. How paying a lower rate for new deposits than for other liabilities impacts a bank's income statement?

where

NI = Bank's net income
A_n = Dollar value of the bank's nth asset
L_m = Dollar value of the bank's mth liability
r_n = Rate earned on the bank's nth asset
r_m = Rate paid on the bank's mth liability
P = Provision for loan losses
NII = Noninterest income earned by the bank, including income from off-balance-sheet activities
NIE = Noninterest expenses incurred by the bank
T = Bank's taxes and extraordinary items
N = Number of assets the bank holds
M = Number of liabilities the bank holds

Net income is the direct result of (1) the amount and mix of assets and liabilities held by the bank taken from the balance sheet and (2) the interest rate on each of them. For example, increasing the dollar value of an asset, all else constant, results in a direct increase in the bank's net income equal to the size of the increase times the rate of interest on the asset. Likewise, decreasing the rate paid on a liability, all else constant, directly increases net income by the size of the rate decrease times the dollar value of the liability on the balance sheet. Finally, changing the mix of assets or liabilities on the balance sheet has a direct effect on net income equal to the size of the rate difference times the dollar value of the asset or liability being changed. For example, suppose that a bank replaces \$100,000 of assets currently yielding 8 percent with assets yielding 10 percent. Net income increases by \$2,000 ((10% − 8%) × \$100,000).

FINANCIAL STATEMENT ANALYSIS USING A RETURN ON EQUITY FRAMEWORK

time series analysis

Analysis of financial statements over a period of time.

cross-sectional analysis

Analysis of financial statements comparing one firm with others.

www.ffiec.gov/UBPR.htm

In recent years, the commercial banking industry has experienced a period of record profits, quite a change from the late 1980s and early 1990s, when banks were failing in record numbers. Despite record profits, many banks have weak and inefficient areas that still need to be addressed. One way to identify weaknesses and problem areas is by analyzing financial statements. In particular, an analysis of selected accounting ratios—ratio analysis—allows a bank manager to evaluate the bank's current performance, the change in its performance over time (**time series analysis** of ratios over a period of time), and its performance relative to that of competitor banks (**cross-sectional analysis** of ratios across a group of firms). A tool available to assist in cross-sectional analysis is the Uniform Bank Performance Report (UBPR) maintained by the Federal Financial Institutions Examination Council. The UBPR summarizes performance of banks for various peer groups (banks similar in size and economic environment), for various size groups, and by state.

Figure 12–4 summarizes the return on equity (ROE) framework.[18] The ROE framework starts with the most frequently used measure of profitability, ROE, and then breaks it down to identify strengths and weaknesses in a bank's performance. The resulting breakdown provides a convenient and systematic method to identify strengths and weaknesses of a bank's profitability. Identification of strengths and weaknesses, and the reasons for them, provides an excellent tool for bank managers as they look for ways to improve profitability. Table 12–4 summarizes the role of ROE and the first two levels of the ROE framework (from Figure 12–4) in analyzing an FI's performance.

The remainder of this chapter applies the ROE framework to our two banks: North Fork Bancorp and Bank of America. All of the ratios discussed as part of the ROE breakdown are

18. The ROE framework is similar to the DuPont analysis that managers of nonfinancial institutions frequently use.

FIGURE 12–4 Classification of Ratios Listed in Tables 12-5 through 12-7

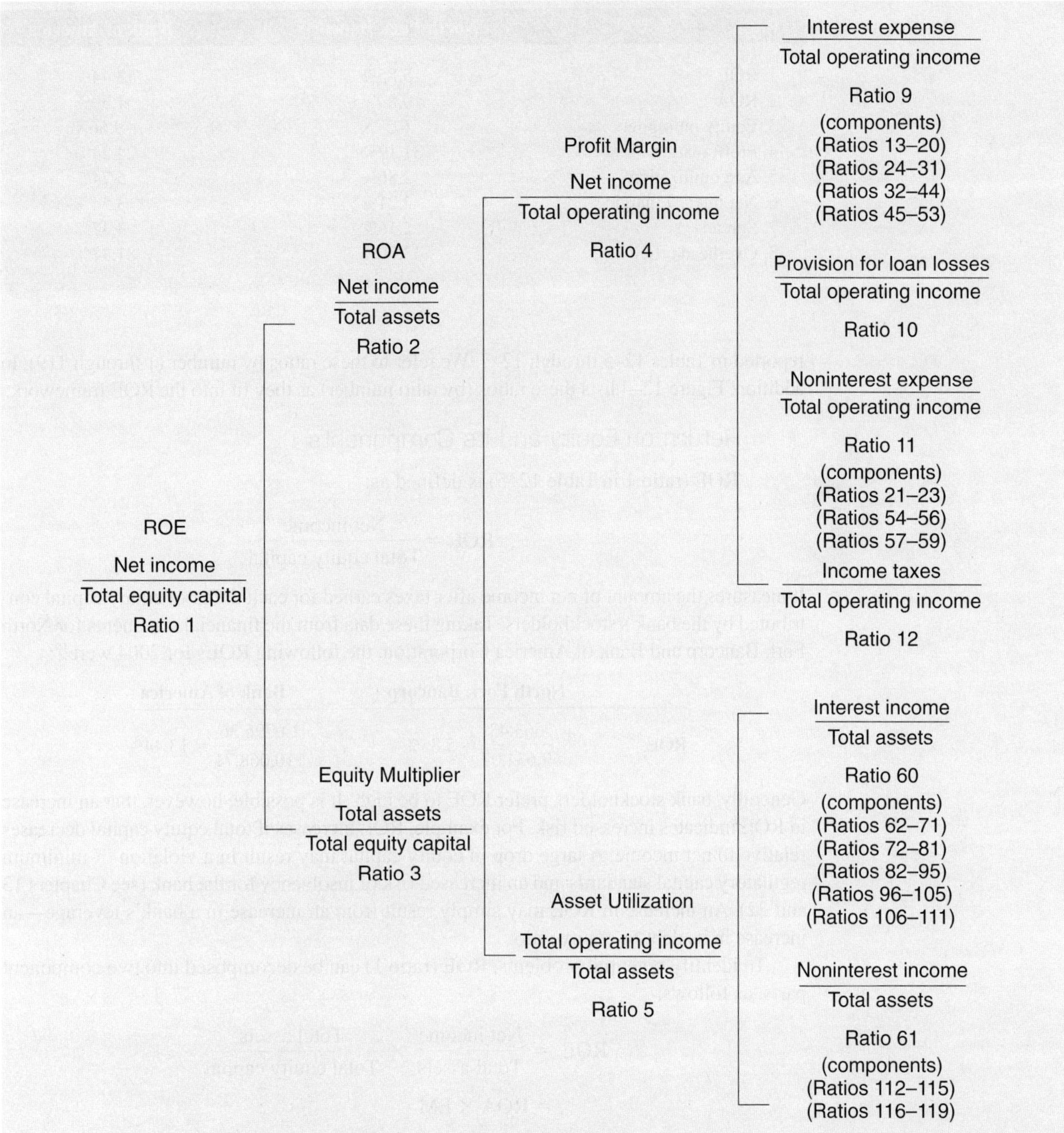

TABLE 12–4 Role of ROE, ROA, EM, PM, and AU in Analyzing Financial Institution Performance

Return on Equity (ROE)—measures overall profitability of the FI per dollar of equity.

Return on Assets (ROA)—measures profit generated relative to the FI's assets.

Equity Multiplier (EM)—measures the extent to which assets of the FI are funded with equity relative to debt.

Profit Margin (PM)—measures the ability to pay expenses and generate net income from interest and noninterest income.

Asset Utilization (AU)—measures the amount of interest and noninterest income generated per dollar of total assets.

TABLE 12–5 Overall Performance Ratios for Two Commercial Banks for 2004

Ratio	North Fork Bancorp	Bank of America
1. ROE	5.85%	13.44%
2. ROA	0.89%	1.39%
3. Equity multiplier	6.57X	9.66X
4. Profit margin	31.12%	24.24%
5. Asset utilization	2.86%	5.74%
6. Net interest margin	2.21%	3.54%
7. Spread	2.16%	3.47%
8. Overhead efficiency	43.96%	81.31%

reported in Tables 12–5 through 12–7. We refer to these ratios by number (1 through 119). In addition, Figure 12–4 lists these ratios (by ratio number) as they fit into the ROE framework.

5

Return on Equity and Its Components

ROE (ratio 1 in Table 12–5) is defined as:

$$\text{ROE} = \frac{\text{Net income}}{\text{Total equity capital}}$$

It measures the amount of net income after taxes earned for each dollar of equity capital contributed by the bank's stockholders. Taking these data from the financial statements for North Fork Bancorp and Bank of America Corporation, the following ROEs for 2004 were[19]:

	North Fork Bancorp	Bank of America
ROE	$\frac{563.43}{9{,}634.07} = 5.85\%$	$\frac{14{,}796.36}{110{,}068.71} = 13.44\%$

Generally, bank stockholders prefer ROE to be high. It is possible, however, that an increase in ROE indicates increased risk. For example, ROE increases if total equity capital decreases relative to net income. A large drop in equity capital may result in a violation of minimum regulatory capital standards and an increased risk of insolvency for the bank (see Chapters 13 and 22). An increase in ROE may simply result from an increase in a bank's leverage—an increase in its debt-to-equity ratio.

To identify potential problems, ROE (ratio 1) can be decomposed into two component parts, as follows:

$$\text{ROE} = \frac{\text{Net income}}{\text{Total assets}} \times \frac{\text{Total assets}}{\text{Total equity capital}}$$

$$= \text{ROA} \times \text{EM}$$

where

ROA (ratio 2) = Return on assets (a measure of profitability linked to the asset size of the bank)

EM (ratio 3) = Equity multiplier (a measure of leverage)

ROA determines the net income produced per dollar of assets; EM measures the dollar value of assets funded with each dollar of equity capital (the higher this ratio, the more leverage or debt the bank is using to fund its assets). The values of these ratios for our two banks in 2004 were:

19. We are using year-end balance sheet data to calculate ratios. The use of these data may bias ratios in that they are data for one day in the year, whereas income statement data cover the full year. To avoid this bias, average values for balance sheet data are often used to calculate ratios.

	North Fork Bancorp	Bank of America
ROA	$\frac{563.43}{63,292.41} = 0.89\%$	$\frac{14,796.36}{1,063,744.22} = 1.39\%$
EM	$\frac{63,292.41}{9,634.07} = 6.57$ times	$\frac{1,063,744.22}{110,068.71} = 9.66$ times

High values for these ratios produce high ROEs, but, as noted, managers should be concerned about the source of high ROEs. For example, an increase in ROE due to an increase in the EM means that the bank's leverage, and therefore its solvency risk, has increased.

Return on Assets and Its Components

A further breakdown of a bank's profitability is that of dividing ROA (ratio 2 in Table 12–5) into its profit margin (PM) and asset utilization (AU) ratio components:

$$\text{ROA} = \frac{\text{Net income}}{\text{Total operating income}} \times \frac{\text{Total operating income}}{\text{Total assets}}$$

$$= \text{PM} \times \text{AU}$$

where

PM (ratio 4) = Net income generated per dollar of total operating (interest and noninterest) income

AU (ratio 5) = Amount of interest and noninterest income generated per dollar of total assets

For our two banks, these are as follows:

	North Fork Bancorp	Bank of America
PM	$\frac{563.43}{1,574.79 + 235.52} = 31.12\%$	$\frac{14,793.36}{41,067.54 + 19,970.73} = 24.24\%$
AU	$\frac{1,574.79 + 235.52}{63,292.41} = 2.86\%$	$\frac{41,067.54 + 19,970.73}{1,063,744.22} = 5.74\%$

Again, high values for these ratios produce high ROAs and ROEs. PM measures the bank's ability to control expenses. The better the expense control, the more profitable the bank. AU measures the bank's ability to generate income from its assets. The more income generated per dollar of assets, the more profitable the bank. Again, bank managers should be aware that high values of these ratios may indicate underlying problems. For example, PM increases if the bank experiences a drop in salaries and benefits. However, if this expense decreases because the most highly skilled employees are leaving the bank, the increase in PM and in ROA is associated with a potential "labor quality" problem. Thus, it is often prudent to break these ratios down further.

Profit Margin. As stated, PM measures a bank's ability to control expenses and thus its ability to produce net income from its operating income (or revenue). A breakdown of PM, therefore, can isolate the various expense items listed on the income statement as follows: (ratios used to decompose the profit margin are listed in Table 12–6)

$$\text{Interest expense ratio (ratio 9)} = \frac{\text{Interest expense}}{\text{Total operating income}}$$

$$\text{Provision for loan loss ratio (ratio 10)} = \frac{\text{Provision for loan losses}}{\text{Total operating income}}$$

$$\text{Noninterest expense ratio (ratio 11)} = \frac{\text{Noninterest expense}}{\text{Total operating income}}$$

$$\text{Tax ratio (ratio 12)} = \frac{\text{Income taxes}}{\text{Total operating income}}$$

SEARCH THE SITE

Go to the Bank of America's Web site at **www.bankofamerica.com.** Find the most recent Balance Sheet and Income Statement from the Annual Report using the following steps.

Click on "About Bank of America"

Under "Shareholders," click on "Annual Report"

Click on the most recent date for "20XX Annual Report"

This will download the most recent Annual Report to your computer. Go to the pages containing the Consolidated Balance Sheet and Consolidated Income Statement.

Questions

1. What is the most recent value of Total Assets for Bank of America? How has this changed since 2004 as reported in Table 12–1?
2. What is the most recent value of Net Income for Bank of America? How has this changed since 2004 as reported in Table 12–3?
3. From the most recent Balance Sheet and Income Statement, calculate the most recent ROA, ROE, Equity Multiplier, Profit Margin, and Asset Utilization Ratios. Which ratio has changed the most since 2004 as reported in Table 12–5?

These ratios measure the proportion of total operating income that goes to pay the particular expense item. The values of these ratios for North Fork Bancorp and Bank of America are as follows:

	North Fork Bancorp	Bank of America
Interest expense ratio	$\frac{379.44}{1{,}574.79 + 235.52} = 20.96\%$	$\frac{11{,}239.61}{41{,}067.54 + 19{,}970.73} = 18.41\%$
Provision for loan loss ratio	$\frac{27.19}{1{,}574.79 + 235.52} = 1.50\%$	$\frac{3{,}555.41}{41{,}067.54 + 19{,}970.73} = 5.82\%$
Noninterest expense ratio	$\frac{535.68}{1{,}574.79 + 235.52} = 29.59\%$	$\frac{24{,}560.99}{41{,}067.54 + 19{,}970.73} = 40.24\%$
Tax ratio	$\frac{304.57}{1{,}574.79 + 235.52} = 16.82\%$	$\frac{6{,}885.90}{41{,}067.54 + 19{,}970.73} = 11.28\%$

The sum of the numerators of these four ratios subtracted from the denominator (total operating income) is the bank's net income.[20] Thus, the lower any of these ratios, the higher the bank's profitability (PM). As mentioned, however, although a low value for any of these ratios produces an increase in the bank's profit, it may be indicative of a problem situation in the bank. Thus, an even more detailed breakdown of these ratios may be warranted. For example, the interest expense ratio can be broken down according to the various interest expense-generating liabilities (ratios 13–20 in Table 12–6; e.g., interest on NOW accounts/total operating income). Additionally, the noninterest expense ratio may be broken down according to its components (ratios 21–23—e.g., salaries and benefits/total operating income). These ratios allow for a more detailed examination of the generation of the bank's expenses.

20. For example, for Bank of America, the denominator of each of the four ratios ($41,067.54 + $19.970.73 = $61,038.27) less the sum of the numerators of the four ratios ($11,239.61 + $3,555.41 + $24,560.99 + $6,885.90 = $46,241.92) is $14,796.36, which is the net income reported for Bank of America in Table 12–3.

TABLE 12-6 Decomposition of Profit Margin for Two Commercial Banks for 2004

Ratio	North Fork Bancorp	Bank of America
Profit Margin Components		
9. Interest expense ratio	20.96%	18.41%
10. Provision for loan loss ratio	1.50	5.82
11. Noninterest expense ratio	29.59	40.24
12. Tax ratio	16.82	11.28
Interest Expenses as a Percentage of Total Operating Income		
13. NOW accounts	0.96%	0.17%
14. MMDAs and other savings	5.47	3.18
15. Foreign deposits	0.00	3.20
16. Retail CDs	1.92	2.55
17. Wholesale CDs	1.73	2.08
18. Fed funds and RPs	5.92	3.47
19. Other borrowed funds	4.86	3.31
20. Subordinated notes and debentures	0.11	0.45
Noninterest Expense as a Percentage of Total Operating Income		
21. Salaries and employee benefits	16.01%	18.21%
22. Expenses of premises and fixed assets	5.57	5.67
23. Other noninterest expenses	8.02	16.35
Liability Yields		
24. NOW accounts	3.05%	0.68%
25. MMDAs and other savings	0.79	0.80
26. Foreign deposits	–	1.78
27. Retail CDs	0.70	2.36
28. Wholesale CDs	1.24	2.16
29. Fed funds and RPs	0.81	1.99
30. Other borrowed funds	1.77	2.35
31. Subordinated notes and debentures	1.08	2.21
Liability Accounts as a Percentage of Total Assets		
32. Demand deposits	3.84%	7.16%
33. NOW accounts	0.90	1.43
34. MMDAs	19.90	22.89
35. Other savings	17.85	9.94
36. Foreign deposits	0.00	10.35
37. Retail CDs	7.82	6.20
38. Core deposits	50.30	57.97
39. Wholesale CDs	3.99	5.52
40. Fed funds and RPs	21.00	10.03
41. Other borrowed funds	7.86	8.06
42. Subordinated notes and debentures	0.29	1.18
43. Purchased funds	33.14	24.79
44. Other liabilities	1.33	6.89
Liability Items as a Percentage of Interest-Bearing Liabilities		
45. NOW accounts	1.13%	1.90%
46. MMDAs	24.99	30.27
47. Other savings	22.42	13.15
48. Foreign deposits	0.00	13.69
49. Retail CDs	9.83	8.20
50. Wholesale CDs	5.01	7.30
51. Fed funds and RPs	26.38	13.27
52. Other borrowed funds	9.87	10.66
53. Subordinated notes and debentures	0.37	1.55
Noninterest Expense as a Percentage of Noninterest Income		
54. Salaries and employee benefits	123.04%	55.67%
55. Expenses of premises and equipment	42.79	17.34
56. Other noninterest income	61.63	49.97
Noninterest Expense as a Percentage of Total Assets		
57. Salaries and employee benefits	0.46%	1.05%
58. Expenses of premises and equipment	0.16	0.33
59. Other noninterest income	0.23	0.94

A different method to evaluate the bank's expense management is to calculate such ratios as deposit yields (ratios 24–31; e.g., interest expense on NOW accounts/dollar value of NOW accounts) or size of investment (e.g., dollar value of NOW accounts/total assets—ratios 32–44—or dollar value of NOW accounts/total interest-bearing liabilities—ratios 45–53). The noninterest expense items can be evaluated using component percentages (ratios 54–56; e.g., salaries and benefits/noninterest income) or size of expense (ratios 57–59; e.g., salaries and benefits/total assets).

Asset Utilization. The AU ratio measures the extent to which the bank's assets generate revenue. The breakdown of the AU ratio separates the total revenue generated into interest income and noninterest income as follows (ratios used to decompose asset utilization are listed in Table 12–7):

$$\text{Asset utilization ratio} = \frac{\text{Total operating income}}{\text{Total assets}} = \begin{matrix}\text{Interest}\\ \text{income ratio}\end{matrix} + \begin{matrix}\text{Noninterest}\\ \text{income ratio}\end{matrix}$$

where

$$\text{Interest income ratio (ratio 60)} = \frac{\text{Interest income}}{\text{Total assets}}$$

$$\text{Noninterest income ratio (ratio 61)} = \frac{\text{Noninterest income}}{\text{Total assets}}$$

which measure the bank's ability to generate interest income and noninterest income, respectively. For the banks represented in Tables 12–1 and 12–3, the values of these ratios are as follows:

	North Fork Bancorp	Bank of America
Interest income ratio	$\frac{1,574.79}{63,292.41} = 2.49\%$	$\frac{41,067.54}{1,063,744.22} = 3.86\%$
Noninterest income ratio	$\frac{235.52}{63,292.41} = 0.37\%$	$\frac{19,970.73}{1,063,744.22} = 1.88\%$

The interest income and noninterest income ratios are not necessarily independent. For example, the bank's ability to generate loans affects both interest income and, through fees and service charges, noninterest income. High values for these ratios signify the efficient use of bank resources to generate income and are thus generally positive for the bank. But some problematic situations that result in high ratio values could exist; for example, a bank that replaces low-risk, low-return loans with high-risk, high-return loans will experience an increase in its interest income ratio. However, high-risk loans have a higher default probability, which could result in the ultimate loss of both interest and principal payments. Further breakdown of these ratios is therefore a valuable tool in the financial performance evaluation process.

The interest income ratio can be broken down using the various components of interest income (ratios 62–71; e.g., income on C&I loans/total assets); or by using asset yields (ratios 72–81; e.g., income on C&I loans/dollar value of C&I loans); or by using size of investment (e.g., dollar value of C&I loans/total assets—ratios 82–95—or dollar value of C&I loans/total earning assets—ratios 96–105). Off-balance-sheet activities can also be measured in terms of the size of the notional values they create in relation to bank assets (ratios 106–111—e.g., loan commitments/total assets). The noninterest income ratio can also be subdivided into the various subcategories (e.g., income from fiduciary activities/total assets—ratios 112–115—or income from fiduciary activities/noninterest income—ratios 116–119).

Other Ratios

A number of other profit measures are commonly used to evaluate bank performance. Three of these are (1) the net interest margin, (2) the spread (ratio), and (3) overhead efficiency.

TABLE 12–7 Decomposition of Asset Utilization for Two Commercial Banks for 2004

Ratio	North Fork Bancorp	Bank of America
Asset Utilization Breakdown		
60. Interest income ratio	2.49%	3.86%
61. Noninterest income ratio	0.37	1.88
Interest Income as a Percentage Total Assets		
62. C&I loans	0.22%	0.55%
63. Real estate loans	1.41	1.30
64. Consumer loans	0.15	0.78
65. Other loans	0.01	0.16
66. Leases	0.01	0.09
67. Deposits at other institutions	0.00	0.03
68. Fed funds and RPs	0.02	0.08
69. U.S. Treasury and agencies	0.01	0.00
70. Mortgage-backed securities	0.56	0.63
71. Municipals and other debt and equity securities	0.10	0.24
Asset Yields		
72. C&I loans	5.08%	6.22%
73. Real estate loans	2.82	4.62
74. Consumer loans	6.10	8.36
75. Other loans	2.14	3.26
76. Leases	4.11	4.71
77. Deposits at other institutions	0.49	1.85
78. Fed funds and RPs	0.38	1.18
79. U.S. Treasury and agencies	0.94	2.43
80. Mortgage-backed securities	2.80	3.91
81. Municipals and other debt and equity securities	3.58	11.21
Asset Items as a Percentage of Total Assets		
82. Cash and balances due from institutions	1.59%	2.29%
83. C&I loans	4.33	8.79
84. Real estate loans	50.11	28.11
85. Consumer loans	2.42	9.31
86. Other loans	0.37	4.92
87. Leases	0.23	1.85
88. Net loans and leases	57.07	52.14
89. Deposits at other institutions	0.36	–0.18
90. Fed funds and RPs	4.22	6.92
91. U.S. Treasury and agencies	1.08	0.03
92. Mortgage-backed securities	20.02	16.23
93. Municipals and other debt and equity securities	2.82	2.12
94. Total investment securities	28.24	27.10
95. Other assets	13.09	18.47
Asset Items as a Percentage of Earning Assets		
96. C&I loans	5.08%	11.10%
97. Real estate loans	58.73	35.48
98. Consumer loans	2.84	11.75
99. Other loans	0.44	6.21
100. Leases	0.27	2.34
101. Deposits at other institutions	0.42	–0.23
102. Fed funds and RPs	4.94	8.73
103. U.S. Treasury and agencies	1.27	0.04
104. Mortgage-backed securities	23.47	20.49
105. Municipals and other debt and equity securities	3.31	2.68

TABLE 12–7 Decomposition of Asset Utilization for Two Commercial Banks for 2004 (continued)

Ratio	North Fork Bancorp	Bank of America
Off-Balance-Sheet Items as a Percentage of Total Assets		
106. Loan commitments	9.43%	53.83%
107. Commercial letters of credit	0.03	0.55
108. Standby letters of credit	0.54	6.11
109. Loans sold	0.00	0.04
110. Derivative securities	11.47	1596.29
111. Total off-balance-sheet items	21.46	1656.82
Noninterest Income as a Percentage of Total Assets		
112. Fiduciary accounts	0.01%	0.09%
113. Service charges	0.16	0.63
114. Trading gains	0.10	0.33
115. Other noninterest income	0.11	0.82
Noninterest Income as a Percentage of Total Noninterest Income		
116. Fiduciary accounts	1.41%	5.03%
117. Service charges	42.47	33.58
118. Trading gains	26.15	17.73
119. Other noninterest income	29.97	43.66

net interest margin

Interest income minus interest expense divided by earning assets.

Net Interest Margin. **Net interest margin** (ratio 6 in Table 12–5) measures the net return on the bank's earning assets (investment securities and loans and leases) and is defined as follows:

$$\text{Net interest margin} = \frac{\text{Net interest income}}{\text{Earning assets}} = \frac{\text{Interest income} - \text{Interest expense}}{\text{Investments securities} + \text{Net loans and leases}}$$

Generally, the higher this ratio, the better. Suppose, however, that a preceding scenario (replacement of low-risk, low-return loans with high-risk, high-return loans) is the reason for the increase. This situation can increase risk for the bank. It highlights the fact that looking at returns without looking at risk can be misleading and potentially dangerous in terms of bank solvency and long-run profitability.

spread

The difference between lending and borrowing rates.

The Spread. The **spread** (ratio 7) measures the difference between the average yield on earning assets and average cost of interest-bearing liabilities and is thus another measure of return on the bank's assets. The spread is defined as:

$$\text{Spread} = \frac{\text{Interest income}}{\text{Earning assets}} - \frac{\text{Interest expense}}{\text{Interest-bearing liabilities}}$$

DO YOU UNDERSTAND?

1. Two scenarios in which a high value of ROE may signal a risk problem for a bank?
2. What ratios ROA can be broken down into?
3. What the *spread* measure means?

The higher the spread, the more profitable the bank, but again, the source of a high spread and the potential risk implications should be considered.

Overhead Efficiency. **Overhead efficiency** (ratio 8) measures the bank's ability to generate noninterest income to cover noninterest expenses. It is represented as:

$$\text{Overhead efficiency} = \frac{\text{Noninterest income}}{\text{Noninterest expense}}$$

overhead efficiency

A bank's ability to generate noninterest income to cover noninterest expense.

In general, the higher this ratio, the better. However, because of the high levels of noninterest expense relative to noninterest income, overhead efficiency is rarely higher than 1 (or in percentage terms, than 100 percent). Further, low operating expenses (and thus low noninterest expenses) can also indicate increased risk if the institution is not investing in the most efficient technology or its back office systems are poorly supported. The values of these ratios for the two banks are as follows:

	North Fork Bancorp	Bank of America
Net interest margin	$\frac{1,195.35}{17,873.25 + 36,127.77} = 2.21\%$	$\frac{29,827.93}{288,292.95 + 554,641.38} = 3.54\%$
Spread	$\frac{1,574.79}{53,997.02} - \frac{379.44}{50,388.29} = 2.16\%$	$\frac{41,067.54}{842,934.33} - \frac{11,239.61}{804,185.77} = 3.47\%$
Overhead efficiency	$\frac{235.52}{535.68} = 43.96\%$	$\frac{19,970.73}{24,560.97} = 81.31\%$

IMPACT OF MARKET NICHE AND BANK SIZE ON FINANCIAL STATEMENT ANALYSIS

Impact of a Bank's Market Niche

As mentioned earlier, in 2004, North Fork Bancorp was a profitable and efficient bank that specialized in real estate loans and low-cost funding methods. Bank of America, on the other hand, operated with a larger and more balanced portfolio of assets and liabilities across both wholesale and retail banking. Keeping the more specialized market niche of North Fork Bancorp in mind, let us make a comparative financial analysis using the ROE framework and the banks' 2004 financial statements.

ROE and Its Components. As stated, the ROE (ratio 1) of 5.85 percent for North Fork Bancorp (NFB) was lower than the 13.44 percent ROE reported for Bank of America (BOA). The breakdown of ROE indicates that NFB's lower profitability was due to its ROA of 0.89 percent compared with that of 1.39 percent for BOA (ratio 2). Further, NFB's equity multiplier or leverage (ratio 3) was lower than that of BOA. NFB's EM of 6.57X translated to an equity-to-asset ratio (= 1/EM) of 15.22 percent, and BOA's EM of 9.66X translated to an equity-to-asset ratio of 10.35 percent. Thus, although both banks appeared to be well capitalized, NFB had more equity. (As we see in the next section, these may be attributed to differences in bank size as well as market niche.)

The more focused orientation of NFB relative to BOA can best be seen by looking at the composition of the asset, and particularly the loan, portfolios (ratios 82 through 95) and the liabilities (ratios 32 through 44) of the two banks. NFB held 50.11 percent of its total assets in the form of real estate loans and 20.02 percent in mortgage-backed securities. Thus, consistent with its niche, a large majority of NFB's assets were tied up in real estate–related assets. BOA, on the other hand, had its asset investments more evenly distributed: 8.79 percent in C&I loans, 28.11 percent in real estate loans, 9.31 percent in consumer loans, and 16.23 percent in mortgage-backed securities.

On the liability side of the balance sheet, NFB issued mainly retail-oriented deposits: MMDAs were 19.90 percent of total assets, other savings were 17.85 percent, and retail CDs were 7.82 percent. BOA again used a broader array of deposits: demand deposits were 7.16 percent, MMDAs were 22.89 percent, other savings were 9.94 percent, foreign deposits were 10.35 percent, and retail CDs were 6.20 percent of total assets. Further, NFB was paying less on its major liabilities relative to BOA (ratios 24–31), particularly those they were using heavily (MMDAs and other savings, retail CDs, and wholesale CDs). MMDAs and other savings at NFB yielded 0.79 in 2004 compared to 0.80 percent at BOA; retail CDs yielded 0.70 percent at NFB and 2.36 percent at BOA; and wholesale CDs yielded 1.24 percent at NFB and 2.16 percent at BOA.

Clearly, NFB has decided to specialize its services in the retail area, while BOA offered the broader spectrum of financial services.

Impact of Size on Financial Statement Analysis

Bank size has traditionally affected the financial ratios of commercial banks, resulting in significant differences across size groups. Large banks' relatively easy access to purchased funds and capital markets compared to small banks' access is a reason for many of these differences. For example, large banks with easier access to capital markets operate with lower amounts of equity capital than do small banks. Also, large banks tend to use more purchased funds (such as fed funds and RPs) and fewer core deposits than do small banks. Large banks tend to put more into salaries, premises, and other expenses than small banks do, and they tend to diversify their operations and services more than small banks do. Large banks also generate more noninterest income (i.e., trading account, derivative security, and foreign trading income) than small banks do and when risky loans pay off, they earn more interest income. As a result, although large banks tend to hold less equity than small banks do, large banks do not necessarily return more on their assets. A study by the Federal Reserve Bank of St. Louis[21] reported that ROA consistently increased for banks grouped by size up to $15 billion in total assets but decreased for banks with more than $15 billion.

Examining ratios for the relatively large Bank of America (BOA) compared to the smaller NFB, we see only some of these size-related effects on accounting ratios. Looking at ROA (ratio 2), BOA is the more profitable overall of the two banks. Notice that BOA is producing the lower income per dollar of total operating income (ratio 4; PM for BOA = 24.24 percent and for NFB = 31.12 percent), but is producing much more operating income per dollar of assets (AU for BOA = 5.74 percent and for NFB = 2.86 percent). The generation of total operating income in the form of interest income (ratio 60) is larger for BOA (interest income ratio for BOA = 3.86 percent and for NFB = 2.49 percent). We do see that, BOA generates much more noninterest income (1.88 percent of total assets) than NFB (0.37 percent of total assets; see ratio 61). This is likely due to BOA's relatively large amount of OBS activities (which is typical of large banks compared with small banks). Indeed, the notional or face value of BOA's off-balance-sheet activities is 1,656.82 percent of its assets on balance sheet compared to NFB's 21.46 percent (see ratios 106 through 111). Notice, too, that BOA's other assets (ratio 95) is 18.47 percent of total assets, compared with 13.09 percent for NFB, and the addition of ratios 21 through 23 indicates that noninterest expenses are much higher for BOA (40.23 percent of total operating income) than for NFB (29.60 percent). Finally, notice that BOA is financing its assets with less equity than NFB. The equity multiplier (ratio 3) for BOA, 9.66X, translates to an equity ratio of 10.35 percent, while that for NFB, 6.57X, translates to an equity ratio of 15.22 percent. Characteristically, because of the size-related differences across the two banks, BOA's ROE (ratio 1) is greater than that of NFB. Further, BOA is using slightly more core deposit and slightly less purchased funds to total assets than NFB (see ratios 38 and 43).

DO YOU UNDERSTAND?

1. How a bank's choice of market niche affects its financial ratios?
2. How a bank's asset size affects its financial ratios?

21. See D. C. Wheelock, "A Changing Relationship between Bank Size and Profitability," in *Monetary Trends,* Federal Reserve Bank of St. Louis, September 1996, p. 1.

SUMMARY

This chapter analyzed the financial statements of commercial banks. The assets, liabilities, and equity capital were described as they appear in the balance sheet. The financial statements of other FIs such as savings banks and credit unions take a similar form. The income and expenses were described as they appear in the income statement. From the items on the financial statements, the profitability of two banks was analyzed using a return on equity (ROE) framework. What might appear as a favorable sign of profitability and performance can sometimes, in fact, indicate risk problems that management should address. Many problems and areas of managerial concern can be identified by performing a detailed breakdown of the financial ratios of banks. Thus, both profitability and risk management are interlinked and should be of concern to managers. The various risks to which FIs are exposed are examined in more detail in the next several chapters.

SEARCH THE SITE

Go to the FDIC Web site at **www.fdic.gov**. Find the total amount of deposits and assets for Wells Fargo and Wachovia using the following steps.

Click on "Analysts."

Click on "Summary of Deposits."

Click on "Find Office."

Enter "Wells Fargo" under Institution Name and click on "Continue."

This will bring up a file that contains the relevant data. Repeat again for Wachovia.

Questions

1. What is the dollar value of total deposits and total assets for each bank?
2. How does the deposit to asset ratio compare for these two banks?

QUESTIONS

1. How does a bank's report of condition differ from its report of income?
2. Match these three types of cash balances with the functions that they serve:

a. Vault cash	(1) Meet legal reserve requirements
b. Deposits at the Federal Reserve	(2) Used to purchase services
c. Deposits at other FIs	(3) Meet customer withdrawals

3. Classify the following accounts into one of the following categories:

a. assets
b. liabilities
c. equity
d. revenue
e. expense
f. off-balance-sheet activities

(1) Services charged on deposit accounts
(2) Retail CDs
(3) Surplus and paid-in capital
(4) Loan commitments
(5) Consumer loans
(6) Federal funds sold

(7) Swaps
(8) Interest on municipals
(9) Interest on NOW accounts
(10) NOW accounts
(11) Commercial letters of credit
(12) Leases
(13) Retained earnings
(14) Provision for loan losses
(15) Interest on U.S. Treasury securities

4. If we examine a typical bank's asset portion of the balance sheet, how are the assets arranged in terms of expected return and liquidity?
5. Repurchase agreements are listed as both assets and liabilities in Table 12–1. How can an account be both an asset and a liability?
6. How does a NOW account differ from a demand deposit?
7. How does a retail CD differ from a wholesale CD?
8. How do core deposits differ from purchased funds?
9. What are the major categories of off-balance-sheet activities?
10. STANDARD &POOR'S Go to the S&P Market Insight Web site at **www.mhhe.com/edumarketinsight** and find the values of assets, liabilities, and equity for Citigroup (C), J.P. Morgan Chase (JPM), Keycorp (KEY), and U.S. Bancorp (USB) using the following steps. Click on "Educational Version of Market Insight." Enter your site ID and click on "Login." Click on "Company." In the box marked "Ticker" enter C and click on "Go!" Click on "Excel Analytics." Click on "Ann. Balance Sheet." This brings up a file that contains the relevant data. Repeat this process using the tickers JPM, KEY, and USB.
11. A bank is considering two securities: a 30-year Treasury bond yielding 7 percent and a 30-year municipal bond yielding 5 percent. If the bank's tax rate is 30 percent, which bond offers the higher tax equivalent yield?
12. A bank is considering an investment in a municipal security that offers a yield of 6 percent. What is this security's tax equivalent yield if the bank's tax rate is 35 percent?
13. How does a bank's annual net income compare with its annual cash flow?
14. How might the use of an end-of-the-year balance sheet bias the calculation of certain ratios?
15. How does the asset utilization ratio for a bank compare to that of a retail company? How do the equity multipliers compare?
16. Smallville Bank has the following balance sheet, rates earned on their assets, and rates paid on their liabilities.

Balance Sheet (in thousands)

Assets		Rate Earned (%)
Cash and due from banks	$ 6,000	4
Investment securities	22,000	8
Repurchase agreements	12,000	6
Loans less allowance for losses	80,000	10
Fixed assets	10,000	0
Other assets	4,000	9
Total assets	$134,000	

Liabilities and Equity		Rate Paid (%)
Demand deposits	$ 9,000	0
NOW accounts	69,000	5
Retail CDs	18,000	7
Subordinated debentures	14,000	8
Total liabilities	110,000	
Common stock	10,000	
Paid-in capital surplus	13,000	
Retained earnings	11,000	
Total liabilities and equity	$134,000	

If the bank earns $120,000 in noninterest income, incurs $80,000 in noninterest expenses, and pays $2,500,000 in taxes, what is its net income?

17. Megalopolis Bank has the following balance sheet and income statement.

Balance Sheet (in millions)

Assets		Liabilities and Equity	
Cash and due from banks	$ 9,000	Demand deposits	$ 19,000
Investment securities	23,000	NOW accounts	89,000
Repurchase agreements	42,000	Retail CDs	28,000
Loans	90,000	Debentures	19,000
Fixed assets	15,000	Total liabilities	$155,000
Other assets	4,000	Common stock	12,000
Total assets	$183,000	Paid-in capital	4,000
		Retained earnings	12,000
		Total liabilities and equity	$183,000

Income Statement

Interest on fees and loans	$ 9,000
Interest on investment securities	4,000
Interest on repurchase agreements	6,000
Interest on deposits in banks	1,000
Total interest income	$20,000
Interest on deposits	$ 9,000
Interest on debentures	2,000
Total interest expense	$11,000
Net interest income	$ 9,000
Provision for loan losses	2,000
Noninterest income	2,000
Noninterest expenses	1,000
Income before taxes	$ 8,000
Taxes	3,000
Net income	$ 5,000

For Megalopolis, calculate:

a. Return on equity
b. Return on assets
c. Asset utilization
d. Equity multiplier
e. Profit margin

f. Interest expense ratio
g. Provision for loan loss ratio
h. Noninterest expense ratio
i. Tax ratio

18. **Using a Spreadsheet to Calculate Financial Statement Ratios:** The 2003 balance sheet and income statements for North Fork Bancorp and Bank of America are located at the book's Web site (**www.mhhe.com/sc3e**). Using these financial statements, calculate the 2003 values of the ratios listed in Tables 12–5 through 12–7.

19. What is the likely relationship between the interest income ratio and the noninterest income ratio?

20. Anytown bank has the following ratios:
    a. Profit margin: 21%
    b. Asset utilization: 11%
    c. Equity multiplier: 12X

    Calculate Anytown's ROE and ROA.

21. A security analyst calculates the following ratios for two banks. How should the analyst evaluate the financial health of the two banks?

	Bank A	Bank B
Return on equity	22%	24%
Return on assets	2%	1.5%
Equity multiplier	11X	16X
Profit margin	15%	14%
Asset utilization	13%	11%
Spread	3%	3%
Interest expense ratio	35%	40%
Provision for loan loss ratio	1%	4%

22. What sort of problems or opportunities might ratio analysis fail to identify?

13 Regulation *of* Commercial Banks

OUTLINE

Chapter NAVIGATOR

1. What types of regulations are commercial banks subject to?
2. What major bank regulations have been passed in the last 20 years?
3. How has commercial banks' reentry into the investment banking business evolved?
4. How and why has the scope of deposits insured by the FDIC changed?
5. How do U.S. regulations on commercial banks compare with those of other countries?
6. Why are commercial banks subject to reserve requirements?
7. What capital regulations must commercial banks meet?

SPECIALNESS AND REGULATION: CHAPTER OVERVIEW

Chapter 1 showed that FIs are special because they provide vital services to various important sectors of the economy. The general areas of FI specialness include the following: information services; liquidity services; price-risk reduction services; transaction cost services; maturity intermediation services; money supply transmission; credit allocation; intergenerational wealth transfers; payment services; and denomination intermediation.

Failure to provide these services or a breakdown in their efficient provision can be costly to both the ultimate providers (households) and users (firms) of funds. Because of the vital nature of the services they provide, commercial banks (CBs) are regulated at the federal level (and sometimes at the state level) to protect against a disruption in the provision of these services and the cost this would impose on the economy and society at large. In this chapter, we provide an overview of the regulations imposed on CBs. We first discuss the history of commercial banks' regulation and then review the specific balance sheet regulations under which commercial banks operate. We also highlight the differences in regulations imposed on domestic versus international commercial banks.

TABLE 13–1 Areas of CB Specialness in Regulation

Safety and Soundness Regulation—layers of regulation have been imposed on CBs to protect depositors and borrowers against the risk of failure.

Monetary Policy Regulation—regulators control and implement monetary policy by requiring minimum levels of cash reserves to be held against commercial bank deposits.

Credit Allocation Regulation—regulations support the CB's lending to socially important sectors such as housing and farming.

Consumer Protection Regulation—regulations are imposed to prevent the CB from discriminating unfairly in lending.

Investor Protection Regulation—laws protect investors who directly purchase securities and/or indirectly purchase securities by investing in mutual or pension funds managed directly or indirectly by CBs (as well as other FIs).

Entry and Chartering Regulation—entry and activity regulations limit the number of CBs in any given financial services sector, thus impacting the charter values of CBs operating in that sector.

TYPES OF REGULATIONS AND THE REGULATORS

1

Six types of regulations seek to enhance the net social benefits of commercial banks' services to the economy: (1) safety and soundness regulation, (2) monetary policy regulation, (3) credit allocation regulation, (4) consumer protection regulation, (5) investor protection regulation, and (6) entry and chartering regulation. These regulations are summarized in Table 13–1. Regulations can be imposed at the federal or the state level and occasionally at the international level, as in the case of bank capital requirements.

Safety and Soundness Regulation

To protect depositors and borrowers against the risk of CB failure—for example, due to a lack of diversification in asset portfolios—regulators have developed layers of protective mechanisms that balance a CB's profitability against its solvency, liquidity, and other types of risk (see Chapter 19). These are illustrated in Figure 13–1. Included in these mechanisms are requirements encouraging CBs to diversify their assets (the first layer of protection). The most obvious way to prevent CB failure is to prevent CBs from investing in an asset portfolio that produces cash flows that are insufficient to make the promised payments to the CB's liability holders. Thus, banks are prohibited from making loans exceeding 10 percent of their

FIGURE 13–1 Layers of Regulation

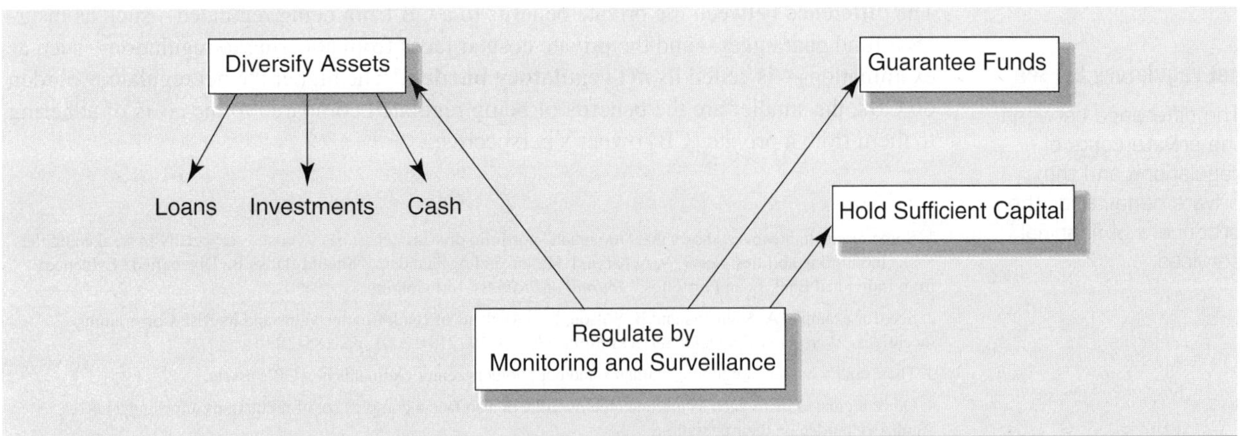

own equity capital funds to any one company or borrower. A bank that has 6 percent of its assets funded by its own capital (and therefore 94 percent by liabilities) can lend no more than 0.6 percent of its assets to any one borrower (i.e., 10 percent of 6 percent). These regulations may result in lower profitability but also lower credit and liquidity risk, and ultimately lower risk of insolvency.[1]

The second layer of protection concerns the minimum level of stockholder capital or equity funds that the owners of a CB need to contribute to the funding of its operations. For example, bank (and thrift) regulators are concerned with the minimum ratio of capital to (risk) assets. The higher the proportion of capital contributed by owners, the greater the protection against insolvency risk for liability claimholders such as depositors.[2] This occurs because losses on the asset portfolio due, for example, to loan defaults are legally borne by the stockholders first and then, only after the equity holders' claims are totally wiped out, by outside liability holders.[3] Consequently, CB regulators can directly affect the degree of risk exposure faced by nonequity claim holders in CBs (such as depositors) by varying the minimum amount of equity capital required to operate and keep a bank open (see discussions below).

www.fdic.gov

The third layer of protection is the provision of guarantee funds such as the Bank Insurance Fund (BIF) for banks (and, as discussed in Chapter 14, the Savings Association Insurance Fund (SAIF) for savings associations). Deposit insurance mitigates a rational incentive depositors otherwise have to withdraw their funds at the first hint of trouble. By protecting CB depositors when a CB collapses and owners' equity or net worth is wiped out, a demand for regulation of insured institutions is created so as to protect the funds' (and taxpayers') resources. For example, the Federal Deposit Insurance Corporation (FDIC) monitors and regulates participants in both BIF and SAIF in return for providing explicit deposit guarantees of up to $100,000 per depositor per bank. Major reforms of FDIC insurance of CB deposits are currently being considered. We discuss these below.

The fourth layer of regulation involves monitoring and surveillance. Regulators subject all CBs to varying degrees of monitoring and surveillance. This involves on-site examination of the CB by regulators as well as the CB's production of accounting statements and reports on a timely basis for off-site evaluation. Just as savers appoint CBs as delegated monitors to evaluate the behavior and actions of ultimate borrowers, society appoints regulators to monitor the behavior and performance of CBs.

Finally, note that regulation is not without costs for those regulated. For example, regulators may require CBs to have more equity capital than private owners believe is in their own best interests. Similarly, producing the information requested by regulators is costly for CBs because it involves the time of managers, lawyers, and accountants. Again, the socially optimal amount of information may differ from a CB's privately optimal amount.

Although regulation may be socially beneficial, it imposes private costs, or a regulatory burden, on individual CB owners and managers. Consequently, regulation attempts to enhance the social welfare benefits and mitigate the social costs of providing CB services. The difference between the private benefits to a CB from being regulated—such as insurance fund guarantees—and the private costs it faces from adhering to regulation—such as examinations—is called its **net regulatory burden.**[4] The higher the net regulatory burden on CBs, the smaller are the benefits of being regulated compared to the costs of adhering to them from a private (CB) owner's perspective.

net regulatory burden

The difference between the private costs of regulations and the private benefits for the producers of financial services.

1. Some research, however, shows that "too much" portfolio diversification has its costs—especially in weakening the banks monitoring abilities. See V. V. Acharya, I. Hasan, and A. Saunders, "Should Banks Be Diversified? Evidence from Individual Bank Loan Portfolios," *Journal of Business,* forthcoming.

2. See, for example, A. Saunders and B. Wilson, "An Analysis of Bank Charter Value and Its Risk Constraining Incentives," *Journal of Financial Services Research,* Vol. 19 (213), 2001, pp. 185–195.

3. Thus, equity holders are junior claimants and debt holders senior claimants to a CB's assets.

4. Other regulated firms such as gas and electric utilities also face a complex set of regulations imposing a net regulatory burden on their operations.

Monetary Policy Regulation

www.federalreserve.gov

outside money

That part of the money supply directly produced by the government or central bank, such as notes and coin.

inside money

That part of the money supply produced by the private banking system.

Another motivation for regulation concerns the special role that banks play in the transmission of monetary policy from the Federal Reserve (the central bank) to the rest of the economy. The central bank directly controls only the quantity of notes and coin in the economy—called **outside money**—whereas the bulk of the money supply is bank deposits—called **inside money.** In theory, a central bank can vary the amount of cash or outside money and directly affect a bank's reserve position as well as the amount of loans and deposits it can create without formally regulating the bank's portfolio. In practice, regulators have chosen to impose formal controls.[5] In most countries, regulators commonly impose a minimum level of required cash reserves to be held against deposits (discussed below). Some argue that imposing such reserve requirements makes the control of the money supply and its transmission more predictable. Such reserves add to a CB's net regulatory burden if they are more than the institution believes are necessary for its own liquidity purposes. In general, all CBs would choose to hold some cash reserves—even noninterest bearing—to meet the liquidity and transaction needs of their customers directly. For well-managed CBs, however, this optimal level is normally low, especially if the central bank (or other regulatory body) does not pay interest on required reserves. As a result, CBs often view required reserves as similar to a tax and as a positive cost of undertaking financial intermediation.[6]

Credit Allocation Regulation

Credit allocation regulation supports the CB's lending to socially important sectors such as housing and farming. These regulations may require a CB to hold a minimum amount of assets in one particular sector of the economy or to set maximum interest rates, prices, or fees to subsidize certain sectors. An example of asset restrictions includes the qualified thrift lender (QTL) test, which requires savings institutions to hold 65 percent of their assets in residential mortgage-related assets to retain a thrift charter. Examples of interest rate restrictions are the usury laws that many states set on the maximum rates that can be charged on mortgages and/or consumer loans, and regulations (now abolished) such as the Federal Reserve Bank's Regulation Q maximums on time and savings deposit interest rates.

Such price and quantity restrictions may be justified for social welfare reasons—especially if society prefers strong (and subsidized) housing and farming sectors. However, they can also be harmful to CBs that must bear the private costs of meeting many of these regulations.

Consumer Protection Regulation

Congress passed the Community Reinvestment Act (CRA) in 1977 and the Home Mortgage Disclosure Act (HMDA) in 1975 to prevent discrimination by lending institutions. For example, since 1975, the HMDA has assisted the public in determining whether banks and other mortgage-lending institutions were meeting the needs of their local communities. HMDA is especially concerned about discrimination on the basis of age, race, sex, or income. Since 1990, examinations for bank compliance with the CRA have become increasingly rigorous. Institutions have been required to disclose publicly their CRA ratings (from outstanding to substantial noncompliance). Since 1992, CBs have had to submit reports to regulators summarizing their lending on a geographic basis, showing the relationship between the demographic area to which they are lending and the demographic data (such as income and percentage of minority population) for that location. Commercial banks also must now report to their chief federal regulator the reasons that they granted or denied credit. Many

5. We discussed these controls in Chapter 4.

6. In the United States, bank reserves held with the central bank (the Federal Reserve Bank, or the Fed) are noninterest bearing. In some other countries, interest is paid on bank reserves—thereby lowering the "regulatory tax" effect. The size of the tax, therefore, depends on the level of interest rates.

www.ffiec.gov

www.federalreserve.gov

www.fdic.gov
www.occ.treas.gov

analysts believed that community and consumer protection laws were imposing a considerable net regulatory burden on CBs without offsetting social benefits that enhance equal access to mortgage and lending markets. To get some idea of the information production cost of regulatory compliance in this area, the Federal Financial Institutions Examination Council processes information on as many as 6 million mortgage transactions from more than 8,000 institutions each quarter. (The council is a federal supervisory body comprising the members of the Federal Reserve, the Federal Deposit Insurance Corporation, and the Office of the Comptroller of the Currency.)

In 1995 CRA regulations were revised to make assessments more performance based, more objective, and less burdensome for covered institutions. The 1977 Act included 12 assessment factors. The revised rules include three measures: lending (the geographic distribution of lending, the distribution of lending across different types of borrowers, the extent of community development lending, and the use of innovative or flexible lending practices to address the needs of low- or moderate-income individuals in the area): investment (the institution's involvement with qualified investments such as providing capital for a community-based investment group that invests in low-income areas); and service (the institution's availability and responsiveness for delivering retail banking services and the extent of community development services and their degree of innovation).

Investor Protection Regulation

A considerable number of laws protect investors who use commercial banks directly to purchase securities and/or indirectly to access securities markets through investing in mutual or pension funds managed by CBs. Various laws protect investors against abuses such as insider trading, lack of disclosure, outright malfeasance, and breach of fiduciary responsibilities. Important legislation affecting investment banks and mutual funds includes the Securities Acts of 1933 and 1934 and the Investment Company Act of 1940. Since CBs are increasingly moving into offering investment banking and mutual fund services following the passage of the Financial Services Modernization Act in 1999, these restrictions will increasingly impact their profits. As with consumer protection legislation, compliance with these acts can impose a net regulatory burden on CBs.

An example of investor protection occurred in 2002 when several commercial banks (e.g., J.P. Morgan Chase and Citigroup) and investment banks (e.g., Merrill Lynch and Morgan Stanley) were investigated for the way their research analysts gave advice to investors. In the spring of 2003 this issue culminated in an agreement between regulators and 10 of the nation's largest financial institutions to pay a record $1.4 billion in penalties to settle charges involving investor abuse. At the heart of the investigation was the changed role of Wall Street analysts. Traditionally, they worked in relative obscurity, writing reports on the financial condition of companies, forecasting earnings, and recommending which stocks investors should buy or sell. With the 1990s stock market boom, however, securities firms and CBs competed to underwrite record numbers of new stocks for large fees. The firms' analysts, instead of simply assessing the stocks, increasingly (and at the expense of investors) promoted them as good investments to buy.

Entry and Chartering Regulation

The entry of CBs is regulated, as are their activities once they have been established. Increasing or decreasing the cost of entry into a financial sector affects the profitability of firms already competing in that industry. Thus, the industries heavily protected against new entrants by high direct costs (e.g., through capital requirements) and high indirect costs (e.g., by restricting the type of individuals who can establish CBs) of entry, produce larger profits for existing firms than those in which entry is relatively easy. In addition, regulations define the scope of permitted activities under a given charter. The broader the set of financial service activities permitted under a charter, the more valuable that charter is likely to be. Thus, barriers to entry and regulations pertaining to the scope of permitted activities affect a CB's *charter value* and the size of its net regulatory burden.

DO YOU UNDERSTAND?

1. The six major types of regulation CBs face?
2. What the layers of protection provided by safety and soundness regulations are? Describe each.
3. What the difference is between inside and outside money?
4. Who the key regulators of commercial banks are?

Regulators

Regulators are responsible for ensuring that CBs are operating in accordance with the regulations discussed above and that the vital services provided by these institutions are carried out safely in a sound and efficient manner. While (like auditors) regulators must analyze and evaluate the business of the CBs they monitor, they do so with special attention to a CB's ability to provide social benefits to the overall economy. Unlike other countries that have one or sometimes two regulators, U.S. commercial banks may be subject to the supervision and regulations of as many as four separate regulators. The key regulators for commercial banks were discussed in Chapter 11. They include the Federal Deposit Insurance Corporation (FDIC), the Office of the Comptroller of the Currency (OCC), the Federal Reserve System (FRS), and state bank regulators. Appendix 13A to this chapter, located at the book's Web site (www.mhhe.com/sc3e), lists the regulators that oversee the various activities of commercial banks (as well as savings institutions (discussed in Chapter 14)).

www.fdic.gov

www.occ.treas.gov

www.federalreserve.gov

In the sections that follow, we describe four facets of the regulatory structure: (1) regulation of product and geographic expansion, (2) the provision and regulation of deposit insurance, (3) balance sheet regulations (reserve requirements and capital regulations), and (4) regulations pertaining to off-balance-sheet activities.

2

REGULATION OF PRODUCT AND GEOGRAPHIC EXPANSION

Historically, commercial banks have been among the most regulated firms in the U.S. economy. Because of the inherent special nature of banking and banking contracts, regulators have imposed numerous restrictions on their products and geographic activities over the last 75 years.

Product Segmentation in the U.S. Commercial Banking Industry

The U.S. financial system has traditionally been segmented along product lines. Regulatory barriers and restrictions have often inhibited a commercial bank's ability to operate in some areas of the financial services industry and expand its product set beyond some limited range. Commercial banks operating in the United States can be compared with those operating in Germany, Switzerland, and the United Kingdom, where a more **universal FI** structure allows individual financial services organizations to offer a far broader range of banking, insurance, securities, and other financial services products.[7]

universal FI
An FI that can engage in a broad range of financial service activities.

3

Commercial and Investment Banking Activities. Since 1863, the United States has experienced several phases of regulating the links between the commercial and investment banking industries. Simply defined, **commercial banking** is the activity of deposit taking and commercial lending; **investment banking** is the activity of underwriting, issuing, and distributing (via public or private placement) securities. Early legislation, such as the 1863 National Bank Act, prohibited nationally chartered commercial banks from engaging in corporate securities activities such as the underwriting and distributing of corporate bonds and equities. As the United States industrialized and the demand for corporate finance increased, however, the largest banks such as National City Bank (a part of today's Citigroup) found ways around this restriction by establishing state-chartered affiliates to do the underwriting. In 1927, the Comptroller of the Currency formally recognized such affiliates as legitimate banking activities.

commercial banking
Banking activity of deposit taking and lending.

investment banking
Banking activity of underwriting, issuing, and distributing securities.

7. For a thorough analysis of universal banking systems overseas, see A. Saunders and I. Walter, *Universal Banking in the U.S.?* (New York: Oxford University Press, 1994); and A. Saunders and I. Walter, eds., *Financial System Design: Universal Banking Considered* (New York: Irwin/McGraw-Hill Professional Publishing, 1996).

TABLE 13–2 Provisions of the Glass-Steagall Act (1933 Banking Act)

The 1933 Glass-Steagall Act imposed a rigid separation between commercial banking and investment banking with three exemptions:

1. The underwriting of new issues of Treasury securities.
2. The underwriting of municipal general obligation bonds.
3. The private placements of corporate debt and equity securities.

After the 1929 stock market crash, the United States entered a major recession, and approximately 10,000 banks failed between 1930 and 1933. A commission of inquiry (the Pecora Commission) established in 1931 began investigating the causes of the crash. Its findings included concerns about the riskiness and conflicts of interest that arise when commercial and investment banking activities are linked (affiliated) in one organization. This resulted in new legislation, the 1933 Banking Act, or the Glass-Steagall Act (summarized in Table 13–2). The Glass-Steagall Act sought to impose a rigid separation (or nonaffiliation) between commercial banking—taking deposits and making commercial loans—and investment banking—underwriting, issuing, and distributing stocks, bonds, and other securities. The act defined three major exemptions to this separation. First, banks were allowed to continue to underwrite new issues of Treasury bills, notes, and bonds. Second, banks were allowed to continue underwriting municipal general obligation (GO) bonds.[8] Third, banks were allowed to continue engaging in private placements (see Chapter 6) of all types of bonds and equities, corporate and noncorporate.

For most of the 1933–1963 period, commercial banks and investment banks generally appeared to be willing to abide by both the letter and spirit of the Glass-Steagall Act. Between 1963 and 1987, however, banks challenged restrictions on their municipal *revenue* bond underwriting activities, commercial paper underwriting activities, discount brokerage activities, and advising activities, including open- and closed-end mutual funds, the underwriting of mortgage-backed securities, and selling annuities.[9] In most cases, the courts eventually permitted these activities for commercial banks.[10]

Section 20 affiliate

A securities subsidiary of a bank holding company through which a banking organization can engage in investment banking activities.

With this onslaught, and the de facto erosion of the Glass-Steagall Act by legal interpretation, the Federal Reserve Board in April 1987 allowed commercial bank holding companies such as J.P. Morgan & Company (now J.P. Morgan Chase), the parent of Morgan Guarantee Trust Company (a commercial bank) to establish separate **Section 20** securities **affiliates** as investment banks. Through these Section 20 affiliates, banks began to conduct all their "ineligible" or "gray area" securities activities, such as commercial paper underwriting, mortgage-backed securities underwriting, and municipal revenue bond underwriting.[11] Note the organizational structure of Citigroup Corp., its bank, and its Section 20 subsidiary (or investment bank) Smith Barney in Figure 13–2. These Section 20 subsidiaries did not violate Section 20 of the Glass-Steagall Act, which restricted affiliations of commercial banks and

8. A municipal general obligation bond is a bond issued by a state, city, or local government whose interest and principal payments are backed by the full faith and credit of that local government—that is, its full tax and revenue base (see Chapter 6).

9. Municipal revenue bonds are riskier than municipal GO bonds since their interest and principal are guaranteed only by the revenue from the projects they finance. One example is the revenue from road tolls of a bond funding the construction of a new section of highway (see Chapter 6).

10. Of the type of issues involved, *discount brokerage* was held to be legal, since it was not viewed as being the same as *full-service brokerage* supplied by securities firms. In particular, a full-service brokerage combines both the agency function of securities purchase along with investment advice (e.g., hot tips). By contrast, discount brokers only carry out the agency function of buying and selling securities for clients; they do not give investment advice. For further discussion of these issues, see M. Clark and A. Saunders, "Judicial Interpretation of Glass-Steagall: The Need for Legislative Action," *The Banking Law Journal* 97 (1980), pp. 721–40; and "Glass-Steagall Revisited: The Impact on Banks, Capital Markets, and the Small Investor," *The Banking Law Journal* 97 (1980), pp. 811–40.

11. In 1989 corporate bonds and in 1990 corporate equities were added to the permitted list.

FIGURE 13–2 **Bank Holding Company and Its Bank and Section 20 Subsidiary**

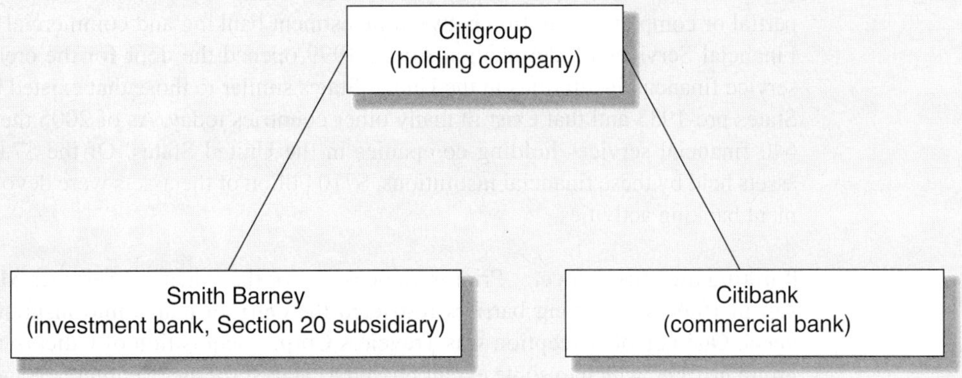

investment banks, since the revenue generated from securities underwriting activities amounted to less than 5 percent (increased later to 10 percent and then 25 percent) of the total revenues generated.[12]

Significant changes occurred in 1997 as the Federal Reserve and the Office of the Comptroller of the Currency (OCC) took actions to expand bank holding companies' permitted activities. In particular, the Federal Reserve allowed commercial banks to acquire directly existing investment banks rather than establish completely new Section 20 investment banking subsidiaries.

The result was a number of mergers and acquisitions between commercial and investment banks in 1997 through 2000. Some of the largest mergers included UBS's $12.0 billion purchase of Paine Webber in 2000, Credit Suisse First Boston's purchase of Donaldson Lufkin Jenrette for $11.5 billion in 2000, Deutsche Bank's $9.7 billion purchase of Banker's Trust in 1999, Citicorp's $83 billion merger with Travelers Group (which owned Smith Barney and Salomon Brothers) in April 1998, and Bankers Trust's April 1997 acquisition of Alex Brown for $1.7 billion. In each case, the banks stated that one motivation for their acquisition was the desire to establish a presence in the securities business since laws separating investment and commercial banking were changing. Also noted as a motivation in these acquisitions was the opportunity to expand business lines, take advantage of economies of scale and scope to reduce overall costs, and merge the customer bases of the respective commercial and investment banks involved in the acquisition.[13, 14]

Finally, in 1999, after years of "homemade" deregulation by banks and securities firms, the U.S. Congress passed the Financial Services Modernization Act, which repealed the Glass-Steagall barriers between commercial banking and investment banking. The bill, touted as the biggest change in the regulation of financial institutions in nearly 70 years, allowed for the creation of a "financial services holding company" that could engage in

12. Legally, as long as less than 50 percent of the affiliate's revenues could be attributable to "ineligible activities," it could not be argued that the affiliate was "principally engaged in such activities"; therefore, an affiliate could not be viewed as violating Section 20 of the Glass-Steagall Act of 1933.

13. The erosion of the product barriers between the commercial and investment banking industries has not been all one way. Large investment banks such as Merrill Lynch have increasingly sought to offer banking products. For example, in the late 1970s, Merrill Lynch created the cash management account (CMA), which allowed investors to own a money market mutual fund with check-writing privileges into which bond and stock sale proceeds could be swept on a daily basis. This account allows the investor to earn interest on cash held in a brokerage account. In addition, investment banks have been major participants as traders and investors in the secondary market for loans to less-developed countries and other loans.

14. However, not all of these mergers reaped the profits management hoped for. For example, in April 2002 FleetBoston announced that the bank would sell off its investment bank subsidiary, Robertson Stephens. FleetBoston stated the sale was a result of sagging profits in the investment banking industry and a desire to concentrate on its core business—lending to medium-size businesses, money management, and retail banking.

banking activities *and* securities underwriting. The bill also allowed large national banks to place certain activities, including some securities underwritings, in direct bank subsidiaries regulated by the Office of the Comptroller of the Currency. Thus, after nearly 70 years of partial or complete separation between investment banking and commercial banking, the Financial Services Modernization Act of 1999 opened the door for the creation of full-service financial institutions in the United States similar to those that existed in the United States pre-1933 and that exist in many other countries today. As of 2005 there were over 640 financial services holding companies in the United States. Of the $7.06 trillion in assets held by these financial institutions, $710 billion of the assets were devoted to investment banking activities.

www.occ.treas.gov

Banking and Insurance. Prior to the passage of the Financial Services Modernization Act in 1999, very strong barriers restricted the entry of banks into insurance, and vice versa. One notable exception was Travelers Corp.'s acquisition of Citicorp to form Citigroup in 1998, which to some extent proved a catalyst for the eventual passage of the 1999 act. Insurance activities can be either of the property-casualty type (e.g., homeowners insurance, auto insurance) or the life/health type (e.g., term life insurance). Moreover, a distinction should be made between a bank selling insurance as an agent by selling other FIs' policies for a fee and a bank acting as an insurance underwriter and bearing the direct risk of underwriting losses itself. In general, the risks of insurance agency activities are quite low in loss potential when compared to insurance underwriting. It might also be noted that certain insurance products—for example, credit life insurance, mortgage insurance, and auto insurance—tend to have natural synergistic links to bank lending.[15]

Prior to the Financial Services Modernization Act of 1999, banks were under stringent restrictions when selling and underwriting almost every type of insurance. For example, national banks were restricted to offering credit-related life, accident, health, or unemployment insurance. Moreover, national banks could act as insurance agents only in towns of fewer than 5,000 people (although they could sell insurance from these offices anywhere in the United States). In addition, the Bank Holding Company Act of 1956 (and its 1970 amendments) and the Garn-St. Germain Depository Institutions Act of 1982 severely restricted bank holding companies from establishing separately capitalized insurance affiliates. Most states also took quite restrictive actions regarding the insurance activities of state-chartered banks. A few states, most notably Delaware, passed liberal laws allowing state-chartered banks to underwrite and broker various types of property-casualty and life insurance. This encouraged large bank holding companies such as Citigroup and Chase to enter Delaware and establish state-chartered banking subsidiaries with their own insurance affiliates.

One "insurance" area in which banks successfully survived legal challenges was the sale of annuities.[16] In 1986, NationsBank (which merged with Bank of America in 1997) began selling annuities and was aggressively challenged in court by the insurance industry. In the meantime, a large number of other banks also began selling annuities. In 1995, the Supreme Court upheld the legality of banks' rights to sell annuities. In its decision, the Supreme Court argued that annuities should be viewed more as investment products than insurance products. Such sales are estimated to add nearly $1 billion a year to bank profits.

Unlike banks, insurance companies are regulated solely at the state level.[17] Although few states explicitly restricted insurance companies from acquiring banks and, therefore, pursuing banking activities, banking laws have historically restricted such expansions. In particular, the Bank Holding Company Act of 1956 severely restricted insurance companies' ability to own, or to be affiliated with, full-service banks.

15. See Saunders and Walter, *Universal Banking in the U.S.?*, for an elaboration of these arguments.

16. An annuity is a life insurance contract that provides a stated periodic payment to the annuity holder until death in exchange for a sum of money paid prior to the start of the annuity period (see Chapter 15).

17. This state level of regulation was reaffirmed by the McCarran-Ferguson Act of 1945. For an excellent discussion of the background to this act, see K. J. Meier, *The Political Economy of Regulation: The Case of Insurance* (Albany, State University of New York Press, 1988).

A great challenge to the Bank Holding Company Act's restrictions on bank–insurance company affiliations came from the 1998 merger between Citicorp and Travelers to create the largest financial services conglomerate in the United States. The primary activity of Travelers was insurance (life and property-casualty), while the primary activity of Citicorp was banking (both also were engaged in securities activities: Citicorp through its Section 20 subsidiary and Travelers through its earlier acquisition of Smith Barney and Salomon Brothers). The Federal Reserve gave initial approval in September 1998. Under the Bank Holding Company Act, the Federal Reserve had up to five years to formally approve the merger. (However, in a turnaround in strategy, Citigroup sold off part of the Travelers Insurance unit in 2002 via the largest initial public offering of the year.)

The Financial Services Modernization Act of 1999 completely changed the landscape for insurance activities as it allowed bank holding companies to open insurance underwriting affiliates and insurance companies to open commercial bank (or savings institutions) as well as securities firm affiliates through the creation of a financial service holding company. With the passage of this act banks no longer have to fight legal battles in states such as Texas and Rhode Island to overcome restrictions on their ability to sell insurance in these states. The insurance industry also applauded the act, as it forced banks that underwrite and sell insurance to operate under the same set of state regulations (pertaining to their insurance lines) as insurance companies operating in that state. Under the new act, a financial services holding company that engages in commercial banking, investment banking, and insurance activities will be functionally regulated. This means that the holding company's banking activities will be regulated by bank regulators (such as the Federal Reserve, FDIC, OCC), its securities activities will be regulated by the SEC, and its insurance activities will be regulated by up to 50 state insurance regulators.

Commercial Banking and Commerce. Although the direct holdings of other firms' equity by national banks has been constrained since 1863, the restrictions on the commercial activities of bank holding companies are a more recent phenomena. In particular, the 1970 amendments to the 1956 Bank Holding Company Act required bank holding companies to divest themselves of nonbank-related subsidiaries over a 10-year period following the amendment. When Congress passed the amendments, bank holding companies owned approximately 3,500 commercial sector subsidiaries ranging from public utilities to transportation and manufacturing firms. Nevertheless, bank holding companies today can still hold up to 4.9 percent of the voting shares in any commercial firm without regulatory approval.[18]

The 1956 Bank Holding Company Act has also effectively restricted acquisitions of banks by commercial firms (as was true for insurance companies before 1999). The major vehicle for a commercial firm's entry into commercial banking has been through **nonbank banks** or nonbank financial service firms that offer banking-type services by divesting a subsidiary "bank" of its commercial loans and/or its demand deposits (as well as any deposit insurance coverage).

nonbank bank

A bank divested of its commercial loans and/or its demand deposits.

The Financial Services Modernization Act of 1999 changed restrictions on ownership limits imposed on financial services holding companies. Commercial banks belonging to a financial service holding company can now take a controlling interest in a nonfinancial enterprise provided that two conditions are met. First, the investment cannot be made for an indefinite period of time. The act did not provide an explicit time limit, but simply states that the investment can be "held for a period of time to enable the sale or disposition thereof on a reasonable basis consistent with the financial viability of the [investment]." Second, the bank cannot become actively involved in the management of the corporation in which it invests. Nevertheless, corporate stocks or equities are still conspicuously absent from most bank balance sheets (see Chapter 12).

18. The Bank Holding Company Act defines *control* as a holding company's equity stake in a subsidiary bank or affiliate that exceeds 25 percent.

DO YOU UNDERSTAND?

1. The rationale for the passage of the Glass-Steagall Act in 1933? What permissible underwriting activities did it identify for commercial banks?
2. Why a 5 percent rather than a 50 percent maximum ceiling was originally imposed on the revenues earned from the eligible underwriting activities of a Section 20 subsidiary?
3. Why a bank that currently specializes in making consumer loans but makes no commercial loans qualifies as a nonbank bank?
4. How the provisions of the National Bank Act of 1863 affected the participation of national banks in establishing nonbank subsidiaries?
5. How the Financial Services Modernization Act of 1999 has opened the doors for the establishment of full-service financial institutions in the United States?
6. How the range of product activities permitted U.S. commercial banks compares to that of banks in other major industrialized countries?

Geographic Expansion in the U.S. Commercial Banking Industry

Geographic expansions can have a number of dimensions. In particular, they can be (1) domestic, (2) within a state or region, or (3) international (participating in a foreign market). Expansions can also be carried out by opening a new office or branch or by acquiring another bank. Historically, in the United States, the ability of commercial banks to expand domestically has been constrained by regulation. By comparison, no special regulations inhibit the ability of commercial firms such as General Motors, IBM, or Sears from establishing new or **de novo offices,** factories, or branches anywhere in the country. Nor are such companies generally prohibited from acquiring other firms—as long as they are not banks. Commercial banks have faced a complex and changing network of rules and regulations covering geographic expansions. Such regulations may inhibit expansions, but they may also create potential opportunities to increase a commercial bank's returns. In particular, regulations may create locally uncompetitive markets with high economic rents that new entrants can potentially exploit. Thus, for the most innovative commercial banks, regulation can provide profit opportunities as well as costs. As a result, regulation acts both as an inhibitor and an incentive to engage in geographic expansions.

Regulatory Factors Impacting Geographic Expansion

Restrictions on Intrastate Banking by Commercial Banks. At the beginning of the last century, most U.S. banks were **unit banks** with a single office. Improving communications and customer needs resulted in a rush to branching. This movement ran into increasing opposition from the smallest unit banks and the largest money center banks. The smallest unit banks perceived a competitive threat to their retail business from the larger branching banks; money center banks feared a loss of valuable correspondent business such as check-clearing and other payment services. As a result, several states restricted banks' ability to branch within the state. Indeed, some states prohibited intrastate (or within-state) branching per se, effectively constraining a bank to unit bank status. Over the years and in a very piecemeal fashion, states have liberalized their restrictions on within-state branching. As of 1997, only six states had laws that restricted *intrastate* banking, usually limiting banks to setting up branches in counties bordering the county in which the bank's head office is established.

de novo office

A newly established office.

unit bank

A bank with a single office.

multibank holding company (MBHC)

A parent banking organization that owns a number of individual bank subsidiaries.

grandfathered subsidiaries

Subsidiaries established prior to the passage of a restrictive law and not subject to that law.

Restrictions on Interstate Banking by Commercial Banks. The defining piece of legislation affecting interstate branching up until 1997 was the McFadden Act, passed in 1927 and amended in 1933. The McFadden Act and its amendments restricted nationally chartered banks' branching abilities to the same extent allowed to state-chartered banks, which essentially prevented all U.S. banks from branching across state lines. Given the McFadden prohibition on interstate branching, bank organizations expanding across state lines between 1927 and 1956 relied on establishing subsidiaries rather than branches. Some of the largest banking organizations established **multibank holding companies** for this purpose. A multibank holding company (MBHC) is a parent company that acquires more than one bank as a direct subsidiary (e.g., First Interstate).

In 1956, Congress recognized the potential loophole to interstate banking posed by the MBHC movement and passed the Douglas Amendment to the Bank Holding Company Act. This act permitted MBHCs to acquire bank subsidiaries only to the extent allowed by the laws of the state in which the proposed bank target resided. Any MBHCs with out-of-state subsidiaries established prior to 1956 were **grandfathered subsidiaries;** that is, MBHCs were allowed to keep them. (One such example was First Interstate.) The passage of the 1956 Douglas Amendment did not close all potential interstate banking loopholoes. Because the

one-bank holding company

A parent banking organization that owns one bank subsidiary and nonbank subsidiaries.

amendment pertained to MBHC acquisitions, it still left open the potential for **one-bank holding company** (OBHC) geographic extensions. An OBHC is a parent bank holding company that has a single bank subsidiary and a number of other nonbank financial subsidiaries. By creating an OBHC and establishing across state lines various nonbank subsidiaries that sell financial services such as consumer finance, leasing, and data processing, a bank could almost replicate an out-of-state banking presence.

In 1970, Congress again acted, recognizing that bankers had creatively innovated yet another loophole to interstate banking restrictions. The 1970 Bank Holding Company Act Amendments effectively restricted the nonbank activities that an OBHC could engage in to those "closely related to banking," as defined by the Federal Reserve under Section 4(c)(8) of the Act. Thus, the year 1970 and the passage of the Bank Holding Company Act Amendments were probably the low point of interstate banking in the United States.

Riegle-Neal Interstate Banking and Branching Efficiency Act of 1994. It has long been recognized that the expansion of nationwide banking through multibank holding companies is potentially far more expensive than through branching. Separate corporations and boards of directors must be established for each bank in an MBHC, and it is hard to achieve the same level of economic and financial integration and synergies as is possible with branches. Moreover, most major banking competitor countries outside of the United States, such as Japan, Germany, France, and the United Kingdom, have nationwide branching.

In the fall of 1994, the U.S. Congress passed an interstate banking law that allowed U.S. and foreign banks to branch interstate by consolidating out-of-state bank subsidiaries into a branch network and/or by acquiring banks or individual branches of banks through acquisition or merger. (The effective beginning date for these new branching powers was June 1, 1997.) Although the act was silent on the ability of banks to establish de novo branches in other states—essentially leaving it to individual states to pass laws allowing de novo branching—under the Riegle-Neal Act a New York bank such as Citibank may purchase, as an example, a single branch of Bank of America in San Francisco. The result of the Riegle-Neal Act is that full interstate banking is becoming a reality in the United States. The relaxation of the branching restrictions, along with recognition of the potential cost, revenue, and risk benefits from geographic expansions are major reasons for the recent merger wave (and increased consolidation) in U.S. banking (see Chapter 11).

DO YOU UNDERSTAND?

1. The difference between the interstate banking restrictions imposed under the 1956 Bank Holding Company Act and those passed under the 1970 Amendments to the Bank Holding Company Act?
2. How the Riegle-Neal Act affected geographic expansion opportunities of banks?

BANK AND SAVINGS INSTITUTION GUARANTEE FUNDS

A key component of the regulatory structure of CBs is deposit insurance and financial guarantees provided to depositors of CBs by regulators. Because the insurance fund that covers deposits of CBs also covers deposits of savings institutions (discussed in Chapter 14), this section discusses the deposit insurance funds as they pertain to both CBs and savings institutions.[19]

FDIC

www.fdic.gov

The FDIC was created in 1933 in the wake of the banking panics of 1930–1933 to maintain the stability of, and public confidence in, the U.S. financial system. Over the period 1933–1979, the FDIC insurance system seemed to work well, failures were few (see Figure 13–3), and the FDIC insurance fund grew in size. Beginning in 1980, however, the number of bank failures increased, with more than 1,039 in the decade ending in 1990

19. In addition to deposit insurance, central banks, such as the Federal Reserve, provide a discount window facility to meet banks' short-term nonpermanent liquidity needs. We discuss the discount window as a mechanism used to ease banks' liquidity problems in Chapter 21.

FIGURE 13–3 Number of Failed Banks by Year, 1934–2005

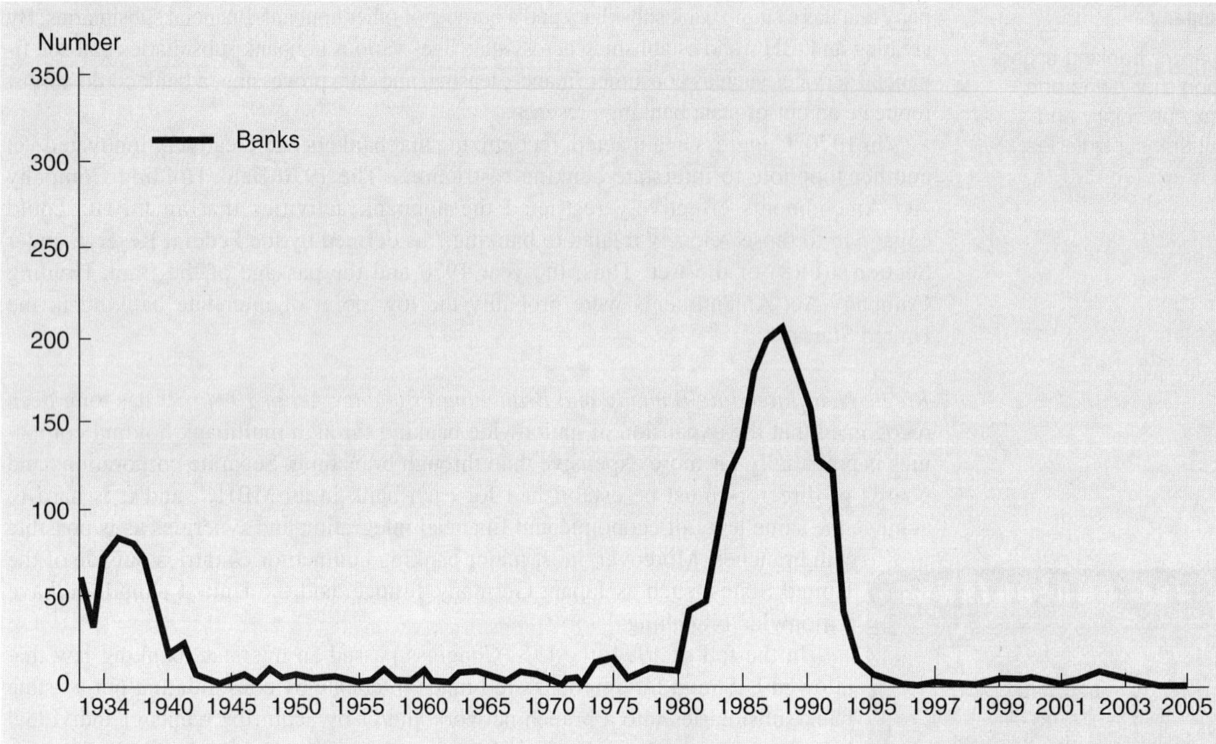

Source: "BIF Closings and Assistance Transactions," various years, FDIC. **www.fdic.gov**

(peaking at 221 in 1988). This number of failures was actually higher than that in the entire 1933–1979 period. Moreover, the costs of each of these failures were often larger than those of the mainly small bank failures that occurred in the 1933–1979 period. As the number and costs of these failures mounted in the 1980s, the FDIC fund was rapidly drained. In response to this crisis, Congress passed the FDIC Improvement Act (FDICIA) in December 1991 to restructure the bank insurance fund and to prevent its potential insolvency.

In the late 1990s, the fund's finances dramatically improved and bank failures decreased significantly, partially in response to record bank profit levels as a result of a very strong U.S. economy (see Chapter 11). Specifically, in September 2004, the FDIC's Bank Insurance Fund (BIF) had reserves of $34.5 billion, and there were only 10 bank failures in 2002, 3 in 2003, and 3 in 2004. At the end of the third quarter of 2004, the fund's reserves stood at a record high and exceeded 1.32 percent of insured bank deposits.[20] As a result of the burgeoning size of the insurance fund and the industry's excellent health, the FDIC assigned a 0 percent annual insurance premium to the nation's safest BIF insured banks (over 90 percent of all banks).

4 The Demise of the Federal Savings and Loan Insurance Corporation (FSLIC) and the FDIC

The Federal Savings and Loan Insurance Corporation (FSLIC) insured the deposits of savings institutions from 1934 to 1989. Like the FDIC, this insurance fund was in relatively good shape until the end of the 1970s. Beginning in 1980, its resources

20. The target size for the fund's reserves has been 1.25 percent of insured deposits.

SEARCH THE SITE

Go to the FDIC Web site at **www.fdic.gov.** Find the number of failed BIF and SAIF member depository institutions for the most recent year using the following steps. Once at the Web site,

Click on "Analysis"

Click on "FDIC Quarterly Banking Profile"

Click on "Quarterly Banking Profile"

Click on "Deposit Insurance Fund Trends"

Click on "Table III-B Selected Indicators, By Fund Membership"

This will bring up a file that contains the relevant data.

Questions

1. How many banks have failed since 2004 as reported in Figure 13–3?
2. Of the total assets held by the failing banks and savings institutions in the last year, calculate the percentage due to failed banks versus failed savings institutions.

began to be depleted as more and more savings institutions failed. Between 1980 and 1988, 581 savings institutions failed. at an estimated cost of $42.3 billion. By 1989, the FSLIC fund had been depleted and the present value of its liabilities exceeded that of its assets.[21] Lacking the resources to close or resolve failing savings institutions, the FSLIC followed a policy of forbearance (or leniency) toward remaining weak and failing savings institutions. This meant that it allowed many badly run savings institutions to stay open and continue to accumulate losses.

In August 1989, Congress passed the Financial Institutions Reform, Recovery, and Enforcement Act (FIRREA), largely in response to the deepening crisis in the savings institution industry and the growing insolvency of the FSLIC. This act restructured the savings association fund and transferred its management to the FDIC.[22] At the same time, the restructured savings association insurance fund was renamed the Savings Association Insurance Fund (SAIF). Currently, the FDIC manages the SAIF separately from the commercial bank fund, which is now called the Bank Insurance Fund (BIF). In September 2004, SAIF had $12.5 billion in reserves, representing 1.33 percent of insured deposits, and only four savings institutions failed in the five-year period 2000–2004. Like BIF-insured banks, the safest SAIF-insured institutions currently pay no insurance premiums. See Figure 13–4 for the organizational structure of FDIC and the number of commercial banks insured by the BIF and SAIF funds.

Reform of Deposit Insurance

On January 1, 1993, the FDIC introduced for the first time a risk-based deposit insurance program. Under this program, which applied equally to all deposit-insured institutions, a bank or thrift's risk would be ranked along a capital adequacy dimension and a supervisory dimension

21. In 1989, 331 savings institutions also failed.

22. At that time, the FSLIC ceased to exist.

FIGURE 13–4 The Structure of FDIC, BIF, and SAIF in 2004

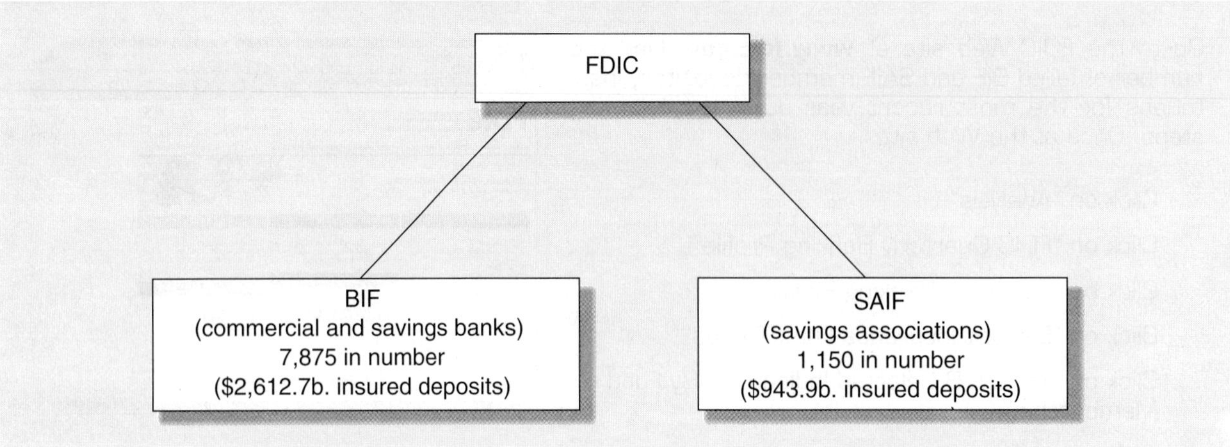

Source: FDIC, *Statistics on Banking,* Third Quarter 2004. **www.fdic.gov**

(the depository institution's CAMELS rating). Since each dimension had three categories, a bank or thrift was placed in any one of nine cells. The best DIs, those in cell 1, which were well-capitalized and had healthy supervisory ratings, paid an annual insurance premium of 23 cents per $100 of deposits, while the worst DIs paid 31 cents. Although the 8 cent differential in insurance premiums between the safest and the riskiest CBs was a first step in risk-based pricing, it was considered to be so small that it did not effectively limit DIs' risk-taking incentives. The average assessment rate in 1993 was 23.2 cents per $100 of deposits.

The improving solvency position of the FDIC (and of the banks and thrifts it insures) has resulted in a considerable reduction in insurance premiums. In 1996 (for BIF-insured DIs) and 1997 (for SAIF-insured DIs) the fee structure for deposit insurance was changed so that the healthiest institutions paid 0 cents per $100 of deposits, while the riskiest paid 27 cents per $100 of deposits. As a result, in September 2004, 92.7 percent of all BIF-insured DIs and 93.3 percent of all SAIF-insured DIs paid the statutory minimum premium, and the average assessment rate was less than 0.1 cent per $100 of deposits.

In the early 2000s, the FDIC identified several weaknesses with the current system of deposit insurance that it felt needed to be corrected.[23] As of March 2005 the U.S. House of Representatives had passed a deposit insurance reform bill. A bill had also been introduced in the Senate but had yet to be passed. Although the two bills differ in a number of details, the proposed changes listed below are common to both. First, the FDIC proposed the merger of the BIF and the SAIF into one insurance fund called the Deposit Insurance Fund. The FDIC argued that the BIF and SAIF offer identical services. Yet, as long as two separate funds existed, the potential for a premium disparity and competitive inequality between banks and thrifts also existed. Moreover, many institutions have both BIF-insured and SAIF-insured deposits as a result of mergers, acquisitions, and the expansion of bank powers. Specifically, more than 40 percent of SAIF-insured deposits are now held by commercial banks. The costs to insured institutions associated with tracking their BIF and SAIF deposits separately could be eliminated by merging both funds. Table 13–3 shows the effects of a possible BIF/SAIF merger at the end of 2004.

Second, the FDIC proposed that the deposit insurance coverage level should be indexed to inflation to maintain its real value. Between 1980 (when the coverage cap was increased to $100,000) and 2001 the real value of deposit insurance coverage had fallen by half. Rather

23. See "Keeping the Promise: Recommendations for Deposit Insurance Reform," FDIC, April 2001.

TABLE 13–3 Merging the BIF and SAIF

	BIF	SAIF	Merged Funds
Bank Data			
Number of fund member banks	7,875	1,150	9,028
Insured deposits (in billions)	$2,612.7	$943.9	$3,556.6
Insurance Fund Data			
Fund balance (in billions)	$34.5	$12.5	$47.0
Reserve ratio*	1.32%	1.33%	1.32%

*Reserve ratio is the amount of reserves on hand as a percentage of total insured deposits.

Source: FDIC Web site. **www.fdic.gov**

than advocating ad hoc increases in deposit insurance coverage levels, as has occurred since 1934, the FDIC proposed a more systematic method of maintaining the real monetary value of coverage through an indexing system. Indexing (for example, based on the CPI—the Consumer Price Index) would increase the predictability and lessen the potential of large sudden increases in insurance premiums and payouts. Both DI owners and depositors would be able to predict the timing and implications of coverage level increases with more accuracy, which would in turn lower the risks of financial planning associated with coverage changes. The FDIC recommended that coverage be adjusted at a maximum interval of every 10 years (and never be allowed to decrease) and then only if the real value of coverage drops below 80 percent of the existing coverage level. While an initial increase in coverage to $130,000 was mentioned, the FDIC, in its 2001 report, stated that the appropriate level of coverage was open to debate and for Congress to ultimately determine.

DO YOU UNDERSTAND?

1. What events led Congress to pass the FDICIA?
2. What events brought about the demise of the FSLIC?
3. The two basic views offered to explain the financial problems of the commercial bank insurance fund during the 1980s?
4. Why interest rate risk was less of a problem for banks than for savings institutions in the early 1980s?
5. What the FDIC proposed in April 2001 for deposit insurance reform?

Third, the FDIC proposed that the current fixed designated minimum reserve ratio of 1.25 percent of insured deposits be replaced with a reserve ratio ranging from 1.00 to 1.50 percent. The FDIC would designate a target for the reserve ratio prior to each calendar year and publish this target for public comment.

Finally, the FDIC was concerned that the current system did not effectively price risk. At the time, regulations restricted the FDIC from charging premiums to well-capitalized and highly rated DIs as long as the insurance fund reserves were above 1.25 percent of insured deposits. As a result (as noted above), over 90 percent of all insured DIs did not pay deposit insurance premiums in the late 1990s and early 2000s. The FDIC argued that it should charge regular premiums for risk regardless of the reserve levels of the fund. One approach for measuring risk, suggested by the FDIC, was to employ a statistical credit-scoring model that uses examination ratings, financial ratios, and, for large banks, certain market signals as inputs to project failure rates. We show this scoring model in Appendix 13B to the chapter, located at the book's Web site (**www.mhhe.com/sc3e**).

Non-U.S. Deposit Insurance Systems

5 Most European countries have historically operated without explicit deposit insurance programs. Despite this, European countries have not seen the 1930s type of bank run and panic experienced in the United States. This is because European governments have often given implicit deposit guarantees at no cost to the largest banks in their countries. This has been possible as the result of the higher degree of concentration of deposits among the largest banks in European countries. However, deposit insurance systems are being increasingly adopted worldwide. One view of this trend toward implementation of explicit deposit programs is that governments are now simply collecting premiums as a fee to offset an obligation (implicit deposit insurance) that they previously offered for free.

Many of these systems offer quite different degrees of protection to depositors compared to the U.S. system. For example, in response to the single banking and capital market in Europe, the European Union (EU) has established a single deposit insurance system covering all EU-located banks. This insures deposit accounts up to 20,000 euros. However, depositors are subject to a 10 percent deductible (loss) to create incentives for them to monitor banks. The idea underlying the EU plan is to create a level playing field for banks across all European Union countries.

BALANCE SHEET REGULATIONS

6 A further form of regulation of CBs pertains to various assets and liabilities on their balance sheets.

Regulations on Commercial Bank Liquidity

Holding relatively small amounts of liquid assets exposes a CB to increased illiquidity and insolvency risk. Excessive illiquidity can result in a CB's inability to meet required payments on liability claims (such as deposit withdrawals) and, at the extreme, its insolvency. Moreover, it can even lead to contagious effects that negatively impact other CBs. Consequently, regulators have often imposed minimum liquid asset reserve requirements on CBs. In general, these requirements differ in nature and scope for various CBs and even according to country. The requirements depend on the illiquidity risk exposure perceived for the CB's type and other regulatory objectives that relate to minimum liquid asset requirements (see Chapter 4). Currently, in accordance with Federal Reserve Regulation D, banks in the United States are required to hold the following "target" minimum reserves against net transaction accounts (transaction accounts minus demand deposit balances due from U.S. Commercial banks and cash items in process of collection):[24]

Less than \$7.0 million	0%
\$7.0 million–\$47.6 million	3
More than \$47.6 million	10

In Appendix 13C located at the book's Web site (**www.mhhe.com/sc3e**), we discuss the details of how to calculate the minimum reserve requirement for a bank.

Regulations on Capital Adequacy (Leverage)

7 The FDICIA of 1991 requires banks (and thrifts, discussed in Chapter 14) to adopt essentially the same (minimum) capital requirements relative to their assets. Some minor differences exist, but the capital requirements for the two industries have essentially converged.[25] A minimum capital ratio effectively constrains the leverage of a CB—since highly leveraged CBs may be more prone to credit, interest rate, and other shocks, and thus, to the risk of failure. Given this, we concentrate on the recent evolution of capital requirements in commercial banking. Since 1987, U.S. commercial banks have faced two different capital requirements: a capital-to-assets ratio and a risk–based capital ratio that is subdivided into a Tier I capital risk–based ratio and a total capital (Tier I plus Tier II capital) risk–based ratio.

24. The Garn-St. Germain Commercial banks Act of 1982 (Public Law 97–320) requires that \$2 million of reservable liabilities of each commercial banks be subject to a zero percent reserve requirement. Each year, the Federal Reserve adjusts the amount of reservable liabilities subject to this zero percent reserve requirement for the succeeding calendar year by 80 percent of the percentage increase in the total reservable liabilities of all depository institutions, measured on an annual basis as of June 30. As of 2005 these were the requirements. The reserve was also reduced from 12 to 10 percent for transaction accounts in April 1992.

25. Credit unions are subject to capital adequacy requirements similar to commercial banks, as required by the National Credit Union Administration (NCUA).

TABLE 13–4 Specifications of Capital Categories for Prompt Corrective Action

Zone	(1) Leverage Ratio		(2) Total Risk-Based Ratio		(3) Tier I Risk-Based Ratio		Capital Directive/ Other
1. Well capitalized	5% or above	and	10% or above	and	6% or above	and	Not subject to a capital directive to meet a specific level for any capital measure
2. Adequately capitalized	4% or above*	and	8% or above	and	4% or above	and	Does not meet the definition of well capitalized
3. Undercapitalized	Under 4%†	or	Under 8%	or	Under 4%		
4. Significantly undercapitalized	Under 3%	or	Under 6%	or	Under 4%		
5. Critically undercapitalized	2% or less	or	2 % or less	or	2% or less		

*3 percent or higher for banks and savings associations that are not experiencing or anticipating significant growth.

†Under 3 percent for composite one-rated banks and savings associations that are not experiencing or anticipating significant growth.

Source: Federal Reserve Board of Governors, September 10, 1993. **www.federalreserve.gov**

capital-to-assets ratio

Ratio of an FI's core capital to its assets.

The Capital-to-Assets Ratio. The **capital-to-assets ratio** measures the ratio of a bank's book value of primary or core capital to the book value of its assets. The lower this ratio, the more highly leveraged the bank is. Primary or core capital is a bank's common equity (book value) plus qualifying cumulative perpetual preferred stock plus minority interests in equity accounts of consolidated subsidiaries.

With the passage of the FDICIA of 1991, a bank's capital adequacy is assessed according to where its capital-to-assets (C), or leverage ratio, places it in one of five target zones listed in the Leverage Ratio column of Table 13–4. The capital-to-assets or leverage ratio is:

$$C = \frac{\text{Core capital}}{\text{Assets}}$$

If a bank's capital-to-assets ratio is 5 percent or higher, it is well capitalized. At 4 percent or more, it is adequately capitalized; at less than 4 percent, it is undercapitalized; at less than 3 percent, it is significantly undercapitalized; and at 2 percent or less, it is critically undercapitalized. Since 1995, less than 0.5 percent of the banking industry assets have been classified as undercapitalized. This compares to 31.3 percent undercapitalized in the fourth quarter of 1990 (i.e., during the 1989–1991 recession). Associated with each zone is a mandatory set of actions as well as a set of discretionary actions for regulators to take. Collectively, these are called "prompt corrective action," or PCA. The idea here is to enforce minimum capital requirements and to limit a regulator's ability to show forbearance to the worst capitalized banks.

prompt corrective action (PCA)

Mandatory action that regulators must take as a bank's capital ratio falls.

Since December 18, 1992, under the FDICIA legislation, regulators must take specific actions—**prompt corrective action (PCA)**—when a bank falls outside zone 1, or the well-capitalized category. If prompt corrective actions are insufficient to save the bank, a receiver must be appointed when a bank's book value of capital-to-assets (leverage) ratio falls to 2 percent or lower.[26] Thus, receivership is mandatory even before the book value ratio falls to 0 percent.

26. Admittedly, managers and stockholders might exploit a number of loopholes and delaying tactics, especially through the courts.

Unfortunately, the leverage ratio as a measure of capital "adequacy" has three problems:

1. **Market Value**—even if a bank is closed when its leverage ratio falls to 2 percent or less, a 2 percent book capital-to-assets ratio could be consistent with a massive negative market value net worth (i.e., the liquidation value of the bank's assets is less than the market value of its liabilities). There is no assurance that depositors and regulators (including taxpayers) are adequately protected against losses.[27]
2. **Asset Risk**—by taking total assets as the denominator of the leverage or capital-to-assets ratio, it fails to consider, even partially, the different credit and interest rate risks of the assets that comprise total assets.
3. **Off-Balance-Sheet Activities**—despite the massive growth in banks' off-balances-heet activities and their associated risks (see Chapters 11 and 19), the leverage or capital-to-assets ratio does not consider these activities.

www.bis.org

Basel (or Basle) Accord

An agreement that requires the imposition of risk-based capital ratios on banks in major industrialized countries.

Risk-Based Capital Ratios. Considering the weaknesses of the simple capital-to-assets ratio just described above, in 1988 U.S. bank regulators formally agreed with other member countries of the Bank for International Settlements (BIS) to implement two new risk-based capital ratios for all commercial banks under their jurisdiction. The BIS phased in and fully implemented these risk-based capital ratios on January 1, 1993, under what has become known as the **Basel** (or **Basle) Accord** (now called Basel I).

The 1993 Basel Agreement explicitly incorporated the different credit risks of assets (both on and off the balance sheet) into capital adequacy measures. This was followed with a revision in 1998 in which market risk was incorporated into risk-based capital in the form of an "add-on" to the 8 percent ratio for credit risk exposure (see Chapter 19). In 2001, the BIS issued a consultative document, "The New Basel Capital Accord," that proposed the incorporation (fully effective in 2007) of operational risk into capital requirements (see Chapter 19) and updated the credit risk assessments in the 1993 agreement. This agreement was adopted in June 2004.[28]

The new Basel Accord or Agreement (called Basel II) consists of three mutually reinforcing pillars (illustrated in Figure 13–5), which together contribute to the safety and soundness of the financial system. Pillar 1 covers regulatory capital requirements for credit, market, and operational risk. The measurement of market risk did not change from that adopted in 1998. In the 2001 consultative document, the BIS proposed a range of options for CBs addressing both credit and operational risk. For the measurement of credit risk, two options were proposed. The first is the standardized approach, and the second is the internal ratings–based (IRB) approach. The Standardized Approach is similar to the 1993 Agreement, but is more risk sensitive. Under the IRB approach, banks are allowed to use their internal estimates of borrower creditworthiness to assess credit risk in their portfolios (using their own internal rating systems and credit scoring models) subject to strict methodological and disclosure standards.[29] Three different approaches are available to measure operational risk: the Basic Indicator, Standardized, and Internal Measurement Approaches.

In Pillar 2, the BIS stressed the importance of the regulatory review process as a critical complement to minimum capital requirements. Specifically, the BIS proposed procedures through which regulators ensure that each bank has sound internal processes in place to assess the adequacy of its capital and set targets for capital that are commensurate with the bank's specific risk profile and control environment. In Pillar 3, the BIS proposal provided detailed guidance on the disclosure of capital structure, risk exposures, and capital adequacy. Such disclosure requirements allow market participants to assess critical information describing the risk profile and capital adequacy of banks.

27. Many savings institutions that were closed with low book capital values in the 1980s had negative net worths on a market value basis exceeding 30 percent.

28. See Basel Committee on Banking Supervision, "The New Basel Capital Accord," January 2001, and International Convergence of Capital Measurement and Capital Standards: A Revised Framework, June 2004, **www.bis.org.**

29. In fact, a Foundations Approach and an Advanced Approach fall under the IRB approach. The approaches differ in the extent to which they allow banks to use their own data to calculate the credit risk sensitivity of their portfolios.

FIGURE 13–5 Basel II Pillars of Capital Regulation

Pillar 1	Pillar 2	Pillar 3
Calculation of regulatory minimum capital requirements	Regulatory supervisory review so as to complement and enforce minimum capital requirements calculated under Pillar 1	Requirements on rules for disclosure of capital structure, risk exposures, and capital adequacy so as to increase FI transparency and enhance market/investor discipline
1. Credit risk: on-balance-sheet and off-balance-sheet (Standardized vs. Internal Ratings-Based Approach) 2. Market risk (Standardized vs. Internal Ratings-Based Approach) 3. Operational risk (Basic Indicator vs. Standardized vs. Advanced Measurement Approach)		

Regulators currently enforce the Basel Accord's risk-based capital ratios as well as the traditional capital-to-assets ratio. Unlike the simple capital-to-assets ratio, the calculation of the two risk-based capital adequacy measures is quite complex. Their major innovation is to distinguish among the size of the different risks of assets on the balance sheet and to identify the risk inherent in instruments off the balance sheet by using a risk-adjusted assets denominator in these capital adequacy ratios. In a very rough fashion, these capital ratios mark to market a bank's on- and off-balance-sheet positions to reflect its overall risk exposure.

Capital. A bank's capital is divided into Tier I and Tier II. Tier I capital is primary or core capital; Tier II capital is supplementary capital. The total capital that the bank holds is defined as the sum of Tier I and Tier II capital less deductions. The definitions of Tier I core capital and Tier II supplementary capital are shown in Table 13–5.

Tier I Capital. Tier I capital is closely linked to a bank's book value of equity, reflecting the concept of the core capital contribution of a bank's owners.[30] Basically, it includes the book value of common equity plus an amount of perpetual (nonmaturing) preferred stock plus minority equity interests held by the bank in subsidiaries minus goodwill. Goodwill is an accounting item that reflects the amount a bank pays above market value when it purchases or acquires other banks or subsidiaries.

Tier II Capital. Tier II capital is a broad array of secondary capital resources. It includes a bank's loan loss reserves up to a maximum of 1.25 percent of risk-adjusted assets plus various convertible and subordinated debt instruments with maximum caps.

Risk-Adjusted Assets. Risk-adjusted assets represent the denominator of the risk-based capital ratio. Two components comprise **risk-adjusted assets:** (1) risk adjusted on-balance-sheet assets and (2) risk adjusted off-balance-sheet assets.

risk-adjusted assets

On- and off-balance-sheet assets whose value is adjusted for approximate credit risk.

30. However, loan loss reserves are assigned to Tier II capital because they often reflect losses that have already occurred rather than losses or insolvency risks that may occur in the future.

TABLE 13-5 Summary Definition of Qualifying Capital for Bank Holding Companies

Components	Minimum Requirements after Transition Period
Core-capital (Tier I)	Must equal or exceed 4 percent of weighted-risk assets
Common stockholders' equity	No limit
Qualifying cumulative and noncumulative perpetual preferred stock	Limited to 25 percent of the sum of common stock, minority interests, and qualifying perpetual preferred stock
Minority interest in equity accounts of consolidated subsidiaries	Organizations should avoid using minority interests to introduce elements not otherwise qualifying for Tier I capital
Less: Goodwill*	
Supplementary capital (Tier II)	Total of Tier II limited to 100 percent of Tier I†
Allowance for loan and lease losses	Limited to 1.25 percent of weighted-risk assets
Perpetual preferred stock	No limit within Tier II
Hybrid capital instruments, perpetual debt, and mandatory convertible securities	No limit within Tier II
Subordinated debt and intermediate-term preferred stock (original weighted-average maturity of five years or more)	Subordinated debt and intermediate-term preferred stock are limited to 50 percent of Tier I; amortized for capital purposes as they approach maturity†
Revaluation reserves (equity and buildings)	Not included; organizations encouraged to disclose; may be evaluated on a case-by-case basis for international comparisons; considered in making an overall assessment of capitalization
Deductions (from sum of Tier I and Tier II)	
Investments in unconsolidated subsidiaries	
Reciprocal holdings of banking organizations' capital securities	As a general rule, one-half of the aggregate investments would be deducted from Tier I capital and one-half from Tier II capital‡
Other deductions (such as other subsidiaries or joint ventures) as determined by supervisory authority	On a case-by-case basis or as a matter of policy after formal rule making
Total capital (Tier I + Tier II − deductions)	Must equal or exceed 8 percent of weighted-risk assets

*Goodwill on the books of bank holding companies before March 12, 1988 would be grandfathered for the transition period.

†Amounts in excess of limitations are permitted but do not qualify as capital.

‡A proportionately larger amount may be deducted from Tier I capital if the risks associated with the subsidiary so warrant.

Source: Federal Reserve Board of Governors, Press Release, January 1989, Attachment II. **www.federalreserve.gov**

total risk–based capital ratio

The ratio of a CB's total capital to its risk-adjusted assets.

tier I (core) capital ratio

The ratio of a CB's core capital to its risk-adjusted assets.

To be adequately capitalized, a bank must hold a minimum total capital (Tier I core capital plus Tier II supplementary capital) to risk-adjusted assets ratio of 8 percent—that is, its **total risk–based capital ratio** is calculated as:

$$\text{Total risk–based capital ratio} = \frac{\text{Total capital (Tier I plus Tier II)}}{\text{Risk-adjusted assets}} \geq 8\%$$

In addition, the Tier I core capital component of total capital has its own minimum guideline. The **Tier I (core) capital ratio** is calculated as follows:

$$\text{Tier I (core) capital ratio} = \frac{\text{Core capital (Tier I)}}{\text{Risk-adjusted assets}} \geq 4\%$$

That is, of the 8 percent total risk–based capital ratio, a bank must hold a minimum of 4 percent in core or primary capital.

In addition to their use to define adequately capitalized banks, risk-based capital ratios—along with the traditional capital-to-assets ratio—also define well-capitalized, undercapitalized, significantly undercapitalized, and critically undercapitalized banks as part of the prompt corrective action program under FDICIA. As with the simple leverage ratio for both the total risk–based capital ratio and the Tier I risk–based capital ratios,

TABLE 13–6 Summary of Prompt Corrective Action Provisions of the Federal Deposit Insurance Corporation Improvement Act of 1991

Zone	Mandatory Provisions	Discretionary Provisions
1. Well capitalized		
2. Adequately capitalized	1. Prohibit brokered deposits, except with FDIC approval	
3. Undercapitalized	1. Suspend dividends and management fees 2. Require capital restoration plan 3. Restrict asset growth 4. Require approval for acquisitions 5. Prohibit brokered deposits	1. Order recapitalization 2. Restrict interaffiliate transactions 3. Restrict deposit interest rates 4. Restrict certain other activities 5. Allow any other action that would better carry out prompt corrective action
4. Significantly undercapitalized	1. Same as for Zone 3 2. Order recapitalization* 3. Restrict interaffiliate transactions* 4. Restrict deposit interest rates* 5. Restrict pay of officers	1. Enforce any Zone 3 discretionary actions 2. Appoint conservatorship or receivership if fails to submit or implement plan or recapitalize pursuant to order 3. Enforce any other Zone 5 provision, if such action is necessary to carry out prompt corrective action
5. Critically undercapitalized	1. Same as for Zone 4 2. Appoint receiver/conservator within 90 days* 3. Appoint receiver if still in Zone 5 four quarters after becoming critically undercapitalized 4. Suspend payments on subordinated debt* 5. Restrict certain other activities	

*Not required if primary supervisor determines action would not serve purpose of prompt corrective action or if certain other conditions are met.

Source: Federal Reserve Board of Governors, Press Release, September 10, 1993. **www.federalreserve.gov**

these five zones—specified in columns (2) and (3) of Table 13–4—assess capital adequacy and the actions regulators are mandated to take as well as those that regulators have the discretion to take.[31] Table 13–6 summarizes these regulatory actions. In Appendix 13D to this chapter located at the book's Web site (**www.mhhe.com/sc3e**), we discuss the details of how to calculate a bank's risk–based capital ratio under both Basel I and Basel II.[32]

31. Most commercial banks keep their capital ratios well above the minimums. One reason for this is that banks have become very dependent on large (greater than $100,000) deposits of commercial firms. Since these deposits are beyond the FDIC insurance limit, banks can attract and retain such deposits only to the extent they can show they are financially sound (i.e., having more than the minimum equity ratio).

32. Since the mid-1980s, a growing number of observers have proposed using subordinate debt (SD) in addition to common stock to provide information on the riskiness of banks. In response to these concerns, the Financial Services Modernization Act of 1999 directed the Federal Reserve and the U.S. Treasury to study and report to Congress on the feasibility and appropriateness of requiring all or some CBs to maintain some portion of their capital in the form of SD. Although the study concluded that a policy of mandatory SD issuance would potentially enhance market discipline and safety and soundness, the Fed and Treasury stated in their 2000 report that additional evidence needed to be gathered before they could support the imposition of a mandatory SD requirement for large CBs. Thus, no final mandate has been implemented. See "The Feasibility and Desirability of Mandatory Subordinated Debt," Board of Governors of the Federal Reserve and U.S. Department of the Treasury, December 2000.

Off-Balance-Sheet Regulations

In the 1980s, increasing losses on loans to less-developed and eastern European countries, increased interest rate volatility, and squeezed interest margins for on-balance-sheet lending (as the result of nonbank competition) led many large commercial banks to seek profitable activities off the balance sheet (OBS). By moving activities off the balance sheet, banks hoped to earn more fee income to offset declining margins or spreads on their traditional lending business. At the same time, they could avoid regulatory costs or taxes since reserve requirements, deposit insurance premiums, and capital adequacy requirements were not levied on off-balance-sheet activities. Thus, banks had both earnings and regulatory "tax-avoidance" incentives to move activities off their balance sheets.

The dramatic increase in OBS activities caused the Federal Reserve to introduce an OBS activity tracking plan in 1983. As part of the quarterly financial reports they file, banks began submitting schedule L, on which they listed the notional dollar size and variety of their OBS activities. In Chapter 12, we discussed four different OBS activities that banks must report to the Federal Reserve each quarter as part of their schedule L section of the financial report (loan commitments, letters of credit, derivative contracts, and loans sold). Further, as described above, the Basel Accord incorporated off-balance-sheet activities in the calculation of required minimum regulatory capital for banks.

DO YOU UNDERSTAND?

1. Why regulators impose reserve requirements on depository institutions?
2. The difference between a bank's leverage ratio and its risk-based capital ratio?
3. What actions regulators must take under prompt corrective action (PCA)?
4. What caused the Federal Reserve to introduce a tracking plan for commercial banks off-balance-sheet activity?

5 FOREIGN VERSUS DOMESTIC REGULATION OF COMMERCIAL BANKS

As discussed earlier in this chapter, many of the product and geographic expansion barriers on U.S. commercial banks have recently been lowered. Despite the loosening of regulations, however, U.S. CBs are still subject to stricter regulations than CBs in foreign countries.

Product Diversification Activities

With the passage of the Financial Services Modernization Act of 1999, the range of nonbank product activities that U.S. banks are permitted to engage in is now more comparable to bank activities allowed in the major industrialized countries.[33]

Global or International Expansion Activities

U.S. CBs have expanded into foreign countries through branches and subsidiaries; this has been reciprocated by the increased entrance of foreign CBs into U.S. financial service markets.

Regulations of U.S. Banks in Foreign Countries. Although some U.S. banking organizations such as Citigroup and J. P. Morgan Chase have had foreign offices since the beginning of the 20th century, the major phase of expansion began in the early 1960s following passage of the Overseas Direct Investment Control Act of 1964. This law restricted U.S. banks' ability to lend to U.S. corporations that wanted to make foreign investments. This law was eventually

33. Many of Japan's postwar regulations were modeled on those of the United States. Thus, Article 65 in Japan separates commercial banking from investment banking in a fashion similar to the pre-1999 Glass-Steagall Act in the United States. In 1992, Japan passed a major deregulation, however, that considerably weakened the historic barriers between commercial and investment banking in that country. Specifically, under the 1992 Comprehensive Financial Reform Law, Japanese banks are permitted to establish subsidiaries to engage in a full range of securities activities. To protect small brokers, however, the law withholds permission to engage in retail equities brokerage. Similarly, in December 2004, Japan's Financial Services Agency (FSA) announced a new set of policies for banking, securities, and insurance firms intended to further deregulate the financial sector. Specifically, the FSA further streamlined the banking, securities, and insurance laws and abandoned unnecessary regulations to better cope with the emergence of financial conglomerates. The changes did not allow for the cross-sector legislation like that of the Financial Services Modernization Act in the United States. However, it did allow banks, securities firms, and insurers to enter one another's business. See "Japan Outlines New Insurance, Banking Rules," *The Wall Street Journal,* December 27, 2004, p. A7.

TABLE 13–7 U.S. Bank Claims Held Outside the United States*

	1990	1995	2000	2001	2004
Total	$320.1	$551.7	$1,027.3	$971.5	$1,473.4
United Kingdom	60.9	82.4	115.6	255.5	383.8
Offshore banking centers†	44.7	99.0	76.3	72.2	39.9

*Billions of dollars held by U.S. offices and foreign branches of U.S. banks (including U.S. banks that are subsidiaries of foreign banks).

†Includes Bahamas, Bermuda, and Cayman Islands.

Source: *Federal Reserve Bulletin,* Table 3.21, various issues and Federal Financial Institutions Examination Council. **www.federalreserve.gov; www.ffiec.gov**

repealed, but it created incentives for U.S. banks to establish foreign offices to service the funding and other business needs of their U.S. clients in other countries. In addition, with certain exceptions, Federal Reserve Regulation K has allowed U.S. banking offices in other countries to engage in the foreign country's permitted banking activities, even if the United States did not permit such activities. For example, U.S. banks setting up foreign subsidiaries can lease real property, act as general insurance agents, and underwrite and deal in foreign corporate securities (up to a maximum commitment of $2 million).

NAFTA

North American Free Trade Agreement.

The 1994, **NAFTA** (North American Free Trade Agreement) enabled U.S. (and Canadian) banks to expand into Mexico, and the December 1997 agreement by 100 countries, reached under the auspices of the World Trade Organization (WTO), heralds an important step toward dismantling barriers inhibiting the entry of foreign banks, insurance companies, and securities firms into emerging market countries.[34]

As a result of these regulatory changes, U.S. banks have been accelerating their foreign business in recent years. U.S. bank claims held outside the country have risen from $320.1 billion in 1990 to $1,473.4 billion in 2004 (Table 13–7). Interestingly, a major segment has been "offshore banking"—issuing loans and accepting deposits. The U.S. bank claims held in the United Kingdom reflect its importance as the center of the Eurodollar market, which is the market for dollar loans and deposits made and held outside the United States.

Political risk concerns among savers in emerging market countries have led to enormous outflows of dollars from those countries, often to U.S. branches and subsidiaries in the Cayman Islands and the Bahamas, which have very stringent bank secrecy rules. Because of the secrecy rules in some foreign countries and the possibility that these rules may result in money laundering and the financing of terrorist activities, the U.S. government enacted the USA Patriot Act of 2001, which amended the Bank Secrecy Act in establishing standards for screening customers who open accounts at financial institutions. The Act prohibits U.S. banks from providing banking services to foreign banks that have no physical presence in any country (so-called shell banks). The bill also added foreign corruption offenses to the list of crimes that can trigger a U.S. money laundering prosecution. Also, federal authorities have the power to subpoena the records of a foreign bank's U.S. correspondent account. Further, the bill makes a depositor's funds in a foreign bank's U.S. correspondent account subject to the same civil forfeiture rules that apply to depositors' funds in other U.S. accounts. Finally, the Act requires U.S. banks to improve their due diligence review in order to guard against money laundering.

In accordance with the Patriot Act, in April 2004 the FBI and federal regulators began a probe into large cash withdrawals from Riggs National Bank by Saudi Arabian citizens/customers and accused Riggs of failing to alert regulators of suspicious transactions. The Office of the Comptroller of the Currency (OCC) also classified Riggs as a "troubled institution" for failing to adequately tighten its money laundering controls despite a request from the OCC to do so. Regulators also pursued a second line of inquiry into

34. See "Accord Is Reached to Lower Barriers in Global Finance," *The New York Times,* December 12, 1997, p. A1.

whether Riggs violated "know your customer" record-keeping laws in its dealings with foreign customers. Treasury Department investigators were looking into the relationship between Riggs and high-risk foreign customers. In January 2005, the Riggs board accepted a plea agreement presented to them by prosecutors in which the bank admitted to one count of violating the Bank Secrecy Act by failing to file reports to regulators on suspicious transfers and withdrawals by clients and agreed to pay a fine of $25 million. In another action, in July 2004, federal and state bank regulators reached an agreement with ABN Amro Bank to correct deficiencies in the bank's program to fight money laundering. The pact required ABN Amro's New York branch to improve policies and practices that had caused certain suspicious transactions in its correspondent banking accounts to go unreported. Just two months later Standard Chartered PLC signed an agreement with regulators stating that it would adhere to the Patriot Act's prohibition on holding accounts for foreign shell banks. Thus, through the middle of the first decade of the 2000s, U.S. regulators are actively pursuing foreign bank violations of the Bank Secrecy and Patriot Acts.

Regulation of Foreign Banks in the United States. Prior to 1978, foreign branches and agencies entering the United States were primarily licensed at the state level. As such, their entry, regulation, and oversight were almost totally confined to the state level. Beginning in 1978 with the passage of the International Banking Act (IBA) and the more recent passage of the Foreign Bank Supervision and Enforcement Act (FBSEA), federal regulators have exerted increasing control over foreign banks operating in the United States.

Pre-IBA. Before the passage in 1978 of the IBA, foreign agencies and branches entering the United States with state licenses had some competitive advantages and disadvantages relative to most domestic banks. On the one hand, as state-licensed organizations, they were not subject to the Federal Reserve's reserve requirements, audits, and exams; interstate branching restrictions (the McFadden Act); or restrictions on corporate securities underwriting activities (the Glass-Steagall Act). However, they had no access to the Federal Reserve's discount window (i.e., lender of last resort); no direct access to Fedwire and, thus, the fed funds market; and no access to FDIC deposit insurance.

Their inability to gain access to deposit insurance effectively precluded them from the U.S. retail banking market and its deposit base. As a result, prior to 1978, foreign banks in the United States largely concentrated on wholesale banking.

Post-IBA. The unequal treatment of domestic and foreign banks regarding federal regulation and the lobbying by domestic banks regarding the unfairness of this situation provided the impetus for Congress to pass the IBA in 1978. The fundamental regulatory philosophy underlying the IBA was one of **national treatment,** a philosophy that attempted to create a level playing field for domestic and foreign banks in U.S. banking markets. As a result of this act, foreign banks were required to hold Federal Reserve–specified reserve requirements if their worldwide assets exceeded $1 billion, and they became subject to Federal Reserve examinations and to both the McFadden and Glass-Steagall Acts. With respect to the latter, an important grandfather provision in the act allowed foreign banks established in the United States prior to 1978 to keep their "illegal" interstate branches and securities-activity operations—that is, interstate and security activity restrictions were applied only to foreign banks entering the United States after 1978.[35]

national treatment

Regulation of foreign banks in the same fashion as domestic banks, or the creation of a level playing field.

If anything, the passage of the IBA accelerated the expansion of foreign bank activities in the United States. A major reason for this was that for the first time, the IBA gave foreign banks access to the Federal Reserve's discount window, Fedwire, and FDIC insurance. In particular, access to FDIC insurance allowed access to retail banking. In 1979 alone, foreign banks acquired four large U.S. banks (Crocker, National Bank of North America, Union Planters, and Marine Midland). In addition, in the early 1980s, the Bank of Tokyo, Mitsubishi

35. For example, in 1978, approximately 60 foreign banks had branches in at least three states. As noted earlier, the McFadden Act prevented domestic banks from interstate branching.

Bank, and Sanwa Bank invested $1.3 billion in California bank acquisitions.[36] Overall, Japanese banks owned more than 25 percent of California bank assets at the end of the 1980s.

The Foreign Bank Supervision Enhancement Act (FBSEA) of 1991. Along with the growth of foreign bank assets in the United States came concerns about foreign banks' rapidly increasing share of U.S. banking markets and about the weakness of regulatory oversight of many of these institutions. Three events focused attention on the weaknesses of foreign bank regulation. The first event was the collapse of the Bank of Credit and Commerce International (BCCI), which had a highly complex international organization structure based in the Middle East, the Cayman Islands, and Luxembourg and had undisclosed ownership stakes in two large U.S. banks. BCCI was not subject to any consolidated supervision by a home country regulator; this quickly became apparent after its collapse, when massive fraud, insider lending abuses, and money-laundering operations were discovered. The second event was the issuance of more than $1 billion in unauthorized letters of credit to Saddam Hussein's Iraq by the Atlanta agency of an Italian bank, Banca Nazionale del Lavoro. The third event was the unauthorized taking of deposit funds by the U.S. representative office of the Greek National Mortgage Bank of New York.

These events and related concerns led to the passage of the FBSEA in 1991. The objective of this act was to extend federal regulatory authority over foreign banking organizations in the United States, especially when these organizations had entered using state licenses. The act's five main features have significantly enhanced the powers of federal bank regulators over foreign banks in the United States:

1. **Entry**—under FBSEA, a foreign banking organization must now have the Fed's approval to establish a subsidiary, branch, agency, or representative office in the United States. The approval applies to both a new entry and an entry by acquisition. To secure Fed approval, the organization must meet a number of standards, two of which are mandatory. First, the foreign bank must be subject to comprehensive supervision on a consolidated basis by a home country regulator. Second, that regulator must furnish all the information that the Federal Reserve requires to evaluate the application. Both standards attempt to avoid the lack of disclosure and lack of centralized supervision associated with BCCI's failure.
2. **Closure**—FBSEA also gives the Federal Reserve authority to close a foreign bank if its home country supervision is inadequate, if it violates U.S. laws, or if it engages in unsound and unsafe banking practices.
3. **Examination**—the Federal Reserve has the power to examine each office of a foreign bank, including its representative offices. Further, each branch or agency must be examined at least once a year.
4. **Deposit Taking**—only foreign subsidiaries with access to FDIC insurance can take retail deposits under $100,000. This effectively rolls back the provision of the IBA that gave foreign branches and agencies access to FDIC insurance.
5. **Activity Powers**—beginning December 19, 1992, state-licensed branches and agencies of foreign banks were not allowed to engage in any activity that was not permitted to a federal branch.

DO YOU UNDERSTAND?

1. What regulatory changes have encouraged the growth of U.S. offshore banking? What factors have deterred U.S. offshore banking?
2. The impact the passage of the International Banking Act of 1978 had on foreign bank activities in the United States?
3. What the five main features of the Foreign Bank Supervision Enforcement Act of 1991 are?

Overall, then, the FBSEA considerably increased the Federal Reserve's authority over foreign banks and added to the regulatory burden or costs of entry into the United States for foreign banks. This has made the post-FBSEA U.S. banking market much less attractive to foreign banks than it had been over the period 1980–1992. Perhaps the strongest punitive action taken so far against a foreign bank was the Federal Reserve's closure of all operations of Daiwa Bank in the United States for six weeks in 1995 for not reporting a bond trader's losses of nearly $1 billion and the resulting four-year prison sentence and $2.57 million fine imposed on the offending trader by a New York court. This closure signaled a willingness of the U.S. banking authorities to be much tougher on foreign banks in the United States in the future.

36. Thus, the newly formed bank—as a result of the 1996 Bank of Tokyo–Mitsubishi Bank merger—controls 70 percent of the Union Bank of San Francisco (a $17 billion bank with 200 branches) and 100 percent of the Bank of California (a $7 billion bank with 50 branches).

SUMMARY

Commercial banks provide services that are vital to all sectors of the economy. Failure to efficiently provide these services can be costly to both the suppliers and users of funds. Consequently, CBs are regulated to protect against a breakdown in the provision of CB services. In this chapter, we reviewed the regulations imposed on CBs. We provided an overview of historical and current regulations on CBs' product offerings and geographic expansion opportunities. The recent loosening of regulations in these areas is likely to result in the emergence of many large U.S. CBs as globally oriented universal banks. We also described regulations on the asset and liability portfolios of CBs. The chapter concluded with a look at foreign CB regulations and the regulation of foreign CBs in the United States.

SEARCH THE SITE

Go to the FDIC Web site at **www.fdic.gov.** Find the most recent reserve balance and reserve ratios held by BIF and SAIF using the following steps. Once at the Web site,

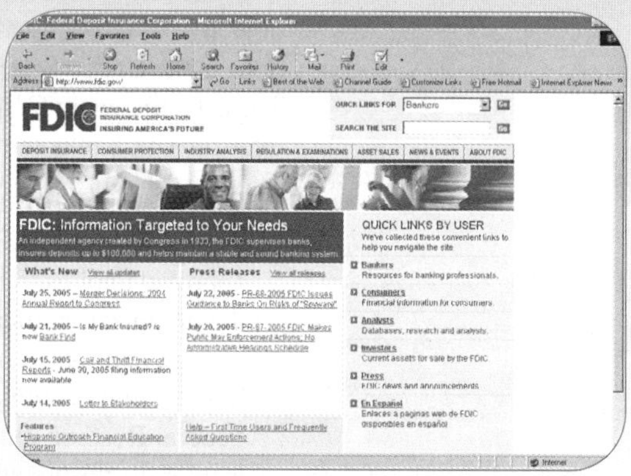

Click on "Analysis."

Click on "FDIC Quarterly Banking Profile."

Click on "Quarterly Banking Profile."

Click on "Deposit Insurance Fund Trends."

Click on "Table I-B Selected Insurance Fund Indicators."

This will bring up a file that contains the relevant data.

Questions

1. How have these values changed since 2004 as reported in the chapter?
2. If BIF and SAIF were combined, as has been proposed by regulators, calculate the total reserve funds held and the combined reserve ratio.

QUESTIONS

1. What forms of protection and regulation are imposed by regulators of CBs to ensure their safety and soundness?
2. How has the separation of commercial banking and investment banking activities evolved through time? How does this differ from banking activities in other countries?
3. A Section 20 subsidiary of a major U.S. bank is planning to underwrite corporate securities and expects to generate $5 million in revenues. It currently underwrites U.S. Treasury securities and general obligation municipal bonds, and earns annual fees of $40 million.
   a. Is the bank in compliance with the laws regulating the turnover of Section 20 subsidiaries?
   b. If it plans to increase underwriting of corporate securities and generate $11 million in revenues, is it in compliance? Would it have been in compliance prior to passage of the Financial Services Modernization Act of 1999?
4. What insurance activities are permitted for U.S. commercial bank holding companies?
5. How did the absence of any U.S. commercial banks from the top 20 world banks likely affect bank industry reform in Congress?
6. What are the new provisions on interstate banking in the Riegle-Neal Interstate Banking and Branching Efficiency Act of 1994?
7. What is the difference between an MBHC and an OBHC? What are the implications of the difference for bank expansion?

8. Why is the market value of equity a better measure of a bank's ability to absorb losses than book value of equity?
9. How is the leverage ratio for a bank defined?
10. What is the significance of prompt corrective action as specified by the FDICIA legislation?
11. Identify and discuss the weaknesses of the leverage ratio as a measure of capital adequacy.
12. What is the Basel Agreement?
13. What is the major feature in the estimation of credit risk under the 1988 Basel capital requirements?
14. What is the total risk–based capital ratio?
15. Identify the five zones of capital adequacy and explain the mandatory regulatory actions corresponding to each zone.
16. What are the definitional differences between Tier I and Tier II capital?
17. What components are used in the calculation of credit risk–adjusted assets?
18. How have the International Banking Act of 1978 and FDICIA of 1991 been detrimental to foreign banks in the United States?
19. What are some of the main features of the Foreign Bank Supervision Enhancement Act of 1991?

The following questions are related to Appendix 13C and 13D material located at the book's Web site (**www.mhhe.com/sc3e**).

20. If the reserve computation period extends from May 18 through May 31, what is the corresponding reserve maintenance period? What accounts for the difference?
21. The average demand deposits of a bank during the most recent reserve computation period has been estimated at $225 million over a 14-day period (Tuesday to Monday) and the corresponding daily vault cash during this period was $4 million. The average daily reserves at the Fed during the 14-day reserve maintenance period has been $16 million.
    a. What are the average daily required reserves to be held by the bank during the maintenance period?
    b. Is the bank in compliance with the requirements?
22. The following net transaction accounts have been documented by a bank for the computation of its reserve requirements (in millions).

	Tuesday 11th	Wednesday 12th	Thursday 13th	Friday 14th	Monday 17th
Demand deposits	$300	$250	$280	$260	$280

	Tuesday 18th	Wednesday 19th	Thursday 20th	Friday 21th	Monday 24th
Demand deposits	$300	$270	$260	$250	$240

The average daily reserves at the Fed for the 14-day reserve maintenance period have been $22.7 million per day and the average vault cash for the computation period has been estimated to be $2 million per day.
    a. What is the amount of the average daily required reserves to be held by the bank during the maintenance period?
    b. Is the bank in compliance with the requirements?
23. What is the contribution to the asset base of the following items under the Basel I (Basel II) requirements? Under the U.S. capital-to-assets rule?
    a. $10 million cash reserves.
    b. $50 million 91-day U.S. Treasury bills.
    c. $25 million cash items in the process of collection.
    d. $5 million U.K. government bonds, AAA rated.
    e. $5 million Australian short-term government bonds, A rated.
    f. $1 million general obligation municipal bonds.
    g. $40 million repurchase agreements (against U.S. Treasuries).
    h. $500 million one- to four-family home mortgages.
    i. $500 million commercial and industrial loans, BBB rated.
    j. $100,000 performance-related standby letters of credit to a blue chip corporation.
    k. $100,000 performance-related standby letters of credit to a municipality issuing general obligation bonds.
    l. $7 million commercial letter of credit to a foreign, A rated corporation.
    m. $3 million five-year loan commitment to an OECD government.
    n. $8 million bankers acceptance conveyed to a U.S., AA rated corporation.
    o. $17 million three-year loan commitment to a private agent.
    p. $17 million three-month loan commitment to a private agent.
    q. $30 million standby letter of credit to back a corporate issue of commercial paper.
    r. $4 million five-year interest rate swap with no current exposure (the counterparty is a private agent).
    s. $4 million five-year interest rate swap with no current exposure (the counterparty is a municipality).
    t. $6 million two-year currency swap with $500,000 current exposure (the counterparty is a private agent).

The following information is for questions 24–27. Consider a bank's balance sheet as follows.

On-Balance-Sheet Items	Category	Face Value
Cash	1	$121,600
Short-term government securities (<92 days)	1	5,400
Long-term government securities (>92 days)	1	414,400
Federal reserve stock	1	9,800
Repos secured by federal agencies	2	159,000
Claims on U.S. depository institutions	2	937,900
Short-term (<1 year) claims on foreign banks	2	1,640,000
General obligations municipals	2	170,000
Claims on or guaranteed by federal agencies	2	26,500

On-Balance-Sheet Items	Category	Face Value
Municipal revenue bonds	3	112,900
Commercial loans, BB+ rated	4	6,645,700
Claims on foreign banks (>1 year)	4	5,800

Off-Balance-Sheet Items	Conversion Factor	Face Value
Guaranteed by U.S. Government: (RiskWeight Category 1)		
Loan commitments, AAA rated		
<1 year	0%	300
1–5 year	50%	1,140
Standby letters of credit, AA rated		
Performance related	50%	200
Other	100%	100
Backed by Domestic Depository Institution: (RiskWeight Category 2)		
Loan commitments, BBB + rated		
<1 year	0%	$ 1,000
>1 year	50%	3,000
Standby letters of credit, AA − rated		
Performance related	50%	200
Other	100%	56,400
Commercial letters of credit, BBB + rated	20%	400
Backed by State or Local Government Revenues: (Risk Weight Category 3)		
Loan commitments, BBB − rated		
>1 year	50%	$ 100
Standby letters of credit, AAA rated		
Performance related	50%	135,400

Off-Balance-Sheet Items	Conversion Factor	Face Value
Extended to Corporate Customers: (Risk Weight Category 4)		
Loan commitments, CCC rated		
<1 year	0%	$2,980,000
>1 year	50%	3,046,278
Standby letters of credit, BBB rated		
Performance related	50%	101,543
Direct credit substitute	100%	485,000
Commercial letters of credit, AA− rated	20%	78,978
Note issuance facilities	50%	20,154
Forward agreements	100%	5,900
Category II Interest Rate Market Contracts: (current exposure assumed to be zero)		
<1year (notional amount)	0%	2,000
>1–5 year (notional amount)	.5%	5,000

24. What is the bank's risk-adjusted asset base under Basel I and Basel II?

25. What are the bank's Tier I and total risk–based capital requirements?

26. Using the leverage-ratio requirement, what is the U.S. bank's minimum regulatory capital requirement to keep it in the well-capitalized zone?

27. What is the bank's capital level if the par value of its equity is $150,000; surplus value of equity is $200,000; and qualifying perpetual preferred stock is $50,000? Does the bank meet Basel (Tier I) capital standards? Does the bank comply with the well-capitalized leverage-ratio requirement?

APPENDIX 13A: Commercial Banks and Their Regulators

View this appendix at www.mhhe.com/sc3e

www.mhhe.com/sc3e

APPENDIX 13B: Proposed Changes to the FDIC's Deposit Insurance Premium Assessments

View this appendix at
www.mhhe.com/sc3e

APPENDIX 13C: Calculating Minimum Required Reserves at U.S. Commercial Banks

View this appendix at
www.mhhe.com/sc3e

APPENDIX 13D: Calculating Risk-Based Capital Ratios

View this appendix at
www.mhhe.com/sc3e

part four

Other Financial Institutions

Part Four of the text provides an overview of key characteristics and regulatory features of the other major sectors of the U.S. financial services industry. We discuss savings institutions, credit unions, and finance companies in Chapter 14, insurance companies in Chapter 15, securities firms and investment banks in Chapter 16, mutual funds in Chapter 17, and pension funds in Chapter 18.

OUTLINE

14

Other Lending Institutions

Savings Institutions, Credit Unions, and Finance Companies

OUTLINE

Chapter NAVIGATOR

1. What is the difference between a savings association, a savings bank, a credit union, and a finance company?
2. What are the main assets and liabilities held by savings institutions?
3. Who regulates savings institutions?
4. How did savings institutions perform in the early 2000s?
5. How are credit unions different from other depository institutions?
6. What are the main assets and liabilities held by credit unions?
7. What are the major types of finance companies?
8. What are the major assets and liabilities held by finance companies?
9. To what extent are finance companies regulated?

OTHER LENDING INSTITUTIONS: CHAPTER OVERVIEW

1

Like commercial banks, the main financial service provided by savings institutions, credit unions, and finance companies is lending. Savings institutions (SIs) comprise two different groups of FIs: savings associations and savings banks. Savings institutions were created in the early 1800s in response to commercial banks' concentration on serving the needs of business (commercial) enterprises rather than the needs of individuals requiring borrowed funds to purchase homes. Thus, the first SIs pooled individual savings and invested them mainly in mortgages and other securities. While today's SIs

FIGURE 14–1 Major Services Offered by Savings Institutions and Credit Unions

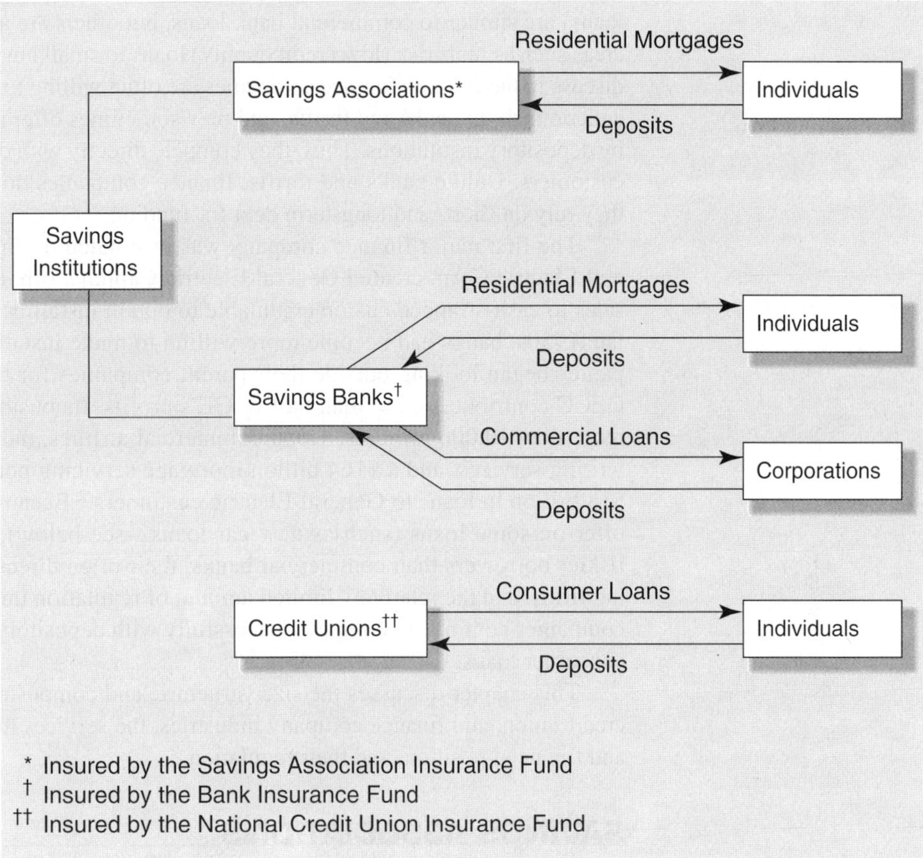

generally perform services similar to commercial banks, they are still grouped separately because they provide important residential mortgage lending and other financial services to households. Historically, savings associations have concentrated primarily on residential mortgages, while savings banks have operated as more diversified institutions, with a large concentration of residential mortgage assets but holding commercial loans, corporate bonds, and corporate stock as well. Credit unions are nonprofit depository institutions mutually organized and owned by their members (depositors). Credit unions have historically focused on consumer loans funded with member deposits. Savings institutions and credit unions together are often referred to as thrifts. Figure 14–1 illustrates the key asset side differences among these three types of depository institutions. Each category includes federally chartered and state-chartered institutions. Table 14–1 shows the number of each type as of year-end 2004.

TABLE 14–1 Number of Savings Institutions and Credit Unions, 2004

Type	Federally Chartered	State Chartered	Total
Savings associations	775 (72.2%)	299 (27.8%)	1,074
Savings banks	40 (11.8%)	299 (88.2%)	339
Credit unions	5,686 (61.7%)	3,524 (38.3%)	9,210

Source: FDIC, *Quarterly Banking Profile,* Fourth Quarter, 2004; and National Credit Union Association, *Quick Facts,* December 2004. **www.fdic.gov; www.ncua.gov**

The primary function of finance companies is also to make loans to both individuals and businesses. Finance companies provide such services as consumer lending, business lending, and mortgage financing. Some finance company loans (e.g., commercial and auto loans) are similar to commercial bank loans, but others are aimed at relatively specialized areas such as high-risk (low credit quality) loans to small businesses and consumers. As we discuss in the chapter, finance companies are often willing to lend to riskier customers than are commercial banks and thrifts, and they sometimes offer rates well below those offered by depository institutions. Thus, they compete directly with depository institutions for loan customers. Unlike banks and thrifts, finance companies do not accept deposits; instead, they rely on short- and long-term debt for funding.

The first major finance company was originated during the Depression when General Electric Corp. created General Electric Capital Corp. (GECC) to finance appliance sales to cash-strapped customers unable to obtain installment credit from banks.[1] By the late 1950s, banks had become more willing to make installment loans, so finance companies began looking outside their parent companies for business. For example, today GECC contributes more than half of GE's profits. Its business today includes leases for more than 10,000 rail cars, 1,000 commercial airlines, more than $30 billion in underwriting services, and a $164 billion mortgage servicing portfolio, along with more than $18 billion in loans to General Electric customers.[2] Because of the attractive rates they offer on some loans (such as new car loans—see below), their willingness to lend to riskier borrowers than commercial banks, their often direct affiliation with manufacturing firms, and the relatively limited amount of regulation imposed on these firms, finance companies continue to compete successfully with depository institutions for business and consumer loans.

This chapter discusses the size, structure, and composition of the savings institution, credit union, and finance company industries, the services they provide, their competitive and financial position, and their regulation.

SAVINGS ASSOCIATIONS

Size, Structure, and Composition of the Industry

The savings associations industry prospered throughout most of the 20th century. Savings associations were historically referred to as savings and loan (S&L) associations. However, in the 1980s, federally chartered savings banks appeared in the United States.[3] These institutions have the same regulators and regulations as the traditional savings and loans. Together they are referred to as savings associations. These specialized institutions made long-term residential mortgages usually backed by the short-term deposits of small savers. This strategy was successful largely because of the Federal Reserve's policy of smoothing or targeting interest rates, especially in the post–World War II period up until the late 1970s (see Chapter 4), and the generally stable and upward-sloping shape of the yield curve or the

1. Installment credit is a loan that is paid back to the lender with periodic payments (installments) consisting of varying amounts of interest and principal (e.g., auto loans, home mortgages, and student loans). Suppose a finance company lent $1,000 to a customer to be repaid in 36 equal installments at the end of each month over the next three years, and the finance company charges the borrower 8 percent interest on the balance of the loan outstanding at the beginning of each month. Accordingly, the borrower must pay the finance company an installment of $31.34 at the end of each month over the next three years to pay off principal and interest on the loan. The installment amount is determined using the following equation as outlined in Chapter 2:

$$\$1{,}000 = PMT\,(PVIFA_{8\%/12,\,3(12)})$$

2. See GECC's Web site, 2004.

3. The term *savings association* has replaced S&L to capture the change in the structure of the industry. In 1978, the Federal Home Loan Bank Board (FHLBB), at the time the main regulator of savings associations, began chartering federal savings banks insured by the Federal Savings and Loan Insurance Corporation (FSLIC). In 1982, the FHLBB allowed S&Ls to convert to federal savings banks with bank (rather than S&L) names. As more and more S&Ls converted to savings banks, the title associated with this sector of the thrift industry was revised to reflect this change.

term structure of interest rates (see Chapter 2). During some periods, such as the early 1960s, the yield curve did slope downward, but for most of the post–World War II period, the upward-sloping yield curve meant that the interest rates on savings associations' 30-year residential mortgage assets exceeded the rates they paid on their short-term deposit liabilities. Moreover, significant shocks to interest rates were generally absent because of the Fed's policy of interest rate smoothing and the fact that the world's economies were far less integrated compared with today's economies.

At the end of the 1970s, slightly fewer than 4,000 savings associations existed, with assets of approximately $0.6 trillion. During the October 1979 to October 1982 period, however, the Federal Reserve radically changed its monetary policy strategy by targeting bank reserves rather than interest rates, in an attempt to lower the underlying rate of inflation (see Chapter 4 for more details). The Fed's restrictive monetary policy actions led to a sudden and dramatic surge in interest rates, with rates on T-bills and bank certificates of deposits rising as high as 16 percent. This increase in short-term rates and the cost of funds had two effects. First, many savings associations faced negative interest spreads or **net interest margins** (interest income minus interest expense divided by earning assets) in funding much of their long-maturity, fixed-rate residential mortgages in their portfolios. For example, a 12 percent, 30-year mortgage was having to be funded by a 15 percent, 3-month CD. Second, they had to pay more competitive interest rates on deposits to prevent **disintermediation** and the reinvestment of these funds in money market mutual fund accounts. Their ability to do this was constrained by the Federal Reserve's **Regulation Q ceilings**, which limited (albeit to a lesser extent for savings institutions than commercial banks) the interest rates that savings associations could pay on traditional passbook savings accounts and retail time deposits that small savers held.[4] Thus, many small depositors, especially the more sophisticated, withdrew their funds from savings association deposit accounts (which were paying less than market interest rates because of Regulation Q) and invested directly in unregulated money market mutual fund accounts (where they could earn market interest rates).

net interest margin

Interest income minus interest expense divided by earning assets.

disintermediation

Withdrawal of deposits from depository institutions to be reinvested elsewhere, e.g., money market mutual funds.

Regulation Q ceiling

An interest ceiling imposed on small savings and time deposits at banks and thrifts until 1986.

Partly to overcome the adverse effects of rising rates and disintermediation on the savings association industry, Congress passed two major acts in the early 1980s revising the permitted scope of savings associations' activities: the Depository Institutions Deregulation and Monetary Control Act (DIDMCA) of 1980 and the Garn–St. Germain Depository Institutions Act (GSGDIA) of 1982; these expanded savings associations' deposit-taking and asset investment powers. On the liability side, savings associations were allowed to offer interest-bearing transaction accounts, called NOW accounts, and to issue more market rate–sensitive liabilities such as money market deposit accounts (MMDAs) to limit disintermediation and to compete with mutual funds. On the asset side of the balance sheet, they were allowed to offer floating- or adjustable-rate mortgages and, to a limited extent, expand into consumer real estate development and commercial lending. Note the structural shifts in savings association balance sheets between 1977 and 1982 in Table 14–2. For many savings associations, the new powers created safer and more diversified institutions.

For a small but significant group, however, whose earnings and shareholders' capital was being eroded in traditional areas of asset and liability business, the new regulations meant the opportunity to take more asset-side risks—which, if they paid off, could return the institution to profitability. For example, with their increased ability to hold riskier assets, Michael Milken, working for Drexel Burnham Lambert, sold junk bonds to savings associations, promising to buy them back or find another buyer when an institution wanted to liquidate its holdings. In doing so, Milken created a web of buyers that helped give the appearance of a market for junk bonds. This allowed Drexel to sell junk bonds at prices generally above their fair market values. Indeed, savings associations held almost 20 percent of junk bonds outstanding in the mid-1980s. When the junk bond market collapsed in the late 1980s and savings association wanted to liquidate their holdings, Milken was unable to

4. In the 1970s, these Regulation Q ceilings were usually set at rates of 5¼ or 5½ percent.

TABLE 14–2 Balance Sheets of Savings Associations (percentage of total assets and liabilities)

Item	1977	1982
Liabilities		
Fixed ceiling liabilities	87.3%	22.0%
Passbook and NOW accounts	33.9	15.6
Fixed ceiling time deposits	53.4	6.4
Market ceiling small time deposits	0.0	52.8
Money market certificates	0.0	28.6
Small saver certificates	0.0	19.3
Other small time deposits	0.0	4.9
Discretionary liabilities	8.6	23.2
Large time deposits	2.1	8.1
FHLB advances	4.7	10.3
Other borrowings	1.8	4.6
Other liabilities	4.0	2.0
Assets		
Mortgage assets	86.0	81.1
Fixed rate	86.0	74.9
Adjustable rate	0.0	6.2
Nonmortgage loans	2.3	2.6
Cash and investments	9.2	11.2
Other assets	2.5	5.1

Source: *Federal Reserve Bulletin,* December 1982. **www.federalreserve.gov**

find sufficient buyers for the bonds. Stuck with these bonds, many savings associations, especially those in California, suffered large losses.[5]

Further, in the mid-1980s, real estate and land prices in Texas and the Southwest collapsed. This was followed by economic downturns in the Northeast and Western states of the United States. Many borrowers with mortgage loans issued by savings associations in these areas defaulted. In other words, the risks incurred by many of these institutions did not pay off. This risk-taking behavior was accentuated by the policies of the federal insurer of savings associations' deposits, FSLIC. It chose not to close capital-depleted, economically insolvent savings associations (a policy of **regulator forbearance**) and to maintain deposit insurance premium assessments independent of the risk taken by the institution (see Chapter 13). As a result, an alarming number (1,248) of savings association failures occurred in the 1982–1992 period (peaking at 316 in 1989), alongside a rapid decline in asset growth of the industry. Figure 14–2 shows the number of failures, mergers, and new charters of **savings institutions** (savings associations and savings banks combined) from 1984 through 2004. Notice the large number of failures from 1987 through 1992 and the decline in the number of new charters.

regulator forbearance

A policy not to close economically insolvent FIs, allowing them to continue in operation.

savings institutions

Savings associations and savings banks combined.

In the 1980s, the large number of savings association failures depleted the resources of the FSLIC to such an extent that by 1989 it was massively insolvent. For example, between 1980 and 1988, 514 thrifts failed, at an estimated cost of $42.3 billion. Moreover, between 1989 and 1992 an additional 734 thrifts failed, at a cost of $78 billion. As a result, Congress passed an additional piece of legislation: the Financial Institutions Reform, Recovery, and Enforcement Act (FIRREA) of 1989. This legislation abolished the FSLIC and created a new savings association insurance fund (SAIF) under the management of the FDIC (with the help of a $100 billion infusion of funds by the U.S. government). FIRREA also replaced the

5. Milken and several other Drexel corporate officials pleaded guilty to six felony counts of federal securities fraud.

FIGURE 14–2 Structural Changes in the Number of Savings Institutions, 1984–2004

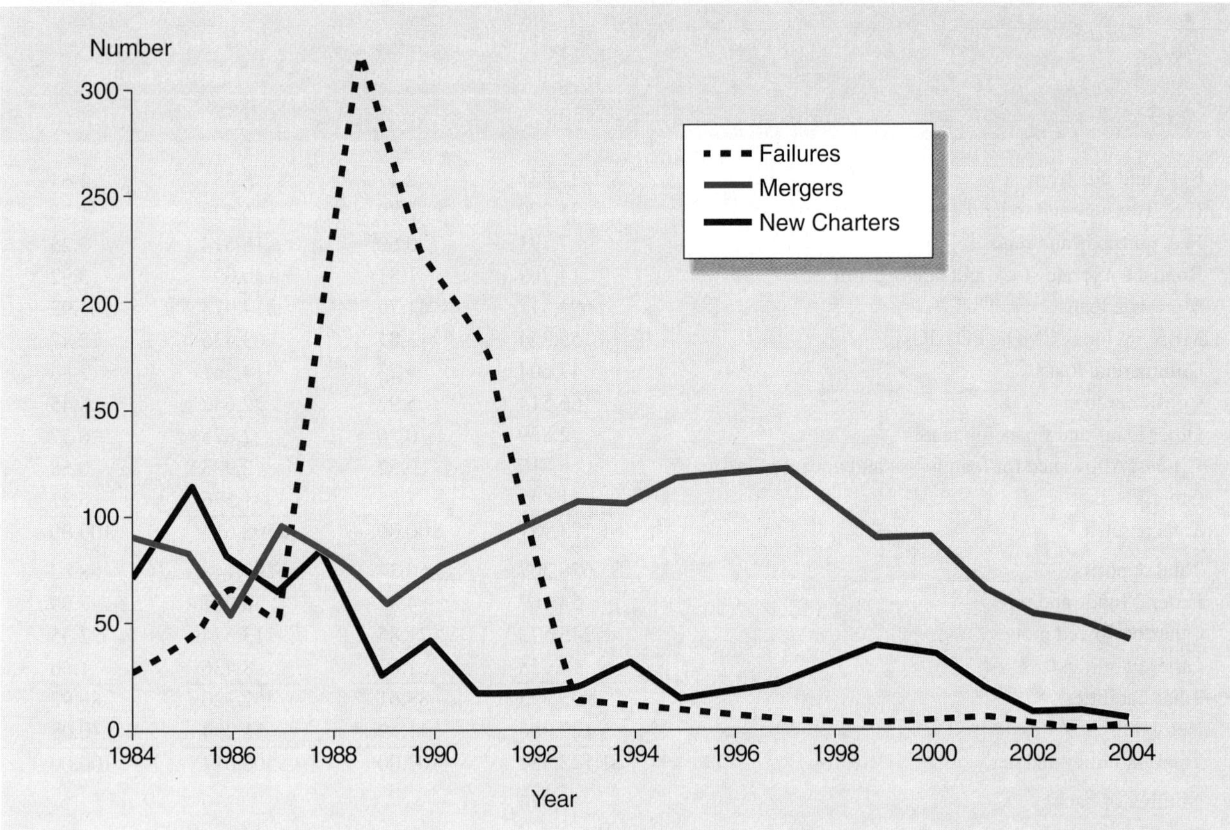

Source: Federal Deposit Insurance Corporation, *Quarterly Banking Profile,* various years, and *Historical Statistics,* various years. **www.fdic.gov**

Federal Home Loan Bank Board with the Office of Thrift Supervision (OTS) as the main regulator of federally chartered savings associations. In addition, the act created the Resolution Trust Corporation (RTC) to close and liquidate the most insolvent savings institutions.[6] The FIRREA also strengthened the capital requirements of savings associations and constrained their non-mortgage-related asset investment powers under a revised qualified thrift lender test, or **QTL test** (discussed below). Following FIRREA, Congress further enacted the Federal Deposit Insurance Corporation Improvement Act (FDICIA). The FDICIA of 1991 introduced risk-based deposit insurance premiums (starting in 1993) in an attempt to limit excessive risk taking by savings association owners. It also introduced a prompt corrective action (PCA) policy, enabling regulators to close thrifts and banks faster (see Chapter 13). In particular, if a savings association's ratio of its owners' equity capital to its assets fell below 2 percent, it had to be closed down or recapitalized within three months.

QTL test

Qualified thrift lender test that sets a floor on the mortgage-related assets that thrifts can hold (currently, 65 percent).

As a result of closing weak savings associations and strengthening their capital requirements, the industry is now significantly smaller in terms of both numbers and asset size. Specifically, the number of savings associations decreased from 2,600 in 1989 to 1,074 in 2004 (by 59 percent) and assets have decreased from $1.2 trillion to $1.1 trillion (by 8 percent) over the same period.

Balance Sheets and Recent Trends

Even in its new smaller state, the future viability of the savings association industry in traditional mortgage lending areas is a matter of debate. This is due partly to intense competition

6. At the time of its dissolution in 1995, the RTC had resolved or closed more than 700 savings associations and savings banks at an estimated cost of $200 billion to U.S. taxpayers.

TABLE 14–3 Assets and Liabilities of Savings Associations and Savings Banks, 2004

	(1) SAIF-Insured Savings Associations		(2) BIF-Insured Savings Banks	
	($ Millions)	(Percent)	($ Millions)	(Percent)
Cash and due from	$ 27,738	2.47%	$ 8,351	1.64%
U.S. Treasury and federal agency obligations	31,270	2.79	6,522	1.28
Federal funds and repos	7,791	0.69	16,514	3.25
Bonds, corporate stock and other securities	14,769	1.31	30,097	5.92
Mortgage loans	694,517	61.79	314,973	61.93
MBS (includes CMOs, POs, IOs)	155,254	13.81	63,436	12.47
Commercial loans	47,604	4.23	14,561	2.86
Consumer loans	66,514	5.92	22,642	4.45
Other loans and financing leases	2,889	0.26	2,875	0.57
Less: Allowance for loan losses and unearned income	5,810	0.52	2,933	0.58
Other assets	81,445	7.25	31,576	6.21
Total assets	$1,123,981	100.00	$508,614	100.00
Total deposits	$ 678,307	60.34	$299,148	58.82
Federal funds and repos	54,162	4.82	36,062	7.09
Other borrowed money	245,573	21.85	113,674	22.35
Other liabilities	17,953	1.60	8,436	1.66
Total liabilities	995,995	88.61	457,320	89.92
Net worth*	127,986	11.39	51,294	10.08
Total liabilities and net worth	$1,123,981	100.00	$508,614	100.00
Number of banks	1,074		339	

*Includes limited life preferred stock for BIF-insured state-chartered savings banks and redeemable preferred stock and minority interest for SAIF-insured institutions and BIF-insured FSBs.

Source: FDIC, *Statistics on Banking,* Fourth Quarter 2004. **www.fdic.gov**

for mortgages from other financial institutions such as commercial banks and specialized mortgage bankers. It is also due to the securitization of mortgages into mortgage-backed security pools by government-sponsored enterprises, which we discuss in Chapters 7 and 24.[7] In addition, long-term mortgage lending exposes FIs to significant credit, interest rate, and liquidity risks.

Column (1) of Table 14–3 shows the balance sheet for the savings association industry in 2004. On this balance sheet, mortgages and mortgage-backed securities (securitized pools of mortgages) represent 75.60 percent of total assets. This compares to 30.87 percent in commercial banks. Figure 14–3 shows the distribution of mortgage-related assets for all savings institutions (savings associations and savings banks) in
2 2004. As noted earlier, the FIRREA uses the QTL test to establish a minimum holding of 65 percent in mortgage-related assets for savings associations.[8] Reflecting the enhanced lending powers established under the 1980 DIDMCA and 1982 GSGDIA, commercial loans and consumer loans amounted to 4.23 and 5.92 percent of savings association assets, respectively, compared to 10.80 percent and 9.78 percent at commercial banks. Finally, savings associations are required to hold cash and investment securities for liquidity purposes and to meet regulator-imposed reserve requirements (see Chapter 13). In 2004, cash and investment securities (U.S. Treasury securities and federal

7. The major enterprises are GNMA, FNMA, and FHLMC.

8. Failure to meet the 65 percent QTL test results in the loss of certain tax advantages and the ability to obtain Federal Home Loan Bank advances (loans).

FIGURE 14–3 **Real Estate Assets as a Percentage of Total Assets at Savings Institutions**

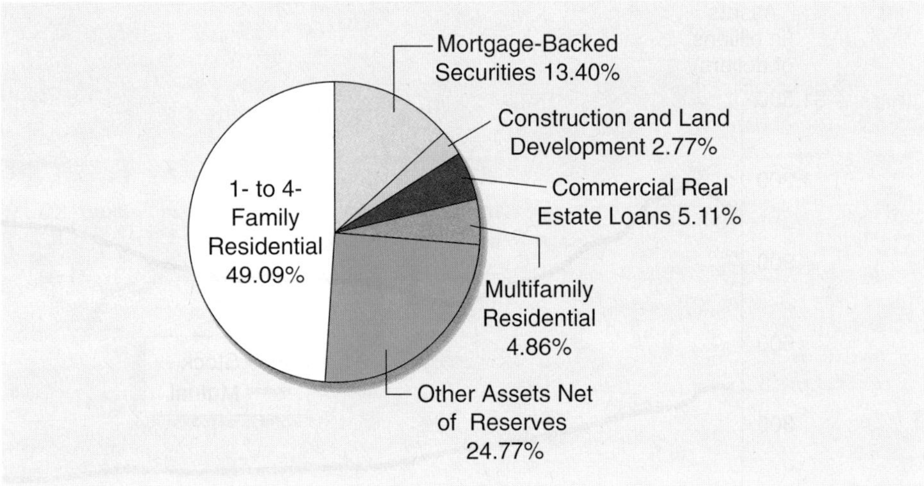

Source: Federal Deposit Insurance Corporation, *Quarterly Banking Profile*, Fourth Quarter 2004. **www.fdic.gov**

agency obligations; federal funds and repos; and bonds, notes, debentures, and other securities) holdings amounted to 7.26 percent of total assets compared to 27.85 percent at commercial banks.

On the liability side of the balance sheet, small time and savings deposits are still the predominant source of funds, with total deposits accounting for 60.34 percent of total liabilities and net worth. This compares to 65.57 percent at commercial banks. The second most important source of funds is borrowing from the 12 Federal Home Loan Banks (FHLBs),[9] which the institutions themselves own. Because of their size and government-sponsored status, FHLBs have access to the wholesale capital market for notes and bonds and can relend the funds borrowed in these markets to savings associations at a small markup over wholesale cost. Other borrowed funds include repurchase agreements and direct federal fund borrowings.

mutual organizations

An Institution in which the liability holders are also the owners—for example, in a mutual savings bank, depositors also own the bank.

www.ots.treas.gov

Finally, net worth is the book value of the equity holders' capital contribution; it amounted to 11.39 percent in 2004. This compares to 10.00 percent at commercial banks. Historically, most savings associations (and savings banks) were established as **mutual organizations** (in which the depositors are the legal owners of the institution and no stock is issued). As a mutual organization, member deposits represent the equity of the savings association. Since they have no stockholders, and thus no demand for equity investment returns, mutual organizations are generally less risky than stock-chartered organizations—mutual savings association managers can concentrate on low-risk investments and the prevention of failure rather than higher-risk investments needed to produce higher required returns on stockholders' investments. However, through time many savings associations (and savings banks) have switched from mutual to stock charters (in which the holders of the stock or equity are the legal owners of the institution rather than depositors as under the mutual charter). This is mainly because stock ownership allows savings institutions to attract capital investment from outside stockholders beyond levels achievable at a mutual institution. Figure 14–4 shows this trend in mutual versus stock charters and asset size for savings institutions from 1988 through 2004.

DO YOU UNDERSTAND?

1. Why the savings association industry prospered throughout most of the 20th century (until the late 1970s)?
2. Why the performance of savings associations deteriorated in the 1970s and 1980s?
3. What was done to rescue the savings associations industry in the 1980s?
4. What the major assets and liabilities of savings associations are?

9. The Federal Home Loan Bank System, established in 1932, consists of 12 regional Federal Home Loan Banks (set up similar to the Federal Reserve Bank system) that borrow funds in the national capital markets and use these funds to make loans to savings associations that are members of the Federal Home Loan Bank. The Federal Home Loan Banks are supervised by the Federal Home Loan Bank Board.

FIGURE 14–4 **Assets and Number of Mutual and Stock Savings Institutions**

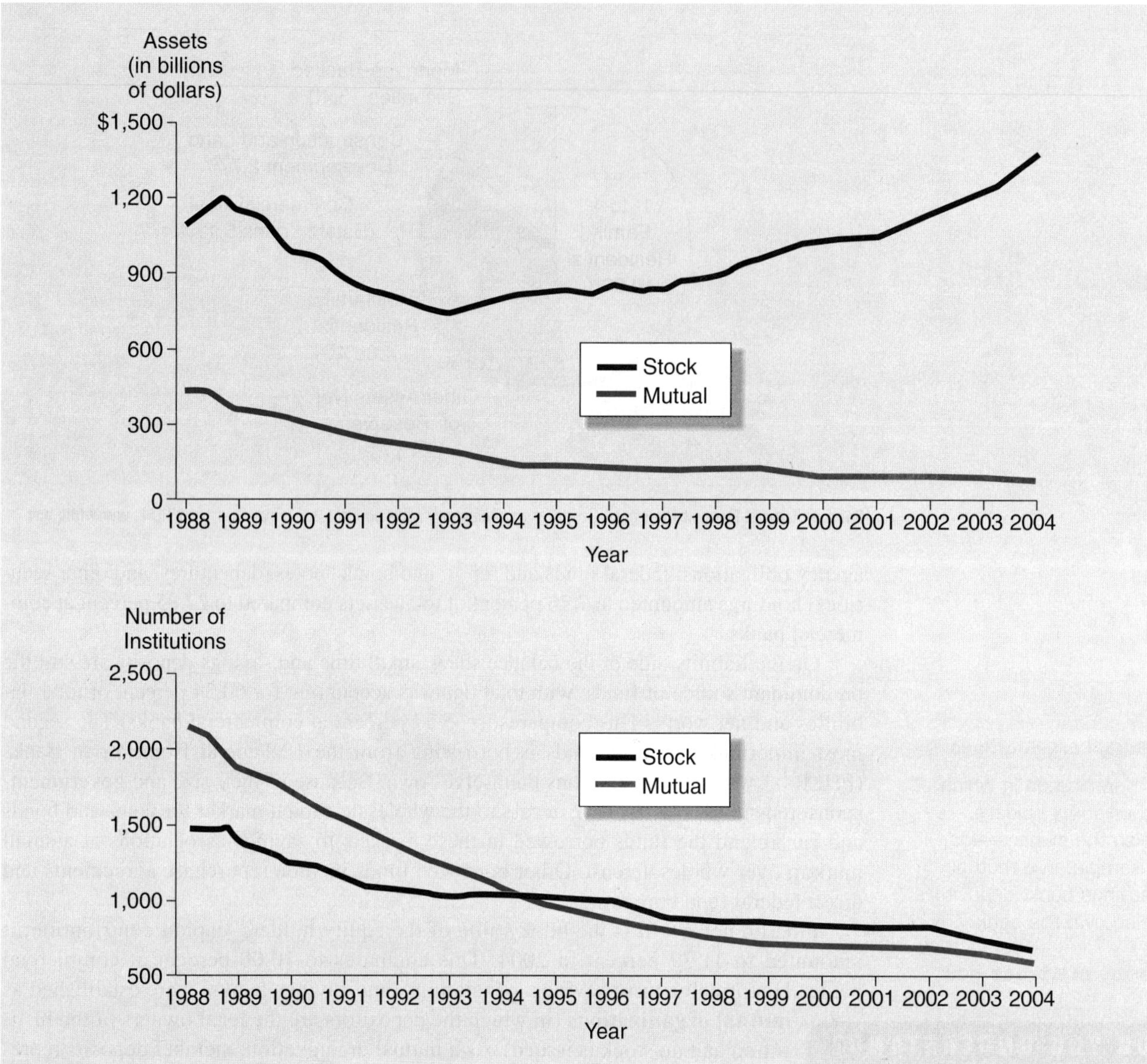

Source: Federal Deposit Insurance Corporation, *Quarterly Banking Profile,* various issues. **www.fdic.gov**

SAVINGS BANKS

Size, Structure, and Composition of the Industry

Traditionally, savings banks were established as mutual organizations in states that permit such organizations. These states were largely confined to the East Coast—for example, New York, New Jersey, and the New England states. As a result, savings banks (unlike savings associations) were not affected by the oil-based economic ups and downs of Texas and the Southwest in the 1980s. The crash in New England real estate values in 1990–1991 presented equally troubling problems for this group, however. Indeed, many of the failures of savings institutions (see Figure 14–2) were of savings banks rather than savings associations. As a result, like savings associations, savings banks have decreased in both size and number. In 2004, 339 savings banks had $509 billion in assets; $299 billion of their deposits are insured by the FDIC under the BIF (Bank Insurance Fund). FDIC insurance under the BIF is just one characteristic that distinguishes savings banks from savings associations, whose deposits are insured under by the FDIC under the SAIF (Savings Association Insurance Fund).

Balance Sheets and Recent Trends

2

Notice the major similarities and differences between savings associations and savings banks in Table 14–3, which shows their respective assets and liabilities as of 2004. Savings banks (in column 2 of Table 14–3) have a heavy concentration (74.40 percent) of mortgage loans and mortgage-backed securities (MBSs). This is slightly less than the savings associations' 75.60 percent in these assets and much more than commercial banks (30.87 percent). Over the years, savings banks have been allowed greater freedom to diversify into corporate bonds and stocks; their holdings in these assets are 5.92 percent compared to 1.31 percent for savings associations. On the liability side, the major difference is that savings banks generally rely less heavily on deposits (58.82 percent of finding) than savings associations (60.34 percent) and therefore savings banks use more borrowed funds (29.44 percent for savings banks versus 26.67 percent for savings associations). Finally, the ratio of the book value of net worth to total assets for savings banks stood at 10.08 percent (compared to 11.39 percent for savings associations and 10.00 percent for commercial banks) in 2004.

DO YOU UNDERSTAND?

1. Where savings banks were originally established?
2. The asset and liability characteristics that differentiate savings banks from savings associations?

REGULATORS OF SAVINGS INSTITUTIONS

3

The three main regulators of savings institutions are the Office of Thrift Supervision (OTS), the FDIC, and state regulators.

The Office of Thrift Supervision. Established in 1989 under the FIRREA, this office charters and examines all *federal* savings institutions. It also supervises the holding companies of savings institutions.

www.ots.treas.gov

The FDIC. The FDIC oversees and manages the Savings Association Insurance Fund (SAIF), which was established in 1989 under the FIRREA in the wake of the FSLIC insolvency. The SAIF provides insurance coverage for savings associations. Savings banks are insured under the FDIC's Bank Insurance Fund (BIF) and are thus also subject to supervision and examination by the FDIC.

www.fdic.gov

Other Regulators. State-chartered savings institutions are regulated by state agencies—for example, the Office of Banks and Real Estate in Illinois—rather than the OTS.

DO YOU UNDERSTAND?

1. Who the regulators of savings institutions are?

SAVINGS ASSOCIATION AND SAVINGS BANK RECENT PERFORMANCE

4

Savings institutions (savings associations and savings banks) experienced record profits in the mid- to late 1990s as interest rates (and thus the cost of funds to savings institutions) remained low and the U.S. economy (and thus the demand for loans) prospered. The result was an increase in the spread between interest income and interest expense for savings institutions and consequently an increase in net income. In 1999, savings institutions reported \$10.7 billion in net income and an annualized ROA of 1.00. Only the \$10.8 billion of net income reported in 1998 exceeded these results. Asset quality improvements were widespread during 1999, providing the most favorable net operating income that the industry had ever reported. However, the downturn in the U.S. economy resulted in a decline in savings institutions' profitability in 2000. Specifically, their ROA and ROE ratios fell slightly in 2000 to 0.92 percent and

TABLE 14–4 Selected Indicators for U.S. Savings Institutions, 1989 through 2004

	2004	2003	2001	2000	1999	1997	1995	1993	1989
Number of institutions	1,365	1,411	1,533	1,589	1,642	1,779	2,030	2,262	3,086
Return on assets (%)	1.19	1.28	1.08	0.92	1.00	0.93	0.77	0.71	−0.39
Return on equity (%)	11.22	13.66	12.73	11.14	11.73	10.84	9.40	9.32	−8.06
Noncurrent assets plus other real estate owned to assets (%)	0.47	0.62	0.66	0.56	0.58	0.95	1.20	2.10	2.78
Asset growth rate (%)	10.96	8.47	6.71	5.99	5.52	−0.21	1.70	−2.85	−11.14
Net operating income growth (%)	14.78	23.03	7.11	3.05	16.62	20.07	13.81	21.16	−58.95
Number of failed institutions	0	0	1	1	1	0	2	8	331

Source: FDIC, *Quarterly Banking Profile,* various issues, and *Historical Statistics,* 1989. **www.fdic.gov**

TABLE 14–5 U.S. Savings Institution Asset Concentration, 1992 versus 2004
(in billions of dollars)

	2004				1992			
	Number	Percent of Total	Assets	Percent of Total	Number	Percent of Total	Assets	Percent of Total
All FDIC-insured savings institutions	1,365		$1,632.6		2,390		$1,030.2	
Under $100 million	450	33.0%	23.1	1.4%	1,109	46.4%	55.9	5.4%
$100 million–$1 billion	765	56.0	249.5	15.3	1,094	45.8	316.2	30.7
$1–$10 billion	97	7.1	192.9	11.8	179	7.5	473.5	46.0
$10 billion or more	53	3.9	1,167.0	71.5	8	0.3	184.5	17.9

Source: *FDIC Quarterly Banking Profile,* Fourth Quarter 1992 and Fourth Quarter 2004. **www.fdic.gov**

11.14 percent, respectively, from their 1999 levels. Despite an economic recession, this downturn was short-lived. Both ROA and ROE increased to record levels each year from 2001 through 2003 and fell only slightly in 2004. One reason for this trend is that in the early 2000s, the industry's net interest margins rose; the cost of funding earning assets declined by 2.70 percent, while the yield on earning assets declined by only 2.35 percent. Table 14–4 presents several performance ratios for the industry from 1989 through 2004.

DO YOU UNDERSTAND?

1. The recent performance of savings institutions?
2. The ways that profit trends for savings institutions have been similar to those of commercial banks in the 1990s and early 2000s?
3. Why profits for savings institutions have outperformed those of commercial banks in the late 1990s and early 2000s?

The savings institutions industry experienced substantial consolidation in the 1990s. For example, the 1998 acquisition of H.F. Ahmanson & Co. by Washington Mutual Inc. for almost $10 billion was the fourth largest bank–thrift merger completed in 1998.[10] Washington Mutual was the third largest savings institution in the United States early in 1997, while Ahmanson was the largest savings institution. In 1997, Washington Mutual bought Great Western to become the largest thrift in the country. Then, in March 1998, Washington Mutual bought Ahmanson to combine the two largest U.S. thrifts. In December 2001, Washington Mutual (still the largest savings institution in the United States) had total assets at $223 billion, ranking seventh of all depository institutions (banks and thrifts). Table 14–5 shows the industry consolidation in number and asset size over the period 1992–2004. Notice that over this period, the biggest savings institutions (over $10 billion) grew in number from 8 to 53

10. Behind Travelers Group–Citicorp ($74 billion), NationsBank–BankAmerica ($62 billion), and BancOne–First Chicago NBD ($30 billion).

SEARCH THE SITE

Go to the FDIC Web site at **www.fdic.gov.** Find the most recent breakdown of U.S. savings institution asset concentrations using the following steps.

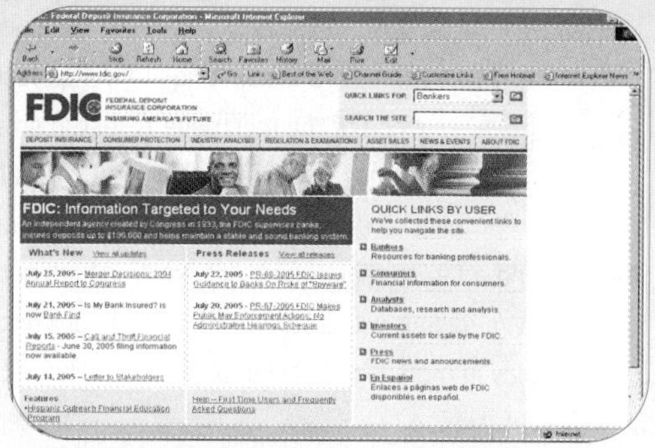

Click on "Analysts"

From there click on "FDIC Quarterly Banking Profile," and then click on "Quarterly Banking Profile," then "Savings Institution Section"

Then click on "TABLE III-B. 200X, FDIC-Insured Savings Institutions"

This will bring the files up on your computer that contains the relevant data.

Questions

1. How has the number and dollar value of assets held by savings institutions changed since 2004 reported in Table 14–5?
2. Calculate the percent of total industry assets held by savings institutions with asset size under $100 million, between $100 million and $1 billion, between $1 billion and $10 billion, and over $10 billion.

and their control of industry assets grew from 17.9 percent to 71.5 percent. Despite the recent resurgence of this industry, as discussed in the In the News box, its future is still uncertain.

CREDIT UNIONS

5

Credit unions (CUs) are classified alongside savings institutions as thrift institutions. Credit unions are not-for-profit depository institutions mutually organized and owned by their members (depositors). They were established in the United States in the early 1900s as self-help organizations intended to alleviate widespread poverty. The first credit unions were organized in the Northeast, initially in Massachusetts. Members paid an entrance fee and put up funds to purchase at least one deposit share. Members were expected to deposit their savings in the CU, and these funds were lent only to other members.

This limit in the customer base of CUs continues today as, unlike commercial banks and savings institutions, CUs are prohibited from serving the general public. Rather, in organizing a credit union, members are required to have a common bond of occupation (e.g., police CUs), association (e.g., university-affiliated CUs), or cover a well-defined neighborhood, community, or rural district. CUs may, however, have multiple groups with more than one type of membership. Each credit union decides the common bond requirements (i.e., which groups it will serve) with the approval of the appropriate regulator (see below). To join a credit union an individual must then be a member of the approved group(s).

The primary objective of credit unions is to satisfy the depository and borrowing needs of their members. CU member deposits (called shares, representing ownership stakes in the CU) are used to provide loans to other members in need of funds. Earnings from these loans are used to pay interest on member deposits. Because credit unions are not-for-profit organizations, their earnings are not taxed. This tax-exempt status allows CUs to offer higher rates on deposits and charge lower rates on some types of loans compared to banks and savings institutions, whose earnings are taxable. This is shown in Figure 14–5 for the period 1991–2004.

IN THE NEWS

A Place for Thrifts

The thrift industry remains a fascinating niche of the mortgage business, with a checkered past, a thriving present, and a future that can't quite be foreseen. We hope it will always have a role to play in mortgage finance, and we expect it will.

While thrifts had a prosperous 2001, as executives meet this week for the midwinter conference of trade group America's Community Bankers in Scottsdale, Ariz., they are reviewing an eventful year. In the past 12 months, for instance, a thrift (Washington Mutual Bank) has reclaimed the top mortgage lending and servicing spot, for the first time since 1988. But thrifts also just endured a big defection (Charter Bank) from their ranks, and last year also saw a high-profile failure at Superior Bank FSB. It's an indication of the complexity of the current environment that the industry has faced charges of being too big and too small simultaneously.

WaMu's spectacular climb has engendered complaints that this thrift has gotten too big, especially in its powerful presence in multiple Federal Home Loan Bank districts. And the Charter Bank decision to become a commercial bank has led to speculations thrifts are becoming too small to remain a separate entity from the community banks' niche. WaMu, of course, is a special case. While a legitimate thrift with a big mortgage portfolio, it also has legitimate claims on being a mortgage bank and commercial bank. You could also argue, that with its mix of portfolio lending, secondary marketing and securitization, it resembles the GSEs (government sponsored agencies) as well. It's possible to believe both that WaMu and big institutions like it should be allowed multiple district memberships, and that the Federal Home Loan Bank System should consider loans-to-one-borrower limitations.

We don't believe the Charter Bank defection will reduce industry mass beyond the minimum survival level, although it is always possible there could be thrift charter changes. But with the potpourri of bank, thrift and credit union regulators as thick as ever despite decades of calls for consolidation, politically there seems to be no special reason to meddle with a niche that is healthy and profitable. And while thrifts remain potent mortgage lenders, they no longer are the specialty shops they were through most of their existence. They now are reaching out to commercial lending as well . . .

Source: *National Mortgage News,* February 11, 2002, p. 4.

DO YOU UNDERSTAND?

1. What some of the major events in the savings institutions industry in 2001 were?
2. Why the savings institutions industry has been criticized as being too big and too small simultaneously?

Size, Structure, and Composition of the Industry

Credit unions are the most numerous of the institutions (9,210 in 2004) that compose the depository institutions segment of the FI industry. Moreover, CUs were less affected by the crisis that affected commercial banks and savings institutions in the 1980s. This is because traditionally more than 40 percent of their assets have been in small consumer loans, often for amounts less than $10,000, which are funded mainly by member deposits. This combination of relatively matched credit risk and maturity in the asset and liability portfolios left credit unions less exposed to credit and interest rate risk than commercial banks and savings institutions. In addition, CUs tend to hold large amounts of government securities (almost 20 percent of their assets in 2004) and relatively small amounts of residential mortgages. CUs' lending activities are funded mainly by deposits contributed by their over 83 million members.

The nation's credit union system consists of three distinct tiers: the top tier at the national level (U.S. Central Credit Union); the middle tier at the state or regional level (corporate credit unions); and the bottom tier at the local level (credit unions). Corporate credit unions are financial institutions that are cooperatively owned by their member credit unions. The 34 corporate credit unions serve their members primarily by investing and lending excess funds (unloaned deposits) that member credit unions place with them. Additional services provided by corporate credit unions include automated settlement, securities safekeeping, data processing, accounting, and payment services. As of 2004, credit unions had over $20 billion (4 percent of total assets) invested in corporate credit unions. The U.S. Central Credit Union serves as a "corporate's corporate"—providing investment and

FIGURE 14–5 Credit Union versus Bank Interest Rates

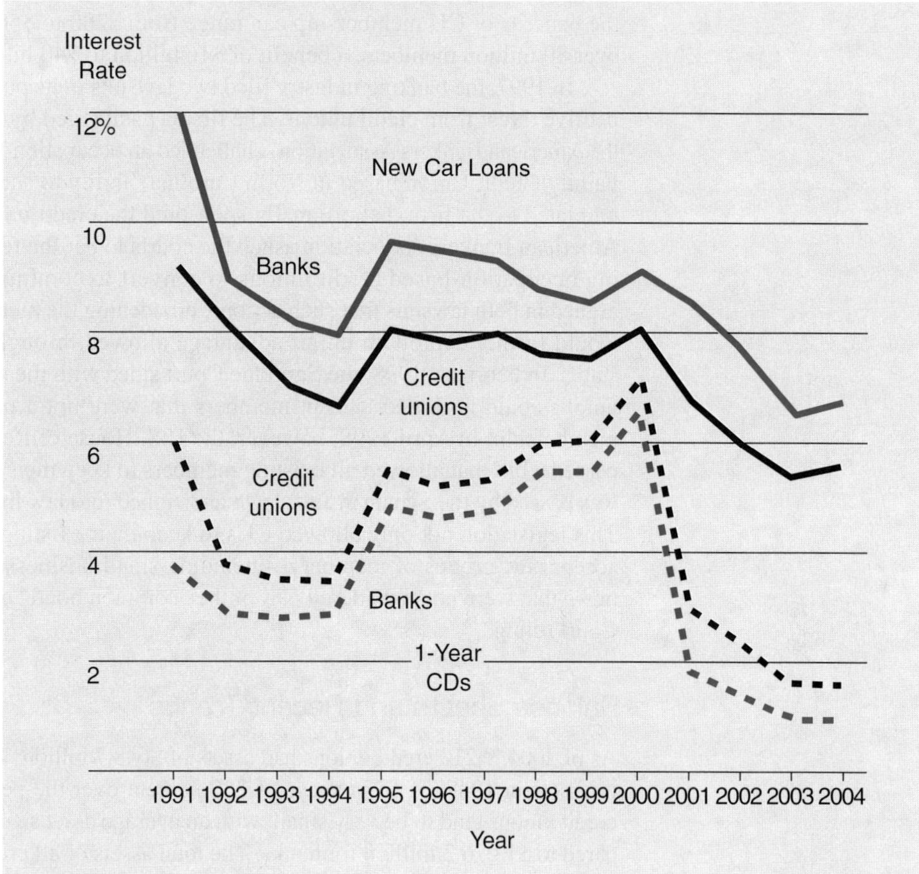

Source: Federal Reserve Board and National Credit Union Administration, various dates. **www.federalreserve.gov; www.ncua.gov**

liquidity services to corporate credit unions. The Central Credit Union acts as a corporate credit unions' main provider of liquidity. It invests their surplus funds and provides financial services and operational support.

In recent years, to attract and keep customers, CUs have expanded their services to compete with commercial banks and savings institutions. For example, many CUs have converted to a common charter from an employer-based charter to expand the eligible customer base. Similarly, CUs now offer mortgages, credit lines, and automated teller machines. Some credit unions also offer business and commercial loans to their employer groups. For example, in the late 1990s, AWANE (Automotive Wholesalers Association of New England) Credit Union's[11] business loans represented 13.6 percent of its lending and the CU participated actively in the Small Business Administration loan programs, which enabled it to sell a portion of those loans. In addition, commercial real estate lending accounted for 29.5 percent of AWANE's total lending.

As CUs have expanded in membership, size, and services, bankers claim that CUs unfairly compete with small banks that have historically been the major lender in small towns and local communities. For example, the American Bankers Association claimed that the tax exemption for CUs gives them the equivalent of a $1 billion a year subsidy. The response of the Credit Union National Association (CUNA) is that any cost to taxpayers from

11. AWANE is a trade association of companies that serve the automotive aftermarket through sales of auto parts and other items. It is the association member companies and firms related to the automotive business, as well as their owners and employees, that AWANE Credit Union serves through its common bond.

CUs' tax-exempt status is more than passed on to their members and society at large through favorable interest rates on deposits and loans. For example, CUNA estimates that the benefits of CU membership can range from $200 to $500 a year per member or, with over 80 million members, a benefit of $16 billion to $40 billion per year.

In 1997, the banking industry filed two lawsuits in its push to restrict the growing competitive threat from credit unions. The first lawsuit (filed by four North Carolina banks and the American Bankers Association) challenged an occupation-based credit union's (the AT&T Family Credit Union based in North Carolina) ability to accept members from companies unrelated to the firm that originally sponsored the credit union. In the second lawsuit, the American Bankers Association asked the courts to bar the federal government from allowing occupation-based credit unions to convert to community-based charters. Bankers argued in both lawsuits that such actions, broadening the membership base of credit unions, would further exploit an unfair advantage allowed through the credit union tax-exempt status. In February 1998, the Supreme Court sided with the banks in its decision that credit unions could no longer accept members that were not a part of the "common bond" of membership. In April 1998, however, the U.S. House of Representatives overwhelmingly passed a bill that allowed all existing members to keep their credit union accounts. The bill was passed by the Senate in July 1998 and signed into law by the president in August 1998. This legislation not only allowed CUs to keep their existing members but allowed CUs to accept new groups of members—including small businesses and low-income communities—that were not considered part of the "common bond" of membership by the Supreme Court ruling.

Balance Sheets and Recent Trends

As of 2004, 9,210 credit unions had assets of $648.7 billion. This compares to $192.8 billion in assets in 1988, or an increase of 230 percent over the period 1988–2004. Individually, credit unions tend to be very small, with an average asset size of $69.0 million in 2004 compared to $1,076.3 million for banks. The total assets of all credit unions are smaller than the largest U.S. banking organization(s). For example, Citigroup had $1,436.6 billion in total assets, J.P. Morgan Chase had $1,138 billion in total assets, and Bank of America had $1,089.3 billion in total assets. This compares to *total* credit union assets of $648.7 billion in 2004.

6 Table 14–6 shows the breakdown of financial assets and liabilities for credit unions as of 2004. Given their emphasis on retail or consumer lending, discussed above, 33.1 percent of CU assets are in the form of small consumer loans (compared to 5.9 percent at savings associations, 4.4 percent at savings banks, and 9.8 percent at commercial banks) and another 31.8 percent are in the form of home mortgages (compared to 75.6 percent at savings associations, 74.4 percent at savings banks, and 30.9 percent at commercial banks). Together these member loans compose 64.9 percent of total assets. Figure 14–6 provides more detail on the composition of the loan portfolio for all CUs. Because of the common bond requirement on credit union customers, few business or commercial loans are issued by CUs.

Credit unions also invest heavily in investment securities (24.3 percent of total assets in 2004 compared to 4.8 percent at savings associations, 10.5 percent at savings banks, and 22.8 percent at commercial banks). Figure 14–7 shows that 55.1 percent of the investment portfolio of CUs is in U.S. government Treasury securities or federal agency securities, while investments in other FIs (such as deposits of banks) totaled 34.4 percent of their investment portfolios. Their investment portfolio composition, along with cash holdings (6.0 percent of total assets), allows credit unions ample liquidity to meet their daily cash needs—such as share (deposit) withdrawals. Some CUs have also increased their off-balance-sheet activities. Specifically, unused loan commitments, including credit card limits and home equity lines of credit, totaled over $83 billion in 2004.

Credit union funding comes mainly from member deposits (86.1 percent of total funding in 2004 compared to 60.3 for savings associations, 58.8 percent for savings banks, and 65.6 for commercial banks). Figure 14–8 presents the distribution of these deposits in

TABLE 14–6 Assets and Liabilities of Credit Unions, 2004

	Billions of Dollars	Percentage
Assets		
Checkable deposits and currency	$ 38.9	6.0%
Time and savings deposits	27.1	4.2
Federal funds and security RPs	3.9	0.6
Open market paper	1.6	0.2
U.S. government securities	125.0	19.3
Treasury	10.0	1.5
Agency	115.0	17.7
Home mortgages	206.3	31.8
Consumer credit	215.0	33.1
Credit market instruments	$617.8	95.2%
Mutual fund shares	3.5	0.6
Miscellaneous assets	27.4	4.2
Total assets	$648.7	100.0%
Liabilities and Equity		
Checkable	$ 71.4	11.0%
Small time and savings	429.0	66.1
Large time	58.4	9.0
Shares/deposits	$558.8	86.1%
Other loans and advances	9.9	1.5
Miscellaneous liabilities	22.3	3.5
Total liabilities	$591.0	91.1%
Total ownership shares	$ 57.7	8.9%

Source: *Federal Reserve Bulletin,* Flow of Fund Accounts, December 2004. **www.federalreserve.gov**

2004. Regular share draft transaction accounts (similar to NOW accounts at other depository institutions—see Chapter 11) accounted for 36.3 percent of all CU deposits, followed by certificates of deposits (22.5 percent of deposits), money market deposit accounts (18.8 percent of deposits), and share accounts (similar to passbook savings accounts at other

FIGURE 14–6 Composition of Credit Union Loan Portfolio, 2004

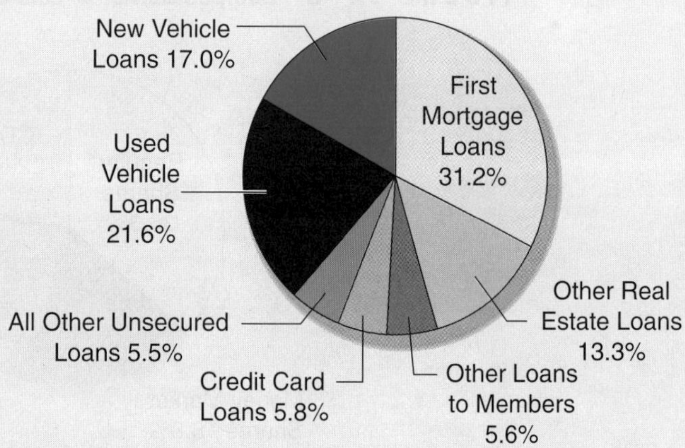

Source: National Credit Union Association, *Year End Statistics,* 2004. **www.ncua.gov**

FIGURE 14–7 Composition of Credit Union Investment Portfolio, 2004

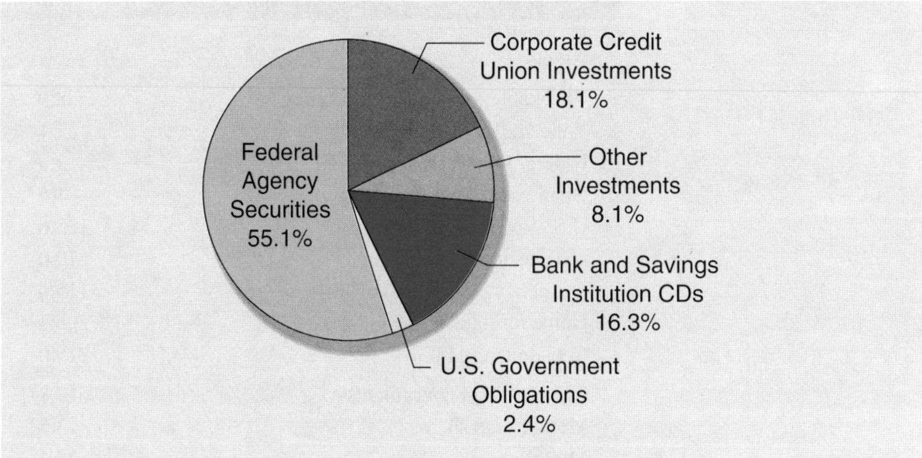

Source: National Credit Union Association, *Year End Statistics*, 2004. **www.ncua.gov**

depository institutions but so named to designate the deposit holders' ownership status) (12.4 percent of deposits). Credit unions tend to hold higher levels of equity than other depository institutions. Since CUs are not stockholder owned, this equity is basically the accumulation of past earnings from CU activities that is "owned" collectively by member depositors. As will be discussed in Chapters 19 and 22, this equity protects a CU against losses on its loan portfolio as well as other financial and operating risks. In 2004, CUs' capital-to-assets ratio was 8.9 percent compared to 11.4 percent for savings associations, 10.1 percent for savings banks, and 10.0 percent for commercial banks.

Regulators

www.ncua.gov

Like savings banks and savings associations, credit unions can be federally or state chartered. As of 2004, 61.7 percent of the 9,210 CUs were federally chartered and subject to National Credit Union Administration (NCUA) regulation (see Table 14–1), accounting for 56.0 percent of the total membership and 55.2 percent of total assets. In addition, through its insurance fund (the National Credit Union Share Insurance Fund, or NCUSIF), the NCUA provides deposit insurance guarantees of up to $100,000 for insured credit unions. Currently, the NCUSIF covers 98 percent of all credit union deposits.

FIGURE 14–8 Composition of Credit Union Deposits, 2004

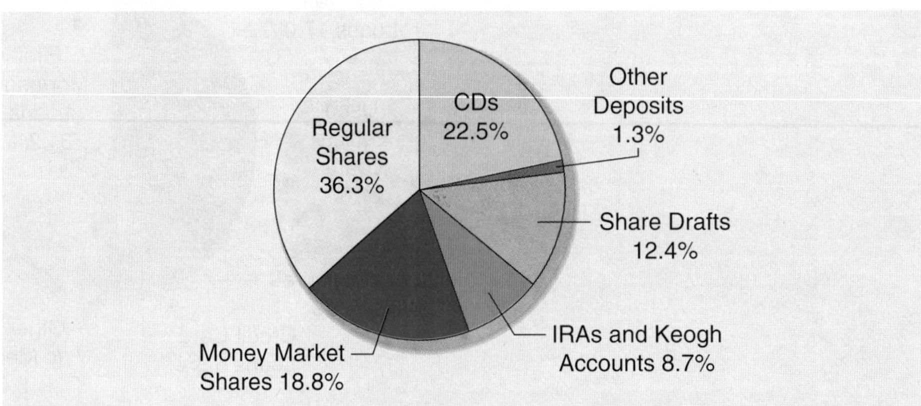

Source: National Credit Union Association, *Year End Statistics*, 2004. **www.ncua.gov**

FIGURE 14–9 Return on Assets for Credit Unions, 1993 through 2004

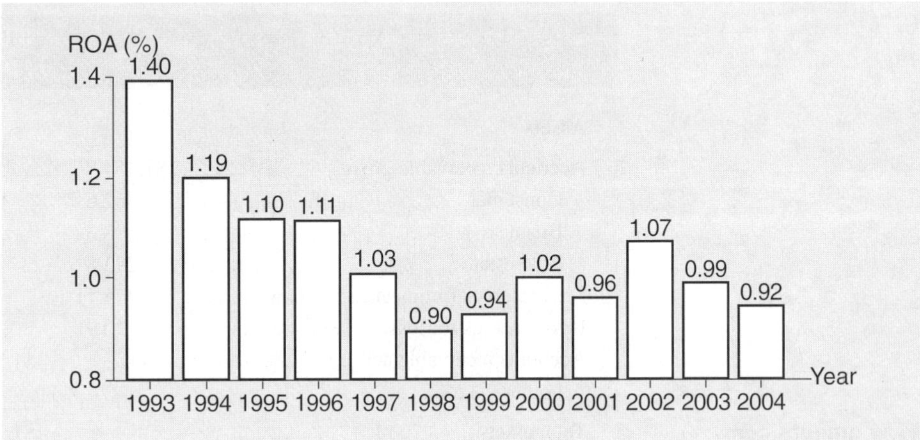

Source: National Credit Union Association, *Midyear Statistics,* 1999, and *Year End Statistics,* various years.
www.ncua.gov

Industry Performance

Like other depository institutions, the credit union industry has grown in asset size in the 1990s and early 2000s. Asset growth from 1999 to 2004 was more than 10 percent annually. In addition, CU membership increased from 63.6 million to over 83.3 million over the 1999–2004 period. Asset growth was especially pronounced among the largest CUs (with assets of over $50 million) as their assets increased by almost 15 percent annually from 1999 through 2004. In contrast, the credit unions with assets between $10 million and $20 million grew by only 12.8 percent and the smallest credit unions decreased in asset size by 3.8 percent. Figure 14–9 shows the trend in ROA for CUs from 1993 through 2004. The industry experienced an ROA of 0.92 percent in 2004 compared to 1.19 percent for savings institutions and 1.31 percent for commercial banks. The decrease in ROA over the period is mostly attributed to earnings decreases at the smaller CUs. For example, the largest credit unions experienced an ROA of 1.18 percent in 2004, while ROA for the smallest credit unions was 0.49 percent. Smaller CUs generally have a smaller and less diversified customer base and have higher overhead expenses per dollar of assets. Thus, their ROAs have been hurt.

Given the mutual-ownership status of this industry, however, growth in ROA (or profits) is not necessarily the primary goal of CUs. Rather, as long as capital or equity levels are sufficient to protect a CU against unexpected losses on its credit portfolio as well as other financial and operational risks, this not-for-profit industry has a primary goal of serving the deposit and lending needs of its members. This contrasts with the emphasis placed on profitability by stockholder-owned commercial banks and savings institutions.

DO YOU UNDERSTAND?

1. How credit unions differ from commercial banks and savings institutions?
2. Why credit unions have prospered in recent years in comparison to savings associations and savings banks?
3. How the credit union industry is organized?
4. Why commercial banks and savings institutions claim that credit unions have an unfair advantage in providing bank services?
5. The main assets and liabilities credit unions hold?

FINANCE COMPANIES

Size, Structure, and Composition of the Industry

At year end 2004, the finance company industry assets stood at $1,745.8 billion (see Table 14–7). GMAC Commercial Mortgage Corp. (GMACCM), a finance company subsidiary of General Motors Acceptance Corp. (GMAC), is in fact the largest business unit of General Motors and the largest commercial mortgage lender in the United States, with a mortgage portfolio of

TABLE 14–7 Assets and Liabilities of U.S. Finance Companies
(September 30, 2004)

	Billions of Dollars		Percent of Total Assets	
Assets				
Accounts receivable gross	$1,354.7		77.6%	
Consumer	462.6		26.5	
Business	598.3		34.3	
Real estate	293.8		16.8	
Less reserves for unearned income	(75.1)		(4.3)	
Less reserves for losses	(20.9)		(1.2)	
Accounts receivable net		$1,258.7		72.1%
All other		487.1		27.9
Total assets		$1,745.8		100.0%
Liabilities and Capital				
Bank loans		$64.1		3.7%
Commercial paper		150.8		8.7
Debt due to parent		112.3		6.4
Debt not elsewhere classified		768.8		44.0
All other liabilities		415.9		23.8
Capital, surplus, and undivided profits		233.9		13.4
Total liabilities and capital		$1,745.8		100.0%

Source: *Federal Reserve Bulletin*, December 2004, Table 1.51. **www.federalreserve.gov**

www.gmacfs.com

www.fordcredit.com

www.hsbcusa.com

www.aigag.com

www.citgroup.com

sales finance institutions

Finance companies specializing in loans to customers of a particular retailer or manufacturer.

more than $160 billion. The company announced in the late 1990s that it had plans to expand its product mix to create one of the world's leading commercial finance companies.

The three major types of finance companies are (1) sales finance institutions, (2) personal credit institutions, and (3) business credit institutions. **Sales finance institutions** (e.g., Ford Motor Credit and Sears Roebuck Acceptance Corp.) specialize in making loans to customers of a specific retailer or manufacturer. Because sales finance institutions can frequently process loans faster and more conveniently (generally at the location of purchase) than depository institutions, this sector of the industry competes directly with depository institutions for consumer loans. **Personal credit institutions** [e.g., Household Finance Corp. and American General Finance, a subsidiary of AIG Corp (an insurance company)] specialize in making installment and other loans to consumers. Personal credit institutions will make loans to customers with low income or a bad credit history, whom depository institutions find too risky to lend to. These institutions compensate for the additional risk by charging higher interest rates than depository institutions and/or accepting collateral (e.g., used cars) that depository institutions do not find acceptable. **Business credit institutions** (e.g., CIT Group and Heller Financial) provide financing to corporations, especially through equipment leasing and **factoring,** in which the finance company purchases accounts receivable from corporate customers at a discount from face value and the finance company assumes the responsibility for collecting the accounts receivable.[12] As a result, the corporate customer no longer has the worry of whether the accounts receivable may be delayed and thus receives cash for sales faster than the time it takes customers to pay their bills. Many large finance companies (e.g., GMAC) perform all three services.

personal credit institutions

Finance companies specializing in installment and other loans to consumers.

business credit institutions

Finance companies specializing in business loans.

factoring

The process of purchasing accounts receivable from corporations (often at a discount), usually with no recourse to the seller should the receivables go bad.

12. The finance company generally checks the credit quality of the customer's accounts receivables before purchasing them. The finance company specializes in bill processing and collections and can take advantage of economies of scale in receivables collection. The selling customer removes the need for a credit department and a credit collection area (thus reducing operating expenses).

TABLE 14–8 The Largest Finance Companies

Company Name	Total Receivables (in millions)
General Electric Capital Corp.	$321,002
General Motors Acceptance Corporation	247,992
Ford Motor Credit Company	188,800
Citigroup Inc.	158,400
MBNA Corp.	118,494
SLM Corp.	90,032
American Express Company	85,000
First USA, Inc.	76,328
Household International, Inc.	71,980
Capital One Financial Corp.	71,245

Source: The Insurance Information Institute.

DO YOU UNDERSTAND?

1. What the three major types of finance companies are? What types of customers does each serve?
2. What a captive finance company is?

captive finance company

A finance company wholly owned by a parent corporation.

The industry is quite concentrated; the 20 largest firms account for more than 75 percent of its assets. In addition, many of the largest finance companies such as GMAC tend to be wholly owned or captive subsidiaries of major manufacturing companies. A major role of a **captive finance company** is to provide financing for the purchase of products manufactured by the parent, as GMAC does for GM cars. Captive finance companies serve as an efficient marketing tool by providing consumer financing to customers of the parent company immediately at the time of purchase. They can also be used to finance distribution or dealer inventories until a sale occurs.

Table 14–8 lists the top ten finance companies (in terms of receivables, or loans outstanding) as of 2004. GECC is the largest finance company with receivables totaling $321.0 billion. Notice that some of the largest finance companies (such as Citigroup and MBNA) are actually subsidiaries of commercial bank (or financial services) holding companies. In late 2000, Associates First Capital, then the fourth largest finance company and the largest consumer finance company, was acquired by Citigroup for $31.1 billion. The acquisition resulted in Citigroup becoming the industry's fourth largest receivables financier with receivables of $158.4 billion in 2004. Additionally, in early 2001, CIT Group Holdings (a business finance company) was purchased by industrial conglomerate Tyco International. Tyco officials stated that the purchase of CIT would provide Tyco customers with financing they need to buy everything from wastewater treatment plants to home security systems, like the GE/GECC model. However, in the wake of several investigations and inquiries regarding the operations of Tyco, in July 2002 Tyco spun off the CIT Group and the company again operates as an independent finance company.

Balance Sheets and Recent Trends

8

Assets. Finance companies provide three basic types of loans: real estate, consumer, and business. The assets and liabilities of finance companies in 2004, are presented in Table 14–7. Business and consumer loans (called *accounts receivable*) are the major assets held by finance companies; they represent 60.8 percent of total assets. In 1975, 92.3 percent of total assets were consumer and business loans (see Figure 14–10). Thus, compared to depository institutions, which hold a large percentage of longer term real estate loans, finance companies hold shorter term consumer and business loans. Over the last 30 years, however, finance companies have replaced consumer and business loans with increasing amounts of real estate loans and other assets, although these loans have not become dominant, as is the case with many depository institutions.

Table 14–9 presents information concerning the industry's loans from 1994 through 2004 for consumer, real estate, and business lending. In recent years, the fastest growing areas of asset activity have been in the nonconsumer finance areas, especially leasing and business lending. In 2004, consumer loans constituted 40.57 percent of all finance company

FIGURE 14–10 Finance Company Assets, 1975 versus 2004

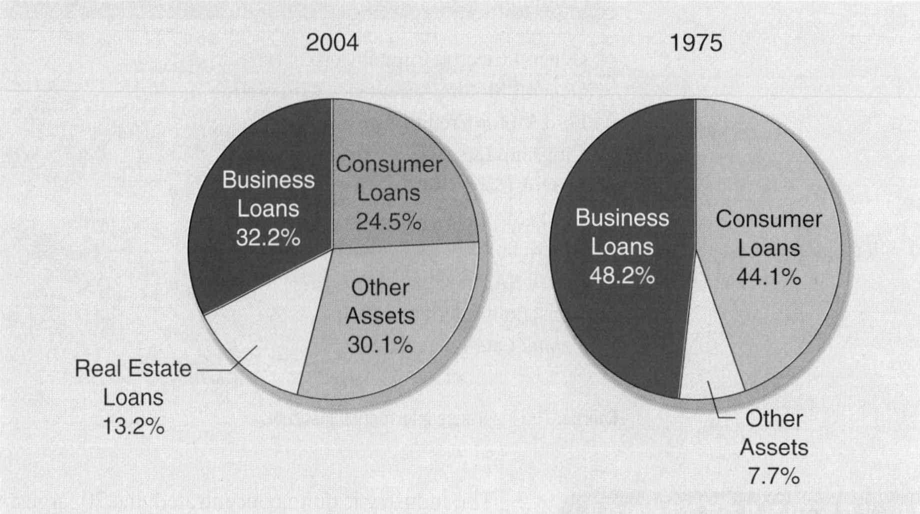

loans, mortgages represented 19.40 percent, and business loans comprised 40.03 percent. This compares to commercial banks with 17.44 percent of their loans in consumer loans, 55.03 percent in mortgages, 19.25 percent in business loans, and 8.28 percent in other loans (e.g., loans to foreign governments).

Consumer Loans. Consumer loans include motor vehicle loans and leases and other consumer loans. Motor vehicle loans and leases are traditionally the major type of consumer loan (71.4 percent of the consumer loan portfolio in 2004). Table 14–10 data indicate that finance companies historically charged higher rates for automobile loans than did commercial banks. From 1994 through 1996, auto finance companies charged interest rates that were from 0.79 to 1.67 percent higher than those of commercial banks. Because new car sales by U.S. firms in 1997 through 1999 were lower than normal, finance companies owned by the major auto manufacturers slashed the interest rates charged on new car loans (some as low as 0.9 percent) over this period. Moreover, after the terrorist attacks in September 2001 the major auto manufacturers lowered new car rates to 0.0 percent in an attempt to boost sales. Some of these 0.0 percent rates continued to be offered into 2005 as the general level of interest rates remained low. However, other than for new auto loans, these types of low rates are rare.

subprime lender

A finance company that lends to high-risk customers.

loan sharks

Subprime lenders that charge unfairly exorbitant rates to desperate, subprime borrowers.

Finance companies generally charge higher rates for consumer loans because they generally attract riskier customers than commercial banks. In fact, customers that seek individual (or business) loans from finance companies are often those who have been refused loans at banks or thrifts.[13] It is, in fact, possible for individuals to obtain a mortgage from a **subprime lender** finance company (a finance company that lends to high-risk customers) even with a bankruptcy in their credit records. Banks rarely make such loans. Most finance companies that offer these mortgages, however, charge rates commensurate with the higher risk, and a few **loan shark** finance companies prey on desperate consumers, charging exorbitant rates as high as 30 percent or more per annum. These predatory lenders often target disadvantaged borrowers who are not aware of the risks they are undertaking with these loans. Predatory lending by loan sharks often leads to the bankruptcy of disadvantaged borrowers.

Other consumer loans include personal cash loans, mobile home loans, and loans to purchase other types of consumer goods such as appliances, apparel, general merchandise, and recreation vehicles. In 2004, other consumer loans made up 28.6 percent of the consumer loan portfolios of finance companies.

Mortgages. Residential and commercial mortgages have become a major component in finance companies' asset portfolios, although they did not generally offer mortgages prior

13. We look at the analysis of borrower (credit) risk in Chapter 20.

TABLE 14–9 Finance Company Loans Outstanding from 1994 through 2004
(in billions of dollars)

	1994	2000	2004	Percent of Total, 2004
Consumer	$248.0	$468.3	$572.5	40.57%
Motor vehicle loans	70.2	141.6	231.2	16.38
Motor vehicle leases	67.5	108.2	62.4	4.42
Revolving*	25.9	37.6	47.4	3.36
Other†	38.4	40.7	84.6	6.00
Securitized assets				
Motor vehicle loans	32.8	97.1	110.2	7.81
Motor vehicle leases	2.2	6.6	4.8	0.34
Revolving	N/A	19.6	22.3	1.58
Other	11.2	17.1	9.6	0.68
Real estate	66.9	198.9	273.7	19.40
One- to four-family	N/A	130.6	188.5	13.36
Other	N/A	41.7	48.3	3.42
Securitized real estate assets‡				
One- to four-family	N/A	24.7	34.3	2.43
Other	N/A	1.9	2.7	0.19
Business	298.6	525.0	565.0	40.03
Motor vehicles	62.0	75.5	89.8	6.36
Retail loans	18.5	18.3	19.6	1.39
Wholesale loans§	35.2	39.7	44.0	3.12
Leases	8.3	17.6	26.2	1.85
Equipment	166.7	283.5	263.2	18.65
Loans	48.9	70.2	70.1	4.97
Leases	117.8	213.3	193.1	13.68
Other business receivables‖	46.2	99.4	116.2	8.23
Securitized assets‡				
Motor vehicles	14.3	37.8	44.9	3.18
Retail loans	1.5	3.2	2.2	0.16
Wholesale loans	12.8	32.5	40.6	2.88
Leases	N/A	2.2	2.0	0.14
Equipment	8.9	23.1	24.0	1.70
Loans	4.7	15.5	11.5	0.81
Leases	4.2	7.6	12.5	0.89
Other business receivables‖	0.5	5.6	27.0	1.91
Total	$613.5	$1,192.2	$1,411.2	100%

* Excludes revolving credit reported as held by depository institutions that are subsidiaries of finance companies.

† Includes personal cash loans, mobile home loans, and loans to purchase other types of consumer goods such as appliances, apparel, boats, and recreation vehicles.

‡ Outstanding balances of pools on which securities have been issued; these balances are no longer carried on the balance sheets of the loan originator.

§ Credit arising from transactions between manufacturers and dealers—that is, floor plan financing.

‖ Includes loans on commercial accounts receivable, factored commercial accounts, and receivable dealer capital; small loans used primarily for business or farm purposes; and wholesale and lease paper for mobile homes, campers, and travel trailers.

Source: Federal Reserve Board, "*Flow of Funds Accounts,*" various issues. **www.federalreserve.gov**

TABLE 14–10 Consumer Credit Interest Rates for 1994 through 2004

Type	1994	1995	1996	1997	2000	2003	2004
Commercial bank new car	8.12%	9.57%	9.05%	9.02%	9.34%	6.93%	6.60%
Auto finance company new car	9.79	11.19	9.84	7.12	6.61	3.40	4.36
Difference in commercial bank versus finance company rate	1.67	1.62	0.79	−1.90	−2.73	−3.53	−2.24

Source: Federal Reserve Board, "*Flow of Funds Accounts,*" various issues. **www.federalreserve.gov**

to 1979 (see Figure 14–10). As explained in Chapter 7, finance companies, which are not subject to as extensive a set of regulations as are banks, are often willing to issue mortgages to riskier borrowers than commercial banks. They compensate for the additional risk by charging higher interest rates. Mortgages include all loans secured by liens on any type of real estate (see Chapter 7). The mortgages in the loan portfolio can be first mortgages, or second mortgages in the form of home equity loans. **Home equity loans** allow customers to borrow on a line of credit secured with a second mortgage on their home. Home equity loans have become very profitable for finance companies since the Tax Reform Act of 1986 was passed, disallowing the tax deductibility of consumers' interest payments other than those made on home mortgages. Also, the bad debt expense and administrative costs of home equity loans are lower than on other finance company loans, and as a result they have become a very attractive product to finance companies.[14] For example, a study by the Consumer Bankers Association found that in 1997–1998 more than 4.2 million households converted $26 billion in credit card debt to home equity loans. Further, in 2004, the average outstanding balance on home equity loans was $70,312, up from $26,627 in 1999.

home equity loan

Loans that let customers borrow on a line of credit secured with a second mortgage on their home.

Finance companies' mortgage portfolios also include **securitized mortgage assets.** Securitization of mortgages involves the pooling of a group of mortgages with similar characteristics, the removal of those mortgages from the balance sheet, and the subsequent sale of cash flows from the mortgage pool to secondary market investors in return for their purchase of bonds (mortgage-backed securities—see Chapters 7 and 24). Thus, securitization of mortgages results in the creation of mortgage-backed securities (e.g., government agency securities, collateralized mortgage obligations), which can be traded in secondary mortgage markets.[15] In addition to income from securitizing mortgage assets, finance companies earn income when they continue to service the original mortgages. **Mortgage servicing** is a fee-related business whereby, after the mortgages are securitized, the flow of mortgage repayments (interest and principal) has to be collected and passed on (by the mortgage servicer) to investors in either whole mortgage loan packages or securitization vehicles such as pass-through securities (see Chapters 7 and 24). In undertaking this intermediation activity, the servicer charges a fee.

securitized mortgage assets

Mortgages packaged and used as assets backing secondary market securities.

mortgage servicing

A fee-related business whereby the flow of mortgage repayments is collected and passed on to investors in whole mortgage loan packages or securitization vehicles.

Business Loans. Business loans represent the largest portion of the loan portfolio of finance companies. Finance companies have several advantages over commercial banks in offering loan services to small-business customers. First, they are not subject to regulations that restrict the type of products and services they can offer (discussed later). Second, because finance companies do not accept deposits, they have no bank-type regulators monitoring their behavior.[16] Third, being (in many cases) subsidiaries of corporate-sector holding companies, finance companies often have substantial industry and product expertise. Fourth—as mentioned with consumer loans—finance companies are more willing to accept risky customers than are commercial banks. Fifth, finance companies generally have lower overheads than banks (e.g., they do not need expensive tellers/branches for deposit taking).

14. A home equity loan is where a house-owner uses his or her house as collateral to borrow money. Should the borrower default, the finance company can seize the house. As a result, home equity finance is among the least risky of the loan products offered by finance companies.

15. Chapter 24 discusses the securitization of mortgages in more detail.

16. Finance companies do, of course, have market participants observing their work and monitoring their activities.

The major subcategories of business loans are retail and wholesale motor vehicle loans and leases (15.9 percent of all business loans in 2004), equipment loans (46.6 percent), other business loans (20.5 percent), and securitized business assets (17.0 percent). Motor vehicle loans consist of retail loans that assist in transactions between the retail seller of the good and the ultimate consumer (i.e., cars purchased by individuals and passenger car fleets purchased by a business for use by its employees). Wholesale loans are loan agreements between parties other than the companies' consumers. For example, GMAC provides wholesale financing to GM dealers for inventory floor plans in which GMAC pays for GM dealers' auto inventories received from GM. GMAC puts a lien on each car on the showroom floor. While the dealer pays periodic interest on the floor plan loan, it is not until the car is sold that the dealer pays for the car.

Business-lending activities of finance companies also include equipment loans, with the finance company either owning or leasing the equipment directly to its industrial customer or providing the financial backing for a working capital loan or a loan to purchase or remodel the customer's facility. Finance companies often prefer to lease equipment rather then sell and finance the purchase of equipment. One reason for this is that repossession of the equipment in the event of default is less complicated when the finance company retains its title (by leasing). Further, a lease agreement generally requires no down payment, making a lease more attractive to the business customer. Finally, when the finance company retains ownership of the equipment (by leasing), it receives a tax deduction in the form of depreciation expense on the equipment. Other business loans include loans to businesses to finance or purchase accounts receivable at a discount (factoring), small farm loans, and wholesale loans and leases for mobile homes, campers, and trailers.

Liabilities and Equity. To finance asset growth, finance companies have relied primarily on short-term commercial paper and other debt instruments (longer-term notes and bonds). Commercial paper is used by finance companies for short-term financing. However, if the finance company remains healthy, these funds can be continually rolled over to create a permanent source of funds. In the past, small or medium-sized finance companies had difficulty qualifying for unsecured commercial paper. As discussed in Chapter 5, only the most creditworthy firms can issue commercial paper. In recent years, however, secured commercial paper has become more popular. Thus, finance companies have access to short-term funds through this market. Finance companies can also obtain long-term funding by issuing debt securities. These long-term debt securities are particularly attractive when interest rates are generally low, as they were in the early 2000s, through the middle of the first decade. Finally, finance companies borrow from commercial banks. These loans can provide a continual source of funds, although some finance companies use bank loans mainly to fund seasonal swings in their business. As data in Table 14–7 indicate, in 2004 commercial paper amounted to $150.8 billion (8.7 percent of total assets); other debt (due to parent holding companies and not elsewhere classified) totaled $881.1 billion (50.4 percent of total assets). Total capital comprised $233.9 billion (13.4 percent of total assets), and loans from banks totaled $64.1 billion (3.7 percent of total assets). In comparison, commercial banks financed 65.6 percent of their assets with deposits, 21.4 percent with other interest-bearing liabilities, 3.0 percent with non-interest bearing liabilities, and 10.0 percent with equity.

As mentioned earlier, unlike banks and thrifts, finance companies cannot accept deposits. Rather, to finance assets, finance companies rely heavily on short-term commercial paper, with many having programs in which they sell commercial paper directly to mutual funds and other institutional investors on a continuous day-by-day basis. Finance companies are now the largest issuers in the short-term commercial paper market. Most commercial paper issues have maturities of 30 days or less, although they can be issued with maturities of up to 270 days (see Chapter 5).[17]

17. Commercial paper issued with a maturity longer than 270 days must be registered with the SEC (i.e., it is treated the same as publicly placed bonds—see Chapter 5).

Industry Performance

Despite an economic slowdown in the United States in the early 2000s, the outlook for the industry as a whole is currently quite bright. Interest rate remain nears historical laws. Mortgage, refinancing is still strong. Loan demand among lower- and middle-income consumers is strong. Because many of these consumers have little savings, no major slowdown in the demand for finance company services is expected. The largest finance companies—those that lend to less risky individual and business customers and with few subprime borrowers (e.g., Household International)—are experiencing strong profits and loan growth. (The industry's assets as a whole grew at a rate of almost 8 percent in 2003 and over 18 percent in 2004.) As such, the most successful finance companies are becoming takeover targets for other financial service as well as industrial firms. For example, as discussed earlier, Citigroup acquired Associates First Capital to create the largest full-service financial institution in the country. In May 2001 American General (the then thirteenth largest finance company) was acquired by American International Group (AIG), one of the country's largest life insurance companies. Finally, in 2003 Household International was acquired by British commercial book HSBC Holdings for $14.9 billion. This acquisition was one of the largest mergers and acquisitions (M&As) of any kind in 2003. These are further examples of the trend toward integration and consolidation among firms in the U.S. financial services sector.

Nevertheless, some analysts predict a shakeout in the market for subprime mortgages as well. For example, Cityscape Financial Corp. of Elmsford, New York, was close to bankruptcy in the late 1990s, as were some of this sector's biggest firms (e.g., Aames Financial Corp., Advanta, and FirstPlus Financial Group). Other leading subprime lenders (e.g., The Money Store and Associates First Capital) ceased trading as they were merged into larger financial institutions. For example, in September 2000 Citigroup announced plans to buy Associates First Capital, the country's second largest subprime lender, for $31.1 billion. These combinations, however, did not necessarily work out. Citigroup incurred regulatory and reputation problems as a result of its acquisition of Associates First Capital. Specifically, the Federal Trade Commission filed a complaint in March 2001 against Associates First Capital and Citigroup alleging systematic and widespread abusive lending practices, deceptive marketing practices, and violating the Truth in Lending Act, the Fair Credit Reporting Act, and the Equal Opportunity Act. The FTC claimed that Associates engaged in widespread deceptive practices, hid essential information from consumers, misrepresented loan terms, and added optional fees to raise the cost of loans to customers. The FTC sought $1 billion in refunds from Citigroup to its customers for the illegal tactics. In September 2002, the FTC agreed to take a $200 million payment from Citigroup to settle allegations of predatory lending. It is problems such as these that may deter future acquisitions, especially of finance companies specializing in the subprime areas.

The U.S. economic downturn in the early 2000s hurt subprime lenders as well. For example, in March 2002 Providian Financial, the leading subprime credit card issuer, sold most of its salable credit card portfolio, while mail order catalogue company Spiegel Group, one of the few retailers to keep its own in-house credit card operations, attempted to sell this division in 2002. In both cases, the credit card portfolio was largely subprime and had been suffering severe credit losses in 2001 and 2002. The problem for subprime lenders started in 1999 and 2000. With the strong economy, these finance companies grew their high-risk accounts aggressively. The economic downturn in 2001 and 2002, combined with increased borrowing by these firms' existing high-risk customers, led to rising levels of delinquencies and losses.

DO YOU UNDERSTAND?

1. How the major assets held by finance companies have changed in the last 30 years?
2. How subprime lender finance company customers differ from consumer loan customers at commercial banks?
3. What advantages finance companies offer over commercial banks to small-business customers?

Another area of this industry that has experienced its ups and downs is finance companies' electronic lending. In the late 1990s electronic lending boomed. Electronic lending allows customers to find, apply for, and close on personal loans (mainly mortgages) completely over the Internet. For example, the first such company, E-Loan, debuted in 1997, initially as a third party, providing an electronic means of matching consumers with lenders (collecting a fee from the lender for bringing the parties together). Upon entering their personal information, customers using electronic lending are presented with multiple options for loans, and sometimes advice on which loan best suits their needs. Customers can keep track of the loan status through the closing—something that often proves difficult when obtaining a loan through the traditional channels. The emphasis with electronic lending is on securing the lowest possible cost for the borrower. While this segment of the industry initially boomed (some estimated that 10 percent of all mortgages would be secured online by 2003), like many dot-com companies, these finance companies took a substantial hit in the early 2000s.

Regulation

9

The Federal Reserve defines a *finance company* as a firm whose primary assets are loans to individuals and businesses.[18] Finance companies, like depository institutions, are financial intermediaries that borrow funds so as to profit on the difference between the rates paid on borrowed funds and those charged on loans. Also like depository institutions, finance companies may be subject to state-imposed usury ceilings on the maximum loan rates assigned to individual customers and are regulated to the extent to which they can collect on delinquent loans (e.g., the legal mechanisms to be followed, such as Chapter 7 and 11 bankruptcy regulations). However, because finance companies do not accept deposits, they are not subject to the extensive oversight by federal and state regulators as are banks or thrifts—even though they offer services that compete directly with those of depository institutions (e.g., consumer installment loans and mortgages—see Table 14–9). The lack of regulatory oversight for these companies enables them to offer a wide scope of "banklike" services and yet avoid the expense of regulatory compliance and the same "net regulatory burden" imposed on banks and thrifts (see Chapter 13).

Nevertheless, since finance companies are heavy borrowers in the capital markets and do not enjoy the same regulatory "safety net" as banks, they need to signal their safety and solvency to investors. Such signals are usually sent by holding much higher equity or capital-to-assets ratios—and therefore, lower leverage ratios—than banks. For example, the 2004 aggregate balance sheet for finance companies (Table 14–7) shows a capital-assets ratio of 13.4 percent. This compares to the capital-to-assets ratio of 10.0 percent reported in Table 11–2 for commercial banks. Larger captive finance companies also use default protection guarantees from their parent companies and/or other guarantees, such as letters of credit or lines of credit purchased for a fee from high-quality commercial or investment banks, as additional protection against insolvency risk and as a device to increase their ability to raise additional funds in the capital and money markets. Thus, this group will tend to operate with lower capital-to-assets ratios than smaller finance companies. Given that regulatory oversight of this industry is relatively light, having sufficient capital and access to financial guarantees are critical to their continued ability to raise funds. Thus, finance companies operate more like nonfinancial, nonregulated companies than the other types of financial institutions examined in this text.

DO YOU UNDERSTAND?

1. Why finance companies are not subject to the same regulations as banks even though they seem to compete in the same lending markets as banks?
2. How finance companies signal solvency and safety to investors?

GLOBAL ISSUES

In contrast to savings institutions in the United States, which must have at least 65 percent of their assets in the form of mortgages (or they lose their tax privileges), savings institutions in Europe were created in the 19th century to channel individuals' savings into the continent's commercial industry. Savings institutions also served as an instrument for providing basic banking services to the poor. The majority of savings institutions in Europe are mutuals (owned by local officials, religious organizations, unions, and deposit holders) rather than stock-owned depository institutions. As a result of the lack of accountability to stockholders, many savings institutions are taking on increasingly more risk as politicians and local businessmen seize upon savings institutions to further their own interests. For example, in November 2004 the Spanish government called on the country's savings banks to bail out the country's ailing shipbuilding industry—a plan blocked by the European Union. Further, Spain's two largest savings banks financed construction of their regional government's unprof-

18. Whereas a bank is defined as an institution that *both* accepts deposits and makes loans.

itable theme park. However, the savings institutions industry worldwide, as in the United States, is very small compared to commercial banks.

Because regulations in most foreign countries are not as restrictive as those in the U.S., finance companies are commonly subsidiaries of commercial banks. For those finance companies owned by commercial banks, their futures are often directly linked to the health of the parent bank. For example, the economic recession in Japan in the late 1990s and the resulting huge volume of nonperforming property loans in Japanese commercial banks depleted Japanese banks' capital and restricted their ability to lend to their finance company subsidiaries, thus constraining their credit market activities. The result has been some attractive opportunities for others. For example, in January 1999 GE Capital Corporation (GECC) agreed to buy (for $7 billion) Japan Leasing Corporation (JLC), the Japanese lending unit of Long-Term Credit Bank of Japan, in the biggest acquisition ever involving a Japanese company. GECC bought only the healthy assets of JLC shortly after its parent, Long-Term Credit Bank, was declared insolvent and nationalized because of huge problems with its nonperforming property loans. Historically assets of a Japanese company, such as JLC, would never have been acquired by a foreign investor like GECC.

SUMMARY

This chapter provided an overview of the major activities of savings institutions, credit unions, and finance companies. Savings institutions and credit unions rely heavily on deposits to fund loans, whereas finance companies do not accept deposits but find themselves mainly with commercial paper and long-term security issues. Historically, while commercial banks have concentrated on commercial or business lending and on investing in securities, savings institutions have concentrated on mortgage lending and credit unions on consumer lending. Finance companies also compete directly with depository institutions for high-quality (prime) loan customers. Further, this industry services those subprime (high-risk) borrowers deemed too risky for depository institutions. These differences are being eroded due to competitive forces, regulation, and the changing nature of financial and business technology, so that the types of interest rate, credit, liquidity, and operational risks faced by commercial banks, savings institutions, credit unions, and finance companies are becoming increasingly similar.

SEARCH THE SITE

Go to the Federal Reserve Board's Web site at **www.federalreserve.gov** and get the latest information on finance company consumer, real estate, and business lending using the following steps.

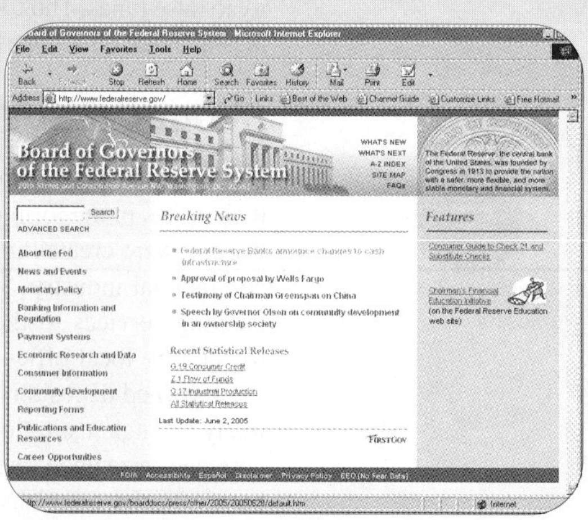

Click on "Economic Research and Data."

Click on "Statistics: Releases and Historical Data."

Click on "Finance Companies."

Click on the most recent date.

This downloads a file onto your computer that contains the relevant data.

Questions

1. How have these data changed since 2004 as reported in Table 14–9.
2. Calculate the percentage of consumer, real estate, business, and other loans to total loans. How have these percentages changed since 2004?

QUESTIONS

1. How do the balance sheets of savings associations and savings banks differ from those of commercial banks? How do their sizes compare?
2. What were the reasons for the crisis of the thrift industry in the late 1970s and early 1980s?
3. What two major pieces of legislation were adopted in the early 1980s to ameliorate the thrift crisis? Explain.
4. What shortcomings in the Depository Institutions Deregulation and Monetary Control Act of 1980 (DIDMCA) and the Garn-St. Germain Depository Institutions Act of 1982 (GSGDIA) contributed to the failure of the SI industry?
5. How did the Financial Institutions Reform, Recovery, and Enforcement Act (FIRREA) of 1989 reverse some of the key features of earlier legislation?
6. What are the main assets and liabilities held by savings associations?
7. What are the similarities and differences among savings institutions (savings associations and savings banks)?
8. What regulatory agencies oversee deposit insurance services to savings associations and saving banks?
9. What happened to the value of the savings institutions' charters in the period of time since October 1979? How did this shift contribute to the crisis in the savings institutions industry?
10. What does it mean when a savings bank is a mutual organization?
11. What is the trend in mutual versus stock charters (in number and asset size) for savings institutions?
12. What explanations can be provided for the recent decline in the size of the savings institutions industry?
13. Go to the S&P Educational Version of Market Insight Web site at **www.mhhe.com/edumarketinsight** and find the most recent balance sheet for Washington Mutual (WM) and Goldent West Financial (GDW) using the following steps. Click on "Educational Version of Market Insight." Enter your site ID and click on "Login." Click on "Company." In the box marked "Ticker:" enter WM and click on "Go!" Click on "Excel Analytics." Click on "FS Ann. Balance Sheet." This brings up a file that contains the relevant data. Repeat this process using the ticker GDW. Compare the ratios of loans to total assets and stockholders' equity to total assets from these balance sheets with those for the savings bank industry listed in Table 14–3.
14. How do credit unions differ from savings institutions?
15. Why were credit unions less affected by the sharp increase in interest rates in the late 1970s and early 1980s than the savings institutions industry?
16. What are the main assets and liabilities held by credit unions?
17. Who are the regulators of credit unions?
18. Why did commercial banks pursue legal action against the credit union industry in the late 1990s? What was the result of this legal action?
19. What are the three types of finance companies and how do they differ from commercial banks?
20. What are the three types of lending services offered by finance companies?
21. How does the amount of equity as a percentage of assets compare for finance companies and commercial banks? What accounts for the difference?
22. What are the major assets and liabilities held by finance companies?
23. What has been the fastest growing area of asset business for finance companies?
24. Why was the reported rate on motor vehicle loans historically higher for a finance company than a commercial bank? Why did this change in 1997?
25. Go to the S&P Educational Version of Market Insight Web site at **www.mhhe.com/edumarketinsight** and find the most recent balance sheet information for Capital One Financial Corp. (COF) and American Express (AXP) using the following steps. Click on "Educational Version of Market Insight." Enter your site ID and click on "Login." Click on "Company." In the box marked "Ticker:" enter COF and click on "Go!" Click on "Excel Analytics." Click on "FS Ann. Balance Sheet." This brings up a file that contains the relevant data. Repeat this process using the ticker AXP. Compare the ratios of consumer loans to total assets, business (commercial) loans to total assets, and real estate (mortgage) loans to total assets from these balance sheets with those for the finance company industry listed in Table 14–7.
26. What advantages do finance companies have over banks in offering services to small-business customers?
27. Why are finance companies less regulated than commercial banks?
28. Why have finance companies begun to offer more mortgage and home equity loans?
29. What is a wholesale motor vehicle loan?
30. What signal does a low debt-to-assets ratio for a finance company send to the capital markets?

15 Insurance Companies

OUTLINE

Chapter NAVIGATOR

1. What are the two types of insurance companies?
2. What are the four basic lines of business performed by life insurance companies?
3. What are the major assets and liabilities of life insurance companies?
4. What are the major regulations governing life insurance companies?
5. What are the major lines of business performed by property–casualty insurance companies?
6. What are the main asset and liability items on property–casualty insurance company balance sheets?
7. Who are the main regulators of property–casualty insurance companies?
8. What are the major trends occurring in the global insurance market?

1 TWO CATEGORIES OF INSURANCE COMPANIES: CHAPTER OVERVIEW

The primary function of insurance companies is to compensate individuals and corporations (policyholders) if a prespecified adverse event occurs, in exchange for premiums paid to the insurer by the policyholder. The insurance industry is classified into two major groups: (1) life and (2) property–casualty. Life insurance provides protection in the event of untimely death, illnesses, and retirement. Property insurance protects against personal injury and liability due to accidents, theft, fire, and other catastrophes. This chapter discusses the main features of insurance companies by concentrating on (1) the size, structure, and composition of the industry in which they operate, (2) their balance sheets and recent trends, and (3) regulations.

LIFE INSURANCE COMPANIES

Size, Structure, and Composition of the Industry

In the early 2000s, the United States had approximately 1,500 life insurance companies, compared to over 2,300 in 1988. The aggregate assets of life insurance companies were \$3.88 trillion at the beginning of 2004, compared to \$1.12 trillion in 1988. The two biggest life insurers in terms of premiums written (Metropolitan Life Insurance Co. and Prudential Insurance Co. of America) wrote 10.4 percent of the industry's \$618.0 billion premiums in 2003. Although not to the extent seen in the banking industry, the life insurance industry has experienced major mergers in recent years (e.g., SunAmerica and AIG, and St. Paul Insurance and USF&G) as competition within the industry and with other FIs has increased. Like consolidation in commercial banking, the consolidation of the insurance industry has mainly occurred to take advantage of economies of scale and scope, and other synergies (see Chapter 11).

Life insurance companies can take the form of a stock or a mutual company. Stock insurance companies are owned by independent shareholders and are publicly traded. Mutual insurance companies have no stock or external owners. Rather, the policyholders are the owners of the company. Traditionally, the largest insurers were mutual companies. However, recently there has been a "demutualization" of the industry as mutual insurance companies have converted to stock organizations. Several reasons are cited for this trend. First, with the financial institutions industry diversifying and merging, insurance companies have needed to acquire other financial institutions to grow and survive. To conduct these acquisitions, the company needs capital. Mutual insurance companies, by definition, cannot issue stock. Thus, to expand, mutual insurance companies have converted to stock insurance companies. Further, stock and stock options have become a more important corporate governance mechanism. Many insurance companies have concluded that to attract and retrain the best managers, they need to offer these managers publicly traded stock in their companies as part of their compensation package.

Life insurance allows individuals to protect themselves and their beneficiaries against the risk of loss of income in the event of death or retirement. By pooling risks of individual customers, life insurance companies can diversify away some of the customer-specific risk and offer insurance services at a cost (premium) lower than any individual could achieve saving funds on his or her own. Thus, life insurance companies transfer income-related uncertainties such as those due to retirement from the individual to a group. Although life insurance may be their core activity area, modern life insurance companies also sell annuity contracts (primarily savings contracts that involve the liquidation of those funds saved over a period of time), manage pension plans (tax-deferred savings plans), and provide accident and health insurance. Figure 15–1 shows the distribution of premiums written for the various lines of insurance in the early 2000s. We discuss these different activity lines below.

In return for insurance premiums, insurance companies accept or underwrite the risk that the prespecified event will occur. The major part of the insurance company underwriting process is deciding which requests for insurance (or risks) they should accept and which ones they should reject. Further, for those risks they accept, they must decide how much they should charge for the insurance. For example, an insurance company would not want to provide life insurance to someone with terminal cancer. Alternatively, the insurer may decide to insure a smoker but charge a higher premium than is charged to a nonsmoker. Thus, the underwriting process is critical to an insurance company's profitability and survival.

adverse selection problem

The problem that customers who apply for insurance policies are more likely to be those most in need of coverage.

One problem that naturally faces life insurance companies (as well as property–casualty insurers) is the **adverse selection problem.** Adverse selection is the problem that customers who apply for insurance policies are more likely to be those most in need of insurance (i.e., someone with chronic health problems is more likely to purchase a life insurance policy than someone in perfect health). Thus, in calculating the probability of having to pay out on an insurance contract and, in turn, determining the insurance premium to charge, insurance companies' use of health (and other) statistics representing the overall population may

FIGURE 15–1 Distribution of Premiums Written on Various Life Insurance Lines

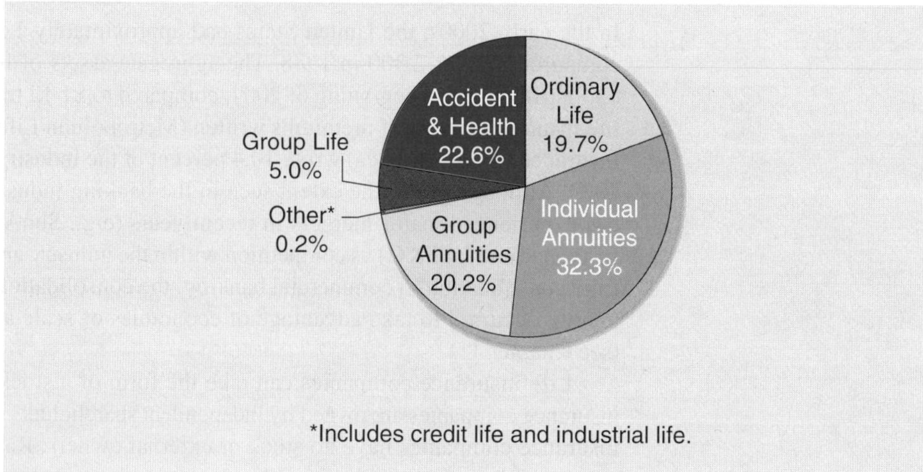

Source: *Best's Aggregates & Averages—Life/Health*, 2004. **www.ambest.com**

not be appropriate (since the insurance company's pool of customers is more prone to health problems than the overall population). Insurance companies deal with the adverse selection problem by establishing different pools of the population based on health and related characteristics (such as income). By altering the pool used to determine the probability of losses to a particular customer's health characteristics, the insurance company can more accurately determine the probability of having to pay out on a policy and can adjust the insurance premium accordingly.

As the various types of insurance policies and services offered are described below, notice that some policies (such as universal life policies and annuities) provide not only insurance features but also savings components. For example, universal life policy payouts are a function of the interest earned on the investment of the policyholder's premiums. Similarly, annuities offer the policyholder a fixed or variable payment each period (generally monthly) for life or over some predetermined future horizon.

2

Life Insurance. The four basic classes or lines of life insurance are distinguished by the manner in which they are sold or marketed to purchasers. These classes are (1) ordinary life, (2) group life, (3) credit life, and (4) other activities. Of the life insurance policies in force in the United States, ordinary life accounts for 59.1 percent, group life for 40.4 percent, and credit life for less than 6 percent of the over \$618.0 billion in premiums written. In recent years sales of basic life insurance policies have declined in the face of competition from annuities and mutual funds. For example, in 2003 net premiums written by insurance companies totaled \$618.0 billion, while sales of annuities[1] totaled \$324.4 billion.

Ordinary Life. Ordinary life insurance policies are marketed on an individual basis, usually in units of \$1,000; policyholders make periodic premium payments in return for insurance coverage. Despite the enormous variety of contractual forms, there are essentially five basic contractual types. The first three are traditional forms of ordinary life insurance, and the last two are newer contracts that originated in the 1970s and 1980s when competition for savings from other segments of the financial services industry, such as mutual funds, increased. The three traditional contractual forms are term life, whole life, and endowment life. The two

1. While life insurance involves different methods of building up an insurance fund, annuities involve different methods of liquidating an insurance fund. We discuss annuities below.

newer forms are variable life and universal life. The key features of each of these contractual forms are identified as follows:

- **Term Life.** This policy is the closest to pure life insurance; it has no savings element attached. Essentially, as long as premium payments are up to date, an individual's beneficiary receives a payout at the time of the individual's death during the coverage period. If the insured individual lives beyond the term of the contract, the contract expires along with any rights to benefits. The term of coverage can vary from as little as 1 year to 40 years or more.
- **Whole Life.** This policy protects the individual over an entire lifetime rather than for a specified coverage period. In return for periodic or level premiums, the individual's beneficiaries receive the face value of the life insurance contract on death. Thus, if the policyholder continues premium payments, the insurance company is certain to make a payment—unlike term insurance, where a payment is made only if death occurs during the coverage period. In the early years of the contract, premiums are larger than those for term life contracts and in the later years they are smaller. The overpayment in the early years creates a cash value for whole life contracts that insured individuals can borrow against (at a stated rate paid to the insurance company).
- **Endowment Life.** This type of policy combines a pure (term) insurance element with a savings element. It guarantees a payout to the beneficiaries of the policy if death occurs during some endowment period (e.g., prior to reaching retirement age). An insured person who lives to the endowment date receives the face amount of the policy.
- **Variable Life.** Unlike traditional policies that promise to pay the insured the fixed or face amount of a policy should a contingency arise, variable life insurance invests fixed premium payments in mutual funds of stocks, bonds, and money market instruments. Usually, policyholders can choose mutual fund investments to reflect their risk preferences. Thus, variable life provides an alternative way to build savings compared to the more traditional policies such as whole life because the value of the policy increases (or decreases) with the asset returns of the mutual fund in which premiums are invested.
- **Universal Life and Variable Universal Life.** A universal life policy allows the insured to change both the premium amounts and the maturity of the life contract, unlike traditional policies that maintain premiums at a given level over a fixed contract period. In addition, for some contracts, insurers invest premiums in money, equity, or bond mutual funds—as in variable life insurance—so that the savings or investment component of the contract reflects market returns. In this case, the policy is called *variable universal life.*

Group Life Insurance. This insurance covers a large number of insured persons under a single policy. Usually issued to corporate employers, these policies may be either *contributory* (where both the employer and employee cover a share of the employee's cost of the insurance) or *noncontributory* (where the employee does not contribute to the cost of the insurance; rather the cost is paid entirely by the employer) for the employees themselves. The principal advantage of group life over ordinary life policies involves cost economies. These occur as the result of mass administration of plans, lower costs for evaluating individuals through medical screening and other rating systems, and reduced selling and commission costs.

Credit Life. This insurance protects lenders against a borrower's death prior to the repayment of a debt contract such as a mortgage or car loan. Usually, the face amount of the insurance policy reflects the outstanding principal and interest on the loan.

Other Life Insurer Activities. Three other major activities of life insurance companies are the sale of annuities, private pension plans, and accident and health insurance.

Annuities. Annuities represent the reverse of life insurance principles. While life insurance involves different contractual methods to *build up* a fund and the eventual payout of a *lump sum* to the beneficiary, annuities involve different methods of *liquidating* a fund over a *long period* of time, such as paying out a fund's proceeds to the beneficiary. As with life insurance contracts, many different types of annuity contracts have been developed. Specifically, they can be sold to an individual or group and on either a fixed or variable basis by being linked to the return on some underlying investment portfolio. Individuals can purchase annuities with a single payment or payments spread over a number of years. Payments may be structured to begin immediately, or they can be *deferred* (for example, to start at retirement). These payments may cease at death or continue to be paid to beneficiaries for a number of years after death. Any interest earned on annuities is tax deferred (i.e., taxes are not paid until the annuity payments are actually made to the beneficiary). In contrast to Individual Retirement Accounts, or IRAs (see Chapter 18), the tax-deferred status of annual annuity contributions are not capped and are not affected by the policyholder's income level. Thus, annuities have become popular with individuals as a mechanism used to save for retirement. Annuity sales in 2003 topped \$275 billion (\$125 billion of which were variable annuities), compared to \$26.1 billion in 1996.[2]

EXAMPLE 15-1 Calculation of the Fair Value of an Annuity Policy

Suppose that a person wants to purchase an annuity today that would pay \$15,000 per year until the end of that person's life. The insurance company expects the person to live for 25 more years and can invest the amount received for the annuity at a guaranteed interest rate of 5 percent.[3] The fair price for the annuity policy today can be calculated as follows:

$$\begin{aligned}\text{Fair value} &= \frac{15{,}000}{1+r} + \frac{15{,}000}{(1+r)^2} + \cdots + \frac{15{,}000}{(1+r)^{25}} \\ &= 15{,}000\left[\frac{1}{1+r} + \frac{1}{(1+r)^2} + \cdots + \frac{1}{(1+r)^{25}}\right] \\ &= 15{,}000\,[PVIF_{r=5\%,n=25}] \\ &= 15{,}000\,[14.0939] \\ &= \$211{,}409\end{aligned}$$

where $PVIFA_{r=5\%,n=25}$ = Present value annuity factor reflecting the present value of \$1 invested at 5 percent over 25 years.

Thus, the cost of purchasing this annuity today would be \$211,409.

Private Pension Funds. Insurance companies offer many alternative pension plans to private employers in an effort to attract this business away from other financial service companies such as commercial banks and securities firms. Some of their innovative pension plans are based on guaranteed investment contracts (GICs). With such plans, the insurer guarantees not only the rate of interest credited to a pension plan over some given period—for example, five years—but also the annuity rates on beneficiaries' contracts. Other plans include immediate participation and separate account plans that follow more aggressive investment strategies than does traditional life insurance, such as investing premiums in special-purpose equity mutual funds. In the early of 2000s, life insurance companies were managing over \$1.5 trillion in pension fund assets, equal to approximately 30 percent of all private pension plans.

Accident and Health Insurance. While life insurance protects against mortality risk, accident and health insurance protect against morbidity or ill-health risk. The rising cost of medical care has made accident and health insurance a top priority for those wanting to

2. As discussed in Chapter 13, life insurers are facing increasingly intense competition from banks in the annuity product market.

3. One possible way to do this would be for the insurer to buy a 25-year maturity zero coupon Treasury bond that has an annual discount yield of 5 percent.

TABLE 15–1 Life Insurance Company Assets
(distribution of assets of U.S. life insurance companies)

Year	Total Assets (in millions)	Government Securities	Corporate Securities		Mortgages	Policy Loans	Miscellaneous Assets*
			Bonds	Stocks			
1917	$5,941	9.6%	33.2%	1.4%	34.0%	13.6%	5.2%
1920	7,320	18.4	26.7	1.0	33.4	11.7	6.5
1930	18,880	8.0	26.0	2.8	40.2	14.9	5.2
1940	30,802	27.5	28.1	2.0	19.4	10.0	6.3
1950	64,020	25.2	36.3	3.3	25.1	3.8	4.1
1960	119,576	9.9	39.1	4.2	34.9	4.4	4.4
1970	207,254	5.3	35.3	7.4	35.9	7.8	5.3
1980	479,210	6.9	37.5	9.9	27.4	8.6	6.6
1990	1,408,208	15.0	41.4	9.1	19.2	4.4	7.8
2000	3,133,900	9.3	39.1	31.5	7.5	3.2	9.4
2004	3,992,700	11.8	43.2	26.4	6.7	2.6	9.3

*Includes cash, checkable deposits, and money market funds.

Note: Beginning with 1962, these data include the assets of separate accounts.

Source: *Federal Reserve Bulletin,* various issues. **www.federalreserve.gov**

have health expenses covered at a reasonable cost.[4] More than $140 billion in premiums were written annually by life and health companies in accident-health in 2004. The major activity line is group insurance, which provides health insurance coverage to corporate employees. Life insurance companies write more than 50 percent of all health insurance premiums. However, the growth in health maintenance organizations (HMOs) (nonregulated providers of health insurance) in the late 1990s has cut into this line of business. Other coverages include credit health plans, whereby individuals have their debt repayments insured against unexpected health contingencies and various types of renewable, nonrenewable, and guaranteed health and accident plans for individuals. In many respects, insurers in accident and health lines face loss exposures that are more similar to those that property–casualty insurers face than those that traditional life insurers face (see the section on property–casualty insurance, which follows shortly).

Balance Sheets and Recent Trends

Assets. Because of the long-term nature of their liabilities (resulting from the long-term nature of life insurance policyholders' claims) and the need to generate competitive returns on the savings elements of life insurance products, life insurance companies concentrate their asset investments at the longer end of the maturity spectrum (e.g., corporate bonds, equities, and government securities). Table 15–1 shows the distribution of life insurance assets. As you can see, in 2004, 11.8 percent of assets were invested in government securities, 69.6 percent in corporate bonds and stocks, and 6.7 percent in mortgages (commercial and home mortgages), with other loans—including **policy loans** (i.e., loans made to policyholders using their policies as collateral)—and miscellaneous assets comprising the remaining assets. Although depository institutions are the major issuers of new mortgages (sometimes keeping the mortgages on their books and sometimes selling them to secondary market investors), insurance companies hold mortgages as investment securities. That is, they purchase many mortgages in the secondary markets (see Chapters 7 and 24). The major trend has been a long-term increase in the

policy loans

Loans made by an insurance company to its policyholders using their policies as collateral.

4. Indeed, the rising cost of health care has made accident and health insurance offered by insurance companies unaffordable to many. As a result, the U.S. government is exploring options for publicly financed health care insurance.

SEARCH THE SITE

Go to the Federal Reserve Board's Web site at **www.federalreserve.gov** and find the most recent distribution of life insurance industry assets for Table 15–1 using the following steps.

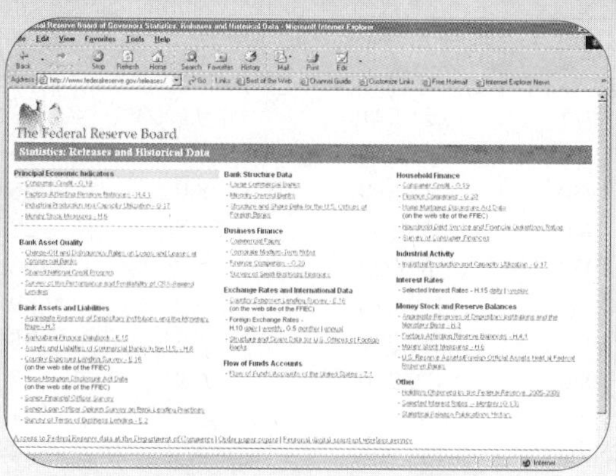

Click on "Economic Research and Data"

Click on "Statistics: Releases and Historical Data"

Click on "Flow of Fund Accounts of the United States." Click on the most recent date

Click on "Level tables"

This will bring the file (Table L.117) onto your computer that contains the relevant data.

Questions

1. How has the value of total assets held by insurance companies changed since 2004 as reported in Table 15–1?
2. Calculate the percentage of this total that represents government securities, corporate securities, mortgages, and policy loans.
3. How has the distribution of the various securities changed since 2004 as reported in Table 15–1? And why?

proportion of bonds and equities[5] and a decline in the proportion of mortgages on life insurer's balance sheets. Thus, insurance company managers must be able to measure and manage the credit risk, interest rate risk, and other risks associated with these securities.

policy reserves

A liability item for insurers that reflects their expected payment commitments on existing policy contracts.

surrender value of a policy

The cash value of a policy received from the insurer if a policyholder surrenders the policy prior to maturity; normally, only a portion of the contract's face value.

separate account

Annuity program sponsored by life insurance companies in which the payoff on the policy is linked to the assets in which policy premiums are invested.

Liabilities. The aggregate balance sheet for the life insurance industry at the beginning of 2004 is presented in Table 15–2. Looking at the liability side of the balance sheet, we see that $1.867 trillion, or 48.2 percent, of total liabilities and capital reflect net **policy reserves.** These reserves are based on actuarial assumptions regarding an insurer's expected future liability or commitment to pay out on present contracts, including death benefits, maturing endowment policies (lump sum or otherwise), as well as the cash **surrender value of policies** (i.e., the cash value paid to the policyholder if the policy is "surrendered" by the policyholder before it matures). Even though the actuarial assumptions underlying policy reserves are normally very conservative, unexpected fluctuations in future payouts can occur; that is, life insurance underwriting is risky. For example, mortality rates—and life insurance payouts—might unexpectedly increase over those defined by historically based mortality tables because of a catastrophic epidemic, as was the case with AIDS in the 1980s. To meet unexpected future losses, a life insurer holds a capital and surplus reserve fund with which to meet such losses. The capital and surplus reserves of life insurers in 2004 totaled $225.7 billion, or 5.8 percent of their total liabilities and capital.[6] **Separate account** business was 30.5 percent of total liabilities and capital in 2004. Legally, separate account funds are invested and held separately from the insurance company's other assets. In particular, these funds may be invested without regard to the usual restrictions (e.g., they may be invested in all stocks, or all bonds).

5. The bull market of the 1980s and 1990s is likely a major reason for the large percentage of assets invested in equities. The need for a more certain stream of cash flows to pay off policies is a major reason for the investment in bonds.

6. An additional line of defense against unexpected underwriting losses is the insurer's investment income from its asset portfolio plus any new premium income flows. Consequently, falling asset values (e.g., due to a stock market decline) can threaten the solvency and safety of firms in the insurance industry.

TABLE 15–2 Life Insurance Industry Balance Sheet as of 2004
(in millions of dollars)

				Percent of Total
Assets				
Bonds			$1,941,081	50.1%
Preferred stock			29,319	0.8
Common stock			64,186	1.7
Mortgage loans			261,072	6.7
Real estate			20,203	0.5
Contract loans			106,249	2.7
Cash and short-term investments			79,435	2.0
Other invested assets			58,628	1.5
Premiums due			21,033	0.5
Accrued investment income			29,630	0.8
Separate account assets			1,186,193	30.6
Other assets			79,675	2.1
Total assets			$3,876,704	100.0%
Liabilities and Capital/Surplus				
Net policy reserves			$1,867,493	48.2%
Policy claims			36,900	0.9
Deposit-type contracts			289,471	7.5
Interest maintenance reserve			14,592	0.4
Commissions, taxes, expenses			26,687	0.7
Securities valuation reserve			31,159	0.8
Other liabilities			201,444	5.2
Separate account business			1,183,257	30.5
Total capital and surplus			225,701	5.8
Capital	$3,714	0.1		
Treasury stock	(322)	0.0		
Paid-in and contributed surplus	87,028	2.2		
Surplus notes and debentures	17,761	0.5		
Unassigned surplus	101,200	2.6		
Other surplus	24	0.0		
Other reserves	16,296	0.4		
Total liabilities and capital/surplus			$3,876,704	100.0%

Source: *Best's Aggregates & Averages, Life-Health* (Oldwick, NJ: A.M. Best Company, 2004), p. 2. Copyrighted by A.M. Best Company. Used with permission. **www.ambest.com**

McCarran–Ferguson Act of 1945

Regulation confirming the primacy of state over federal regulation of insurance companies.

The returns on life insurance policies written as part of separate account business depend, then, on the return on the funds invested in separate account assets. Another important life insurer liability, guaranteed investment contracts or GICs (7.5 percent of total liabilities and capital), are short- and medium-term debt instruments sold by insurance companies to fund their pension plan business (see deposit-type contracts in Table 15–2).

Regulation

The most important legislation affecting the regulation of life insurance companies is the **McCarran–Ferguson Act of 1945,** which confirms the primacy of state over federal regulation of insurance companies. Thus, unlike the depository institutions we discussed in Chapters 11 through 13, which can be chartered at either the federal or state levels, a life insurer is chartered entirely at the state level. In addition to chartering, state insurance commissions supervise and examine insurance companies using a coordinated examination system

www.naic.org

developed by the National Association of Insurance Commissioners (NAIC). Regulations cover areas such as insurance premiums, insurer licensing, sales practices, commission charges, and the types of assets in which insurers may invest. An example of state insurance regulatory actions is the 1997 case of Prudential Insurance Company. Prudential's policyholders filed and settled (for $410 million) a class action lawsuit claiming that Prudential's sales representatives defrauded customers by talking them into using the built-up cash values held in older life insurance policies to buy newer, costlier policies. A task force of state insurance regulators from 45 states conducted an 18-month "deceptive sales practices" investigation. The report resulting from this investigation was instrumental in determining the legal settlement.

In early 2004 the prospect of the federal government gaining a role in the regulation of the insurance industry gained momentum. The chairman of the House Committee on Financial Services spelled out plans for 2004 legislation that would create a council of federal and state officials to oversee insurance (life as well as property–casualty) nationally with a presidential appointee as its head. The legislation would force states to adopt uniform standards and permit the market to determine insurance prices rather than have them determined by state regulators, as is generally the case. For several years state regulators have been trying to simplify and speed their procedures on rates, conditions of coverage, and approval of new insurance products. But progress has been slow. The results have been complaints that cumbersome and costly state regulations have been failing to meet the needs of both insurance companies and their customers. Many of the nation's biggest insurers have been campaigning for a dual system, which would create a federal regulator but also permit companies to choose whether to be regulated at the federal level or the state level. The proposal has met resistance from the states, consumer groups, and some members of Congress.[7]

insurance guarantee fund

A fund of required contributions from within-state insurance companies to compensate insurance company policyholders in the event of failure.

www.ins.state.ny.us

Other than supervision and examination, states also promote life **insurance guarantee funds.** Unlike banks and thrifts, life insurers have no access to a federal guarantee fund. These state guarantee funds differ in a number of important ways from deposit insurance. First, although these programs are sponsored by state insurance regulators, they are actually run and administered by the private insurance companies themselves.

Second, unlike SAIF or BIF, in which the FDIC has established a permanent reserve fund by requiring banks to pay annual premiums in excess of payouts to resolve failures (see Chapter 13), no such permanent guarantee fund exists for the insurance industry—with the sole exception of the property–casualty and life guarantee funds in the state of New York. This means that contributions are paid into the guarantee fund by surviving firms in a state only after an insurance company has actually failed.

DO YOU UNDERSTAND?

1. The difference between a life insurance contract and an annuity contract?
2. What the different forms of ordinary life insurance are?
3. Why life insurance companies invest in long-term assets?
4. What the major source of life insurance underwriting risk is?
5. Who the main regulators of the life insurance industry are?

Third, the size of the required contributions that surviving insurers make to protect policyholders in failed insurance companies differs widely from state to state. In those states that have guarantee funds, each surviving insurer is normally levied a pro rata amount, according to the size of its statewide premium income. This amount either helps pay off small policyholders after the assets of the failed insurer have been liquidated or acts as a cash injection to make the acquisition of a failed insurer attractive. The definition of small policyholders varies among states in the range from $100,000 to $500,000.

Finally, because no permanent fund exists, and the annual pro rata payments to meet payouts to failed insurer policyholders are often legally capped, a delay usually occurs before small policyholders receive the cash surrender values of their policies or other payment obligations from the guarantee fund. This contrasts with deposit insurance, which normally provides insured depositors immediate coverage of their claims up to $100,000.

As discussed in Chapter 13, a piece of legislation that will have a major impact on the insurance (both life insurance and property–casualty insurance) industry in the future is the Financial Services Modernization Act of 1999. This legislation allows insurance companies, commercial banks, and investment banks to engage in each other's business. In addition to the new opportunities this bill has brought to the insurance industry, industry leaders praised the legislation for its requirement that commercial banks and investment

7. See "New Momentum for Letting U.S. Help Regulate Nation's Insurers," *The New York Times,* March 18, 2004, p. B8.

banks entering the insurance business would be subject to insurance regulations of the state in which they operate. This creates a level playing field for the regulation of the insurance activities of insurance companies, banks, and securities firms.

The year 2004 saw the first action against an insurance company involving alleged unethical practices. In a sweeping investigation of variable annuity sales, federal and state regulators prepared a case against Conseco, asserting that the insurer provided advantages to big investors that could increase profits but hurt small investors. Until recently, many variable annuities permitted almost unlimited movement of money among asset pools in which annuity funds were invested. Regulators asserted that in the early 2000s companies had increasingly imposed limits on asset pool movements by smaller investors (annuity holders). Regulators were also investigating a number of other insurance companies and brokerage companies for similar practices.

PROPERTY–CASUALTY INSURANCE COMPANIES

Size, Structure, and Composition of the Industry

Currently, some 3,200 companies sell property–casualty (P&C) insurance, and approximately half of these firms write P&C business in all or most of the United States. The U.S. P&C insurance industry is quite concentrated. Collectively, the top 10 firms have a 45 percent share of the overall P&C market measured by premiums written, and the top 200 firms make up over 95 percent of the industry premiums written.[8] In 2004, the top firm (State Farm) wrote 10.3 percent of all P&C insurance premiums, while the second-ranked insurer, American International Group (AIG), wrote 6.0 percent of all premiums (i.e., a joint total of 16.3 percent of premiums). In contrast, in 1985, the top two firms wrote 14.5 percent of the total industry insurance premiums. Thus, the industry leaders appear to be increasing their domination of this financial services sector. As with commercial banks, much of this consolidation is coming through mergers and acquisitions. For example, in late 2003 St. Paul Companies acquired Travelers Property Casualty Corporation in a $16.4 billion stock swap to create St. Paul Travelers. The acquisition moved the combined companies into the number three position (based on total assets) among all PC insurers. The total assets of the P&C industry as of the beginning of 2004 were $1,174 billion, or approximately 30 percent of the life insurance industry's assets.

P&C Insurance. Property insurance involves insurance coverages related to the loss of real and personal property. Casualty—or perhaps more accurately, liability—insurance offers protection against legal liability exposures. However, distinctions between the two broad areas of property and liability insurance are becoming increasingly blurred. This is due to the tendency of P&C insurers to offer multiple activity line coverages combining features of property and liability insurance into single policy packages—for example, homeowners multiple peril insurance. The following describes the key features of the main P&C lines. Note, however, that some P&C activity lines (e.g., auto insurance) are marketed as one product to individuals and another to commercial firms, while other lines (e.g., boiler and machinery insurance targeted at commercial purchasers) are marketed to one specific group. To understand the importance of each line in premium income (so-called **premiums written**) and losses incurred in 2003, review Table 15–3. The following data show the P&C lines (and their changing importance to the P&C industry):

premiums written
The entire amount of premiums on insurance contracts written.

- **Fire Insurance and Allied Lines** protect against the perils of fire, lightning, and removal of property damaged in a fire (2.0 percent of all premiums written in 2003 versus 16.6 percent in 1960).
- **Homeowners Multiple Peril (MP) insurance** protects against multiple perils of damage to a personal dwelling and personal property (e.g., fire, lightning, windstorm, hail, explosion, theft, weight of ice or snow) as well as liability coverage against the financial consequences of legal liability resulting from injury to others. Thus, it combines features of both property and liability insurance (10.8 percent of all premiums written in 2003; 5.2 percent in 1960).

8. *Best's Review,* August 2004.

TABLE 15–3 Property and Casualty Insurance
(industry underwriting by lines, 2004)

Line	Premiums Written*	Percent of Total Premiums Written	Losses Incurred†
Fire	$ 9,071,576	2.0%	38.7%
Allied lines	7,091,646	1.6	48.4
Multiple peril (MP) crop	3,382,048	0.8	87.1
Farm owners MP	2,151,891	0.5	61.0
Homeowners MP	48,376,292	10.8	59.5
Commercial MP—nonliability	19,028,777	4.3	45.4
Commercial MP—liability	12,398,328	2.8	57.7
Mortgage guarantee	4,309,078	1.0	41.7
Ocean marine	2,447,516	0.5	63.1
Inland marine	10,787,788	2.4	43.3
Financial guarantee	3,120,411	0.7	6.0
Medical malpractice	10,142,575	2.3	81.1
Earthquake	1,805,733	0.4	14.3
Federal flood	1,618,485	0.4	37.7
Group accident and health	7,219,768	1.6	71.0
Other accident and health	3,215,624	0.7	66.0
Workers' compensation	49,862,964	11.2	74.8
Other liability	48,105,076	10.8	76.6
Product liability	3,707,256	0.8	100.3
Private passenger auto liability	90,752,265	20.3	66.6
Commercial auto liability	21,442,909	4.8	61.4
Private passenger auto PD	64,253,042	14.4	58.3
Commercial auto PD	7,561,673	1.7	47.9
Aircraft	2,431,315	0.5	41.8
Fidelity	1,192,373	0.3	37.7
Surety	3,889,105	0.9	51.3
Federal employees health	884,690	0.2	93.6
Burglary and theft	118,026	0.0	24.4
Boiler and machinery	1,179,079	0.3	22.4
Credit	820,605	0.2	42.1
Other lines	3,621,305	0.8	71.6
Totals	$445,989,219	100.0%	62.9%

*In thousands.

†To premiums earned.

Source: *Best's Review, August 2004,* p. 47. Copyrighted by A.M. Best Company. Used with permission. **www.ambest.com**

- **Commercial Multiple Peril Insurance** protects commercial firms against perils similar to homeowners multiple peril insurance (7.0 percent of all premiums written in 2003; 0.4 percent in 1960).
- **Automobile Liability and Physical Damage (PD) insurance** provides protection against (1) losses resulting from legal liability due to the ownership or use of the vehicle (auto liability) and (2) theft or damage to vehicles (auto physical damage) (41.3 percent of all premiums written in 2003; 43.0 percent in 1960).
- **Liability Insurance (other than auto)** provides protection to either individuals or commercial firms against nonautomobile-related legal liability. For commercial firms, this includes protection against liabilities relating to their business operations (other than personal injury to employees covered by workers' compensation insurance) and product liability hazards (14.4 percent of all premiums written in 2003; 6.6 percent in 1960).

Balance Sheets and Recent Trends

6

The Balance Sheet and Underwriting Risk. The balance sheet of P&C firms at the beginning of 2004 is shown in Table 15–4. Similar to life insurance companies, P&C insurers invest the majority of their assets in long-term securities, although the proportion held in common stock is lower than that of life insurance companies. Overall the maturity of their assets (and liabilities) tends to be shorter than that for life insurance companies. Bonds ($624.8 billion), preferred stock ($9.2 billion), and common stock ($126.6 billion) represented 66.3 percent of total assets in 2004. Looking at their liabilities, we can see that major component is the loss reserves set aside to meet expected payments that have already occurred but not yet been paid from *underwriting* the P&C lines described above and the loss adjustment expense, which relates to expected administrative and related costs of adjusting (settling) these claims ($445.4 billion). This item represents 37.9 percent of total liabilities and capital. **Unearned premiums** (a set-aside reserve that contains the portion of a premium that has been paid at the start of the coverage period and therefore before insurance coverage has been provided) are also a major liability and are equal to 15.0 percent of total liabilities and capital.

unearned premium

Reserves set aside that contain the portion of a premium that has been paid before insurance coverage has been provided.

To understand how and why the loss reserve—which is the largest liability component—on the balance sheet is established, we need to understand the risks of underwriting P&C insurance. In particular, P&C underwriting risk results when the premiums generated on a given

TABLE 15–4 Property–Casualty Industry Balance Sheet as of 2004*
(in millions of dollars)

			Percent of Total	
Assets				
Invested assets		$ 967,704		82.4%
Bonds	$642,839		54.7%	
Preferred stocks	9,205		0.8	
Common stocks	126,560		10.8	
Real estate investment	1,510		0.1	
Cash and short-term investments	89,251		7.6	
Investments in affiliates	58,445		5.0	
Real estate, office	7,956		0.7	
Other invested asset	31,938		2.7	
Premium balance		106,691		9.1
Accrued interest		8,655		0.7
All other assets		91,278		7.8
Total assets		$1,174,328		100.0%
Liabilities and Capital/Surplus				
Losses and loss adjustment expenses		$ 445,422		37.9%
Unearned premiums		176,311		15.0
Other liabilities		178,854		15.3
Conditional reserve funds		19,892		1.7
Policyholders' surplus		353,849		30.1
Capital and assigned surplus	$146,907		12.5	
Surplus notes	9,589		0.8	
Unassigned surplus	197,353		16.8	
Total liabilities and capital/surplus		$1,174,328		100.0%

*Excludes state funds.

Source: *Best's Aggregates & Averages, Property–Casualty* (Oldwick, NJ: A.M. Best Company, 2004), p. 2. Copyrighted by A.M. Best Company. Used with permission. **www.ambest.com**

insurance line are insufficient to cover (1) the claims (losses) incurred insuring the risk and (2) the administrative expenses of providing that insurance coverage (legal expenses, commissions, taxes, etc.), after taking into account (3) the investment income generated between the time when the premiums are received to the time when losses are covered. Thus, underwriting risk may result from (1) unexpected increases in loss rates (or loss risk), (2) unexpected increases in expenses (or expense risk), and/or (3) unexpected decreases in investment yields or returns (investment yield/return risk). Next, we look more carefully at each of these three areas of P&C underwriting risk.

Loss Risk. The key feature of claims loss risk is the actuarial *predictability* of losses relative to premiums earned. This predictability depends on a number of characteristics or features of the perils insured, specifically:

- **Property versus Liability.** In general, the maximum levels of losses are more predictable for property lines than for liability lines. For example, the monetary value of the loss or damage to an auto is relatively easy to calculate, but the upper limit on the losses to which an insurer might be exposed in a product liability line—for example, asbestos damage to workers' health under other liability insurance—might be difficult if not impossible to estimate.
- **Severity versus Frequency.** In general, loss rates are more predictable on low-severity, high-frequency lines than on high-severity, low-frequency lines. For example, losses in fire, auto, and homeowners peril lines tend to be expected to occur with high frequency and to be independently distributed across any pool of insured customers. Thus, only a limited number of customers are affected by any single event. Furthermore, the dollar loss of each event in the insured pool tends to be relatively small. Applying the law of large numbers, the expected loss potential of such lines—the **frequency of loss** times the extent of the damage (**severity of loss**)—may be estimable within quite small probability bounds. Other lines, such as earthquake, hurricane, and financial guarantee insurance tend to insure very low-probability (frequency) events. Here, many policyholders in the insured pool are affected by any single event (i.e., their risks are correlated) and the severity of the loss could be potentially enormous. This means that estimating expected loss rates (frequency times severity) is extremely difficult in these coverage areas. This higher uncertainty of losses forces P&C firms to invest in more *short-term assets* and hold a larger percentage of capital and reserves than life insurance firms do.

frequency of loss

The probability that a loss will occur.

severity of loss

The size of a loss.

- **Long Tail versus Short Tail.** Some liability lines suffer from a long-tail risk exposure phenomenon that makes estimation of expected losses difficult. This **long-tail loss** arises in policies for which the insured event occurs during a coverage period but a claim is not filed or made until many years later. The delay in the filing of a claim is in accordance with the terms of the insurance contract and often occurs because the detrimental consequences of the event are not known for a period of time after the event actually occurs. Losses incurred but not reported have caused insurers significant problems in lines such as medical malpractice and other liability insurance where product damage suits (e.g., the Dalkon shield case and asbestos cases) have been filed many years after the event occurred and the coverage period expired.[9]

long-tail loss

A loss for which a claim is made some time after a policy was written.

- **Product Inflation versus Social Inflation.** Loss rates on all P&C property policies are adversely affected by unexpected increases in inflation. Such increases were triggered, for example, by the oil price shocks of 1973 and 1978. However, in addition to a systematic unexpected inflation risk in each line, line-specific inflation risks may also exist. The inflation risk of property lines is likely to reflect the approximate underlying inflation risk of the economy.

9. In some product liability cases, such as those involving asbestos, the nature of the risk being covered was not fully understood at the time many of the policies were written. For example, in the 1940s manufacturers began using asbestos as an insulator and fire retardant in products such as insulation and floor tiles. Thirty years later it was learned that exposure to asbestos could cause cancer.

Liability lines, however, may be subject to social inflation, as reflected by juries' willingness to award punitive and other damages at rates far above the underlying rate of inflation. Such social inflation has been particularly prevalent in commercial liability and medical malpractice insurance and has been directly attributed by some analysts to faults in the U.S. civil litigation system. In the early 2000s, through the middle of the first decade, many regulators and doctors argued that unwarranted lawsuits and skyrocketing jury awards were having a crippling effect on the insurance premiums paid by small physician practices throughout the nation. For example, according to the *Cook County (Illinois) Jury Verdict Reporter,* the number of claims reported by ISMIE Mutual (an insurance company that covered physicians in the area) increased 46 percent between 2000 and 2003. In Cook County, the average jury verdict went up 314 percent, from $1.07 million in 1998 to $4.45 million in 2003. The average jury award for noneconomic damages increased 247 percent. Many states took actions to cap these growing awards. For example, the Georgia Senate proposed legislation that would cap medical malpractice jury awards for a victim's pain and suffering at $250,000, which could be increased to $750,000 in multidefendant cases.

loss ratio

A measure of pure losses incurred to premiums earned.

premiums earned

Premiums received and earned on insurance contracts because time has passed with no claim filed.

The **loss ratio** measures the actual losses incurred on a specific policy line. It measures the ratio of losses incurred to **premiums earned** (premiums received and earned on insurance contracts because time has passed without a claim being filed). Thus, a loss ratio of less than 100 means that premiums earned were sufficient to cover losses incurred on that line. Aggregate loss ratios for the period 1951–2004 are shown in Table 15–5 and Figure 15–2. Notice the steady increase in industry loss ratios over the period, increasing from the 60 percent range in the 1950s to the 70 and 80 percent range in the 1980s, 1990s, and beyond 2000. For example, in 2001 the aggregate loss ratio on all P&C lines was 88.4. This includes, however, loss adjustment expenses (LAE)—see below—as well as "pure" losses. The (pure) loss ratio, net of LAE, in 2003 was was 62.9 (see Table 15–3). Rather than bearing all the loss risk themselves, insurance companies can protect themselves from large losses by buying insurance from other

TABLE 15–5 Property–Casualty Industry Underwriting Ratios

Year	Loss Ratio*	Expense Ratio†	Combined Ratio	Dividends to Policyholders‡	Combined Ratio after Dividends
1951	60.3	34.0	94.3	2.6	96.9
1960	63.8	32.2	96.0	2.2	98.1
1965	70.3	30.4	100.7	1.9	102.6
1970	70.8	27.6	98.4	1.7	100.1
1975	79.3	27.3	106.6	1.3	107.9
1980	74.9	26.5	101.4	1.7	103.1
1985	88.7	25.9	114.6	1.6	116.3
1990	82.3	26.0	108.3	1.2	109.6
1995	78.9	26.1	105.0	1.4	106.4
1997	72.8	27.1	99.9	1.7	101.6
2000	81.4	27.8	109.2	1.3	110.5
2001	88.4	26.9	115.3	0.7	116.0
2002	81.1	25.6	106.7	0.5	107.2
2003	72.8	26.8	99.6	0.5	100.1
2004	74.4	24.9	98.1	0.5	97.6

*Losses and adjustment expenses incurred to premiums earned.

†Expenses incurred (before federal income taxes) to premiums written.

‡Dividends to policyholders to premiums earned.

Source: *Best's Aggregates & Averages, Property–Casualty* (Oldwick, NJ: A.M. Best Company, 1994), p. 158; *Best's Review,* various issues; Copyrighted by A.M. Best Company. Used with permission. **www.ambest.com**

FIGURE 15–2 Property–Casualty Industry Underwriting Ratios

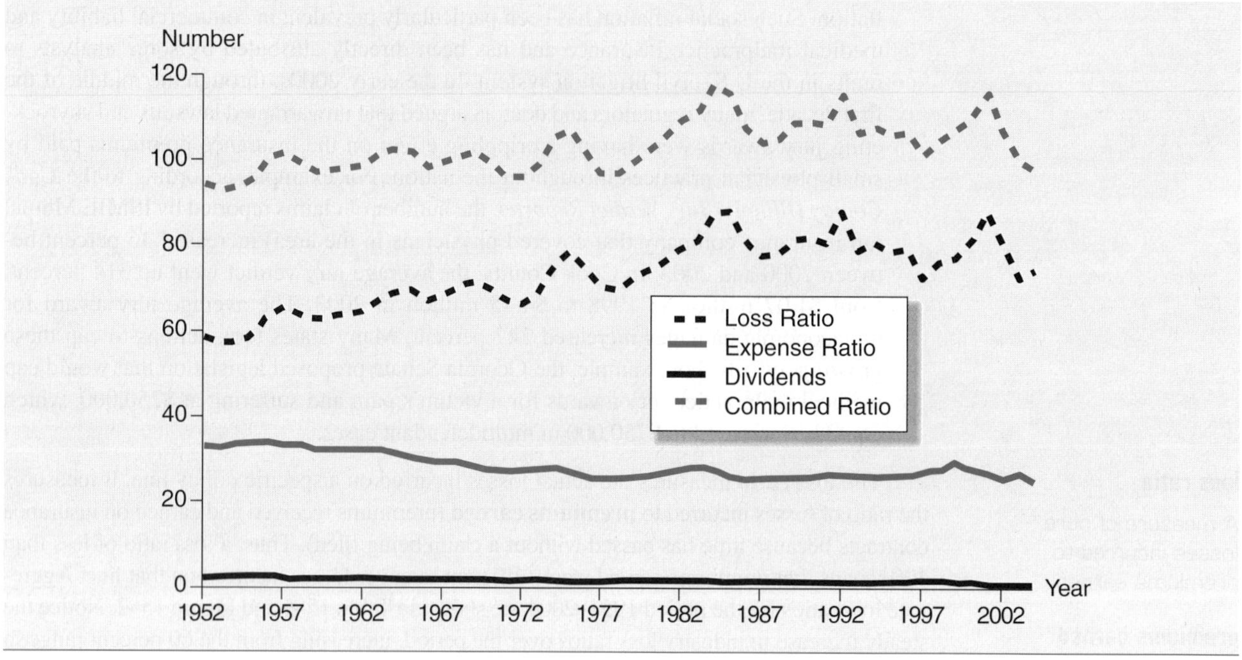

insurance companies, called reinsurance. Like insurance, reinsurance is based on the pooling of risks. A reinsurer diversifies risk of the individual policies by writing many unrelated policies for different insurance companies, so that the potential overall loss from the pool of reinsurance policies is small relative to the reinsurer's capital. Approximately 10 percent of all insurance worldwide is reinsured. Small insurance companies reinsure more frequently than large companies and, because of the larger and less predictable losses, property–casualty companies reinsure more than life insurers.

Expense Risk. The two major sources of expense risk to P&C insurers are (1) loss adjustment expenses (LAE) and (2) commissions and other expenses. LAE relate to the costs surrounding the loss settlement process; for example, many P&C insurers employ adjusters who determine the liability of an insurer and the size of an adjustment or settlement to make. The other major area of expense involves the commission costs paid to insurance brokers and sales agents and other operating expenses related to the acquisition of business. As mentioned above, the loss ratio reported in Table 15–5 and Figure 15–2 includes LAE. The expense ratio reported in Table 15–5 includes the commission and other expenses for P&C insurers during the 1951–2004 period. Notice in this table that, in contrast to the increasing trend in the loss ratio, the expense ratio decreased over the period shown. Despite this trend, expenses continue to account for a significant portion of the overall costs of operations. In 2004, for example, commission and other expenses amounted to 24.9 percent of premiums written. Clearly, sharp rises in commissions and other operating costs can rapidly render an insurance line unprofitable.

combined ratio

A measure of the overall underwriting profitability of a line; equals the loss ratio plus the ratios of loss-adjusted expenses to premiums earned as well as commission and other acquisition costs to premiums written plus any dividends paid to policyholders as a proportion of premiums earned.

A common measure of the overall underwriting profitability of a line, which includes the loss, loss-adjusted expenses, and expense ratios, is the **combined ratio.** Technically, the combined ratio is equal to the loss ratio plus the ratios of LAE to premiums written, and commissions and other expenses to premiums written. The combined ratio after dividends adds dividends paid to policyholders as a portion of premiums earned to the combined ratio. If the combined ratio is less than 100, premiums alone are sufficient to cover both losses and expenses related to the line.

If premiums are insufficient and the combined ratio exceeds 100, the P&C insurer must rely on investment income on premiums for overall profitability. For example, in 2001, the combined ratio before dividend payments was 115.3, indicating that premiums alone were insufficient to cover the costs of both losses and expenses related to writing P&C insurance. Conversely, in 2003 a drop in losses incurred on premiums written resulted in a combined ratio before dividends of 99.6, the first year premiums covered losses since 1979. Table 15–5 presents the combined ratio and its components for the P&C industry for the years 1951–2004. We see that the trend over this period is toward decreased profitability. The industry's premiums generally covered losses and expenses until the 1980s. Since then, premiums have generally been unable to cover losses and expenses (i.e., combined ratios have been consistently higher than 100).

Investment Yield/Return Risk. As discussed above, when the combined ratio is higher than 100, overall profitability can be ensured only by a sufficient investment return on premiums earned. That is, P&C firms invest premiums in assets between the time they receive the premiums and the time they make payments to meet claims. For example, in 2000, net investment income to premiums earned (or the P&C insurers' investment yield) was 13.1 percent. As a result, the overall average profitability (or **operating ratio**) of P&C insurers was 97.4. It was equal to the combined ratio after dividends (110.5, see Table 15–5) minus the investment yield (13.1). Since the operating ratio was less than 100, P&C insurers were profitable overall in 2000. However, in 2001, even though net investment income to premiums earned was 14.0 percent, the overall average profitability of P&C insurers (the operating ratio) was 102 percent, meaning that underwriting P&C insurance was unprofitable. As discussed further below, 2001 was the first full year net loss experienced by the P&C industry in the post-1950 period. Thus, the behavior of interest rates and default rates on P&C insurers' investments is crucial to the P&C insurers' overall profitability. That is, measuring and managing credit and interest rate risk are key concerns of P&C managers, as they are for all FI managers.

operating ratio

A measure of the overall profitability of a P&C insurer; equals the combined ratio minus the investment yield.

EXAMPLE 15-2 Calculation of P&C Company Profitability

Suppose that an insurance company's loss ratio is 79.8 percent, its expense ratio is 27.9 percent, and the company pays 2 percent of its premiums earned to policyholders as dividends. The combined ratio (after dividends) for this insurance company is equal to:

$$\begin{array}{ccccccc} \text{Loss ratio} & + & \text{Expense ratio} & + & \text{Dividend ratio} & = & \text{Combined ratio after dividends} \\ 79.8 & + & 27.9 & + & 2.0 & = & 109.7 \end{array}$$

Thus, expected losses on all P&C lines, expenses, and dividends exceeded premiums earned by 9.7 percent. As a result, without considering investment income, the P&C insurer is not profitable.

Suppose, however, that the company's investment portfolio yielded 12 percent; the operating ratio and overall profitability of the P&C insurer would then be:

$$\begin{aligned} \text{Operating ratio} &= \text{Combined ratio after dividends} - \text{Investment yield} \\ &= 109.7 \text{ percent} \qquad\qquad\qquad - 12.0 \text{ percent} \\ &= 97.7 \text{ percent} \end{aligned}$$

and:

$$\begin{aligned} \text{Overall profitability} &= 100 \text{ percent} - \text{Operating ratio} \\ &= 100 \text{ percent} - 97.7 \text{ percent} \\ &= 2.3 \text{ percent} \end{aligned}$$

As can be seen, the high investment returns (12 percent) make the P&C insurer profitable overall.

Given the importance of investment returns to P&C insurers' profitability, combined with the need for a predictable stream of cash flows to meet required payouts on their insurance policies, the balance sheet in Table 15–4 indicates that bonds—both treasury and corporate—dominate the asset portfolios of P&C insurers. For example, bonds represented 54.7 percent of total assets and 66.4 percent ($642,839m./$967,704m.) of financial assets (unaffiliated investments) in 2004.

Finally, if losses, LAE, and other expenses are higher and investment yields are lower than expected, resulting in operating losses, P&C insurers carry a significant amount of surplus reserves (policyholder surplus) to reduce the risk of insolvency. In 2004, the ratio of policyholder surplus to assets was 30.1 percent.

Recent Trends. While catastrophes should be random, the period 1987–2004 was characterized by a number of catastrophes of historically high severity. This is shown in Figure 15–3. As a result, the period 1987–2004 was not very profitable for the P&C industry. In particular, the combined ratio (the measure of loss plus expense risk) increased from 104.6 in 1987 to 116.0 in 2001, which was the highest ratio since 1985. (Remember that a combined ratio higher than 100 is bad in that it means that losses, expenses, and dividends totaled *more* than premiums earned.) The major reason for this rise was a succession of catastrophes from Hurricane Hugo in 1989, the San Francisco earthquake in 1991, the Oakland fires of 1991, to the losses (of more than $15 billion) incurred in Florida as a result of Hurricane Andrew in 1991. In the terminology of P&C insurers, the industry was in the trough of an **underwriting cycle**—that is, underwriting conditions were difficult. An example of how bad things were in this industry was that Lloyd's of London (arguably one of the world's most well-known and respected insurers) posted a £510 million loss in 1991.[10,11]

underwriting cycle

A pattern that the profits in the P&C industry tend to follow.

In 1993, the industry showed signs of improvement, with the combined ratio after dividends falling to 106.9. In 1994, however, the ratio rose again to 108.4, partly as a result of the Northridge earthquake with estimated losses of $7 billion to $10 billion. A drop in disaster-related losses caused the industry ratio to fall back to 101.6 in 1997. However, major losses associated with El Nino (e.g., Hurricane Georges and Midwest storms) drove the combined ratio after dividends back to 105.6 in 1998. The combined ratio after dividends increased even further to 107.9 in 1999 and 110.5 in 2000. Part of these increases is attributable to an increase in amounts paid on asbestos claims. In 1999, $3.4 billion was paid out on these claims, the largest payout ever. The Insurance Services Office, Inc., estimates that the combined ratio for 1999, 107.9, would have been one percentage point lower without these claims. Also affecting the current profitability of the insurance industry (both life/health and PC) has been the introduction of technology and insurance services offered on the Internet. In 2000, insurers spent more than $12 billion on technological investments, equal to about 4 percent of premiums written and 16 percent of their controllable expenses. The investment in technology was intended to both manage customer relations and reduce operating costs (by some estimates as much as 70 percent).

www.iso.com

The year 2001 saw yet another blow to the insurance industry and the world with terrorist attacks on the World Trade Center and the Pentagon. Estimates of the costs of these attacks to insurance companies were as high as $40 billion. It was estimated that only 10 percent of the September 11 losses were reported in 2001 and yet the losses attributed to the terrorist attacks added an estimated 4 percentage points to the combined ratio after dividends of 116.0. Because of the tremendous impact these attacks had on the health of the U.S. insurance industry, the Bush administration proposed that the U.S. government pay the majority of the losses of the insurance industry due to the attacks. The proposal capped insurers' liabilities at 10 percent of claims over $1 billion (the federal government would pay the other 90 percent) for as many as three years after a terrorist-related event. Despite this bailout of the industry, many insurers did not survive 2001 and those that did were forced to increase premiums significantly.[12]

10. Lloyd's associations do not directly write insurance contracts. Rather, they provide services, including underwriting insurance contracts, for members of the association who write insurance as individuals or corporations.

11. As Lloyd's management explained, the loss was a result of four years of unprecedented disaster claims. As a result of their losses, a group of Lloyd's investors sued the company for negligence in their business operations (some of which in the early 2000s were still working their way through the legal system).

12. See also "The Risk That Nobody Wants," *The Economist,* November 17, 2001, pp. 66–68.

FIGURE 15–3 **U.S. Catastrophes, 1949–2004**

Catastrophe	Year	Amount U.S. $(millions)	Catastrophe	Year	Amount U.S. $(millions)
Terrorist attack on WTC and Pentagon	2001	$40,000	Hurricane Fran	1995	$1,600
			Hurricane Frederic	1979	1,575
Florida hurricanes	2004	21,600	Wind, hail, tornadoes	1974	1,395
Hurricane Andrew	1992	15,900	Minnesota storms	1998	1,300
Northridge earthquake	1994	7,200	Freeze	1983	1,280
Hurricane Hugo	1989	4,939	Oakland fire	1991	1,273
Asbestos claims	1999	3,400	Hurricane Cecelia	1970	1,169
Midwest tornadoes	2003	3,100	Wind	1950	1,136
Hurricane Georges	1998	2,900	California earthquake	1989	1,130
Hurricane Betsy	1965	2,346	Midwest drought	2000	1,100
Hurricane Opal	1995	2,100	Texas hailstorm	1995	1,100
Blizzard of 1996	1996	2,000	Hurricane Isabel	2003	1,000
Hurricane Iniki	1992	1,646	Midwest storms	1998	1,000
Blizzard of 1993	1993	1,625	Hurricane Alicia	1983	983
Hurricane Floyd	1999	1,600	L.A. riots	1992	797

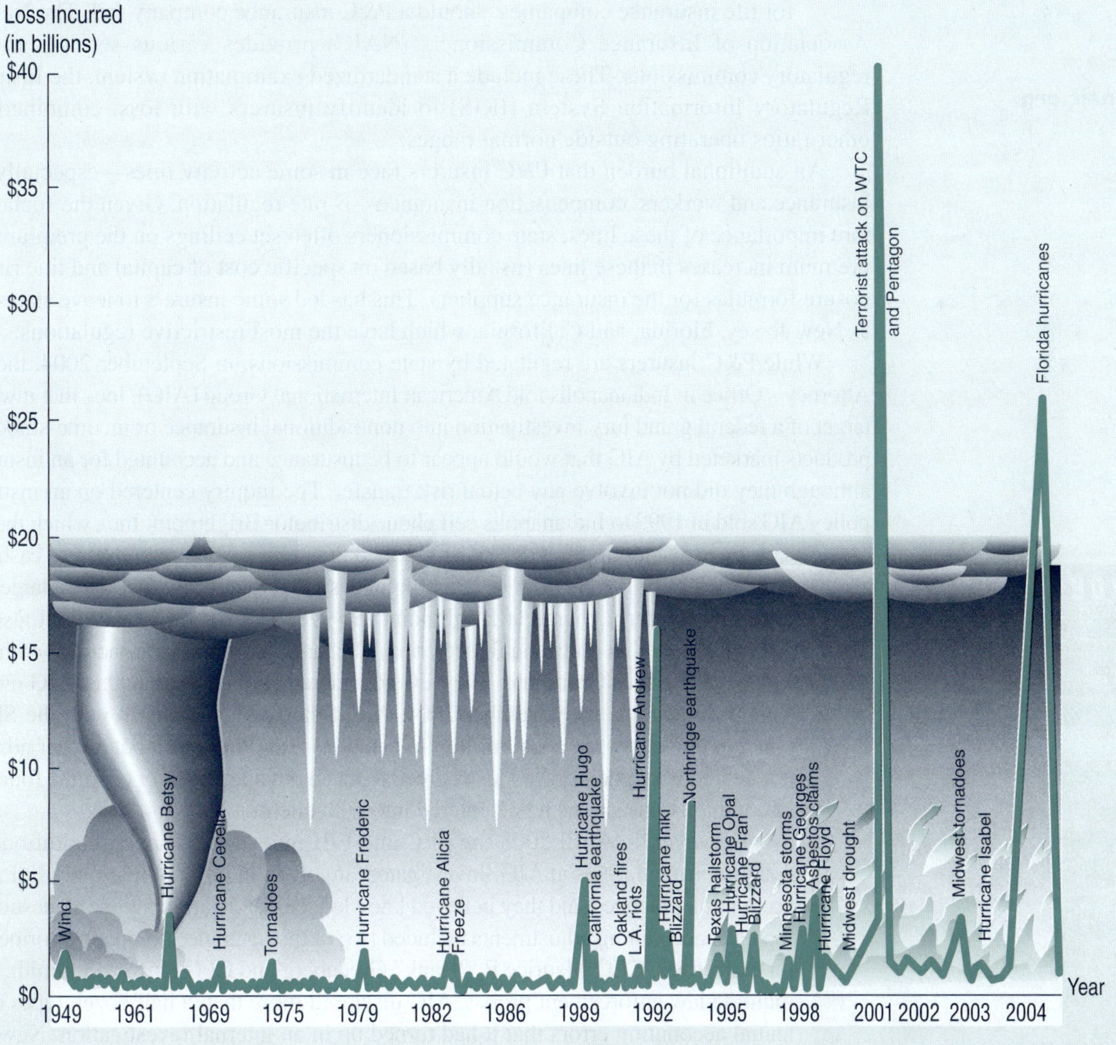

Source: Richard L. Sandor, Centre Financial Products, 1949–1994; author's research, 1995–2004.

After several tumultuous years, 2003 and 2004 saw profitability in the PC industry improve. The combined ratio after dividends was 100.1 in 2003, down sharply from 107.2 in 2002, and much better than most analysts and industry experts expected. The 2003 results were the best since 1979, when the combined ratio was 100.6. Then in 2004 the combined ratio after dividends fell to 97.6, despite losses from Florida hurricanes totaling $21.6 billion. This marked the first year since 1978 that the industry showed a profit from purely insurance-based activities (i.e., ignoring the return on the investment of premiums written on policies as discussed above). Despite the decrease in the combined ratio to 100.1 and 97.6, it is important to note that in the 2000s, a combined ratio of 100 is not what it was 25 years ago. The industry's combined ratio of 100.6 in 1979 resulted in a 15.5 percent ROE for the industry, in large part because of much higher interest rates at that time relative to today. In 2003 and 2004, the industry saw a 9.4 and 9.9 percent ROE, respectively. Insurers would have needed a combined ratio of 94.3 to produce a 15 percent ROE given the prevailing market interest rates and investment returns on premiums written. It might be noted that the average yield on 10-year Treasury securities in 1979 was 9.43 percent, compared to only 4.01 percent in 2003.

Regulation

7

Similar to life insurance companies, P&C insurers are chartered at the state level and regulated by state commissions. In addition, state guarantee funds provide (some) protection to policyholders, in a manner similar to that described earlier for life insurance companies, should a P&C insurance company fail. The National Association of Insurance Commissioners (NAIC) provides various services to state regulatory commissions. These include a standardized examination system, the Insurance Regulatory Information System (IRIS) to identify insurers with loss, combined, and other ratios operating outside normal ranges.

www.naic.org

An additional burden that P&C insurers face in some activity lines—especially auto insurance and workers' compensation insurance—is rate regulation. Given the social welfare importance of these lines, state commissioners often set ceilings on the premiums and premium increases in these lines (usually based on specific cost of capital and line risk exposure formulas for the insurance supplier). This has led some insurers to leave states such as New Jersey, Florida, and California, which have the most restrictive regulations.

While P&C insurers are regulated by state commissions, in September 2004, the U.S. Attorney's Office in Indianapolis told American International Group (AIG), Inc., that it was the target of a federal grand jury investigation into nontraditional insurance or income-smoothing products marketed by AIG that would appear to be insurance and accounted for an insurance, although they did not involve any actual risk transfer. The inquiry centered on an insurance policy AIG sold in 1999 to Indianapolis cell phone distributor Brightpoint Inc., which the SEC accused of accounting fraud. The SEC called that transaction a round trip of cash from Brightpoint to AIG and back to Brightpoint designed to improperly offset a larger than expected quarterly charge at Brightpoint in 1998. The Justice Department also told AIG that one of its units could face criminal charges over past transactions with PNC Financial Services Group Inc. The SEC considered civil charges against AIG over the same transactions. In November 2004, AIG finalized a settlement with the SEC in which it agreed to pay $126 million in penalties and other costs but neither admitted nor denied wrongdoing. AIG also agreed to let an outside reviewer examine four years of complex transactions it had entered into with clients.

However, in April 2005 the SEC and FBI investigated several additional accounting irregularities at AIG. Investigators involved in the multiple probes of AIG's accounting practices said they believed knowledge of and participation in questionable top level accounting adjustments included two of the insurance company's former senior executives, CEO Maurice R. "Hank" Greenberg and CFO Howard I. Smith. Amid multiple law enforcement probes, AIG disclosed more than a half dozen types of potential accounting errors that it had turned up in an internal investigation. New York Attorney General Eliot Spitzer suggested that Mr. Greenberg could face criminal

DO YOU UNDERSTAND?

1. Why P&C insurers hold more capital and reserves than life insurers do?
2. Why life insurers' assets are, on average, longer in maturity than P&C insurers' assets?
3. What the main lines of insurance offered by P&C insurers are?
4. What the components of the combined ratio are?
5. How the operating ratio differs from the combined ratio?
6. Why the combined ratio tends to behave cyclically?

charges over what he called overwhelming evidence of a billion dollar fraud at a company run with an iron fist by a CEO who did not tell the public the truth.

Similarly, as was the case with other sectors of the FI industry, PC insurance companies came under scrutiny for alleged inconsistencies in fees paid to brokers and consultants for arranging certain policies. For example, Marsh & McLennan Cos. (the country's largest insurance broker) said it received $845 million in controversial fees from insurance companies in 2003. The fees, called contingent commissions, came under fire in a lawsuit filed by New York Attorney General Eliot Spitzer in October 2004. The lawsuit alleged that Marsh pursued these fees, which led some employees of the company to steer their clients to insurers paying higher contingent commissions and to rig the bidding process in such a way that clients were overcharged. In January 2005, Robert Stearns, a former Marsh broker, pleaded guilty to criminal charges for his part in the alleged rigging of fees for large insurance contracts. Stearns was the first Marsh employee to plead guilty in connection with the lawsuit. Then in February 2005, Marsh reached an $850 million settlement of civil fraud charges with the New York State's Attorney General's Office and the state insurance department in a pact that included an apology to the firm's clients.

GLOBAL ISSUES

8

Like the other sectors of the financial institutions industry, the insurance sector is becoming increasingly global. Table 15–6 lists the top 10 countries in terms of total premiums written in 2004 (in U.S. dollars) and the percentage share of the world market. Table 15–7 lists the top 10 insurance companies worldwide by total revenues.

TABLE 15–6 The World's Top Countries in Terms of Insurance Premiums Written

Rank	Country	Premiums Written (in billions of U.S. $)	Share of World Market
	Panel A: Life Insurers		
1	United States	$480.9	28.8%
2	Japan	381.3	22.8
3	United Kingdom	154.8	9.3
4	France	105.4	6.3
5	Germany	76.7	4.6
6	Italy	71.7	4.3
7	South Korea	42.0	2.5
8	China	32.4	1.9
9	Netherlands	25.4	1.5
10	Switzerland	24.7	1.5
	Panel B: Property–Casualty Insurers		
1	United States	$574.6	45.3%
2	Japan	97.5	7.7
3	Germany	94.1	7.4
4	United Kingdom	91.9	7.2
5	France	58.2	4.6
6	Italy	40.1	3.2
7	Canada	36.3	2.9
8	Spain	27.0	2.1
9	Netherlands	24.9	2.0
10	Australia	18.0	1.4

Source: Swiss Re, sigma, no. 3/2004.

TABLE 15–7 World's Largest Insurance Companies by Total Revenues

Rank	Company	Revenues (in millions of U.S.$)	Home Country
	Panel A: Life Insurers		
1	ING Group	$88,102	Netherlands
2	AXA Group	62,051	France
3	Nippon Life Insurance	61,175	Japan
4	Assicurazioni Generali	55,105	Italy
5	Aviva	53,723	United Kingdom
6	Dai-Ichi Mutual Life	46,445	Japan
7	Sumitomo Life Insurance	42,220	Japan
8	Prudential	39,410	United Kingdom
9	MetLife	33,967	United States
10	Aegon	26,803	Netherlands
	Panel B: Property–Casualty Insurers		
1	Allianz	$74,178	Germany
2	American International Group	44,637	United States
3	Munich Re Group	41,974	Germany
4	State Farm Insurance	40,656	United States
5	Berkshire Hathaway	39,962	United States
6	Zurich Financial Services	38,400	Switzerland
7	Allstate	26,959	United States
8	Millea Holdings	26,018	Japan
9	Swiss Reinsurance	24,028	Switzerland
10	Royal & Sun Alliance	20,953	United Kingdom

Source: Insurance Information Institute Web site, 2004. **www.iii.org**

In both tables, Panel A lists the data for life insurers and Panel B lists the data for P&C insurers. While North America, Japan, and western Europe dominate the global market, all regions are engaged in the insurance business and many insurers are engaged internationally.

Globalization has certainly affected the U.S. insurance market. In the early 2000s, insurers headquartered outside the United States accounted for over 10 percent of all premiums written in the United States. Because of less stringent regulations, such as lower capital regulations, many insurance companies have set up offices in the Cayman Islands and the Bahamas. Indeed, estimates indicate that 44 percent of the insurance companies selling life insurance in the Caribbean are from outside the region. The pressure of the global economy, the inability of local insurers to serve all domestic customers, and domestic demand for better economic performance have caused governments around the world to introduce and accelerate insurance market reform. This includes improving insurance and insurance supervision by formulating common principles and practices across nations. One consequence of these changes is that there have been a number of mergers of insurance companies across countries, such as the Dutch ING Group's 2000 acquisitioin of the U.S.-based insurer Aetnia for $7.75 billion.

As with commercial banks, Japanese non–life insurance companies suffered severe losses in the early 2000s. In 2003, six of the nine major non–life insurance groups saw their net premiums drop from the preceding year. The main factor in the decline was the sluggish performance of automobile insurance, which accounts for roughly half of the revenue for these firms. The total net premiums of the nine groups declined 0.5 percent on the year to ¥4.9 trillion (U.S. $46.4 billion). Life insurers did not fare much better. In 2004, many Japanese life insurers took steps to boost reserves and repair their capital bases after two very difficulty years. The sector is expected to continue facing problems due to asset deflation, low interest rates, and a shrinking market for life insurance products.

SUMMARY

This chapter examined the activities and regulation of insurance companies. The first part of the chapter described the various classes of life insurance and recent trends in this sector. The second part discussed property–casualty companies. The various lines that comprise property–casualty insurance are becoming increasingly blurred as multiple activity line coverages are offered. Both life and property–casualty insurance companies are regulated at the state rather than the federal level.

SEARCH THE SITE

Go to the Insurance Information Institute's Web site at **www.iii.org** and use the following steps to find the most recent data on the world's largest life insurance companies by total revenue.

Click on the "Facts and Statistics"

Click on "International Facts"

This will bring the file onto your computer that contains the relevant data.

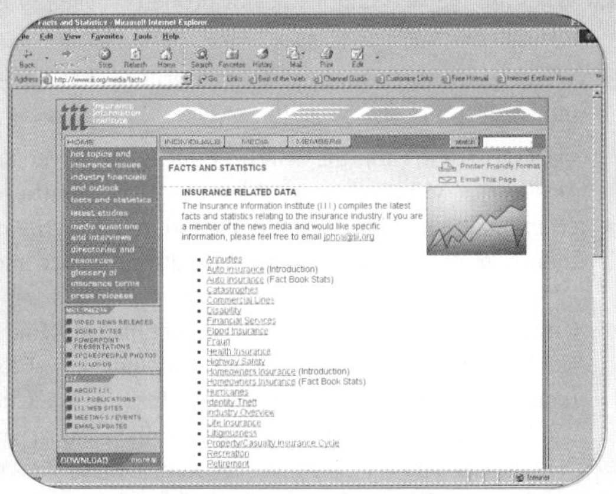

Questions

1. What are total revenues and assets of the top 10 life insurance companies? Property-casualty companies? How have these values changed since 2004 reported in Table 15–7?
2. What countries are the major writers of life and property-casualty insurance worldwide? Has this changed since 2004?

QUESTIONS

1. How does the primary function of an insurance company compare with that of a depository institution?
2. Contrast the balance sheet of depository institutions with those of life insurance firms.
3. How has the composition of the assets of U.S. life insurance companies changed over time?
4. What are the similarities and differences among the four basic lines of life insurance products?
5. Explain how annuities represent the reverse of life insurance activities.
6. How can you use life insurance and annuity products to create a steady stream of cash disbursements and payments so as to avoid either the payment or receipt of a single lump sum cash amount?
7. If an insurance company decides to offer a corporate customer a private pension fund, how would this change the balance sheet of the insurance company?
8. How does the regulation of insurance companies compare with that of depository institutions?
9. **a.** Calculate the annual cash flows (annuity payments) from a fixed-payment annuity if the present value of the 20-year annuity is $1 million and the annuity earns a guaranteed annual return of 10 percent. The payments are to begin at the end of the current year.

   b. Calculate the annual cash flows (annuity payments) from a fixed-payment annuity if the present value of the 20-year annuity is $1 million and the annuity earns a guaranteed annual return of 10 percent. The payments are to begin at the end of five years.
10. You deposit $10,000 annually into a life insurance fund for the next 10 years, at which time you plan to retire. Instead of a lump sum, you wish to receive annuities for the next 20 years. What is the annual payment you expect to receive beginning in year 11 if you assume an interest rate of 8 percent for the whole time period?

11. Suppose a 65-year-old person wanted to purchase an annuity from an insurance company that would pay $20,000 until the end of that person's life. The insurance company expected that this person would live for 15 more years and it would be willing to pay 6 percent on the annuity. How much should the insurance company ask this person to pay for the annuity? A second 65-year-old person wants the same $20,000 annuity, but this person is much healthier and is expected to live for 20 years. If the same 6 percent interest rate applies, how much should this healthier person be charged for the annuity?
12. How do life insurance companies earn profits? How does investment in junk bonds increase their returns and what are the drawbacks?
13. How have the product lines based on net premiums written by insurance companies changed over time?
14. What are the two major lines of property–casualty (P&C) insurance firms?
15. What are the three sources of underwriting risk in the P&C industry?
16. STANDARD &POOR'S Go to the S&P Educational Version of Market Insight Web site at **www.mhhe.com/edumarketinsight** and identify the Industry Description and Industry Constituents for Life & Health Insurance and then Property & Casualty Insurance using the following steps. Click on "Educational Version of Market Insight." Enter your site ID and click on "Login." Click on "Industry." From the Industry list, select "Life & Health Insurance." Click on "Go!" Click on "GICS Sub-Industry Profile" and, separately, "GICS Sub-Industry Constituents." Repeat these steps selecting Property & Casualty from the Industry List.
17. How do increases in unexpected inflation affect P&C insurers?
18. **a.** If the simple loss ratio on a line of property insurance is 73 percent, the loss adjustment expense is 12.5 percent, and the ratio of commissions and other acquisitions expenses is 18 percent, is this line profitable?
    b. How does your answer to part (a) change if investment yields of 8 percent are added?
19. An insurance company's projected loss ratio is 77.5 percent and its loss adjustment expense ratio is 12.9 percent. It estimates that commission payments and dividends to policyholders will add another 16 percent. What is the minimum yield on investments required in order to maintain a positive operating ratio?
20. STANDARD &POOR'S Go to the S&P Educational Version of Market Insight Web site at **www.mhhe.com/edumarketinsight** and find the most recent balance sheet for Allstate Corporation (ALL) and Cigna (CI) using the following steps. Click on "Educational Version of Market Insight." Enter your site ID and click on "Login." Click on "Company." Enter ALL in the "Ticker:" box and click on "Go!" Click on "FS Ann. Balance Sheet." This will download the balance sheet for Allstate, which contains the balances for total equity and total assets. Repeat the process by entering CI in the "Ticker:" box to get information on Cigna. Compare the equity ratio for these companies from these balance sheets with that for the property and casualty insurance industry listed in Table 15–4.
21. Which of the insurance lines listed below will be charged a higher premium by insurance companies and why?
    a. Low-severity, high-frequency lines versus high-severity, low-frequency lines.
    b. Long-tail versus short-tail lines.
22. An insurance company collected $3.6 million in premiums and disbursed $1.96 million in losses. Loss adjustment expenses amounted to 6.6 percent and dividends paid to policyholders totaled 1.2 percent. The total income generated from their investments was $170,000 after all expenses were paid. What is the net profitability in dollars?
23. STANDARD &POOR'S Go to the S&P Educational Version of Market Insight Web site at **www.mhhe.com/edumarketinsight** and look up the Industry Financial Highlights as posted by S&P for the Life & Health Insurance and then Property & Casualty Insurance industry using the following steps. Click on "Educational Version of Market Insight." Enter your site ID and click on "Login." Click on "Industry." From the Industry list, select "Life & Health Insurance." Click on "Go!" Click on any/all of the items listed under "GICS Sub-Industry Financial Highlights." Repeat these steps selecting Property & Casualty from the Industry List.

16

Securities Firms *and* Investment Banks

Chapter NAVIGATOR

1. What are the different types of securities firms and investment banks?
2. What are the major activity areas in which securities firms and investment banks engage?
3. What are the major assets and liabilities held by securities firms?
4. Who are the main regulators of securities firms and investment banks?

OUTLINE

SERVICES OFFERED BY SECURITIES FIRMS VERSUS INVESTMENT BANKS: CHAPTER OVERVIEW

Securities firms and investment banks primarily help net suppliers of funds (e.g., households) transfer funds to net users of funds (e.g., businesses) at a low cost and with a maximum degree of efficiency. Unlike other types of FIs, securities firms and investment banks do not transform the securities issued by the net users of funds into claims that may be "more" attractive to the net suppliers of funds (e.g., banks and their creation of bank deposits). Rather, they serve as brokers intermediating between fund suppliers and users.

Investment banking involves transactions such as the raising of debt and equity securities for corporations or governments. This includes the origination, underwriting, and placement of securities in money and capital markets for corporate or government issuers. Securities services involve assistance in the trading of securities in the secondary markets (brokerage services or market making). Together these services are performed by the securities firms and investment banking industry. The largest companies in this industry perform multiple services (e.g., underwriting and brokerage services). These full-line firms are generally called investment banks. Many other firms concentrate their services in one area only (either securities trading or securities underwriting)—that is, some firms in the industry specialize in the purchase, sale, and brokerage of existing securities (the retail side of the business) and are called securities firms, while other firms specialize in originating, underwriting, and distributing issues of new securities (the commercial side of the business) and are called investment banks.

Investment banking also includes corporate finance activities such as advising on mergers and acquisitions (M&As), as well as advising on the restructuring of existing corporations.

FIGURE 16–1 **Total Values of Mergers and Acquisitions Managed by Investment Banks, 1990–2004**
(in billions of dollars)

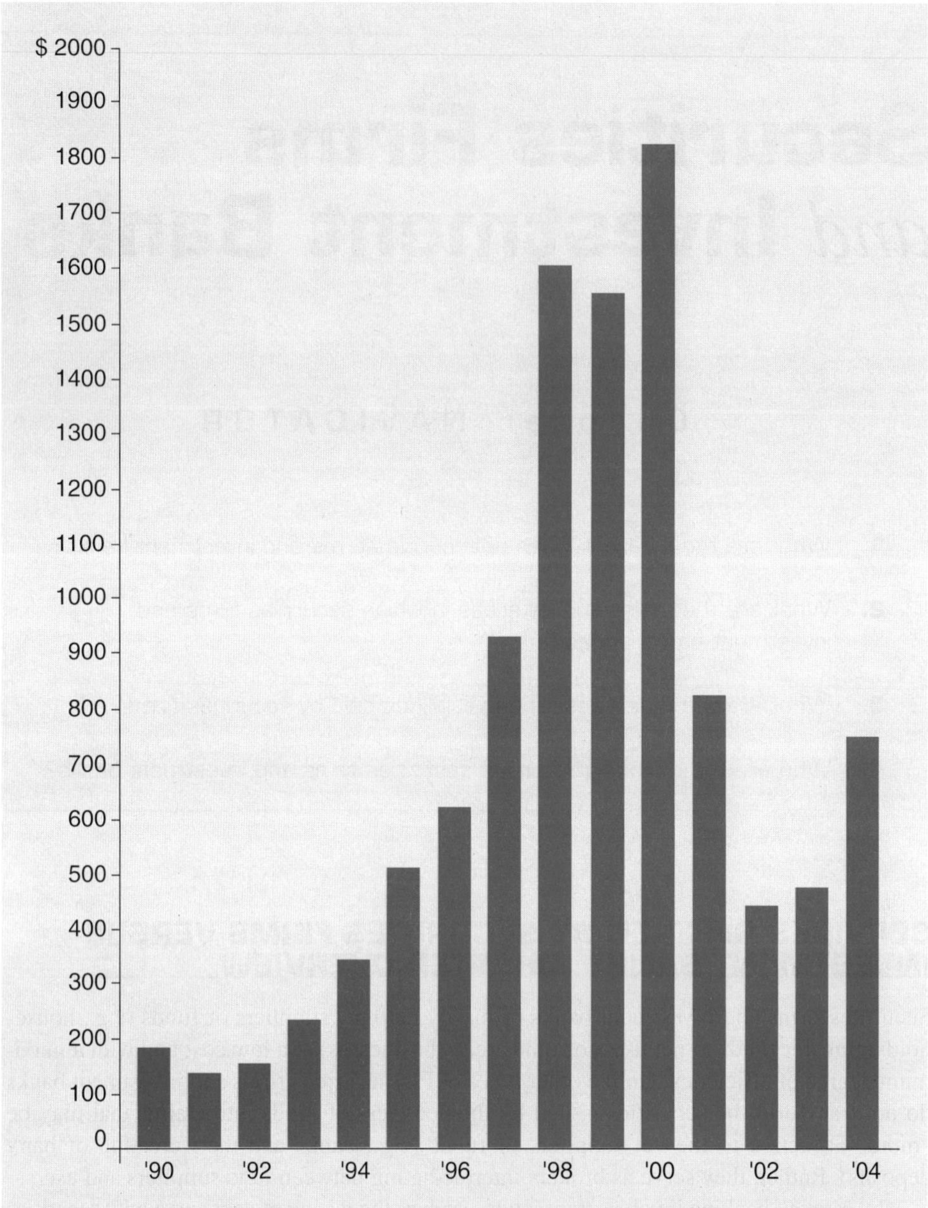

Source: Thomson Financial Web site, 2005. **www.tfibcm.com**

Figure 16–1 reports M&As managed by investment banks for the period 1990–2004. For most of this period there was a boom in this line of business. Total dollar volume (measured by market value of the target firm, i.e., transaction value) of domestic M&As increased from less than $200 billion in 1990 to $1.83 trillion in 2000.[1] The investment bank Goldman Sachs alone managed over $800 billion worth of mergers in 2000, followed by Credit Suisse First Boston with $611 billion and Morgan Stanley with $578 billion. This merger wave was not restricted to the United States. For example, in 2000 there were over

1. This reflected more than 10,800 deals in 2000.

36,700 merger and acquisition deals globally, valued at over $3.49 trillion. Nevertheless, reflecting the downturn in the U.S. economy, M&A transactions fell 53 percent in 2001 to $819 billion on only 7,525 deals (the first time since 1995 there were fewer than 10,000 deals). Similarly, worldwide M&As fell to $1.74 trillion in 2001. Domestic M&A activity bottomed out at $458 billion in 2002 (while worldwide activity fell to $1.20 trillion) before recovering (along with the economy) to $465 billion in the United States (and $1.21 trillion worldwide) in 2003. M&A activity then soared in 2004 to $748 billion in the United States and to more than $1.52 trillion worldwide. Interestingly, M&As involving financial institutions led the way with deals including J.P. Morgan Chase's acquisition of Bank One for $60.0 billion and Bank of America's acquisition of FleetBoston Financial for $49 billion. This chapter presents an overview of (1) the size, structure, and composition of the industry; (2) the key activities of securities firms and investment banks; (3) the industry's balance sheet and recent trends; and (4) its regulation.

SIZE, STRUCTURE, AND COMPOSITION OF THE INDUSTRY

Because of the emphasis on securities trading and underwriting (e.g., security brokerage) rather than longer-term investment in securities, the size of the industry is usually measured by the equity capital of the firms participating in the industry rather than by "asset size." Securities trading and underwriting is a financial service that requires relatively little investment in assets or liability funding (such as the issuance of loans funded through deposits or payments on insurance contracts funded through insurance premiums). Rather, securities trading and underwriting is a profit-(equity-) generating activity that does not require that FIs actually hold or invest in the securities they trade or issue for their customers. Accordingly, asset value is not traditionally the main measure of the size of a firm in this industry. Equity capital in this industry amounted to $168.0 billion in of 2004, supporting total assets of $5.11 trillion.

Beginning in 1980 and until the stock market crash of October 19, 1987, the number of firms in the industry expanded dramatically, from 5,248 in 1980 to 9,515 in 1987. The aftermath of the crash included a major shakeout, with the number of firms declining to 6,285 by 2004, or by 31 percent since 1987. Concentration of business among the largest firms over this period has increased dramatically. The largest investment bank in 1987, Salomon Brothers, held capital of $3.21 billion. By 2004, the largest independent investment bank, Morgan Stanley, held capital of $28.9 billion—nine times as much. Some of the significant growth in size has come through M&As among the top-ranked firms in the industry. Table 16–1 lists major U.S. securities industry M&A transactions, many of which involve repeated ownership changes. Notice from this table that 16 of the largest 20 mergers in the industry occurred in 1997 through 2004. Notice, too, how many recent M&As are interindustry mergers among financial service firms (e.g., insurance companies and investment banks). Recent regulatory changes such as the Financial Services Modernization Act of 1999 (discussed briefly here and in detail in Chapter 13) have been the major cause of such mergers.

The firms in the industry can be categorized into three major types. These types are not necessarily mutually exclusive in the sense that a small firm may engage in more than one type of activity engaged in by larger firms. First are the largest firms, the diversified financial service or national full-line investment banks that service both retail customers (especially by acting as **broker-dealers**—assisting in the trading of existing securities, or secondary market transactions) and corporate customers (by securities **underwriting**—assisting in the issue of new securities, or primary market transactions). The major national full-line firms (ranked by capital) are Merrill Lynch and Morgan Stanley. In 1997, Morgan Stanley, ranked sixth in capital size, and Dean Witter, Discover, ranked fifth in capital size, merged to create the then largest securities firm in the world. These firms generally receive the largest percentage of their revenues from brokerage commissions on securities transactions as well as fees from underwriting activities. National full-line firms generally employ a large number of employees and operate a national branch network.

broker-dealers

Firms that assist in the trading of existing securities.

underwriting

Assisting in the issue of new securities.

TABLE 16–1 Major U.S. Securities Industry Merger and Acquisition Transactions

Rank	Deal	Price (in billions of dollars)	Year
1.	Citicorp merges with Travelers Group (which owns Smith Barney and Salomon)	$83.0	1998
2.	J. P. Morgan acquires Bank One*	60.0	2004
3.	Bank of America acquires Fleet Boston*	49.3	2003
4.	Chase acquires J. P. Morgan*	35.0	2000
5.	UBS acquires Paine Webber Group	12.0	2000
6.	Credit Suisse First Boston acquires Donaldson Lufkin Jenrette	11.5	2000
7.	Dean Witter merges with Morgan Stanley†	10.2	1997
8.	Deutsche Bank acquires Bankers Trust*	10.1	1998
9.	Travelers Group acquires Salomon Inc.	9.0	1997
10.	Goldman Sachs acquires Spear, Leeds & Kellogg	6.5	2000
11.	Sears spins off Dean Witter, Discover	5.0	1993
12.	Lehman Brothers acquires Neuberger Berman	2.9	2003
13.	Bankers Trust acquires Alex Brown	2.1	1997
14.	Mellon Bank acquires Dreyfus	1.8	1993
15.	American Express spins off Lehman Bros. Holdings	1.6	1994
16.	Fleet Financial acquires Quick and Reilly	1.6	1997
17.	Chase acquires Hambrecht & Quist	1.3	1998
18.	Primerica acquires Shearson	1.2	1993
19.	NationsBank acquires Montgomery Securities	1.2	1997
20.	First Union acquires EverenCapital	1.2	1999

*These organizations owned section 20 securities subsidiaries and/or established financial service holding companies (FSHCs) under the Financial Services Modernization Act.

†Value of Dean Witter, Discover shares to be exchanged for Morgan Stanley stock, based on closing price of $40.625 on February 5, 1997.

Source: *The Wall Street Journal,* various issues.

discount broker

A stockbroker that conducts trades for customers but does not offer investment advice.

Second are the national full-line firms that specialize more in corporate finance or primary market activities and are less active in trading securities, or secondary market activities. A good example of this is Goldman Sachs. These firms usually focus on underwriting and distributing common stock and corporate and municipal debt, arranging private placements, acting as advisers in mergers and acquisitions, and providing other corporate services.

Third is the rest of the industry, which includes five subclasses or categories of firms that perform a mix of primary and secondary market services to a particular segment of the financial markets:

1. Specialized investment bank subsidiaries of commercial bank holding companies (such as J. P. Morgan Chase).
2. Specialized **discount brokers** (such as Charles Schwab), which effect trades for customers without offering investment advice or tips.[2]
3. Regional securities firms, which are often classified as large, medium, and small and concentrate on servicing customers in a particular region such as New York or California.

DO YOU UNDERSTAND?

1. How securities firms and investment banks fit into the intermediation process?
2. The trend in the number of securities firms and investment banks since 1980?
3. What categories of firms exist in the securities firm and investment banking industry?
4. What the difference is between brokerage services and underwriting services?

2. Discount brokers usually charge lower commissions than do full-service brokers such as Merrill Lynch.

4. Specialized electronic trading securities firms (such as E*Trade), which provide a platform for customers to trade without the use of a broker. Rather, trades are enacted on a computer via the Internet.
5. Venture capital firms, which pool money from individual investors and other FIs (e.g., insurance companies) to fund relatively small and new businesses (e.g., biotechnology).[3]

2

SECURITIES FIRM AND INVESTMENT BANK ACTIVITY AREAS

Securities firms and investment banks engage in as many as seven key activity areas: investing, investment banking, market making, trading, cash management, mergers and acquisitions, and other service functions.[4] As we describe each of these below, note that while each activity is available to a firm's customers independently, many of the activities can be and are conducted simultaneously (such as mergers and acquisitions, issuing debt and equity, and advisory services) for a firm's customers. Since 1975 when fixed fees or commissions on securities trades were abolished, commissions or fees charged by securities firms and investment banks for their various services have been negotiated between the firm and the customer based on the total bundle of services provided, from executing trades to research and advice, etc.

Investing

Investing involves managing pools of assets such as closed- and open-end mutual funds (in competition with commercial banks, life insurance companies, and pension funds). Securities firms can manage such funds either as agents for other investors or as principals for themselves and their stockholders. The objective in funds management is to select asset portfolios to beat some return-risk performance benchmark such as the S&P 500 index. Since this business generates fees that are based on the size of the pool of assets managed, it tends to produce a more stable flow of income than does either investment banking or trading (discussed next).

Investment Banking

Investment banking refers to activities related to underwriting and distributing new issues of debt and equity securities. New issues can be either first-time issues of a company's debt or equity securities or the new issues of a firm whose debt or equity is already trading—seasoned issues (see Chapter 9 for a detailed discussion). Table 16–2 lists the top five underwriters of debt and equity in 2004 based on the dollar value of issues underwritten. The top five underwriters represented 36.6 percent of the industry total, suggesting that the industry is dominated by a small number of "top tier" underwriting firms. Top tier rating and the implied reputation this brings has a huge effect in this business. At times, investment banks have refused to participate in an issue because their name would not be placed where they desired it on the "tombstone" advertisement announcing an issue (see Chapter 6).

private placement

A securities issue placed with one or a few large institutional investors.

Securities underwriting can be undertaken through either public or private offerings. In a private offering, an investment banker acts as a **private placement** agent for a fee, placing the securities with one or a few large institutional investors such as life insurance companies.[5] In a public offering, the securities may be underwritten on a best efforts or a firm commitment basis, and the securities may be offered to the public at large. With best

3. Venture capital firms generally play an active management role in the firms in which they invest, often including a seat on the board of directors, and hold significant equity stakes. This differentiates them from traditional banking and securities firms.

4. See Ernest Bloch, *Inside Investment Banking,* 2nd ed. (Burr Ridge, IL: McGraw-Hill/Irwin, 1989) for a similar list.

5. Issuers of privately placed securities are not required to register with the SEC since the placements (sales of securities) are made only to large, sophisticated investors.

TABLE 16–2 Top Underwriters of Global Debt and Equity, Ranked by All Issues, 2004
(in billions of dollars)

Rank	Underwriter	Value	Number of Issues	Market Share*
1.	Citigroup/Salomon Smith Barney	$534.5	1,892	9.4%
2.	Morgan Stanley	413.6	1,334	7.3
3.	J.P. Morgan Chase	385.8	1,492	6.8
4.	Merrill Lynch	374.3	1,564	6.6
5.	Lehman Brothers	369.6	1,292	6.5
Top 5		$2,077.8	7,574	36.6%
Industry total		$5,693.0	20,066	100.0%

*Based on value of issues underwritten.
Source: Thompson Financial Web site 2005. **www.tfibcm.com**

efforts underwriting, investment bankers act as *agents* on a fee basis related to their success in placing the issue with investors. In firm commitment underwriting, the investment banker acts as a *principal,* purchasing the securities from the issuer at one price and seeking to place them with public investors at a slightly higher price. Finally, in addition to investment banking operations in the corporate securities markets, the investment banker may participate as an underwriter (primary dealer) in government, municipal, and mortgage-backed securities. See Chapters 6, 7, and 9 for a detailed discussion of these services. Table 16–3 shows the top ranked underwriters for 2003 and 2004 in the different areas of securities underwriting.

Market Making

Market making involves the creation of a secondary market in an asset by a securities firm or investment bank. Thus, in addition to being primary dealers in government securities and underwriters of corporate bonds and equities, investment bankers make a secondary market in these instruments. Market making can involve either agency or principal transactions. *Agency transactions* are two-way transactions on behalf of *customers*—for example, acting as a *stockbroker* or dealer for a fee or commission (as discussed in Chapter 8). On the NYSE, a market maker in a stock such as IBM may, upon the placement of orders by its customers, buy the stock at $78 from one customer and immediately resell it at $79 to another customer.

TABLE 16–3 Who's Number 1 in Each Market

	Full Year 2004		Full Year 2003	
Type	Amount in Billions	Top-Ranked Manager	Amount in Billions	Top-Ranked Manager
Global debt	$5,187.0	Citigroup/SSB	$4,972.7	Citigroup/SSB
Convertible debt	98.4	Morgan Stanley	164.8	J.P. Morgan
Investment-grade debt	688.6	Citigroup/SSB	665.0	Citigroup/SSB
Mortgage debt	729.3	Bear Stearns	915.9	UBS
Asset-backed securities	856.7	Citigroup/SSB	604.5	J.P. Morgan
IPOs	44.9	Morgan Stanley	14.1	Goldman Sachs
Municipal new issues	356.2	UBS	379.4	Citigroup/SSB
Syndicated loans	1,339.0	J.P. Morgan	983.9	J.P. Morgan
Equity	505.1	Morgan Stanley	388.8	Goldman Sachs

Source: Thomson Financial Web site, 2005. **www.tfibcm.com**

SEARCH THE SITE

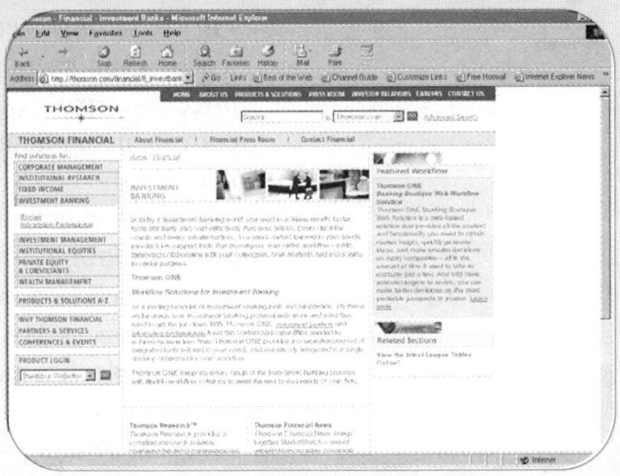

Go to the Thomson Financial-Investment Banking and Capital Markets Group Web site and find the latest information available for top underwriters of various securities.

Go to the Thomson Financial-Investment Banking and Capital Markets Group Web site at **www.tfibcm.com.**

Click on "View the latest League Tables Online!"

Click on "Debt & Equity."

Click on "Global/US Capital Markets Press Release."

This will download a file on to your computer that will contain the most recent information on top underwriters for various securities.

Questions

1. What is the most recent dollar volume of global debt, municipals, and equity underwritten?
2. How have these amounts changed in the last year?
3. Who are the lead underwriters in each market?
4. What percentage of the overall market have the top firms underwritten?

The \$1 difference between the buy and sell price is usually called the bid-offer spread and represents a large proportion of the market maker's profit. In *principal transactions,* the market maker seeks to profit on the price movements of securities and takes either long or short inventory positions for its own account. (Or the market maker may take an inventory position to stabilize the market in the securities.[6]) In the example above, the market maker would buy the IBM stock at \$78 and hold it in its own portfolio in expectation of a price increase. Normally, market making can be a fairly profitable business; however, in periods of market stress or high volatility, these profits can rapidly disappear. For example, on the NYSE, market makers, in return for having monopoly power in market making for individual stocks (e.g., IBM), have an "affirmative obligation" to buy stocks from sellers even when the market is crashing. This caused a number of actual and near bankruptcies for NYSE market makers at the time of the October 1987 market crash. On NASDAQ, which has a system of competing market makers, liquidity was significantly impaired at the time of the crash and a number of firms had to withdraw from market making. Finally, the recent decimalization of equities markets in the United States (i.e., expressing quotes in integers of 1 cent (e.g., \$50.32) rather than rounding to eights (e.g., $\$50^3/_8$)) has cut into traders' profits, as has competition from Internet-based exchanges such as The Island ECN and GlobeNet ECN.

Trading

Trading is closely related to the market-making activities performed by securities firms and investment banks just described; a trader takes an active net position in an underlying instrument or asset. There are at least six types of trading activities:

1. ***Position Trading***—involves purchases of large blocks of securities on the expectation of a favorable price move. Position traders maintain long or short positions for intervals of up to several weeks or even months. Rather than attempting to profit from very short

6. In general, full-service investment banks can become market makers in stocks on the National Association of Securities Dealers Automated Quotation (NASDAQ), but they have been prevented until recently from acting as market-making specialists on the NYSE.

term movements in prices, as day traders do, position traders take relatively longer views of market trends. Such positions also facilitate the smooth functioning of the secondary markets in such securities.

2. ***Pure Arbitrage***—entails buying an asset in one market at one price and selling it immediately in another market at a higher price. Pure arbitrageurs often attempt to profit from price discrepancies that may exist between the spot, or cash, price of a security and its corresponding futures price. Some important theoretical pricing relationships in futures markets should exist with spot markets and prices (see Chapter 10). When these relationships get out of line, pure arbitrageurs enter the market to exploit them.
3. ***Risk Arbitrage***—involves buying securities in anticipation of some information release—such as a merger or takeover announcement or a Federal Reserve interest rate announcement. It is termed *risk arbitrage* because if the event does not actually occur—for example, if a merger does not take place or the Federal Reserve does not change interest rates—the trader stands to lose money.[7]
4. ***Program Trading***—is defined by the NYSE as the simultaneous buying and selling of a portfolio of at least 15 different stocks valued at more than \$1 million, using computer programs to initiate such trades. Program trading is a type of pure arbitrage trading in that it is often associated with seeking to profit from differences between the cash market price (e.g., the Standard & Poor's 500 Stock Market Index) and the *futures* market price of a particular instrument.[8] Because computers are used to continuously monitor stock and futures prices—and can even initiate buy or sell orders—these trades are classified separately as *program trading*.
5. ***Stock Brokerage***—involves the trading of securities on behalf of individuals who want to transact in the money or capital markets. To conduct such transactions, individuals contact their broker (such as Merrill Lynch), who then sends the orders to its representative at the exchange to conduct the trades (see Chapter 9). Large brokerage firms often will own several seats on the floor of a stock exchange (e.g., NYSE), through which their commission brokers (see Chapter 9) trade orders from the firm's clients or for the firms own account.
6. ***Electronic Brokerage***—offered by major brokers, involves direct access, via the Internet, to the trading floor therefore bypassing traditional brokers. Many securities firms and investment banks offer online trading services to their customers as well as direct access to a client representative (stockbroker). Thus, customers may now conduct trading activities from their homes and offices through their accounts at securities firms. Because services provided by a typical brokerage firm are bypassed, the cost per share is generally lower and the price may be advantageous compared with trading directly on the exchanges. Users of the system can often use the network to discover existing size and quotes of offers to buy or sell. Interested parties can then negotiate with each other using the system's computers. In the early 2000s, more than 100 purely electronic securities trading firms also were in existence. These firms, where at least \$5,000 is generally required to open an account, offer investors (often day traders) a desk and a computer with high-speed access to the stock markets.[9] An estimated 5 million people used the facilities offered by electronic trading firms in the early 2000s. Accordingly, technology risk is an increasingly important issue for these FIs (see Chapter 19).

Securities trading can be conducted on behalf of a customer as an agent or on behalf of the firm as a principal. When trading at the retail level occurs on behalf of customers, it

7. A good example of heavy losses from such activities were those sustained by the hedge fund Long-Term Capital Management (LTCM) in 1998 with reported losses close to \$4 billion.

8. An example is investing cash in the S&P index and selling futures contracts on the S&P index. Since stocks and futures contracts trade in different markets, their prices are not always equal. Moreover, program trading can occur between cash markets in other assets—for example, commodities.

9. A day trader takes positions that are held for short time periods in the hope of (stock) price appreciation. Holding periods may vary from a few seconds to many hours.

is often called brokerage (or stock brokering). Further, as noted previously, many securities firms and investment banks offer online trading services to their customers as well as direct access to a client representative (stockbroker). For example, a recent survey by the Securities Industry Association found that in 2001, some 39 percent of all equity investors used the Internet to conduct an equity transaction. This compares to 19 percent just three years earlier in 1998.[10]

Cash Management

cash management account

Money market mutual fund sold by investment banks that offer check-writing privileges.

Securities firms and investment banks offer bank deposit–like **cash management accounts** (CMAs) to individual investors and, since the 1999 Financial Services Modernization Act, deposit accounts themselves (Merrill Lynch being the first to offer a direct deposit account in June 2000 via the two banks it owns). Most of these accounts allow customers the ability to write checks against some type of mutual fund account (e.g., money market mutual fund). These accounts can even be covered directly or indirectly by federal deposit insurance from the FDIC. CMAs were instrumental in this industry's efforts to provide commercial banking services prior to the passage of the 1999 Financial Services Modernization Act.

Mergers and Acquisitions

As noted earlier, investment banks frequently provide advice on, and assistance in, mergers and acquisitions. For example, they assist in finding merger partners, underwrite any new securities to be issued by the merged firms, assess the value of target firms, recommend terms of the merger agreement, and even assist target firms in preventing a merger (for example, writing restrictive provisions into a potential target firm's securities contracts). As mentioned in the chapter overview, mergers and acquisitions activity topped $1.83 trillion in 2000, and then plummeted by 53 percent to $819 in 2001 before recovering to $833.6 billion in 2004. Table 16–4 lists the top 10 investment bank merger advisers ranked by dollar volume of the mergers in which they were involved. Table 16–5 lists the top 10 investment banks ranked by dollar volume of worldwide M&A activity. Notice that many of the top U.S. ranked investment banks reported in Table 16–4 are also top ranked for worldwide activity in Table 16–5.

DO YOU UNDERSTAND?

1. What the key areas of activities for securities firms are?
2. What the difference is between a best efforts and a firm commitment offering?
3. What the six trading activities performed by securities firms are?

Other Service Functions

Other service functions include custody and escrow services, clearance and settlement services, and research and advisory services—for example, giving advice on divestitures, spin-offs, and asset sales. In addition, investment banks are making increasing inroads into traditional bank service areas such as small-business lending and the trading of loans (see Chapters 7 and 24). In performing these functions, investment banks normally act as agents for a fee. As mentioned previously, fees charged are often based on the total bundle of services performed for the client by the firm. The portion of the fee or commission allocated to research and advisory services is called soft dollars. When one area in the firm such as an investment adviser uses client commissions to buy research from another area in the firm, it receives a benefit because it is relieved from the need to produce and pay for the research itself. Thus, advisers using soft dollars face a conflict of interest between their need to obtain research and their clients' interest in paying the lowest commission rate available. Because of the conflict of interest that exists, the SEC (the primary regulator of investment banks and securities firms, see following) requires these firms to disclose soft dollar arrangements to their clients.

Nevertheless, in 2001 tremendous publicity was generated concerning conflicts of interest in a number of securities firms between analysts' research recommendations on stocks to buy or not buy and whether the firm played a role in underwriting the securities of the firm the analysts were recommending. For example, after an investigation by the New York State

10. See Investment Company Institute and Securities Investor Association, "Equity Ownership in America, 2002."

TABLE 16-4 Ten Largest U.S. Mergers and Acquisition Firms Ranked by Value of Mergers, 2004

Rank	Investment Bank	Value (billions of dollars)	Number of Deals
1.	Goldman Sachs	$269.5	145
2.	Lehman Brothers	189.9	117
3.	J.P. Morgan Chase	173.3	124
4.	Merrill Lynch	161.3	85
5.	Citigroup/Salomon Smith Barney	156.7	147
6.	Morgan Stanley	137.9	124
7.	Bank of America Securities	117.8	72
8.	Lazard	109.5	57
9.	UBS Warburg	95.6	88
10.	Credit Suisse First Boston	93.7	112
Industry total		$748.4	6,689

Source: Thomson Financial Web site, 2005. **www.tfibcm.com**

Attorney General, Merrill Lynch agreed to pay a fine of $100 million and to follow procedures more clearly separating analysts' recommendations (and their compensation) from the underwriting activities of the firm. As we discuss below, a number of other major Wall Street firms were subsequently placed under investigation. The investigation was triggered by the dramatic collapse of many new technology stocks while analysts were still making recommendations to buy or hold them.

RECENT TRENDS AND BALANCE SHEETS

Recent Trends

In this section, we look at the balance sheet and trends in the securities firm and investment banking industry since the 1987 stock market crash. Trends in this industry depend heavily

TABLE 16-5 Ten Largest Worldwide Mergers and Acquisition Firms Ranked by Total Credit Lent, 2004

Rank	Investment Bank	Credit Lent (billions of dollars)	Number of Deals
1.	Goldman Sachs	$500.2	290
2.	Morgan Stanley	355.2	277
3.	J.P. Morgan Chase	321.9	324
4.	Merrill Lynch	317.0	200
5.	Citigroup/Salomon Smith Barney	282.8	308
6.	Lehman Brothers	239.2	167
7.	UBS	204.0	247
8.	Lazard	187.9	184
9.	Credit Suisse First Boston	166.8	242
10.	Rothschild	145.4	226
Industry total		$1,516.1	20,723

Source: Thomson Financial Web site, 2005. **www.tfibcm.com**

FIGURE 16–2 **Commission Income as a Percentage of Total Revenues**

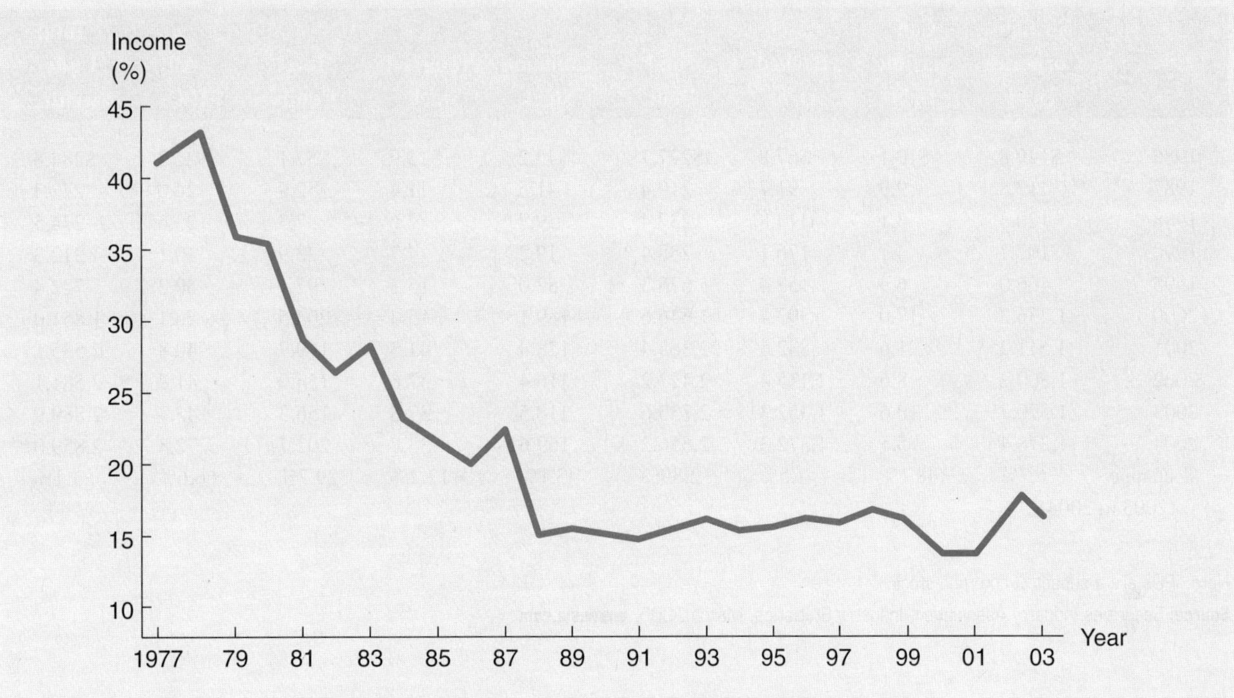

Source: Securities and Exchange Commission and Standard & Poor's *Industry Surveys,* various issues.

on the state of the stock market. For example, a major effect of the 1987 stock market crash was a sharp decline in stock market trading volume and, thus, in the brokerage commissions earned by securities firms over the 1987–1991 period (see Figure 16–2).[11] Commission income began to recover only in 1992 with record stock market trading volumes being achieved in 1995 through 2000 (when the Dow Jones and S&P indexes hit new highs—see Chapter 9.) As stock market values plummeted in 2001 and 2002, so did commission income. However, improvements in the U.S. economy in 2003 and 2004 resulted in an increase in stock market values and trading and thus commission income. However, the increase in the popularity (around 2005) of electronic communication networks (ECNs) should result in further decreases in commission income. As discussed in Chapter 9, ECNs are computerized systems that automatically match orders between buyers and sellers and serve as an alternative to traditional market making and floor trading services provided by brokers. Since ECNs do not involve brokers, commission income will decrease with the increased use of ECNs.

Also affecting the profitability of the investment banking industry was the decline in bond and equity underwriting during the 1987–1990 period. This was partly a result of the stock market crash, partly a result of a decline in M&As, and partly a reflection of investor concerns about junk bonds[12] following the Michael Milken/Ivan Boesky–Drexel Burnham

11. The decline in brokerage commissions actually began as early as 1977 following the abolition of fixed commissions on securities trades by the Securities and Exchange Commission (SEC) in May 1975 and the fierce competition for wholesale commissions and trades that followed. Although a sharply increased volume of equities trading in 1992 returned commissions to 1987 levels, this may be a temporary phenomenon.

12. A junk bond is a bond that rating agencies such as Standard & Poor's (S&P) and Moody's classify as being excessively risky, having below investment grade quality.

TABLE 16-6 U.S. Corporate Underwriting Activity
(in billions of dollars)

	Straight Corporate Debt	Convertible Debt	Asset-Backed Debt	Total Debt	Common Stock	Preferred Stock	Total Equity	All IPOs	Total Underwriting
1986	$149.8	$10.1	$67.8	$227.7	$43.2	$13.9	$57.1	$22.3	$284.8
1987	117.8	9.9	91.7	219.4	41.5	11.4	52.9	24.0	272.3
1988	120.3	3.1	113.8	237.4	29.7	7.6	37.3	23.6	274.5
1990	107.7	4.7	176.1	288.4	19.2	4.7	23.9	10.1	312.3
1995	466.0	6.9	152.4	625.3	82.0	15.1	97.1	30.2	722.4
2000	1,236.2	17.0	393.4	1,646.6	189.1	15.4	204.5	76.1	1,851.0
2001	1,511.2	21.6	832.5	2,365.4	128.4	41.3	169.7	40.8	2,535.1
2002	1,300.2	8.6	1,115.4	2,427.2	116.4	37.6	154.0	41.2	2,581.1
2003	1,370.7	10.6	1,352.3	2,733.6	118.5	37.8	156.3	43.7	2,889.9
2004	1,278.4	5.5	1,372.3	2,656.2	169.6	33.2	202.7	72.8	2,859.0
% change (2003 to 2004)	−6.7%	−48.1%	1.5%	−2.89%	43.1%	−12.2%	29.7%	66.6%	−1.1%

Note: IPOs are a subset of common stock.

Source: Securities Industry Association, Industry Statistics, March 2005. **www.sia.com**

Lambert scandal, which resulted in that firm's failure in 1989.[13] Between 1991 and 2001, however, the securities industry showed a resurgence in underwriting activity and profitability.[14] For example, domestic underwriting activity over the 1990–2001 period grew from $312 billion in 1990 to $2,535.1 billion in 2001 (see Table 16–6). Two principal reasons for this have been the attractiveness of corporate debt issues to corporate treasurers due to relatively low long-term interest rates and the growth in the asset-backed securities market as a result of increased securitization of mortgages (as well as the growth of mortgage debt).

As a result of enhanced trading profits, and growth in new issues underwriting, pretax profits for the industry has topped $10 billion in recent years: $12.2 billion in 1997; $16.3 billion in 1999; and 21.0 billion in 2000 (see Figure 16–3).[15] This is despite the collapse of Russian ruble and bond markets in 1998, economic turmoil in Asia in 1997, and economic uncertainty in the United States in the early 2000s. Indeed, despite a downturn in the U.S. economy toward the end of 2000, pretax profits in the securities industry soared to an all-time high of $21.0 billion in 2000.

The continued slowdown of the U.S. economy in 2001, an accompanying drop in stock market values, and terrorist attacks on the World Trade Center in September 2001, however, brought an end to these record profits. Industry pretax profits for 2001 fell 51 percent to $10.4 billion. The Bank of New York alone estimated its costs associated with the terrorist

13. Drexel was once the most influential firm on Wall Street because of its pioneering work under Michael Milken in the junk bond market. Drexel went bankrupt, however, after its corporate officials pleaded guilty to six felony counts of federal securities fraud. Drexel and Milken were found to have "plundered" the savings institutions industry by manipulating the market for junk bonds. The essence of the legal action involved the fact that Milken, working for Drexel, used savings institutions to create a web of buyers that helped give the appearance of a market for junk bonds. The fraudulent market allowed Drexel to sell junk bonds at prices above their fair market values; savings institutions held almost 20 percent of junk bonds outstanding, and when the junk bond market collapsed, many savings institutions, especially those in California, suffered large losses.

14. Revenue for the securities industry rose from $69 million in 1990 to $228 billion in 1999, $331 billion in 2000, and $273 billion in 2001.

15. This information is from the Securities Industry Association. The dip in pretax profits in 1994 coincides with the increase in interest rates and the resulting drop in new securities issues during this year.

FIGURE 16–3 **Securities Industry Pretax Profits, 1990–2004**
(in billions of dollars)

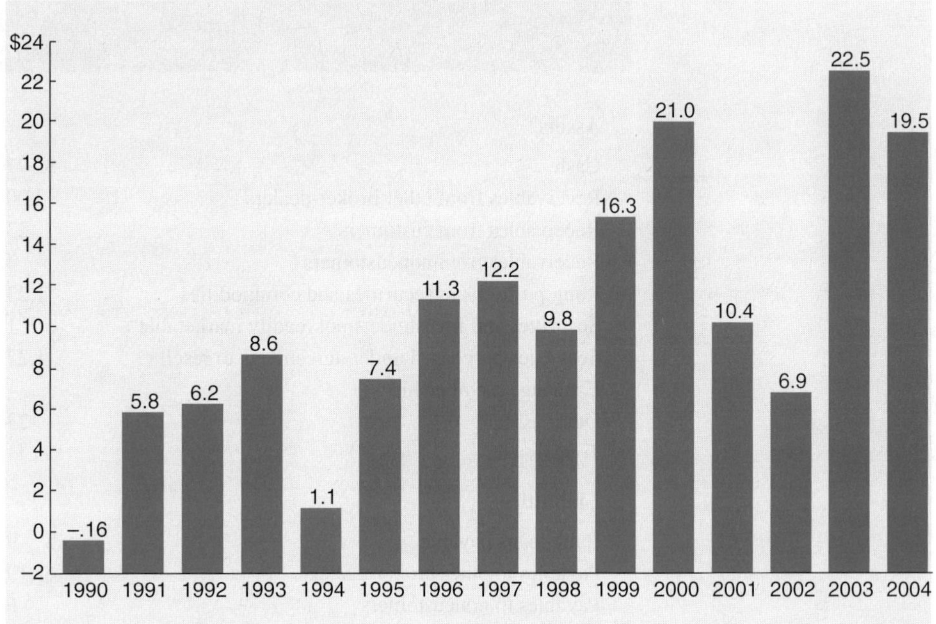

Source: Securities Industry Association, various years. **www.sia.com**

attacks at $125 million. Citigroup estimated it lost $100 million to $200 million in business from branches that were closed and because of the four days the stock market did not trade. Morgan Stanley, the largest commercial tenant in the World Trade Center, said the cost of property damage and relocation of its employees was $150 million.

The slow rate of recovery of the U.S. economy (along with the decline in stock market trading and the fall in M&As and related activities) hampered the ability of the industry to generate profit growth in 2002. As a result, 2002 pretax profits for securities firms were the lowest since 1995, $6.9 billion. Further, employment declined by 793,700 jobs in May 2003 (a decline of 5.6 percent from the high in March 2001). Moreover, as discussed earlier and below, the securities industry was rocked by several allegations of securities law violations as well as a loss of investor confidence in Wall Street and corporate America as a result of a number of corporate governance failures and accounting scandals including Enron, Merck, WorldCom, and other major U.S. corporations.

However, with the recovery of the U.S. economy in late 2002, 2003, and 2004, the U.S. securities industry again earned record profits as revenue growth strengthened and became more broadly based. Domestic underwriting surged to $2,859.0 billion in 2004, from $2,535.1 billion in 2001 (see Table 16–6). Further, the industry maintained its profitability mainly through deep cuts in expenses. Total expenses fell 10.4 percent from 2002 levels, largely due to lower interest expenses. Interest expense fell from $48.4 billion in 2002 to $37.5 billion in 2003 and $44.2 billion in 2004. Operating expenses, excluding interest expense, fell 4.1 percent in 2003 and 14.3 percent in 2004, reflecting the success of cost controls and continued high rates of productivity growth in the securities industry. The results for 2003 were record pretax profits of $22.5 billion and for 2004 profits of $19.5 billion (see Figure 16–3).

Balance Sheet

3

The consolidated balance sheet for the industry is shown in Table 16–7. Looking at the asset portfolio, long positions in securities and commodities accounted for 24.11 percent of assets; reverse repurchase agreements—securities purchased under agreements to resell (i.e., the broker gives a short-term loan to the repurchase

TABLE 16–7 Assets and Liabilities of Broker-Dealers as of 2004
(in millions of dollars)

		Percent of Total Assets
Assets		
Cash	$ 70,261.9	1.38%
Receivables from other broker-dealers	2,006,759.2	39.26
Receivables from customers	232,072.4	4.54
Receivables from noncustomers	45,579.2	0.89
Long positions in securities and commodities	1,232,369.6	24.11
Securities and investments not readily marketable	14,719.3	0.29
Securities purchased under agreements to resell	1,273,470.7	24.92
Exchange membership	1,076.1	0.02
Other assets	234,765.6	4.59
Total assets	$5,111,074.2	100.00
Liabilities		
Bank loans payable	$ 93,651.6	1.83
Payables to other broker-dealers	1,193,745.7	23.36
Payables to noncustomers	67,720.8	1.32
Payables to customers	546,099.3	10.68
Short positions in securities and commodities	611,860.2	11.97
Securities sold under repurchase agreements	1,915,891.4	37.49
Other nonsubordinated liabilities	421,243.7	8.24
Subordinated liabilities	92,827.3	1.82
Total liabilities	$4,943,039.9	96.71
Capital		
Equity capital	$ 168,034.3	3.29
Number of firms	6,285	

Source: *Focus Report,* Office of Economic Analysis, U.S. Securities and Exchange Commission, 2004, Washington, D.C. **www.sec.gov**

DO YOU UNDERSTAND?

1. What the trend in profitability in the securities industry has been over the last 15 years?
2. What the major assets held by broker-dealers are?
3. Why broker-dealers tend to hold less equity capital than do commercial banks and thrifts?

agreement seller, see Chapter 5)—accounted for 24.92 percent of assets. Because of the extent to which this industry's balance sheet consists of financial market securities, the industry is subjected to particularly high levels of market risk and interest rate risk. Further, to the extent that many of these securities are foreign-issued securities, FI managers must be concerned with foreign exchange risk and sovereign risk as well (see Chapter 19).

With respect to liabilities, repurchase agreements—securities sold under agreement to repurchase—were the major source of funds (these are securities temporarily lent in exchange for cash received). Repurchase agreements amounted to 37.49 percent of total liabilities and equity. The other major sources of funds were securities and commodities sold short for future delivery and broker-call loans from banks. Equity capital amounted to only 3.29 percent of total assets. These levels are generally below the levels held by commercial banks (9.96 percent in 2004). One reason for their lower equity capital levels is that securities firm and investment bank balance sheets contain mostly tradable (liquid) securities compared to the relatively illiquid loans that represent a significant portion of banks' asset portfolios. Firms in this industry are required by the SEC to maintain a minimum net worth (capital) to assets ratio of 2 percent.

4 REGULATION

The primary regulator of the securities industry is the Securities and Exchange Commission (SEC), established in 1934. The National Securities Markets Improvement Act (NSMIA) of 1996 reiterated the primacy of the SEC in this capacity. Prior to NSMIA, most securities firms were subject to regulation from both the SEC and the state in which they operated. NSMIA provides that states may still require securities firms to pay fees and file documents submitted to the SEC, but most of the regulatory burden imposed by states has been removed. States are also now prohibited from requiring registration of securities firms' transactions. Thus, NSMIA effectively gives the SEC primary regulatory jurisdiction over securities firms. However, the early 2000s saw a reversal of this trend toward the dominance of the SEC with states—especially their attorneys general—increasingly intervening through securities-related investigations. As noted earlier, several highly publicized securities violations resulted in criminal cases brought against securities law violators by state prosecutors. In particular, the New York State attorney general forced Merrill Lynch to pay a $100 million penalty because of allegations that Merrill Lynch analysts gave investors overly optimistic reports about the stock of its investment banking clients.

www.sec.gov

Subsequent to these investigations the SEC instituted rules requiring Wall Street analysts to vouch that their stock picks are not influenced by investments banking colleagues and that analysts disclose details of their compensation that would flag investors to any possible conflicts. If evidence surfaces that analysts falsely attested to the independence of their work, it could be used to bring enforcement actions. Violators will face a wide array of sanctions, including fines and other penalties, such as a temporary suspension or even a permanent bar from the securities industry.

This conflict of interest issue culminated in the spring of 2003 with an agreement between state and federal regulators and 10 of the nation's largest securities firms with the latter agreeing to pay a record $1.4 billion in penalties to settle charges involving investor abuses. The long awaited settlement centered on charges that securities firms routinely issued overly optimistic stock research to investors in order to gain favor with corporate clients and win their investment banking business. The agreement also settled charges that at least two big firms, Citigroup and Credit Suisse First Boston, improperly allocated IPO shares to corporate executives to win banking business from their firms. The investigations of the SEC and other regulators, including the NASD, the NYSE, and state regulators, unveiled multiple examples of how Wall Street stock analysts tailored their research reports and ratings to win investment banking business. The Wall Street firms agreed to the settlement without admitting or denying any wrongdoing. The agreement also forced brokerage companies to make structural changes in the way they handle research—preventing, for example, analysts from attending certain investment banking meetings. The agreement also requires that securities firms have separate reporting and supervisory structures for their research and banking operations and that analysts' pay be tied to the quality and accuracy of their research rather than the amount of investment banking business they generate. Table 16–8 lists the 10 firms involved in the settlement and the penalties assessed. Within days of this agreement, however, Bears Stearns, one of the 10 firms involved in the settlement, was accused of using its analysts to promote a new stock offering (see the Ethical Debates box).

DO YOU UNDERSTAND?

1. Why Bear Stearns' sales staff e-mail of May 2, 2003, was in violation of the settlement agreed to by the securities firm industry?

Along with these changes instituted by the SEC, the U.S. Congress passed the Sarbanes-Oxley Act, a corporate governance and accounting oversight bill, in July 2002. This bill created an independent auditing oversight board under the SEC, increased penalties for corporate wrongdoers, forced faster and more extensive financial disclosure, and created avenues of recourse for aggrieved shareholders. The goal of the legislation was to prevent deceptive accounting and management practices and bring stability to jittery stock markets battered in the summer of 2002 by corporate governance scandals of Enron, Global Crossings, Tyco, WorldCom, and others. Indeed, after WorldCom's failure, its investors filed a class action lawsuit against Wall Street securities firms that helped finance WorldCom before it was forced to

Bear Stearns Used Analyst to Tout IPO Despite Pact with Regulators

Days after agreeing to a sweeping settlement aimed at overhauling the way Wall Street does business, Bear Stearns Cos. reverted to the practice of using an analyst to promote a new stock offering. When questions about the episode were raised by The Wall Street Journal, Bear Stearns took the embarrassing step of delaying the initial public offering of stock in credit card processing firm iPayment Inc., and the securities firm said it would bar the analyst from covering iPayment. Bear Stearns also called the Securities and Exchange Commission and the New York Attorney General's office to tell them about the incident and apologize . . .

Letting stock research analysts participate in company- or investment-banking-sponsored road shows is expressly forbidden under the regulatory pact the 10 securities firms announced with regulators April 28. Documents released in the settlement revealed how firms had routinely used analysts as de facto marketers, having them cite bullish views on IPO candidates during "pitches" to win lucrative underwriting business, and later having them deliver glowing forecasts in roadshow presentations to investors before the offering.

Virtually before the ink was dry on the settlement, Bear Stearns sales people on May 2 e-mailed institutional investors a link to a prerecorded "net roadshow" for iPayment, one of the few stock issues planned by Wall Street in two months amid the worst IPO famine in the U.S. in recent years. In the video clip, Mr. Kissane, a top Bear Sterns computer-services-industry analyst, called it his "pleasure" to introduce three top executives of iPayment and dubbed the Nashville, Tenn., company a smart investment. "I think iPayment represents a great way for investors to play a proven winning strategy in the merchant processing space focused on small business, which I just think is a tremendous growth opportunity," he said.

Source: *The Wall Street Journal,* May 12, 2003, p. A1, by Ann Davis.

declare the largest bankruptcy in U.S. history. The securities firms collected about $84 million in fees for underwriting the $17 billion of WorldCom bonds they had sold in 2000 and 2001. In March 2005, J.P. Morgan Chase agreed to pay $2 billion to settle the investor lawsuit. Altogether, 14 investment banks agreed to pay about $6 billion (the largest payment, $2.85 billion, coming from Citigroup) to settle the case, a record for a securities fraud class action suit. The WorldCom civil suit represented the latest class action lawsuit filed by investors against Wall Street firms that courted and helped finance high-flying companies that later failed (others included Enron and Italian dairy giant Parmalat, where an accounting fraud left the company with about $19 billion in debt it could not pay off).

In addition to investigating and prosecuting securities law violations, the SEC also sets rules governing securities firms' underwriting and trading activities. For example, with respect to underwriting, SEC Rule 144A defines the boundaries between the public offering of securities and the private placement of securities (see Chapter 9). SEC Rule 415 on

TABLE 16–8 Securities Firm Penalties Assessed for Trading Abuses

Firm	Penalty (in millions)
Citigroup	$400
Credit Suisse First Boston	200
Merrill Lynch	200
Morgan Stanley	125
Goldman Sachs	110
Bear Stearns	80
J.P. Morgan Chase	80
Lehman Brothers	80
UBS Warburg	80
Piper Jaffray	32.5

Source: Authors' research.

shelf registration

Allows firms that plan to offer multiple issues of stock over a two-year period to submit one registration statement summarizing the firm's financing plans for the period.

shelf registrations allows large corporations to register their new issues with the SEC up to two years in advance.[16] With respect to trading activities, in 1996, the SEC charged the NASD with ignoring illegal behavior on the NASDAQ stock market and demanded that the self-regulatory organization change its oversight function. The SEC and U.S. Justice Department found anticompetitive practices by Wall Street firms that raise prices for buying customers while lowering prices when selling. Specifically, from taped telephone conversations between traders and from other sources, the SEC found that market makers rarely used odd one-eighth quotes (e.g., 12⅜), suggesting that dealers secretly worked together to keep spreads wider than they would be in a more competitive market, for example, quoting 12½ to buy rather than 12⅜, thus making an extra one-eighth of a $1 profit. The SEC report also showed that NASD officials knew about these practices on the market as far back as 1990, yet failed to do anything. In lieu of a financial penalty, the NASD promised to spend $100 million over the next five years to improve the enforcement of trading rules. Further, 30 brokerage firms, including Merrill Lynch, Goldman Sachs, and Morgan Stanley, Dean Witter, Discover & Company, in December 1997 acknowledged wrongdoing and agreed to pay about $900 million to end a civil suit contending they schemed with one another for years to fix prices on the NASDAQ stock market.

While the SEC sets the overall regulatory standards for the industry, two self-regulatory organizations are involved in the day-to-day regulation of trading practices. These are the New York Stock Exchange (NYSE) and the National Association of Securities Dealers (NASD)—the latter responsible for trading in the over-the-counter markets such as NASDAQ. The NYSE and NASD monitor trading abuses (such as insider trading), trading rule violations, and securities firms' capital (solvency positions)—such as the 2 percent net worth to assets minimum capital ratio. For example, in July 2003, the NYSE fined a veteran floor trader at Fleet Specialist Inc. $25,000 for allegedly mishandling customer orders in General Motors stock when they fell sharply on June 27, 2002 after rumors circulated that the automaker had accounting problems. Instead of buying the stock, the trader sold 10,000 shares from Fleet's own account when another known seller was on the floor.

www.nyse.com

www.nasd.com

Securities firms and investment banks have historically been strongly supportive of efforts to combat money laundering, and the industry has been subject to federal laws that impose extensive reporting and record-keeping requirements. However, the U.S.A. Patriot Act, passed in response to the September 11, 2001 terrorist attacks, included additional provisions that financial services firms must implement. Since taking effect in October 2003, the new rules impose three requirements on firms in the industry. First, firms must verify the identity of any person seeking to open an account. Second, firms must maintain records of the information used to verify the person's identity. Third, firms must determine whether a person opening an account appears on any lists of known or suspected terrorists organizations. The new rules are intended to deter money laundering without imposing undue burdens that would constrain the ability of firms to serve their customers.

Finally, the Securities Investor Protection Corporation (SIPC) protects investors against losses of up to $500,000 on securities firm failures. This guarantee fund was created following the passage of the Securities Investor Protection Act in 1970 and is financed by premium contributions from member firms. The fund protects investor accounts in the event that a member firm cannot meet its financial obligations to customers. The fund does not, however, protect against losses on customers' accounts due to poor investment choices that reduce the value of their portfolio.

www.sipc.org

DO YOU UNDERSTAND?

1. What the major result of NSMIA is?
2. What two organizations monitor trading abuses?

While not a primary regulator of securities firms and investment banks, the Federal Reserve, as overseer of the financial system as a whole, also comments on rules and regulations governing the industry and suggests changes to be made. For example, in late 2000, the Federal Reserve called for the securities industry to shorten the time

16. They are called *shelf* offerings because after registering the issue with the SEC, the firm can take the issue "off the shelf" and sell it to the market when conditions are the most favorable—for example, in the case of debt issues, when interest rates are low.

it takes to complete stock trades. Federal Reserve Chairman Alan Greenspan stated that rising volumes of stock trading were straining the capacity of brokerage firms to settle trades in a timely fashion. Delays between the purchase of a stock to completion of the paperwork increases risk to the financial system. The Fed worried that when stock prices plunge, large banks may be vulnerable if investors to whom banks have lent money are unable to come up with more collateral for those loans. A shorter time for the completion of stock sales would lower the risk of defaults on any one trade. Mr. Greenspan noted that the Securities Industry Association, an industry trade group, had been working to shorten the settlement time to one day after the stock sale instead of the current three days.

GLOBAL ISSUES

Much more so than other sectors of the financial institutions industry, securities firms and investment banks operate globally. This can be seen in Table 16–1 where many recent mergers (such as Deutsche Bank's acquisition of Bankers Trust) involve non-U.S. securities firms. Also, Table 16–3 showed that UBS, a Swiss-based investment bank, was the top underwriter of U.S. municipal securities and the second leading underwriter of U.S. mortgage-backed securities. Indeed, in May 2004 UBS announced a further incursion into U.S. financial markets with the creation of a dedicated wealth group aimed at the provision of investment services to the wealthy, exploiting the well-known Swiss advantage in the provision of so-called private banking to high–net worth individuals.[17] Accordingly, as domestic securities trading and underwriting grew in the 1990s so did foreign securities trading and underwriting. Figures 16–4 and 16–5 show the foreign transactions in U.S. securities and U.S. transactions in foreign securities from 1991 to 2004. For example, foreign investors' transactions involving U.S. stocks increased from $211.2 billion in 1991 to $4,054.6 billion in 2004, an increase of 1,733 percent. Similarly, U.S. investors transactions involving stocks listed on foreign exchanges grew from $152.6 billion in 1991 to $1,803.1 billion in 2004, an increase of 1,082 percent.

FIGURE 16–4 **Foreign Transactions in U.S. Securities Markets**
(in billions of dollars)

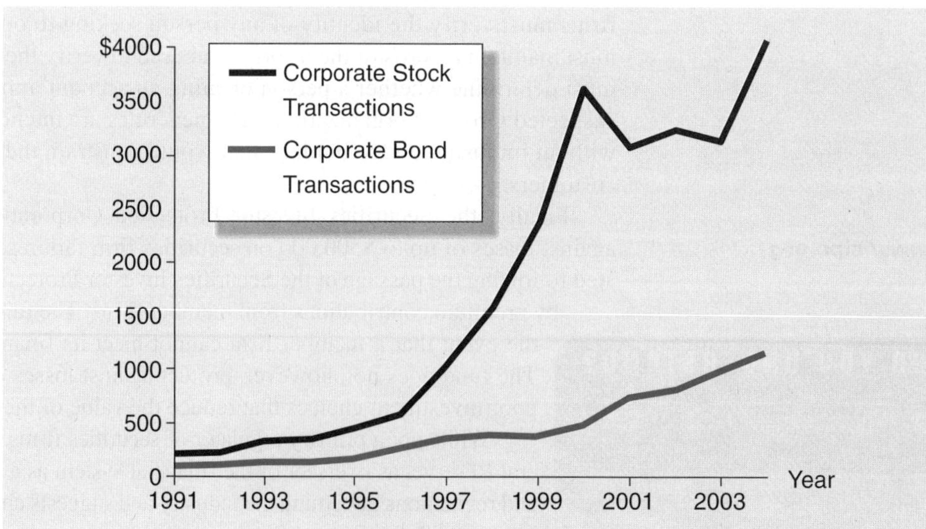

Source: *Treasury Bulletin,* U.S. Treasury, various issues. **www.ustreas.gov**

17. See "Wall Street Fights over the Rich," by Robert Frank, *The Wall Street Journal,* May 19, 2004, p. C1.

FIGURE 16–5 **U.S. Transactions in Foreign Securities Markets**
(in billions of dollars)

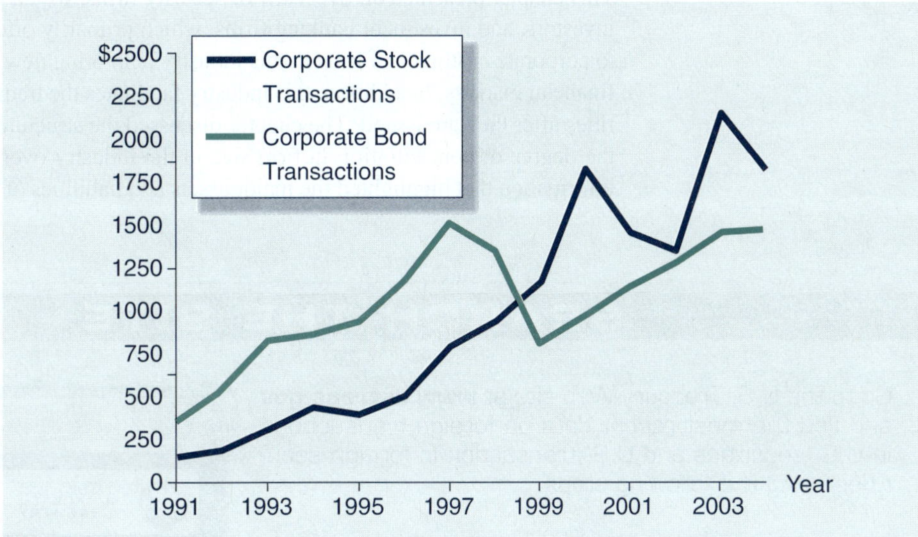

Source: *Treasury Bulletin,* U.S. Treasury, various issues. **www.ustreas.gov**

DO YOU UNDERSTAND?

1. What the trends in foreign transactions in U.S. securities and U.S. transactions in foreign securities in the 1990s and early 2000s have been?
2. What the trends in international securities offerings in the late 1990s and early 2000s have been?
3. Why foreign banks operating in the United States compete with both U.S. commercial banks and investment banks?

Table 16–9 reports the total dollar value of international security offerings from 1995 to 2004. In nine years total international offerings increased from $367.7 billion to $1,789.7 billion. Of the amounts in 2004, U.S. security issuers offered $383.6 billion in international markets, up from $93.0 billion in 1995. Nevertheless, concerns about U.S. accounting practices as a result of recent scandals, the burdensome nature of reporting accounting figures using U.S. accounting standards as well as their own local accounting standards, the decline in the U.S. stock market, and the fall in the value of the U.S. dollar against the euro, pound sterling, and yen were all working to weaken the attractiveness of U.S. markets to foreign investors and issuers in the early 2000s.

TABLE 16–9 **Value of International Security Offerings**
(in billions of dollars)

Type of Offering	1995	2000	2001	2002	2003	2004
Total International Offerings						
Floating-rate debt	$ 63.0	$ 356.8	$ 301.7	$ 199.0	$ 384.4	$ 644.4
Straight debt	250.4	715.4	808.6	800.1	983.4	924.6
Convertible debt	0.0	16.7	35.5	10.1	20.9	6.2
Equity	54.3	316.7	148.0	103.0	120.0	214.5
Total offerings	$367.7	$1,405.6	$1,293.8	$1,112.2	$1,508.6	$1,789.7
International Offerings by U.S. Issuers						
Floating-rate debt	$ 26.5	$ 162.4	$ 63.6	$ 22.4	$ 79.1	$ 124.7
Straight debt	56.9	390.3	480.6	415.6	358.9	257.0
Convertible debt	0.0	0.3	10.1	0.0	4.0	0.0
Equity	9.6	70.5	24.1	1.2	2.5	1.9
Total offerings	$ 93.0	$ 623.5	$ 578.4	$ 439.2	$ 444.5	$ 383.6

Source: "Quarterly Review: International Banking and Financial Market Developments," Bank for International Settlements, various issues. **www.bis.org**

SUMMARY

This chapter presented an overview of security firms, which primarily offer retail services to investors, and investment banking firms, which primarily offer activities and services related to corporate customers. Firms in this industry help bring new issues of debt and equity to the financial markets. In addition, this industry facilitates the trading and market making of securities after they are issued. The chapter discussed the structure of the industry and changes in the degree of concentration in firm size in the industry over the last decade. Balance sheet information that highlighted the major assets and liabilities of the firms was also analyzed.

SEARCH THE SITE

Go to the U.S. Treasury Web site at **www.ustreas.gov** and find the most recent data on foreign transactions in U.S. securities and U.S. transaction in foreign securities using the following steps.

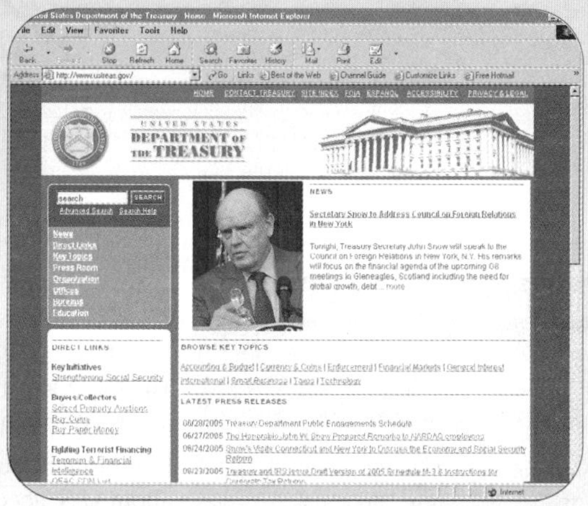

Click on "Bureaus."

Click on "Financial Management Services (FMS)."

Under "Statements & Reports," click on "Treasury Bulletin (quarterly)."

Click on "Capital Movements Tables (Section V)."

This will download a file on to your computer that will contain the most recent information on foreign transactions (Grand Total listed at the bottom of Table V-5).

Questions

1. What is the most recent dollar value of foreign stock and bond transactions in U.S. securities markets?
2. What is the most recent dollar value of U.S. investor stock and bond transactions in foreign securities markets?
3. How have these number changed since 2004 as reported in Figures 16–4 and 16–5?

QUESTIONS

1. In what ways are securities firms and investment banks financial intermediaries?
2. How has the size of the securities firm and investment banking industry changed since the late 1980s?
3. What are the different firms in the securities industry and how do they differ from each other?
4. Contrast the activities of securities firms with depository institutions and insurance firms.
5. What are the seven key activity areas of security firms and how were they impacted by the stock market crash of 1987?
6. What is the difference between pure arbitrage and risk arbitrage? If an investor observes the price of a stock trading in one exchange to be different from another exchange, what form of arbitrage is applicable and how could the investor participate in that arbitrage?
7. What three factors accounted for the resurgence in profits for securities firms from 1991 to 2000? Are firms that trade in fixed-income securities more or less likely to have volatile profits? Why or why not?
8. What factors contributed to the significant decrease in profit for securities firms in the early 2000s and the resurgence in profit in the middle of the first decade of the 2000s?
9. Go to the S&P Educational Version of Market Insight Web site at **www.mhhe.com/edumarketinsight** and identify the Industry Description and Industry Constituents for Investment Banking & Brokerage using the following steps. Click on "Educational Version of

Market Insight." Enter your site ID and click on "Login." Click on "Industry." From the Industry list, select "Investment Banking & Brokerage." Click on "Go!" Click on "Industry Profile" and, separately, "Industry Constituents."

10. STANDARD &POOR'S Go to the S&P Educational Version of Market Insight Web site at **www.mhhe.com/edumarketinsight** and look up the Industry Financial Highlights as posted by S&P for Investment Banking & Brokerage using the following steps. Click on "Educational Version of Market Insight." Enter your site ID and click on "Login." Click on "Industry." From the Industry list, select "Investment Banking & Brokerage." Click on "Go!" Click on any/all of the items listed under "Industry Financial Highlights."
11. Explain the difference between the investing and investment banking activities performed by securities firms and investment banks.
12. How does a public offering differ from a private placement?
13. How does a best efforts underwriting differ from a firm commitment underwriting? If you operated a company issuing stock for the first time, which type of underwriting would you prefer? Why might you still choose the alternative?
14. How do agency transactions differ from principal transactions for market makers?
15. Why have brokerage commissions earned by securities firms fallen since 1977?
16. What was the largest single asset and largest single liability of securities firms in 2004?
17. STANDARD &POOR'S Go to the S&P Educational Version of Market Insight Web site at **www.mhhe.com/edumarketinsight** and look up the most recent balance sheet for Merrill Lynch (MER) and Morgan Stanley Dean Witter (MWD) using the following steps. Click on "Educational Version of Market Insight." Enter your site ID and click on "Login." Click on "Company," Enter "MER" in the "Ticker:" box and click on "Go!" Click on "Excel Analytics." Click on "FS Ann. Balance Sheet." This will download the balance sheet for Merrill Lynch which contains the balances for Total Equity and Total Assets. Repeat the process by entering MWD in the "Ticker:" box to get information on Morgan Stanley Dean Witter. Compare the equity ratios for these firms with that for the broker-dealer industry listed in Table 16–7.
18. What benefits could a commercial banker obtain by getting into the investment banking business?
19. An investor notices that an ounce of gold is priced at $318 in London and $325 in New York. What action could the investor take to try to profit from the price discrepancy? Which of the six trading activities would this be? What might be some impediments to the success of the transaction?
20. An investment banker agrees to underwrite a $5,000,000 bond issue for the JCN corporation on a firm commitment basis. The investment banker pays JCN on Thursday and plans to begin a public sale on Friday. What type of interest rate movement does the investment bank fear while holding these securities?
21. An investment banker pays $23.50 per share for 3,000,000 shares of the KDO company. It then sells these shares to the public for $25. How much money does KDO receive? What is the investment banker's profit? What is the stock price of KDO?
22. The MEP company has issued 5,000,000 new shares. Its investment banker agrees to underwrite these shares on a best efforts basis. The investment banker is able to sell 4,200,000 shares for $54 per share. It charges MEP $1.25 per shares sold. How much money does MEP receive? What is the investment banker's profit. What is the stock price of MEP?
23. Which type of security accounts for the most underwritings in the United States?
24. What was the significance of the National Securities Markets Improvement Act of 1996?
25. What have been the trends in global securities trading and underwriting in the 1990s and early 2000s?

www.mhhe.com/sc3e

17

Mutual Funds

OUTLINE

Chapter NAVIGATOR

1. How has the mutual fund industry grown through time?
2. What is the difference in long-term mutual funds and money market mutual funds?
3. What is a mutual fund prospectus?
4. How is the net asset value of a mutual fund investment calculated?
5. Who are the main regulators of mutual funds?
6. What is the dollar value of mutual funds outstanding globally?

MUTUAL FUNDS: CHAPTER OVERVIEW

Mutual funds are financial intermediaries that pool the financial resources of investors and invest those resources in (diversified) portfolios of assets. Open-end mutual funds (the majority of mutual funds) sell new shares to investors and redeem outstanding shares on demand at their fair market values. Thus, they provide opportunities for small investors to invest in a diversified portfolio of financial securities. Mutual funds are also able to enjoy economies of scale by incurring lower transaction costs and commissions.

The first mutual fund was established in Boston in 1924. The industry grew very slowly at first, so that by 1970, 360 funds held about $50 billion in assets. Since then, the number of funds and the asset size of the industry have increased dramatically. This growth is attributed to the advent of money market mutual funds in 1972 (as investors looked for ways to earn market rates on short-term funds when regulatory ceilings constrained the interest rates they earned on bank deposits), to tax-exempt money market mutual funds first established in 1979, and to an explosion of special-purpose equity, bond, emerging market, and derivative funds (as capital market values soared in the 1990s). Money market mutual funds invest in securities with an original maturity under one year, while long-term funds invest in securities with an original maturity generally over one year.

TABLE 17–1 Growth of Mutual Funds for Various Years from 1940 to 2004*

Year	Total Net Assets (in billions)	Number of Shareholder Accounts† (in thousands)	Number of Funds
2004	$8,106.9	267,363	8,044
2003	7,414.4	260,882	8,126
2002	6,390.4	251,224	8,244
2001	6,975.0	248,816	8,305
2000	6,964.7	244,839	8,155
1999	6,846.3	226,346	7,791
1998	5,525.2	194,078	7,314
1997	4,468.2	170,363	6,684
1996	3,525.8	150,042	6,248
1995	2,811.3	131,219	5,725
1994	2,155.3	114,383	5,325
1993	2,070.0	93,214	4,534
1992	1,642.5	79,931	3,824
1991	1,393.2	68,332	3,403
1990	1,065.2	61,948	3,079
1980	134.8	12,088	564
1970	47.6	10,690	361
1960	17.0	4,898	161
1950	2.5	939	98
1940	0.5	296	68

*Data pertain to conventional fund members of the Investment Company Institute.

†Number of shareholder accounts includes a mix of individual and omnibus accounts.

Source: Investment Company Institute, *2005 Investment Company Fact Book,* Copyright © 2005 by the Investment Company Institute (**www.ici.org**). Reprinted with permission.

The tremendous increase in the market value of financial assets such as equities in the 1990s[1] and the relatively low transaction cost opportunity that mutual funds provide to investors (particularly small investors) who want to hold such assets (through either direct mutual fund purchases or contributions to retirement funds sponsored by employers and managed by mutual funds—see Chapter 18) have caused the mutual fund industry to boom, although the dramatic decline in the equity markets in the early 2000s eroded some of this growth. Shareholder services offered by mutual funds include free exchanges of investments between a mutual fund company's funds, automatic investing, check-writing privileges on many money market funds and some bond funds, automatic reinvestment of dividends, and automatic withdrawals. At year-end 2004, more than 8,000 different mutual funds held total assets of $8.11 trillion. This chapter presents an overview of the services offered by mutual funds and highlights their rapid growth in the last decade.

1 SIZE, STRUCTURE, AND COMPOSITION OF THE INDUSTRY

Historical Trends

Table 17–1 documents the tremendous increase in mutual funds for various years from 1940 though 2004. For example, total assets invested in mutual funds increased from $0.4 billion in 1940 to $8,106.9 billion in 2004. In addition, the number of mutual funds

1. For example, the S&P index reported a return of more than 28 percent in 1998 and 1999.

SEARCH THE SITE

Go to the Investment Company Institute Web site and find the latest information available for Total Net Assets, Number of Funds, and Number of Shareholder Accounts in U.S. mutual funds.

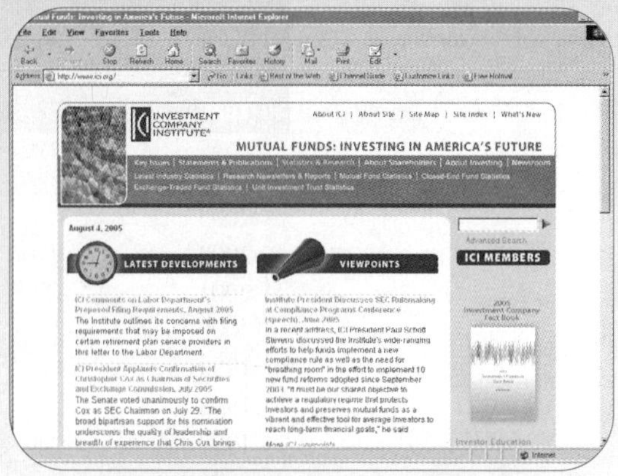

Go to the Investment Company Institute Web site at **www.ici.org.**

Click on "Statistics & Research."

Click on "Mutual Fund Statistics."

Click on "Mutual Fund Fact Book."

Click on, the most recent year "20XX Mutual Fund Fact Book."

This will download a file on to your computer that will contain the most recent information on U.S. mutual funds. In the Data Section of the Fact Book go to the table listing Industry Total Net Assets, Number of Funds, Number of Share Classes, and Number of Shareholder Accounts.

Questions

1. What is the most recent value for Total Net Assets, Number of Funds, and Number of Shareholder Accounts?
2. How has each of these changed since 2004 reported in Table 17–1?
3. Is the trend in Net Assets increasing or decreasing? Why?

increased from 68 in 1940 to 8,044 in 2004.[2] The majority of this increase occurred during the bull market run in the 1990s (total mutual fund assets in 1990 were $1,065.2 billion). As the U.S. economy and stock markets faltered in the early 2000s, mutual fund growth slowed as well. Table 17–2 lists the net new investment in long-term mutual funds and the return on the New York Stock Exchange (NYSE) composite index from 1985 through 2004. Notice that net new cash flows into long-term mutual funds is highly correlated with the return on the NYSE stock index.

As Figure 17–1 illustrates, in terms of asset size, even with the slowdown in growth in the early 2000s the mutual fund (money market and long-term mutual funds) industry is larger than the insurance industry and just a bit smaller than the commercial banking industry. This makes mutual funds the second most important FI group in the United States as measured by asset size.

Other types of FIs have noticed the tremendous growth in this area of FI services and have sought to directly compete by either buying existing mutual fund groups or managing mutual fund assets for a fee. For example, banks' share of all mutual fund assets managed had grown to 20 percent in 2004. Much of this growth has occurred through banks' buying mutual fund companies, for example, Mellon buying Dreyfus, as well as converting internally managed trust funds into open-end mutual funds. Insurance companies are also beginning to enter this market. In March 2001, for example, State Farm began offering a family of 10 mutual funds nationwide. The funds are available from more than 9,000 registered State Farm agents, on the Internet, or by application sent in response to phone requests made to a toll-free number. As of 2004, insurance companies managed 14 percent of the mutual fund industry's assets.

2. Most mutual fund companies offer more than one type of fund.

TABLE 17–2 Net New Cash Flows to Equity Mutual Funds versus Annual Returns on the NYSE Composite Index

	Net New Cash Flows to Equity Mutual Funds*	Return on NYSE Composite Index
1985	$6.6	26.80%
1986	20.4	13.97
1987	19.2	−0.25
1988	−14.9	13.00
1989	6.8	24.82
1990	12.9	−7.46
1991	39.9	27.12
1992	79.0	4.69
1993	127.3	7.86
1994	114.5	−3.14
1995	124.4	31.31
1996	216.9	19.06
1997	227.1	30.31
1998	156.9	16.55
1999	187.6	9.15
2000	309.4	1.01
2001	32.0	−10.21
2002	−27.6	−19.83
2003	152.3	25.36
2004	177.9	12.57

*In billions of dollars.

Source: For the net New Cash Flows to Equity Mutual Funds: Investment Company Institute, *2005 Investment Company Fact Book,* Copyright © 2005 by the Investment Company Institute (**www.ici.org**). Reprinted by permission.

Low barriers to entry in the U.S. mutual fund industry have allowed new entrants to offer funds to compete for investor attention and have kept the industry from being increasingly concentrated. As a result, the share of industry assets held by the largest mutual fund sponsors has changed little since 1990. For example, the largest 25 companies that sponsor mutual funds managed 72 percent of the industry's assets in 2004, compared to 76 percent of the industry's assets in 1990. The composition of the list of the 25 largest fund sponsors, however, has changed, with 7 of the largest fund companies in 2004 not among the largest in 1990.

equity funds

Funds consisting of common and preferred stock securities.

bond funds

Funds consisting of fixed income capital market debt securities.

hybrid funds

Funds consisting of stock and bond securities.

money market mutual funds

Funds consisting of various mixtures of money market securities.

Different Types of Mutual Funds

The mutual fund industry is usually considered to have two sectors: short-term funds and long-term funds. Long-term funds comprise **equity funds** (composed of common and preferred stock securities), **bond funds** (composed of fixed-income securities with a maturity of over one year), and **hybrid funds** (composed of both stock and bond securities). Short-term funds comprise taxable **money market mutual funds** (MMMFs) and tax-exempt money market mutual funds (containing various mixes of those money market securities with an original maturity of less than one year, discussed in Chapter 5). Tables 17–3 and 17–4 report the growth of bond and equity as well as hybrid mutual funds relative to money market mutual funds from 1980 through 2004. As can be seen, the 1990s saw a strong trend toward investing in equity mutual funds, reflecting the rise in share values during the 1990s. As a result, in 1999, some 74.2 percent of all mutual fund assets were in long-term funds while the remaining funds, 25.8 percent, were in money market mutual funds. However, in the early 2000s, as interest rates rose, the U.S. economy

FIGURE 17–1 Financial Assets of Major Financial Intermediaries, 1990 and 2004
(in trillions of dollars)

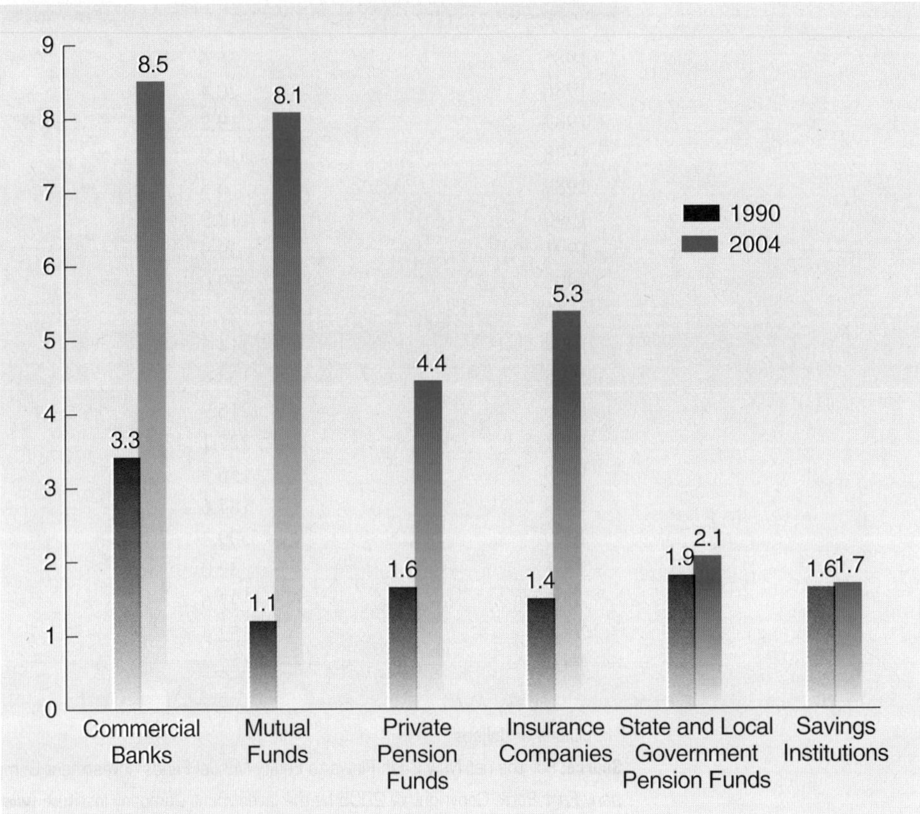

Source: Federal Reserve Board, Statistical Releases, "Flow of Fund Accounts," March 1991 and March 2005. **www.federalreserve.gov**

weakened, and stock returns fell, the growth of money market funds increased relative to the growth of long-term funds. In 2002, some 62.1 percent of all mutual fund assets were in long-term funds; the remaining funds, or 37.9 percent, were in money market mutual funds. In 2003 and 2004, as the U.S. economy recovered and stock values increased, the share of long-term funds grew to 74.3 percent of all funds, while money market funds decreased to 25.7 percent.

A growing number of the long-term mutual funds (approximately 25 percent) are index funds in which fund managers buy securities in proportions similar to those included in a specified major stock index (such as the S&P 500 Index). That is, index funds are designed to match the performance of a stock index. Because little research or aggressive management is necessary for index funds, management fees (discussed below) are lower and returns are often higher than more actively managed funds. Exchange-traded funds (ETFs) are long-term mutual funds that are also designed to replicate a particular stock market index. However, unlike index funds, ETFs are traded on a stock exchange at prices that are determined by the market. ETFs include funds such as SPDRs traded by the AMEX and Vanguard's Large-Cap VIPERS funds.[3] Like index funds, the share price of an ETF

3. SPDRs, Standard & Poor's Depository Receipts, hold a portfolio of the equity securities that comprise the Standard & Poor's 500 Composite Stock Price Index. SPDRs seek investment results that, before expenses, generally correspond to the price and yield performance of the Standard & Poor's 500 Composite Stock Price Index. Vanguard Large-Cap Index Participation Equity Receipts (VIPERs) seek to track the performance of a benchmark index that measures the investment return of large-capitalization stocks.

TABLE 17–3 Growth in Long-Term versus Short-Term Mutual Funds from 1980 through 2004 *(in billions of dollars)*

	1980	1990	1995	1999	2000	2002	2004	Percent Growth 1990–2004
A. Equity, Hybrid, and Bond Mutual Funds								
Holdings at market value	$61.8	$608.4	$1,852.8	$4,538.5	$4,434.6	$3,638.4	$5,435.3	793.4%
Household sector	45.7	456.7	1,247.8	3,112.8	3,094.3	2,326.3	3,570.4	681.8
Nonfinancial corporate business	1.5	9.7	45.7	128.9	129.2	97.0	128.9	1,228.9
State and local governments	0.0	4.8	35.0	25.6	26.4	24.2	28.3	489.6
Commercial banking	0.0	1.9	2.3	11.1	13.8	19.6	18.0	847.4
Credit unions	0.0	1.4	2.8	2.5	2.2	3.5	3.1	121.4
Bank personal trusts and estates	6.4	62.7	253.5	460.6	387.0	339.1	413.1	558.9
Life insurance companies	1.1	30.7	27.7	43.3	48.1	76.6	99.6	224.4
Private pension funds	7.1	40.5	228.5	753.8	733.6	752.0	1,173.7	2,798.0
B. Money Market Mutual Funds								
Total assets	$76.4	$493.3	$741.3	$1,578.8	$1,812.1	$2,223.9	$1,879.9	281.1%
Household sector	62.1	338.6	450.1	873.2	1,006.4	1,084.7	893.7	163.9
Nonfinancial business	7.0	26.3	77.0	178.3	228.2	446.1	378.2	1,338.0
Bank personal trusts and estates	2.2	26.0	33.6	53.7	57.4	54.1	41.9	61.2
Life insurance companies	1.9	18.1	22.8	133.8	142.3	159.8	120.7	566.9
Private pension funds	2.6	17.8	37.5	75.1	79.6	82.8	85.1	378.1
Funding corporations	0.6	36.6	120.2	264.7	298.2	396.4	360.2	884.2

Source: Federal Reserve Bulletin, "Flow of Fund Accounts," various issues. **www.federalreserve.gov**

changes over time in response to a change in the stock prices underlying a stock index. Further, since both ETFs and index funds are intended to track a specific index, management of the funds is relatively simple and management fees are lower than those for actively managed mutual funds. Unlike index funds, however, ETFs can be traded during the day, they can be purchased on margin, and they can be sold short by an investor who expects a drop in the underlying index value. Because ETFs behave like stocks, investors are subject to capital gains taxes only when they sell their shares. Thus, ETF investors can defer capital gains for as long as they hold the ETF.

Money market mutual funds provide an alternative investment opportunity to interest-bearing deposits at commercial banks, which may explain the increase in MMMFs in the 1980s and early 2000s when the spread earned on MMMFs investments relative to deposits was mostly positive. Figure 17–2 illustrates the net cash flows invested in taxable money market mutual funds and the interest rate spread between MMMFs and the average rate on

TABLE 17–4 Number of Mutual Funds, 1980, 1990, 2000, and 2004

Year	Equity	Hybrid	Bond	Taxable Money Market	Tax-Exempt Money Market	Total
1980*	288	N/A	170	96	10	564
1990	1,099	193	1,046	506	235	3,079
2000	4,385	523	2,208	703	336	8,155
2004	4,550	510	2,041	639	304	8,044

*Data from 1980 is not comparable to current classification. All funds were reclassified in 1984.

Source: Investment Company Institute, *2005 Investment Company Fact Book,* Copyright © 2005 by the Investment Company Institute (**www.ici.org**). Reprinted with permission.

FIGURE 17–2 **Interest Rate Spread and Net New Cash Flow to Taxable Retail Money Market Funds, 1985–2005**

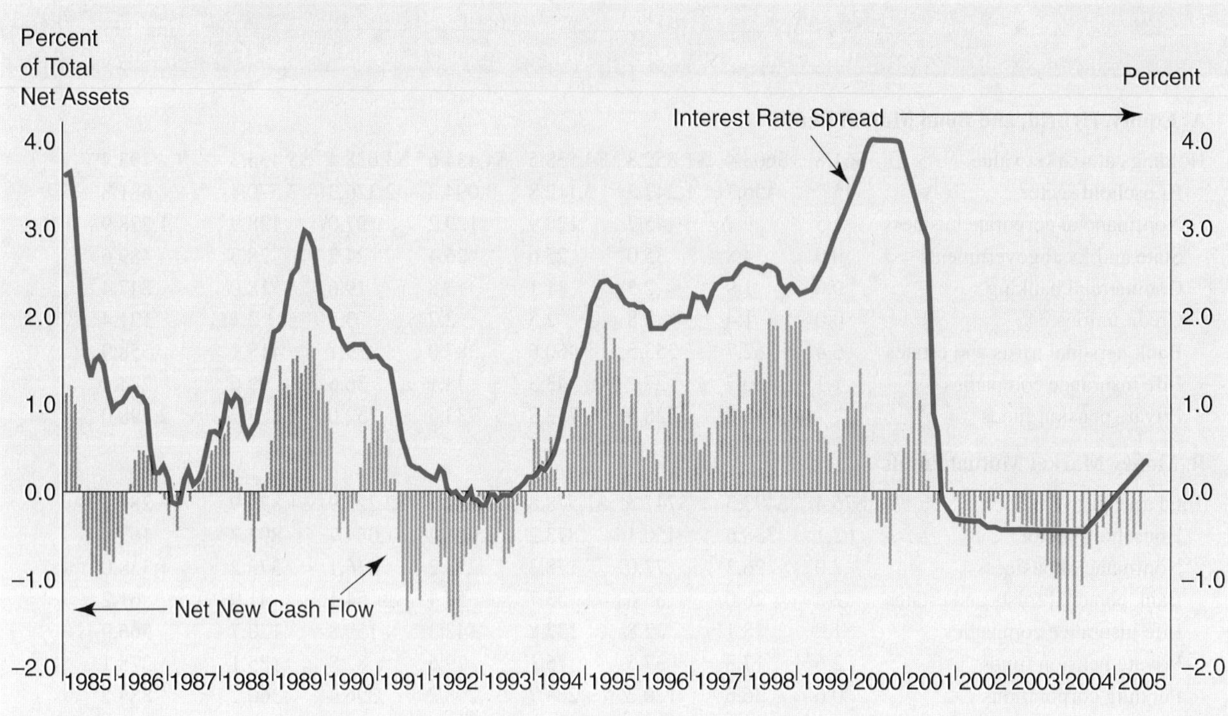

Note: Net new cash flow is a measured as a percentage of previous month-end taxable retail money market fund assets and is shown as a six-month moving average. The interest rate spread is the difference between the taxable retail money market fund yield and the average interest rate on money market deposit accounts; the series is plotted with a six-month lag.

Source: Investment Company Institute, *2005 Investment Company Fact Book,* Copyright © 2005 by the Investment Company Institute (**www. ici.org**). Reprinted with permission.

savings deposits from 1985 through 2004. Both investments are relatively safe and earn short-term returns. The major difference between the two is that interest-bearing deposits (below $100,000) are fully insured by the FDIC but, because of bank regulatory costs (such as reserve requirements, capital adequacy requirements, and deposit insurance premiums), generally offer lower returns than noninsured MMMFs.[4] Thus, the net gain in switching to MMMFs is a higher return in exchange for the loss of FDIC deposit insurance coverage. Many investors appeared willing to give up FDIC insurance coverage to obtain additional returns in the late 1980s, mid- and late-1990s. Despite this growth, the decline in the relative importance of short-term funds and the increase in the relative importance of long-term funds in the 1990s reflect the dramatic rise in equity returns over the 1990–2000 period even though MMMF interest spreads over bank deposits were mostly positive. However, a period of low interest rates that began in 2001 and persisted through 2004 resulted in a large relative drop in investments in MMMFs. Many individual and institutional investors moved assets from MMMFs to bank and thrift deposits as well as into equities and bonds.

Table 17–4 reports the growth in this industry in terms of the number of mutual funds in 1980, 1990, 2000, and 2004. All categories of funds have increased in number in this time period, from a total of 564 in 1980 to 8,044 in 2004. *Tax-exempt* money market funds first became available in 1979. This was the major reason for their relatively small number (10 funds) in 1980. Also, the number of equity funds boomed in the 1990s: equity funds numbered 4,550 in 2004, up from 1,099 in 1990, while bond funds numbered 2,041 in 2004, up from 1,046 in 1990.

4. Some mutual funds are covered by private insurance and/or by implicit or explicit guarantees from mutual fund management companies.

TABLE 17–5 Selected Characteristics of Household Owners of Mutual Funds*

	2004	1995
Demographic Characteristics:		
Median age	48 years	44 years
Median household income	$68,700	$60,000
Median household financial assets	$125,000	$50,000
Percent of households:		
Married or living with a partner	71	71
Four-year college degree or more	56	58
Employed	77	80
Fund types owned:		
Equity	80	73
Bond	44	49†
Hybrid	34	N/A
Money market	49	52

*Characteristics of primary financial decision maker in the household.

†This number is for bond and income funds.

Source: Investment Company Institute, *Profile of Mutual Fund Shareholders,* Copyright © 2004 by the Investment Company Institute (**www.ici.org**). Reprinted with permission.

Notice that in Table 17–3, households (i.e., small investors) own the majority of both long- and short-term funds, 65.7 percent for long-term mutual funds and 47.5 percent for short-term mutual funds in 2004. This is to be expected, given that the rationale for the existence of mutual funds is to achieve superior diversification through fund and risk pooling compared to what individual small investors can achieve on their own. Consider that wholesale CDs sell in minimum denominations of $100,000 each and often pay higher interest rates than passbook savings accounts or small time deposits offered by depository institutions. By pooling funds in a money market mutual fund, small investors can gain access to wholesale money markets and instruments and, therefore, to potentially higher interest rates and returns.

As of 2004, some 53.9 million U.S. households (48.1 percent) owned mutual funds. This was down from 56.3 million (52.0 percent) in 2001. Table 17–5 lists some characteristics of household mutual fund owners as of 2004. Most are long-term owners, with 49 percent making their first purchases before 1990. Forty-nine percent of all mutual fund holders are members of the baby boom generation (born between 1946 and 1964), 23 percent are from the "silent generation" (born before 1946), 24 percent are generation Xers (born between 1965 and 1976), and 4 percent are generation Yers (born after 1976). Interestingly, the number of families headed by a person with less than a college degree investing in mutual funds is 44 percent. In 75 percent of married households owning mutual funds, the spouse also worked full- or part-time. The bull markets of the 1990s and the low transaction costs of purchasing mutual fund shares, as well as the diversification benefits achievable through mutual fund investments, are again the likely reasons for these trends. The typical fund-owning household has $48,000 invested in a median number of four mutual funds. Finally, more than a quarter of investors who conducted equity fund transactions used the Internet for some or all of these transactions. This compares to 6 percent in 1998. Notice from Table 17–5 that 2004 has seen a slight increase in the median age of mutual fund holders (from 44 to 48 years) and a large increase in median household financial assets owned (from $50,000 to $125,000). Further, holdings of equity funds have increased from 73 to 80 percent of all households.

Mutual Fund Prospectuses and Objectives

3

Regulations require that mutual fund managers specify the investment objectives of their funds in a prospectus available to potential investors. This prospectus includes a list of the securities that the fund holds. Many "large" company funds, aiming to diversify across company size, held stocks of relatively "small" companies in the late 1990s, contrary to their stated objectives. Some fund managers justified the inclusion of seemingly "smaller" companies by changing their definition of what a large company is. For example, one fund manager stated his definition of a small company as one that has less than $1 billion in equity capital versus a large company that has more than $1 billion (the median size of equity capital of firms in the S&P 500 index is $28 billion). The point here is that investors need to read a prospectus carefully before making an investment.

The aggregate figures for long-term funds tend to obscure the fact that many different funds fall into this group of funds. Table 17–6 classifies 12 major categories of investment objectives for mutual funds, with the assets allocated to each of these major categories in 2004. The fund objective provides general information about the types of securities the mutual fund holds as assets. For example, "capital appreciation" funds hold securities (mainly equities) of the highest growth and highest-risk firms. Again, within each of these 12 categories of mutual funds are a multitude of different funds offered by mutual fund companies (see also the mutual fund quote section below). Historically, mutual funds have had to send out lengthy prospectuses describing their objectives and investments. In 1998, the SEC adopted a new procedure in which key sections of all fund prospectuses must be written in "plain English" instead of overly legal language. The idea is to increase the ability of investors to understand the risks related to the investment objectives or profile of a fund.

Table 17–7 lists the largest 20 mutual funds in total assets held in January 2005, including the fund objective, 12-month and five-year returns, net asset value (NAV—see later), and

TABLE 17–6 Total Net Asset Value of Mutual Funds by Investment Classification

Classification	Combined Assets (in billions of dollars)	Percent of Total
Total net assets	**$8,106.87**	**100.0%**
Capital appreciation	2,158.42	26.6%
World equity	689.67	8.5
Total return	1,535.98	19.0
Total equity funds	**$4,384.07**	**54.1%**
Total hybrid funds	**$519.29**	**6.4%**
Corporate bond	224.63	2.8%
High-yield bond	155.62	1.9
World bond	36.76	0.4
Government bond	210.83	2.6
Strategic income	334.76	4.1
State municipal	145.10	1.8
National municipal	182.62	2.3
Total bond funds	**$1,290.32**	**15.9%**
Taxable funds	1,602.84	19.8
Tax-exempt funds	310.35	3.8
Total money market funds	**$1,913.19**	**23.6%**

Source: Investment Company Institute, *2005 Investment Company Fact Book,* Copyright © 2005 by the Investment Company Institute (**www.ici.org**). Reprinted with permission.

TABLE 17–7 The Largest Mutual Funds in Assets Held

Name of Fund	Objective	Total Assets (in millions)	Total Return 12 month	Total Return 5 year	NAV	Initial Fees
Vanguard Index: 500	Growth/Income	$81,804.8	10.74%	−2.38%	111.64	0.00%
American Funds: InvCoA	Growth/Income	63,633.0	9.78	3.28	30.75	5.75
Fidelity Magellan	Growth	62,550.0	7.49	−3.87	103.79	0.00
American Funds: WshMut	Growth/Income	61,398.1	9.77	5.42	30.78	5.75
American Funds: Growth	Extreme Growth	58,163.7	11.95	1.81	27.38	5.75
Fidelity Invest: Contra	Growth	42,839.7	15.07	1.62	56.74	0.00
Dodge & Cox Stock	Multicap value	41,436.2	19.17	12.40	130.22	0.00
American Funds: Inc	Balanced	40,768.0	12.83	9.40	18.56	5.75
American Funds: Eupac	International	35,639.1	19.69	−0.17	35.63	5.75
Fidelity Lw-Prcd Stock	Growth	34,416.1	22.24	19.45	40.25	0.00
Vangaurd Instl Indx: Instl	Balanced	33,209.3	10.87	−2.26	110.71	0.00
American Funds: NewPer	International	32,599.7	14.27	2.22	27.72	5.75
Fidelity Invest: Grw/Inc	Growth/Income	31,300.9	9.84	−0.99	38.21	0.00
Vanguard Tot Stk Inx; Inv	Growth	30,433.2	12.52	−1.44	28.77	0.00
American Funds CIB; A	Balanced	30,345.9	17.43	11.10	53.26	5.75
American Funds Bal; A	Balanced	28,004.1	8.92	9.47	18.00	5.75
Vanguard: Windsor II	Multicap value	27,918.7	18.31	7.63	30.73	0.00
Vanguard: Wellington	Balanced	27,503.0	11.17	7.53	30.19	0.00
Fidelity: Eq/Inc	Equity/Income	25,549.9	11.29	4.31	52.78	0.00
American Funds CWFI; A	Global	25,136.4	19.42	8.24	33.89	5.75

Source: *The Wall Street Journal,* January 6, 2005. Reprinted by permission of *The Wall Street Journal* **www.wsj.com**

any initial fees (discussed below). Vanguard's Index: 500 (which is designed to replicate the performance of the S&P 500 Index) was the largest fund at the time. Vanguard, Fidelity, and American Funds offered 19 of the top 20 funds measured by asset size. Many of the top funds list either growth or growth and income as the fund's objective, and all of the top 20 funds performed well, in terms of return, in 2004. The downturn in the U.S. economy and the general drop in stock market values, however, hurt fund returns in the five years from 2000 to 2004. Six of the top 20 funds listed in Table 17–7 experienced negative five-year returns (from January 2000 through December 2004), Fidelity's Magellan Fund being the worst performer with a return of −3.87 percent for the five years. It should be noted that prospectuses rarely mention the risk of returns (e.g., the fund's total return risk or, alternatively, its systematic risk or "beta").[5] In 1998, the SEC adopted an initiative requiring mutual funds to disclose more information about their return risk as well as the returns themselves. The SEC's rule is intended to better enable investors to compare return-risk trade-offs from investing in different mutual funds.

www.fidelity.com

www.vanguard.com

www.americanfunds.com

Investor Returns from Mutual Fund Ownership

The return for the investor from investing in mutual fund shares reflects three aspects of the underlying portfolio of mutual fund assets. First, the portfolio earns income and dividends on those assets. Second, capital gains occur when the mutual fund sells an asset at prices higher than the original purchase price of the asset. Third, capital appreciation in the underlying values of its existing assets adds to the value of mutual fund shares. With respect to capital

5. Beta measures covariability of the returns on a specific investment (e.g., a mutual fund) with the returns on the market portfolio (e.g., the S&P 500 Index).

marked to market

Asset and balance sheet values are adjusted to reflect current market prices.

NAV

The net asset value of a mutual fund—equal to the market value of the assets in the mutual fund portfolio divided by the number of shares outstanding.

appreciation, mutual fund assets are normally **marked to market** daily. This means that the managers of the fund calculate the current value of each mutual fund share by computing the daily market value of the fund's total asset portfolio and then dividing this amount by the number of mutual fund shares outstanding. The resulting value is called the net asset value **(NAV)** of the fund. This is the price that investors obtain when they sell shares back to the fund that day or the price they pay to buy new shares in the fund on that day.

EXAMPLE 17-1 Calculation of NAV on an Open-End Mutual Fund

Suppose today a mutual fund contains 1,000 shares of Sears, Roebuck currently trading at \$37.75, 2,000 shares of Exxon/Mobil currently trading at \$43.70, and 4,500 shares of Citigroup currently trading at \$46.67. The mutual fund has 15,000 shares outstanding held by investors. Thus, today, the fund's NAV[6] is calculated as:

$$\text{NAV} = \frac{\text{Total market value of assets under management}}{\text{Number of mutual fund shares outstanding}}$$

$$= (1{,}000 \times \$37.75 + 2{,}000 \times \$43.70 + 4{,}500 \times \$46.67) \div 15{,}000 = \$13.01$$

If tomorrow Sears's shares increase to \$45, Exxon/Mobil's shares increase to \$48, and Citigroup's shares increase to \$50, the NAV (assuming the number of shares outstanding remains the same) would increase to:

$$\text{NAV} = (1{,}000 \times \$45 + 2{,}000 \times \$48 + 4{,}500 \times \$50) \div 15{,}000 = \$14.40$$

open-end mutual fund

A fund for which the supply of shares is not fixed but can increase or decrease daily with purchases and redemptions of shares.

Mutual funds are **open end** in that the number of shares outstanding fluctuates daily with the amount of share redemptions and new purchases. With open-end funds, investors buy and sell shares from and to the mutual fund company. Thus, the demand for shares determines the number of shares outstanding, and the market value of the underlying securities held in the mutual fund divided by the number of shareholders outstanding determines the NAV of shares.

EXAMPLE 17-2 Calculation of NAV of an Open-End Mutual Fund When the Number of Shares Increases

Consider the mutual fund in Example 17–1, but suppose that today 1,000 additional investors buy one share each of the mutual fund at the NAV of \$13.01. This means that the fund manager has \$13,010 additional funds to invest. Suppose that the fund manager decides to use these additional funds to buy additional shares in Sears. At today's market price, the manager could buy 344 additional shares (\$13,010/\$37.75) of Sears. Thus, its new portfolio of shares has 1,344 in Sears, 2,000 in Exxon/Mobil, and 1,500 in Citigroup. Given the same rise in share values as assumed in Example 17-1, tomorrow's NAV will now be:

$$\text{NAV} = (1{,}344 \times \$45 + 2{,}000 \times \$48 + 1{,}500 \times \$50) \div 16{,}000 = \$14.47$$

Note that the fund's value changed over the month due to both capital appreciation and investment size. A comparison of the NAV in Example 17–1 with the one in this example indicates that the additional shares and the profitable investments made with the new funds from these shares resulted in a slightly higher NAV than had the number of shares remained static (\$14.47 versus \$14.40).

6. We omit any fees that the mutual fund company charges for managing the mutual fund. These fees and their impact on returns are discussed later in the chapter.

closed-end investment companies

Specialized investment companies that have a fixed supply of outstanding shares but invest in the securities and assets of other firms.

REIT

A real estate investment trust; a closed-end investment company that specializes in investing in mortgages, property, or real estate company shares.

Open-end mutual funds can be compared with regular corporations traded on stock exchanges and to **closed-end investment companies**, both of which have a fixed number of shares outstanding at any given time. For example, real estate investment trusts (**REITs**) are closed-end investment companies that specialize in investing in real estate company shares and/or in buying mortgages.[7] For most closed-end company funds, investors generally buy and sell the company's shares on a stock exchange as they do for corporate stocks. Since the number of shares available for purchase, at any moment in time, is fixed, the NAV of the fund's shares is determined by the value of the underlying shares as well as by the demand for the investment company's shares themselves. When demand for the investment company's shares is high, because the supply of shares in the fund is fixed the shares can trade for more than the NAV of the securities held in the fund's asset portfolio. In this case, the fund is said to be *trading at a premium* (i.e., more than the fair market value of the securities held). When demand for the shares is low, the value of the closed-end fund's shares can fall to less than the NAV of its assets. In this case, its shares are said to be *trading at a discount* (i.e., less than the fair market value of the securities held).

EXAMPLE 17-3 Market Value of Closed-End Mutual Fund Shares

Because of high demand for a closed-end investment company's shares, the 50 shares (N_S) are trading at \$20 per share (P_S). The market value of the equity-type securities in the fund's asset portfolio, however, is \$800, or \$16 (\$800 ÷ 50) per share. The market value balance sheet of the fund is shown below:

Assets		Liabilities and Equity	
Market value of asset portfolio	\$800	Market value of closed-end fund shares ($P_S \times N_S$)	\$1,000
Premium	\$200		

The fund's shares are trading at a premium of \$4 (200 ÷ 50) per share.

Because of low demand for a *second* closed-end fund, the 100 shares outstanding are trading at \$25 per share. The market value of the securities in this fund's portfolio is \$3,000, or each share has a NAV of \$30 per share. The market value balance sheet of this fund is:

Assets		Liabilities and Equity	
Market value of asset portfolio	\$3,000	Market value of closed-end fund shares (100 × \$25)	\$2,500
Discount	−\$500		

www.morningstar.com

www.lipperweb.com

Mutual fund investors can get information on the performance of mutual funds from several places. For example, for a comprehensive analysis of mutual funds, Morningstar, Inc. offers information on over 10,000 open-end and closed-end funds. Morningstar does not own, operate, or hold an interest in any mutual fund. Thus, it is recognized as a leading provider of unbiased data and performance analysis (e.g., returns) for the industry. Similarly, Lipper Analytical services, a subsidiary of Reuters, tracks the performance of more than 115,000 funds worldwide.

Mutual Fund Costs

Mutual funds charge shareholders a price or fee for the services they provide (i.e., management of a diversified portfolio of financial securities). Two types of fees are incurred by

7. Many closed-end funds are specialized funds investing in shares in Latin American countries such as Argentina, Brazil, or Mexico. The shares of these closed-end funds are traded on the NYSE or in the over-the-counter market. The total market value of funds invested in closed-end funds was \$254.4 billion at the end of 2004. This compares to \$8,101.0 billion invested in open-end funds at that time.

investors: sales loads and fund operating expenses. We discuss these next. The total cost to the shareholder of investing in a mutual fund is the sum of the annualized sales load and other fees charged.

load fund

A mutual fund with an up-front sales or commission charge that the investor must pay.

no-load fund

A mutual fund that does not charge up-front sales or commission charges on the sale of mutual fund shares to investors.

Load versus No-Load Funds. An investor who buys a mutual fund share may be subject to a one-time sales or commission charge, sometimes as high as 8.5 percent. In this case, the fund is called a **load fund.**[8] Funds that market shares directly to investors and do not use sales agents working for commissions (and have no up-front commission charges) are called **no-load funds.**

The argument in favor of load funds is that they provide the investor with more personal attention and advice on fund selection than no-load funds. The cost of increased personal attention may not be worthwhile, however. For example, Table 17–7 lists initial fees for the largest U.S. stock funds in 2005. Notice that only American Funds group assesses a load fee on mutual fund share purchases. After adjusting for this fee the 12-month returns on the nine American Funds mutual funds fall from 19.69 percent to 8.92 percent (among the highest returns earned by the largest funds) and from 13.94 percent to 3.17 percent (among the lowest of the returns on these funds). As Figure 17–3 indicates, investors increasingly recognized this cost disadvantage for load funds in the 1990s as stock market values increased broadly and dramatically.[9] In 1985, load funds represented almost 70 percent of mutual fund sales and no-load funds represented just over 30 percent. By 1998 new sales of no-load mutual fund shares actually exceeded those of load fund shares and by 2002 total assets invested in no-load funds exceeded those invested in load funds.

The demand for no-load funds by mutual fund investors has not gone unnoticed. Many companies, particularly discount brokers, now offer mutual fund "supermarkets" through which investors can buy and sell the mutual funds shares offered by several different mutual fund sponsors. The most important feature of a fund "supermarket" is its non-transaction fee program, whereby an investor may purchase mutual funds with no transaction fees from a large number of fund companies. The broker is generally paid for services from the

FIGURE 17–3 Load versus No-Load Fund Assets as a Share of Fund Assets

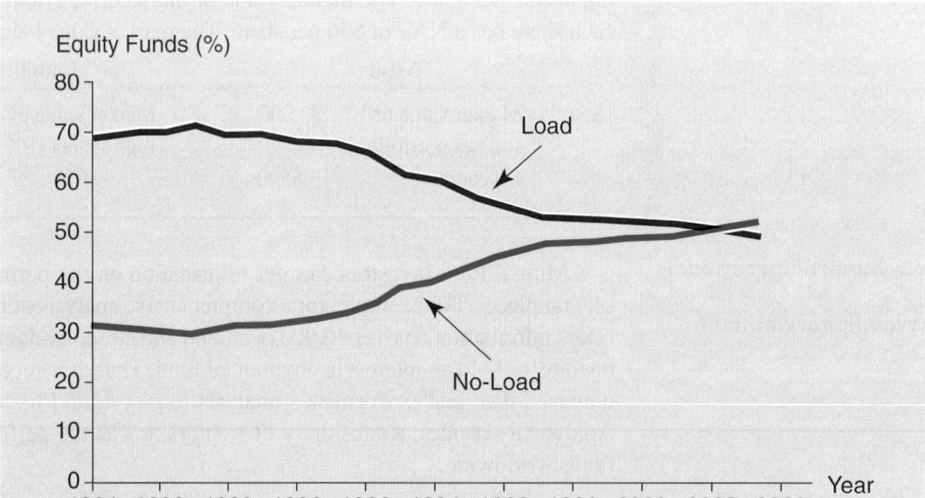

Source: Investment Company Institute, *2004 Mutual Fund Fact Book* (Washington, D.C.: Investment Company Institute, 2004). Reprinted by permission of the Investment Company Institute. **www.ici.org**

8. Another kind of load, called a *back-end load,* is sometimes charged when mutual fund shares are sold by investors. Back-end loads, also referred to as deferred sales charges, are an alternative way to compensate the fund managers or sales force for their services.

9. Load fees can be reduced by purchasing shares through a discount broker.

fund's 12b-1 fees (discussed below). The non-transaction fee fund offerings at a discount broker often number in the thousands, providing an investor the convenience of purchasing no-load funds from different families at a single location.

12b-1 fees

Fees relating to the distribution costs of mutual fund shares.

Fund Operating Expenses. In contrast to one-time up-front load charges on the initial investment in a mutual fund, annual fees are charged to cover fund-level expenses calculated as a percentage of the fund assets. One type of fee (called a management fee) is charged to meet operating costs (such as administration and shareholder services). In addition, mutual funds generally require a small percentage of investable funds—as a fee—to meet fund-level marketing and distribution costs. Such annual fees are known as **12b-1 fees** after the SEC rule covering such charges.[10] A 2004 survey conducted by the Investment Company Institute found that funds use most of these 12b-1 fees (92 percent) to compensate financial advisers and other financial intermediaries for assisting fund investors (responding to customer inquiries and providing information on investments) before and after they purchase fund shares.[11] Because these fees, charged to cover fund operating expenses, are paid out of the fund's assets, investors indirectly bear these expenses. These fees are generally expressed as a percentage of the average net assets invested in the fund.

EXAMPLE 17-4 Calculation of Mutual Fund Costs

The cost of mutual fund investing to the shareholder includes both the one-time sales load and any annual fees charged. Suppose an individual invests \$10,000 in a load mutual fund. The load fee entails an up-front commission charge of 4 percent of the amount invested and is deducted from the original funds invested. Thus, the individual's actual investment, after the load fee is deducted, is:

$$\$10{,}000\,(1 - .04) = \$9{,}600$$

In addition, annual fund operating expenses are 0.85 percent (representing a management fee of 0.75 percent and a 12b-1 fee of 0.10 percent). The annual fees are charged on the average net asset value invested in the fund and are recorded at the end of each year. Investments in the fund return 5 percent each year paid on the last day of the year. If the investor reinvests the annual returns paid on the investment, after one year the operating fees deducted and the value of the investment are:

$$\text{Annual operating expenses} = \text{average net asset value} \times \text{annual operating expenses}$$

$$= [\$9{,}600 \div \$9{,}600(1.05)]/2 \times .0085 = \$83.640$$

$$\text{Value of investment at end of year 1} = \$9{,}600(1.05) - \$83.640 = \$9{,}996.360$$

The investor's return on the mutual fund investment after one year is:

$$(\$9{,}996.360 - \$10{,}000)/\$10{,}000 = -0.04\%$$

In year 2, the investor's fees deducted and investment value at the end of the year are:

$$\text{Annual operating expenses} = [\$9{,}996.360 \div \$9{,}996.360(1.05)]/2 \times .0085 = \$87.093$$

$$\text{Value of investment at end of year 2} = \$9{,}996.360(1.05) - \$87.093 = \$10{,}409.085$$

After two years the investor has paid a total of \$400 in load fees and \$170.733 in operating expenses, and he has made \$409.085 above the original \$10,000 investment. The investor's annual return on the mutual fund is 2.02 percent.[12]

10. 12b-1 fees cannot exceed 1 percent of a fund's average net assets per year and may include a service fee of up to 0.25 percent. No-load funds cannot have a 12b-1 fee of more than 0.25 percent.

11. "How Mutual Funds Use 12b-1 Fees," *Fundamentals* 14, no.2, Investment Company Institute, February 2005, pp. 1–4.

12. That is, $\$10{,}000 = \$10{,}409.085(PVIF_{i,2}) => i = 2.02\%$

Funds sold through financial professionals such as brokers have recently adopted alternative payment methods. These typically include an annual 12b-1 fee based on asset values that may also be combined with a front-end or back-end sales charge. In many cases, funds offer several different share classes (all of which invest in the same underlying portfolio of assets), but each share class may offer investors different methods of paying for broker services. Indeed, in 2002, over half of all mutual funds had two or more share classes, compared to 1980 when all funds had only one share class. Most funds sold in multiple classes offer investors three payment plans through three share classes (A, B, and C), each having different mixes of sales loads and 12b-1 fees.

Class A shares represent the traditional means for paying for investment advice. That is, Class A shares carry a front-end load that is charged at the time of purchase as a percentage of the sales price. The front-end load on Class A shares is charged on new sales and is not generally incurred when Class A shares are exchanged for another mutual fund within the same fund family. In addition to the front-end load, Class A shares usually have an annual 12b-1 fee that is used to compensate brokers and sales professionals for ongoing assistance and service provided to fund shareholders. The 12b-1 fee for Class A shares is typically between 25 and 35 basis points of the portfolio's assets.

Unlike Class A shares, *Class B shares* are offered for sale at the NAV without a front-end load. Class B share investors pay for advice and assistance from brokers through a combination of annual 12b-1 fees (usually 1 percent) and a back-end load. The back-end load is charged when shares are redeemed (sold) and is typically based on the lesser of the original cost of the shares or the market value at the time of sale. After six to eight years, Class B shares typically convert to Class A shares, lowering the level of the annual 12b-1 fees from 1 percent to that of A shares.

Class C shares are offered at the NAV with no front-end load, and typically recover distribution costs through a combination of annual 12b-1 fees of 1 percent and a back-end load, set at 1 percent in the first year of purchase. After the first year no back-end load is charged on redemption. The Class C shares usually do not convert to Class A shares, and thus the annual 1 percent payment to the broker continues throughout the period of time that the shares are held.

www.vanguard.com

As discussed below, the lack of complete disclosure and the inability of most mutual fund investors to understand the different fees charged for various classes of mutual fund shares came under scrutiny in the early 2000s. Indeed, the potential for overcharging fees to various classes of mutual fund shareholders led to the SEC creating new rules pertaining to these charges (see below).

DO YOU UNDERSTAND?

1. Where mutual funds rank in terms of asset size of all FI industries?
2. What the difference is between short-term and long-term mutual funds?
3. What the trends as to the number of mutual funds have been since 1980?
4. What the three largest mutual fund companies are? How have their funds performed in recent years?
5. What the difference is between open-end and closed-end mutual funds?

Mutual Fund Share Quotes

Table 17–8 presents mutual fund quotes from *The Wall Street Journal* for Vanguard Index Funds as of January 6, 2005. The majority of mutual funds in the United States are held by fund groups or families. These fund families offer a variety of different types of equity bond, hybrid, and money market funds as well as annuities and other products. Vanguard's Index Fund family offers funds that replicate a variety of equity, bond, and global indexes. The quotes include information on each fund's name; its objective; the fund's asset size; its NAV; its fourth quarter 2004, and one- through five-year returns and ratings (A through E); its maximum initial and exit sales charges; and annual expenses. The maximum initial charge is listed as "No" or "0.00" for each of the Vanguard Index Funds, meaning that they are all no-load funds. Fund returns are ranked by total return within each investment objective defined by *The Wall Street Journal*: A = top 20 percent; B = next 20 percent; C = middle 20 percent; D = next 20 percent; and E = bottom 20 percent.[13] For example, Vanguard's 500 Index had a one-year (as of January 6, 2005) return of 10.7 percent and a rank of A. Thus, the return on this fund, 10.7 percent, was one of the top 20 percent of returns on *all* mutual funds (Vanguard's and all other

13. Other rating agencies such as Morningstar have their own rating system. All methods, however, rate funds relative to other funds *with the same* investment objective.

TABLE 17–8 Money Mutual Fund Quote

Fund Name	INV obj	Assets ($mil)	NAV 12/31	4th qtr	Performance & Rank One Year	Three Year	Five Year	Max Initial sls cg	Ann exp as %
Vanguard Index FDS ☎ 800-662-7447									
500	SP	81805	111.64	9.2	10.7A	3.5A	−2.4A	NO	0.18
Balanced	BL	4536	19.45	6.5	9.3B	5.8B	2.4C	NO	0.22
CalSoc	LC	312	8.02	9.6	8.3C	2.3B	NS	NO	0.25
DevMkt	IL	1117	9.20	15.2	20.3B	12.0B	NS	NO	
EmerMkt	EM	2895	14.68	18.7	26.1B	22.6C	5.3B	0.00	0.53
Europe	EU	8620	25.99	15.9	20.9C	11.2C	0.1C	0.00	0.32
Extnd	MC	5253	31.36	14.0	18.7B	11.7B	1.4E	0.00	0.26
Growth	LG	7522	26.41	9.4	7.2C	1.0B	−6.9B	NO	0.23
ITBond	IB	3393	10.68	1.0	5.2A	7.2A	8.7A	NO	0.20
LarCaplx	LC	38	21.41	9.6	NS	NS	NS	NO	NA
LTBond	AB	1240	11.82	2.2	8.4A	9.4A	10.5A	NO	0.20
MidCp	MC	4925	15.64	14.8	20.4A	11.3B	10.1A	NO	0.26
Pacific	PR	3732	9.38	13.9	18.8A	14.3C	−4.0D	0.00	0.39
REIT	SE	4381	18.79	15.0	30.7B	22.5B	21.2B	NO	0.24
SmCap	SC	5996	26.82	13.9	19.9B	11.8C	7.0D	0.00	0.27
SmGth	SG	1348	15.16	14.8	16.1A	11.9A	7.2A	0.00	0.27
SmVal	SV	2753	13.97	13.0	23.6B	13.3D	15.1D	0.00	0.27
STBond	SB	3779	10.14	0.1	1.7C	3.7B	5.7B	NO	0.20
TotBd	IB	19046	10.27	1.0	4.2B	5.5D	7.2C	NO	0.22
TotIntl	IL	7986	12.60	15.6	20.8B	12.9B	−0.6B	0.00	
TotSt	XC	30433	28.77	10.3	12.5B	5.3C	−1.4D	0.00	0.20
Value	LV	3455	21.35	9.8	15.3A	6.4B	2.4D	NO	0.23

Notes: SP = replicates the S&P 500 Index; BL = balanced fund; EM = emerging market fund; EU = European region fund; MC = middle-sized company fund; LG = large, growth company fund; SG = small, growth company fund; SV = small, undervalued company fund; XC = growth fund; LV = large undervalued fund; IL = Canadian and International small cap fund; PR = Pacific region fund; LC = large company fund; SC = small company fund; AB = long-term corporate debt A-rated fund; SB = short-term investment grade debt fund; SE = funds that invest in companies restricted to specific sectors such as gold health, biotech, etc; and IB = intermediate-term investment-grade debt fund.

Source: *The Wall Street Journal,* January 6, 2005, p. R21. Reprinted by permission of *The Wall Street Journal* © 2005 Dow Jones & Company, Inc. All Rights Reserved Worldwide. **www.wsj.com**

mutual fund companies) with an objective to replicate the S&P 500 Index. The return on the S&P 500 Index over the same period was 8.99 percent.

BALANCE SHEETS AND RECENT TRENDS

Long-Term Funds

Note the asset distribution of long-term mutual funds in Table 17–9. As might be expected, it reflects the relative popularity of bonds and equities at various times. Underscoring the attractiveness of equities in 2004 was the fact that corporate equities represented more than 68.0 percent of total long-term mutual fund asset portfolios in 2004, while corporate and foreign bonds were the next most popular assets (11.5 percent of the asset portfolio). In contrast, consider the distribution of assets in 1990 when the equity markets were not doing well and the economy was in recession. Corporate equities made up only 38.3 percent of long-term mutual fund portfolios, with U.S. government securities and municipals comprising the largest asset group at 44.8 percent of total assets.

TABLE 17–9 Distribution of Assets in Long-Term Mutual Funds from 1990 through 2004
(in billions of dollars)

	1990	1995	2000	2004	Percent Change 1990 through 2004
Total financial assets	$608.4	$1,852.8	$4,434.6	$5,435.3	793.4%
Security RPs	6.1	50.2	106.4	108.6	16.8
Credit market instruments	360.1	771.3	1,097.8	1,624.2	351.0
Open-market paper	28.5	50.2	106.4	90.3	216.8
Treasury securities	87.1	205.3	123.7	150.2	72.4
Agency securities	72.6	109.9	275.3	466.4	542.4
Municipal securities	112.6	210.2	230.5	294.5	161.5
Corporate and foreign bonds	59.3	195.7	361.9	622.9	950.4
Corporate equities	233.2	1,024.9	3,226.9	3,697.2	1,485.4
Miscellaneous assets	8.9	6.3	3.5	5.1	−42.7

Source: Federal Reserve Board Web site, "Flow of Fund Accounts," various issues. **www.federalreserve.gov**

Money Market Funds

Look at the distribution of assets of money market mutual funds from 1990 through 2004 in Table 17–10. At year-end 2004, $1,243,3.2 billion (66.1 percent of total assets) were invested in short-term (under one year to maturity) financial securities—such as foreign deposits, domestic checkable deposits and currency, time and savings deposits, repurchase agreements (RPs or repos), open-market paper (mostly commercial paper), and U.S. government securities. Short-maturity asset holdings reflect the objective of these funds to retain the depositlike nature of the share liabilities they issue. In fact, most money market mutual fund shares have their values fixed at $1. Asset value fluctuations due to interest rate changes and any small default risk and capital gains or losses are adjusted for by increasing or reducing the number of $1 shares owned by the investor.

EXAMPLE 17–5 Calculation of Number of Shares Outstanding in a Money Market Mutual Fund

Because of a drop in interest rates, the market value of the assets held by a particular MMMF increases from $100 to $110.[14] The market value balance sheet for the mutual fund before and after the drop in interest rates is:

(a) Before interest rate drop:

Assets		Liabilities and Equity	
Market value of MMMF assets	$100	Market value of MMMF fund shares (100 shares × $1)	$100

(b) After interest rate drop:

Assets		Liabilities and Equity	
Market value of MMMF assets	$110	Market value of MMMF fund shares (110 shares × $1)	$110

14. As discussed in Chapter 2, the value of fixed-income securities such as T-bills, CDs, and so on will rise in value whenever yields (interest rates) fall. That is, there is an inverse relationship between market value and interest rates for most MMMFs since they specialize in holding (short-term) fixed-income securities.

TABLE 17–10 Distribution of Assets in Money Market Mutual Funds from 1990 through 2004
(in billions of dollars)

	1990	1995	2000	2004	Percent Change 1990 through 2004
Total financial assets	$493.3	$741.3	$1,812.1	$1,879.9	281.1%
Foreign deposits	26.7	19.7	91.1	75.4	183.4
Checkable deposits and currency	11.2	−3.5	2.2	0.6	−94.6
Time and savings deposits	21.9	52.3	142.4	174.1	695.0
Security RPs	58.2	87.8	183.0	239.2	311.0
Credit market instruments	371.3	545.5	1,290.9	1,260.8	239.6
Open-market paper	204.0	235.5	608.6	395.3	93.8
Treasury securities	44.9	70.0	90.4	96.4	114.7
Agency securities	36.4	90.8	185.2	262.2	620.3
Municipal securities	84.0	127.7	244.7	318.8	279.5
Corporate and foreign bonds	2.0	21.5	161.9	188.1	9,305.0
Miscellaneous assets	4.0	43.4	102.5	129.7	3,142.5

Source: Federal Reserve Board Web site, "Flow of Fund Accounts," various issues. **www.federalreserve.gov**

The interest rate drop results in 10 (110 − 100) new equity-type shares that are held by investors in the MMMF, reflecting the increase in the market value of the MMMF's assets of $10 (i.e., 10 new shares of $1 each).

5 REGULATION

www.sec.gov

www.nasd.com

Because mutual funds manage and invest small investor savings, this industry is heavily regulated. Indeed, many regulations have been enacted to protect investors against possible abuses by mutual fund managers. The SEC is the primary regulator of mutual funds. Specifically, the Securities Act of 1933 requires a mutual fund to file a registration statement with the SEC and sets rules and procedures regarding a fund's prospectus that it sends to investors. In addition, the Securities Exchange Act of 1934 makes the purchase and sale of mutual fund shares subject to various antifraud provisions. This act requires mutual funds to furnish full and accurate information on all financial and corporate matters to prospective fund purchasers. The 1934 Act also appointed the National Association of Securities Dealers (NASD) to supervise mutual fund share distributions. In 1940, Congress passed the Investment Advisers Act and Investment Company Act. The Investment Company Act established rules to prevent conflicts of interest, fraud, and excessive fees or charges for fund shares.

DO YOU UNDERSTAND?

1. What the major assets held by mutual funds have been in the 1990s and early 2000s?
2. How the asset distribution for money market mutual funds and long-term mutual funds differs?

In recent years, the Insider Trading and Securities Fraud Enforcement Act, of 1988 has required mutual funds to develop mechanisms and procedures to avoid insider trading abuses. In addition, the Market Reform Act of 1990, passed in the wake of the 1987 stock market crash, allows the SEC to introduce circuit breakers to halt trading on exchanges and to restrict program trading when it deems necessary. Finally, the National Securities Markets Improvement Act (NSMIA) of 1996 (discussed in Chapter 16) also applies to mutual fund companies. Specifically, the NSMIA exempts mutual fund sellers from oversight by state securities regulators, thus reducing their regulatory burden.

Despite the many regulations imposed on mutual fund companies, several allegations of trading abuses and improper assignment of fees were revealed and prosecuted in the early 2000s. The abusive activities fell into four general categories: market timing, late trading, directed brokerage, and improper assessment of fees to investors.

Putnam Claims Ex-CEO Hid Abuses to Stay in Power

Putnam Investments claims ousted Chief Executive Lawrence Lasser concealed improper trading at the mutual fund firm to "maintain his power and absolute control," and to preserve his compensation—more than $100 million over five years—according to an arbitration claim that the company filed in a dispute over his exit package. In November, Putnam's parent, Marsh & McLennan Cos., removed Mr. Lasser as CEO shortly after federal and state regulators accused Putnam of allowing fund managers to trade rapidly in Putnam funds, skimming profits from long-term shareholders. Putnam has said that Mr. Lasser, who ruled it for 18 years and built the firm into an investment titan, knew about the fund-manager trading in 2000, but didn't tell fund trustees, who represent shareholders. In a letter to the chairman of the Putnam funds' trustees, Mr. Lasser disputes that account and has claimed he is being made "a scapegoat."...

In harsh language, the SEC's enforcement section called Putnam's conduct "egregious" and "a massive breach of fiduciary duty."... In the brief, SEC enforcement attorneys said Mr. Lasser and Putnam had concealed the trading until last year to protect a valuable franchise, and they noted that once the trading was disclosed, investors withdrew $54 billion from Putnam in the fourth quarter of 2003 . . . the SEC attorneys quoted at length from Putnam's arbitration complaint against Mr. Lasser to paint the company's behavior in a harsher light. "When it came time for Mr. Lasser to respond to evidence of market timing by Putnam employees, Lasser made a conscious decision to stick his head in the sand," the SEC quoted Putnam as saying in its arbitration filing . . . "Mr. Lasser knew that if the market-timing trades were revealed to the Putnam trustees or to anyone at [Marsh], he could be forced to surrender the absolute control with which he had managed Putnam for years," according to Putnam's complaint.

Source: *The Wall Street Journal*, March 24, 2004, p. Cl, by John Hechinger. Reprinted by permission of *The Wall Street Journal*

Market timing is short-term trading of mutual funds that seeks to take advantage of short-term discrepancies between the price of a mutual fund's shares and out-of-date values on the securities in the fund's portfolio. It is especially common in international funds, where traders can exploit differences in time zones. Typically market timers hold a fund for only a few days. For example, when Asian markets close with losses but are expected to rebound the following day, market timers can buy a U.S. mutual fund, investing in Asian securities after the loss on that day, and then sell the shares for a profit the next day. This single-day investment dilutes the profits of the fund's long-term investors, while market timers profit without much risk. The Ethical Debates box highlights one particularly flagrant case in which a mutual fund allowed selected traders to engage in market timing.

Late trading allegations involved cases in which some investors were able to buy or sell mutual fund shares long after the price had been set at 4:00 p.m. Eastern time each day (i.e., after the close of the NYSE and NASDAQ). Under existing rules, investors had to place an order with their broker or another FI by 4:00 p.m. But the mutual fund company might receive the order much later—sometimes as late as 9:00 p.m.—allowing large investors to call their broker back after the market closed and alter or cancel the order.

Directed brokerage arrangements between mutual fund companies and brokerage houses may afford brokers the opportunity to improperly influence investors on their funds recommendations. For example, some mutual fund companies agreed to direct orders for stock and bond purchases and sales to brokerage houses that agreed to promote sales of the mutual fund company's products.

Finally, the disclosure of 12b-1 fees seemingly allows brokers to *improperly assess fees* by tricking investors into believing they are buying no-load funds. Before 12b-1 fees, all funds sold through brokers carried front-end load fees. As discussed earlier, with 12b-1 fees, fund companies introduced share classes, some of which carried back-end loads that declined over time and others that charged annual fees of up to 1 percent of asset values. Fund classes that charged annual 12b-1 fees would see performance decrease by that amount and thus not perform as well as an identical fund that carried a lower 12b-1 fee.

TABLE 17–11 Mutual Fund Investigations in the Early 2000s

Company	Charge	Results
Alliance Capital	Market timing	$250 million settlement; 2 employees fired
Bank of America	Market timing/ Late trading	$515 million settlement; 3 employees fired; several more employees resigned
Bank One	Market timing	2 managers resigned
Bear Steams	Market timing	6 employees fired
Canary Capital	Market timing/ Late trading	$40 million settlement
Charles Schwab	Late trading	2 employees fired
Citigroup	Market timing/ Late trading	5 employees fired
Federated Investors	Market timing	Actions pending
Fred Alger & Co.	Market timing/ Late trading	Vice-chairman convicted of felony and fined $400,000; 2 employees fired
Janus Capital	Market timing	$226 million settlement; CEO and others resign; fee reductions of $125 million
Merrill Lynch	Market timing	3 employees fired
MFS Investment Management	Market timing	$225 million settlement; fee reductions of $125 million
Millennium Partners	Late trading	Fund trader pleads guilty and sentenced to up to 4 years in prison
Morgan Stanley	Directed brokerage/ Improper fees	$50 million settlement
PBHG Funds	Market timing	Cofounders resign
Pilgrim, Baxter & Associates	Market timing	2 founders resign
Prudential Securities	Market timing	12 employees fired; 7 employees facing charges
Putnam Investments	Market timing/ Improper fees	$110 million settlement; CEO resigns; 6 fund managers resign
Security Trust	Market timing	Company closed; CEO, president, and head of trading operations charged with grand larceny and fraud
Strong Capital Management	Market timing	$140 million settlement; chairman of mutual fund unit resigns: fee reductions of $35 million

Source: Author's research.

The shareholder, however, saw only the fund's raw return (before annual fees) and not the dollar amount of the fee paid. Further, brokers often overcharged customers by failing to provide discounts to fund investors who qualified to receive them. Since discount policies differ from fund to fund, brokers did not always realize which customers qualified for them. Table 17–11 lists some of the mutual fund companies at the center of these abuses, the abuses they were accused of, and outcomes of some of the investigations.

As a result of these illegal and abusive activities, new rules and regulations were imposed (in 2004 and 2005) on mutual fund companies. The rules were intended to give investors more information about conflicts of interest, improve fund governance, and close legal loopholes that some fund managers had abused. Many of these new rules involve changes in the way mutual funds operate, including requirements that funds have an independent board headed by an independent chairman. Specifically, the SEC required an increase in the percentage of independent board members to 75 percent from the previous level of 50 percent. The SEC saw independent directors as those who better serve as watchdogs guarding investors' interests. Further, the Sarbanes-Oxley Act of 2002 requires public companies, including mutual fund companies, to make sure their boards' audit committees have at least one individual who is familiar with generally accepted accounting principles (GAAP) and has experience with internal auditing controls, preparing or auditing financial statements of "generally comparable issuers," and applying GAAP principles for estimates, accruals, and reserves.

The SEC also took steps to close a loophole that allowed improper trading to go unnoticed at some mutual funds. Prior to the new rules, the SEC required that funds report trading by senior employees in individual stocks but not in shares of mutual funds they manage. The SEC now requires portfolio managers to report trading in funds they manage. Investment advisers also have to protect information about stock selections and client holdings and transactions. The SEC and other regulators had found that advisory personnel revealed confidential information about fund portfolio holdings so that others could exploit the funds.

To address the problem of market timing, the SEC now requires funds to provide expanded disclosure of the risks of frequent trading in fund shares and of their policies and procedures regarding such activities. Mutual funds also now have to be more open about their use of fair value pricing (a practice of estimating the value of rarely traded securities or updating the values of non-U.S. securities that last traded many hours before U.S. funds calculate their share prices each day) to guard against stale share prices that could produce profits for market timers. The market timing provisions also require mutual funds to explain when they use fair value pricing. Fair value pricing is one of the most effective ways of combating the market timing that was most common in some mutual funds holding non-U.S. stocks. Many mutual funds had rarely used fair value pricing. Further, new SEC rules require brokers to tell investors about any payments, compensation, or other incentives they receive from fund companies, including whether they were paid more to sell a certain fund. Such conflicts would have to be disclosed before a sale was completed.

To ensure that the required rule changes take place, starting October 5, 2004, the SEC required that mutual funds hire chief compliance officers to monitor whether a mutual fund company follows the rules. The chief compliance officer will report directly to mutual fund directors, and not to executives of the fund management company. To further insulate the chief compliance officer from being bullied into keeping quiet about improper behavior, only the fund board can fire the compliance officer. Duties of the compliance officer include policing personal trading by fund managers, ensuring accuracy of information provided to regulators and investors, reviewing fund business practices such as allocating trading commissions, and reporting any wrongdoing directly to fund directors.

Finally, the new SEC rules call for shareholder reports to include the fees shareholders paid, as well as management's discussion of the fund's performance over that period. As of September 1, 2004, mutual fund companies must provide clear information to investors on brokerage commissions and discounts, including improved disclosure on up-front sales charges for broker-sold mutual funds. Investors now get a document showing the amount they paid for a fund, the amount their broker was paid, and how the fund compares with industry averages based on fees, sales loads, and brokerage commissions. As of December 2004, mutual funds must provide to investors summary information in a fund prospectus on eligibility for fee discounts and explain what records investors may need to show brokers to demonstrate they qualify for discounts.

The SEC has also proposed that mutual funds or their agents receive all trading orders by 4:00 p.m. Eastern time, when the fund's daily price is calculated. This "hard closing,"

DO YOU UNDERSTAND?

1. Who the primary regulator of mutual fund companies is?
2. How the NSMIA affected mutual funds?

which would require fund orders to be in the hands of the mutual fund companies by 4:00 p.m., is intended to halt late trading abuses. This proposal had not yet been passed as of mid-2004 because some argued that the change would cause significant problems for investors who buy funds through brokers. The move requires deadlines several hours earlier at intermediaries such as brokerage firms, forcing them to place orders as early as 10:00 a.m., so their requests are processed on the same day. Thus, mutual fund investors using brokers for their trades would have less flexibility than direct mutual fund investors.

GLOBAL ISSUES

6 As discussed throughout the chapter, mutual funds have been the fastest-growing sector in the U.S. financial institutions industry throughout the 1990s and into the early 2000s. Worldwide investment in mutual funds is shown in Table 17–12. While not as striking as the growth in U.S. funds, worldwide (other than in the United States) investments in mutual funds have increased over 395 percent from $1.626 trillion in 1992 to $8.046 trillion in 2004. This compares to growth of over 290 percent in U.S. funds. As this industry developed in countries throughout the world, the number of mutual funds worldwide (other than in the United States) increased almost 155 percent from 18,183 in 1992 to 46,335 in 2004. Much more established in the United States, mutual funds increased 116 percent over this period.

As may be expected, the worldwide mutual fund market is most active in those countries with the most sophisticated securities markets (e.g., Japan, France, Australia, and the United Kingdom). However, in the late 1990s and early 2000s, the faltering Japanese economy resulted in a decrease in both the assets invested in and the number of mutual funds. Assets invested in Japanese mutual funds fell from $502.8 billion in 1999 to $399.5 billion in 2004 (a drop of 21.5 percent) and the number of funds fell from 3,444 to 2,884 (16.3 percent) over the two-year period. Some U.S. FIs saw this decline in the Japanese market as an opportunity. U.S. FIs, such as PaineWebber Group (forming an alliance with Yasuda Life Insurance Co.) and Merrill Lynch (buying the assets of failed Japanese brokerage firm Yamaichi Securities), entered the Japanese mutual fund market in the late 1990s and early 2000s. The U.S. FIs saw Japan as a potentially profitable market for mutual fund sales, noting that about 60 percent of Japan's savings were in low-yielding bank deposits or government-run institutions.[15] The worldwide economic downturn in 2001–2002 also affected the global mutual fund industry. Assets invested in non-U.S. mutual funds fell from $4.91 trillion in 1999 to $4.68 trillion in 2001. As the worldwide economic situation improved in 2003 and 2004, so did assets invested in mutual funds, rising to $8.05 trillion by the end of 2004.

DO YOU UNDERSTAND?

1. What the trends in the assets invested in worldwide mutual funds during the 1990s and early 2000s have been?

Although U.S. mutual fund companies sponsor funds abroad, barriers to entry overseas are typically higher than in the United States. The U.S. mutual fund industry has worked to lower the barriers that prevent U.S. mutual fund firms from marketing their services abroad more widely and to improve competition in the often diverse fund markets around the world. The U.S. mutual fund industry has, for example, worked to achieve a true cross-border market for mutual fund companies in Europe and to ensure that publicly offered mutual fund companies can be used as funding vehicles in the retirement fund market in Europe and Japan. The industry has also sought to reduce barriers for U.S. mutual fund sponsors seeking to offer mutual fund company products in China and other Asian countries.

15. It might be noted that, as many European countries move away from state-sponsored pension plans to privately funded pension plans and retirement vehicles, the rate of growth in mutual funds in these countries is likely to rapidly accelerate.

TABLE 17–12 Worldwide Assets of Open-End Investment Companies*
(in millions of U.S. dollars)

Non-U.S. Countries	1999	2000	2001	2002	2003	2004
Argentina	$ 6,990	$ 7,425	$ 3,751	$ 1,021	$ 1,916	$ 2,355
Australia	371,207	341,955	334,016	356,304	518,411	635,073
Austria	56,254	56,549	55,211	66,877	87,982	103,707
Belgium	65,461	70,313	68,661	74,983	98,724	118,373
Brazil	117,758	148,538	148,189	96,729	171,596	220,586
Canada	269,825	279,511	267,863	248,979	338,369	413,772
Chile	4,091	4,597	5,090	6,705	8,552	12,588
Costa Rica	N/A	919	1,577	1,738	2,754	1,053
Czech Republic	1,473	1,990	1,778	3,297	4,083	4,860
Denmark‡	27,558	32,485	33,831	40,153	49,533	64,799
Finland	10,318	12,698	12,933	16,516	25,604	37,658
France	656,132	721,973	713,378	845,147	1,148,446	1,370,954
Germany	237,312	238,029	213,662	209,168	276,319	295,997
Greece	36,397	29,154	23,888	26,621	38,394	43,106
Hong Kong	182,265	195,924	170,073	164,322	255,811	343,638
Hungary	1,725	1,953	2,260	3,992	3,936	4,966
India	13,065	13,507	15,284	20,364	29,800	32,846
Ireland	95,174	137,024	191,840	250,116	360,425	467,620
Italy	475,661	424,014	359,879	378,259	478,734	511,733
Japan	502,752	431,996	343,907	303,191	349,148	399,462
Korea	167,177	110,613	119,439	149,544	121,663	177,417
Liechtenstein	N/A	N/A	N/A	3,847	8,936	12,543
Luxembourg	661,084	747,117	758,720	803,869	1,104,112	1,396,131
Mexico	19,468	18,488	31,723	30,759	31,953	35,157
Netherlands	94,539	93,580	79,165	84,211	93,573	89,749[a]
New Zealand	8,502	7,802	6,564	7,505	9,641	11,171
Norway	15,107	16,228	14,752	15,471	21,994	29,907
Philippines	117	108	211	474	792	952
Poland	762	1,546	2,970	5,468	8,576	12,014
Portugal	19,704	16,588	16,618	19,969	26,985	30,514
Romania	N/A	8	10	27	36	159
Russia	177	177	297	372	851	1,347
Slovakia	N/A	N/A	N/A	N/A	1,061	2,168
South Africa	18,235	16,921	14,561	20,983	34,460	54,006
Spain	207,603	172,438	159,899	179,133	255,344	317,538
Sweden	83,250	78,085	65,538	57,992	87,746	107,064
Switzerland	82,512	83,059	75,973	82,622	90,772	94,407
Taiwan	31,153	32,074	49,742	62,153	76,205	77,328
Turkey	N/A	N/A	N/A	6,002	14,157	18,112
United Kingdom	375,199	361,008	316,702	288,887	396,523	492,726
Total non-U.S.	**$ 4,916,001**	**$ 4,916,006**	**$ 4,679,953**	**$ 4,933,770**	**$ 6,663,914**	**$ 8,045,556**
Total U.S.	**$ 6,846,339**	**$ 6,964,667**	**$ 6,974,951**	**$ 6,390,360**	**$ 7,414,084**	**$ 8,106,873**
Total world	**$11,762,345**	**$11,871,061**	**$11,654,904**	**$11,324,130**	**$14,048,318**	**$16,152,429**

[a]Data as of 09/30/2004.

*Funds of funds are not included except for France, Italy, and Luxembourg in 2004. Data include home-domiciled funds, except for Hong Kong, Korea, and New Zealand, which include home and foreign-domiciled

‡Before 2003, data include special funds reserved for institutional investors.

Note: Components may not add to total because of rounding. N/A = not available.

Source: Investment Company Institute, *2005 Investment Company Fact Book*, Copyright © 2005 by the Investment Company Institute (**www.ici.org**). Reprinted with permission.

SUMMARY

This chapter presented an overview of the mutual fund industry. Mutual funds pool funds from individuals and corporations and invest in diversified asset portfolios. Due to the tremendous increase in the value of financial assets such as equities in the 1990s and the cost-effective opportunity that mutual funds offer for small investors to participate in these markets, mutual funds have increased tremendously in size, number of funds, and number of shareholders. The chapter also discussed the two major categories of mutual funds—short-term and long-term open-end funds—highlighting the differences in their growth rates and the composition of their assets. The chapter also illustrated the calculation of the net asset values (NAV) of mutual fund shares.

SEARCH THE SITE

Go to the Investment Company Institute Web site at **www.ici.org** and look up the most recent data on worldwide asset values of mutual funds using the following steps.

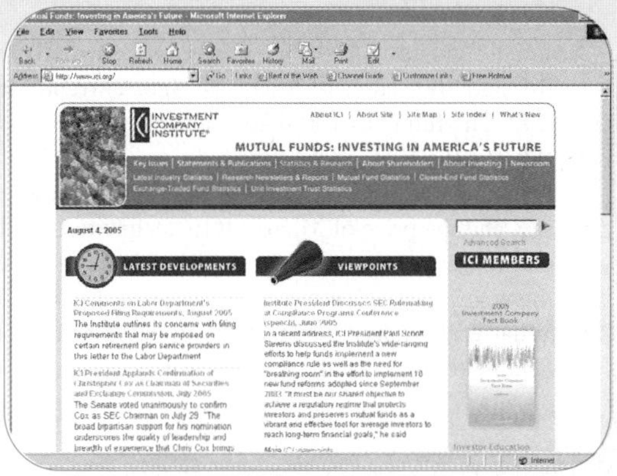

Under "Statistics & Research," click on the "Mutual Fund Statistics."

Click on "Mutual Fund Fact Book."

Click on the most recent year for "XXXX Mutual Fund Fact Book."

Go to the "Data Section."

This section contains the relevant data. The data on asset values and number of mutual funds is among the first few pages.

Questions

1. How have these values increased since those for 2004 reported in Table 17–12?
2. Which countries have seen the largest increases in the dollar value of assets in mutual funds?
3. How has the percentage of worldwide assets in U.S. mutual funds versus non-U.S. mutual funds changed since 2004 reported in Table 17–12?

QUESTIONS

1. What is a mutual fund? In what sense is it a financial intermediary?
2. What benefits do mutual funds have for individual investors?
3. What are money market mutual funds? In what assets do these funds typically invest? What factors caused the strong growth in this type of fund since the late 1970s?
4. What are long-term mutual funds? In what assets do these funds usually invest? What factors caused the strong growth in this type of fund during the 1990s and the decline in growth in the early 2000s?
5. Using the data in Table 17–3, discuss the growth and ownership holding over the last 25 years of long-term funds versus money market funds.
6. How does the risk of short-term funds differ from that of long-term funds?
7. What are the economic reasons for the existence of mutual funds?
8. What are the principal demographics of household owners of mutual funds?
9. What change in regulatory guidelines occurred in 1998 that had the primary purpose of giving investors a better understanding of the risks and objectives of a mutual fund?
10. What are the three components of the return that an investor receives from a mutual fund?
11. How is the net asset value (NAV) of a mutual fund determined? What is meant by the term *marked-to-market daily?*

12. An investor purchases a mutual fund for $50. The fund pays dividends of $1.50, distributes a capital gain of $2, and charges a fee of $2 when the fund is sold one year later for $52.50. What is the net rate of return from this investment?
13. What is the difference between open-end and closed-end mutual funds? Which of them tend to be more specialized?
14. Open-end Fund A has 100 shares of ATT valued at $100 each and 50 shares of Toro valued at $50 each. Closed-end Fund B has 75 shares of ATT and 100 shares of Toro. Both funds have 100 shares outstanding.
    a. What is the NAV of each fund using these prices?
    b. Assume that another 100 shares of ATT valued at $100 are added to Fund A. What is the effect on Fund A's NAV if the prices remain unchanged?
    c. If the price of ATT stock increases to $105 and the price of Toro stock declines to $45, how does that impact the NAV of both funds? Assume that Fund A has only 100 shares of ATT.
15. A mutual fund has 200 shares of Fiat, Inc., currently trading at $14, and 200 shares of Microsoft, Inc., currently trading at $140. The fund has 100 shares outstanding.
    a. What is the NAV of the fund?
    b. If investors expect the price of Fiat shares to increase to $18 and the price of Microsoft to decline to $110 by the end of the year, what is the expected NAV at the end of the year?
    c. What is the maximum that the price of Microsoft can decline to maintain the NAV as estimated in (a)?
16. How might an individual's preference for a mutual fund's objective change over time?
17. An investor purchases a mutual fund share for $100. The fund pays dividends of $3, distributes a capital gain of $4, and charges a fee of $2 when the fund is sold one year later for $105. What is the net rate of return from this investment?
18. What is a 12b-1 fee? Suppose that you have a choice between two mutual funds, one a load fund with no annual 12b-1 fees, and the other a no-load fund with a maximum 12b-1 fee. How would the length of your expected holding period influence your choice between these two funds?
19. Suppose an individual invests $20,000 in a load mutual fund for two years. The load fee entails an up-front commission charge of 2.5 percent of the amount invested and is deducted from the original funds invested. In addition, annual fund operating expenses (or 12b-1 fees) are 0.55 percent. The annual fees are charged on the average net asset value invested in the fund and are recorded at the end of each year. Investments in the fund return 7 percent each year paid on the last day of the year. If the investor reinvests the annual returns paid on the investment, calculate the annual return on the mutual funds over the two-year investment period.
20. Why did the proportion of equities in long-term mutual funds increase from 38.3 percent in 1990 to 72.8 percent in 2000 and decrease back to 68.0 percent in 2004? How might an investor's preference for a mutual fund's objective change over time?
21. Who are the primary regulators of the mutual fund industry? How do their regulatory goals differ from those of other types of financial institutions?
22. Discuss the improper trading abuses and improper assignment of fees for which mutual funds were prosecuted in the early 2000s.

APPENDIX 17A: Hedge Funds

View this appendix at www.mhhe.com/sc3e

www.mhhe.com/sc3e

18

Pension Funds

Chapter NAVIGATOR

1. What is the difference between a private pension fund and a public pension fund?
2. What is the difference between a defined benefit and defined contribution pension fund?
3. What are the different types of private pension funds?
4. What are the different types of public pension funds?
5. What are the main regulations governing pension funds?
6. What are the major issues for pension funds in the global markets?

OUTLINE

PENSION FUNDS DEFINED: CHAPTER OVERVIEW

Pension funds are similar to life insurance companies (discussed in Chapter 15) and mutual funds (discussed in Chapter 17) in that all three attract small savers' funds and invest them in the financial markets to be liquidated at a later date. Indeed, as discussed in this chapter, insurance companies and mutual funds are the main providers of pension funds. Pension funds are unique, however, in that they offer savings plans through which fund participants accumulate tax deferred savings during their working years before withdrawing them during their retirement years. Funds originally invested in and accumulated in a pension plan are exempted from current taxation. Rather, tax payments are not made until funds are actually distributed to the fund participant, often later in his or her life.

Pension funds were first established in the United States in 1759 to benefit the widows and children of church ministers. It was not until 1875 that the American Express Company established the first corporate pension fund. By 1940, only 400 pension funds were in existence, mainly for employees in the railroad, banking, and public utilities industries. Since then, the industry has boomed, so that currently over 700,000 pension funds now exist. In 2004, U.S. households had 26.2 percent of their financial assets invested in pension funds, compared to just over 5 percent in 1950.

TABLE 18–1 Pension Fund Reserves, 1990–2004
(in billions of dollars)

	1990	1995	2000	2004
Federal government	$ 250.5	$ 374.8	$ 704.9	$1,024.0
Private pension funds				
Life insurance companies	596.0	997.3	1,456.1	2,002.8
Other private pension funds	1,601.1	2,681.4	4,582.6	4,490.6
State and local government retirement funds	931.0	1,535.9	2,331.5	2,120.4
Total	$3,378.6	$5,589.4	$9,075.1	$9,637.8

Source: Federal Reserve Board, "Flow of Fund Accounts," various issues. **www.federalreserve.gov**

1 The pension fund industry comprises two distinct sectors. **Private pension funds** are those funds administered by a private corporation (e.g., insurance company, mutual fund). Because pension funds are such a large percentage of the insurance industry's business (see below), they are often listed separately from other private pension funds. **Public pension funds** are those funds administered by a federal, state, or local government (e.g., Social Security). At the end of 2004, total financial assets invested in pension funds were $9,637.8 billion: $6,493.4 billion in private funds (including life insurance companies), $2,120.4 billion in state and local government funds, and $1,024.0 billion in federal government funds (see Table 18–1). Growth of private funds was particularly significant in the 1990s as the long-term viability of the major public pension fund, Social Security, came into question.

private pension funds

Funds administered by a private corporation.

public pension funds

Funds administered by a federal, state, or local government.

This chapter provides an overview of the pension fund industry. In particular, we examine the size, structure, and composition of the industry. We also describe recent trends in private and public pension fund growth as well as the differences between these two major types of funds. Finally, we describe the major regulations under which the industry operates.

SIZE, STRUCTURE, AND COMPOSITION OF THE INDUSTRY

In this section, we describe the various characteristics of pension funds, including insured versus noninsured pension funds and defined benefit versus defined contribution pension funds. We then present an overview of the private pension funds and public pension funds that comprise this industry.

Insured versus Noninsured Pension Funds

A **pension plan** governs the operations of a pension fund. Pension funds administered by life insurance companies (over 20 percent of the industry's assets) are termed **insured pension funds.** The designation as an insured pension fund is not necessarily derived from the type of administrator but from the classification of assets in which pension fund contributions are invested. Specifically, no separate pool of assets backs the pension plan. Rather, pension plan funds are pooled and invested in the general assets of the insurance company. The amount of the insurance company's assets devoted to pension funds is reported on the liability side of the balance sheet under "pension fund reserves." For example, in December 2005 (see Table 18–2), life insurance companies managed a total of $2,002.8 billion in pension fund assets (reported in the liability account as "pension fund reserves"). These reserves represented 48.1 percent of the industry's total liabilities and equity. Pension fund assets were distributed among various assets on life insurance companies' balance sheets (e.g., U.S. government securities, corporate and foreign bonds, corporate equities), rather than being reported as a separate pool of pension fund assets segregated from other life insurance assets.

pension plan

Document that governs the operations of a pension fund.

insured pension fund

A pension fund administered by a life insurance company.

TABLE 18–2 Life Insurance Company Balance Sheet, December 2004
(in billions of dollars)

Total Assets	**$4,159.9**	**100.0%**
Checkable deposits and currency	40.1	1.0
Money market fund shares	120.7	2.9
Credit market instruments	2,675.0	64.3
Open market paper	70.7	1.7
Treasury securities	75.0	1.8
Agency securities	371.8	8.9
Municipal securities	28.0	0.7
Corporate and foreign bonds	1,753.7	42.2
Policy loans	106.0	2.5
Mortgages	270.0	6.5
Corporate equities	1,091.5	26.2
Mutual fund shares	99.6	2.4
Miscellaneous assets	132.7	3.2
Total Liabilities	**$3,905.1**	**93.9%**
Other loans and advances	11.1	0.3
Life insurance reserves	1,067.3	25.7
Pension Fund Reserves	**2,002.8**	**48.1**
Taxes payable	28.1	0.7
Miscellaneous liabilities	796.0	19.1

Source: Federal Reserve Board, "Flow of Fund Accounts," March 10, 2005. **www.federalreserve.gov**

noninsured pension fund

A pension fund administered by a financial institution other than a life insurance company.

Noninsured pension funds are managed by a trust department of a financial institution appointed by the sponsoring business, participant, or union. Trustees invest the contributions and pay the retirement benefits in accordance with the terms of the pension fund. In contrast to insured pension funds, assets managed in noninsured pension funds are owned by the sponsor and are thus segregated and listed as separate pools of assets on the trustees' balance sheet. While the day-to-day investment decisions for a noninsured pension fund are controlled by the trustee, the sponsor of the pension fund normally specifies general guidelines the trustee should follow.

Premiums paid into insured pension funds, and the assets purchased with these premiums, become the legal property of the insurance company managing the pension funds. In contrast, premiums paid into noninsured pension funds, and the assets purchased with these premiums, are the legal property of the sponsoring corporation. Because insurance companies, as the asset owners (of insured pension funds), incur the risk associated with value fluctuations in their pension fund assets, they generally concentrate their asset investments in less risky securities (bonds and mortgages). Noninsured pension fund managers, by contrast, do not incur the risk associated with asset value fluctuations. Thus, the trustees overseeing these pension funds generally invest pension premiums received in more risky securities (e.g., equities). As a result, noninsured pension funds generally offer the potential for higher rates of return but are also more risky than insured pension funds. However, the higher rates of return allow the employee to reduce contributions necessary to achieve a given amount of funds at retirement.

2 Defined Benefit versus Defined Contribution Pension Funds

Pension funds can also be distinguished by the way contributions are made and benefits are paid. A pension fund is either a defined benefit fund or a defined

defined benefit pension fund

Pension fund in which the employer agrees to provide the employee with a specific cash benefit upon retirement.

flat benefit formula

Pension fund that pays a flat amount for every year of employment.

career average formula

Pension fund that pays retirement benefits based on the employee's average salary over the entire period of employment.

final pay formula

Pension fund that pays retirement benefits based on a percentage of the average salary during a specified number of years at the end of the employee's career times the number of years of service.

contribution fund. In a **defined benefit pension fund,** the corporate employer (or fund sponsor) agrees to provide the employee a specific cash benefit upon retirement, based on a formula that considers such factors as years of employment and salary during employment. The formula is generally one of three types: flat benefit, career average, or final pay formula. These three types of defined benefit funds are discussed in more detail next.

Flat Benefit Formula. A **flat benefit formula** pays a flat amount for every year of employment.

EXAMPLE 18-1 Calculation of Retirement Benefit for a Defined Benefit Fund under a Flat Benefit Formula

An employee with 20 years of service at a company is considering retirement at some point in the next 10 years. The employer uses a flat benefit formula by which the employee receives an annual benefit payment of $2,000 times the number of years of service. For retirement now, in 5 years, and in 10 years, the employee's annual retirement benefit payment is:

	Retirement Benefit
Retire now	$2,000 × 20 = $40,000
Retire in 5 years	$2,000 × 25 = $50,000
Retire in 10 years	$2,000 × 30 = $60,000

Career Average Formula. Two variations of **career average formulas** exist; both base retirement benefits on the average salary over the entire period of employment. Under one formula, retirees earn benefits based on a percentage of their average salary during the entire period they belonged to the pension fund. Under the alternative formula, the retirement benefit is equal to a percentage of the average salary times the number of years employed.

EXAMPLE 18-2 Calculation of Retirement Benefit under a Defined Benefit Fund Using a Career Average Formula

An employee with 20 years of service at a company is considering retirement some time in the next 10 years. The employer uses a career average benefit formula by which the employee receives an annual benefit payment of 4 percent of his career average salary times the number of years of service. For retirement now, in 5 years, and in 10 years, the employee's annual retirement benefit payment is:

	Average Salary	Retirement Benefit
Retire now	$48,000	$48,000 × .04 × 20 = $38,400
Retire in 5 years	$50,000	$50,000 × .04 × 25 = $50,000
Retire in 10 years	$52,000	$52,000 × .04 × 30 = $62,400

Final Pay Formula. A **final pay formula** pays a retirement benefit based on a percentage of the average salary during a specified number of years at the end of the employee's career times the number of years of service.

EXAMPLE 18-3 Calculation of Retirement Benefit under a Defined Benefit Fund Using a Final Pay Formula

An employee with 20 years of service at a company is considering retirement at some time in the next 10 years. The employer uses a final pay benefit formula by which the employee receives an annual benefit payment of 2.5 percent of her average salary during her last five years of service times her total years employed. For retirement now, in 5 years, and in 10 years, the employee's (estimated) annual retirement benefit payment is:

	Average Salary during Last Five Years of Service	Retirement Benefit
Retire now	\$75,000	\$75,000 × .025 × 20 = \$37,500
Retire in 5 years	\$80,000*	\$80,000 × .025 × 25 = \$50,000
Retire in 10 years	\$85,000*	\$85,000 × .025 × 30 = \$63,750

*These are based on estimates of the employee's future salary.

fully funded

A pension fund that has sufficient funds available to meet all future payment obligations.

underfunded

A pension fund that does not have sufficient funds available to meet all future promised payments.

overfunded

A pension fund that has more than enough funds available to meet the required future payouts.

defined contribution benefit fund

Pension fund in which the employer agrees to make a specified contribution to the pension fund during the employee's working years.

Notice that of the three benefit formulas, the final pay formula usually produces the biggest retirement benefit increases as years of service increase. This formula generally provides better protection against erosion of pension income by inflation; benefit payments are based on the employee's career-end salary, which is generally the highest and often reflects current levels of price and wage inflation. This type of plan is also generally more costly to the employer.

Under defined benefit pension funds, the employer should set aside sufficient funds to ensure that it can meet the promised payments. When sufficient funds are available, the pension fund is said to be **fully funded.** Frequently, pension funds do not have sufficient funds available to meet all future promised payments, in which case the fund is said to be **underfunded.** While underfunding is not illegal, the pension fund is required by law to meet all of its payment obligations (see discussion below). Occasionally, pension funds have more than enough funds available to meet the required future payouts. In this case, the fund is said to be **overfunded.**

With a **defined contribution pension fund,** the employer (or plan sponsor) does not precommit to providing a specified retirement income. Rather, the employer contributes a specified amount to the pension fund during the employee's working years. The final retirement benefit is then based on total employer contributions, any additional employee contributions, and any gains or losses on the investments purchased by the fund with these contributions. For *fixed-income funds,* a minimum rate of return is often guaranteed, with the possibility of higher returns if fund assets earn above minimum rates of return. For *variable-income funds,* all investment profits and losses are passed through to fund participants. Thus, defined contribution funds provide benefits to employees in the form of higher potential returns than offered by defined benefit funds, but employees also must accept the increased risk of uncertain pension fund payouts.

Private Pension Funds

Private pension funds are created by private entities (e.g., manufacturing, mining, or transportation firms) and are administered by private corporations (financial institutions). Of the \$6,493.4 billion of financial assets in private pension funds in 2004, life insurance companies administered \$2,002.8 billion, mutual funds administered \$1,173.7 billion, and other financial institutions such as banks administered \$3,316.9 billion. Private fund contributions come from fund participants and/or their employers.

Defined contribution funds are increasingly dominating the private pension fund market. Indeed, many defined benefit funds are converting to defined contribution funds. Figure 18–1,

FIGURE 18–1 Pension Fund Assets, 1977–2004

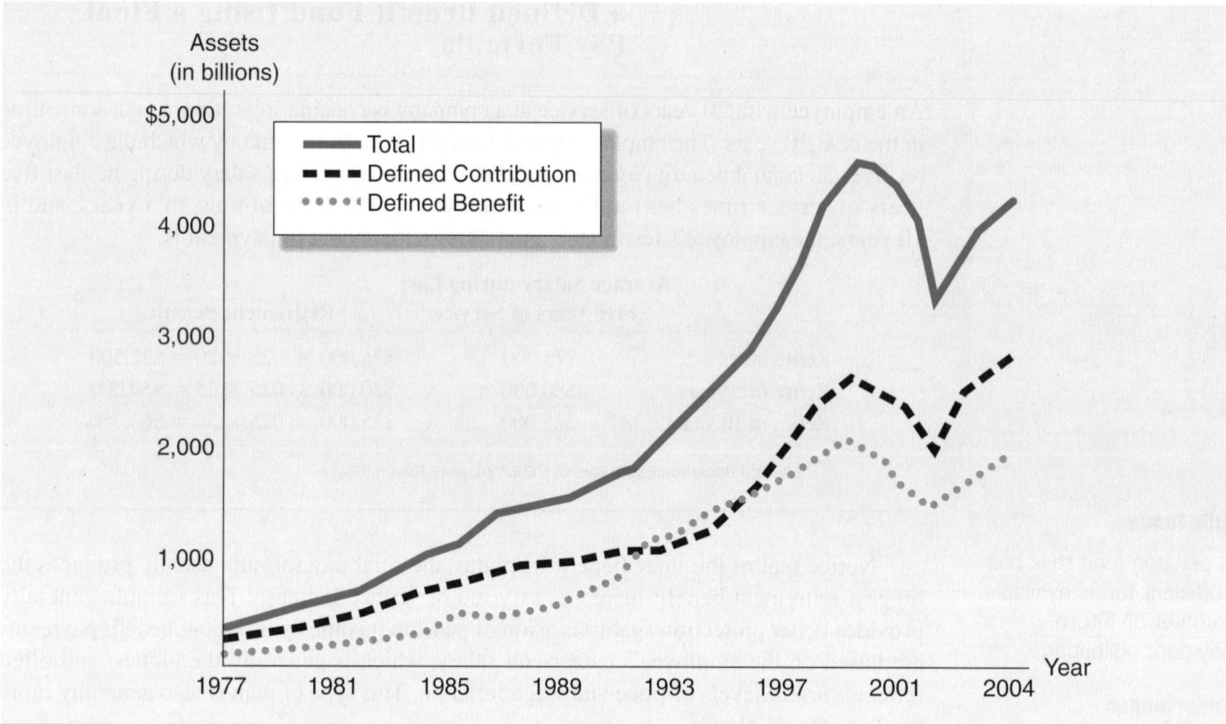

Source: Department of Labor, Pension and Welfare Benefits Administration, *Private Pension Plan Bulletin,* Winter 2001–2002, and Federal Reserve Board, *Flow of Fund Accounts,* various issues. **www.dol.gov/dol/pwba; www.federalreserve.gov**

shows private pension fund assets from 1997 to 2004. From Figure 18–1 note that as equity market values fell in 2001, pension fund asset values, particularly for defined contribution funds, fell as well. As the economy recovered and equity market values increased in 2003 and 2004, so did the value of pension fund assets. As we discuss below, this is because the main asset held by private pension funds is corporate equities. Note also that defined contribution funds are increasing in importance relative to defined benefit funds. Figure 18–2 shows the acquisition of new financial assets in defined benefit and defined contribution funds from 1990 through 2004. In 11 of the 15 years, defined benefit funds actually experienced a reduction in new assets held, while defined contribution funds saw a continuous increase in new asset investments. One reason for this shift is that defined contribution funds do not require the employer to guarantee retirement benefits, and thus corporate stockholders and managers do not need to monitor the pension fund's performance once the required contributions are made.

3

Types of Private Pension Funds. Private defined benefit and defined contribution pension funds come in various types. Employees may participate in 401(k) and 403(b) plans, individual retirement accounts (IRAs), and Keogh accounts.

401(k) and 403(b) plans

Employer-sponsored plans that supplement a firm's basic retirement plan.

401(k) and 403(b) Plans. **401(k) and 403(b) plans** are employer-sponsored plans that supplement a firm's basic retirement plan, allowing for both employee and employer contributions (e.g., Supplementary Retirement Accounts offered by TIAA-CREF). 401(k) plans are offered to employees of taxable firms, while 403(b) plans are for employees of certain tax exempt employers (e.g., hospitals and educational institutions). Contributions to these plans are taken on a pretax basis and thus reduce the employee's taxable salary. Both the contributions and earnings then grow tax deferred until they are withdrawn. Most of these plans are transferable to another 401(k) or 403(b) plan, or an IRA,

SEARCH THE SITE

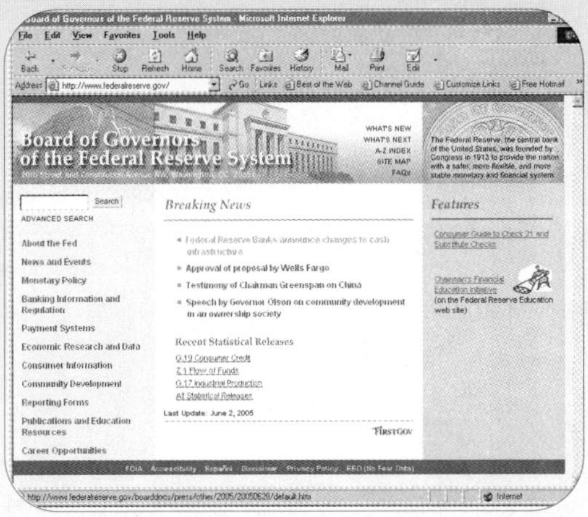

Go to the Federal Reserve Board's Web site at **www.federalreserve.gov.** Find the most recent information on the net flow of funds to defined benefit and defined contribution pension funds using the following steps.

Click on "Economic Research and Data."

Click on "Statistics: Releases and Historical Data."

Click on "Flow of Funds Accounts of the United States: Releases."

Click on the most recent date.

Click on "Supplementary Tables."

This will bring up the file onto your computer with the relevant data in Table F.119.b and F.119.c.

Questions

1. How has the flow of funds to defined benefit and defined contribution pension funds changed since 2004 reported in Figure 18–2?
2. Is the flow of funds into these two types of pension funds currently positive or negative? Why would these trends occur?

FIGURE 18–2 **Net Acquisition of Financial Assets, Defined Benefit and Defined Contribution Funds**
(in billions of dollars)

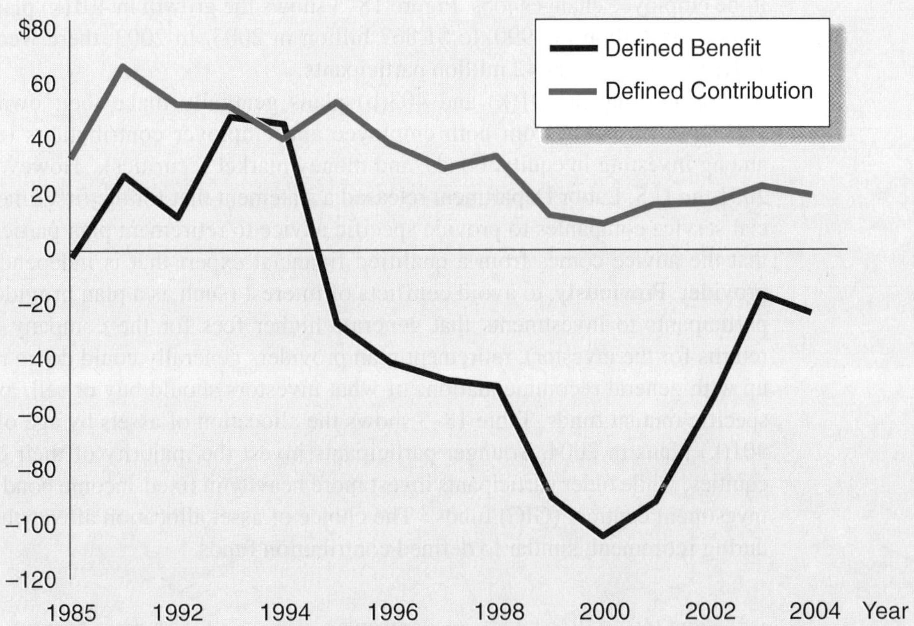

Source: Federal Reserve Board, "Flow of Fund Accounts," various issues. **www.federalreserve.gov**

FIGURE 18–3 Assets in 401(k) Plans

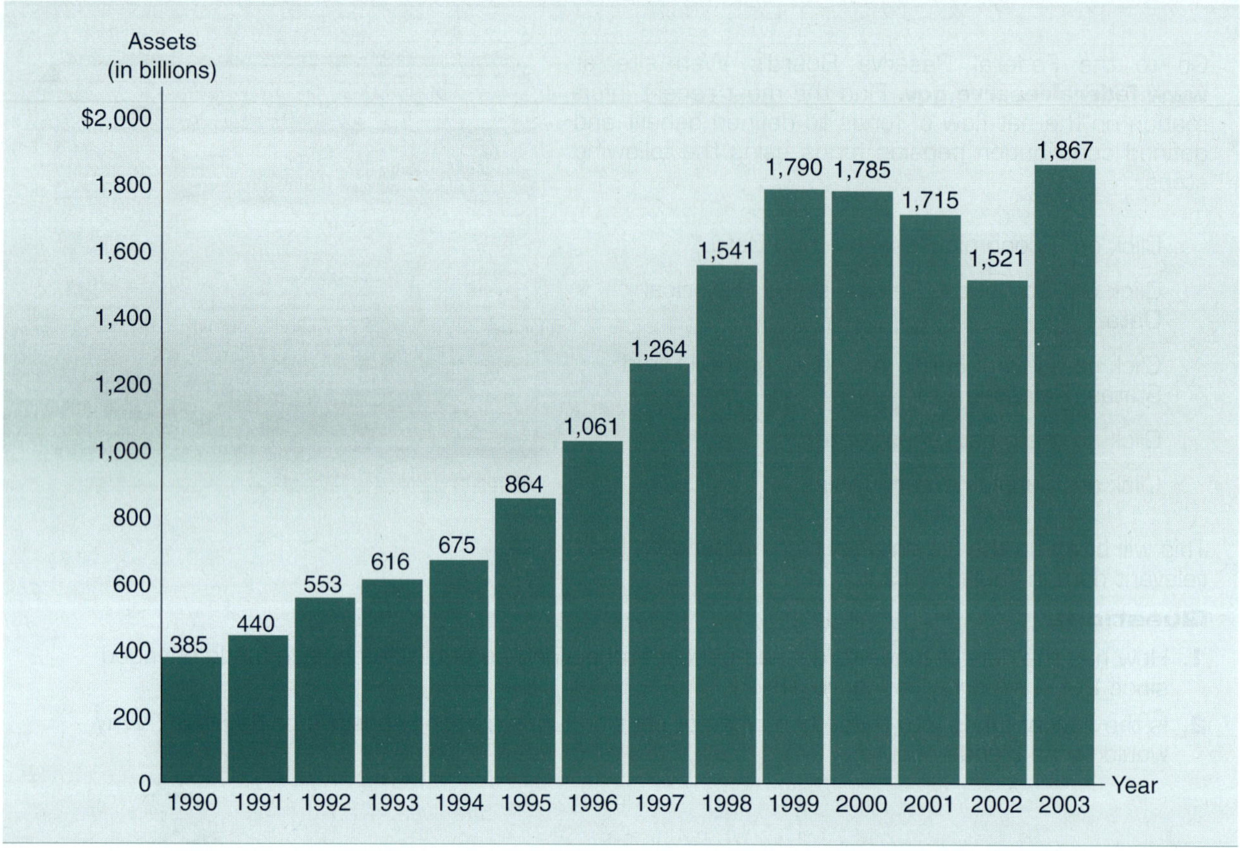

Source: Investment Company Institute, *Mutual Fund Fact Book,* various years. Reprinted by permission of the Investment Company Institute. **www.ici.org**

if the employee changes jobs. Figure 18–3 shows the growth in 401(k) plans in the 1990s: from $385 billion in 1990, to $1,867 billion in 2003. In 2003, there were over 300,000 401(k) plans and over 42 million participants.

Participants in 401(k) and 403(b) plans generally make their own choice of the allocation of assets from both employee and employer contributions (e.g., the choice among investing in equity, bonds, and money market securities).[1] However, in December 2001 the U.S. Labor Department released a statement that for the first time allowed financial service companies to provide specific advice to retirement plan participants provided that the advice comes from a qualified financial expert that is independent of the plan provider. Previously, to avoid conflicts of interest (such as a plan provider steering plan participants to investments that generate higher fees for the company and reduce net returns for the investor), retirement plan providers generally could do no more than come up with general recommendations of what investors should buy or sell, avoiding naming specific mutual funds. Table 18–3 shows the allocation of assets by age of participants in 401(k) plans in 2004. Younger participants invest the majority of their contributions in equities, while older participants invest more heavily in fixed-income bond and guaranteed investment contract (GIC) funds.[2] The choice of asset allocation affects the fund's payout during retirement, similar to defined contribution funds.

1. See "401(k) Investors to Get Advice Soon," *The Wall Street Journal,* June 10, 2002, p. C15.

2. A GIC is a long-term liability issued by insurance companies. A GIC guarantees not only a rate of interest over some given period but also the annuity rate on a beneficiary's contract (see Chapter 15).

TABLE 18–3 401(k) Asset Allocation by Age

Age Cohort	Equity Funds	Bond Funds	Company Stock	Money Funds	Balanced Funds	GICs	Other or Unknown
20s	51.3%	9.0%	14.4%	5.8%	11.8%	6.1%	1.6%
30s	54.2	8.1	16.0	4.2	9.8	5.9	1.9
40s	48.6	8.6	17.5	4.3	9.8	9.3	2.0
50s	42.0	10.2	16.9	4.8	9.6	14.3	2.1
60s	35.1	12.5	14.0	5.6	8.5	22.1	2.3
All	44.6	9.8	16.4	4.7	9.5	12.9	2.1

Source: Investment Company Institute and Employee Benefit Research Institute, *401(k) Plan Asset Allocation, Account Balances, and Loan Activity,* August 2004. Reprinted by permission of the Investment Company Institute. **www.ici.org**

EXAMPLE 18–4 Calculating the Return on a 401(k) Plan

An employee contributes 10 percent of his \$75,000 salary into the company's 401(k) plan. The company matches 40 percent of the first 6 percent of the employee's salary. The employee is in the 31 percent tax bracket and the 401(k) plan expects to yield an 8 percent rate of return. The employee's own contribution and his plan return for one year are calculated as follows.

1. Employee's gross contribution = \$75,000 × .10 = \$ 7,500
2. Tax savings = \$7,500 × .31 = \$ 2,325
3. Employee's net of tax contribution \$ 5,175
4. Employer's contribution = \$75,000 × .40 × .06 = \$ 1,800
5. Total 401(k) plan investment at year's start \$ 9,300
6. 1-year earnings = \$9,300 × .08 = \$ 744
7. Total 401(k) investment at year-end \$10,044 (= (1) + (4) + (6))
   Employee's 1-year return = (\$10,044 − \$5,175)/\$5,175 = 94.09%

Assuming the employee's salary, tax rate, and 401(k) yield remain constant over a 20-year career, when the employee retires, the 401(k) will be worth:

$$\$9{,}300(FVIFA_{8\%,\,20}) = \$425{,}586$$

The employee's net of tax contributions over the period is \$5,175 × 20 = \$103,500.

The allocation of a fund's assets across different types of securities can have a significant effect on the fund's returns and risks.

EXAMPLE 18–5 Impact of Asset Allocation on a 401(k) Plan Return

An employee contributes \$10,000 to a 401(k) plan each year, and the company matches 20 percent of this annually, or \$2,000. The employee can allocate the contributions among equities (earning 10 percent annually), bonds (earning 6 percent annually), and money market securities (earning 4 percent annually). The employee expects to work at the company 30 years. The employee can contribute annually along one of the three following patterns:[3]

3. In reality, the employee has a larger number of possible choices in terms of fund asset allocation.

	Option 1	Option 2	Option 3
Equities	60%	50%	40%
Bonds	40%	30%	50%
Money market securities	0%	20%	10%
	100%	100%	100%

The terminal value of the 401(k) plan, assuming all returns and contributions remain constant (at $12,000) over the 30 years,[4] will be:

Option 1:

$$12{,}000(.6)(FVIFA_{10\%,\,30}) + 12{,}000(.4)(FVIFA_{6\%,\,30}) = \$1{,}563{,}836$$

Option 2:

$$12{,}000(.5)(FVIFA_{10\%,\,30}) + 12{,}000(.3)(FVIFA_{6\%,\,30}) + 12{,}000(.2)(FVIFA_{4\%,\,30}) = \$1{,}406{,}177$$

Option 3:

$$12{,}000(.4)(FVIFA_{10\%,\,30}) + 12{,}000(.5)(FVIFA_{6\%,\,30}) + 12{,}000(.1)(FVIFA_{4\%,\,30}) = \$1{,}331{,}222$$

Notice that Option 1, which includes the largest investment in equities, produces the largest terminal value for the 401(k) plan, while Option 3, with the smallest investment in equities, produces the smallest terminal value. However, as discussed in Chapter 3, equity investments are riskier than bond and money market investments. Thus, the larger the portion of funds invested in equities, the higher the return risk of the pension plan—that is, the more uncertain the final (terminal) value of the plan. For example, suppose the economy slumped and equity investments only earned a 3 percent annual return over the 30 years the employee worked. In this case, the terminal value of the 401(k) plan would be:

Option 1:

$$12{,}000(.6)(FVIFA_{3\%,\,30}) + 12{,}000(.4)(FVIFA_{6\%,\,30}) = \$722{,}022$$

Option 2:

$$12{,}000(.5)(FVIFA_{3\%,\,30}) + 12{,}000(.3)(FVIFA_{6\%,\,30}) + 12{,}000(.2)(FVIFA_{4\%,\,30}) = \$704{,}666$$

Option 3:

$$12{,}000(.4)(FVIFA_{3\%,\,30}) + 12{,}000(.5)(FVIFA_{6\%,\,30}) + 12{,}000(.1)(FVIFA_{4\%,\,30}) = \$770{,}013$$

In this case, Option 3, which involves the smallest investment in risky equities, produces the largest terminal value for the 401(k) plan.

individual retirement accounts (IRAs)

Self-directed retirement accounts set up by employees who may also be covered by employer-sponsored pension plans.

Individual Retirement Accounts. **Individual retirement accounts (IRAs)** are self-directed retirement accounts set up by employees who may also be covered by employer-sponsored pension plans as well as self-employed individuals. Contributions to IRAs are made strictly by the employee. IRAs were first allowed in 1981 as a method of creating a tax-deferred retirement account to supplement an employer-sponsored plan. As of 2004, a maximum of $4,000 may be contributed to an IRA per year, and nonworking spouses may contribute an additional $4,000 as long as the couple's adjusted gross income is less than $150,000 and neither person is covered by an employer-sponsored

4. For simplicity, we assume that the employee's contribution remains constant over the 30 years. Realistically, as an employee's salary increases over his or her working years, contributions to the retirement funds increase as well.

TABLE 18–4 Differences between a Roth IRA and Traditional IRA

Terms	Roth IRA	Traditional IRA
Eligibility	Adjusted gross income (AGI) under: Single: $110,000. Married (filing jointly): $160,000.	Anyone not participating in a company-sponsored retirement plan or contributing to a company-sponsored retirement plan with AGI under: Single: $34,000 Married (filing jointly): $54,000
Annual contributions	Maximum $4,000 for single with AGI of $110,000 or less. Maximum $6,000 for married, filing jointly, with AGI of $160,000 or less.	The lesser of $4,000 or 100% of earned income.
Withdrawals and distributions	No mandatory withdrawal age. Cannot make withdrawals until age $59\frac{1}{2}$. No income tax on withdrawals after age $59\frac{1}{2}$. Take a lump sum or withdraw in installments.	Must begin to withdraw required minimum distribution (RMD) amount of your account no later than when you turn $70\frac{1}{2}$. Cannot make withdrawals until age $59\frac{1}{2}$. Take a lump sum or withdraw in installments.
Deductions	No deductions allowed.	Contribution is fully deductible under specified conditions.
Taxes and limitations	Cannot make withdrawals until age $59\frac{1}{2}$. No income tax on withdrawals after age $59\frac{1}{2}$.	Cannot make withdrawals until age $59\frac{1}{2}$. Must start withdrawing by age $70\frac{1}{2}$ to avoid penalties. Pay regular income tax on withdrawals of all earnings and pretax dollars you contributed.
Conversions	Conversion from traditional IRA allowed if AGI is $110,000 or less. Direct rollovers from qualified retirement plan to a Roth IRA prohibited.	Direct rollovers from qualified retirement plans to IRAs are tax free.

pension plan. This maximum contribution increases to $5,000 in 2008. After 2008, the limit will be indexed annually in $500 increments, adjusted for the cost of living.[5] IRAs may also be used by employees changing jobs. Any funds held by an employee in the old employer's pension fund may be invested in a tax-qualified IRA to maintain the tax deferred status. In 2004, IRA account assets were greater than $3.0 trillion.

In 1998, a new type of IRA, a Roth IRA, was established. Like a regular IRA, in 2005 Roth IRAs allow a maximum of $4,000 after-tax contribution per individual ($8,000 per household) and the cap will increase as that on regular IRAs increases. Unlike a regular IRA, contributions to a Roth IRA are taxed in the year of contribution, and withdrawals from the account are tax free (provided funds have been invested for at least five years and the account holder is at least $59\frac{1}{2}$ years old). Roth IRAs are available only to individuals with an adjusted gross income of less than $110,000 or households less than $160,000. Table 18–4 summarizes the main differences between a Roth IRA and a traditional IRA.

Most IRA contributions are invested in mutual funds purchased through a broker or a mutual fund company. Choices of funds include stocks, bonds, futures, and U.S. Treasuries. Depository institutions usually handle CDs for their IRA customers. Whether a Roth IRA is a better option than a traditional IRA depends on the individual's expectation of his or her future tax bracket. Traditionally, retirees moved into a lower tax bracket. However, recently

5. Individuals over 50 years of age can contribute $4,500 per year in 2005, $5,000 in 2006 and 2007, and $6,000 in 2008. If an employee's earnings exceed the limit, he or she can still invest in an IRA. However, the contribution is not tax deductible.

more retirees maintain high levels of income even in retirement. These individuals may be better off paying taxes on their IRA contributions during their working years (as under a Roth IRA). There are many Web sites available that calculate the advantage of a Roth IRA versus a traditional IRA for individuals (e.g., **www.quicken.com**).

Keogh Accounts. A Keogh account is a retirement account available to self-employed individuals. Contributions by the individual may be deposited in a tax-deferred account administered by a life insurance company, a bank, or other financial institution. As with 401(k) plans, the participant in a Keogh account is given some discretion as to how the funds are to be invested.

The two types of Keogh plans are profit-sharing and money-sharing plans. Money-sharing plans require a mandatory contribution (at a constant percentage of the employee's income) each year whether the individual has profits or not. Profit-sharing plan contributions can vary by year. The most attractive feature of a Keogh retirement plan is the high maximum contribution allowed. Money-sharing plan contributions can be as high as the lesser of $41,000 or 25 percent of the individual's self-employment income. Profit-sharing plan contributions can vary from 0 to 20 percent of the individual's income, up to $41,000.[6]

Public Pension Funds

1 Pension funds sponsored by the federal or state and local governments are referred to as public pension funds. In 2004, these funds managed assets of more than $3.1 trillion.

4 **State or Local Government Pension Funds.** Employees of state or local governments may contribute to pension funds sponsored by these employers. Most of these are funded on a "pay as you go" basis, meaning that contributions collected from current employees are the source of payments to the current retirees. As a result of the increasing number of retirees relative to workers, some of these pension funds (e.g., New York City) have experienced a situation in which contributions have not been high enough to cover the increases in required benefit payments (or the pension funds are what we called earlier "underfunded"). Some state and local governments have proposed tax increases to address this underfunding. Others have considered modifying the "pay as you go" method of funding contributions to operate their funds more like private pension funds. Without some modifications, many of the state and local government funds will increasingly be unable to maintain their promised payments to retirees, especially as the longevity of the population increases.

4 **Federal Government Pension Funds.** The federal government sponsors two types of pension funds. The *first type* are funds for federal government employees: civil service employees, military personnel, and railroad employees. Civil service funds cover all federal employees who are not members of the armed forces. This group is not covered by Social Security. Similar to private pension funds, the federal government is the main contributor to the fund, but participants may contribute as well. In addition to Social Security, career military personnel receive retirement benefits from a federal government–sponsored military pension fund. Contributions to the fund are made by the federal government, and participants are eligible for benefits after 20 years of military service. Employees of the nation's railroad system are eligible to participate in the federal railroad pension system. Originated in the 1930s, contributions are made by railroad employers, employees, and the federal government.

The *second type* of fund, and the largest federal government pension fund, is Social Security. Also known as the Old Age and Survivors Insurance Fund, Social Security provides retirement benefits to almost all employees and self-employed individuals in the

6. Keogh contribution caps are linked to the cost of living. In 2004, the cap was $41,000.

TABLE 18–5 Financial Assets Held by Private Pension Funds, 1975 and 2004*
(in billions)

	1975		2004	
Total financial assets	$244.3	100.00%	$4,444.4	100.00%
Checkable deposits and currency	4.4	1.77	10.4	0.23
Time and savings deposits	14.5	5.84	152.3	3.43
Money market mutual shares	0.0	0.00	85.1	1.91
Security RPs	4.3	1.73	33.3	0.75
Credit market instruments	71.3	28.70	712.0	16.02
Open market paper	9.1	3.66	37.9	0.85
Treasury securities	12.4	4.99	92.7	2.08
Agency securities	5.5	2.22	240.4	5.41
Corporate and foreign bonds	41.9	16.87	331.0	7.45
Mortgages	2.4	0.96	10.0	0.23
Corporate equities	108.0	43.48	1,690.0	38.03
Mutual fund shares	2.8	1.13	1,173.7	26.41
Miscellaneous assets	43.1	17.35	587.5	13.22

Source: Federal Reserve Board, "Flow of Fund Accounts," various issues. **www.federalreserve.gov**

DO YOU UNDERSTAND?

1. What the difference is between an insured and a noninsured pension fund?
2. What the differences are between a flat benefit and final pay benefit formula for a defined benefit pension fund?
3. What a defined contribution pension fund is?
4. What the major federally sponsored pension funds are?

United States. Social Security was established in 1935 with the objective of providing minimum retirement income to all retirees. Social Security is funded on a pay as you go basis; current employer and employee Social Security taxes are used to pay benefits to current retirees. Historically, Social Security tax contributions have generally exceeded disbursements to retirees. Any surpluses are held in a trust fund that can be used to cover required disbursements in years when contributions are insufficient to cover promised disbursements. Contributions, also known as the FICA tax, are a specified percentage of an individual's gross income—in 2005 it was 7.65 percent (for employees and 15.30 percent for self-employed individuals) of the first $87,900 earned—and are matched with equivalent employer contributions.[7]

As the percentage of the population that is retired has increased, and the percentage of the population that is working has decreased, Social Security tax revenue has dropped relative to benefits being paid out (i.e., Social Security is an underfunded pension fund). Based on current trends, Social Security payouts are expected to exceed revenues by 2018, and the Social Security system will be bankrupt (annual contributions and trust fund assets will be insufficient to cover required disbursements to retirees) by 2042. As a result, the federal government is currently considering new methods and ideas (discussed later) for fully funding the Social Security system.

FINANCIAL ASSET INVESTMENTS AND RECENT TRENDS

Employer and employee contributions made to pension funds are invested in financial assets. These investments are tracked by the Federal Reserve because of the increasing importance of pension funds as participants in national and international security markets.

Private Pension Funds

Financial assets (pension fund reserves) held by private pension funds in 1975 and 2004 are reported in Table 18–5. Financial assets held by pension funds totaled $244.3 billion in 1975 and $4,444.4 billion in 2004 (a 1,719 percent increase in 30 years). In 2004, some

7. Self-employed individuals contribute at twice the rate of employees, because employers pay a matched amount. The combined rate of the employee and employer is equal to the self-employment contribution rate.

FIGURE 18–4 **Financial Assets in Defined Benefit and Defined Contribution Pension Funds**

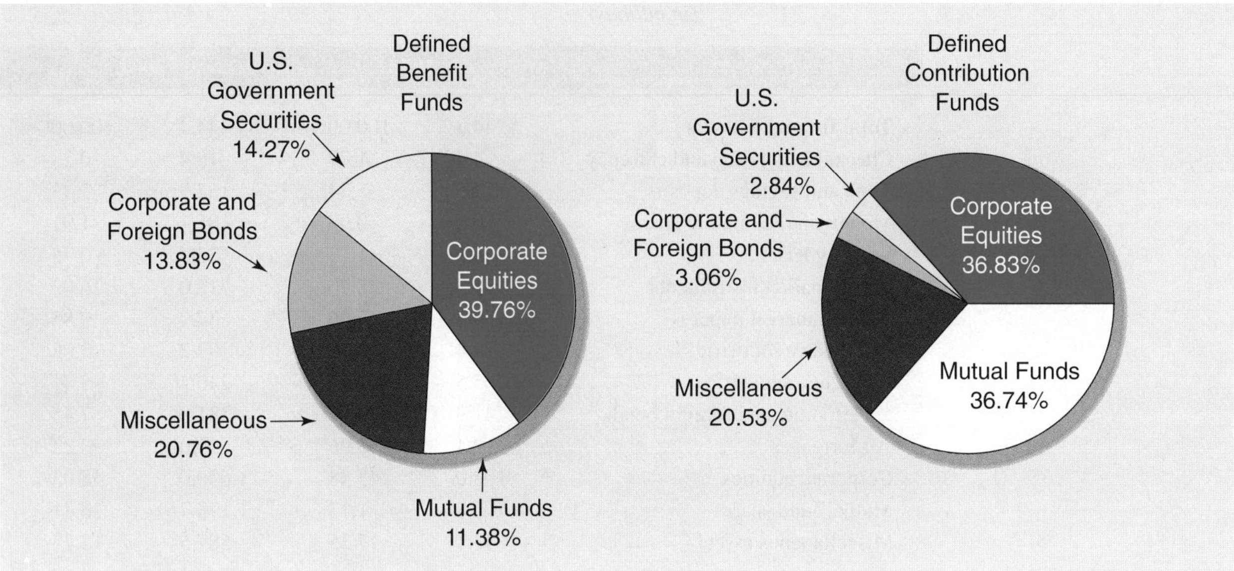

Source: Federal Reserve Board, "Flow of Fund Accounts," March 10, 2005. **www.federalreserve.gov**

64.54 percent of pension fund assets were in corporate equities or equity mutual funds shares. This compares to 44.61 percent in 1975. In fact, pension funds are the largest institutional investor in the U.S. stock market. Certainly the booming stock market was a major reason for the increased investment in equities by pension funds in the 1990s. For example, in 1999 corporate equities and equity mutual fund shares composed 64.71 percent of private pension fund assets. The fall in stock market values in 2001–2002 resulted in a drop in this percentage to 55.87 percent at the end of 2002.

Figure 18–4 shows differences between defined benefit and defined contribution fund investment portfolio allocations. In 2004, defined benefit funds had 28.10 percent of their funds invested in U.S. government securities and bonds compared to 5.90 percent for defined contributions funds. Also, defined benefit funds had 39.76 percent of their assets invested in corporate equities compared to 36.83 percent by defined contribution funds. In contrast, defined contribution funds had 36.74 percent of their funds invested in mutual fund shares compared to 11.38 percent for defined benefit funds.

Defined benefit pension funds offer employees a guaranteed payout, while defined contribution funds do not. The promise made of a guaranteed retirement payment is likely a major reason for the larger percentage of investments in fixed-income securities made by defined benefit funds. Defined contribution funds do not offer a guaranteed retirement payout—thus, defined contribution fund administrators are more likely to invest in risky equities and equity mutual fund shares. The introduction of equities into these funds helps to reduce the funding contributions required of the plan sponsor.

Public Pension Funds

Financial assets held by state and local government pension funds in 1975 and 2004 are reported in Table 18–6. Like private pension funds, state and local pension funds held most of their assets in corporate equities (58.13 percent in 2004). Second in importance were U.S. government securities and bonds (30.83 percent in 2004). In 1975, only 23.32 percent of pension fund assets were in equities and 66.03 percent were in U.S. government securities and bonds.

Social Security contributions are invested in relatively low-risk, low-return Treasury securities. This, along with the fact that the growth of the population is slowing, and the percentage of the population in retirement is increasing, has led to questions regarding the

TABLE 18–6 Financial Assets Held by State and Local Government Pension Funds, 1975 and 2004*
(in billions)

	1975		2004	
Total financial assets	$104.0	100.00%	$2,072.4	100.00%
Checkable deposits and currency	0.3	0.29	7.7	0.37
Time and savings deposits	1.2	1.15	0.9	0.04
Security RPs	0.0	0.00	38.8	1.87
Credit market instruments	78.2	75.05	708.2	34.17
Open market paper	0.0	0.00	47.3	2.28
Treasury securities	2.5	2.40	146.7	7.08
Agency securities	5.3	5.09	159.0	7.67
Municipal securities	1.9	1.82	0.9	0.04
Corporate and foreign bonds	61.0	58.54	333.2	16.08
Mortgages	7.5	7.20	21.2	1.02
Corporate equities	24.3	23.32	1,204.7	58.13
Miscellaneous assets	0.2	0.19	112.1	5.41

Source: Federal Reserve Board, "Flow of Fund Accounts," various issues. **www.federalreserve.gov**

www.ssa.gov

long-term viability of the Social Security fund (and the Social Security system in general). To bolster public confidence, the Social Security system was restructured in the mid-1990s by raising contributions and reducing retirees' benefits. For example, full retirement age was 65 for many years. However, beginning with individuals born in 1938 or later, that age will gradually increase until it reaches 67 for people born after 1959. Further, the wage contribution increases virtually each year (e.g., contributions as a percentage of an employee's income was 6.2 percent of the first $72,600 in 1998 and 7.65 percent of $87,900 in 2005).

DO YOU UNDERSTAND?

1. What the major financial assets held by private pension funds are?
2. What the major financial assets held by public pension funds are?

In the late 1990s, several proposals were also introduced as possible ways of bolstering the Social Security fund's resources. Many politicians proposed that all, or a portion, of any U.S. government budget surplus[8] be transferred to Social Security. In addition, investing in securities issued by private companies was proposed. For example, in December 2001 the Bush administration's Presidential Commission on Social Security Reform proposed changes to the Social Security system that included personal retirement accounts. In his 2005 State of the Union address President Bush again called for a review of the options to permanently strengthen Social Security. In his address, the president again stated that personal retirement accounts must be a part of a comprehensive solution for Social Security's problems. Personal retirement accounts would allow workers to take a small portion (up to 4 percent) of their payroll taxes and put it in a fund that invests in corporate stocks and bonds. The funds would be limited in terms of the allowable risk so that they meet minimum safety and soundness requirements. These accounts, similar to those available to all federal government workers (discussed above), would hold only broadly diversified low-cost mutual funds. Building value over time, these accounts would provide retirement benefits to supplement those paid from the traditional Social Security program. By building assets, this program would reduce the financial pressure on the Social Security system—along with the pressure to increase taxes or reduce benefits. Moreover, these personal accounts would give workers greater ownership and control over their retirement savings. Since the accounts would be the worker's legal property, if he or she dies before using up the account, it could be passed on to a spouse or children. For many workers, particularly younger ones, the current Social Security system is a very risky

8. That is, the difference between federal revenues and expenditures.

"investment," since without reform they are unlikely to recoup the contributions they pay into the program. For that reason, many young workers are attracted to the idea of personal accounts as part of the Social Security system program. To ease the transition to a personal retirement system, participation would be phased in according to the age of the worker. In the first year of implementation, workers between the ages of 40 and 54 would have the option of establishing personal retirement accounts. In the second year, workers between the ages of 26 and 54 would be given the option, and by the end of the third year, all workers older than 54 who want to participate in personal retirement accounts would be able to do so.

Such funding was touted as a permanent solution for keeping the Social Security fund solvent. Other proposals suggested federally sponsored alternatives to Social Security (e.g., bumping up IRA and 401(k) limits), hoping to take some of the pressure off having to maintain "minimum" levels of Social Security retirement income. Despite several proposals for reform, to date no change has been agreed upon by politicians, largely due to the war on terrorism and the economic downturn in the United States. These two events appear to have changed the government's budget strategy. Initiatives associated with these events have resulted in much larger expenditures and caused the nation to operate with a budget deficit (expenditures minus receipts (such as taxes)) since 2002. In fact, in 2004 the U.S. government had to spend an estimated $164 billion in Social Security money to fund government operations.

REGULATION

5

The major piece of regulation governing private pension funds is the Employee Retirement Income Security Act (ERISA) of 1974 (also called the Pension Reform Act). While ERISA does not mandate that employers establish pension funds for their employees, it does require them to meet certain standards if a fund is to be eligible for tax-deferred status. ERISA was passed when many workers, who had contributed to pension funds for years, were failing to receive their pension benefits in a timely fashion. ERISA charged the Department of Labor with the task of overseeing pension funds. The principal features of ERISA involve pension plan funding, vesting of benefits, fiduciary responsibility, pension fund transferability, and pension fund insurance.

www.dol.gov

Funding. Prior to ERISA, there were no statutory requirements forcing defined benefit fund administrators to adequately fund their pension funds. Specifically, funds sometimes operated such that employees' annual contributions to pension funds were insufficient to meet promised annual pension obligations. ERISA established guidelines for funding and set penalties for fund deficiencies. Contributions to pension funds must be sufficient to meet all annual costs and expenses and to fund any unfunded historical liabilities over a 30-year period. Further, any new underfunding arising from low investment returns or other losses had to be funded over a 15-year period. For some companies the required obligations resulting from ERISA were significant. For example, after ERISA was enacted, General Motors had to put $7.3 billion into its underfunded pension funds, while Ford Motor Company had to add $3.3 billion. Indeed, this provision of ERISA is one reason many companies switched from defined benefit to defined contribution retirement plans, as discussed earlier. Large declines in stock market values also led to huge increases in underfunded pension funds. Underfunded pension liabilities surged to $450 billion in 2004, the largest value ever (see Figure 18–5). Not all of this underfunding posed a major risk to participants and the pension insurance fund, however. Most companies that sponsored defined benefit plans were financially healthy and would be able to meet their pension obligations to their workers. However, the amount of underfunding in pension plans sponsored by financially weaker employers was also at an all-time high in 2004. Noninvestment grade companies were estimated to have sponsored pension plans with $96 billion in underfunding, almost three times as large as the amount recorded at the end of 2002.

FIGURE 18–5 Total Underfunding of Insured Single-Employer Plans
(in billions of dollars)

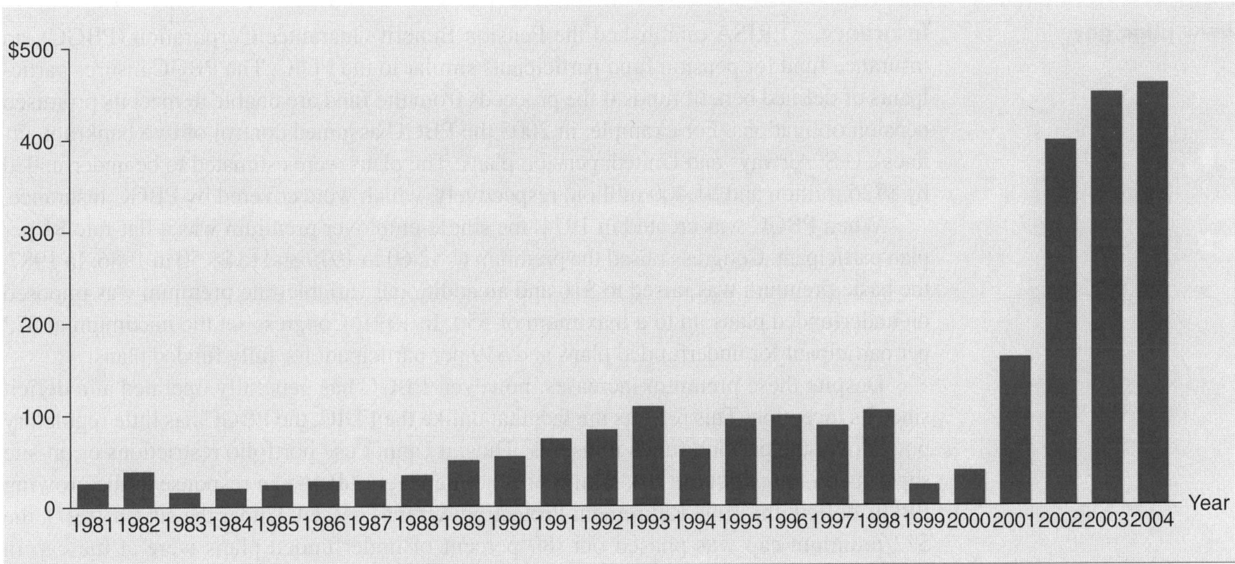

Source: PBGC Web site, March 2005. **www.pbgc.gov**

vested employee

An employee who is eligible to receive pension benefits because he or she has worked for a stated period of time.

Vesting of Benefits. Frequently, while employers start contributing to an employee's pension fund as soon as the employee is eligible to participate, benefits may not be paid to the employee until he or she has worked for the employer for a stated period of time (or until the employee is **vested**). For example, prior to ERISA, some plans required their employees to work 15 and even 25 years before they were eligible to receive pension benefits. ERISA requires that a plan must have a minimum vesting requirement, and sets a maximum vesting period of 10 years.

Fiduciary Responsibilities. A pension plan fiduciary is a trustee or investment adviser charged with management of the pension fund. ERISA set standards governing the pension fund management. Specifically, ERISA required that pension fund contributions be invested with the same diligence, skill, and care as a "prudent person" in like circumstances (the *prudent-person rule*). Fund assets are required to be managed with the sole objective of providing the promised benefits to participants. To ensure that a fund operates in this manner, ERISA requires pension funds to report on the current status (e.g., market value of assets held, income and expenses of the fund) of the pension fund.

Despite ERISA's fiduciary standards governing pension fund management, in 2002 Congress moved to implement changes in pension and corporate governance rules after the Enron failure caused thousands of workers to lose their retirement savings, which were heavily weighted in company stock. Enron matched its employees' 401(k) contributions with company stock, but barred workers from selling this stock until age 50. Further, when Enron's stock price was rising, employees included more shares of the company's stock in their pension funds. However, as the stock price plunged when Enron's accounting problems were revealed, management barred employees from selling their shares of Enron. It was estimated that Enron employees lost $3 billion in retirement funds after the energy trader filed for bankruptcy and its stock price fell to less than $1 dollar (from a high of over $80). Historically, labor laws limited the assets of traditional pension funds that may be held in employer stock or property to 10 percent. But Congress exempted 401(k) funds from that provision, hoping to encourage employers to offer retirement plans.

Transferability. ERISA allowed employees to transfer pension credits from one employer's fund to another's when switching jobs.

www.pbgc.gov

Insurance. ERISA established the Pension Benefit Guarantee Corporation (PBGC), an insurance fund for pension fund participants similar to the FDIC. The PBGC insures participants of defined benefit funds if the proceeds from the fund are unable to meet its promised pension obligations. For example, in 2005 the PBGC assumed control of two bankrupt airlines', U.S. Airways and United, pension plans. The plans were estimated to be underfunded by $726 million and $1,400 million, respectively, which were covered by PBGC insurance.

When PBGC was created in 1974, the single-employer premium was a flat-rate $1 per plan participant. Congress raised the premium to $2.60 in 1979 and to $8.50 in 1986. In 1987, the basic premium was raised to $16 and an additional variable-rate premium was imposed on underfunded plans up to a maximum of $50. In 1991, Congress set the maximum at $72 per participant for underfunded plans and $19 per participant for fully funded plans.

Despite these premium increases, however, PBGC has generally operated at a deficit since its inception. This reflects the fact that unlike the FDIC, the PBGC has little regulatory power over the pension funds it insures. Thus, it cannot use portfolio restrictions or on-site supervision to restrict the risk taking of fund managers.[9] Partly in response to the growing PBGC deficit, the 1994 Retirement Protection Act was passed. Under the act (in 1997), the $72 premium cap was phased out (80 percent of underfunded plans were at the cap in 1997). Thus, underfunded programs are now subjected to even higher premiums (some as high as several hundred dollars per participant).[10] Thus, like the FDIC in 1993 the PBGC has changed to a more overtly risk-based premium plan. As a result of these changes, in 2000 the PBGC's insurance fund operated at a record surplus of $9.7 billion.[11] However, bankrupties of several large companies (e.g, United Airlines, LTV Steel, Bethlehem Steel) in the early 2000s resulted in the agency posting a deficit of $23.3 billion and a call for additional reform at the beginning of 2005.

DO YOU UNDERSTAND?

1. Why ERISA was passed?
2. What the major features introduced by ERISA are?

A proposal put forth by the Bush administration in January 2005 called for an increase in annual premiums paid by companies to $30 per worker from $19 and the imposition of automatic increases in premiums each year, which would be tied to average wage increases of U.S. workers. Companies with troubled plans would pay higher premiums, based on the extent that their pension plans are underfunded. In addition, the administration proposed giving companies between 7 and 10 years (rather than the current 20 years) to make up shortfalls in their defined benefit pension plans. The proposal also called for companies to be required to tell investors and employees well before any pension plan becomes significantly underfunded, to give interested parties a chance to pressure companies to increase pension plan funding. As of 2005, the PBGC has not needed taxpayer funds to cover its obligations; however, some analysts have warned that a bailout funded by taxpayers is not out of the question if no reform of the insurance program is enacted.

GLOBAL ISSUES

Pension systems around the world take many forms. For example, even within Europe there is wide variation in pension systems. The United Kingdom, the Netherlands, Ireland, Denmark, and Switzerland all have a tradition of state- (or public-) funded pension schemes (where the pension plans have sufficient funds to cover required payouts for various numbers of years), while Spain, Portugal, and Italy have less developed pension systems, and France uses a pay-as-you-go pension system. The systems of other countries vary greatly in their details. However, the extent to which the contributions a person makes to the system during his or her working years are linked to the benefits that person receives in retirement is one

9. To the extent that regulation restricts the asset and liability activities of a firm or FI, these restrictions are similar to imposing an "implicit" premium or tax on the activities of the firm.

10. Underfunded plans pay a surcharge of $9 per participant per $1,000 of underfunding.

11. See *Pension Insurance Data Book,* Pension Benefit Guarantee Corp., Spring 2002.

6

characteristic that distinguishes systems. For example, France and Germany are among the countries where the relationship between the benefits people receive in retirement and the taxes they pay during their working years is relatively weak. Such countries have typically offered generous benefits to those who take early retirement. As a result, many of these countries have begun to experience problems in the financing of public pensions and they have had to undertake reforms that strengthen the link between contributions and benefits. At the other extreme are countries such as Sweden, Italy, the United Kingdom, and Chile, which impose a tight relationship between a person's payments into the system and the benefits received during retirement. Some of these countries have strengthened this link by shifting some of the financing of state pensions into private sources. Although these countries are relatively well prepared to handle the problem of an aging population, several are considering reforming their systems.

Reforms of pension systems in other countries have included benefit reductions, measures to encourage later retirement, and expansions of private funding for government pensions. For example, in many countries reforms include raising the age at which a person is eligible for pension benefits. This type of reform recognizes increased life expectancy. Finland has already taken the step of indexing its full pension retirement age to life expectancy, and several countries have taken steps to encourage people to remain in the labor force as they get older. Some have done so by strengthening the link between contributions and benefits. For example, Sweden has introduced notional accounts by which participants can see their potential pension benefits rise as they work longer and contribute more to the system. Other countries have taken steps to reduce payments to persons who retire before the established retirement age. Many countries have traditionally offered generous benefits to people who choose to retire early, although early retirees typically receive a smaller annual pension than persons who wait until they are older to retire. However, the difference in retirement payments in many countries has not been sufficient to discourage large numbers of people from retiring early.

The British pension system is the most reliant on private finance of any high-income country. The relatively heavy use of private pension plans within the state pension system means that state pension spending in Britain accounted for only 5.5 percent of GDP in the early 2000s. In contrast, across other European countries, the average expenditure on state pensions was over 10 percent of GDP during this period and is expected to rise to nearly 14 percent by 2040. By comparison, in the U.S. expenditure on Social Security benefits was 4.3 percent of GDP in the early 2000s. Chile has moved quickly into a primarily private state pension system in recent years. Thanks to the rapid growth of Chile's economy during the 1980s and 1990s, individuals have seen average annual returns of more than 10 percent per year on their private retirement savings accounts under the Chilean system. The perceived success of the Chilean reforms has led other countries to make similar reforms to their own state pension systems. As of 2004, eleven other Latin American countries had adopted some version of the Chilean model.

DO YOU UNDERSTAND?

1. How retirement systems in other countries vary?
2. The pension reforms undertaken in other countries?

SUMMARY

This chapter provided an overview of the pension fund industry. Pension funds provide a way of accumulating retirement funds similar to life insurance contracts and mutual funds. Pension funds, however, have a tax advantage in that an employee's contributions to pension funds are exempt from current taxation. The chapter reviewed the types of funds offered by private companies (financial institutions) and by federal and state or local governments. Given the problems with the funding of public pension funds and the phenomenal increase in stock market values, growth in private pension funds has been larger than any other type of financial institution in the 1990s. We looked at the distribution of asset investments for both private and public pension funds and highlighted their differences. The chapter also reviewed the major piece of regulation governing the industry, ERISA, and the role played by the Pension Benefit Guarantee Corporation (PBGC).

www.mhhe.com/sc3e

SEARCH THE SITE

Go to the Federal Reserve Board's Web site at **www.federalreserve.gov.** Find the most recent pension reserve levels for the federal government, life insurance companies, private pension funds, and state and local government retirement funds using the following steps.

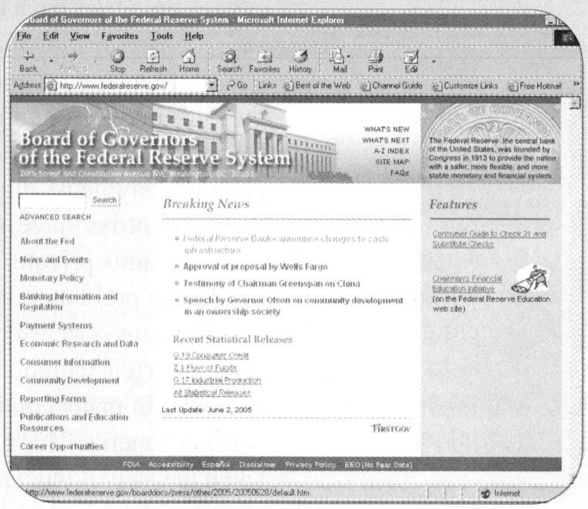

Click on "Economic Research and Data."

Click on "Statistics: Releases and Historical Data."

Click on "Flow of Funds Accounts of the United States: Releases."

Click on the most recent date.

Click on "Level Tables."

This will bring up the file onto your computer with the relevant data in Table L.225.

Questions

1. How have these values changed since 2004 reported in Table 18–1?
2. Which of these areas has seen the largest and smallest increase in pension reserve levels since 2004?

QUESTIONS

1. Describe the difference between a private pension fund and a public pension fund.
2. Describe the difference between an insured pension fund and a noninsured pension fund. What type of financial institutions would administer each of these?
3. Describe the difference between a defined benefit pension fund and a defined contribution pension fund.
4. What are the three types of formulas used to determine pension benefits for defined benefit pension funds? Describe each.
5. Your employer uses a flat benefit formula to determine retirement payments to its employees. The fund pays an annual benefit of \$2,500 per year of service. Calculate your annual benefit payments for 25, 28, and 30 years of service.
6. An employer uses a career average formula to determine retirement payments to its employees. The annual retirement payout is 5 percent of the employees' career average salary times the number of years of service. Calculate the annual benefit payment under the following scenarios.

Years Worked	Career Average Salary
30	\$60,000
33	62,500
35	64,000

7. **eXcel** **Using a Spreadsheet to Calculate Pension Benefit Payments:** Your employer uses a career average formula to determine retirement payments to its employees. You have 20 years of service at the company and are considering retirement some time in the next 10 years. Your average salary over the 20 years has been \$50,000 and you expect this to increase at a rate of 1 percent per year. Your employer uses a career average formula by which you receive an annual benefit payment of 5 percent of your career average salary times the number of years of service. Calculate the annual benefit if you retire now, in 2 years, 5 years, 8 years, and 10 years.

Retire	Average Salary	=>	The Payment Will Be
Now	\$50,000		50,000 × .05 × 20 = \$50,000
In 2 years	51,005		51,005 × .05 × 22 = \$56,105
In 5 years	52,551		52,551 × .05 × 25 = \$65,688
In 8 years	54,143		54,143 × .05 × 28 = \$78,800
In 10 years	55,231		55,231 × .05 × 30 = \$82,847

8. **eXcel** **Using a Spreadsheet to Calculate Pension Benefit Payments:** Your employer uses a final pay formula to determine retirement payments to its employees. You have 20 years of service at the company and are considering retirement some time in the next

www.mhhe.com/sc3e

10 years. Your employer uses a final pay formula by which you receive an annual benefit payment of 4 percent of your average salary over the last three years of service times the number of years employed. Calculate the annual benefit if you retire now, in 2 years, 5 years, 8 years, and 10 years using the estimated annual salary during the last three years of service listed below.

Retire	Average Salary	=>	The Payment Will Be
Now	$50,000		50,000 × .04 × 20 = $40,000
In 2 years	51,005		51,005 × .04 × 22 = $44,884
In 5 years	52,551		52,551 × .04 × 25 = $52,551
In 8 years	54,143		54,143 × .04 × 28 = $60,640
In 10 years	55,231		55,231 × .04 × 30 = $66,277

9. An employer uses a final pay formula to determine retirement payouts to its employees. The annual payout is 3 percent of the average salary over the employees' last three years of service times the total years employed. Calculate the annual benefit under the following scenarios.

Years Worked	Average Salary during Last Three Years of Service
17	$40,000
20	$47,000
22	$50,000

10. What have the trends been for assets invested in defined benefit versus defined contribution pension funds in the last two decades?

11. Describe the trend in assets invested in 401(k) plans in the 1990s and early 2000s.

12. Your company sponsors a 401(k) plan into which you deposit 12 percent of your $60,000 annual income. Your company matches 50 percent of the first 5 percent of your earnings. You expect the fund to yield 10 percent next year. If you are currently in the 31 percent tax bracket, what is your annual investment in the 401(k) plan and your one-year return?

13. Using the information in question 12, and assuming all variables remain constant over the next 25 years, what will your 401(k) fund value be in 25 years (when you expect to retire)?

14. What is the difference between an IRA and a Keogh account?

15. Describe the "pay as you go" funding method that is used by many federal and state or local government pension funds. What is the problem with this method that may damage the long-term viability of such funds?

16. Describe the different pension funds sponsored by the federal government.

17. What are the major assets held by private pension funds in 1975 versus 2004? Explain the differences.

18. How do the financial asset holdings of defined benefit pension funds differ from those of defined contribution pension funds? Explain the differences.

19. What was the motivation for the passage of ERISA?

20. Describe the major features of ERISA.

www.mhhe.com/sc3e

part five

Risk Management *in* Financial Institutions

Part Five concludes the text by examining risks facing a modern FI and FI managers, and the various strategies for managing these risks. In Chapter 19, we preview the risk measurement and management chapters that follow with an overview of the risks facing a modern FI. In Chapter 20, we look at credit risk on individual loans and bonds and how these risks adversely affect an FI's profit and value. Chapter 21 covers liquidity risk in FIs. In Chapter 22, we investigate the effects of interest rate risk and the mismatching of asset and liability maturities on FI risk exposure. At the core of FI risk insulation is the size and adequacy of the FI owners' capital stake, which is also a focus of Chapter 22. The management of risk off the balance sheet is examined in Chapter 23, which highlights various new markets and instruments that have emerged to allow FIs to better manage risk. Finally, Chapter 24 explores ways of removing credit risk from the loan portfolio through asset sales and securitization.

OUTLINE

19 Types *of* Risks Incurred *by* Financial Institutions

OUTLINE

Chapter NAVIGATOR

1. What are the major risks faced by financial institutions?
2. How is insolvency risk a consequence of the other types of risk?
3. How are the various risks faced by financial institutions related?

1 WHY FINANCIAL INSTITUTIONS NEED TO MANAGE RISK: CHAPTER OVERVIEW

As has been mentioned in previous chapters, a major objective of FI management is to increase the FI's returns for its owners. This often comes, however, at the cost of increased risk. As discussed in Chapter 12, regulators' evaluation of the overall safety and soundness of a depository institution (DI) is summarized in the CAMELS rating assigned to the DI.[1] This chapter overviews the various risks facing FIs: credit risk, liquidity risk, interest rate risk, market risk, off-balance-sheet risk, foreign exchange risk, country or sovereign risk, technology risk, operational risk, and insolvency risk. Table 19–1 presents a brief definition of each of these risks. As will become clear, the effective management of these risks is central to an FI's performance. Indeed, it can be argued that the main business of FIs is to manage these risks.

While over the last decade U.S. financial institution profitability has been robust, the risks of financial intermediation have increased as the U.S. and overseas economies have become more integrated. For example, weak economic conditions outside the United States—especially in Asia and South America—have presented great risks for those FIs that operate in and lend to foreign markets and customers. Even those FIs that do not have foreign customers can be exposed to foreign exchange and sovereign risk if their domestic customers have business dealings with foreign countries. As a result, FI managers must devote significant time to understanding and managing the various risks to which their FIs are exposed. By the end of this chapter, you will have a basic understanding of the variety and

1. Where C = capital adequacy, A = asset quality, M = management, E = earnings, L = liquidity, and S = sensitivity to market risk, and ratings range from 1 (Best) to 5 (Worst).

TABLE 19–1 Risks Faced by Financial Institutions

1. **Credit Risk**—the risk that promised cash flows from loans and securities held by FIs may not be paid in full.
2. **Liquidity Risk**—the risk that a sudden and unexpected increase in liability withdrawals may require an FI to liquidate assets in a very short period of time and at low prices.
3. **Interest Rate Risk**—the risk incurred by an FI when the maturities of its assets and liabilities are mismatched and interest rates are volatile.
4. **Market Risk**—the risk incurred in trading assets and liabilities due to changes in interest rates, exchange rates, and other asset prices.
5. **Off-Balance-Sheet Risk**—the risk incurred by an FI as the result of its activities related to contingent assets and liabilities.
6. **Foreign Exchange Risk**—the risk that exchange rate changes can affect the value of an FI's assets and liabilities denominated in foreign currencies.
7. **Country or Sovereign Risk**—the risk that repayments by foreign borrowers may be interrupted because of interference from foreign governments or other political entities.
8. **Technology Risk**—the risk incurred by an FI when its technological investments do not produce anticipated cost savings.
9. **Operational Risk**—the risk that existing technology or support systems may malfunction, that fraud may occur that impacts the FI's activities, and/or external shocks such as hurricanes and floods occur.
10. **Insolvency Risk**—the risk that an FI may not have enough capital to offset a sudden decline in the value of its assets relative to its liabilities.

complexity of the risks facing managers of modern FIs. In the remaining chapters of the text, we look at the management of the most important of these risks in more detail

CREDIT RISK

credit risk

The risk that the promised cash flows from loans and securities held by FIs may not be paid in full.

Credit risk arises because of the possibility that promised cash flows on financial claims held by FIs, such as loans and bonds, will not be paid in full. Virtually all types of FIs face this risk. However, in general, FIs that make loans or buy bonds with long maturities are more exposed than are FIs that make loans or buy bonds with short maturities. This means, for example, that banks, thrifts, and life insurance companies are more exposed to credit risk than are money market mutual funds and property–casualty insurance companies, since banks, thrifts, and life insurance companies tend to hold longer maturity assets in their portfolios than mutual funds and property–casualty insurance companies. If the principal on all financial claims held by FIs were paid in full on maturity and interest payments were made on their promised payment dates, FIs would always receive back the original principal lent plus an interest return—that is, they would face no credit risk. Should a borrower default, however, both the principal loaned and the interest payments expected to be received are at risk.

Many financial claims issued by individuals or corporations and held by FIs promise a limited or fixed upside return (principal and interest payments to the lender) with a high probability, but they also may result in a large downside risk (loss of loan principal and promised interest) with a much smaller probability. Some examples of financial claims issued with these return-risk trade-offs are fixed-coupon bonds issued by corporations and bank loans. In both cases, an FI holding these claims as assets earns the coupon on the bond or the interest promised on the loan if no borrower default occurs. In the event of default, however, the FI earns zero interest on the asset and may well lose all or part of the principal lent, depending on its ability to lay claim to some of the borrower's assets through legal bankruptcy and insolvency proceedings. Accordingly, a key role of FIs involves screening and monitoring loan applicants to ensure that FI managers fund the most creditworthy loans (see Chapter 20).

EXAMPLE 19-1 Impact of Credit Risk on an FI's Equity Value

Consider an FI with the following balance sheet:

Cash	$20m.	Deposits	$90m.
Gross loans	80m.	Equity (net worth)	10m.
	$100m.		$100m.

Suppose that the managers of the FI recognize that $5 million of its $80 million in loans is unlikely to be repaid due to an increase in credit repayment difficulties of its borrowers. Eventually, the FI's managers must respond by charging off or writing down the value of these loans on the FI's balance sheet. This means that the value of loans falls from $80 million to $75 million, an economic loss that must be charged off against the stockholder's equity capital or net worth (i.e., equity capital falls from $10 million to $5 million). Thus, both sides of the balance sheet shrink by the amount of the loss:

Cash		$20m.	Deposits	$90m.
Gross loans	80m.		Equity after charge-off	5m.
Less: Loan loss	−5m.			
Loans after charge-off		75m.		
		$95m.		$95m.

The effects of credit risk are evident in Figures 19–1 and 19–2, which show commercial bank charge-off (or write-off) rates (loans charged off as a percentage of total loans) for various types of loans. Notice, in particular, the high rate of charge-offs experienced on credit

FIGURE 19–1 **Charge-Off Rates for Commercial Bank Lending Activities, 1984–2004**

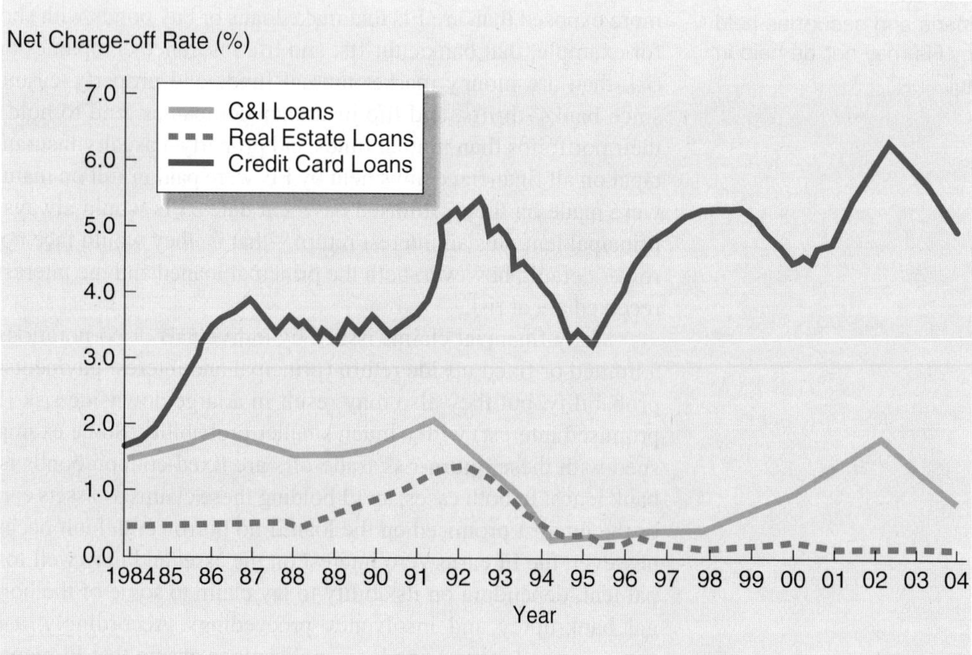

Source: FDIC, *Quarterly Banking Profile*, various issues. **www.fdic.gov**

FIGURE 19–2 **Credit Card Loss Rates and Personal Bankruptcy Filings, 1984–2004**

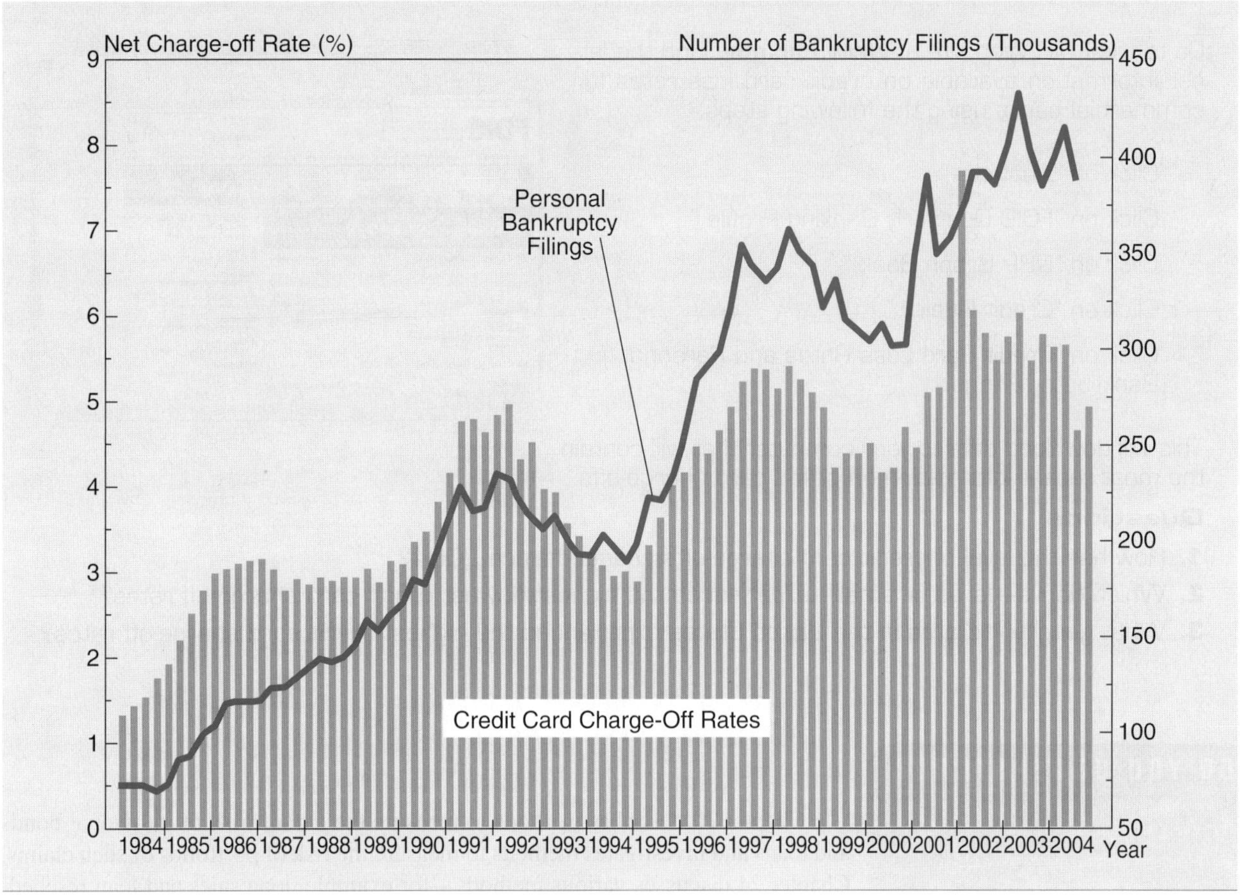

Source: FDIC, *Quarterly Banking Profile,* Fourth Quarter 2004. **www.fdic.gov**

card loans throughout this period. Indeed, credit card charge-offs by commercial banks increased persistently from the mid-1980s until late 1991 and again from 1995 through early 1997. While high relative to real estate and commercial and industrial (C&I) loan charge-off rates, by February 1997, credit card charge-offs leveled off, and they even declined in 1998 and 1999. With the downturn in the U.S. economy and an impending change in bankruptcy laws making it more difficult to declare bankruptcy, credit card charge-offs rose rapidly in 2001 and remained high through 2004. Despite these losses, credit card loans (including unused balances) extended by commercial banks continued to grow, from \$1.856 trillion in March 1997 to \$3.897 trillion in December 2004.

firm-specific credit risk

The risk of default for the borrowing firm associated with the specific types of project risk taken by that firm.

systematic credit risk

The risk of default associated with general economywide or macroconditions affecting all borrowers.

The potential loss an FI can experience from lending suggests that FIs need to collect information about borrowers whose assets are in their portfolios and to monitor those borrowers over time. Thus, managerial (monitoring) efficiency and credit risk management strategies directly affect the returns and risks of the loan portfolio. Moreover, one of the advantages that FIs have over individual investors is their ability to diversify credit risk exposures by exploiting the law of large numbers in their asset investment portfolios. Diversification across assets, such as loans exposed to credit risk, reduces the overall credit risk in the asset portfolio and thus increases the probability of partial or full repayment of principal and/or interest. In particular, diversification reduces individual **firm-specific credit risks,** such as the risk specific to holding the bonds or loans of Enron or WorldCom, while still leaving the FI exposed to **systematic credit risk,** such as factors that simultaneously increase the default risk of all firms in the economy (e.g., an economic recession).

SEARCH THE SITE

Go to the FDIC Web site at **www.fdic.gov.** Find the latest information available on credit card loss rates for commercial banks using the following steps.

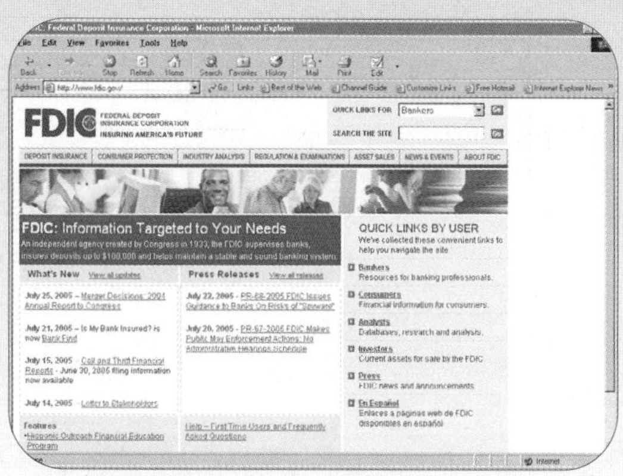

Click on "Analysts."

Click on "FDIC Quarterly Banking Profile."

Click on "QBP Graph Book."

Click on "Credit Quality."

Click on "Credit Card Loss Rates and Personal Bankruptcy Filings."

This will download data to your computer that will contain the most recent information on credit card charge-offs.

Questions

1. How has the level of credit card charge-offs changed since 2004?
2. Which banks—large or small—experienced the highest/lowest credit card charge-off rates?
3. What geographic area in the United States experienced the highest credit card charge-off rates?

DO YOU UNDERSTAND?

1. Why credit risk exists for FIs?
2. How diversification affects an FI's credit risk exposure?

Chapter 20 describes methods to measure the default risk of individual bonds and loans and investigates methods to measure the risk of portfolios of such claims. Chapter 24 discusses various methods—for example, loan sales and loan reschedulings—to manage and control credit risk exposures better.

LIQUIDITY RISK

liquidity risk

The risk that a sudden and unexpected increase in liability withdrawals may require an FI to liquidate assets in a very short period of time and at low prices.

Liquidity risk arises when an FI's liability holders, such as depositors or insurance policyholders, demand immediate cash for the financial claims they hold with an FI or when holders of off-balance-sheet loan commitments (or credit lines) suddenly exercise their right to borrow (draw down their loan commitments). In recent years, the Federal Reserve has expressed concerns about both liability side and asset side liquidity risk.[2] For example, when liability holders demand cash immediately—that is, "put" their financial claim back to the FI—the FI must either borrow additional funds or sell assets to meet the demand for the withdrawal of funds. The most liquid asset of all is cash, which FIs can use directly to meet liability holders' demands to withdraw funds. Although FIs limit their cash asset holdings because cash earns no interest, low cash holdings are generally not a problem. Day-to-day withdrawals by liability holders are generally predictable, and large FIs can normally expect to borrow additional funds to meet any sudden shortfalls of cash in the money and financial markets (see Chapter 22).

At times, however, FIs face a liquidity crisis. For example, at the end of 1999 the Fed was concerned that fear of year 2000 computer problems would result in unusually large deposit withdrawals from depository institutions, which could create liquidity problems for the global financial payments system if not addressed. As a preventative step, by

2. See "Regulators Press for Safeguards," and "Years of Living Dangerously Set to Haunt Banks," *Financial Times*, June 4, 2001.

September 1999 the Fed had ordered the printing of almost $700 billion dollars that would be made available to depository institutions to prevent such a problem from arising. In addition to an unusual or unexpected need for cash, a lack of confidence by liability holders in an FI may lead liability holders to demand larger withdrawals than usual. When all, or many, FIs face abnormally large cash demands, the cost of purchased or borrowed funds rises and the supply of such funds becomes restricted. As a consequence, FIs may have to sell some of their less liquid assets to meet the withdrawal demands of liability holders. This results in a more serious liquidity risk, especially as some assets with "thin" markets generate lower prices when the sale is immediate than when an FI has more time to negotiate the sale of an asset. As a result, the liquidation of some assets at low or "fire-sale" prices (the price the FI receives if the assets must be liquidated immediately at less than their fair market value) could threaten an FI's profitability and solvency. Good examples of such illiquid assets are bank loans to small firms. Serious liquidity problems may eventually result in a "run" in which all liability claimholders seek to withdraw their funds simultaneously from an FI because they fear that it will be unable to meet their demands for cash in the near future. This turns the FI's liquidity problem into a solvency problem and can cause it to fail.[3]

EXAMPLE 19-2 Impact of Liquidity Risk on an FI's Equity Value

Consider the simple FI balance sheet in Table 19–2. Before deposit withdrawals, the FI has $10 million in cash assets and $90 million in nonliquid assets (such as small business loans). These assets were funded with $90 million in deposits and $10 million in owner's equity. Suppose that depositors unexpectedly withdraw $15 million in deposits (perhaps due to the release of negative news about the profits of the FI) and the FI receives no new deposits to replace them. To meet these deposit withdrawals, the FI first uses the $10 million it has in cash assets and then seeks to sell some of its nonliquid assets to raise an additional $5 million in cash. Assume that the FI cannot borrow any more funds in the short-term money markets (see Chapter 5), and because it cannot wait to get better prices for its assets in the future (as it needs the cash now to meet immediate depositor withdrawals), the FI has to sell any nonliquid assets at 50 cents on the dollar. Thus, to cover the remaining $5 million in deposit withdrawals, the FI must sell $10 million in nonliquid assets, incurring a loss of $5 million from the face value of those assets. The FI must then write off any such losses against its capital or equity funds. Since its capital was only $10 million before the deposit withdrawal, the loss on the fire-sale of assets of $5 million leaves the FI with $5 million.

DO YOU UNDERSTAND?

1. Why an FI might face a sudden liquidity crisis?
2. What circumstances might lead an FI to liquidate assets at fire-sale prices?

Chapter 21 examines the nature of normal, abnormal, and run-type liquidity risks and their impact on banks, thrifts, insurance companies, and other FIs in more detail. In addition, it looks at ways in which an FI can measure liquidity risk and better manage liquidity and liability risk exposures. Finally, Chapter 13 discussed the roles of deposit insurance and other liability guarantees in deterring deposit or other liability runs in depository institutions.

3. The situation of several Ohio savings institutions in 1985 is an extreme example of liquidity risk. A group of 70 Ohio savings institutions were insured by a private fund, the Ohio Deposit Guarantee Fund (ODGF). One of these savings banks, Home State Savings Bank (HSSB), had invested heavily in a Florida-based government securities dealer, EMS Government Securities, Inc., which eventually defaulted on its debts to HSSB (note the interaction between credit risk and liquidity risk). This in turn made it difficult for HSSB to meet deposit withdrawals of its customers. HSSB's losses from the ESM default were, in fact, so large that the ODGF could not cover them. Not only was HSSB unable to cover the deposit withdrawals, but also other Ohio savings institutions insured by ODGF were inundated with deposit withdrawals to the extent that they could not cover them as well. As a result, ODGF-insured institutions were temporarily closed and the Ohio state legislature had to step in to cover depositors' claims.

TABLE 19–2 Adjusting to a Deposit Withdrawal Using Asset Sales *(in millions)*

Before the Withdrawal				After the Withdrawal			
Assets		Liabilities/Equity		Assets		Liabilities/Equity	
Cash assets	$ 10	Deposits	$ 90	Cash assets	$ 0	Deposits	$75
Nonliquid assets	90	Equity	10	Nonliquid assets	80	Equity	5
	$100		$100		$80		$80

INTEREST RATE RISK

Chapter 1 discussed asset transformation as a special or key function of FIs. *Asset transformation* involves an FI buying primary securities or assets and issuing secondary securities or liabilities to fund the assets. The primary securities that FIs purchase often have maturity characteristics different from the secondary securities that FIs sell. In mismatching the maturities of its assets and liabilities as part of its asset transformation function, an FI potentially exposes itself to **interest rate risk.**

interest rate risk

The risk incurred by an FI when the maturities of its assets and liabilities are mismatched and interest rates are volatile.

EXAMPLE 19–3 Impact of an Interest Rate Increase on an FI's Profit When the Maturity of Assets Exceeds the Maturity of Liabilities

Consider an FI that issues $100 million of liabilities with one year to maturity to finance the purchase of $100 million of assets with a two-year maturity. We show this in the following time lines:

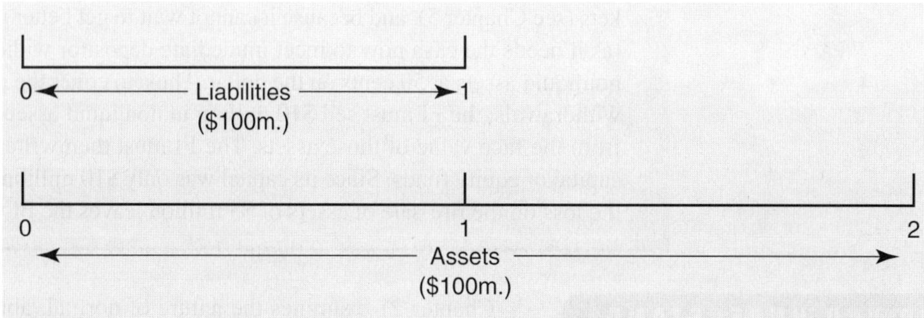

Suppose that the cost of funds (liabilities) for the FI is 9 percent per year and the interest return on the assets is 10 percent per year. Over the first year, the FI can lock in a profit spread of 1 percent (10 percent − 9 percent) times $100 million by borrowing short term (for one year) and lending long term (for two years). Thus, its profit is $1 million (.01 × 100m.).

Its profit for the second year, however, is uncertain. If the level of interest rates does not change, the FI can *refinance* its liabilities at 9 percent and lock in a 1 percent or $1 million profit for the second year as well. The risk always exists, however, that interest rates will change between years 1 and 2. If interest rates rise and the FI can borrow new one-year liabilities at only 11 percent in the second year, its profit spread in the second year is actually negative; that is, 10 percent − 11 percent = −1 percent, or the FI loses $1 million (−.01 × 100m.). The positive spread earned in the first year by the FI from holding assets with a longer maturity than its liabilities is offset by a negative spread in the second year. Note that if interest rates were to rise by more than 2 percent in the second period, the FI would stand to make losses over the two-year period as a whole. As a result, when an FI holds longer-term assets relative to liabilities, it potentially exposes itself to **refinancing risk.** Refinancing risk is a type of interest rate risk in that the cost of refinancing can be more than the return earned on asset investments. The classic example of this mismatch in recent years was demonstrated by U.S. savings institutions in the 1980s (see Chapters 13 and 14).

refinancing risk

The risk that the cost of rolling over or reborrowing funds will rise above the returns being earned on asset investments.

EXAMPLE 19-4 Impact of an Interest Rate Decrease When the Maturity of an FI's Liabilities Exceeds the Maturity of Assets

An alternative balance sheet structure would have the FI borrowing $100 million for a longer term than the $100 million of assets in which it invests. This is shown as follows:

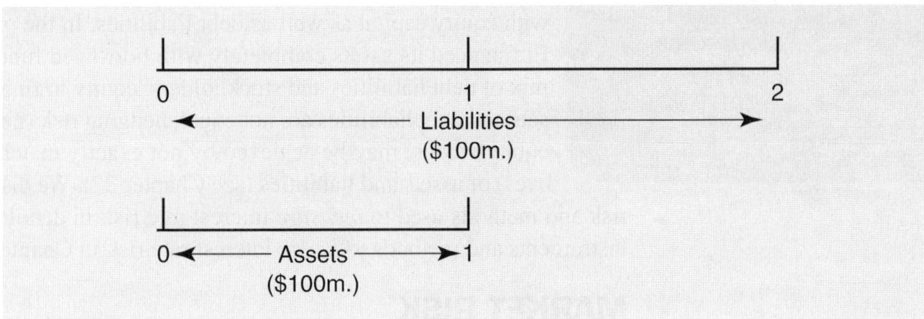

In this case, the FI is also exposed to an interest rate risk; by holding shorter term assets relative to liabilities, it faces uncertainty about the interest rate at which it can *reinvest* funds in the second period. As before, suppose that the cost of funds for the FI is 9 percent per year over the two years and the interest rate on assets is 10 percent in the first year. Over the first year, the FI can lock in a profit spread of 1 percent, or $1 million. If in the second year interest rates on $100 million invested in new one-year assets decreases to 8 percent, the FI's profit spread is negative 1 percent (8 percent − 9 percent), or the FI loses $1 million (−.01 × $100m.). The positive spread earned in the first year by the FI from holding assets with a shorter maturity than its liabilities is offset by a negative spread in the second year. Thus, the FI is exposed to **reinvestment risk;** by holding shorter term assets relative to liabilities, it faced uncertainty about the interest rate at which it could reinvest funds borrowed over a longer period. In recent years, good examples of this exposure are banks operating in the Euromarkets that have borrowed fixed-rate deposits while investing in floating-rate loans—loans whose interest rates are changed or adjusted frequently.

reinvestment risk

The risk that the returns on funds to be reinvested will fall below the cost of funds

In addition to a potential refinancing or reinvestment effect, an FI faces *market value* or *present-value* uncertainty as well when interest rates change. Remember that the economic or fair market value of an asset or liability is conceptually equal to the present value of the current and future cash flows on that asset or liability. Therefore, rising interest rates increase the discount rate on future asset (liability) cash flows and reduce the market price or present value of that asset or liability. Conversely, falling interest rates increase the present value of the cash flows from assets and liabilities. Moreover, mismatching maturities by holding longer term assets than liabilities means that when interest rates rise, the economic or present value of the FI's assets fall by a larger amount than do its liabilities.[4] This exposes the FI to the risk of economic loss and potentially to the risk of insolvency.

4. As discussed in Chapter 3, this is because this discounting effect is more powerful the more future cash flows there are (i.e., the longer the maturity of the asset or liability).

If holding assets and liabilities with mismatched maturities exposes FIs to interest rate risk, the FIs can seek to hedge or protect themselves against interest rate risk by matching the maturity of their assets and liabilities.[5] This has resulted in the general philosophy that matching maturities is somehow the best policy for FIs averse to risk. Note, however, that matching maturities is not necessarily consistent with an active asset transformation function for FIs. That is, FIs cannot be asset transformers (i.e., transforming short-term deposits into long-term loans) and direct balance sheet matchers or hedgers at the same time. Although it does reduce exposure to interest rate risk, matching maturities may reduce the FI's profitability because returns from acting as specialized risk-bearing asset transformers are reduced. As a result, some FIs emphasize asset–liability maturity mismatching more than others. For example, banks and savings institutions traditionally hold longer term assets than liabilities, whereas life insurance companies tend to match the long-term nature of their liabilities with long-term assets. Finally, matching maturities hedges interest rate risk only in a very approximate rather than complete fashion. The reasons for this are technical, relating to the difference between the average life (or duration) and maturity of an asset or liability and whether the FI partly funds its assets with equity capital as well as debt liabilities. In the preceding simple examples, the FI financed its assets completely with borrowed funds. In the real world, FIs use a mix of debt liabilities and stockholders' equity to finance asset purchases. When assets and debt liabilities are not equal, hedging risk (i.e., insulating FIs' stockholder's equity values) may be achieved by not exactly matching the maturities (or average lives) of assets and liabilities (see Chapter 22). We discuss the *causes* of interest rate risk and methods used to *measure* interest rate risk in detail in Chapter 22. We discuss the instruments and methods to *hedge* interest rate risk in Chapters 10 and 23.

DO YOU UNDERSTAND?

1. What refinancing risk is? What type of FI best illustrated this concept in the 1980s?
2. Why a rise in the level of interest rates adversely affects the market value of both assets and liabilities?
3. What the concept of maturity matching means?

MARKET RISK

market risk

The risk incurred in trading assets and liabilities due to changes in interest rates, exchange rates, and other asset prices.

Market risk arises when FIs actively trade assets and liabilities (and derivatives) rather than holding them for longer term investment, funding, or hedging purposes. Market risk is closely related to interest rate and foreign exchange risk in that as these risks increase or decrease, the overall risk of the FI is affected. However, market risk adds another dimension of risk: trading activity. Market risk is the incremental risk incurred by an FI when interest rate and foreign exchange risks are combined with an active trading strategy, especially one that involves short trading horizons such as a day.[6]

Conceptually, an FI's trading portfolio can be differentiated from its investment portfolio on the basis of time horizon and liquidity. The trading portfolio contains assets, liabilities, and derivative contracts that can be quickly bought or sold on organized financial markets. The investment portfolio (or in the case of banks, the "banking book") contains assets and liabilities that are relatively illiquid and held for longer periods. Table 19–3 shows a hypothetical breakdown between banking book and trading book assets and liabilities. Note that capital produces a cushion against losses on either the banking or trading books (see Chapter 22). As can be seen the banking book contains the majority of loans and deposits plus other illiquid assets. The trading book contains long and short positions in instruments such as bonds, commodities, foreign exchange, equities, and derivatives.

As discussed in Chapters 11 through 18, the traditional roles of many financial institutions have changed in recent years. For example, for large commercial banks such as money center banks, the decline in income from traditional deposit taking and lending activities has been matched by an increased reliance on income from trading. Similarly, the decline in underwriting and brokerage income for large investment banks has also been met by more active and

5. This assumes that FIs can directly "control" the maturity of their assets and liabilities. As interest rates fall, many mortgage borrowers seek to "prepay" their existing loans and refinance at a lower rate. This prepayment risk—which is directly related to interest rate movements—can be viewed as a further interest rate–related risk (see Chapters 7 and 24).

6. This market or trading risk is not the same as the concept of "market risk" used in asset portfolio management [often called beta (β) risk].

TABLE 19-3 The Investment (Banking) Book and Trading Book of a Commercial Bank

	Assets	Liabilities
Banking book	Loans	Capital
	Other illiquid assets	Deposits
Trading book	Bonds(long)	Bonds (short)
	Commodities (long)	Commodities (short)
	FX (long)	FX (short)
	Equities (long)	Equities (short)
	Derivatives* (long)	Derivatives (short)

*Derivatives are off-balance-sheet (as discussed in Chapter 10).

aggressive trading in securities, derivatives, and other assets. Mutual fund managers, who actively manage their asset portfolios, are also exposed to market risk. Of course, with time, every asset and liability can be sold. While bank regulators have normally viewed tradable assets as those being held for horizons of less than one year, private FIs take an even shorter-term view. In particular, FIs are concerned about the fluctuation in value—or value at risk (VAR)—of their trading account assets and liabilities for periods as short as one day—so-called daily earnings at risk (DEAR)—especially if such fluctuations pose a threat to their solvency.

To see the type of risk involved in active trading, consider the case of Barings, the 200-year-old British merchant bank that failed as a result of trading losses in February 1995. In this case, the bank (or, more specifically, one trader, Nick Leeson) was betting that the Japanese Nikkei Stock Market Index would rise by buying futures on that index (some $8 billion worth). However, for a number of reasons—including the Kobe earthquake—the index actually fell. As a result, over a period of one month, the bank lost over $1.2 billion on its trading positions, rendering the bank insolvent.[7] That is, the losses on its futures positions exceeded the bank's own equity capital resources. Of course, if the Nikkei Index had actually risen, the bank would have made very large profits and might still be in business. Another good example involves the trading losses incurred by commercial banks, investment banks, and mutual funds in Russian assets as a result of the dramatic decline in the value of the Russian ruble from 6 to $1 to 16 to $1 in August and September 1998. Finally, market risk was incurred by commercial banks, investment banks, mutual funds, and other FIs as U.S. equity markets fell dramatically in value in July 2002. For example, in a two-week period (from July 9, 2002 to July 20, 2002) the Dow Jones Industrial Average sank 1,255.64 points, 13.54 percent, from 9,274.90 to 8,019.26.

DO YOU UNDERSTAND?

1. What trading or market risk is?
2. What modern conditions have led to an increase in market risk for FIs?

Trading or market risk is the risk that when an FI takes an open or unhedged long (buy) or short (sell) position in bonds, equities, commodities, and derivatives, prices may change in a direction opposite to that expected. As a result, as the volatility of asset prices increases, the market risks faced by FIs that adopt open trading positions increase. This requires FI management (and regulators) to establish controls or limits on positions taken by traders as well as to develop models to measure the market risk exposure of an FI on a day-to-day basis.

OFF-BALANCE-SHEET RISK

off-balance-sheet risk

The risk incurred by an FI as the result of activities related to contingent assets and liabilities.

One of the most striking trends involving modern FIs has been the growth in their off-balance-sheet (OBS) activities and thus, their **off-balance-sheet risks.** While most OBS risk is related to interest rate risk, credit risk, and foreign exchange risk, OBS items introduce some unique risks that must be managed by FIs. Indeed, the 1995 failure of the U.K. investment bank Barings, the legal problems of Bankers Trust (relating to swap deals involving Procter & Gamble and Gibson Greeting Cards) in 1995, the $2.6 billion loss incurred by Sumitomo Corp.

7. In 1995 Barings was acquired as a subsidiary of ING, a Dutch bank, and was fully integrated into ING in 2000.

(of Japan) in 1996 from commodity futures trading, and the $1.5 billion in losses and eventual bankruptcy (in 1995) of Orange County, California, have all been linked to FI off-balance-sheet activities in derivatives. For example, in May 1998 Credit Suisse First Boston paid $52 million to Orange County to settle a lawsuit alleging that it had been partly responsible for that county's investments in risky securities and derivatives transactions. Twenty other banks and securities firms have been similarly sued. Further, in addition to increasing an FI's risk, OBS activities can hedge or reduce the interest rate, credit, and foreign exchange risks of FIs. That is, OBS activities have both risk-increasing and risk-reducing attributes.

While all FIs to some extent engage in off-balance-sheet activities, most attention has been drawn to the activities of banks, especially large banks. The value of on-balance-sheet items for commercial banks in December 2004 was $8.413 trillion, while the face or notional value of off-balance-sheet items was $94.114 trillion. By contrast, off-balance-sheet activities have been less of a concern to smaller depository institutions and many insurance companies. An off-balance-sheet activity, by definition, does not appear on an FI's current balance sheet since it does not involve holding a current primary claim (asset) or the issuance of a current secondary claim (liability). Instead, off-balance-sheet activities affect the *future shape* of an FI's balance sheet since they involve the creation of contingent assets and liabilities that give rise to their potential placement in the future on the balance sheet. As such, accountants place them "below the bottom line" on an FI's balance sheet.

letter of credit

A credit guarantee issued by an FI for a fee on which payment is contingent on some future event occurring, most notably default of the agent that purchases the letter of credit.

A good example of an off-balance-sheet activity is the issuance of standby **letter of credit** guarantees by insurance companies and banks to back the issuance of municipal bonds. Many state and local governments could not issue such securities without bank or insurance company letter of credit guarantees that promise principal and interest payments to investors should the municipality default on its obligations in the future. Thus, the letter of credit guarantees payment should a municipal government (e.g., New York state) face financial problems in paying either the promised interest and/or principal payments on the bonds it issues. If a municipal government's cash flow is sufficiently strong so as to pay off the principal and interest on the debt it issues, the letter of credit guarantee issued by the FI expires unused. Nothing appears on the FI's balance sheet today or in the future. The fee earned for issuing the letter of credit guarantee appears on the FI's income statement (see Chapter 12).

The ability to earn fee income while not loading up or expanding the balance sheet has become an important motivation for FIs to pursue off-balance-sheet business. Unfortunately, this activity is not risk free. Suppose the municipal government defaults on its bond interest and principal payments. Then the contingent liability or guaranty the FI issued becomes an actual or real liability that appears on the FI's balance sheet. That is, the FI has to use its own equity to compensate investors in municipal bonds. Indeed, significant losses in off-balance-sheet activities can cause an FI to fail, just as major losses due to balance sheet default and interest rates risks can cause an FI to fail.

Letters of credit are just one example of off-balance-sheet activities. Others include loan commitments by banks; mortgage servicing contracts by savings institutions; and positions in forwards, futures, swaps, and other derivative securities held by almost all large FIs (see Chapter 12). Although some of these activities are structured to reduce an FI's exposure to credit, interest rate, or other risks, mismanagement or speculative use of these instruments can result in major losses to FIs.

EXAMPLE 19-5 Impact of Off-Balance-Sheet Risk on an FI's Equity Value

Consider Table 19–4. In Panel A, the value of the FI's net worth (E) is calculated in the traditional way as the difference between the market values of its on-balance-sheet assets (A) and liabilities (L):

$$E = A - L$$
$$10 = 100 - 90$$

TABLE 19–4 Valuation of an FI's Net Worth with and without Consideration of Off-Balance-Sheet Activities

Assets		Liabilities	
Panel A: Traditional Valuation of an FI's Net Worth			
Market value of assets (A)	100	Market value of liabilities (L)	90
		Net worth (E)	10
	100		100
Panel B: Valuation of an FI's Net Worth with On- and Off-Balance-Sheet Activities Valued			
Market value of assets (A)	100	Market value of liabilities (L)	90
		Net worth (E)	5
Market value of contingent assets (CA)	50	Market value of contingent liabilities (CL)	55
	150		150

Under this calculation, the market value of the stockholders' equity stake in the FI is 10 and the ratio of the FI's capital to assets (or capital–assets ratio) is 10 percent. Regulators and FIs often use this ratio as a simple measure of solvency (see Chapter 13 for more details).

A more accurate picture of the FI's economic solvency should consider the market values of both its on-balance-sheet and OBS activities (Panel B of Table 19–4). Specifically, the FI manager should value contingent or future asset and liability claims as well as current assets and liabilities. In our example, the current market value of the FI's contingent assets (CA) is 50; the current market value of its contingent liabilities (CL) is 55. Since CL exceeds CA by 5, this difference is an additional obligation, or claim, on the FI's net worth. That is, stockholders' true net worth (E) is really:

$$
\begin{aligned}
E &= (A - L) + (CA - CL) \\
&= (100 - 90) + (50 - 55) \\
&= 5
\end{aligned}
$$

rather than 10 when we ignored off-balance-sheet activities. Thus, economically speaking, contingent assets and liabilities are contractual claims that directly impact the economic value of the equity holders' stake in an FI. Indeed, from both the stockholders' and regulators' perspectives, large increases in the value of OBS liabilities can render the FI economically insolvent just as effectively as losses due to mismatched interest rate gaps and default or credit losses from on-balance-sheet activities.

DO YOU UNDERSTAND?

1. Why FIs are motivated to pursue off-balance-sheet business? What are the risks?
2. Why letter of credit guarantees are an off-balance-sheet item?

We detailed the specific nature of the risks of off-balance-sheet activities and instruments more fully in Chapter 12. We also look at how some of these instruments (forwards, futures, swaps, and options) can be used to manage risk in Chapter 23.

FOREIGN EXCHANGE RISK

FIs have increasingly recognized that both direct foreign investment and foreign portfolio investment can extend the operational and financial benefits available from purely domestic investments. Thus, U.S. pension funds that held approximately 5 percent of their assets in foreign securities in the early 1990s now hold close to 10 percent of their assets in foreign securities. Japanese pension funds currently hold more than 30 percent of their assets in foreign securities plus an additional 10 percent in foreign currency deposits. At the same time, many large U.S. banks, investment banks, and mutual funds have become more global in their orientation. To the extent that the returns on domestic and foreign investments are imperfectly correlated, FIs can reduce risk through domestic-foreign activity/investment diversification.

The returns on domestic and foreign direct investments and portfolio investments are not perfectly correlated for two reasons. The first is that the underlying technologies of various economies differ, as do the firms in those economies. For example, one economy may be agriculturally based and another industry based. Given different economic infrastructures, one economy could be expanding while another is contracting—in the late 1990s, for example, the U.S. economy was rapidly expanding while the Japanese economy was contracting. The second reason is that exchange rate changes are not perfectly correlated across countries—the dollar–euro exchange rate may be appreciating while the dollar–yen exchange rate may be falling.

One potential benefit to an FI from becoming increasingly global in its outlook is an ability to expand abroad directly through branching or acquisitions or by developing a financial asset portfolio that includes foreign as well as domestic securities. Even so, foreign investment activities expose an FI to **foreign exchange risk.** Foreign exchange risk is the risk that exchange rate changes can adversely affect the value of an FI's assets and liabilities denominated in foreign currencies.

foreign exchange risk

The risk that exchange rate changes can affect the value of an FI's assets and liabilities denominated in foreign currencies.

Chapter 8 introduced the basics of FX markets and risks by discussing how events in other countries affect an FI's return-risk opportunities. Foreign exchange risks can occur either directly as the result of trading in foreign currencies, making foreign currency loans (a loan in British pounds to a corporation), buying foreign-issued securities (British pound–denominated bonds or euro-denominated government bonds), or issuing foreign currency–denominated debt (British pound–denominated certificates of deposit) as a source of funds.

To understand how foreign exchange risk arises, suppose that a U.S. FI makes a loan to a British company in pounds sterling (£). Should the British pound depreciate in value relative to the U.S. dollar, the principal and interest payments received by U.S. investors would be devalued in dollar terms. Indeed, were the British pound to fall far enough over the investment period, when cash flows are converted back into dollars, the overall return could be negative. That is, on the conversion of principal and interest payments from pounds into dollars, foreign exchange losses can offset the promised value of local currency interest payments at the original exchange rate at which the investment occurred.

In general, an FI can hold assets denominated in a foreign currency and/or issue foreign liabilities. Consider a U.S. FI that holds £100 million British pound loans as assets and funds £80 million of them with British pound certificates of deposit. The difference between the £100 million in pound loans and £80 million in pound CDs is funded by dollar CDs (i.e., £20 million pounds worth of dollar CDs). See Figure 19–3. In this case, the U.S. FI is net long £20 million in British assets; that is, it holds more foreign assets than liabilities. The U.S. FI suffers losses if the exchange rate for pounds falls or depreciates against the dollar over this period. In dollar terms, the value of the British pound loan assets falls or decreases in value by more than the British pound CD liabilities do. That is, the FI is exposed to the risk that its net foreign assets may have to be liquidated at an exchange rate lower than the one that existed when the FI entered into the foreign asset-liability position.

FIGURE 19–3 The Foreign Asset and Liability Position: A Net Long Asset Position in Pounds

FIGURE 19–4 **The Foreign Asset and Liability Position: Net Short Asset Position in Pounds**

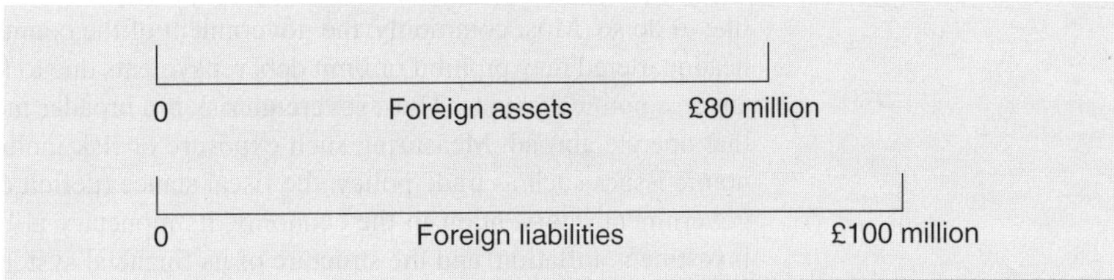

Instead, the FI could have £20 million more foreign liabilities than assets; in this case, it would be holding a net short position in foreign assets, as shown in Figure 19–4. Under this circumstance, the FI is exposed to foreign exchange risk if the pound appreciates against the dollar over the investment period. This occurs because the value of its British pound liabilities in dollar terms rose faster than the return on its pound assets. Consequently, to be approximately hedged, the FI must match its assets and liabilities in each foreign currency.

Note that the FI is fully hedged only if we assume that it holds foreign assets and liabilities of exactly the same maturity. Consider what happens if the FI matches the size of its foreign currency book (British pound assets = British pound liabilities = £100 million in that currency) but mismatches the maturities so that the pound sterling assets are of six-month maturity and the liabilities are of three-month maturity. The FI would then be exposed to foreign interest rate risk—the risk that British interest rates would rise when it has to roll over its £100 million British CD liabilities at the end of the third month. Consequently, an FI that matches both the size and maturities of its exposures in assets and liabilities of a given currency is hedged or immunized against foreign currency and foreign interest rate risk. To the extent that FIs mismatch their portfolio and maturity exposures in different currency assets and liabilities, they face both foreign currency and foreign interest rate risks. As already noted, if foreign exchange rate and interest rate changes are not perfectly correlated across countries, an FI can diversify away part, if not all, of its foreign currency risk.

Extreme foreign exchange risk was evident in 1997 when a currency crisis occurred in Asia. The crisis began on July 2, when an economic crisis in Thailand resulted in a nearly 50 percent drop in the value of the Thai baht relative to the U.S. dollar. This drop led to contagious falls in the value of other Asian currencies and eventually affected currencies outside of Asia (e.g., the Brazilian real and Russian ruble). As a result of these currency devaluations, the earnings of some major U.S. FIs were adversely impacted. For example, in November 1997, Chase Manhattan Corp. announced a $160 million loss for October 1997 from foreign currency trading and holdings of foreign currency bonds. Similarly, in 1998, J.P. Morgan was forced to discharge about 700 employees (nearly 5 percent of its workforce) partly as a result of losses experienced when Asian currency values dropped in 1997 and 1998. In addition, the stability of the Japanese banking system has been questioned, given its foreign currency loan and investment exposures in troubled Asian countries, including Indonesia, South Korea, and Thailand.

DO YOU UNDERSTAND?

1. Why the returns on domestic and foreign portfolio investments are not, in general, perfectly correlated?

COUNTRY OR SOVEREIGN RISK

country or sovereign risk

The risk that repayments from foreign borrowers may be interrupted because of interference from foreign governments.

A globally oriented FI that mismatches the size and maturities of its foreign assets and liabilities is exposed to foreign currency risk. Even beyond this risk, and even when investing in dollars, holding assets in a foreign country can expose an FI to an additional type of foreign investment risk called **country or sovereign risk.** Country or sovereign risk is different from the type of credit risk that is faced by an FI that purchases domestic assets such as the bonds and loans of domestic corporations. For example, when a domestic corporation is unable or unwilling to repay a loan, an FI usually has recourse to the domestic bankruptcy court and eventually may recoup at least a portion of its original investment when the assets of the defaulted firm are liquidated or restructured. By comparison, a foreign corporation may be unable to repay the principal or interest on a loan even if it would like to do so. Most commonly, the government of the country in which the corporation is headquartered may prohibit or limit debt repayments due to foreign currency shortages and adverse political events. Thus, sovereign risk is a broader measure of the risk faced by FIs that operate abroad. Measuring such exposure or risk includes an analysis of macroeconomic issues such as trade policy, the fiscal stance (deficit or surplus) of the government, government intervention in the economy, its monetary policy, capital flows and foreign investment, inflation, and the structure of its financial system.

For example, in 1982, the Mexican and Brazilian governments announced a debt moratorium (i.e., a delay in their debt repayments) to Western creditors. The largest U.S. banks had made substantial loans to these countries and their government-owned corporations (such as Pemex, the Mexican state-run oil company). As a result, banks such as Citicorp (now Citigroup) eventually had to make additions to their loan loss reserves to meet expected losses on these loans. In 1987 alone, Citicorp set aside more than $3 billion to cover expected losses (again, note the interaction between credit risk and country risk) on South American loans made in 1982 or earlier. More recently, in the late 1990s, U.S., European, and Japanese banks had enhanced sovereign risk exposures to countries such as Russia, Thailand, South Korea, Malaysia, and Indonesia. Financial support given to these countries by the International Monetary Fund (IMF), the World Bank, and the U.S., Japanese, and European governments enabled the banks largely to avoid the full extent of the losses that were possible. Nevertheless, Indonesia had to declare a moratorium on some of its debt repayments, while Russia defaulted on payments on its short-term government bonds. In 1999, some banks agreed to settle their claims with the Russian government, receiving less than 5 cents for every dollar owed. Finally, in 2001, the government of Argentina, which had pegged its peso to the dollar on a one-to-one basis since the early 1990s, had to default on its government debt largely because of an overvalued peso and the adverse effect this had on its exports and foreign currency earnings. In December 2001, Argentina ended up defaulting on $130 billion in government-issued debt and, in 2002, passed legislation that led to defaults on $30 billion of corporate debt owed to foreign creditors. Argentina's economic problems continued into the middle of the first decade of the 2000s. In September 2003, it defaulted on a $3 billion loan to the IMF, and in 2005 Argentina announced that it was offering its creditors about 30 cents on the dollar from its 2001 debt restructuring of $103 billion. The offer was nonnegotiable and the lowest amount on a dollar-denominated debt default ever. Yet about three-quarters of the bondholders were expected to accept the offer.

DO YOU UNDERSTAND?

1. How an FI can be subject to sovereign risk even if it lends to the highest quality foreign corporations?
2. How an FI can discipline a country that threatens not to repay its loans?

In the event of restrictions or outright prohibitions on the payment of debt obligations by sovereign governments, the FI claimholder has little if any recourse to local bankruptcy courts or to an international civil claims court. The major leverage available to an FI, so as to ensure or increase repayment probabilities, is its control over the future supply of loans or funds to the country concerned. Such leverage may be very weak, however, in the face of a country's collapsing currency and government.

TECHNOLOGY AND OPERATIONAL RISK

www.bis.org

Technology and operational risks are closely related and in recent years have caused great concern to FI managers and regulators alike. The Bank for International Settlements (BIS), the principal organization of cental banks in the major economies of the world, defines operational risk (inclusive of technological risk) as "the risk of loss resulting from inadequate or failed internal processes, people, and systems or from external events."[8] A number of FIs

8. See Basel Committee on Bank Supervision, *Sound Practices for the Management and Supervision of Operational Risk*, Bank for International Settlements, July 2002, p. 27. **www.bis.org**

add reputational risk and strategic risk (e.g., due to a failed merger) as part of a broader definition of operational risk.

Technological innovation has been a major concern of FIs in recent years (see Chapter 11). In the 1980s and 1990s, banks, insurance companies, and investment companies sought to improve their operational efficiency with major investments in internal and external communications, computers, and an expanded technological infrastructure. For example, most banks provide depositors with the capabilities to check account balances, transfer funds between accounts, manage finances, pay bills, and more from their home personal computer. At the wholesale level, electronic transfers of funds through the automated clearing houses (ACH) and wire transfer payment networks such as the Clearing House Interbank Payments Systems (CHIPS) have been developed. Indeed, a global financial service firm such as Citigroup has operations in more than 100 countries connected in real time by a proprietary satellite system.

The major objectives of technological expansion are to lower operating costs, increase profits, and to capture new markets for an FI. In current terminology, the object is to allow the FI to exploit, to the fullest extent possible, potential economies of scale and economies of scope in selling its products (see Chapter 11). For example, an FI could use the same information on the quality of customers stored in its computers to expand the sale of both loan products and insurance products—the same information (e.g., age, job, size of family, or income) can identify both potential loan and life insurance customers.

technology risk

The risk incurred by an FI when its technological investments do not produce anticipated cost savings.

Technology risk occurs when technological investments do not produce the anticipated cost savings in the form of either economies of scale or economies of scope. Diseconomies of scale, for example, arise because of excess capacity, redundant technology, and/or organizational and bureaucratic inefficiencies (red tape) that become worse as an FI grows in size. Diseconomies of scope arise when an FI fails to generate perceived synergies or cost savings through major new technology investments. Technological risk can result in major losses in an FI's competitive efficiency and ultimately result in its long-term failure. Similarly, gains from technological investments can produce performance superior to an FI's rivals as well as allow it to develop new and innovative products enhancing its long-term survival chances.

operational risk

The risk that existing technology or support systems may malfunction or break down.

Operational risk is partly related to technology risk and can arise when existing technology malfunctions or "back-office" support systems break down. For example, in 2001 a failure of a back-office system (the downside of operational risk) was evident when Citibank's (the bank subsidiary of Citigroup) ATM system crashed for an extended period. Citibank's 2,000 nationwide ATMs, its debit card system, and its online banking functions went down for almost two business days. In September 2004, a third of Wachovia Securities' brokers, sales assistants, and other employees were blocked from logging on to their computers. As the week wore on, the technology breakdowns escalated, with many frustrated brokers unable to view clients' accounts, place trades, or wire funds from their computers without using a backup system. Most recently, in February 2005 Bank of America announced that it had lost computer backup tapes containing personal information such as names and Social Security numbers on about 1.2 million federal government employee charge cards as the tapes were being transported to a data-storage facility for safekeeping. Bank of America could not rule out the possibility of unauthorized purchases using the lost data, but it said the account numbers, names, addresses, and other tape contents were not easily accessible without highly sophisticated equipment and technological expertise. Even though such computer and data problems are rare, their occurrence can cause major dislocations for the FIs involved and potentially disrupt the financial system in general.

DO YOU UNDERSTAND?

1. How operational risk is related to technology risk?
2. How technological expansion can help an FI better exploit economies of scale and economies of scope?

Operational risk is not exclusively the result of technological failure. Other sources of operational risk can result in direct costs (e.g., loss of income), indirect costs (e.g., client withdrawals and legal costs), and opportunity costs (e.g., forgone business opportunities) that reduce an FI's profitability and market value. For example, employee fraud, misrepresentations, and account errors comprise a type of operational risk that often negatively effects the reputation of an FI (see Chapter 16). Indeed, several highly publicized securities violations by employees of major investment banks resulted in criminal cases brought against securities law violators by state and federal prosecutors in 2004–2005. For example, the New York State attorney general forced Merrill Lynch to pay a $100 million penalty because of allegations that Merrill Lynch brokers misrepresented the value of the stock of its investment banking clients.

2 INSOLVENCY RISK

Insolvency risk is a consequence or an outcome of one or more of the risks described above: interest rate, market, credit, off-balance-sheet, technological, foreign exchange, sovereign, and liquidity. Technically, insolvency occurs when the capital or equity resources of an FI's owners are driven to, or near to, zero due to losses incurred as the result of one or more of the risks described above. Consider the case of the 1984 failure of Continental Illinois National Bank and Trust. Continental's strategy in the late 1970s and early 1980s had been to pursue asset growth through aggressive lending. Continental's loan portfolio grew at an average rate of 19.8 percent per year from 1977 to 1981. The downturn in the U.S. economy at the beginning of the 1980s resulted in the default of many of these loans (credit risk). In addition, Continental had a very small core deposit base, relying instead on purchased and borrowed funds such as fed funds, RPs, and Eurodollar deposits. The increasing number of defaults in Continental's loan portfolio fueled concerns about the bank's ability to meet its liability payments, resulting in the refusal by a number of major lenders to renew or roll over the short-term funds they had lent to Continental (liquidity risk). The substantial defaults on Continental's loans combined with its inability to obtain new, or retain existing, funds resulted in the rapid deterioration of Continental's capital position (insolvency risk). Continental was unable to survive, and the FDIC assumed control in 1984.

insolvency risk

The risk that an FI may not have enough capital to offset a sudden decline in the value of its assets relative to its liabilities.

In general, the more equity capital to borrowed funds an FI has—that is, the lower its leverage—the better able it is to withstand losses due to risk exposures such as adverse liquidity changes, unexpected credit losses, and so on. Thus, both the management and regulators of FIs focus on an FI's capital (and its "adequacy") as a key measure of its ability to remain solvent and grow in the face of a multitude of risk exposures. Chapter 13 discusses the issue of what is considered to be an adequate level of capital to manage an FI's overall risk exposure.

DO YOU UNDERSTAND?

1. When insolvency risk occurs?
2. How insolvency risk is related to credit risk and liquidity risk?

3 OTHER RISKS AND INTERACTION AMONG RISKS

This overview chapter concentrated on 10 major risks continuously impacting an FI manager's decision-making process and risk management strategy. These risks were interest rate risk, foreign exchange risk, market risk, credit risk, liquidity risk, off-balance-sheet risk, technology risk, operational risk, country or sovereign risk, and insolvency risk. Even though the discussion generally described each independently, in reality these risks are interdependent. For example, when interest rates rise, corporations and consumers find maintaining promised payments on their debt more difficult. Thus, over some range of interest rate movements, credit and interest rate risks are positively correlated. Furthermore, the FI may have been counting on the funds from promised payments on its loans for liquidity management purposes. Thus, liquidity risk is also correlated with interest rate and credit risks. The inability of a customer to make promised payments also affects the FI's income and profits and, consequently, its equity or capital position. Thus, each risk and its interaction with other risks ultimately affects solvency risk. The interaction of the various risks also means that FI managers face making complicated trade-offs. In particular, as they take actions to manage one type of risk, FI managers must consider the possible impact of such actions on other risks.

Various other risks also impact an FI's profitability and risk exposure. Discrete risks include a sudden change in taxation, such as the Tax Reform Act of 1986, which subjected banks to a minimum corporate tax rate of 20 percent (the alternative minimum tax) and limited their ability to expense the cost of funds used to purchase tax-free municipal bonds.

Such changes can affect the attractiveness of some types of assets over others, as well as the liquidity of an FI's balance sheet. For example, banks' demand for municipal bonds fell quite dramatically following the 1986 tax law change. As a result, the municipal bond market became quite illiquid for a time.

Changes in regulatory policy constitute another type of discrete or event-type risk. These include lifting the regulatory barriers to lending or to entry or on products offered (see Chapter 13). The 1994 regulatory change allowing interstate banking after 1997 is one example, as is the 1999 Financial Services Modernization Act. Other discrete or event risks involve sudden and unexpected changes in financial market conditions due to war, revolution, or sudden market collapse, such as the 1929, 1987, and 2002 stock market crashes or the September 2001 terrorist attacks in the United States.[9] These can have a major impact on an FI's risk exposure. Other event risks include theft, malfeasance, and breach of fiduciary trust; all of these can ultimately cause an FI to fail or be severely harmed. Yet, each is difficult to model and predict.

More general macroeconomic risks such as increased inflation, inflation volatility, and unemployment can directly and indirectly impact an FI's level of interest rate, credit, and liquidity risk exposure. For example, inflation was very volatile during the period 1979–1982 in the United States and interest rates reflected this volatility. During periods in which an FI faces high and volatile inflation and interest rates, its interest rate risk exposure from mismatching its balance sheet maturities tends to rise. Its credit risk exposure also rises because borrowing firms with fixed-price product contracts often have difficulty keeping up their loan interest payments when inflation and interest rates rise abruptly.

DO YOU UNDERSTAND?

1. What the term event risk means?
2. What some examples of event and general macroeconomic risks that impact FIs are?

9. Event risks of this type can also be viewed as a component or type of operational risk.

SUMMARY

This chapter provided an overview of the major risks that modern FIs face. FIs face *interest rate risk* when the maturities of their assets and liabilities are mismatched. They incur *market risk* for their trading portfolios of assets and liabilities if adverse movements in the prices of these assets or liabilities occur. They face *credit risk* or default risk if their clients default on their loans and other obligations. They encounter *liquidity risk* as a result of excessive withdrawals of liabilities by customers. Modern-day FIs also engage in significant amount of off-balance-sheet activities, thereby exposing them to *off-balance-sheet risks*—changing values of their contingent assets and liabilities. If FIs conduct foreign business, they are subject to *foreign exchange risk.* Business dealings in foreign countries or with foreign companies also subject FIs to *sovereign risk.* The advent of sophisticated technology and automation increasingly exposes FIs to both *technological* and *operational risks.* FIs face *insolvency risk* when their overall equity capital is insufficient to withstand the losses that they incur as a result of such risk exposures. The effective management of these risks—including the interaction among them—determines the ability of a modern FI to survive and prosper over the long run. The chapters that follow analyze these risks in greater detail, beginning with those risks incurred on the balance sheet.

QUESTIONS

1. What is the difference between firm-specific credit risk and systematic credit risk? How can an FI alleviate firm-specific credit risk?
2. In the 1980s, many thrifts that failed had made loans to oil companies located in Louisiana, Texas, and Oklahoma. When oil prices fell, these companies, the regional economy, and the thrifts all experienced financial problems. What types of risk were inherent in the loans that these thrifts had made?
3. What is the difference between refinancing risk and reinvestment risk? If an FI funds long-term assets with short-term liabilities, what will be the impact of an interest rate increase on earnings?

www.mhhe.com/sc3e

SEARCH THE SITE

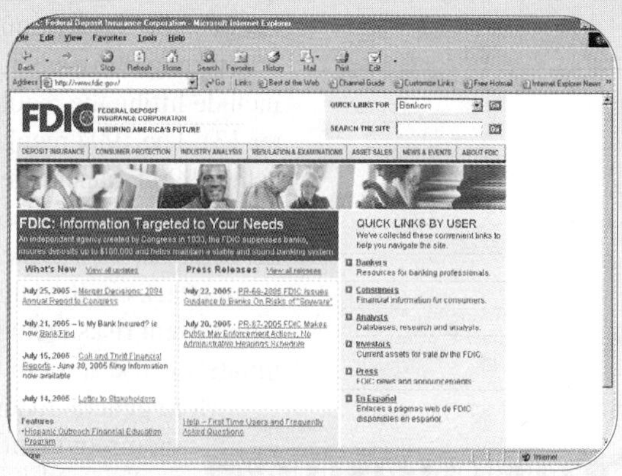

Go to the FDIC Web site at **www.fdic.gov**. Find the most recent breakdown for charge-off rates for C&I loans of commercial banks using the following steps.

Click on "Analysts."

From there click on "FDIC Quarterly Banking Profile."

Click on "Quarterly Banking Profile," and then click on "Commercial Bank Section."

Then click on "TABLE V-A. Loan Performance, FDIC-Insured Commercial Banks."

This will bring the files up on your computer that contains the relevant data.

Questions

1. How has the charge-off rate changed since 2004 reported in Figure 19–1?
2. Compare the charge-off rate of C&I loans with real estate and credit card loans. Which has changed the most since 2004?

4. The sales literature of a mutual fund claims that the fund has no risk exposure since it invests exclusively in default risk–free federal government securities. Is this claim true? Why or why not?
5. What does the term market value risk mean?
6. Consider two bonds, a 10-year premium bond with a coupon rate higher than its required rate of return and a zero coupon bond that pays only a lump sum payment after 10 years with no interest over its life. Which do you think would have more interest rate risk—that is, which bond's price would change by a larger amount for a given change in interest rates? Explain your answer.
7. Consider the following income statement for WatchoverU Savings Inc. (in millions):

Assets		Liabilities	
Floating-rate mortgages (currently 10% annually)	$ 50	NOW accounts (currently 6% annually)	$ 70
30-year fixed-rate loans (currently 7% annually)	50	Time deposits (currently 6% annually)	20
		Equity	10
Total	$100		$100

   a. What is WatchoverU's expected net interest income at year end?
   b. What will be the net interest income at year end if interest rates rise by 2 percent?

8. If a bank invested $50 million in a two-year asset paying 10 percent interest per annum and simultaneously issued a $50 million one-year liability paying 8 percent interest per annum, what would be the impact on the bank's net interest income if, at the end of the first year, all interest rates increased by 1 percentage point?
9. A money market mutual fund bought $1,000,000 of two-year Treasury notes six months ago. During this time, the value of the securities has increased, but for tax reasons the mutual fund wants to postpone any sale for two more months. What type of risk does the mutual fund face for the next two months?
10. Corporate bonds usually pay interest semiannually. If a company decided to change from semiannual to annual interest payments, how would this affect the bond's interest rate risk?
11. Off-balance-sheet risk encompasses several of the other nine sources of risk exposure (e.g., interest rate risk, credit risk, and foreign exchange rate risk). Discuss.
12. If international capital markets are well integrated and operate efficiently, will banks be exposed to foreign exchange risk? What are the sources of foreign exchange risk for FIs?
13. A U.S. insurance company invests $1,000,000 in a private placement of British bonds. Each bond pays £300 in interest per year for 20 years. If the current exchange rate is £1.5612 for U.S.$1, what is the nature of the insurance company's exchange rate risk? Specifically, what type of exchange rate movement concerns this insurance company?

14. If you expect the Swiss franc to depreciate in the near future, would a U.S.-based FI in Basel, Switzerland, prefer to be net long or net short in its asset positions? Discuss.

15. Assume that a bank has assets located in Germany worth €150 million earning an average of 8 percent on its assets. It also holds €100 in liabilities and pays an average of 6 percent per year. The current spot rate is €0.9891 for U.S.$1. If the exchange rate at the end of the year is €1.4391 for U.S.$1,

a. What happened to the dollar? Did it appreciate or depreciate against the euro (€)?

b. What is the effect of the exchange rate change on the net interest margin (interest received minus interest paid) in dollars from its foreign assets and liabilities?

c. What is the effect of the exchange rate change on the value of the assets and liabilities in dollars?

16. Six months ago, Qualitybank, Ltd., issued a $100 million, one-year-maturity CD, denominated in British pounds (Euro CD). On the same date, $60 million was invested in a £-denominated loan and $40 million in a U.S. Treasury bill. The exchange rate on this date was £1.5382 for U.S.$1. If you assume no repayment of principal and if today's exchange rate is £1.1905 for U.S.$1:

a. What is the current value of the Euro CD principalin dollars and pounds?

b. What is the current value of the British loan principal in dollars and pounds?

c. What is the current value of the U.S. Treasury bill in dollars and pounds?

d. What is Qualitybank's profit/loss from this transaction in dollars and pounds?

17. Suppose you purchase a 10-year AAA-rated Swiss bond for par that is paying an annual coupon of 8 percent and has a face value of 1,000 Swiss francs (SF). The spot rate is U.S. $0.66667 for SF1. At the end of the year, the bond is downgraded to A A and the yield increases to 10 percent. In addition, the SF depreciates to U.S. $0.74074 for SF1.

a. What is the loss or gain to a Swiss investor who holds this bond for a year?

b. What is the loss or gain to a U.S. investor who holds this bond for a year?

18. What is the difference between technology risk and operational risk? How does internationalizing the payments system among banks increase operational risk?

19. Bank 1, with $130 million in assets and $20 million in costs, acquires Bank 2, which has $50 million in assets and $10 million in costs. After the acquisition, the bank has $180 million in assets and $35 million in costs. Did this acquisition produce economies of scale or economies of scope?

20. Characterize the risk exposure(s) of the following FI transactions by choosing one or more of the following:

a. Credit risk
b. Interest rate risk
c. Off-balance-sheet risk
d. Foreign exchange rate risk
e. Country/sovereign risk
f. Technology risk

(1) A bank finances a $10 million, six-year, fixed-rate commercial loan by selling one-year certificates of deposit.

(2) An insurance company invests its policy premiums in a long-term municipal bond portfolio.

(3) A French bank sells two-year fixed-rate notes to finance a two-year fixed-rate loan to a British entrepreneur.

(4) A Japanese bank acquires an Austrian bank to facilitate clearing operations.

(5) A mutual fund completely hedges its interest rate risk exposure using forward contingent contracts.

(6) A bond dealer uses his own equity to buy Mexican debt on the less developed countries (LDC) bond market.

(7) Asecurities firm sells a package of mortgage loans as mortgage-backed securities.

21. STANDARD &POOR'S Go to the S&P Educational Version of Market Insight Web site at **www.mhhe.com/edumarketinsight** and find the most recent balance sheet for Bank of America (BAC), MBNA (KRB), and J.P. Morgan Chase (JPM) using the following steps. Click on "Educational Version of Market Insight." Enter your site ID and click on "Login." Click on "Company." Enter "BAC" in the "Ticker:" box and click on "Go!" Click on "Excel Analytics." Click on "FS Ann. Balance Sheet." This will download the balance sheet for Bank of America which contains the balances for total assets and stockholders equity. Repeat the process by entering "KRB" in the "Ticker:" box to get information on MBNA and "JPM" in the "Ticker:" box to get information on J.P. Morgan Chase.

a. Calculate the capital ratios for the three banks from the balance sheets.

b. Compare the capital of the banks. Which bank has the least/most solvency risk?

22. Discuss the interrelationships among the different sources of FI risk exposure.

www.mhhe.com/sc3e

20 Managing Credit Risk *on the* Balance Sheet

OUTLINE

Chapter NAVIGATOR

1. What has been the trend in nonperforming loans at commercial banks?
2. How does a financial institution evaluate a mortgage loan application?
3. What is a credit-scoring model?
4. What type of analysis is involved in mid-market commercial and industrial lending?
5. How are large commercial and industrial loans analyzed?
6. How do you calculate the return on a loan?

CREDIT RISK MANAGEMENT: CHAPTER OVERVIEW

In Chapter 19, we provided a basic description of the risks that emanate from financial markets as well as from the traditional activities of financial institutions. In the next three chapters, we provide a more detailed analysis of four of these risks. We also discuss how these risks can be managed. Specifically, we look at the measurement and management of credit risk, liquidity risk, interest rate risk, and insolvency risk. We start our analysis with credit risk.

As discussed in Chapter 1, financial institutions (FIs) are special because of their ability to transform financial claims of household savers efficiently into claims issued to corporations, individuals, and governments. FIs' ability to evaluate information and control and monitor borrowers allows them to transform these claims at the lowest possible cost to all parties. One specific type of financial claim transformation discussed in Chapter 1 is credit allocation. FIs transform claims of household savers (in the form of deposits) into loans issued to corporations, individuals, and governments. The FI accepts the credit risk on these loans in exchange for a fair return sufficient to cover the cost of funding paid (e.g., covering the cost of borrowing, or issuing deposits) to household savers, the credit risk involved in lending, and a profit margin reflecting competitive conditions. In this chapter we examine various approaches used to measure credit risk. In Chapter 24 we look at methods (such as loan sales and securitization) of reducing the impact of credit risk on the FIs' balance sheet.

FIGURE 20–1 Nonperforming Asset Ratio for U.S. Commercial Banks

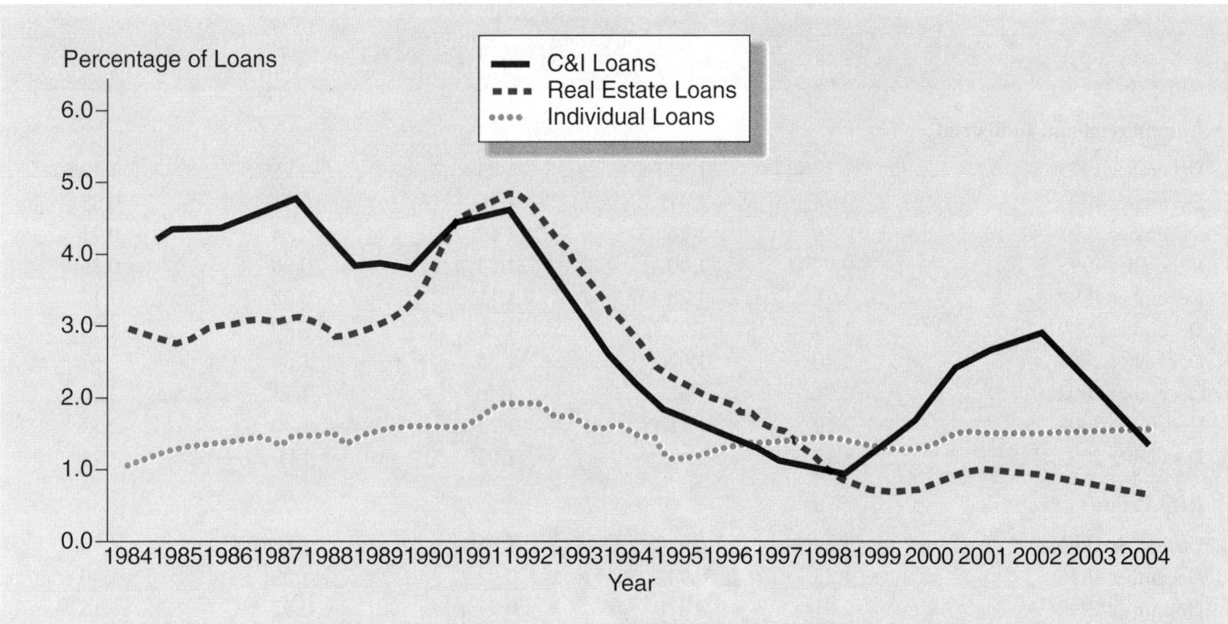

Source: Federal Deposit Insurance Corporation, *Quarterly Banking Profile,* various issues. **www.fdic.gov**

junk bond

A bond rated as speculative or less than investment grade (below Baa by Moody's and BBB by S&P) by bond-rating agencies such as Moody's.

Over the past twenty-five years, the credit quality of many FIs' lending and investment decisions has attracted a great deal of attention. For most of the 1980s, tremendous problems occurred with bank and thrift residential and farm mortgage loans. In the late 1980s and early 1990s, attention shifted to the problems relating to commercial real estate loans (to which banks, thrifts, and insurance companies were all exposed) and to **junk bonds** (bonds rated as speculative or less than investment-grade securities by rating agencies such as Moody's or S&P—see Chapter 6 for the assignment and meaning of bond ratings). In the late 1990s, concern shifted to the rapid increase in auto loans and credit cards as well as the declining quality in commercial lending standards as high-yield business loan delinquencies started to increase. In the late 1990s and early 2000s, attention has focused on problems with telecommunication companies, new technology companies, and a variety of sovereign countries including at various times Argentina, Brazil, South Korea, Thailand, Russia, and Uruguay.

1

Nevertheless, the credit quality of most FIs improved throughout the last decade. For example, for FDIC-insured commercial banks, the ratio of nonperforming loans to assets declined significantly from 1992 to 2000 (see Figure 20–1).[1] The recession in the U.S. economy in the early 2000s led to a reversal in this trend as nonperforming loan rates increased, particularly on commercial and industrial (C&I) loans. However, the nonperformance of loans in all categories was still below that of the early 1990s. As the U.S. economy improved in the 2000s, nonperforming loan rates fell. Indeed, notice from Figure 20–1 and Table 20–1 the percentage of nonperforming C&I loans fell below that of loans to individuals mainly due to the relatively high rate of credit card defaults by individuals. Nonperforming loan ratios grouped according to banks' asset sizes are shown in Table 20–1.[2] Notice that during the late 1990s nonperforming business loans were larger in smaller banks (with assets less than $1 billion), yet it was the large banks that experienced the largest increases in nonperforming loans in the 2000s. Further, nonperforming loans to individuals have consistently been larger in those banks with more than $1 billion in assets.

1. In addition, the increased securitization or sale of loans (see Chapter 24) has caused banks to hold loans for shorter periods of time, thus reducing the potential for credit quality problems.

2. *Nonperforming loans* are defined as loans past due 90 days or more and loans that are not accruing interest due to problems of the borrower.

TABLE 20–1 Nonperforming Loans as a Percentage of Total Loans
Insured Commercial Banks by Consolidated Assets

Quarter	All Banks	$0–$100 million	$100 million–$1 billion	$1 billion–$10 billion	$10 billion +
Commercial and Industrial					
December 1995	1.19%	1.32%	1.23%	0.98%	1.13%
December 1996	0.98	1.41	1.26	0.91	0.83
December 1997	0.86	1.26	1.19	0.84	0.71
December 1998	0.99	1.40	1.24	0.90	0.89
December 1999	1.18	1.28	1.11	0.93	1.17
December 2000	1.67	1.21	1.20	1.39	1.73
December 2001	2.40	1.62	1.35	1.68	2.67
December 2002	2.92	1.62	1.46	1.73	3.36
December 2003	2.10	1.71	1.27	1.40	2.35
December 2004	1.17	1.47	1.03	1.00	1.21
Real Estate					
December 1995	1.39%	0.98%	1.06%	1.18%	1.78%
December 1996	1.23	0.94	0.92	1.28	1.40
December 1997	1.01	0.87	0.77	0.97	1.15
December 1998	0.91	0.87	0.71	0.84	1.02
December 1999	0.79	0.73	0.59	0.70	0.89
December 2000	0.81	0.75	0.64	0.70	0.91
December 2001	0.96	0.97	0.83	0.84	1.04
December 2002	0.89	1.00	0.83	0.88	0.91
December 2003	0.86	0.96	0.79	0.80	0.88
December 2004	0.65	0.84	0.62	0.60	0.67
Loans to Individuals					
December 1995	1.22%	0.72%	0.64%	1.14%	1.56%
December 1996	1.36	0.84	0.79	1.42	1.50
December 1997	1.46	0.86	0.78	1.53	1.62
December 1998	1.52	0.92	0.81	1.54	1.69
December 1999	1.42	0.79	0.88	1.13	1.65
December 2000	1.40	0.87	0.87	1.15	1.56
December 2001	1.50	1.00	0.97	1.22	1.65
December 2002	1.51	1.01	0.97	1.07	1.65
December 2003	1.52	1.01	0.88	1.11	1.63
December 2004	1.46	0.94	0.90	0.93	1.56

Source: Federal Deposit Insurance Corporation, *Quarterly Banking Profile*, various issues. **www.fdic.gov**

Larger banks are more likely than smaller banks to accept riskier loans, such as sovereign and syndicated loans (large loans that main banks put together in a package, i.e., as part of a syndicate). Moreover, larger banks undertake more off-balance-sheet activities (e.g., derivatives trading) than small banks. Thus, they are exposed to the risk that the counterparties to such contracts might default (a special type of credit risk called counterparty risk). Accordingly, credit analysis by FI managers is now more important than ever before.[3]

Figure 20–2 presents the probability distribution of dollar returns from an FI investing in risky loans or bonds. The distribution indicates a high probability (but less than 1) of repayment of principal and promised interest in full (point *A*). Problems with a borrower's cash flows can result in varying degrees of default risk. These range from partial or complete

3. This is one of the reasons for bank regulators' new approach to setting capital requirements against credit risk (see Chapter 13).

SEARCH THE SITE

Go to the FDIC Web site at **www.fdic.gov.** Find the most recent breakdown for nonperformance rates for C&I, real estate, and individual loans based on the size of the lending institution using the following steps.

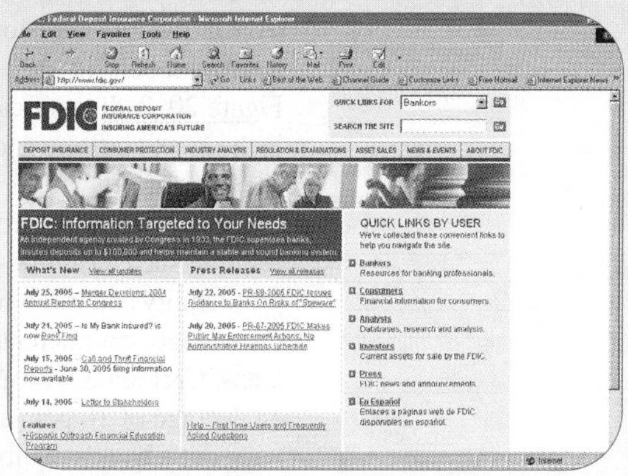

Click on "Analysis."

From there click on "FDIC Quarterly Banking Profile."

Click on "Quarterly Banking Profile," and then click on "Commercial Bank Section."

Then click on "TABLE V-A. Loan Performance, FDIC-Insured Commercial Banks."

This will bring the files up on your computer that contain the relevant data.

Questions

1. How has the nonperformance rate changed since 2004 reported in Table 20–1?
2. Compare the nonperformance rate of C&I loans with real estate and credit card loans for the smallest (less than $100 million in asset size) and the largest (more than $10 billion in asset size) banks. Which has changed the most since 2004?

default on interest payments (the range between point *A* and point *B*) and, if the problems are extreme, partial or complete default on the principal lent, as well (the range between point *B* and point *C*). Notice too that the probability of a complete default of principal and interest (point *C*) is small (but greater than 0). Because the probability of partial or complete default on bond and loan interest and principal exists, FIs must estimate expected default risk on these assets and demand risk premiums on them to compensate for that risk exposure.

The potential loss an FI can experience from lending suggests that FIs need to collect information about borrowers whose assets are in their portfolios and monitor those borrowers

FIGURE 20–2 **The Probability Distribution of Dollar Returns on Risky Debt (Loans/Bonds)**

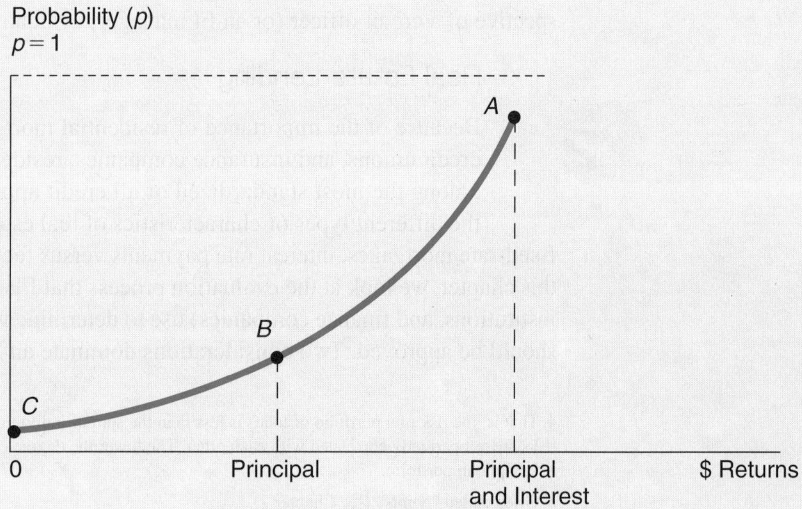

over time. Thus, managerial efficiency and credit risk management strategies directly affect the return and risks of the loan portfolio. Moreover, the credit risk distribution in Figure 20–2 is for the investment in a single asset exposed to default risk. One of the advantages that FIs have over individual investors is the ability to diversify some credit risk by exploiting the law of large numbers in their asset investment portfolios (see Chapter 1). In the framework of Figure 20–2, diversification across assets exposed to credit risk reduces the overall credit risk in the asset portfolio and thus increases the probability of partial or full repayment of principal and/or interest.[4]

A credit quality problem, in the worst case, can cause an FI to become insolvent, or it can result in such a significant drain on earnings and net worth that it can adversely affect the FI's profitability and its ability to compete with other domestic and international FIs. For example, on average, commercial banks hold 60 percent of their assets in the form of loans (mortgage loans, C&I loans, consumer loans, and other loans), while they finance their total assets with an average of 10 percent equity (see Chapter 11). Large losses on these loans could quickly wipe out a bank's equity capital. Consider an FI with the following balance sheet:

Cash	$20m.	Deposits	$90m.
Gross loans	80m.	Equity (net worth)	10m.
	$100m.		$100m.

Suppose that the managers of the FI recognize that $10 million of its $80 million in loans are unlikely to be repaid due to an increase in credit repayment difficulties of its borrowers. Eventually, the FI's managers must respond by charging off or writing down the value of these loans on the FI's balance sheet. This means that the value of loans falls from $80 million to $70 million, an economic loss that must be charged off against the stockholder's equity capital or net worth (i.e., equity capital falls from $10 million to zero). Thus, both sides of the balance sheet shrink by the amount of the loss:

Cash		$20m.	Deposits	$90m.
Gross loans	80m.		Equity after charge-off	0m.
Less: Loan loss	−10m.			
Loans after charge-off		70m.		
		$90m.		$90m.

We discuss credit analysis next.

CREDIT ANALYSIS

This section discusses credit analysis for real estate lending, consumer and small-business lending, mid-market commercial and industrial lending, and large commercial and industrial lending. It also provides insights into the credit risk evaluation process from the perspective of a credit officer (or an FI manager) evaluating a loan application.

Real Estate Lending

2 Because of the importance of residential mortgages to banks, savings institutions, credit unions, and insurance companies, residential mortgage loan applications are among the most standardized of all credit applications. In Chapter 7, we outlined the different types of characteristics of real estate loans (e.g, adjustable-rate versus fixed-rate mortgages, interest rate payments versus fee payments,[5] and down payments). In this chapter, we look at the evaluation process that FIs (such as commercial banks, savings institutions, and finance companies) use to determine whether a real estate loan application should be approved. Two considerations dominate an FI's decision to approve a mortgage

4. That is, the risk of a portfolio of loans is less than the sum of individual risks of each loan because individual loans' risks are not perfectly correlated with each other. The lower the degree of correlation among loans' risks, the lower the risk of a loan portfolio.

5. Often called "points" (see Chapter 7).

loan application (1) the applicant's ability and willingness to make timely interest and principal repayments and (2) the value of the borrower's collateral.

Ability and willingness of the borrower to repay debt outstanding is usually established by application of qualitative and quantitative models. The character of the applicant is also extremely important. Stability of residence, occupation, family status (e.g., married, single), previous history of savings, and credit (or bill payment) history are frequently used in assessing character. The loan officer must also establish whether the applicant has sufficient income. In particular, the loan amortization (i.e., principal payments) should be reasonable when compared with the applicant's income and age. The loan officer should also consider the applicant's monthly expenditures. Family responsibilities and marital stability are also important. Monthly financial obligations relating to auto, personal, and credit card loans should be ascertained, and an applicant's personal balance sheet and income statement should be constructed.

GDS (gross debt service) ratio

Total accommodation expenses (mortgage, lease, condominium, management fees, real estate taxes, etc.) divided by gross income.

TDS (total debt service) ratio

Total accommodation expenses plus all other debt service payments divided by gross income.

Two ratios are very useful in determining a customer's ability to maintain mortgage payments: the **GDS (gross debt service)** and the **TDS (total debt service)** ratios. Gross debt service ratio is the customer's total annual accommodation expenses (mortgage, lease, condominium, management fees, real estate taxes, etc.) divided by annual gross income. Total debt service ratio is the customer's total annual accommodation expenses plus all other debt service payments divided by annual gross income. These can be represented as follows:

$$\text{GDS} = \frac{\text{Annual mortage payments} + \text{Property taxes}}{\text{Annual gross income}}$$

$$\text{TDS} = \frac{\text{Annual total debt payments}}{\text{Annual gross income}}$$

As a general rule, for an FI to consider an applicant, the GDS and TDS ratios must be less than an acceptable threshold. The threshold is commonly 25 to 30 percent for the GDS and 35 to 40 percent for the TDS ratios.[6]

EXAMPLE 20-1 Calculation of the GDS and TDS Ratios

Consider two customers who have applied for a mortgage from an FI with a GDS threshold of 25 percent and a TDS threshold of 40 percent.

Customer	Gross Annual Income	Monthly Mortgage Payments	Annual Property Taxes	Monthly Other Debt Payments
1	$150,000	$3,000	$3,500	$2,000
2	60,000	500	1,500	200

The GDS and TDS ratios for the mortgage applicants are as follows:

Customer	GDS	TDS
1	$\frac{3{,}000(12) + 3{,}500}{150{,}000} = 26.33\%$	$\frac{3{,}000(12) + 3{,}500 + 2{,}000(12)}{150{,}000} = 42.33\%$
2	$\frac{500(12) + 1{,}500}{60{,}000} = 12.50\%$	$\frac{500(12) + 1{,}500 + 200(12)}{60{,}000} = 16.50\%$

Despite a higher level of gross income, Customer 1 does not meet the GDS or TDS thresholds because of relatively high mortgage, tax, and other debt payments. Customer 2, while earning less, has fewer required payments and meets both the FI's GDS and TDS thresholds.

6. The numerator of the GDS is often increased to include home heating and property taxes. When the GDS ratio is used for consumer credit, rent is substituted for mortgage payments.

FIs often combine the various factors affecting the ability and willingness to make loan repayments into a single credit score. A **credit-scoring system** (illustrated below) is a quantitative model that uses observed characteristics of the applicant to calculate a "score" representing the applicant's probability of default (versus repayment). Credit-scoring systems are developed by using borrower characteristics (e.g., income, age, loan payment history) for some past period. The credit-scoring model weights each characteristic to identify a boundary number (score) or range such that if past loan customers had an overall credit score (derived from the weighted characteristics) greater than the boundary number (score) they did not default on the loan, whereas if they had a credit score less than the boundary number they defaulted on the loan. The boundary number or range is derived by statistical analysis, such as logit or discriminant analysis.[7] Assuming new loan customers act like past customers, the credit-scoring system can then be used to calculate a credit score for new loan applicants and assign them to a high or low default risk group. The applicant's total score must be above the boundary score or range to be considered acceptable for a loan.

credit-scoring system

A mathematical model that uses observed loan applicant's characteristics to calculate a score that represents the applicant's probability of default.

The theory behind credit scoring is that by selecting and combining different economic and financial characteristics, an FI manager may be able to separate good from bad loan customers based on the characteristics of borrowers who have defaulted in the past. One advantage of a credit-scoring system is that a loan applicant's credit quality is expressed as a single numerical value, rather than as a judgmental assessment of several separate factors. This is beneficial for FIs that must evaluate small loan applicants quickly, at low cost, and consistently and who would otherwise have to employ many more credit analysts (each of whom might well apply inconsistent standards across different loan applicants as well as adding to the FI's labor costs).

If the FI uses a scoring system, the loan officer can give an immediate answer— yes, maybe, or no—and the reasons for that answer. A maybe occurs in borderline cases or when the loan officer is uncertain of the classification of certain input information. A credit-scoring system allows an FI to reduce the ambiguity and turnaround time and increase the transparency of the credit approval process.

EXAMPLE 20-2 Credit Scoring of a Real Estate Loan

An FI uses the following credit-scoring model to evaluate real estate loan applications:

Characteristic	Characteristic Values and Weights				
Annual gross income	<$10,000	$10,000–$25,000	$25,000–$50,000	$50,000–$100,000	>$100,000
Score	0	15	35	50	75
TDS	<50%	35%–50%	15%–35%	5%–15%	>5%
Score	0	10	20	35	50
Relations with FI	None	Checking account	Savings account	Both	
Score	0	30	30	60	
Major credit cards	None	1 or more			
Score	0	20			
Age	<25	25–60	>60		
Score	5	30	35		

7. For example, those credit scoring systems based on a statistical technique called discriminant analysis are also referred to as discriminant analysis models. Discriminant analysis places borrowers into two groups (defaulting and nondefaulting) and, by seeking to maximize the difference in the variance of the characteristics (e.g., income) between these groups while minimizing the variance within each group, seeks to derive appropriate weights for the characteristics that discriminate between the defaulting and nondefaulting groups. This is the discriminant function that results from discriminant analysis.

Characteristic	Characteristic Values and Weights		
Residence	Rent	Own with mortgage	Own outright
Score	5	20	50
Length of residence	<1 year	1–5 years	>5 years
Score	0	20	45
Job stability	<1 year	1–5 years	>5 years
Score	0	25	50
Credit history	No record	Missed a payment in last 5 years	Met all payments
Score	0	−15	50

The loan is automatically rejected if the applicant's total score is less than 120 (i.e., applicants with a score of 120 or less have, in the past, mainly defaulted on their loan); the loan is automatically approved if the total score is greater than 190 (i.e., applicants with a score of 190 or more have, in the past, mainly paid their loan in complete accordance with the loan agreement). A score between 120 and 190 is reviewed by a loan committee for a final decision.

A loan customer listing the following information on the loan application receives the following points:

Characteristic	Value	Score
Annual gross income	$67,000	50
TDS	12%	35
Relations with FI	None	0
Major credit cards	4	20
Age	37	30
Residence	Own/mortgage	20
Length of residence	$2\frac{1}{2}$ years	20
Job stability	$2\frac{1}{2}$ years	25
Credit history	Met all payments	50
Total score		250

The real estate loan for this customer would be automatically approved.

perfecting collateral

The process of ensuring that collateral used to secure a loan is free and clear to the lender should the borrower default on the loan.

foreclosure

The process of taking possession of the mortgaged property in satisfaction of a defaulting borrower's indebtedness and forgoing claim to any deficiency.

power of sale

The process of taking the proceedings of the forced sale of a mortgaged property in satisfaction of the indebtedness and returning to the mortgagor the excess over the indebtedness or claiming any shortfall as an unsecured creditor.

Verification of the borrower's financial statements is essential. If the answer is yes to a loan application, the loan officer states that the FI is prepared to grant the loan subject to a verification of his or her creditworthiness and obtains the applicant's permission to make all necessary inquiries. The collateral provided by the mortgage is normally considered only after the loan officer has established that the applicant can service the loan. If collateral secures a loan, the FI must make sure that its claim, should the borrower default, is free and clear from other claims. This process is referred to as **perfecting** a security interest in the **collateral.** Even if collateral secures the loan, no FI should become involved in a loan that is likely to go into default. In such a case, the FI would at best seize the property in a **foreclosure** (where the FI takes possession of the mortgaged property in satisfaction of the defaulting borrower's indebtedness, forgoing claim to any deficiency) or **power of sale** (where the FI takes the proceedings of the forced sale of a mortgaged property in satisfaction of the indebtedness and returns to the mortgagor the excess over the indebtedness or claims any shortfall as an unsecured creditor).

Before an FI accepts a mortgage, it must satisfy itself regarding the property involved in the loan by doing the following:

- Confirming the title and legal description of the property.
- Obtaining a surveyor's certificate confirming that the house is within the property boundaries.

- Checking with the tax office to confirm that no property taxes are unpaid.
- Requesting a land title search to determine that there are no other claims against the property.
- Obtaining an independent appraisal to confirm that the purchase price is in line with the market value.

Consumer (Individual) and Small-Business Lending

The techniques used for mortgage loan credit analysis are very similar to those applied to individual and small-business loans. Individual consumer loans are scored like mortgages, often without the borrower ever meeting the loan officer. Unlike mortgage loans for which the focus is on a property, however, nonmortgage consumer loans focus on the individual's ability to repay. Thus, credit-scoring models for such loans would put more weight on personal characteristics such as annual gross income, the TDS score, and so on.

Small-business loans are more complicated because the FI is frequently asked to assume the credit risk of an individual whose business cash flows require considerable analysis, often with incomplete accounting information available to the credit officer. The payoff for this analysis is also small, by definition, because loan principal amounts are usually small. A $50,000 loan with a 3 percent interest spread over the cost of funds provides only $1,500 of gross revenues before loan loss provisions, monitoring costs, and allocation of overheads. This low profitability has caused many FIs to build small business scoring models similar to, but more sophisticated than, those used for mortgages and consumer credit. These models often combine computer-based financial analysis of borrower financial statements with behavioral analysis of the owner of the small business.

Mid-Market Commercial and Industrial Lending

In recent years, mid-market commercial and industrial lending has offered some of the most profitable opportunities for credit-granting FIs. Although definitions of mid-market corporates vary, they typically have sales revenues from $5 million to $100 million a year, have a recognizable corporate structure (unlike many small businesses), but do not have ready access to deep and liquid capital markets (as do large corporations).

4 Credit analysis of a mid-market corporate customer differs from that of a small business because, while still assessing the character of the firm's management, its main focus is on the business itself. The credit process begins with an account officer gathering information by meeting existing customers, checking referrals, and meeting with new business prospects. Having gathered information about the credit applicant, an account officer decides whether it is worthwhile to pursue the new business, given the applicant's needs, the FI's credit policies, the current economy, and the competitive lending environment. If it is, the account officer structures and prices the credit agreement with reference to the FI's credit granting policy. This includes several areas of analysis, including the five Cs of credit, cash flow analysis, ratio analysis, and financial statement comparisons (described below). At any time in this process, conditions could change or new information could be revealed, significantly changing the borrower's situation and forcing the account officer to begin the process again.

Once the applicant and an account officer tentatively agree on a loan, the account officer must obtain internal approval from the FI's credit risk management team. Generally, even for the smallest mid-market credit, at least two officers must approve a new loan customer. Larger credit requests must be presented formally (either in hard copy or through a computer network) to a credit approval officer and/or committee before they can be signed. This means that, during the negotiations, the account officer must be very well acquainted with the FI's overall credit philosophy and current strategy.

Five C's of Credit. To analyze the loan applicant's credit risk, the account officer must understand the customer's character, capacity, collateral, conditions, and capital (sometimes referred to as the *five Cs of credit*). Character refers to the probability that the loan applicant will try to honor the loan obligations. Capacity is a subjective judgment regarding applicant's ability to pay the FI according to the terms of the loan. Collateral is represented by assets that the loan applicant offers as security backing the loan. Conditions refer to any general economic trends or special developments in certain geographic regions or sectors of the economy that might affect the applicant's ability to meet the loan obligations. Capital is measured by the general financial condition of the applicant as indicated by an analysis of the applicant's financial statements and his or her leverage. Some important questions that provide information on the five Cs follow.

Production (measures of capacity and conditions)

- On what production inputs does the applicant depend?
- To what extent does this cause supply risk?
- How do input price risks affect the applicant?
- How do costs of production compare with those of the competition?
- How does the quality of goods and services produced compare with those of the competition?

Management (measures of character and conditions)

- Is management trustworthy?
- Is management skilled at production? Marketing? Finance? Building an effective organization?
- To what extent does the company depend on one or a few key players?
- Is there a successful plan?
- Are credible and sensible accounting, budgeting, and control systems in place?

Marketing (measures of conditions)

- How are the changing needs of the applicant's customers likely to affect the applicant?
- How creditworthy are the applicant's customers?
- At what stage of their life cycles are the applicant's products and services?
- What are the market share and share growth of the applicant's products and services?
- What is the applicant's marketing policy?
- Who are the applicant's competitors? What policies are they pursuing? Why are they able to remain in business?
- How is the applicant meeting changing market needs?

Capital (measures of capital and collateral)

- How much equity is currently funding the firm's assets?
- How much access does the firm have to equity and debt markets?
- Will the company back the loan with the firm's assets?

Cash Flow Analysis. As an initial step of the loan analysis, FIs require corporate loan applicants to provide cash flow information, which provides the FI with relevant information about the applicant's cash receipts and disbursements to compares with the principal and interest payments on the loan. *Cash receipts* include any transaction that results in an increase in cash assets (i.e., receipt of income, decrease in a noncash asset, increase in a liability, and increase in an equity account). *Cash disbursements* include any transaction that results in a decrease in cash assets (i.e., cash expenses, increase in a noncash asset, decrease in a liability, and decrease in equity).[8] The cash flow statement (or cash-based income statement) reconciles changes in the cash account over some period according to three cash flow activities: operating, investing, and financing activities. Operating activities include net income, depreciation, and changes in current assets and current liabilities other than cash and short-term debt. Investing activities include investments in or sales of fixed assets. Financing activities include cash raised by issuing short-term debt, long-term debt, or stock. Also, since dividends paid or cash used to buy back outstanding stock or bonds reduces the applicant's cash, such transactions are included as financing activities.

When evaluating the cash flow statement, FIs want to see that the loan applicant can pay back the loan with cash flows produced from the applicant's operations. FIs do not (except as a last resort) want the loan applicant to pay back the loan by selling fixed assets or issuing additional debt. Thus, the cash flows from the operating activities section of the cash flow statement are most critical to the FI in evaluating the loan applicant.

EXAMPLE 20-3 Computation of Cash Flow Statement

Consider the financial statement for the loan applicant presented in Table 20–2. The cash flow statement reconciles the change in the firm's cash assets account from 2007 to 2008 as equal to −$61 (see the first row of panel A). Construction of the cash flow statement begins with all cash flow items associated with the operating activities of the applicant. Panel A of Table 20–3 shows that the cash flows from operations total −$78. Next, cash flows from investment activities (i.e., fixed-asset investments and other nonoperating investments of the firm) are calculated in Table 20–3, Panel B as −$168. Finally, cash flows from financing activities are shown in Panel C as $185. The sum of these cash flow activities, reported in Panel D, −$61, equals the change in the cash account from 2007 to 2008 (Table 20–2, Panel A, first row). Given that the loan should be repaid from cash flows from operations, which are negative, i.e., −$78, this loan applicant will likely be rejected.

Importantly, cash flows generated from operations, as in the preceding example, are the source of cash used to repay the loan to the FI, and thus they play a key role in the credit decision process.

Ratio Analysis. In addition to cash flow information, an applicant requesting specific levels of credit substantiates these business needs by presenting historical audited financial statements and projections of future needs. Historical financial statement analysis can be useful in determining whether cash flow and profit projections are plausible on the basis of the history of the applicant and in highlighting the applicant's risks.

Calculation of financial ratios is useful when performing financial statement analysis on a mid-market corporate applicant. Although stand-alone accounting ratios are used for determining the size of the credit facility, the analyst may find relative ratios more informative when determining how the applicant's business is changing over time (i.e., time series analysis) or how the applicant's ratios compare to those of its competitors (i.e., cross-sectional analysis). Ratios are particularly informative when they differ either from an industry average (or FI-determined standard of what is appropriate) or from the applicant's own past history. An optimal value is seldom given for any ratio because no two companies are identical. A ratio that differs from an industry average or an FI-determined standard, however, normally raises a "flag" and causes the account officer to investigate further. For example, a ratio that shifts radically from accounting period to accounting period may reveal a company weakness.

8. For example, if a firm issues new bonds (increasing liabilities), it will have a(n) (increased) cash flow from the purchasers of the newly issued bonds. Similarly, a sale of new equity (such as common stock) will create a positive cash inflow to the firm from purchasers of the equity.

TABLE 20–2 Financial Statements Used to Construct a Cash Flow Statement
(in thousands of dollars)

Panel A : Balance Sheets

Assets	2007	2008	Change from 2007 to 2008	Liabilities/Equity	2007	2008	Change from 2007 to 2008
Cash	$ 133	$ 72	$ (61)	Notes payable	$ 657	$ 967	$ 310
Accounts receivable	1,399	1,846	447	Accounts payable	908	1,282	374
Inventory	1,255	1,779	524	Accruals	320	427	107
Current assts	2,787	3,697	910	Current liabilities	1,885	2,676	791
Gross fixed assets	876	1,033	157	Long-term debt	375	300	(75)
Less: depreciation	(277)	(350)	(73)	Common stock	700	700	0
Net fixed assets	599	683	84	Retained earnings	465	754	298
Temporary investments	39	50	11	Total	$3,425	$4,430	$1,005
Total assets	$3,425	$4,430	$1,005				

Panel B: Income Statement

	2008
Net sales (all on credit)	$12,430
Cost of goods sold	(8,255)
Gross profit	4,175
Cash operating expenses	(3,418)
Depreciation	(73)
Operating profit	684
Interest expense	(157)
Taxes	(188)
Net income	339
Dividends	(50)
Change in retained earnings	$ 289

Hundreds of ratios could be calculated from any set of accounting statements. The following are a few that most credit analysts find useful. Values of the ratios using the 2008 financial statements in Table 20–2 are also presented.

Liquidity Ratios

$$\text{Current ratio} = \frac{\text{Current assets}}{\text{Current liabilities}} = \frac{3{,}697}{2{,}676} = 1.38 \text{ times}$$

$$\text{Quick ratio (acid-test ratio)} = \frac{\text{Current assets} - \text{Inventory}}{\text{Current liabilities}} = \frac{3{,}679 - 1{,}779}{2{,}676} = 0.72 \text{ times}$$

Liquidity provides the defensive cash and near-cash resources for firms to meet claims for payment. Liquidity ratios express the variability of liquid resources relative to potential claims. When considering the liquidity of a loan applicant, high levels of liquidity effectively guard against liquidity crises but at the cost of lower returns on investment. Note that a company with a very predictable cash flow can maintain low levels of liquidity without much liquidity risk. Account officers frequently request detailed cash flows from an applicant that specify exactly when cash inflows and outflows are anticipated.

TABLE 20–3 Cash Flow Statement
(in thousands of dollars)

		Cash Flow Impact
Panel A: Cash Flow from Operating Activities		
Net sales	\$12,430	↑
Change in accounts receivable	(447)	↓
Cash receipts from sales	11,983	
Cost of goods sold	(8,255)	↓
Change in inventory	(524)	↓
Change in accounts payable	374	↑
Cash margin	3,578	
Cash operating expenses	(3,418)	↓
Change in accruals	107	↑
Cash before interest and taxes	267	
Interest expense	(157)	↓
Taxes	(188)	↓
Cash flows from operations	(78)	
Panel B: Cash Flow from Investing Activities		
Change in gross fixed assets	(157)	↓
Change in temporary investments	(11)	↓
Cash flows from investing activities	(168)	
Panel C: Cash Flows from Financing Activities		
Retirement of long-term debt	(75)	↓
Change in notes payable	310	↑
Change in common stock	0	—
Dividends paid	(50)	↓
Cash flow from financing activities	185	
Panel D: Net Increase (Decrease) in Cash		
	(61)*	

*This is equal to the change in cash for 2007–2008 reported in Panel A of Table 20–2.

Asset Management Ratios

$$\text{Number of days sales in receivables} = \frac{\text{Accounts receivable} \times 365}{\text{Credit sales}} = \frac{1{,}846 \times 365}{12{,}430} = 54.21 \text{ days}$$

$$\text{Number of days in inventory} = \frac{\text{Inventory} \times 365}{\text{Cost of goods sold}} = \frac{1{,}779 \times 365}{8{,}255} = 78.66 \text{ days}$$

$$\text{Sales to working capital} = \frac{\text{Sales}}{\text{Working capitals}} = \frac{12{,}430}{3{,}697 - 2{,}676} = 12.17 \text{ times}$$

$$\text{Sales to fixed assets} = \frac{\text{Sales}}{\text{Fixed assets}} = \frac{12{,}430}{683} = 18.20 \text{ times}$$

$$\text{Sales to total assets (assets turnover)} = \frac{\text{Sales}}{\text{Total assets}} = \frac{12{,}430}{4{,}430} = 2.81 \text{ times}$$

The asset management ratios give the account officer clues to how well the applicant uses its assets relative to its past performance and the performance of the industry. For example, ratio analysis may reveal that the number of days that finished goods are in inventory is increasing. This suggests that finished goods inventories, relative to the sales they support, are not being used as well as in the past. If this increase is the result of a deliberate policy to increase inventories to offer customers a wider choice and if it results in higher future sales volumes or increased margins that more than compensate for increased capital tied up in inventory, the increased relative size of finished goods inventories is good for the applicant and, thus, the FI. An FI should be concerned, on the other hand, if increased finished goods inventories are the result of declining sales but steady purchases of supplies and production. Inventory aging schedules give more information than single ratios and should be requested by the account officer concerned about deteriorating ratios.

What a loan applicant often describes in words differs substantially from what the ratio analysis reveals. For example, a company that claims to be a high-volume producer but has low sales-to-assets ratios relative to the industry bears further investigation. In discussing the analysis with the applicant, the account officer not only gains a better appreciation of the applicant's strategy and needs but also may help the applicant better understand the company relative to financial and industry norms.

Debt and Solvency Ratios

$$\text{Debt-to-asset ratio} = \frac{\text{Short-term liabilities} + \text{Long-term liabilioties}}{\text{Total assets}} = \frac{2{,}676 + 300}{4{,}430} = 67.18\%$$

$$\text{Times in interest earned ratio} = \frac{\text{Earnings available to meet interest charges}}{\text{Interest charges}} = \frac{684}{157} = 4.36 \text{ times}$$

$$\text{Cash-flow-to-debt ratio} = \frac{\text{EBIT} + \text{Depreciation}}{\text{Debt}} = \frac{684 + 73}{2{,}676 + 300} = 25.44\%$$

EBIT

Earnings before interest and taxes.

where **EBIT** represents earnings before interest and taxes.

Debt and solvency ratios give the account manager an idea of the extent to which the applicant finances its assets with debt versus equity. Specifically, the lower the debt-to-asset ratio, the less debt and more equity the applicant uses to finance its assets (i.e., the bigger the applicant's equity cushion). Similarly, the higher the times interest earned ratio and the cash-flow-to-debt, the more equity and less debt the applicant uses to finance its assets.

Adequate levels of equity capital are as critical to the health of a credit applicant as they are to the health of FIs. The account officer analyzing a credit application or renewal wishes to know whether a sufficient equity cushion exists to absorb fluctuations in the loan applicant's earnings and asset values and sufficient cash flow exists to make debt service payments. Clearly, the larger the fluctuations or variability of cash flows, the larger is the need for an equity cushion. Note that from a secured debtor's point of view (e.g., a bank lender), the unsecured creditors and subordinate lenders (such as subordinate bond holders) form part of the quasi-equity cushion in liquidation. The secured creditor must make sure, however, that it enjoys true seniority in cash payment so that the firm's assets are not liquidated in paying down the claims of the subordinate (junior) creditors and equity holders.

Whether a debt burden is too large can be analyzed with the help of a fixed-charge coverage ratio. This ratio measures the dollars available to meet fixed-charge obligations (earnings available to meet fixed charges). A value of 1 for this ratio means that $1 of earnings is available to meet each dollar of fixed-charge obligations. A value of less (greater) than 1 means that the applicants has less (more) than $1 of earnings available to pay each dollar of fixed-charge obligations. This ratio can be tailored to the applicant's situation, depending on what really constitutes fixed charges that must be paid. One version of it follows: (EBIT + Lease payments)/[Interest + Lease payments + Sinking fund/$(1 - T)$], where T is the marginal tax rate.[9] Here, it is assumed that sinking fund payments must be made.[10] They are adjusted by the division of $(1 - T)$ into a before-tax

9. Another version adds to the denominator investments for replacing equipment that is needed for the applicant to remain in business.

10. *Sinking funds* are required periodic payments into a fund that is used to retire the principal amounts on bonds outstanding.

cash outflow so they can be added to other before-tax cash outflows. The variability of cash flows (the cash flow ratio) provides a clue as to how much higher than 1 a fixed-charge coverage ratio should be.

The cash-flow-to-debt ratio is a variant of the fixed-charge coverage ratio. It measures the cash flow available for debt service in proportion to the debt principal being serviced and can be compared to the interest rate on the debt. If this ratio is equal to the interest rate on the debt, the applicant's cash flows are just sufficient to pay the required interest on the debt principal. The more the ratio exceeds the interest rate on the debt, the larger is the debt-service cushion.

Profitability Ratios

$$\text{Gross margin} = \frac{\text{Gross profit}}{\text{Sales}} = \frac{4{,}175}{12{,}430} = 33.59\%$$

$$\text{Operating profit margin} = \frac{\text{Operating profit}}{\text{Sales}} = \frac{684}{12{,}430} = 5.50\%$$

$$\text{Return on assets} = \frac{\text{EAT}}{\text{Total assests}} = \frac{339}{4{,}430} = 7.65\%$$

$$\text{Return on equity} = \frac{\text{EAT}}{\text{Total equity}} = \frac{339}{1{,}475} = 22.98\%$$

$$\text{Dividend payout} = \frac{\text{Dividends}}{\text{EAT}} = \frac{50}{339} = 14.75\%$$

EAT

Earnings after taxes.

where **EAT** represents earnings after taxes, or net income.

For all but the dividend payout ratio, the higher the value of the ratio, the higher the profitability of the firm. The dividend payout ratio measures how much of the profit is retained in the firm versus paid out to the stockholders as dividends. The lower the dividend payout ratio, the more profits (percentage wise) are retained in the firm. A profitable firm that retains its earnings increases its level of equity capital as well as its creditworthiness. The analyst should be concerned about large swings in profitability as well as profit trends.[11]

Cautions with Ratio Analysis. While ratio analysis provides useful information about a loan applicant's financial condition, it also has limitations that require care and judgment in its use. For example, many firms operate in more than one industry. For these companies, it is difficult to construct a meaningful set of industry averages. Further, different accounting practices can distort industry comparisons. For example, the loan applicant may be using straight line depreciation for its fixed assets, while industry competitors are using an accelerated cost recovery method (ACRS), which causes depreciation to accrue quickly. ACRS methods will cause fixed asset values to be written down quickly and leave their book value lower than straight line depreciation. This can distort the analysis of fixed asset-based ratios. In addition, it is sometimes difficult to generalize whether a particular value for a ratio is good or bad. For example, a high current ratio can be a sign of a highly liquid firm or one that holds excessive cash. FI loan officers need to be aware of the problems with ratio analysis in analyzing the loan applicant's financial statements and making a loan decision. Finally, concerns about how earnings are reported in recent high-profile cases such as Enron and WorldCom have accentuated the weakness of FIs relying totally on ratio analysis in making credit decisions. For example, in August 2002 J.P. Morgan Chase announced the creation of

11. *Market value ratios* such as the growth rate in the share price, price–earnings ratio, and dividend yield are also valuable indicators if they are available. For a mid-market corporation, however, they are probably unavailable since the debt and equity claims of most mid-market corporations are not publicly traded. The account officer may find it informative to substitute a similar listed firm (a comparability test).

a Policy Review Office that, separately from the results of ratio analysis, would examine proposed financial deals in light of potential risks to the bank's reputation.[12]

Common-Size Analysis and Growth Rates. In addition to the ratios listed above, an analyst can compute sets of ratios by dividing all income statement amounts by total sales revenue and all balance sheet amounts by total assets. These calculations yield common-size financial statements that can be used to identify changes in corporate performance. Year-to-year growth rates also give useful ratios for identifying trends. Common-size financial statements may provide quantitative clues as to the direction that the firm is moving and that the analysis should take.

Having reviewed the financial and other conditions of the applicant, the FI can include loan covenants (similar to bond covenants discussed in Chapter 6) as a part of the loan agreement. Loan covenants reduce the risk of the loan to the lender. They can include a variety of conditions such as maintenance of various ratios at or within stated ranges, key-person insurance policies on employees critical to the success of the project funded by the loan, and so on.

conditions precedent

Those conditions specified in the credit agreement or terms sheet for a credit that must be fulfilled before drawings are permitted.

Following Approval. The credit process does not end when the applicant signs the loan agreement. As is the case for mortgage loans, before allowing a drawdown (the actual release of the funds to the borrower) of a mid-market credit, the account officer must make sure that **conditions precedent** have been cleared. Conditions precedent are those conditions specified in the credit agreement or terms sheet for a credit that must be fulfilled before drawdowns are permitted. These include various title searches, perfecting of collateral, and the like. Following drawdown, the credit must be monitored throughout the loan's life to ensure that the borrower is living up to its commitments and to detect any deterioration in the borrower's creditworthiness so as to protect the FI's interest in the loan being repaid in full with the promised interest return.

Typically, the borrower's credit needs will change from time to time. A growing company has an expanding need for credit. A company moving into the international arena needs foreign exchange. A contractor may have periodic guarantee requests. Even if the credit agreements being offered do not change, a corporation's credit needs are usually reviewed on an annual basis to ensure that they comply with the terms of the original credit agreement. FIs typically wish to maintain close contact with customers to meet their ongoing financial service requirements—both credit and noncredit—so that the relationship will develop into a permanent, mutually beneficial one (the customer relationship effect).

Large Commercial and Industrial Lending

5

An FI's bargaining strength is severely diminished when it deals with large creditworthy corporate customers. Large corporations are able to issue debt and equity directly in the capital markets as well as to make private placements of securities. Also, they typically maintain credit relationships with several FIs and have significant in-house financial expertise. They manage their cash positions through the money markets by issuing their own commercial paper (see Chapter 5) to meet fund shortfalls and use excess funds to buy Treasury bills, banker's acceptances, and other companies' commercial paper. Moreover, large corporate clients are not seriously restricted by international borders but have operations and access to international capital markets and FIs in many parts of the world. Large corporate clients are very attractive to FIs because, although spreads and fees are small in percentage terms, the transactions are often large enough to make them very profitable as long as a default does not occur and they offer the potential for cross-selling other FI products to the client.

Specifically, the FI's relationship with large corporate clients goes beyond lending. The FI's role as broker, dealer, and adviser to a corporate client may rival or exceed the importance of its role as a lender. A large corporate client is likely to investigate several avenues for obtaining credit and to compare, for example, the flexibility and cost of a bond, a private placement, and borrowing from different FIs. The client may periodically poll FIs

12. See "J.P. Morgan to Review Deals for Risks to Bank's Reputation," *The Wall Street Journal,* August 13, 2002, p. C5.

to determine opportune times to tap financial markets, even if this means inventorying funds.[13] The FI's loan account officer must often liaise with the FI's investment banker to obtain information and indicative pricing on new security issues. Clearly, the amount of time this involves means that an FI's senior corporate account officer manages far fewer accounts than colleagues providing mid-market credits.

In providing a credit service to large corporations, credit management remains an important issue. Large corporations frequently use loan commitments (a contractual commitment to loan to a firm a certain maximum amount at a given interest rate), performance guarantees (such as letters of credit—see Chapter 5), and term loans, as do mid-market corporates. If the FI is contracting in spot and forward foreign exchange or swaps, or is engaging in other derivative activities with the corporate client as a counterparty, it must do so within the credit limits established by a regular credit review process.

An additional complicating factor is that large corporate accounts often consist of several related corporate entities under a common management. For example, a holding company may wholly own, control, or have substantial stakes in various operating subsidiaries. A subsidiary's credit risk may be better than, the same as, or worse than that of a holding company as a whole. An FI lending to a holding company with no assets other than its equity stake in its subsidiaries puts itself in a subordinate lending position relative to the lenders to the operating subsidiaries, which have direct claims over those subsidiaries' operating assets.

An account officer preparing a credit review for a large corporate customer often faces a complex task. The standard methods of analysis that we introduced when discussing mid-market corporates applies to large corporate clients but with additional complications. The corporate business often crosses more than one business activity and location. Hence, industry comparisons are difficult at best. Additional analytical aids are available to account officers. Specifically, large corporations are tracked by rating agencies and market analysts, who can provide account officers with a great deal of information to aid in their credit analysis. Also, because of these customers' additional complexities and large credit risk exposures, FIs can use sophisticated credit-scoring models in the credit review process based on accounting and/or financial market data. We discuss two such credit-scoring models below.

Credit-Scoring Models. Credit-scoring models use data on observed borrower characteristics either to calculate the probability of default or to sort borrowers into different default risk classes. By selecting and combining different economic and financial borrower characteristics, an FI manager may be able to:

1. Numerically establish which factors are important in explaining default risk.
2. Evaluate the relative degree or importance of these factors.
3. Improve the pricing of default risk.
4. Screen high-risk loan applicants.
5. Calculate any reserves needed to meet expected future loan losses.

To employ credit-scoring models in this manner, the FI manager must identify objective economic and financial measures of risk for any particular class of borrower. After data are identified, a statistical technique quantifies or scores the default risk probability or default risk classification.

Altman's Z-Score. E. I. Altman developed a Z-score model for analyzing publicly traded manufacturing firms in the United States. The indicator variable Z is an overall measure of the borrower's default risk classification. This classification, in turn, depends on the values of various financial ratios of the borrower (X_j) and the weighted importance of these ratios based on the observed experience of defaulting versus nondefaulting borrowers derived from a discriminant analysis model.[14]

13. Or opening new lines of credit (loan commitments)—see below.

14. E. I. Altman, "Managing the Commercial Lending Process," in *Handbook of Banking Strategy,* ed. R. C. Aspinwall and R. A. Eisenbeis (New York: John Wiley & Sons, 1985), pp. 473–510. See also footnote 7 in this chapter for a discussion of this technique. Other models include linear probability models and logit models. See A. Saunders and M.M. Cornett, *Financial Institutions Management: A Risk Management Approach,* 5th ed. (New York: McGraw-Hill, 2006).

www.capis.com

Altman's credit-scoring model takes the following form:

$$Z = 1.2X_1 + 1.4X_2 + 3.3X_3 + 0.6X_4 + 1.0X_5$$

where

X_1 = Working capital/Total assets ratio
X_2 = Retained earnings/Total assets ratio
X_3 = Earnings before interest and taxes/Total assets ratio
X_4 = Market value of equity/Book value of long-term debt ratio
X_5 = Sales/Total assets ratio.

The higher the value of Z, the lower the borrower's default risk classification.[15] Thus, low or negative Z values may be evidence that the borrower is a member of a relatively high default risk class.

EXAMPLE 20-4 Calculation of Altman's Z-Score

Suppose that the financial ratios of a potential borrowing firm took the following values:

$$X_1 = .2$$
$$X_2 = 0$$
$$X_3 = -.20$$
$$X_4 = .10$$
$$X_5 = 2.0$$

The ratio X_2 is zero and X_3 is negative, indicating that the firm has had negative earnings or losses in recent periods. Also, X_4 indicates that the borrower is highly leveraged. However, the working capital ratio (X_1) and the sales/assets ratio (X_5) indicate that the firm is reasonably liquid and is maintaining its sales volume. The Z-score provides an overall score or indicator of the borrower's credit risk since it combines and weights these five factors according to their past importance in explaining (discriminating between) borrower default and borrower repayment. For the borrower in question:

$$Z = 1.2(.2) + 1.4(0) + 3.3(-.20) + .6(.10) + 1.0(2.0)$$
$$Z = .24 + 0 - .66 + .06 + 2.0$$
$$Z = 1.64$$

According to Altman's credit-scoring model, any firm with a Z-score of less than 1.81 should be considered a high default risk, between 1.81 and 2.99 an indeterminate default risk, and greater than 2.99 a low default risk. Thus, the FI should not lend to this borrower until it improves its earnings performance.

Use of the Z-score model to make credit risk evaluations has a number of problems. The first problem is that this model usually discriminates only among three cases of borrower behavior: high, indeterminate, and low default risk. As discussed in Chapter 19, in the real world various gradations of default exist, from nonpayment or delay of interest payments (nonperforming assets) to outright default on all promised interest and principal payments. This problem suggests that a more accurate or finely calibrated sorting among borrowers may require defining more classes in the scoring model.

The second problem is that there is no obvious economic reason to expect that the weights in the Z-score model—or, more generally, the weights in any credit-scoring model—will be constant over any but very short periods. The same concern also applies to the scoring model's explanatory variables (X_j). Specifically, due to changing financial market conditions, other borrower-specific financial ratios may come to be increasingly relevant in explaining default risk probabilities.

15. Working capital is Current assets − Current liabilities.

The third problem is that these models ignore important, hard-to-quantify factors that may play a crucial role in the default or no-default decision. For example, the reputation of the borrower and the nature of long-term borrower–lender relationships could be important borrower-specific characteristics, as could macro factors such as the phase of the business cycle. Credit-scoring models often ignore these variables. Moreover, traditional credit-scoring models rarely use publicly available information, such as the prices of the outstanding public debt and equity of the borrower.[16]

www.kmv.com

www.moodys.com

A fourth problem relates to the infrequency (e.g., quarterly or annually) with which accounting variables are updated. This allows scores to be changed at generally infrequent intervals.

DO YOU UNDERSTAND?

1. The credit quality problems faced by FIs in the last two decades?
2. What a credit-scoring system is?
3. What a title search accomplishes?
4. Why large corporations do not rely heavily on FIs to fulfill their financing needs?
5. Why FIs have separate checks on account officers' granting credit?
6. Why an account officer must be well versed in the FI's credit policy before talking to potential borrowers?
7. Why a credit officer should be concerned if a borrower's number of days' receivables increases beyond the industry norm?
8. What the major problems with the Z-score model of credit risk are?

KMV Credit Monitor Model. In recent years, following the pioneering work on options by Merton, Black, and Scholes, we now recognize that when a firm raises funds either by issuing bonds or by increasing its bank loans, it holds a very valuable default or repayment option.[17] That is, if a borrower's investments fail to pay off, so that it cannot repay its bondholders or the loan to the FI, it has the option to default on its debt repayments and turn any remaining assets over to the debtholder. Because of limited liability, the borrower's loss is limited, on the downside, by the amount of equity that is invested in the firm.[18] On the other hand, if things go well, the borrower can keep most of the upside returns on asset investments after the promised principal and interest on the debt have been paid. The KMV Corporation (purchased by Moody's in 2002) has turned this relatively simple idea into a credit-monitoring model. Many of the largest U.S. banks are now using this model to determine the expected default frequency (EDF), that is the probability of default, of large corporations.[19]

The expected default frequency that is calculated reflects the probability that the market value of the firm's assets will fall below the promised repayments on debt liabilities in one year. If the value of a firm's assets falls below its debt liabilities, it can be viewed as being economically insolvent. Simulations by KMV have shown that this model outperforms both accounting-based models and S&P rating changes as predictors of corporate failure and distress.[20] An example for Enron Corp., which filed for Chapter 11 bankruptcy protection in December 2001, is shown in Figure 20–3.[21] Note that the KMV score (EDF) is rising faster than the rating agency is downgrading the firm's debt. Indeed, the rating agency is very slow to react to, if not totally insensitive to, the increase in Enron's risk. Thus, the KMV EDF score gives a better "early warning" of impending default.[22]

CALCULATING THE RETURN ON A LOAN

6

An important element in the credit management process, once the decision to make a loan has been made, is its pricing. This includes adjustments for the perceived credit risk or default risk of the borrower. This section demonstrates two ways to calculate the return on a loan: the traditional *return on assets approach* and a newer

16. However, it might be noted that the X_4 variable in Altman's Z-score model includes a market value of equity measure (i.e., the price of the firm's shares times the number of its shares outstanding) as part of the leverage ratio.

17. R. C. Merton, "On the Pricing of Corporate Debt: The Risk Structure of Interest Rates," *Journal of Finance* 29 (1974), pp. 449–70; and F. Black and M. Scholes, "The Pricing of Options and Corporate Liabilities," *Journal of Political Economy* 81 (1973), pp. 737–59.

18. Given limits to losses in personal bankruptcy, a similar analysis can be applied to retail and consumer loans.

19. See KMV Corporation, *Credit Monitor* (San Francisco: KMV Corporation, 1994).

20. KMV currently provides EDFs for more than 25,000 U.S. and foreign companies worldwide (basically every corporation whose equity is traded on a stock market). In addition it has a private-firm model that maps private firms (whose equity is not publicly traded) into a public-firm equivalent. For more information see the KMV Corp. Web site.

21. Note a KMV EDF score varies from a minimum of zero percent to a maximum of 20 percent per annum.

22. One reason for this is that the KMV score is extracted from stock market data that is highly sensitive to new information about a firm's future prospects.

FIGURE 20–3 KMV and S&P Ratings for Enron Corp Inc.

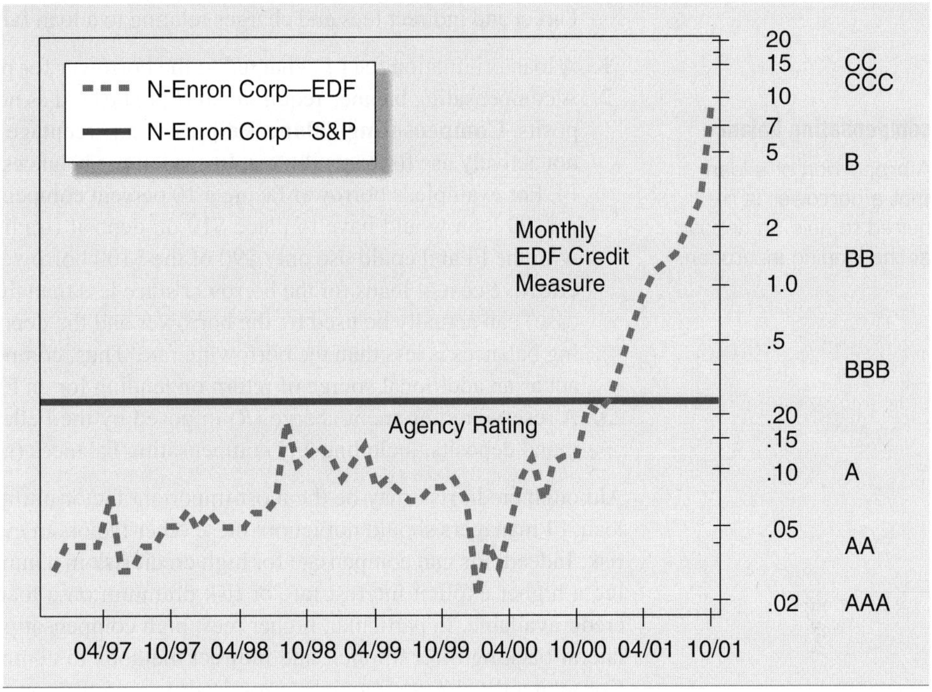

Source: KMV Corporation, San Francisco, California. **www.moodyskmv.com**

approach used by many FIs including banks, thrifts, and insurance companies called *risk-adjusted return on capital* (RAROC) which considers loan returns in the context of the risk of the loan to the FI. While we demonstrate the return calculations using examples of commercial and industrial loans, the techniques can be used to calculate the return on other loans (such as credit card or mortgage loans) as well.

Return on Assets (ROA)

A number of factors impact the promised return that an FI achieves on any given dollar loan (asset) amount. These factors include the following:

1. The interest rate on the loan.
2. Any fees relating to the loan.
3. The credit risk premium (m) on the loan.
4. The collateral backing the loan.
5. Other nonprice terms (such as compensating balances and reserve requirements).

In this section, we consider an example of how to calculate the promised return on a C&I loan. Suppose that an FI makes a spot one-year, $1 million loan. The loan rate is set at as follows:

LIBOR

The London Interbank Offered Rate, the rate for interbank dollar loans in the foreign or Eurodollar market of a given maturity.

$$\begin{aligned} \text{Base lending rate } (BR) &= 12\% \\ + \text{ Risk premium } (m) &= \underline{\ \ 2\ \ } \\ BR + m &= 14\% \end{aligned}$$

The base lending rate (BR) could reflect the FI's weighted average cost of capital or its marginal cost of funds, such as the commercial paper rate, the federal funds rate, or **LIBOR**—the London Interbank Offered Rate, which is the rate for interbank dollar loans in the foreign or Eurodollar market of a given maturity. Alternatively, it could reflect the **prime lending rate.** Traditionally, the prime rate has been the rate charged to the bank's lowest risk customers. Now it is more a rate to which positive or negative risk premiums

prime lending rate

The base lending rate periodically set by banks.

can be added. In other words, FIs now charge their best and largest borrowers below prime rate to compete with the commercial paper market.

Direct and indirect fees and charges relating to a loan fall into three general categories:

1. A loan origination fee (f) charged to the borrower for processing the application.
2. A compensating balance requirement (b) to be held as noninterest-bearing demand deposits. **Compensating balances** represent a percentage of a loan that a borrower cannot actively use for expenditures. Instead, these balances must be kept on deposit at the FI. For example, a borrower facing a 10 percent compensating balance requirement on a \$100 loan would have to place \$10 on deposit (traditionally in a demand deposit) with the FI and could use only \$90 of the \$100 borrowed. This requirement raises the effective cost of loans for the borrower since less than the full loan amount (\$90 in this case) can actually be used by the borrower and the deposit rate earned on compensating balances is less than the borrowing rate. Thus, compensating balance requirements act as an additional source of return on lending for an FI.[23]
3. A reserve requirement charge (R) imposed by the Federal Reserve on the bank's demand deposits, including any compensating balances (see Chapter 13).

compensating balance

A proportion of a loan that a borrower is required to hold on deposit at the lending institution.

Although credit risk may be the most important factor ultimately affecting the return on a loan, FI managers should not ignore these other factors in evaluating loan profitability and risk. Indeed, FIs can compensate for high credit risk in a number of ways other than charging a higher explicit interest rate or risk premium on a loan or restricting the amount of credit available. In particular, higher fees, high compensating balances, and increased collateral backing offer implicit and indirect methods to compensate an FI for lending risk. Consequently, the contractually promised gross return on the loan, k, per dollar lent (or $1 + k$)—or ROA per dollar lent—will equal:[24]

$$1 + k = 1 + \frac{f + (BR + m)}{1 - b(1 - R)}$$

This formula may need some explanation. The numerator is the promised gross cash inflow to the FI per dollar lent, reflecting direct fees f plus the loan interest rate $(BR + m)$ discussed above. In the denominator, for every \$1 in loans that the FI lends, it retains b as noninterest-bearing compensating balances. Thus, $1 - b$ represents the net proceeds of each \$1 of loans received by the borrower from the FI, ignoring reserve requirements. However, since b (compensating balances) are held by the borrower at the FI as demand deposits, the Federal Reserve requires the FI to hold noninterest-bearing reserves at the rate R against these compensating balances. Thus, the FI's net benefit from requiring compensating balances must consider the cost of holding higher noninterest-bearing reserves. The net outflow by the FI per \$1 of loans is, thus, $1 - b(1 - R)$, or 1 minus the reserve-adjusted compensating balance requirement.

EXAMPLE 20-5 Calculation of ROA on a Loan

Suppose a bank does the following:

1. Sets the loan rate on a prospective loan at 14 percent (where $BR = 12\%$ and $m = 2\%$).
2. Charges a ⅛ percent (or 0.125 percent) loan origination fee (f) to the borrower.
3. Imposes a 10 percent compensating balance requirement (b) to be held as non-interest-bearing demand deposits.

23. They also create a more stable supply of deposits and, thus, mitigate liquidity problems.

24. This formula ignores present value aspects that could easily be incorporated. For example, fees are earned in up-front undiscounted dollars, while interest payments and risk premiums are normally paid on loan maturity and, thus, should be discounted by the FI's cost of funds.

4. Sets aside reserves (R) at a rate of 10 percent of deposits, held at the Federal Reserve (i.e. the Fed's cash-to-deposit reserve ratio is 10 percent).

Placing the numbers from our example into this formula, we have:

$$1 + k = 1 + \frac{.00125 + (.12 + .02)}{1 - (.10)(.9)}$$

$$1 + k = 1 + \frac{.14125}{.91}$$

$$1 + k = 1.1552, \text{ or } k = 15.52\%$$

This is, of course, larger than the simple promised interest return on the loan, BR + m = 14 percent.

In the special case in which fees (f) are zero and the compensating balance (b) is zero:

$$f = 0$$
$$b = 0$$

the contractually promised return formula reduces to:

$$1 + k = 1 + (BR + m)$$

That is, the credit risk premium is the fundamental factor driving the promised return on a loan, once the base rate on the loan has been set.

Note that as commercial lending markets have become more competitive, both origination fees (f) and compensating balances (b) have become less important. For example, when compensating balances are still required, banks may now allow them to be held as time deposits and earn interest. As a result, borrowers' opportunity losses from compensating balances have been reduced to the difference between the loan rate and the compensating balance time-deposit rate. In addition, compensating balance requirements are very rare on international loans such as Eurodollar loans.[25]

RAROC Models

An increasingly popular model used to evaluate the return on a loan to a large customer is the risk-adjusted return on capital (RAROC) model. Bankers Trust (acquired by Deutsche Bank in 1998) pioneered RAROC, which has now been adopted by virtually all the large banks in the United States and Europe, although with some proprietary differences among them.

The essential idea behind RAROC is that rather than evaluating the actual or promised annual cash flow on a loan as a percentage of the amount lent (or ROA), as described in the last subsection, the lending officer balances the loan's expected income against the loan's expected risk.[26] Thus, rather than dividing expected annual loan income by assets lent, it is divided by some measure of asset (loan) value at risk or what is often called value (or capital) at risk, since loan losses have to be written against an FI's capital (see Chapter 12):

$$\text{RAROC} = \frac{\text{One-Year income on a loan}}{\text{Loan (asset) risk or value at risk}}$$

25. As mentioned above, the ROA model can also be applied to other than commercial and industrial loans. For example, a consumer loan could be priced using a risk premium (m) over some base rate (BR) and fees are generally charged on a consumer loan (e.g., annual fees for credit card provision). However, consumer loans do not require compensating balance requirements. Thus, the gross return on a consumer loan would be $1 + k = 1 + f + (BR + m)$.

26. Since loan defaults are charged to the FI's capital or equity account, the loan's risk is also a measure of "risk capital," or capital at risk. Note, however, that in general, smaller loans have their risk controlled more through the quantity of credit granted rather than price. That is, all small borrowers passing a given FI's credit scoring test may be charged the same interest rate. Those failing the test may be denied credit.

A loan is approved by the FI only if RAROC is sufficiently high relative to a benchmark return on equity capital (e.g., the ROE after tax required by its stockholders or ROE (1 − t)), where ROE measures the return stockholders require on their equity investment in the FI. The idea here is that a loan should be made only if the risk-adjusted return on the loan adds to the FI's equity value as measured by the ROE required by the FI's stockholders. Thus, for example, if an FI's tax-adjusted ROE is 15 percent, a loan should be made only if the estimated RAROC is higher than the 15 percent required by the FI's stockholders as a reward for their investment. Alternatively, if the RAROC on an existing loan falls below an FI's RAROC benchmark, the lending officer should seek to adjust the loan's terms (e.g., via the required loan rate or fees) to make it "profitable" again.

One problem in estimating RAROC is the measurement of loan risk (the denominator in the RAROC equation). In calculating RAROC, most FIs divide one-year loan income by a loan risk measure calculated as the product of an "unexpected" default rate and the proportion of the loan that cannot be recaptured on a borrower's default—the so-called loss given default. The denominator in the RAROC equation is, therefore, an estimate of the unexpected overall loss on the loan in extreme conditions such as the worst year in the next 100 years, which is the product of the unexpected default rate and the loss given default.

DO YOU UNDERSTAND?

1. What factors impact the rate of return on loans issued by FIs?
2. What the difference between the ROA and the RAROC on a loan is?

EXAMPLE 20-6 Calculation of RAROC

Suppose a borrower of $100,000 has risk characteristics that put her in a risk class that has experienced an average historical default rate of 0.2 percent. However, one year in every 100 (or 1 percent of the time), such as in a major recession, the bank expects 4 percent of these types of loans to default. This 4 percent can be viewed as the unexpected or 1 in 100 years default rate.[27] Moreover, upon default, the FI has historically recovered only 20 percent of the defaulted loans. As a result, the loss given default is 80 percent. Accordingly, for this borrower, the loan loss risk per dollar lent is 0.032 (.04 × .80), or the value (or capital) at risk to the FI (the denominator of the RAROC equation) is $100,000(.04 × .80) = $3,200.[28] Thus:

$$\text{RAROC} = \frac{\text{One-year income on a loan}}{\text{Dollar value of a loan} \times \text{Unexpected default rate} \times \text{Loss given default}}$$

Suppose the cost of funds for the FI is 9.20 percent and the loan rate is 10 percent on the $100,000 loan. After adjusting for fees of 0.5 percent, the expected one-year income on the loan, or the numerator of the RAROC equation, is $100,000 times 0.3 cents per dollar lent (10% − 9.20% − .50%), or 0.003. The extreme case loss rate for borrowers of this type is 4 percent (i.e., the default that has or is projected to occur once in every 100 years), and the dollar proportion of loans of this type that cannot be recaptured on default (loss given default) has historically been 80 percent. Then:

$$\text{RAROC} = \frac{100{,}000(.003)}{(100{,}000)(.04)(.8)} = \frac{300}{3{,}200} = 9.375\%$$

If the FI's after-tax ROE is less than 9.375 percent (e.g., it is 9 percent), the loan can be viewed as being profitable. If the tax-adjusted ROE is higher than 9.375 percent (e.g., 12 percent), it should be rejected and/or the loan officer should seek higher spreads and fees on the loan.[29]

27. The extreme loss rate is usually calculated by taking the average annual loss rate over some historical period and estimating the annual standard deviation of loan loss rates around that mean. If the standard deviation is multiplied by 2.33, as long as loan loss rates are normally distributed, this reflects the 99th percentile worst-loss case scenario. In practice, loss rates are not normally distributed, so many FIs use higher multiples of σ. For example, Bank of America uses a multiple of $6 \times \sigma$.

28. Again, unexpected losses are written off against the bank's capital. Traditionally, loan loss reserves have been viewed as the reserve against losses.

29. For more on RAROC, see A. Saunders and L. Allen, *Credit Risk Measurement: New Approaches to Value at Risk and Other Paradigms,* 2nd ed. (New York: John Wiley & Sons, 2002).

SUMMARY

This chapter provided an in-depth look at the measurement and on-balance-sheet management of credit risks. The chapter then discussed the role of credit analysis and how it differs across different types of loans, especially mortgage loans, individual loans, mid-market corporate loans, and large corporate loans. Both qualitative and quantitative approaches to credit analysis were discussed, as well as methods to evaluate the risk of loan portfolios.

SEARCH THE SITE

Go to the FDIC Web site at **www.fdic.gov**. Find the most recent breakdown for nonperformance rates for C&I loans of commercial banks using the following steps.

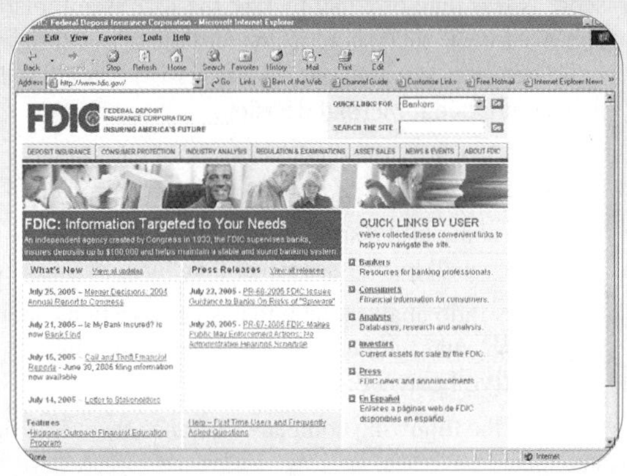

Click on "Analysts."

From there click on "FDIC Quarterly Banking Profile."

Click on "Quarterly Banking Profile," and then click on "Commercial Bank Section."

Then click on "TABLE V-A. Loan Performance, FDIC-Insured Commercial Banks."

This will bring up on your computer the files that contain the relevant data.

Questions

1. How has the nonperformance rate changed since 2004 reported in Figure 20–1?
2. Compare the nonperformance rate of C&I loans with real estate and credit card loans. Which has changed the most since 2004?

QUESTIONS

1. Why is credit risk analysis an important component of FI risk management?
2. How does an FI evaluate its credit risks with respect to consumer and commercial loans?
3. Jane Doe earns $30,000 per year and has applied for an $80,000, 30-year mortgage at 8 percent interest, paid monthly. Property taxes on the house are expected to be $1,200 per year. If her bank requires a gross debt service ratio of no more than 30 percent, will Jane be able to obtain the mortgage?
4. Suppose you are a loan officer at Carbondale Local Bank. Joan Doe listed the following information on her mortgage application:

Characteristic	Value
Annual gross income	$45,000
TDS	10%
Relations with FI	Checking account
Major credit cards	5
Age	27
Residence	Own/Mortgage
Length of residence	$2\frac{1}{2}$ years
Job stability	$5\frac{1}{2}$ years
Credit history	Missed 2 payments 1 year ago

Use the information below to determine whether or not Joan Doe should be approved for a mortgage from your bank.

Characteristic	Characteristic Values and Weights				
Annual gross income	<$10,000	$10,000–$25,000	$25,000–$50,000	$50,000–$100,000	>$100,000
Score	0	10	20	35	60
TDS	>50%	35%–50%	15%–35%	5%–15%	<5%
Score	−10	0	20	40	60
Relations with FI	None	Checking account	Savings account	Both	
Score	0	10	10	20	
Major credit cards	None	Between 1 and 4	5 or more		
Score	0	20	10		
Age	<25	25–60	>60		
Score	5	25	35		
Residence	Rent	Own with mortgage	Own outright		
Score	5	20	50		

www.mhhe.com/sc3e

Characteristic	Characteristic Values and Weights		
Length of residence	<1 year	1–5 years	>5 years
Score	0	25	40
Job stability	<1 year	1–5 years	>5 years
Score	0	25	50
Credit history	No record	Missed a payment in last 5 years	Met all payments
Score	0	−15	40

The loan is automatically rejected if the applicant's *total* score is less than or equal to 120; the loan is automatically approved if the total score is greater than or equal to 190. A score between 120 and 190 (noninclusive) is reviewed by a loan committee for a final decision.

5. In what ways does the credit analysis of a mid-market borrower differ from that of a small-business borrower?

6. What are some of the special risks and considerations when lending to small businesses rather than large businesses?

7. How does ratio analysis help to answer questions about the production, management, and marketing capabilities of a prospective borrower?

8. Consider the following company's balance sheet and income statement.

Balance Sheet

Assets		Liabilities and Equity	
Cash	$ 4,000	Accounts payable	$30,000
Accounts receivable	52,000	Notes payable	12,000
Inventory	40,000		
Total current assets	96,000	Total current liabilities	42,000
Fixed assets	44,000	Long-term debt	36,000
		Equity	62,000
Total assets	$140,000	Total liabilities and equity	$140,000

Income Statement

Sales (all on credit)	$200,000
Cost of goods sold	130,000
Gross margin	70,000
Selling and administrative expenses	20,000
Depreciation	8,000
EBIT	42,000
Interest expense	4,800
Earnings before tax	37,200
Taxes	11,160
Net income	$ 26,040

For this company, calculate the following:

a. Current ratio.
b. Number of days' sales in receivables.
c. Sales to total assets.
d. Number of days in inventory.
e. Debt ratio.
f. Cash-flow debt ratio.
g. Return on assets.
h. Return on equity.

9. In Question 8, how might we determine whether these ratios reflect a well-managed, creditworthy company?

10. Industrial Corporation has an income-to-sales (profit margin) ratio of .03, a sales-to-assets (asset utilization) ratio of 1.5, and a debt-to-asset ratio of .66. What is Industrial's return on equity?

11. Consider the coefficients of Altman's Z-score. Can you tell by the size of the coefficients which ratio appears most important in assessing the creditworthiness of a loan applicant? Explain.

12. The following is ABC Inc.'s balance sheet (in thousands):

Assets		Liabilities	
Cash	$ 20	Accounts payable	$ 30
Accounts receivable	90	Notes payable	90
Inventory	90	Accruals	30
		Long-term debt	150
Plant and equipment	500	Equity	400
Total	$700		$700

Also assume that sales equal \$500, cost of goods sold equals \$360, interest payments equal \$62, taxes equal \$56, and net income equals \$22. Assume the beginning retained earnings is \$0, the market value of equity is equal to its book value, and the company pays no dividends.

a. Calculate Altman's Z-score for ABC Inc. if ABC has a 50 percent dividend payout ratio and the market value of equity is equal to its book value. Recall the following:

Net working capital = Current assets − Current liabilities

Current assets = Cash + Accounts receivable + Inventories

Current liabilities = Accounts payable + Accruals + Notes payable

EBIT = Revenues − Cost of goods sold − Depreciation

Taxes = (EBIT − Interest)(Tax rate)

Net income = EBIT − Interest − Taxes

Retained earnings = Net income (1 − Dividend payout ratio)

b. Should you approve ABC Inc.'s application to your bank for \$500,000 for a capital expansion loan?

c. If ABC's sales were \$450,000, taxes were \$16,000, and the market value of equity fell to one-quarter of its book value (assume cost of goods sold and interest are unchanged), how would that change ABC's income statement? ABC's tax liability can be used to offset tax liabilities incurred by the other divisions of the firm. Would your credit decision change?

d. What are some of the shortcomings of using a discriminant function model to evaluate credit risk?

13. Why could a lender's expected return be lower when the risk premium is increased on a loan?

14. Countrybank offers one-year loans with a stated rate of 10 percent but requires a compensating balance of 10 percent. What is the true cost of this loan to the borrower?

15. Metrobank offers one-year loans with a 9 percent stated rate, charges a ¼ percent loan origination fee, imposes a 10 percent compensating balance requirement, and must pay a 6 percent reserve requirement to the Federal Reserve. What is the return to the bank on these loans?

16. An FI is planning a loan of $5,000,000 to a firm in the steel industry. It expects to charge an up-front fee of 0.10 percent and a service fee of 5 basis points. The loan has a maturity of 8 years. The cost of funds (and the RAROC benchmark) for the FI is 10 percent. Assume that the FI has estimated the risk premium on the steel manufacturing sector to be approximately 0.18 percent, based on two years of historical data. The current market interest rate for loans in this sector is 10.1 percent. The 99th (extreme case) loss rate for borrowers of this type has historically run at 3 percent, and the dollar proportion of loans of this type that cannot be recaptured on default has historically been 90 percent. Using the RAROC model, should the FI make the loan?

The following questions are related to the appendix material.

17. How does loan portfolio risk differ from individual loan risk?

18. Explain how modern portfolio theory can be applied to lower the credit risk of an FI's portfolio.

19. A bank has two loans of equal size outstanding, A and B, and the bank has identified the returns they would earn in two different states of nature, 1 and 2, representing default and no default, respectively.

	State	
	1	2
Security A	.02	.14
Security B	.00	.18

If the probability of state 1 is .2 and the probability of state 2 is .8, calculate:

a. The expected return of each security.
b. The expected return on the portfolio in each state.
c. The expected return on the portfolio.

APPENDIX 20A: Loan Portfolio Risk and Management

View this appendix at
www.mhhe.com/sc3e

www.mhhe.com/sc3e

21

Managing Liquidity Risk *on the* Balance Sheet

OUTLINE

Chapter NAVIGATOR

1. What are the causes of liquidity risk?
2. What two methods do financial institutions use to manage liquidity risk?
3. How do banks measure liquidity risk?
4. What are the components of a liquidity plan?
5. Why do abnormal deposit drains occur?
6. To what extent are insurance companies exposed to liquidity risk?
7. To what extent are mutual funds exposed to liquidity risk?

LIQUIDITY RISK MANAGEMENT: CHAPTER OVERVIEW

This chapter looks at the problems created by liquidity risk. Unlike other risks that threaten the very solvency of an FI, liquidity risk is a normal aspect of the everyday management of an FI. In extreme cases, liquidity risk problems develop into solvency risk problems (see In The News box). Moreover, some FIs are more exposed to liquidity risk than others. At one extreme, depository institutions are highly exposed; at the other extreme, mutual and pension funds and property–casualty insurance companies have relatively low liquidity risk exposure. We examine the reasons for these differences in this chapter.

CAUSES OF LIQUIDITY RISK

1

There are two types of liquidity risk. The first type arises when an FI's liability holders, such as depositors or insurance policyholders, seek to cash in or withdraw their financial claims. The second type arises when commitments made by the FI and recorded off the balance sheet, such as loan commitments, are exercised by the commitment holder. Upon exercise, the loan commitment becomes an asset (a loan) on the FI's balance sheet.

Public's Confidence in Bank System Tested

The weekend run on Bank of New England (BNE) and its subsequent seizure by the government underscore the public's fragile confidence in the banking system. While the large increase in troubled loans announced last Friday apparently prompted large withdrawals, the insolvency of Rhode Island's private deposit insurance fund earlier in the week and large losses reported in the national deposit fund played a role as well. "The psychological atmosphere in New England following the Rhode Island debacle is not good," said William Isaac, head of the Secura Group, a Washington consulting firm. Bert Ely, a financial consultant based in Alexandria, VA, chalked it up to "jitteriness, uncertainty and confusion . . . I think we're asking too much of people to worry about how sound their bank is," he said. Ely called the seizure a "terrible comment on the bank regulatory process."

To some extent, the run and seizure were unexpected, even though analysts noted that Bank of New England has been the nation's largest problem bank for the past year. The bank also had recently worked out a deal to swap some of its debt for equity. Yet, analysts said, failure may have been inevitable. "Failure was in the cards," said Gerard Cassidy, a banking analyst with Tucker Anthony based in Portland, Maine. "And the FDIC played them this weekend." "They were somewhat of an aberration in their lending and the way they ran the institution," said Ely . . . "They were not representative of the New England banks, and New England is not representative of the rest of the country." After years as the region's most aggressive real estate lender, BNE was particularly hard hit when that market headed south, analysts said. The large increase in troubled loans BNE reported Friday was mainly due to real estate and effectively wiped out its capital . . .

All of BNE's depositors will be covered by deposit insurance, regardless of the amount. By contrast, the larger depositors at Freedom National Bank in Harlem, formerly the nation's largest minorityowned bank, got only 50 cents for each $1 above $100,000. But some of that money may be recovered after assets are sold, according to regulators.

Source: *Investor's Daily*, January 8, 1991, p. 1, Karen Padley **www.investors.com**

DO YOU UNDERSTAND?

1. What the main reasons were for the failure of Bank of New England?

With respect to the first type of liquidity risk, when liability holders withdraw their financial claims, the FI needs to meet these withdrawals by borrowing additional funds or selling assets so as to generate cash. Although most assets can be turned into cash eventually, for some assets this can only be done at high transaction costs or unexpectedly low prices. For example, FIs selling stock securities during the week of September 17, 2001 (as markets opened following the September 11, 2001, terrorist attacks) were forced to do so at unexpectedly low values. For example, on September 21, 2001, the Dow Jones Industrial Average dropped to 8235.81. Had FIs been able to wait until October 2001 to sell securities, they would have found stock prices had recovered significantly. By October 3, 2001, the DJIA had increased 887.97 points to 9123.78. Thus, some assets may be liquidated only at low or **fire-sale prices.** If asset sale prices are insufficient to meet all the cash liquidity needs to meet liability withdrawals, the FI is effectively insolvent.

fire-sale price

The price received for an asset that has to be liquidated (sold) immediately.

To understand the connection between liquidity risk and insolvency risk, consider the simple FI balance sheet in Table 21–1. Before deposit withdrawals, the FI has $10 million in cash assets and $90 million in nonliquid assets. These assets were funded with $90 million in deposits and $10 million in owner's equity. Suppose that depositors unexpectedly withdraw $20 million in deposits (perhaps due to the release of negative news about the profits of the FI) and the FI receives no new deposits to replace them. To meet these deposit withdrawals, the FI first uses the $10 million it has in cash assets and then seeks to sell some of its nonliquid assets to raise an additional $10 million in cash. Suppose also that the FI cannot borrow any more funds in the short-term money markets (see Chapter 5), and because it cannot wait to get better prices for its assets in the future (as it needs the cash now

TABLE 21-1 Adjusting to a Deposit Withdrawal Using Asset Sales *(in millions)*

Before the Withdrawal				After the Withdrawal			
Assets		**Liabilities/Equity**		**Assets**		**Liabilities/Equity**	
Cash assets	$ 10	Deposits	$ 90	Cash assets	$ 0	Deposits	$70
Nonliquid assets	90	Equity	10	Nonliquid assets	70	Equity	0
	$100		$100		$70		$70

to meet immediate depositor withdrawals), the FI has to sell any nonliquid assets at 50 cents on the dollar. Thus, to cover the remaining $10 million in deposit withdrawals, the FI must sell $20 million in nonliquid assets, incurring a loss of $10 million from the face value of those assets. The FI must then write off any such losses against its capital or equity funds. Since its capital was only $10 million before the deposit withdrawal, the loss on the fire-sale of assets of $10 million leaves the FI economically insolvent (i.e., with zero equity capital or net worth).

The second type of liquidity risk arises directly from the effect on the asset side of the balance sheet due to unexpected loan demand that cannot be fulfilled because of a lack of funds or to an exercise of off-balance-sheet loan commitments. As we described in Chapter 12, a loan commitment allows a customer contractually to borrow (take down) funds on demand from an FI. When a borrower draws on its loan commitment contracts, it creates a need for liquidity by the FI, since the FI is contractually obliged to supply (loanable) funds to the customer immediately. As was the case for liability withdrawals, an FI can meet such liquidity needs by running down its cash assets, selling off other assets to raise cash, or borrowing additional funds in the money markets.

DO YOU UNDERSTAND?

1. What the sources of liquidity risk are?
2. What the phrase "liquidating assets at fire-sale prices" means?

LIQUIDITY RISK AND DEPOSITORY INSTITUTIONS

Liability Side Liquidity Risk

As discussed in Chapter 11, a depository institution's balance sheet typically has a large amount of short-term liabilities, such as demand deposits and other transaction accounts, which fund relatively long-term, relatively illiquid assets such as commercial loans and mortgages. Demand deposit accounts and other transaction accounts are contracts that give the holders the right to put their financial claims back to the depository institution on any given day and demand immediate repayment of the face value in cash.[1] Thus, an individual demand deposit account holder with a balance of $10,000 can demand cash to be repaid immediately in cash as can a corporation with $100 million in its demand deposit account. In theory, at least, a depository institution that has 20 percent of its liabilities in demand deposits and other transaction accounts must stand ready to pay out the entire amount by liquidating an equivalent amount of assets (or borrowing additional funds) on any given banking day.

In reality, a depository institution knows that *normally* only a small proportion of its demand deposits will be withdrawn on any given day. Most demand deposits remain with

1. Accounts with this type of put option include demand deposits, NOW accounts (checking accounts with minimum balance requirements), and money market accounts (checking accounts with minimum balance and restrictions as to the number of checks written). We describe these accounts in more detail in Chapter 12. Banks typically liquidate savings account contracts immediately upon request of the customer. Many savings account contracts, however, give a bank some powers to delay withdrawals by requiring notification of withdrawal a certain number of days before withdrawal or by imposing penalty fees such as loss of interest.

FIGURE 21–1 Distribution of an FI's Net Deposit Drains (cash outflows)

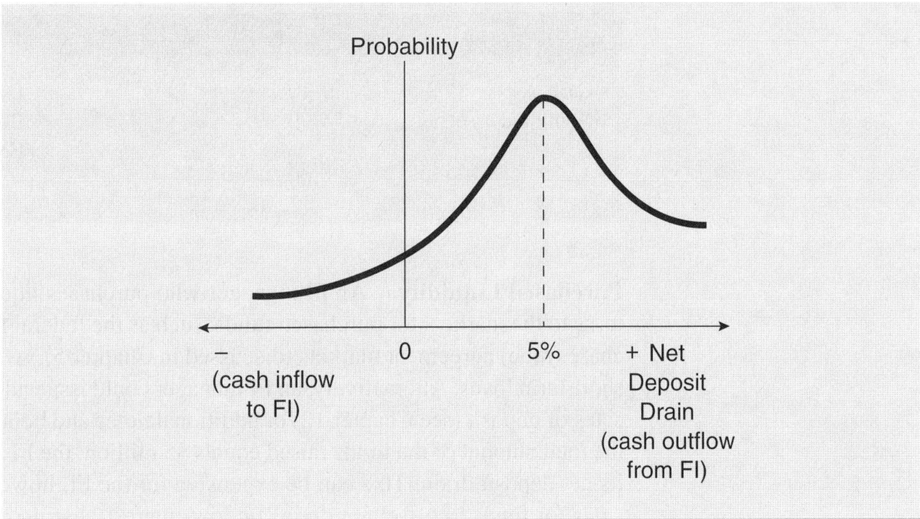

core deposits

Deposits that provide a relatively stable, long-term funding source to a depository institution.

net deposit drain

The amount by which cash withdrawals exceed additions; a net cash outflow.

the FI, thus behaving as **core deposits** on a day-by-day basis, providing a relatively stable or long-term source of funding for the depository institution. Moreover, deposit withdrawals may in part be offset by the inflow of new deposits. The depository institution manager must monitor the resulting net deposit withdrawals or **net deposit drains**. Specifically, over time a depository institution manager can normally predict—with a good degree of accuracy—the probability of different-sized net deposit drains (the difference between deposit withdrawals and deposit additions) on any given banking day.

Consider the distribution of net deposit drains shown in Figure 21–1. This distribution is assumed to be strongly peaked at the 5 percent net (deposit) withdrawal level—this FI expects approximately 5 percent of its net deposit funds to be withdrawn on any given day with the highest probability. A net deposit drain means that an FI is receiving insufficient additional deposits (and other cash inflows) to offset deposit withdrawals, which means that the liability side of its balance sheet is contracting (see Table 21–2, which illustrates a 5 percent, equal to $5 million, net deposit drain).

2

An FI can manage a drain on deposits in two major ways: (1) purchased liquidity management and/or (2) stored liquidity management. Traditionally, FI managers relied on *stored liquidity* as the primary mechanism of liquidity management. Today, many FIs—especially the largest banks with access to the money market and other nondeposit markets for funds—rely on *purchased liquidity*, whereas smaller FIs—such as community banks—more often look to *stored liquidity*.

TABLE 21–2 The Effect of Net Deposit Drains on the Balance Sheet
(in millions)

Before the Drain				After the Drain			
Assets		Liabilities/Equity		Assets		Liabilities/Equity	
Cash assets	$ 10	Deposits	$ 70	Cash assets	$ 5	Deposits	$65
Nonliquid assets	90	Borrowed funds	10	Nonliquid assets	90	Borrowed funds	10
		Equity	20			Equity	20
	$100		$100		$95		$95

TABLE 21-3 **Adjusting to a Deposit Drain by Purchasing Funds** *(in millions)*

Assets		Liabilities/Equity	
Cash assets	\$ 10	Deposits	\$ 65
Nonliquid assets	90	Borrowed funds	15
		Equity	20
	\$100		\$100

Purchased Liquidity. An FI manager who purchases liquidity to offset a deposit drain turns to the markets for purchased funds, such as the federal funds market and/or the repurchase (repo) agreement markets (discussed in Chapter 5),[2] which are interbank markets for short-term loans. Alternatively, an FI manager could issue additional fixed-maturity certificates of deposit (see Chapter 12) or additional notes and bonds.[3] In our example, as long as the total amount of the funds raised equals \$5 million, the FI in Table 21–2 could fully fund its net deposit drain. This can be expensive for the FI, however, since it is paying *market rates* for funds to offset net drains on low-interest-bearing deposits.[4] Thus, the higher the cost of purchased funds relative to the rates earned on assets, the less attractive this approach to liquidity management becomes. Further, since most of these funds are not covered by deposit insurance, their availability may be limited should the FI incur insolvency difficulties[5]. Table 21–3 shows the FI's balance sheet if it responds to deposit drains by using purchased liquidity techniques.

Note that purchased liquidity has allowed the FI to maintain its overall balance sheet size of \$100 million without disturbing the size and composition of the asset side of its balance sheet—that is, the complete adjustment to the deposit drain occurs on the liability side of the balance sheet. In other words, purchased liquidity management can insulate the asset side of the balance sheet from normal drains on the liability side of the balance sheet. This is one of the reasons for the enormous growth of FI-purchased liquidity techniques and associated purchased fund markets such as fed funds, repurchase agreements, and CDs. (We described and discussed these instruments and markets in Chapter 5.)

Stored Liquidity. Instead of meeting the net deposit drain by purchasing liquidity in the money markets, the FI could use or sell off some of its assets (or utilize its stored liquidity). U.S. banks traditionally have held or "stored" cash reserves in their vaults and at the Federal Reserve for this very purpose. The Federal Reserve sets a minimum requirement for the cash reserves that banks must hold (see Chapter 13).[6] Even so, banks still tend to hold cash reserves in excess of the minimum required amount to meet liquidity drains.

2. Securities companies and institutional investors use the repo market extensively for liquidity management purposes.

3. The *discount window* is also a source of funds. See the section "Bank Runs, the Discount Window, and Deposit Insurance" in this chapter for more discussion of the role of the discount window.

4. Although checking accounts pay no explicit interest, other transaction accounts such as NOW and money market accounts do. However, the rates paid are normally slow to adjust to changes in market interest rates and lie below purchased fund rates.

5. For example, in 1984 Continental Illinois Bank, headquartered in Chicago and at the time the nation's eighth largest bank, had a very small core deposit base as a result of restrictions on bank branching within the state. As a result, it had to rely extensively on borrowed funds such as fed funds, RPs, and Eurodollar deposits. As these borrowings grew, concerns about the bank's ability to meet its payment commitments increased—especially in view of a worsening loan portfolio. This resulted in the eventual refusal of a number of large money market lenders (such as Japanese banks) to renew or roll over their borrowed funds on maturity. With the rapid withdrawal of such borrowed funds, Continental Illinois was unable to survive and was eventually taken over by the FDIC.

6. Currently, the Fed requires a minimum 3 percent cash reserve on the first \$47.6 million and 10 percent on the rest of a bank's demand deposit and transaction account holdings. The \$47.6 million figure is adjusted annually along with the increase or decrease in bank deposits. The first \$7.0 million of the \$47.6 million is not subject to reserve requirements. See Chapter 13.

TABLE 21–4 Composition of an FI's Balance Sheet *(in millions)*

Assets		Liabilities/Equity	
Cash assets	$ 9	Deposits	$ 70
Nonliquid assets	91	Borrowed funds	10
		Equity	20
	$100		$100

TABLE 21–5 Reserve Asset Adjustment to Deposit Drain *(in millions)*

Assets		Liabilities/Equity	
Cash assets	$ 4	Deposits	$65
Nonliquid assets	91	Borrowed funds	10
		Equity	20
	$95		$95

Suppose in our example that on the asset side of the balance sheet the FI normally holds $9 million of its assets in cash (of which $3 million is to meet Federal Reserve minimum reserve requirements and $6 million is an "excess" cash reserve). We depict the situation before the net drain in liabilities in Table 21–4. As depositors withdraw $5 million in deposits, the FI meets this by using the excess cash stored in its vaults or held on deposit at other FIs or at the Federal Reserve. If the reduction of $5 million in deposit liabilities is met by a $5 million reduction in cash assets held by the FI, its balance sheet is as shown in Table 21–5.

When the FI uses its cash as the liquidity adjustment mechanism, both sides of its balance sheet contract. In this example, both the FI's total assets and liabilities/equity shrink from $100 to $95 million. The cost to the FI of using stored liquidity, apart from decreased asset size,[7] is that it must hold excess noninterest-bearing assets in the form of cash on its balance sheet.[8] Thus, the cost of using cash to meet liquidity needs is the forgone return (or opportunity cost) of being unable to invest these funds in loans and other higher income-earning assets.

Finally, note that although stored liquidity management and purchased liquidity management are alternative strategies for meeting deposit drains, an FI can combine the two methods by using some purchased liquidity management and some stored liquidity management to meet any given deposit drain. Moreover, an FI can sell off its noncash assets to generate additional cash reserves to meet liquidity needs.

EXAMPLE 21–1 Impact of Stored Liquidity versus Purchased Liquidity Management on an FI's Net Income

Suppose an FI has the following balance sheet:

Assets		Liabilities and Equity	
Cash	$1 m. (equal to required reserves)	Core deposits	$ 6 m.
Loans	9 m.	Subordinated debt	2 m.
		Equity	2 m.
	$10 m.		$10 m.

7. There is no empirical evidence supporting a significant positive correlation between a bank's asset size and its profits.

8. FIs could hold highly liquid interest-bearing assets such as T-bills, but they are still less liquid than cash, and immediate liquidation may result in some small capital value losses and transaction costs.

The average cost of core deposits is 6 percent and the average yield on loans is 8 percent. Increases in interest rates are expected to cause a net drain of \$2 million in core deposits over the next six months. New short-term debt (such as subordinated debt) can be obtained at a cost of 7.5 percent. If the FI uses stored liquidity management to manage liquidity risk, it reduces its loan portfolio (selling loans for cash) to offset this expected decline in deposits. Assuming there is no capital loss on the sale of the loans, the FI's net income will change as follows:[9]

Decrease in interest income-loans	−.08 × \$2m =	−\$160,000
Decrease in interest expense-core deposits	−(−.06) × \$2m =	\$120,000
Change in net income		−\$ 40,000

If the FI uses purchased liquidity management to manage liquidity risk, it issues short-term, subordinated debt to pay off the expected decline in deposits. In this case, the FI's net income will change by:

Decrease in interest expense-core deposits	−(−.06) × \$2m =	\$120,000
Increase in interest expense-short-term debt	−.075 × \$2m =	−\$150,000
Change in net income		−\$ 30,000

The FI is more profitable if it manages the drain in core deposits using purchased liquidity management. The decrease in net income is \$30,000 versus \$40,000 if it uses stored liquidity management.

Asset Side Liquidity Risk

Just as deposit drains can cause an FI liquidity problems, so can loan requests, resulting from the exercise, by borrowers, of loan commitments and other credit lines, that cannot be funded immediately. For example, in 2001 regulators found that U.S. banks' unused loan commitments to "on-hand liquidity" had grown from a ratio of 3.5 in 1994 to 11 in the early 2000s.[10] Thus, at that time, loan commitments outstanding were dangerously high for banks as well as other DIs. Table 21–6 shows the effect of a \$5 million exercise of a loan commitment by a borrower. As a result, the FI must fund \$5 million in additional loans on the balance sheet. Consider the Before columns in Table 21–6 (the balance sheet before the commitment exercise) and the After columns (as the loan is added to the balance sheet after the exercise). In particular, the exercise of the loan commitment means that the FI needs to provide \$5 million immediately to the borrower (other assets increase from \$91 to \$96 million). This can be done either by purchased liquidity management (borrowing an additional \$5 million in the money market and lending these funds to the borrower) or by stored liquidity management (decreasing the FI's excess cash assets from \$9 million to \$4 million). We present these two policies in Table 21–7. The next section illustrates several methods for measuring an FI's liquidity "exposure" that take into account its excess cash reserves and its ability to raise additional purchased funds.

Measuring a Bank's Liquidity Exposure

3 **Sources and Uses of Liquidity.** As discussed above, an FI's liquidity risk can arise either from a drain on deposits or from new loan demands, and the subsequent need to meet these demands by liquidating assets or borrowing funds. Therefore, a bank manager must be able to measure its liquidity position on a daily basis, if possible. A useful tool is a *net liquidity statement,* which lists sources and uses of liquidity and, thus, provides a measure of a bank's net liquidity position. Such a statement for a hypothetical U.S. money center bank is presented in Table 21–8.

9. If the FI can only sell loans at a capital loss (i.e., it must sell \$2.5m. in book value of loans to raise \$2m. in cash needed to meet the deposit withdrawals), its net income will decrease further by the amount of the capital loss (or in this case by another \$0.5m.).

10. See "Years of living Dangerously Set to Haunt Banks," *Financial Times,* June 4, 2001, p. 24.

TABLE 21-6 The Effects of a Loan Commitment Exercise
(in millions)

Before				After			
Cash assets	$ 9	Deposits	$ 70	Cash assets	$ 9	Deposits	$ 70
Nonliquid assets	91	Borrowed funds	10	Nonliquid assets	96	Borrowed funds	10
		Equity	20			Equity	20
	$100		$100		$105		$100

TABLE 21-7 Adjusting the Balance Sheet to a Loan Commitment Exercise
(in millions)

Purchase Liquidity Management				Stored Liquidity Management			
Cash assets	$ 9	Deposits	$ 70	Cash assets	$ 4	Deposits	$ 70
Nonliquid assets	96	Borrowed funds	15	Nonliquid assets	96	Borrowed funds	10
		Equity	20			Equity	20
	$105		$105		$100		$100

The bank can obtain liquid funds in three ways. First, it can sell its liquid assets such as T-bills immediately with little price risk and low transaction costs. Second, it can borrow funds in the money/purchased funds market up to a maximum amount (this is an internal guideline based on the manager's assessment of the credit limits that the purchased or borrowed funds market is likely to impose on the bank). Third, it can use any excess cash reserves over and above the amount held to meet regulatory imposed reserve requirements. The bank's *sources* of liquidity total $14,500 million. Compare this to the bank's *uses* of liquidity—in particular, the amount of borrowed or purchased funds it has already utilized (e.g., fed funds, RPs borrowed) and the amount of cash it has already borrowed from the Federal Reserve through discount window loans. These total $7,000 million. As a result, the bank has a positive net liquidity position of $7,500 million. These liquidity sources and uses can be tracked easily on a day-by-day basis.

Peer Group Ratio Comparisons. Another way to measure a bank's liquidity exposure is to compare certain of its key ratios and balance sheet features—such as loans to deposits, borrowed funds to total assets, and commitments to lend to assets ratios—with those for banks of a similar size and geographic location (see Chapter 12). A high ratio of loans to deposits and borrowed funds to total assets means that the bank relies heavily on the short-term

TABLE 21-8 Net Liquidity Position
(in millions)

Sources of Liquidity	
1. Total cash-type assets	$ 2,000
2. Maximum borrowed funds limit	12,000
3. Excess cash reserves	500
Total	$14,500
Uses of Liquidity	
1. Funds borrowed	$ 6,000
2. Federal Reserve borrowing	1,000
Total	$ 7,000
Total net liquidity	$ 7,500

TABLE 21–9 Liquidity Exposure Ratios for Two Banks, 2004 Values

	North Fork Bancorp	Bank of America
Borrowed funds to total assets	33.14%	24.79%
Core deposits to total assets	50.30	57.97
Loans to deposits	105.13	82.12
Commitments to lend to total assets	9.99	60.49

money market rather than on core deposits to fund loans. This could mean future liquidity problems if the bank is at or near its borrowing limits in the purchased funds market. Similarly, a high ratio of loan commitments to assets indicates the need for a high degree of liquidity to fund any unexpected takedowns of these loans by customers—high-commitment banks often face more liquidity risk exposure than do low-commitment banks.

Table 21–9 lists the 2004 values of these ratios for the banks we reviewed in Chapter 12: North Fork Bancorp (NFB) and Bank of America Corporation (BAC). Neither of these banks relied heavily on borrowed funds (short-term money market instruments) to fund loans. Their ratio of borrowed funds to total assets was 33.14 percent and 24.79 percent, respectively. Their ratio of core deposits (the stable deposits of the FI, such as demand deposits, NOW accounts, MMDAs, other savings accounts, and retail CDs) to total assets, on the other hand, was 50.30 percent and 57.97 percent, respectively. Furthermore, NFB had a ratio of loan commitments to total assets of only 9.99 percent, while BAC had a much greater ratio of 60.49 percent. Thus, BAC was exposed to substantially greater liquidity risk from unexpected takedowns of these commitments.

Liquidity Index. A third way to measure liquidity risk is to use a liquidity index. This index measures the potential losses a bank could suffer from a sudden or fire-sale disposal of assets compared to the amount it would receive at a fair market value established under normal market conditions. The larger the differences between immediate fire-sale asset prices (P_i) and fair market prices (P_i^*), the less liquid is the bank's portfolio of assets. Define an index I such that:

$$I = \sum_{i=1}^{N} [(w_i)(P_i/P_i^*)]$$

where

w_i = Percentage of each asset in the FI's portfolio
$\Sigma w_i = 1$
P_i = Price it gets if an FI liquidates asset i today
P_i^* = Price it gets if an FI liquidates asset i at the end of the month

EXAMPLE 21–2 Calculation of the Liquidity Index

Suppose that a bank has two assets: 50 percent in one-month Treasury bills and 50 percent in real estate loans. If the bank must liquidate its T-bills today (P_1), it receives \$99 per \$100 of face value; if it can wait to liquidate them on maturity (in one month's time), it will receive the fair market price of \$100 per \$100 of face value (P_1^*). If the bank has to liquidate its real estate loans today, it receives \$85 per \$100 of face value (P_2); liquidation at the end of one month (closer to maturity) will receive the fair market price of \$92 per \$100 of face value (P_2^*). Thus, the one-month liquidity index value for this bank's asset portfolio is:

$$\begin{aligned} I &= (\tfrac{1}{2})(.99/1.00) + (\tfrac{1}{2})(.85/.92) \\ &= 0.495 + 0.462 \\ &= 0.957 \end{aligned}$$

Suppose alternatively that a slow or thin real estate market causes the bank to be able to liquidate the real estate loans at only \$65 per \$100 of face value (P_2) on an immediate sale. The one-month liquidity index for the bank's asset portfolio is:

$$I = (\tfrac{1}{2})(.99/1.00) + (\tfrac{1}{2})(.65/.92)$$
$$= 0.495 + 0.353$$
$$= 0.848$$

The value of the one-month liquidity index decreases due to the larger discount on the immediate or fire-sale price—from the fair (full value) market price of real estate—over the one-month period. The larger the discount from fair value, the smaller the liquidity index or higher the liquidity risk the bank faces.[11]

financing gap

The difference between a bank's average loans and average (core) deposits.

Financing Gap and the Financing Requirement. A fourth way to measure liquidity risk exposure is to determine the bank's financing gap. As we discussed earlier, even though demand depositors can withdraw their funds immediately, they do not do so in normal circumstances. On average, most demand deposits stay at banks for quite long periods, often two years or more.[12] Thus, a banker often thinks of the average deposit base, including demand deposits, as a core source of funds that over time can fund a bank's average amount of loans. We define a **financing gap** as the difference between a bank's average loans and average (core) deposits, or:

$$\text{Financing gap} = \text{Average loans} - \text{Average deposits}$$

If this financing gap is positive, the bank must find liquidity to fund the gap. This funding can come via either purchased liquidity management (i.e., borrowing funds) or stored liquidity management (i.e., liquidating assets), as discussed above. Thus:

$$\text{Financing gap} = -\text{Liquid assets} + \text{Borrowed funds}$$

We can write this relationship as:

$$\text{Financing gap} + \text{Liquid assets} = \text{Financing requirement (borrowed funds)}$$

financing requirement

The financing gap plus a bank's liquid assets.

As expressed in this fashion, the liquidity and managerial implications of the **financing requirement** (the financing gap plus a bank's liquid assets) are that the level of core deposits and loans as well as the amount of liquid assets determines the bank's borrowing or purchased fund needs.[13] In particular, the larger a bank's financing gap and liquid asset holdings, the higher the amount of funds it needs to borrow in the money markets and the greater is its exposure to liquidity problems from such a reliance.

The balance sheet in Table 21–10 indicates the relationship between the financing gap, liquid assets, and the borrowed funds financing requirement. This is seen in the following equation:

$$\underset{(\$5\text{ million})}{\text{Financing gap}} + \underset{(\$5\text{ million})}{\text{Liquid assets}} = \underset{(\$10\text{ million})}{\text{Financing requirement}}$$

A widening financing gap can warn of future liquidity problems for a bank since it may indicate increased deposit withdrawals (core deposits falling below \$20 million in Table 21–10) and increasing loans due to more exercise of loan commitments (loans rising above \$25 million). If the bank does not reduce its liquid assets—they stay at \$5 million—the manager

11. The liquidity index is always between 0 and 1. The liquidity index for this bank could be compared with similar indexes calculated for a group of similar banks.

12. See Federal Reserve Board of Governors, "Risk-Based Capital and Interest Rate Risk," press release, July 30, 1992.

13. The bank holds cash and liquid assets to meet day-to-day variations in the actual level of deposits and loans. On any given day, however, cash and liquid asset balances may exceed those needed to meet daily variations in deposits and loans. These excess balances may be run down to fund the financing gap.

TABLE 21–10 The Financing Requirement of a Bank
(in millions)

Assets		Liabilities	
Loans	$25	Core deposits	$20
	Financing gap	(5)	
Liquid assets	5	**Financing requirement (borrowed funds)**	10
Total	$30	Total	$30

must resort to more money market borrowings. As these borrowings rise, sophisticated lenders in the money market may be concerned about the bank's creditworthiness. They may react by imposing higher risk premiums on borrowed funds or establishing stricter credit limits by not rolling over funds lent to the bank. If the bank's financing requirements dramatically exceed such limits, it may become insolvent. A good example of an excessive financing requirement resulting in bank insolvency is the failure of Continental Illinois in 1984 (see Chapter 19). This possibility of insolvency also highlights the need for bank managers to engage in active liquidity planning to avoid such crises.

www.bis.org

BIS Approach: Maturity Ladder/Scenario Analysis. In February 2000, recognizing that liquidity is crucial to the ongoing viability of a depository institution (DI), the Bank for International Settlements (BIS) outlined a Maturity Laddering method for measuring liquidity risk and, specifically, net funding (financing) requirements.[14] At a minimum, liquidity measurement involves assessing all cash inflows against its outflows as outlined in Table 21–11. Once identified, a maturity ladder model allows a comparison of cash inflows and outflows on a day-to-day basis and/or over a series of specified time periods. Daily and cumulative net funding requirements can then be determined from the maturity ladder.

For the DI in Table 21–11, for example, excess cash of $4 million is available over the one-day time horizon. However, a cumulative net cash shortfall of $46 million exists over the next month. The DI will need to immediately start planning to obtain additional funding to fill this net funding requirement. Over the six-month period, the DI has cumulative excess cash of $1,104 million. If these expectations hold true, the DI will need to find a place to invest these excess funds until they are needed.

The relevant time frame for active liquidity management is generally quite short, including intraday liquidity. However, the appropriate time frame will depend on the nature of a DI's business. DIs that rely on short-term funding concentrate primarily on managing their liquidity in the very short term (e.g., the BIS recommends a five-day horizon for such DIs). DIs that are less dependent on short-term funding might actively manage their net funding requirements over a slightly longer period. In addition, DIs should analyze and monitor their liquidity positions over the longer term. Typically a DI may find substantial funding gaps in distant periods and thus need to plan ways to fill these gaps by influencing the maturity of transactions to offset the future funding gap.

While liquidity is typically managed under normal conditions, the BIS cautions that DIs must also be prepared to manage liquidity under abnormal conditions. Analyzing liquidity thus entails generating and analyzing various "what if" scenarios. Under each scenario, the DI should try to account for any significant positive or negative liquidity swings that could occur. These scenarios should take into account factors both internal (bank specific) and external (market related). Under the BIS Scenario Analysis, a DI needs to assign a timing of cash flows for each type of asset and liability by assessing the probability of the behavior of

14. See "Sound Practices for Managing Liquidity in Banking Organizations," Basel Committee on Banking Supervision, BIS, Basel, Switzerland, February 2000.

TABLE 21–11 Net Funding Requirement Using the BIS Maturity Laddering Model
(in millions of dollars)

	1 day	1 month	6 months
Cash Inflows			
Maturing assets	$10	$150	$1,500
Saleable nonmaturing assets	12	250	4,000
Access to deposit liabilities	15	200	2,000
Established credit lines	12	100	750
Ability to securitize	5	50	400
	$54	$750	$8,650
Cash Outflows			
Liabilities falling due	$30	$490	$4,500
Committed lines of credit that can be drawn on and other contingent liabilities	16	300	2,960
Cash outflows from unanticipated events	4	10	40
	$50	$800	$7,500
Net funding requirement	$4	($50)	$1,150
Cumulative net funding requirement	$4	($46)	$1,104

those cash flows under the scenario being examined. Accordingly, the timing of cash inflows and outflows on the maturity ladder can differ among scenarios, and the assumptions may differ quite sharply. For example, a DI may believe, based upon its historical experience, that its ability to control the level and timing of future cash flows from a stock of saleable assets in a DI-specific funding crisis would deteriorate little from normal conditions. However, in a market crisis, this capacity may fall off sharply if few institutions are willing or able to make cash purchases of less liquid assets.

The evolution of a DI's liquidity profile under each scenario can be portrayed graphically as in Figure 21–2. A stylized liquidity graph enables the evolution of the cumulative net excess or shortage of funds to be compared under the major scenarios (e.g., normal conditions, general market crisis conditions, DI-specific crisis conditions). The DI can use this profile to provide additional insights into how consistent and realistic the assumptions are for its liquidity. For example, in Figure 21–2, a high-quality DI (Panel A) may look very liquid under normal circumstances and remain so in a general market crisis (i.e., the DI has excess funds available to meet its liquidity needs, cumulative funding is positive), but may suffer a liquidity crisis only in a DI-specific crisis (i.e., the DI does not have sufficient funds to meet its liquidity needs, cumulative funding is negative). In contrast, a lower quality DI (Panel B) might be equally illiquid in a general and a DI-specific crisis. Because a DI's future liquidity position can be affected by factors that cannot always be accurately predicted, it is critical that assumptions used to determine its funding requirements be reviewed and revised frequently.

Liquidity Planning. Liquidity planning is a key component in measuring (and being able to deal with) liquidity risk and its associated costs. Specifically, liquidity planning allows managers to make important borrowing priority decisions before liquidity problems arise. Such forward planning can lower the cost of funds (by determining an optimal funding mix) and can minimize the amount of excess reserves that a bank needs to hold.

4 A liquidity plan has a number of components. The first component is the delineation of managerial details and responsibilities. Responsibilities are assigned to key management personnel should a liquidity crisis occur; the plan identifies those

FIGURE 21–2 Cumulative Excess or Shortages of Funds for a High-Quality and a Low-Quality DI under Various Market Conditions

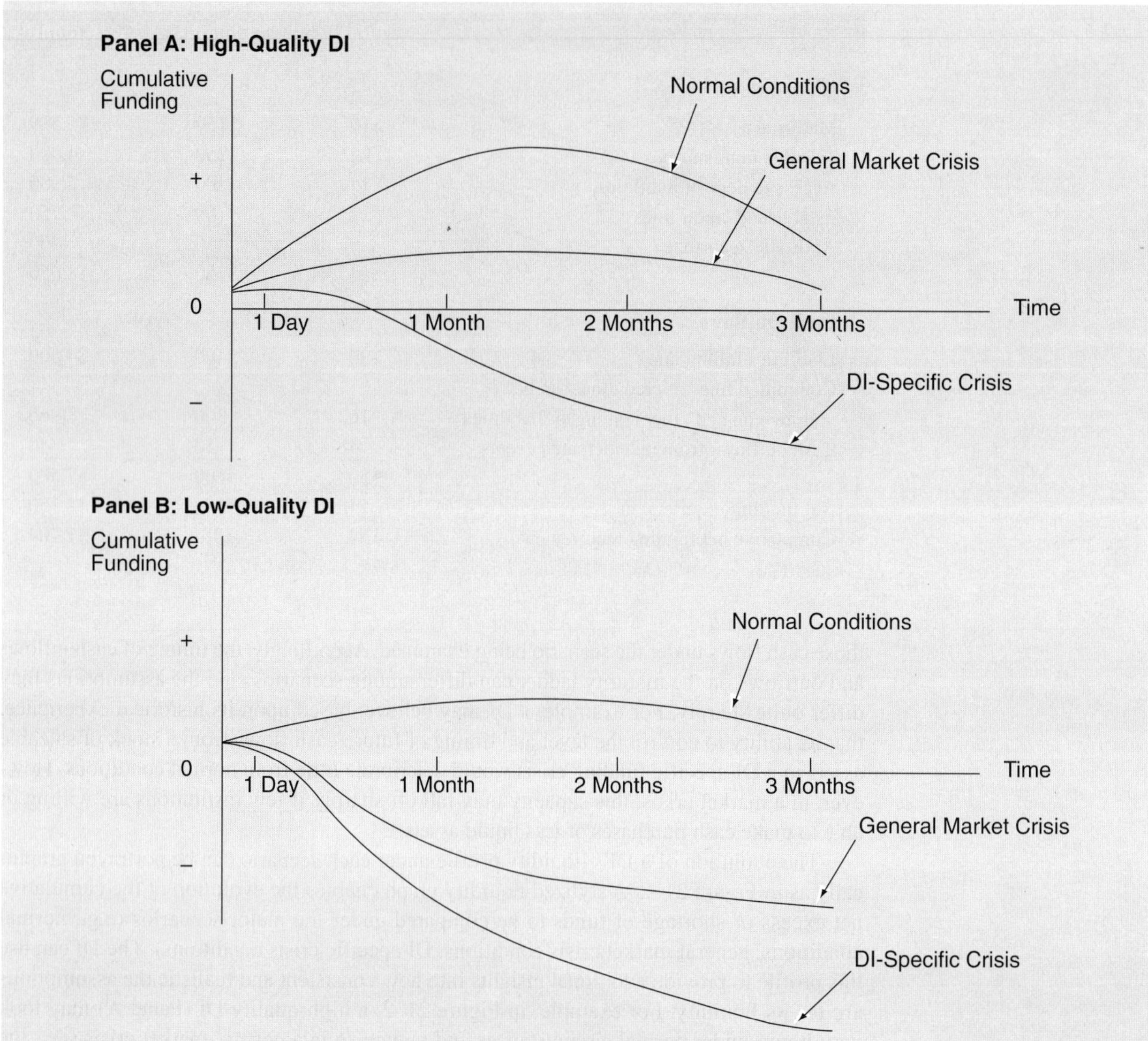

www.federalreserve.gov

www.fdic.gov

www.ots.treas.gov

managers responsible for interacting with various regulatory agencies such as the Federal Reserve, the FDIC, and Office of Thrift Supervision (OTS). It also specifies areas of managerial responsibility in disclosing information to the public, including depositors. The second component of a liquidity plan is a detailed list of fund providers most likely to withdraw as well as the pattern of fund withdrawals. For example, in a crisis, financial institutions such as mutual funds and pension funds are more likely than correspondent banks and small business corporations to withdraw funds quickly from banks and thrifts. In turn, correspondent banks and small corporations are more likely than individual depositors to withdraw funds quickly. This makes liquidity exposure sensitive to the effects of future funding composition changes. In addition, FIs such as depository institutions face particularly heavy seasonal withdrawals of deposits in the quarter before Christmas. The third component of liquidity planning is the identification of the size of potential deposit and fund withdrawals over various time horizons in the future (one week, one month, one quarter, etc.) as well as alternative private market funding sources to meet such withdrawals (e.g., emergency loans from other FIs and the Federal Reserve). The fourth component of the plan sets internal limits on separate subsidiaries' and branches' borrowings as well as bounds for acceptable risk premiums to pay in

TABLE 21–12 Deposit Distribution and Possible Withdrawals Involved in a Bank's Liquidity Plan
(in millions)

Deposits	$250
From:	
Mutual funds	60
Pension funds	50
Correspondent banks	15
Small businesses	70
Individuals	55

Expected Withdrawals	Average	Maximum
One week	$40	$105
One month	55	140
Three months	75	200

The Sequence of Deposit Withdrawal Funding	One Week	One Month	Three Months
1. New deposits	$10	$35	$75
2. Investment portfolio asset liquidation	50	60	75
3. Borrowings from other FIs	30	35	45
4. Borrowings from Fed	15	10	5

each market (fed funds, RPs, CDs, etc.). In addition, the plan details a sequencing of assets for disposal in anticipation of various degrees or intensities of deposit/fund withdrawals. Such a plan may evolve from a bank's asset-liability management committee and may be relayed to various key departments of the bank (e.g., the money desk and the treasury department) that play vital day-to-day roles in liability funding.

Consider, for example, Table 21–12. The data are for a bank that holds $250 million in deposits from mutual funds, pension funds, correspondent banks, small businesses, and individuals. The table includes the average and maximum expected withdrawals over the next one-week, one-month, and one-quarter periods. The liquidity plan for the bank outlines how to cover expected deposit withdrawals should they materialize. In this case, the bank will seek to cover expected deposit withdrawals over the next three months first with new deposits, then with the liquidation of marketable securities in its investment portfolio, then with borrowings from other FIs, and finally, if necessary, with borrowings from the Federal Reserve.

Liquidity Risk, Unexpected Deposit Drains, and Bank Runs

Under normal banking conditions, and with appropriate management planning, neither net deposit withdrawals nor the exercise of loan commitments poses significant liquidity problems for banks. For example, even in December and the summer vacation season, when net deposit withdrawals are high, banks anticipate these *seasonal* effects by holding larger than normal excess cash reserves or borrowing more than normal on the wholesale money markets.

5 Major liquidity problems can arise, however, if deposit drains are abnormally large and unexpected. Abnormal deposit drains may occur for a number of reasons, including:

1. Concerns about a bank's solvency relative to that of other banks.
2. Failure of a related bank, leading to heightened depositor concerns about the solvency of surviving banks (*a contagion effect*).
3. Sudden changes in investor preferences regarding holding nonbank financial assets (such as T-bills or mutual fund shares) relative to bank deposits.

In such cases, sudden and unexpected surges in net deposit withdrawals risk triggering a **bank run,** which could force a bank into insolvency.

bank run

A sudden and unexpected increase in deposit withdrawals from a bank.

Deposit Drains and Bank Run Liquidity Risk. At the core of bank run liquidity risk is the fundamental and unique nature of the demand deposit contract. Specifically, demand deposit contracts are first-come, first-served contracts in the sense that a depositor's place in line determines the amount he or she will be able to withdraw from a bank. For example, suppose that a bank has 100 depositors, each of whom deposited $1. Suppose that each has a reason to believe—correctly or incorrectly—that the bank has assets worth only $90 on its balance sheet. A frequent reason for depositors to believe this is the announcement of trouble in the bank's loan portfolio (refer again to In The News box).

As a result, each depositor has an incentive to be the first to go to the bank and withdraw his or her $1 deposit because the bank pays depositors sequentially as it liquidates its assets. If it has $90 in assets, it can pay in full only the first 90 depositors in the line. The 10 depositors at the end of the line get *nothing at all*.[15] Thus, demand deposits are in essence either full-pay or no-pay contracts.

Because demand deposit contracts pay in full only a certain proportion of depositors when a bank's assets are valued at less than its deposits—and because depositors realize this—any line outside a bank encourages other depositors to join the line immediately even if they do not need cash today for normal consumption purposes. Thus, even the bank's core depositors, who really do not need to withdraw deposits for current consumption needs, rationally seek to withdraw their funds immediately when they observe a sudden increase in the lines at their bank.

The incentives for depositors to run first and ask questions later creates a fundamental instability in the banking system, in that an otherwise sound bank can be pushed into insolvency and failure by unexpectedly large depositor drains and liquidity demands. This is especially so in periods of contagious runs or **bank panics** (such as the panic involving the Ohio savings banks in 1985 discussed in Chapter 19 and the Russian banking crisis of 1998) when depositors lose faith in the banking system as a whole and engage in a run on all banks in a banking system.

bank panic

A systemic or contagious run on the deposits of the banking industry as a whole.

Bank Runs, the Discount Window, and Deposit Insurance

Regulators have recognized the inherent instability of the banking system due to the all-or-nothing payoff features of deposit contracts. As a result, regulatory mechanisms are in place to ease banks' liquidity problems and to deter bank runs and panics. The two major liquidity risk insulation mechanisms are *deposit insurance* and the *discount window*.

Deposit Insurance. Because of the serious effects that a contagious run on banks could have on the economy (e.g., inability to transfer wealth from period to period, inability to implement monetary policy, inability to allocate credit to various sectors of the economy in special need of financing—see Chapter 1), government regulators of depository institutions have established guarantee programs offering deposit holders varying degrees of insurance protection to deter runs. Specifically, if a deposit holder believes his or her claim is totally secure, even if the bank is in trouble, the holder has no incentive to run. The deposit holder's place in line no longer affects his or her ability to retrieve funds deposited in the bank.

www.fdic.gov

When the deposit insurance contract was introduced in 1933, the level of coverage per depositor was $2,500. This coverage cap gradually rose over the years to $100,000 in 1980.[16] The $100,000 cap concerns a depositor's beneficial interest and ownership of

15. We assume no deposit insurance exists that guarantees payment of deposits or no discount window borrowing is available to fund a temporary need for funds. The presence of deposit insurance and the discount window alters the incentive to engage in a bank run, as we describe later in this chapter.

16. In 2001 the FDIC proposed an increase in the cap to $130,000 and then maintaining the real value of coverage through an indexing system such as indexing coverage based on the consumer price index (see Chapter 13).

TABLE 21–13 Deposit Ownership Categories

- Individual ownership, such as a simple checking account.
- Joint ownership, such as the savings account of a husband and wife.
- Revocable trusts, in which the beneficiary is a qualified relative of the settlor, and the settlor has the ability to alter or eliminate the trust.
- Irrevocable trusts whose beneficial interest is not subject to being altered or eliminated.
- Employee benefit plans whose interests are vested and thus not subject to being altered or eliminated.
- Public units—accounts of federal, state, and municipal governments.
- Corporations and partnerships.
- Unincorporated businesses and associates.
- Individual retirement accounts (IRAs).
- Keogh accounts.
- Executor or administrator accounts.
- Accounts held by banks in an agency or fiduciary capacity.

Source: U.S. Department of the Treasury, "Modernizing the Financial System: Recommendations for Safer More Competitive Banks" (Washington, D.C.: Treasury Department, February 1991). **www.ustreas.gov**

deposited funds. In actuality, by structuring deposit funds in a bank or thrift in a particular fashion, a depositor can achieve many times the $100,000 coverage cap on deposits. To see this, consider the different categories of deposit fund ownership available to an individual shown in Table 21–13. Each of these categories represents a distinct accumulation of funds toward the $100,000 insurance cap; the coverage ceiling is *per bank.* We give an example of how depositors can raise the coverage level by adopting certain strategies.

EXAMPLE 21-3 Calculation of Insured Deposits

A married couple with one child and with individual retirement account (IRA) and Keogh private pension plans for both the husband and the wife at the bank could accrue a total coverage cap of $800,000 as a family: his individual deposit account, her individual deposit account, their joint deposit account, their child's deposit account held in trust, his IRA account, his Keogh account, her IRA account, and her Keogh account. By expanding the range of ownership in this fashion, the coverage cap for a family per bank can rapidly approach $1 million or more.

While the healthy U.S. economy of the 1990s and early 2000s resulted in few DI failures and no runs, recall from Chapters 11 and 14 that the 1980s was a period in which some 3,000 banks and savings institutions failed. Although deposit insurance coverage guaranteed the safety and soundness of small depositors' funds at these DIs, some large uninsured depositors were concerned that an impending bank failure might result in a run on deposits. Should DI failures again occur in these numbers, the likely result would be bank runs by the most anxious depositors, despite the existence of highly credible deposit insurance in the United States. Any runs of this type would require significant liquidity management on the part of the failing DI's managers as well as regulators.

www.federalreserve.gov

The Discount Window. In addition to deposit insurance, central banks such as the Federal Reserve have traditionally provided a discount window facility to meet banks' short-term nonpermanent liquidity needs (see the discussion in Chapters 4 and 13). Suppose that a bank has an unexpected deposit drain near the end of a reserve requirement period but cannot meet its reserve target (see Chapter 13). It can seek to borrow from the central bank's discount

TABLE 21–14 The Spread between the Discount Rate and the Fed Funds Rate

	1990	1993	1996	1999	2000	2001	2002	2003	2004
Federal funds	8.10	3.02	5.30	4.97	6.24	3.88	1.67	1.13	1.35
Discount window	6.98	3.00	5.02	4.62	5.73	3.40	1.17	2.12	2.34

Source: Federal Reserve Board Web site. **www.federalreserve.gov**

window facility. Alternatively, discount window loans can also meet short-term seasonal liquidity needs due to crop-planting cycles. Normally, banks make such loans by discounting short-term high-quality securities such as Treasury bills and banker's acceptances with the central bank. The interest rate at which such securities are discounted is called the *discount rate* and is set by the central bank.

In the wake of the terrorist attacks of September 11, 2001, the Federal Reserve's discount window supplied funds to the banking system in unprecedented amounts. The magnitude of destruction resulting from the attacks caused severe disruptions to the U.S. banking system, particularly in DIs' abilities to send electronic payments. The physical disruptions caused by the attacks included outages of telephone switching equipment in lower Manhattan's financial district, impaired records processing and communications systems at individual banks, the evacuation of buildings that were the sites for the payment operations of several large DIs, and the suspended delivery of checks by air couriers. These disruptions left some DIs unable to execute payments to other DIs through the Fed's Fedwire system (see Chapter 13), which in turn resulted in an unexpected shortfall of funds for other DIs. The Federal Reserve took several steps to address the problems in the payments system on and after September 11, 2001. Around noon on the eleventh, the Board of Governors of the Fed released a statement saying that the Fed was open and operating, and that the discount window was available to meet liquidity needs of all FIs.[17] The Fed staff also contacted FIs frequently during the next few days, encouraging them to make payments and to consider the use of the discount window to cover unexpected shortfalls that they might encounter. Thus, the Fed's discount window was a primary tool used to restore payments coordination during this period.

In the United States, the central bank had traditionally set the discount rate below market rates, such as the overnight bank-determined federal funds rates, shown in Table 21–14.[18] The volume of outstanding discount loans was ordinarily small, however, because the Fed prohibited DIs from using discount window loans to finance sales of fed funds or to finance asset expansion. In January 2003, the Fed implemented changes to its discount window lending that increased the cost of borrowing but eased the terms. Specifically, three lending programs are now offered through the Fed's discount window. *Primary credit* is available to generally sound depository institutions on a very short-term basis, typically overnight, at a rate above the Federal Open Market Committee's (FOMC) target rate for federal funds. For example, in May 2005, the fed funds rate was 3.00 percent and the primary credit rate at the discount window was 4.00 percent. Primary credit may be used for any purpose, including financing the sale of fed funds. Primary credit may be extended for periods of up to a few weeks to depository institutions in generally sound financial condition that cannot obtain temporary funds in the financial markets at reasonable terms. *Secondary credit* is available to depository institutions that are not eligible for primary credit. It is extended on a very short-term basis, typically overnight, at a rate that is above the primary credit rate. For example, in May 2005, the primary

17. Nonbank FIs—especially securities firms—were also promised access to discount window borrowing.

18. As the level of market rates drops, however, fed fund rates can lie below the discount rate. This occurred in October 1992, when the fed funds rate was 2.96 percent and the discount rate was 3 percent.

credit rate at the discount window was 4.00 percent and the secondary credit rate was 4.50 percent. Secondary credit is available to meet backup liquidity needs when its use is consistent with a timely return to a reliance on market sources of funding or the orderly resolution of a troubled institution. *Secondary credit* may not be used to fund an expansion of the borrower's assets. The Federal Reserve's *seasonal credit* program is designed to assist small depository institutions in managing significant seasonal swings in their loans and deposits. Seasonal credit is available to depository institutions that can demonstrate a clear pattern of recurring intrayearly swings in funding needs (such as banks that are located in farming communities, which are subject to crop cycles). Eligible institutions are also often located in tourist areas. Under the seasonal program, borrowers may obtain longer term funds from the discount window during periods of seasonal need so that they can carry fewer liquid assets during the rest of the year and make more funds available for local lending. In May 2005, the fed funds rate was 3.00 percent and the seasonal credit rate at the discount window was 2.95 percent.

DO YOU UNDERSTAND?

1. The benefits and costs of using (*a*) liability management and (*b*) reserve or cash assets to meet a deposit drain?
2. What the major sources of FI liquidity are? What the two major uses are?
3. What factors determine a bank's financing requirement?
4. How to measure liquidity risk?

These changes were not intended to change the Fed's use of the discount window to implement monetary policy, but would significantly increase the discount rate while making it easier for a DI to get a discount window loan. By increasing banks' use of the discount window as a source of funding, the Fed hopes to reduce volatility in the fed funds market as well. The policy changes also allow healthy banks to borrow from the Fed regardless of the availability of private funds such as interbank fed funds and repos. Previously, the Fed required borrowers to prove they could not get funds from the private sector, which put a stigma on discount window borrowing. With the changes, the Fed will lend to all banks, but the subsidy will be gone.

LIQUIDITY RISK AND INSURANCE COMPANIES

6

Life Insurance Companies

Like depository institutions, life insurance companies hold cash reserves and other liquid assets in order to meet policy payments and cancellations (surrenders) and other working capital needs that arise in the course of writing insurance. Least predictable among these is the early cancellation of an insurance policy which results in the insurer having to pay the insured the **surrender value** of that policy.[19] In the normal course of business, premium income and returns on an insurer's asset portfolio are sufficient to meet the cash outflows required when policyholders surrender their policies early (see Chapter 15). When premium income is insufficient to meet surrenders, however, a life insurer can sell some of its relatively liquid assets, such as government bonds. In this case, bonds act as a buffer or reserve asset source of liquidity for the insurer. Nevertheless, a drop in market values of insurers' financial assets such as the drop in the market values of many securities in 2001 and 2002 resulted in investment losses for insurance companies that raised the possibility of increased insurance company failures.

surrender value

The amount that an insurance policyholder receives when cashing in a policy early.

Concerns about the solvency of an insurer can result in a run in which new premium income dries up and existing policyholders as a group seek to cancel their policies by cashing them in early. To meet exceptional demands for cash, a life insurer could be forced to liquidate other assets in its portfolio, such as commercial mortgage loans and other securities, potentially at fire-sale prices.[20] Forced asset liquidations can push an insurer, like a bank, into insolvency.

19. A surrender value is usually some proportion or percentage less than 100 percent of the face value of the insurance contract. The surrender value continues to grow as funds invested in the policy earn interest (returns). Earnings to the policyholder are taxed if and when the policy is actually surrendered or cashed in before the policy matures. Some insurance companies have faced run problems resulting from their sale of guaranteed investment contracts (GICs). A GIC, similar to a long-term, fixed-rate bank deposit, is a contract between an investor and an insurance company. As market interest rates rose in the 1980s, many investors withdrew their funds early and reinvested elsewhere in higher return investments. This created both liquidity and refinancing problems for life insurers that supplied such contracts and eventually led to restrictions on withdrawals.

20. Life insurers also provide a considerable amount of loan commitments, especially in the commercial property area. As a result, they face asset side loan commitment liquidity risk in a similar fashion to banks.

Property–Casualty Insurance Companies

As discussed in Chapter 15, property–casualty (PC) insurers sell policies insuring against certain contingencies impacting either real property or individuals. These contingencies are relatively short term and unpredictable, unlike those covered by life insurers. With the help of mortality tables, claims on life insurance policies are generally predictable. PC claims (such as the estimated $40 billion in insurance losses associated with the September 11, 2001 terrorist attacks) are virtually impossible to predict. Thus, PC insurers have a greater need for liquidity than life insurers. As a result, PC insurers tend to hold shorter term, more liquid assets than do life insurers. PC insurers' contracts and premium-setting intervals are usually relatively short term as well, so that problems caused by policy surrenders are less severe. PC insurers' greatest liquidity exposure occurs when policyholders cancel or fail to renew policies with an insurer because of pricing, competition, or safety and solvency concerns. This may cause an insurer's premium cash inflow, when added to its investment returns, to be insufficient to meet its policyholders' claims. Alternatively, large unexpected claims may materialize as a result of disasters such as the Florida hurricanes in 2004 and the terrorist attacks on the World Trade Center in 2001.[21]

Guarantee Programs for Life and Property–Casualty Insurance Companies

Both life insurance and property–casualty insurance companies are regulated at the state level (see Chapter 15). Unlike banks and thrifts, neither life nor PC insurers have a federal guarantee fund. Beginning in the 1960s, most states began to sponsor state guarantee funds for firms selling insurance in that state.[22] As discussed in Chapter 15, these state guarantee funds differ in a number of important ways from deposit insurance. First, although these programs are sponsored by state insurance regulators, they are actually run and administered by the private insurance companies themselves. Second, unlike the Savings Association Insurance Fund and the Bank Insurance Fund, in which the FDIC established a permanent fund by requiring DIs to pay annual premiums to the fund in excess of insurance fund payouts to resolve failures, no permanent guarantee fund exists for the insurance industry, with the sole exception of the PC and life guarantee funds for the state of New York. This means that contributions are paid into the guarantee fund by surviving firms only *after* an insurance company has failed. Third, the size of the required contributions that surviving insurers make to protect policyholders in failed insurance companies differs widely from state to state. In those states that have no permanent guarantee fund, each surviving insurer is normally levied a pro rata amount, according to the size of its statewide premium income. This amount either helps pay off small policyholders after the assets of the failed insurer have been liquidated or acts as a cash injection to make the acquisition of a failed insurer attractive. The definition of small policyholders generally varies across states from $100,000 to $500,000. Finally, because no permanent fund exists and the annual pro rata contributions are often legally capped, a delay usually occurs before small policyholders receive the cash surrender values of their policies or other payment obligations from the guarantee fund. This contrasts with deposit insurance, where insured depositors normally receive immediate coverage (payout) of their claims For example, the failure of Executive Life Insurance in 1991 left approximately $117.3 million in outstanding claims in Hawaii. But the Hawaii life

DO YOU UNDERSTAND?

1. What is likely to be a life insurance company's first source of liquidity when premium income is insufficient?
2. Whether a life insurance company can be subjected to a run, and if so, under what circumstances?
3. What the greatest cause of liquidity exposure that property–casualty insurers face is?
4. Why the liquidity risk of property–casualty insurers is, in general, smaller than that of life insurers?
5. How state-sponsored guarantee funds for insurance companies differ from deposit insurance?

21. Claims also may arise in long-tail lines when a contingency takes place during the policy period but a claim is not lodged until many years later. As mentioned in Chapter 15, the claims regarding damage caused by asbestos contacts are in this category.

22. However, Louisiana, New Jersey, and Washington, D.C. have no fund for life insurance industry failures, and Colorado has only recently established one. New York has a permanent fund into which insurers pay premiums regardless of the failure rate.

insurance guarantee fund can raise only $13.1 million a year due to legal caps on surviving firms' contributions. This means that surviving firms took nine years to meet the claims of Executive Life policyholders in Hawaii. In May 1999, Martin Frankel fled to Italy after he allegedly stole $215 million from seven insurance companies he controlled. Frankel was eventually found and extradited to the United States for trial, yet, as of 2005, insurance commissioners in five states involved were still trying to compensate policyholders, stating that some policyholders would not receive full payment on their policies.

Thus, the private nature of insurance industry guarantee funds, their lack of permanent reserves, and low caps on annual contributions mean that they provide less credible protection to claimants than do bank and thrift insurance funds. As a result, the incentives for insurance policyholders to engage in a run, should they perceive that an insurer has asset quality problems or insurance underwriting problems, is quite strong even in the presence of such guarantee funds.

LIQUIDITY RISK AND MUTUAL FUNDS

7 Mutual funds sell shares as liabilities to investors and invest the proceeds in assets such as bonds and equities. Open-end mutual funds must stand ready to buy back issued shares from investors at their current market price or net asset value (see Chapter 17). Thus, at a given market price, P, the supply of open-end fund shares is perfectly elastic. The price at which an open-end mutual fund stands ready to sell new shares or redeem existing shares is the net asset value (NAV). As discussed in Chapter 17, the NAV is the current or market value of the fund's assets less any accrued liabilities divided by the number of shares in the fund.

A mutual fund's willingness to provide instant liquidity to shareholders while it invests funds in equities, bonds, and other long-term instruments could expose it to liquidity problems similar to those depository institutions face when the number of withdrawals (or in this case, mutual fund shares redeemed) rises to abnormally high or unexpected levels. At year-end 2004 long-term mutual funds held $240.5 billion in liquid assets (open market paper and Treasury securities), or 4.42 percent of total assets ($5,435.3 billion). Indeed, mutual funds can be subject to dramatic liquidity needs if investors become nervous about the true value of a mutual fund's assets.[23] If the market value of the underlying assets falls and is expected to continue to fall, fund holders will want to liquidate their positions as fast as possible. For example, for the week ended July 19, 2002, mutual fund investors withdrew a record $12.2 billion from stock funds.

Indeed, mutual funds can be subject to dramatic liquidity runs if investors become nervous about the NAV of the mutual funds' assets. However, the fundamental difference in the way that mutual fund contracts are valued compared to the valuation of bank deposit contracts reduces the incentives for mutual fund shareholders to engage in depositlike runs. Specifically, if a mutual fund were to be closed and liquidated, its assets would be distributed to fund shareholders on an equal or pro rata basis rather than on the first-come, first-served basis employed under deposit and insurance policy contracts. To illustrate this difference, we can compare the incentives for mutual fund investors to engage in a run with those of DI depositors. Table 21–15 shows a simple balance sheet of an open-end mutual fund and a DI. When they perceive that a DI's assets are valued below its liabilities, depositors have an incentive to engage in a run on the DI to be first in line to withdraw. In the example in Table 21–15, only the first 90 DI depositors would receive $1 back for each $1 deposited. The last 10 would receive nothing at all.

Now consider the mutual fund with 100 shareholders who invested $1 each for a total of $100 with assets worth $90. If these shareholders tried to cash in their shares, none

23. For example, the value of assets held by mutual funds specializing in the equities of Asian countries such as Indonesia and Thailand as well as Russia during the emerging market crises of 1997–1998.

TABLE 21–15 Run Incentives of DI Depositors versus Mutual Fund Investors

Depository Institution		Open-End Mutual Fund	
Assets	**Liabilities**	**Assets**	**Liabilities**
Assets $90	$100 Deposits (100 depositors with $1 deposits)	Assets $90	$100 Shares (100 shareholders with $1 shares)

would receive $1. Instead, a mutual fund values its balance sheet liabilities on a market value basis; the price of any share liquidated by an investor is:

$$P = \frac{\text{Value of assets}}{\text{Shares outstanding}} = \text{NAV}$$

Thus, unlike deposit contracts that have fixed face values of $1, the value of a mutual fund's shares reflects the changing value of its assets divided by the number of shares outstanding.

In Table 21–15, the value of each shareholder's claim is:

$$P = \frac{\$90}{100} = \$0.90$$

DO YOU UNDERSTAND?

1. What the impact would be on a bank's liquidity needs if it offered deposit contracts of an open-end mutual fund type rather than the traditional all-or-nothing demand deposit contract?
2. How the incentives of a mutual fund's investors to engage in runs compare with the incentives of bank depositors?

That is, each mutual fund shareholder participates in the fund's loss of asset value on a pro rata, or proportional, basis. Technically, whether first or last in line, each mutual fund shareholder who cashes in shares on any given day receives the same net asset value per share of the mutual fund. In this case, it is 90 cents, representing a loss of 10 cents per share for all shareholders. All mutual fund shareholders realize this and know that investors share asset losses on a pro rata basis. As a result, being first in line to withdraw mutual fund shares, on any given day, has no overall advantage.[24] Of course, rapidly falling asset values will result in a greater incentive for investors to cash in their shares as quickly as possible before values fall any further. However, this rush, or run, by investors is due to a drop in the underlying value of their investments and not the threat of receiving nothing because they are not first in line to cash in.

24. For example, in the case of a bank run discussed earlier in the chapter, rather than the first 90 claimholders receiving full payment ($1 each) and the last 10 nothing, in the case of a mutual fund liquidation each of the 100 shareholders would receive a payout of $0.90 (or 90 cents) in this example.

SUMMARY

This chapter provided an in-depth look at the measurement and on-balance-sheet management of liquidity risks. Liquidity risk is a common problem that FI managers face. Well-developed policies for holding liquid assets or having access to markets for purchased funds are normally adequate to meet liability withdrawals. Very large withdrawals, however, can cause asset liquidity problems to be compounded by incentives for liability claimholders to engage in runs at the first sign of a liquidity problem. The incentives for depositors and life insurance policyholders to engage in runs can push normally sound FIs into insolvency.

SEARCH THE SITE

Go to the Federal Reserve Board's Web site at **www.federalreserve.gov** and find the most recent data for the fed funds rate and the discount window rate using the following steps.

Click on "Economic Research and Data."

Click on "Statistics: Releases and Historical Data."

Under Interest Rates, click on "weekly."

Click on the most recent date.

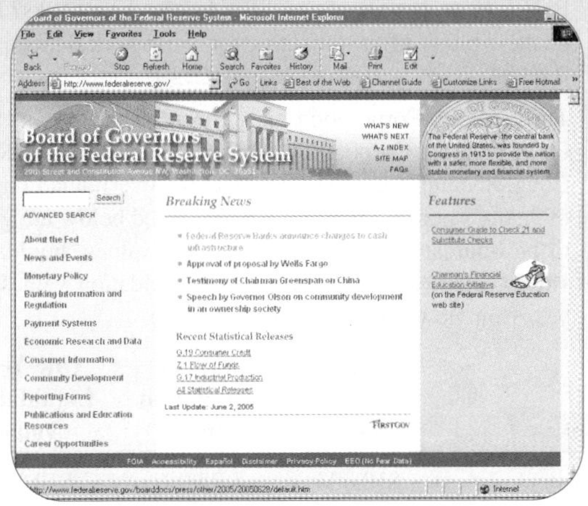

Questions

1. Using information in this file, update Table 21–14.
2. Calculate the percentage change in each rate since 2004 as reported in Table 21–14. Which rate has increased/or decreased more? Why?

QUESTIONS

1. How does the asset side reason for liquidity risk differ from the liability side reason?
2. The probability distribution of the net deposit drain of an FI has been estimated to have a mean of 2 percent and a standard deviation of 1 percent.
   a. Is this FI increasing or decreasing in size? Explain.
   b. If an FI has a net deposit drain, what are the two ways it can offset this drain of funds? How do the two methods differ?
3. How is asset side liquidity risk likely to be related to liability side liquidity risk?
4. Why would an FI be forced to sell assets at fire-sale prices?
5. The AllStarBank has the following balance sheet:

Assets (in millions)		Liabilities	
Cash	$ 30	Deposits	$ 90
Other assets	140	Borrowed funds	40
	$170	Other liabilities	40
			$170

Its largest customer decides to exercise a $15 million loan commitment. Show how the new balance sheet changes if AllStar uses (*a*) asset management or (*b*) liability management.

6. Assume that an FI has assets of $10 million consisting of $1 million in cash and $9 million in loans. It has core deposits of $6 million. It also has $2 million in subordinated debt and $2 million in equity. Increases in interest rates are expected to result in a net drain of $2 million in core deposits over the year.
   a. The average cost of deposits is 6 percent and the average cost of loans is 8 percent. The FI decides to reduce its loan portfolio to offset this expected decline in deposits. What is the cost and what will be the total asset size of the firm from this strategy after the drain?
   b. If the cost of issuing new short-term debt is 7.5 percent, what is the cost of offsetting the expected drain if it increases its liabilities? What will be the total asset size of the FI from this strategy after the drain?
7. Consider the balance sheet for an FI listed below:

Assets (in millions)		Liabilities	
Cash	$10	Deposits	$68
Loans	50	Equity	7
Securities	15		

The FI is expecting a $15 million net deposit drain. Show the FI's balance sheet if under these two conditions:
   a. The FI purchases liabilities to offset this expected drain.
   b. The stored liquidity method is used to meet the liquidity shortfall.

8. What are five measures of liquidity risk?
9. STANDARD &POOR'S Go to the S&P Educational Version of Market Insight Web site at **www.mhhe.com/edumarketinsight.** Click on "Educational Version of Market Insight." Enter your site ID and click on "Login." Click on "Company." Find the most recent balance sheets for Mellon Financial Corp. (MEL), Wachovia Corp. (WB), and Suntrust Banks Inc. (STI). Enter "MEL" in the "Ticker," box and click on "Go!" Click on "Excel analytics." Click on "FS Ann. Balance Sheet." This will download the balance sheet for Mellon Financial. From these balance sheets, calculate the following liquidity ratios: loans to deposits and borrowed funds to total assets using the balances for total loans, total deposits, total borrowed funds, and total assets. Repeat

www.mhhe.com/sc3e

the process by entering "WB" in the "Ticker:" box to get information on Wachovia Corp. Repeat the process by entering "STI" in the "Ticker:' box to get information on Suntrust Banks. How do these ratios differ for the three banks? How do these ratios differ from those for North Fork Bancorp and Bank of America reported in Table 21–9?

10. The Acme Corporation has been acquired by the Conglomerate Corporation. To help finance the takeover, Conglomerate is going to liquidate the overfunded portion of Acme's pension fund. The assets listed below are going to be liquidated. Listed are their face values, liquidation values today, and their anticipated liquidation values one year from now (their fair market values).

Asset	Face Value	Current Liquidation Value	One-Year Liquidation Value
IBM stock	$10,000	$ 9,900	$10,500
GE bonds	5,000	4,000	4,500
Treasury securities	15,000	13,000	14,000

Calculate the one-year liquidity index for these securities.

11. An FI has the following assets in its portfolio: $20 million in cash reserves with the Fed, $20 million in T-bills, $50 million in mortgage loans, and $10 million in fixed assets. If it needs to dispose of its assets at short notice, it will receive only 99 percent of the fair market value of the T-bills, 90 percent of the fair market value of its mortgage loans, and 0 percent of the fair market value of the fixed assets. Calculate the liquidity index using the above information.

12. A bank has $10 million in T-bills, a $5 million line of credit to borrow in the repo market, and $5 million in cash reserves with the Fed in excess of its required reserve requirements. It has also borrowed $6 million in federal funds and $2 million from the Federal Reserve's discount window to meet seasonal demands.

a. What is the bank's total available (sources of) liquidity?

b. What are the bank's total uses of liquidity?

c. What is the net liquidity of the bank and what conclusions can you derive from the result?

13. What are the several components of an FI's liquidity plan? How can the plan help an FI reduce liquidity shortages?

14. The Plainbank has $10 million in cash and equivalents, $30 million in loans, and $15 in core deposits. Calculate (*a*) the financing gap and (*b*) the financing requirement.

15. What changes were made to discount window borrowing by U.S. DIs in 2003? How did these changes affect a DI's ability to borrow from the Fed's discount window to manage liquidity risk?

16. Why is access to the discount window of the Federal Reserve less effective as a deterrent for bank runs than deposit insurance?

17. How is the liquidity problem faced by mutual funds different from those of banks and insurance companies?

18. A mutual fund has the following assets in its portfolio: $40 million in fixed-income securities and $40 million in stocks at current market values. In the event of a liquidity crisis, it can sell its assets at a 96 percent discount if they are disposed of in two days. It will receive 98 percent if disposed of in four days. Two shareholders, Aand B, own 5 percent and 7 percent of equity (shares), respectively.

a. Market uncertainty has caused shareholders to sell their shares back to the fund. What will the two shareholders receive if the mutual fund must sell all its assets in two days? In four days?

b. How does this differ from a bank run? How have bank regulators mitigated the problem of bank runs?

19. A mutual fund has $1 million in cash and $9 million invested in securities. It currently has 1 million shares outstanding.

a. What is the NAV of this fund?

b. Assume that some of the shareholders decide to cash in their shares of the fund. How many shares, at its current NAV, can the fund take back without resorting to a sale of assets?

c. As a result of anticipated heavy withdrawals, it sells 10,000 shares of IBM stock currently valued at $40. Unfortunately, it receives only $35 per share. What is the net asset value after the sale? What are the fund's cash assets after the sale?

d. Assume after the sale of IBM shares, 100,000 shares are sold back to the fund. What is the current NAV? Is there a need to sell more stocks to meet this redemption?

20. What is the greatest cause of liquidity exposure that property–casualty insurers face?

22

Managing Interest Rate Risk *and* Insolvency Risk *on the* Balance Sheet

OUTLINE

Chapter NAVIGATOR

1. What is the repricing gap model used to measure interest rate risk?
2. What are the weaknesses of the various interest rate risk models?
3. What is the duration gap model used to measure interest rate risk?
4. How does capital protect against credit risk and interest rate risk?
5. What causes the discrepancies between the book value and market value of equity?

INTEREST RATE AND INSOLVENCY RISK MANAGEMENT: CHAPTER OVERVIEW

In this third chapter on managing risk on an FI's balance sheet, we provide a detailed analysis of interest rate risk and insolvency risk. Chapter 19 established the fact that while performing their asset-transformation functions, financial institutions (FIs) often mismatch the maturities of their assets and liabilities. In so doing, they expose themselves to interest rate risk. For example, in the 1980s, a large number of thrifts suffered economic insolvency (i.e., the net worth or equity of their owners was eradicated) when interest rates unexpectedly increased. As discussed in the In the News box, an unprecedented wave of mortgage refinancings in 2001 and early 2002 increased interest rate risk at many New England thrifts to the extent that some regulators noted concerns about these thrifts' financial health.

This chapter analyzes two methods used to measure an FI's interest rate risk exposure: the repricing model and the duration model. The repricing model examines the impact of interest rate changes on an FI's net interest income (NII). However, as we explain later in the chapter, the FI's duration gap is a more comprehensive measure of interest rate risk

FDIC Sees a Pocket of Risk in New England's Thrifts

Earnings at New England thrifts will be hit particularly hard if the federal funds rate starts to rise, according to the Federal Deposit Insurance Corp. Dan Frye, the Boston regional manager of the FDIC's division of insurance, said an "unprecedented wave of mortgage refinancing" last year has heightened interest rate risk at all thrifts, which still rely primarily on interest from real estate loans for income. He is particularly concerned about New England, where thrifts make up such a large share of the banking market. In Massachusetts alone, 81 percent of the state's 225 institutions are thrifts. In Connecticut, the region's second most populous state, 64 percent of the institutions are thrifts.

Net interest margins have been declining steadily at New England savings banks, and many are holding long-term, fixed-rate mortgages "in an effort to keep their margins from falling any further," Mr. Frye wrote in the FDIC's "Regional Outlook" report for the first quarter, released last month. The refinancing boom left many of those thrifts with high concentrations of fixed-rate, 15- and 30-year mortgages—booked while interest rates were spiraling downward to levels not seen since the Eisenhower administration. Now Mr. Frye is worried about what happens when rates start rising. "I've been monitoring this situation for a while." . . . At the end of the third quarter the FDIC reported that long-term assets exceeded 40 percent of total earning assets at more than half of New England's thrifts. Six years earlier only 10 percent of its savings banks reported long-term asset concentrations higher than 40 percent of earning assets. Financial institutions typically seek to avoid putting a larger number of long-term mortgages on their books because of the difficulty involved in matching them with funding sources of comparable maturity. The problem is, with interest rates so low, there has been virtually no demand for the adjustable-rate mortgages that lenders prefer to make. "No one is looking for adjustable rates now," said William P. Morrisey, a senior vice president of the $433 million asset Central Bancorp Inc. in Somerville, Mass. "It's a fact of the market. When rates are low, people want to lock them in."

However, Mr. Frye said market forces were no excuse for the jump in long-term assets on thrifts' books. "I understand that no one wants an adjustable rate when you can lock in a lower rate, but that doesn't mean that banks had to hold all those mortgages. . . They could have sold them on the secondary market." But for many New England savings banks, selling mortgages was easier said than done, given the margin pressures they faced. For several years net interest margins at the region's thrifts have trended downward. In 1994 the FDIC said only 15 percent of New England thrifts reported net interest margins lower than 3.5 percent. By Sept. 30, 2001, that percentage had increased to 48 percent.

A declining net interest margin is a huge problem for small thrifts, many of which, given the one dimensional nature of their operations, cannot offset any loss of interest income with additional fees or noninterest income. Even so, Mr. Frye insisted that the region's community banks and thrifts would have been better off selling their long-term assets, even if it meant taking a loss. To explain why, he outlined a worst-case scenario during an interview last week. Beginning this year the Federal Reserve starts steadily increasing the federal funds rate, the benchmark lenders use to calculate their own interest rates. Banks and thrifts are forced to increase the rates they pay for deposits in response. At the same time a reinvigorated stock market begins siphoning money out of bank accounts and back into equities. This would put banks and thrifts, particularly those in New England, in a classic squeeze. They would be forced to pay progressively higher rates to replace the deposits they lost, but that higher cost money would still be funding the low rate, long-term mortgages they added to their books during the 1998 and 2001 refinancing booms. . .

After dropping 13 times in 17 months between May 2000 and October 2002, to a low of 6.1 percent, the average rate for a 15-year fixed-rate mortgage has jumped in three of the past five months and hit 6.52 percent last month, according to Freddie Mac. Predictably, the number of borrowers seeking to refinance their mortgages has plummeted and will likely continue to drop, according to the Mortgage Bankers Association. . . That means all those fixed-rate mortgages worrying Mr. Frye are clinging more tightly to banks' books precisely when the federal funds rate—and with it banks' cost of funds—is expected to begin rising. The steeper the rate rise, the more pronounced the erosion, he said. . . .

Source: *The American Banker,* April 10, 2002, p. 1, by John Reosti.
www.americanbanker.com

exposure than the repricing gap. We also discuss in this chapter the measurement and on-balance-sheet management of interest rate risk.[1]

Insolvency risk is the result or consequence or an outcome of excessive amounts of one or more of the risks taken by an FI (e.g., liquidity risk, credit risk, and interest rate risk). Technically, insolvency occurs when the internal capital or equity resources of an FI's owners are at or near zero as a result of bad balance sheet outcomes due to one or more of these risks.

DO YOU UNDERSTAND?

1. What the trend has been in the issuance of long-term, fixed-rate mortgages at New England thrifts in the late 1990s and early 2000s?
2. Why New England thrifts' net interest margins would decrease if interest rates start rising?

INTEREST RATE RISK MEASUREMENT AND MANAGEMENT

In this section, we analyze two methods used to measure an FI's interest rate risk: the repricing model and the duration gap model. The repricing model, sometimes called the funding gap model, concentrates on the impact of interest rate changes on an FI's net interest income (NII), which is the difference between an FI's interest income and interest expense (see Chapter 12), and thus the FI's profits. This contrasts with the market value–based duration gap model, which incorporates the impact of interest rate changes on the overall market value of an FI's balance sheet and ultimately on its owners' equity or net worth. Until recently, U.S. bank regulators had been content to base their evaluations of bank interest rate risk exposures on the repricing model alone. As discussed later in this chapter, regulators and other analysts now recognize the serious weaknesses of the repricing gap model. As a result, while the repricing gap is still used to measure interest rate risk in most FIs, it is increasingly being used in conjunction with the duration gap model.[2]

Repricing Model

The **repricing** or **funding gap** model is essentially a book value accounting cash flow analysis of the interest income earned on an FI's assets and the interest expense paid on its liabilities (or its net interest income) over some particular period. For example, until recently, the Fed required quarterly reporting by commercial banks of repricing gaps for assets and liabilities with these maturities:[3]

repricing or funding gap

The difference between those assets whose interest rates will be repriced or changed over some future period (RSAs) and liabilities whose interest rates will be repriced or changed over some future period (RSLs).

1. One day
2. More than 1 day to 3 months
3. More than 3 months to 6 months
4. More than 6 months to 12 months
5. More than 1 year to 5 years
6. More than 5 years

The gap in each maturity bucket (or bin) is calculated by estimating the difference between the rate-sensitive assets (RSAs) and rate-sensitive liabilities (RSLs) on its balance sheet. **Rate sensitivity** means that the asset or liability is repriced (either because it matures and the funds will be rolled over into a new asset or liability, or because it is a financial instrument with a variable interest rate) at or near current market interest rates within the maturity horizon of the bucket under consideration.

rate sensitivity

The time to repricing of an asset or liability.

Refer to Table 22–1 to see how the assets and liabilities of an FI might be categorized into each of the six buckets according to their time to repricing. Although the cumulative repricing gap over the whole balance sheet must be zero by definition, the advantage of the

1. In Chapter 23, we examine how derivative securities can be used to hedge interest rate risk.

2. W. G. Brawley, J. H. Gilkeson, and C. K. Ruff in "International Measures of Interest Rate Risk: Are Income and Economic Value Approaches Different?" Federal Reserve Bank of Altanta, WP, 2001, examine 300 small- to medium-size banks. They find the correlation between the net interest income and equity value measures of interest rate risk to be approximately 0.6.

3. The BIS has recently proposed that banks report the value of the equity or net worth at risk due to interest rate changes to bank examiners and supervisors. This measure is based on the duration gap measure presented below. See "Principles for the Management and Supervision of Interest Rate Risk," Bank for International Settlements, Basel, Switzerland, January 2001.

TABLE 22–1 Repricing Gaps for an FI
(in millions of dollars)

	Assets	Liabilities	Gaps
1. 1 day	$ 20	$ 30	$−10
2. More than 1 day–3 months	30	40	−10
3. More than 3 months–6 months	70	85	−15
4. More than 6 months–12 months	90	70	+20
5. More than 1 year–5 years	40	30	+10
6. More than 5 years	10	5	+5
	$260	$260	0

repricing model lies in its information value and its simplicity in pointing to an FI's net interest income exposure (or profit exposure) to interest rate changes in each different maturity bucket.[4]

For example, suppose that an FI's report indicates a negative $10 million difference between assets and liabilities being repriced in one day (or the one-day bucket). Assets and liabilities that are repriced each day are likely to be interbank borrowings on the federal funds or repurchase agreement markets (see Chapter 5). Thus, a negative gap (RSA < RSL) indicates that a rise in these short-term rates would lower the FI's net interest income since the FI has more rate-sensitive liabilities than assets in that bucket. In other words, assuming equal changes in interest rates on RSAs and RSLs, interest expense will increase by more than interest revenue. Specifically, let:

ΔNII_i = Change in net interest income in the i th maturity bucket
GAP_i = Dollar size of the gap between the book value of rate-sensitive assets and rate-sensitive liabilities in maturity bucket i
ΔR_i = Change in the level of interest rates impacting assets and liabilities in the ith maturity bucket

Then:

$$\Delta NII_i = (GAP_i)\Delta R_i = (RSA_i - RSL_i)\Delta R_i$$

In this first bucket, if the gap is negative $10 million and short-term interest rates (such as the fed funds and/or repo rates) rise by 1 percent, the annualized change in the FI's future net interest income is:

$$\Delta NII_i = (-\$10 \text{ million}) \times .01 = -\$100{,}000$$

This approach is very simple and intuitive. We will see later in this section, however, that market or present-value losses (and gains) also occur on assets and liabilities when interest rates change. These effects are not accounted for in the funding gap model because asset and liability values are reported at their *historic* book values rather than on a market value basis. Thus, in this model, interest rate changes affect only the current interest income earned and interest expence paid on an asset or liability.[5]

The FI manager can also estimate cumulative gaps (CGAP) over various repricing categories or buckets. A common cumulative gap of interest is the one-year repricing gap estimated from Table 22–1 as:

$$\text{CGAP} = (-\$10\text{m.}) + (-\$10\text{m.}) + (-\$15\text{m.}) + \$20\text{m.} = -\$15 \text{ million}$$

4. We include equity capital as a long-term (over five years) liability.

5. For example, a 30-year bond purchased 10 years ago when rates were 13 percent would be reported as having the same book (accounting) value as when rates were 7 percent. Using market values, capital gains and losses would be reflected on the balance sheet as rates change.

TABLE 22–2 Simple Bank Balance Sheet and Repricing Gap
(in millions of dollars)

Assets		Liabilities	
1. Cash and due from	$ 5	**1.** Two-year time deposits	$ 40
2. Short-term consumer loans (one-year maturity)	50	**2.** Demand deposits	40
3. Long-term consumer loans (two-year maturity)	25	**3.** Passbook savings	30
4. Three-month T-bills	30	**4.** Three-month CDs	40
5. Six-month T-notes	35	**5.** Three-month banker's acceptances	20
6. Three-year T-bonds	60	**6.** Six-month commercial paper	60
7. 10-year fixed-rate mortgages	20	**7.** One-year time deposits	20
8. 30-year floating-rate mortgages	40	**8.** Equity capital (fixed)	20
9. Premises	5		
	$270		$270

If ΔR_i is the average interest rate change affecting assets and liabilities that can be repriced within a year, the cumulative effect on the bank's net interest income is:

$$\begin{aligned}\Delta NII &= \left(\sum_{i=\text{1-day}}^{\text{1-year}} RSA_i - \sum_{i=\text{1-day}}^{\text{1-year}} RSL_i\right)\Delta R_i \\ &= (CGAP)\Delta R_i \\ &= (-\$15 \text{ million})(.01) = -\$150{,}000\end{aligned}$$

We next look at an example of calculating the cumulative one-year gap using an FI in the form of a commercial bank. Remember that the manager considers whether each asset or liability will, or can, have its interest rate changed within the next year. If it will or can, it is a rate-sensitive asset or liability; if not, it is a rate-insensitive asset or liability.

Measuring and Managing Interest Rate Risk Using the Repricing Gap. Consider the simplified bank balance sheet in Table 22–2. Rather than the original maturities, the reported maturities are those remaining on different assets and liabilities at the time the repricing gap is estimated.

Rate-Sensitive Assets. Looking down the asset side of the balance sheet in Table 22–2, we see the following one-year rate-sensitive assets (RSAs):

1. *Short-term consumer loans: $50 million,* which are repriced at the end of the year and just make the one-year cutoff.
2. *Three-month T-bills: $30 million,* which are repriced on maturity (rollover) every three months.
3. *Six-month T-notes: $35 million,* which are repriced on maturity (rollover) every six months.
4. *30-year floating-rate mortgages: $40 million,* which are repriced (i.e., the mortgage rate is reset) every nine months. Thus, these long-term assets are RSAs in the context of the repricing model with a one-year repricing horizon.

Summing these four items produces total one-year RSAs of $155 million. The remaining $115 million of assets are not rate sensitive over the one-year repricing horizon—that is, a change in the level of interest rates will not affect the size of the interest income generated by these assets over the next year.[6] The $5 million in the cash and due from category and

6. We are assuming that the assets are noncallable over the year and that there will be no prepayments (runoffs, see below) on the mortgages within a year.

the $5 million in premises are nonearning assets. Although the $105 million in long-term consumer loans, three-year Treasury bonds, and 10-year, fixed-rate mortgages generate interest income, the size of revenue generated will not change over the next year, since the interest rates or coupons earned on these assets are not expected to change (i.e., they are fixed over the next year).

Rate-Sensitive Liabilities. Looking down the liability side of the balance sheet in Table 22–2, we see that the following liability items clearly fit the one-year rate or repricing sensitivity test:

1. *Three-month CDs: $40 million,* which mature in three months and are repriced on rollover.
2. *Three-month bankers acceptances: $20 million,* which mature in three months and are repriced on rollover.
3. *Six-month commercial paper: $60 million,* which mature and are repriced every six months.
4. *One-year time deposits: $20 million,* which are repriced at the end of the one-year gap horizon.

Summing these four items produces one-year rate-sensitive liabilities (RSLs) of $140 million. The remaining $130 million is not rate sensitive over the one-year period. The $20 million in equity capital and $40 million in demand deposits (see the following discussion) do not pay interest and are therefore classified as noninterest paying. The $30 million in passbook savings (see the following discussion) and $40 million in two-year time deposits generate interest expense over the next year, but the level of the interest expense generated will not change if the general level of interest rates change. Thus, we classify these items as rate-insensitive liabilities.

The four repriced liabilities ($40 + $20 + $60 + $20) sum to $140 million, and the four repriced assets ($50 + $30 + $35 + $40) sum to $155 million. Given this, the cumulative one-year repricing gap (CGAP) for the bank is:

$$\begin{aligned} \text{CGAP} &= (\text{One-year RSA}) - (\text{One-year RSL}) \\ &= \text{RSA} - \text{RSL} \\ &= \$155 \text{ million} - \$140 \text{ million} = \$15 \text{ million} \end{aligned}$$

Interest rate sensitivity can also be expressed as a percentage of assets (A):

$$\frac{CGAP}{A} = \frac{\$15 \text{ million}}{\$270 \text{ million}} = .056 = 5.6\%$$

Expressing the repricing gap in this way is useful since it tells us (1) the direction of the interest rate exposure (positive or negative CGAP) and (2) the scale of that exposure as indicated by dividing the gap by the asset size of the institution. In our example, the bank has a CGAP equal to 5.6 percent of the value of its total assets.

Equal Changes in Rates on RSAs and RSLs. The CGAP provides a measure of a bank's interest rate sensitivity. Table 22–3 highlights the relation between CGAP and changes in NII when interest rate changes for RSAs are equal to interest rate changes for RSLs. For

TABLE 22–3 Impact of CGAP on the Relation between Changes in Interest Rates and Changes in Net Interest Income, Assuming Rate Changes for RSAs Equal Rate Changes for RSLs

Row	CGAP	Change in Interest Rates	Change in Interest Income		Change in Interest Expense	Change in NII
1	>0	↑	↑	>	↑	↑
2	>0	↓	↓	>	↓	↓
3	<0	↑	↑	<	↑	↓
4	<0	↓	↓	<	↓	↑

example, when CGAP (or the gap ratio) is positive (or the bank has more RSAs than RSLs), NII will rise when interest rates rise (row 1, Table 22–3), since interest income increases more than interest expense does.

EXAMPLE 22-1 Impact of Rate Changes on Net Interest Income When CGAP Is Positive

Suppose that interest rates rise by 1 percent on both RSAs and RSLs. The CGAP would project the expected annual change in net interest income (ΔNII) of the bank as approximately:

$$\begin{aligned}\Delta NII &= CGAP \times \Delta R \\ &= (\$15 \text{ million}) \times .01 \\ &= \$150{,}000\end{aligned}$$

Similarly, if interest rates fall equally for RSAs and RSLs (row 2, Table 22–3), NII will fall when CGAP is positive. As rates fall, interest income falls by more than interest expense. Thus, NII falls. Suppose that for our bank, rates fall by 1 percent. The CGAP predicts that NII will fall by:

$$\begin{aligned}\Delta NII &= CGAP \times \Delta R \\ &= (\$15 \text{ million}) \times (-.01) \\ &= -\$150{,}000\end{aligned}$$

It is evident from this equation that the larger the absolute value of CGAP, the larger the expected change in NII (i.e., the larger the increase or decrease in the FI's interest income relative to interest expense). In general, when CGAP is positive, the change in NII is positively related to the change in interest rates. Conversely, when CGAP (or the gap ratio) is negative, if interest rates rise by equal amounts for RSAs and RSLs (row 3, Table 22–3), NII will fall (since the bank has more RSLs than RSAs). Thus, an FI would want its CGAP to be positive when interest rates are expected to rise.

Similarly, if interest rates fall equally for RSAs and RSLs (row 4, Table 22–3), NII will increase when CGAP is negative. As rates fall, interest expense decreases by more than interest income. In general then, when CGAP is negative, the change in NII is negatively related to the change in interest rates. Thus, an FI would want its CGAP to be negative when interest rates are expected to fall. We refer to these relationships as **CGAP effects.**

CGAP effect

The relation between changes in interest rates and changes in net interest income.

Unequal Changes in Rates on RSAs and RSLs. The previous section considered changes in net interest income as interest rates changed, assuming that the change in rates on RSAs was exactly equal to the change in rates on RSLs (in other words, assuming the interest rate spread between rates on RSAs and RSLs remained unchanged). This is not often the case; rather, rate changes on RSAs generally differ from those on RSLs (i.e., the spread between interest rates on assets and liabilities changes along with the levels of these rates). See Figure 22–1, which plots monthly CD rates (liabilities) and prime lending rates (assets) for the period 1990–March 2005. Notice that although the rates generally move in the same direction, they are not perfectly correlated. In this case, as we consider the impact of rate changes on NII, we have a spread effect in addition to the CGAP effect.[7]

EXAMPLE 22-2 Impact of Spread Effect on Net Interest Income

To understand spread effect, assume for a moment that RSAs equal RSLs equals \$155 million. Suppose that rates rise by 1.2 percent on RSAs and by 1 percent on RSLs (i.e., the spread

7. The spread effect therefore presents a type of "basis" risk for the FI. The FI's net interest income varies as the difference (basis) between interest rates on RSAs and interest rates on RSLs vary. We discuss basis risk in detail in Chapter 23.

SEARCH THE SITE

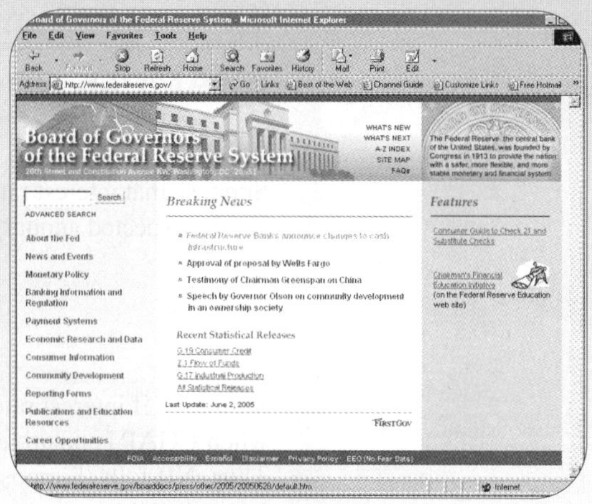

Go to the Federal Reserve Board's Web site at **www.federalreserve.gov** and find the latest information available on three-month CD rates versus the prime rate using the following steps.

Click on "Economic Research and Data."

Click on "Statistics: Releases and Historical Data."

Under "Other" click on "Selected Interest Rates-Monthly."

Click on "It is historical data."

To get monthly CD rates, under "CDs (secondary market), 3-month," click on "Monthly."

This will download data to your computer that will contain the most recent information on three-month CD rates. Repeat these steps to get the bank prime loan rate.

Questions

1. How have prime rates and CD rates changed since early 2005 as reported in Figure 22–1?
2. Calculate the spread between the prime rate and CD rate since early 2005. How has the spread changed over the last several years?

FIGURE 22–1 Three-Month CD Rates versus Prime Rate for 1990–March 2005

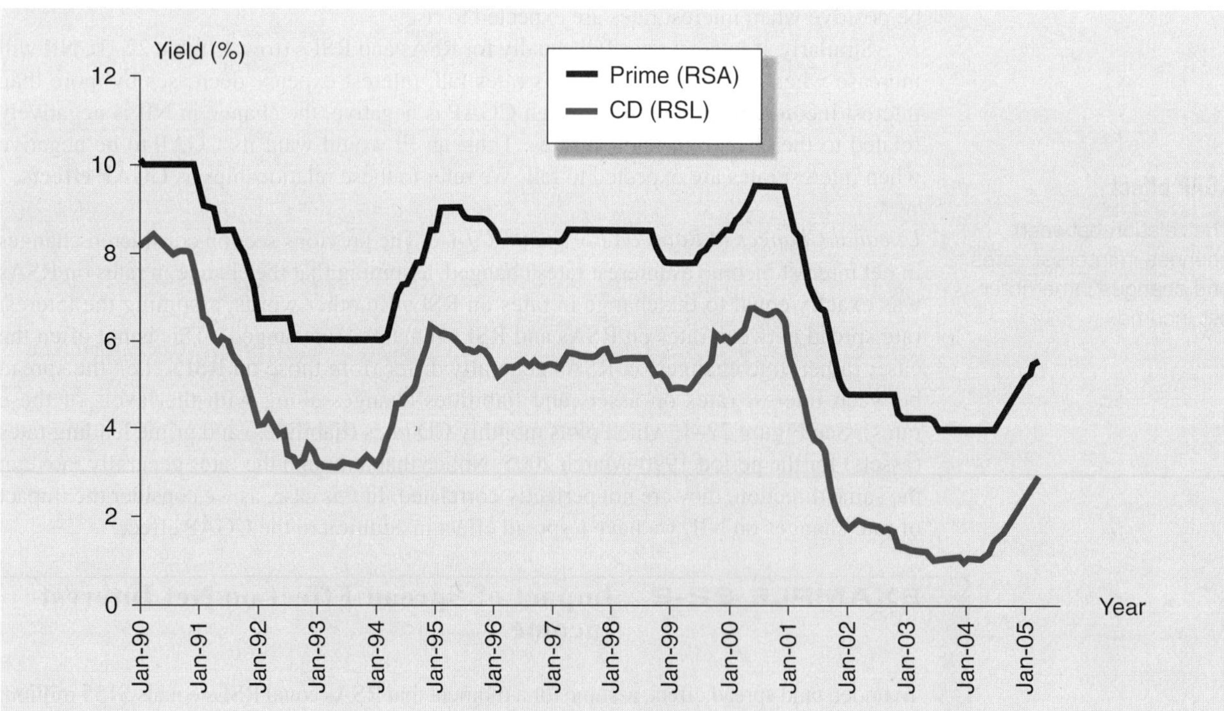

RSA = Rate-sensitive assets.

RSL = Rate-sensitive liabilities.

Source: *Federal Reserve Bulletin*, various issues. **www.federalreserve.gov**

between the rate on RSAs and RSLs increases by 1.2 percent − 1 percent = 0.2 percent). The resulting change in NII is calculated as:

$$\begin{aligned}\Delta NII &= (RSA \times \Delta R_{RSA}) - (RSL \times \Delta R_{RSL})\\ &= \Delta\text{Interest income} - \Delta\text{Interest expense}\\ &= (\$155 \text{ million} \times 1.2\%) - (\$155 \text{ million} \times 1.0\%)\\ &= \$155 \text{ million } (1.2\% - 1.0\%)\\ &= \$310{,}000\end{aligned}$$

If the spread between the rate on RSAs and RSLs increases, when interest rates rise (fall), interest income increases (decreases) by more (less) than interest expense. The result is an increase in NII. Conversely, if the spread between the rates on RSAs and RSLs decreases, when interest rates rise (fall), interest income increases (decreases) less (more) than interest expense, and NII decreases. In general, the **spread effect** is such that, regardless of the direction of the change in interest rates, a positive relation occurs between changes in the spread (between rates on RSAs and RSLs) and changes in NII. Whenever the spread increases (decreases), NII increases (decreases).

spread effect

The effect that a change in the spread between rates on RSAs and RSLs has on net interest income (NII) as interest rates change.

See Table 22–4 for various combinations of CGAP and spread changes and their effects on NII. The first four rows in Table 22–4 consider a bank with a positive CGAP; the last four rows consider a bank with a negative CGAP. Notice in Table 22–4 that the CGAP and spread effects can both have the same effect on NII. In these cases, FI managers can accurately predict the direction of the change in NII as interest rates change (rows indicated with one arrow under the "Change in NII" column). When the two work in opposite directions, however, the change in NII cannot be predicted without knowing the size of the CGAP and expected change in the spread (rows indicated by two arrows, ↑↓, under the "Change in NII" column).

The repricing gap is the measure of interest rate risk most often used by FIs. The repricing gap model is conceptually easy to understand and can easily be used to forecast changes in profitability for a given change in interest rates. The repricing gap can be used to allow an FI to structure its assets and liabilities or to go off the balance sheet to take advantage of a projected interest rate change. However, the repricing gap model has some major weaknesses that have resulted in regulators calling for the use of more comprehensive models (e.g., the duration gap model) to measure the interest rate risk of an FI. We next discuss some of the major weaknesses of the repricing model.

Weakness of the Repricing Model. The repricing model has four major weaknesses: (1) it ignores market value effects of interest rate changes, (2) it ignores cash flow patterns within a maturity bucket, (3) it fails to deal with the problem of

TABLE 22–4 Impact of CGAP on the Relation between Changes in Interest Rates and Changes in Net Interest Income, Allowing for Different Rate Changes on RSAs and RSLs

Row	CGAP	Change in Interest Rates	Change in Spread	Change in NII
1	>0	↑	↑	↑
2	>0	↑	↓	↑↓
3	>0	↓	↑	↑↓
4	>0	↓	↓	↓
5	<0	↑	↑	↑↓
6	<0	↑	↓	↓
7	<0	↓	↑	↑
8	<0	↓	↓	↑↓

rate-insensitive asset and liability cash flow runoffs and prepayments, and (4) it ignores cash flows from off-balance-sheet activities. This section discusses each of these weaknesses.

Market Value Effects. As discussed in the next section, interest rate changes have a market (or present) value effect in addition to an income effect on asset and liability values. That is, the present value of the cash flows on assets and liabilities changes, in addition to the immediate interest received or paid on them, as interest rates change. In fact, the present values (and, where relevant, the market prices) of virtually all assets and liabilities on an FI's balance sheet change as interest rates change. As such, the repricing gap is only a *partial* and short-term measure of an FI's true overall interest rate risk exposure.

Cash Flow Patterns within a Maturity Bucket. The problem of defining buckets over a range of maturities ignores information regarding the distribution of assets and liabilities within that bucket. For example, the dollar values of RSAs and RSLs within any maturity bucket range may be equal; however, on average, liabilities may be repriced toward the end of the bucket's range and assets may be repriced toward the beginning, in which case a change in interest rates will have an effect on asset and liability cash flows that will not be accurately measured by the repricing gap approach.

runoff

Periodic cash flow of interest and principal amortization payments on long-term assets such as conventional mortgages that can be reinvested at market rates.

The Problem of Runoffs and Prepayments. Even if an asset or liability is rate insensitive, virtually all assets and liabilities pay some interest and/or principal back in any given year. As a result, the FI receives a cash flow or **runoff** from its rate-insensitive portfolio that can be reinvested at current market rates; that is, most assets and liabilities (e.g., long-term mortgages) pay some principal and/or interest back to the FI in any given year. This runoff cash flow component of a rate-insensitive asset and liability is itself rate *sensitive.* The FI manager can easily deal with this in the repricing gap model by identifying for each asset and liability item the estimated dollar cash flow that will be run off within the next year and adding these amounts to the value of rate-sensitive assets and liabilities.

Similarly, the repricing model assumes that there is no prepayment of RSAs and RSLs. In reality, however, cash flows from RSAs and RSLs do not act in such a predictable fashion. For example, a mortgage may be paid off early, either to buy a new house or to refinance the mortgage should interest rates fall. For a variety of reasons, mortgage borrowers relocate or refinance their mortgages (especially when current mortgage rates are below mortgage coupon rates). This propensity to prepay means that realized cash flows on RSAs and RSLs can often deviate substantially from the stated or expected cash flows in a no-prepayment world. As with runoffs, the FI manager can deal with prepayments in the repricing gap model by estimating the amount of prepayment on each asset and liability within the next year and adding these amounts to the values of RSAs and RSLs.

Cash Flows from Off-Balance-Sheet Activities. The RSAs and RSLs used in the repricing model generally include only assets and liabilities listed on the balance sheet. Changes in interest rates will affect the cash flows on many off-balance-sheet instruments as well. For example, an FI might have hedged its interest rate risk with an interest rate futures contract (see Chapter 23). As interest rates change, these futures contracts—as part of the marking-to-market process—produce a daily cash flow (either positive or negative) for the FI that may offset any on-balance-sheet gap exposure. These offsetting cash flows from futures contracts are ignored by the simple repricing model and should (and could) be included in the model.

Duration Model

3

In Chapter 3, we demonstrated how to calculate duration and showed that the duration measure has economic meaning as the interest sensitivity of an asset or liability's value to small changes in interest rates. That is:

$$D = -\frac{\%\Delta \text{ in the market value of a security}}{\Delta R/(1+R)}$$

For FIs, the major relevance of duration is its use as a measure of interest rate risk exposure. The duration model can be used instead of the repricing model discussed above to evaluate an FI's overall interest rate exposure—to measure the FI's **duration gap.**

duration gap

A measure of overall interest rate risk exposure for an FI.

The Duration Gap for a Financial Institution. To estimate the overall duration gap of an FI, we first determine the duration of an FI's asset portfolio (A) and the duration of its liability portfolio (L). Specifically, the duration of a portfolio of assets or liabilities is the market value weighted average of the durations of the components of the portfolio. These can be calculated as:

$$D_A = X_{1A}\, D_1^A + X_{2A} D_2^A + \cdots + X_{nA}\, D_n^A$$

and:

$$D_L = X_{1L}\, D_1^L + X_{2L} D_2^L + \cdots + X_{nL}\, D_n^L$$

where

$$X_{1j} + X_{2j} + \cdots + X_{nj} = 1$$
$$j = A, L$$

The X_{ij}'s in the equation represent the market value proportions of each asset or liability held in the respective asset and liability portfolios. Thus, if new 30-year Treasury bonds were 1 percent of a life insurer's portfolio and D_1^A, the duration of those bonds, was equal to 9.25 years, $X_{1A}\, D_1^A = 0.01(9.25) = 0.0925$. More simply, the duration of a portfolio of assets or liabilities is a market value weighted average of the individual durations of the assets or liabilities on the FI's balance sheet.[8]

Consider an FI's simplified market value balance sheet:

Assets ($)	**Liabilities/Equity ($)**
Assets (A) = $100	Liabilities (L) = $ 90
	Equity (E) = 10
$100	$100

From the balance sheet:

$$A = L + E$$

and:

$$\Delta A = \Delta L + \Delta E$$

or:

$$\Delta E = \Delta A - \Delta L$$

That is, when interest rates change, the change in the FI's equity or net worth (E) equals the difference between the change in the market values of assets and liabilities on each side of the balance sheet.

Since $\Delta E = \Delta A - \Delta L$, we need to determine how ΔA and ΔL—the changes in the market values of assets and liabilities on the balance sheet—are related to their duration.[9] From the duration model (assuming annual compounding of interest):

$$\frac{\Delta A}{A} = -D_A \frac{\Delta R}{(1 + R)}$$

8. This derivation of an FI's duration gap closely follows G. G. Kaufman, "Measuring and Managing Interest Rate Risk: A Primer," *Economic Perspective* (Chicago: Federal Reserve Bank of Chicago, 1984), pp. 16–29.

9. In what follows, we use the Δ (change) notation instead of d (derivative notation) to recognize that interest rate changes tend to be discrete rather than infinitesimally small. For example, in real-world financial markets, the smallest observed rate change is usually one basis point, or 1/100 of 1 percent.

and:

$$\frac{\Delta L}{L} = -D_L \frac{\Delta R}{(1 + R)}$$

Here we have simply substituted $\Delta A/A$ or $\Delta L/L$, the percentage change in the market values of assets or liabilities, for $\Delta P/P$, the percentage change in any single bond's price, and D_A or D_L, the duration of the FI's asset or liability portfolio, for D_i, the duration on any given bond, deposit, or loan. The term $\Delta R/(1 + R)$ reflects the shock to interest rates as before.[10] To show dollar changes, these equations can be rewritten as:

$$\Delta A = A \times -D_A \times \frac{\Delta R}{(1 + R)}$$

and:

$$\Delta L = L \times -D_L \times \frac{\Delta R}{(1 + R)}$$

Since $\Delta E = \Delta A - \Delta L$, we can substitute these two expressions into this equation. Rearranging and combining these equations[11] results in a measure of the change in the market value of equity:

$$\Delta E = -(D_A - kD_L) \times A \times \frac{\Delta R}{(1 + R)}$$

where

$k = L/A =$ Measure of the FI's leverage—the amount of borrowed funds or liabilities rather than owners' equity used to fund its asset portfolio

10. For simplicity, we assume that the interest rate changes are the same for both assets and liabilities. This assumption is standard in Macauley duration analysis (see Chapter 3).

11. $$\Delta E = \left[A \times (-D_A) \times \frac{\Delta R}{(1 + R)}\right] - \left[L \times (-D_L) \times \frac{\Delta R}{(1 + R)}\right]$$

Assuming that the level of interest rates and expected shock to interest rates are the same for both assets and liabilities:

$$\Delta E = [(-D_A)A + (D_L)L] \frac{\Delta R}{(1 + R)}$$

or:

$$\Delta E = -(D_A A - D_L L) \frac{\Delta R}{(1 + R)}$$

To rearrange the equation in a slightly more intuitive fashion, we multiply and divide both the terms $D_A A$ and $D_L L$ by A (assets):

$$\Delta E = -[(A/A)D_A - (L/A)D_L] \times A \times [\Delta R/(1 + R)]$$

Therefore:

$$\Delta E = -[D_A - (L/A)D_L] \times A \times [\Delta R/(1 + R)]$$

and thus:

$$\Delta E = -(D_A - kD_L) \times A \times [\Delta R/(1 + R)]$$

where

$$k = L/A$$

The effect of interest rate changes on the market value of an FI's equity or net worth (ΔE) breaks down into three effects:

1. *The leverage-adjusted duration gap* $= D_A - kD_L$. This gap is measured in years and reflects the degree of duration mismatch in an FI's balance sheet. Specifically, the larger this gap *in absolute terms,* the more exposed the FI is to interest rate risk.
2. *The size of the FI.* The term A measures the size of the FI's assets. The larger the asset size of the FI, the larger the dollar size of the potential net worth exposure from any given interest rate shock.
3. *The size of the interest rate shock* $= \Delta R/(1 + R)$. The larger the shock, the greater the FI's exposure.[12]

Given this, we express the exposure of the net worth of the FI as:

$$\Delta E = -\text{Adjusted duration gap} \times \text{Asset size} \times \text{Interest rate shock}$$

Interest rate shocks are largely external to the FI and often result from changes in the Federal Reserve's monetary policy or from international capital movements (as discussed in Chapter 4). The size of the duration gap and the size of the FI, however, are largely under the control of its management.

The next section uses an example to explain how a manager can utilize information on an FI's duration gap to restructure the balance sheet to immunize stockholders' net worth against interest rate risk (i.e., set the balance sheet up *before* a change in interest rates, so that ΔE is nonnegative for a forecasted change in interest rates). The general rules we illustrate are as follows. If the duration gap (DGAP) is negative, there is a positive relation between changes in interest rates and changes in the market value of the FI. Thus, if interest rates increase (decrease), the market value of the FI increases (decreases). If the DGAP is positive, there is a negative relation between changes in interest rates and changes in the market value of the FI. Thus, if interest rates decrease (increase), the market value of the FI increases (decreases).

EXAMPLE 22-3 Duration Gap Measurement and Exposure

Suppose that the FI manager calculates that:

$$D_A = 5 \text{ years}$$
$$D_L = 3 \text{ years}$$

Then the manager learns from an economic forecasting unit that rates are expected to rise from 10 to 11 percent in the immediate future; that is:

$$\Delta R = 1\% = .01$$
$$1 + R = 1.10$$

The FI's initial balance sheet is assumed to be:

Assets ($ millions)	Liabilities ($ millions)
A = $100	L = $ 90
	E = 10
$100	$100

12. We assume that the level of rates and the expected shock to interest rates are the same for both assets and liabilities. This assumption is standard in Macauley duration analysis. Although restrictive, this assumption can be relaxed. Specifically, if ΔR_A is the shock to assets and ΔR_L is the shock to liabilities, we can express the duration gap model as:

$$\Delta E = -\left[\left(D_A \times A \times \frac{\Delta R_A}{1 + R_A}\right) - \left(D_L \times L \times \frac{\Delta R_L}{1 + R_L}\right)\right]$$

The FI manager calculates the potential loss to equity holders' net worth (E) if the forecast of rising rates proves true:

$$\Delta E = -(D_A - kD_L) \times A \times \frac{\Delta R}{(1+R)}$$

$$= -[5 - (.9)(3)] \times \$100 \text{ million} \times \frac{.01}{1.1} = -\$2.09 \text{ million}$$

The FI could lose \$2.09 million in net worth if rates rise by 1 percent. The FI started with \$10 million in equity, so the loss of \$2.09 million is almost 21 percent of its initial net worth. The market value balance sheet after the rise in rates by 1 percent then appears as follows:[13]

Assets ($ millions)	Liabilities ($ million)
A = \$95.45	L = \$87.54
	E = 7.91
\$95.45	\$95.45

Even though the rise in interest rates would not push the FI into economic insolvency, it reduces the FI's net worth-to-assets ratio from 10 (10/100) to 8.29 percent (7.91/95.45). To counter this effect, the manager might reduce the FI's adjusted duration gap. In an extreme case, this gap might be reduced to zero:

$$\Delta E = (0) \times A \times \Delta R/(1+R) = 0$$

To do this, the FI should not directly set $D_A = D_L$, which ignores the fact that the FI's assets (A) do not equal its borrowed liabilities (L) and that k (which reflects the ratio L/A) is not equal to 1. To see the importance of factoring in leverage (or L/A), suppose that the manager increases the duration of the FI's liabilities to five years, the same as D_A. Then:

$$\Delta E = -[5 - (.9)(5)] \times \$100 \text{ million} \times (.01/1.1) = -\$0.45 \text{ million}$$

The FI is still exposed to a loss of \$0.45 million if rates rise by 1 percent.

An appropriate strategy involves changing D_L until:

$$D_A = kD_L = 5 \text{ years}$$

For example:

$$\Delta E = -[5 - (.9)5.55] \times \$100 \text{ million} \times (.01/1.1) = 0$$

In this case, the FI manager sets $D_L = 5.55$ years, or slightly longer than $D_A = 5$ years, to compensate for the fact that only 90 percent of assets are funded by borrowed liabilities,

13. These values are calculated as follows:

$$\frac{\Delta A}{A} = -5\left(\frac{.01}{1.1}\right) = -.04545 = -4.545\%$$

$$100 + (-.04545)100 = 95.45$$

and:

$$\frac{\Delta L}{L} = -3\left(\frac{.01}{1.1}\right) = -.02727 = -2.727\%$$

$$90 + (-.02727)90 = 87.54$$

with the other 10 percent funded by equity. Note that the FI manager has at least three other ways to reduce the adjusted duration gap to zero:

1. *Reduce D_A*. Reduce D_A from 5 years to 2.7 years [equal to kD_L, or (.9)(3)] so that

$$(D_A - kD_L) = [2.7 - (.9)(3)] = 0$$

2. *Reduce D_A and increase D_L*. Shorten the duration of assets and lengthen the duration of liabilities at the same time. One possibility is to *reduce* D_A to 4 years and to *increase* D_L to 4.44 years so that

$$(D_A - kD_L) = [4 - (.9)(4.44)] = 0$$

3. *Change k and D_L*. Increase k (leverage) from .9 to .95 and increase D_L from 3 years to 5.26 years so that:

$$(D_A - kD_L) = [5 - (.95)(5.26)] = 0$$

The preceding example demonstrated how the duration model can be used to immunize an FI's entire balance sheet against interest rate risk, i.e., so that the value of the FI's equity is unaffected by changes in interest rates.

2

Difficulties in Applying the Duration Model to Real-World FI Balance Sheets. Critics of the duration model have often claimed that it is difficult to apply in real-world situations. However, duration measures and immunization strategies are useful in most real-world situations. In fact, the model recently proposed by the Federal Reserve and the Bank for International Settlements (BIS)[14] to monitor bank interest rate risk taking is heavily based on the duration model. We next consider the various criticisms of the duration model and discuss ways in which a modern FI manager would deal with these criticisms in practice.

Duration Matching Can Be Costly. Critics charge that although in principle an FI manager can change D_A and D_L to immunize the FI against interest rate risk, restructuring the balance sheet of a large and complex FI can be both time-consuming and costly. This argument may have been true historically, but the growth of purchased funds, asset securitization, and loan sales markets has considerably eased the speed and lowered the transaction costs of major balance sheet restructurings. (See Chapter 24 for a discussion of these strategies.) Moreover, an FI manager could still manage risk exposure using the duration model by employing techniques other than direct portfolio rebalancing to immunize against interest rate risk. Managers can obtain many of the same results of direct duration matching by taking offsetting (hedging) positions in the markets for derivative securities, such as futures, forwards, options, and swaps (Chapter 23).

Immunization Is a Dynamic Problem. Even though assets and liabilities are duration matched today, the same assets and liabilities may not be matched tomorrow. This is because the duration of assets and liabilities change as they approach maturity, and, most importantly, the rate at which their durations change through time may not be the same on the asset and liability sides of the balance sheet. As a result, the manager has to continuously restructure the balance sheet to remain immunized. In theory, the strategy requires the portfolio manager to rebalance the portfolio continuously to ensure that the durations of its assets and liabilities are matched. Because continuous rebalancing may not be easy to do and involves costly transaction fees, most FI managers seek to be only

14. In 1993, the BIS proposed a duration gap model to measure the interest rate risk of the whole balance sheet. This was reaffirmed in 1999 (see Basel Committee on Banking Supervision, "A New Capital Adequacy Framework," Basel, June 1999, and Chapter 13) and 2001 (see "Principles for the Management and Supervision of Interest Rate Risk," Basel, January 2001). Since 1998, the Federal Reserve has been using a duration gap model as part of the standardized model to measure a bank's interest rate risk exposure in its trading (or market) portfolio—see Chapter 19.

FIGURE 22–2 Duration Estimated versus True Bond Price

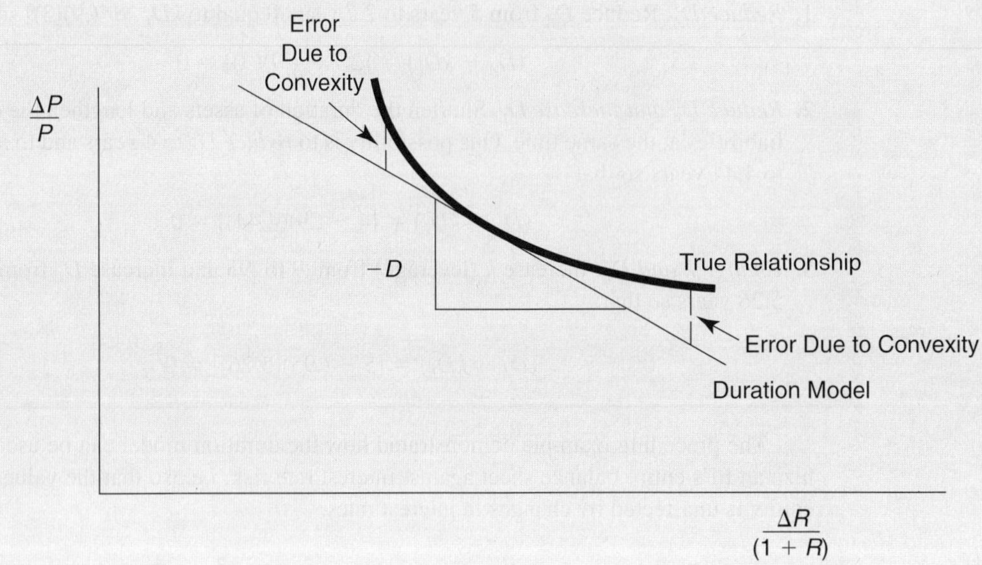

approximately dynamically immunized against interest rate changes by rebalancing at discrete intervals, such as quarterly. That is, FI managers accept the trade-off between being perfectly immunized and the transaction costs of maintaining an immunized balance sheet dynamically.

Large Interest Rate Changes and Convexity. Duration measures the price sensitivity of fixed-income securities for small changes in interest rates of the order of one basis point (or one-hundredth of 1 percent). But suppose that interest rate shocks are much larger, of the order of 2 percent or 200 basis points. In this case, duration becomes a less accurate predictor of how much the prices of securities will change and, therefore, a less accurate measure of the interest rate sensitivity and the interest rate gap of an FI. Figure 22–2 is a graphic representation of the reason for this. Note the change in an asset's or liability's price, such as that of a bond, due to yield (interest rate) changes according to the duration model and the "true relationship," as calculated directly, using the exact present value calculation for a bond.

DO YOU UNDERSTAND?

1. How FIs can change the size and the direction of their repricing gap?
2. What four major weaknesses of the repricing model are?
3. What a runoff means?
4. Why critics argue that the duration model is difficult to apply in real-world situations? How these arguments can be countered?
5. What convexity is?

Specifically, the duration model predicts that the relationship between an interest rate change (or shock) and a bond's price change will be proportional to the bond's duration (D). By precisely calculating the true change in the bond's price, however, we would find that for large interest rate increases, duration overpredicts the *fall* in the bond's price, and for large interest rate decreases, it underpredicts the *increase* in the bond's price. That is, the duration model predicts symmetric effects for rate increases and decreases on the bond's price. As Figure 22–2 shows, in actuality, the capital *loss* effect of rate increases tends to be smaller than the capital *gain* effect of rate decreases. This is the result of the bond's price-yield relationship exhibiting a property called **convexity** rather than linearity, as assumed by the basic duration model (see the more detailed discussion in Chapter 3). Nevertheless, an FI manager sufficiently concerned about the impact of large rate changes on the FI's balance sheet can capture the convexity effect by directly measuring it and incorporating it into the duration gap model.[15]

convexity

The degree of curvature of the price-yield curve around some interest rate level.

15. Technically speaking, convexity can be viewed as the *rate of change* of the bond's value with respect to any interest rate change, whereas duration measures the *change* in a bond's value with respect to a change in interest rates.

TABLE 22–5 Duration of a Four-Year Bond with an 8 Percent Coupon Paid Annually and a 10 Percent Yield

t	CF_t	$PVIF_{10\%,t}$	*PVIF* of *CF*	*PVIF* of $C \times t$
1	80	0.9091	72.727	72.727
2	80	0.8264	66.116	132.231
3	80	0.7513	60.105	180.316
4	1,080	0.6830	737.655	2,950.618
			$936.603	$3,263.165

$$D = \frac{3{,}263.165}{936.603} = 3.484 \text{ years}$$

EXAMPLE 22–4 The Impact of Convexity for Large Interest Rate Changes

Consider a four-year bond that pays 8 percent coupons annually and has a yield to maturity of 10 percent. Table 22–5 shows that the market value of this bond is $936.603 and the duration of this bond is 3.484 years. Suppose interest rates change such that the yield to maturity on the bond increases to 12 percent. The true market value of the bond decreases to:

$$V_b = 80\,(PVIFA_{12\%,4}) + 1{,}000(PVIF_{12\%,4})$$
$$= 80\,(3.03735) + 1{,}000\,(.63552) = \$878.508$$

This is a drop of $58.095. According to the duration model, however, the change in the bond's value is:

$$P = 936.603 \times (-3.484) \times (.02/1.10) = -\$59.330$$

or the new bond value is $877.273.

The difference in these two values, $1.235 ($878.508 − $877.273), is due to the convexity in the "true" market value calculation versus the linearity in the duration model. This linearity assumption leads to inaccuracies in the duration value calculations that increase with the size of the interest rate change.[16]

INSOLVENCY RISK MANAGEMENT

In the previous two chapters and in this chapter, we have examined three major areas of risk exposure facing a modern FI manager. To ensure survival, an FI manager needs to protect the institution against the risk of insolvency—to shield it from those risks that are sufficiently large to cause the institution to fail. The primary means of protection against the risk of insolvency and failure is an FI's equity capital. However, capital also serves as a source of funds and as a necessary requirement for growth under the existing minimum capital-to-assets ratios set by regulators. FI managers may often prefer low levels of capital because they allow the institution to generate a higher return on equity for the firm's stockholders. The moral hazard problem of deposit insurance (see Chapter 13) exacerbates this tendency. However, this strategy results in a greater chance of insolvency.

16. Even allowing for convexity, there still may be a very small difference between the true change in the value of a bond and the value change predicted by the duration model adjusted for convexity. This is because convexity itself varies as the level of interest rates changes. In practice, few investors or fund managers concern themselves with this issue.

Since regulators are more concerned with the safety of the financial system than stockholder returns, there is a need for minimum capital requirements (Chapter 13 discussed the regulatory requirements on an FI's capital). In the remainder of this chapter, we focus on how various risks affect the level of an FI's capital.

Capital and Insolvency Risk

Capital. To understand how an FI's equity capital protects against insolvency risk, we must define *capital* more precisely. The problem is that equity capital has many definitions: an economist's definition of capital may differ from an accountant's definition, which in turn may differ from a regulator's definition. Specifically, the economist's definition of an FI's capital, or owners' equity stake, is the difference between the market values of its assets and its liabilities. This is also called an FI's **net worth** (see Chapter 12). This is the *economic* meaning of capital, but regulators and accountants have found it necessary to adopt definitions that depart by a greater or lesser degree from economic net worth. The concept of an FI's economic net worth is really a *market value accounting* concept. With the exception of the investment banking industry, regulatory- and accounting-defined capital and required leverage ratios are based in whole or in part on historical or **book value** accounting concepts.

net worth

A measure of an FI's capital that is equal to the difference between the market value of its assets and the market value of its liabilities.

book value

Value of assets and liabilities based on their historical costs.

We begin by looking at the role of economic capital or net worth as a device to protect against two of the major types of risk described in the previous chapters and in this chapter: credit risk and interest rate risk. We then compare this market value concept with the book value concept of capital. Because it can actually distort an FI's true solvency position, the book value of capital concept can be misleading to managers, owners, liability holders, and regulators alike. We also examine some possible reasons FI regulators continue to rely on book value concepts when such economic value transparency problems exist.

4

The Market Value of Capital. To understand how economic net worth insulates an FI against the risk of insolvency, consider the following example. Table 22–6 presents a simple balance sheet, where an FI's assets and liabilities are valued in market value terms. On a **market value** or **mark-to-market value basis,** asset and liability values are adjusted each day to reflect current market conditions. Thus, the economic value of the FI's equity is $10 million, which is the difference between the market value of its assets and liabilities, and it is economically solvent. Let's consider the impact of two classic types of FI risk—credit and interest rate—on this FI's net worth.

market value or mark-to-market value basis

Balance sheet values that reflect current rather than historical prices.

Market Value of Capital and Credit Risk. The balance sheet in Table 22–6 indicates that the FI (such as a finance company) has $20 million in long-term loans. Suppose that as the result of a recession, a number of its borrowers have cash flow problems and are unable to keep up their promised loan repayment schedules. A decline in the current and expected future cash flows on loans lowers the market value of the FI's loan portfolio below $20 million. Suppose that loans are really worth only $12 million (the price the FI would receive if it could sell these loans in a secondary market). This means the market value of the loan portfolio has fallen from $20 million to $12 million. The revised market value balance sheet is presented in Table 22–7.

TABLE 22–6 An FI's Market Value Balance Sheet
(in millions of dollars)

Assets		Liabilities	
Long-term securities	$ 80	Liabilities (short-term floating-rate deposits)	$ 90
Long-term loans	20	Net worth	10
	$100		$100

TABLE 22–7 An FI's Market Value Balance Sheet after a Decline in the Value of Loans
(in millions of dollars)

Assets		Liabilities	
Long-term securities	$80	Liabilities	$90
Long-term loans	12	Net worth	2
	$92		$92

TABLE 22–8 An FI's Market Value Balance Sheet after a Major Decline in the Value of the Loan Portfolio
(in millions of dollars)

Assets		Liabilities	
Long-term securities	$80	Liabilities	$90
Long-term loans	8	Net worth	−2
	$88		$88

The loss of $8 million in the market value of loans appears on the liability side of the balance sheet as a loss of $8 million of the FI's net worth—the loss of asset value is directly charged against the equity owners' capital or net worth. As you can see, the liability holders are fully protected because the total market value of their $90 million in liability claims is still $90 million. This is due to the fact that liability holders legally are senior claimants and equity holders are junior claimants to the FI's assets. Consequently, equity holders bear losses on the asset portfolio first. In fact, in this example, liability holders are hurt only when losses on the loan portfolio exceed $10 million (which was the FI's original net worth). Let's consider a larger credit risk shock in which the market value of the loan portfolio plummets from $20 million to $8 million, a loss of $12 million (see Table 22–8).

This larger loss renders the FI insolvent; the market value of its assets ($88 million) is now less than the value of its liabilities ($90 million). The owners' net worth stake has been completely wiped out—reduced from $10 million to −$2 million, resulting in a negative net worth. Therefore, this hurts liability holders, but only a bit. Specifically, the equity holders bear the first $10 million of the $12 million loss in value of the loan portfolio. Only after the equity holders are completely wiped out do the liability holders begin to lose. In this example, the economic value of their claims on the FI has fallen from $90 million to $88 million, or a loss of $2 million (a percentage loss of 2.22 percent). After insolvency, the remaining $88 million in assets is liquidated and distributed to deposit holders. Note here that we are ignoring insurance guarantees afforded to some FI (e.g., bank) liability holders.[17]

This example clearly demonstrates the concept of net worth or capital as an "insurance" fund protecting liability holders against insolvency risk. The larger the FI's net worth relative to the size of its assets, the more insolvency protection its liability holders and, in some cases, liability guarantors such as the FDIC have. This is the reason that regulators focus on capital requirements such as the ratio of net worth to assets in assessing an FI's insolvency risk exposure and in setting deposit insurance premiums (see Chapter 13).

Market Value of Capital and Interest Rate Risk. Consider the market value balance sheet in Table 22–6 before interest rates rise. As we discussed earlier in the chapter, rising interest rates reduce the market value of the FI's long-term fixed-income assets and loans, while floating-rate instruments find their market values largely unaffected if interest rates on such

17. In the presence of deposit insurance, the insurer, such as the FDIC, bears some of the depositors' losses; for details, see Chapter 13.

TABLE 22–9 An FI's Market Value Balance Sheet after a Rise in Interest Rates
(in millions of dollars)

Assets		Liabilities	
Long-term securities	$75	Liabilities	$90
Long-term loans	17	Net worth	2
	$92		$92

securities are instantaneously reset.[18] Suppose that a rise in interest rates reduces the market value of the FI's long-term securities investments to $75 million from $80 million and the market value of its long-term loans to $17 million from $20 million. Because all deposit liabilities are assumed to be short-term floating-rate deposits, their market values are unchanged at $90 million.

After the shock to interest rates, the market value balance sheet is represented in Table 22–9. The loss of $8 million in the market value of the FI's assets is once again reflected on the liability side of the balance sheet by an $8 million decrease in net worth to $2 million. Thus, as for increased credit risk, the equity holders first bear losses in asset values due to adverse interest rate changes. Only if the fall in the market value of assets exceeds $10 million are the liability holders, as senior claimants to the FI's assets, adversely affected.

These examples show that market valuation of the balance sheet produces an economically accurate picture of net worth and, thus, an FI's solvency position. The equity holders directly bear the credit risk and interest rate risks that result in losses in the market value of assets and liabilities in the sense that such losses are charges against the value of their ownership claims in the FI. As long as the owners' capital or equity stake is adequate, or sufficiently large, liability holders (and implicitly regulators that back the claims of liability holders) are protected against insolvency risk. If regulators were to close an FI before its economic net worth became zero, neither liability holders, nor those regulators guaranteeing the claims of liability holders, would stand to lose. Thus, many academics and analysts advocate the use of market value accounting and market value of capital closure rules for all FIs, especially because the book value of capital rules are closely associated with the savings institutions disaster in the 1980s (discussed in Chapter 13).[19] To see why book value of capital rules may incorrectly measure insolvency risk, consider the same credit and interest rate risk scenarios discussed above, but this time in a world where book value accounting and capital regulations hold sway.

4

The Book Value of Capital. Table 22–10 uses the same initial balance sheet as in Table 22–6 but assumes that assets and liabilities are now valued at their historical book values. In Table 22–10, the $80 million in long-term securities and $20 million in long-term loans reflect the historic or original book values of those assets—that is, they reflect the (historic) values at the time the loans were made and securities were purchased, which may have been many years ago when the economy was in a different stage of the business cycle and interest rates were at different levels. Similarly, on the liability side, the $90 million in liabilities also reflects their

18. This is because the interest rate increase is incorporated in the revised coupon rate on the floating-rate loan as well as its yield to maturity (on discount rate), leaving its market value unchanged, while the coupon rate on a fixed-income loan cannot change. Rather, for the fixed-income loan, the interest rate increase can only be incorporated in the yield to maturity (discount rate), which in turn affects the market value (see Chapter 3).

19. Three regulatory concerns expressed in the banking industry about market value accounting that slow this from happening are (1) market value accounting (MVA) is difficult to implement, especially for small commercial banks and thrifts; (2) MVA introduces an unnecessary degree of variability into an FI's earnings because paper capital gains and losses are passed through the income statement; and (3) FIs would be less willing to accept long-term asset exposure with MVA, since they are continually marked to market.

TABLE 22–10 An FI's Book Value Balance Sheet
(in millions of dollars)

Assets		Liabilities	
Long-term securities	$ 80	Short-term liabilities	$ 90
Long-term loans	20	Equity	10
	$100		$100

historic cost, so that the equity of the FI is now the book value of the stockholders' claims rather than the market value of those claims. For example, the book value of capital—the difference between the book value of an FI's assets and the book value of its liabilities—usually comprises the following three components in banking:

1. **Par Value of Shares**—the face value of the common shares issued by the FI (the par value is usually $1 per share) times the number of shares outstanding.
2. **Surplus Value of Shares**—the difference between the price the public paid for common shares when originally offered (e.g., $5 per share) and their par values (e.g., $1) times the number of shares outstanding.
3. **Retained Earnings**—the accumulated value of past profits not yet paid in dividends to shareholders. Since these earnings could be paid in dividends, they are part of the equity owners' stake in the FI.

Consequently for an FI, Book value of its capital = Par value + Surplus + Retained earnings. As the example in Table 22–10 is constructed, the book value of capital equals $10 million. However, invariably, the book value of equity *does not equal* the market value of equity (the difference between the market value of assets and liabilities). This inequality between the book and market values of equity can be best understood by examining the effects of the same credit and interest rate shocks on the FI, but assuming book value rather than market value accounting methods.

The Book Value of Capital and Credit Risk. Suppose that some of the $20 million in loans are in difficulty due to the inability of businesses to maintain their repayment schedules. We assumed in Table 22–7 that the revaluation of the promised cash flows of loans leads to an immediate downward adjustment of the loan portfolio's market value from $20 million to $12 million, and a market value loss of $8 million. By contrast, under historic book value accounting methods, such as generally accepted accounting principles (GAAP), FIs have more discretion in reflecting and timing the recognition of loan loss on their balance sheets, and thus of the impact of such losses on capital. Indeed, managers of FIs may well resist writing down the values of bad assets as long as possible to try to present a more favorable picture to depositors, shareholders, and regulators. Such resistance might be expected if managers believe that the recognition of such losses could threaten their careers. Similarly, FI managers can selectively sell assets to inflate their reported capital. For example, managers can sell assets that have market values above their book values, resulting in an increase in the book value of capital. Only pressure from auditors and regulators such as bank, thrift, and insurance examiners may force loss recognition and write-downs of the values of problem assets. In recent years, on-site examinations of property insurance companies have occurred as infrequently as once every three years, while insurance regulators analyze off-site balance sheet information as infrequently as once every 18 months. Although bank call report data and on-site examinations are now more frequent,[20]

www.fasb.org

20. The FDIC Improvement Act of 1991 requires examinations at least annually for large and troubled banks and every 18 months for smaller, healthy banks. Banks produce call reports (balance sheet and income statement data) quarterly.

the tendency is still to delay writing down the book values of loans. In Japan, the financial crisis of the late 1990s resulted in the Finance Ministry calling for banks to discontinue their delay in writing off many of the nonperforming loans in their portfolios.

Book Value of Capital and Interest Rate Risk. Although book value accounting systems recognize credit risk problems, albeit only partially and usually with a long and discretionary time lag, their failure to recognize the impact of interest rate risk is even more extreme. In the market value accounting example in Table 22–9, a rise in interest rates lowered the market values of long-term securities and loans by $8 million and led to a fall in the market value of net worth from $10 million to $2 million. In a book value accounting world, when all assets and liabilities reflect their original cost of purchase, the rise in interest rates has no effect on the value of assets, liabilities, or the book value of equity—the balance sheet remains unchanged. Table 22–10 reflects the position both before and after the interest rate rise. This was the case for those thrifts that continued to report long-term fixed-rate mortgages at historic book values even though interest rates rose dramatically in the early 1980s and, therefore, continued to record a positive book capital position. On a market value net worth basis, however, their mortgages were worth far less than the book values shown on their balance sheets.[21] Indeed, more than half of the firms in the industry were economically insolvent, many massively so.[22]

5

The Discrepancy between the Market and Book Values of Equity. The degree to which the book value of an FI's capital deviates from its true economic market value depends on a number of factors, especially:

1. **Interest Rate Volatility**—the higher the interest rate volatility, the greater the discrepancy.
2. **Examination and Enforcement**—the more frequent are on-site and off-site examinations and the stiffer the examiner/regulator standards regarding charging off problem loans, the smaller the discrepancy.
3. **Loan Trading**—the more loans that are traded, the easier it is to assess the true market value of the loan portfolio.

market-to-book ratio

A ratio that shows the discrepancy between the stock market value of an FI's equity and the book value of its equity.

In actual practice, we can get an idea of the discrepancy between book values (BV) and market values (MV) of equity for large publicly traded FIs even when the FI does not mark its balance sheet to market. Specifically, in an efficient capital market, the FI's stock price reflects the market value of the FI's outstanding equity shares. This valuation is based on the FI's current and expected future net earnings or dividend flows. The market value (MV) of equity per share is therefore:

$$MV = \frac{\text{Market value of equity ownership in shares outstanding}}{\text{Number of shares}}$$

By contrast, the historical or book value of the FI's equity per share (BV) is equal to:

$$BV = \frac{\text{Par value of equity} + \text{Surplus value} + \text{Retained earnings}}{\text{Number of shares}}$$

The ratio MV/BV is often called the **market-to-book ratio** and shows the degree of discrepancy between the market value of an FI's equity capital as perceived by investors in the stock market and the book value of capital on its balance sheet. The higher the

DO YOU UNDERSTAND?

1. Why an FI can be economically insolvent when its book value of net worth is positive?
2. What the major components of an FI's book value of equity are?
3. Whether book value accounting for loan losses is backward or forward looking?
4. What a market-to-book ratio that is less than 1 implies about an FI's performance?
5. What the arguments against the use of market valve accounting are?

21. Note that although book values were not directly affected by changes in interest rates, the increase in interest rates resulted in shrinking spreads and accounting earnings. As a result, the rise in interest rates did not leave the book value accounting results entirely unaffected.

22. See L. J. White, *The S and L Debacle* (New York: Oxford University Press, 1991), p. 89.

TABLE 22–11 Market-to-Book Value Ratios for U.S. Banks and Savings Institutions

Bank Name	Market-to-Book Ratio
Bank of America	1.8X
Bank of New York	2.3
BankNorth Group	2.3
BB&T	2.0
Comerica	1.9
Deutsche Bank	1.3
Golden West Financial	2.7
J.P. Morgan Chase	1.2
KeyCorp	1.9
MBNA Corp.	1.9
Mellon Financial	2.9
National City	1.7
PNC Financial	2.0
Providian Financial	1.8
State Street Corp.	2.5
SunTrust Banks	1.7
U.S. Bancorp	2.7
Wachovia Corp.	1.7
Wells Fargo	2.7

Source: Standard & Poor's Educational Version of Market Insight, May 2005.

market-to-book ratio, the more the book value of capital understates an FI's true equity or economic net worth position as perceived by investors in the capital market. Table 22–11 lists the market-to-book ratios for selected U.S. banks and savings institutions. The values range from a low of 1.2 time for J.P. Morgan Chase to 2.9 times for Mellon Financial.

Arguments against Market Value Accounting. The first argument against market value (MV) accounting it that it is difficult to implement. This may be especially true for small commercial banks and thrifts with large amounts of nontraded assets such as small loans in their balance sheets. When market prices or values for assets cannot be determined accurately, marking to market may be done only with error. A counterargument to this that the error resulting from the use of market valuation of nontraded assets is still likely to be less than that resulting from the use of original book or historical valuation since the market value approach does not require all assets and liabilities to be traded. As long as current and expected cash flows on an asset or liability and an appropriate discount rate can be specified, approximate market values can always be imputed. Further, with the increase of loan sales and asset securitization (see Chapter 24), indicative market prices are available on an increasing variety of loans.

A second argument against market value accounting is that it introduces an unnecessary degree of variability into an FI's earnings—and thus net worth—because paper capital gains and losses on assets are passed through the income statement. Critics argue that reporting unrealized capital gains and losses is distortionary if the FI actually plans to hold these assets to maturity. FI managers argue that in many cases, they do hold loans and other assets to maturity and, therefore, never actually realize capital gains or losses. Further, regulators have argued that they may be forced to close banks too early under the prompt corrective action requirements imposed by the FDIC Improvement Act (FDICIA) of 1991 (see Chapter 13), especially if an interest rate spike is only temporary (as much empirical evidence shows) and capital losses on securities can be quickly turned into capital gains as rates fall again. The counterargument is that FIs are increasingly trading, selling, and securitizing assets rather than holding them to maturity. Further, the failure to reflect capital gains and losses from interest rate changes means that the FI's equity position fails to reflect its true interest rate risk exposure.

A third argument against market value accounting is that FIs are less willing to accept longer-term asset exposures, such as mortgage loans and C&I loans, if these assets must be continually marked to market to reflect changing credit quality and interest rates. For example, as discussed earlier in the chapter, long-term assets are more interest rate sensitive than are short-term assets. The concern is that market value accounting may interfere with FIs' special functions (see Chapter 1) as lenders and monitors and may even result in (or accentuate) a major credit crunch. Of the three arguments against market value accounting, this one is probably the most persuasive to regulators concerned about small business finance and economic growth.

SUMMARY

This chapter provided an in-depth look at the measurement and on-balance-sheet management of interest rate and insolvency risks. The chapter first introduced two methods to measure an FI's interest rate gap and thus its risk exposure: the repricing model and the duration model. The repricing model concentrates only on the net interest income effects of rate changes and ignores balance sheet or market value effects. As such it gives a partial, but potentially misleading, picture of an FI's interest rate risk exposure. The duration model is superior to the simple repricing model because it incorporates the effects of interest rate changes on the market values of assets and liabilities. The chapter concluded with an analysis of the role of an FI's capital in insulating it against credit, interest rate, and other risks. According to economic theory, shareholder equity capital or economic net worth should be measured on a market value basis as the difference between the market value of an FI's assets and liabilities. In actuality, regulators use a mixture of book value and market value accounting rules. For example, FIs are required to mark-to-market investment securities held as trading assets, while being able to carry most loans at their book values. This mix of book value and market value accounting for various assets and liabilities creates a potential distortion in the measured net worth of the FI.

SEARCH THE SITE

Go to the FDIC's Web site at **www.fdic.gov** and find the most recent data for assets and equity capital of all insured banks for the five most recent years available using the following steps.

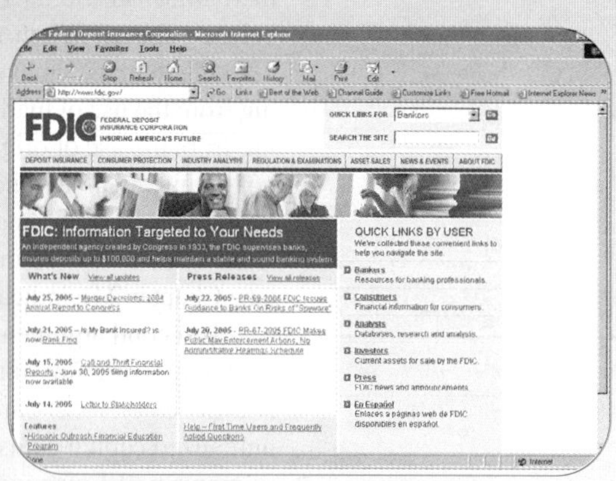

Click on "Analysts."

Under "Trends & Statistics," click on "Statistics on Banking."

Click on "Run Reports."

This will bring the files up on your computer that contain the relevant data for the most current year. Repeat the process, changing the "Report Date" to the four prior years under "Statistics on Banking."

Questions

1. By how much has the ratio of equity to assets changed over this period?
2. Calculate the percentage change in the equity-to-assets ratio for each year.
3. What do your answers to questions 1 and 2 say about the solvency of banks over the five-year period?

www.mhhe.com/sc3e

QUESTIONS

1. Why is the length of time selected for repricing assets and liabilities important when using the repricing model?
2. Calculate the repricing gap and impact on net interest income of a 1 percent increase in interest rates for the following positions:
   a. Rate-sensitive assets = \$100 million; Rate-sensitive liabilities = \$50 million.
   b. Rate-sensitive assets = \$50 million; Rate-sensitive liabilities = \$150 million.
   c. Rate-sensitive assets = \$75 million; Rate-sensitive liabilities = \$70 million.
   d. What conclusions can you draw about the repricing model from the above results?
3. Consider the repricing model.
   a. What are some of its weaknesses?
   b. How have large banks solved the problem of choosing the optimal time period for repricing?
4. Which of the following assets or liabilities fit the one-year rate or repricing sensitivity test?
   a. 91-day U.S. Treasury bills.
   b. 1-year U.S. Treasury notes.
   c. 20-year U.S. Treasury bonds.
   d. 20-year floating-rate corporate bonds with annual repricing.
   e. 30-year floating-rate mortgages with repricing every two years.
   f. 30-year floating-rate mortgages with repricing every six months.
   g. Overnight fed funds.
   h. 9-month fixed-rate CDs.
   i. 1-year fixed-rate CDs.
   j. 5-year floating-rate CDs with annual repricing.
   k. Common stock.
5. If a bank manager was quite certain that interest rates were going to rise within the next six months, how should the bank manager adjust the bank's repricing gap to take advantage of this anticipated rise? What if the manager believed rates would fall?
6. What is the difference between book value accounting and market value accounting? How do interest rate changes affect the value of bank assets and liabilities under the two methods?
7. If you use duration only to immunize your portfolio, what three factors affect changes in an FI's net worth when interest rates change?
8. Consider the following.
   a. Calculate the leverage-adjusted duration gap of an FI that has assets of \$1 million invested in 30-year, 10 percent semiannual coupon Treasury bonds selling at par and whose duration has been estimated at 9.94 years. It has liabilities of \$900,000 financed through a two-year, 7.25 percent semiannual coupon note selling at par.
   b. What is the impact on equity values if all interest rates fall 20 basis points—that is, $\Delta R/(1 + R/2) = -0.0020$?
9. If interest rates rise and an investor holds a bond for a time longer than the duration, will the return earned exceed or fall short of the original required rate of return?
10. Use the data provided for Gotbucks Bank, Inc., to answer this question.

Gotbucks Bank, Inc. (in \$ millions)

Assets		Liabilities	
Cash	\$ 30	Core deposits	\$ 20
Federal funds	20	Federal funds	50
Loans (floating)	105	Euro CDs	130
Loans (fixed)	65	Equity	20
Total assets	\$220	Total liabilities and equity	\$220

Notes to the balance sheet: Currently, the fed funds rate is 8.5 percent. Variable-rate loans are priced at 4 percent over LIBOR (currently at 11 percent). Fixed-rate loans are selling at par and have five-year maturities with 12 percent interest paid annually. Core deposits are all fixed rate for two years at 8 percent paid annually. Euros currently yield 9 percent.

   a. What is the duration of Gotbucks Bank's (GBI) fixed-rate loan portfolio if the loans are priced at par?
   b. If the average duration of GBI's floating-rate loans (including fed fund assets) is .36 year, what is the duration of the bank's assets? (Note that the duration of cash is zero.)
   c. What is the duration of GBI's core deposits if they are priced at par?
   d. If the duration of GBI's Euro CD and fed fund liabilities is .401 year, what is the duration of the bank's liabilities?
   e. What is GBI's duration gap? What is its interest rate risk exposure? If *all* yields increase by 1 percent, what is the impact on the market value of GBI's equity? (That is, $\Delta R/(1 + R) = .01$ for all assets and liabilities.)
11. An insurance company issued a \$90 million one-year, zero-coupon note at 8 percent add-on annual interest (paying one coupon at the end of the year) and used the proceeds to fund a \$100 million face value, two-year commercial loan at 10 percent annual interest. Immediately after these transactions were (simultaneously) undertaken, all interest rates went up 1.5 percent.
   a. What is the market value of the insurance company's loan investment after the changes in interest rates?
   b. What is the duration of the loan investment when it was first issued?
   c. Using duration, what is the expected change in the value of the loan if interest rates are predicted to increase to 11.5 percent from the initial 10 percent?
   d. What is the market value of the insurance company's \$90 million liability when interest rates rise by 1.5 percent?
   e. What is the duration of the insurance company's liability when it is first issued?
12. Use the following balance sheet information to answer this question.

Balance Sheet ($ thousands) and Duration (in years)

	Duration	Amount
T-bills	0.5	$ 90
T-notes	0.9	55
T-bonds	4.393	176
Loans	7	2,724
Deposits	1	2,092
Federal funds	0.01	238
Equity		715

Notes: Treasury Bonds are five-year maturities paying 6 percent semiannually and selling at par.

a. What is the average duration of all the assets?
b. What is the average duration of all the liabilities?
c. What is the FI's leverage-adjusted duration gap? What is the FI's interest rate risk exposure?
d. If the entire yield curve shifted upward 0.5 percent (i.e., $\Delta R/(1 + R) = .0050$), what is the impact on the FI's market value of equity?
e. If the entire yield curve shifted downward 0.25 percent (i.e., $\Delta R/(1 + R) = -.0025$), what is the impact on the FI's market value of equity?

13. If a bank manager was quite certain that interest rates were going to rise within the next six months, how should the bank manager adjust the bank's duration gap to take advantage of this anticipated rise? What if the manager believed rates would fall?

14. What are the criticisms of using the duration model to immunize an FI's portfolio?

15. Consider the following.
a. What is the duration of a two-year bond that pays an annual coupon of 10 percent and whose current yield to maturity is 14 percent? Use $1,000 as the face value.
b. What is the expected change in the price of a bond if interest rates are expected to decline by 0.5 percent?

16. What are some of the arguments for and against the use of market value versus book value of capital?

17. Why is the market value of equity a better measure of a bank's ability to absorb losses than book value of equity?

18. STANDARD &POOR'S Go to the S&P Educational Version of Market Insight Web site at **www.mhhe.com/edumarketinsight** and find the most recent market-to-book values for Mellon Financial Corp. (MEL), Wachovia Corp. (WB), and Suntrust Banks Inc. (STI) using the following steps. Click on "Educational Version of Market Insight." Enter your site ID and click on "Login." Click on "Company." Enter "MEL" in the "Ticker:" box and click on "Go!" Click on "Financial Hlts." This will download information for Mellon Financial. The market-to-book ratio is listed as "Price/Book" under "Valuation." Repeat these steps for Wachovia Corp. and Suntrust Banks. How do these ratios differ from those for 2004 reported in Table 22–11? How do these values differ from the industry average and what do these differences say about the performance and market valuation of the banks?

19. Consider the following income statement for WatchoverU Savings Inc. (in millions):

Assets		Liabilities	
Floating-rate mortgages (currently 10% p.a.)	$60	Demand deposits (currently 6% p.a.)	$105
30-year fixed-rate loans (currently 7% p.a.)	90	Time deposits (currently 6% p.a.)	$ 25
		Equity	20
Total	$150		$150

a. What is WatchoverU's expected net interest income at year end?
b. What will be the net interest income at year end if interest rates rise by 2 percent?
c. Using the one-year cumulative repricing gap model, what is the expected net interest income for a 2 percent increase in interest rates?

20. Use the following information about a hypothetical government security dealer named J.P. Groman. (Market yields are in parentheses; amounts are in millions.)

Assets		Liabilities	
Cash	$ 10	Overnight repos	$170
1-month T-bills (7.05%)	75	Subordinated debt	
3-month T-bills (7.25%)	75	7-year fixed (8.55%)	150
2-year T-notes (7.50%)	50		
8-year T-notes (8.96%)	100		
5-year munis (floating rate) (8.20% reset every six months)	25	Equity	15
Total	$335		$335

a. What is the repricing or funding gap if the planning period is 30 days? 91 days? 2 years? (Recall that cash is a noninterest-earning asset.)
b. What is the impact over the next 30 days on net interest income if all interest rates rise by 50 basis points?
c. The following one-year runoffs are expected: $10 million for two-year T-notes, $20 million for the eight-year T-notes. What is the one-year repricing gap?
d. If runoffs are considered, what is the effect on net interest income at year end if interest rates rise by 50 basis points?

23

Managing Risk *with* Derivative Securities

Chapter NAVIGATOR

1. How can risk be hedged with forward contracts?
2. How can risk be hedged with futures contracts?
3. What is the difference between a microhedge and a macrohedge?
4. How can risk be hedged with option contracts?
5. How can risk be hedged with swap contracts?
6. How do the different hedging methods compare?

OUTLINE

DERIVATIVE SECURITIES USED TO MANAGE RISK: CHAPTER OVERVIEW

Chapters 20 through 22 described ways financial institutions (FIs) measure and manage various risks on the balance sheet. Rather than managing risk by making on-balance-sheet changes, FIs are increasingly turning to off-balance-sheet instruments such as forwards, futures, options, and swaps to hedge these risks. As the use of these derivatives has increased, so have the fees and revenues FIs have generated. For example, revenue from derivatives transactions at commercial banks averaged $11.27 billion per year from 1999 to 2004. We discussed the basic characteristics of derivative securities and derivative securities markets in Chapter 10. This chapter considers the role that derivative securities contracts play in managing an FI's interest rate risk, foreign exchange, and credit risk exposures. Although large banks and other FIs are responsible for a significant amount of derivatives trading activity, FIs of all sizes have used these instruments to hedge their asset-liability risk exposures.

FORWARD AND FUTURES CONTRACTS

To present the essential nature and characteristics of forward and futures contracts, we first review the comparison of these derivative contracts with spot contracts (see also Chapter 10).

spot contract

An agreement to transact involving the immediate exchange of assets and funds.

Spot Contract. A **spot contract** is an agreement between a buyer and a seller at time 0, when the seller of the asset agrees to deliver it immediately for cash and the buyer agrees to pay in cash for that asset.[1] Thus, the unique feature of a spot contract is the immediate and simultaneous exchange of cash for securities, or what is often called *delivery versus payment.* A spot bond quote of $97 for a 20-year maturity bond means that the buyer must pay the seller $97 per $100 of face value for immediate delivery of the 20-year bond.[2]

forward contract

An agreement to transact involving the future exchange of a set amount of assets at a set price.

Forward Contract. A **forward contract** is a contractual agreement between a buyer and a seller, at time 0, to exchange a prespecified asset for cash at some later date. For example, in a three-month forward contract to deliver 20-year bonds, the buyer and seller agree on a price and amount today (time 0), but the delivery (or exchange) of the 20-year bond for cash does not occur until three months hence. If the forward price agreed to at time 0 was $97 per $100 of face value, in three months' time the seller delivers $100 of 20-year bonds and receives $97 from the buyer. This is the price the buyer must pay and the seller must accept no matter what happens to the spot price of 20-year bonds during the three months between the time the contract was entered into and the time the bonds are delivered for payment. As of December 2004, commercial banks held $7.97 trillion in forward contracts off their balance sheets.

Forward contracts often involve underlying assets that are nonstandardized (e.g., six-month pure discount bonds). As a result, the buyer and seller involved in a forward contract must locate and deal directly with each other to set the terms of the contract rather than transacting the sale in a centralized market. Accordingly, once a party has agreed to a forward position, canceling the deal prior to expiration is generally difficult (although an offsetting forward contract can normally be arranged).

futures contract

An agreement to transact involving the future exchange of a set amount of assets for a price that is settled daily.

marked to market

Describes the prices on outstanding futures contracts that are adjusted each day to reflect current futures market conditions.

Futures Contract. A **futures contract** is usually arranged by an organized exchange. It is an agreement between a buyer and a seller at time 0 to exchange a standardized, prespecified asset for cash at some later date. As such, a futures contract is very similar to a forward contract. The difference relates to the price, which in a forward contract is fixed over the life of the contract ($97 per $100 of face value with payment in three months), but a futures contract is **marked to market** daily. This means that the contract's price and the future contract holder's account are adjusted each day as the futures price for the contract changes. Therefore, actual daily cash settlements occur between the buyer and seller in response to this marking-to-market process, i.e., gains and losses must be realized daily. This can be compared to a forward contract for which cash payment from buyer to seller occurs only at the end of the contract period.[3] In December 2004, commercial banks held $3.41 trillion in futures contracts off their balance sheets.

Hedging with Forward Contracts

naive hedge

A hedge of a cash asset on a direct dollar-for-dollar basis with a forward or futures contract.

1

To understand the usefulness of forward contracts in hedging an FI's interest rate risk, consider a simple example of a **naive hedge** (a hedge of a cash asset on a direct dollar-for-dollar basis with a forward or futures contract). Suppose that an FI portfolio manager holds a 20-year, $1 million face value government bond on the balance sheet. At time 0, the market values these bonds at $97 per $100 of face value, or $970,000 in total. Assume that the manager receives a forecast that interest rates are expected to rise by 2 percent from their current level of 8 percent to 10 percent over the

1. Technically, physical settlement and delivery may take place one or two days after the contractual spot agreement in bond markets. In equity markets, delivery and cash settlement normally occur three business days after the spot contract agreement, so-called T+3.

2. Throughout this chapter, as we refer to the prices of various securities, we do not include the transaction fees charged by brokers and dealers for conducting trades for investors and hedgers.

3. Another difference between forwards and futures is that forward contracts are bilateral contracts subject to counterparty default risk, but the default risk on futures is significantly reduced by the futures exchange guaranteeing to indemnify counterparties against credit or default risk.

next three months. Knowing that if the predicted change in interest rates is correct, rising interest rates mean that bond prices will fall, the manager stands to make a capital loss on the bond portfolio. Having read Chapters 3 and 22, the manager is an expert on duration and has calculated the 20-year maturity bond's duration to be exactly nine years. Thus, the manager can predict a capital loss, or change in bond values (ΔP), from the duration equation of Chapter 3:[4]

$$\frac{\Delta P}{P} = -D \times \frac{\Delta R}{1 + R}$$

where

$$\begin{aligned} \Delta P &= \text{Capital loss on bond} = ? \\ P &= \text{Initial value of bond position} = \$970{,}000 \\ D &= \text{Duration of the bond} = 9 \text{ years} \\ \Delta R &= \text{Change in forecast yield} = .02 \\ 1 + R &= 1 \text{ plus the current yield on 20-year bond} = 1.08 \end{aligned}$$

$$\frac{\Delta P}{\$970{,}000} = -9 \times \left(\frac{.02}{1.08}\right)$$

$$\Delta P = -9 \times \$970{,}000 \times \left(\frac{.02}{1.08}\right) = -\$161{,}667$$

As a result, the FI portfolio manager expects to incur a capital loss on the bond of \$161,667—as a percentage loss ($\Delta P/P$) = 16.67%—or a drop in price from \$97 per \$100 face value to \$80.833 per \$100 face value. To offset this loss—in fact, to reduce the risk of capital loss to zero—the manager may hedge this position by taking an off-balance-sheet hedge, such as selling \$1 million face value of 20-year bonds for forward delivery in three months' time.[5] Suppose that at time 0, the portfolio manager can find a buyer willing to pay \$97 for every \$100 of 20-year bonds delivered in three months' time.

Now consider what happens to the FI portfolio manager if the gloomy forecast of a 2 percent rise in interest rates is accurate. The portfolio manager's bond position has fallen in value by 16.67 percent, equal to a capital loss of \$161,667. After the rise in interest rates, however, the manager can buy \$1 million face value of 20-year bonds in the spot market at \$80.833 per \$100 of face value, a total cost of \$808,333, and deliver these bonds to the forward contract buyer. Remember that the forward contract buyer agreed to pay \$97 per \$100 of face value for the \$1 million of face value bonds delivered, or \$970,000. As a result, the portfolio manager makes a profit on the forward transaction of:

\$970,000	−	\$808,333	=	\$161,667
(price paid by forward buyer to forward seller)		(cost of purchasing bonds in the spot market at t = month 3 for delivery to the forward buyer)		

As you can see, the on-balance-sheet loss of \$161,667 is exactly offset by the off-balance-sheet gain of \$161,667 from selling the forward contract. In fact, for any change in interest rates, a loss (gain) on the balance sheet is offset by a partial or complete gain (loss) on the forward contract. Indeed, the success of a hedge does not hinge on the manager's ability to accurately forecast interest rates. Rather, the reason for the hedge is the lack of ability to perfectly predict interest rate changes. The hedge allows the FI manager to protect

4. For simplicity, we ignore issues relating to convexity here (see Chapter 22).

5. Since a forward contract involves the delivery of bonds at a future time period, it does not appear on the balance sheet, which records only current and past transactions. Thus, forwards are one example of off-balance-sheet items (see Chapter 12).

against interest rate changes even if they are not perfectly predicted. Thus, the FI's net interest rate exposure is zero, or, in the parlance of finance, it has **immunized** its assets against interest rate risk.

immunize

To fully hedge or protect an FI against adverse movements in interest rates (or asset prices).

Hedging with Futures Contracts

Even though some hedging of interest rate risk does take place using forward contracts—such as forward rate agreements commonly used by insurance companies and banks prior to mortgage loan originations—most FIs hedge interest rate risk either at the micro level (called *microhedging*) or at the macro level (called *macrohedging*) using futures contracts. Before looking at futures contracts, we explain the difference between microhedging and macrohedging.

microhedging

Using a futures (forward) contract to hedge a specific asset or liability.

Microhedging. An FI is **microhedging** when it employs a futures or a forward contract to hedge a particular asset or liability risk. For example, we earlier considered a simple example of microhedging asset-side portfolio risk in which an FI manager wanted to insulate the value of the institution's bond portfolio fully against a rise in interest rates. An example of microhedging on the liability side of the balance sheet occurs when an FI, attempting to lock in a cost of funds to protect itself against a possible rise in short-term interest rates, takes a short (sell) position in futures contracts on CDs or T-bills. In microhedging, the FI manager often tries to pick a futures or forward contract whose underlying deliverable asset closely matches the asset (or liability) position being hedged. The earlier example of exactly matching the asset in the portfolio with the deliverable security underlying the forward contract (20-year bonds) was unrealistic. Because such exact matching often cannot be achieved, the usual situation produces a residual "unhedgeable" risk termed **basis risk.** This risk occurs mainly because the prices of the assets or liabilities that an FI wishes to hedge are imperfectly correlated over time with the prices on the futures or forward contract used to hedge risk.

basis risk

A residual risk that occurs because the movement in a spot (cash) asset's price is not perfectly correlated with the movement in the price of the asset delivered under a futures or forward contract.

macrohedging

Hedging the entire duration gap of an FI.

Macrohedging. **Macrohedging** occurs when an FI manager wishes to use futures or other derivative securities to hedge the entire balance sheet duration gap. This contrasts with microhedging in which an FI manager identifies specific assets and liabilities and seeks individual futures and other derivative contracts to hedge those individual risks. Note that macrohedging and microhedging can lead to quite different hedging strategies and results. In particular, a macrohedge takes a whole portfolio view and allows for individual asset and liability interest sensitivities or durations to net out each other. This can result in a very different aggregate futures position than when an FI manager disregards this netting or portfolio effect and hedges only individual asset and liability positions on a one-to-one basis.[6]

The Choice between Microhedging and Macrohedging. Several factors affect an FI's choice between microhedging and macrohedging interest rate risk. These include risk-return considerations, accounting rules, and for depository institutions, federal regulation.

Risk-Return Considerations. Ideally, an FI would like to reduce its interest rate or other risk exposures to their lowest possible level by buying or selling sufficient futures to offset the interest rate risk exposure of its whole balance sheet or cash positions in each asset and liability. For example, this reduction might be achieved by macrohedging the duration gap. However, since reducing risk also reduces expected return, not all FI managers seek to do this.

Rather than taking a fully hedged position, many FIs choose to bear some interest rate risk as well as credit and FX risks because of their comparative advantage as FIs (see Chapter 1).

6. P. H. Munter, D. K. Clancy, and C. T. Moores found that macrohedges provided better hedge performance than microhedges in a number of different interest rate environments. See "Accounting for Financial Futures: A Question of Risk Reduction," in *Advances in Accounting* (1986), pp. 51–70. See also R. Stoebe, "Macrohedging Bank Investment Portfolios," *Bankers Magazine*, November–December 1994, pp. 45–48.

For example, an FI manager may generate expectations regarding future interest rates before deciding on a futures position. As a result, the manager may selectively hedge only a portion of its balance sheet position, or microhedge. Alternatively, the FI manager may decide to remain unhedged or even to overhedge by selling more futures than the cash or on-balance-sheet position requires, although regulators may view this as speculative. Thus, the fully hedged position becomes one of several choices depending, in part, on managerial interest rate expectations, managerial objectives, and the nature of the return-risk tradeoff from hedging.

www.fasb.org

Accounting Rules and Hedging Strategies. The Financial Accounting Standards Board (FASB)—the main regulator of accounting standards—has made a number of rulings regarding the accounting and tax treatment of futures transactions.[7] In hedge accounting, a futures position is a hedge transaction if it can be linked to a particular asset or liability. An example is using a T-bond futures contract to hedge an FI's holdings of long-term bonds as investments. In 1997, the FASB required that all gains and losses on derivatives used to hedge assets and liabilities on the balance sheet be recognized *immediately* as earnings, together with the offsetting gain or loss on the hedged item. Thus, the 1997 ruling effectively requires derivatives to be marked to market. Additionally, U.S. companies that hold or issue derivatives must report their trading objectives and strategies in public document disclosures such as annual reports.[8] Because of the volatility in earnings that futures introduce as they are marked to market, an FI manager may choose to selectively hedge only a portion of the FI's balance sheet positions (microhedge) rather than take large positions on futures contracts needed to hedge the entire balance sheet (macrohedge).

www.federalreserve.gov

www.fdic.gov

www.occ.treas.gov

Policies of Bank Regulators. The main bank regulators—the Federal Reserve, the FDIC, and the Comptroller of the Currency—have issued uniform guidelines for banks taking positions in futures and forwards. These guidelines require a bank to (1) establish internal guidelines regarding its hedging activity, (2) establish trading limits, and (3) disclose large contract positions that materially affect a bank's risk to shareholders and outside investors. Overall, regulatory policy is to encourage the use of futures for hedging and to discourage their use for speculation, although on a practical basis, it is often difficult to distinguish between the two.

Finally, as Chapter 13 discusses, futures contracts are not subject to the risk-based capital requirements imposed by regulators on depository institutions; by contrast, over-the-counter forward contracts are potentially subject to capital requirements because of the presence of counterparty risk (see below). Other things being equal, the risk-based capital requirements favor the use of futures over forwards. To the dismay of some legislators in Congress and regulators, the use of derivative securities in some nondepository FIs—especially hedge funds—remains virtually unregulated.[9]

Microhedging with Futures. The number of futures contracts that an FI should buy or sell in a microhedge depends on the interest rate risk exposure created by a particular asset or liability on the balance sheet. The key is to take a position in the futures market to offset a loss on the balance sheet due to a move in interest rates with a gain in the futures market. Table 23–1 shows part of an interest rate futures quote from *The Wall Street Journal* for January 10, 2005 (see also Table 10–5). In this list, a June 2005 Eurodollar futures contract can be bought (long) or sold (short) on January 10, 2005, for 96.72 percent of the face value of the Eurodollar CD contract, or the yield on the Eurodollar CD contract deliverable in

7. *FASB Statement No. 80,* "Accounting for Futures Contracts" (1984) is probably the most important.

8. See "Called to Account," *Risk Magazine*, August 1996, pp. 15–17.

9. See "Long-Term Capital Management: Regulators Need to Focus Greater Attention on Systematic Risk," GAO/GGD-00-3 (October 1999).

TABLE 23–1 Futures Contracts on Interest Rates, January 10, 2005

Interest Rate Futures

	OPEN	HIGH	LOW	SETTLE	CHG	LIFETIME HIGH	LIFETIME LOW	OPEN INT
Treasury Bonds (CBT)-$100,000; pts 32nds of 100%								
Mar	112-09	112-15	112-00	112-11	8	114-02	100-25	612,141
June	111-16	111-20	111-10	111-16	8	113-07	100-00	18,941
Sept	109-31	109-31	109-31	110-26	8	111-02	109-31	195
Est vol 147,946; vol Fri 379,969; open int 631,291, +18,215.								

	OPEN	HIGH	LOW	SETTLE	CHG	YIELD	CHG	OPEN INT
Eurodollar (CME)-$1,000,000; pts of 100%								
Jan	97.34	97.34	97.33	97.33	...	2.67	...	74,450
Feb	97.18	97.18	97.18	97.18	...	2.82	...	8,016
Mar	97.06	97.06	97.03	97.04	-.01	2.96	.01	1,072,293
June	96.74	96.74	96.71	96.72	-.01	3.28	.01	1,167,365
Sept	96.48	96.49	96.44	96.47	-.01	3.53	.01	1,080,285
Dec	96.29	96.30	96.24	96.27	-.02	3.73	.02	807,488
Mr06	96.17	96.18	96.12	96.15	-.01	3.85	.01	603,927
June	96.08	96.08	96.03	96.06	-.01	3.94	.01	427,781
Sept	95.99	96.01	95.95	95.98	-.01	4.02	.01	312,914
Dec	95.90	95.93	95.86	95.89	-.01	4.11	.01	271,139
Mr07	95.83	95.85	95.79	95.82	-.01	4.18	.01	180,265
June	95.76	95.76	95.72	95.74	-.01	4.26	.01	160,047
Sept	95.68	95.69	95.65	95.67	-.01	4.33	.01	125,473
Dec	95.60	95.60	95.56	95.59	...	4.41	...	120,327
Mr08	95.53	95.54	95.50	95.52	...	4.48	...	96,701
June	95.45	95.46	95.43	95.44	...	4.56	...	103,718
Sept	95.37	95.38	95.35	95.36	...	4.64	...	95,510
Dec	95.28	95.28	95.26	95.27	...	4.73	...	85,283
Mr09	95.21	95.22	95.19	95.20	...	4.80	...	66,313
June	95.12	95.13	95.10	95.12	.01	4.88	-.01	59,362
Sept	95.04	95.05	95.02	95.04	.01	4.96	-.01	50,398
Dec	94.94	94.96	94.93	94.95	.01	5.05	-.01	29,002
Mr10	94.88	94.90	94.88	94.89	.01	5.11	-.01	13,739
June	94.81	94.83	94.81	94.83	.02	5.17	-.02	9,478
Sept	94.74	94.76	94.74	94.76	.03	5.24	-.03	7,788
Dec	94.65	94.67	94.65	94.67	.03	5.33	-.03	7,959
Mr11	94.60	94.62	94.60	94.62	.02	5.38	-.02	5,967
June	94.55	94.57	94.55	94.57	.02	5.43	-.02	5,432
Sept	94.50	94.52	94.50	94.52	.02	5.48	-.02	4,408
Dec	94.42	94.44	94.42	94.44	.03	5.56	-.03	2,010
Est vol 394,719; vol Fri 2,178,312; open int 7,062,495, +164,238.								

Source: *The Wall Street Journal*, January 11, 2005, p. C11. Reprinted by permission of *The Wall Street Journal*. **www.wsj.com**

June 2005 will be 3.28 percent (100% − 96.72%). The minimum contract size on one of these futures is $1,000,000, so a position in one contract can be taken at a price of $967,200.

The subsequent profit or loss from a position in June 2005 Eurodollar futures taken on January 10, 2005, is graphically described in Figure 23–1. A short position in the futures will produce a profit when interest rates rise (meaning that the value of the underlying Eurodollar contract decreases). Therefore, a short position in the futures market is the appropriate hedge when the FI stands to lose on the balance sheet if interest rates are expected to rise (e.g., the FI holds Eurodollar CDs in its asset portfolio).[10] In fact, if the FI is perfectly hedged, any loss in value from a change in the yield on an asset on the balance sheet over the period of the hedge is exactly offset by a gain on the short position in the Eurodollar futures contract (see Figure 23–2). A long position in the futures market produces a profit when interest rates fall (meaning that the value of the underlying Eurodollar CD contract increases).[11] Therefore, a long position is the appropriate hedge when the FI stands to lose on the balance sheet if interest rates are expected to fall.[12] Table 23–2 summarizes the long and short position. Appendix 23A to this chapter located at the book's Web site (**www.mhhe.com/sc3e**) presents mathematical details and numerical examples of hedging with futures contracts.

DO YOU UNDERSTAND?

1. The difference between a futures contract and a forward contract?
2. What the major differences between a spot contract and a forward contract are?
3. How a naive hedge works?
4. What is meant by the phrase "an FI has immunized its portfolio against a particular risk"?
5. When a futures position is a hedge transaction according to FASB rules?

10. We assume that the balance sheet has no liability of equal size and maturity (or duration) as the CD. If the FI has such a liability, any loss in value from the CD could be offset with an equivalent decrease in value from the liability. In this case, there is no interest rate risk exposure and thus there is no need to hedge.

11. Notice that if rates move in an opposite direction from that expected, losses are incurred on the futures position—that is, if rates rise and futures prices drop, the long hedger loses. Similarly, if rates fall and futures prices rise, the short hedger loses.

12. This might be the case when the FI is financing itself with long-term, fixed-rate certificates of deposit.

FIGURE 23–1 Profit or Loss on a Futures Position in Eurodollar Futures, Taken on January 10, 2005

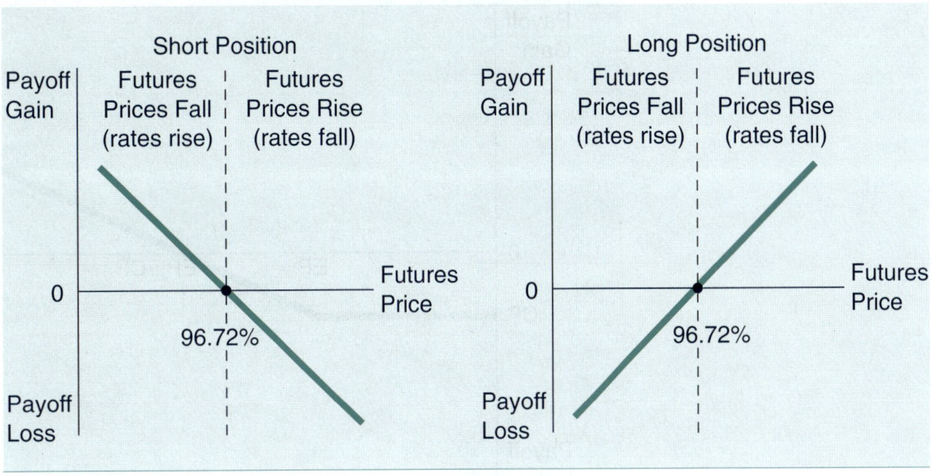

FIGURE 23–2 FI Value Change On and Off the Balance Sheet from a Perfect Short Hedge

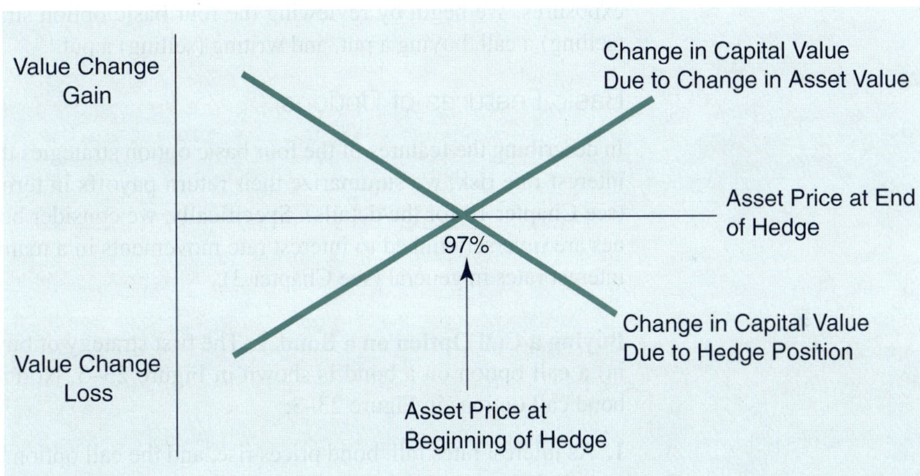

TABLE 23–2 Summary of Gains and Losses on Microhedges Using Futures Contracts

Type of Hedge	Change in Interest Rates	Cash Market	Futures Market
Long hedge (buy)	Decrease	Loss	Gain
Short hedge (sell)	Increase	Loss	Gain

OPTIONS

This section discusses the role of options in hedging interest rate risk. FIs have a wide variety of option products to use in hedging, including exchange-traded options, over-the-counter (OTC) options, options embedded in securities, and caps, collars, and floors (see Chapter 10). Not only have the types of option products increased in recent years but the use of options has increased as well. In December 2004, commercial banks held $3.13 trillion in

FIGURE 23–3 **Payoff Function for the Buyer of a Call Option on a Bond**

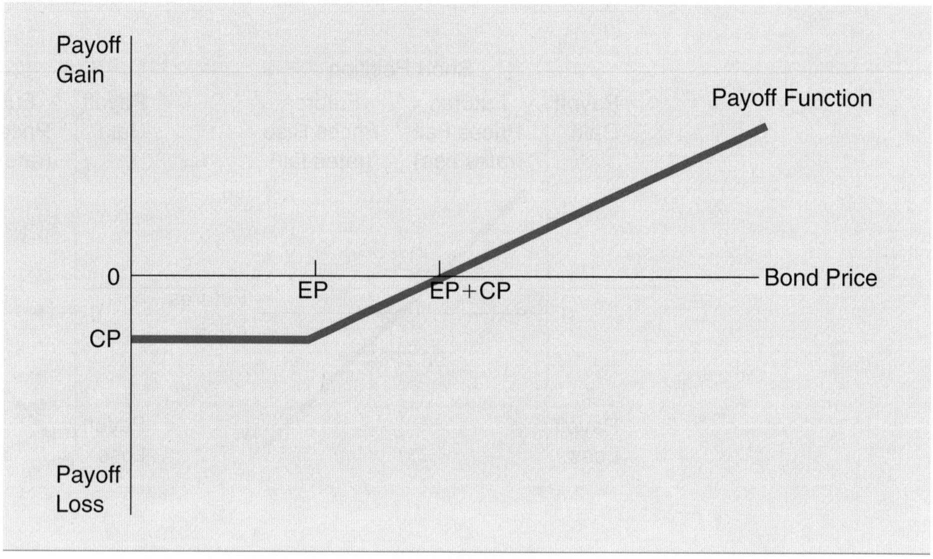

exchange trade options and $14.62 trillion in OTC options as part of their off-balance-sheet exposures. We begin by reviewing the four basic option strategies: buying a call, writing (selling) a call, buying a put, and writing (selling) a put.[13]

Basic Features of Options

In describing the features of the four basic option strategies that FIs might employ to hedge interest rate risk, we summarize their return payoffs in terms of interest rate movements (see Chapter 10 for the details). Specifically, we consider bond options whose payoff values are inversely linked to interest rate movements in a manner similar to bond prices and interest rates in general (see Chapter 3).

Buying a Call Option on a Bond. The first strategy of buying (or taking a long position in) a call option on a bond is shown in Figure 23–3. Notice two important things about bond call options in Figure 23–3:

1. As interest rates fall, bond prices rise, and the call option buyer has a large profit potential; the more rates fall (the higher bond prices rise), the larger the profit on the exercise of the option.
2. As interest rates rise, bond prices fall and the potential for a negative payoff (loss) for the buyer of the call option increases. If rates rise so that bond prices fall below the exercise price, EP, the call buyer is not obligated to exercise the option. Thus, the buyer's losses are truncated by the amount of the up-front premium payment (call premium, CP) made to purchase the call option.

Thus, buying a call option is a strategy to take when interest rates are expected to fall. Notice that unlike interest rate futures, whose prices and payoffs move symmetrically with changes in the level of interest rates, the payoffs on bond call options move asymmetrically with changes in interest rates.[14] As we discuss below, this often results in options being the preferred hedging instruments over futures contracts.

13. The two basic option contracts are *puts* and *calls*. However, an FI could potentially be a buyer or seller (writer) of each.

14. This does not necessarily mean that options are less risky than spot or futures positions. Options can, in fact, be riskier than other investments since they exist for only a limited period of time and are leveraged investments (i.e., their value is only a fraction of the underlying security). To compare an option position to a spot position one must consider an equal dollar investment in the two positions over a common period of time.

FIGURE 23–4 Payoff Function for the Writer of a Call Option on a Bond

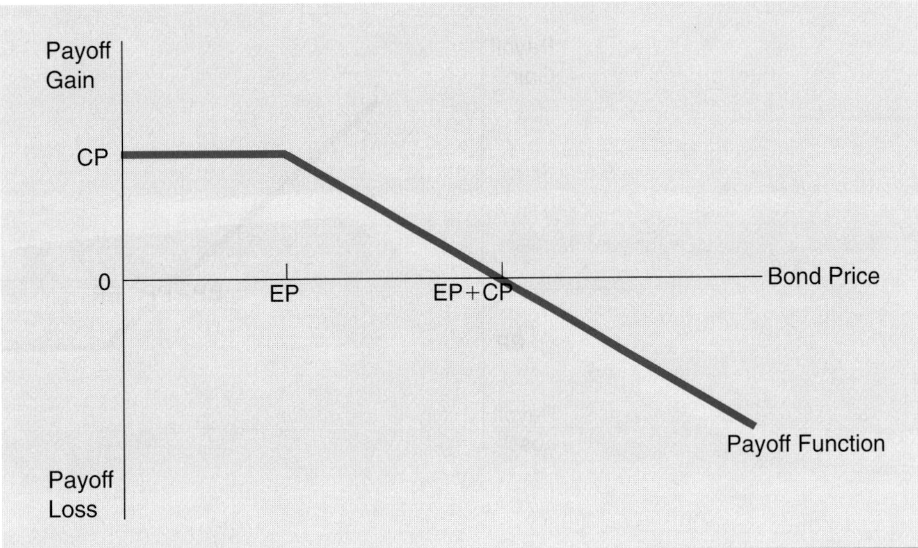

Writing a Call Option on a Bond. The second strategy is writing (or taking a short position in) a call option on a bond shown in Figure 23–4. Notice two important things about this payoff function:

1. When interest rates rise and bond prices fall, the potential for the writer of the call to receive a positive payoff or profit increases. The call buyer is less likely to exercise the option, which would force the option writer to sell the underlying bond at the exercise price, EP. However, this profit has a maximum equal to the call premium (CP) charged up front to the buyer of the option.
2. When interest rates fall and bond prices rise, the probability that the writer will take a loss increases. The call buyer will exercise the option, forcing the option writer to sell the underlying bonds. Since bond prices are theoretically unbounded in the upward direction, although they must return to par at maturity, these losses could be very large.

Thus, writing a call option is a strategy to take when interest rates are expected to rise. Caution is warranted, however, because profits are limited but losses are unlimited. As discussed below, this results in the writing of a call option being unacceptable as a strategy to use when hedging interest rate risk.

Buying a Put Option on a Bond. The third strategy is buying (or taking a long position in) a put option on a bond, shown in Figure 23–5. Note the following:

1. When interest rates rise and bond prices fall, the probability that the buyer of the put will make a profit from exercising the option increases. Thus, if bond prices fall, the buyer of the put option can purchase bonds in the bond market at that price and put them (sell them) back to the writer of the put at the higher exercise price. As a result, the put option buyer has unlimited profit potential; the higher the rates rise, the more the bond prices fall, and the larger the profit on the exercise of the option.
2. When interest rates fall and bond prices rise, the probability that the buyer of a put will lose increases. If rates fall so that bond prices rise above the exercise price, EP, the put buyer does not have to exercise the option. Thus, the maximum loss is limited to the size of the up-front put premium (PP).

Thus, buying a put option is a strategy to take when interest rates are expected to rise.

FIGURE 23–5 **Payoff Function for the Buyer of a Put Option on a Bond**

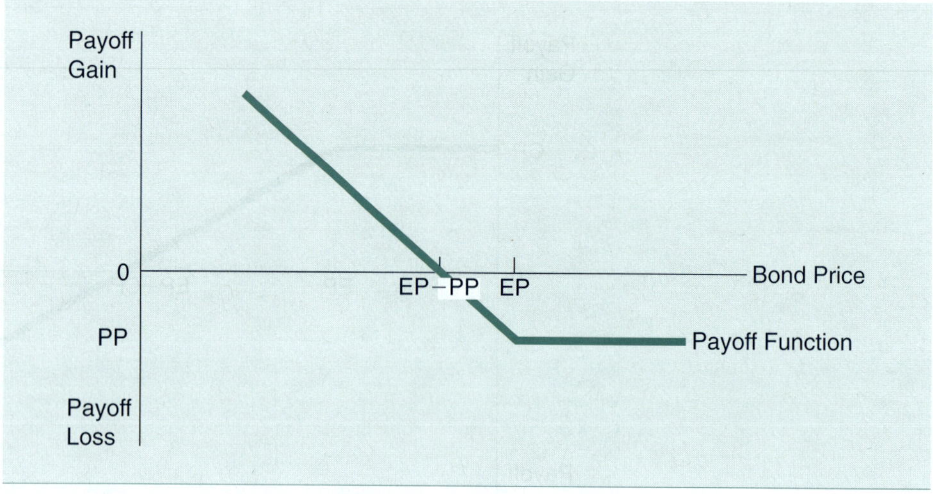

Writing a Put Option on a Bond. The fourth strategy is writing (or taking a short position in) a put option on a bond, shown in Figure 23–6. Note the following:

1. When interest rates fall and bond prices rise, the writer has an enhanced probability of making a profit. The put buyer is less likely to exercise the option, which would force the option writer to buy the underlying bond. However, the writer's maximum profit is constrained to equal the put premium (PP).
2. When interest rates rise and bond prices fall, the writer of the put is exposed to potentially large losses. The put buyer will exercise the option, forcing the option writer to buy the underlying bond at the exercise price, EP. Since bond prices are theoretically unbounded in the downward direction, these losses can be unlimited.

Thus, writing a put option is a strategy to take when interest rates are expected to fall. However, profits are limited and losses are potentially unlimited (i.e., the investor could potentially lose his or her entire investment in the option). As with the writing of a call option (and discussed below), this results in the writing of a put option being unacceptable as a strategy to use when hedging interest rate risk.

FIGURE 23–6 **Payoff Function for the Writer of a Put Option on a Bond**

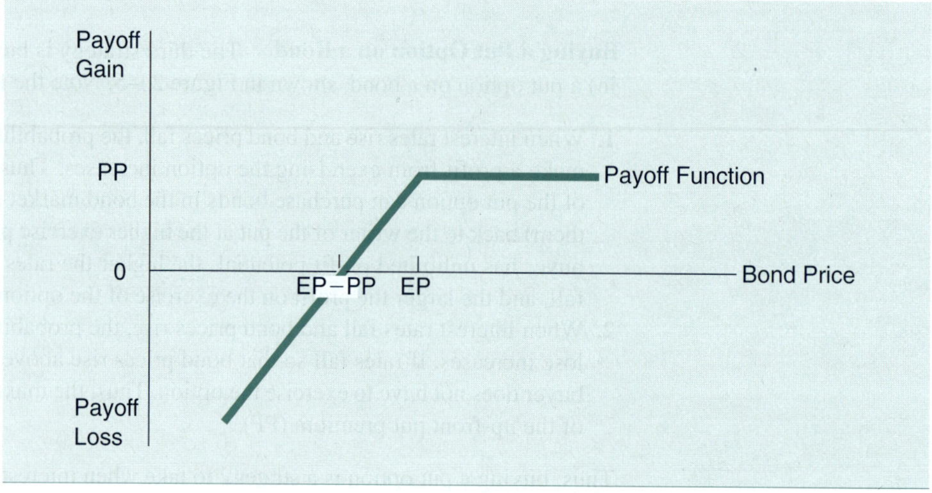

Actual Interest Rate Options

www.cbt.com
www.cme.com
www.liffe.com

FIs have a wide variety of OTC and exchange-traded options available. Table 23–3, from Table 10–8 and *The Wall Street Journal*'s business section, reports exchange-traded interest rate futures options traded on the Chicago Board of Trade (CBT) and the Chicago Mercantile Exchange (CME) on January 10, 2005. We discussed these contracts and the operations of the markets in detail in Chapter 10.

Hedging with Options

Figures 23–7 and 23–8 describe graphically the way that buying a put option on a bond can potentially hedge the interest rate risk exposure of an FI that holds bonds as part of its asset investment portfolio. Figure 23–7 shows the gross payoff of a bond and the payoff from buying a put option on it. In this case, any losses on the bond (as rates rise and bond values decrease) are offset with profits from the put option that was bought (points to the left of point X in Figure 23–7). If rates fall, the bond value increases, yet the accompanying losses on the purchased put option positions are limited to the option premiums paid (points to the right of point X). Figure 23–8 shows the net overall payoff from the bond investment combined with the put option hedge. Note in Figure 23–8 that buying a put option truncates the downside losses on the bond following interest rate rises to some maximum amount and scales down the upside profits by the cost of bond price risk insurance—the put premium—leaving some positive upside profit potential. Notice too that the combination of being long in the bond and buying a put option on a bond mimics the payoff

TABLE 23–3 Futures Options on Interest Rates, January 10, 2005

STRIKE | CALLS-SETTLE | PUTS-SETTLE

Interest Rate

T-Bonds (CBT)
$100,000; points and 64ths of 100%

Price	Feb	Mar	Apr	Feb	Mar	Apr
110	2-27	2-52	...	0-05	0-30	1-09
111	1-36	2-05	2-02	0-14	0-47	1-34
112	0-54	1-29	1-33	0-32	1-07	2-01
113	0-22	0-61	1-06	1-00	1-39	...
114	0-07	0-37	0-49	1-49	2-15	...
115	0-02	0-22	0-33	2-44	2-63	...

Est vol 40,597;
Fr vol 27,753 calls 37,460 puts
Op int Fri 242,355 calls 343,663 puts

T-Notes (CBT)
$100,000; points and 64ths of 100%

Price	Feb	Mar	Apr	Feb	Mar	Apr
109	...	2-33	...	0-01	0-08	0-34
110	1-28	1-43	1-23	0-03	0-18	0-55
111	0-39	0-63	0-53	0-14	0-38	1-21
112	0-08	0-31	0-29	0-47	1-06	...
113	0-01	0-12	0-15	1-39	1-51	...
114	0-01	0-04	0-07	...	2-43	...

Est vol 192,801 Fr 122,929 calls 162,054 puts
Op int Fri 907,025 calls 1,235,899 puts

5 Yr Treas Notes (CBT)
$100,000; points and 64ths of 100%

Price	Feb	Mar	Apr	Feb	Mar	Apr
10800	0-63	...	...	0-02	0-13	0-33
10850	0-35	0-50	0-45	0-06	0-22	0-46
10900	0-15	0-32	0-30	0-18	0-34	...
10950	0-04	0-17	0-19	0-39	0-52	1-20
11000	0-01	0-09	...	1-04	1-12	...
11050	0-01	0-04	...	1-35	1-39	...

Est vol 77,636 Fr 17,815 calls 57,440 puts
Op int Fri 174,627 calls 497,173 puts

Eurodollar (CME)
$ million; pts. of 100%

Price	Jan	Feb	Mar	Jan	Feb	Mar
9675	...	...	.290	.000	.000	.000
9700	.040	.057	.065	.000	.017	.025
9725	.000	.005	.010	.210	.215	.220
9750	.000	.000	.000	.460	...	.460
9775	.000	...	.000	...	...	.710
9800	.000	...	.000	.960	...	.960

Est vol 809,507;
Fr vol 207,031 calls 664,280 puts
Op int Fri 5,123,572 calls 5,237,907 puts

Source: *The Wall Street Journal*, January 11, 2005, p. C11. Reprinted by permission of *The Wall Street Journal*. **www.wsj.com**

FIGURE 23–7 Buying a Put Option to Hedge the Interest Rate Risk on a Bond

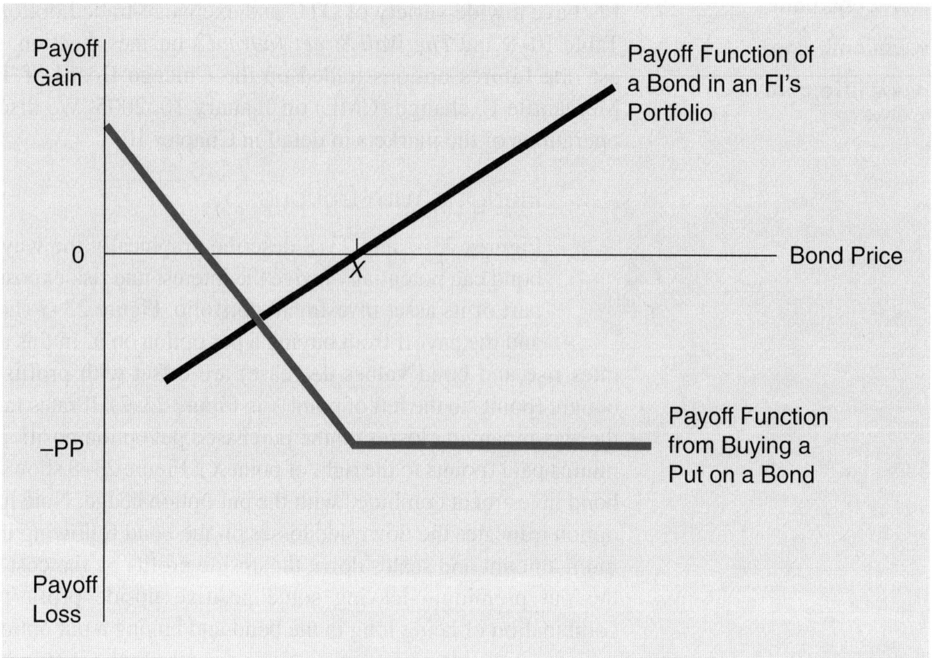

function of buying a call option (compare Figures 23–3 and 23–8). Conversely, an FI can buy a call option on a bond to hedge interest rate risk exposure from a bond that is part of the FI's liability portfolio. Option contracts can also be used to hedge the aggregate duration gap exposure (macrohedge), foreign exchange risk, and credit risk of an FI as well. Appendix 23B to this chapter located at the book's Web site (**www.mhhe.com/sc3e**) presents mathematical details and numerical examples of hedging with options.

Caps, Floors, and Collars

As discussed in Chapter 10, caps, floors, and collars are derivative securities that have many uses, especially in helping an FI hedge interest rate risk exposure as well as risks

FIGURE 23–8 Net Payoff of Buying a Bond Put and Investing in a Bond

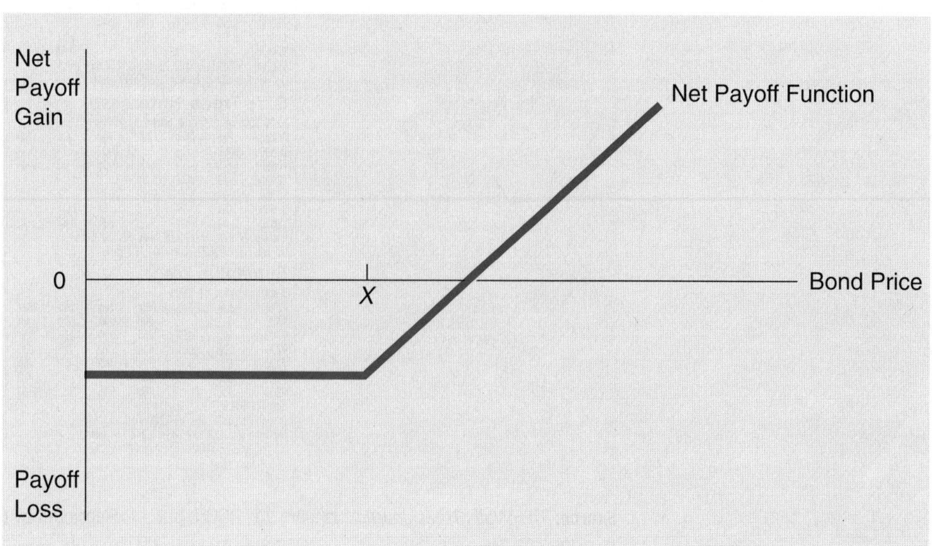

unique to its individual customers. Buying a cap means buying a call option or a succession of call options on interest rates. Specifically, if interest rates rise above the cap rate, the seller of the cap—usually a bank—compensates the buyer—for example, another FI—in return for an up-front premium. As a result, buying an interest rate cap is like buying insurance against an (excessive) increase in interest rates.

Buying a floor is similar to buying a put option on interest rates. If interest rates fall below the floor rate, the seller of the floor compensates the buyer in return for an up-front premium. As with caps, floor agreements can have one or many exercise dates.

A collar occurs when an FI takes a simultaneous position in a cap and a floor, such as buying a cap and selling a floor. The idea here is that the FI wants to hedge itself against rising rates but wants to finance the cost of the cap. One way to do this is to sell a floor and use the premiums on the floor to pay the premium on the purchased cap. Thus, these three over-the-counter instruments are special cases of options; FI managers use them like options to hedge the interest rate risk of an FI's portfolios.

In general, FIs purchase interest rate caps if they are exposed to losses when interest rates rise. Usually, this happens if they are funding assets with floating-rate liabilities such as notes indexed to the LIBOR (or some other cost of funds) and they have fixed-rate assets or they are net long in bonds, or—in a macrohedging context—their duration gap is greater than zero, or $D_A - kD_L > 0$. By contrast, FIs purchase floors when they have fixed costs of debt and have variable rates (returns) on assets or they are net short in bonds, or $D_A - kD_L < 0$. Finally, FIs purchase collars when they are concerned about excessive volatility of interest rates or more commonly to finance cap or floor positions. Appendix 23C to this chapter located at the book's Web site (**www.mhhe.com/sc3e**) presents details and examples of hedging with calls, floors, and collars.

RISKS ASSOCIATED WITH FUTURES, FORWARDS, AND OPTIONS

Financial institutions can be either users of derivative contracts for hedging and other purposes or dealers that act as counterparties in trades with customers for a fee. At the end of 2004, approximately 680 banks were users of derivatives, with three big dealer banks (J.P. Morgan Chase, Bank of America, and Citigroup) accounting for some 90 percent of the $87,880 billion derivatives held by the user banks. However, these securities entail risk for the user banks. For example, Allied Irish Banks suffered a $750 million loss on its derivative positions due to trades by a rogue employee in the early 2000s. This section discusses the various types of risk involved with futures, forwards, and options trading.

Contingent credit risk is likely to be present when FIs expand their positions in forward, futures, and option contracts. This risk relates to the fact that the counterparty to one of these contracts may default on payment obligations, leaving the FI unhedged and having to replace the contract at today's interest rates, prices, or exchange rates. Further, such defaults are most likely to occur when the counterparty is losing heavily on the contract and the FI is in the money on the contract. This type of default risk is much more serious for forward contracts than for futures contracts. This is so because forward contracts are nonstandard contracts entered into bilaterally by negotiating parties such as two FIs and all cash flows are required to be paid at one time (on contract maturity). Thus, they are essentially over-the-counter arrangements with no external guarantees should one or the other party default on the contract. For example, the contract seller might default on a forward foreign exchange contract that promises to deliver £10 million in three months' time at the exchange rate $1.70 to £1 if the cost to purchase £1 for delivery is $1.90 when the forward contract matures. By contrast, futures contracts are standardized contracts guaranteed by organized exchanges such as the New York Futures Exchange (NYFE). Futures contracts, like forward contracts, make commitments to deliver

DO YOU UNDERSTAND?

1. How interest rate increases affect the payoff from buying a call option on a bond? How they affect the payoff from writing a call option on a bond?
2. How interest rate increases affect the payoff from buying a put option on a bond? How they affect the payoff from writing a put option on a bond?
3. What the outcome is if an FI hedges by buying put options on futures and interest rates rise (i.e., bond prices fall)?
4. The difference between a cap, a floor, and a collar used to hedge interest rate risk?
5. The risks involved with hedging with forwards, futures, and options?

foreign exchange (or some other asset) at some future date. If a counterparty were to default on a futures contract, however, the exchange assumes the defaulting party's position and payment obligations. Thus, unless a systematic financial market collapse threatens the exchange itself, futures are essentially default risk free.[15] In addition, default risk is reduced by the daily marking to market of future contracts. This prevents the accumulation of losses and gains that occur with forward contracts.

Option contracts can also be traded by an FI over the counter (OTC) or bought/sold on organized exchanges. If the options are standardized options traded on exchanges, such as bond options, they are virtually default risk free. If they are specialized options purchased OTC such as interest rate caps, some element of default risk exists.

SWAPS

The market for swaps has grown enormously in recent years—the value of swap contracts outstanding by U.S. commercial banks was $56.41 trillion in December 2004. The five generic types of swaps, in order of their notional principal, are *interest rate swaps, currency swaps, credit risk swaps, commodity swaps,* and *equity swaps* (see Chapter 10).[16] The instrument underlying the swap may change, but the basic principle of a swap agreement is the same in that it involves the transacting parties restructuring asset or liability cash flows in a preferred direction. In this section, we consider the role of the two major generic types of swaps—interest rate and currency—in hedging FI risk. We then examine the credit risk characteristics of these instruments.

Hedging with Interest Rate Swaps

5

To explain the role of a swap transaction in hedging FI interest rate risk, we use a simple example. Consider two FIs: the first is a money center bank that has raised $100 million of its funds by issuing four-year, medium-term notes with 10 percent annual fixed coupons rather than relying on short-term deposits to raise funds (see Table 23–4). On the asset side of its portfolio, the bank makes commercial and industrial (C&I) loans whose rates are indexed to annual changes in the London Interbank Offered Rate (LIBOR). Banks often index most large commercial and industrial loans to either LIBOR or the federal funds rate in the money market.

As a result of having floating-rate loans and fixed-rate liabilities in its asset-liability structure, the money center bank has a negative duration gap; the duration of its assets is shorter than that of its liabilities.

$$D_A - kD_L < 0$$

One way for the bank to hedge this exposure is to shorten the duration or interest rate sensitivity of its liabilities by transforming them into short-term floating-rate liabilities that better match the rate sensitivity of its asset portfolio. The bank can make changes either on or off the balance sheet. On the balance sheet, the bank could attract an additional $100 million in short-term deposits that are indexed to the LIBOR rate (at, say, LIBOR plus 2.5 percent) in a manner similar to its loans. The proceeds of these deposits would be used to pay off the medium-term notes. This reduces the duration gap between the bank's assets and liabilities. Alternatively, the bank could go off the balance sheet and sell an interest rate swap—that is, enter into a swap agreement to make the floating-rate payment side of a swap agreement.

The second party of the swap is a thrift institution (savings bank) that has invested $100 million in fixed-rate residential mortgages of long duration. To finance this residential mortgage portfolio, the savings bank had to rely on short-term certificates of deposit

15. More specifically, the default risk of a futures contract is less than that of a forward contract for at least four reasons: (1) daily marking to market of futures, (2) margin requirements on futures that act as a security bond, (3) price limits that spread extreme price fluctuations over time, and (4) default guarantees by the futures exchange itself.

16. There are also *swaptions,* which are options to enter into a swap agreement at some preagreed contract terms (e.g., a fixed rate of 10 percent) at some time in the future in return for the payment of an up-front premium.

TABLE 23–4 Money Center Bank Balance Sheet

Assets		Liabilities	
C&I loans (rate indexed to LIBOR)	$100 million	Medium-term notes (coupons fixed at 10% annually)	$100 million

TABLE 23–5 Savings Bank Balance Sheet

Assets		Liabilities	
Fixed-rate mortgages	$100 million	Short-term CDs (one year)	$100 million

with an average duration of one year (see Table 23–5). On maturity, these CDs must be rolled over at the current market rate.

Consequently, the savings bank's asset-liability balance sheet structure is the reverse of the money center bank's:

$$D_A - kD_L > 0$$

The savings bank could hedge its interest rate risk exposure by transforming the short-term floating-rate nature of its liabilities into fixed-rate liabilities that better match the long-term maturity (duration) structure of its assets. On the balance sheet, the thrift could issue long-term notes with a maturity equal or close to that on the mortgages (at, say, 12 percent). The proceeds of the sale of the notes can be used to pay off the CDs and reduce the repricing gap. Alternatively, the thrift can buy a swap—that is, take the fixed-payment side of a swap agreement.

The opposing balance sheet and interest rate risk exposures of the money center bank and the savings bank provide the necessary conditions for an interest rate swap agreement between the two parties. This swap agreement can be arranged directly between the parties. However, it is likely that an FI—another bank or an investment bank—would act as either a broker or an agent, receiving a fee for bringing the two parties together or to intermediate fully by accepting the credit risk exposure and guaranteeing the cash flows underlying the swap contract. By acting as a principal as well as an agent, the FI can add a credit risk premium to the fee. However, the credit risk exposure of a swap to an FI is somewhat less than that on a loan (this is discussed later in this chapter). Conceptually, when a third-party FI fully intermediates the swap, that FI is really entering into two separate swap agreements, one with the money center bank and one with the savings bank.

plain vanilla

A standard agreement without any special features.

For simplicity, we consider an example below of a **plain vanilla** fixed-floating rate swap (a standard swap agreement without any special features) in which a third-party intermediary acts as a simple broker or agent by bringing together two DIs with opposing interest rate risk exposures to enter into a swap agreement or contract.

EXAMPLE 23–1 Expected Cash Flows on an Interest Rate Swap

In this example, the notional (or face) value of the swap is $100 million—equal to the assumed size of the money center bank's medium-term note issue—and the four-year maturity is equal to the maturity of its note liabilities. The annual coupon cost of these note liabilities is 10 percent. The money center bank's problem is that the variable return on its assets may be insufficient to cover the cost of meeting these fixed coupon payments if market interest rates *fall*. By comparison, the fixed returns on the savings bank's mortgage asset portfolio may be insufficient to cover the interest cost of its CDs should market rates

TABLE 23–6 Financing Cost Resulting from Interest Rate Swap
(in millions of dollars)

	Money Center Bank	Savings Bank
Cash outflows from balance sheet financing	−10% × \$100	−(CD Rate) × \$100
Cash inflows from swap	10% × \$100	(LIBOR + 2%) × \$100
Cash outflows from swap	−(LIBOR + 2%) × \$100	−10% × \$100
Net cash flows	−(LIBOR + 2%) × \$100	−(8% + CD Rate − LIBOR) × \$100
Rate available on		
Variable-rate debt	LIBOR + 2½%	
Fixed-rate debt		12%

FIGURE 23–9 Fixed–Floating Rate Swap

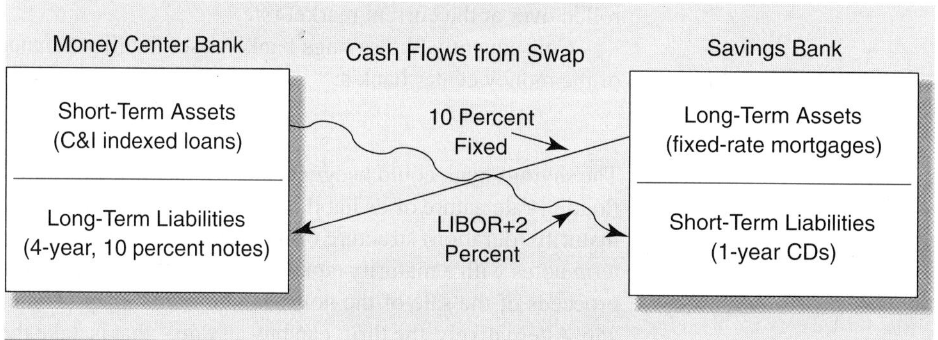

rise. As a result, the swap agreement might dictate that the savings bank send fixed payments of 10 percent per annum of the notional \$100 million value of the swap to the money center bank to allow the money center bank to cover fully the coupon interest payments on its note issue. In return, the money center bank sends annual payments indexed to the one-year LIBOR to help the savings bank cover the cost of refinancing its one-year renewable CDs. Suppose that the money center bank agrees to send the savings bank annual payments at the end of each year equal to one-year LIBOR plus 2 percent.[17] We depict this fixed–floating rate swap transaction in Figure 23–9; the expected net financing costs for the FIs are listed in Table 23–6.

As a result of the swap, the money center bank has transformed its four-year, fixed-rate liability notes into a variable-rate liability matching the variability of returns on its C&I loans. Further, through the interest rate swap, the money center bank effectively pays LIBOR plus 2 percent for its financing. Had it gone to the debt market, the money center bank would pay LIBOR plus 2.5 percent (a savings of .5 percent with the swap). The savings bank also has transformed its variable-rate CDs into fixed-rate payments similar to those received on its fixed-rate mortgages—it has successfully microhedged.

Note in Example 23–1 that in the absence of default/credit risk, only the money center bank is really fully hedged. This happens because the annual 10 percent payments it receives from the savings bank at the end of each year allows it to meet the promised 10 percent coupon rate payments to its note holders regardless of the return it receives on its

17. These rates implicitly assume that this is the cheapest way each party can hedge its interest rate exposure. For example, LIBOR plus 2 percent is the lowest-cost way that the money center bank can transform its fixed-rate liabilities into floating-rate liabilities.

variable-rate assets. By contrast, the savings bank receives variable-rate payments based on LIBOR plus 2 percent. It is quite possible that the CD rate that the savings bank must pay on its deposit liabilities does not exactly track the LIBOR-indexed payments sent by the money center bank—that is, the savings bank is subject to basis risk exposure on the swap contract. This basis risk can come from two sources. First, CD rates do not exactly match the movements of LIBOR rates over time since the former are determined in the domestic money market and the latter in the Eurodollar market. Second, the credit/default risk premium on the savings bank's CDs may increase over time; thus, the plus 2 percent add-on to LIBOR may be insufficient to hedge the savings bank's cost of funds. The savings bank might be better hedged by requiring the money center bank to send it floating payments based on U.S. domestic CD rates rather than on LIBOR. To do this, the money center bank would probably require additional compensation since it would then bear basis risk. Its asset returns would be sensitive to LIBOR movements while its swap payments were indexed to U.S. CD rates.

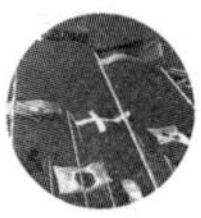

Currency Swaps

currency swap

A swap used to hedge against foreign exchange rate risk from mismatched currencies on assets and liabilities.

Swaps are long-term contracts that can also be used to hedge an FI's exposure to currency risk. The following section considers a plain vanilla example of how **currency swaps** can immunize FIs against foreign exchange rate risk when they mismatch the currencies of their assets and liabilities.

Fixed-Fixed Currency Swaps. Consider a U.S. FI with all of its fixed-rate assets denominated in dollars. It is financing part of its asset portfolio with a £50 million issue of four-year, medium-term British pound notes that have a fixed annual coupon of 10 percent. By comparison, an FI in the United Kingdom has all its assets denominated in pounds; it is partly funding those assets with a \$100 million issue of four-year, medium-term dollar notes with a fixed annual coupon of 10 percent.

These two FIs are exposed to opposing currency risks. The U.S. FI is exposed to the risk that the dollar will depreciate against the pound over the next four years, which would make it more costly to cover the annual coupon interest payments and the principal repayment on its pound-denominated notes. On the other hand, the U.K. FI is exposed to the risk that the dollar will appreciate against the pound, making it more difficult to cover the dollar coupon and principal payments on its four-year, \$100 million note issue from the pound cash flows on its assets.

The FIs can hedge the exposures either on or off the balance sheet. Assume that the dollar/pound exchange rate is fixed at \$2/£1. On the balance sheet, the U.S. FI can issue \$100 million in four-year, medium-term dollar notes (at, say, 10.5 percent). The proceeds of the sale can be used to pay off the £50 million of four-year, medium-term pound notes. Similarly, the U.K. FI can issue £50 million in four-year, medium-term pound notes (at, say, 10.5 percent), using the proceeds to pay off the \$100 million of four-year, medium-term dollar notes. Both FIs have taken actions on the balance sheet so that they are no longer exposed to movements in the exchange rate between the two currencies.

EXAMPLE 23-2 Expected Cash Flows on a Fixed–Fixed Currency Swap

Off the balance sheet, the U.K. and U.S. FIs can enter into a currency swap by which the U.K. FI sends annual payments in pounds to cover the coupon and principal repayments of the U.S. FI's pound note issue, and the U.S. FI sends annual dollar payments to the U.K. FI to cover the interest and principal payments on its dollar note issue.[18] We summarize this

18. In a currency swap, it is usual to include both principal and interest payments as part of the swap agreement. (For interest rate swaps, it is usual to include only interest rate payments.) The reason for this is that both principal and interest are exposed to foreign exchange risk.

TABLE 23–7 Financing Costs Resulting from the Fixed–Fixed Currency Swap Agreement
(in millions of dollars)

	U.S. FI	U.K. FI
Cash outflows from balance sheet financing	−10% × £50	−10% × $100
Cash inflows from swap	10% × £50	10% × $100
Cash outflows from swap	−10% × $100	−10% × £50
Net cash flows	−10% × $100	−10% × £50
Rate available on		
Dollar-denominated notes	10.5%	
Pound-denominated notes		10.5%

FIGURE 23–10 Fixed–Fixed Pound/Dollar Currency Swap

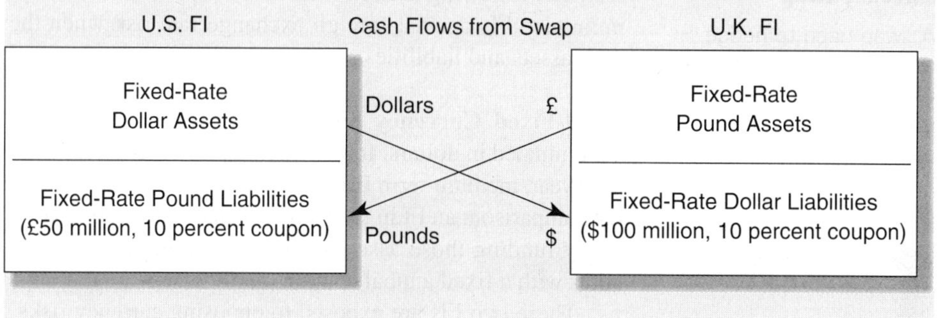

currency swap in Figure 23–10 and Table 23–7. As a result of the swap, the U.K. FI transforms fixed-rate dollar liabilities into fixed-rate pound liabilities that better match the pound fixed-rate cash flows from its asset portfolio. Similarly, the U.S. FI transforms fixed-rate pound liabilities into fixed-rate dollar liabilities that better match the fixed-rate dollar cash flows from its asset portfolio. Further, both FIs transform the pattern of their payments at a lower rate than had they made changes on the balance sheet. Both FIs effectively obtain financing at 10 percent while hedging against exchange rate risk. Had they gone to the market, they would have paid 10.5 percent to do this. In undertaking this exchange of cash flows, the two parties normally agree on a fixed exchange rate for the cash flows at the beginning of the period.[19] In this example, the fixed exchange rate is $2/£1.

By combining an interest rate swap of the fixed–floating type described earlier with a currency swap, we can also produce a fixed–floating currency swap that is a hybrid of the two plain vanilla swaps we have considered so far.

Credit Risk Concerns with Swaps

www.bis.org

The growth of the over-the-counter (OTC) swap market was one of the major factors underlying the imposition of the BIS risk-based capital requirements in January 1993 (see Chapter 13). The fear was that in a long-term OTC swap-type contract, the losing or

19. As with interest rate swaps, this exchange rate reflects the contracting parties' expectations as to future exchange rate movements.

www.isda.org

out-of-the-money counterparty would have incentives to default on such contracts to deter current and future losses. Consequently, the BIS (with significant input and support from the global trade association the International Swaps and Derivatives Association (ISDA), which sets codes and standards for swap markets) imposed a risk-based capital requirement for banks to hold against their interest rate, currency, and other swaps.

This raises the following questions. What, exactly, is the default risk on swaps? Is it high or low? Is it the same as or different from the credit risk on loans? In fact, the credit risk on swaps and the credit risk on loans differ in three major ways, so that the credit risk on a swap is much less than that on a loan of equivalent dollar size.[20] We discuss these differences next.

Netting and Swaps. One factor that mitigates the credit risk on swaps is the netting of swap payments. On each swap payment date, one party makes a fixed payment and the other makes a floating payment. In general, however, each party calculates the net difference between the two payments, and one party makes a single payment for the net difference to the other. This netting of payments implies that the default exposure of the in-the-money party is limited to the net payment rather than either the total fixed or floating payment itself.

For instance, in Example 23–1, if the LIBOR rate on the first swap payment date is 3.5 percent, from Table 23–6 the money center bank's cash inflows and cash outflows from the swap are \$10m. (= 10% × \$100m.) and \$5.5m. (= (3.5% + 2%) × \$100m.), respectively. Conversely, the savings bank's cash inflows and outflows from the swap are \$5.5m. and \$10m., respectively. Rather, than have both FIs receive cash *and* pay cash, the cash flows from the swap are netted. Thus, the savings bank pays a net cash flow of \$4.5m. to be received by the money center bank.

DO YOU UNDERSTAND?

1. What the difference between an interest rate swap and a currency swap is?
2. What the major differences between the credit risk on swaps and the credit risk on loans are?

Payment Flows Are Interest, not Principal. Currency swaps involve swaps of interest and principal, but interest rate swaps involve swaps of interest payments only measured against some notional (or face) principal value. This suggests that the default risk on such interest rate swaps is less than on a regular loan, in which both its interest and principal payments are exposed to credit risk.

Standby Letters of Credit. When swaps are made between parties of different credit standings so that one party perceives a significant risk of default by the other party, the poor-quality credit risk party may be required to buy a standby letter of credit (or another form of performance guarantee) from a third-party high-quality (AAA-rated) FI so that should default occur, the standby letter of credit party would provide the swap payments in lieu of the defaulting party.[21]

6 COMPARISON OF HEDGING METHODS

As described above, an FI has many alternative derivative instruments with which it can hedge a particular risk. In this section, we look at some general features of the different types of contracts that may lead to an FI preferring one derivative instrument over another. We summarize these in Table 23–8.

Writing versus Buying Options

Many FIs prefer to buy rather than write options. Of the two reasons for this, one is economic and the other is regulatory.

20. As with loans, swap participants deal with the credit risk of counterparties by setting bilateral limits on the notional amount of swaps entered into (similar to credit rationing on loans) and adjusting the fixed and/or floating rates by including credit risk premiums. For example, a low credit-quality, fixed-rate payer may have to pay an additional spread to a high credit-quality, floating-rate payer.

21. Another solution employed by market participants is to use collateral to mark to market a swap contract in a way similar to marking futures to market to prevent credit risk building up over time. Remember that a swap contract is like a succession of forward contracts.

TABLE 23–8 Comparison of Hedging Methods

Writing versus Buying Options

- Writing options truncates upside profit potential while downside loss potential is unlimited.
- Buying options truncates downside loss potential while upside profit potential is unlimited.
- Commercial banks are prohibited by regulators from writing options in certain areas of risk management.

Futures versus Options Hedging

- Futures hedging produces symmetric gains and losses when interest rates move against the on-balance-sheet securities, *as well as* when interest rates move in favor of on-balance-sheet securities.
- Options hedging protects the FI against value losses when interest rates move against the on-balance-sheet securities, but, unlike with futures hedging, does not fully reduce value gains when interest rates move in favor of on-balance-sheet securities.

Swaps versus Forwards, Futures, and Options

- Futures, and most options, are standardized contracts with fixed principal amounts. Swaps (and forwards) are OTC contracts negotiated directly by the counterparties to the contract.
- Futures contracts are marked to market daily. Swaps and forwards require payments only at times specified in the swap or forward agreement.
- Swaps can be written for relatively long time horizons. Futures and option contracts do not trade for more than two or three years into the future and active trading in these contracts generally extends to contracts with a maturity of less than one year.
- Swap and forward contracts are subject to default risk. Most futures and option contracts are not subject to default risk.

Economic Reasons for Not Writing Options. In writing an option, the upside profit potential is truncated but the downside losses are not. On an *expected* basis, the writing of an appropriate call or put option would lead to a fair rate of return. However, the *actual* price or interest rate movement on the underlying asset may move against the option writer. It is this actual price or rate change that leads to the possibility of unlimited losses. Although such risks may be offset by writing a large number of options at different exercise prices and/or hedging an underlying portfolio of bonds, the writer's downside risk exposure may still be significant. Figure 23–11 indicates this. An FI is long in a bond in its portfolio and seeks to hedge the interest rate risk on that bond by writing a bond call option. Note that writing the call may hedge the FI when rates fall and bond prices rise—that is, the increase in the value of the bond is offset by losses on the written call. When the reverse occurs and interest rates rise, the FI's profits from writing the call may be insufficient to offset the loss on its bonds. This occurs because the upside profit (per call written) is truncated and equals the premium income (C). If the decrease in the bond value is larger than the premium income (to the left of point A in Figure 23–11), the FI is unable to offset the associated capital value loss on the bond with profits from writing options.

By contrast, hedging the FI's risk by buying a put option on a bond generally offers the manager a more attractive alternative. Refer again to Figures 23–7 and 23–8. The net overall payoff from the bond investment combined with the put option hedge truncates the downside losses on the bond following interest rate rises to some maximum amount and scales down the upside profits by the put premium.

naked options

Option positions that do not identifiably hedge an underlying asset or liability.

Regulatory Reasons. Many FIs also buy options rather than write options for regulatory reasons. Regulators consider writing options, especially **naked options,** which do not identifiably hedge an underlying asset or liability position, to be risky because of their unlimited loss potential. Indeed, bank regulators prohibit commercial banks from writing puts or calls in certain areas of risk management.

FIGURE 23–11 Writing a Call Option to Hedge the Interest Rate Risk on a Bond

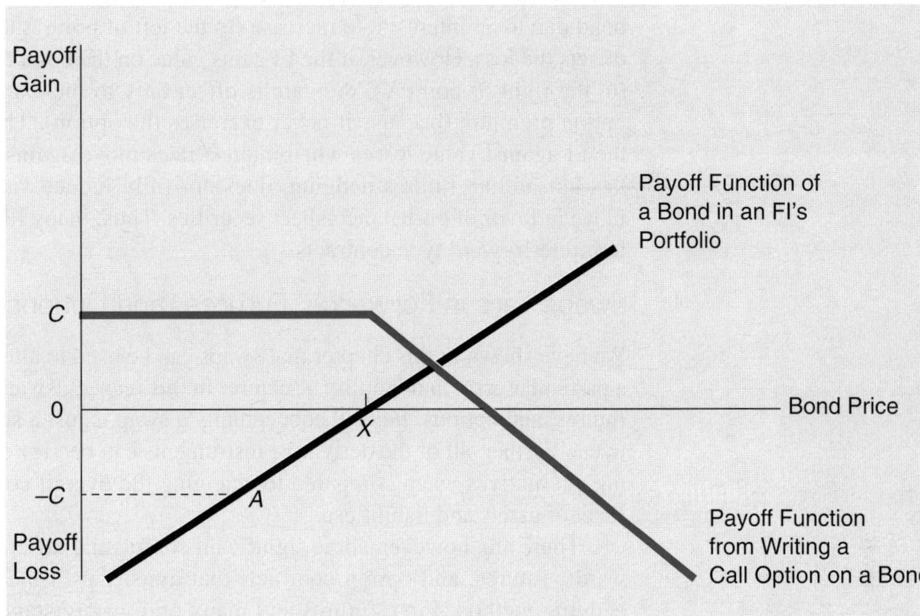

Futures versus Options Hedging

To understand the factors that impact the choice between using futures rather than options contracts to hedge, compare the payoff gains illustrated in Figure 23–12 (for futures contracts) with those in Figure 23–7 (for option contracts). A hedge with futures contracts produces symmetric gains and losses with interest rate increases and decreases. That is, if the FI in Figure 23–12 loses value on the bond resulting from an interest rate increase (to the left of point X), it enjoys a gain on the futures contract to offset this loss. If the FI gains value on the bond due to an interest rate decrease (to the right of point X), a loss on the futures contract offsets this gain.

FIGURE 23–12 Buying a Futures Contract to Hedge the Interest Rate Risk on a Bond

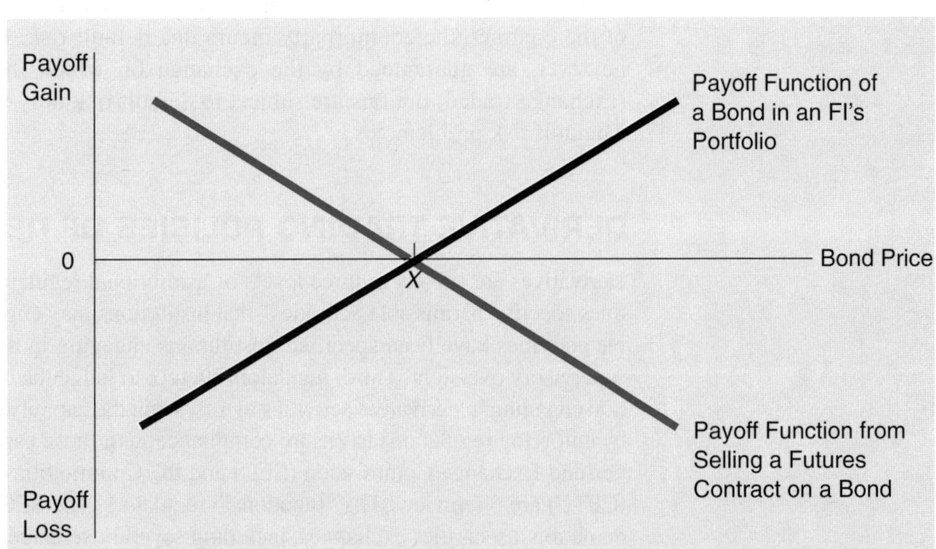

By comparison, a hedge with an option contract offsets losses but only partly offsets gains—gains and losses from hedging with options are no longer symmetric for interest rate increases and decreases. For example, in Figure 23–7, if the FI loses value on the bond due to an interest rate increase (to the left of point X), a gain on the option contract offsets the loss. However, if the FI gains value on the bond due to an interest rate decrease (to the right of point X), the gain is offset only to the extent that the FI loses the fixed option premium (because it never exercises the option). Thus, the option hedge protects the FI against value losses when interest rates move against the on-balance-sheet securities but, unlike futures hedging, does not fully reduce value gains when interest rates move in favor of on-balance-sheet securities. Thus, many FIs prefer option-type contracts to future/forward type contracts.

Swaps versus Forwards, Futures, and Options

We have shown in this chapter that swaps can be used to alter the cash flows of an FI from a particular asset and liability structure. In this respect, swaps are comparable to forwards, futures, and options. Indeed, conceptually a swap is just a succession of forward rate contracts. Further, all of the derivative instruments can be viewed as relatively low-cost hedging alternatives when compared to changing the overall composition of the FI's balance sheet of assets and liabilities.

There are, however, some significant contractual differences between swaps and forwards, futures, and option contracts that assist the FI manager in his or her choice of hedging method. First, futures and many options are standardized contracts with fixed principal amounts. Swaps (and forwards), on the other hand, are OTC contracts negotiated directly by the counterparties to the contract. This feature allows for flexibility in the principal amount of the swap contract. Second, futures contracts are marked to market daily, while swaps and forwards require payments only at times specified in the swap or forward agreement. Thus, hedging risk exposure with futures can result in large cash inflows and outflows for the FI if price movements result in margin calls at the end of the day as a result of this marking-to-market process. Third, swaps can be written for relatively long time horizons, sometimes as long as 20 years. Futures and option contracts do not trade for more than two or three years into the future and active trading in these contracts generally extends to contracts with a maturity of less than one year. Thus, swaps provide the FI with better long-term contractual protection against risk exposures than futures and options. Finally, swap and forward contracts are subject to default risk, while most futures and option contracts are not. Swap and forward contracts are negotiated between two counterparties, and should one party fail to abide by the terms of the contract, the counterparty incurs this default risk. Futures and option contracts, however, are guaranteed by the exchange on which they trade. Thus, futures and (exchange-traded) options are subject to default risk only when the entire exchange has a default risk problem.

DO YOU UNDERSTAND?

1. What the economic reasons are that FIs do not write options?
2. What the regulatory reasons are that an FI might choose to buy options rather than write them?
3. What the differences are between swaps, forwards, futures, and option contracts in hedging risk exposure on an FI's balance sheet?

DERIVATIVE TRADING POLICIES OF REGULATORS

Derivatives are subject to three levels of institutional regulation. First, regulators of derivatives specify "permissible activities" that institutions may engage in. Second, once permissible activities have been specified, institutions engaging in those activities are subjected to supervisory oversight. Third, regulators attempt to judge the overall integrity of each institution engaging in derivative activities by assessing the capital adequacy of the institutions and by enforcing regulations to ensure compliance with those capital requirements. The Securities and Exchange Commission (SEC) and the Commodities Futures Trading Commission (CFTC) are often viewed as "functional" regulators. The SEC regulates all securities traded on national securities exchanges, including several exchange-traded derivatives. The SEC's regulation of derivatives includes price reporting requirements and margin requirements. The CFTC also has jurisdiction over all exchange-traded derivative securities. It therefore regulates all national futures exchanges, as well as all futures and options on futures. The CFTC's regulations include minimum capital requirements for traders, reporting and transparency requirements, antifraud and antimanipulation regulations, and minimum standards for clearinghouse organizations.

The main bank regulators—the Federal Reserve, the FDIC, and the Comptroller of the Currency—also have issued uniform guidelines for banks taking positions in futures and forwards. These guidelines require a bank to (1) establish internal guidelines regarding its hedging activity, (2) establish trading limits, and (3) disclose large contract positions that materially affect bank risk to shareholders and outside investors. Overall, the policy of regulators is to encourage the use of futures for hedging and to discourage their use for speculation, although on a practical basis distinguishing between the two is often difficult.

As of January 1, 2000, the main regulator of accounting standards (the FASB) required all FIs (and nonfinancial firms) to reflect the mark-to-market value of their derivative positions in their financial statements. This means that FIs must immediately recognize all gains and losses on such contracts and disclose those gains and losses to shareholders and regulators. Further, firms must show whether they are using derivatives to hedge risks connected to their business or whether they are just taking an open risky position.

Finally, as noted in Chapter 13, exchange-traded futures contracts are not subject to risk-based capital requirements; by contrast, OTC forward contracts are potentially subject to capital requirements. Other things being equal, the risk-based capital requirements favor the use of futures over forwards.

In contrast to futures and options markets, swap markets are governed by very little regulation; no central governing body oversees swap market operations. However, because commercial banks are the major swap dealers, the swap markets are subject, indirectly, to regulations imposed by the Federal Reserve, the FDIC, and other bank regulatory agencies charged with monitoring bank risk. To the extent that swap activity is part of a bank's overall business, swap markets are monitored for abuses and the risk exposure they add to the bank.

DO YOU UNDERSTAND?

1. The three levels of regulation to which derivatives are subject?
2. Who the main regulators of derivative trading by FIs are?

SUMMARY

This chapter analyzed the risk-management role of forwards, futures, options, and swaps. These (off-balance-sheet) derivative securities provide FIs with a low-cost alternative to managing risk exposure directly on the balance sheet. We first looked at the use of forwards and futures contracts as hedging instruments. We saw that while they are close substitutes, they are not perfect substitutes. A number of characteristics such as maturity, liquidity, flexibility, marking to market, and capital requirements differentiate these products and make one or the other more attractive to any particular FI manager. We next discussed the use of option-type contracts available to FI managers to hedge interest rate risk. In particular, we noted that the unique nature of the asymmetric payoff structure of option-type contracts often makes them more attractive to FIs than other hedging instruments such as forwards and futures. We then evaluated the role of swaps as risk-management vehicles for FIs. We analyzed the major types of swaps, such as interest rate and currency swaps. Swaps have special features of long maturity, flexibility, and liquidity that make them attractive alternatives relative to shorter-term hedging vehicles such as futures, forwards, and options. Finally, we outlined the regulatory procedures governing derivatives.

www.mhhe.com/sc3e

SEARCH THE SITE

Go to the Web site of the Office of the Comptroller of the Currency at **www.occ.treas.gov** and find the most recent data on the notional amount of the various types of derivatives contracts outstanding at commercial banks using the following steps.

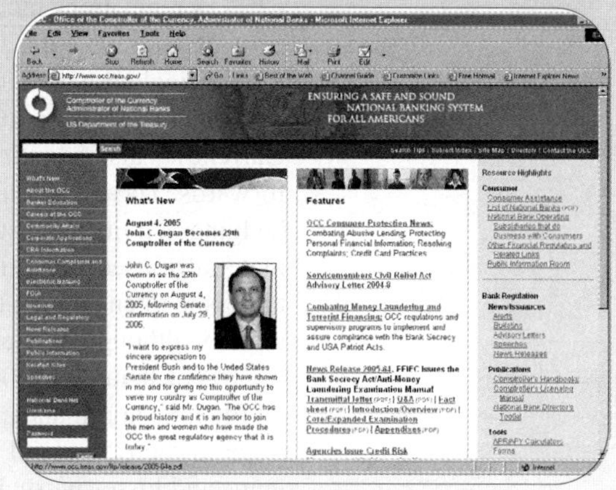

Click on "Publications."

Click on "Qrtrly. Derivative Fact Sheet."

Click on the most recent date.

Click on "Tables."

This will bring the file onto your computer that contains the relevant data.

Questions

1. What is the total notional amount of derivatives outstanding?
2. What is the notional amount of forwards, futures, options, and swaps outstanding?
3. What are the three largest banks dealing in derivatives and what percentage of the total derivatives market does each comprise?

QUESTIONS

1. What are some of the major differences between futures and forward contracts?
2. In each of the following cases, indicate whether it would be appropriate for an FI to buy or sell a forward contract to hedge the appropriate risk.
   a. A commercial bank plans to issue CDs in three months.
   b. An insurance company plans to buy bonds in two months.
   c. A thrift is going to sell Treasury securities next month.
   d. A U.S. bank lends to a French company; the loan is payable in euros.
   e. A mutual fund plans to sell its holding of stock in a German company.
   f. A finance company has assets with a duration of 6 years and liabilities with a duration of 13 years.
3. Suppose that you purchase a Treasury bond futures contract at $95 per $100 of face value.
   a. What is your obligation when you purchase this futures contract?
   b. If an FI purchases this contract, in what kind of hedge is it engaged?
   c. Assume that the Treasury bond futures price falls to 94. What is your loss or gain?
   d. Assume that the Treasury bond futures price rises to 97. Mark your position to market.
4. Answer the following.
   a. What is the duration of a 20-year 8 percent coupon (paid semiannually) Treasury bond (deliverable against the Treasury bond futures contract) selling at par?
   b. What is the impact on the Treasury bond price if interest rates increase 50 basis points annually (25 basis points semiannually)?
   c. What is the meaning of the following Treasury bond futures price quote: 101-13?
5. An FI holds a 15-year, $10,000,000 par value, bond that is priced at 104 and yields 7 percent. The FI plans to sell the bond but for tax purposes must wait two months. The bond has a duration of eight years. The FI's market analyst is predicting that the Federal Reserve will raise interest rates within the next two months and doing so will raise the yield on the bond to 8 percent. Most other analysts are predicting no change in interest rates, so presently plenty of two-month forward contracts for 15-year bonds are available at 104. The FI would like to hedge against this interest rate forecast with an appropriate position in a forward contract. What will this position be? Show that if rates rise by 1 percent as forecast, the hedge will protect the FI from loss.
6. Answer the following:
   a. What are the two ways to use call and put options on T-bonds to generate positive cash flows when interest rates decline?
   b. When and how can an FI use options on T-bonds to hedge its assets and liabilities against interest rate declines?
   c. Is it more appropriate for FIs to hedge against a decline in interest rates with long calls or short puts?

7. In each of the following cases, indicate whether it is appropriate for an FI to buy a put or a call option in order to hedge the appropriate risk.
   a. A commercial bank plans to issue CDs in three months.
   b. An insurance company plans to buy bonds in two months.
   c. A thrift plans to sell Treasury securities next month.
   d. A U.S. bank lends to a French company; the loan is payable in euros.
   e. A mutual fund plans to sell its holding of stock in a German company.
   f. A finance company has assets with a duration of 6 years and liabilities with a duration of 13 years.
8. Consider Table 23–3. What are the prices paid for the following futures options:
   a. March T-bond calls at 112.
   b. April 5-year T-note puts at 10850.
   c. March Eurodollar calls at 9700.
9. Consider Table 23–3 again.
   a. What happens to the price of a call when:
      (1) The exercise price increases?
      (2) The time until expiration increases?
   b. What happens to the price of the put when these two variables increase?
10. Suppose that an FI manager writes a call option on a T-bond futures contract with an exercise price of 114 at a quoted price of 0-55. What type of opportunities or obligations does the manager have?
11. Suppose that a pension fund manager anticipates the purchase of a 20-year 8 percent coupon T-bond at the end of two years. Interest rates are assumed to change only once every year at year end. At that time, it is equally probable that interest rates will increase or decrease 1 percent. When purchased in two years, the T-bond will pay interest semiannually. Currently, it is selling at par.
    a. What is the pension fund manager's interest rate risk exposure?
    b. How can the pension fund manager use options to hedge that interest rate risk exposure?
12. Distinguish between a swap *seller* and a swap *buyer*.
13. An insurance company owns $50 million of floating-rate bonds yielding LIBOR plus 1 percent. These loans are financed by $50 million of fixed-rate guaranteed investment contracts (GICs) costing 10 percent. A finance company has $50 million of auto loans with a fixed rate of 14 percent. They are financed by $50 million of debt with a variable rate of LIBOR plus 4 percent. If the finance company is going to be the swap buyer and the insurance company the swap seller, what is an example of a feasible swap?
14. A commercial bank has $200 million of floating-rate loans yielding the T-bill rate plus 2 percent. These loans are financed by $200 million of fixed-rate deposits costing 9 percent. A savings association has $200 million of mortgages with a fixed rate of 13 percent. They are financed by $200 million of CDs with a variable rate of T-bill plus 3 percent.
    a. Discuss the type of interest rate risk each FI faces.
    b. Propose a swap that would result in each FI having the same type of assets and liabilities (i.e., one has fixed assets and fixed liabilities, and the other has assets and liabilities all tied to some floating rate).
    c. Show that this swap would be acceptable to both parties.
    d. What are some practical difficulties in arranging this swap?
15. A British bank issues a $100 million, three-year Eurodollar CD at a fixed annual rate of 7 percent. The proceeds of the CD are lent to a British company for three years at a fixed rate of 9 percent. The spot exchange rate of pounds for U.S. dollars is £1.50/US$.
    a. Is this expected to be a profitable transaction ex ante? What are the cash flows if exchange rates are unchanged over the next three years? What is the risk exposure of the bank's underlying cash position? How can the British bank reduce that risk exposure?
    b. If the U.S. dollar is expected to appreciate against the pound to £1.65/$1, £1.815/$1, and £2.00/$1 over the next three years, respectively, what will be the cash flows on this transaction?
    c. If the British bank swaps U.S. dollar payments for British pound payments at the current spot exchange rate, what are the cash flows on the swap? What are the cash flows on the entire hedged position? Assume that the U.S. dollar appreciates at the same rates as in part (*b*).
16. Bank 1 can issue five-year CDs at an annual rate of 11 percent fixed or at a variable rate of LIBOR + 2 percent. Bank 2 can issue five-year CDs at an annual fixed rate of 13 percent or at a variable rate of LIBOR + 3 percent.
    a. Is a mutually beneficial swap possible between the two banks?
    b. What is the comparative advantage of the two banks?
    c. What is an example of a feasible swap?
17. How does hedging with options differ from hedging with forward or futures contracts?
18. Contrast the use of financial futures options with the use of options on cash instruments to construct interest rate hedges.
19. Consider the following FI's balance sheet:

Assets ($000)		Liabilities ($000)	
Duration = 10 years	$950	Duration = 2 years	$860
		Equity	90

    a. What is the FI's duration gap?
    b. What is the FI's interest rate risk exposure?
    c. How can the FI use futures and forward contracts to macrohedge?
20. A bank purchases a six-month $1 million Eurodollar deposit at an interest rate of 6.5 percent per year. It invests the funds in a six-month Swedish krona bond paying 7.5 percent per year. The current spot rate of U.S. dollars for Swedish krona is $0.18/SKr.
    a. The six-month forward rate on the Swedish krona is being quoted at $0.1810/SKr. What is the net spread earned on this investment if the bank covers its foreign exchange exposure using the forward market?
    b. At what forward rate will the spread be only 1 percent per year?

APPENDIX 23A: Hedging with Futures Contracts

View this appendix at
www.mhhe.com/sc3e

APPENDIX 23B: Hedging with Options

View this appendix at
www.mhhe.com/sc3e

APPENDIX 23C: Hedging with Caps, Floors, and Collars

View this appendix at
www.mhhe.com/sc3e

www.mhhe.com/sc3e

Managing Risk *with* Loan Sales *and* Securitization

OUTLINE

Chapter NAVIGATOR

1. What are the purposes of loan sales and securitizations?
2. What characteristics describe the bank loan sale market?
3. What factors encourage and deter loan sales growth?
4. What are the major forms of asset securitization?
5. Can all assets be securitized?

1 WHY FINANCIAL INSTITUTIONS SELL AND SECURITIZE LOANS: CHAPTER OVERVIEW

Loan sales and **securitization**—the packaging and selling of loans and other assets backed by loans issued by the FI—are one of the mechanisms that FIs have used to hedge their credit risk, interest rate risk, and liquidity risk exposures. In addition, loan sales and securitization have allowed FI asset portfolios to become more liquid, provided an important source of fee income (with FIs acting as servicing agents for the assets sold), and helped to reduce the adverse effects of regulatory "taxes" such as capital requirements, reserve requirements, and deposit insurance premiums on FI profitability. Loan sales involve splitting up larger loans and loan portfolios, where as loan securitization involves the grouping of smaller loans into larger pools. While loan sales have been in existence for many years, the use of loan sales (by removing existing loans from the balance sheet) is increasingly being recognized as a valuable tool in an FI manager's portfolio of credit risk management techniques. In Chapter 1, we discussed the role of FIs as both asset transformers and asset brokers. By increasingly relying on loan sales and securitization, FIs such as depository institutions have begun moving away from being strictly asset transformers that originate and hold assets to maturity toward becoming more reliant on servicing and other fees. This makes depository institutions look increasingly similar to securities firms and investment banks in terms of the enhanced importance of asset brokerage over asset transformation functions.

In Chapter 7, we discussed the basics of asset sales and securitization and the markets in which these securities trade. This chapter investigates the role of loan sales and

TABLE 24–1 Basic Description of Loan Sales and Other Forms of Mortgage Securitization

Loan Sale—an FI originates a loan and subsequently sells it.

Pass-Through Securities—mortgages or other assets originated by an FI are pooled and investors are offered an interest in the pool in the form of pass-through certificates or securities. Examples of pass-through securities are Government National Mortgage Association (GNMA) or Federal National Mortgage Association (FNMA) securities.

Collateralized Mortgage Obligations (CMOs)—similar to pass-throughs, CMOs are securities backed by pools of mortgages or other assets originated by an FI. Pass-throughs give investors common rights in terms of risks and returns, but CMOs assign varying combinations of risk and return to different groups of investors in the CMO by repackaging the pool.

Mortgage-Backed Bonds (MBBs)—a bond issue backed by a group of mortgages on an FI's balance sheet. With MBBs, the mortgages remain on the FI's balance sheet, and funds used to pay the MBB holders' coupons and principal repayments may or may not come from the collateralized mortgages.

other forms of asset securitization in improving the return–risk trade-off for FIs. It describes the process associated with loan sales and the major forms, or vehicles, of asset securitization and analyzes their unique characteristics. Table 24–1 presents a definition of the loan sale and securitization mechanisms that this chapter discusses.

LOAN SALES

loan sales and securitization

The packaging and selling of loans and other assets backed by securities issued by an FI.

correspondent banking

A relationship between a small bank and a large bank in which the large bank provides a number of deposit, lending, and other services.

highly leveraged transaction (HLT) loan

A loan that finances a merger and acquisition; a leveraged buyout results in a high leverage ratio for the borrower.

FIs have sold loans among themselves for more than 100 years. In fact, a large part of **correspondent banking** involves small FIs making loans that are too big for them to hold on their balance sheets—either for lending concentration risk or capital adequacy reasons—and selling (or syndicating) parts of these loans to large FIs with whom they have had a long-term deposit-lending correspondent relationship. In turn, the large banks often sell (or syndicate) parts of their loans called *participations* to smaller FIs. The syndicated loan market—that is, the market for buying and selling loans once they have been originated—can be segmented into three categories: market makers, active traders, and occasional sellers/investors. Market makers are generally the large commercial banks (e.g., J.P. Morgan Chase) and investment banks (e.g., Morgan Stanley), which commit capital to create liquidity and take outright positions in the markets. Institutions that actively engage in primary loan origination have an advantage in trading on the secondary market, mainly because of their acquired skill in accessing and understanding loan documentation. Active traders are mainly investment banks, commercial banks, and vulture funds (see below). Other financial institutions such as insurance companies also trade but to a lesser extent. Occasional participants are either sellers of loans (who seek to remove loans from their balance sheets to meet regulatory constraints or to manage their exposures) or buyers of loans (who seek exposure to sectors or countries, especially when they do not have the critical size to do so in the primary loan markets).[1]

Even though this market has existed for many years, it grew slowly until the early 1980s when it entered a period of spectacular growth, largely due to expansion in **highly leveraged transaction (HLT) loans** to finance leveraged buyouts (LBOs) and mergers and

1. See E. I. Altman, A. Gande, and A. Saunders, "International Efficiency of Loans versus Bonds: Evidence from Secondary Market Prices," New York University Working Paper, 2004.

FIGURE 24–1 Recent Trends in the Loan Sales Market

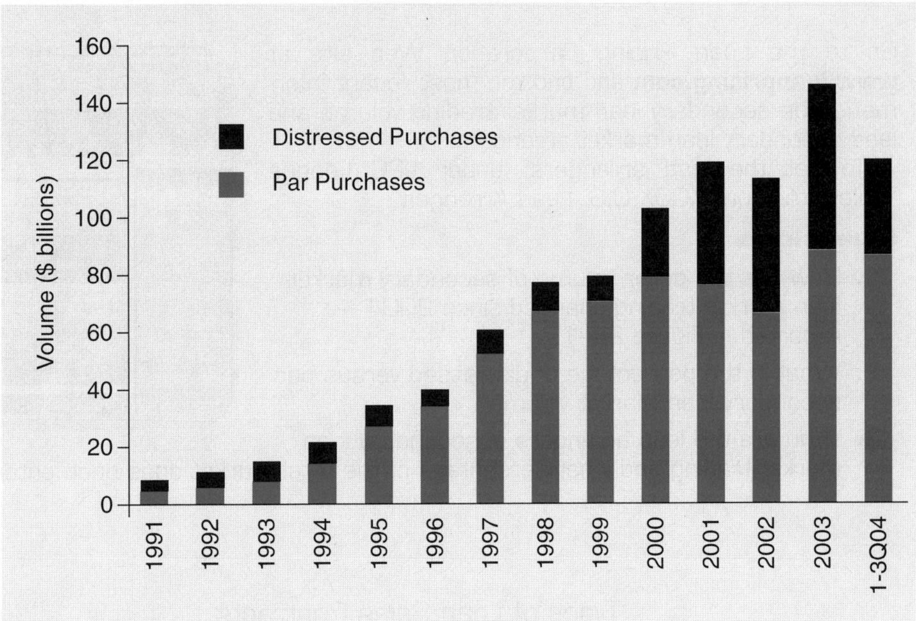

Source: Loan Pricing Corporation Web site, April 2005. **www.loanpricing.com**

acquisitions (M&As). Specifically, the volume of loans sold by U.S. banks increased from less than $20 billion in 1980 to $285 billion in 1989. In the early 1990s, the volume of loan sales declined almost as dramatically, along with the decline in LBO and M&A activity. In 1991, the volume of loan sales had fallen to approximately $10 billion. In the late 1990s, the volume of loan sales expanded again, partly due to an expanding economy and a resurgency in M&As.[2] For example the loan market research firm Loan Pricing Corporation reported secondary trading volume in 1999 was more than $79 billion. Loan sales continued to grow to almost $120 billion in the early 2000s as FIs sold distressed loans (loans trading below 90 cents on the dollar). Triggered by an economic slowdown, distressed loan sales jumped from 11 percent of total loan sales in 1999 to 36 percent in 2001, and 42 percent in 2002. As the U.S. economy improved in the first decade of the 2000s, the percentage of distressed loan sales fell. In the first three quarters of 2004 distressed loans were just 28 percent of total loan sales. Figure 24–1 shows recent trends in the loan sales market.

loan sale

Sale of loan originated by a bank with or without recourse to an outside buyer.

recourse

The ability of a loan buyer to sell the loan back to the originator should it go bad.

A **loan sale** occurs when an FI originates a loan and sells it with or without recourse to an outside buyer. If the loan is sold without recourse, the FI not only removes it from its balance sheet (purchasing new investments with the freed-up funds) but also has no explicit liability if the loan eventually goes bad. The loan buyer (not the FI that originated the loan) bears all the credit risk. If, however, the loan is sold with **recourse,** under certain conditions the buyer can put the loan back to the selling FI; therefore, the FI retains a contingent (credit risk) liability. As an example, Green Point Financial Corp. issued in excess of $19.4 billion in mortgage loans in the first half of 2004. Over the same period, Green Point had sold over $14.6 billion of these loans to secondary market investors and recorded revenues of $295 million for the period from its mortgage division. In practice, most loan sales are without recourse because a loan sale is technically removed from the balance sheet only when the buyer has no future credit risk claim on the FI. Loan sales usually involve no creation of new types of securities, such as those described later in the chapter when we consider the securitization activities of FIs.

2. Also, the composition of loan sales is changing, with increasing amounts of commercial real estate loans being sold.

SEARCH THE SITE

Go to the Loan Pricing Corporation Web site at **www.loanpricing.com** and find the most recent information on secondary loan market trading volume and lead secondary loan market arrangers.

To get the lead arrangers, under LPC League Tables, click on "XQOX U.S. Lead Arranger."

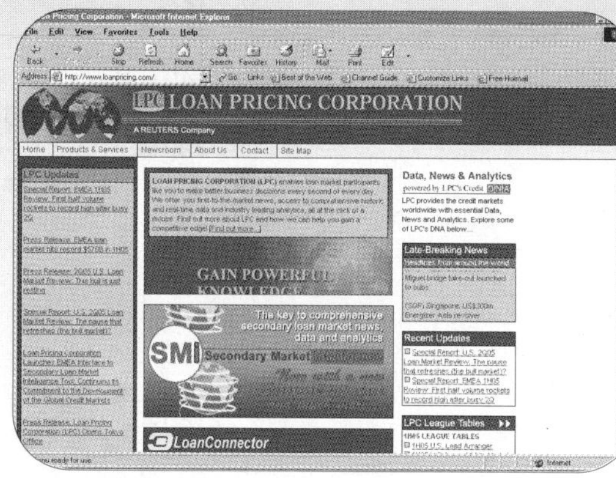

Questions

1. How has the dollar volume of secondary market loan market trading changed since 2004 reported in Figure 24–1?
2. What is the percentage of distressed versus par secondary loan market volume?
3. Who are the lead arrangers of secondary loan market trading and what percentage of the total market does each entail?

Types of Loan Sales Contracts

The two basic types of loan sales contracts are *participations* and *assignments*. Currently, assignments represent the bulk of loan sales.

participation in a loan

The act of buying a share in a loan syndication with limited contractual control and rights over the borrower.

Participations. The unique characteristics of **participations in loans** are:

- The holder (buyer) is not a party to the underlying (primary) credit agreement, so that the initial contract between loan seller (which may be a syndicate of FIs) and borrower remains in place after the sale.
- The loan buyer can exercise only partial control over changes in the loan contract's terms. The holder can vote on only material changes to the loan contract, such as the interest rate or collateral backing.

The economic implication of these characteristics is that the buyer of the loan participation has a double risk exposure—to the borrower as well as to the original lender (or lenders). Specifically, if the selling FI fails, the loan participation bought by an outside party may be characterized as an unsecured obligation of the FI rather than a true sale. Alternatively, the borrowers' claims against a failed selling FI may be netted against its loans, reducing the amount of loans outstanding and adversely impacting the buyer of a participation in those loans. As a result of these exposures, the buyer bears a double monitoring cost as well.

assignment

The purchase of a share in a loan syndication with some contractual control and rights over the borrower.

Assignments. Because of the monitoring costs and the risks involved in participations, loans are sold on an assignment basis in more than 90 percent of the cases on the U.S. domestic market. The key features of an **assignment** are:

- All ownership rights are transferred on sale, meaning that the loan buyer holds a direct claim on the borrower.
- U.S. domestic loans are normally transferred with a Uniform Commercial Code filing, meaning there is documentation of a change of ownership in which the buyer has first claim on the borrower's assets in the event of bankruptcy.

Although ownership rights are generally much clearer in a loan sale by assignment, contractual terms frequently limit the seller's (e.g., an FI's) scope regarding to whom the loan can be sold. A loan sale by assignment means the borrower (e.g., IBM) must negotiate any changes on the loan with an FI it may have had no prior relationship with or knowledge of. To protect the borrower (IBM), the original loan contract may require either the FI agent or the borrower (IBM) to agree to the sale.[3] The loan contract may also restrict the sale to a certain class of institutions, such as those that meet certain net worth/net asset size conditions (say, Allstate Insurance Company). Currently, the trend appears to be toward originating loan contracts with very limited assignment restrictions. This is true in both the U.S. domestic and less developed country (LDC) loan sales markets. The most tradable loans are those that can be assigned without buyer restrictions. In evaluating ownership rights, the buyer of the loan (Allstate) also needs to verify the original loan contract and to establish the full implications of the purchase regarding the buyer's (Allstate's) rights to collateral if the borrower (IBM) defaults. Because of these contractual problems, trading frictions, and costs, some loan sales take as long as three months to complete, although for most loan sales the developing market standard is that loan sales should be completed within 10 days.

2 The Loan Sale Market

The U.S. loan sale market has three segments; two involve sales and trading of domestic loans, and the third involves sales of **LDC** (less developed country) **loans** (loans that have been made to certain Asian, African, and Latin American countries).

LDC loan

Loans made to a less developed country (LDC).

Traditional Short-Term Segment. In the traditional short-term segment of the market, FIs sell loans with short maturities, often one to three months. This market has characteristics similar to that of the market for commercial paper (see Chapter 5) in that loan sales have similar maturities and issue sizes. Loan sales, however, usually have yields that are 1 to 10 basis points above those of commercial paper of a similar rating and, unlike commercial paper, are secured by the assets of the borrowing firm. The key characteristics of the loans bought and sold in the short-term loan sale market are similar to those of commercial paper. That is:

- The loans are secured by assets of the borrowing firm or other external guarantors.
- They have been made to investment-grade borrowers or better.
- They are issued for a short term (90 days or less).
- They are sold in units of $1 million and up.
- Loan rates are closely tied to the commercial paper rate.

Traditional short-term loan sales dominated the market until 1984 and the emergence of the HLT and LDC loan markets. The growth of the commercial paper market (see Chapter 5) has also reduced the importance of this market segment.

HLT Loan Sales. With the increase in M&As and LBOs financed via HLTs, especially from 1985 to 1989, a new segment in the loan sales market, HLT loan sales or highly leveraged loan market, appeared.[4] One measure of the increase in HLTs is that between January 1987 and September 1994, the loan market research firm Loan Pricing Corporation reported 4,122 M&A deals with a combined dollar amount in new-issue HLT loans estimated at $593.5 billion. HLT loans mainly differ according to whether they are nondistressed (bid price exceeds 90 cents per $1 of loans) or distressed (bid price is less than 90 cents per $1 of loans or the borrower is in default).

www.loanpricing.com

Virtually all HLT loans have the following characteristics:

- They are secured by assets of the borrowing firm (usually given senior security status).
- They have long maturity (often three- to six-year maturities).
- They have floating rates tied to the London Interbank Offered Rate (LIBOR), the prime rate, or a CD rate (HLT rates are normally 200–275 basis points above these rates).
- They have strong covenant protection.

3. An FI agent is an FI that distributes interest and principal payments to lenders in loan syndications with multiple lenders.

4. What constitutes an HLT loan has often caused dispute. In October 1989, however, the three U.S. federal bank regulators adopted a definition of an HLT as a loan that (1) involves a buyout, acquisition, or recapitalization and (2) either doubles the company's liabilities and results in a leverage ratio higher than 50 percent, results in a leverage ratio higher than 75 percent, or is designated as an HLT by a syndication agent.

financial distress

The state when a borrower is unable to meet a payment obligation to lenders and other creditors.

vulture fund

A specialized fund that invests in distressed loans.

Nevertheless, HLTs tend to be quite heterogeneous with respect to the size of the issue, the interest payment date, interest indexing, and prepayment features. After origination, some HLT borrowers such as Macy's and El Paso Electric suffered periods of **financial distress**[5] in that they were unable to make timely payments on many of the bonds they had issued and loans they had outstanding. As a result, a distinction between the market for distressed and nondistressed HLTs is usually made.

The Buyers. Of the wide array of potential buyers, some are interested in only a certain segment of the market for regulatory and strategic reasons. In particular, an increasingly specialized group of buyers of distressed HLT loans includes investment banks and **vulture funds.** For the nondistressed HLT market and the traditional U.S. domestic loan sales market, the five major buyers are other domestic banks, foreign banks, insurance companies and pension funds, closed-end bank loan mutual funds, and nonfinancial corporations.

Investment Banks. Investment banks are predominantly buyers of HLT loans because (1) analysis of these loans[6] utilizes investment skills similar to those required for junk bond trading and (2) investment banks are often closely associated with the HLT borrower in underwriting the original junk bond/HLT deals. As such, large investment banks—for example, Merrill Lynch and Goldman Sachs—are relatively more informed agents in this market, either by acting as market makers or in taking short-term positions on movements in the market prices of these loans.

Vulture Funds. Vulture funds are specialized investment funds established to invest in distressed loans, often with an agenda that does not include helping the distressed firm survive. These investments can be active, especially for those seeking to use the loans purchased for bargaining in a restructuring deal, which generates restructuring returns that strongly favor the loan purchaser. Alternatively, such loans may be held as passive investments or high-yield securities in a well-diversified portfolio of distressed securities. Investment banks, in fact, manage many vulture funds. Most secondary market trading in U.S. loan sales occurs in this segment of the market.

The common perception of vulture funds is that after picking up distressed loans at a discount, they force firms to restructure or are quick to realize the break-up value of the firm—for example, turning a 50 cent on the dollar investment into a 70 cent on the dollar investment (i.e., 20 cents on the dollar profit). Thus, a vulture fund's reputation is often not a congenial one. A possible reason for this adverse reputation is that while banks are looking for a return of loan principal in a restructuring, vulture funds are looking for a return on capital invested. That is, vulture funds are transaction driven, not relationship based. Unlike banks, vulture funds are rarely interested in making decisions based on developing and maintaining long-term relationships with the corporation in question. Nevertheless, they provide an exit strategy for investors and creditors, and they enable assets to be liquidated in an orderly manner.

Other Domestic Banks. Interbank loan sales are at the core of the traditional market and historically have revolved around correspondent banking and regional banking/branching restrictions. Restrictions on nationwide banking in the past led banks to originate regionally undiversified and borrower-undiversified loan portfolios. Small banks often sold loan participations to their large correspondents to improve regional/borrower diversification and to avoid regulatory imposed single-borrower loan concentration ceilings. (A loan to a single borrower should not exceed 10 percent of a bank's capital.) This arrangement also worked in the other direction, with the larger banks selling participations to smaller banks.

The traditional interbank market, however, has been shrinking as a result of three factors. First, the traditional correspondent banking relationship is breaking down as markets

5. Thus, an HLT may be distressed or nondistressed.

6. Junk bonds are noninvestment-grade bonds (i.e., those issued with a credit rating of BB or below by Standard & Poor's or Bal or below by Moody's)—see Chapter 6.

become more competitive. Second, concerns about counterparty risk and moral hazard have increased. In particular, moral hazard is the risk that the selling bank will seek to offload its "bad" loans (via loan sales) keeping the "good" loans in its portfolio. An extreme example of this is Penn Square, a small Texas bank, which sold many risky (energy-based) loans to its larger correspondent bank, Continental Illinois, in the early 1980s. Not only did Penn Square fail, but in 1984 Continental Illinois, then the eighth largest bank in the United States, also failed as a result of losses on these loans. Third, the barriers to nationwide banking are being eroded, particularly following the full implementation of interstate banking in 1997 (after the passage of the Riegle-Neal Interstate Banking and Branching Efficiency Act in 1994) and the (continuing) contraction in the number of small banks (see Chapter 13).

Foreign Banks. Foreign banks remain the dominant buyer of domestic U.S. loans. Because of the cost of branching, the loan sales market allows foreign banks to achieve a well-diversified domestic U.S. loan portfolio without developing a nationwide banking network. However, renewed interest in asset **downsizing,** especially among Japanese banks, has caused this source of demand to contract.

downsizing

Shrinking an FI's asset size.

Insurance Companies and Pension Funds. Subject to meeting liquidity and credit quality restrictions (such as buying only BBB-rated borrowers or above), insurance companies (such as Aetna) and pension funds are important buyers of long-term loans.

Closed-End Bank Loan Mutual Funds. First established in 1988, these leveraged mutual funds, such as Merrill Lynch Prime Fund, invest in domestic U.S. bank loans. Although they could purchase loans in the loan sales market, the largest funds have moved into primary loan syndications as well because of the attractive fee income available. These mutual funds increasingly participate in funding loans originated by commercial banks. Indeed, some money center banks, such as J.P. Morgan Chase, have actively encouraged closed-end fund participation in primary loan syndications.

Nonfinancial Corporations. Some corporations—primarily the financial services arms of the very largest U.S. and European companies (e.g., GE Capital and ITT Finance)—buy loans. This activity amounts to no more than 5 percent of total U.S. domestic loan sales.

The Sellers. The sellers of domestic loans and HLT loans are major money center banks, small regional or community banks, foreign banks, and investment banks.

Major Money Center Banks. The largest money center banks have dominated loan selling. In recent years, market concentration in loan selling has been accentuated by the increase in HLTs (and the important role that major money center banks have played in originating loans in HLT deals) as well as growth in real estate loan sales.

Small Regional or Community Banks. As mentioned earlier, small banks sell loans and loan participations to larger FIs for diversification and regulatory purposes. Although they are not a major player in the loan sales market, small banks have found loan sales to be essential for diversifying their credit risk.

Foreign Banks. To the extent that foreign banks are sellers rather than buyers of loans, these loans come from branch networks such as the Japanese-owned banks in California or through selling loans originated in their home country in U.S. loan sales markets.

Investment Banks. Investment banks such as Salomon Smith Barney (a subsidiary of Citigroup) act as loan sellers either as part of their loan origination activities—since the passage of the Financial Services Modernization Act in 1999—or as active traders in the market. Again, these loan sales are generally confined to large HLT transactions.

Secondary Market for Less Developed Country Debt

Since the mid-1980s, a secondary market for trading less developed country (LDC) debt has developed among large commercial and investment banks in New York and London. The volume of trading grew dramatically from around $2 billion per year in 1984 to almost $6 trillion in 1997 (trading in Brazilian debt alone accounted for $1.44 trillion). Trading declined to $4.2 billion in 1998 after the Russian debt defaults and again in 1999 after Ecuador's failure to pay interest on its Brady bonds (see below). The early 2000s were characterized by increasing trading activity and growing investor confidence in emerging market debt, sparked in large part by Brazil's rapid economic recovery, Mexico's upgraded credit rating to investment grade, and Russia's successful debt restructuring. Like domestic loan sales, the removal of LDC loans from the balance sheet allows an FI to free up assets for other investments. Further, being able to sell these loans—even if at a price below the face value of the original loan—may signify that the FI's balance sheet is sufficiently strong to bear the loss. In fact, a number of studies have found that announcements of FIs writing down the value of LDC loans—prior to their charge-off and sale—has a positive effect on FI stock prices.

The major cost of LDC loan sales is the loss itself (the tax-adjusted difference between the face value of the loan and its market value at the time of the sale). In addition, many FIs engaged in LDC loan sales in 1987 and 1988 after taking big loan-loss reserve additions in May and June 1987. Beginning in 1988, and in particular in the period 1991–1993, the secondary market loan prices of many LDC countries rose in value. However, an economic crisis in southeast Asia, South America, and Russia in the late 1990s sent prices back down. This suggests an additional cost related to loan sales—the optimal timing of such sales (the point when FIs can minimize losses from such sales).

Trading in LDC loans often takes place in the high-yield (or junk bond) departments of participating FIs. These reflect programs in the early to mid-1990s under which U.S. and other FIs exchanged their dollar loans for dollar bonds issued by the relevant countries. These bonds have a much longer maturity than that promised on the original loans and a lower promised original coupon (yield) than the interest rate on the original loan. These loans-for-bond restructuring programs, also called *debt-for-debt swaps*, were developed under the auspices of the U.S. Treasury's Brady Plan and other international organizations such as the IMF. Once FIs swapped loans for bonds, they could sell them in the secondary market. By converting loans into **Brady bonds** (a bond that is swapped for an outstanding loan to an LDC—see Chapter 6), an FI's ownership of an LDC's assets becomes more liquid[7] because these bonds were usually partially collateralized (backed) by U.S. governments securities such as U.S. Treasury bonds. These bond-for-loan swap programs sought to restore LDCs' creditworthiness and thus the value of FI holdings of such debt by creating longer-term, lower fixed-interest but more liquid securities in place of shorter-term, floating-rate loans. In recent years, many of the more successful emerging market LDCs have repurchased collateralized Brady bonds and replaced them with dollar bonds with no explicit collateral backing—as a result, the price of these bonds reflects the creditworthiness of the issuing country and spreads over U.S. Treasury bonds, for countries like Argentina and Brazil, have often risen to well over 15 and 23 percent, respectively.

Brady bond

A bond that is swapped for an outstanding loan to an LDC.

3 Factors Encouraging Future Loan Sales Growth

The introduction to this chapter stated that one reason that FIs sell loans is to manage their credit risk better. Loan sales remove assets (and credit risk) from the balance

7. A Brady bond is usually created on an interest rate rollover date. On that date, floating-rate loans are usually converted into fixed-rate coupon bonds on the books of an agent bank. The agent bank is the bank that keeps the records of loan ownership and distributed interest payments made by the LDC to individual bank creditors. Once converted, the bonds can start trading.

DO YOU UNDERSTAND?

1. What the reasons are for the rapid growth and subsequent decline in loan sales over the last two decades?
2. Which loans should have the highest yields—loans sold with recourse or loans sold without recourse?
3. What the two basic types of loan sale contracts by which loans can be transferred between seller and buyer are? Describe each.
4. What institutions are the major buyers in the traditional U.S. domestic loan sales market? What institutions are the major sellers in this market?
5. What some of the economic and regulatory reasons are that FIs choose to sell loans?
6. What some of the factors are that will likely encourage loan sales growth in the future?
7. What some of the factors are that will likely deter the growth of the loan sales market in the future?

sheet[8] and allow an FI to achieve better asset diversification. Other than credit risk management, however, FIs are encouraged to sell loans for a number of other economic and regulatory reasons.

Fee Income. An FI can often report any fee income earned from originating loans as current income, but interest earned on direct lending can be accrued (as income) only over time (see Chapter 12). As a result, originating and quickly selling loans can boost an FI's reported income under current accounting rules.

Liquidity Risk. In addition to credit risk, holding loans on the balance sheet can increase the overall illiquidity of an FI's assets. This illiquidity is a problem because FI liabilities tend to be highly liquid. Asset illiquidity can expose the FI to harmful liquidity problems when depositors unexpectedly withdraw their deposits. To mitigate a liquidity problem, an FI's management can sell some of its loans to outside investors (see Chapter 21). Thus, the FI loan market has created a secondary market that has significantly reduced the illiquidity of loans held as assets on the balance sheet.

Capital Costs. The capital adequacy requirements imposed on FIs are a burden as long as required capital exceeds the amount the FI believes to be privately beneficial. Thus, FIs struggling to meet a required capital-to-assets (K/A) ratio can boost this ratio by reducing assets (A) rather than boosting capital (K)—see Chapter 13. One way to downsize or reduce A and boost the K/A ratio is through loan sales.

Reserve Requirements. Regulatory requirements, such as noninterest-bearing reserves that a bank must hold at the central bank, represent a form of tax that adds to the cost of funding the loan portfolio. Regulatory taxes such as reserve requirements create an incentive for banks to remove loans from the balance sheet by selling them without recourse to outside parties.[9] Such removal allows banks to shrink both their assets and deposits and, thus, the amount of reserves they have to hold against their deposits.

Factors Deterring Future Loan Sales Growth

3

The loan sales market has experienced a number of up-and-down phases in recent years. Notwithstanding the value of loan sales as a credit risk management tool and other reasons described above, a number of factors may deter the market's growth and development in the future. We discuss these next.

Access to the Commercial Paper Market. Since 1987, large banks have enjoyed much greater powers to underwrite commercial paper directly, without experiencing legal challenges by the securities industry claiming that underwriting by banks is contrary to the Glass-Steagall Act. These underwriting powers were expanded in 1999 with the passage of the Financial Services Modernization Act, which eliminated Glass-Steagall restrictions on underwriting activities such as commercial paper underwriting (see Chapter 13). This means that the need to underwrite or sell short-term bank loans as an imperfect substitute for commercial paper underwriting has now become much less important. In addition, more and more smaller middle markets are gaining direct access to the commercial paper market. As a result, such firms have less need to rely on bank loans to finance their short-term expenditures, with fewer loan originations generally resulting in fewer loans being sold.

8. However, if FIs primarily sell high-quality loans, the average quality of the remaining loans may actually decrease.

9. Under current reserve requirement regulations (Regulation D, amended May 1986), bank loan sales with recourse are regarded as a liability and hence are subject to reserve requirements. The reservability of loan sales extends to a bank issuing a credit guarantee and a recourse provision. Loans sold without recourse (or credit guarantees by the selling bank) are free of reserve requirements. With the elimination of reserve requirements on nontransaction accounts and the lowering of reserve requirements on transaction accounts in 1991, the reserve tax effect is likely to become a less important feature driving bank loan sales (as well as the recourse/nonrecourse mix) in the future.

fraudulent conveyance

A transaction such as a sale of securities or transference of assets to a particular party that is determined to be illegal.

Legal Concerns. A number of legal concerns are currently hampering the loan sale market's growth, especially for distressed loans. In particular, although FIs are normally secured creditors, other creditors may attack this status through **fraudulent conveyance** proceedings if the borrowing firm enters bankruptcy. Fraudulent conveyance is any transfer of assets (such as a loan sale) at less than fair value made by a firm while it is insolvent. Fraudulent conveyance prevents an insolvent firm from giving away its assets or selling them at unreasonably low prices and thereby depriving its remaining creditors of fair treatment on liquidation or bankruptcy. For example, fraudulent conveyance proceedings have been brought against the secured lenders to firms such as Revco, Circle K, Allied Stores, and RJR Nabisco. In these cases, the sale of loans to a particular party were found to be illegal. As discussed above, contractual terms in loan contracts can limit the loan originator's scope regarding to whom the loan can be sold. Fraudulent conveyance proceedings are challenges of loan sales as defined in the original loan contract. Such lawsuits represent one of the factors that have slowed the growth of the distressed loan market.

LOAN SECURITIZATION

4

Loan securitization is useful in improving the risk–return trade-off for FIs. This section discusses the three major forms of securitization—the pass-through security, collateralized mortgage obligation (CMO), and mortgage-backed bonds—and analyzes their unique characteristics. Although depository institutions mainly undertake loan securitization, the insurance industry has also entered into this area. In addition, although all three forms of securitization originated in the real estate lending market, these techniques are currently being applied to loans other than mortgages—for example, credit card loans, auto loans, student loans, and commercial and industrial (C&I) loans. The Bond Market Association, a bond industry trade group representing over 260 member and associate securities firms, banks, and government agencies, reported that over $2,131.9 billion of mortgage-backed securities were issued in 2003 and $1,019.1 billion were issued in 2004.

www.bondmarkets.com

Pass-Through Security

FIs frequently pool the mortgages and other loans they originate and offer investors an interest in the pool in the form of *pass-through certificates* or *securities*. Pass-through mortgage securities "pass through" promised payments by households of principal and interest on pools of mortgages created by financial institutions to secondary market investors (mortgage-backed security bond holders) holding an interest in these pools. We illustrate this process in Figure 24–2. After a financial institution accepts mortgages (step 1 in Figure 24–2),

FIGURE 24–2 Pass-Through Mortgage Security

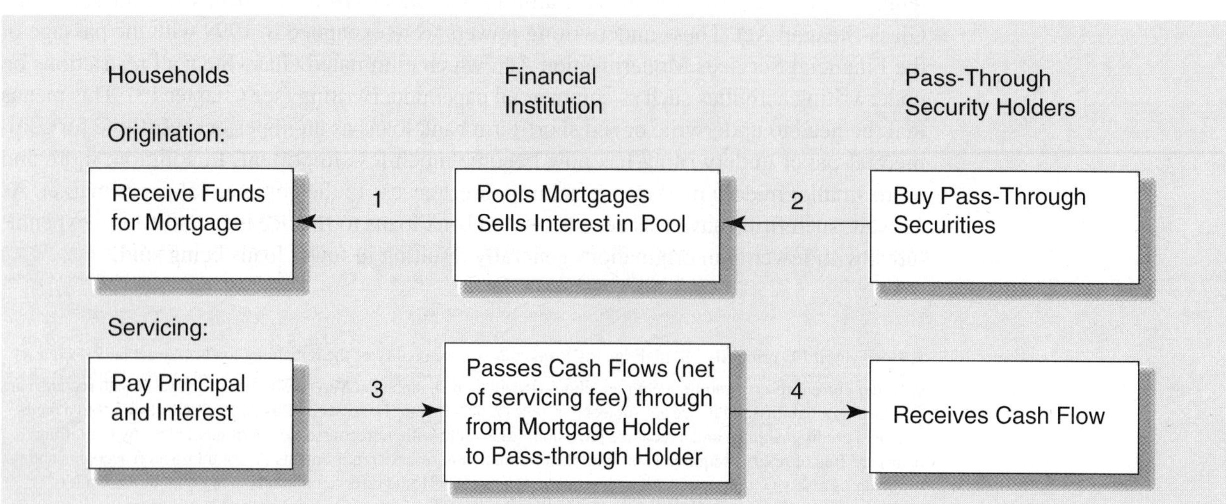

it pools them and sells interests in these pools to pass-through security holders (step 2 in Figure 24–2). Each pass-through mortgage security represents a fractional ownership share in a mortgage pool. Thus, a 1 percent owner of a pass-through mortgage security issue is entitled to a 1 percent share of the principal and interest payments made over the life of the mortgages underlying the pool of securities. The originating financial institutions (e.g., bank or mortgage company) or a third-party servicer receives principal and interest payments from the mortgage holder (step 3 in Figure 24–2) and passes these payments (minus a servicing fee) through to the pass-through security holders (step 4).

Although many different types of loans (and other assets) on FIs' balance sheets are currently being securitized as pass-throughs, the original use of this type of securitization is a result of government-sponsored programs to enhance the liquidity of the residential mortgage market. These programs indirectly subsidize the growth of home ownership in the United States. We begin by analyzing the government-sponsored securitization of residential mortgage loans. Three government agencies or government-sponsored enterprises (introduced in Chapter 7) are directly involved in the creation of mortgage-backed pass-through securities. Informally, they are known as Ginnie Mae (GNMA), Fannie Mae (FNMA), and Freddie Mac (FHLMC).

www.ginniemae.gov

www.fanniemae.com

www.freddiemac.com

The Incentives and Mechanics of Pass-Through Security Creation. In beginning to analyze the securitization process, we trace the mechanics of a mortgage pool securitization to provide insights into the return–risk benefits of this process to the mortgage-originating FI, as well as the attractiveness of these securities to investors. Given that more than $3.6 trillion of mortgage-backed securities are outstanding—a large proportion sponsored by GNMA—we analyze the creation of a GNMA pass-through security next.[10]

Suppose that an FI has just originated 1,000 new residential mortgages in its local area. The average size of each mortgage is $100,000. Thus, the total size of the new mortgage pool is:

$$1{,}000 \times \$100{,}000 = \$100 \text{ million}$$

Each mortgage, because of its small size, receives credit risk insurance protection from the FHA. This insurance costs a small fee to the originating FI. In addition, each of these new mortgages has an initial stated maturity of 30 years and a mortgage rate—often called the *mortgage coupon*—of 9 percent per year. Suppose that the FI originating these loans relies mostly on liabilities such as demand deposits as well as its own capital or equity to finance its assets. Under current capital adequacy requirements, each $1 of new residential mortgage loans must be backed by some capital. Since residential mortgages fall into the 50 percent risk weight category under the risk-based capital standards and the risk-based capital requirement is 8 percent (see Chapter 13), the FI capital needed to back the $100 million mortgage portfolio is:

$$\text{Capital requirement} = \$100 \text{ million} \times .5 \times .08 = \$4 \text{ million}$$

We assume that the remaining $96 million needed to fund the mortgages comes from the issuance of demand deposits. Current regulations require that for every dollar of demand deposits held by the FI, a 10 percent cash reserve has to be held at the Federal Reserve Bank or in the vault (see Chapter 13). Assuming that the FI funds the cash reserves on the asset side of the balance sheet with demand deposits, the bank must issue $106.67 ($96/(1 − .1)) in demand deposits (i.e., $96 to fund mortgages and $10.67 to fund the required cash reserves on these demand deposits). The reserve requirement on demand deposits is essentially an additional tax, over and above the capital requirement, on funding the FI's residential mortgage portfolio. Note that since a 0 percent reserve requirement currently exists on CDs and time deposits, the FI needs to raise fewer funds if it uses CDs to fund its mortgage portfolio.

Given these considerations, the FI's initial postmortgage balance sheet may look like the one in Table 24–2. In addition to the capital and reserve requirement taxes, the FI also

10. At the end of the first quarter 2004, outstanding mortgage pools were $3.547 trillion, with GNMA pools amounting to $442.3 billion; FNMA, $1,895.8 billion; and FHLMC, $1,209.2 billion.

TABLE 24–2 FI Balance Sheet
(in millions of dollars)

Assets		Liabilities	
Cash reserves	$ 10.67	Demand deposits	$106.67
Long-term mortgages	100.00	Capital	4.00
	$110.67		$110.67

must pay an annual insurance premium to the FDIC based on the size of its deposits (see Chapter 13). Assuming a deposit insurance premium of 27 basis points,[11] the fee would be:

$$\$106.67 \text{ million} \times .0027 = \$288{,}000$$

Although the FI is earning a 9 percent mortgage coupon on its mortgage portfolio, it is facing three levels of regulatory taxes:

www.federalreserve.gov

www.fdic.gov

1. Capital requirements
2. Reserve requirements
3. FDIC insurance premiums

Thus, one incentive to securitize is to reduce the regulatory "tax" burden on the FI to increase its after-tax return.

In addition to facing regulatory taxes on its residential mortgage portfolio earnings, the FI in Table 24–2 has two risk exposure problems:

1. *Interest Rate Risk Exposure.* The FI funds the 30-year mortgage portfolio from (short-term) demand deposits; thus, it has a maturity mismatch (see Chapters 19 and 22). This is true even if the mortgage assets have been funded with short-term CDs, time deposits, or other purchased funds.
2. *Liquidity Risk Exposure.* The FI is holding an illiquid asset portfolio of long-term mortgages and no excess reserves; as a result, it is exposed to the type of potential liquidity problems discussed in Chapter 21, including the risk of having to conduct mortgage asset "fire sales" to meet large unexpected demand deposit withdrawals.

One possible solution to these interest rate and liquidity risk problems is to lengthen the FI's on-balance-sheet liabilities by issuing longer-term deposits or other liability claims such as medium-term notes. Another solution is to engage in interest rate swaps to transform the FI's liabilities into those of a long-term, fixed-rate nature (see Chapter 23). These techniques, however, do not resolve the problem of regulatory taxes and the burden they impose on the FI's returns.

In contrast, creating GNMA pass-through securities can largely resolve the interest rate and liquidity risk problems on the one hand and reduce the burden of regulatory taxes on the other. This requires the FI to securitize the $100 million in residential mortgages by issuing GNMA pass-through securities. In our example, the FI can do this since each of the 1,000 underlying mortgages has FHA/VA mortgage insurance, the same stated mortgage maturity of 30 years, and coupons of 9 percent. Therefore, they are eligible for securitization under the GNMA program if the FI is an approved lender (which we assume it is—see Chapter 7).

The steps followed in this securitization process are summarized in Figure 24–3. The FI begins the securitization process by packaging the $100 million in mortgage loans. The packaged mortgage loans are removed from the balance sheet by placing them with a third-party trustee off the balance sheet. This third-party trustee may be another FI of high

11. As of 2005, this was the fee charged to the lowest-quality banks.

FIGURE 24–3 **Summary of a GNMA Pass-Through**

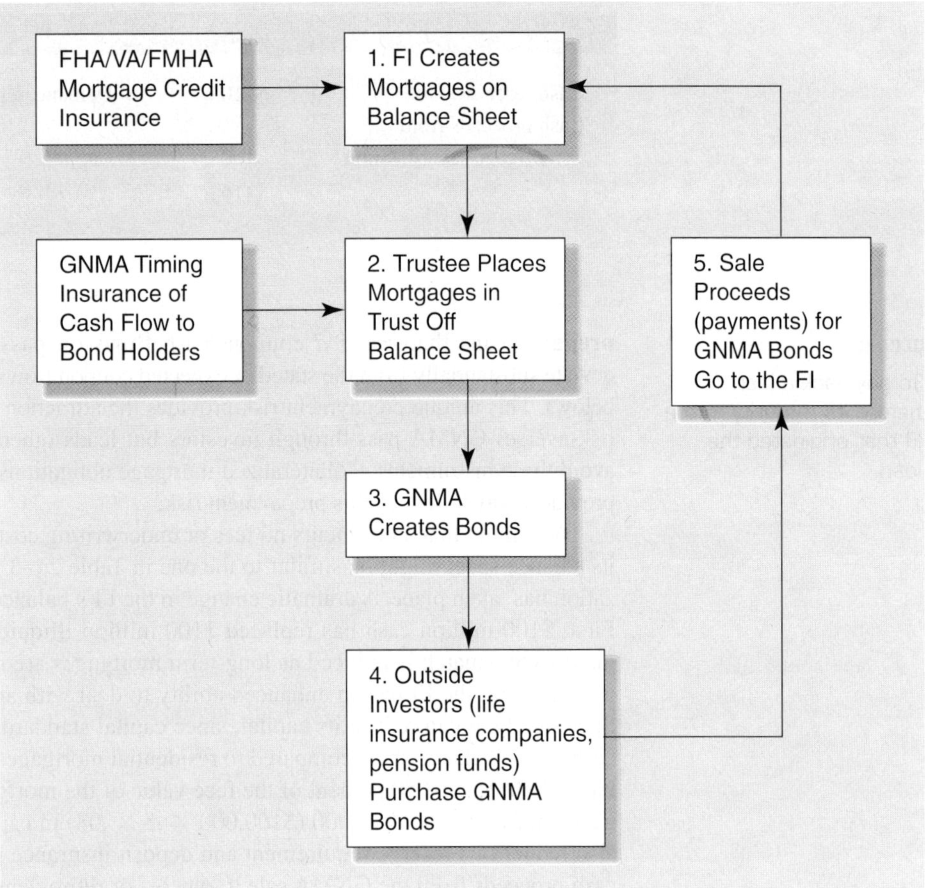

creditworthiness or a legal trustee. Next, the FI determines that (1) GNMA will guarantee, for a fee, the timing of interest and principal payments on the bonds issued to back the mortgage pool and (2) the FI itself will continue to service the pool of mortgages for a fee, even after they are placed in trust. Then, GMNA issues pass-through securities backed by the underlying $100 million pool of mortgages. These GNMA securities or pass-through bonds are sold to outside investors in the capital market, and the proceeds (net of any underwriting fees) go to the originating FI.

Prepayment Risk on GNMA Pass-Throughs. Mortgage loan securitization reduces (or removes) the regulatory tax burden, interest rate risk exposure, and liquidity risk exposure that FIs face when they issue mortgages. It does, however, introduce a new risk—so-called prepayment risk—to the pass-through security holder. Following the sale, each mortgagee makes a payment every month to the FI. The FI aggregates these payments and passes the funds through to GNMA bond investors via the trustee net of servicing fee and insurance fee deductions. Most fixed-rate mortgages are **fully amortized** over the mortgage's life. This means that so long as the mortgagee does not seek to prepay the mortgage early within the 30-year period, either to buy a new house or to refinance the mortgage should interest rates fall, bond holders can expect to receive a constant stream of payments each month analogous to the stream of income on fixed-coupon, fixed-income bonds. In reality, however, mortgagees do not act in such a predictable fashion. For a variety of reasons, they relocate or refinance their mortgages (especially when current mortgage rates are below mortgage coupon rates). This propensity to

full amortization

The equal, periodic repayment on a loan that reflects part interest and part principal over the life of the loan.

TABLE 24–3 The FI's Balance Sheet Postsecuritization
(in millions of dollars)

Assets		Liabilities	
Cash reserves	$ 10.67	Demand deposits	$106.67
Cash proceeds from mortgage securitization	100.00	Capital	4.00
	$110.67		$110.67

prepay
To pay back a loan before its maturity to the FI that originated the loan.

prepay means that *realized* coupons/cash flows on pass-through securities can often deviate substantially from the stated or expected coupon flows in a no-prepayment world (see below). This unique prepayment risk provides the attraction of pass-throughs to some (less risk-averse) GNMA pass-through investors but leads other more risk-averse investors to avoid these instruments. Collateralized mortgage obligations, discussed in the next section, provide a way to reduce this prepayment risk.

Assuming that an FI incurs no fees or underwriting costs in the securitization process, its balance sheet might be similar to the one in Table 24–3 immediately after the securitization has taken place. A dramatic change in the FI's balance sheet exposure has occurred. First, $100 million cash has replaced $100 million illiquid mortgage loans. Second, the maturity mismatch is reduced as long-term mortgages are replaced by cash (a short-term asset). Third, the FI has an enhanced ability to deal with and reduce its regulatory taxes. Specifically, it can reduce its capital, since capital standards require none be held against cash on the balance sheet compared to residential mortgages, which require 8 percent capital be held against 50 percent of the face value of the mortgage (i.e., on a $100,000 mortgage, an FI must hold $4,000 ($100,000 × .5 × .08) in capital—see Chapter 13). The FI also reduces its reserve requirement and deposit insurance premiums if it uses part of the cash proceeds from the GNMA sale to pay off or retire demand deposits and downsize its balance sheet.

Of course, keeping an all- or highly liquid asset portfolio and/or downsizing is a way to reduce regulatory taxes, but these strategies are hardly likely to enhance an FI's profits. The real logic of securitization is that the FI can use cash proceeds from the mortgage/GNMA sale to create or originate new mortgages, which in turn can be securitized. In so doing, the FI is acting more as an asset (mortgage) broker than a traditional asset transformer, as we discussed in Chapter 1. The advantage of being an asset broker is that the FI profits from mortgage pool servicing fees plus up-front points and fees from mortgage origination. At the same time, the FI no longer must bear the illiquidity and maturity mismatch risks and regulatory taxes that arise when it acts as an asset transformer and holds mortgages to maturity on its balance sheet. Put more simply, the FI's profitability becomes more fee dependent than interest rate spread dependent.

Prepayment Risk on Pass-Through Securities. As we discussed above, the cash flows on the pass-through directly reflect the interest and principal cash flows on the underlying mortgages minus service and insurance fees. However, over time, mortgage rates change. As coupon rates on new mortgages fall, there is an increased incentive for individuals in the pool to pay off old, high-cost mortgages and refinance at lower rates. However, refinancing involves transaction costs and recontracting costs. As a result, mortgage rates may have to fall by some amount below the current coupon rate before there is a significant increase in prepayment in the pool. This was particularly evident from the early 2000s to the middle of the first decade as new residential mortgage rates fell to their lowest levels in 30 years. Figure 24–4 plots the prepayment frequency of a pool of mortgages in relation to the spread between the current mortgage coupon rate (Y) and the mortgage coupon rate (r)

FIGURE 24–4 The Prepayment Relationship

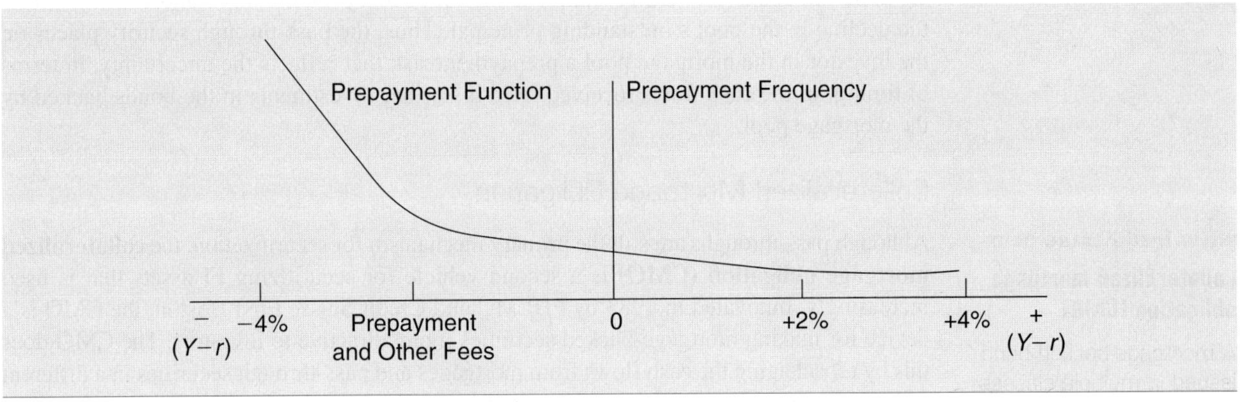

in the existing pool. Notice when the current mortgage rate (Y) is above the rate in the pool ($Y > r$), mortgage prepayments are small, reflecting monthly forced turnover as people have to relocate because of jobs, divorces, marriages, and other considerations. Even when the current mortgage rate falls below r, those remaining in the mortgage pool do not rush to prepay because up-front refinancing, contracting, and penalty costs are likely to outweigh any present value savings from lower mortgage rates. However, as current mortgage rates continue to fall, the propensity for mortgage holders to prepay increases significantly. Conceptually, mortgage holders have a very valuable call option on the mortgage when this option is in the money. That is, when current mortgage rates fall sufficiently lower so that the present value savings of refinancing outweigh the exercise price (the cost of prepayment penalties and other fees and costs), the mortgage will be called by the mortgage holder.

Since the FI has sold the mortgage cash flows to GNMA investors and must by law pass through all payments received (minus servicing and guaranty fees), investors' cash flows directly reflect the rate of prepayment. As a result, instead of receiving an equal monthly cash flow, *PMT*, as is done under a no-prepayment scenario, the actual cash flows (*CF*) received on these securities by investors fluctuate monthly with the rate of prepayments (see Figure 24–5).

In a no-prepayment world, each month's cash flows are the same: $PMT_1 = PMT_2 = \cdots = PMT_{360}$. However, in a world with prepayments each month's realized cash flows from the mortgage pool can differ. In Figure 24–5 we show a rising level of cash flows from month 2 onward peaking in month 60, reflecting the effects of early prepayments by some of the 1,000 mortgagees in the pool. This leaves less outstanding principal and interest to be paid in later years. For example, if 300 mortgagees fully prepay by month 60, only 700 mortgagees will remain in the pool at that date. The effect of prepayments is to lower dramatically the principal and interest cash flows received in the later months

FIGURE 24–5 The Effects of Prepayments on Pass-Through Bondholders' Cash Flows

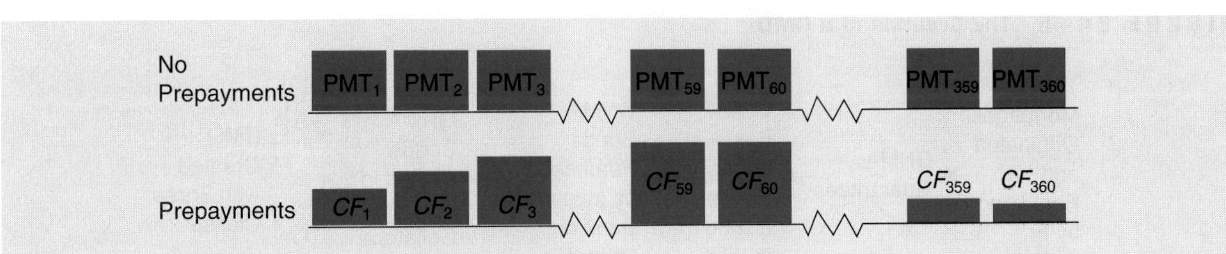

of the pool's life. For instance, in Figure 24–5, the cash flow received by GNMA bondholders in month 360 is very small relative to month 60 and even months 1 and 2. This reflects the decline in the pool's outstanding principal. Thus, the pass-through security places on the investor in the mortgage pool a prepayment risk that reflects the uncertainty, in terms of timing, of the cash flows received from his or her investments in the bonds backed by the mortgage pool.

Collateralized Mortgage Obligation

www.freddiemac.com

collateralized mortgage obligation (CMO)

A mortgage-backed bond issued in multiple classes or tranches.

Although pass-throughs are still the primary mechanism for securitization, the **collateralized mortgage obligation (CMO)** is a second vehicle for securitizing FI assets that is used increasingly. Innovated in 1983 by FHLMC and Credit Suisse First Boston, the CMO is a device for making mortgage-backed securities more attractive to investors. The CMO does this by repackaging the cash flows from mortgages and pass-through securities in a different fashion to attract different types of investors with different degrees of aversion to "prepayment risk." A pass-through security gives each investor a pro rata share of any promised and prepaid cash flows on a mortgage pool; the CMO is a multiclass pass-through with a number of different bond holder classes or tranches differentiated by the order in which each class is paid off. Unlike a pass-through, each bond holder class has a different guaranteed coupon just as a regular T-bond has, but more importantly, the allocation of early cash flows due to mortgage prepayments is such that at any one time, all prepayments go to retire the principal outstanding of only one class of bond holders at a time, leaving the other classes' prepayment protected for a period of time. Thus, a CMO serves as a way to distribute or reduce prepayment risk.

Creation of CMOs. CMOs can be created either by packaging and securitizing whole mortgage loans or, more usually, by placing existing pass-throughs in a trust off the balance sheet. The trust or third-party FI holds the GNMA pass-throughs as collateral against issues of new CMO securities. The trust issues these CMOs in three or more different classes. For example, the first CMO that Freddie Mac issued in 1983, secured by 20,000 conventional home mortgages worth $1 billion, had three classes: A, $215 million; B, $350 million; and C, $435 million. We show a three-class or tranche CMO in Figure 24–6.

Class A CMO holders will be the least prepayment protected since after paying any guaranteed coupons to the three classes of bondholders, A, B, and C, all remaining cash flows from the mortgage pool have to be used to repurchase the principal outstanding of class A bond holders. Thus, these bonds have the shortest average life with a minimum of prepayment protection. They are, therefore, of great interest to investors seeking short-duration mortgage-backed assets to reduce the duration of their mortgage-related asset portfolios. In recent years depository institutions have been large buyers of CMO class A securities.

After class A bonds have been retired, remaining cash flows (after coupon payments) are used to retire the bonds of class B. As a result, class B holders will have higher prepayment protection than class A and expected durations of five to seven years, depending on the level of interest rates. Pension funds and life insurance companies primarily purchase these bonds, although some depository institutions buy this bond class as well.

FIGURE 24–6 The Creation of a CMO

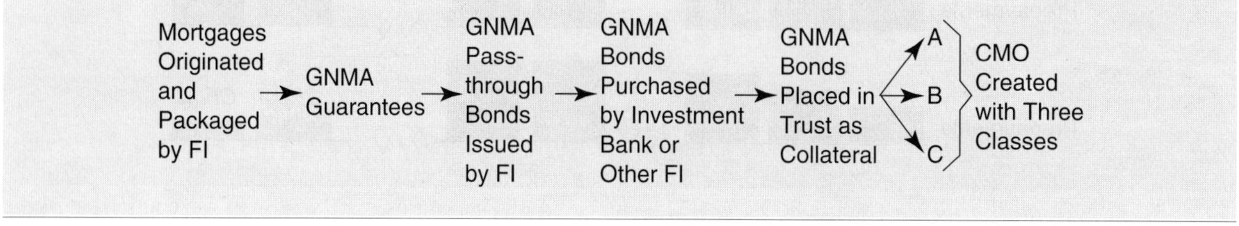

Class C holders will have the greatest prepayment protection. Because of their long expected duration, class C bonds are highly attractive to insurance companies and pension funds seeking long-term duration assets to match their long-term duration of liabilities. Indeed, because of their failures to offer prepayment protection, regular GNMA pass-throughs may not be very attractive to these institutions. Class C CMOs, with their high but imperfect degree of prepayment protection, may be of greater interest to the managers of these institutions.

EXAMPLE 24–1 Calculation of Payments to Three Classes of CMO Bond Holders

Suppose that an investment bank buys a $150 million issue of GNMAs and places them in trust as collateral. It then issues a CMO with the following three classes:

Class A: Annual fixed coupon 7 percent, class size $50 million.
Class B: Annual fixed coupon 8 percent, class size $50 million.
Class C: Annual fixed coupon 9 percent, class size $50 million.

Suppose that in month 1 the promised amortized cash flows (R) on the mortgages underlying the GNMA pass-through collateral are $1 million, but an additional $1.5 million cash flow results from early mortgage prepayments. Thus, in the first month, the cash flows available to pay promised coupons to the three classes of bond holders is:

$$R + \text{Prepayments} = \$1 \text{ million} + \$1.5 \text{ million} = \$2.5 \text{ million}$$

This cash flow is available to the trustee, who uses it in the following fashion:

1. **Coupon Payments.** Each month (or more commonly, each quarter or half-year), the trustee pays the guaranteed coupons to the three classes of bond holders at annualized coupon rates of 7 percent, 8 percent, and 9 percent, respectively. Given the stated principal of $50 million for each class, the class A (7 percent annual coupon) bond holders receive approximately $291,667 in coupon payments in month 1; the class B (8 percent annual coupon) receive approximately $333,333 in month 1; and the class C (9 percent annual coupon) receive approximately $375,000 in month 1. Thus, the total promised coupon payments to the three classes amounts to $1,000,000 (equal to R, the no-prepayment principal and interest cash flows in the GNMA pool).
2. **Principal Payments.** The trustee has $2.5 million available to pay as a result of promised mortgage payments plus early prepayments, but the total payment of coupon interest amounts to only $1 million. For legal and tax reasons, the remaining $1.5 million must be paid to the CMO bond holders. The unique feature of the CMO is that the trustee pays this remaining $1.5 million to class A bond holders only. This retires early some of these bond holders' principal outstanding. At the end of month 1, only $48.5 million ($50 million − $1.5 million) of class A bonds remains outstanding, compared to $50 million of class B and $50 million of class C. These payment flows are shown graphically in Figure 24–7.

Suppose that in month 2 the promised amortized cash flows (R) on the mortgages underlying the GNMA pass-through collateral are $991,250, but again an additional $1.5 million cash flow results from early mortgage prepayments. Thus, in month 2, the cash flows available to pay promised coupons to the three classes of bondholders is:

$$R + \text{Prepayments} = \$991{,}250 + \$1.5 \text{ million} = \$2{,}491{,}250$$

This cash flow is available to the trustee, who uses it in the following fashion:

1. **Coupon Payments.** The trustee pays the guaranteed coupons to the three classes of bond holders at annualized coupon rates of 7 percent, 8 percent, and 9 percent, respectively. Given the remaining principal of $48.5 million for class A (7 percent annual coupon) bonds, these bondholders receive approximately $282,917 in coupon payments

FIGURE 24–7 Allocation of Cash Flows to Owners of CMO Classes

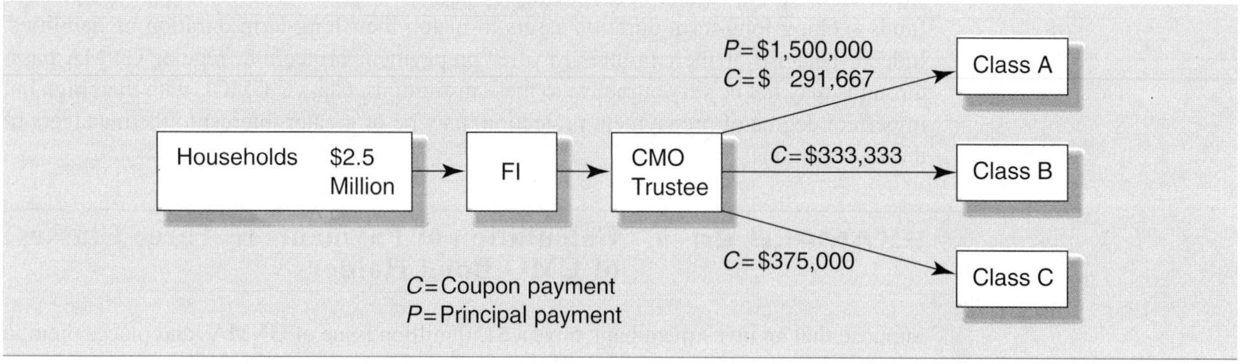

in month 2. The \$50 million for class B bonds (8 percent annual coupon) again receive approximately \$333,333 in month 2; and the \$50 million for class C bonds (9 percent annual coupon) again receive approximately \$375,000 in month 2. Thus, the total promised coupon payments to the three classes amounts to \$991,250 (equal to R, the no-prepayment principal and interest cash flows in the GNMA pool).

2. **Principal Payments.** The trustee has \$2,491,250 million available to pay as a result of promised mortgage payments plus early prepayments. Again, the remaining \$1.5 million must be paid to the CMO bond holders. The unique feature of the CMO is that the trustee pays this remaining \$1.5 million to class A bond holders only. This retires early some of these bond holders' principal outstanding. At the end of month 2, only \$47 million (\$48.5 million − \$1.5 million) of class A bonds remains outstanding, compared to \$50 million of class B and \$50 million of class C.

This continues until the full amount of the principal of class A bonds is paid off. Once this happens, any subsequent prepayments go to retire the principal outstanding to class B bond holders and, after they are paid off, to class C bond holders.

Clearly, issuing CMOs is often equivalent to engaging in double securitization. An FI packages mortgages and issues a GNMA pass-through. An investment bank such as Goldman Sachs or another CMO issuer such as FHLMC, a commercial bank, or a savings bank may buy this entire issue or a large part of it. Goldman Sachs, for example, then places these GNMA securities as collateral with a trust and issues three new classes of bonds backed by the GNMA securities as collateral. (These trusts are sometimes called real estate mortgage investment conduits (REMICs)). As a result, the investors in each CMO class have a claim to the GNMA collateral should the issuer fail. The investment bank or other issuer creates the CMO to make a profit by repackaging the cash flows from the single-class GNMA pass-through into cash flows more attractive to different groups of investors. The sum of the prices at which the three CMO bond classes can be sold normally exceeds that of the original pass-through:

$$\sum_{i=1}^{3} P_{iCMO} > P_{GNMA}$$

Gains from repackaging come from the way CMOs restructure prepayment risk to make it more attractive to different classes of investors. Specifically, under a CMO, each class has a guaranteed or fixed coupon.[12] By restructuring the GNMA as a CMO, an FI can offer investors who buy bond class C a high degree of mortgage prepayment protection compared to a pass-through; those who buy class B receive an average degree of

12. Coupons may be paid monthly, quarterly, or semiannually.

FIGURE 24–8 Principal Balance Outstanding to Classes of Three-Class CMO

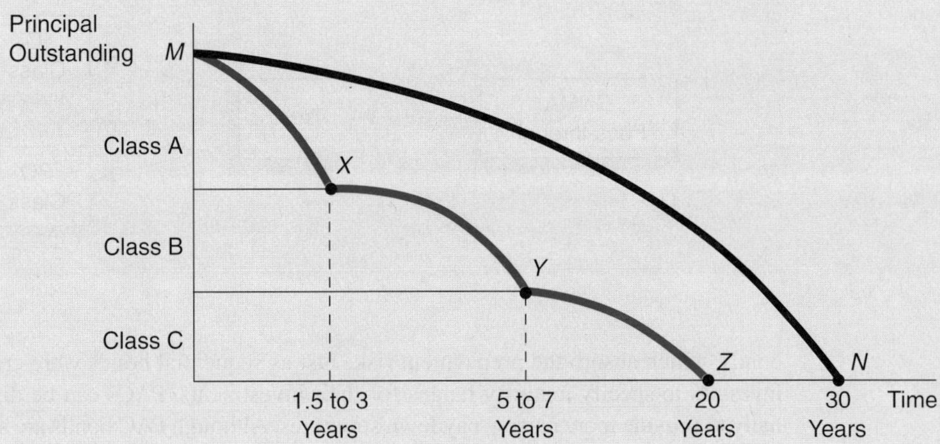

prepayment protection; those who buy class A have virtually no prepayment protection. Thus, CMOs redistribute prepayment risk among investors.

Figure 24–8 illustrates the typical pattern of outstanding principal balances for a three-tranche (class) CMO over time. With no prepayment, the outstanding principal balance is represented in Figure 24–8 by the curved line *MN*. Given any positive flow of prepayments, within a few years, the class A bonds clearly would be fully retired, point *X* in Figure 24–8. In practice, this often occurs between 1.5 and 3 years after issue. After the trustee retires class A, only classes B and C remain. As the months pass, the trustee uses any excess cash flows over and above the promised coupon payments to class B and C bond holders to retire bond class B's principal. Eventually, all of the principal on class B bonds is retired (point *Y* in Figure 24–8)—in practice, five to seven years after CMO issue. After class B bonds are retired, all remaining cash flows are dedicated to paying the promised coupon of class C bond holders and retiring the full amount of principal on class C bonds (point *Z* in Figure 24–8). In practice, class C bonds can have an average life of as long as 20 years.

CMOs can always have more than three classes described above. Indeed, issues of up to 17 different classes have been made. Clearly, the 17th-class bond holders would have an enormous degree of prepayment protection, since the first 16 classes would have had their bonds retired before the principal outstanding on this bond class would be affected by early prepayments. In addition, trustees have created other special types of classes as products to attract investor interest. Frequently, CMO issues contain a Z class as the last regular class. The Z implicitly stands for zero, but these are not really zero-coupon bonds. This class has a stated coupon such as 10 percent and accrues interest for the bond holder on a monthly basis at this rate. The trustee does not pay this interest, however, until all other classes of bonds are fully retired. When the other classes have been retired, the Z class bond holder receives the promised coupon and principal payments plus accrued interest payments. Thus, the Z class has characteristics of both a zero-coupon bond (no coupon payments for a long period) and a regular bond.

Another type of CMO class that is partially protected from prepayment risk is a planned amortization class, or PAC class. A PAC is designed to produce constant cash flows within a range (or band) of prepayment rates. The greater predictability of the cash flows on these classes of bonds occurs because they must satisfy a principal repayment schedule, compared to other CMO classes in which principal repayment might or might not occur. PAC bondholders have priority over all other classes in the CMO issue in receiving principal payments from the underlying mortgages. Thus, the greater certainty of the cash flows for the PAC bonds comes at the expense of the non-PAC classes, called support

FIGURE 24–9 IO/PO Strips

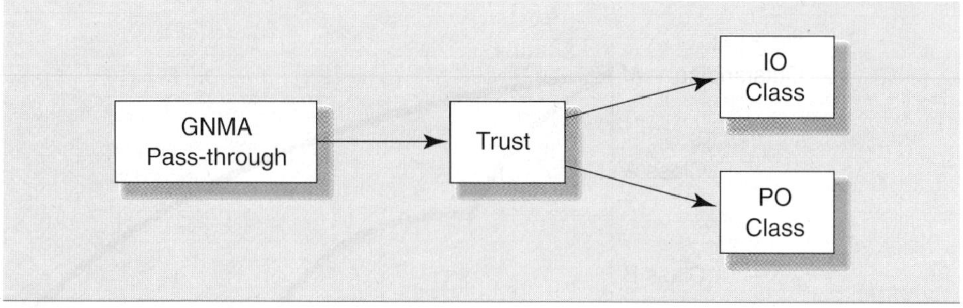

bonds, which absorb the prepayment risk. Just as sequential bonds were created to allow investors to specify maturity ranges for their investments, PACs can be divided sequentially to provide more narrow paydown structures. Although PAC bonds are somewhat protected from prepayment risk, they are not completely risk free. If prepayments are fast enough or slow enough, the cash flows of the PAC bonds will change.[13]

One drawback of CMOs is that originators may not be able to pass through all interest payments on a tax-free basis when they issue multiple debt securities. This creates a tax problem for various originators. A provision of the 1986 Tax Reform Act authorized the creation of a new type of mortgage-backed security called a REMIC (real estate mortgage investment conduit). A REMIC allows for the pass-through of all interest and principal payments before taxes are levied. Today, most CMOs are created as REMICs because of this tax advantage.

As noted above, CMOs are attractive to secondary mortgage market investors because they can choose a particular CMO class that fits their maturity needs. While there is no guarantee that the CMO securities will actually mature in exact accordance with the horizon desired by the investor, the CMO significantly increases the probability of receiving cash flows over a specified horizon. For example, a third-class CMO holder knows that he or she will not be paid off until all first- and second-class holders are paid in full.

Mortgage Pass-Through Strips. The mortgage pass-through strip is a special type of CMO with only two classes of securities. The fully amortized nature of mortgages means that any given monthly payment contains an interest component and a principal component. Beginning in 1987, investment banks and other financial institution issuers stripped out the interest component from the principal component and sold each payment stream separately to different bond class investors. They sold an interest only (IO) class and a principal only (PO) class. We show this stripping of the cash flows in Figure 24–9.

IO strips

A CMO whose owner has a claim to the present value of interest payments by the mortgagees in the GNMA pool.

The owner of an **IO strip** has a claim to the interest payments made by the mortgage holder in the GNMA pool—that is, to the IO segments of each month's cash flows received from the underlying mortgage pool. An IO strip has no par value. If interest rates decrease slightly, the value of an IO strip increases (e.g., its present value increases as interest rates decrease). However, an IO investor receives interest only on the amount of the principal outstanding. Thus, he or she hopes prepayments on the mortgage will not occur. If interest rates fall significantly, mortgage borrowers will prepay their mortgages (and refinance them at the lower rate). When prepayments occur, the amount of interest payments the IO investor receives falls as the outstanding principal in the mortgage pool falls. In absolute terms, the number of IO payments the investor receives is likely to shrink. For example, the investor might receive only 100 monthly IO payments instead of the expected 360 in a

13. The PAC band is the range of constant prepayment speeds defined by a minimum and maximum under which the scheduled payments will remain unchanged. The minimum and maximum prepayment speeds are stated in the contract governing the CMO. As long as the prepayment speed remains within this stated range, the PAC payments are known and guaranteed. If prepayment falls outside of the stated range, cash flows on the PAC can vary.

FIGURE 24–10 Price-Yield Curves of IO/PO Strips

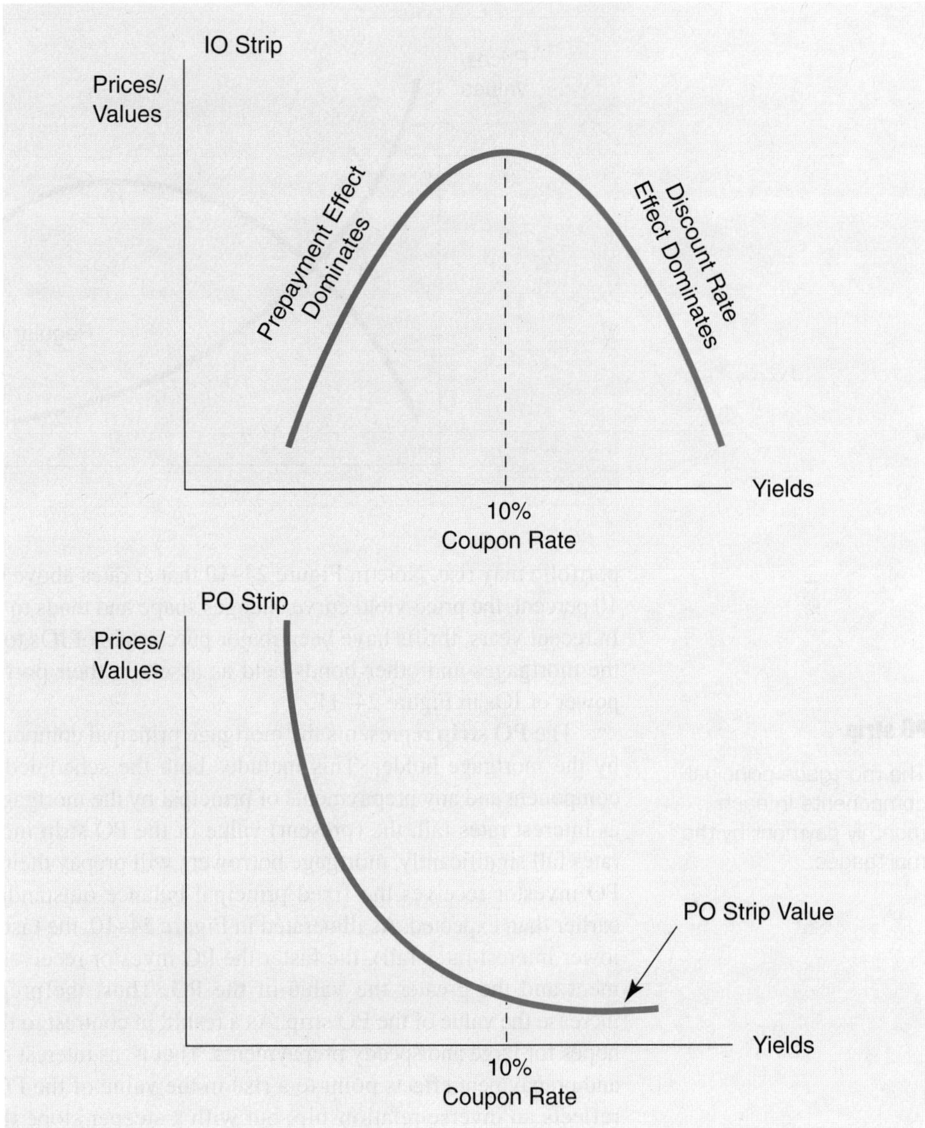

no-prepayment world of a 30-year mortgage. The decrease in *total* payments reduces the value of the IO, counteracting the positive effect a decrease in interest rates has on the present value of the remaining payments on the IO. If prepayments are large, the IO investor may not recover his or her initial investment in the IO strip.

Note the price-yield curve in Figure 24–10 for an IO strip on a pass-through bond with 10 percent mortgage coupon rates. If interest rates rise above 10 percent, mortgage prepayments will be relatively low. Thus, the discount effect of interest rates dominates the determination of price of the IO. However, one can expect that as interest rates fall below the mortgage coupon rate of the bonds in the pool, 10 percent, prepayments increase. Thus, the prepayment effect gradually dominates the discount effect, so that over some range the price or value of the IO bond falls as interest rates fall. This means that as current interest rates fall (rise), IO values or prices fall (rise). As a result the IO is a rare example of a negative duration asset that is very valuable as a portfolio-hedging device when included with regular bonds whose price-yield curves show the normal inverse relationship. That is, while as interest rates rise the value of the regular bond portfolio falls, the value of an IO

FIGURE 24–11 Hedging with IOs

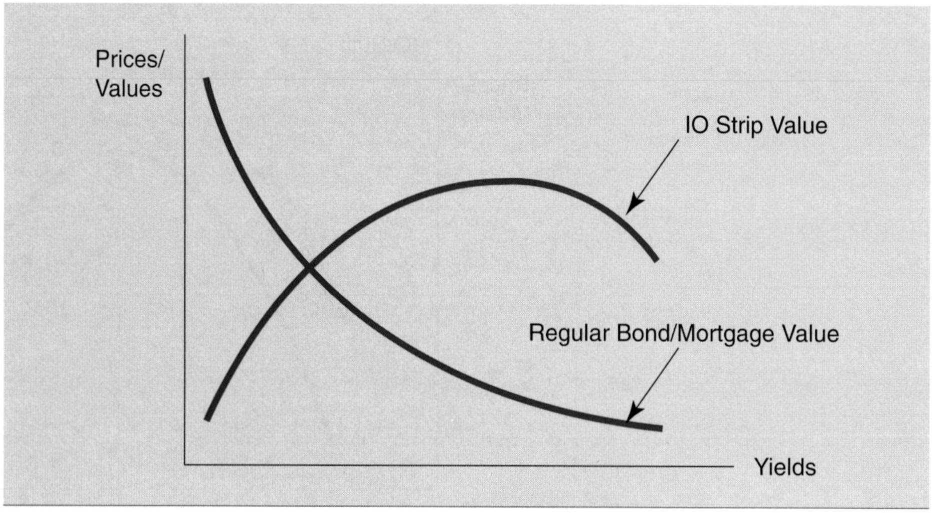

portfolio may rise. Note in Figure 24–10 that at rates above the pool's mortgage coupon of 10 percent, the price-yield curve changes shape and tends to perform like any regular bond. In recent years, thrifts have been major purchasers of IOs to hedge the interest rate risk on the mortgages and other bonds held as assets in their portfolios. We depict the hedging power of IOs in Figure 24–11.

PO strip

The mortgage principal components in each monthly payment by the mortgagee.

The **PO strip** represents the mortgage principal components in each monthly payment by the mortgage holder. This includes both the scheduled monthly amortized principal component and any prepayments of principal by the mortgage holder. As with any security, as interest rates fall, the (present) value of the PO strip increases. In addition, if interest rates fall significantly, mortgage borrowers will prepay their mortgages. Consequently, the PO investor receives the fixed principal balance outstanding on the pool of mortgages earlier than expected. As illustrated in Figure 24–10, the faster prepayments occur (i.e., the lower interest rates fall), the faster the PO investor receives a return on his or her investment and the greater the value of the PO. Thus, the prepayment effect also works to increase the value of the PO strip. As a result, in contrast to the IO investor, the PO investor hopes for large and speedy prepayments. That is, as interest rates fall, both the discount rate and prepayment effects point to a rise in the value of the PO strip. The price–yield curve reflects an inverse relationship, but with a steeper slope than for normal bonds; that is, PO strip bond values are very interest rate sensitive, especially for yields below the stated mortgage coupon rate. We show this in Figure 24–10 for a 10 percent PO strip. (Note that a regular coupon bond is affected only by the interest rate effect.) As you can see, when yields fall below 10 percent, the market value or price of the PO strip can increase very fast. At rates above 10 percent, it tends to behave like a regular bond (as the incentive to prepay disappears).

The IO/PO strip is a classic example of financial engineering. From a given GNMA pass-through bond, two new bonds have been created. Each class is attractive to different investors and investor segments. The IO is attractive to banks and thrifts as an on-balance-sheet hedging vehicle—as interest rates increase, the gain in value on an IO can offset the loss in value from mortgages and other bonds in the bank or thrift's asset portfolio (see Figure 24–11). The PO is attractive to those financial institutions that wish to increase the interest rate sensitivity in their portfolios in expectation of falling interest rates and to investors or traders who wish to take a speculative position regarding the future course of interest rates. Their high and complex interest sensitivity has resulted in major traders such as J.P. Morgan Chase and Merrill Lynch, as well as many investors such as hedge funds, suffering considerable losses on their investments in these instruments when interest rates move unexpectedly against them.

Mortgage-Backed Bond

mortgage- (asset-) backed bonds

Bonds collateralized by a pool of assets.

As discussed in Chapter 7, **mortgage- (asset-) backed bonds** (MBBs) differ from pass-throughs and CMOs in two key dimensions. First, while pass-throughs and CMOs help FIs remove mortgages from their balance sheets, MBBs normally remain on the balance sheet. Second, pass-throughs and CMOs have a direct link between the cash flows on the underlying mortgages and the cash flows on the bond instrument issued. By contrast, the relationship for MBBs is one of collateralization—the cash flows on the mortgages backing the bond are not necessarily directly connected to interest and principal payments on the MBB.

An FI issues an MBB to reduce risk to the MBB holders, who have a first claim to a segment of the FI's mortgage assets. The FI segregates a group of mortgage assets on its balance sheet and pledges this group of assets as collateral against the MBB issue. A trustee normally monitors the segregation of assets and ensures that the market value of the collateral exceeds the principal owed to MBB holders. That is, FIs back most MBB issues by excess collateral. This excess collateral backing of the bond, in addition to the priority rights of the bond holders, generally ensures the sale of these bonds with a high investment grade credit rating. In contrast, the FI, when evaluated as a whole, could be rated as BB or even lower. A high credit rating results in lower coupon payments than would be required if significant default risk had lowered the credit rating. To explain the potential benefits and the sources of any gains to an FI from issuing MBBs, we examine the following simple example.

EXAMPLE 24-2 Gains to an FI from Issuing MBBs

Consider an FI with $20 million in long-term mortgages as assets. It is financing these mortgages with $10 million in short-term uninsured deposits (e.g., wholesale deposits over $100,000) and $10 million in insured deposits (e.g., retail deposits of $100,000 or less). In this example, we ignore the issues of capital and reserve requirements. Look at the balance sheet structure shown in Table 24–4.

This balance sheet poses problems for the FI manager. First, the FI has significant interest rate risk exposure due to the mismatch of the maturities of its assets and liabilities. Second, because of this interest rate risk and the potential default and prepayment risk on the FI's mortgage assets, uninsured depositors are likely to require a positive and potentially significant risk premium to be paid on their deposits. By contrast, the insured depositors may require approximately the risk-free rate on their deposits because they are fully insured by the FDIC (see Chapter 21).

To reduce its interest rate risk exposure and to lower its funding costs, the FI can segregate $12 million of the mortgages on the asset side of its balance sheet and pledge them as collateral backing a $10 million long-term MBB issue. Because the $10 million in MBBs is backed by mortgages worth $12 million, the mortgage-backed bond issued by the FI may cost less to issue, in terms of required yield, than uninsured deposit rates currently being paid—it may well be rated AA while uninsured deposits might be rated BB. The FI can then use the proceeds of the $10 million bond issue to replace the $10 million of uninsured deposits.

Consider the FI's balance sheet after the issue of the MBBs (Table 24–5). It might seem that the FI has miraculously engineered a restructuring of its balance sheet that has resulted in a better match of the maturities of its assets and liabilities and a decrease in funding costs. The bond issue has lengthened the average maturity of liabilities by replacing short-term wholesale deposits with long-term MBBs and has lowered funding costs because AA-rated bond coupon rates are below BB-rated uninsured deposit rates. This outcome, however, occurs only because the insured depositors do not worry about risk exposure since they are 100 percent insured by the FDIC. The result of the MBB issue and the segregation of $12 million of assets as collateral backing the $10 million bond issue is that the insured deposits of $10 million are now backed by only $8 million in free or unpledged assets. If smaller depositors were not insured by the FDIC, they would surely demand very high risk premiums for holding these risky deposits. The implication of this is that the FI

TABLE 24–4 Balance Sheet of Potential MBB Issuer
(in millions of dollars)

Assets		Liabilities	
Long-term mortgages	$20	Insured deposits	$10
		Uninsured deposits	10
	$20		$20

TABLE 24–5 FI's Balance Sheet after MBB Issue
(in millions of dollars)

Assets		Liabilities	
Collateral (maket value of segregated mortgages)	$12	MBB issue	$10
Other mortgages	8	Insured deposits	10
	$20		$20

gains only because the FDIC is willing to bear enhanced credit risk through its insurance guarantees to depositors.[14] As a result, the FI is actually gaining at the expense of the FDIC. Consequently, it is not surprising that the FDIC is concerned about the growing use of this form of securitization by risky banks and thrifts.

DO YOU UNDERSTAND?

1. What the three forms of asset securitization are? What are the major differences in the three forms?
2. How a simple bank balance sheet would change when a pass-through mortgage is securitized? Assume the mortgage is funded with demand deposits and capital and reserve regulations are in force.
3. Why an investor in a securitized asset who is concerned about prepayment risk would prefer a CMO over a pass-through security?
4. Why an AAA-rated FI would ever issue mortgage-backed bonds? Explain your answer.

MBB issuance also has a number of costs. First, MBBs tie up mortgages on the FI's balance sheet for a long time, thus decreasing the asset portfolio's liquidity. Further, the balance sheet becomes more illiquid due to the need to collateralize MBBs to ensure a high-quality credit risk rating for the issue; in our example, the overcollateralization was $2 million. Second, the MBB issuer (the FI) is subject to any prepayment risk on the mortgages underlying the MBB. Third, the FI continues to be liable for capital adequacy and reserve requirement taxes by keeping the mortgages on the balance sheet. Because of these costs, MBBs are the least used of the three basic vehicles of securitization.

SECURITIZATION OF OTHER ASSETS

The major use of the three securitization vehicles—pass-throughs, CMOs, and mortgage-backed bonds—has been to package fixed-rate residential mortgage assets. The standard features on mortgages have made the packaging and securitization of these securities relatively easy. But these techniques can and have been used for other assets, including the following:

- Automobile loans.
- Credit card receivables (CARDs)
- Small-business loans guaranteed by the Small Business Administration
- Commercial and industrial loans
- Student loans
- Mobile home loans

14. The FDIC does not make the risk-based deposit insurance premium to banks and thrifts sufficiently large to reflect this risk.

TABLE 24–6 Benefits versus Costs of Securitization

Benefits	Costs
1. New funding source (bonds versus deposits).	**1.** Public/private credit risk insurance and guarantees.
2. Increased liquidity of bank loans.	**2.** Overcollateralization.
3. Enhanced ability to manage the maturity gap and thus interest rate risk.	**3.** Valuation and packaging (the cost of asset heterogeneity).
4. A savings to the issuer, if off balance sheet, on reserve requirements, deposit insurance premiums, and capital adequacy requirements.	

- Junk bonds
- Time share loans
- Adjustable rate mortgages[15]

CAN ALL ASSETS BE SECURITIZED?

DO YOU UNDERSTAND?

1. Whether or not all assets and loans can be securitized? Explain your answer.

The extension of securitization technology to assets other than fixed-rate residential mortgages raises questions about the limits of securitization and whether all assets and loans can eventually be securitized. Conceptually, the answer is that they can, so long as doing so is profitable or the benefits to the FI from securitization outweigh its costs. With heterogeneous loans, it is important to standardize the salient features of loans. Default risks, if significant, have to be reduced by diversification. Expected maturities have to be reasonably similar. As mechanisms are developed to overcome these difficulties, it is perfectly reasonable to expect securitization to grow. Table 24–6 summarizes the overall benefits versus the costs of securitization.

From Table 24–6, given any set of benefits, the more costly and difficult it is to find asset packages of sufficient size and homogeneity, the more difficult and expensive it is to securitize. For example, C&I loans have maturities running from a few months to eight years; in addition, they have varying interest rate terms (fixed, LIBOR floating, federal funds-rate floating) and fees. In addition, C&I loans contain different contractual covenants (covering items such as dividend payments by firms) and are made to firms in a wide variety of industries. Given this, it is often difficult for investors, insurers, and bond rating agencies to value C&I loan pools.[16] The more difficult it is to value such asset pools, the higher are the costs of securitization. The potential boundary to securitization may well be defined by the relative degree of homogeneity of an asset type or group—the more homogeneous or similar are the assets in any pool, the easier they are to securitize. Thus, it is not surprising that 30-year fixed-rate residential mortgages were the first assets to be securitized, since they are the most homogeneous of all assets on FI balance sheets (i.e., have similar maturities and interest rates). Moreover, the existence of secondary markets for houses provides price information that allows for reasonably accurate market valuations of the underlying asset to be made by originators, insurers, and investors in the event of mortgage defaults.

15. At the end of 2004, securitized automobile loans totaled $232.1 billion, credit card receivables totaled $390.7 billion, student loans totaled $115.2 billion, and mobile homes totaled $42.2 billion.

16. Despite this, there has been some securitization of C&I loans. These are called collateralized loan obligations (CLOs). A CLO is modeled on the CMO. An FI collects a diversified pool of loans, places them in a trust, and usually issues three tranches of securities against the pool: usually a senior tranche, a subordinated tranche, and a tranche that has features similar to the residual tranche of CMOs. Most issues so far have involved securitizing highly leveraged loans to finance mergers and acquisitions.

SUMMARY

Loan sales provide a simple alternative to the full securitization of loans through bond packages. In particular, they provide a valuable tool to an FI that wishes to manage its credit risk exposure better. Recently, by increasingly relying on securitization, banks and thrifts have begun to move away from being asset transformers to become asset brokers. Thus, over time, we can expect the traditional differences between commercial banking and investment banking to diminish as more and more loans and assets are securitized. This chapter discussed the increasing role of loan sales in addition to the legal and regulatory factors that are likely to affect the future growth of this market. The chapter also discussed three major forms of securitization—pass-through securities, collateralized mortgage obligations (CMOs), and mortgage-backed bonds—and described recent innovations in the securitization of other FI assets.

SEARCH THE SITE

Go to the Bond Markets Association Web site at **www.bondmarkets.com** and find the most recent level of mortgage-backed securities using the following steps.

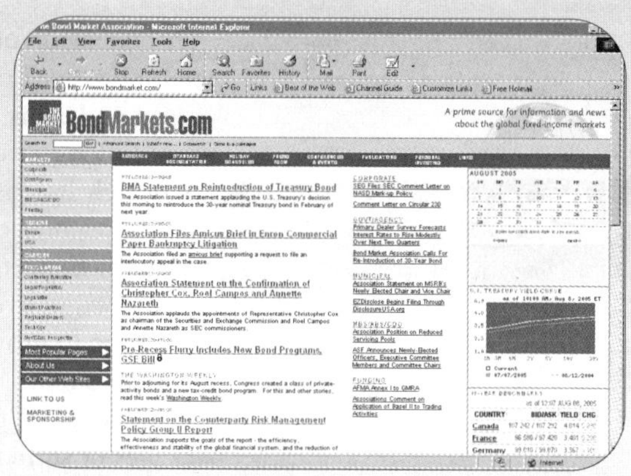

Click on "MBS/ABS/CDO."

Click on "Statistical Data."

Under MBS/ABS, click on "Issuance of Agency Mortgage-Backed Securities" and "Asset Backed Securities Outstanding by Major Types of Credit."

The information on the most current levels of mortgage-backed securities is on these two pages.

Questions

1. What is the total amount of agency mortgage-backed securities outstanding? Calculate the percentage of this amount issued by GNMA, FNMA, and FHLMC.
2. What is the total amount of asset-backed securities outstanding? Calculate the percentage of this amount backed by automobile loans, credit card loans, home equity loans, manufactured home loans, and student loans.

QUESTIONS

1. What is the difference between loans sold with recourse and without recourse from the perspective of both sellers and buyers?
2. What are some of the key features of short-term loan sales? How have banks used this sector of the loan market to circumvent Glass-Steagall limitations?
3. Why are yields higher on loan sales than they are for similar maturity and issue size commercial paper issues?
4. What is the difference between loan participations and loan assignments?
5. Why have FIs been very active in loan securitization issuance of pass-through securities while they have reduced their volume of loan sales? Under what circumstances would you expect loan sales to dominate loan securitization?
6. Who are the buyers and sellers of U.S. loans? Why do they participate in this activity?

7. A bank has made a three-year $10 million dollar loan that pays annual interest of 8 percent. The principal is due at the end of the third year.
   a. The bank is willing to sell this loan with recourse at an 8.5 percent discount rate. What should it receive for this loan?
   b. The bank also has the option to sell this loan without recourse at a discount rate of 8.75 percent. What should it expect for selling this loan?
   c. If the bank expects a ½ percent probability of default on this loan over its three-year life, is it better off selling this loan with or without recourse? It expects to receive no interest payments or principal if the loan is defaulted.
8. City Bank has made a 10-year, $2 million HLT loan that pays annual interest of 10 percent per year. The principal is expected at maturity.
   a. What should it expect to receive from the sale of this loan if the current market rate on loans is 12 percent?
   b. The prices of loans of this risk are currently being quoted in the secondary market at bid-offer prices 88–89 cents (on each dollar). Translate these quotes into actual prices for the above loan.
   c. Do these prices reflect a distressed or nondistressed loan? Explain.
9. What role do reserve requirements play in the decision to sell a loan with or without recourse?
10. What are the three levels of regulatory taxes faced by FIs when making loans? How does securitization reduce the levels of taxation?
11. How will a move toward market value accounting affect the market for loan sales?
12. An FI is planning to issue $100 million in commercial loans. It will finance all of it by issuing demand deposits.
    a. What is the minimum capital required if there are no reserve requirements?
    b. What is the minimum demand deposits it needs to attract in order to fund this loan if you assume there is a 10 percent average reserve requirement on demand deposits, all reserves are held in the form of cash, and $8 million of funding is through equity?
    c. Show a simple balance sheet with total assets and total liabilities and equity if this is the only project funded by the bank.
13. How do loan sales and securitization help an FI manage its interest rate and liquidity risk exposures?
14. What are the differences between CMOs and MBBs?
15. Consider $200 million of 30-year mortgages with a coupon of 10 percent paid quarterly.
    a. What is the quarterly mortgage payment?
    b. What are the interest repayments over the first year of life of the mortgages? What are the principal repayments?

    Construct a 30-year CMO using this mortgage pool as collateral. There are three tranches (where A offers the least protection against prepayment and C offers the most). A $50 million tranche A makes quarterly payments of 9 percent; a $100 million tranche B makes quarterly payments of 10 percent; and a $50 million tranche C makes quarterly payments of 11 percent.
    c. Assuming no amortization of principal and no prepayments, what are the total promised coupon payments to the three classes? What are the principal payments to each of the three classes for the first year?
    d. If, over the first year, the trustee receives quarterly prepayments of $10 million on the mortgage pool, how are the funds distributed?
    e. How can the CMO issuer earn a positive spread on the CMO?
16. Assume an FI originates a pool of short-term real estate loans worth $20 million with maturities of five years and paying interest rates of 9 percent (paid annually).
    a. What is the average payment received by the FI (both principal and interest) if no prepayment is expected over the life of the loans?
    b. If the loans are converted into real estate certificates and the FI charges a 50 basis points servicing fee (including insurance), what are the payments expected by the holders of the securities, if no prepayment is expected?
17. How do FIs use securitization to manage their interest rate, credit, and liquidity risks?
18. Why do buyers of class C tranches of collateralized mortgage obligations (CMOs) demand a lower return than do purchasers of class A tranches?

REFERENCES

Acharaya, V. V., I. Hassan, and A. Saunders. "Should Banks Be Diversified? Evidence from Individual Bank Loan Portfolios," *Journal of Business,* forthcoming.

Allen, L., and A. Saunders. "Bank Window Dressing: Theory and Evidence." *Journal of Banking and Finance,* 1992, pp. 585–624.

Altman, E. I. "Managing the Commercial Lending Process." *Handbook of Banking Strategy,* R. C. Aspinwall and R. A. Eisenbeis, eds. (New York: John Wiley & Sons, 1985), pp. 473–510.

Altman, E. I., A. Gande, and A. Saunders. "International Efficiency of Loans versus Bonds: Evidence from Secondary Market Prices," New York University, working paper, 2004

Altman, E. I., and B. Karlin, "Default and Returns on High-Yield Bond Analysis through 2003 and Default Outlook," New York University Salomon Center, working paper, May 2004.

American Banker, February 15, 1989, p. 1; April 10, 2002, p. 1.

Asset Securitization Report. "Europe at an Interesting Crossroads," November 2004.

Bank for International Settlements. "A New Capital Adequacy Framework," June 1999.

———. "The New Basel Capital Accord," January 2002.

———. "Working Paper on Regulatory Treatment of Operational Risk," September 2001.

———. "Sound Practices for Managing Liquidity in Banking Organizations," February 2000.

———. "Principals for the Management and Supervision of Interest Rate Risk," January 2001.

———. *"International Convergence of Capital Measurement and Capital Standards." A Revised Framework, June 2004.*

The Banker, May 2000, pp. 110–111.

Berger, A. N., Q. Dai, S. Ongena, and D. C. Smith. "To What Extent Will the Banking Industry Be Globalized? A Study of Bank Nationality and Reach in 20 European Nations," Federal Reserve Board, working paper, May 2002.

Best's Review, August 2001, p. 47; May 2001.

Black, F., and M. Scholes. "The Pricing of Options and Corporate Liabilities," *Journal of Political Economy* 81 (May–June 1973), pp. 637–654 and 737–759.

Bloch, E. *Inside Investment Banking,* 2nd ed. (Burr Ridge, IL: McGraw-Hill/Irwin, 1989).

Brawley, W. G., J. H. Gilkeson, and C. K. Ruff. "International Measures of Interest Rate Risk: Are Income and Economic Value Approaches Different?" Federal Reserve Bank of Atlanta, 2004.

Brealey, R. A., S. C. Myers, and A. J. Marcus. *Fundamentals of Corporate Finance* (New York: McGraw-Hill, 1999), pp. 225–229.

Buerkle, T. "What's Wrong with the ECB?" *Institutional Investor,* September 2001, p. 64.

Clark, J. A. "Economies of Scale and Scope at Depository Financial Institutions: A Review of the Literature," Federal Reserve Bank of Kansas City, *Economic Review,* September-October 1988, pp. 16–33.

Clark, M., and A. Saunders. "Judicial Interpretation of Glass-Steagall: The Need for Legislative Action," *The Banking Law Journal,* 1980, pp. 721–740.

———. "Glass-Steagall Revisited: The Impact on Banks, Capital Markets, and the Small Investor," *The Banking Law Journal* 97, 1980, pp. 811–840.

Cox, J., and M. Rubenstein, *Options Markets* (Englewood Cliffs, NJ: Prentice-Hall, 1985).

Department of Treasury. "Uniform Price Auctions: Update of the Treasury Experience," October 1998.

The Economist, December 4, 2004, p. 56.

Ellis, K., R. Michaely, and M. O'Hara. "When the Underwriter Is the Market Maker: An Examination of Trading in the IPO Aftermarket," *Journal of Finance,* June 2002, pp. 1039–1074.

Elton, E. J., and M. J. Gruber. *Modern Portfolio Theory and Investment Analysis,* 6th ed. (New York: John Wiley & Sons, 1998), Chapter 2.

FASB Statement No. 80. "Accounting for Futures Contracts," FASB, 1984.

Federal Deposit Insurance Corporation. "Keeping the Promise: Recommendations for Deposit Insurance Reform," April 2001.

———. *DOS Manual of Examination Policies,* February 2000.

Federal Reserve Board. "Risk-Based Capital and Interest Rate Risk," July 30, 1992.

———. *"The Feasibility and Desirability of Mandatory Subordinate Debt," December 2000.*

Financial Times, June 4, 2001; June 16, 2004, p. 48; October 8, 2004, p. 45.

Furst, K., W. W. Lang, and D. E. Nolle. "Internet Banking: Developments and Prospects," Office of the Comptroller of the Currency, Economic and Policy Analysis, working paper 2000-9, September 2000.

Gande, A., M. Puri, and A. Saunders. "Bank Entry, Competition and the Market for Corporate Securities Underwriting," *Journal of Financial Economics* 54, no. 2 (October 1999), pp. 165–196.

General Accounting Office. "Long-Term Capital Management: Regulators Need to Focus Greater Attention on Systematic Risk," GAO/GGD-00-3, October 1999.

Gorton, G., and R. Rosen. "Banks and Derivatives," University of Pennsylvania Wharton School, working paper, February 1995.

Higgins, B. "Is a Recession Inevitable This Year?" *Economic Review,* Federal Reserve Bank of Kansas City, January 1988, pp. 3–16.

Ibbotson Associates' Stocks, Bonds, Bills and Inflation 2004 Yearbook (Chicago: Ibbotson Associates, 2004).

Institutional Investor. "The Institutional Investor Guide to Foreign Exchange as an Asset Class," February 2004, p. 4.

International Herald Tribune, May 22, 2002, p. 12.

Investment Company Institute. "How Mutual Funds Use 12b-1 Fees," *Fundamentals* 14, no. 2 February 2005, pp. 1–4.

Investor's Daily. January 8, 1991, p. 1.

Kaufman, G. G. "Measuring and Managing Interest Rate Risk: A Primer," *Economic Perspective* (Chicago: Federal Reserve Bank of Chicago, 1984), pp. 16–29.

Kiplinger's Personal Finance. "Online Trading: Investors Take Charge," January 28, 2003, p. 28.

KMV Corporation. *Credit Monitor* (San Francisco: KMV Corporation, 1994).

Lee, I., S. Lockhead, J. Ritter, and Q. Zhao. "The Cost of Raising Capital." *Journal of Financial Research,* Spring 1996, pp. 59–74.

Meier, K. J. *The Political Economy of Regulation: The Case of Insurance* (Albany, NY: State University of New York Press, 1988).

Merton, R. C. "On Option Pricing of Corporate Debt: The Risk Structure of Interest Rates," *Journal of Finance* 29 (1974), pp. 447–470.

Munter, P. H., D. K. Clancy, and C. T. Moores. "Accounting for Financial Futures: A Question of Risk Reduction," *Advances in Accounting,* 1986, pp. 51–70.

National Mortgage News, February 11, 2002, p. 4.

Neely, C. G. "September 11, 2001," *Monetary Trends,* November 2001, p. 1.

The New York Times, April 25, 2002, p. C2; July 5, 1996, pp. D1–D3; October, 5, 1998, pp. C1–C4; March 18, 2004, p. B8.

Office of the Comptroller of the Currency. *Bank Derivatives Report,* First Quarter 2002; Third Quarter 2004.

Risk Magazine, "Called to Account," August 1996, pp. 15–17.

Sarkar, A., and K. Li. "Should U.S. Investors Hold Foreign Stocks?" *Current Issues,* Federal Reserve Bank of New York, March 2002.

Saunders, A., and L. Allen. *Credit Risk Measurement: New Approaches to Value at Risk and Other Paradigms,* 2nd. ed. (New York: John Wiley & Sons, 2002).

Saunders, A., and M.M. Cornett. *Financial Institutions Management: A Risk Managements Approach,* 5th ed. (New York: McGraw-Hill, 2006).

Saunders, A., and I. Walter. *Universal Banking in the U.S.?* (New York: Oxford University Press, 1994).

Saunders, A., and B. Wilson. "An Analysis of Bank Charter Value and Its Risk Constraining Incentive," *Journal of Financial Services Research,* 2001, pp. 185–195.

Silber, W. L. "Marketmaker Behavior in an Auction Market: An Analysis of Scalpers in Futures Markets." *Journal of Finance*, September 1984, pp. 937–953.

Stoebe, R. "Macrohedging Bank Investment Portfolios," *Bankers Magazine,* November-December 1994, pp. 45–48.

U.S. Department of Justice. "Horizontal Merger Guideline," April 2, 1992.

U.S. General Accounting Office. "Mutual Funds: Impact on Bank Deposits and Credit Availability," GAO/GGD-95-230, Washington, DC: Government Printing Offices, 1995.

______. GAO/GGD-94-23, 1994, p. 57.

U.S. Treasury, Bureau of Public Debt, November 8, 2004; November 19, 2004.

The Wall Street Journal. January 9, 2002, p. A10; June 10, 2002, p. C15; August 13, 2002, p. C5; May 15, 2002, p. A1; July 2, 2002, p. A2; November 26, 2003, p. C12; April 25, 2003, p. C1; January 20, 2004, p. A12; February 26, 2004, p. C5; March 24, 2004, p. C1; March 29, 2004, p. A2; April 28, 2004, p. A1; May 11, 2004, p. A3; May 19, 2004, p. C1; May 25, 2004, p. C14; July 16, 2004, p. A3; September 23, 2004, p. A3.

Wheelock, D. C. "A Changing Relationship between Bank Size and Profitability." *Monetary Trends*, Federal Reserve Bank of St. Louis, September 1996, p. 1.

White, L. J. *The S and L Debacle* (New York: Oxford University Press, 1991).

INDEX